Routledge
Encyclopedia of
PHILOSOPHY

General Editor
EDWARD CRAIG

London and New York

First published 1998
by Routledge
...ew Fetter Lane, London EC4P 4EE
Simultaneously published in the USA and Canada
by Routledge
29 West 35th Street, New York, NY 10001

©1998 Routledge

Typeset in Monotype Times New Roman by
Routledge

Printed in England by
T J International Ltd, Padstow, Cornwall, England

Printed on acid-free paper which conforms to ANS1.Z39, 48-1992 and ISO 9706 standards

British Library Cataloguing-in-Publication Data
A catalogue record for this book is available from the British Library

Library of Congress Cataloguing-in-Publication Data
Routledge encyclopedia of philosophy / general editor, Edward Craig.
p. cm.
Includes bibliographical references and indexes.
ISBN 0415-07310-3 (boxed set : alk. paper)
1. Philosophy–Encyclopedias.
I. Craig, Edward. II. Routledge (Firm) III. Title Encyclopedia of philosophy.
B51.R68 1998
100–DC21
97-4549
CIP

ISBN: 0415-07310-3 (10-volume set)
ISBN: 0415-18706-0 (volume 1)
ISBN: 0415-18707-9 (volume 2)
ISBN: 0415-18708-7 (volume 3)
ISBN: 0415-18709-5 (volume 4)
ISBN: 0415-18710-9 (volume 5)
ISBN: 0415-18711-7 (volume 6)
ISBN: 0415-18712-5 (volume 7)
ISBN: 0415-18713-3 (volume 8)
ISBN: 0415-18714-1 (volume 9)
ISBN: 0415-18715-X (volume 10)

ISBN: 0415-16916-X (CD-ROM)
ISBN: 0415-16917-8 (10-volume set and CD-ROM)

Contents

Using the *Encyclopedia*

List of entries

Volume 1   A posteriori – Bradwardine, Thomas

Volume 2   Brahman – Derrida, Jacques

Volume 3   Descartes, René – Gender and science

Volume 4   Genealogy – Iqbal, Muhammad

Volume 5   Irigaray, Luce – Lushi chunqiu

Volume 6   Luther, Martin – Nifo, Agostino

Volume 7   Nihilism – Quantum mechanics, interpretation of

Volume 8   Questions – Sociobiology

Volume 9   Sociology of knowledge – Zoroastrianism

Volume 10   Index

List of contributors, their affiliations and entries

Below is an alphabetical listing of authors, with their affiliations and the titles of entries they have contributed. Where no departmental affiliation is listed, the author is a member of a department of philosophy.

Professor José Luis Abellán
Universidad Complutense de Madrid
Spain
Spain, philosophy in

Mr Reuben Abel
Larchmont, New York
USA
Schiller, Ferdinand Canning Scott

Professor Peter Achinstein
Johns Hopkins University
USA
Crucial experiments
Demarcation problem

Dr Christopher Adair-Toteff
College of Arts and Sciences
University of South Florida
USA
Hartmann, Karl Robert
  Eduard von
Vaihinger, Hans

Revd Professor Marilyn McCord
Adams
Yale Divinity School
USA
Evil, problem of
Hell

Professor Jonathan E. Adler
*Brooklyn College and The Graduate
School*
City University of New York
USA
Rationality of belief

Professor Dr Jan A. Aertsen
Thomas-Institut
University of Cologne
Germany
Meister Eckhart

Professor Salman Albdour
University of Jordan
Jordan
al-Juwayni, Abu'l Ma'ali
Ibn Hazm, Abu Muhammad 'Ali

Professor Jeffrey C. Alexander
Department of Sociology
*University of California, Los
Angeles*
USA
Sociology, theories of

Professor Philip S. Alexander
*Department of Religions and
Theology*
University of Manchester
UK
Midrash

Dr Keimpe A. Algra
University of Utrecht
Netherlands
Posidonius

Dr T.R.S. Allan
*Reader in Legal and Constitutional
Theory*
Pembroke College
University of Cambridge
UK
Rule of law (Rechtsstaat)

Professor Diogenes Allen
Stuart Professor of Philosophy
Theology Department
Princeton Theological Seminary
USA
Justification, religious
Nygren, Anders
Sanctification

Dr R.T. Allen
Loughborough, Leicestershire
UK
Polanyi, Michael

Professor Henry E. Allison
Boston University
USA
Eberhard, Johann August
Spinoza, Benedict de

Professor Brenda Almond
University of Hull
UK
Applied ethics

Professor William P. Alston
Syracuse University
USA
Empiricism
Internalism and externalism in
  epistemology
Religion, history of philosophy of
Religious experience
Religious language

Dr David Ambuel
*Department of Classics, Philosophy
and Religion*
Mary Washington College
USA
Ontology in Indian philosophy

v

Professor Roger T. Ames
*Professor of Philosophy
and Director of the Center for
Chinese Studies
University of Hawaii
USA*
Chinese philosophy
Confucius
Dao
Daoist philosophy
De
East Asian philosophy
Qi
Sunzi
Tian
Xin (heart and mind)
Xing
Yin-yang
You-wu
Zhi
Zhuangzi

Professor Paul Anderer
*Professor of Japanese Literature
Department of East Asian
Languages and Culture
Columbia University, City of New
York
USA*
Literature, philosophy in modern
    Japanese

Dr Robert Andrews
*The Franciscan Institute
St Bonaventure University
USA*
Brinkley, Richard
Peter of Auvergne

Professor G. Aldo Antonelli
*Michigan State University
USA*
Definition

Professor Carol Any
*West Hartford, Connecticut
USA*
Russian literary formalism

Professor K. Anthony Appiah
*Professor of Afro-American Studies
and Philosophy
Chair, African Studies
Harvard University
USA*
African philosophy
African traditional religions
Cabral, Amilcar
Ethical systems, African
Fanon, Frantz
Pan-Africanism

Professor Roger Ariew
*Virginia Polytechnic Institute and
State University
USA*
Aristotelianism in the 17th century

Professor Allan Arkush
*Judaic Studies Department
Binghamton University
USA*
Mendelssohn, Moses

Professor Richard Arneson
*University of California, San Diego
USA*
Paternalism
Work, philosophy Of

Professor Nicholas Asher
*University of Texas at Austin
USA*
Anaphora
Discourse semantics

Professor E.J. Ashworth
*University of Waterloo
Canada*
Bruno, Giordano
Language, Renaissance
    philosophy of
Lipsius, Justus
Logic, medieval
Logic, Renaissance
Paracelsus (Philippus Aureolus
    Theophrastus Bombastus von
    Hohenheim)
Patrizi da Cherso, Francesco
Paul of Venice
Renaissance philosophy

Dr George N. Atiyeh
*Head, Near East Section, African
and Middle Eastern Division
Library of Congress
USA*
Ibn Massara, Muhammad ibn
    'Abd Allah
al-Sijistani, Abu Sulayman
    Muhammad

Ms Elspeth Attwooll
*Department of Jurisprudence,
School of Law
University of Glasgow
Scotland, UK*
Jhering, Rudolf von
Legal idealism

Professor Robert Audi
*University of Nebraska
USA*
Reasons for belief

Professor Shlomo Avineri
*Faculty of Social Sciences
The Hebrew University of Jerusalem
Israel*
Hess, Moses

Professor Michael Ayers
*Wadham College
University of Oxford
UK*
Burthogge, Richard
Locke, John
Substance

Professor Kent Bach
*San Francisco State University
USA*
Ambiguity
Content, indexical
Content: wide and narrow
Performatives
Speech acts

Professor John B. Bacon
*Department of Traditional and
Modern Philosophy
University of Sydney
Australia*
Logical and mathematical terms,
    glossary of

Professor Neera K. Badhwar
University of Oklahoma
USA
Friendship

Dr Patrick Baert
Fellow and Director of Studies in
Social and Political Sciences
New Hall and King's College
University of Cambridge
UK
Bourdieu, Pierre

Professor Timothy Bahti
Program in Comparative Literature
University of Michigan
USA
De Man, Paul

Professor Annette Baier
Distinguished Service Professor,
Emeritus
University of Pittsburgh
USA
Hume, David

Dr A.J. Baker
Rozelle, New South Wales
Australia
Anderson, John

Professor Judith Baker
Glendon College
York University
Canada
Grice, Herbert Paul

Professor David Bakhurst
Queen's University
Canada
Asmus, Valentin Ferdinandovich
Il'enkov, Eval'd Vasil'evich
Marxist philosophy, Russian and
  Soviet

Professor Thomas Baldwin
Head of the Department of
Philosophy
University of York
UK
Analytical philosophy
McTaggart, John McTaggart Ellis
Merleau-Ponty, Maurice
Moore, George Edward

Professor Terence Ball
Professor of Political Science
University of Minnesota
USA
Green political philosophy
Mill, James

Professor Zenon Bańkowski
Professor of Legal Theory
Centre for Law and Society
University of Edinburgh
Scotland, UK
Kelsen, Hans
Norms, legal

Professor Michael Banton
Professor Emeritus of Sociology
University of Bristol
UK
Race, theories of

Professor Peter Barker
Professor of the History of Science
University of Oklahoma
USA
Hertz, Heinrich Rudolf

Professor Jonathan Barnes
Université de Genève
France
Academy
Antiochus
Arcesilaus
Carneades
Philo of Larissa

Dr Samuel Barnish
Lecturer in the History of the Later
Roman Empire and Early Medieval
Europe
Royal Holloway and Bedford New
College
University of London
UK
Encyclopedists, medieval

Professor Brian Barry
Professor of Political Science
Department of Government
London School of Economics
University of London
UK
Justice
Justice, international

Professor David Basinger
Roberts Wesleyan College
USA
Miracles
Process theism

Professor Kenneth Baynes
State University of New York at
Stony Brook
USA
Habermas, Jürgen

Professor George Bealer
University of Colorado – Boulder
USA
Analyticity
Intensional entities

Professor John Beatty
Department of Ecology, Evolution
and Behavior
University of Minnesota – St Paul
USA
Ecology

Professor Tom L. Beauchamp
Georgetown University
USA
Value judgments in social science

Professor William Bechtel
Philosophy-Neuroscience-
Psychology Program
Washington University
USA
Vitalism

Professor Lawrence C. Becker
William R. Kenan, Jr, Professor in
the Humanities
College of William and Mary
USA
Reciprocity

Dr Barbara G. Beddall
Private Scholar
Pennsylvania
USA
Wallace, Alfred Russel

Professor John Beer
Peterhouse
University of Cambridge
UK
Eliot, George

Professor David Beetham
Department of Politics
University of Leeds
UK
Legitimacy

Professor Frederick Beiser
Indiana University
USA
Cambridge Platonism
Culverwell, Nathaniel
Hamann, Johann Georg
Herder, Johann Gottfried
Humboldt, Wilhelm von
Romanticism, German
Schlegel, Friedrich von

Professor Charles R. Beitz
Dean for Academic Affairs
Bowdoin College
USA
International relations,
    philosophy of

Professor J.L. Bell
University of Western Ontario
Canada
Boolean algebra

Professor Richard Bellamy
Department of Politics
University of Reading
UK
Croce, Benedetto
Gentile, Giovanni
Gramsci, Antonio
Green, Thomas Hill

Professor Mara Beller
Barbara Druss Dibner Professor in
History and Philosophy of Science
The Hebrew University of Jerusalem
Israel
Bohr, Niels
Heisenberg, Werner

Professor Andrew Belsey
Centre for Applied Ethics
University of Wales, Cardiff
UK
Journalism, ethics of

Professor Marvin Belzer
Chair, Department of Philosophy
Bowling Green State University
USA
Deontic logic

Dr Yemima Ben-Menahem
The Hebrew University of Jerusalem
Israel
Putnam, Hilary

Dr Phil Linos Benakis
Athens
Greece
Byzantine philosophy

Professor Ermanno Bencivenga
University of California, Irvine
USA
Free logics

Professor David Benfield
Department of Philosophy and
Religion
Montclair State University
USA
Chisholm, Roderick Milton

Professor Ted Benton
Department of Sociology
University of Essex
UK
Naturalism in social science

Dr Mariateresa Fumagalli Beonio-
Brocchieri
Cattedra di Storia della Filosofia
Medievale
Università degli Studi di Milano
Italy
Durandus of St Pourçain

Professor Robert Bernasconi
Moss Professor of Philosophy
The University of Memphis
USA
Levinas, Emmanuel

Professor J.M. Bernstein
W. Alton Jones Professor of
Philosophy
Vanderbilt University
USA
Adorno, Theodor Wiesengrund
Horkheimer, Max

Professor Christopher J. Berry
Politics Department
University of Glasgow
Scotland, UK
Enlightenment, Scottish
Human nature, science of, in the
    18th Century

Professor María Teresa Bertelloni
Departmento de Humanidades
Universidad de Puerto Rico –
Mayagüez
USA
Existentialist thought in Latin
    America
Phenomenology in Latin America

Professor Mauricio Beuchot
Instituto de Investigaciones
Filológicas
Universidad Nacional Autónoma de
México
Báñez, Domingo

Dr Rajeev Bhargava
Centre for Political Studies
Nehru University
India
Holism and individualism in
    history and social science

Professor Sibajiban Bhattacharyya
Emeritus Professor
Calcutta University
India
Definition, Indian concepts of
God, Indian conceptions of

Dr Joël Biard
Directeur de recherches
Centre National de la Recherche
Scientifique
France
Albert of Saxony
Major, John

Professor Cristina Bicchieri
Professor of Philosophy and Social
and Decision Sciences
Carnegie Mellon University
USA
Decision and game theory

Professor Myriam Bienenstock
Institut de Philosophie
Université de Tours
France
Rosenzweig, Franz

Dr G.M. Bierman
Gonville and Caius College
University of Cambridge
UK
Linear logic

Dr John C. Bigelow
Monash University
Australia
Functionalism in social science
Particulars
Universals

Professor Purushottama Bilimoria
Melbourne University
Australia
Kauṭṭilya
Testimony in Indian philosophy

Professor Anne D. Birdwhistell
Professor of Philosophy and Asian
Civilization
Philosophy and Religion Program
Richard Stockton College of New
Jersey
USA
Lu Xiangshan
Shao Yong

Professor P.B.H. Birks
Regius Professor of Civil Law
All Souls College and the University
of Oxford
UK
Roman law

Dr Alison H. Black
Greenock, Renfrewshire
UK
Wang Fuzhi

Professor Deborah L. Black
University of Toronto
Canada
Aesthetics in Islamic philosophy
Logic in Islamic philosophy

Professor Simon Blackburn
Edna J. Koury Distinguished
Professor of Philosophy
University of North Carolina,
Chapel Hill
USA
Collingwood, Robin George
Communication and intention
Meaning and communication
Projectivism
Supervenience

Professor Patricia A. Blanchette
University of Notre Dame
USA
Realism in the philosophy of
   mathematics

Professor Kalman Bland
Department of Religion
Duke University
USA
Delmedigo, Elijah

Professor Ned Block
Professor of Philosophy and
Psychology
New York University
USA
Holism: mental and semantic
Mind, computational theories of
Semantics, conceptual role

Dr David Bloor
Science Studies Unit
University of Edinburgh
Scotland, UK
Sociology of knowledge

Professor Margaret A. Boden
Professor of Philosophy and
Psychology
University of Sussex
UK
Artificial intelligence

Professor James Bohman
University of St Louis
USA
Systems theory in social science

Professor Sissela Bok
Distinguished Fellow
Harvard Center for Population and
Development Studies
USA
Truthfulness

Professor John Bolt
Professor of Systematic Theology
Calvin Theological Seminary
USA
Dooyeweerd, Herman

Dr Pierrette Bonet
Education Nationale
Université Paris IV (Paris-
Sorbonne)
France
Ravaisson-Mollien, Jean-Gaspard
   Félix Lacher

Professor Laurence BonJour
University of Washington
USA
Knowledge and justification,
   coherence theory of

Professor Jack A. Bonsor
St Patrick's Seminary
USA
Rahner, Karl

Professor Patrizia Borsellino
Facoltà di Guiresprudensa
Università degli Studi di Milano
Italy
Bobbio, Norberto

Dr E.P. Bos
Facultat der Wijsbegeerte
Rijksuniversiteit Leiden
Netherlands
Marsilius of Inghen

Mr Curtis V. Bostick
Division for Late Medieval and
Reformation Studies
University of Arizona
USA
Hus, Jan

Professor Aryeh Botwinick
Professor of Political Science
Temple University
USA
Theology, Rabbinic

Professor Andrew Bowie
Anglia Polytechnic University
UK
Schelling, Friedrich Wilhelm
  Joseph von

Professor Peter J. Bowler
Department of Social Anthropology
The Queen's University of Belfast
Northern Ireland
Darwin, Charles Robert

Professor Bernard Boxill
University of North Carolina,
Chapel Hill
USA
Affirmative action

Dr Nicholas Boyle
Magdalene College
University of Cambridge
UK
Goethe, Johann Wolfgang von

Dr David Braddon-Mitchell
Australian National University
Behaviourism, analytic
Belief

Associate Professor James Bradley
Memorial University of
Newfoundland
Canada
Whitehead, Alfred North

Professor David Braine
Old Aberdeen
Scotland, UK
Grace
Negative theology
Sacraments

Professor Dr Jozef Brams
Hoger Instituut voor Wijsbegeerte
Belgium
Translators

Professor Peg Brand
Department of Philosophy/
Women's Studies Program
Indiana University
USA
Langer, Susanne Katherina
  Knauth

Professor R. Bracht Branham
Professor of Classics and
Comparative Literature
Emory University
USA
Cynics
Diogenes of Sinope
Lucian

Professor Stephen E. Braude
University of Maryland, Baltimore
County
USA
Paranormal phenomena

Professor David Braybrooke
Centennial Commission Chair in the
Liberal Arts
Professor of Government and
Professor of Philosophy
University of Texas at Austin
USA
Social science, contemporary
  philosophy of

Professor Daniel Breazeale
University of Kentucky
USA
Fichte, Johann Gottlieb

Professor Elizabeth Bredeck
Lecturer in German
Department of Literature
University of California, San Diego
USA
Mauthner, Fritz

Professor Andrew Brennan
University of Western Australia
Environmental ethics

Mr Arthur Brittan
Department of Sociology
University of York
UK
Symbolic interactionism

Professor Thomas Brockelman
Le Moyne College
USA
Lacan, Jacques

Dr Jens Brockmeier
Fachbereich Erziehungswissenschaft
Freie Universität Berlin
Germany
Wundt, Wilhelm

Professor Dr Johannes Bronkhorst
Section de langues et civilisations
orientales
Université de Lausanne
Switzerland
Bhartṛhari
Language, Indian theories of
Patañjali

Professor Bruce W. Brower
Tulane University
USA
Contextualism, epistemological

Dr Beverley Brown
Chair in Law
University of East London
UK
Law, philosophy of
Legal discourse

Professor Charlotte R. Brown
Illinois Wesleyan University
USA
Common-sense ethics
Paley, William
Wollaston, William

Professor John H. Brown
University of Maryland
USA
Art, abstract
Beauty

Professor Stuart Brown
The Open University
UK
Helmont, Franciscus Mercurius van

Professor Stephen F. Brown
Department of Theology
Boston College
USA
Chatton, Walter
Clarembald of Arras
Gregory of Rimini
Matthew of Aquasparta
Richard of Middleton

Professor Anthony Brueckner
University of California, Santa
Barbara
USA
Deductive closure principle

Professor Jacques Brunschwig
Professor Emeritus
Université de Paris I
France
Anaxarchus
Pyrrho
Timon

Mr Christopher Bryant
Ivybridge, Devon
UK
Brown, Thomas

Dr Thomas L. Bryson
Associate Executive Director
American Academy of Religion
USA
Ramakrishna movement

Dr Jan K. Brzezinski
University of Toronto
Canada
Gauḍīya Vaiṣṇavism
Rāmānuja

Professor Jeffrey Bub
University of Maryland
USA
Quantum measurement problem

Professor Allen Buchanan
Joel Feinberg Professor of
Philosophy
University of Wisconsin – Madison
USA
Community and
    communitarianism

Professor Malcolm Budd
University College, University of
London
UK
Aesthetic attitude
Aesthetics
Art, value of
Formalism in art

Dr Bernd Buldt
Universität Konstanz
Germany
Infinitary logics

Professor Robert W. Burch
Texas A&M University
USA
Royce, Josiah

Professor John P. Burgess
Princeton University
USA
Constructible universe
Forcing
Set theory

Professor Dr Walter Burkert
Klassisch-Philologisches seminar der
Universität Zürich
Switzerland
Orphism

Dr Charles Burnett
The Warburg Institute
University of London
UK
Islamic philosophy: transmission
    into Western Europe

Mr M.F. Burnyeat
All Souls College
University of Oxford
UK
Dissoi logoi

Professor David Burrell
Theodore M. Hesburgh Professor in
Arts and Letters
University of Notre Dame
USA
Causality and necessity in Islamic
    thought
Platonism in Islamic philosophy

Professor Mark S. Burrows
Andover Newton Theological School
USA
Gerson, Jean

Professor John Bussanich
University of New Mexico
USA
Nemesius
Suso, Henry
Tauler, John
Themistius
Ulrich of Strasbourg

Professor Robert E. Buswell, Jr
Department of East Asian
Languages and Cultures
University of California, Los
Angeles
USA
Chinul
Ûisang

Dr Jeremy Butterfield
All Souls College
University of Oxford
UK
Determinism and indeterminism

Professor Robert E. Butts
Professor Emeritus
Talbot College
University of Western Ontario
Canada
Science, 19th century philosophy of

Professor José Ignacio Cabezón
Associate Professor of Theology
Iliff School of Theology
USA
mKhas grub dge legs dpal bzang po

Dr Caroline Cahm
Southsea, Hampshire
UK
Kropotkin, Pëtr Alekseevich

Dr Norman Calder
Department of Middle Eastern
Studies
University of Manchester
UK
Law, Islamic philosophy of

Mr Robert R. Calder
University of Strathclyde
UK
Kemp Smith, Norman

Professor Craig Calhoun
Department of Sociology
New York University
USA
Taylor, Charles

Professor Alex Callinicos
Department of Politics
University of York
UK
Althusser, Louis Pierre
Lukács, Georg
Marcuse, Herbert
Trotsky, Leon

Professor Cristian S. Calude
Director, The Centre for Discrete
Mathematics and Theoretical
Computer Science
University of Auckland
New Zealand
Computability and information

Professor Keith Campbell
University of Sydney
Australia
Epiphenomenalism

Professor Stewart Candlish
University of Western Australia
Bradley, Francis Herbert
Mind, bundle theory of
Private language argument

Dr Margaret Canovan
Reader in Politics
University of Keele
UK
Totalitarianism

Professor Mirella Capozzi
Dipartimento di filosofia e scienze
sociali
Università di Siena
Italy
Logic in the 17th and 18th
  centuries

Professor Claudia Falconer Card
University of Wisconsin
USA
Rectification and remainders

Professor Allen Carlson
University of Alberta
Canada
Nature, aesthetic appreciation of

Professor David Carroll
Department of French and Italian
University of California – Irvine
USA
Lyotard, Jean-François

Professor Nancy Cartwright
Department of Philosophy, Logic
and Scientific Method
London School of Economics
University of London
UK
Causation
Neurath, Otto

Professor Terrell Carver
Department of Politics
University of Bristol
UK
Engels, Friedrich

Dr Roberto Casati
Centre National de la Recherche
Scientifique
France
Dreaming

Dr Jordi Cat
Centre for Philosophy of Natural
and Social Sciences
London School of Economics
University of London
UK
Neurath, Otto
Unity of science

Dr Jeremy Catto
Oriel College
University of Oxford
UK
Wyclif, John

Professor Horacio Cerutti-
Guldberg
Universidad Nacional Autónoma de
México
and Formerly, President of
Asociacion Filosofia de Mexico
Liberation philosophy
Mexico, philosophy in

Professor Yông-ho Ch'oe
Department of History
University of Hawaii
USA
Chông Yagyong (Tasan)
Sirhak
Tonghak

Professor Henry Chadwick
Oxford
UK
Boethius, Anicius Manlius
  Severinus
Clement of Alexandria

Professor Ruth Chadwick
Head of Centre and Professor of
Moral Philosophy
Centre for Professional Ethics
University of Central Lancashire
UK
Genetics and ethics
Professional ethics

Professor Agnes Chalier
Cambridge
UK
Wang Chong

Dr J.A.I. Champion
Department of History
Royal Holloway College
University of London
UK
Toland, John

Professor Leo S. Chang
Professor of Political Science
Regis College
USA
Han Feizi
Legalist philosophy, Chinese

Professor Tina Chanter
University of Memphis
USA
Irigaray, Luce
Kristeva, Julia

Dr Tim Chappell
University of Manchester
UK
Utilitarianism

Professor Christopher Cherniak
Committee on History and
Philosophy of Science
University of Maryland
USA
Rational beliefs

Professor Catherine Chevalley
Université François Rabelais
France
Helmholtz, Hermann von

Professor Roderick M. Chisholm
Brown University
USA
Brentano, Franz Clemens
Commonsensism

Dr Gaetano Chiurazzi
l'Università di Torino
Italy
Italy, philosophy in

Professor Sungtaek Cho
Program in Korean Studies
Department of Comparative Studies
State University of New York at
Stony Brook
USA
Buddhist philosophy, Korean

Dr Youssef Choueiri
Department of Arabic and Islamic
Studies
University of Exeter
UK
Islamic Fundamentalism

Mr Simon Christmas
Gonville and Caius College
University of Cambridge
UK
Intensionality

Dr Emilios A. Christodoulidis
Law Faculty
University of Edinburgh
Scotland, UK
Dworkin, Ronald

Professor Maudemarie Clark
Department of Philosophy and
Religion
Colgate University
USA
Nietzsche, Friedrich

Professor C.A.J. Coady
University of Melbourne
Australia
Australia, philosophy in
Testimony
Violence

Professor Nino B. Cocchiarella
Indiana University
USA
Property theory
Theory of types

Professor Lorraine Code
York University
Canada
Feminist epistemology

Professor Jean L. Cohen
Professor of Political Science
Columbia University
USA
Civil society

Professor Richard J. Cohen
Associate Director
Department of South Asia Regional
Studies
University of Pennsylvania
USA
Vallabhācārya

Professor Stewart Cohen
Arizona State University
USA
Scepticism

Professor Ted Cohen
University of Chicago
USA
Artistic taste

Professor Dan Cohn-Sherbok
Department of Theology and
Religious Studies
University of Wales
UK
Bible, Hebrew

Professor Jules L. Coleman
Yale Law School
USA
Law, economic approach to

Professor Marcia L. Colish
Department of History
Oberlin College
USA
Lombard, Peter

Mr Andrew Collier
University of Southampton
UK
Critical realism

Dr Finn Collin
Department of Education,
Philosophy and Rhetoric
University of Copenhagen
Denmark
Schütz, Alfred

Professor Gary L. Comstock
Religious Studies Program and
Bioethics Program
Iowa State University
USA
Agricultural ethics

Professor Earl Conee
University of Rochester
USA
Memory, epistemology of
Normative epistemology

Professor Tom Conley
Department of Romance Languages
Harvard University
USA
Certeau, Michel de

Professor Verena Andermatt
Conley
Committee on Degrees in Literature
Harvard University
USA
Cixous, Hélène

Dr Alessandro D. Conti
La Maddalena
Italy
Kilwardby, Robert

Professor Francis H. Cook
Associate Professor Emeritus
Department of Religious Studies
University of California, Riverside
USA
Fazang

Professor David E. Cooper
University of Durham
UK
Existentialist ethics
Marcel, Gabriel

Dr John Cooper
Faculty of Oriental Studies
University of Cambridge
UK
al-Dawani, Jalal al-Din
Mulla Sadra (Sadr al-Din
  Muhammad al-Shirazi)
al-Razi, Fakhr al-Din
al-Sabzawari, al-Hajj Mulla Hadi
al-Suhrawardi, Shihab al-Din
  Yahya
al-Tusi, Khwajah Nasir

Professor John M. Cooper
Princeton University
USA
Owen, Gwilym Ellis Lane
Socrates

Professor Charles A. Corr
Department of Philosophical
Studies
Southern Illinois University at
Edwardsville
USA
Wolff, Christian

Professor Roger Cotterrell
Faculty of Laws
Queen Mary and Westfield College,
University of London
UK
Social theory and law

Professor John Cottingham
University of Reading
UK
Impartiality

Mr L.S. Cousins
Formerly Senior Lecturer in
Comparative Religion
University of Manchester
UK
Buddha
Nirvāṇa

Professor Fiona Cowie
Division of Humanities and Social
Sciences
California Institute of Technology
USA
Language, innateness of

Professor Collett Cox
Department of Asian Languages and
Literature
University of Washington
USA
Buddhism, Ābidharmika schools of

Dr Edward Craig
Churchill College
University of Cambridge
UK
Fatalism
Metaphysics
Monism
Ontology
Pluralism
Private states and language
Realism and antirealism
Relativism
Solipsism

Dr Tim Crane
University College, University of
London
UK
Content, non-conceptual
Intentionality

Professor Richard Creath
Arizona State University
USA
Carnap, Rudolf

Professor Mark Crimmins
University of Michigan
USA
Language, philosophy of
Semantics

Dr Roger Crisp
St Anne's College
University of Oxford
UK
Ethics
Fact/value distinction
Moral particularism
Utilitarianism
Virtue ethics

Professor David A. Crocker
Senior Research Scholar
Institute for Philosophy and Public
Policy
School of Public Affairs
University of Maryland
USA
Development ethics

Professor Donald A. Crosby
Colorado State University
USA
Nihilism

Dr George Crowder
Department of Politics
Flinders University
Australia
Anarchism

Dr Paul Crowther
Corpus Christi College
University of Oxford
UK
Sublime, the

Professor A.S. Cua
Professor Emeritus
The Catholic University of America
USA
Confucian philosophy, Chinese
Xunzi

Professor Jonathan Culler
Professor of English and
Comparative Literature
Cornell University
USA
Structuralism

Dr Garrett Cullity
Department of Moral Philosophy
University of St Andrews
Scotland, UK
Moral judgment

Professor Randall R. Curren
University of Rochester
USA
Education, history of philosophy of
Education, philosophy of

Professor Gregory Currie
Flinders University of South
Australia
Australia
Art works, ontology of
Artistic forgery
Film, aesthetics of
Narrative
Photography, aesthetics of

Professor James T. Cushing
Department of Physics
University of Notre Dame
USA
Conservation principles
Electrodynamics

Professor Andrew Cutrofello
Loyola University of Chicago
USA
Derrida, Jacques

Professor Jan Czerkawski
Department of History of Polish
Philosophy
Catholic University of Lublin
Poland
Poland, philosophy in

Professor Hamid Dabashi
Department of Middle East
Languages and Cultures
Columbia University
USA
Mir Damad, Muhammad Baqir

Professor Thorild Dahlquist
Uppsala University
Sweden
Hägerström, Axel Anders Theodor

Dr Chris Daly
Keele University
UK
Natural kinds

Professor Jonathan Dancy
Reading University
UK
Moral realism

Professor Lindley Darden
University of Maryland, College
Park
USA
Genetics

Professor Stephen Darwall
University of Michigan
USA
Price, Richard

Dr George Davie
Reader Emeritus
University of Edinburgh
Scotland, UK
Kemp Smith, Norman

Dr Stephen Davies
University of Auckland
New Zealand
Art, definition of
Art, performing
Artistic expression

Professor Michael Davis
Center for the Study of Ethics in the
Professions
Illinois Institute of Technology
USA
Engineering and ethics

Professor Stephen T. Davis
Claremont McKenna College
USA
Eschatology

Professor Wayne A. Davis
Georgetown University
USA
Implicature

Professor John W. Dawson, Jr
Professor of Mathematics
Pennsylvania State University
USA
Gödel, Kurt

Dr Avner de-Shalit
Department of Political Science
The Hebrew University
Israel
Future generations, obligations to

Professor Peter Dear
Department of History
Cornell University
USA
Mersenne, Marin

Professor David DeGrazia
George Washington University
USA
Suffering

Professor C.F. Delaney
University of Notre Dame
USA
Knowledge, tacit

Professor William A. Dembski
Research Fellow, Center for the
Renewal of Science and Culture
Discovery Institute
Seattle, Washington
USA
Randomness

Professor Nicholas Dent
University of Birmingham
UK
Conscience
Rousseau, Jean-Jacques

Mr Nicholas Denyer
Trinity College
University of Cambridge
UK
Diodorus Cronus
Philo the Dialectician

Dr Madhav M. Deshpande
*Professor of Sanskrit and
Linguistics
Department of Asian Languages and
Cultures
University of Michigan
USA*
Interpretation, Indian theories of
Meaning, Indian theories of

Professor Michael Detlefsen
*University of Notre Dame
USA*
Gödel's theorems
Hilbert's programme and
  formalism
Logical and mathematical terms,
  glossary of
Mathematics, foundations of

Professor Max Deutscher
*School of History, Philosophy and
Politics
Macquarie University
Australia*
Le Doeuff, Michèle
Memory

Professor Harry Deutsch
*Illinois State University
USA*
Demonstratives and indexicals

Professor Michael Devitt
*University of Maryland
USA*
Reference

Dr Peter Dews
*University of Essex
UK*
Communicative rationality

Professor George di Giovanni
*McGill University
Canada*
Jacobi, Friedrich Heinrich
Reinhold, Karl Leonhard

Professor Michael R. Dietrich
*History and Philosophy of Science
Program
University of California, Davis
USA*
Molecular biology

Professor Mary G. Dietz
*Department of Political Science
University of Minnesota
USA*
Machiavelli, Niccolò

Professor John Dillon
*Regius Professor of Greek
School of Classics
Trinity College, University of Dublin
Ireland*
Alcinous
Apuleius
Calcidius
Celsus
Damascius
Numenius
Platonism, Early and Middle
Plutarch of Chaeronea
Speusippus
Xenocrates

Professor Randall R. Dipert
*Department of English/Philosophy
U.S. Military Academy
USA*
Logic in the 19th century
Logic machines and diagrams

Professor Idit Dobbs-Weinstein
*Vanderbilt University
USA*
Abravanel, Judah ben Isaac

Mr Peter Dolník
*University of Sydney
Australia*
Church, Alonzo

Dr Frank Döring
*University of Cincinnati
USA*
Counterfactual conditionals

Professor William C. Dowling
*Department of English
Rutgers University
USA*
American philosophy in the 18th
  and 19th centuries

Professor Stephen M. Downes
*University of Utah
USA*
Constructivism

Professor John P. Doyle
*St Louis University
USA*
Collegium Conimbricense
Fonseca, Pedro da
John of St Thomas
Soto, Domingo de
Suárez, Francisco
Toletus, Franciscus

Professor James Dreier
*Brown University
USA*
Stevenson, Charles Leslie

Professor Fred Dretske
*Stanford University
USA*
Information theory and
  epistemology

Professor Georges B.J. Dreyfus
*Department of Religion
Williams College
USA*
rGyal tshab dar ma rin chen
Sa skya paṇḍita

Professor Shadia B. Drury
*Department of Political Science
University of Calgary
Canada*
Strauss, Leo

Professor R.A. Duff
*University of Stirling
Scotland, UK*
Crime and punishment
Responsibility

Professor Stephen D. Dumont
*University of Toronto
Canada*
Duns Scotus, John

Dr Francis Dunlop
*Honorary Lecturer
School of Economics and Social
Studies
University of East Anglia
UK*
Scheler, Max Ferdinand

Dr Robert Dunn
University of Wollongong
Australia
Intention

Mr John Dunne
Research Fellow
Section de langues et civilisations
orientales
Université de Lausanne
Switzerland
Nominalism, Buddhist doctrine of

Professor Edwin M. Duval
Department of French
Yale University
USA
Rabelais, François

Dr Neil Duxbury
Faculty of Law
University of Manchester
UK
Frank, Jerome
Legal realism

Professor David Ludovic
Dyzenhaus
Associate Professor of Law and
Philosophy
Faculty of Law
University of Toronto
Canada
Schmitt, Carl

Dr Patricia A. Easton
The Claremont Graduate School
USA
Desgabets, Robert
Le Grand, Antoine

Professor Marcia Eaton
University of Minnesota
USA
Aesthetic concepts

Dr Roger Eatwell
Reader in European Politics
University of Bath
UK
Fascism

Dr Sten Ebbesen
Institute for Greek and Latin
University of Copenhagen
Denmark
Averroism
Boethius of Dacia
Brito, Radulphus
Language, medieval theories of

Professor Paul Edwards
Professor Emeritus
Brooklyn College, City University of
New York
USA
Suicide, ethics of

Professor Frances Egan
Rutgers University
USA
Vision

Dr Abdelwahab El-Affendi
London
UK
Islamic theology

Professor Catherine Z. Elgin
Lexington, Massachusetts
USA
Goodman, Nelson

Professor Rachel Elior
Professor of Jewish Mysticism
Department of Jewish Thought
The Hebrew University of Jerusalem
Israel
Hasidism

Professor David Ellenson
I.H. and Anna Grancell Professor of
Jewish Religious Thought
Jewish Institute of Religion
Hebrew Union College
USA
Kaplan, Mordecai

Professor Lester Embree
Florida Atlantic University
USA
Phenomenological movement

Professor Caryl Emerson
Slavic Languages and Literatures
Department
Princeton University
USA
Mamardashvili, Merab
  Konstantinovich

Professor Roger L. Emerson
Professor of History
University of Western Ontario
Canada
Home, Henry (Lord Kames)

Professor Kent Emery, Jr
Medieval Institute
University of Notre Dame
USA
Denys the Carthusian
Richard of St Victor
Thomas à Kempis

Professor Eyjólfur Kjalar Emilsson
University of Oslo
Norway
Plotinus

Professor Dorothy Emmet
Professor Emeritus
University of Manchester
UK
Alexander, Samuel
Processes

Professor H. Tristram
Engelhardt, Jr
Department of Medicine, Baylor
College of Medicine
and Department of Philosophy, Rice
University
USA
Medicine, philosophy of

Professor Pascal Engel
Université de Caen
and CREA, École Polytechnique
France
Propositions, sentences and
  statements

Professor Dr Michael Erler
Institut für Klassische Philologie
Universität Würzburg
Germany
Diogenes of Oenoanda
Lucretius
Philodemus

Professor Elizabeth Deeds Ermarth
Saintsbury Professor, English
Department
University of Edinburgh
Scotland, UK
Postmodernism

Professor Stephen L. Esquith
Michigan State University
USA
Slavery

Dr Juan Carlos Torchia Estrada
Former Executive Secretary for
Education, Science and Culture
Organization of American States
Washington, DC
USA
Argentina, philosophy in

Professor Girard J. Etzkorn
Professor Emeritus
The Franciscan Institute
St Bonaventure University
USA
Marston, Roger
Pecham, John

Dr Colin Evans
Birkbeck College, University of
London
UK
Taine, Hippolyte-Adolphe

Professor C. Stephen Evans
Calvin College
USA
Existentialist theology

Dr Mark Evans
Department of Political Theory and
Government
University of Wales, Swansea
UK
Self-realization

Professor C.W.F. Everitt
W.W. Hansen Experimental Physics
Laboratory
Stanford University
USA
Maxwell, James Clerk

Professor Regis A. Factor
Department of Goverment
University of South Florida
USA
Weber, Max

Professor Majid Fakhry
Georgetown University
USA
Ethics in Islamic philosophy
Greek philosophy: impact on
    Islamic philosophy

Professor K.T. Fann
Atkinson College
Canada
Johnson, Alexander Bryan

Ms Claire Farrimond
Trinity College
University of Cambridge
UK
Medieval philosophy, Russian

Professor John L. Farthing
Professor of Religion and Classical
Languages
Hendrix College
USA
Biel, Gabriel

Professor Susan L. Feagin
University of Missouri – Kansas
City
USA
Tragedy

Professor R.J. Fechner
Professor of History
Adrian College
USA
Witherspoon, John

Professor Laurent Fedi
Douai, France
Renouvier, Charles Bernard

Professor Ronald J. Feenstra
Heritage Professor of Systematic
and Philosophical Theology
Calvin Theological Seminary
USA
Calvin, John
Reprobation

Professor Solomon Feferman
Department of Mathematics
Stanford University
USA
Ordinal logics

Professor Joel Feinberg
University of Arizona
USA
Coercion
Freedom and liberty

Professor Fred Feldman
University of Massachusetts at
Amherst
USA
Death

Professor Richard Feldman
University of Rochester
USA
Charity, principle of
Epistemology and ethics

Professor Seymour Feldman
Rutgers University
USA
Crescas, Hasdai
Gersonides

Professor Paul B. Fenton
Département des études arabes et
orientales
Université de Paris IV – Sorbonne
France
Ibn Ezra, Moses ben Jacob
Maimonides, Abraham ben Moses

Professor Peter Fenves
Department of German
Northwestern University
USA
Alterity and identity, postmodern
    theories of
Nancy, Jean-Luc

Professor Arthur Fine
Northwestern University
USA
Bell's theorem
Einstein, Albert
Fictionalism
Scientific realism and antirealism

Professor John Finnis
Professor of Law and Legal
Philosophy
and Fellow of University College
University of Oxford
UK
and Biolchini Professor of Law
University of Notre Dame
USA
Natural law

Professor Menachem Fisch
The Cohn Institute for the History
and Philosophy of Science and Ideas
Tel Aviv University
Israel
Whewell, William

Professor Owen Flanagan
Professor of Philosophy,
Psychology, and Neurobiology
Adjunct Professor in the Graduate
Program in Literature
and Chair of Philosophy
Duke University
USA
Moral development
Skinner, Burrhus Frederick

Professor Thomas P. Flint
University of Notre Dame
USA
Omniscience

Dr Luciano Floridi
Wolfson College
University of Oxford
UK
Fardella, Michelangelo
Huet, Pierre-Daniel

Professor Richard Foley
Rutgers University
USA
Justification, epistemic

Professor Dagfinn Føllesdal
University of Oslo, Norway
Stanford University, USA
Husserl, Edmund
Scandinavia, philosophy in

Professor Graeme Forbes
Tulane University
USA
Logic, philosophy of
Proper names

Dr J.D. Ford
Gonville and Caius College
University of Cambridge
UK
Grotius, Hugo
Pufendorf, Samuel
Sovereignty

Professor Peter Forrest
University of New England
Australia
Mereology
Quantum logic

Professor Eckart Förster
Stanford University
USA
Beck, Jacob Sigismund

Professor Andrew O. Fort
Department of Religion
Texas Christian University
USA
Śaṅkara

Dr Eli Franco
Institut für Kultur und Geschichte
Indiens und Tibets
Universität Hamburg
Germany
Gautama, Akṣapāda
Materialism, Indian school of
Nyāya-Vaiśeṣika

Professor Åke Frändberg
Faculty of Law
Uppsala University
Sweden
Legal concepts

Dr Daniel Frank
Porter Fellow in Medieval Jewish
History
Oxford Centre for Hebrew and
Jewish Studies
UK
Karaism

Professor Daniel H. Frank
Professor of Philosophy
and Director of Judaic Studies
Program
University of Kentucky
USA
Albo, Joseph
Ibn Gabirol, Solomon
Political philosophy in classical
    Islam

Professor Allan Franklin
Department of Physics
University of Colorado
USA
Mechanics, Aristotelian

Professor Julian H. Franklin
Professor Emeritus of Political
Sciences
Columbia University
USA
Bodin, Jean

Professor Paul Franks
Assistant Professor of Philosophy
and Adjunct Member of the Jewish
Studies Program Faculty
Indiana University, Bloomington
USA
German idealism
Maimon, Salomon

Dr Robert L. Frazier
Christ Church
University of Oxford
UK
Duty
Intuitionism in ethics

Professor Alfred J. Freddoso
University of Notre Dame
USA
Molina, Luis de
Molinism

Dr Michael Freeden
Mansfield College
University of Oxford
UK
Ideology

Professor Samuel Freeman
University of Pennsylvania
USA
Contractarianism
Rawls, John

Professor R.G. Frey
Bowling Green State University
USA
Bioethics
Butler, Joseph

Professor Michael Friedman
Department of History and
Philosophy of Science
Indiana University
USA
Logical positivism

Dr Ulf Friedrichsdorf
Fakultät für Mathematik
Universität Konstanz
Germany
Dynamic logics

Dr Delia Frigessi
Torino
Italy
Cattaneo, Carlo

Professor David Frisby
Department of Sociology
University of Glasgow
Scotland, UK
Simmel, Georg

Dr André Fuhrmann
Universität Konstanz
Germany
Non-monotonic logic

Professor Richard Fumerton
University of Iowa
USA
Knowledge by acquaintance and
    description
Phenomenalism

Dr Jason Gaiger
Art History Department
The Open University
UK
Lebensphilosophie

Dr Gedeon Gál
The Franciscan Institute
St Bonaventure University
USA
Alexander of Hales

Mr Roger Gallie
University of Nottingham
UK
Reid, Thomas

Professor C.R. Gallistel
Department of Psychology
University of California, Los
Angeles
USA
Behaviourism, methodological and
    scientific
Learning

Dr Andrá Gallois
University of Queensland
Australia
De re/de dicto
Sense-data

Dr Jonardon Ganeri
University of Nottingham
UK
Gadādhara

Professor Daniel Garber
Lawrence Kimpton Distinguished
Service Professor in Philosophy
University of Chicago
USA
Clauberg, Johannes
Descartes, René
Henricus Regius
Leibniz, Gottfried Wilhelm

Mr Patrick Gardiner
Magdalen College
University of Oxford
UK
Kierkegaard, Søren Aabye

Dr Brian Garrett
Australian National University
Personal identity
Persons

Professor James W. Garson
University of Houston
USA
Intensional logics

Professor Eugene Garver
Regents Professor of Philosophy
St John's University
USA
Rhetoric

Professor Tom Gaskill
Southern Illinois University at
Carbondale
USA
al-'Amiri, Abu'l Hasan
    Muhammad ibn Yusuf

Dr Stephen Gaukroger
University of Sydney
Australia
Clarke, Samuel
Fludd, Robert

Professor Charles Genequand
Faculté des Lettres
Université de Genève
Switzerland
al-Tawhidi, Abu Hayyan

Professor Vincent Geoghegan
Department of Politics
The Queen's University of Belfast
Northern Ireland
Bloch, Ernst Simon

Professor Alexander George
Amherst College
USA
Frege, Gottlob

Professor Raymond Geuss
University of Cambridge
UK
Critical theory

Dr John Gibbins
University of Teeside
UK
Grote, John

Professor Roger F. Gibson
Washington University
USA
Radical translation and radical
  interpretation

Professor Ronald N. Giere
University of Minnesota
USA
Naturalized philosophy of science

Professor Margaret Gilbert
University of Connecticut
USA
Social norms

Mr Didier Gil
Le Comte de Nice
France
Boutroux, Émile

Professor Brendan S. Gillon
Department of Linguistics
McGill University
Canada
Inference, Indian theories of
Negative facts in classical Indian
  philosophy

Professor Clark Glymour
Valtz Family Professor of
Philosophy
University of California, San Diego
USA
Learning

Professor Peter Godfrey-Smith
Stanford University
USA
Fodor, Jerry Alan
Semantics, teleological

Dr Stephen J. Goldberg
Department of Art
University of Hawaii
USA
Aesthetics, Chinese

Dr Mark Goldie
Churchill College
University of Cambridge
UK
Harrington, James

Professor Alan H. Goldman
University of Miami
USA
Artistic interpretation

Professor Alvin I. Goldman
Regents Professor
University of Arizona
USA
Reliabilism

Dr M.M. Goldsmith
Victoria University of Wellington
New Zealand
and formerly Professor of Political
Theory at University of Exeter
UK
Mandeville, Bernard

Dr José Luis Gómez-Martínez
Department of Romance Languages
and Literatures
University of Georgia
USA
Literature, philosophy in Latin
  American

Dr David C. Gooding
Department of Psychology
Faculty of Humanities and Social
Sciences
University of Bath
UK
Thought experiments

Dr L.E. Goodman
Vanderbilt University
USA
Halevi, Judah
Ibn Paquda, Bahya
Jewish philosophy
Maimonides, Moses
Saadiah Gaon

Professor Russell B. Goodman
University of New Mexico
USA
American philosophy in the 18th
  and 19th centuries
Emerson, Ralph Waldo

Professor Peter Goodrich
Corporation of London Professor
of Law
Birkbeck College, University of
London
UK
Legal hermeneutics
Selden, John

Professor Alison Gopnik
Department of Psychology
University of California, Berkeley
USA
Cognition, infant
Piaget, Jean

Professor William M. Gordon
School of Law
University of Glasgow
Scotland, UK
Bartolus of Sassoferrato (or
  Saxoferrato)

Mr Justin Gosling
St Edmund Hall
University of Oxford
UK
Hedonism

Dr H.B. Gottschalk
School of Classics
University of Leeds
UK
Heraclides of Pontus

Professor James Gouinlock
Emory University
USA
Dewey, John

Professor Timothy Gould
Metropolitan State College of
Denver
USA
Thoreau, Henry David

Dr Barry Gower
University of Durham
UK
Oken, Lorenz

Professor Daniel W. Graham
Brigham Young University
USA
Vlastos, Gregory

Professor Gordon Graham
*Regius Professor of Moral
Philosophy*
King's College
University of Aberdeen
Scotland, UK
History, philosophy of

Professor I. Grattan-Guinness
*Professor in the History of
Mathematics and Logic*
*School of Mathematics and
Statistics*
Middlesex University
UK
Analysis, philosophical issues in

Dr Tim S. Gray
Department of Politics
University of Newcastle upon Tyne
UK
Spencer, Herbert

Professor Leslie Green
York University
Canada
Authority
Power

Professor Mitchell Green
University of Virginia
USA
Imperative logic

Professor Kent Greenawalt
School of Law
Columbia University
USA
Civil disobedience

Professor Mario A. Di Gregorio
Dipartimento di Culture Comparate
Università di L'Aquila
Italy
Huxley, Thomas Henry

Professor Peter N. Gregory
Program for the Study of Religion
*University of Illinois at Urbana-
Champaign*
USA
Awakening of faith in Mahāyāna
Zongmi

Professor Philip T. Grier
Dickinson College
USA
Il'in, Ivan Aleksandrovich

Professor David Ray Griffin
Professor of Philosophy of Religion
*Claremont School of Theology and
The Claremont Graduate School*
USA
Process philosophy

Professor J.P. Griffin
*White's Professor of Moral
Philosophy*
Corpus Christi College
University of Oxford
UK
Happiness

Professor Nicholas Griffin
McMaster Univerity
Canada
Neutral monism
Russell, Bertrand Arthur William

Dr Allen C. Guelzo
*Grace F. Kea Professor of American
History*
Department of History
Eastern College
USA
Pietism

Dr Rita Guerlac
Independent Scholar
Ithaca, New York
USA
Vives, Juan Luis

Professor Charles B. Guignon
University of Vermont
USA
Existentialism

Professor Ingemund Gullvåg
Professor Emeritus
*Norwegian University of Science
and Technology*
Norway
Næss, Arne

Professor Colin Gunton
*Department of Theology and
Religious Studies*
*King's College, University of
London*
UK
Atonement

Professor Anil Gupta
Rudy Professor of Philosophy
Indiana University
USA
Tarski's definition of truth

Professor G. Gutheil
Skidmore College
USA
Cogntive development

Professor Gary Gutting
University of Notre Dame
USA
Foucault, Michel
French philosophy of science
Post-structuralism
Post-structuralism in the social
    sciences

Professor Paul Guyer
*Florence R.C. Murray Professor in
the Humanities*
University of Pennsylvania
USA
Kant, Immanuel

Professor Knud Haakonssen
Boston University
USA
Cumberland, Richard
Smith, Adam
Thomasius (Thomas), Christian

Professor Dr Alexander Haardt
Ruhr-Universität Bochum
Germany
Shpet, Gustav Gustavovich

Dr Ralph Häfner
*Fachrichtung Geschichte der
Philosophie und der
Geisteswissenschaften*
Freie Universität Berlin
Germany
Jungius, Joachim

Professor Roger Haight
Weston Jesuit School of Theology
USA
Liberation theology

Professor Theodore Hailperin
Mathematics Department
Lehigh University
USA
Boole, George

Dr Vinit Haksar
University of Edinburgh
Scotland, UK
Moral agents

Professor Wilhelm Halbfass
Professor of Indian Philosophy
Department of Asian and Middle
Eastern Studies
University of Pennsylvania
USA
Karma and rebirth, Indian
    conceptions of

Professor John J. Haldane
Department of Moral Philosophy
University of St Andrews
Scotland, UK
Architecture, aesthetics of
Ferrier, James Frederick
Thomism

Professor Bob Hale
University of Glasgow
Scotland, UK
Abstract objects

Professor David L. Hall
University of Texas at El Paso
USA
Chinese Philosophy
Dao
Daoist Philosophy
De
Qi
Tian
Xin (heart and mind)
Xing
You-Wu
Zhi

Dr Barry Hallen
Fellow
W.E.B. Du Bois Institute
Harvard University
USA
Aesthetics, African
Yoruba epistemology

Professor Ilpo Halonen
University of Helsinki
Finland
Epistemic logic

Professor G.M. Hamburg
Professor of History
University of Notre Dame
USA
Liberalism, Russian

Dr Andy Hamilton
University of Durham
UK
Mach, Ernst

Dr Alan Hamlin
Reader in Economics
University of Southampton
UK
Social choice

Professor Guyton B. Hammond
Professor Emeritus
Religious Studies Program
Virginia Polytechnic Institute and
State University
USA
Tillich, Paul

Professor Iain Hampsher-Monk
Professor of Political Theory
University of Exeter
UK
Burke, Edmund
Political philosophy, history of

Professor Jean Hampton
Deceased – formerly of the
University of Arizona
USA
Rationality, practical

Professor Michael Hand
Texas A&M University
USA
Semantics, game-theoretic

Professor James Hankins
Professor of History
Harvard University
USA
Ficino, Marsilio
Pico della Mirandola, Giovanni
Platonism, Renaissance

Professor R.J. Hankinson
University of Texas
USA
Aenesidemus
Agrippa
Galen
Hellenistic medical epistemology
Hippocratic medicine
Pyrrhonism
Sextus Empiricus

Professor Robert Hanna
York University
Canada
Conceptual analysis

Dr Chad Hansen
Chair Professor of Chinese
Philosophy
University of Hong Kong
Logic in China

Professor Russell L. Hanson
Department of Political Science
Indiana University Bloomington
USA
Republicanism

Professor Sandra G. Harding
University of California, Los
Angeles
USA
Gender and science
Postcolonial philosophy of science

Professor Russell Hardin
Department of Politics
New York University
USA
Rational choice theory

Professor R.M. Hare
*White's Professor of Moral
Philosophy Emeritus
Corpus Christi College
University of Oxford
UK*
Prescriptivism

Professor William L. Harper
*University of Western Ontario
Canada*
Newton, Isaac

Professor David Harrah
*Emeritus Professor
University of California, Riverside
USA*
Questions

Dr Rom Harré
*Psychology Department
Georgetown University
USA*
Behaviourism in the social sciences
Bentley, Richard

Dr Horton Harris
*Cambridge
UK*
Strauss, David Friedrich

Professor Jay M. Harris
*Harry Austryn Wolfson Professor of
Jewish Studies
Near Eastern Languages and
Civilizations
Harvard University
USA*
Enlightenment, Jewish
Krochmal, Nachman

Professor John Harris
*Centre for Social Ethics and Policy
University of Manchester
UK*
Life and death

Dr Olivia Harris
*Goldsmith's College, University of
London
UK*
Lévi-Strauss, Claude

Dr Ross Harrison
*King's College
University of Cambridge
UK*
Bentham, Jeremy
Democracy
Transcendental arguments
Williams, Bernard Arthur Owen

Professor Charles Hartman
*Professor of East Asian Studies
State University of New York at
Albany
USA*
Han Yu

Professor D. Hartman
*Shalom Hartman Institute
Israel*
Leibowitz, Yeshayahu
Soloveitchik, Joseph B.

Professor W.D. Hart
*University of Illinois at Chicago
USA*
Löwenheim-Skolem theorems and
  non-standard models
Meaning and verification

Dr Edeltraud Harzer Clear
*Department of Asian Studies
University of Texas at Austin
USA*
Cosmology and cosmogony, Indian
  theories of
Hindu philosophy
Mādhava

Professor William Hasker
*Huntington College
USA*
Creation and conservation,
  religious doctrine of
Occasionalism
Providence

Dr Riffat Hassan
*Louisville, Kentucky
USA*
Iqbal, Muhammad

Professor Gary Hatfield
*University of Pennsylvania
USA*
Scientific method

Mr Jeffrey Hause
*St John's Seminary College
USA*
Francis of Meyronnes
Origen

Dr Roger Hausheer
*Department of Modern Languages
Bradford University
UK*
Meinecke, Friedrich

Professor Daniel Hausman
*University of Wisconsin
USA*
Economics and ethics
Economics, philosophy of

Professor Richard P. Hayes
*Faculty of Religious Studies
McGill University
Canada*
Buddhist philosophy, Indian
Dignāga
Indian and Tibetan philosophy
Potentiality, Indian theories of
Vasubandhu

Professor A.P. Hazen
*University of Melbourne
Australia*
Non-constructive rules of inference

Professor John M. Headley
*Distinguished University Professor
Department of History
University of North Carolina at
Chapel Hill
USA*
Campanella, Tommaso

Dr Jane Heal
*Faculty of Philosophy and St John's
College
University of Cambridge
UK*
Wittgenstein, Ludwig Josef Johann

Professor Peter Heath
*Professor of Philosophy (Emeritus)
University of Virginia
USA*
Dodgson, Charles Lutwidge (Lewis
  Carroll)

Dr Stephen Heath
Fellow of Jesus College
University of Cambridge
UK
Tel Quel School

Professor Richard Heck
Harvard University
USA
Frege, Gottlob

Professor Michael Heidelberger
Humboldt-Universität zu Berlin
Germany
Büchner, Friedrich Karl Christian
   Ludwig (Louis)
Naturphilosophie

Professor Steven Heine
Religious Studies Department
Florida International University
USA
Kumazawa Banzan

Professor J.W. Heisig
Nanzan Institute for Religion and
Culture
Nanzan University
Japan
Kyoto school
Miki Kiyoshi
Nichiren

Ms Laura Hengehold
Loyola University of Chicago
USA
Subject, postmodern critique of the

Dr Ann-Mari Henschen-Dahlquist
Uppsala University
Sweden
Hägerström, Axel Anders Theodor

Dr Heinrich Herre
Institut für Informatik
Universität Leipzig
Germany
Formal languages and systems

Professor David Heyd
The Hebrew University of Jerusalem
Israel
Population and ethics

Professor James Higginbotham
Professor of General Linguistics
Somerville College
University of Oxford
UK
Adverbs

Dr M.A. Higton
Faculty of Divinity
Cambridge University
UK
Luther, Martin

Professor David R. Hilbert
University of Illinois at Chicago
USA
Colour, theories of

Professor R. Kevin Hill
Northwestern University
USA
Genealogy

Professor Thomas E. Hill, Jr
University of North Carolina at
Chapel Hill
USA
Respect for persons

Professor Himi Kiyoshi
Professor of Philosophy and
Religion
Nara University of Commerce
Japan
Nishi Amane
Tanabe Hajime

Professor Jaakko Hintikka
Boston University
USA
Epistemic logic
Quantifiers

Dr Angela Hobbs
University of Warwick
UK
Antiphon
Callicles
Physis and nomos
Thrasymachus

Professor Harold Hodes
Sage School of Philosophy
Cornell University
USA
Recursion-theoretic hierarchies
Turing reducibility and Turing
   degrees

Professor Wilfrid Hodges
School of Mathematical Sciences
Queen Mary and Westfield College
University of London
UK
Model theory

Dr Frank J. Hoffman
West Chester University
USA
Gandhi, Mohandas Karamchand

Professor Joshua Hoffman
University of North Carolina
USA
Omnipotence

Dr George B. Hogenson
Psychotherapist
Chicago, Illinois
USA
Jung, Carl Gustav

Professor David Holdcroft
University of Leeds
UK
Saussure, Ferdinand de
Structuralism in linguistics

Professor Axel Honneth
Goethe Universität Frankfurt
Germany
Frankfurt School
Recognition

Dr Brad Hooker
University of Reading
UK
Moral expertise

Professor C.A. Hooker
University of Newcastle
Australia
Laws, natural

Professor Christopher Hookway
University of Sheffield
UK
Peirce, Charles Sanders

Dr Bernard Hoose
Heythrop College
University of London
UK
Charity
Innocence

Dr John Hope Mason
School of Humanities
Middlesex University
UK
Encyclopedists, 18th-century

Mr H.M. Höpfl
Department of Politics
Lancaster University
UK
Voegelin, Eric

Dr James Hopkins
King's College, University of
London
UK
Freud, Sigmund
Psychoanalysis, post-Freudian

Professor Jasper Hopkins
University of Minnesota
USA
Anselm of Canterbury
Nicholas of Cusa

Dr R.D. Hopkins
University of Birmingham,
Edgbaston
UK
Depiction

Professor Jennifer Hornsby
Birkbeck College
University of London
UK
Action

Professor Norbert Hornstein
Linguistics Program
University of Maryland
USA
Chomsky, Noam

Professor Dr Rolf-Peter
Horstmann
Humboldt-Universität zu Berlin
Germany
Hegel, Georg Wilhelm Friedrich

Mr John Horton
Department of Politics
Keele University
UK
Toleration

Professor John Horty
University of Maryland
USA
Common-sense reasoning,
    theories of

Professor Paul Horwich
University College, University of
London
UK
Conventionalism
Time travel

Professor Don Howard
University of Notre Dame
USA
Duhem, Pierre Maurice Marie
Einstein, Albert
Le Roy, Édouard Louis Emmanuel
    Julien
Planck, Max Karl Ernst Ludwig

Dr Jane Howarth
Furness College
Lancaster University
UK
Phenomenology, epistemic issues in

Professor Robert Howell
State University of New York at
Albany
USA
Fiction, semantics of

Dr Christina Howells
Wadham College
University of Oxford
UK
Sartre, Jean-Paul

Professor Paul Hoyningen-Huene
Universität Konstanz
Germany
Kuhn, Thomas Samuel

Mrs Pamela M. Huby
University of Liverpool
UK
Theophrastus

Dr Gerard J. Hughes
Vice-Principal
Heythrop College, University of
London
UK
Prudence

Professor John A. Hughes
Department of Sociology
Lancaster University
UK
Experiments In Social Science

Professor David L. Hull
Northwestern University
USA
Taxonomy

Professor Monte S. Hull
Lake Forest College
USA
Mujō

Professor Mark Hulliung
Department of Politics
Brandeis University
USA
Helvétius, Claude-Adrien
Montesquieu, Charles Louis de
    Secondat

Professor Lloyd Humberstone
Monash University
Australia
Many-valued logics, philosophical
    issues in

Professor Paul Humphreys
Corcoran Department of Philosophy
University of Virginia
USA
Probability, interpretations of

Dr Geoffrey Hunt
European Centre for Professional Ethics
Faculty of Science, University of East London
UK
Labriola, Antonio
Nursing ethics

Professor Thomas Hurka
University of Calgary
Canada
Perfectionism

Dr Rosalind Hursthouse
The Open University
UK
Reproduction and ethics

Dr Sarah Hutton
Faculty of Humanities, Languages and Education
University of Hertfordshire
UK
Cockburn, Catharine
Conway, Anne
Cudworth, Ralph
Masham, Damaris
Norris, John

Dr Drew A. Hyland
Trinity College
USA
Sport and ethics
Sport, philosophy of

Dr Alec Hyslop
La Trobe University
Australia
Other minds

Professor Shotaro Iida
Vancouver, British Columbia
Canada
Wŏnch'ŭk

Professor Shams C. Inati
Villanova University
USA
Epistemology in Islamic
    philosophy
Ibn 'Adi, Yahya
Ibn Bajja, Abu Bakr Muhammad
    ibn Yahya ibn as-Say'igh
Ibn ar-Rawandi
Ibn Tufayl, Abu Bakr Muhammad
Soul in Islamic philosophy

Dr Sohail Inayatullah
The Communication Centre
Queensland University of Technology
Australia
Political philosophy, Indian

Professor Brad Inwood
Department of Classics
University of Toronto
Canada
Epictetus
Hierocles
Marcus Aurelius
Musonius Rufus
Seneca, Lucius Annaeus

Mr Michael Inwood
Trinity College
University of Oxford
UK
Hartmann, Nicolai
Hermeneutics

Professor F. Abiola Irele
Professor of African, French and Comparative Literature
Department of Black Studies
The Ohio State University
USA
African philosophy, francophone

Professor T.H. Irwin
Susan Linn Sage Professor of Philosophy and Humane Letters
Sage School of Philosophy
Cornell University
USA
Aristotle

Professor Charles Issawi
Bayard Dodge Professor of Near Eastern Studies, Emeritus
Princeton University
USA
Ibn Khaldun, 'Abd al-Rahman

Professor Philip J. Ivanhoe
Departments of Philosophy and Asian Languages and Cultures
University of Michigan
USA
Cheng
History, Chinese theories of
Li
Mohist philosophy
Neo-Confucian philosophy
Ti and yong
Xin (trustworthiness)

Professor Frank Jackson
Research School of Social Sciences
Australian National University
Australia
Armstrong, David Malet
Belief
Indicative conditionals
Mind, identity theory of
Mind, philosophy of
Passmore, John Arthur
Smart, John Jamieson Carswell

Dr Klaus Jacobi
Albert-Ludwigs-Universität
Germany
Gilbert of Poitiers

Professor Margaret C. Jacob
Professor of the History of Science
University of Pennsylvania
USA
Illuminati

Dr Susan James
University of Cambridge
UK
Feminism

Professor Dale Jamieson
University of Colorado
and Henry R. Luce Professor in

*Human Dimensions of Global
Change*
Carleton College
USA
Animal language and thought

Dr Christopher Janaway
*Birkbeck College, University of
London*
UK
Schopenhauer, Arthur

Dr Hannes Jarka-Sellers
Sage School of Philosophy
Cornell University
USA
Liber de causis
Pseudo-Dionysius

Professor Ian C. Jarvie
Distinguished Research Professor
York University
Canada
Popper, Karl Raimund

Professor R. Jeffrey
Princeton University
USA
Hempel, Carl Gustav

Dr Jeremy Jennings
*Department of Political Science and
International Studies*
University of Birmingham
UK
Sorel, Georges

Professor Dr Hans Joas
John F. Kennedy Instituts
Freie Universität Berlin
Germany
Mead, George Herbert

Professor Paul F. Johnson
*Division of Humanities and Fine
Arts*
St Norbert College
USA
Condillac, Etienne Bonnot De
D'Alembert, Jean Le Rond

Professor Mark D. Johnston
Department of Foreign Languages
Illinois State University
USA
Llull, Ramon

Professor Karen Jones
Cornell University
USA
Trust

Professor Peter Jones
Professor of Political Philosophy
University of Newcastle
UK
Freedom of speech

Professor Roger Jones
Adjunct Assistant Professor
University of Kentucky
USA
Optics

Professor W. Gareth Jones
School of Modern Languages
University of Wales, Bangor
UK
Enlightenment, Russian

Professor David Joravsky
Professor of History
Northwestern University
USA
Bogdanov, Aleksandr
   Aleksandrovich
Partiinost'
Russian Empiriocriticism
Vygotskii, Lev Semënovich

Professor Mark D. Jordan
The Medieval Institute
University of Notre Dame
USA
Aristotelianism, medieval
Augustinianism
Gerard of Cremona
Hugh of St Victor
John of La Rochelle
John of Paris
John of Salisbury
Neckham, Alexander
Pseudo-Grosseteste

Professor Mario Jori
Instituto di Dirritto Pubblico
Università di Cagliari
Italy
Legal positivism

Dr Raphael Jospe
The Open University of Israel
Ibn Ezra, Abraham
Ibn Falaquera, Shem Tov

Professor Michael Jubien
University of California, Davis
USA
Kripke, Saul Aaron
Ontological commitment

Professor Yukio Kachi
University of Utah
USA
Shōtoku Constitution

Professor Charles H. Kahn
University of Pennsylvania
USA
Gorgias
Hippias
Prodicus
Protagoras
Socratic Dialogues
Sophists

Professor Michael C. Kalton
Director, Liberal Studies
University of Washington, Tacoma
USA
Confucian Philosophy, Korean
Han Wônjin
Yi Hwang
Yi Kan

Professor Mark Kaplan
*University of Wisconsin –
Milwaukee*
USA
Induction, epistemic issues in

Professor Ivan Karp
*National Endowment for the
Humanities Professor*
Institute of African Studies
Emory University
USA
Ethnophilosophy, African

Professor Thomas P. Kasulis
Comparative Studies
The Ohio State University
USA
Dōgen
Fa
Japanese Philosophy
Kūkai
Logic in Japan
Motoori Norinaga
Sengzhao

Professor Steven T. Katz
Director, Center for Judaic Studies
and Professor of Religion
Boston University
USA
Holocaust, the

Professor Leslie S. Kawamura
Department of Religious Studies,
Faculty of Humanities
University of Calgary
Canada
Buddhism, Mādhyamika: India
   and Tibet

Professor Russell Keat
Department of Politics
University of Edinburgh
Scotland, UK
Scientific realism and social science
Socialism

Professor Michael H. Keefer
Department of English
University of Guelph
Canada
Agrippa Von Nettesheim, Henricus
   Cornelius

Professor F.C. Keil
Department of Psychology
Cornell University
USA
Cognitive development

Professor John Kekes
State University of New York at
Albany
USA
Evil

Professor Stephen H. Kellert
Hamline University
USA
Chaos theory

Professor Menachem Kellner
Dean of students and Wolfson
Professor of Jewish Thought
University of Haifa
Israel
Duran, Profiat
Duran, Simeon ben Tzemach

Dr Aileen Kelly
Lecturer in Slavonic Studies
and Fellow of King's College
University of Cambridge
UK
Bakunin, Mikhail Aleksandrovich
Herzen, Aleksandr Ivanovich
Russian philosophy
Signposts movement

Professor Salim Kemal
Chair of Philosophy
University of Dundee
Scotland, UK
Ibn Sina, Abu 'Ali al-Husayn

Dr Kiki Kennedy-Day
New York
USA
al-Kindi, Abu Yusuf Ya'qub ibn
   Ishaq
Aristotelianism in Islamic
   philosophy

Professor John Peter Kenney
Dean of the College and Professor of
Religious Studies
St Michael's College
USA
Marius Victorinus
Patristic philosophy
Tertullian, Quintus Septimus
   Florens

Professor Bonnie Kent
Columbia University
USA
Bonaventure
Gerard of Odo

Reverend Dr Ian Ker
Tutor in Theology
University of Oxford
UK
Newman, John Henry

Professor Dr Eckhard Kessler
Institut für Geistesgeschichte und
Philosophie der Renaissance
Universität München
Germany
Cardano, Girolamo
Telesio, Bernardino
Zabarella, Jacopo

Professor David Kettler
Professor Emeritus, Trent
University
Canada
Scholar in Residence, Bard College
USA
Ferguson, Adam

Dr Hafiz A. Ghaffar Khan
Director
Georgia Islamic Institute
USA
Shah Wali Allah (Qutb al-Din
   Ahmad al-Rahim)

Professor Jaegwon Kim
Brown University
USA
Reduction, problems of

Professor Harold Kincaid
University of Alabama
USA
Positivism in the social sciences

Dr E.F. Kingdom
Department of Sociology, Social
Policy and Social Work Studies
University of Liverpool
UK
Feminist jurisprudence

Professor Jeffrey C. King
University of California, Davis
USA
Quantification and inference

Professor Richard Kinsey
Retired – formerly of Centre for

*Criminology and The Social and
Philosophical Study of Law
University of Edinburgh
Scotland, UK*
Renner, Karl

Professor Richard L. Kirkham
*Georgia State University
USA*
Truth, coherence theory of
Truth, correspondence theory of
Truth, deflationary theories of
Truth, pragmatic theory of

Mr Christopher Kirwan
*Exeter College
University of Oxford
UK*
Manicheism
Pelagianism

Professor Philip Kitcher
*University of California at San
Diego
USA*
Explanation

Professor Patricia Kitcher
*University of California at San
Diego
USA*
Psychoanalysis, methodological
  issues in

Professor Peter Kivy
*State University of New Jersey
USA*
Hanslick, Eduard

Dr Martha Klein
*Pembroke College
University of Oxford
UK*
Praise and blame

Professor Peter D. Klein
*Rutgers University
USA*
Certainty
Epistemology
Knowledge, concept of

Professor George L. Kline
*Milton C. Nahm Professor Emeritus
of Philosophy
Bryn Mawr College
USA*
Leont'ev, Konstantin Nikolaevich
Losev, Aleksei Fëdorovich

Professor Noretta Koertge
*History and Philosophy of Science
Department
Indiana University Bloomington
USA*
Chemistry, philosophical aspects of

Professor Hilary Kornblith
*University of Vermont
USA*
Introspection, epistemology of

Professor Christine M. Korsgaard
*Chair, Department of Philosophy
Harvard University
USA*
Good, theories of the
Teleological ethics

Professor Carolyn Korsmeyer
*State University of New York at
Buffalo
USA*
Feminist aesthetics

Professor Peter Kosso
*Northern Arizona University
USA*
Observation

Dr Erik C.W. Krabbe
*University of Groningen
Netherlands*
Dialogical Logic

Dr Matthew H. Kramer
*Faculty of Law
University of Cambridge
UK*
Holmes, Oliver Wendell, Jr

Professor Richard Kraut
*Northwestern University
USA*
Egoism and altruism

Dr Angèle Kremer-Marietti
*Docteur d'Etat ès Lettres et
Sciences Humaines
Département de Philosophie à
lUniversité d'Amiens
Faculté Libre de Philosophie
Comparée à Paris
France*
Comte, Isidore-Auguste-Marie-
  François-Xavier

Professor Norman Kretzmann
*Susan Linn Sage Professor Emeritus
of Philosophy
Sage School of Philosophy
Cornell University
USA*
Aquinas, Thomas
Eternity
Kilvington, Richard
Medieval philosophy

Professor Peter Kroes
*Department of Philosophy and
Social Sciences
University of Technology Delft
Netherlands*
Technology, philosophy of

Professor Martin Krygier
*Department of Law
University of New South Wales
Australia*
Common law

Professor Arthur Kuflik
*University of Vermont
USA*
Moral standing

Professor Steven T. Kuhn
*Georgetown University
USA*
Modal logic

Professor Theo A.F. Kuipers
*University of Groningen
Netherlands*
Confirmation theory

Dr Chandran Kukathas
Department of Politics
Australian Defence Force Academy
Australia
Hayek, Friedrich August von
Rand, Ayn

Professor Bruce Kuklick
Nichols Professor of History
University of Pennsylvania
USA
Paine, Thomas

Dr K.S. Kumar
School of Information Technology
Bond University
Australia
Arya Samaj
Brahmo Samaj

Professor Wolfgang Künne
Universitänt Hamburg
Germany
Bolzano, Bernard

Professor Jonathan L. Kvanvig
Texas A&M University
USA
Paradoxes, epistemic

Professor Will Kymlicka
University of Ottawa
Canada
Citizenship

Professor Massimo La Torre
Professor of Law
European University Institute
Italy
Fuller, Lon Louvois
Radbruch, Gustav

Dr A.R. Lacey
King's College, University of
London
UK
Bergson, Henri-Louis

Professor John Lachs
Centennial Professor of Philosophy
Vanderbilt University
USA
Santayana, George

Professor Michael LaFargue
Acting Director of East Asian
Studies
Lecturer in Religion and Philosophy
University of Massachusetts Boston
USA
Daodejing

Dr Eerik Lagerspetz
Turku University
Finland
Social sciences, prediction in

Dr Joy Laine
Macalester College
USA
Mind, Indian Philosophy Of
Udayana
Uddyotakara
Vātsyāyana

Professor Peter Lamarque
Ferens Professor of Philosophy
University of Hull
UK
Fictional entities

Professor Karel Lambert
Research Professor of Logic and
Philosophy of Science
University of California, Irvine
USA
Free logics, philosophical issues in

Dr Y. Tzvi Langermann
University and National Library
The Hebrew University
Israel
al-Baghdadi, Abu 'l-Bakarat
Ibn Kammuna

Dr Alfred Langewand
Institut für Pädagogik
Ludwig Maximilians Universität
Germany
Herbart, Johann Friedrich

Professor Charles Larmore
Columbia University
USA
Bayle, Pierre
Right and good

Professor Daniel J. Lasker
Norbert Blechner Professor of
Jewish Values
Jewish Thought Division,
Department of History
Ben-Gurion University of the Negev
Israel
Israeli, Isaac Ben Solomon

Professor D.C. Lau
Department of Chinese Literature
Chinese University of Hong Kong
Confucius

Dr Larry Laudan
San Miguel De Allende
Mexico
Underdetermination

Dr Rachel Laudan
San Miguel De Allende
Mexico
Geology, philosophy of

Professor Shaughan Lavine
University of Arizona
USA
Predicate calculus
Second- and higher-order logics

Professor Ronald Laymon
The Ohio State University
USA
Idealizations

Professor Alison Laywine
McGill University
Canada
Knutzen, Martin
Swedenborg, Emanuel

Professor Allan Lazaroff
New York University
USA
Voluntarism, Jewish

Professor Živan Lazović
University of Belgrade
Yugoslavia
South Slavs, philosophy of

Dr Michèle Le Doeuff
*Centre de Recherches sur les Arts et
le Language
Centre National de la Recherche
Scientifique
France
UK*
Suchon, Gabrielle

Dr Robin Le Poidevin
*University of Leeds
UK*
Change
Continuants

Dr A.L. Le Quesne
*Shrewsbury
UK*
Carlyle, Thomas

Professor Oliver Leaman
*Liverpool John Moores University
UK*
Abravanel, Isaac
al-Afghani, Jamal al-Din
Anti-Semitism
Averroism, Jewish
Duran, Profiat
Ibn Hazm, Abu Muhammad 'Ali
Ibn Khaldun, 'Abd al-Rahman
Ibn Miskawayh, Ahmad ibn
    Muhammad
Ibn Rushd, Abu 'l Walid
    Muhammad
Illuminationist philosophy
Islam, concept of philosophy in
Islamic philosophy
Islamic philosophy, modern
al-Juwayni, Abu'l Ma'ali
Kabbalah
Meaning in Islamic philosophy

Professor Mary R. Lefkowitz
*Department of Greek and Latin
Wellesley College
USA*
Egyptian philosophy: influence on
    ancient Greek thought

Professor Brian Leftow
*Fordham University
USA*
God, concepts of
Immutability
Necessary Being
Omnipresence
Simplicity, Divine
Voluntarism

Professor Thomas M. Lennon
*University of Western Ontario
Canada*
Bernier, François
Régis, Pierre-Sylvain

Dr David Leopold
*Lecturer in Politics
Merton College
University of Oxford
UK*
Cousin, Victor
Saint-Simon, Claude-Henri de
    Rouvroy, Comte de
Staël-Holstein, Anne-Louise-
    Germaine, Mme de
Stirner, Max

Professor Ernie Lepore
*Center for Cognitive Science
Rutgers University
USA*
Davidson, Donald
Searle, John

Professor J.H. Lesher
*Professor of Philosophy and Classics
University of Maryland
USA*
Xenophanes

Professor Alan M. Leslie
*Professor of Psychology
Center for Cognitive Science
Rutgers University
USA*
Mind, child's theory of

Professor Isaac Levi
*Columbia University
USA*
Nagel, Ernest

Professor Joseph Levine
*Department of Philosophy and
Religion
North Carolina State University
USA*
Colour and qualia

Professor Janet Levin
*University of Southern California
USA*
Qualia

Professor Henry S. Levinson
*Department of Religious Studies
University of North Carolina at
Greensboro
USA*
Jewish philosophy, contemporary

Professor Jerrold Levinson
*University of Maryland
USA*
Emotion in response to art
Erotic art
Gurney, Edmund
Humour
Music, aesthetics of

Professor Dr Ze'ev Levy
*Professor Emeritus
University of Haifa
Israel*
Baumgardt, David
Ha'am, Ahad
Zionism

Professor Alain de Libera
*École pratique des hautes études
France*
Albert the Great

Dr Menno Lievers
*Utrecht University
Netherlands*
Molyneux problem

Dr Reginald Lilly
*Department of Philosophy and
Religion
Skidmore College
USA*
Postmodernism, French critics of

Professor Françoise Lionnet
*Miller Research Professor in
Literature*
*Department of French and
Comparative Literature*
Northwestern University
USA
Todorov, Tzvetan

Professor Elisabeth A. Lloyd
*Program in Logic and Methodology
of Science*
University of California, Berkeley
USA
Evolution, theory of
Models

Professor Barry Loewer
Rutgers University
USA
Mental causation
Probability theory and
 epistemology
Supervenience of the mental

Professor Maurice Loi
École Normale Supérieure
France
Brunschvicg, Léon

Professor A.A. Long
Department of Classics
University of California
USA
Cratylus
Heraclitus
Nous
Psychē

Professor John Longeway
Department of Humanities
University of Wisconsin – Parkside
USA
Heytesbury, William
John of Damascus
Peter of Spain
William of Sherwood

Professor Eric Lormand
University of Michigan
USA
Consciousness

Professor Robert B. Louden
University of Southern Maine
USA
Examples in ethics

Professor Martin Loughlin
Professor of Law
University of Manchester
UK
Dicey, Albert Venn
Millar, John

Dr John A. Loughney
Westfield State College
USA
Cultural identity

Professor Michael J. Loux
University of Notre Dame
USA
Nominalism

Mr Stephen Lovell
*School of Slavonic and East
European Studies, University of
London*
UK
Nihilism, Russian

Dr Sabina Lovibond
Worcester College
University of Oxford
UK
Wittgensteinian ethics

Professor John A. Lucy
Committee on Human Development
University of Chicago
Sapir-Whorf hypothesis

Professor John C. Luik
The Niagara Institute
Canada
Humanism

Professor Eva Lundgren-Gothlin
*Department of History of Ideas and
Science*
Göteborg University
Sweden
Beauvoir, Simone de

Professor Steven Luper
Trinity University
USA
Belief and knowledge
Naturalized epistemology

Professor Dan Lusthaus
Department of Religion
Florida State University
USA
Buddhism, Yogācāra school of
Buddhist philosophy, Chinese
Sāṅkhya

Professor Matthias Lutz-
Bachmann
*Johann Wolfgang Goethe-
Universität Frankfurt*
Germany
Religion, critique of
Theology, political

Dr Colin Lyas
University of Lancaster
UK
Art criticism
Art, understanding of

Professor William G. Lycan
*University of North Carolina at
Chapel Hill*
USA
Dennett, Daniel Clement
Theoretical (epistemic) virtues

Dr Richard John Lynn
Department of East Asian Studies
University of Alberta
Canada
Yijing

Professor William Lyons
*School of Mental and Moral
Science*
Trinity College Dublin
Ireland
Ryle, Gilbert

Professor Jim MacAdam
Professor Emeritus
Champlain College
Trent University
Canada
Prichard, Harold Arthur

Professor Neil MacCormick
Regius Professor of Public Law
Centre for Law and Society
University of Edinburgh
Scotland, UK
Frank, Jerome
Hart, Herbert Lionel Adolphus
Hohfeld, Wesley Newcomb
Law, philosophy of
Legal reasoning and interpretation
Llewellyn, Karl Nickerson
Pothier, Robert Joseph
Pound, Roscoe
Renner, Karl
Savigny, Friedrich Karl von
Villey, Michel
Weinberger, Ota

Dr Graham MacDonald
Senior Lecturer, Department of
Interdisciplinary Human Studies
University of Bradford
UK
Ayer, Alfred Jules

Professor Scott MacDonald
Sage School of Philosophy
Cornell University
USA
Grosseteste, Robert
Illumination
Medieval philosophy
Natural theology
Philip the Chancellor
William of Auxerre

Professor Moshé Machover
King's College, University of
London
UK
Analysis, nonstandard

Dr Penelope Mackie
University of Birmingham
UK
Existence

Professor Edward Mackinnon
California State University
USA
Hanson, Norwood Russell

Dr Peter Mack
Department of English
University of Warwick
UK
Agricola, Rudolph
Melanchthon, Philipp
Ramus, Petrus

Professor Ian Maclean
All Souls College
University of Oxford
UK
Libertins
Moralistes
Pascal, Blaise

Professor Edward H. Madden
Professor Emeritus
State University of New York at
Buffalo
USA
Ducasse, Curt John
Stewart, Dugald
Common Sense School

Professor Patrick Maher
University of Illinois at Urbana-
Champaign
USA
Inductive inference

Professor Edward P. Mahoney
Duke University
USA
Aristotelianism, Renaissance
Cajetan (Thomas de Vio)
James of Viterbo
John of Jandun
Nifo, Agostino
Vernia, Nicoletto

Professor Stephen Maitzen
Dalhousie University
Canada
Tennant, Frederick Robert

Professor Dr Ulrich Majer
Institut für Wissenschaftsgeschichte
Universität Göttingen
Germany
Cantor, Georg
Kronecker, Leopold

Dr Stephen Makin
University of Sheffield
UK
Zeno of Elea

Professor Rudolf A. Makkreel
Charles Howard Candler Professor
of Philosophy
Emory University
USA
Dilthey, Wilhelm

Professor Jonathan W. Malino
Guilford College
USA
Jewish philosophy, contemporary

Professor Peter T. Manicas
University of Hawaii
USA
Social science, history of
  philosophy of

Professor Richard N. Manning
Ohio University
USA
Functional explanation

Professor James W. Manns
University of Kentucky
USA
Buffier, Claude

Professor William E. Mann
University of Vermont
USA
Damian, Peter
David of Dinant
Theological virtues
Vital du Four

Professor John C. Maraldo
Department of History, Philosophy
and Religious Studies
University of North Florida
USA
Buddhist Philosophy, Japanese
Nishida Kitarō

Dr John Marenbon
Trinity College
University of Cambridge
UK
Carolingian renaissance
Chartres, School of
Thierry of Chartres
William of Conches

Professor Joseph Margolis
Temple University
USA
Structuralism in literary theory

Professor Peter J. Markie
University of Missouri – Columbia
USA
Rationalism

Professor Charles Marks
University of Washington
USA
Split brains

Professor Steven P. Marrone
Department of History
Tufts University
USA
Henry of Ghent
William of Auvergne

Dr Graeme Marshall
University of Melbourne
Australia
Pleasure

Professor John Marshall
History Department
University of Denver
USA
Latitudinarianism
Socinianism

Professor Genoveva Martí
University of California, Riverside
USA
Sense and reference

Dr Oscar R. Martí
Center for Ethics and Values,
Institute of Humanities
California State University,
Northridge
USA
Analytical philosophy in Latin
    America
Positivist thought in Latin America

Dr M.G.F. Martin
University College, University of
London
UK
Bodily sensations
Perception

Professor Mike W. Martin
Chapman University
USA
Self-deception, ethics of

Professor Rex Martin
University of Kansas, USA
and Professor of Political Theory
and Government
University of Wales, Swansea
UK
Rights

Professor A.P. Martinich
University of Texas at Austin
USA
Metaphor
Ordinary language philosophy

Professor Martin E. Marty
Divinity School
University of Chicago
USA
Niebuhr, Helmut Richard
Niebuhr, Reinhold

Mr Jonathan Maskit
Northwestern University
USA
Bataille, Georges

Professor D.A. Masolo
University of Louisville
USA
Ethnophilosophy, African

Dr Andrew Mason
University of Reading
UK
Solidarity

Dr Freya Mathews
La Trobe University
Australia
Ecological philosophy

Dr Matt Matravers
Department of Politics
University of York
UK
Justice
Justice, international

Professor Gareth B. Matthews
University of Massachusetts
USA
Augustine

Professor George I. Mavrodes
Professor Emeritus
University of Michigan
USA
Monotheism
Prayer
Predestination

Professor Timothy McCarthy
University of Illinois at Urbana-
Champaign
USA
Logical constants

Professor David Charles McCarty
USA
Combinatory logic
Constructivism in mathematics
Intuitionism
Lambda calculus
Logical and mathematical terms,
    glossary of

Professor Sally McConnell-Ginet
Professor of Linguistics
Cornell University
USA
Language and gender

Professor Charles J. McCracken
Michigan State University
USA
Johnson, Samuel

Professor John McDowell
University of Pittsburgh
USA
Evans, Gareth

Professor Graham McFee
Chelsea School of Physical
Education
University of Brighton
UK
Dance, aesthetics of

Professor Vann McGee
Department of Linguistics and
Philosophy
Massachusetts Institute of
Technology
USA
Inductive definitions and proofs
Semantic paradoxes and theories of
   truth

Professor Colin McGinn
Rutgers University
USA
Secondary qualities

Dr Marie McGinn
University of York
UK
Criteria

Professor A.S. McGrade
University of Connecticut
USA
Hooker, Richard
Marsilius of Padua

Professor Ralph McInerny
University of Notre Dame
USA
Garrigou-Lagrange, Réginald
Maritain, Jacques

Professor Thomas J. McKay
Syracuse University
USA
Modal logic, philosophical issues in

Professor Antony McKenna
Institut Claude Longeon
Université Jean Monnet Saint-
Étienne
France
Clandestine literature
Port-Royal

Professor Richard McKirahan
E.C. Norton Professor of Classics
and Philosophy
Pomona College
USA
Anaximander
Anaximenes
Archē
Thales

Professor Colin McLarty
Case Western Reserve University
USA
Category theory, applications to
   the foundations of mathematics
Category theory, introduction to

Professor Brian P. McLaughlin
Rutgers University
USA
Anomalous monism
Connectionism
Perception, epistemic issues in
Semantics, informational

Mr Grant McLeod
Department of Private Law
University of Edinburgh
Scotland, UK
Gaius
Justinian

Professor Ernan McMullin
Director Emeritus
Program in History and Philosophy
of Science
University of Notre Dame
USA
Copernicus, Nicolaus
Cosmology
Galilei, Galileo
Kepler, Johannes

Dr T. McNair
Heartland Community College
Bloomington, Illinois
USA
Tucker, Abraham

Professor David McNaughton
Keele University
UK
Consequentialism
Deontological ethics
Ross, William David
Shaftesbury, Third Earl of
   (Anthony Ashley Cooper)

Dr Michael S. McPherson
President
Macalester College
USA
Economics and ethics

Professor John R. McRae
Department of Religious Studies
Indiana University
USA
Platform Sutra
Zhi Dun

Professor Dr Günter Meckenstock
Schleiermacher-Forschungsstelle
Universität Kiel
Germany
Schleiermacher, Friedrich Daniel
   Ernst

Dr Marek Mejor
Head of the Department of South
Asia
Oriental Institute
Warsaw University
Poland
Suffering, Buddhist views of
   origination of
Vasubandhu

Dr Abraham Melamed
Department of Jewish History and
Thought
University of Haifa
Israel
Alemanno, Yohanan ben Isaac

Professor Alfred R. Mele
Vail Professor of Philosophy
Davidson College
USA
Self-deception

Dr Joseph Melia
University of York
UK
Possible worlds

Professor D.H. Mellor
University of Cambridge
UK
Campbell, Norman Robert
Events
Ramsey, Frank Plumpton

Professor Andrew N. Meltzoff
Professor of Psychology
University of Washington
USA
Cognition, infant

Professor Susan Mendus
Politics Department
University of York
UK
Feminist political philosophy
Pornography

Professor Christopher Menzel
Texas A&M University
USA
Logical form

Professor Christia Mercer
Columbia University
USA
Digby, Kenelm
Keckermann, Bartholomew

Professor Daniel D. Merrill
Oberlin College
USA
De Morgan, Augustus
Venn, John

Professor Hugo Meynell
Department of Religious Studies
University of Calgary
and Fellow of The Royal Society of
Canada
Canada
Lonergan, Bernard Joseph Francis

Professor Alan Milchman
Queen's College
City University of New York
USA
Blanchot, Maurice

Dr Alexander Miller
University of Birmingham
UK
Objectivity

Dr David Miller
Nuffield College
University of Oxford
UK
Desert and merit
Market, ethics of the
Nation and nationalism
Pareto principle
Political philosophy
Social democracy

Professor Richard W. Miller
Cornell University
USA
Marxist philosophy of science

Dr J.R. Milton
King's College, University of
London
UK
Bacon, Francis
Chillingworth, William

Professor Kenneth Minogue
Professor Emeritus
Government Department
London School of Economics,
University of London
UK
Oakeshott, Michael Joseph

Professor Robert N. Minor
Professor of Religious Studies
University of Kansas
USA
Radhakrishnan, Sarvepalli
Tagore, Rabindranath

Professor Carl Mitcham
Pennsylvania State University
USA
Technology and ethics

Professor Bengt Molander
NTNU Norwegian University of
Science and Technology, Trondheim
Norway
Praxeology

Dr Robert N. Moles
Senior Lecturer
Faculty of Law
Australian National University
Austin, John

Dr George Molland
Department of History and
Economic History
University of Aberdeen
Scotland, UK
Henry of Harclay
Oresme, Nicole

Professor John Monfasani
Department of History
State University of New York at
Albany
USA
George of Trebizond
Humanism, Renaissance
Petrarca, Francesco
Valla, Lorenzo

Mr Alan Montefiore
Emeritus Fellow of Balliol College
Academic Visitor in the Department
of Philosophy, Logic and Scientific
Method
University of Oxford
UK
Responsibilities of scientists and
   intellectuals

Dr A.W. Moore
St Hugh's College
University of Oxford
UK
Antirealism in the philosophy of
   mathematics
Infinity

Professor F.C.T. Moore
Chair of Philosophy
University of Hong Kong
Bonnet, Charles
Cabanis, Pierre-Jean
Maine de Biran, Pierre-François

Professor Gregory H. Moore
Department of Mathematics and Statistics
McMaster University
Canada
Axiom of choice
Logic in the early 20th century
Paradoxes of set and property

Professor James Moore
Professor of Political Science
Concordia University
Canada
Carmichael, Gershom

Professor James H. Moor
Dartmouth College
USA
Turing, Alan Mathison

Professor Dermot Moran
University College Dublin
Ireland
Eriugena, Johannes Scottus
Platonism, medieval

Professor Parviz Morewedge
Institute of Global Cultural Studies and Philosophy
State University of New York at Binghamton
USA
Islamic philosophy, modern

Professor Charles G. Morgan
University of Victoria
Canada
Fuzzy logic
Many-valued logics

Professor Michael L. Morgan
Indiana University
USA
Fackenheim, Emil Ludwig

Professor John Morreall
Religious Studies
University of South Florida
USA
Comedy

Professor Margaret C. Morrison
University of Toronto
Canada
Experiment

Professor Gary Saul Morson
Frances Hooper Professor of the Arts and Humanities
Department of Slavic Languages
Northwestern University
USA
Bakhtin, Mikhail Mikhailovich
Dostoevskii, Fëdor Mikhailovich
Tolstoi, Count Lev Nikolaevich

Professor Paul K. Moser
Loyola University of Chicago
USA
A posteriori
A priori

Professor Lenny Moss
Genetic Science in Society Fellow
Department of Philosophy and Eccles Institute for Human Genetics
University of Utah
USA
Life, origin of

Professor Glenn W. Most
Professor of Greek, Universität Heidelberg
Germany
Professor of Social Thought, University of Chicago
USA
Epicharmus
Hesiod
Homer
Katharsis
Mimēsis

Dr H.O. Mounce
University of Wales, Swansea
UK
Cournot, Antoine Augustin
Hamilton, William

Professor Richard J. Mouw
Professor of Christian Philosophy and Ethics
Fuller Theological Seminary
USA
Religion and morality

Dr Laura Mues de Schrenk
Academia Mexicana de Derechos Humanos
Universidad Nacional Autónoma de Mexico
Latin America, pre-Columbian and indigenous thought in

Dr Stephen Mulhall
University of Essex
UK
Cavell, Stanley

Professor Paul E. Muller-Ortega
Department of Religion and Classics
University of Rochester
USA
Abhinavagupta

Professor Kevin Mulligan
Université de Genève
Switzerland
Predication

Professor Daniele Mundici
Dipartimento di Scienze dell' Informazione
Università degli Studi di Milano
Italy
Computability theory

Professor Colin Munro
Department of Public Law
University of Edinburgh
Scotland, UK
Bryce, James

Professor Donald J. Munro
Professor Emeritus of Philosophy and of Chinese
Department of Asian Languages and Culture
University of Michigan
USA
Marxism, Chinese

Professor Stephen R. Munzer
Professor of Law
University of California, Los Angeles
USA
Property

Professor Roman Murawski
*Faculty of Mathematics and
Computer Science
Adam Mickiewicz University
Poland*
Tarski, Alfred

Professor Murray G. Murphey
*University of Pennsylvania
USA*
Franklin, Benjamin
Jefferson, Thomas

Professor Claudia Eisen Murphy
*University of Toronto
Canada*
Hildegard of Bingen

Professor Jeffrie G. Murphy
*Regents' Professor of Law and
Philosophy
Arizona State University
USA*
Forgiveness and mercy

Professor Liam B. Murphy
*Assistant Professor of Law
New York University
USA*
Help and beneficence

Professor Nancey Murphy
*Associate Professor of Christian
Philosophy
Fuller Theological Seminary
USA*
Religion and science

Mr Sean Eisen Murphy
*Department of Medieval Studies
Cornell University
USA*
Bernard of Clairvaux
Joachim of Fiore

Professor Alan Musgrave
*University of Otago
New Zealand*
Social relativism

Professor Steven Nadler
*University of Wisconsin – Madison
USA*
Arnauld, Antoine
Cordemoy, Géraud de
Foucher, Simon
La Forge, Louis de
Malebranche, Nicolas

Professor Nagatomo Shigenori
*Department of Religion
Temple University
USA*
Kuki Shūzō
Linji

Professor Kojiro Nakamura
*Tokyo
Japan*
al-Ghazali, Abu Hamid

Professor Terry Nardin
*Department of Political Science
University of Wisconsin –
Milwaukee
USA*
War and peace, philosophy of

Dr Seyyed Hossein Nasr
*Islamic Studies Department
George Washington University
USA*
Mystical philosophy in Islam

Professor Stephen Neale
*University of California, Berkeley
USA*
Descriptions
Syntax

Dr Karen Neander
*Johns Hopkins University
USA*
Mental illness, concept of

Dr Mark T. Nelson
*University of Leeds
UK*
Moral scepticism

Dr Thomas Nemeth
*Old Bridge, New Jersey
USA*
Neo-Kantianism, Russian

Professor Ian Richard Netton
*Professor of Arabic Studies
University of Leeds
UK*
al-Farabi, Abu Nasr
Ikhwan Al-Safa'
Neoplatonism in Islamic
  philosophy

Mr Peter P. Nicholson
*Department of Politics
University of York
UK*
Bosanquet, Bernard
General will
State, the

Professor James W. Nickel
*University of Colorado
USA*
Discrimination

Professor Thomas Nickles
*University of Nevada, Reno
USA*
Discovery, logic of

Professor Ilkka Niiniluoto
*University of Helsinki
Finland*
Von Wright, Georg Henrik

Professor Helen Nissenbaum
*University Center for Human Values
Princeton University
USA*
Information technology and ethics
Technology and ethics

Ubai Nooruddin
*New York
USA*
Orientalism and Islamic philosophy

Professor Wayne Norman
*University of Ottawa
Canada*
Federalism and confederalism

Professor Alan Norrie
*Drapers' Professor of Law
Queen Mary and Westfield College,
University of London
UK*
Critical legal studies

Professor Christopher Norris
University of Wales, Cardiff
UK
Deconstruction

Professor David Fate Norton
McGill University
Canada
Hutcheson, Francis

Professor John D. Norton
Department of History and
Philosophy of Science
University of Pittsburgh
USA
Einstein, Albert

Professor Peter Nosco
East Asian Languages and Culture
University of Southern California
USA
Confucian philosophy, Japanese

Professor David Novak
Bronfmann Professor of Jewish
Thought
Department of Religious Studies
University of Virginia
USA
Heschel, Abraham Joshua

Professor Martha C. Nussbaum
Ernst Freund Professor of Law and
Ethics
University of Chicago
USA
Love
Morality and emotions

Professor Michael Nylan
East Asian Studies
Bryn Mawr College
USA
Dong Zhongshu
Jia Yi
Yang Xiong
Zheng Xuan

Mr Clive Nyman
Southport
UK
Anti-Semitism

Professor David K. O'Connor
University of Notre Dame
USA
Xenophon

Professor Anthony O'Hear
Interdisciplinary Human Studies
University of Bradford
UK
Conservatism
Culture
Tradition and traditionalism

Dr J. O'Leary-Hawthorne
Arizona State University
USA
Imagination

Professor Eileen O'Neill
University of Massachusetts
USA
Astell, Mary
Cavendish, Margaret Lucas
Elisabeth of Bohemia
Schurman, Anna Maria van

Dr John O'Neill
Lancaster University
UK
Socialism
Theory and practice

Dr Onora O'Neill
The Principal, Newnham College
University of Cambridge
UK
Constructivism in ethics
Kantian ethics
Practical reason and ethics
Universalism in ethics
Vulnerability and finitude

Professor Thomas Oberdan
Department of Philosophy and
Religion
Clemson University
USA
Schlick, Friedrich Albert Moritz

Professor Steve Odin
University of Hawaii
USA
Watsuji Tetsurō

Professor Mark Okrent
Department of Philosophy and
Religion
Bates College
USA
Being

Dr Alex Oliver
Queens' College
University of Cambridge
UK
Facts
Logical Atomism
Value, ontological status of

Professor Amy A. Oliver
Department of Language and
Foreign Studies
The American University
USA
Feminist thought in Latin America
Latin America, philosophy in
Marginality

Professor Dorothea E. Olkowski
University of Colorado
USA
Deleuze, Gilles

Dr Hans-Ludwig Ollig
Frankfurt
Germany
Neo-Kantianism

Professor Frances Olsen
School of Law
University of California, Los
Angeles
USA
Privacy

Professor Elsayed M.H. Omran
Center for Arab and Islamic Studies
Villanova University
USA
al-Afghani, Jamal al-Din
Ibn Sab'in, Muhammad ibn 'Abd
  al-Haqq

Dr Graham Oppy
Monash University
Australia
Propositional Attitudes

Professor Alex Orenstein
*Philosophy Department and The
Graduate Center
City University of New York
UK*
Quine, Willard Van Orman

Professor Nelson R. Orringer
*Department of Modern and
Classical Languages
University of Connecticut
USA*
Ortega y Gasset, José
Unamuno y Jugo, Miguel de

Professor Marco Orrú
*Deceased – formerly of the
University of South Florida
USA*
Durkheim, Émile

Professor Margaret J. Osler
*Department of History
University of Calgary
Canada*
Gassendi, Pierre

Dr William Outhwaite
*School of European Studies
University of Sussex
UK*
Theory and observation in social
    sciences

Professor Gene Outka
*Dwight Professor of Philosophy and
Christian Ethics
Department of Religious Studies
Yale University
USA*
Situation ethics

Dr Anthony Pagden
*Harry C. Black Professor of History
Johns Hopkins University
USA*
Absolutism
Vitoria, Francisco de

Professor Peter Pagin
*Stockholm University
Sweden*
Intuitionistic logic and antirealism

Professor David A. Pailin
*Department of Religion and
Theology
University of Manchester
UK*
Herbert, Edward (Baron Herbert
    of Cherbury)

Professor Claude Panaccio
*Université du Québec à Trois
Rivières
Canada*
William of Ockham

Professor David Papineau
*King's College, University of
London
UK*
Functionalism

Professor George S. Pappas
*The Ohio State University
USA*
Epistemology, history of

Professor B. Parekh
*Department of Politics
University of Hull
UK*
Arendt, Hannah

Professor Rohit Parikh
*Doctoral programs in Computer
Science, Philosophy and
Mathematics
City University of New York
Graduate Center
and Brooklyn College, City
University of New York
USA*
Church's theorem and the decision
    problem

Professor Graham Parkes
*University of Hawaii
USA*
Nishitani Keiji

Professor Sung Bae Park
*Program in Korean Studies,
Department of Comparative Studies
State University of New York at
Stony Brook
USA*
Sôsan Hyujông
Wônhyo

Professor Terence Parsons
*University of California
USA*
Montague, Richard Merett

Dr Robert Pasnau
*St Joseph's University
USA*
Aureol, Peter
Crathorn, William
Holcot, Robert
Olivi, Peter John

Professor Enrico Pattaro
*Centro Interdipartinentale di
Ricerca in Filosofia del Diritto e
Informatica Giuridica
Università degli Studi di Bologna
Italy*
Ross, Alf

Dr Aleksandar Pavković
*School of History, Philosophy and
Politics
Macquarie University
Australia*
South Slavs, philosophy of

Mr James Pavlin
*Graduate Student
Department of Middle Eastern
Studies
New York University
USA*
Ibn Taymiyya, Taqi al-Din

Professor Steven Payne
*Institute of Carmelite Studies
Washington, DC
USA*
Mysticism, history of
Mysticism, nature of

Dr Volker Peckhaus
Der Universität Erlangen-Nürnberg
Germany
Gentzen, Gerhard Karl Erich
Zermelo, Ernst

Professor Aleksander Peczenik
Law School
Lund University
Sweden
Olivecrona, Karl
Petrażycki, Leon

Dr R.P. Peerenboom
Honolulu, Hawaii
USA
Law and ritual in Chinese
    philosophy

Professor Jeffry Pelletier
University of Alberta
Canada
Mass terms

Professor László Perecz
Department for Legal Sciences
Technical University of Budapest
Hungary
Hungary, philosophy in

Dr Michela Pereira
Dipartimento di Filosofia e Scienze
Sociali
Università di Siena
Italy
Alchemy

Dr Mary Anne Perkins
Faculty of Human Sciences
Kingston University
UK
Coleridge, Samuel Taylor

Professor Dominik Perler
Der Georg-August Universität
Germany
Alighieri, Dante
Hervaeus Natalis
Nicholas of Autrecourt

Dr Roy W. Perrett
Massey University
New Zealand
Causation, Indian theories of

Professor John R. Perry
Henry Waldgrave Stuart Professor
of Philosophy
Director of Center for the Study of
Language and Information
Stanford University
USA
Semantics, possible worlds
Semantics, situation

Professor Philip Pettit
Research School of Social Sciences
Australian National University
Desire
Social laws

Professor David Phillips
University of Houston
USA
Emotive meaning

Professor Stephen H. Phillips
Professor of Philosophy and Asian
Studies
University of Texas at Austin
USA
Aurobindo Ghose
Awareness in Indian thought
Brahman
Epistemology, Indian Schools Of
Error and illusion, Indian
    conceptions of
Gaṅgeśa
Knowledge, Indian views of
Monism, Indian
Sense perception, Indian views of
Vedānta

Dr Mark Philp
Oriel College
University of Oxford
UK
Corruption
Godwin, William

Dr Mario Piccinini
Vicenza
Italy
Gioberti, Vincenzo

Professor Michel Piclin
Saint-Pierre-les-Elbeuf
France
Lachelier, Jules

Professor Martin L. Pine
Professor of History
Queens College, City University of
New York
USA
Pomponazzi, Pietro

Dr Thomas Pink
Kings College, University of London
UK
Will, the

Dr Anna Pintore
Instituto di Filosophia e Sciologia
del Dirri
Italy
Institutionalism in law

Professor Alvin Plantinga
John A. O'Brien Professor of
Philosophy
University of Notre Dame
USA
God, arguments for the existence of
Religion and epistemology

Lord Raymond Plant
Master, St Catherine's College
University of Oxford
UK
Political philosophy, nature of

Dr Olaf Pluta
Ruhr-Universität Bochum
Germany
Ailly, Pierre d'

Professor Leon Pompa
Emeritus Professor
University of Birmingham
UK
Vico, Giambattista

Professor Richard H. Popkin
Professor Emeritus
Washington University, St Louis
Adjunct Professor of History and
Philosophy
University of California, Los
Angeles
USA
Charron, Pierre
Montaigne, Michel Eyquem de
Sanches, Francisco
Scepticism, Renaissance

Professor Roy Porter
*The Wellcome Institute for the
History of Medicine*
London
UK
Hartley, David
Johnson, Dr Samuel

Professor Mark Poster
History Department
University of California, Irvine
USA
Baudrillard, Jean

Dr Michael Potter
Fitzwilliam College
University of Cambridge
UK
Arithmetic, philosophical issues in
Set theory, different systems of

Dr Karin Preisendanz
*Institut für Kultur und Geschichte
Indiens und Tibets*
Universität Hamburg
Germany
Gautama, Akṣapāda
Materialism, Indian school of
Nyāya-Vaiśeṣika

Professor Dr Ulrich K. Preuß
*Zentrum für Europäische
Rechtspolitik*
Universität Bremen
Germany
Constitutionalism

Mr A.W. Price
*Birkbeck College, University of
London*
UK
Hare, Richard Mervyn

Professor Graham Priest
University of Queensland
Australia
Numbers
Paraconsistent logic

Dr John Procopé
*Deceased – formerly of
Cambridge, UK*
Hermetism

Professor Dr Francesco del Punta
Classe di Lettere e Filosofia
Scuola Normale Superiore
Italy
Giles of Rome

Professor Richard L. Purtill
Western Washington University
USA
Lewis, Clive Staples

Professor Ruth Anna Putnam
Wellesley College
USA
James, William

Professor Zenon W. Pylyshyn
*Board of Governors Professor of
Cognitive Science*
*Rutgers Center for Cognitive
Science*
Rutgers University
USA
Cognitive architecture
Modularity of mind

Dr Ato Quayson
*Faculty of English and Pembroke
College*
University of Cambridge
UK
Postcolonialism

Professor Philip L. Quinn
*John A. O'Brien Professor of
Philosophy*
University of Notre Dame
USA
Asceticism
Religious pluralism
Self-control
Sin

Professor James Rachels
*University of Alabama at
Birmingham*
USA
Animals and ethics

Professor Peter Railton
University of Michigan
USA
Analytic ethics

Professor Lisa Raphals
*Assistant Professor of History and
Asian Studies*
Bard College
USA
Chinese classics

Mr John D. Ray
Reader in Egyptology
University of Cambridge
UK
Egyptian cosmology, ancient

Dr Stephen Read
*Department of Logic and
Metaphysics*
University of St Andrews
Scotland, UK
Relevance logic and entailment

Professor Andrews Reath
University of California, Riverside
USA
Autonomy, ethical

Professor Franois Recanati
Directeur de recherche, CREA
CNRS / École Polytechnique
France
Pragmatics

Professor Michael Redhead
*Department of History and
Philosophy of Science*
University of Cambridge
UK
Relativity theory, philosophical
   significance of

Dr Walter B. Redmond
Austin, Texas
USA
Latin America, colonial thought in

Professor Pietro Redondi
Università di Bologna
Italy
Koyré, Alexander

Professor T.J. Reed
Queen's College
University of Oxford
UK
Schiller, Johann Christoph
   Friedrich

Dr Andrew Reeve
Department of Politics
University of Warwick
UK
Representation, political

Dr Bryan Stephenson Rennie
Department of Religion, History,
Philosophy and the Classics
Westminster College
USA
Eliade, Mircea

Professor Ferruccio Franco
Repellini
Università degli Studi di Milano
Italy
Ptolemy

Dr Nicholas Rescher
University of Pittsburgh
USA
Fallibilism

Dr Greg Restall
School of History, Philosophy and
Politics
Macquarie University
Australia
Logical laws

Professor Georges Rey
University of Maryland
USA
Concepts
Eliminativism
Folk psychology
Language of thought
Mind, computational theories of
Mind, philosophy of
Semantics, informational
Skinner, Burrhus Frederick
Unconscious mental states

Professor Nicholas V. Riasanovsky
Sidney Hellman Ehrman Professor
of History
University of California, Berkeley
USA
Eurasian movement
Pan-Slavism

Professor Mark Richard
Tufts University
USA
Compositionality
Quantifiers, substitutional and
    objectual
Scope

Professor Robert C. Richardson
University of Cincinnati
USA
Vitalism

Dr Caterina Rigo
Jerusalem
Israel
Hillel ben Samuel of Verona
Immanuel ben Solomon of Rome
Judah ben Moses of Rome

Professor Patrick Riley
Professor of Political and Moral
Philosophy
Department of Government
Harvard University
USA
Fénelon, François de Salignac de la
    Mothe
Gerdil, Giancinto Sigismondo

Professor Arthur Ripstein
University of Toronto
Canada
Multiculturalism

Dr Augustin Riska
Notre Dame College
St John's University
USA
Avenarius, Richard

Professor James Risser
Seattle University
USA
Barthes, Roland

Dr Julian Roberts
Universität München
Germany
Benjamin, Walter
Honour
Lorenzen, Paul

Professor Isabelle Robinet
Département de Chinois
Université de Provence-Aix-
Marseille
France
Guanzi

Professor Daniel N. Robinson
Professor of Psychology and
Adjunct Professor of Philosophy
Georgetown University
USA
Du Bois-Reymond, Emil
Fechner, Gustav Theodor

Mr Howard Robinson
University of Liverpool
UK
Materialism in the philosophy of
    mind

Professor Jenefer M. Robinson
University of Cincinnati
USA
Artistic style

Dr Neal Robinson
Lecturer in Islamic Studies
Leeds University
UK
'Abduh, Muhammad
Ash'ariyya and Mu'tazila
Ibn al-'Arabi, Muhyi al-Din

Ms Teresa Rodriguez de Lecea
Instituto de Filosofía
Consejo Superior de Investigaciones
Científicas
Spain
Krause, Karl Christian Friedrich

Professor G.A.J. Rogers
University of Keele
UK
Bold, Samuel
Charleton, Walter
Glanvill, Joseph

Professor Michael David Rohr
Rutgers University
USA
Rorty, Richard McKay

Professor Richard Rorty
University of Virginia
USA
Pragmatism

Professor Connie S. Rosati
West Bloomfield, Michigan
USA
Ideals

Professor Alan Rosenberg
Queen's College, City University of
New York
USA
Blanchot, Maurice

Professor Alex Rosenberg
University of Georgia
USA
Social science, methodology of
Sociobiology

Professor Jay F. Rosenberg
University of North Carolina
USA
Sellars, Wilfrid Stalker

Professor Gary Rosenkrantz
University of North Carolina
USA
Omnipotence

Dr Michael Rosen
Lincoln College
University of Oxford
UK
Marx, Karl

Professor Bernice Glatzer
Rosenthal
Professor of History
Fordham University
USA
Bulgakov, Sergei Nikolaevich
Nietzsche: impact on Russian
 thought
Rozanov, Vasilii Vasil'evich
Russian religious-philosophical
 renaissance
Shestov, Lev (Yehuda Leib
 Shvartsman)

Professor David M. Rosenthal
Professor of Philosophy and

Coordinator, Concentration in
Cognitive Science
The Graduate School and University
Center
City University of New York
USA
Dualism

Professor Sandra B. Rosenthal
Loyola University
USA
Lewis, Clarence Irving

Professor Brian Rosmaita
Kent State University
USA
Neumann, John Von

Dr Angus Ross
University of East Anglia
UK
Society, concept of

Professor H.D. Roth
Department of Religious Studies
and East Asian Studies
Brown University
USA
Huainanzi
Yangzhu

Professor Michael S. Roth
The Getty Centre for the History of
Art and the Humanities
USA
Kojève, Alexandre

Professor Joseph Rouse
Wesleyan University
USA
Heideggerian philosophy of science

Professor William L. Rowe
Purdue University
USA
Agnosticism
Atheism
Deism
Freedom, divine

Professor Young-chan Ro
Department of Philosophy &
Religious Studies
George Mason University
USA
Yi Yulgok

Professor David-Hillel Ruben
Department of Philosophy, Logic
and Scientific Method
London School of Economics,
University of London
UK
Explanation in history and social
 science
Social sciences, philosophy of

Professor Tamar Rudavsky
The Ohio State University
USA
Ibn Tzaddik, Joseph ben Jacob

Professor William Ruddick
New York University
USA
Family, ethics and the

Professor Dr T.S. Rukmani
Chair in Hindu Studies
Department of Religion
Concordia University
Canada
Self, Indian theories of

Professor Ian Rumfitt
University of Michigan at Ann
Arbor
USA
Meaning and understanding
Presupposition

Dr Erika Rummel
Department of History
Wilfrid Laurier University
Canada
Erasmus, Desiderius

Professor David T. Runia
Chair of Ancient and Medieval
Philosophy
Leiden University
Netherlands
Diogenes Laertius
Doxography
Philo of Alexandria

Professor Donald Rutherford
Emory University
USA
Universal language

Professor Alan Ryan
Department of Politics
University of Princeton
USA
Systems theory in social science

Professor T.A. Ryckman
Northwestern University
USA
General relativity, philosophical
  responses to
Geometry, philosophical issues in
Weyl, Hermann

Dr Kurt Salamun
Karl-Franzens-Universität Graz
Austria
Jaspers, Karl

Professor Merrilee H. Salmon
Department of History and
Philosophy of Science
University of Pittsburgh
USA
Anthropology, philosophy of

Professor Wesley C. Salmon
University of Pittsburgh
USA
Reichenbach, Hans

Professor Jerry Samet
Brandeis University
USA
Nativism

Professor Norbert M. Samuelson
Professor of Jewish Philosophy
Temple University
USA
Ibn Daud, Abraham

Professor Gabriel Sandu
University of Helsinki
Finland
Quantifiers

Ziauddin Sardar
London, UK
Science in Islamic philosophy

Professor Lyman Tower Sargent
Department of Political Science
University of Missouri – St Louis
USA
Communism
Utopianism

Professor Rose-Mary Sargent
Merrimack College
USA
Boyle, Robert

Professor Dr Hans-Martin Sass
Ruhr Universität
Germany
Feuerbach, Ludwig Andreas
Ruge, Arnold

Professor Geoffrey Sayre-McCord
Gillian Cell Professor of Philosophy
University of North Carolina at
Chapel Hill
USA
Moral knowledge

Professor Kenneth M. Sayre
University of Notre Dame
USA
Information theory

Professor James P. Scanlan
Emeritus Professor
The Ohio State University
USA
Berdiaev, Nikolai Aleksandrovich
Lossky, Nicholas Onufrievich
Russian Materialism: 'The 1860s'
Vysheslavtsev, Boris Petrovich

Professor Michael Scanlan
Oregon State University
USA
Post, Emil Leon

Professor T.M. Scanlon
Alford Professor of Natural
Religion, Moral Philosophy and
Civil Polity
Harvard University
USA
Moral justification
Promising

Professor Margaret Schabas
York University
Canada
Keynes, John Maynard

Professor Kenneth F. Schaffner
University Professor of Medical
Humanities
George Washington University
USA
Medicine, philosophy of

Professor Theodore R. Schatzki
University of Kentucky
USA
Structuralism in social science

Professor Naomi Scheman
University of Minnesota
USA
Linguistic discrimination

Professor Dr Hermann S. Schibli
Lehrstuhl für Alte Geschichte
Universität Passau
Germany
Archytas
Neo-Pythagoreanism
Philolaus
Pythagoras
Pythagoreanism

Professor Frederick F. Schmitt
University of Illinois at Urbana-
Champaign
USA
Social epistemology

Dr Malcolm Schofield
St. John's College
University of Cambridge
UK
Alcmaeon
Anaxagoras
Antisthenes
Diogenes of Apollonia
Empedocles
Plato

Professor Robert E. Schofield
Professor Emeritus
Department of History
Iowa State University
USA
Priestley, Joseph

Dr Martin Schönfeld
University of South Florida
USA
Fontenelle, Bernard de
Tschirnhaus, Ehrenfried
   Walther von

Professor Peter A. Schouls
Massey University
New Zealand
Revolution

Professor Dr Peter Schroeder-Heister
Wilhelm-Schickard-Institut
Universität Tübingen
Germany
Formal languages and systems

Dr Bart Schultz
University of Chicago
USA
Grote, John
Sidgwick, Henry

Professor David A. Schum
George Mason University
USA
Legal evidence and inference

Professor Ofelia Schutte
University of Florida
USA
Marxist thought in Latin America

Dr Paul Schweizer
Centre for Cognitive Science
University of Edinburgh
Scotland, UK
Matter, Indian conceptions of
Modal operators

Professor Giovanni Scibilia
Università di Pavia
Italy
Lacoue-Labarthe, Philippe

Dr Jean-Loup Seban
La Chapelle Royale
Brussels, Belgium
Barth, Karl
Boehme, Jakob
Bonhoeffer, Dietrich
Brunner, Emil
Bultmann, Rudolf
Tindal, Matthew
Troeltsch, Ernst Peter Wilhelm

Dr Sonia Sedivy
University of Toronto
Canada
Nagel, Thomas

Professor David Sedley
Christ's College
University of Cambridge
UK
Ancient Philosophy
Aretē
Ariston of Chios
Atomism, ancient
Chrysippus
Cleanthes
Dialectical school
Epicureanism
Epicurus
Hellenistic philosophy
Megarian school
Melissus
Parmenides
Presocratic philosophy
Stoicism
Zeno of Citium

Professor Kenneth Seeskin
Northwestern University
USA
Jewish philosophy in the early 19th
   century

Dr Gabriel Segal
King's College, University of
London
UK
Indirect discourse
Methodological individualism

Professor Michael J. Seidler
Department of Philosophy and
Religion
Western Kentucky University
USA
Crusius, Christian August

Dr James D. Sellmann
College of Arts and Sciences
University of Guam
Lushi chunqiu

Dr Robert Service
School of Slavonic and East
European Studies, University of
London
UK
Lenin, Vladimir Il'ich

Professor Dudley Shapere
Reynolds Professor of the
Philosophy and History of Science
Wake Forest University
USA
Incommensurability
Matter

Professor Ian Shapiro
Professor of Political Science
Yale University
USA
Human Nature

Professor Stewart Shapiro
The Ohio State University at
Newark
USA
and University of St Andrews
Scotland, UK
Church's thesis
Second-order logic, philosophical
   issues in

Professor R.W. Sharples
Department of Greek and Latin
University College, University of
London
UK
Alexander of Aphrodisias
Peripatetics
Strato

Professor David Shatz
Yeshiva University
USA
Prophecy

Professor Robert Shaver
University of Manitoba
USA
Enthusiasm

Professor Thomas Sheehan
Loyola University of Chicago
USA
Heidegger, Martin

Professor Richard Sher
Department of Humanities
New Jersey Institute of Technology
USA
Blair, Hugh

Professor Christopher Shields
Associate Professor of Philosophy
and Classics
University of Colorado at Boulder
USA
Language, ancient philosophy of

Professor Rob Shields
Sociology and Anthropology
Carleton University
Canada
Lefebvre, Henri

Professor Robert K. Shope
University of Massachusetts
USA
Gettier problems

Dr Kristin Shrader-Frechette
Distinguished Research Professor
University of South Florida
USA
Risk
Risk assessment

Professor Shun Kwong-loi
University of California, Berkeley
USA
Wang Yangming

Professor Richard M. Shusterman
Temple University
USA
Poetry

Professor Alan Sidelle
University of Wisconsin
USA
Necessary truth and convention

Professor Mark Siderits
Illinois State University
USA
Nāgārjuna

Dr L.A. Siedentop
Keble College
University of Oxford
UK
Tocqueville, Alexis de

Professor Wilfried Sieg
Carnegie Mellon University
USA
Computability theory
Proof theory

Professor Michael Silverthorne
Department of History
McGill University
Canada
Carmichael, Gershom

Dr N.E. Simmonds
Reader in Jurisprudence
Corpus Christi College
University of Cambridge
UK
Blackstone, William
Law and morality

Professor A. John Simmons
University of Virginia
USA
Consent
Obligation, political

Professor Lawrence H. Simon
Bowdoin College
USA
Rationality and cultural relativism

Professor Peter Simons
University of Leeds
UK
Brentano, Franz Clemens
Identity of indiscernibles
Meinong, Alexius

Professor Ira Singer
Hofstra University
USA
Morality and identity

Professor Georgette Sinkler
University of Illinois at Chicago
USA
Bacon, Roger

Dr Lucas Siorvanes
King's College, University of
London
UK
Chaldaean Oracles
Hypatia
Iamblichus
Neoplatonism
Porphyry
Proclus

Professor David A. Sipfle
William H. Laird Professor of
Philosophy and the Liberal Arts
Carleton College
USA
Meyerson, Émile

Professor Lawrence Sklar
University of Michigan
USA
Thermodynamics
Time

Professor John Skorupski
Department of Moral Philosophy
University of St Andrews
UK
Mill, John Stuart
Morality and ethics

Reverend Robert Slesinski
University of Scranton
USA
Florenskii, Pavel Aleksandrovich

Professor Michael Slote
University of Maryland
USA
Moral psychology

Dr Robin Small
Faculty of Education
Monash University, Clayton
Australia
Dühring, Eugen Karl

Professor Timothy Smiley
University of Cambridge
UK
Consequence, conceptions of
Multiple-conclusion logic

Dr A.D. Smith
University of Essex
UK
Primary–secondary distinction

Professor Barry Smith
State University of New York at
Buffalo
USA
Axiology
Gestalt psychology
Reinach, Adolf

Dr Barry C. Smith
Birkbeck College, University of
London
UK
Language, conventionality of
Language, social nature of
Meaning and rule-following

Dr Frederick M. Smith
School of Religion
University of Iowa
USA
Heaven, Indian conceptions of

Dr G.W. Smith
Department of Politics
University of Lancaster
UK
Law, limits of

Professor George E. Smith
Tufts University
USA
Newton, Isaac

Professor Michael Smith
Senior Fellow
Research School of Social Sciences
Australian National University
Australia
Emotivism
Reasons and causes

Professor Nicholas D. Smith
Michigan State University
USA
Slavery
Wisdom

Mr Nicholas J.J. Smith
University of Sydney
Australia
Epiphenomenalism

Mr Peter Smith
University of Sheffield
UK
Broad, Charlie Dunbar

Professor Quentin Smith
Western Michigan University
USA
Tense and temporal logic

Dr Paul F. Snowdon
Exeter College
University of Oxford
UK
Strawson, Peter Frederick

Professor Elliott Sober
Hans Reichenbach Professor
University of Wisconsin – Madison
USA
Evolution and ethics
Evolutionary theory and social
    science
Innate knowledge
Simplicity (in scientific theories)

Professor Alan Soble
University of New Orleans
USA
Sexuality, philosophy of

Professor Robert C. Solomon
University of Texas at Austin
USA
Emotions, nature of
Emotions, philosophy of

Ms Fiona Somerset
University of Oxford
UK
Dietrich of Freiberg
Gerbert of Aurillac
John of Mirecourt
Thomas of York

Professor Johann P. Sommerville
Department of History
University of Wisconsin – Madison
USA
Filmer, Sir Robert

Dr Jayandra Soni
Fachgebiet Indologie
Philipps-Universität
Germany
Jaina philosophy
Mahāvīra
Manifoldness, Jaina theory of

Dr Kate Soper
History, Philosophy and
Contemporary Studies
University of North London
UK
Nature and convention

Professor Richard Sorabji
King's College, University of
London
UK
Aristotle commentators

Professor Tom Sorell
University of Essex
USA
Business ethics
Hobbes, Thomas

Professor Ernest Sosa
Romeo Elton Professor of Natural
Theology
Brown University
USA
Foundationalism

Professor James South
Marquette University
USA
Aristotelianism, Renaissance

Dr Beverley Southgate
*Reader Emeritus in the History of
Ideas*
University of Hertfordshire
UK
Sergeant, John
White, Thomas

Professor Peter Spirtes
Carnegie-Mellon University
USA
Statistics and social science

Professor Gayatri Chakravorty
Spivak
*Avalon Foundation Professor of the
Humanities*
*Department of English and
Comparative Literature*
Columbia University
USA
Feminist literary criticism

Professor Alan Sponberg
*Professor of Asian Philosophy and
Religion*
University of Montana
USA
Ambedkar, Bhimrao Ramji

Professor T.L.S. Sprigge
Professor Emeritus
University of Edinburgh
Scotland, UK
Absolute, the
Idealism
Panpsychism

Professor David A. Sprintzen
*C.W. Post College of Long Island
University*
USA
Camus, Albert

Professor George J. Stack
Professor Emeritus
*State University of New York at
Brockport*
USA
Lange, Friedrich Albert
Materialism

Dr Friedrich Stadler
*Director of the Vienna Circle
Institute*
Austria
Vienna Circle

Professor Allen Stairs
University of Maryland
USA
Parapsychology
Quantum mechanics,
  interpretation of

Professor B. Stanosz
Warsaw
Poland
Kotarbiński, Tadeusz

Professor Paul G. Stanwood
Professor of English
University of British Columbia
Canada
Law, William

Professor Cynthia A. Stark
University of Utah
USA
Self-respect

Professor Daniel Statman
Bar-Ilan University
Israel
Moral luck

Professor Christopher Stead
Ely Professor of Divinity, Emeritus
University of Cambridge
UK
Eusebius
Gnosticism
Logos
Pneuma

Professor Howard Stein
University of Chicago
USA
Dedekind, Julius Wilhelm Richard
Logicism

Professor Peter Stein
Queens' College
University of Cambridge
UK
Jurisprudence, historical

Professor Dr Ernst Steinkellner
*Institut für Tibetologie und
Buddhismuskunde*
Universität Wien
Austria
Dharmakīrti

Professor Lawrence S. Stepelevich
Villanova University
USA
Bauer, Bruno
Cieszkowski, August von

Professor Antoni B. Stępień
Catholic University of Lublin
Poland
Ingarden, Roman Witold
Poland, philosophy in

Dr Kim Sterelny
Victoria University of Wellington
New Zealand
Reductionism in the philosophy of
  mind
Species

Professor Josef Stern
University of Chicago
USA
Arama, Isaac ben Moses
Nahmanides, Moses

Dr Robert Stern
University of Sheffield
UK
Hegelianism

Professor Daniel B. Stevenson
Department of Religious Studies
University of Kansas
USA
Zhiyi

Professor P.F. Stevens
Harvard University
USA
Linnaeus, Carl von

Dr Helen Steward
Balliol College
University of Oxford
UK
Akrasia

Professor M.A. Stewart
Research Professor in the History of Philosophy
University of Lancaster
UK
Oswald, James

Professor Stephen P. Stich
Rutgers University
USA
Cognitive pluralism
Epistemic relativism
Folk psychology

Ms Valerie Stoker
South Asia Regional Studies
University of Pennsylvania
USA
Madhva

Dr Martin Stone
Lecturer in the Philosophy of Religion
King's College, University of London
UK
Casuistry

Dr Philip Stratton-Lake
Keele University
UK
Hope

Dr Galen Strawson
Jesus College
University of Oxford
UK
Free will

Professor Sarah Stroumsa
Department of Arabic Language and Literature and Department of Jewish Thought
The Hebrew University
Israel
al-Muqammas, Daud

Professor David J. Stump
University of San Francisco
USA
Poincaré, Jules Henri

Professor Eleonore Stump
St Louis University
USA
Aquinas, Thomas
Eternity
Religion, philosophy of

Professor Nicholas L. Sturgeon
Sage School of Philosophy
Cornell University
USA
Naturalism in ethics

Professor Fred Gillette Sturm
University of New Mexico
USA
Brazil, philosophy in

Dr Scott C. Styles
Faculty of Law
University of Aberdeen
Scotland, UK
Stair, James Dalrymple, Viscount

Professor Marjorie Suchocki
Dean, School of Theology
Claremont University
USA
Feminist theology

Mr Jeffrey M. Suderman
Department of History
University of Western Ontario
Canada
Campbell, George

Professor David Sullivan
Metropolitan State College of Denver
USA
Lotze, Rudolf Hermann

Professor Claude Sumner
Addis Ababa University
Ethiopia
Ethiopia, philosophy in

Professor Frederick Suppe
Professor of Philosophy and Chairperson of History and Philosophy of Science
University of Maryland, College Park
USA
Bridgman, Percy William
Operationalism
Theories, scientific

Professor Patrick Suppes
Lucie Stern Professor of Philosophy, Emeritus
Center for the Study of Language and Information
Stanford University
USA
Measurement, theory of

Professor Marshall Swain
The Ohio State University
USA
Knowledge, causal theory of
Knowledge, defeasibility theory of

Professor Richard Swedberg
Professor of Sociology
University of Stockholm
Sweden
Schumpeter, Joseph Alois

Professor Zeno Swijtink
Sonoma State University
USA
Beth's theorem and Craig's theorem

Professor Richard Swinburne
Oriel College
University of Oxford
UK
Revelation
Soul, nature and immortality of the

Dr Philip J. Swoboda
Assistant Professor of History
Lafayette College
USA
Frank, Semën Liudvigovich

Professor Edith Dudley Sylla
Department of History
North Carolina State University
USA
Bradwardine, Thomas
Burley, Walter
Natural philosophy, medieval
Oxford Calculators

Professor Zoltán Gendler Szabó
Sage School of Philosophy
Cornell University
USA
Language, early modern
 philosophy of

Professor John A. Taber
University of New Mexico
USA
Duty And Virtue, Indian
 Conceptions Of
Mīmāṃsā
Universals, Indian theories of

Dr Guglielmo Tamburrini
Research Scientist
Instituto di Cibernetica
Consiglio Nazionale delle Ricerche
Italy
Turing machines

Dr Michael Tanner
University of Cambridge
UK
Aesthetics and ethics
Art and morality
Opera, aesthetics of

Dr John Tasioulas
School of Law
University of Glasgow
Scotland, UK
Justice, equity and law

Dr Liba Taub
Whipple Museum of the History of
Science
University of Cambridge
UK
Eudoxus

Professor Michael Tavuzzi
Pontificia Università S. Tommaso
Italy
Capreolus, Johannes
Silvestri, Francesco

Professor Barry Taylor
University of Melbourne
Australia
Dummett, Michael Anthony
 Eardley

Mr C.C.W. Taylor
Corpus Christi College
University of Oxford
UK
Democritus
Eudaimonia
Leucippus

Professor Jacqueline Taylor
Tufts University
USA
Moral sense theories

Professor Kenneth A. Taylor
Stanford University
USA
Propositional attitude statements

Professor Paul Taylor
University of Cape Town
South Africa
Art and truth
Artist's intention

Professor Paul Teller
University of California, Davis
USA
Field theory, quantum

Professor Victor Terras
Professor emeritus
Department of Slavic Languages
and Literatures
Brown University
USA
Belinskii, Vissarion Grigorievich
Schellingianism

Dr Udo Thiel
Faculty of Arts
Australian National University
Overton, Richard

Dr J.M.M.H. Thijssen
Katholieke Universiteit Nijmegen
Netherlands
Eternity of the world, medieval
 views of

Professor Canon Anthony C.
 Thistelton
Professor of Christian Theology and
Head of Department
Department of Theology
University of Nottingham
UK
Hermeneutics, Biblical

Dr Alan Thomas
King's College, University of
London
UK
Axiology
MacIntyre, Alasdair
Values

Professor Paul Thom
Faculty of Arts
Australian National University
Logic, ancient

Dr John B. Thompson
Jesus College
University of Cambridge
UK
Ricoeur, Paul

Professor Kirill Ole Thompson
Foreign Languages and Literature
Department
National Taiwan University
Zhang Zai
Zhou Dunyi
Zhu Xi

Professor Michael Thompson
University of Pittsburgh
USA
Anscombe, Gertrude Elizabeth
 Margaret

Dr Christopher Thornhill
Department of German
King's College, University of
London
UK
Historicism

Professor J.E. Tiles
Department of Philosophy
University of Hawai'i at Mānoa
USA
Pragmatism in ethics

Professor Mary Tiles
University of Hawaii
USA
Bachelard, Gaston
Cantor's theorem
Continuum hypothesis

Professor Tom J.F. Tillemans
Section de langues et civilisations
orientales
Faculté des Lettres, Université de
Lausanne
Switzerland
Tibetan philosophy
Tsong kha pa Blo bzang grags pa

Professor Hoyt Cleveland Tillman
Professor of History
Arizona State University
USA
Cheng Hao
Cheng Yi

Professor Mark Timmons
University of Memphis
USA
Logic of ethical discourse

Mr Ian Tipton
University of Wales, Swansea
UK
Berkeley, George

Professor Hava Tirosh-Samuelson
Associate Professor of Religious
Studies
Indiana University
USA
Messer Leon, Judah
Shem Tov Family

Professor William Mills Todd III
Curt Hugo Reisinger Professor of
Slavic Languages and Literatures
and Professor of Comparative
Literature
Harvard University
USA
Moscow-Tartu School

Professor Robert B. Todd
Department of Classics
University of British Columbia
Canada
Cleomedes

Professor Rosemarie Tong
Thatcher Professor of Philosophy
and Medical Humanities
Davidson College
USA
Feminist ethics

Mr John Torrance
Hertford College
University of Oxford
UK
Marxism, Western

Professor Roberto Torretti
Santiago
Chile
Space
Spacetime

Professor Dabney Townsend
Professor of Philosophy and Dean of
Arts and Sciences
Armstrong Atlantic State University
Department of Philosophy and
Humanities
University of Texas
USA
Alison, Archibald
Baumgarten, Alexander Gottlieb
Gerard, Alexander
Lessing, Gotthold Ephraim

Dr Cecilia Trifogli
Classe di Lettere e Filosofia
Scuola Normale Superiore
Italy
Giles of Rome

Dr Voula Tsouna
Pomona College
USA
Aristippus the Elder
Cyrenaics
Socratic schools

Professor John Allen Tucker
Associate Professor of History
University of North Florida
USA
Fujiwara Seika
Itō Jinsai
Ogyū Sorai
Tominaga Nakamoto

Professor Mary Evelyn Tucker
Associate Professor of Religion
Bucknell University
USA
Kaibara Ekken

Mr H. Tudor
Department of Politics
University of Durham
UK
Bernstein, Eduard
Kautsky, Karl Johann
Lassalle, Ferdinand
Luxemburg, Rosa

Professor Raimo Tuomela
Academy Professor
Academy of Finland
University of Helsinki
Finland
Social action

Professor Stephen P. Turner
University of South Florida
USA
Weber, Max

Professor Martin M. Tweedale
University of Alberta
Canada
Abelard, Peter
Roscelin of Compiègne
William of Champeaux

Professor William Twining
Quain Professor of Jurisprudence
Emeritus
University College, University of
London
UK
Llewellyn, Karl Nickerson

Professor Michael Tye
Temple University
USA
Imagery
Mental states, adverbial theory of
Vagueness

Professor A.M. Ungar
State University of New York at
Albany
USA
Herbrand's theorem
Natural deduction, tableau and
  sequent systems

Dr Suzanne Uniacke
University of Wollongong
Australia
Double effect, principle of

Professor Taitetsu Unno
Jill Ker Conway Professor of
Religion
Smith College
USA
Shinran

Professor J.O. Urmson
Emeritus Professor
Stanford University
USA
Austin, John Langshaw

Professor Alasdair Urquhart
University of Toronto
Canada
Complexity, computational

Professor Robert Van Gulick
Syracuse University
USA
Chinese Room Argument

Professor Peter van Inwagen
John Cardinal O'Hara Professor of
Philosophy
University of Notre Dame
USA
Incarnation and Christology
Lewis, David Kellogg
Resurrection
Trinity

Professor Bryan W. Van Norden
Vassar College
USA
Mencius

Professor Thomas Vargish
English Department
University of Maryland
USA
Modernism

Professor Paul Varley
Sen Professor of Japanese Cultural
History
University of Hawaii
USA
Bushi philosophy
Shintō

Professor Gregory Velazco y
Trianosky
Olivet College
USA
Supererogation

Professor Theo Verbeek
Rijksuniversiteit Utrecht
Netherlands
Geulincx, Arnold
Le Clerc, Jean
Rohault, Jacques

Professor Donald Phillip Verene
Charles Howard Candler Professor
of Metaphysics and Moral
Philosophy
Emory University
USA
Cassirer, Ernst

Professor Richard Vernon
Department of Political Science
University of Western Ontario
Canada
Proudhon, Pierre-Joseph

Professor Guido Verucci
Professore Ordinario di Storia
Moderna
Dipartimento di Storia Facoltà di
Lettere e Filosofia
Università di Roma tor Vergata
Italy
Rosmini-Serbati, Antonio

Professor Graziella Federici
Vescovini
Professore titolare di Storia della
Filosofia
Università di Firenze
Italy
Blasius of Parma

Dr Albert Visser
Utrecht University
Netherlands
Provability logic

Professor Meera Viswanathan
Associate Professor of Comparative
Literature and East Asian Studies
Brown University
USA
Aesthetics, Japanese
Kokoro

Professor Jonathan Vogel
Amherst College
USA
Inference to the best explanation

Professor Candace Vogler
University of Chicago
USA
Taylor, Harriet

Professor Barbara Von Eckardt
Associate Dean, College of Arts and
Sciences
University of Nebraska – Lincoln
USA
Introspection, psychology of

Dr Alexander von Rospatt
Institut für Indologie und
Zentralasienwissenschaften
Universität Leipzig
Germany
Momentariness, Buddhist
  doctrine of

Professor William J. Wainwright
University of Wisconsin –
Milwaukee
USA
Edwards, Jonathan

Dr Michael B. Wakoff
University of Wisconsin – Parkside
USA
Theosophy

Professor Jeremy Waldron
Laurance S. Rockefeller University
and Professor of Politics, Princeton
University
USA
Liberalism
Neutrality, political

Dr Andrzej Walicki
O'Neill Professor of History
University of Notre Dame
USA
Chaadaev, Pëtr Iakovlevich
Chernyshevskii, Nikolai
  Gavrilovich
Hegelianism, Russian
Hessen, Sergei Iosifovich
Lavrov, Pëtr Lavrovich
Mikhailovskii, Nikolai
  Konstantinovich
Positivism, Russian
Slavophilism
Solov'ëv, Vladimir Sergeevich

Mr Nicholas Walker
Former Research Fellow
Magdalene College
University of Cambridge
UK
Hegelianism
Hölderlin, Johann Christian
  Friedrich

Professor Paul E. Walker
Chicago, Illinois
USA
al-Razi, Abu Bakr Muhammad ibn
  Zakariyya'

Dr Ralph C.S. Walker
Magdalen College
University of Oxford
UK
Contingency

Professor R. Jay Wallace
Humboldt-Universität zu Berlin
Germany
Moral motivation
Moral sentiments

Professor Robert L. Walters
Professor Emeritus
Department of French
University of Western Ontario
Canada
Du Châtelet-Lomont, Gabrielle-
  Émilie

Professor Douglas Walton
University of Western Australia
Fallacies
Formal and informal logic

Dr Robert Wardy
St. Catharine's College
University of Cambridge
UK
Categories

Sir Geoffrey Warnock
Deceased – formerly of
Wiltshire, UK
Ordinary language philosophy,
  school of

Professor Corey Washington
University of Maryland
USA
Use/mention distinction and
  quotation

Professor W.C. Watt
Professor Emeritus
Department of Cognitive Sciences
University of California
USA
Semiotics

Professor Albert Weale
Department of Government
University of Essex
UK
Equality
Needs and interests
Public interest
Welfare

Professor R.K. Webb
Professor of History (Emeritus)
University of Maryland Baltimore
County
USA
Martineau, Harriet

Professor Tu Wei-ming
East Asian Languages and
Civilizations
Harvard University
USA
Daxue
Self-cultivation in Chinese
  philosophy
Zhongyong

Professor Ota Weinberger
Graz
Austria
Weyr, František

Dr Paul Weindling
Wellcome Unit for the History of
Medicine
University of Oxford
UK
Haeckel, Ernst Heinrich

Professor Michael A. Weinstein
Department of Political Science
Purdue University
USA
Anti-positivist thought in Latin
  America

Professor Daniel M. Weinstock
Université de Montréal
Canada
Moral pluralism

Professor Paul J. Weithman
University of Notre Dame
USA
Religion and political philosophy

Professor Kathleen Wellman
Associate Professor of History
Southern Methodist University
USA
La Mettrie, Julien Offroy de

Professor Dag Westerståhl
Stockholm University
Sweden
Quantifiers, generalized

Professor Merold Westphal
Fordham University
USA
Phenomenology of religion
Postmodern theology

Professor Winthrop Wetherbee
English Department
Cornell University
USA
Bernard of Tours
Isaac of Stella

Dr N.E. Wetherick
Formerly of the Department of
Psychology
University of Aberdeen
Scotland, UK
Psychology, theories of

Professor Howard Wettstein
University of California, Riverside
USA
Ritual

Professor Linda Wetzel
Georgetown University
USA
Type/token distinction

Dr James D. White
Institute of Russian and East
European Studies
University of Glasgow
Scotland, UK
Plekhanov, Georgii Valentinovich

Professor John White
History and Philosophy
Institution of Education, University
of London
UK
Moral education

Professor Stephen A. White
Associate Professor of Classics
University of Texas
USA
Cicero, Marcus Tullius
Panaetius

Professor Stephen K. White
Department of Political Science
Virginia Polytechnic Institute
USA
Postmodernism and political
  philosophy

Professor Peter M. Whiteley
Department of Anthropology
Sarah Lawrence College
USA
Native American philosophy

Professor Margaret Whitford
French Department
Queen Mary and Westfield College,
University of London
UK
Feminism and psychoanalysis

Professor Stanisław Wielgus
Department of History of Polish
Philosophy
Catholic University of Lublin
Poland
Poland, philosophy in

Professor Geoffrey Wigoder
Jerusalem
Israel
Bar Hayya, Abraham

Professor Daniel Wikler
Madison Medical School
University of Wisconsin
USA
Medical ethics

Professor Christian Wildberg
Department of Classics
Princeton University
USA
Ammonius, son of Hermeas
Philoponus
Simplicius

Professor Charity Cannon Willard
Professor Emerita, Ladycliff
College
USA
Christine de Pizan

Dr Alan Williams
Department of Religions and Theory
University of Manchester
UK
Zoroastrianism

Professor Bernard Williams
All Souls College
University of Oxford
UK
Berlin, Isaiah
Virtues and vices

Professor C.J.F. Williams
Emeritus Professor
University of Bristol
UK
Prior, Arthur Norman

Professor David Williams
Department of French
University of Sheffield
UK
Condorcet, Marie-Jean-Antoine
  Nicolas Caritat de
Voltaire (François-Marie Arouet)

Professor Michael Williams
Charles and Emma Morrison
Professor of Humanities
and Professor of Philosophy
Northwestern University
USA
Doubt
Feyerabend, Paul Karl

Dr Paul Williams
Centre for Buddhist Studies
Department of Theology and
Religious Studies
University of Bristol
UK
Buddhist concept of emptiness
Mi bskyod rdo rje

Bishop Rowan Williams
Emeritus Professor
University of Oxford
UK
Weil, Simone

Dr Stephen G. Williams
Worcester College
University of Oxford
UK
Meaning and truth

Professor Thomas Williams
University of Iowa
USA
Farrer, Austin Marsden

Dr Timothy Williamson
University of Edinburgh
Scotland, UK
Identity

Professor Mark Wilson
The Ohio State University
USA
Field theory, classical
Mechanics, classical

Professor Kenneth P. Winkler
Class of 1919 Professor of
Philosophy
Wellesley College
USA
Browne, Peter
Collier, Arthur
Collins, Anthony
More, Henry

Professor John Winnie
Department of History and
Philosophy of Science
Indiana University
USA
Computer science

Professor John F. Wippel
The Catholic University of America
USA
Godfrey of Fontaines
Siger of Brabant

Professor Kwasi Wiredu
University of South Florida
USA
African philosophy, anglophone
Akan philosophical psychology

Dr Robert Wokler
Reader in The History of Political
Thought
University of Manchester
UK
Buffon, Georges Louis Leclerc,
    Comte de
Diderot, Denis
Enlightenment, continental
Monboddo, Lord (James Burnett)

Professor Jan Woleński
Jagiellonian University
Poland
Ajdukiewicz, Kazimierz
Leśniewski, Stanisław
Łukasiewicz, Jan
Twardowski, Kazimierz

Mr Jonathan Wolff
University College, University of
London
UK
Libertarianism
Nozick, Robert

Professor Susan Wolf
Johns Hopkins University
USA
Life, meaning of

Professor Nicholas P. Wolterstorff
Noah Porter Professor of
Philosophical Theology
Yale University
USA
Faith
Frei, Hans

Professor David B. Wong
Brandeis University
USA
Moral relativism

Professor Allen W. Wood
Yale University
USA
Alienation
Dialectical materialism
Fries, Jacob Friedrich

Professor Dennis Wood
Department of French Studies,
School of Modern Languages
University of Birmingham
UK
Constant de Rebeque, Henri-
    Benjamin

Dr Andrew Woodfield
University of Bristol
UK
Teleology

Dr Paul Wood
Department of History
University of Victoria
Canada
Aberdeen Philosophical Society
Beattie, James
Turnbull, George

Professor Rega Wood
Yale University
USA
Richard Rufus of Cornwall
Wodeham, Adam

Professor Paul Woodruff
University of Texas
USA
Thucydides

Dr Julian F. Woods
Montreal
Canada
Fatalism, Indian

Professor James Woodward
Department of Humanities and
Social Sciences
California Institute of Technology
USA
Statistics

Dr John Worrall
Department of Philosophy, Logic
and Scientific Method
London School of Economics,
University of London
UK
Lakatos, Imre
Science, philosophy of

Professor John S. Wright
Professor of Black Studies
University of Minnesota
USA
Amo, Anton Wilhelm

Professor Kathleen Wright
Haverford College
USA
Gadamer, Hans-Georg

Dr Tamra Wright
Jews' College, University of London
UK
Buber, Martin

Professor Alison Wylie
University of Western Ontario
Canada
Archaeology, philosophy of
Feminism and social science

Professor Stephen Yablo
University of Michigan, Ann Arbor
USA
Essentialism

Professor Keith E. Yandell
University of Wisconsin
USA
Bowne, Borden Parker
Inge, William Ralph
Loisy, Alfred
Oman, John Wood
Otto, Rudolf
Pantheism
Personalism
Ramsey, Ian Thomas
Rashdall, Hastings
Reincarnation
Salvation
Steiner, Rudolf
Teilhard de Chardin, Pierre
Temple, William
Thielicke, Helmut

Professor Robin D.S. Yates
Departments of East Asian Studies
and History
McGill University
Canada
Mozi

Professor Yü Ying-shih
East Asian Studies
Princeton University
USA
Dai Zhen

Dr Nissim Yosha
Institute for Jewish Studies
The Hebrew University
Israel
Herrera, Abraham Cohen de

Mr George M. Young
North Berwick, Maine
USA
Fëdorov, Nikolai Fëdorovich

Professor Michiko Yusa
Professor of Japanese and East
Asian Studies
Department of Foreign Languages
Western Washington University
USA
Zeami

Professor Linda Zagzebski
Loyola Marymount University
USA
Goodness, perfect
Heaven
Limbo
Purgatory
Virtue epistemology

Dr Taras D. Zakydalsky
Canadian Institute of Ukrainian
Studies
University of Alberta
Canada
Skovoroda, Hryhorii Savych

Dr Michael Zank
Assistant Professor of Religion
Boston University
USA
Cohen, Hermann

Ms Susan Khin Zaw
Faculty of Arts
The Open University
UK
Wollstonecraft, Mary

Professor Hossein Ziai
Department of Near Eastern
Languages and Cultures
University of California, Los
Angeles
USA
Illuminationist philosophy

Professor Marek Zirk-Sadowski
Department of Law
University of Łódź
Poland
Wróblewski, Jerzy

Dr Noam J. Zohar
Senior Lecturer, Bar Ilan University
and Shalom Hartman Institute
Israel
Bioethics, Jewish
Halakhah

Professor Günter Zöller
University of Iowa
USA
Lambert, Johann Heinrich
Lichtenberg, Georg Christoph
Tetens, Johann Nicolaus

Dr Josef Zumr
Institute of Philosophy
Czech Academy of Sciences
Czech Republic
Comenius, John Amos
Czech Republic, philosophy in
Masaryk, Thomáš Garrigue
Patočka, Jan
Slovakia, philosophy in

Professor Jack Zupko
Emory University
USA
Buridan, John

Professor Jan Zygmunt
Department of Logic
University of Wrocław
Poland
Polish logic

Using the Index

The index lists alphabetically the key concepts, names, countries and contributors in Volumes 1 to 9.

Each index entry gives the volume and page numbers (separated by a colon) where the reference occurs, (for example, 1:75–8). Numbers in bold type indicate the volume and pages of a whole entry devoted to a particular topic or philosopher. For example, the index entry on Wittgenstein begins:

Wittgenstein, Ludwig Josef Johann **9:757–70**

References to the topic in general are given first of all, followed by an alphabetical breakdown by sub-topic. For example, the index entry on quantum mechanics begins:

quantum mechanics
    Bell's theorem 1:712–15
    Bohr, N. 1:820
    causal laws 5:187
    chaos theory 2:278
    chemistry applications 2:298–9

Topics indexed under a different heading are referred to by *see*:

Sinn und Bedeutung *see* sense and reference

Entries of related interest are indicated by *see also*. For example:

Action *see also* acts; divine action; karma; moral motivation; praxis

Countries are indexed by contemporary state names. Biographical entries of ancient and modern philosophers born and/or who worked in a particular region are included under the name of the modern state. For example:

Italy **5:34–42**
    Alemanno, Y. 1:161–3
    Alighieri, Dante 1:181–5
    Aquinas, T. 1:326–50
    Archytas 1:366–9

In addition, pre-modern philosophers are often also referred to under their historical region, city-state etc.

All entries are also indexed under contributor name, and such instances are indicated by a dagger (†). For example:

Kretzmann, Norman
    Aquinas, T. †1:326–50

Running heads refer to the first and last full references appearing on each double-page span.

The publishers would like to acknowledge the work of Indexing Specialists of Hove, UK who compiled the index.

Index

A

a posteriori **1:1–3**
see also a priori
a priori distinction (by
Quine, W.V.) 1:235
coherentism 1:1–2
empirical warrant 1:1
foundationalism 1:2–3
innate knowledge 4:796
rationality of belief 8:62
a priori **1:3–6**
see also a posteriori; analytic truth;
necessary truth; synthetic a priori
knowledge
a posteriori distinction
(Quine, W.V.) 1:235
analytic-synthetic distinction 1:4,
8:6
anthropological knowledge of
(Fries, J.F.) 3:798
certainty 1:5
concepts 2:508
Eleatic philosophy 1:263
empiricism 3:302, 5:668
foundationalism 2:333
innate knowledge 4:795–6
legal (Reinach, A.) 8:180–1
necessity distinction (Kripke, S.A.)
5:302–3
necessity/contingency distinction
1:4
partial entailment (Ramsey, F.P.)
8:45
rationality of belief 8:61–2
scepticism (Mill, J.S.) 6:360,
6:364–5
science
demarcation problem 2:863–4
naturalized philosophy of 6:728,
6:729, 6:730
science (Carnap, R.) 2:208
space and time (Kant, I.) 5:184–5
synthetic (Kant, I.) 5:183–4, 5:790,
5:791
a/theology
Taylor, M.C. 7:585
Aarnio, A. 5:530, 8:492
Aaron ben Elijah of Nicomedia 5:208
Aarsleff, H. 4:527, 5:378, 8:472
Abbagnano, Nicola 5:39

al-'Abbasi 4:638
Abbey, E. 1:128
Abbott, E.A. 1:632
Abbott, S. 4:697
Abdel Haleem, M. 5:30
abduction 7:274–5, 9:478
'Abduh, Muhammad **1:6–8**, 5:30–1
Abe, Masao 3:111, 6:594, 7:16
Abed, A. 6:239
Abed, S.B. 1:385, 5:711, 6:239
Abel, G. 5:652
Abel, Reuben
Schiller, F.C.S. †8:522–4
Abelard, Peter **1:8–15**
atonement 1:539
Bernard of Clairvaux 1:754
Heloise 1:8–9
limbo 5:636
logic 1:8, 1:9, 1:10–11, 5:748
nominalism 7:19, 7:22
paganism (William of Conches)
9:731
Theologia 1:9
universals 1:11, 7:434–5, 9:729
vocalism 5:392
will 9:724
Abelé, J. 5:482
Abeles, F. 3:108
Abellán, José Luis
Spain, philosophy in †9:70–7
Abercrombie, N. 7:286
Aberdeen Philosophical Society **1:15**
Aberth, O. 2:634, 2:638
Abhayadeva
commentaries
Jainism 5:55
Abhidharma see Ābhidharmika
Schools of Buddhism
Abhidharmakośa see Vasubandhu
Ābhidharmika Schools of Buddhism
(Abhidharma) **2:53–8**
see also Dārṣṭāntika; Sarvāstivāda;
Theravāda
causality 2:98, 2:256
consciousness 2:72–3
cosmology and cosmogony 2:683
emptiness 2:77–8, 2:79
exegesis 2:54–5
ontology 2:55–6

perception 2:56–7
reductionism 6:638–9
Vasubandhu 2:65–6
Abhinavagupta **1:15–19**
Indian and Tibetan philosophy
4:738
nonduality 1:16–17
recognition 1:17
Tantra 1:17–18
Abhyankar, K.V. 4:837
ability
logic of 6:431–2
Abimbola, W. 9:833
Abiodun, R. 1:64–5
Abir-Am, P. 6:459, 6:460
abolitionism
punishment 2:705, 2:709–10
abortion
ethics 1:778–9, 8:276–7, 8:279
rights
feminist jurisprudence 3:609
Roman Catholicism 4:798
Abraham ben David, Rabbi see Ibn
Daud, Abraham
Abraham ibn Ezra see Ibn Ezra,
Abraham
Abraham, N. 2:900
Abraham, W.E. 1:97, 1:211, 3:449
Abraham, W.J. 6:415
Abrahamov, B. 8:115
Abrahamsen, A. 2:576–7, 6:394
Abrahamson, M.R. 5:301
Abrams, M.H. 1:68, 1:509, 7:476
Abramson, N. 4:785
Abravanel, Isaac **1:19–23**, 5:89
Abravanel, Judah ben Isaac **1:23–7**,
5:89
absence
see also nonexistence
causation
Indian theories of 7:606
Absolute, the **1:27–9**
dialectic (McTaggart, J.M.E.) 6:25
Jo-nang-pa School 9:403
positive philosophy
(Schelling, F.W.J. von) 8:509,
8:515–16
real intuition (Krause, K.) 5:299
reality (Bradley, F.H.) 1:860–1

transcendental idealism 2:67
true compassion (Shinran) 8:747–8
as true self (Radhakrishnan, S.)
 8:23–4
Vysheslavtsev, B.P. 9:675–6
Wissenschaftslehre (theory of
 science) 3:645, 3:648
absolute being
 Scheler, M.F. 8:507
absolute consciousness
 Abhinavagupta 1:16–17
absolute idealism 4:665–7
 Anglo-American 1:28, 4:667
 Bosanquet, B. 1:846–7
 German 1:27–8, 4:665–7
 human freedom 1:852
 panpsychism 7:197
 Reid, T. 9:136
absolute immanence
 actualism (Gentile, G.) 4:21
absolute immanentism
 epistemology (Lossky, N.O.) 5:833,
 5:834–5
absolute knowledge
 Hegel, G.W.F. 4:267
absolute nothingness
 Kyoto School 5:327–8
 Nishida Kitarō 5:78, 5:714–15,
 7:14
 Tanabe Hajime 9:261
absolute scales
 measurement theory 6:243
Absolute Spirit
 Hegel, G.W.F. 5:436
absolutes
 existentialism 3:500
absolutism **1:29–32**
 see also sovereignty
 contractarianism (Locke, J.) 2:661
 legal concepts 5:495
 public law (Bodin, J.) 1:796–7
 truthfulness 9:483
abstemiousness
 Jewish pietism (Ibn Paquda) 4:635
abstract art *see* art, abstract
abstract objects **1:32–5**
 abstract–concrete distinction 1:32,
 1:33
 dance
 type/token analysis 2:775
 fictional entities 3:666
 intensional logics 4:810
 materialism 6:177
 metaphysics 6:339
 nonexistence of (Kotarbiński, T.)
 5:293–4
 rGyal tshab dar ma rin chen 8:304

structuralism in social science
 9:185, 9:188
abstraction
 critique of Cajetan, T. 8:776–7
 economics 3:213
 experience (Locke, J.) 5:665,
 5:670–1
 Ibn Sina 4:649
 ideas (Hume, D.) 4:546
 legal (Holmes, O.W.) 4:493, 4:494
 Locke, J.
 critique by Berkeley, G. 1:739,
 1:741–2
 practical to theoretical shift
 (Heidegger, M.) 4:324
 thought experiments 9:393, 9:396
abstractive cognition
 Aureol, P. 1:565
 Chatton/Campsall debate 2:293
 Duns Scotus, J. 3:154, 3:165–6
 Gilbert of Poitiers 4:70
 John of Mirecourt 5:112
absurd, the
 existentialism 3:498–9
 Camus, A. 2:194
 meaning of life 5:630, 5:631–2
Abu Rabi, I. 1:7
Abu Ridah, M. 4:67
Abubacer *see* Ibn Tufayl
Abulafia, Abraham 5:174
Abunaser (al-)Farabi *see* al-Farabi,
 Abu Nasr
Academic scepticism 1:263–4, 3:373
 see also Academy
 Aenesidemus 1:50
 Antiochus 1:299, 1:300
 Arcesilaus 1:351–4
 Augustine 1:544–5
 Carneades 2:215–16, 2:215–19,
 2:218–19
 Cicero, M.T. 2:357
 critiques of
 Middle Platonism 7:422
 Philo of Larissa 7:362–3
 divination (Panaetius) 7:189
 Epictetus 3:339
 Foucher, S. 3:714–15, 3:716
 Platonism 7:422
 Plutarch of Chaeronea 7:465
 Pyrrhonism 7:850
 Stoic defence of cognitive certainty
 7:849, 9:142, 9:151–2
Academy **1:36**
 see also Academic scepticism
 early
 God 7:425–6

establishment of
 Plato 1:263, 7:402
 language
 philosophy of 5:361
 mathematics emphasis
 Plato 7:423
 Speusippus 9:89
 membership of 1:415
 Platonism
 Early and Middle 7:421–2,
 7:425–6
 God 7:425–6
 Speusippus **9:89–91**
 Stoic-Peripatetic syncretism
 (Antiochus) 1:300–1
 Xenocrates 9:806
Academy, New *see* Academic
 scepticism
Academy, Old *see* Old Academy
acceptance
 epistemology 7:211–12, 7:708
accessibility
 modal logic 6:418, 6:420
accidents
 causes (Duns Scotus, J.) 3:161–2
 individuation (Duns Scotus, J.)
 3:164–5
 Islamic philosophy
 Ash'ariyya/Mu'tazila
 comparison 1:520
 Mulla Sadra 6:595–6
 al-Suhrawardi 9:221–2
 medieval metaphysics 6:273–4
 as qualities (Rohault, J.) 8:342
 substance
 Brentano, F. 2:14
 Duns Scotus, J. 3:154, 3:159
 Godfrey of Fontaines 4:120–1
accommodation
 cognitive development (Piaget, J.)
 7:384, 7:385
accountability
 see also responsibility
 Chinese Legalism 5:534, 5:537
 free will (Kant, I.) 7:645–6
 moral 6:520–1
 professional ethics 7:735
Achilles argument
 Zeno of Elea 9:843, 9:849
Achinstein, Peter
 crucial experiments †2:735–6
 explanation 3:524
 models 6:446
 science
 demarcation problem †2:863–7
 theories 9:351
Ackah, C.A. 3:434

Acker, W.R.B. 1:74
Ackerman, B.A. 3:238, 6:820, 7:528
Ackerman, J. 1:508, 1:509
Ackerman, R.J. 3:517, 7:539
Ackermann, Wilhelm
  completeness problem 4:108, 4:116
  decision problem 2:349
  logic
    early twentieth century 5:737
    second- and higher-order 8:595,
      8:603
    predicate calculus 7:665
    proof theory 7:751
    relevance logic and entailment
      8:200–1, 8:203
    set theory 8:713, 8:715
Ackermann function 2:483–4
Ackrill, J.L. 1:434
Acmeism
  Nietzsche, F.W. 6:866
acquaintance
  knowledge by **5:259–63**
  Russell, B.A.W. 8:399
  sense-data 3:379
acquired intellect
  Albert the Great 1:148, 1:150–1
  immortality (Gersonides) 4:50
  Islamic philosophy 9:42–3
    al-Farabi 3:556
    Ibn Bajja 4:606
    rational soul 9:42, 9:43
acrasia see akrasia
Acta Comeniana 2:440
act-consequentialism *see*
  consequentialism
acting-intuiting
  Nishida Kitarō 5:714–15
action **1:37–41**
  see also acts; divine action; karma;
    moral motivation; praxis
  akrasia 1:139–42
  analysis of (Aquinas, T.) 1:339
  attributes of
    Ash'ariyya/Mu'tazila
      comparison 1:522
  awareness of (Maine de Biran, P.-
    F.) 6:51–2
  capacity (Spinoza, B. de) 9:101–2
  causality/motive distinction
    (Stewart, D.) 9:137
  causes 1:39–40, 8:124–6
  communicative (Habermas, J.)
    4:195
  criteria of
    Pyrrhonism 7:852
  Daoism 2:789–90

decision theory (Ramsey, F.P.)
  8:44, 8:46
distanciation (Ricouer, P.) 8:320
divine *see* divine action
essence distinction
  Ibn Massara 4:627–8
events distinction 1:37
evil 3:464
explanation
  history and social science
    3:528–30
fatalism 3:563–4
formal-finalistic theory of 9:702
free will 3:749–50, 9:721–2
  Indian fatalism 3:565–7
  Kant, I. 5:191–2
  al-Razi, Fakhr al-Din 8:114
good/evil
  Wolff, C. 9:780
holism 4:483, 4:487
incontinent (*akrasia*)
  Aristotle 1:428
Indian fatalism 3:567
individuation 1:37–8
instrumental
  Habermas, J. 4:195
intention 1:280–1, 4:812–15
intentional 4:814–15
interpretation 8:865
karma and rebirth
  Indian philosophy 5:209, 5:212,
    5:213, 5:214
language of (Austin, J.L.) 1:572,
  1:573
mental causation 6:407
moral 6:565
  Ross, W.D. 8:365–7
  Wollaston, W. 9:787–8
moral realism 6:536–7
motivation 3:30, 8:174–5
  Freud, S. 3:786, 3:789, 3:790–1
narrative 6:656
ontological categories
  Indian philosophy 7:123
as particulars 3:462
passions (Hume, D.) 4:543, 4:551
plausibility (Carneades) 2:219
political
  Arendt, H. 1:370–1, 1:372
  Machiavelli, N. 7:510
practical reason 7:613, 7:614–15
praxeology 7:647–8
prescriptivism 7:667–70
product distinction
  (Twardowski, K.) 9:509
propositional attitudes 7:781

Pyrrhonian Scepticism
  (Arcesilaus) 1:353–4
Rabbinic theology 9:334–5
rational
  satisficing 8:96
  theories of reason 8:90, 8:93
reasons 8:124–6
  causes relationship
    (Davidson, D.) 2:800–1
Schopenhauer, A. 8:549, 8:550
self-cultivation
  Wang Yangming 8:623
social 8:869
  explanation in social science
    3:529–30
  Habermas, J. 4:195–6
  joint action 8:822–3
  joint intention 8:822–3
  Reinach, A. 8:181–2
  Weber, M. 8:886, 9:695–6
speculation relationship
  (Comte, A.) 2:498
strategic (Habermas, J.) 4:195
subjective meaning 8:841
supererogation 9:232–4
Wang Yangming 9:683
wayward causal chains 8:126–7
will 9:720–4
yoga relationship
  Indian philosophy 3:183, 3:186
active intellect
  Abravanel, I. 1:21
  Aristotle 1:171–2
  ethics 3:438, 3:441
  al-Farabi 3:555, 3:556
  Gersonides 4:49–50
  al-Ghazali 4:65
  Hillel ben Samuel of Verona 4:432
  Ibn Sina 4:649, 4:650, 4:651
  Judah ben Moses of Rome 5:129
  Kabbalah 5:174
  Mulla Sadra 6:597
  prophecy 1:21, 7:768
Acton, E. 4:410
Acton, H.B. 3:57, 6:110
Acton, Lord
  nation and nationalism 6:661
actor networks
  scientific constructivism 2:625,
    2:628
acts
  basic 1:38–9
  belief relationship (Albo, J.) 1:153
actual entities
  see also enduring individuals
  process theism 7:716–18
actual idealism *see* actualism

actual intellect 3:556, 9:42
actual sin *see* sin, actual
actualism
    critical realism 2:721
    existence of God (Kant, I.) 4:88
    Gentile, G. 4:20, 4:21–2
actuality
    eternal objects (Whitehead, A.N.) 9:716
Acworth, R. 7:43
Aczel, P.
    intensional entities 4:806
    non-constructive rules of inference 7:29
    set theory 8:714, 8:715
ad baculum fallacy 3:544
ad hominem argument 1:353
ad hominem fallacy 3:544
ad ignorantiam fallacy 3:544
ad misericordiam fallacy 3:544
ad populum fallacy 3:544
ad verecundiam fallacy 3:544
Adair-Toteff, Christopher
    Hartmann, K.R.E. von †4:238–40
    Vaihinger, H. †9:566–8
Adam (Biblical)
    see also Fall, The
    language
        origins of 5:413
Adam, A. 5:621, 6:77
Adam, C. 4:353–4
Adam Kadmon 4:397, 4:398
Adams, C.C. 1:7
Adams, D. 9:215
Adams, Ernest 1:357, 4:741, 4:742, 7:34
Adams, F. 3:662
Adams, H. 7:476
Adams, H.P. 9:605
Adams, James Luther 9:412
Adams, J.L. 2:368
Adams, Marilyn McCord
    Anselm of Canterbury 1:296
    Chatton, W. 2:293–4
    Duns Scotus, J. 3:168
    epistemology 3:381
    eternity 3:426
    evil 3:466
    evil, problem of †3:466–72
    forgiveness and mercy 3:700
    hell †4:329–33
    Henry of Harclay 4:362–3
    morality and religion 8:221, 8:223
    omniscience 7:112
    reprobation 8:275
    sin 8:795
    voluntarism 9:664

William of Ockham 9:747
Wodeham, A. 9:776
Adams, R. 3:421, 7:237
Adams, R.M.
    divine freedom 3:761
    evil 3:466
    evil, problem of 3:469, 3:471–2
    Leibniz, G.W. 5:561
    Molina, L. de 6:465
    necessary being 6:746
    religion, history of philosophy of 8:246
    religion and morality 8:223
    theological virtues 9:330
Adams, W.Y. 1:357
Adamson, R. 3:652
Adamson, W.L. 4:154
adaptation
    see also Darwinism; evolutionary theory
    biological functionalism 3:815
    natural selection 3:476
    sociobiology 8:894
Addas, C. 4:605, 4:629
Addis, S. 2:781
Addison, J. 8:144, 9:204
addition theory
    forms (Duns Scotus, J.) 2:141
Adelard of Bath 9:455
Adelmann, D. 2:402
adequate object
    Duns Scotus, J. 3:159–60
adjectives
    paronymy (Anselm of Canterbury) 1:289–90
adjudication
    equity (Dworkin, R.M.) 5:152
    indeterminacy
        legal realism 5:523–4
Adkins, A.W.H. 1:374, 3:27, 4:502
Adler, J.A. 8:737, 9:831
Adler, J.E. †8:86–90
Adler, Max 6:143
Adorno, Theodor Wiesengrund
1:41–6
    aesthetics 1:44
        art and morality 1:456
        music 6:612
    capitalism 6:97, 6:98
    communicative rationality 2:461
    critical theory 2:722–8, 3:732–3, 3:735, 3:736
    Hegelianism 4:292
    Hölderlin, J.C.F. 4:482
    Horkheimer, M. 4:511
    Lyotard, J.-F. 6:11

Marxism
    Western 6:144
    morality and art 1:456
    negative dialectics 1:42, 1:44
    social science 8:846
    theology, political 9:332
    totalitarianism 9:444
Adotevi, Stalinas 1:112, 1:114
Adrastus of Aphrodisias 2:175
adultery 8:718
adulthood
    cultural identity 2:745
Advaita Vedānta School of Hindu philosophy
    see also Vedānta
    analogy
        knowledge 5:282, 5:283–4
    appearance
        causation 2:251, 2:254–5
    ātman 6:402
        Brahman relationship 9:590, 9:591–2
    awareness 1:605, 1:606, 1:607–8
    Brahman 2:3–4
    Brahmasūtra 4:438
    circumstantial implication
        knowledge 5:282
    conflict with Vedānta Schools 9:591–2
    God 4:102, 4:103–4
    heaven 4:256
    illusion
        mystical awareness 3:410
    karma and rebirth 5:213
    Mādhava 6:28, 6:29–30
    meaning 4:436
    monism 6:475–8
    non-dualism 9:589
    pantheism 7:202
    Ramakrishna Movement 8:39–41
    reincarnation 8:183, 8:185
    salvation 8:447–8, 8:449
    Śaṅkara 8:458–61
    self
        theories of 8:610
    self-certificationalism 3:388, 3:391
adverbial realism *see* realism, adverbial
adverbial theory of mental states *see* mental states, adverbial theory of
adverbs **1:46–50**
    ambiguities 1:47–9
    event predicate theory 6:316
    extensionality 1:49
    ontological commitment
        (Davidson, D.) 2:803–4

predicate operator theory
6:315–16
scope
ambiguity of 9:251–2
types 1:46–7
advertising
semiology (Baudrillard, J.) 1:662
advocacy
social science 9:577–8
Aegidius Romanus *see* Giles of Rome
Aelred of Rievaulx 3:795, 3:796–7
Aenesidemus **1:50–1**
Pyrrhonian Scepticism 1:129,
7:848, 7:849, 7:850, 7:853
Aertsen, Jan A.
Aquinas, T. 1:346
medieval Platonism 7:437
Meister Eckhart †6:286–8
Aeschines 9:20
aesthetic attitude **1:51–5**
characterization 1:53–4
non-aesthetic attitudes 1:52–3
particularity 1:54
reality of 1:54
aesthetic concepts **1:55–9**
contextual contructs 1:58
eighteenth-century views 1:55–6
Sibley, F. 1:56–7
subjectivity versus objectivity 1:55,
1:56
taste 1:55–7
aesthetic realism 1:57–8
Chernyshevskii, N.G. 2:304
film 3:673, 3:674–5, 3:676
aesthetics **1:59–61**
see also art; beauty; style, artistic;
taste
African **1:61–5**
anthropology 1:62–3
art history 1:63
négritude 1:62
Yoruba culture 1:63–4
analytic 1:67–8
anthropodicy (Florenskii, P.A.)
3:681
appreciation 1:59
architecture **1:361–6**
art works
ontology of 1:480–4
attitude 1:59–60
autonomy relationship (Kant, I.)
5:193–4
Baumgarten, A.G. 1:669–72
beauty 1:680–4
Belinskii, V.G. **1:709–12**, 4:304,
8:521

characteristics/relation distinction
(Anderson, J.) 1:266
Chinese **1:68–75**
common-sense philosophy
(Reid, T.) 8:171–2, 8:176–7
concepts 1:59
Ingarden, R.W. 4:789, 4:790–1
Confucianism 2:320, 2:324
consciousness (Cohen, H.) 6:781–2
content (Belinskii, V.G.) 1:711,
1:712
dance **2:774–7**
deconstruction (Lyotard, J.-F.) 6:8
educational philosophy 3:234
environmental 6:732, 6:735
ethics (Kierkegaard, S.) 5:238–9
ethics relationship **1:65–8**
expressionism (Ducasse, C.J.)
3:141
feminist **3:593–6**
film **3:673–7**
forgery 1:498–501
German Romanticism 8:349–50
God
appearance of (Cousin, V.)
2:691
Goodman, N. 4:137–8
Hegelian 2:304, 4:304
history 1:67
ideology (Man, P. de) 2:838
imagination (Kant, I.) 4:707
immediacy (Santayana, G.) 8:467,
8:469
immoralism (Nietzsche, F.W.)
5:568
internal sense 4:36, 4:500
intuition (Croce, B.) 2:730–1
Islamic philosophy **1:75–9**, 5:15
Japanese **1:79–91**
aesthetic ideals 1:80, 1:87–9
expressive-affective capacity
1:80, 1:83–5
kokoro 5:291–2
nature 1:80–3
poetry 1:84, 1:88, 1:89
religion 1:85–7
self-expressive reality 5:72
transience 6:593
Jewish
Saadiah Gaon 8:439
judgments 1:511–12
katharsis 5:218–19
literary theory (Man, P. de) 2:812
Maritain, J. 6:103
mimēsis 6:381–2
mode of living
Kuki Shūzō 5:320–1

Watsuji Tetsurō 9:692
modern
critique by Adorno, T.W. 1:44
moral freedom (Kant, I.) 5:178
morality relationship
(Tolstoi, L.N.) 9:438–9
music **6:606–15**
nature 6:731–5
ontological definition (Foht, I.)
9:52
order
Chinese philosophy 2:317
organic
Belinskii, V.G. 1:710
Grigor'ev, A. 8:521
passions relationship (Burke, E.)
2:137–8
of production (Schleiermacher, F.)
8:535
rationalist (Lessing, G.E.) 5:576
religious experience (Il'in, I.A.)
4:694
Romantic (Schlegel, F. von)
8:529–31
Russian
literary formalism 8:412
realism 2:304, 8:416–17
realism (Lunacharskii, A.)
8:407–8
Schellingianism 8:521
Russian nihilism 7:7
Schiller, J.C.F. 8:524–8
style *see* style, artistic
taste *see* taste
theological (Edwards, J.) 3:240,
3:243
truth relationship (Hamann, J.G.)
4:216–17
universal integration
(Solov'ëv, V.S.) 9:30
will-less perception
(Schopenhauer, A.) 8:546,
8:550–1
Afanasyev, V.G. 3:57
affection for the just
Duns Scotus, J. 3:155, 3:167
affects *see* emotions
el-Affendi, Abdel Wahab
Islamic theology †5:25–31
political philosophy
Indian 7:524
Affifi, A.E. 4:605
affinity (*bandhutā*) theory
self
Indian theories of 8:607
affirmative action **1:91–4**
al-Afghani, Jamal al-Din **1:94–5**

Afghanistan
  al-Afghani **1:94–5**
Africa **1:95–7**
  aesthetics **1:61–5**
  Akan philosophical psychology
    1:138–9
  Amo, A.W. **1:210–11**
  Anglophone philosophy
    1:97–1:108
    indigenous African
      philosophers 1:104–5
    négritude 1:98–9
    socialism 1:99–1:101
    synthesis with Western thought
      1:105–6
    typology of current trends
      1:102–4
  art 1:58
  Augustine of Hippo **1:541–59**
  Cabral, A. **2:168–71**
  Carneades **2:215–20**
  Egyptian philosophy, ancient
    3:250–4
  ethical systems in **3:430–5**
  Ethiopian philosophy **3:442–5**
  ethnophilosophy **3:446–50**
  Fanon, F. **3:552–4**
  Francophone philosophy **1:108–17**
    Anglophone relationship 1:113
    transition to modernity 1:108
  Marius Victorinus **6:105–7**
  pan-Africanism **7:191–4**
  Tertullian, Q.S.F. **9:307–9**
  traditional religions in **1:117–21**
  Yoruba epistemology **9:832–4**
Africans
  influence on Brazilian philosophy
    2:8–9
Afrocentrism
  Egyptian influence on ancient
    Greek thought 3:253
'after-death experiences' 9:48
afterlife 8:249
  see also eternal life; soul,
    immortality of
  African ethical systems 3:431–2
  Ash'arites versus Mu'tazilites 4:64
  deism (Butler, J.) 2:157–8, 2:159
  divine goodness
    (Mendelssohn, M.) 6:305
  happiness (Ibn Rushd) 4:642
  imaginal world (Mulla Sadra)
    6:598
  Indian philosophy
    Vedic thought 5:211–12
  intellect (al-Kindi) 5:251

meaninglessness of life
  (Schopenhauer, A.) 2:822
personal identity (Butler, J.) 2:159
punishment (Ibn Sina) 4:652
reward
  al-'Amiri 1:207, 1:208
  Ibn Sina 4:652
  al-Razi, Abu Bakr 8:111
as social control (Ibn Rushd)
  4:641, 4:642
soul
  Bar Hayya, A. 1:650
  Hillel ben Samuel of Verona
    4:432–3
  Ibn Tzaddik, J. 4:660, 4:662
survival of personal identity 3:415
world of images
  Ibn al-'Arabi 4:604
agape
  see also charity; love
  Christian theology 2:280–1, 7:68
    Niebuhr, R. 6:843
    Nygren, A. 7:68
  friendship relationship 3:795
  respect for persons 8:285
Agathocles the Sicilian 6:18–19
ageing
  Epicureanism 3:90
agency
  action 1:40
  bodily movement (Reid, T.) 8:174
  causality
    Reid, T. 8:173
    Stewart, D. 9:137
  determinism
    Alexander of Aphrodisias
      critique 1:173–4
  explanation of nature
    African traditional religions
      1:118
  first/second order (Aquinas, T.)
    9:721–2
  free will 3:749–50
  freedom
    Indian fatalism 3:565, 3:566,
      3:567
  genealogy (Foucault, M.) 9:198
  God
    Jewish philosophy 5:96, 5:98,
      9:665–6
  individualism
    social science 4:484
  intentionality (Heidegger, M.)
    4:324
  Islamic philosophy 2:242–3
  moral 7:677–8, 9:277
  power 7:611

agent cause see efficient causes
agent intellect
  see also active intellect
  Albert the Great 1:151
  Aquinas, T. 1:336, 1:339
  Aristotle
    Themistius' interpretation 9:325
  conjunction with soul
    Ibn Bajja 4:605, 4:606, 4:607
  dialectic psychology
    (Melanchthon, P.) 6:291
  happiness
    Averroism 1:597
  intelligible forms (Ibn Bajja) 4:606
  Islamic philosophy 3:386
  John of Jandun 5:107
  monopsychism
    Averroism 1:596
  nature of (Dietrich of Freiberg)
    3:70
  possible intellect (Toletus, F.) 9:435
  rational soul
    Islamic philosophy 9:42–3
  Renaissance philosophy
    (Silvestri, F.) 8:776–7
  soul
    Matthew of Aquasparta 6:201
    Paul of Venice 7:266
  theoretical intellect
    Islamic philosophy 3:386
  William of Auvergne 9:726
agent sense
  Nifo, A. 6:869
  Renaissance Aristotelianism
    1:407–8
agents
  moral 2:890–1, **6:499–504**
    see also moral luck; moral
    standing
    autonomy 6:569
    collectivity 6:502–3
    deontology 2:890–1
    duty 3:179, 3:181
    free will 3:749–50
    Kantian view 6:501–2
    mental illness 6:313–14
    recipients distinction 6:499
    relativity 2:890–1
    responsibility 8:287–90, 8:291
    self (Taylor, C.) 9:277
    Soviet Marxism 6:158
    universalism in ethics 9:536
    utilitarianism 9:553
    virtue ethics 9:623
    will 9:722–3
  rational
    autonomy 1:587–8

will 9:720–2
aggadah 4:411, 6:648
aggregates
    mathematics (Mill, J.S.) 6:363
    particulars 7:237
aggregation
    social choice 8:824–5
aggressivity
    ego alienation (Lacan, J.) 5:337
agnosticism **1:121–3**
    negative theology 6:761–2
    Protagoras 7:788–9, 7:790
Agrarian Law
    Harrington, J. 4:232–3
agreement
    see also consent; promising
    contractarianism 2:658–9
    social rules 8:835
    verification
        pragmatism 5:65
agreement–disagreement dichotomy
    holism 4:491–2
Agricola, Rudolph **1:123–6**
    logic 5:770, 5:772
    maxims 5:770
    Ramus, P. 8:52–3
    topics 1:124–5
agricultural ethics **1:126–8**
    see also bioethics; environmental
    ethics; green political philosophy
    animals 1:127
    developing countries
        industrialization 1:126–7
    farming 1:127–8
    social justice 1:126–7
Agriculturalists
    Lushi chunqiu 5:864
Agrippa **1:129**, 7:851–2
Agrippa von Nettesheim, Henricus
    Cornelius **1:130–33**
    feminism 1:131
        influence on Descartes, R. 1:132
    scepticism 1:131
    verbal magic 1:131
Aguilar, J.A.V. 2:120
Aguinis, Marcos 5:655, 5:656
Ahearne, J. 2:269
Ahlberg, L.-O. 5:355
Ahlefeld, H. 9:561
Ahmad, Aijaz 7:581
Ahndung see religion, experiential
Ahura Mazdā 9:872, 9:873
AI *see* artificial intelligence
aid
    development ethics 1:126, 1:127,
        3:40

AID *see* artificial insemination by
    donor
Aiken, W.
    ethics 1:128, 3:43, 3:552
    help and beneficence 4:344
Ailly, Pierre d' **1:133–5**
    theories of language 5:390, 5:401
Ainsworth, M.D.S. 7:822
air
    divine nature of (Anaximenes)
        7:470–1
    intelligence (Diogenes of
        Apollonia) 3:88
    as primary substance
        (Anaximenes) 1:259, 1:260,
        1:261
Airaksinen, T. 7:736, 9:690
Aires Ramos da Silva, Matias
    2:9–2:11
Aiton, E.J. 5:561
Aizawa, K. 2:576
Ajdukiewicz, Kazimierz **1:135–8**
    Kotarbiński, T. 5:295
    logical semantics 7:486
    Polish logic 7:496–7
    syntax 9:252
Ajita, Keśakambala 6:179
Ajzenberg, A. 5:491
Akaike, H. 8:782–3
Akamatsu Tsunihiko 6:358–9
Akan philosophical psychology
    1:138–9
Akbarian tradition 6:619
Akhlaq-e Jalali (al-)Dawani
Akhtar, S. 5:9
Akhtar, W. 8:441
Akkerman, F. 1:126
akrasia **1:139–42**
    see also self-control; will,
        weakness of
    Aristotle 8:611
    Augustine 1:548, 1:554–5
    moral motivation 6:524
    moral psychology 6:532–3
    practical rationality 8:101
Aksakov, Ivan 8:811
Aksakov, Konstantin 8:809
Akṣapāda Gautama/Gotama *see*
    Gautama, Akṣapāda
Alain of Lille 3:306, 7:437
'alam al-amthal (world of images)
    4:604, 6:598
'alam al-khayal (world of
    imagination) 4:702
Aland, K. 6:5
Alanen, Lilli 8:492
Alarco, Luis Felipe 3:512, 3:513

al-'Alawi, J.D. 4:608
Albalag, Isaac 1:599–600
Albdour, Salman
    Ibn Hazm †4:620–1
    al-Juwayni †5:169–70
Albee, E. 9:493
Alberdi, Juan Bautista 1:375–6,
    1:378, 7:566, 7:568
Albernini, Coriolano 1:376
Albert the Great **1:145–52**
    Aquinas, T. 1:147–8, 1:149–50,
        1:328
    Aristotelianism 1:394, 1:399,
        1:400, 1:402
    David of Dinant 2:800
    illuminationism 4:699–700
    limbo 5:636
    Pseudo-Dionysius 7:807
    soul
        union with intellect 1:147–8
    Thomism 9:381
    Ulrich of Strasbourg 9:517
    world of forms
        medieval Platonism 7:436
Albert of Saxony (Albert of
    Rickmersdorf) **1:143–5**
Albert, H. 7:539
Alberti, A. 4:517
Alberti, L.B. 1:361–2, 1:365–6
Albertus Magnus *see* Albert the
    Great
Albertus Parvus *see* Albert of Saxony
Albigensians *see* Cathars
Albinus 7:428
Albistur, M. 9:212
Albo, Joseph **1:152–5**
    Duran, S. 3:172
    Jewish philosophy 5:89
Albritton, R. 2:713
alchemy **1:155–9**
    Aristotelianism 1:157, 2:295
    Islamic
        Hermetism 6:617
    Jung, C.G. 5:134
    matter 1:155, 1:156–7, 6:194
    medieval natural philosophy 6:693
    Newton, I. 6:827
Alcibiades 9:19, 9:20
Alcinous **1:159–60**
    God, concepts of 4:101
    perfect-being theology 4:97
    Plutarch of Chaeronea 7:470
Alcmaeon **1:160–1**
Alcoff, L. 3:592, 3:601, 8:223
Alcuin of York 2:220, 2:221, 2:222,
    6:692
Alegría, Ciro 5:655, 5:656

Alegría, Claribel 5:655
Alejandro, J.M. 9:195
Aleksandrov, G.F. 1:526, 6:158
Alemanno, Yohanan ben Isaac
  1:161–3, 5:89
Alembert, Jean le Rond d' **1:163–8**
  Cartesianism 1:164, 1:166
  Encyclopédie 1:165, 1:166, 3:303–4
  Enlightenment 1:164, 3:317
  humanism 4:529, 4:532
  organic unity 1:166–7
  unity of science 9:532
Alesse, F. 7:190
Alexander of Aphrodisias **1:169–76**
  active intellect 1:171–2
  agent intellect 9:325
  ancient logic 5:692
  Aristotelianism 1:407, 1:408
  free will 3:751
  Ibn Sina 4:654
  immortality of the intellect
    (Gersonides) 4:50
  soul
    nature of 1:171–2
Alexander the Great
  Aristotle's tutorship of 1:415
Alexander of Hales **1:176–8**
  John of La Rochelle 5:109–10
Alexander, Bernát 4:569, 4:571
Alexander, H.G. 2:380
Alexander, I. 9:662
Alexander, Jeffrey C.
  social science
    philosophy history 8:856
    systems theory 9:256
  sociology
    theories of †9:2–8
Alexander, L. 3:105
Alexander, P. 1:856, 7:687
Alexander, P.S.
  midrash †6:353–5
Alexander, R.D. 3:475, 3:487, 8:896
Alexander, Samuel **1:168–9**, 1:576–7,
  1:582
Alexander, T. 3:51
Alexander, W.M. 4:217
Alexandria
  Ammonius, son of Hermeas
    1:208–10
  Hellenistic philosophy 1:263–4
  Hypatia **4:596–7**
  Neoplatonism 6:804
  Philo of Alexandria **7:357–61**
  Philoponus **7:371–8**
  Platonic school (Eudorus) 7:422
Alexy, R. 5:530
Alfarabi *see* al-Farabi, Abu Nasr

Alfonso da Costa, Newton Carneiro
  2:11
Alfred of Shareshill (Sarashel) 5:22,
  9:456
Algazel *see* al-Ghazali, Abu Hamid
algebra
  abstract (Whitehead, A.N.) 9:714
  analytic geometry (Descartes, R.)
    3:1, 3:2
  Boolean *see* Boolean algebra
  Cantor, G. 2:196–7
  Dedekind, J.W.R. 2:840–1
  of logic (Boole, G.) 1:841
  seventeenth-century 5:718
Algeria
  Augustine of Hippo **1:541–59**
algorithms
  artificial intelligence 1:485
  computability 2:351–2, 7:573
  computational theories of mind
    6:391
  genetic 1:491
  glossary 5:795
  learning 2:575, 5:483, 5:486
Algra, Keimpe
  ancient philosophy 1:265
  Posidonius †7:555–8
Alhazen *see* Ibn Hazm, Abu
  Muhammad 'Ali
alienation **1:178–81**
  Cartesian dualism
    German Romanticism 8:351
  Chinese Marxism 6:139–40
  competition
    sport ethics 9:111
  everydayness (Lefebvre, H.) 5:490
  existentialist Marxism (Sartre, J.-
    P.) 6:145
  feminism (Beauvoir, S. de) 1:686
  Feuerbach, L. 1:179
  Hegel, G.W.F. 1:179
  labour 1:180, 9:795
  language (Lacan, J.) 5:337
  marginality 6:100
  market ethics 6:109–10
  Marx, K. 1:179–81, 6:121–2
    human communal nature 6:122
    political philosophy
      history of 7:516
    private property 7:759
    species-being 6:118, 6:122
  self-enriching (Solov'ëv, V.S.)
    9:28–9
  socialism 8:882
  spectator problem (Marcel, G.)
    6:92

Alighieri, Dante **1:181–5**
  languages 5:403
  limbo of the sages 5:637
  love 5:845
  morality and emotions 6:561,
    6:563
  natural philosophy 1:183, 1:184
  political philosophy 1:183–4
  purgatory 7:838
Alison, Archibald **1:185–7**
Alkindus *see* al-Kindi, Abu Yusuf
  Ya'qub ibn Ishaq
Allais, M. 2:834, 8:101
Allan, D. 3:632
Allan, D.J. 2:694
Allan, T.R.S.
  rule of law †8:387–91
Allard, M. 4:646, 5:170
Allberry, C.R.C. 6:77
allegory
  Bible 3:778, 4:390–1
  Frei, H. 3:757, 3:778
  exegesis
    Arama, I. 1:350
    Origen 7:161
  medieval language theories 5:395
  Qur'an (Ibn Rushd) 4:643
  use of (Prodicus) 7:731, 7:732
Allen, Diogenes
  justification, religious †5:165–8
  Nygren, A. †7:67–9
  sanctification †8:454–8
Allen, Douglas 3:263
Allen, E.B. 4:404
Allen, G.E. 9:642
Allen, G.W. 3:272
Allen, M.J.B. 3:658, 7:392
Allen, N.W. 7:381
Allen, R.E. 7:420, 7:672, 9:852
Allen, R.G.D. 8:68, 8:74
Allen, R.L. 8:556
Allen, R.T.
  Polanyi, M. †7:489–92
Allers, R. 7:208
Allison, Henry E.
  Eberhard, J.A. †3:196
  Kant, I. 5:196
  Spinoza, B. de †9:91–9:107
Allison, J.W.F. 5:141
Allistel, C.
  learning †5:483–7
Allony, N. 4:212–13
All-Unity
  human development
    (Solov'ëv, V.S.) 9:28–9
Almeder, R. 7:224, 8:337

Almond, Brenda
applied ethics †1:317–25
Almond, G.A. 9:256
Almond, P.C. 7:175
Alon, I. 2:244, 3:442, 3:558
Alpago, Andrew 5:24
Alpern, K.D. 8:279–80
Alperson, P. 1:471, 6:612
Alquié, F. 6:65
alreadiness (*Gewesenheit*) 4:310
Alsdorf, L. 6:81
Alston, William P.
emotive meaning 3:291
empiricism †3:298–303
enthusiasm 3:332
epistemic justification 3:381,
5:164, 8:130
epistemology
and ethics 3:370
normative 7:37
religion 8:218
evil, problem of 3:472
faith 3:543
foundationalism 3:723
God, concepts of 4:101
internalism-externalism distinction
†4:821–6
introspection 4:842
knowledge 5:266, 5:275
mysticism 6:632
omnipresence 7:107
omniscience 7:112
perception 7:298
pragmatics 7:630
realism
mathematics 8:123
reliabilism 8:208
religious experience †8:250–5
religious language †8:255–60
religious philosophy
history of †8:238–4
religious pluralism 8:262–3
alterity
see also Other
community (Blanchot, M.) 1:783
heterology (Certeau, M. de) 2:268
Latin American liberation
philosophy 5:610, 5:612
postmodern theories of **1:187–92**
within selfhood (Levinas, E.)
5:580–1
structuralist literary theory
(Todorov, T.) 9:426
Altesor, Homero 7:350–1
Altham, J.E.J. 5:764, 9:752
Althaus, P. 6:5

Althusser, Louis Pierre **1:192–6**
French anti-postmodernism 7:594
ideology 4:682, 4:685
Marx, K. 6:132
Marxism
philosophy of science 6:150
Western 6:142, 6:145, 6:146
Montesquieu, C.L. 6:494
social science 8:856, 9:187, 9:188
structuralism 9:187, 9:188
Altman, Andrew 8:391
Altmann, Alexander
Cohen, H. 2:402
Herrera, A. Cohen de 4:400
Israeli, I. 5:34
Jewish Enlightenment 3:323
Maimon, S. 6:38
Mendelssohn, M. 6:307
Messer Leon 6:334
prophecy 7:770
altruism **3:246–8**
business ethics 2:152
egoism opposition (Kant, I.) 5:182
Epicureanism 3:347
eudaimonia 3:451
hedonism 4:258
intelligence relationship
(Comte, A.) 2:500
moral motivation 6:525
moral psychology 6:531–2
reductionism (Parfit, D.) 6:573
socialism 8:881, 8:882
sociobiology 8:892–5
Alvarez, A. 9:228
Alverny, M.-T. d' 5:24
Aman, K. 3:43
Amann, E. 4:41
Amaterasu 8:748, 8:750, 8:751
Ambedkar, Bhimrao Ramji **1:196–7**
Indian and Tibetan philosophy
4:738
ambiguity **1:197–201**
adverbs 1:47–9
compositionality 2:476–7
de re/de dicto 2:815, 3:20–1
descriptions 3:21, 3:23
Gestalt psychology 4:52–3
implicature 4:724
Islamic philosophy 4:644–5,
6:237–8
medieval language theories 5:389,
5:399–401
quantifiers 7:880
Ambrose, A. 6:498
Ambrosoli, L. 2:241

Ambuel, David
ontology in Indian philosophy
†7:118–12
Ameghino, Florentino 1:378
Amengual, G. 3:639
America *see* Canada; Latin America;
see also United States of America
American Institutionalists
economics 3:214
American personalism *see*
personalism
American postulate theorists 5:732–3
Ameriks, Karl 5:196
Amerio, R. 2:190
Ames, Roger T.
Chinese aesthetics 1:74
Chinese Confucianism 2:548
Chinese philosophy †2:315–28,
5:454
Confucius 2:570
dao †2:778–9
Daoist philosophy †2:783–95
de †2:809–10
East Asian Philosophy †3:192–6
fa 3:533
Huainanzi 4:514
qi †7:862–3
self-deception 8:631
Sunzi †9:230–2
tian †9:400–2
xin (heart-and-mind) †9:815–16
xing †9:817–18
yin-yang †9:831–2
you-wu †9:834–5
zhi †9:858
Zhuangzi †9:865–7
Amida Buddha
enlightenment 2:103
forty-eight vows 8:747–8
Japan 5:73
Shinran 8:747–8
Amin, O. 1:7
Amin Razavi, M. 9:223
al-'Amiri, Abu'l Hasan Muhammad
ibn Yusuf **1:207–8**, 3:557
Amita
devotional Buddhism
China 2:89
Ammonius, son of Hermeas
1:208–10, 1:435–6
amnesia 6:296
Amo, Anton Wilhelm 1:96, **1:210–11**
Amor Divino e Caneca, Frei Joaquim
do 2:10
Amor Ruibal, Angel 9:75, 9:76
Ampe, A. 9:374

ampliation
  medieval language 5:399
Amrine, F. 6:740
Amsel, A. 5:487
Anabaptism
  ethics 8:222
anachrony
  film aesthetics 3:675–6
Anacker, S. 2:74, 9:586
analectic philosophy
  Latin American liberation
    philosophy 5:611, 5:612
Analects see Confucius
analogy
  Aquinas, T. 2:171–2, 6:760, 8:776
    causation 1:334
  attribution 5:414
  being (Henry of Ghent) 3:157
  Capreolus, J. 2:200
  equivocal terms 5:414
  inference
    other minds 7:171–2
  Islamic philosophy 6:237–8
  knowledge of God (Browne, P.)
    2:29
  language
    medieval 5:400
    Renaissance philosophy of
      5:414–15
  proportionality 5:414
  religious statements 8:259
  scientific theory (Maxwell, J.C.)
    6:208
  by similarity (Carnap, R.) 2:533–4
  as source of knowledge
    Indian philosophy 5:281–2, 7:63
  theory formation (Campbell, N.R.)
    2:193
Analysis
  analytic philosophy 1:227
analysis **1:216–20**
  see also philosophical analysis
  arithmetization of 5:847
  conceptual 1:236, 1:774, 2:508,
    2:518–22
  epistemological
    analytic philosophy 1:225
  fuzzy 3:824
  infinite
    contingent truth (Leibniz, G.W.)
      5:554
  Krause, K. 5:299
  logic
    analytic philosophy 1:224–5
  mathematical (Weyl, H.) 9:706–7
  method of 1:224, 1:226–7
  nonstandard **1:211–16**, 7:52

psychological (Lachelier, J.)
    5:338–9
  scientific method 8:577–8
  self-construction
    (Whitehead, A.N.) 9:717
  social
    organicist theories 9:253–4
analytic
  glossary 5:795–7
analytic behaviourism *see*
    behaviourism, analytic
analytic ethics **1:220–3**
  emotivism 1:221
  intuitionism 1:220–1
  noncognitivism 1:221–2
analytic geometry 4:30–1
  Descartes, R. 3:1, 3:2, 3:15
  Spinoza, B. de 9:92
analytic psychology
  Jung, C.G. 5:131–5
analytic truth
  conservation laws (Meyerson, É.)
    6:349, 6:350–49
  Lewis, C.I. 5:586–7
analytical languages
  sophismata
    Oxford Calculators 7:181–2
analytical philosophy **1:223–9**
  see also ordinary language
    philosophy
  aesthetics 1:67–8
  Argentina 1:377
  classical Greek philosophy
    (Vlastos, G.) 9:650–2
  Dodgson, C.L. 3:107
  Latin America **1:229–34**, 5:427
  Mexico 6:346
  natural laws 5:473–4
  speech acts (Searle, J.) 8:590
  technology 9:285
analyticity **1:234–9**
  a priori 1:4
  conceptual role semantics 8:655
  meaning (Lewis, C.I.) 5:586–7
  modal logic 6:429
  necessity 5:303, 6:748, 6:749
  propositions (Bolzano, B.) 1:826
  Quine, W.V. 2:213, 2:520, 8:10–12
analytic/synthetic distinction
  holism 4:490–1
  logic of ethical discourse 5:760
  Quine, W.V. 1:226, 1:227, 8:6,
    8:10–11
Ānandavardhana
  linguistic meaning 4:437
anaphora **1:239–44**
  see also pronouns

discourse representation theory
    3:93–5, 3:96–7
  Montague grammar 3:92
  reference 8:154, 8:161
  scope 8:588
anarchism **1:244–9**
  Bakunin, M.A. 1:646–7
  drawbacks to 9:121
  environmental ethics 3:333–4
  feminist 1:247
  justifications 1:585
  Kropotkin, P.A. 5:313–14
  libertarianism 5:618
  mystical (Berdiaev, N.A.) 8:770
  philosophical 1:244
  philosophical (Godwin, W.) 4:122,
    4:124
  political obligation 7:76, 7:79–80
  post-war 1:247
  Tolstoi, L.N. 9:439
  transition theories 1:246–7
  types of 1:246
anarcho-capitalism 5:618
Anastos, M. 2:164
anātma-vāda see no-self theory
Anawati, G. 5:31, 5:170
Anaxagoras **1:249–54**, 1:263
  creation 1:252–3
  matter 6:193
  mind as first cause 1:249, 1:252–3
  mind–matter dualism 1:252
  monism (Diogenes of Apollonia)
    3:88
  nous 7:43
Anaxarchus **1:254–5**
Anaximander **1:255–9**, 1:263
  archē 1:360
  astronomy 1:257–8
  cosmogony 1:256–7
  kosmos (world)
    origin of 1:257–8
  life
    origin of 1:258
Anaximander of Miletus
  infinity 4:772–3
Anaximenes **1:259–62**, 1:263
  pneuma (spirit) 7:470
ancestor worship
  China 4:447, 9:401
  Japan 2:105
Ancient Learning School *see kogaku*
ancient logic **5:687–93**
ancient philosophy **1:262–5**
  see also Egypt; Greek philosophy,
    ancient; Roman philosophy
  Athenian schools
    decline of 1:264

epistemology 3:371–2
language **5:356–61**
pagan
    Christian banning of 1:262,
    1:264–5
Patristic philosophy distinction
    1:265
Ancient Studies (*kogaku*)
    Confucianism, Japanese 2:549,
    2:553, 2:554
Anckaert, L.
    Rosenzweig, F. 8:361
Ancona Costa, C. D' 1:151–2, 5:598
Anderer, Paul
    Japanese philosophy in modern
    literature †5:657–60
Anderson, A.J. 1:268
Anderson, Alan Ross 5:789, 7:210,
    8:200–2, 8:203
Anderson, B. 6:661
Anderson, C.A. 2:349, 4:810, 8:404
Anderson, C.G. 3:525
Anderson, E. 4:134, 4:674, 6:110
Anderson, Francis 1:575
Anderson, G.W. 1:769
Anderson, J.K. 9:814
Anderson, J.L. 8:196, 8:198
Anderson, John **1:266–9**
    Andersonianism 1:577
    Australia, philosophy in 1:574,
    1:577–8, 1:582
Anderson, L. 1:840
Anderson, M.L. 3:592
Anderson, P.
    absolutism 1:31
    Althusser, L.P. 1:195
    Cambridge Platonism 2:185
    Marxism
        Western 6:146
    Trotsky, L. 9:466
Anderson, R. 7:822
Anderson, T. 5:505
Andersson, G. 3:642, 7:539
Andlau, B. 4:348
Andrada e Silva, José Bonifacio de
    2:9
Andre, J. 6:110
André, Y. 6:65
Andresen, C. 2:264
Andreski, S. 6:720
Andreu, P. 9:36
Andrews, P.B. 4:377
Andrews, Robert
    Brinkley, R. †2:19–21
    Peter of Auvergne †7:321–4

androcentrism
    scientific research 3:861–2,
    3:863–4, 3:867
    social sciences 3:588–90, 3:591
Andronicus of Rhodes 1:435, 7:304
Anesaki, M. 8:753
Anesaki Masaharu 6:829
Angel, E. 3:502
angels
    divine action (Ibn Daud, A.) 4:609
    identity 4:678
    Illuminationist philosophy (al-
    Suhrawardi) 9:221, 9:222
    Kabbalah 5:172
    medieval natural philosophy
    6:692, 6:694, 6:701
anger
    Aristotle 3:286–7
Anglet, K. 9:332
Anglo-American philosophy
    absolute idealism 1:28, 4:667
Angra Manyu (Hostile Spirit)
    Zoroastrianism 9:872, 9:873
anguish
    existential 3:510
animal behaviour
    innate releasing mechanisms 6:674
    learning 1:697–8
animal navigation
    scientific behaviourism critique
    8:800–1
animalism
    persons 7:318, 7:319
animals
    action
        will 9:723–4
    ethics **1:273–6**
        see also bioethics
        agricultural 1:126, 1:127
        duty towards 3:179
        environmental 3:333, 3:334–5
        moral standing 6:499, 6:550,
        6:551–3
        suffering 9:213–14
    human nature distinction 4:526–7
    language and thought **1:269–73,**
    5:372
        Condillac, É.B. de 5:376–7
        Davidson, D. 1:271, 2:804
    needless slaughter of (al-Razi, Abu
    Bakr) 8:111
    sociobiology 8:892–5
animism
    Japan 5:69
    Native American philosophy 6:663
Anjou, E. d' 3:315

Anjuman-e-Himayat-e-Islam (Society
    for the Support of Islam) 4:864
Ankori, Z. 5:208
Annaṃbhaṭṭa 3:826, 4:765
Annas, G.J.
    genetics and ethics 4:19
Annas, J.
    Arcesilaus 1:354
    eudaimonia 3:451
    happiness 4:229
    Hellenistic philosophy 4:336
    language
        ancient philosophy of 5:361
    moral scepticism 6:545
    Philodemus 7:367
    pleasure 7:450
    Pyrrhonism 7:854
Annas, J.E.
    Strato 9:163
Annicerians
    Cyrenaics 2:760, 2:762
Annis, David
    concept of knowledge 5:275
    defeasibility theory of knowledge
    5:278, 5:279
    epistemic justification 8:830, 8:832
    epistemological contextualism
    2:649
anomalous monism **1:276–80**, 2:801
    psychological anomalism 1:278–9
    psychophysical identity 1:276–7
    supervenience 1:279
Anschauung see intuition
Anscombe, Gertrude Elizabeth
    Margaret **1:280–3**
    Anselm of Canterbury 1:296
    bodily sensations 1:795
    causation 2:250
    consequentialism 2:606
    desire 3:33
    double effect principle 3:121
    duty 3:182
    institutionalism in law 4:802
    intentionality 4:820
    logical atomism 5:775
    pleasure 7:450
    practical reason and ethics 7:618
    promising 7:742
    right and good 8:324–5
    sacraments 8:445
    testimony 9:313
    Trinity 9:461
    virtue theory 9:623, 9:625
    Wittgenstein, L. 9:769
Ansell-Pearson, K. 6:861
Anselm of Canterbury **1:283–97**
    atonement 1:536, 1:540

Augustinianism 1:561
Cur deus homo 1:283, 1:285
    Incarnation 1:283–4, 1:293–4
    rational argument 1:285, 1:286
    satisfaction doctrine 1:284
De processione Spiritus Sancti
    1:293
divine foreknowledge 1:294
eternity 3:426
faith 3:542
freedom of choice 1:290–2
God
    concepts of 4:96–7, 4:101
    existence arguments 1:283,
        1:286–9, 1:831, 4:92
        ontological 4:86, 4:87–9,
        8:242
Incarnation 1:283–4, 1:292–4
language 5:395–6, 5:397
medieval Platonism 7:435
mercy 3:700
Monologion 1:286–7
    rational argument 1:284, 1:285,
        1:286, 1:294–5
monotheism 6:481, 6:482–3
natural theology 6:712
necessary being 6:743, 6:745, 6:746
omnipotence 8:243
omnipresence 7:105, 7:107
original sin 8:793–4, 8:795
perfections
    pure 3:158
predestination 1:294
predication 9:774
Proslogion 1:283, 1:286, 1:287–9
purgatory 7:837–8
rational argument 1:285–6,
    1:294–5
religion
    philosophy history 8:246
satisfaction doctrine 1:284,
    1:293–4, 1:538
Trinity 1:292–3
true being 1:333
truth 1:290–1
will 9:663
Anstoß
    'the I' (Fichte, J.G.) 3:648–9
Antarvyāptivāda
    Tibet 9:407
antecedentialism 3:26
anthropic principle
    see also God, existence of
    cosmology 2:679
anthropocentrism
    aesthetics (Chernyshevskii, N.G.)
        2:304

green political philosophy 4:160,
    4:161
mechanical philosophy
    (Fontenelle, B. de) 3:691
moral standing 6:552–3
anthropodicy 3:681
anthropology
    African aesthetic culture 1:62–3
    African Francophone philosophy
        1:110, 1:113
    Cixous, H. 2:373
    cognitive 1:297
    cultural relativism 8:81
    Dewey, J. 3:45–6
    ethnophilosophy critique 3:448
    guilt/shame cultures 6:567–9
    kinship (Lévi-Strauss, C.) 5:583
    of language
        Monboddo 6:473–4
    materialism (Chernyshevskii, N.G.)
        2:304–5
    monogenetic (Buffon, G.L.L.)
        2:122
    morality 6:562
    objectivity 1:298
    philosophy of **1:297–9**
    plasticity (Herder, J.G.) 4:382
    relativism 6:539, 6:541
    Renaissance (Pico della
        Mirandola, G.) 7:389
    Russian nihilism 7:7
    structuralism 7:600–1, 9:175, 9:186
    symbolic 1:297–8
    theological (Brunner, E.) 2:30,
        2:31–2
anthropomorphism
    see also anti-anthropomorphism
    Chinese philosophy 9:401
    cosmic design
        Hume, D. 4:559–60
    critique of
        Xenophanes 9:809
    of God
        Kabbalah 5:173
        Maimonides, M. 6:42–3, 6:46
    sociobiology 8:893–4
anthroposophy 9:133
anti-anthropomorphism
    Philo of Alexandria 7:256
anti-Aristotelianism
    Patrizi, F. 7:262–3
anticipation
    see also prolēpsis
    interpretation contrast (Bacon, F.)
        1:628
anti-determinism
    Cudworth, R. 2:740

Dostoevskii, F.M. 3:116–17
anti-essentialism 3:417–18
    see also essentialism; social
        constructionism
anti-formalism
    Fuller, L.L. 3:801–2
anti-foundationalism
    see also foundationalism
anti-Hegelianism
    unity (Deleuze, G.) 2:857
anti-humanism
    anti-postmodernist critique 7:595
    Marxism 1:192, 1:193–4, 7:594
anti-individualism
    computational theory of vision
        6:342–3
    mental content, wide 6:341–2
Antilles, French
    Fanon, Frantz **3:552–4**
anti-naturalism
    see also naturalism
    human uniqueness 6:719
    scientific realism 8:586–7
    social science 8:863, 8:865
antinomies
    see also paradoxes
    metaphysical (Kant, I.) 5:188–9
    Russell, B.A.W. 7:216
Antioch, School of 4:391
    see also John Chrysostom
Antiochus of Ascalon **1:299–301**
    influence on Romans 1:299–300,
        1:301
    Old Academy
        Platonism 7:422
Antiphon **1:301–3**
    physis and *nomos* debate 7:381,
        7:382
anti-Platonism
    mathematical realism 8:121–2
    Renaissance 7:441–2
anti-positivism
    Argentina 1:376
    knowledge (Nietzsche, F.W.) 6:849
    Latin America **1:304–7**, 5:427
anti-postmodernism **7:593–6**
anti-rationalism
    morality (Hume, D.) 4:556
antirealism 6:655–6, **8:115–19**
    see also realism; scientific
        antirealism; scientific realism
    coherence theory of truth 9:470,
        9:471
    conventionalism 2:667–8
    Dummett, M.A.E. 3:149, 3:152–3
    epistemic paradoxes 7:213
    law of excluded middle 8:118

mathematics **1:307–11**
  bivalence 4:856, 4:859–60
  intuitionism 4:851–2
  meaning (Dummett, M.A.E.)
    6:227
  metaphysics 6:340
  narrative 6:655–6
  objectivity 7:73, 7:74–5
  occasionalism 7:89
  pragmatism 7:636
  realism 6:655–6
    law of excluded middle 8:118
    pragmatism 7:636
  relativism 8:190
  Roscelin of Compiègne 8:356
  scientific **8:581–4**
  Strawson, P.F. 9:170
  truth conditions 6:224–5
anti-reductionism
  Nagel, T. 6:644–5
anti-scholasticism
  Renaissance scepticism 8:502
anti-Semitism **1:311–14**
  see also Holocaust
  Fries, J.F. 3:799
  Zionism 9:868
anti-slavery movement 1:210, 7:191–2
Antisthenes **1:314–17**
  Cynics 2:754, 9:21
anti-subjectivism
  see also subject, postmodern
  critique of the
  freedom 9:197
antitheory
  ethics 3:488
  moral particularism relationship
    6:528
antitraditionalism
  history of 9:445
anti-universability
  African ethical systems 3:431
anti-utopianism 9:559
antivoluntarism
  theological (Cudworth, R.) 2:740
Antonaci, A. 7:264
Antonelli, Gian Aldo
  definition †2:845–9
Antony, L. 3:602
Any, Carol
  Russian literary formalism
    †8:409–14
Anzaldua, G. 3:613–14
Apáczai, Csere János 4:568, 4:571
Apamea (Syria)
  Numenius **7:54–6**
apatheia
  emotion 3:285, 3:287

apeiron (infinite matter) 1:255,
  1:256–7
Apel, Karl-Otto
  communicative rationality 2:459,
    2:461–2
  Hegelianism 4:295, 4:296
  Wright, G.H. von 9:669
apocatastasis
  moral duty (Unamuno y Jugo, M.
    De) 9:520
apoha theory of language 9:407,
  9:547–8
Apollinarianism
  Christology 4:727
apologetics
  natural theology 6:711
apologists
  early Christian 7:257
  Nemesius 6:763
  Tertullian, Q.S.F. 9:307–8
apophatic way see negative theology
App, U. 5:646
apparent existence see esse apparens
appearance
  causation
    Indian theories of 2:251,
      2:254–5
  reality distinction
    Buddhism 2:76, 2:77–8
  reproduction of
    photography 7:379
  sense experience as 3:300, 3:301
appearances (phainomena)
  Aristotle 1:416, 1:426
  Philo of Larissa 7:362–3
appearances (phantasiai)
  Carneades 2:218–19
apperception
  awareness
    Indian theories of 1:607–8
  Wundt, W. 9:799
appetite
  rational
    desire distinction (Aristotle)
      1:426
    will 9:720–1
Appiah, Kwame Anthony
  Africa †1:95–7
    aesthetics 1:65
    Anglophone philosophy 1:106
    ethical systems †3:430–5
    ethnophilosophy 3:447, 3:449
    traditional religions †1:117–21
  Akan philosophical psychology
    1:139
  Cabral, A. †2:168–71
  Fanon, F. †3:552–4

indicative conditionals 4:742
pan-Africanism †7:190–4
postcolonialism 7:581
Yoruba epistemology 9:833–4
Appleby, J. 1:205
applied ethics **1:318–25**, 3:437
  critiques of 1:319–20
  method 1:319
  theoretical ethics distinction
    1:318–19
applied philosophy
  Passmore, J.A. 7:247–8
applied rationalism
  French philosophy of science
    3:780–1
appreciation
  aesthetics 1:51–4, 1:473, 1:474–5
    art criticism 1:461, 1:496
    emotion 3:279
appreciative self
  Iqbal, M. 4:864–5
approximation
  fallibilism 3:546–7
  idealization 4:670–2
Apuleius 1:262, **1:325–6**
Apuleius of Madaura
  logic 5:747
Aquinas, Thomas **1:326–50**
  see also Thomism
  adequate object of the intellect
    (Duns Scotus, J.) 3:159
  analogy (Silvestri, F.) 8:776
  Aristotelian–Christian synthesis
    1:432
  Aristotelianism 1:394, 1:399–400,
    1:402
    Platonism distinction 7:436
  Aristotle 1:327, 1:330–1, 1:333
  Aristotle commentators 1:436
  atonement 1:538, 1:540
  beatific vision 4:251
  beauty 1:363
  casuistry 2:228
  Catholicism 8:39
  common-sense 2:582–3
  conscience 2:580, 2:581
  consciousness 2:583
  critique of
    Pecham, J. 7:267, 7:268
  David of Dinant 2:799, 2:800
  divine simplicity 4:142, 8:787
  double effect principle 3:120, 3:121
  educational philosophy 3:225,
    3:228
  epistemology 3:373–4, 3:381
  eschatology 3:416

essence–existence relationship
  Dietrich of Freiberg 3:70
  Siger of Brabant 8:765–6
eternity 2:697, 3:424, 3:426
  Matthew of Aquasparta 6:201
  Siger of Brabant 8:767
ethics 1:339–41, 3:489–90
  animals 1:274, 1:275–6
  applied 1:324
  Gerard of Odo 4:39
evil 3:466, 4:141–2, 8:244
faith 3:538, 3:541–2, 3:543, 8:245
Franciscan attacks on 5:113
friendship 3:795, 3:797
Giles of Rome 1:347, 4:73
God
  concepts of 4:94, 4:101
  existence of 4:85–6, 4:87, 4:92,
    8:240–1
  infinite being 3:160
  knowledge of 1:831
grace 4:147–9, 4:151
heaven 4:250, 4:251, 4:252
hell 4:330
hermeneutics
  biblical 4:391, 4:394
illuminationism 4:699, 4:700
immutability 4:710, 4:712, 4:713
Incarnation 4:150
intellectualism 9:663
intentionality 4:817
Islamic/Jewish philosophy 1:327
Job, Book of
  commentaries on 1:329–30
justice, equity and law 5:147, 5:152
justification doctrine 5:168
knowledge (Rahner, K.) 8:35
limbo 5:636, 5:637
Maritain, J. 6:101–3
modern interpretations 8:36
monotheism 6:483
moral standing 6:553
natural law 2:444–5, 5:465, 6:687
  political-religious authority
    conflict 8:224, 8:226
natural philosophy 1:407, 6:705
  Christian–Aristotelian synthesis
    6:699–700
natural theology 1:341–4, 6:708,
  6:709, 6:712
necessary being 6:743, 6:744–5,
  6:747
negative theology 6:759–61, 6:762
omnipotence 7:102, 8:243
omnipresence 7:106, 7:107
perfect goodness 4:140, 4:141,
  4:143

Peter of Auvergne 7:321–2
Platonism
  Aristotelian distinction 7:436
political authority 8:225–6
political philosophy 7:508–9
positive law 6:688
predestination 7:656
prophecy 7:767, 7:769, 7:770
prudence 7:802, 7:803
Pseudo-Dionysius 7:807
purgatory 7:838–9
religion
  language 8:259
  natural knowledge 8:216
  philosophy history 8:246
  political philosophy 8:229
reprobation 7:656, 8:273–4, 8:275
resurrection 8:295
revelation 8:299, 8:300
sacraments 8:443, 8:445
salvation 4:150
sanctification 8:457
scholastic method 1:328
sexuality 8:721–2, 8:727
Simplicius 8:790
slavery 8:804, 8:805
soul 9:44, 9:45, 9:46, 9:48
suicide 9:226, 9:228
Summa contra gentiles 1:329,
  1:341–2, 8:776
Summa theologiae (Synopsis of
  Theology) 1:331–2, 1:339–41,
  1:342–4
  applied ethics 1:324
  beatific vision 4:251
  commentary by Cajetan 2:172,
    2:173
  commentary by Toletus, F.
    9:433–5
  common sense 2:583
  conscience 2:580, 2:581
  double effect principle 3:120,
    3:121
  eternity 3:424
  negative theology 6:760
  perfect goodness 4:141
  prudence 7:802, 7:803
  as scholastic disputation 6:273
  sexuality 8:721–2, 8:727
supererogation 9:232, 9:234
teleological physics 8:241
testimony 9:313
theological virtue 9:326–8,
  9:327–8, 9:330
  faith 9:328–9
Thomism 9:380–2
truthfulness 9:484

unconscious mental states 9:522
universals (Crathorn, W.) 2:692–3
virtues and vices 9:627
war 8:226
war and peace 9:686–7, 9:690
will 9:721, 9:724–5
  intellectualism 9:663
  Matthew of Aquasparta
    6:201–2
Åqvist, L. 8:3
Arabic philosophy *see* Islamic
  philosophy
Araki, Kengo 5:177
Arama, Isaac ben Moses **1:350–1**,
  5:89
Aranci, G. 7:392
Aranguren, José Luis 9:75
Āraṇya, Svāmī Hariharānanda 2:257,
  8:466–7
Āraṇyakas
  inference
    Indian theories of 4:760
Arapura, J.G. 8:25
Arato, A. 2:371, 3:735, 5:859, 9:7
Arbaugh, G.B. 5:243
Arbaugh, G.H. 5:243
Arberry, A.J. 8:300
Arbib, M. 6:812
Arblaster, A. 5:604
Arbuckle, G. 3:112
L'Arc (journal) 2:860, 6:11
Arcesilaus **1:351–4**
  Academic scepticism 1:263–4
  Ariston of Chios 1:381
  Pyrrhonian Scepticism 1:352–4
  Stoicism
    critique of 1:353
archaeological method of knowledge
  Foucault, M. 3:708, 3:710–11
archaeology **1:354–9**
  evidence 1:356–7
  explanation 1:355–6
  inference 1:356
  meta-archaeology 1:354–5
Archambault, P. 1:852
Archard, D. 6:324, 8:805–6
Archaud, D. 3:552
archē (beginning)
  Chinese philosophy
    xing 9:817
archē (principle) **1:359–61**
  Aristotle's six meanings of 1:360
  etymology of 1:359–60
  incommensurability 1:360–1
  science 1:360–1
Archer, M. 2:722

archetypes
    perception (Johnson, S.) 5:125
    theory of (Jung, C.G.) 5:132, 5:133
architectonic philosophy
    Peirce, C.S. 7:276, 7:277
architecture
    aesthetics of 1:61, **1:361–6**
    beauty 1:362, 1:363–4
    cognitive **2:392–3**
        computational theories of mind
            2:392–3
        connectionism 2:571, 2:573,
            2:575–6
    Gothic 1:363
    postmodernism 1:365
Archytas **1:367–9**
    mathematics 1:367–8
    music 1:368
    politics 1:368–9
árdal, Páll S. 4:561
Ardao, A. 7:568–9
Ardigò, Roberto 5:37, 5:40
Ardley, G. 7:170
Arefayne Hagos 3:445
Arendt, Hannah **1:369–73**
    forgiveness 8:136, 8:140
    phenomenological movement
        7:340
    power 7:611, 7:612
    revolution 8:303
    totalitarianism 9:443–4
    truthfulness 9:484
    violence 9:617
Arendzen, J.P. 4:252, 7:839
Arens, K. 1:594
Arens, K.M. 6:206
aretē (virtue) **1:373–4**
    components of 1:373–4
    educational philosophy 3:223,
        3:224
    as function of the soul 1:373
    Socrates 9:10–11, 9:14–15
Arethas of Patras 2:161
Arfa, M. 4:610
Argentina
    academic repression 5:611
    analytic philosophy 1:231
    existentialism 3:511–14
    phenomenology 7:349
    philosophy in **1:374–9**
        colonial period 1:375
        nineteenth century 1:374,
            1:375–6
        twentieth century 1:374–5,
            1:376–8
        positivism 7:566–7
Argerami, O. 3:429

Arguedas, Alcides 5:654, 5:656
Arguedas, J.M. 5:656
argument
    see also debate
    Ābhidharmika Schools 2:55
    ad hominem
        Arcesilaus 1:353
    Buddhism
        Tibet 9:407
    covering-law model of explanation
        3:521–2
    deduction
        Aristotle 1:417
    dialectic
        Arcesilaus 1:352, 1:353
        Socrates 9:11–14
        Stoicism 9:150
    disputation in medieval
        scholasticism 6:272–3
    eliminative
        crucial experiments 2:735–6
    glossary 5:797
    Hindu philosophy 4:434
    inference
        Indian theories of 4:761–2
    inferential logic
        Stoicism 9:151
    'limited and unlimited'
        Zeno of Elea 9:845–6
    logic
        formal and informal 3:702
    ontological 7:117
    predicate calculus 7:657
    private language 9:452–3
    rational (Anselm of Canterbury)
        1:284, 1:285–6, 1:294–5
    slingshot 3:536–7
    soritical (Carneades) 2:216
    third man 9:541
    transcendental **9:452–4**
    twofold (*dissoi logoi*) **3:106–7**
    validity of
        ancient logic 5:687, 5:690
        predicate calculus 7:658–9
        second-order logic 8:591–2
argumentation
    Chinese philosophy 2:322–3
        Confucianism 2:537, 2:545–7
        Mohist 6:456
        Sengzhao 8:683
    informal logic 3:702
    Islamic philosophy 5:706,
        5:710–11
    legal discourse 5:498
Arianism
    natural theology (Clarke, S.) 2:378
Aries, Phillipe 5:644

Ariew, Roger
    Aristotelianism in the seventeenth
        century †1:386–93
    Duhem, P.M.M. 3:146
Arisaka, Y. 7:16
Aristippus the Elder **1:379–80**, 9:21
Aristippus the Younger 2:760, 2:762
aristocracy
    republicanism 8:281
Ariston of Chios **1:380–2**
    Stoicism
        Arcesilaus 1:352
Aristophanes
    Clouds 7:731, 9:9, 9:18, 9:33–4
    Prodicus 7:731
    Socrates 9:9, 9:18
    Sophists 9:33–4
    tradition 9:445
Aristotelianism
    see also Averroism; Peripateticism
    alchemy 1:157
    Alexander of Aphrodisias
        1:169–70
    business ethics 2:151–2
    Christianity and
        Averroism 1:595, 1:596
        natural philosophy 6:698–701
        naturalist perfectionism 4:521
        Olivi, P.J. 7:95
        Philoponus 7:375–6
        White, T. 9:712–13
    critiques of
        Arama, I. 1:350
        Crescas, H. 2:700, 2:701–2
        Descartes, R. 3:4
        medieval philosophy 1:394,
            1:398–9, 1:400–1
        Nicholas of Autrecourt 6:829,
            6:830–1
        Peter Lombard 5:821–2
        Philoponus 7:372–4
    defence of (Ibn Shem Tov, I.) 8:738
    eternity of the world
        Averroism 1:597
        Maimonides, M. 6:44
        Nahmanides, M. 6:648–9
    ethics
        liberalism relationship 5:439
        MacIntyre, A. 6:22, 6:23
    Galilei, G. 3:836
    impartiality 4:714, 4:716–17
    influence on
        Neoplatonism 6:798–9
        Western philosophy 1:263

Islamic philosophy **1:382–6**,
    5:13–14
    Albert the Great 1:145, 1:146,
        1:147–51
    Ash'ariyya 5:29
    al-Farabi 3:555
    Ibn Miskawayh 4:630
    Ikhwan al-Safa' 4:686, 4:687
    influence on medieval
        philosophy 6:272
    logic 4:64, 5:706, 5:708–11
    poetics and rhetoric 1:77
Jewish philosophy
    Abravanel, J. 1:23, 1:25–6
    Arama, I. 1:350
    Crescas, H. 2:700, 2:701–2
    Ibn Daud, A. 4:608–9
    Ibn Shem Tov, I. 8:738
    Karaism 5:208
    Maimonides, M. 6:44
    Messer Leon 6:331–2, 6:333
Karaism 5:208
knowledge (Sergeant, J.) 8:698–9
logic
    empirical judgment (Jungius, J.)
        5:135, 5:136
    essentialism 3:419
    form 5:781–2, 5:783–4
    Islamic philosophy 4:64, 5:706,
        5:708–11
    medieval philosophy 6:274–5
    Messer Leon 6:331–2, 6:333
logic (Abelard, P.) 1:8, 1:10
mechanical philosophy (Digby, K.)
    3:72
mechanism
    matter 8:231
medieval **1:393–404**
    adequate object of the intellect
        (Duns Scotus, J.) 3:159
        Albert the Great 1:145,
            1:146, 1:147–51
    ambiguities of extension
        1:394–5
    Augustinian opposition to
        1:559, 1:561–3
    Jenry of Ghent 4:355
    Kilwardby, R. 5:245, 5:248
    Byzantine philosophy 2:163
    Christianity conflict
        Averroism 1:595, 1:596
        natural philosophy
            6:698–701
        Olivi, P.J. 7:95
    critiques of 1:394, 1:398–9,
        1:400–1
    Encyclopedists 3:306

Henry of Ghent 4:357–8
    indivisibles (Chatton, W.) 2:293
    logic 6:274–5
    Richard Rufus of Cornwall
        8:314, 8:315–16
    sacramental theology
        Peter Lombard 5:821
        William of Auvergne 9:726
methodological (Keckermann, B.)
    5:225
mitigated scepticism (Gassendi, P.)
    3:850, 3:851–2
natural philosophy
    medieval
        Christianity conflict
            6:698–701
philosophy/theology distinction
    (Maritain, J.) 6:102
Platonism synthesis (Abravanel, J.)
    1:23, 1:25–6
prime mover argument (Peter
    Lombard) 5:821
radical *see* Averroism
Renaissance **1:404–13**
    see also Averroism; Scotism;
        Thomism
    absolute demonstration
        (*demonstratio potissima*)
        (Vernia, N.) 9:596
    Collegium Conimbricense
        2:406–7
    critiques of
        Ficino, M. 3:654–5
        Vives, J.L. 9:647
    demonstration 1:406
    ethics 1:411–12
    George of Trebizond 4:35
    humanism 4:539
        classical texts recovery 4:533,
            4:537
    immortality 1:409–10
    intellective soul (Vernia, N.)
        9:597
    logic 5:769
    metaphysical hierarchy
        1:410–11
    natural philosophy 1:406–7
    Nifo, A. 6:867–70
    Plato–Aristotle controversy
        7:443–4
        George of Trebizond 4:34,
            4:35
        Pico della Mirandola, G.
            7:390
    Pomponazzi, P. 7:529–31
    scepticism (Sanches, F.) 8:451,
        8:452–3

scholasticism 8:265–6
    scientific methodology 1:406
    Telesio, B. 9:297–9
    virtue (Valla, L.) 9:570
seventeenth century **1:386–93**
substance
    Peter Lombard 5:821–2
    Thomism 9:381
    virtue ethics 6:533, 9:624
Aristotle **1:414–35**
    active intellect 4:651
    akrasia 1:140–1, 1:142
    Albert the Great 1:145, 1:146,
        1:147–51
    Alcmaeon 1:161
    Alexander of Hales 1:176–7
    altruism and egoism 3:222, 3:224,
        3:229
    Ammonius, son of Hermeas
        1:208–9
    Antisthenes 1:316, 1:317
    appearance (*phantasia*) 1:426
    appearances (*phainomena*) 1:416
    Aquinas, T. 1:327, 1:330–1, 1:333,
        1:341
    archē 1:360–1
    aretē 1:373–4
    argument
        deduction 1:417
    arrow argument (Zeno of Elea)
        9:843, 9:849–51
    art
        morality 1:456
        truth 1:457, 1:459
        value of 1:480
    atomism 1:535, 3:342, 3:343, 3:349
    Bacon, R. 1:633
    being 1:702
        property/entity debate 1:700
        and substance 1:422
        Vaiśesika comparison 9:545
    blame 6:567, 6:570
    Boethius, A.M.S. 1:801, 1:805,
        1:806–7, 6:270
    Bonaventure 6:750
    casuistry 2:228
    categorical divisions 1:418
    Categories
        categorical divisions 1:418
        commentaries on (Philoponus)
            7:372
        critique of (Plotinus) 7:460–1
        De Interpretatione relationship
            Islamic philosophy 5:709
        denomination 5:390
        logic 5:687

medieval translations of 1:394,
1:396
necessary existence 4:650–1
Porphyrian interpretation of
9:729
categories 2:229–30, 2:232
classification 2:230
Indian philosophy comparison
7:119–20
substance 2:230
Valla, L. 9:571
catharsis 3:278, 9:448–9
causation and explanation
1:419–20
certainty 2:265, 2:267
change
potentiality 1:420–1
substance 1:418–19
Christianity conflict
natural philosophy 6:691
civil society (*politike koinonia*)
2:369, 2:371
comedy 2:435
commentaries on **1:435–7**
Alexander of Aphrodisias
1:169, 1:170–1, 1:172–4
Islamic philosophy 4:157–8,
4:639, 5:22–3
Philoponus 7:372–4
seventeenth century 1:387–8
Simplicius 8:788, 8:789–90
consequence 2:599–600
conservatism 2:608, 2:610, 2:614
contextualism
epistemological 2:649
continuity 2:655
contradiction principle
(Łukasiewicz J.) 5:861
corpus chronology 1:415–16
cosmology 2:677–8
Cratylus 2:694
critiques of
Bonaventure 1:828, 1:831
Crescas, H. 2:700, 2:701–2,
2:703
Plotinus 7:460–1
De Anima (On the soul)
commentary
Cajetan 2:172, 2:173
Nico, A. 6:869
Toletus, F. 9:435
exegesis
Themistius 9:325
knowledge 3:372, 3:381
perception 2:583

De Interpretatione (On
Interpretation)
Categories relationship
Islamic philosophy 5:709
language 5:359–60
medieval translations of 1:394,
1:396, 5:390
modal logic 6:418–19
semantics 5:688
deduction 1:417
demonstrative science 1:417–18,
6:708
desire and voluntary action
1:426–7
dialectic
Owen, G.E.L. 7:178
Ramus, P. 8:51, 8:52–3
Renaissance logic 5:769–70
dialectical school 3:58
divine infinity (Duns Scotus, J.)
3:162–3
divine simplicity 8:787
doxography 3:126
dreaming 3:129
educational philosophy 3:222,
3:224, 3:229
egoism and altruism 3:248
emotions 3:285, 3:286–7, 3:289
empiricism
limitations of 1:832
'episodic' universe criticism
(Speusippus) 9:89–90
equality 3:395
eternity 3:424
eternity of the world
Gersonides 4:48
medieval views of 3:427–8
ethical life 6:23
ethics
animals 1:274
applied 1:320–1
examples in 3:488, 3:490
flourishing 8:338–9
human good 1:427
Islamic philosophy 3:439–40
eudaimonia 3:450–1
see also happiness
practical reason 7:616
virtue ethics 9:622, 9:623, 9:625
Eudoxus 3:453
explanation 1:419–20
faith 3:541, 3:542
fallacies 3:544, 3:545
fatalism 3:564
form
substance 1:422–3
foundationalism 5:275

free will 3:751
friendship 3:794–5, 3:797, 9:330
God 1:424
concepts of 4:101
Denys the Carthusian 2:885
existence of 4:92
first mover 4:85
immutability argument 4:711
necessary existence 8:240
good life 4:162
good, theories of the 4:130, 4:134
gratitude 8:138, 8:140
happiness 1:429–30, 4:227, 4:229
see also eudaimonia
Augustinianism synthesis 5:248
substantive ideals 4:673, 4:674
hedonism 4:259
Heidegger, M. 4:309
homonyms 5:358–9
honour 4:504
human nature 4:521, 4:525
ideal states 1:430
imagination 4:708
immutability 4:710, 4:713
impartiality 4:716–17
imperfect states 1:430–1
infinity 4:773–4, 4:775, 4:777
actual–potential distinction
4:773–4
influence of
Christianity
existence of God 8:240
Islamic philosophy 1:77,
3:439–40, 4:157–8
Latin America 5:425, 5:427
medieval philosophy 6:269,
6:271
Platonism 7:423
Thomism 9:381
Western philosophy 1:263
instrumental action 1:431
intentionality 4:817
John of Jandun 5:106, 5:107
justice 5:146, 5:148–9, 5:151–2
katharsis 5:218–19
knowledge 1:417–18
perceptual 3:372
scientific 3:372, 3:381
scientific 3:372
scientific 3:372, 3:381
scientific 3:372
language 5:358–60, 5:361
medieval theories of 5:389–90,
5:399
and thought 1:416–17
Leucippus 5:578, 5:579
life, origin of 5:634

logic 5:687–9, 5:692
    formal and informal 3:702
    Łukasiewicz, J. 5:862
    modal 6:418–19
    syllogism 5:688–9, 5:691–2
logical form 5:785
logical laws 5:786, 5:789
logos 5:818
love 5:843, 5:845
mathematics 1:423–4
matter 6:192–4
    four elements 2:295, 2:296
mechanics 6:249–51
Megarian school 6:279
memory 6:299
metaphor 6:337
Metaphysics 1:421–2
    commentaries by
        Fonseca, P. da 3:689
        Nico, A. 6:870
        Duns Scotus, J. 3:155–6
        God 1:424
metaphysics 1:421–2, 6:338
mimēsis 6:382
modal logic 6:418–19, 6:425
moral education 6:507, 6:508,
    6:509
moral luck 6:521
moral particularism 6:528
moral philosophy 6:103
moral sentiments 6:548, 6:550
moral standing 6:553
morality
    emotions 6:558, 6:559–60, 6:563
natural justice 5:464–5
natural law 6:687, 6:689–90
natural philosophy
    medieval 6:275, 6:276, 6:692–4,
        6:698
        Christianity conflict 6:691
        commentaries 6:690–1,
            6:693, 6:695
        cosmology 6:695–8
nature classification
    Linnaeus, C. von 5:649
nature and convention 8:847,
    8:848–9
necessary existence 6:743, 6:744
    Islamic philosophy 4:650–1
Nicomachean Ethics
    akrasia 1:140, 1:142
    blame 6:567, 6:570
    conservatism 2:610
    examples in ethics 3:488, 3:490
    friendship 3:794–5, 3:797
    Gerard of Odo 4:38–9

good, theories of the 4:130,
    4:134
happiness 4:227, 4:229
human nature 4:521
justice 5:148–9, 5:151–2
moral sentiments 6:548, 6:550
pleasure 7:448–9
practical reasoning/rationality
    8:91
prescriptivism 7:667–8, 7:670
prudence 7:802, 7:803–4
teleological ethics 2:604, 2:606
nous 7:43–4
omnipresence 7:107
Organon 5:687–8
    Islamic philosophy 5:706, 5:709,
        5:710
    medieval translations of 1:394,
        1:396
    order of books
        Islamic philosophy 5:709,
            5:710
particulars 7:236
Paul of Venice 7:265–6
perception 1:425–6, 2:583
perfect goodness 4:140–1
Peri hermeneias see Aristotle *De
    Interpretatione*
Peter of Auvergne 7:322
Physics
    commentaries
        Simplicius 8:789–90
        Toletus, F. 9:434
    divine infinity 3:162–3
    mechanics 6:249–51
    prime mover 3:160–1
physis and *nomos* debate 7:382
Plato
    harmonization with (Porphyry)
        7:546–7, 7:548
    influence of 7:417
    misrepresentation of (Francis of
        Meyronnes) 3:724–5
Platonism 1:264
    medieval 7:431, 7:434
pleasure 7:448–9, 7:450–1
Poetics
    Arabic to Latin translations
        5:22–3
    Islamic philosophy 1:77
    katharsis 5:219
    mimēsis 6:382
    tragedy 1:431, 9:448
poetics 1:431
    Islamic philosophy 1:77
poetry 7:474, 7:476
poetry defence 7:473–4

political philosophy
    history of 7:506
    Islamic philosophy 7:518,
        7:519–20
Politics
    ideal states 1:430
    imperfect states 1:430–1
    Islamic political philosophy
        7:518–20
    Suárez, F. 9:195
possible worlds (Crescas, H.) 2:703
Posterior Analytics
    archē 1:360–1
    demonstration analysis 1:406
    epistemology 3:372, 3:381
    scientific method 8:577, 8:580
    syllogistic theory
        Islamic philosophy 5:710,
            5:711
practical rationality 8:91
praise and blame 7:645, 7:646
prescriptivism 7:667–8, 7:670
prime mover argument (Duns
    Scotus) 3:160–1
Prior Analytics
    semantics 5:688
    semiotics 8:676
    syllogisms 8:603
        Islamic philosophy 5:710
processes 7:722, 7:723
proper sensibles 7:684
property 7:758
prophecy 7:767–8, 7:770
prudence 7:802, 7:803–4
psychē (soul) 7:810, 7:811
Pythagoreanism 7:860–1
rational choice theory 8:65, 8:73
ratios of velocity 1:863–4
relation
    Indian ontology comparison
        7:125–6
religion, history of philosophy of
    8:246
Renaissance logic 5:769
Rhetoric
    instrumental action 1:431
rhetoric 1:431, 8:307, 8:309
    Islamic philosophy 1:77
scientific method 8:577, 8:580
self-control 8:611, 8:612, 8:613
self-realization 8:632–3, 8:634
semantics 5:688
semiotics 8:676, 8:679
Siger of Brabant 8:765, 8:766
signification 5:359–60
slavery 8:804, 8:806

social science
  history of philosophy of 8:856
Socrates 9:18
Socratic dialogues 9:19
soul 9:48
  and body 1:424–5
  doctrine of 1:407
  inseparability of 9:44–5
space 9:64
Spinoza, B. de comparison 9:103
sport 9:113
Strato 9:163
substance 1:418–19, 1:422–3,
  9:205–6, 9:210
suicide 9:228
syllogisms 8:603
  Islamic philosophy 5:710
technology 9:285–6
teleology 9:295, 9:296, 9:297
  ethics 2:604, 2:606
  explanation (Ravaisson-
    Mollien, F.) 8:104
Thales 9:322
Themistius 9:324–5
theological virtues 9:330
Theophrastus
  critique of 9:338
  as pupil and successor 9:337–9
theory and practice 9:358
thought and language 1:416–17
Topics
  logic 5:687
  Renaissance logic 5:769–70
tragedy 1:431, 9:447–9, 9:451
  katharsis 5:218–19
translations of 5:748
  Arabic to Latin 5:22–3
  Greek to Arabic 4:156–7
  Latin to French
    seventeenth century 1:387
  medieval 1:393–4, 1:396–8,
    6:270, 9:455–6
    Boethius, A.M.S. 1:395–6,
      1:805
    William of Moerbeke 1:400
  Renaissance 5:769
  Western
    marginality 6:100
truth
  correspondence theory of 9:472,
    9:474
universals 1:423, 9:540, 9:541,
  9:542
  William of Auvergne 9:726
utopianism 9:558
value 9:582
virtue 1:428–9

virtues and vices 9:626, 9:627–30
voluntary action and desire
  1:426–7
will 9:721, 9:725
William of Ockham 9:735–6
wisdom 9:753, 9:754
women 3:576, 3:583
Zeno of Elea 9:847–52
Aristoxenus 7:420
arithmetic **1:437–41**
  cardinal 8:703–4
  completeness of *see* Gödel's
    theorems
  consistency of
    Gentzen, G.K.E. 4:24
    Hilbert's programme 4:425–7
  formal theory of (Frege, G.)
    3:774–5
  geometry distinction 6:181–3,
    6:184
  Gödel, K. 4:105–6
  Kronecker, L. 5:312
  logical proofs (Frege, G.) 3:772–3
  logicism 5:812, 5:813–14
  mathematics
    foundations of 5:847
  ordinal 8:702, 8:703
arithmetic hierarchy *see* recursion-
  theoretic hierarchies
arithmetical hierarchy theorem
  8:142–3
Arkoun, M. 3:442, 4:632, 5:20
Arkush, A.
  Jewish Enlightenment 3:323
  Mendelssohn, M. †6:304–7
Arminius, Jacobus 7:286, 7:395, 8:274
Armitage, A. 2:672
Armogathe, D. 9:212
Armogathe, J.-R. 3:29, 8:342
Armstrong, A.H.
  ancient philosophy 1:265
  logos 5:819
  medieval philosophy 6:276
  Neoplatonism 6:803
  Neo-Pythagoreanism 6:809
  patristic philosophy 7:261
  Plotinus 7:462
Armstrong, David Malet **1:441–3**
  analytic behaviourism 1:692
  Anderson, J. 1:268
  artist's intention 1:515
  Australian materialism 1:578–9,
    1:582
  belief 1:706
  bodily sensations 1:795
  causal theory of knowledge 5:266
  colour theories 2:431

  consciousness 2:594
  empiricism 3:303
  epistemic justification 5:164
  facts 3:537
  identity theory of mind 6:174,
    6:177, 6:399
  information theory 4:785
  intensional entities 4:806
  introspection 4:842, 4:845
  Lewis, D.K. 5:593
  materialism 6:173
  natural laws 5:474
  naturalized epistemology 6:727
  nominalism 7:22
  particulars 7:237–8
  perception 7:298
  possible worlds 7:572
  Ramsey, F.P. 8:49
  reductionism, philosophy of mind
    8:153
  reliabilism 5:275
  sense-data 8:698
  universals 9:543
Armstrong, S. 2:514
Armstrong, T.J. 3:713
Arnaldez, R. 4:621, 4:629, 8:115
Arnauld, Antoine **1:443–8**
  analytic philosophy 1:227
  decision and game theory 2:834
  intensional entities 4:806
  language
    early modern philosophy of
      5:373, 5:377
  Leibniz, G.W. debate 5:543–4
  Malebranche, N. debate 6:57,
    6:60–1, 6:65–6, 7:553
  Port-Royal 7:553
Arndt, H.W.
  logic in the seventeenth and
    eighteenth centuries 5:720
Arneson, Richard J.
  freedom and liberty 3:756
  human nature 4:525
  paternalism †7:250–2
  work
    philosophy of †9:794–7
Arnett, W.E. 8:470
Arnholm, C.J. 7:94
Arnim, H. von
  Ariston of Chios 1:382
  Chrysippus 2:346
  Cleanthes 2:383
  Stoicism 9:159
  Zeno of Citium 9:842
Arnold, E.V. 3:339, 6:95, 6:616, 8:682
Arnold, Matthew 2:749, 7:476
Arnold, N.S. 6:110

Arnold, Thomas W. 4:867
Arnold, Thurman 5:524
Arnold, W.J. 7:829
Aronson, E. 1:695
Aronson, R. 8:479
Arouet, François-Marie *see* Voltaire
arousal
    artistic expression 1:494–5
    musical expressiveness 4:189–90
    sexual 8:719, 8:720
Arrighetti, G. 3:351
arrow argument
    Zeno of Elea 9:843, 9:849–51
Arrow, K.J. 8:64, 8:73, 9:705
ars contextualis (art of
    contextualizing) 2:316–17, 2:326,
    3:193–4
Arsenijević, Miloš 9:53–4
art
    see also aesthetics; style, artistic;
        taste
    abstract **1:448–52**
        emotional response to 3:277–8
        nonfigurative abstraction 1:450
        schematizing abstraction
            1:449–50
    aesthetics 1:59, 1:60–1, 3:279
        intuition (Ravaisson-
            Mollien, F.) 8:104–5
        Japanese 1:80, 1:83–5
    African 1:63
    artist's intention **1:513–16**
    aura
        Benjamin, W. 1:717–18
    Chinese **1:68–75**
    critical theory (Adorno, T.W.)
        2:727
    criticism **1:460–3**, 1:474–5, 1:513,
        1:514
    dance **2:774–7**
    as deception 9:481
    definitions of **1:464–8**
        functionalism 1:465–6
        proceduralism 1:466
        properties 1:464–5
        recursive 1:466–8
    disclosure (Heidegger, M.)
        4:317–19
    elevated contemplation
        (Schopenhauer, A.) 8:551
    emotion in response to 1:61,
        3:273–81
        aesthetics 3:279
        fiction paradox 3:274–7
        music 3:277–8
        tragedy 3:278

emotions in response to
    expression 1:458, 1:492–8
    Japan 1:82, 1:83–5
    erotic **3:406–9**
    ethics 1:65–8
    expression 1:61, **1:493–8**
        arousal theory 1:494–5
        art works 1:497
        Collingwood, R.G. 2:414
        Croce, B. 2:730, 2:731
        Ducasse, C.J. 3:141
        emotional 1:492–8
        expression theory 1:495–6
        fiction 1:496–7
    forgery **1:499–502**
    formalism **3:706–8**
    freedom of speech 3:763
    hermeneutics (Gadamer, H.-G.)
        3:828, 3:829–30
    history 1:506
    human conduct (Dewey, J.) 3:46,
        3:49
    Impressionism (Merleau-
        Ponty, M.) 6:323–4
    interpretation **1:502–5**
        incompatibility 1:504–5
        intention 1:503–4
        meaning 1:503
    lyrical nature of (Croce, B.)
        2:730–1
    melancholy (Benjamin, W.) 1:717
    morality **1:452–6**, 9:439
    nature relationship (Alison, A.)
        1:186
    performing 1:61, 1:83, **1:468–72**
    political identity (Benjamin, W.)
        1:717–18
    politics relationship
        (Belinskii, V.G.) 1:709, 1:711,
        1:712
    practice/theory relationship
        African culture 1:64
    representational
        emotional response to 3:274–7
    Romantic aestheticism 8:349–50
    Russian nihilism 7:7
    Russian Symbolism 8:425
    Schiller, J.C.F. 8:524–8
    semantic theory of
        (Langer, S.K.K.) 5:354–5
    sociopolitical analysis
        (Helvétius, C.-A.) 4:347–8
    style *see* style, artistic
    styles of (Hegel, G.W.F.) 4:276
    symbolism
        Benjamin, W. 1:717
        Goodman, N. 4:136–7

taste *see* taste
theory critique (Nietzsche, F.W.)
    6:846–7
transcendental idealism
    (Schelling, F.W.J. von) 8:509,
    8:512
and truth 1:85–6, **1:456–9**, 1:505
understanding of **1:472–6**
    categories 1:473
    contextual evaluation 1:474
    morality relationship 1:474
universal character of (Croce, B.)
    2:731
value of 1:60, **1:476–80**
    Hume, D. 1:477–8
    incommensurability 1:477
    Ingarden, R.W. 4:790–1
    Kant, I. 1:477–8
    Plato 1:478–9
art of contextualizing *see ars
    contextualis*
The Art of Warfare *see Sunzi*
art works
    dance as 2:774
    ontology of **1:480–5**
        aesthetics 1:60
        autographic/allographic
            distinction 1:480, 1:483–4
        contextualism 1:482–3
        physical objects 1:481–2
        structuralism 1:482–3
        type/token distinction 1:482
        types 1:482
    artefacts
        theories of
            poetry 7:474–5
    artha (meaning) 6:239–43
    Arthaśāstra see Kauṭilya
    Arthur, C.J. 3:312
    artifacts
        technology 9:285
    artificial insemination by donor
        (AID) 1:779, 8:276, 8:277–9
    artificial intelligence (AI) **1:485–92**
        see also Chinese room argument;
            computation
        classical 1:485, 1:486–9
        cognitive psychology 7:827
        common-sense reasoning
            theories of **2:451–3**
        computational models of vision
            9:632, 9:634–7
        computational theories of mind
            2:392–3, 6:390–4
        connectionism 1:485–6, 1:489–90,
            2:574–5

discovery
  logic of 3:100–1
  evolutionary 1:491
  materialism 6:172
  neo-Heideggerian challenge
    1:491–2
  strong
    limitations of
      Chinese room argument
        2:328–9
      Turing machines 9:494
artificial intelligence in medicine
  (AIM) 6:267
artists
  expressive-affective capacity
    Japanese aesthetics 1:80, 1:83–5
  intention 1:473, **1:513–16**, 1:503–4
Arvon, H. 3:639
Arya Samaj (The Association of
  Nobles) **1:516–17**
Āryadeva
  Mādhyamika Buddhism 2:59
  India and Tibet 2:63
Aryadeva see Mādhyamika
al-A'sam, A. 4:638
Asaṅga 2:64–5, 4:762
Asante, K.M. 3:449
ascetic ideal
  Nietzsche, F.W.
    eternal recurrence 6:858–9
    morality 6:855–6
    Übermensch 6:857
    values 6:845, 6:851
asceticism **1:517–19**
  critiques of
    Rabbinic theology 9:334
    Tagore, R. 9:258
  duty
    Indian concepts of 3:183, 3:185,
      3:186
  Eastern Orthodoxy 8:455–6
  ethics
    Jainism 5:48–9, 5:52–3
  Ikhwan al-Safa' 4:685–6, 4:688
  Illuminationist philosophy 9:221
  Jainism
    Mahāvīra 6:33
  Jewish philosophy
    Ibn Falaquera 4:616
  Jewish pietism
    Ibn Paquda 4:635
  opposition to
    al-Razi, Abu Bakr 8:111
  Roman Catholicism 8:455–6
  Rozanov, V.V. 8:383
  Yoga 4:439
Asch, S. 1:695

Aschheim, S. 3:563
Asclepiades see Hellenistic
  philosophy, medical
  epistemology
Asea munje yônguso
  sirhak 8:797
Asenjo, F.G. 7:210
asexuality
  species classification 9:80
Asfar see Mulla Sadra
Ash, M.G. 4:53
al-Ash'ari
  causality and necessity 2:244
  human freedom 2:242–3
  Mu'tazila critique 1:520, 1:523
    divine justice 1:522
    essence 1:521–2
    Qur'anic anthropomorphisms
      1:521
Ash'ariyya **1:519–23**
  emergence 5:25
  al-Ghazali 4:63
  'ilm al-kalam 5:29
  al-Juwayni 5:169–70
  moral language 4:641
  resurrection 4:65
  science 8:562, 8:563
  value judgments (al-Juwayni)
    5:170
Ashcraft, R. 3:229, 4:525, 5:435
Ashcroft, Bill 7:578–9, 7:581
Asher, Nicholas
  anaphora †1:239–44
  discourse semantics †3:91–9
Asheri, M. 3:563
Ashlock, P.D. 9:275
Ashtiyani, S. 6:411
Ashton, R. 3:267
Ashworth, A.J. 2:710, 8:293
Ashworth, E.J.
  Aquinas, T. 1:346
  Bruno, G. †2:34–9
  Cajetan 2:174
  Fonseca, P. da 3:690
  John of St Thomas 5:120
  language
    Renaissance philosophy of
      †5:411–15
  Lipsius, J. †5:650–2
  logic
    medieval †5:746–59
    Renaissance †5:766–72
    seventeenth and eighteenth
      century 5:720
  Nifo, A. 6:871
  Paracelsus †7:205–8
  Patrizi, F. †7:261–5

Paul of Venice †7:265–6
  Renaissance philosophy †8:264–7
  Soto, D. de 9:39
  Toletus, F. 9:435
  Wyclif, J. 9:804
Asian philosophy, East **3:192–6**
as-if
  see also fictionalism
  Vaihinger, H. 9:567
Asín Palacios, M. 4:629
Askol'dov, S. 5:838
Asmis, E. 3:349, 6:95, 7:367
Asmus, Valentin Ferdinandovich
  1:523–7
Aspasia 9:19, 9:20
Aspasius 1:435
Aspect, A. 1:716
Aspelin, G. 2:743
Aspray, W. 6:812
Assaf, S. 4:612
assent
  see also tasdiq
  evident/inevident (John of
    Mirecourt) 5:111–12
  imaginative
    poetic language (Ibn Sina)
      4:652
assertions
  bivalence theory
    (Dummett, M.A.E.) 3:151
  indicative conditionals 4:741–2
  metaphor comparison 6:336
assimilation
  cognitive development (Piaget, J.)
    7:384, 7:385
  Judaism
    nationhood
      Ha'am, Ahad 4:193
      Zionism 9:868, 9:869
Assmann, J. 3:250
association
  aesthetic taste (Alison, A.) 1:186
  of ideas
    Alison, A. 1:186
    Hume, D. 4:543–4
    Tucker, A. 9:491
  learning theory 5:483, 5:484
  passions (Hume, D.) 4:550
associationism
  behaviourism 5:484–5
  causation
    Hume, D. 2:245–6, 4:547
  etiology
    Mill, J.S. 6:360, 6:368
  Hume, D.
    critique by Kemp Smith, N.
      5:229

learning
 James, W. 5:484
psychology
 scientific 7:826
Ast, Friedrich 4:385, 4:388
Astat (Eustathius) 4:156
Astbury, W.T. 6:458
Astell, Mary **1:527–30**
 Masham, D. 6:168
Astrada, Carlos
 Latin America
  existentialist thought 3:511,
   3:513
  Marxism 6:164
  phenomenology 7:349, 7:351
astral bodies
 Steiner, R. 9:133–4
astrology
 critiques of
  Oresme, N. 7:155–6
 critiques of Panaetius 7:189
 Jewish philosophy
  Ibn Ezra, A. 4:611–12
  Nahmanides, M. 6:649
 Kepler, J. 5:232
 medieval natural philosophy
  6:693, 6:697
astronomy
 Anaximander 1:257–8
 Boethius, A.M.S. 1:802, 1:804,
  1:806
 Copernican
  Kepler, J. 5:231, 5:232
 Galilei, G. 3:835–41
 geometric modelling (Eudoxus)
  3:452–3
 Heraclides of Pontus 4:363
 Islam 8:562, 8:563
 materialism (Laplace, P.) 6:172
 mathematical (Copernicus, N.)
  2:671–2
 medieval natural philosophy
  6:695–6, 6:698
 Philolaus 7:367, 7:369–70
 planetary motion
  Endoxus 3:452–3
  Kepler, J. 5:231
 Ptolemaic cosmology
  rejection of (Proclus) 7:729
 Ptolemy 7:830, 7:831
 Ramus, P. 8:54
 Stoicism (Cleomedes) 2:385
 Thales 9:324
Atanasijević, Ksenija 9:51, 9:54
atemporality
 divine foreknowledge 8:243
 eternality 3:422–4

providence 7:801
Ateneo de la Juventud (Athenaum of
 thought)
 Mexican philosophy 6:345
Athanasian Creed
 see also Nicene Creed
 Incarnation 4:726, 4:727
 Trinity 9:457
Athanasius 1:537, 1:540, 8:457
a-theism
 Strauss, D.F. 9:164–5
atheism **1:530–4**
 critiques of
  Bentley, R. 1:725
  Charron, P. 2:288
 definition of 1:530–1
 Holocaust
  evil 4:495–6
 Indian
  potentiality arguments 7:604–5
 Islamic philosophy (Ibn ar-
  Rawandi) 4:637
 justification for 1:530, 1:531–4
 linguistic relativism (Mauthner, F.)
  6:205
 materialist (Priestley, J.) 7:683
 morality (Bayle, P.) 1:673
 negative theology 6:761–2
 Prodicus 7:732
 singularity 6:483
 taxonomy (Cudworth, R.) 2:741
 toleration (Locke, J.) 5:677–8
 will to truth (Nietzsche, F.W.)
  6:852
Athenagoras of Athens
 Apology 7:257
 divine simplicity 8:787
Athens
 see also Academy
 Antisthenes **1:314–17**
 Early and Middle Platonism
  7:421–2
 Epicurus **3:350–1**
 philosophical centre 1:263, 1:264
  decline of 1:264
 Plato **7:399–421**
 Socrates **9:8–9**
 Thucydides **9:398–9**
 Xenophon **9:810–15**
atheology
 natural 6:711
Atherton, C. 5:361, 9:159
Atherton, M. 1:749
Atienza, M. 5:530
Atiyah, M. 2:481, 4:32
Atiyah, P.S. 7:742

Atiyeh, George N.
 Ibn Massara †4:627–30
 al-Sijistani †8:774–6
Atkins, S. 3:607, 3:610
Atkinson, D. 9:258
Atkinson, M. 7:462–3
Atkinson, R.F. 4:458
Atkinson, Ti-Grace 8:727
Atlas, J.D. 1:200
Atlas, S. 6:38
ātman (self)
 Buddhism
  emptiness 2:76–8
  Nyāya debate
   Udayana 9:512–13
 Hinduism 4:434
  Advaita Vedānta 6:402
  Brahman relationship 8:605,
   8:606, 8:607
  Advaita Vedānta/theistic
   Vedānta disputes 9:590,
   9:591–2
  mysticism 6:621–2
  Śaṅkara 6:622, 8:459
  Nyāya-Vaiśeṣika 8:608
  Upaniṣadic theories of mind
   6:400–1
atomic physics
 chemistry
  bonding 2:298–9
  sub-atomic particles discovery
   2:296–9
 quantum theory (Bohr, N.) 1:820
atomic swerve
 Epicureanism 2:218, 3:343, 3:348
atomism
 see also atomism, ancient;
  corpuscularianism; logical
  atomism; particulate matter
 astronomy opposition 6:698
 Blasius of Parma 1:786
 change (Nicholas of Autrecourt)
  6:831
 chemistry
  ancient Greek 2:294, 2:295
  nineteenth century 2:296–8
  thermodynamics 2:296, 2:297–8
 Christianized (Gassendi, P.)
  3:850–1, 3:853
 concepts 2:514
 critical theory 2:725
 critiques of (Vasubandhu) 9:585
 Descartes, R. 3:14
 extension
  Cordemoy, G. de 2:673
  Desgabets, R. 3:28

Gassendi, P. 3:848–9, 3:850–1,
3:852–3
Gestalt psychology 4:51, 4:52
indiscerpibility (More, H.) 6:578–9
Islamic philosophy 2:243
Mu'tazila 1:520
Karaism 5:207
language 5:357
Leibniz, G.W. rejection 5:556
matter 6:193, 6:194
Jainism 5:49
meaning/belief content 4:488–9,
4:492
natural philosophy (Gassendi, P.)
3:852–3
Nyāya 7:604
Nyāya-Vaiśeṣika 7:58, 7:121–2
Planck, M.K.E.L. 7:396–7
primary–secondary distinction
(Locke, J.) 7:685
substance 9:205
taxonomy of (Cudworth, R.) 2:741
Vaiśeṣika 4:439, 7:604, 7:605–6
atomism, ancient **1:534–5**
see also Democritus
change
Diodorus Cronus 3:84, 9:848
chemistry 2:294, 2:295
critique of
Galen 3:833
Epicureanism 3:340, 3:342–4
Charleton, W. 2:286
Marcus Aurelius 6:94–5
minima 3:342–3
motion 3:343, 3:348
Greek philosophy
Vaiśeṣika contrast 7:606
Heraclides of Pontus 4:363
Leucippus 5:578–9
materialism 6:171
Melissus 6:295
Pyrrhonism 7:853
Zeno of Elea 9:844, 9:845
atomization
Tocqueville, A. de 9:424
atonement **1:536–41**
see also justification, religious
doctrine of
Bible 1:536–8
Calvinism 2:180
evil, problem of 1:540
moral blame 6:568
moral responsibility 1:540
pietism 7:395
satisfaction doctrine 1:538
substitution 1:537, 1:539–40
universality 1:540

Atran, S. 2:395
attention
Wundt, W. 9:799
Attfield, R. 2:418, 3:43, 7:302
Atticus 7:422, 7:428
attitudes
see also propositional attitudes
aesthetic **1:51–5**
social 8:823
attributes
conception of
Reid, T. 8:175–6
God *see* God, attributes
infinite
Spinoza, B. de 9:94
Attwooll, Elspeth
Jhering, R. von †5:100–2
legal idealism †5:510–14
Atwell, J.E. 8:553
Atwell, R.R. 7:839
Aubrey, J. 2:308, 4:476
Aubry, D. 4:517–18
Audi, Robert
epistemological belief †8:127–30
foundationalism 5:275
intention 4:815
intuitionism in ethics 4:856
practical reason and ethics 7:618
religion and political philosophy
8:229
Ross, W.D. 8:367
audiences
performing art 1:469–70
Auerbach, D. 4:427
Aufbau see world, logical structure
Auffret, D. 5:290
Aufklärung see Enlightenment,
German
Augustijn, C. 3:401
Augustine of Hippo **1:541–59**
absolutism 9:483, 9:484
African philosophy 1:96
Augustinianism 1:559, 1:560
Campanella, T. 2:190
Confessiones libri tredecim
(Confessions)
evil, problem of 1:543, 1:551
metaphysics 1:550–1
Platonism 7:431–2
religion 1:553
soul 7:260
Contra academicos (Against the
academics) 1:543, 1:544, 1:545
conversion to Christianity 1:543
De Civitate Dei (The City of God)
3:305, 9:646, 9:753, 9:754
De Doctrina Christiana (On

Christian doctrine) 8:677–8,
8:679
De genesi ad litteram (On the
literal meaning of Genesis)
1:546, 1:550, 1:553–4
De libero arbitrio (Free choice of
the will) 1:544–5, 1:548, 1:549
De trinitate (The Trinity) 1:286,
1:287, 5:390
divine ideas
Francis of Meyronnes 3:724
educational philosophy 3:222–3,
3:225, 3:228–9
emotions 3:289
Encyclopedists, medieval 3:305,
3:308
epistemology 1:546, 1:550, 1:553–4
eternity 3:424, 3:426, 3:427
evil 1:543, 1:551, 3:466, 4:141
faith 3:542, 6:709–10
forgiveness 3:699
free will 1:544–5, 1:548, 1:549,
3:751
friendship 3:795, 3:797
God, concepts of 4:101
grace 4:147, 4:150
happiness 5:248
hell 4:330
history
philosophy of 4:458
hope 4:507, 4:509, 9:329
illuminationism 4:698, 4:699, 4:700
immutability 4:710, 4:711–12,
4:713
influenced by
Plato 1:541–2, 7:259–60
influence of
Anselm of Canterbury 1:286,
1:287
medieval philosophy 6:271,
6:275
Platonism 7:431–2, 7:437
influenced by
ancient philosophy 1:265
justification doctrine 5:166, 5:168
language 5:390
limbo 5:636
love 5:843–5
Manicheism 6:74, 6:75–6, 6:77
memory 6:297, 6:299
metaphysics 1:550–1
mysticism 6:624
natural theology 6:712
Neoplatonism (Marius Victorinus)
6:105
omnipresence 7:106, 7:107
original sin 8:792, 8:793–5

originality 1:542
Pelagianism 7:284–5, 7:286
perfect goodness 4:143
perfect-being theology 4:96, 4:97–8
political philosophy 7:507–8,
    8:224, 8:225, 8:229
political theology 9:332
prophecy 7:770
providence 7:798, 7:799, 7:801
purgatory 7:837, 7:839
reprobation 8:273, 8:275
rhetoric 8:308, 8:309
scepticism 3:373, 3:381
semiotics 8:676, 8:677–8, 8:679
sexuality 8:720–1, 8:727
situation ethics 8:798, 8:799
slavery 8:804, 8:806
speech in the mind 5:390
Stoicism
    critique of 6:561
temporality 9:413
testimony 9:313
text availability 1:560–1
theological virtues 9:330
Trinity 8:245, 9:457, 9:461
vital attention
    Vital du Four 9:638–9
wisdom 9:753, 9:754
Augustinian religious orders
    Augustinianism 1:563, 1:564
        Latin America 5:422, 5:423
Augustinian-Boethian doctrine 5:390,
    5:395–6
Augustinianism 1:559–65
    Aristotelianism conflict 1:559,
        1:561–3, 5:245–6, 9:726
    Augustine
        relation to 1:559, 1:560
    Gregory of Rimini 4:170–1
    Grosseteste, R. 4:179
    Hugh of St Victor 4:519
    influence of 1:560–1
    Kilwardby, R. 5:245–6
    primary object of the intellect
        Duns Scotus, J. 3:159
    William of Auvergne 9:726
Aumann, R. 2:834
Aumont, J. 3:676
Aune, Bruce 5:196
aura
    art 1:717–18
Aureol, Peter 1:565–7
    Duns Scotus, J. 2:293
Aurnague, M. 3:98
Aurobindo Ghose 1:567–9
    Indian monism 6:479
    nationalism 7:524

Neo-Vedānta movement 9:592–3
Auroux, S. 5:720
Ausdruck see expression
Ausland, H.W. 7:847
Austin, John 1:569–71
    legal norms 7:39, 7:41
    legal positivism 5:519
    political authority 1:585, 1:586
    science of law 8:874–5
    sovereignty 9:57, 9:58, 9:59
Austin, John Langshaw 1:571–4
    adverbs 1:49
    analytic philosophy 1:227
    conceptual analysis 2:522
    correspondence theory of truth
        9:170, 9:473, 9:474–5
    criteria (Cavell, S.) 2:258
    critique (Ayer, A.J.) 1:618
    deconstruction 2:839
    happiness 4:229
    illocutionary acts 7:621, 7:630
    imperative logic 4:720
    knowledge
        corrigibility 3:379
    non-cognitivism 3:366–7, 3:370
    ordinary language philosophy
        7:144, 7:145, 7:146–7, 7:151–2
    perception 7:292, 7:297, 7:298
    performatives 7:302–3, 7:304
    rational beliefs 8:62, 8:63
    rhetoric 8:309
    sense-data 8:698
    speech acts 5:409, 9:82–3, 9:86
Austin, R.W.J. 4:605
Austin, S. 7:234
Australia 1:574–8
    Anderson, J. 1:265–9, 1:574,
        1:577–8
    Armstrong, D.M. 1:441–3
    environmental philosophy 1:575,
        1:581
    feminism 1:581
    idealism 1:576
    materialism 1:574, 1:578–80
    moral philosophy 1:580
    Passmore, J.A. 7:247–8
    philosophy in
    Scottish influence 1:575, 1:576
    religion, philosophy of 1:581
    Smart, J.J.C. 8:813–15
    Wittgenstein, L.
        influence of 1:574, 1:578
Austria
    Brentano, F. 2:12–17
    Buber, M. 2:42–8
    Feyerabend, P.K. 3:640–2
    Freud, S. 3:786–94

Hayek, F.A. 4:245–9
Kelsen, H. 5:226–7
Mach, E. 6:13–16
Meinong, A. 6:282–6
Neurath, O. 6:813–16
Popper, K.R. 7:533–40
Renner, K. 8:267–8
Schlick, F.A.M. 8:539–44
Shütz, A. 8:559–61
Twardowski, K. 9:507–9
Vienna Circle 9:606–13
Wittgenstein, L. 9:757–70
Authentic Person
    Daoism 9:866
authenticity
    existentialism 3:493, 3:498,
        3:499–500
        Beauvoir, S. de 1:685, 1:686
        ethics 3:502, 3:504–5
        Latin America 3:510–11
    Heidegger, M. 4:311
    self-deception 8:629–30
author
    see also authorship
    death of the 1:657, 4:393
    intention 4:386
    narrator distinction 6:654–5
authoritarianism
    Bolshevism (Bogdanov, A.A.)
        1:817
    family system ethics (Watsuji
        Tetsurō) 9:692
authority 1:584–6
    absolute 1:29–31
        sovereignty 9:56–7
    biblical
        Chillingworth, W. 2:307–8
        Spinoza, B. de 9:92, 9:106
    Chinese Legalism 5:531, 5:533–4
    consent theory 2:598
    divine see divine authority
    divine right theories 1:585
    duty (Locke, J.) 5:680–2
    imperial
        Renaissance 7:509
        Roman 7:507, 7:508
    justifications 1:585–6
    law
        Hooker, R. 4:504–5
    of moral facts 6:535–6
    moral obligation (Locke, J.) 5:679
    natural right theory 7:512–13
    nature and forms 1:584–5
    papal
        John of Paris 5:113–14
        Marsilius of Padua 6:112, 6:113

William of Ockham 9:732,
9:734, 9:745
patriarchalism
Filmer, R. 3:677, 3:678
political 7:501
Enlightenment 8:227–8
ethical autonomy 1:587
Herder, J.G. 4:384
Hume, D. 4:556–8
'ilm al-kalam 5:27
Marsilius of Padua 6:112–13
Molina, L. de 6:464
religion conflict 8:224, 8:225–6
Suárez, F. 9:192–3
trust 9:469
rejection of (Descartes, R.) 3:4–5
religious
Hooker, R. 4:505–6
Marsilius of Padua 6:112
secular conflict 7:504, 7:507–8,
7:510–11
Suárez, F. 9:193
temporal conflict (Giles of
Rome) 4:75
Wyclif, J. 9:802, 9:803
resistance to
Reformation 7:510–11
of rules 5:526
source of
medieval philosophy 7:509
supreme
religion (Hooker, R.) 4:505–6
textual
Chinese classics 2:310, 2:311,
2:313
Vitoria, F. de 9:643–4
authorization
political representation 8:272
authorship
evidence of 8:298
autism
child's theory of mind 6:385,
6:386–7, 6:388
folk psychology 3:686, 3:687
autognosis
Latin America 5:427
autoinfanticide
time travel 9:417–18
automata
formal languages 3:703
autonomy
see also free will; freedom; liberty
aesthetics relationship (Kant, I.)
5:193–4
axiology 1:611
Chinese Marxism 6:140

citizenship (Tocqueville, A. de)
9:423, 9:424
democracy 2:868
design argument (Kant, I.) 5:194–5
educational philosophy 3:235
epistemic 9:310–11, 9:312
ethical **1:586–92**
anarchism 1:244
critical reflection 1:589–90
definition 1:591
duty 3:181
education 6:506–7
genetic counselling 4:17
intuitionism 4:854, 4:855
Jesus Christ
atonement 1:539
Kant, I. 5:178
Kant, I. 5:189, 5:193–5
liberalism 5:439
logic of ethical discourse 5:761
moral agents 6:499, 6:501, 6:569
naturalism 6:714, 6:715–16
normative aspects 1:590–1
nursing ethics 7:57
pornography 7:544
rational agents 1:587–8
religion 8:221
self-governance 1:586–7,
1:588–9
technology 9:282–3
euthanasia 5:628
halakhic man (Soloveitchik, J.B.)
9:26
individual
Stirner, M. 9:141
law relationship 8:389–90
literature
Russian 8:412–13
musical faculty 4:189
paternalism 7:250, 7:251–2
professional *see* professional ethics
reason (Kant, I.) 5:177–8, 5:189
self-respect 8:635–6
social contract 2:662–3
solidarity conflict 9:23, 9:24
technology 9:282–3
transcendental idealism
Kant, I. 5:196
vulnerability and finitude 9:670
welfare 9:705
autopoiesis
social systems 9:255
Auyang, S.Y. 3:673
Avakumovic, I. 5:314
Avalokitavrata 2:59–60
Avatamsakasūtra (Flower Garland
Scripture) 9:516, 9:870, 9:871

Avé-Lallemant, R.C.B. 5:137
Avempace *see* Ibn Bajja
Avenarius, Richard **1:592–5**
Kemp Smith, N. 5:228
natural world concept (Husserl, E.)
4:583, 4:586
Avendaugh/Avendauth *see* Ibn Daud,
Abraham
Averintsev, S. 5:832
Averroes *see* Ibn Rushd
Averroism **1:595–8**
active intellect (Gersonides) 4:50
Aristotle (Nifo, A.) 6:868, 6:869
Augustinian opposition to
(Marston, R.) 6:114
Christianity conflict 1:332, 1:596–7
definition of 1:595–6
eternity of the world 1:597
Jewish **1:598–602**, 5:87
Delmedigo, E. 2:861
Latin
Albert the Great 1:146, 1:150
Aquinas, T. 1:332
medieval Aristotelianism
1:400–1
Themistius 9:325
medieval Platonism 7:437
motion (Vernia, N.) 9:597
soul (Paul of Venice) 7:266
Vernia, N. 9:596, 9:597
Avesta 9:872–3
Avicebrol *see* Ibn Gabirol, Solomon
Avicebron *see* Ibn Gabirol, Solomon
Avicenna *see* Ibn Sina
Avineri, Shlomo
community and
communitarianism 2:471
Hess, M. †4:413–15
Zionism 9:869–70
Avramides, A. 2:458
Awakened One *see* Buddha
awakening
Buddhism 2:96, 9:405–6
Awakening of Faith in Mahāyāna
1:603–4, 2:84–5
awareness
Chinese philosophy
self-cultivation 8:623–5
focal 5:286
Indian philosophy **1:605–8**, 5:281
mystical 3:410
Nyāya reliabilism 3:389–90
of self 6:475, 6:476–7
sense perception 8:690, 8:691
veridicality 3:409, 3:411–12
introspection, psychology of
4:843–4

Kyoto School 5:325–6
reflexive (Dilthey, W.) 3:78
subsidiary 5:286
verbalizable
    Gaṅgeśa 8:694
awe
    religious 7:354–5, 8:339
Axelrod, R.
    decision and game theory 2:834
    public interest 7:834
    rational choice theory 8:73
    reciprocity 8:131
    sociobiology 8:896
axiology **1:608–12**
    Austro-German school of
        phenomenology 1:609
    British tradition 1:609–10
    Latin America 1:305
axiom of choice *see* choice, axiom of
axiom of infinity *see* infinity, axiom of
axiom schema 5:798
axiom of separation *see* separation,
    axiom of
axioms
    archē 1:360
    of constructibility 2:623–4
    definability of concepts 1:760–1
    Frege, G. 5:725
    glossary 5:797
    Hilbert, D. 4:424–5, 5:732–3
    knowledge
        Locke, J. 5:668
        More, H. 6:577–8
    multiple-conclusion logic 6:603–4
    Ramsey sentences 8:45

set theory 8:711–15
Ayer, Alfred Jules **1:614–19**
    a posteriori 1:2, 1:3
    a priori 1:5
    analytic philosophy 1:227, 1:238
        Latin America 1:230, 1:232
    concepts 2:514
    conventionalism 2:668
    critiques of
        Austin, J.L. 1:572, 1:574
        Church, A. 1:615–16
    emotivism 3:291, 3:293
    empiricism 3:303
    ethics 1:223, 6:716
    explanation in history and social
        science 3:530
    fact/value distinction 3:538
    foundationalism 5:275
    good, theories of the 4:134–5
    knowledge criteria 1:617
    logical positivism 5:794
    meaning and verification 6:235
    moral knowledge 6:519
    moral scepticism 6:545
    natural theology 6:712
    necessary truths 6:748, 6:749
    neutral monism 6:817
    normative epistemology 7:37
    objectivity 7:75
    ordinary language philosophy
        7:152–3
    Paine, T. 7:186
    perception 7:298
    phenomenalism 3:379, 3:381, 7:333
    pragmatism 7:638

prescriptivism 7:670
psychological certainty 1:707,
    1:709
religious language 6:710
sense-data 8:695–6, 8:698
Stevenson, C.L. 9:135
Strawson, P.F. 9:174
substance 9:207, 9:210
value, ontological status of 9:581
verificationism 1:614, 1:615–16
    perception 1:616–17
Ayers, Michael R.
    Burthogge, R. †2:144–6
    Digby, K. 3:74
    epistemology, history of 3:381
    Keckermann, B. 5:225
    Locke, J. †5:665–87
    Molyneux problem 6:468
    natural kinds 6:684
    substance †9:205–11
Aylmer, G.E. 2:375
Ayrault, R. 8:351, 8:531
al-Azmeh, A. 4:626
Azouvi, F. 2:168, 6:52
Azpilcueta, Martín de 9:72, 9:76
Aztec (Nahuatl) civilization
    concept of God 5:430
    culture 5:429
    philosophcal methodology 6:344,
        6:345
    thought 5:428–9, 5:430–1, 6:344,
        6:345
    translations of 5:429, 5:430–1
Azuela, Mariano 5:654, 5:656

B

Ba'al Shem Tov *see* Israel Ben Eliezer, Rabbi
Baasner, R. 5:624
Babbit, S.M. 7:157
Babeuf, Françoise Emile 2:462
Babić, Jovan 9:54
Babut, D. 7:470
Bacalar Oliveira, J. 2:408
Bach, Kent
 ambiguity †1:197–201
 content
  indexical †2:639–40
  wide and narrow †2:643–6
 performatives †7:302–4
 pragmatics 7:630–1
 speech acts †9:81–7
Bachelard, Gaston 1:620–4
 alchemy 1:158
 French philosophy of science 3:779–85
Bacher, W. 4:612
Bachrach, P. 7:612
Back, L. 8:21
Backes, I. 9:518
Backhouse, R. 3:219
backpropagation 2:573, 2:574–5
Bacon, Francis 1:624–32
 crucial experiments 2:735, 2:736
 educational philosophy 3:229
 Herzen, A.I. 4:405, 4:408
 idols of the mind 1:628–9
 induction 1:624, 1:628, 1:629–30, 4:758
 method 1:627–8, 8:578, 8:580
 normative epistemology 7:35, 7:37–8
 technology and ethics 9:281, 9:283
 teleology 9:297
 universal language 9:534, 9:535
Bacon, J. 1:443
Bacon, Roger 1:632–6
 Alexander of Hales 1:177, 1:178
 education 1:634
 language 1:635, 5:390, 5:391, 5:396–7
 Liber de causis commentary 5:598
 natural philosophy 6:704, 6:705
 projectile motion 8:315
 science 1:634–5

Badaloni, N. 2:190
Bādarāyaṇa 4:438, 9:590–1, 9:593
Badawi, A.-R. 4:159, 5:597, 7:430
Badawi, M.A.Z. 1:7
Badham, L. 3:416
Badham, P. 3:416
Badhwar, Neera K.
 friendship †3:794–7
Badinter, E. 2:531
Badinter, R. 2:531
Baensch, O. 5:351
Baer, R.A. 7:361
Baer, Y. 4:213
Baert, Patrick
 Bourdieu, P. †1:848–50
Baertschi, B. 6:53
al-Baghdadi, Abu'l-Barakat 1:636–8, 5:88
Bahti, Timothy
 Man, P. de †2:810–13
Baier, Annette C.
 Hume, D. †4:543–62
 justice
  international 5:156
 morality 6:527, 6:550, 6:563
 trust 9:467–8, 9:469
 virtues and vices 9:630
Baier, Kurt 1:582, 3:238, 5:632
Bailes, K.E. 1:820, 8:408–9
Bailey, C. 3:351, 5:579
Bailin, S. 3:238
Baillargeon, R. 2:391, 6:675
Baillet, A. 3:18
Baillie, D. 8:445
Bailyn, B. 1:205
Bain, A. 2:504, 6:360, 9:279–80
Bainton, R.H. 6:5
Baird, D. 3:102
Baird, R.D. 3:263
Bakar, O. 8:564
Baker, A.J.
 Anderson, J. †1:265–9
 Australia, philosophy in 1:582
Baker, C.E. 3:764
Baker, Donald 2:565, 8:797, 9:827
Baker, G.P. 9:769–70
Baker, Judith
 Grice, H.P. †4:172–7
 trust 9:469

Baker, K.M. 2:531, 4:527
Baker, L.R. 3:265, 6:310–11
Baker, R. 6:264, 8:727
Baker, T. 2:475
Bakewell, M. 3:108
Bakhtin, Mikhail Mikhailovich 1:638–45
 dialogue 1:638, 1:640
 Dostoevskii, F.M. 3:119
 double voiced utterances 1:641
 heteroglossia 1:640–1
 novels, theories of 1:638–9, 1:643–4
 polyphony 1:642–3
Bakhurst, David
 Asmus, V.F. †1:523–7
 Il'enkov, E.V. †4:688–92
 Marxist philosophy, Russian and Soviet †6:150–6
Bakirir, G. 2:577
Bakunin, M. 1:246, 1:247–8
Bakunin, Mikhail Aleksandrovich 1:645–7
 Hegelianism
  Russian 4:302–3, 4:306
 materialism
  Russian 8:416, 8:417–18
 Plekhanov, G.V. 7:452
Balayé, S. 9:118
Balazs, Etienne 8:613, 8:625
Baldry, H.C. 9:842
Baldwin, James 6:100, 6:101
Baldwin, R. 6:817
Baldwin, Thomas
 analytic philosophy †1:223–9
 existentialist ethics 3:505
 McTaggart, J.M.E. †6:24–8
 Merleau-Ponty, M. †6:320–5
 Moore, G.E. †6:494–9
 state 9:122
Balens, D. 7:210
Balguy, John 4:591, 4:593
Baljon, J.M.S. 4:213
Ball, John 4:553
Ball, Terence
 green political philosophy †4:159–66
 Mill, J. †6:359–60
Ballard, D.H. 2:577

Ballard, G. 1:529, 6:168
Ballentine, L.E. 1:716, 7:893
Balmes, Abram de 5:23
Baltes, M. 7:428
Balthasar, H.U. von 1:655
Balz, A.G.A. 2:382, 2:674, 5:332, 8:342
Balzer, W. 3:219, 3:222, 4:672
Ban Gu 2:311, 4:449
Banach, S. 9:263
Banach-Tarski paradox 1:613, 9:263
Banerjee, M. 8:385
Baneth, D.H. 4:213, 4:623
Báñez, Domingo **1:647–9**
  de auxiliis 9:72, 9:76
  God's grace 6:462–3
  Thomism 9:383
Bańkowski, Zenon
  Kelsen, H. †5:226–7
  legal norms †7:38–41
Banton, Michael
  discrimination 3:105
  race
    theories of †8:18–21
Bantu philosophy 1:110, 1:111, 3:446
Bao Xi 1:69
baptism 5:636, 5:637, 8:455, 8:793
Bar Hayya, Abraham **1:649–51**, 5:88
Bar Hiyya, Abraham *see* Bar Hayya, Abraham
Baran, H. 6:587
Baranova-Shestova, N. 8:746
Barata-Moura, J. 3:639
Baratta, A. 8:22
Baratz, M.S. 7:612
Baraut, C. 5:104
barbarism
  Latin American literature 5:653–5
Barbata, A. 3:559
Barber, B. 2:871
Barber, K.F. 6:285
Barber, W.H. 3:133, 9:662
Barbier, M. 9:645
Barbour, Ian 7:714, 8:232, 8:235, 8:259
Bardenhewer, O. 5:597
Bardili, C.G. 8:188
Bardo, S.R. 3:867
bare particulars, doctrine of 7:236
Bareau, A. 2:57
Barendregt, H. 2:433, 5:349
Barfoot, M. 4:501
Bārhaspatyas *see* Lokāyata
Bar-Hillel, Y. 7:220, 7:630–1, 8:715
Barker, E. 7:188
Barker, John 4:56, 4:58, 5:279

Barker, Peter
  Duhem, P.M.M. 3:146
  Hertz, H.R. †4:400–2
Barker, S.F. 2:448
Barker-Benfield, G.J. 9:791
Barkow, J.H. 3:487
Barlow, John Perry 4:778–9, 4:781
Barlow, M. 1:736
Barnard, F.M. 2:749–50, 4:384, 8:856, 9:380
Barnes, A. 1:505, 5:476
Barnes, B. 5:318, 8:856, 9:2, 9:579
Barnes, Jonathan
  Academy †1:36
  Agrippa 1:129
  Ammonius, son of Hermeas 1:209
  Anaximander 1:259
  Anaximenes 1:262
  ancient logic 5:692
  ancient philosophy 1:265
  Antiochus †1:299–301
  Antiphon 1:303
  Arcesilaus †1:351–4
  Aristotle 1:434
  atomism, ancient 1:535
  Carneades †2:215–20
  Cicero, M.T. 2:360
  Cleomedes 2:386
  Democritus 2:877
  Diogenes of Apollonia 3:89
  dissoi logoi (twofold argument) 3:107
  existence 3:492
  Galen 3:835
  Hellenistic philosophy 4:336, 4:337
  Heraclitus 4:369
  Leucippus 5:578–9
  Melissus 6:295
  moral scepticism 6:545
  Parmenides 7:234
  Peripatetics 7:305
  Philo of Larissa †7:361–3
  Presocratics 7:671
  Pyrrhonism 7:854
  relativism 8:190
  war and peace 9:690
  Xenophanes 9:810
  Zeno of Elea 9:852
Barnes, R.H. 6:669
Barnhart, R.M. 1:74
Barnikol, E. 1:667
Barnish, Samuel
  Encyclopedists, medieval †3:304–9
Barnouw, J. 9:321
Barocelli, F. 1:787
Baron, H. 4:540
Baron, M. 6:533

Baron, R. 4:520
Baron, S. 7:455
Baron, S.W. 4:213, 6:48
Baron-Cohen, S. 3:687, 6:386, 6:389
Barr, A.H., Jr 1:452
Barr, M. 5:640
Barreau, H. 1:736
Barrès, Maurice 1:109–10, 1:114
Barreto, Oscar 7:351
Barreto de Meneses, Tobias 2:10, 7:567, 7:569
Barrett, K.C. 7:822
Barrett, R.B. 8:13–14
Barrientos García, J. 9:39
Barrios de Chungara, D. 3:628
Barrow, J.D. 2:651
Barry, B.
  equality 3:395
  Godwin, W. 4:125
  justice †5:141–7
    international †5:153–7
  law and morality 5:441, 5:442
  needs and interests 6:755
  neutrality
    political 6:820
  obligations to future generations 3:821, 3:822
  political philosophy
    nature of 7:528
  population and ethics 7:542, 7:543
  public interest 7:834
  rational choice theory 8:73
  Rawls, J. 8:109
  reciprocity 8:131
  state 9:122
Barry, Sister M. Inviolata 1:347
Barry, N. 4:249, 5:619
Barth, E.M. 3:61
Barth, Karl **1:651–6**
  agapeleros distinction 2:280, 2:282
  atonement 1:540
  Bonhoeffer, D. 1:837
  Brunner, E. 2:33
  Bultmann, R. 2:130
  dialectical theology 1:651, 1:652–3
  existentialist theology 3:507–8, 3:509
  Hegelianism 4:295
  natural theology 6:711, 6:712
  omnipresence 7:107
  reprobation 8:275
  revelation 8:297
  theology of the Word 1:651, 1:653–4
Barthes, Roland **1:656–8**
  hermeneutics
    biblical 4:390, 4:393

narrative 6:656
rhetoric 8:309
structuralism 7:598–9, 9:183,
  9:184, 9:188
Bartholomew of Messina 9:456
Bartholomew, D.J. 7:801
Bartholomew, M. 4:595
Bartlett, E. 6:268
Bartley, W.W. 3:108, 7:539
Bartolus of Sassoferrato **1:658–9**,
  7:509
Bartra, R. 6:348
Bartram, G. 1:718
Bartsch 6:387–8
Bartsch, H.-W. 4:394
Baruch, E. Hoffman 5:308
Barwise, J.
  anaphora 1:243
  Beth's theorem and Craig's
    interpolation theorem 1:762–3
  facts 3:537
  inductive definitions and proofs
    4:755
  logic
    early twentieth century 5:735–6
    infinitary 4:771
    intensional 4:807, 4:810
    second-order 8:603
  logical constants 5:780
  model theory 6:442
  pragmatics 7:631
  quantifiers
    generalized 7:877
  semantic paradoxes and theories
    of truth 8:648
  set theory 8:708
  situation semantics 8:671–2
Barwise-Moschovakis-Gandy
  theorem 4:755
Barz, R. 9:575
Barzun, J. 5:67
Bashō 1:88–9
basho see logic of place
basic ecclesial communities
  liberation theology 5:615
Basil of Caesarea (Basil the Great)
  7:259, 7:837
Basinger, David
  miracles †6:411–16
  process theism †7:716–20
Basinger, R. 6:415
al-Basir, Yusuf 5:207, 5:208
Basso, K.H. 6:669–70
Bastid, P. 2:617–18
Bataille, Georges **1:659–61**
  dialectics of desire 1:188, 1:190
  Hegelianism 4:299

Bataille, P. 8:20
Batard, Y. 2:345
Bateman, B.W. 5:235
Bateson, Gregory 3:201
Batkin, N. 7:380
Batsap Nyimadrak *see* Pa tshab Nyi
  ma grags
Battail, J.-F. 2:674
Batterman, R.W. 2:279
Battersby, C. 3:596
Battin, M.P. 9:228–9
Bauch, Bruno 6:777, 6:788, 6:789
Baudrillard, Jean **1:662–3**
  alterity and identity 1:190–1
Baudry, L. 9:747
Bauer, Bruno **1:664–7**
  Gospel 1:664
  Hegelianism 4:283
Bauer, E. 7:890
Bauer, J. 6:48
Bauer, Otto 6:143
Bauer, W. 7:472
Baum, G. 5:47–8
Bauman, Z. 9:7
Baumanns, P. 3:652
Baumgardt, David **1:667–9**
  Jewish philosophy 5:90
  Maimon, S. 6:38
Baumgarten, Alexander Gottlieb
  1:669–72
Baumgarten, H.-U. 9:321
Baumgartner, M. 3:652, 9:727
Baumgartner, W. 2:17
Baur, Ferdinand Christian 4:282,
  4:296
Bausola, A. 5:40
Bavarian Academy of Sciences
  Historical Commission (1966)
  4:240
ha-Bavli *see* al-Muqammas, Daud
Baxter, Andrew 1:749
Bayer, D. 8:59
Bayesian confirmation theory 2:534
  experiments 3:517
  idealization 4:670
  learning 5:485
  medicine
    prognoses/diagnoses 6:266–7
  risk 8:331, 8:332
  scientific theories
    simplicity 8:781–2
  statistics 9:124–5
  subjectivity 9:125–6
Bayesian epistemology
  see also probabilism
  acceptance 7:708
  criticisms of 7:705, 7:709–10

epistemic justification 5:162
paradoxes 7:212
problem of priors 7:709–10
rational belief 7:705, 7:708, 8:87
scientific method 7:707, 7:708–9,
  7:708
Bayle, Pierre **1:672–7**
  Berkeley, G. 1:739–40
  epistemology 3:381
  Foucher, S. 3:717
  Port-Royal 7:553
  religion, critique of 8:238
Bayles, M. 4:236, 7:542
Bayne, R. 1:823
Baynes, K.
  Habermas, J. †4:193–200
Bazala, Albert 9:51, 9:54
Bazin, A. 3:676, 7:380–1
Bealer, G.
  analyticity †1:234–9
  Church, A. 2:349
  concepts 2:514
  correspondence theory of truth
    9:475
  empiricism 3:303
  property theory 7:766
  unconscious mental states 9:525–6
Bealer, George
  intensional entities †4:803–7
Beardsley, E. 4:720
Beardsley, M.C.
  art
    artist's intention 1:513, 1:516
    criticism 1:463
    definition of 1:466, 1:468
    interpretation 1:505
    understanding of 1:475
  music
    aesthetics of 6:612
  poetry 7:475, 7:476
Beardsworth, T. 8:251, 8:255
Beasley, W.G. 4:452
beatific vision
  Ash'ariyya/Mu'tazila comparison
    1:521
  al-Ghazali 4:65
  heaven 4:249, 4:251
  intuitive cognition (Duns
    Scotus, J.) 3:166
  purgatory 7:838
beatitude
  natural rights (Carmichael, G.)
    2:206–7
Beattie, J.
  African traditional religions 1:118,
    1:120

Beattie, James **1:677–80**
  Common Sense School 1:679
  common-sense ethics 1:678–9,
    2:450
Beatty, John
  ecology †3:202–5
  genetics 4:15
Beauchamp, T.C. 2:448
Beauchamp, Tom L.
  ethics
    bioethics 1:776
    business 2:153
    journalism 5:128
    medical 6:263
    nursing 7:56, 7:57
    professional 7:736
  Hume, D. 4:561
  social science
    methodology of 8:867
    value judgments in †9:575–80
  suicide 9:229
Beaude, J. 3:29
beauty **1:680–4**
  see also aesthetics
  aesthetic attitude 1:52
  African aesthetics 1:62, 1:63–4
  architecture 1:362, 1:363–4
  art and morality 1:453
  connoisseurs (Kant, I.) 1:65, 1:66
  contemporary views 1:683
  contextual 1:58
  Daoism 2:790
  dependent 1:683
  empirical investigation into 1:511
  of God (Edwards, J.) 3:240, 3:243
  Hume, D. 1:510–11
  intelligible
    Islamic philosophy 1:75–7
  intrinsic properties 1:681–2
  Islamic philosophy 1:75–7
    al-Farabi 1:76
    Ibn Sina 1:76–7
    intelligible 1:75–7
  Japanese aesthetics 1:80, 1:87, 1:88
  Kant, I. 1:511
  Lessing, G.E. 5:575, 5:576, 5:577
  love 5:844–5, 7:411–12
  as moral character
    African aesthetics 1:62, 1:63–4
  music 4:189–90, 6:611–12
  nature
    Alison, A. 1:186
    Fechner, G.T. 3:571
    Kant, I. 5:193–4
    Shintō 8:749
  Nō performers (Zeami) 9:840
  objectivity 1:511–12

projectivism 7:738
realism 1:682–3
relativism 1:683
Schiller, J.C.F. 8:526–8
sensible (Ibn Sina) 1:76–7
sources of (Burke, E.) 2:137
spiritual sense (Edwards, J.)
  3:243–4
subjectivism 1:681, 1:683
the sublime 5:194, 8:176–7
supervenience 9:238
transience
  Japanese Buddhism 6:593
value of (Alexander, S.) 1:168–9
works of art 1:478
Beauvoir, Simone de **1:684–7**
  existentialism
    ethics 3:505
    phenomenology 7:338–9, 7:340
  feminism 3:580–1, 3:583
    Le Doeuff, M. 5:477, 5:478
    literary criticism 3:613
'because' (causal)
  slingshot argument 3:536–7
Beccaria, Cesare 3:326, 4:526, 4:527,
  5:40
Bechtel, William
  computational theories of mind
    6:394
  connectionism 2:576–7
  vitalism †9:639–43
Beck, F.A.G. 3:229
Beck, Jacob Sigismund **1:687–9**
Beck, Lewis White
  Crusius, C.A. 2:739
  educational philosophy 3:229
  Kant, I. 5:196
  Lambert, J.H. 5:351
  Tetens, J.N. 9:321
Beck, L.J. 3:18
Becker, G.S. 3:219, 8:73
Becker, Lawrence C.
  impartiality 4:717
  property 7:759, 7:760
  reciprocity †8:130–2
  trust 9:469
Becker, O. 7:340
Beckmann, J.P. 9:747
Beckner, Morton 3:805
Bedani, G. 9:605
Bedau, H. 2:368–9
Beddall, B.G.
  Wallace, A.R. †9:678–9
Bedekar, V.M. 3:567
Bedeutung see meaning

Bedeutungsfunktion see function,
  significative
Bedford, Errol 3:282, 3:285, 3:289
Bedford, Jessie *see* Godfrey, E.
Bedford, R.D. 4:375
Bedouelle, G. 2:201, 3:174
Beecher, H. 5:629–30
Beeckman, Isaac 3:2, 3:18
Beer, A. 5:232
Beer, G. 3:267
Beer, John
  George Eliot †3:266–7
Beer, M. 2:886
Beer, P. 5:232
Beeson, M.J. 2:354, 2:638, 4:852,
  6:188
Beetham, David
  legitimacy †5:538–41
Beethoven, Ludwig von 1:454–5
Begriffsjurisprudenz (conceptual
  jurisprudence) 5:495
Beha, H.M. 6:202
behaviour
  see also behaviourism
  art's influence on 1:454
  belief
    language of thought hypothesis
      1:704–5
  Chinese Legalism
    self-interest 5:531, 5:532–3
    standard 5:532
  classical AI 1:488, 8:800
  communication (Mead, G.H.)
    6:210–11
  dialectical concept of (Merleau-
    Ponty, M.) 6:321
  emotions 3:282
  rational choice theory 8:71–3
  replication of
    classical artificial intelligence
      1:488
  rules of
    Chinese Confucianism 2:542–3
  self-destructive (Dostoevskii, F.M.)
    3:115
behaviour therapy
  psychology
    theories of 7:828–9
behaviourism
  analytic **1:689–93**, 6:174, 8:117
    animal language and thought
      1:271
    eliminativism 3:263
    emotions 3:282
    ethics 1:67–8
    folk psychology 3:686
    functionalism 3:282, 3:806

mental states 6:395–6, 6:404
neutral monism
    (Russell, B.A.W.) 8:400
ontology 7:117–18
private language argument
    7:697
propositional attitudes 2:882
reductionism 6:395–6, 8:145,
    8:150
Ryle, G. 8:428, 8:430
Wittgenstein, L. 9:766
epistemological (Rorty, R.)
    8:353–4
methodological 1:689, 1:690,
    1:696–9
animal language and thought
    1:271
language
    acquisition 4:52
    Bloomfield, L. 9:178
    Quine, W.V. 8:12–13
in social science and psychology
    (Taylor, C.) 9:276
radical *see* behaviourism, scientific
1:696–9
associationism 5:484–5
classical/operant conditioning
    5:484
economics 8:71–2
introspection 4:844
operationalism 7:133–4
psychology 7:824, 7:826,
    7:828–9
Skinner, B.F. 8:799–801
in social psychology 1:693–4
in social sciences **1:693–6**, 1:694
in sociology 1:694
testability 8:861
verbal (Sellars, W.S.) 8:638, 8:639,
    8:640
Behler, E. 4:43–4, 8:351
Beidelman, T.O. 3:434
Beierwaltes, W. 5:598, 7:437
Beilharz, P. 9:466
Beiner, R. 2:365
being **1:699–702**
see also categories; *Dasein*;
    existence; God; metaphysics;
    ontology
as act/actuality (Báñez, D.) 1:648
alienation from (Marcel, G.) 6:92
analogy (Duns Scotus, J.) 3:158
anthropodicy (Florenskii, P.A.)
    3:681
Aquinas, T. 1:333–4
attribution
    Fonseca, P. da 3:689

Suárez, F. 9:189, 9:190–1
as being
Godfrey of Fontaines 4:119
Siger of Brabant 8:765
beings distinction (Nicholas of
    Cusa) 6:834
changelessness (Parmenides)
    7:229, 7:230–3
Chinese philosophy 2:316, 2:786,
    9:817
    see also you-wu
in common (Nancy, J.-L.) 6:651–2
Dasein (being-in-the-world) *see*
    Dasein
degrees of
    Neoplatonism 6:800–1
emanation (Mir Damad,
    Muhammad Baqir) 6:409
entity
    Aristotle 1:700
    Heidegger, M. 4:307
    Parmenides 1:700
    Quine, W.V. 1:700–1
esse est percipi (to be is to be
    perceived) (Berkeley, G.) 1:740,
    1:743
essence–existence distinction
    Henry of Ghent 4:356
    Kilwardby, R. 5:247
existence distinction 4:702
existence as property 1:700–1
fictional characters 3:659–62
futility of
    pre-Columbian thought 5:431
God relationship (Meister
    Eckhart) 6:287
hierarchy of
    Ibn Khaldun 4:626
    Nifo, A. 6:869–70
Ibn al-'Arabi 4:603
Ibn Massara 4:628
Ibn Sina 2:242
immobility (Parmenides) 7:231–2
indefinability (Lotze, R.H.) 5:841
indivisibility (Parmenides) 7:231
intentionality 1:702
levels of
    Neoplatonism (Proclus) 7:726
mobile (John of St Thomas) 5:119
modes of (Frank, S.L.) 3:727–8
multivocity (Aristotle) 1:417, 1:418
nature of (Schelling, F.W.J. von)
    8:513, 8:514–15, 8:516
necessary *see* necessary being
necessary conditions of 1:699
    Heidegger, M. 1:701–2
    Husserl, E. 1:701–2

Kant, I. 1:701
    Quine, W.V. 1:701
Nishida Kitarō 5:715
non-being (Eriugena) 3:403
non-things (Brentano, F.) 2:14
not-being
    Gorgias 4:144, 4:145
    Parmenides 7:230
objects 6:283–4
ontology
    Hartmann, N. 4:242
    Ingarden, R.W. 4:790
onto-typo-logy (Lacoue-
    Labarthe, P.) 5:340
origin of ideas (Rosmini-
    Serbati, A.) 8:362–3
phenomenology 7:346
Platonic (Owen, G.E.L.) 7:178
pre-eternality (Mir Damad,
    Muhammad Baqir) 6:409–10
as primary object of the intellect
    (Duns Scotus, J.) 3:158–60
Rahner, K. 8:37
Santayana, G. 8:468
self-realization (Jaspers, K.) 5:80
singularity (Parmenides) 7:232
speculative (Whitehead, A.N.)
    9:716
spheres of (Scheler, M.F.) 8:507
Stoicism 9:142, 9:145
substance (Aristotle) 1:422
temporality
    Heidegger, M. 4:309
    Ingarden, R.W. 4:790
that-which-is (Parmenides)
    7:230–3
thought
    logic of origin (Cohen, H.)
    2:399
three orders of (Conway, A.) 2:670
three paths (Parmenides) 7:230
Ulrich of Strasbourg 9:518
universal science of (Aristotle)
    1:421–2
univocity of
    Duns Scotus, J. 2:293, 3:154,
    3:157–8
    Henry of Ghent 4:358–9
    Wolff, C. 9:781–2
being for-itself
    consciousness (Sartre, J.-P.) 8:473,
    8:475–6
being in-itself
    consciousness (Sartre, J.-P.) 8:473,
    8:475–6
being in time
    Ingarden, R.W. 4:790

being-in-the-world (*Dasein*) *see*
 Dasein
beings of reason (*entia rationis*) 3:689,
 5:413–14, 9:189, 9:191
being-time
 Dōgen
  mujō 6:593–4
Beiser, Frederick C.
 Cambridge Platonism †2:182–5
 Culverwell, N. †2:750–2
 Eberhard, J.A. 3:196
 German idealism 4:44
 Hamann, J.G. †4:213–17
 Hegel, G.W.F. 4:279
 Herder, J.G. †4:378–84
 Humboldt, W. von †4:541–3
 Jacobi, F.H. 5:48
 Kant, I. 5:196
 Maimon, S. 6:38
 Reinhold, K.L. 8:188
 Romanticism, German †8:348–52
 Schlegel, F. von †8:529–31
Beisser, A. 9:115, 9:116
Beitz, Charles R.
 international relations †4:826–33
 justice
  international 5:156
 nation and nationalism 6:661
 state 9:122
Bekoff, M. 1:273
Beld, A. van den 6:166
Belfiore, E.S. 5:219, 6:382
Belgium
 Denys the Carthusian **2:884–7**
 Geulincx, A. **4:59–61**
 Godfrey of Fontaines **4:119–22**
 Helmont, F.M. van **4:340–2**
 Henry of Ghent **4:354–60**
 Irigaray, L. **5:1–4**
 Lipsius, J. **5:650–2**
 Man, P. de **2:810–13**
belief **1:703–6**
 see also a posteriori; a priori;
  cognitive pluralism; cognitivism;
  faith; foundationalism;
  justification, epistemic;
  probabilism; religious belief; web
  of belief
 accidentally reliable 9:620–1
 agreement of (James, W.) 5:65
 analytic behaviourism
  (Dennett, D.C.) 2:882
 animal language and thought
  1:271
 causal theory of knowledge 8:205
 certainty **2:264–7**, 7:35
 coherent systems of 3:722–3, 5:159

commonsensism 2:453–5
conceptual content 2:640, 2:641
conditional upon intellect
 (Aristotle) 1:426
de relde dicto **2:815–17**
degrees of 7:705, 7:706–8
 Locke, J. 5:676
 Ramsey, F.P. 8:46
  Ramsey, F.P. 8:44, 8:45–6
desire relationship 3:30, 3:32
duty *see* doxastic conduct
emotions 3:283, 6:559
empirical (Holcot, R.) 4:478
epistemic appearances 7:295
epistemic relativism 3:360–1
epistemic/non-epistemic
 distinction 5:158
external 3:299–300
false
 child's theory of mind 6:385–8
 fixation of (Peirce, C.S.) 7:271–3
folk psychology
 connectionism 2:575
 habits of (Lewis, C.I.) 5:588
 holism (Davidson, D.) 2:804–5,
  8:33–4
human nature relationship
 (Home, H.) 4:499
ideas (Spinoza, B. de) 9:97
identity of
 mental holism 4:488–93
incommensurability 4:735
indexical 2:879–81
individuation of
 informational semantics
  8:659–61
induction 4:745–52, 6:723
infallibility
 Descartes, R. 4:843, 4:844
 indubitability distinction 5:159
information-caused 4:787–8
innate 4:795, 4:796
intention 4:812
interaction
 perception 7:295–6
introspection 4:840, 4:841
introspective awareness 4:843
justified
 Nāgājuna 2:96–7
knowledge relationship **1:706–9**,
 5:267–8
 eliminativism thesis 1:706,
  1:708–9
 entailment thesis 1:706–7
 identity thesis 1:706, 1:707
 incompatibility thesis 1:706,
  1:707–8

Locke, J. 5:674–5
 separability thesis 1:706, 1:708
 sociology of 9:1
 Yoruba epistemology 9:832–3
legitimacy (Weber, M.) 9:695
management practices 6:725–6
as a map (Armstrong, D.M.) 1:442
Marxist philosophy of science
 6:148–9
memory 5:259
moral
 evil 3:465
 Williams, B.A.O. 9:751–2
moral attitudes 6:534, 6:538
moral judgment 6:511–12
moral sentiments 6:548, 6:549
myth of the given 5:159
neutral monism (Russell, B.A.W.)
 8:400
objective (James, W.) 5:60
other minds 7:171, 7:172–3
paradoxes 7:212
perception 7:294
perceptual
 cognitive spontaneity 5:256–7
 justificatory efficacy 4:822
 knowledge 7:294
 sense-data 7:291
personal identity (Parfit, D.) 6:572
persons
 self-reflection 7:318–19
practice relationship
 Torah 3:170
pretheoretical 4:136
propositional
 Chinese philosophy 5:695, 5:697
 Hume, D. 6:230
Pyrrhonian Scepticism 7:854
radical interpretation
 (Davidson, D.) 2:804–5, 8:32–4
rational **8:61–4**
 Carneades 2:219
 Condorcet, M.J.A.N. 2:529–30
rationality of cultural relativism
 8:82, 8:83, 8:84–5
rationality of **8:86–90**
reasons for **8:127–30**
reliabilism 8:204–5
religious *see* religious belief
revision
 non-monotonic logic 7:33
scientific
 constructivism 2:625, 2:626
self-deception 8:627–8
self-evident
 a priori 1:5
sense-data theory 7:297

social relativism 8:836
teleological theory 8:673, 8:674
trust 9:468
truth conditions (Ramsey, F.P.)
8:46–7
truth-generating capacity 3:360–1
underdetermination 9:528–9
warranted 5:268–72
web of
conventionalism 2:667
Belinskii, Vissorion Grigorievich
1:709–12
Russian Hegelianism 4:303, 4:304,
4:306
Bell, C. 1:463, 1:475, 3:708
Bell, Daniel 2:471
Bell, David 4:586, 4:685, 4:820
Bell, J.A. 1:356, 1:357
Bell, J.M. 6:263
Bell, J.N. 4:656
Bell, John L.
Boolean algebra †1:843–6
category theory 2:238
numbers 7:53
quantum logic 7:885
Bell, John S.
Bell's theorem 1:716
optics 7:138–9
quantum measurement problem
7:890
quantum mechanics,
interpretation of 7:893–4
Bell, R.H. 9:701
Bellah, R.N. 7:91, 9:692
Bellamy, Edward 2:463, 2:464, 9:559,
9:561
Bellamy, Richard
Croce, B. †2:728–35
Gentile, G. †4:19–23
Gramsci, A. †4:151–5
Green, T.H. †4:166–70
Hegelianism 4:300
Bellarmine, Robert 6:466, 8:226–7,
8:229
Beller, Mara
Bohr, N. †1:820–2
Heisenberg, W. †4:327–9
Bellerate, B.M. 2:201, 8:777
Bello, Andres 5:653
Bello, I.A. 6:807
Bellomo, M. 1:659
Bell's theorem **1:712–16**
Bell inequalities
quantum mechanics 1:712–15
Belmond, S. 6:115
Belnap, N.D.
conventionalism 2:668

definition 2:848, 2:849
deflationary theories of truth 9:477
logic
imperative 4:720
many-valued 6:83
paraconsistent 7:210
relevance logic and entailment
8:200–2, 8:203
logical constants 5:779, 5:780
logical laws 5:789
non-constructive rules of inference
7:29
ontological commitment 7:116
questions 8:3
revision theory
semantic paradoxes 8:646–7,
8:648
Tarski's definition of truth 9:269
belonging, sense of
cultural identity 2:745
Belsey, Andrew
journalism ethics †5:126–8
Beltrametti, E. 7:885–6
Beltrami, Eugenio 1:760
Belvakar, S.K. 8:610
Belyi, Andrei 8:413
Belzer, Marvin
deontic logic †2:887–90
Bem, D.J. 7:227
Ben Yehiel, Judah see Messer Leon
Bénabou, J. 2:236
Benacerraf, P.
arithmetic 1:440
category theory 2:236
Frege, G. 3:772, 3:777
Gödel's theorems 4:114
mathematics
antirealism 1:310
constructivism in 2:638
foundations of 2:236, 6:188–9
realism 8:123
numbers 7:53
reduction 8:148
set theory 8:708
Benakis, L.G.
Byzantine philosophy †2:160–5
Benardete, J.A. 4:777
Bence, György 4:571
Bencivenga, E.
free logic †3:738–9, 3:743
Ben-David, S. 8:334, 8:337
Benden, M. 2:739
Bender, J. 5:259
Bendersky, J.W. 3:563, 8:545, 9:332
Benedict, Ruth
conscience 2:581
guilt/shame contrast 8:139, 8:140

moral relativism 6:541
morality and ethics 6:570
beneficence **4:342–4**
duty 2:890
egoism 3:246–7
gratitude 8:138–9
prima facie duties (Ross, W.D.)
8:366
benevolence
see also ren
beauty (Edwards, J.) 3:242–3
charity 2:281
civic virtue (Franklin, B.) 3:737
Confucianism 5:322, 6:303
divine
prayer 7:650–2
moral sense (Hutcheson, F.) 4:588,
4:590
self-love distinction (Butler, J.)
2:155, 2:156
universal (Cumberland, R.) 2:752
as a virtue (Witherspoon, J.) 9:756
Benfield, David
Chisholm, R.M. †2:332–5
Benhabib, S.
critical theory 2:728
Frankfurt School 3:735
Habermas, J. 4:199
Horkheimer, M. 4:511–12
religious ethics 8:223
Benítez, M. 2:375–6
Benjamin, A. 5:308, 6:11
Benjamin, J. 3:587
Benjamin, Walter **1:716–18**
Frankfurt School 3:735
historicism 4:445
hope 4:508
theology, political 9:332
Ben-Jochannan, Y.A.A. 3:253
Ben-Menahem, Yemima
Putnam, H. †7:839–44
Benn, S.I. 3:756, 7:693, 9:24
Benner, P. 7:57
Bennett, Charles H. 2:481
Bennett, D. 3:336
Bennett, Jonathan
Anscombe, G.E.M. 1:282
communication and intention
2:458
conscience 2:581
duty 3:182
events 3:463
Grice, H.P. 4:177
infinity 4:777
Kant, I. 5:196
meaning and communication
6:213

Spinoza, B. de 9:107
Bennett, T. 8:413
Bennett, W.L. 5:499
Bennington, G. 6:11
Benot, Y. 3:68–9
Ben-Shammai, H. 5:208
Benson, H.H. 9:18
Benson, R. 2:410–11
Bentham, Jeremy **1:718–25**
  asceticism critique 1:518, 1:519
  Baumgardt, D. 1:668
  Blackstone, W. 1:780–1
  common law 2:444, 2:445
  ethics
    animals and 1:274, 1:276
    applied 1:321, 1:324
    universalism in 9:538
  fictional entities 3:664
  government 1:721, 1:723–4
  happiness 4:228, 4:229
  hedonism 4:259
  Helvétius, C.-A. 4:345–6
  human nature 4:521–2, 4:525,
    4:526, 4:527
  impartiality 4:714
  interest 1:722
  legal hermeneutics 5:508
  legal positivism 5:519
  legislation 1:719, 1:721–2
  legitimacy 5:541
  liberalism 5:604
  moral agents 6:501, 6:503
  moral standing 6:553
  morality
    and religion 8:220, 8:223–4
  paraphrasis 1:722–3
  pleasure 7:449, 7:450–1
  practical reasoning/rationality
    8:93, 8:101
  property 7:758–9
  public interest 7:834
  public reasoning 1:722
  punishment and reward 1:719,
    1:721–2
  religion
    and morality 8:220–1663,
    8:223–4
  utilitarianism 7:515, 9:556
  utility principle 1:718–19, 1:720–1
  welfare 9:703, 9:705
Benthem, J.F. van
  Beth's theorem and Craig's
    interpolation theorem 1:763
  modal logic 6:425
  paradoxes of set and property
    7:220
  possible worlds semantics 8:668

quantifiers
  generalized 7:877
Bentler, P. 9:132
Bentley, Richard **1:725–6**
  Collins, A. 2:416, 2:418
Benton, R. 6:425
Benton, Ted
  Althusser, L.P. 1:195
  social science 8:856
    naturalism †6:717–21
    scientific realism 8:587
Benussi, V. 4:52–3
Benvenista, E. 1:114, 6:656
Beran, H. 2:598, 6:661, 7:80
Berdiaev, Nikolai Aleksandrovich
  1:726–32
  Leont'ev, K.N. 5:570
  liberalism 5:609
  moral consciousness 1:729
  Neo-Kantianism 6:795, 6:797
  Nietzsche, F.W. 6:864, 6:866
  objectification of history 1:728
  Signposts movement 8:770, 8:772,
    8:773
  Slavophilism 8:811
  Solov'ëv, V.S. 9:32
  Ungrund ('the groundless')
    doctrine 1:727–8
Bereshit Rabba (exegetical
  commentary) 6:354
Berg, J. 1:827
Berg, M. 5:3
Bergamaschi, C. 8:364
Berge, M. 9:272
Bergé, P. 2:279
Berger, D. 6:650
Berger, Fred R. 6:375, 8:138, 8:140
Berger, J. 3:409
Berger, P. 3:43, 9:356
Bergfleth, G. 1:661
Bergin, A.E. 7:813, 7:816
Berglar, P. 2:50
Bergman, A. 7:823
Bergman, S.H. 6:38, 8:361
Bergmann, G. 1:227, 7:134
Bergson, Henri-Louis **1:732–7**
  African philosophy, Francophone
    1:109–10
  comedy 2:437
  duration 1:733
  élan vital 1:735
  humour 4:563–4, 4:566
  Lossky, N.O. 5:835
  Maritain, J. 6:102
  phenomenology 7:340, 7:350,
    7:353, 7:355
  process philosophy 1:734, 7:722–3

Ravaisson-Mollien, F. 8:104
time 2:857
Bergström, Lars 8:491
Berkeley, E.M. 5:68
Berkeley, George **1:737–50**
  Ajdukiewicz, K. 1:136–7
  Browne, P. 2:30
  coherence theory of truth 9:472
  Collier, A. 2:410
  Collins, A. 2:418–19
  concepts 2:511, 2:514–15
  epistemology
    history of 3:370–7, 3:381
  Fardella, M. 3:559–60
  Foucher, S. 3:717
  idealism 1:737, 1:740–5, 4:663–4,
    4:668, 8:60
    common sense conciliation
      9:136
  infinity 4:774
  Johnson, S. 5:125
  language 5:377
  Locke, J. 3:377, 5:375–6
  Malebranche, N. 6:65
  Molyneux problem 6:468
  monism
    idealist 6:475
  nominalism 7:20–1, 7:22
  occasionalism 7:89
  omnipresence 7:105
  ontology 7:117
  phenomenalism 3:377, 7:331, 7:333
  primary–secondary distinction
    7:685–6
  soul 9:48
  *Three Dialogues between Hylas and
    Philonous* 1:744–5
  *A Treatise concerning the
    Principles of Human Knowledge*
    idealism 1:741–4
  vision 1:740–1, 9:632, 9:637
Berkhof, Louis 7:656, 8:275
Berki, R. 8:885
Berkouwer, G.C. 7:801, 8:457
Berkovits, E. 4:207
Berkowitz, A.J. 8:737
Berkowitz, L. 1:695
Berkson, W. 7:539
Berleant, A. 6:735
Berlin, Isaiah **1:750–3**
  Austin, J.L. 1:574
  conservatism 2:614
  Constant de Rebecque, H.-B.
    2:618
  culture 2:749
  freedom 3:756–7
  Green, T.H. 4:170

Hamann, J.G. 4:217
Hegelianism
Russian 4:306
Herder, J.G. 4:384
Herzen, A.I. 4:410
Hess, M. 4:415
liberalism 5:604, 5:609
liberty 1:750, 1:752, 3:754, 3:756–7
Machiavelli, N. 6:22
moral pluralism 6:530–1
nation and nationalism 6:661
political philosophy
nature of 7:528
Russian philosophy 8:422
self-realization 8:634
social science 8:856
Tolstoi, L.N. 9:439
totalitarianism 9:443, 9:444
value pluralism 1:750, 1:751–2
Vico, G. 9:606
Berman, D. 1:749, 2:30, 2:376, 2:419
Berman, H.J. 5:509, 5:524
Berman, M. 3:201
Berman, S. 2:177
Bermant, G. 3:210
Bernal, J.D. 5:634–5, 6:458
Bernal, Martin 3:253, 7:581
Bernard of Arezzo 6:830
Bernard of Chartres 2:290, 2:291,
7:434, 7:437
Bernard of Clairvaux **1:753–5**
Bernard of Clairveaux
mysticism 6:624
Bernard of Tours (Bernardus
Silvestris) **1:755–6**
Bernard of Chartres 2:290
Chartres school 2:291
natural philosophy 6:705
Platonism
medieval 7:436
Bernard, H. 1:299
Bernard, P. 1:255
Bernardus Silvestris *see* Bernard of
Tours
Bernasconi, R.
Buber, M. 2:47
Bernasconi, Robert
Levinas, E. †5:579–82
Bernays, J. 5:219
Bernays, P.
completeness problem 4:114, 4:116
computability theory 2:490
Herbrand's theorem 4:378
Hilbert's programme and
formalism 4:428
logic 5:733–4, 5:736

mathematics
antirealism 1:310
foundations of 6:189
realism 8:123
Post, E.L. 7:575
proof theory 7:745, 7:746, 7:749,
7:751
quantifiers 7:873
Bernet, R. 4:586
Bernhard, F. 9:218
Bernheim, B.D. 2:834
Bernier, François **1:756–8**
Bernoulli, Daniel 2:823–4, 2:834
Bernstein, A.E. 7:839
Bernstein, A.R. 1:214
Bernstein, Eduard **1:758–60**
communism 2:464
Kautsky, K.J. controversy 5:223
Lassalle, F. 5:420
Luxemburg, R. 6:6
Marxism
Western 6:142–3
social democracy 8:828
Bernstein, Felix 7:217
Bernstein, J.M.
Adorno, T.W. †1:41–6
Horkheimer, M. †4:510–12
recognition 8:134
Bernstein, M.A. 1:645
Bernstein, R. 4:199
Berry, Christopher J.
Enlightenment, Scottish †3:327–30
human nature, eighteenth-century
science of †4:526–7
Berry, George 7:218
Berry, Wendell 1:127–8, 4:165
Berryman, P. 5:656
Bertefflany, L. von 8:472
Bertelloni, María Teresa
Latin America
existentialist thought †3:509–14
phenomenology †7:348–52
Berthelot, R. 1:736, 4:299
Berthrong, J. 9:401
Bertman, M.S. 5:378, 9:690
Bertocci, P.A. 5:355, 7:318
Bertola, E. 5:24, 5:822
Bertolini, S. 9:212
Bérubé, C. 4:359, 6:202–3, 7:96
Berzelius, Jacob J. 9:640, 9:641–3
BESHT *see* Israel Ben Eliezer, Rabbi
Besoli, S. 5:842
Besomi, O. 9:573
Bessarion, Cardinal 7:443–4, 7:447
Besser, G.R. 9:118
best of all possible worlds *see* possible
worlds, best of all

Besterman, T. 9:662
Beth, Everet 9:351
Beth, Evert W. 4:850, 6:682, 7:220
Bethge, E. 1:837
Beth's theorem **1:760–4**, 2:847
Bett, R. 2:219, 7:847
Bettan, I. 1:351
Bettenson, H. 4:732
Betti, Emilio 3:831, 5:508–9
Bettoni, E. 6:203, 7:96
Beuchelt, E. 9:801
Beuchot, Mauricio
Báñez, D. †1:647–9
Latin America, colonial thought in
5:425–6
Soto, D. de 9:39
Beutler, R. 7:55
Beversluis, J. 5:590
Bevilacqua, V. 1:680, 1:782, 2:192
Beyleveld, D. 5:519
Beyreuther, E. 7:395
Bhabha, Homi 7:580, 7:581
Bhaduri, S. 2:257, 7:64
Bhagavad Gītā
asceticism 1:518, 1:519
Brahman 2:4
duty and virtue 3:183, 3:186–7
fatalism 3:567
monism 6:479
mysticism 6:622
Rāmānuja 8:44
self
theories of 8:610
Vedānta Schools
theistic 9:589–90, 9:593
Bhaktivedanta Swami, A.C. 3:859
Bharati, A. 8:41
Bhargava, Rajeev
holism and individualism in
history and social science
†4:482–8
Bhartiya, M.C. 2:257
Bhartṛhari **1:764–6**
Indian and Tibetan philosophy
4:738
interpretation 4:836, 4:837
language 4:436, 5:379, 5:380,
5:381–2, 5:383
sense perception 8:693
meaning 6:240, 6:242
sentential understanding 4:434
universals 9:545–6, 9:548
Bhaskar, Roy
critical realism 2:720–1, 2:722
social science
naturalism 6:720
philosophy of history 8:856

scientific realism 8:587
  theory and observation 9:356
Bhāskara 4:438
Bhatt, B. 5:56, 6:81
Bhatt, G.P. 3:392, 6:381
Bhāṭṭa 6:242, 6:377, 6:379, 6:380,
  9:544–5
Bhattacharya, D.C. 3:826, 3:846
Bhattacharya, G. 8:694
Bhattacharya, K. 3:846
Bhattacharya, R.S. 4:440
Bhattacharyya, K.C. 3:567–8, 9:318,
  9:593
Bhattacharyya, Sibajiban
  awareness
    in Indian thought 1:608
  definition
    Indian concepts of †2:849–52
  Gaṅgeśa 3:846
  God, Indian conceptions of
    †4:102–5
  Hindu philosophy 4:440
  Indian epistemology 3:392
  knowledge
    Indian views of 5:285
  Nyāya-Vaiśeṣika 7:66
  ontology in Indian philosophy
    7:127–8
  sense perception
    Indian views of 8:694
Bhāvaviveka 2:60
Bhavya see Bhāvaviveka
Bhedābhedavāda 4:438
bi (obscuration) 9:819–20
Biagini, H. 1:378
Biagio Pelacani da Parma see Blasius
  of Parma
Biagioli, M. 3:841
Bianchi, H. 2:710
Bianchi, L. 1:151, 8:768
Biard, Joël
  Ailly, P. d' 1:135
  Albert of Saxony †1:143–5
  language
    medieval theories of 5:403–4
  Major, J. †6:54–6
Biardeau, M. 6:243, 6:403
bias
  see also androcentrism; objectivity
  random number generators 8:57
  value judgments in social science
    9:577
Bibago, Abraham 9:665–6
Bible
  see also Bible, Hebrew;
    Ecclesiastes; exegesis, biblical;
    Genesis; Gospels; hermeneutics,

biblical; New Testament; Scripture
  atonement 1:536–8
  creation 2:695, 2:696, 4:95–6
  critiques of
    Eliot, G. 3:266
    Spinoza, B. de 9:92, 9:106
  exegesis see exegesis, biblical
  heaven 4:250
  hell 4:329, 4:332
  Hellenistic Jewish thought 7:255–6
  hermeneutics 4:389–95
  infallibility 2:307
  inner nature of 8:802, 8:803
  interpretation
    existential 2:128
    Luther, M. 6:3
    mythological (Strauss, D.F.)
      9:164–5
  justification doctrine 5:165–6
  language
    origins of 5:372
  metaphors and allegories 5:395
  moral directives 8:220
  mythological interpretation
    (Strauss, D.F.) 9:164–5
  negative theology 6:759
  purgatory 7:837
  reprobation 8:273
  revelation 5:677, 8:297–300
  scientific reality 8:230, 8:231
  sin 8:791–2
  universal language 9:533–4
Bible, Hebrew 1:766–9
  see also Pentateuch
  creation doctrine 2:695, 2:696
  halakhah 4:205–6
  heaven 4:250
  Hellenistic Judaism 7:255
  hermeneutics 4:390–1
    Buber, M. 2:45
    Hillel ben Samuel of Verona
      4:431–2
    New Testament interpretation
      of 4:390
  justification doctrine 5:165
  midrash 6:353–4
  negative theology 6:759
  original sin 8:793
  prophetic monotheism 7:97
  providence 7:797–8, 7:797
  as revelation 8:298–300
  sin 8:791–2
  slavery 8:804
biblical hermeneutics see
  hermeneutics, biblical

biblical law
  Jewish philosophy
    halakhah 4:205
Bibó, István 4:570–1
Bicchieri, Cristina
  decision and game theory
    †2:823–35
  social sciences
    prediction in 8:872
Bichat, Xavier 9:640, 9:643
biconditionals 5:798
Biddle, John 9:458
Biederman, Irving 9:636–8
Biedermann, Alois Emanuel 4:282–3,
  4:296
Biel, Gabriel 1:769–72, 6:1–2
Bielefeldt, C. 3:111
Bienenstock, M.
  Rosenzweig, F. †8:357–62
Bieri, P. 9:454
Bierman, G.M.
  linear logic †5:638–41
Biermann, K.-R. 5:312
Biesterfeldt, H.H. 1:208
Big Bang cosmology 2:679–80, 2:699,
  8:233
Bigelow, John C.
  functional explanation 3:805
  functionalism in social science
    †3:813–18
  mental illness
    concepts of 6:314
  natural laws 5:474
  particulars †7:235–8
  universals †9:539–44
Bigg, C. 2:385
Bigongiari, D. 1:346
bijection 5:798
Bijker, W.E. 9:283, 9:287
Bijlert, V.A. van 3:53
Bilbao, Francisco 7:568, 7:569–8
Bilimoria, Purushottama
  Kauṭilya †5:220–2
  testimony in Indian philosophy
    †9:314–19
Billanovich, G. 7:329
Billerbeck, M. 2:758
Billig, J. 4:306
Billington, J.H. 3:326, 6:357
Billot, F.-M. 1:36
Binder, H. 3:149
Binder, T. 6:166
Binkley, R. 7:214
Binkley, T. 5:355
Binmore, K. 2:665, 2:834
Binswanger, L. 3:713

biocentrism 4:161–2
  see also bioethics; ecology;
  environment; environmental ethics
bioethics **1:772–6**
  see also animals, ethics; ecology;
  environmental ethics; medical
  ethics; nursing ethics
  casuistry application 2:228
  expertise 1:322–3
  Jewish **1:776–80**
    abortion 1:778–9
    euthanasia 1:777–8
    medicine 1:777
    organ donation 1:779
    triage 1:778
  medicine, philosophy of 6:266,
    6:267–8
  moral standing 1:774–5
  Singer, P. 1:574–5, 1:580, 1:583–4
  technology and ethics 9:282
biology
  see also botany; classification;
  ecology; evolutionary theory;
  genetics; life, origin of; natural
  history; sociobiology; species;
  taxonomy; vitalism
  causation and explanation
    (Aristotle) 1:420
  Descartes, R. 3:15–16
  developmental
    vitalism 9:641–2
  evolution 3:483–4
  evolutionary
    ecology relationship 3:203–4
  family ethics 3:549–50
  functional explanation 3:524,
    3:815–17
  innateness 4:795
  molecular 6:458–61
  Pythagoreanism (Philolaus) 7:370
  social science parallels 8:862–3
  species 9:78–80
  theological issues 8:232–3
Bion of Borysthenes 2:756
Bion, W.R. 7:819, 7:822
biotic community 4:160, 4:161–2
Birch, Anthony H. 8:270–1, 8:272
Birch (Pope-Henessy), U. 8:559
Bird, G. 5:67
Bird, T. 8:803
Birdwhistell, Anne D.
  Chinese neo-Confucianism 6:776
  Lu Xiangshan †5:851–3
  Shao Yong †8:736–7
Birkenmajer, A. 7:488
Birkhoff, G. 7:882, 7:886–5, 9:351

Birks, Peter B.H.
  Roman law/civilian tradition
    †8:343–8
Birley, A. 6:95
birth rate
  death rate balance 7:540
al-Biruni 8:562, 8:563–4
Biscaretti di Ruffia, P. 4:802
Bischoff, B. 2:222
Bishop constructivism see new
  constructivism
Bishop, Errett 2:635, 2:638
Bishop, J. 8:127
Bissinger, A. 9:785
Bitō, Masahide 7:91
Bitzer, L. 2:192–3
bivalence
  fuzzy logic 3:822, 3:823
  intuitionistic logic 4:856–7,
    4:858–9
  law of
    determinism
      Epicureanism 3:348
  many-valued logic 5:861, 6:81–2,
    6:84, 6:85–6
  realism 3:152, 4:856–7, 4:859–62
  truth conditions 4:856–7, 4:861
  truth-concepts 3:151
Bjarup, J. 7:94
bKa'-brgyud-pas 9:405
Black, Alison H.
  neo-Confucianism 6:776
  Shao Yong 8:737
  Wang Fuzhi †9:680–2
Black, Antony J. 7:517, 8:229, 9:122
Black, Deborah L.
  aesthetics in Islamic Philosophy
    †1:75–9
  al-Farabi 3:558
  logic in Islamic philosophy
    †5:706–13
black Latinos
  marginality 6:99
Black liberation theology 5:614
Black, Max
  fuzzy logic 3:823, 3:824
  identity of indiscernibles 4:680
  induction 4:751
  many-valued logics 6:83
  metaphor 6:337
  models 6:446
  Sapir-Whorf Hypothesis 8:472–3
Blackall, E.A. 9:785
Blackburn, Simon
  Collingwood, R.G. †2:411–15
  communication
    and intention †2:455–9

  and meaning †6:212–14
  emotivism 3:291, 3:293
  meaning
    and communication †6:212–14
    and rule-following 6:219
  modal logic 6:432
  moral judgment 6:512, 6:514
  naturalism in ethics 6:716
  objectivity 7:75
  ontological status of value 9:580–1
  projectivism †7:737–40
  propositions 7:788
  Stevenson, C.L. 9:135
  supervenience †9:235–8
  supervenience of the mental 9:239
Blackham, H.J. 3:501
Blackloism 8:698–9, 9:712, 9:713
Blackmore, J. 6:16
Blackstone, William **1:780–1**
  common law 2:445
  suicide 9:225, 9:226, 9:229
Blackwell, R.J. 9:785–6
Blackwell, T. 3:329
Blackwood, R.T. 5:122
Blair, Ann 1:391–3
Blair, Hugh **1:781–2**
  Enlightenment, Scottish 1:781–2,
    3:329
  Wollstonecraft, M. 9:791
Blaise of Parma see Blasius of Parma
Blake, J. 7:557
Blake, R. 4:846
Blakemore, D. 4:725
Blakey, M.L. 1:358
Blalock, H.M. 9:132
blame **7:644–7**
  see also rectification; remainders
  desert 7:645
  information technology and ethics
    4:781
  moral sentiments 6:564, 6:566–9
  morality of 9:750–1:4
  responsibility 8:291, 8:292
  shame contrast 6:567–9, 6:570
  transgression 6:569
Blamey, S.R. 6:90
Blanché, R. 5:720, 9:711
Blanchet, L. 2:190
Blanchette, Patricia A.
  realism, mathematics †8:119–23
Blanchot, Maurice **1:782–4**
  Nancy, J.-L. 6:653
Blanckaert, C. 2:122
Bland, K.P.
  Delmedigo, E. †2:861–3
  Jewish Averroism 1:602
Bland, Tony 5:627–8

Blane, G. 6:265, 6:268
Blank, G. 7:822
Blank, R. 7:822
Blanshard, Brand
    coherence theory of justification
        and knowledge 5:254, 5:259
    coherence theory of truth 9:470–1,
        9:472
    religion and epistemology 8:218
    wisdom 9:754
Blasius of Parma (Blasius de
    Pelacanis) **1:784–7**
Blass, A. 5:640
Blattner, W. 4:327
Blatz, C. 1:128
Blaug, Mark 3:219, 3:221
Blaut, J.M. 7:577
Blavatsky, Helena Petrovna 9:363,
    9:364–5
Blegvad, M. 8:492
Bleich, J.D. 1:779, 3:172
blessedness
    Saadiah Gaon 8:437
    Spinoza, B. de 9:104
blessings
    Jewish ritual 8:340
Blier, S.P. 1:65
Bligh, E.W. 3:74
blind truth ascriptions
    deflationary theories of truth 9:476
blindness
    Molyneux problem 6:467–8
blindsight
    absent qualia
        functionalism 2:425
    phenomenal consciousness
        2:590–1
    unconscious mental states
        (Weiskrantz, L.) 9:522, 9:524,
        9:525, 9:527
Bloch, Ernst Simon **1:787–90**
    communism 2:463
    hope 4:507, 4:508, 4:509
    Lukács, G. 5:859
    religion, critique of 8:238
    utopianism 9:560, 9:561
Bloch, O.R. 2:376, 3:857
Block, Ned
    behaviourism
        analytic 1:692
    computational theories of mind
        †6:390–4
    concepts 2:515
    conceptual role semantics
        †8:652–7
    consciousness 2:594

content
    wide and narrow 2:645
    eliminativism 3:265
    functionalism 3:813
        colour and qualia 2:427
    holism
        mental and semantic †4:488–93
    intelligence 3:238
    mental causation 6:311
    mental imagery 4:704, 4:705
    qualia 2:427, 7:867
    reductionism, philosophy of mind
        8:153
    semantics
        informational 8:661
    Turing, A.M. 9:495
    type/token distinction 9:511
Blok, A. 1:712
Blok, W.J. 9:264
Blondel, F. 1:363–4, 1:366
Bloom, A. 8:376, 8:748, 9:168
Bloom, H. 9:184
Bloom, I. 3:800, 5:43, 7:91, 9:818
Bloomfield, Leonard 9:177, 9:178,
    9:181
Bloor, David
    constructivism 2:628, 2:629
    sociology of knowledge †9:1–2
Bloss, S. 7:253
Blount, C. 2:380
Blum, Lawrence A.
    friendship 3:796, 3:797
    moral psychology 6:533
    morality and emotions 6:563
    virtue ethics 9:625
    vulnerability and finitude 9:670
Blumberg, Albert 9:608, 9:611
Blumberg, M.S. 1:698, 5:487
Blumenthal, H.J. 4:599, 7:463, 9:326
Blumer, H. 9:245
Blund, W. 5:650
Blustein, J. 3:551
Blyden, Edward Wilmot 7:192–3,
    7:194
Bo Zhuyi 1:86
Board of Ethic Review 3:315
Boas, Franz 1:298, 1:299, 8:470–1,
    8:473
Boas, G. 2:692, 6:53, 6:350
Boase, A.M. 6:489
Bobbio, Norberto **1:790–2**
    Cattaneo, C. 2:241
    legal positivism 5:514, 5:516,
        5:519–20
    political philosophy
        Italy 5:39, 5:40
Bobik, J. 2:174

Bocheński, I.M. (Józef M.)
    dialectical materialism 3:57
    inference
        Indian theories of 4:762, 4:765
    logic
        Polish 7:493, 7:497
        seventeenth-and eighteenth-
            century 5:720
Bock, G. 2:190
Bodde, D. 2:327, 5:454, 5:865
Boden, M.A.
    artificial intelligence †1:485–92
    Turing, A.M. 9:495
Bodhiruci 2:83
bodhisattva
    dependent origination 9:217–18
    Japanese Buddhism 2:103–4
    Shinran 8:748
bodies
    active (Deleuze, G.) 2:857–8
    causal inference (Hume, D.) 4:548,
        4:549
    corpuscularianism (Boyle, R.)
        1:855–6
    Epicureanism 3:340, 3:341–2
    meaning-events (Deleuze, G.)
        2:858
    motion (Hobbes, T.) 4:459, 4:468,
        4:469
    natural (Hobbes, T.) 4:465
    politic (Hobbes, T.) 4:465, 4:474–5
    qualities of (Mu'tazila) 1:520
bodily sensations **1:792–5**
    see also pain; pleasure
Bodin, Jean **1:795–9**
    absolutism 1:30, 1:31
    public law 1:796–7
    slavery 8:806
    social science
        history of philosophy of 8:850,
            8:857
    sovereignty 7:511, 9:56, 9:57, 9:59
Bodnár, J. 8:813
body
    see also embodiment; mind–body
        problem
    Cartesian conception
        Leibniz, G.W. 5:546
    causation
        La Forge, L. de 5:331–2
        occasionalist view 7:87–8
    corporeal substance
        (Leibniz, G.W.) 5:547–8,
            5:555–6
    extension (Descartes R.) 3:14
    glorified (Aquinas, T.) 4:250

matter distinction (Cordemoy, G.
  de) 2:673
phenomenology 6:322–3, 7:346–7
qi 7:862
sexual concepts 8:718–19
soul relationship *see* soul, body
  relationship
Boehm, R. 4:586
Boehme, Jakob **1:799–801**, 2:124,
  9:363
Boehner, P. 1:178, 1:566, 9:747
Boeotia
  Plutarch of Chaeronea **7:464–70**
Boethius, Anicius Manlius Severinus
  1:801–13
  ancient philosophy
    influence on other philosophies
    1:265
  Aquinas, T. 1:328–9
  Aristotle 1:393–4, 1:395–7,
    1:436–7, 9:455
  Christian doctrine 1:802, 1:804,
    1:807–8
  De consolatione philosophiae (On
    the Consolation of Philosophy)
    1:801, 1:803–6, 1:808–10, 1:812
    Carolingian renaissance
    2:221–2
  translation of 1:803
  Encyclopedists, medieval 3:306,
    3:308
  eternity 3:422–3, 3:424, 3:426
  God
    concepts of 4:101, 8:243
    concepts of
      perfect goodness 4:141, 4:143
      perfect-being 4:96
  immutability 4:710, 4:712, 4:713
  imposition 5:390, 5:391
  logic 1:806–7, 5:747, 5:769, 5:770
  natural philosophy 6:691
  patristic philosophy 7:260
  Platonism
    medieval 7:433, 7:434
  possibility definitions (Philo the
    Dialectician) 7:364–5
  religion, history of philosophy of
    8:246
  Roman Empire decline
    effect on medieval philosophy
    6:270
  theological discourse (Gilbert of
    Poitiers) 4:71
  theological influence
    medieval philosophy 6:275
  universals 7:18, 9:541, 9:543
  Valla, L. 1:801, 1:805, 9:570, 9:571

Boethius of Dacia **1:813–16**
  Averroism 1:597–8
  eternity of the world 3:429
  ethics 1:814
  grammar 1:814–15
  natural philosophy 6:699, 6:705
Boettner, L. 7:656
Boff, Leonardo 5:614, 5:615, 5:616
Bogdan, R.J. 1:443, 2:334, 8:492
Bogdanov, Aleksandr
  Aleksandrovich **1:816–20**
  empiriocriticism 1:817, 8:405–7,
    8:421
  Lenin, V.I. 1:816–17, 5:565
  Marxism 6:153, 6:158
  Nietzsche, F.W. 6:864, 6:865
  Plekhanov, G.V. 7:453
  proletarian culture 1:818
Bogen, J. 3:517, 7:86
Bogen, J.E. 9:109
Boghossian, P.A.
  analyticity 1:238
  eliminativism 3:265
  meaning and rule-following 6:219
  objectivity 7:75
  private language argument 7:698
  semantics
    informational 8:661
Bogomil 6:76
Bogomils *see* Cathars
Bogue, R. 2:860
Boh, I. 3:359
Bohatec, J. 2:382
Bohemia
  see also Czech Republic;
    Czechoslovak Republic
  Hus, J. **4:573–4**
Böhler, D. 7:648
Bohm, David
  determinism and indeterminism
    3:39
  ecological philosophy 3:201
  quantum measurement problem
    7:890
  quantum mechanics 7:893, 7:894
Bohman, James
  systems theory in social science
    †9:253–6
Böhme, G. 6:740
Bohnert, H. 4:720
Bohr, Niels **1:820–2**
  Heisenberg, W. 4:328
  quantum mechanics 7:892, 7:894
  spectroscopy
    optics 7:138
Boi, L. 9:64
Boirel, R. 2:41

Bois, H. 3:149
Boisvert, R. 3:51
Bok, Sissela
  applied ethics 1:324
  truthfulness †9:480–5
Bol, Peter K. 2:303, 8:737, 9:831
Boland, L. 3:220
Bolc, L. 5:863
Bold, Samuel **1:822–3**
Boldt-Irons, L.A. 1:661
Boler, J. 3:168
Bolívar, Simón 5:653, 5:656
Bollack, J. 3:298
Bolland, G.J.P.J. 4:286–7
Bolle, K.W. 1:568
Bollen, K. 9:132
Bollert, K. 4:8
Bollinger, L. 9:432
Bollnow, O.F. 5:488
Bolshakoff, S. 8:811
Bolshevism
  critique of
    Shestov, L. 8:742
  empiriocriticism 6:151, 6:153–5
  Nietzsche, F.W. 6:864–5
  Russian intellectuals' response to
    8:427
  Signposts movement 8:772
Bolt, John
  Dooyeweerd, H. †3:113–14
Boltanski, L. 9:7
Bolton, M. 2:387
Bolton, R. 5:361
Boltzmann, Ludwig 9:367, 9:369
Boltzmann machine 2:574
Boltzmann's constant 7:396
Bolyai, J. 4:29
Bolzano, Bernard **1:823–8**
  analyticity 1:238, 1:826
  consequence 2:600–1, 2:602
  Czech Republic, philosophy in
    2:766
  infinity 4:777
  ontology 1:824–5
  truth
    degrees of validity 1:825–6
Bolzoni, L. 2:190
Bombyk, M. 3:593
Bonafede, G. 6:115
Bonansea, B.M. 1:834, 2:190, 3:169
Bonardel, F. 1:158
Bonastrug de Porta *see* Nahmanides,
  Moses
Bonaventure **1:828–35**
  Aristotelianism 1:400
  eternity of the world 1:831–2

God
existence of 1:831
happiness 1:828, 1:830, 1:833–4
illuminationism 4:699, 4:700
Itinerarium mentis in Deum
(Journey of the Mind to God)
1:829, 1:830
limbo 5:636
mysticism 1:828, 1:830
natural philosophy 6:705
Platonism
medieval 7:436–7
Richard of St Victor 8:313
virtue 1:833–4
Bonß, W. 4:511–12
Bondeli, M. 8:188
Bonet, Pierrette
Ravaisson-Mollien, F. †8:103–6
Bonevac, D. 1:106
Bonfil, R. 6:334
Bonhoeffer, Dietrich **1:835–8**
Bonhöffer, A. 3:339
Boniface VIII, Pope 3:155, 4:73
Bonilla y San Martin, A. 9:650
Bonitz, H. 1:434
BonJour, Laurence
a posteriori 1:3
coherence theory of justification
and knowledge 3:381, †5:253–9,
5:275
'Doxastic Presumption' 5:258
empiricism 3:300, 3:303
epistemology
naturalized 6:723, 6:727
normative 7:38
internalism–externalism
distinction 4:825
justification 5:164
knowledge by acquaintance/
description 5:262
Bonner, G.I. 7:286
Bonnet, Charles **1:838–40**
epiphenomenalism 3:354
vitalism 9:641–2
Bonnet, G. 1:840
Bonnot, Étienne *see* Condillac,
Étienne
Bonsiepen, W. 6:740
Bonsor, Jack
Rahner, K. †8:35–9
Boobbyer, P. 3:729
Book of Causes see Liber de causis
Book of Changes see Yijing
Book of Common Prayer
Hooker, R. 4:505
Book of the Dead 3:249
Book of the Master Guan see Guanzi

Book of Rites see Lijing
Bookchin, Murray
anarchism 1:248
environmental ethics 3:333–4
green political philosophy 4:161,
4:165
social ecology 3:200–1
Boole, George **1:841–3**
logic 5:727
algebra of 1:843, 1:844, 1:846,
5:724
mathematics
primacy of 8:566
Boolean algebra **1:843–6**
Boole, G. 1:841
De Morgan, A. 2:813–14
history of 5:724–5
quantum logic 7:883, 7:884, 7:885
Venn, J. 9:595
Boolean-valued models method
set theory 1:845–6
Boolos, George
computer science 2:495
consequence 2:602–3
Frege, G. 3:777
Gödel, K. 4:107
Gödel's theorems 4:114
mathematical models 6:446
modal logic 6:425
natural deduction, tableau and
sequent systems 6:682
provability logic 7:796
set theory 8:715
universals 9:543
Boone, S.A. 1:65
Boorse, Christopher 6:312, 6:314
Boorstin, D. 1:205, 5:85
Boorstin, D.J. 1:781
Boot, W.J. 3:800
Booth, W.C. 6:656–7
Boothby, R. 5:338
Borch-Jacobsen, M. 1:191
Bordo, S. 3:269, 3:587, 3:602
Bordwell, D. 3:676
Borel, É. 2:481, 8:59
Borgeaud, Ph. 7:164
Börger, E. 7:664
Borges, Jorge Luis 5:655
Boring, E.G. 1:698, 3:572, 9:801
Borker, R.A. 5:367
Borkowski, L. 5:863
Bormida, Marcelo 7:351
Bornheim, Gerd A. 3:511–12, 3:513
Bornstein, Benedykt 7:487, 7:488
Borochov, Ber 9:868–9, 9:870
Boros, L. 5:637
Borowik, P. 5:863

Borsari, S. 2:734
Borsellino, Patrizia
Bobbio, N. †1:790–2
Borst, C.V. 6:399
Bos, Egbert Peter
Marsilius of Inghen †6:110–12
Bos, H.J.M. 1:220
Bosanquet, Bernard **1:846–8**
coherence theory of justification
5:259
general will 4:11
Grote, J. 4:184
Hegelianism 4:289
Temple, W. 9:301
Bosanquet, H. 1:848
Bosch, J. 7:214
Bosco, U. 1:184
Boscovich, Roger Joseph (Bošković,
Rudjer Josip)
chemistry
philosophical aspects of 2:297,
2:299
mechanics
classical 6:253, 6:259
non-extended atom 9:50, 9:54
scientific hypotheses 9:139
Böss, O. 3:456
Bossi, M. 6:742
Bossuet, J.B. 1:30, 1:31, 8:229
Bossy, J. 2:38
Bostad, I. 8:491
Bostick, Curtis V.
Hus, J. †4:573–4
Boström, Christopher Jacob 8:485
Boswell, James 5:123, 5:469
Boswell, John 8:727
botany
Linnaeus, C. von 5:647–8
Theophrastus 9:337, 9:339
Botero, Giovanni 5:40
Bots, H. 5:476
Bottazzini, U. 1:220
Bottin, F. 7:266
Bottomore, T. 6:146, 6:164, 8:885
Botwinick, A.
Rabbinic theology †9:333–7
Boubarki, N. 8:715
Boucher, D. 2:415
Boudot, M. 1:736
Bougerol, J.G. 1:834
Bouglé, C. 5:339
Bouillier, Francisque 1:391–3, 3:18,
5:481, 8:342
Bouju, Théophraste 1:386, 1:389,
1:390
Boullée, Étienne-Louis 1:362, 1:364,
1:366

boundaries
  continuum problem (Brentano, F.)
    2:14–15
Boundas, C.V. 2:860
Bourbaki, N. 9:64
Bourdieu, Pierre **1:848–50**
  habitus 1:849
  legal discourse 5:499
  objectivism/subjectivism dualism
    1:849
  social science 8:857
  sociology
    theories of 9:6–7
  structuralism in social science
    9:188
Bourgeois, P.L 8:322
bourgeoisie
  Cattaneo, C. 2:239–40
  Hegel, G.W.F. 4:274–5
  revolutionary potential of 2:170
Bourke, V.J. 9:386, 9:388, 9:664, 9:666
Bouterwek, F. 8:188
Boutroux, Émile **1:850–2**
Bouvère, Karel L. de 1:763
Bouwsma, O.K. 1:498, 7:147
Bouyer, Louis 6:626
Bovo of Corvey 2:222–3
Bowen, A.C. 3:453
Bower, A. 1:680
Bower, T.G.R. 2:391, 7:818, 7:822
Bowerbank, S. 2:263
Bowersock, G.W. 6:803
Bowie, Andrew
  Hegelianism 4:300
  Romanticism, German 8:351
  Schelling, F.W.J. von †8:509–20
Bowie, N. 2:153
Bowlby, John 5:845, 7:822
Bowler, Peter J.
  Darwin, C.R. †2:795–9
Bowman, A.A. 5:230
Bowne, Borden Parker **1:852–3**
  causality 7:316–17
  personalism 7:315, 7:318
  space 7:316
  time 7:316
Box, M.A. 4:561
Boxill, Bernard
  affirmative action †1:91–4
  discrimination 3:105
  self-respect 8:637
Boyancé, P. 5:855
Boyarin, D. 6:354
Boyce Gibson, W.R. 1:576
Boyce, M. 9:874

Boyd, R.
  evolutionary theory and social
    science 3:487
  inference to the best explanation
    4:769
  logic of ethical discourse 5:764
  naturalism in ethics 6:716
  sociobiology 8:896
Boyd White, J. 5:499
Boyde, P. 1:184–5
Boyer, C.B. 3:70, 4:32, 5:727, 7:53
Boyle, James 2:716, 2:719
Boyle, J.M. 6:690, 9:690
Boyle, Nicholas
  Goethe, J.W. von †4:125–9
Boyle, Robert **1:853–7**
  More, H. 6:580, 6:582
  primary–secondary distinction
    7:687
Boys-Stones, G. 1:382
Bozzolo, C. 2:345
Braakhuis, H.A.G. 5:249, 5:404,
    6:111–12, 9:749
Braaten, C.E. 2:130
Bracciolini, Poggio 4:536
Brachmachari, M.N.B. 3:859
bracketing *see* phenomenology,
    epistemic issues in
Bradbury, M. 6:449
Braddon-Mitchell, David
  analytic behaviourism †1:689–93
  belief †1:702–6
  mind, philosophy of 6:407
  propositional attitudes 7:786
Bradie, M. 3:487
Bradish, N.C. 8:699
Bradley, A.C. 3:708, 7:476, 9:450–1
Bradley, Francis Herbert **1:857–63**
  the Absolute 1:27, 1:28, 1:29
  coherence theory of justification
    5:259
  coherence theory of truth 9:472
  ethics 1:858–9
  Hegelianism 4:289
  idealism 4:668, 6:496
  logic 1:859–60
  monism 1:861, 6:474, 6:475
  Moore, G.E. 6:496
  moral agents 6:500, 6:503
  perfectionism 7:301
  reality 1:860–1
  Russell, B.A.W. 8:393
  testimony 9:313
  truth 1:860
Bradley, J. 4:300
Bradley, James
  Whitehead, A.N. †9:713–20

'Bradley problem' 3:845, 6:478
Bradley Studies 1:862
Bradshaw, G. 3:102
Bradwardine, Thomas **1:863–7**
  indivisibilism 4:361
  liar paradox 5:757
  motion quantification 7:181
  natural philosophy 6:702
  Pelagianism 1:563–4, 7:285–6
  ratios 7:155
  reprobation 8:274, 8:275
Brady, I. 1:346, 7:269
Brady, R.T. 7:210, 8:204
Braham, W.E. 1:139
Brahe, Tycho 5:231
Brahmā
  lifespan
    cosmology and cosmogony
      Indian theories of 2:683
Brahmagupta 7:48–9
Brahman **2:1–5**
  the Absolute 1:28
  ātman relationship 8:605, 8:606,
    8:607
    mysticism 6:621–2
    reincarnation 8:185
    Śaṅkara 8:459
  concepts of
    Advaita Vedānta 8:610
    Aurobindo Ghose 1:567–8
    Rāmānuja 8:42
    Vedānta School 9:589–90,
      9:591, 9:592
  enlightenment
    Advaita Vedānta 8:449
  individual relationship with
    Vedānta School disputes 9:590,
      9:591–2
  īśvara (Śaṅkara) 8:460
  monism 6:475, 6:477, 6:478
  mysticism 6:622
  nonduality (Śaṅkara) 8:459–60
  as pure existence (Rāmānuja) 8:43
  reality (Radhakrishnan, S.) 8:23–4
  reincarnation 8:183, 8:184
  revelation (Rāmānuja) 8:43
  superimposition 4:435
    Advaita Vedānta 4:438
    Śaṅkara 3:410, 8:459
  universals 9:545–6
Brāhmaṇas 4:760
Brahmanism
  see also Brahman; Hindu
  philosophy
  Brahmo Samaj movement 2:5–6
  caste system (Ambedkar, B.R.)
    1:196

duty and virtue 3:184
epistemology 3:390–1
Brahmasūtra see BādarāyaṇaBrahmo
    Samaj (Society of Brahma)
    2:5–7
Braidotti, R. 3:585, 3:587
brain
    see also neurology; split brains
    emotions 3:282
    identity theory of mind 3:352,
        6:394–9, 8:814
    memory 6:298–9
    mind relationship
        Dennett, D.C. 2:883
        Hartley, D. 4:236, 4:237
    organizational levels
        computational theories of mind
            6:393–4
    parallel processing 1:486
    structure
        learning processes 5:484
brain death 5:626–7
Braine, David
    grace †4:146–51
    negative theology †6:759–63
    sacraments †8:442–5
brain-in-a-vat thought experiment
    8:493, 8:494
Braithwaite, J. 2:710
Braithwaite, R.B.
    explanation 3:524
    natural laws 5:474
    natural theology 6:712
    religious language 6:710, 8:259
    teleology 9:297
    Whitehead, A.N. 9:718
Brams, Jozef
    translators †9:455–7
Bramstead, E.K. 5:604
Bramwell, A. 4:165
Branch, M.A. 6:166
Branch, T. 5:304
branching logic 6:267, 8:658
Brand, D.J. 5:597
Brand, M. 1:41
Brand, P.Z.
    aesthetic concepts 1:58
    feminist aesthetics 3:596
    Langer, S.K.K. †5:354–6
Brandeis, L. 7:693
Brandom, R. 7:638
Brandon, R.N. 4:15
Brandon, S.F.G. 8:451
Brandt Bolton, M. 6:468
Brandt, R. 2:402
Brandt, Richard B.
    analytic ethics 1:223

gratitude 8:140
happiness 4:229
hedonism 4:259
ideals 4:674
moral justification 6:516
Native American philosophy 6:670
supererogation 9:234
Brandwood, L. 7:420
Branham, R.B.
    Cynics †2:753–9
    Diogenes of Sinope †3:90–1
    Lucian †5:853–4
Brann, E. 4:708
Brann, R. 4:213
Branning, D. 1:716
Brantlinger, Patrick 7:581
Bras, M. 3:98
Brathwaite, Edward 6:100
Bratman, Michael 3:33, 4:814–15,
    8:101
Braude, Stephen E.
    paranormal phenomena †7:221–4
Braun, D. 2:881
Braun, H.-J. 2:227, 3:639
Braybrooke, David
    needs and interests 6:755
    social science
        contemporary philosophy of
            †8:838–47
Brazil **2:7–12**
    analytical philosophy 1:231
    colonialism 2:8
    existentialism 3:511–12
    independence 2:9–2:10
    phenomenology 7:349
    positivism 7:567–8
    precalabrian civilization 2:7
Brazill, W.J. 1:667, 4:300, 8:387
Breazeale, D.
    Fichte, J.G. †3:642–53
    German idealism 4:44
    Reinhold, K.L. 8:188
Brecht, Bertolt 9:451
Brecht, G. 7:220
Brecht, M. 6:5
Bredeck, E.
    Mauthner, F. †6:203–6
Bree, G. 2:196
Bréhier, É. 2:346, 6:104, 8:679
Breines, P. 5:859
Breinlinger, K. 2:391–2, 2:395
Brelage, M. 2:402, 6:792
Breloer, B. 5:221
Brenk, F.E. 7:470
Brennan, Andrew
    bundle theory of mind 6:384
    ecological philosophy 3:201

environmental ethics †3:332–6
Brennan, M. 3:405
Brennan, T. 3:587
Brenner, A. 3:146
Brenner, J.H. 9:869
Brent, J. 7:283
Brentano, Franz Clemens **2:12–17**
    Aristotle commentators 1:436
    Chisholm, R.M. 2:333, 2:334–5
    descriptive psychology 9:508
    emotions 3:289
    Husserl, E. 4:576–7, 4:586
    intentionality 1:609, 1:611,
        2:13–14, 4:817, 4:820
    mental phenomena 2:13, 2:593,
        2:594
    phenomenology 7:340, 7:347
    truth 2:15
    value, theory of 2:15–16
    Vygotskii, L.S. 9:674
Brentjes, B. 1:211
Bressan, A. 8:603
Brest, P. 3:105
Bretall, R.W. 6:844
Bretherton, I. 7:822
Brethren of Purity *see* Ikhwan al-
    Safa'
Breton, A. 8:73
Breuer, Joseph 3:787
Brewer, J. 3:632
Brewka, G. 7:34
Brewster, D. 2:504
Brezik, V.B. 9:386
Bṛhaspati 6:179
Bricke, John 4:561
Bricker, P. 6:828, 7:572
bricolage 2:268–9
bridge laws 8:146–7
Bridges, C.B. 4:15
Bridges, D. 2:638, 6:189
Bridgman, Percy William **2:17–19**
    general relativity 4:8
    operationalism 7:131–2, 7:134
Brierly, J.L. 4:832
Briggs, Jean 6:563
Bright, J. 1:769
Brightman, Edgar Sheffield 7:317,
    7:318
Brightman, R.A. 6:670
Brillouin, L. 4:785–6
Bringmann, W.G. 9:801
Brink, D.O.
    axiology 1:611
    beauty 1:683
    logic of ethical discourse 5:764
    moral justification 6:516
    moral knowledge 6:519

moral realism 6:538
Brink, J. 6:812
Brinkley, Richard **2:19–21**
Brinton, C. 8:303
Brisson, L. 2:481, 3:253, 7:164, 7:549
Britain *see* Great Britain
British empiricists *see* Hume, D.;
　　Locke, J.; Mersenne, M.
Brito, Radulphus **2:21–3**
Brittan, Arthur
　symbolic interactionism †9:243–5
Brittan, Gordon G., Jr 5:196, 9:353
Britton, K. 2:26
Broad, Charlie Dunbar **2:23–6**
　Alexander, S. 1:169
　Butler, J. 2:160
　epiphenomenalism 3:354
　Hägerström, A.A.T. 4:204
　Leibniz, G.W. 3:381, 5:561
　McTaggart, J.M.E. 6:27–8
　paranormal phenomena 7:224
　Prichard, H.A. 7:682
　sense-data 3:300–1, 5:275
　Sidgwick, H. 8:763
　time 9:416
Broadbent, Donald 2:577
Broadie, A. 3:632, 5:758, 6:56
Broadie, S.W. 1:434, 6:533, 7:804,
　9:630
Broccolini, G. 4:419
Brochard, V. 7:847, 9:420
Brock, D. 6:263, 7:252
Brock, W.H. 2:299
Brockelman, Thomas
　Lacan, J. †5:336–8
Brockliss, Lawrence W.B. 1:391–3
Brockmeier, Jens
　Wundt, W. †9:798–802
Broderick, A. 4:802
Brodick, J. 6:465
Brody, B.A. 4:680
Brody, H. 1:776
Brody, J. 4:518–17
Broido, M. 6:352
Brom, L. van den 7:107
Bromberger, S.
　causation 2:250
　explanation 3:522–3, 3:524
　questions 8:3
　scientific theories 9:351–2
　type/token distinction 9:511
Brome, V. 5:134
Bronkhorst, Johannes
　Bhartṛhari †1:764–6
　language
　　Indian theories of †5:379–84
　Nyāya-Vaiśeṣika 7:64

Patañjali †7:248–50
Bronner, S.E. 6:7
Brons, B. 7:808
Bronstein, Lev Davidovich *see*
　Trotsky, Leon
Brontë, Charlotte 3:613
Brook, Andrew 5:196
Brook, R.J. 1:749
Brooke, Roger
　Jung, C.G. 5:134
Brooks, D.R. 9:276
Broome, J. 8:101, 9:566
Brotz, H. 7:194
Broughton, R.S. 7:227
Broussais, François-Joseph-Victor
　6:265, 6:268
Brouwer, L.E.J.
　infinity 4:776, 4:777
　intuitionistic logic 4:857–8, 4:859,
　　4:862
　mathematics
　　constructivism 2:635–6, 2:638
　　foundations of 6:189
　　intuitionism 4:847–9, 4:852,
　　　6:183–4, 8:120
　　　arithmetic 1:439
　　　realism 8:123
　paradoxes of set and property
　　7:219
　proof theory 7:750
Brouwer's theorem 2:636, 4:848–9
Brouzeng, P. 3:146
Brower, Bruce
　contextualism
　　epistemological †2:646–50
Brower, R. 1:90
Brown, Beverley A.
　law †5:464–8
　legal discourse †5:496–9
　philosophy of social science,
　　contemporary theories 8:846
Brown, Charlotte
　common-sense ethics †2:448–51
　Paley, W. †7:186–8
　Wollaston, W. †9:786–8
Brown, Chris 5:156
Brown, D. 7:838, 7:839, 9:461, 9:526
Brown, D.M. 8:753–4
Brown, H. 4:518
Brown, J.
　Duns Scotus, J. 3:168
Brown, James H.
　ecology 3:205
Brown, James R.
　social epistemology 8:832
　sociology of knowledge 9:2
　thought experiments 9:396

Brown, John
　Culverwell, N. 2:752
Brown, John H.
　art, abstract †1:448–52
　beauty †1:680–4
Brown, L. 5:361
Brown, Mark 6:426, 6:431–2
Brown, Penelope 5:367
Brown, Peter G. 3:210
Brown, Peter R. 1:558, 8:338
Brown, R.
　Australia, philosophy in 1:582–3
　Passmore, J.A. 7:248
　social laws 8:834
Brown, R.F.
　Boehme, J. 1:801
Brown, Roger
　Humboldt, W. von 4:543
Brown, Stephen F.
　Chatton, W. †2:292–4
　Clarembald of Arras †2:376–8
　Duns Scotus, J. 3:168
　eternity of the world
　　medieval views of 3:429
　Gregory of Rimini †4:170–2
　Matthew of Aquasparta †6:200–3
　Richard of Middleton †8:310–12
Brown, Stuart
　Conway, A. 2:670
　Helmont, F.M. van †4:340–2
　Islamic philosophy
　　modern 5:20
　Malebranche, N. 6:66
Brown, Thomas **2:26–9**
　Common Sense School 2:27
　substance dualism 2:26, 2:28
Brown, V. 8:821
Brown, W.M. 9:112
Browne, Peter **2:29–30**
Browne, T.D.K. 3:74
Browning, D. 7:714
Brownlie, I 4:832
Brownsword, R. 5:519
Bruce, J.P. 9:864
Brucker, Jakob 9:363, 9:365
Brueckner, Anthony
　charity principle 2:285
　deductive closure principle
　　†2:842–5
　transcendental arguments 9:454
Brués, Guy de 8:502
Bruford, W.H. 4:129
Brummer, R. 5:664
Brundell, B. 3:857
Bruner, Jerome S. 1:695, 6:451, 9:801
Bruni, G. 4:77
Bruni, Leonardo 1:411

Brunner, Emil **2:30–4**
 eristic theology 2:31
 existentialist theology 3:509
 natural theology 2:31
 theology of crisis 2:30–1
Brunner, F. 4:620
Brunner, H.H. 2:33
Bruno, Giordano **2:34–9**
 cosmology 2:36
 imagination 2:35–6
 magic 2:35–6
 memory
  art of 2:35–6
 pantheism 7:202–3
 space 9:64
 unity of nature 5:34–5, 5:40
Bruns, G.L. 4:388
Brunschvicg, Léon 1:851–2, **2:39–41**
Brunschwig, Jacques
 Anaxarchus †1:254–5
 Hellenistic philosophy 4:336
 Pyrrho †7:844–8
 Stoicism 9:159
 Timon †9:419–20
Brunton, P. 9:365
Brush, C.B. 1:677, 6:489
Brush, S.G. 6:210, 9:369
Bruun, H.H. 9:698
Bruyère, N. 8:54
Bruyère-Robinet, N. 8:54
Bryant, C.J.
 Brown, T. †2:26–9
Bryce, James **2:41–2**
 historical jurisprudence 5:140,
  5:141
Brykman, G. 9:429
Bryson, Thomas L.
 Ramakrishna Movement †8:39–42
Bryson, V. 3:620
Brzezinski, Jan
 Gauḍīya Vaiṣṇavism †3:857–9
 Rāmānuja †8:42–4
Brzezinski, Z. 9:443, 9:444
bSam-yas (Samyay), Great Debate of
 9:405–6
Bub, Jeffrey
 quantum measurement †7:886–90
 quantum mechanics,
  interpretation of 7:894
Bubacz, B. 1:558
Bubeck, D. 3:551
Buber, Martin **2:42–8**
 Brunner, E. 2:33
 hermeneutics 2:45
 Ich und Du 2:43–5
 Jewish philosophy 5:85, 5:90, 5:91,
  5:95

 mysticism 2:42, 2:43
 Rosenzweig, F. 8:360, 8:361
 utopianism 9:561
 Zionism 9:869, 9:870
Buchanan, Allen E.
 communitarianism †2:464–71
 economics and ethics 3:210
 market ethics 6:110
 medical ethics 6:263
 nation and nationalism 6:661
 Pareto principle 7:228
 paternalism 7:252
 reciprocity 8:131
 socialism 8:885
Buchanan, J.M.
 contractarianism 2:665
 economics
  philosophy of 3:220
 libertarianism 5:619
 rational choice theory 8:73
 social choice 8:825–6
Buchdahl, Gerd 5:196, 6:758
Buchholz, W. 7:750
Büchner, Friedrich Karl Christian
 Ludwig (Louis) **2:48–51**
 materialism 2:48, 2:49
Büchner, Ludwig 6:173, 8:415, 8:418
Bucholtz, M. 5:367
Buchwald, J.Z. 3:260, 4:402, 6:210
Buck-Morss, S. 1:46, 1:718
Budapest School 4:570
Budd, Malcolm
 aesthetic attitude †1:51–5
 aesthetics †1:59–61
 art
  emotion in response to 3:280
  expression 1:498
  and truth 1:459
  value of †1:476–80
 formalism 3:706–8
 Gurney, E. 4:191
 Hanslick, E. 4:224
 meaning and rule-following 6:219
 music
  aesthetics of 6:612
 Wittgenstein, L. 9:770
Buddecke, W. 1:801
Buddha **2:51–3**
 see also Amida Buddha; Buddha
  Dainichi
 Ambedkar, B.R. 1:196, 1:197
 authority of (Dharmakīrti) 2:97
 central teachings 2:92–3
 God 6:480–1
 human nature 2:93–4
 Indian and Tibetan philosophy
  4:738

 inference 4:761
 levels of teaching
  Chinese interpretation 2:86
 light
  Pure Land Buddhism 8:747
 manifoldness, Jaina theory of 6:78
 nature of 2:95–6
 self 7:521
 suffering
  dependent origination 9:215–16
 Tiantai
  Zhiyi 9:860
 truth
  art 1:85–6
  Yogācāra Buddhism 2:64
Buddha Dainichi 5:71, 5:318, 5:319
Buddhadāsa Bikkhu 2:80
Buddhaghosa 2:57
buddhahood
 ab initio
  Great Debate of bSam-yas
   9:405–6
 attainability
  Japanese Buddhism 2:102–4
 Chan Buddhism 8:621
 degrees of 2:96
 Pure Land Buddhism 8:747–8
 suffering
  dependent origination 9:216
 universal
  Japanese Buddhism 2:103
buddha-nature 2:95–6
 emptiness
  Buddhist concept of 2:79
 impermanence 6:593–4
 inherence of
  China 2:83
 li 5:594
 self-cultivation
  Chinese philosophy 8:620, 8:622
 Zongmi 9:871
Buddhapālita 2:60
buddhas
 awakening 2:96
buddhi (pure intellect)
 Sāṅkhya 6:200, 8:463–4, 8:466
Buddhist philosophy
 see also Ābhidharmika Schools;
 Buddha; Chan; Chogye; dGa'-ldan-
 pa; dGe-lugs-pa; emptiness; Karma,
 bKa'-brgyud (Kagyü); Mādhyamika;
 Mahāyāna; Shingon; Theravada;
 Vaibhāṣika; Vātsīputrīya-Sāṃmatīya;
 Yogācāra; Zen
  Chinese 2:66, **2:80–92**, 2:315, 2:325
   *Awakening of Faith in
    Mahāyāna* 1:603

Confucianism 2:326
Daoism 3:532–3, 9:866
Fazang 3:568–9
li 5:594
mysticism 6:622–3
neo-Confucianism 6:764–7
poetry 1:68, 1:70
self-cultivation 8:619–21
Sengzhao 8:682–4
xin 9:816
Zhi Dun 9:859
Zhiyi 9:859, 9:860–1
Zongmi 9:870–1
Confucianism
China 2:326
Korea 2:114–15, 2:116
Confucianism assimilation
Japan 2:551
consciousness
psychology 2:583
Daoism
China 3:532–3, 9:866
deities
relations to other religions
8:750–1
East Asian Philosophy 3:195
emotions 3:285
God
concept of 6:480–1
Indian **2:92–9**, 4:737, 4:738
awareness 1:606
Buddha-nature 2:95–6
causation
inference 4:761–2
cosmology and cosmogony
2:681, 2:683
critique of Śaivism
Abhinavagupta defence 1:17
dependent origination 2:252,
9:215–18
Dharmakīrti 3:51–3
emptiness **2:76–80**
epistemology 2:96–7, 3:388–9
ethics 2:94–5
fa 3:532–3
heaven 4:254
human nature 2:93–4
illusion 3:410
karma and rebirth 5:211,
5:213–15, 5:216, 5:217
matter 7:605
meaning 6:240, 6:243
metaphysics 2:97–9
mind 6:399, 6:401–2
momentariness **6:469–73**,
7:605–6
mysticism 6:622

Nāgārjuna 6:638–40
nominalism **7:23–7**
non-identity
causation 2:251, 2:252, 2:255–6
Nyāya debate 7:121, 9:512–13,
9:587–8
reality (Bhartṛhari) 1:764–5
salvation 8:447–9
sense perception 8:689–90,
8:692–3
social emancipation 1:196,
1:197
testimony 5:280, 9:315
universals 9:544, 9:546, 9:547
virtue 3:185–6
Japanese **2:99–106**, 5:68, 5:70
absolute nothingness
Kyoto School 5:327
aesthetics 1:80, 1:85–6
*Awakening of Faith in
Mahāyāna* 1:603
categories 2:101–2
emptiness
mujō 6:592–3
Fujiwara Seika 3:800
government 2:550
impermanence 6:591–4
kokoro 5:291, 5:292
mysticism 6:622–3
Nichiren 6:828–9
Nishitani Keiji 7:16–17
pure experience
Kyoto School 5:323–4
Shintō 2:103–4, 8:750–1
Tominaga Nakamoto 9:440
Watsuji Tetsurō 9:691
Zeami 9:839–40
Korean **2:106–18**
*Awakening of Faith in
Mahāyāna* 1:603
Chinul 2:329–31
Confucianism 2:114–15, 2:116
Kyo/Sôn dispute 9:36
Ûisang 9:516
Wônhyo 9:793
mystical experiences 6:622–3,
8:254
nirvāṇa **7:8–12**
particulars 7:235–6
processes 7:722
reincarnation
enlightenment 8:184
escape from 8:183
voidism 8:185
renunciation 3:183, 3:185
suffering 9:214
theosophy 9:364

Tibetan 2:66, **9:402–9**
enlightenment path
Great Debate of bSam-yas
9:405–6
Karma bKa'-brgyud (Kagyü)
school
Mi bskyod rdo rje 6:351–2
rGyal tshab dar ma rin chen
8:304–5
Sa skya paṇḍita 8:433–4
Tsong kha pa Blo bzang grags
pa 9:487–90
Budziszewski, J. 9:432
Buffier, Claude **2:118–20**
common-sense philosophy
2:119–20
first truths 2:119
Buffière, F. 4:502
Buffon, Georges Louis Leclerc,
Comte de **2:120–3**
evolutionary theory 2:120, 2:121–2
human nature, science of in the
eighteenth century 4:526–7
Bufford, S. 5:355–6
Buford, T.O. 7:173
Buhl, G. 1:827
Bühler, G. 3:187
Bühler, K. 7:631
Buhr, M. 4:509
Buickerood, J.G. 5:720
Buijs, J. 6:48
Buitenen, J.A.B. van 8:43–4, 9:594
Bukharin, N.I. 6:158–9
Bukowski, T. 3:429, 7:269
Buldt, Bernd
infinitary logic †4:769–72
Bulgakov, Sergei Nikolaevich **2:123–6**
Signposts movement 8:770, 8:771
Sophiology 2:125
Bulgaria
Kristeva, J. **5:305–8**
Todorov, T. **9:425–7**
Bull, H. 4:186
Bull, R.A. 6:425
Bullard, R.D. 8:333
*Bulletin de la Société française de
philosophie* 6:350
Bullough, D. 2:223
Bullough, E. 1:54–5
Bultmann, Rudolf **2:126–31**
existentialist theology 3:508, 3:509
faith 3:543
hermeneutics, biblical 4:392, 4:394
Strauss, D.F. 9:166
Bunder, M. 2:433
bundle theory of mind **6:382–5**
Hume, D. 6:231

phenomenalism 7:331
Bunge, Carlos Octavio 1:376
Bunge, Mario 1:229, 1:231, 1:232,
    7:539
Bunt, H. 6:170
Bunyan, John 8:457–8
Burali-Fori, Cesare 7:215
Burali-Forti's paradox *see* largest
    ordinal, paradox of
Burana, Johannes 5:23
Burbank J. 8:773
Burch, Robert W.
    Peirce, C.S. 7:283
    Royce, J. †8:377–81
bureaucracy
    Chinese Legalism 5:531, 5:534–5,
        5:537
    sociological theory (Weber, M.)
        9:3, 9:4
Burge, Tyler
    anti-individualism
        computational theory of vision
            6:341, 6:342–3
    concepts 2:515
    content
        indexical 2:639, 2:640
        wide and narrow
            twin earth experiments
                2:644–5
    de re/de dicto belief 2:817
    hierarchy theory 9:266–7
    holism and individualism in
        history and social science 4:487
    indirect discourse 4:744, 4:745
    language
        social nature of 5:418–19
    materialism 6:176–7
    mental causation 6:311
    proper names 7:756
    reference 8:157, 8:163
    semantic paradoxes and theories
        of truth 8:648
    sense and reference 8:687
Burger, C. 4:47
Burger, P. 6:741
Burgess, G. 2:445–6
Burgess, John P.
    constructible universe †2:622–4
    forcing †3:693–7
    set theory †8:700–9
    tense logic 9:307
Burgess, R.G. 3:238
Burgos, Elizabeth 5:655, 5:656
Burgundio of Pisa 9:456
Burian, R. 4:15
Buridan, John 2:131–6
    Albert of Saxony 1:143, 1:144

Aristotelianism 1:401
    connotation 5:398
    consequences 5:755–6
    epistemology 2:133
    ethics 2:134
    Gerard of Odo 4:39
    logic 2:132, 5:750, 5:752
    Marsilius of Inghen comparison
        6:110–11
    metaphysics 2:132–3
    natural philosophy 2:133–4
    nominalism 2:141–2, 5:392, 6:54
    propositions 5:401
    supposition theory 5:754
    transitivity of signification 5:391,
        5:392
Burkard, F. 1:772
Burkard, F.-P. 2:17
Burke, Edmund 2:136–40
    aesthetic concepts 1:55, 1:58
    architecture
        aesthetics of 1:364, 1:366
    conservatism 2:608, 2:610–11,
        2:614
    French Revolution
        natural rights 7:514–15
        party politics 2:136, 2:138
        political representation 8:271,
            8:272
    religious conservatism 8:224, 8:228
    Schiller, J.C.F. 8:529
    the sublime 2:136, 2:137–8, 9:204
    tradition and traditionalism
        9:445–6, 9:447
    trans-generational community
        3:820
    Wollstonecraft, M. 9:791
Burke, K. 8:306, 8:309, 9:245
Burke, M.L. 8:41
Burke, P. 7:517
Burke, T.E. 7:539
Burkert, Walter
    Archytas 1:369
    Egyptian influence on ancient
        Greek thought 3:253–4
    Orphism †7:163–5
    Pythagoras 7:856
    Pythagoreanism 7:861
Burkhard, F. 5:491
Burkhardt, H. 6:170, 6:319
Burki, S.J. 3:44
Burks, A.W. 6:446, 9:352
Burley, Walter 2:141–4
    language 5:401–2, 7:181–2
    natural philosophy 6:704
    obligations 5:757
    syllogism 5:752

Burnaby, J. 7:69
Burnet, Gilbert 4:590–1
Burnet, J. 1:269–8, 9:653
Burnett, Charles
    Islamic philosophy, transmission
        into Western Europe †5:21–5
Burnett, James *see* Monboddo, Lord
Burns, J.H. 6:56, 7:517
Burns, N.T. 7:177
Burns, R. 2:193
Burnyeat, M.F.
    dissoi logoi (twofold argument)
        †3:106–7
    doubt 3:124
    Hellenistic philosophy 4:336, 4:337
    perception 7:292
    Plato 7:420
    Protagoras 7:790
    Pyrrhonism 7:854
    scepticism 3:381
    Stoicism 9:159
    Strauss, L. 9:168
    testimony 9:313
Buroker, J.V. 5:378, 9:64
Burr, D. 7:96
Burr, J.R. 8:491
Burrell, David B.
    Aquinas, T. 1:347
    Aristotelianism in Islamic
        philosophy 1:385
    causality and necessity in Islamic
        thought †2:241–4
    creation and conservation
        religious doctrine of 2:699
    Platonism in Islamic philosophy
        †7:429–30
Burrows, Mark S.
    Gerson, J. †4:45–7
Bursill-Hall, G.L. 5:404
Burski, Adam 7:485
Burthogge, Richard 2:144–6
Burton, E.W. 7:472
Burton, S.J. 5:530
Burtt, E.A. 5:297, 6:582
Busa, R. 1:347
Busch, E. 1:655
Bush, S. 1:74
Bush, U.T. 1:594
bushi philosophy 2:146–50, 5:76
bushidō see bushi philosophy
Bushnell, Horace 8:457
Busia, K.A. 1:139
Business Council for Sustainable
    Development 2:153
business ethics 2:150–4
Buss, S.R. 4:377

Bussanich, John
  Nemesius †6:763–4
  Plotinus 7:463
  Suso, H. †9:240–1
  Tauler, J. †9:269–71
  Themistius †9:324–6
  Ulrich of Strasbourg †9:517–18
Busson, H. 2:289, 6:489
Buswell, Robert E., Jr
  Buddhism
    Chinese 2:92
  Buddhist philosophy
    Korean 2:118
  Chinul †2:329–32, 2:331–2
  Ûisang †9:516–17
  Yogācāra Buddhism 2:74–5
Butler, Joseph **2:154–60**
  conscience 2:580, 2:581
  decision and game theory 2:834
  deism 2:154, 2:157–9
  forgiveness and mercy 3:700–1
  good, theories of the 4:135

  moral motivation 2:157, 6:527
  psychological egoism 3:247, 3:248
  rectification and remainders 8:140
  revelation 2:158, 8:300
  self-deception 8:629, 8:631
  soul 9:48
  system of parts 2:154–7
Butler, Judith
  Beauvoir, S. de 1:687
  feminism and psychoanalysis
    3:586, 3:587
  feminist literary criticism 3:613
  Hegelianism 4:300
  Kojève, A. 5:290–1
  language and gender 5:367
  moral psychology 6:533
  subject
    postmodern critique of 9:200
Butler, R.J. 1:227–8
Butterfield, Jeremy
  determinism and indeterminism
    †3:33–9

Butterworth, C.E. 5:24, 7:520
Butterworth, G. 2:391
Butts, Robert E.
  Galilei, G. 3:841
  Kant, I. 5:196
  science, nineteenth century
    philosophy of †8:565–72
Buzzetti, D. 5:758
Bychkov, V. 3:682
Byerly, H. 5:474
Bykhovskii, B.E. 1:526, 6:158
Byrne, A. 2:431
Byrne, P. 2:855
Byrne, P.M. 3:429, 6:705
Byzantine philosophy **2:160–5**
  Aristotelianism 2:163
  Greek affinity with 2:161, 2:162,
    2:164
  Neoplatonism 2:163
Byzantium
  Diogenes Laertius **3:86–7**
  Proclus **7:723–31**

C

Cabada Castro, M. 3:639
Cabala *see* Kabbalah
Cabanis, Pierre-Jean **2:166–8**
Cabaud, J. 9:701
Cabeen, D.C. 4:518–17
Cabet, Étienne
  communism 2:462, 2:463, 2:464
  utopianism 9:557, 9:559, 9:561
Cabezón, José Ignacio
  Buddhism
    emptiness concept 2:80
    mKhas grub dge legs dpal bzang
      po †6:416–17
    Tibetan philosophy 9:408
Cabinis, J. 6:173
Cabral, Amílcar **2:168–71**
  African philosophy 1:97
Cacciari, M. 5:40
Cach J. 2:440
Cadden, J. 6:705
Cady, L. 5:852
Cage, J. 6:607
Cahan, D. 4:340
Cahill, J. 1:74
Cahm, Caroline
  Kropotkin, P.A. †5:313–14
Cahn, S. 1:93, 3:238
Cai Zongqi 8:684
Caillat, C. 4:256
Cailliet, É. 2:168
Cain, A.J. 5:650
Cain, J.A. 4:15
Cain, M. 8:878
Caird, E. 2:752, 4:300
Cairnes, J.E. 3:214, 3:220
Cairns, J. 6:460
Cairns, J.W. 8:347
Cairola, J. 6:115
Caitanya 3:857–8, 4:738
Caizzi, F.D. 1:303
Cajetan of Thienne 1:409
Cajetan (Cardinal Thomas de Vio)
  2:171–5
  abstraction (Silvestri, F.) 8:776–7
Cajori, F. 5:745, 7:53, 9:852
Calabresi, Guido 7:758, 7:760
Calcidius **2:175–6**
  translations by 6:691, 7:432–3,
    9:455

calculability *see* computation
calculation (*logismos*)
  Archytas 1:368–9
calculus 7:881
  see also first-order logic; predicate
    calculus; predicate logic; second-
    order logic; sentential logic
  differential and integral 1:216–17
  Leibniz, G.W. 5:542, 5:554
  logical
    formal languages and systems
      3:704–6
    logic
      seventeenth and eighteenth
        century 5:718–20
    Newtonian (Berkeley, G.) 1:746–7
Calder, Norman
  law, Islamic philosophy of
    †5:457–60
Calder, Robert R.
  Kemp Smith, N. †5:227–31
Caldwell, B. 3:220
Caldwell, W. 4:240
Calhoun, C.
  Bourdieu, P. 1:850
  emotions 3:285, 3:289
  Habermas, J. 4:199
  sociology
    theories of 9:7
  Taylor, C. †9:276–9
Callahan, C. 5:525
Callahan, D. 6:263–4
Callahan, J.C. 8:806
Callan, E. 3:238
Callebaut, A. 7:269
Callen, D. 6:612
Callicles **2:176–7**
  physis and *nomos* debate 7:381
Callicott, J.B.
  agricultural ethics 1:128
  ecological philosophy 3:201
  environmental ethics 3:336
  green political philosophy 4:165
  moral standing 6:553–4
calligraphy
  Chinese 1:68–9, 1:71–2, 1:73, 1:74
Callinicos, Alex
  Althusser, L.P. †1:192–6
  Lukács, G. †5:856–9

Marcuse, Herbert †6:95–9
Marx, K. 6:132
Trotsky, L. †9:464–6
Callus, D.A. 4:182, 5:24, 8:317
Calude, Christian
  computability and information
    †2:477–82
Calvenus Taurus 7:422, 7:428
Calvert, P. 8:303
Calvin, John **2:177–82**, 8:249
  atonement 1:538–9, 1:540, 2:180
  creation doctrine 2:179
  hermeneutics
    biblical 4:391
  influence of 2:181
  Pelagianism 7:286
  predestination 2:177, 2:180, 7:656
  providence 2:179–80
  religious epistemology 2:178–9,
    8:216
  reprobation 8:274, 8:275
  sacraments 8:444, 8:445
  salvation 2:180
  sanctification 8:457, 8:458
  socio-political thought 2:180–1
  supererogation 9:234
  voluntarism
    Cambridge Platonism critique
      2:184–5
  will 9:724, 9:725
Calvinism
  see also Calvin, John
  Charron, P. 2:288
  Culverwell, N. 2:750–1
  Dooyeweerd, H. 3:113–14
  Edwards, J. 1:201
  ethics 8:222
  pietism 7:395
  political philosophy 7:510–11
  predestination 7:653
  providence 7:797, 7:799, 7:800
Camacho, L. 3:43
Cambours Ocampo, Arturo 7:349,
  7:351–49
Cambridge change 2:274–5
  see also see also Russell, Bertrand
Cambridge Metaphysical Club 1:203
Cambridge Platonism **2:182–5**
  see also Latitudinarianism

Conway, A. 2:669–70
Cudworth, R. 2:739–43
Culverwell, N. 2:751
Cameron, A. 8:791–0
Cameron, D. 5:367
Cameron, R. 6:77
Cameron, S. 1:205, 9:392
Camic, C. 8:821
Camp, J.L., Jr 9:477
Campanella, Giovanni Domenico *see*
  Campanella, Tommaso
Campanella, Tommaso **2:186–91**
  epistemology 2:186–7, 5:35, 5:40
  ethics 2:188–9
  philosophy of nature 2:187–8
  politics 2:189
  South Slavs, philosophy of 9:54
Campanini, M. 4:67
Campbell, A.H. 9:119
Campbell, B. 9:365
Campbell, C.A. 1:862, 3:751,
  6:501–2, 6:503
Campbell, Donald T.
  evolutionary epistemology 6:724,
    6:727
  evolutionary theory and social
    science 3:487, 3:520
  logic of discovery of 3:101–2
Campbell, George **2:191–3**
  Aberdeen Philosophical Society
    1:15
  Enlightenment, Scottish 2:191,
    3:329
Campbell, J. 2:431, 3:51, 9:174
Campbell, J.M. 1:540
Campbell, Keith
  analytic behaviourism 1:692
  Armstrong, D.M. 1:443
  epiphenomenalism †3:351–4
  particulars 7:238
  qualia 1:579
Campbell, L. 6:210
Campbell, Lewis 7:403–4, 7:420
Campbell, Norman Robert **2:193–4**
  models 6:446
  scientific theories 9:352
Campbell, R. 1:296, 8:101
Campbell, R.H. 3:329, 8:821
Campbell, T.D. 8:821
Campo, Heimeric de 1:402
Camporeale, S. 9:573
Campos, J.J. 7:818, 7:822
Campsall, Richard 2:293
Camurati, M. 5:656
Camus, Albert **2:194–6**
  ethics
    existentialist 3:505

sport 9:110
existentialism 3:494, 3:500, 3:501
  meaning of life 5:631, 5:632
  nihilism 7:2, 7:3, 7:4
  totalitarianism 9:444
Canada
  Lonergan, B.J.F. **5:822–5**
  Taylor, C. **9:276**
Cāṇakya *see* Kauṭilya
Candidus Wizo 2:223
Candlish, Stewart
  Bradley, F.H. †1:857–63
  bundle theory of mind †6:382–5
  private language argument
    †7:693–8
Candrakīrti 2:60–1, 6:351–2
Candramati 7:64
Caneva, K.L. 6:740
Canfield, J.V. 6:384, 7:698, 9:770
Canguilhem, Georges 3:779, 3:781–6
Cannabrava, Euryalo 3:512, 3:513
cannibalism 5:431
Canning, J. 1:659
Cannon, W.B. 3:282, 3:285, 7:723
Cannon, W.F. 8:571
Cano, Melchor 9:71, 9:76
canonical system (Post, E.L.) 7:573–4
Canovan, Margaret
  Arendt, H. 1:372
  totalitarianism †9:442–4
Cantor, Georg **2:196–9**
  Bolzano, B. 1:827
  continuum hypothesis 2:654,
    2:655–6, 2:657, 8:705
  Dedekind, J.W.R. 2:842
  Frege, G. 3:777
  infinity 4:775–6, 4:777
  mathematical analysis 1:218
  measurement, theory of 6:249
  proof theory 7:743
  Russell, B.A.W. 8:394
  set theory 8:700, 8:702, 8:708
    non-standard models 5:847
    paradoxes 7:215–16, 7:220
  transfinite numbers 7:50–1
Cantor's theorem **2:199–200**
  glossary 5:798
Canziani, G. 2:376
Čapek, K. 6:166
Čapek, M. 1:736, 9:416
Capiński, M. 1:215
capital punishment
  Camus, A. 2:194–5
  Jewish philosophy
    halakhah 4:206
  Roman Catholicism 4:798

capitalism
  alienation 1:180
  business ethics 2:153
  commodity fetishism
    Lukács, G. 5:857–8
    Marx, K. 6:128–9
  critiques of
    Frankfurt School 6:95–6, 6:97
    Lukács, G. 6:96–7
    Marcuse, H. 6:95–6, 6:97
    socialist 8:879, 8:881–4
    Weil, S. 9:700
  defence of
    Rand, A. 8:55
  demise of
    Kautsky, K.J. 5:222
    Luxemburg, R. 6:6–7
    Schumpeter, J.A. 8:555
  division of labour 9:795
  economic failings 8:881
  laissez-faire 7:692
  Marx, K. 6:118, 6:127–8, 6:131,
    7:516, 8:853
    fetishism of commodities
      6:128–9
  Marxism
    ideology 4:681–2
    Latin America 6:160, 6:162,
      6:163, 6:164
  private property 7:759
  race
    theories of 8:19
  social democracy 8:827–8
  solidarity 9:23–4
  technology and ethics 9:281
Caplan, A. 6:267–8
Capozzi, Mirella
  logic in the seventeenth and
    eighteenth centuries †5:716–22
Cappelletti, A.J. 1:378
Cappuyns, M. 3:405
Capra, F. 3:201
Capreolus, Johannes **2:200–2**, 9:382
Caputo, J. 4:327, 7:340
Caputo, J.D. 7:586
Cara, F. 8:90
Carabelli, A.M. 5:235
Carabelli, G. 9:429
Carboncini, S. 2:739
Card, Claudia
  forgiveness and mercy 3:701
  lesbian sadomasochism 8:726,
    8:727
  rectification and remainders
    †8:134–41
Cardano, Girolamo **2:202–4**

Cardano, Hieronymus *see* Cardano, Girolamo
cardinal numbers
  see also largest cardinal
  glossary 5:798
  set theory 7:51–2, 8:702, 8:703–4
    axioms 8:706–7
cardinal virtues
  prudence 7:802
cardinality
  of the continuum 2:199–200, 2:654, 2:656
  infinite
    model of 4:109
  value theory 8:64, 8:72, 8:73
Cardona, G. 4:765, 7:250
Cardoso, Fernando Henrique 5:655, 5:656
care
  charity 2:281
  feminine ethics 3:603–4
  nursing ethics 7:56–7
Carey, J.J. 9:412
Carey, S. 2:394, 2:395
Cargill Thompson W.D.J. 6:5
Carlen, Pat 5:497–8, 5:499
Carlisle, R.B. 8:447
Carlson, A.
  nature
    aesthetic appreciation of †6:731–5
Carlson, E.A. 4:15
Carlson, M. 1:471–2
Carlyle, R.W. 8:229
Carlyle, Thomas **2:205–6**
Carman, J.B. 8:44, 8:451
Carmichael, Gershom **2:206–8**
  beatitude 2:206–7
Carnap, Rudolf **2:208–15**
  adverbs 1:49–50
  analytic philosophy 1:226, 1:228, 1:238
    critique (Quine, W.V.) 2:213, 8:11
    Latin America 1:230, 1:232
  arithmetic 1:440–1
  causation 2:247, 2:250
  concepts 2:515
  confirmation theory 2:532–4, 2:535
    logical probabilities 2:212–13
  consequence 2:603
  conventionalism 2:668
    linguistic 2:667
  definitions 2:209, 2:846, 2:848
  descriptions 3:23
  essentialism 3:421

general relativity
  Kantian interpretation 4:7
  philosophical responses to 4:8
Hempel, C.G. 4:352
inference
  inductive 4:758
  non-constructive rules of 7:29
intensional entities 4:806
logic
  early twentieth century 5:736
  modal 6:419, 6:425
  multiple-conclusion 6:604
logical positivism 5:793–4
  relativity 5:791, 5:792–3, 5:794
logicism 5:816
Mach, E. 6:16
mathematics
  foundations of 6:189
  meaning and verification 6:231, 6:235
metalanguages 2:210–11
modal logic 6:419, 6:425
modal operators 6:435
models 6:446
Naturphilosophie 6:740
necessary truth and convention 6:749
Neo-Kantian epistemology
  science 9:344–6
nominalism 7:21, 7:22
operationalism 7:134–5
possible worlds semantics 7:787, 7:788, 8:663, 8:668
predicate calculus 7:664
prescriptivism 7:670
probability 7:705, 7:710
propositional attitude statements 7:778
rationality 8:63
realism/antirealism 8:119
reduction 8:148
Reichenbach, H. 8:170–1
relativity
  logical positivism 5:791, 5:792–3, 5:794
Russell, B.A.W. 8:402
science 9:352
  demarcation problem 2:866
  unity of 9:531, 9:532
types
  theory of 9:361
Vienna Circle 2:209–10, 9:608–11, 9:612
Carneades **2:215–20**
  Academic scepticism 1:263–4, 2:215–16, 2:218–19
  Alexander of Aphrodisias 1:173

  ethics 2:217
  Stoicism 2:216, 2:217–18
Carney, F.S. 3:573
Carney, J.D. 1:468
Carolingian renaissance **2:220–3**
  Encyclopedists, medieval 3:307
  logic revival 2:221
  predestination 2:222
Caroll, R.T. 5:435
Caroti, S. 6:705, 7:157
Carpi, D. 6:334
Carr, A.E. 8:39
Carr, D. 6:509, 8:846
Carr, E.H. 1:647, 4:410, 9:229
Carr, K. 7:4
Carraud, V. 7:246
Carré, J.-R. 3:693
Carrier, L.S. 5:266
Carrió, G.R. 1:232
Carrithers, M. 2:53
Carro, V.D. 9:39
Carroll, David
  African Francophone philosophy 1:114
  Lyotard, J.-F. †6:7–6:12
Carroll, Lewis *see* Dodgson, C.L.
Carroll, N.
  art
    definition of 1:468
    emotion in response to 3:280
  film
    aesthetics of 3:676
  humour 4:566
  narrative 6:657
Carroll, P.N. 5:125
Carruthers, P.
  a posteriori 1:3
  a priori 1:5
  bundle theory of mind 6:384–5
  consciousness 2:594
  nativism 6:675
  Wittgenstein, L. 9:770
Carson, M.F. 5:865
Carson, Rachel 1:321, 1:324
Carstanjen, F. 1:594
Carston, R. 7:631
Cartan, E. 4:32
Carter, A. 3:843
Carter, R. 1:509
Carter, R.E. 5:715
Cartesian Circle 3:10–11, 8:79
Cartesian dualism *see* dualism, Cartesian
Cartesianism
  see also Descartes, R.; Geulincx, A.
  animal language and thought 1:270, 5:372

Aristotelianism
  seventeenth century 1:390–1
behaviourism 1:694
clandestine literature 2:375
Clauberg, J. 2:380–1
conservation law 5:555
Cordemoy, G. de 2:672–4
critiques of
  Elisabeth of Bohemia 3:268
  Foucher, S. 3:713, 3:715–16
  Huet, P.-D. 4:514, 4:515
  Leibniz, G.W. 5:555
  Marcel, G. 6:92
demonstration (Vico, G.) 9:599,
  9:601
Desgabets, R. 3:27–8
Fardella, M. 3:558–9
La Forge, L. de 5:331–2
Le Clerc, J. 5:475–6
Le Grand, A. 5:479–80
life, origin of 5:633
Malebranche, N. 6:58–9, 6:62–3
materialism
  consciousness 2:883
  perception 8:640
persons 7:318, 7:320
Port-Royal 7:550, 7:552–3
projectivism 7:738
religion relationship 6:580
Rohault, J. 8:342
science (Alembert, J. le R. d')
  1:164, 1:166
worldview 3:197–8
Cartwright, Nancy
causation †2:244–51
explanation 3:524
idealizations 4:672
inference to the best explanation
  4:769
natural laws 5:472, 5:474
Neurath, O. †6:813–16
parapsychology 7:227
pragmatic virtues 9:343
science 9:352
  realism/antirealism 8:582–3,
    8:584
  unity of 9:532
Cartwright, R. 9:461
Cartwright, R.L. 7:116, 7:788
Carus, P. 2:781
Cārvāka
  see also Lokāyata
  causation 2:251, 2:253
  inference 5:280
  materialism 7:605
  sense perception 8:691

Carvalho Mont'Alverne, Francisco
  José de 2:10
Carver, Terrell
  Engels, F. †3:309–13
  social science
    philosophy of history 8:857
Cary, Sir Lucius 2:308
Casado, F. 5:59
Casalla, Mario 5:610–11
Casares, Jorge 3:511, 3:513
Casas, Bartolomé de las 5:421, 5:426
Casati, Roberto
  dreaming †3:127–9
  Gestalt psychology 4:54
Casaubon, Meric 3:332
Case, T.J. 3:204–5
case-reasoning (casuistry)
  bioethics 2:228
  moral theology 2:228
Casey, E. 4:708
Casey, J. 8:293
Caso, Antonio
  Latin America
    analytical philosophy 1:230,
      1:232
    anti-positivism 1:306, 1:307
    phenomenology 7:350, 7:351
Caspar, M. 5:232
Casper, B. 8:361
Cassam, Q. 7:321
Cassell, E. 9:214
Cassian, John 7:285, 7:286
Cassidy, D.C. 4:329
Cassinelli, G. 7:885–6
Cassio, A.C. 3:337
Cassiodorus 3:306–7, 3:308
Cassirer, Ernst 2:223–7
  Baumgarten, A.G. 1:672
  Cambridge Platonism 2:185
  Condillac, É.B. de 2:527
  Cudworth, R. 2:743
  Enlightenment, continental 3:319
  general relativity
    Kantian interpretation 4:6
    philosophical responses to 4:8
  German idealism 4:44–5
  Geulincx, A. 4:61
  Lessing, G.E. 5:577
  Neo-Kantianism 6:777, 6:783–4,
    6:789–90
Cassirer, H. 1:540–1, 5:168
Cassuto, U. 4:710
Castagnino, Raúl 7:349, 7:351
Castañeda, Hector-Neri
  adverbs 1:49
  analytical philosophy
    Latin America 1:229

imperative logic 4:720
indexicals 2:881
Sellars, W.S. 8:642
caste
  critiques of
    Arya Samaj movement 1:516
    Brahmo Samaj movement 2:5
  duty, Indian concepts of 3:183,
    3:184
  liberation from saṃsāra 8:460
  political philosophy 7:523
  sacrificial metaphor 2:681–2
  social emancipation
    (Ambedkar, B.R.) 1:196–7
Castellanos, Rosario 3:625, 3:628
Castiglione, D. 6:74
Castro, José de 2:8
Castro-Gómez, S. 5:612
casuistry 2:227–9
  applied ethics 1:319
  as case-reasoning 2:227, 2:228
  as dialectic method 2:227, 2:228
  as moral laxism 2:227–8
  Tolstoi, L.N. 9:438
Cat, Jordi
  Neurath, O. †6:813–16
  unity of science †9:530–3
catallaxy
  Hayek, F.A. 4:247
Catalonia
  Llull, R. 5:662–4
  Nahmanides, M. 6:647–51
Catania, A.C. 1:698
catastrophism
  geology 4:26, 4:27
categorematic terms
  see also syncategorematic terms
  conceptual analysis 2:519
  infinity 4:773–4
  syncategorematic distinction 7:19
categorial conversion
  African Marxism (Nkrumah, K.)
    1:100
categorical imperative
  Kant, I.
    duty 5:201
    ethics
      autonomy 1:588
      universalism 9:538, 9:539
    formulations of 5:189–90
    freedom 5:191–2
    impartiality 4:716
    moral stage development 6:504
    reasoning
      moral 5:201, 8:100
      practical 7:617–18
    respect for persons 8:285

Zionism (Leibowitz, Y.) 5:563
categorical propositions
  glossary 5:798
  spicular notation
    De Morgan, A. 2:813
categorical syllogism
  Wolff, C. 9:781
Categories see Aristotle
categories **2:229–33**
  see also category mistake;
    classification
  Aristotelian 2:229–30
    Aquinas, T. 1:333
    divisions of 1:418
    medieval natural philosophy
      6:702
    Porphyry 7:546, 9:729
    Roscelin of Compiègne 8:356
    substance 9:206
    Valla, L. 9:571
  art evaluation 1:473
  artificial neural networks
    connectionism 2:570
  Chinese philosophy 2:318,
    6:456–7, 9:834–5
    see also lei
  concepts 2:505
  conditions of existence
    (Anderson, J.) 1:267
  dialectical method (Hegel, G.W.F.)
    4:269
  doctrine of signs (John of St
    Thomas) 5:118–19
  Eastern philosophy 2:232
  Graham, A.C. 2:229, 2:232
  grammatical
    criteria (Wittgenstein, L.)
      2:712–13
    Port-Royalists 5:373–4
    structuralism 9:178
  Illuminationist philosophy (al-
    Suhrawardi) 4:701, 9:221–2
  Indian philosophy *see* ontology,
    Indian philosophy
  Jewish philosophy (Maimon, S.)
    6:35–6, 6:37
  Kant, I. 2:229, 2:231–2, 5:185–6
    judgment 5:185–6
    objectification 4:338–9
    schemata 5:186
  language
    discrimination 5:641–2
    linguistic relativism 2:232
    Sapir-Whorf Hypothesis
      8:470–2
  legal
    feminist jurisprudence 3:608–9

logical/ontological
  abstract objects 1:32–3
  metaphysics 6:338
  Neo-Kantian
    Cohen, H. 6:781
    Hartmann, K.R.E. von 4:239
    Natorp, P. 6:783
  Nyāya 4:439
  Nyāya-Vaiśeṣika 7:60
  objectification (Kant, I.) 4:338–9
  Ryle, G. 2:229, 2:230–1
  speculative metaphysics
    (Whitehead, A.N.) 9:716–17
  Stoicism 9:147–8
  syntactic (Ajdukiewicz, K.) 1:137
  theory of (Peirce, C.S.) 7:270,
    7:276–8
  universality 2:232
  Vaiśeṣika 4:438–9
category of categories 2:235
category mistake
  Ryle, G. 2:230–1, 8:428, 8:430–1
category theory **2:237–9**
  intuitionism 4:851
  mathematics
    foundations of **2:233–7**
Cathars (Albigensians, Bogomils)
  Manicheism 6:76
catharsis
  see also katharsis
  Aristotle 9:448–9
Catherine of Alexandria 6:624
Catherine the Great 3:326
Catherine of Siena 6:625
Catholic Modernism 5:819
Catholic Reformation *see* Counter-
  Reformation
Catholicism *see* Roman Catholicism
Caton, C.E. 7:147, 7:153
Cattaneo, Carlo **2:239–41**
  Italy 5:36, 5:40
Catto, Jeremy
  Wyclif, J. †9:802–5
Catton, W.R. 4:165, 6:720
Cauchy, A.L.
  analysis 1:217–20
Cauchy, A.-L.
  mechanics
    classical 6:258, 6:259
causa sui (self-caused) 3:744, 3:747,
  9:92–3
causal of reference *see* historical
  chain theory
causal theory of knowledge *see*
  knowledge, causal theory of
causal theory of objects
  phenomenalism 7:333

causality **2:244–51**
  see also causes; dependent
    origination; determinism; end
    cause; mental causation;
    occasionalism
  abstract objects 1:33, 1:34–5
  action
    Davidson, D. 2:801
    Stewart, D. 9:137
    Wright, G.H. von 9:668
  adequate (Weber, M.) 9:694–5
  analogies (Aquinas, T.) 1:334
  antinomies (Kant, I.) 5:188–9
  associationism (Hume, D.) 2:245–6
  atomic swerve 3:343
  bodily movement (Reid, T.) 8:174
  Buddhism 2:93, 2:97–8
  Buddhist/Nyāya debate 9:512–13
  Cartesianism (Clauberg, J.) 2:381
  causal determinism 6:531
  causal explanation
    history and social science 3:526,
      3:527–8, 3:529
    Meyerson, É 6:349–50
  causal laws 2:247–8, 8:832–3
    intentionality 8:863–5
    normative law distinction
      7:38–9
  causal powers 2:249–50
  chaos theory 2:279
  children's reasoning about
    (Piaget, J.) 7:383–4, 7:385
  concepts 2:510
  concomitance (Cavendish, M.L.)
    2:261
  connectionist networks 2:572
  constant conjunction (Glanvill, J.)
    4:81
  correlation 2:247
  creation
    Jewish philosophy 8:436–7
  critiques of
    Pyrrhonism 7:853
  design argument
    Hume, D. 4:559–60
    Kant, I. 5:194
  disease 6:267
  divine
    Cicero, M.T. 2:358
    Spinoza, B. de 9:95, 9:96
  divine theophanies (Eriugena, J.S.)
    3:403–4
  dual theory 7:88
  dualism (La Forge, L. de) 5:331–2
  economics 3:213
  efficient
    Duns Scotus, J. 3:160–3

William of Ockham 9:742, 9:743
emanation
    Mir Damad, Muhammad Baqir 6:409
    Neoplatonism 2:242
emptiness
    Buddhism 2:78–9
etiological necessity (Ducasse, C.J.) 3:139
facts 3:536–7
four causes (Galen) 3:832, 3:834
free will
    compatibilism 1:614, 1:617–18
freedom (Hartmann, N.) 4:241
functionalism in social science 3:527
generalizations (Ramsey, F.P.) 8:47
geology 4:26–7
Gestalt psychology 4:53
Henry of Ghent 3:160
hierarchical ontology (Plotinus) 7:460–1
Hindu philosophy 4:435
Hume, D. 2:27, 3:139
incommensurability 4:735
indeterministic (Broad, C.D.) 2:24–5
Indian theories of 2:56, 2:57, **2:251–7**, 7:122–3
inference
    Hume, D. 4:544, 4:546–8
    Indian theories of 4:761
inference systems 2:607, 4:224
Islamic philosophy **2:241–4**
    al-Ghazali 4:65, 4:640
    Ibn Rushd 4:640
    Ikhwan al-Safa' 4:686
    Islamic fundamentalism 5:12
    meaning 6:237–8
    necessity (Ibn Sina) 4:650
    resurrection (al-Ghazali) 4:65
karma and rebirth 5:213–14
law of (Schopenhauer, A.) 8:547
law of universal (Mill, J.S.) 6:365, 6:367, 6:368
lawfulness (*Gesetzlichkeit*) (Helmholtz, H. von) 4:339
legal significance of (Hart, H.L.A.) 4:235
logic of infinity (Wodeham, A.) 9:774–5
meaning
    Hume, D. 6:230–1
    Islamic philosophy 6:237–8
mental *see* mental causation
mind (Brown, T.) 2:28

miracles 6:411–12, 6:414, 6:415
momentariness
    Buddhism 6:469, 6:472
motion (Cavendish, M.L.) 2:261
multivocity (Aristotle) 1:417, 1:419–20
Native American philosophy 6:665
natural laws 5:470, 5:471
naturalized epistemology 6:722
nature-nurture debate 8:895
necessity (Ibn Sina) 4:650
occasionalist critique of 7:87–9
paranormal phenomena 7:221–2, 7:223–4
perception of 4:499
perceptual knowledge 7:295, 7:296, 7:297
personalism (Bowne, B.P.) 7:316–17
physical (Leibniz, G.W.) 5:548
pragmatic theory of truth 9:478–9
predestination 7:655–6
pre-existent effect (Śaṅkara) 8:460
probabilistic
    sociobiology 8:895
processes 7:721
psychical (Wundt, W.) 9:799–800
psychoanalytic methodology 7:813
resurrection (al-Ghazali) 4:65
Sāṅkhya 8:465–6
scepticsm (Nicholas of Autrecourt) 6:830
science
    Popper, K.R. 7:534
    top-down 8:234
scientific explanation 3:523
singular 2:248–9
spacetime (Reichenbach, H.) 8:169
supervenience
    mental/physical properties 9:239
'theoretician's dilemma'
    scientific behaviourism 8:800
thought experiments 9:393
time 9:415
time travel 9:417–18
types of (Reid, T.) 8:173–4
universe (Hartmann, K.R.E. von) 4:239
voluntarism 9:663, 9:664
causation *see* causality
causes
    action 1:39–40
    efficient
        action
            Reid, T. 8:174

    existence
        Reid, T. 8:173–4
        Hobbes, T. 4:466
    essentially-ordered (Duns Scotus, J.) 3:161–2
    exemplar (Duns Scotus, J.) 3:160, 3:163
    final
        Descartes, R. rejection 3:15
        Leibniz, G.W. 5:549, 5:556
        material–efficient relation (Aristotle) 1:420
        Spinoza, B. de 9:91
    infinite regress (Duns Scotus, J.) 3:161–2
    proximate (Spinoza, B. de) 9:92–3
    and reasons 2:800–1, **8:124–7**
    teleological/mechanistic distinction 3:802
    ultimate
        Liber de causis 5:595–6
Causey, R.L. 8:148
Caute, D. 3:554
Cavallin, J. 9:509
Cavalli-Sforza, L. 3:487
Cave, J.D. 3:263
Cavell, M. 3:793
Cavell, Stanley **2:257–60**
    aesthetics
        film 3:676
        music 6:612
    American philosophy
        eighteenth and nineteenth century 1:205
    criteria 2:713
    doubt 3:124
    Emerson, R.W. 3:272
    love 5:845
    poetry 7:476
    promising 7:742
    Thoreau, H.D. 9:390, 9:392
    value 9:583
    Wittgenstein, L. 9:770
Cavendish, Margaret Lucas **2:260–4**
Caws, P. 8:479, 9:177, 9:181, 9:184
Ceadel, M. 9:690
Cech, T.R. 5:635
celestial spheres (Alighieri, Dante) 1:184
cells
    life, origin of 5:634
Celsus of Alexandria **2:264**, 2:384
Ceñal, R. 3:690, 9:196
censorship
    see also freedom, of speech; journalism; pornography

art
 morality 1:454
 Plato 1:479
 clandestine literature 2:374–5
 intellectual freedom (Kant, I.)
  5:195–6
central state identity theory *see*
 identity theory of mind
centralism
 Chinese Marxism 6:136–7
centrality
 self-cultivation
  Chinese philosophy 8:619
 Zhongyong 9:861
Centre for Contemporary Cultural
 Studies, University of Birmingham
 3:614
Cercidas 2:756–7
Cercle philosophique de Prague 2:767
cerebral hemispheres
 split brain studies 9:108–9
cerebral theory (Comte, A.) 2:503–4
Cerezo Galán, P. 7:168
certainty **2:264–7**
 see also belief; doubt; scepticism
 a priori 1:5
 antiscepticism (White, T.) 9:712
 cogito argument (Descartes, R.)
  3:1, 3:7–8
 cognitive
  Stoic–Academic debate 7:849,
   9:142, 9:151–2
 degrees of
  Wodeham, A. 9:773
 demonstration
  philosophical method
   (Wolff, C.) 9:778–80, 9:781
  Vico, G. 9:601
 divine illumination 1:828, 1:833
 doubt **3:122–5**
  method of (Descartes, R.)
   3:374–5, 7:35
 epistemic
  Yoruba epistemology 9:832–3
 epistemic duty (Locke, J.) 8:212–13
 illative sense (Newman, J.H.) 6:822
 mathematics (Mersenne, M.)
  6:327–8
 metaphysical/moral distinction
  (Chillingworth, W.) 2:307–8
 moral
  Latitudinarianism 5:433
 objective
  propositional 2:267
 perception (Nicholas of
  Autrecourt) 6:829, 6:830
 propositional 2:265–7

psychological 1:707, 2:264–5
rationalism 8:79
religious 8:209, 8:213–14, 8:698,
 8:699
science, demarcation problem
 2:864, 2:865–6
transcendental idealism (Kant, I.)
 5:182
Certeau, Michel de **2:268–9**
 mysticism, nature of 6:632
certification
 reliabilism
  Nyāya 3:390
certitude
 al-Farabi 5:711
 moral relativism 6:541
Cerutti-Guldberg, Horacio
 Argentina, philosophy in 1:378
 liberation philosophy †5:610–13
 Mexico, philosophy in †6:344–8
Cesa, C. 3:639
Césaire, A. 1:114
Cessario, R. 2:201
Chaadaev, Pëtr Iakovlevich **2:270–3**
 Russian Idea 8:419
 Russian Schellingianism 8:521–2
Chaba Chögyi sengge *see* Phya pa
 Chos kyi seng ge
Chabal, P. 2:170
Chadwick, D. 4:19
Chadwick, Henry
 Augustine 1:558
 Boethius, A.M.S. †1:801–13
 Clement of Alexandria †2:383–5
 Manicheism 6:77
 patristic philosophy 7:261
Chadwick, Ruth
 ethics
  genetics †4:16–19
  journalism 5:128
  professional †7:733–7
 Kant, I. 5:196
Chaitin, G.J.
 computability and information
  2:480, 2:481–2
 computer science 2:495
 Gödel's theorems 4:114–15
Chakrabarti, A. 9:314, 9:318
Chakrabarti, S.K. 2:6
Chakravarti, P. 8:467
Chakravarty, R. 3:859
Chalcedon
 Xenocrates **9:806–7**
Chalcedon Council 4:726–8
Chalcidius *see* Calcidius
Chalcis
 Iamblichus **4:598–9**

Chaldaean Oracles **2:273–4**
 Sudiae Lexicon 2:274
Chalier, Agnes
 Wang Chong †9:679–80
Chalikova, Viktoriia 9:561
Chalmers, D. 2:587, 2:594
Chambers, R. 4:595
Chamfort, de
 moralistes 6:557
Champion, J.A.I.
 Toland, J. †9:427–9
Chan, A.K.L. 2:781–2
Chan Buddhism
 see also Sôn Buddhism; Zen
  Buddhism
 China 2:88–9
 Linji 5:645
 mysticism 6:622–3
 Platform Sutra 7:398–9
 self-cultivation 8:621
 Zongmi 9:870–1
Chan Wing-tsit
 Cheng Hao 2:301
 Chinese Confucianism 2:547,
  6:776, 2:327
 Daodejing 2:781
 Daxue 2:809
 fa 3:533
 li 5:595
 Lu Xiangshan 5:852
 self-cultivation 8:613, 8:621, 8:625
 Xunzi 9:820
 Zhongyong 9:862
 Zhou Dunyi 9:863
 Zhu Xi 9:864–5
chance
 randomness 8:56, 8:59
 simulation of
  computers 8:56–7
Chandrasekharan, K. 9:707
Chang, C. 2:547, 5:852, 9:684
Chang, C.C. 1:763, 5:851, 6:83
Chang, Chung-yuan 2:795
Chang, K.C. 4:452
Chang, Leo S.
 Chinese Legalist philosophy
  †5:531–8
 Han Feizi †4:219–20
Chang, S. 9:858
Chang Tsai *see* Zhang Zai
change **2:274–6**
 see also eternity of the world;
  immutability; impermanence;
  momentariness
 African tradition 3:448
 Aristotelianism
  eternity 1:597

atomism (Diodorus Cronus) 3:84
Cambridge change 2:274–5
causality 2:275
cognitive development 2:394–5
continuants 2:275–6, 2:652
cycle of (Empedocles) 3:293,
    3:294–5
divine action
    atheistic potentiality argument
        7:605
    etiological theory of biological
        function 3:816
    events 3:462
    experience of God 8:50
    feminist theology 3:623
    historical
        Kojève, A. 5:289, 5:290
        self concepts 9:277
    knowledge of (Dewey, J.) 3:47
    metaphysics 6:339
    momentariness
        Buddhism 6:469–70, 6:471–2
    natural philosophy (William of
        Ockham) 9:741–2
    in nature (Aristotle) 1:418–19
    patterns of (Shao Yong) 8:736
    potentiality (Aristotle) 1:420–1
    power 7:610–13
    scientific paradigms
        incommensurability 4:733
    social
        neo-structuralism 9:187
    socioeconomic
        development ethics 3:39–42
    substantial motion (Mulla Sadra)
        6:597
    technological
        dynamics 9:286–7
    that-which-is (Melissus) 6:294–5
    time 2:274, 2:275–6
        relationism 9:414
Chanter, Tina
    Irigaray, L. †5:1–4
    Kristeva, J. †5:305–8
Chaos
    Cosmos comparison 2:316
    Daoism 2:791
chaos theory 2:276–80
    definition 2:276–7
    determinism/predictability
        distinction 6:254
    divine action 8:233–4
    Poincaré, J.H. 7:478–9
Chapman, J.W. 1:93, 7:693
Chapman, R.W. 5:123
Chappell, D. 9:861

Chappell, T.D.J.
    Thrasymachus 9:398
    utilitarianism †9:551–7
Chappell, V. 3:18
Chappius, M. 1:135
Chapple, C. 8:467
character
    ethology
        Mill, J.S. 6:368
    will relationship
        good, theories of the 4:132–3
        Mill, J.S. 6:369–70
characterization
    art works 1:494, 1:496–7
    comedy 2:436–7
    literary criticism (Schlegel, F. von)
        8:530
charity 2:280–2
    animals and ethics 1:274
    beneficence 4:342
    benevolence 2:281
    Christian love 2:280–1
    conceptual role semantics 8:653
    faith 3:539, 3:542
    justice (Leibniz, G.W.) 5:557–8
    virtue
        Aquinas, T. 9:627
        Hume, D. 4:552
charity, principle of 2:282–5
    animal language and thought
        1:271–2
    belief and knowledge 1:707
    Collingwood, R.G. 2:412
    critical thinking 2:283
    Davidson, D. 2:802, 8:33–4
    epistemology 2:283–5
    intentional systems 2:283
    radical translation 2:283–5, 8:80,
        8:83
    scepticism 2:283–5
    Wilson, N. 8:27
Charlemagne, Emperor 2:220, 8:226
Charles, D. 1:434
Charleton, Walter 2:286–7
Charlton, D.G. 9:260
Charron, J.D. 2:289
Charron, Pierre 2:287–90
    De la sagesse
        scepticism 2:288–90, 8:503
    wisdom 9:754
Charron, W.C. 9:435
Chartres, School of 2:290–2
    Clarembald of Arras 2:376–7
    Encyclopedists, medieval 3:306
Charvet, J. 8:376
Chase, A. 3:726
Chase, C. 2:812

Chase, Martha 6:458
Chastain, C. 8:163
chastity 4:554
Chatelaine, E. 2:800
Châtillon, J. 4:520, 8:314
Chatman, S. 6:657
Chatterjee, M. 3:843
Chatterjee, P. 8:41
Chatterjee, S.C. 4:105, 8:610
Chatton, Walter 2:292–4
    Gregory of Rimini 4:171
    indivisibilism (Bradwardine, T.)
        1:864
    Wodeham, A. 9:773, 9:774, 9:775
Chattopadhyaya, D.P. 4:439, 6:180–1
Chaucer, Geoffrey 9:449
Chaudhuri, R. 3:859
Chaumartin, F.-R. 8:682
Chauviré, R. 1:798
Cheetham, M. 1:452
Chejne, A. 4:621
Chellas, B.F. 2:889–90, 4:720, 6:425
Chelpanov, Georgii 6:794, 6:797
chemistry 2:294–300
    alchemy 1:156, 1:157
    atomism
        ancient Greek 2:294, 2:295
        nineteenth century 2:296–8
        thermodynamics 2:296, 2:297–8
    corpuscularianism
        Boyle, R. 1:853, 1:855–6
        Descartes, R. 2:295–6
    Duhem, P.M.M. 3:143
    matter 6:195
    quantum mechanics 2:298–9
    vitalism 9:640–1
Ch'en, J. 6:140
Ch'en, K. 2:92
Chemparathy, G. 7:64
Chen Baisha see Chen Xianzhang
Chen Beixi 5:43
Chen Chun 9:400
Chen Daqi 2:539, 2:547
Chen Duxiu 6:134, 6:135
Chen Xianzhang (Chen Baisha)
    6:771–2
cheng (integrity or sincerity) 2:300,
    4:221, 9:862–3
Cheng Hao 2:300–2
    Cheng Yi 2:302
    neo-Confucianism 6:769
    self-cultivation 8:622–3
Cheng Hsnan see Zheng Xuan
Ch'eng I see Cheng yi
Ch'eng Ming-tao see Cheng Hao
Cheng Yi 2:302–3
    cheng 2:300

Cheng Hao 2:301
emotion
   self-cultivation 8:623
Korean Confucianism 2:563–4
li 5:594–5
neo-Confucianism 6:769
xin (trustworthiness) 9:816
Yijing 9:829–30
Ch'eng Yi-ch'uan *see* Cheng yi
Chengguan 2:87, 9:870
Cheng-Zhu School of neo-
  Confucianism 2:325–6, 2:556,
  2:558–9, 6:771
Chenu, M.-D. 1:347, 5:249, 6:705,
  7:437
Chern, S.-S. 4:32
Cherniak, Christopher
  rational beliefs †8:61–4
Cherniss, H. 7:428, 7:437–8, 9:90,
  9:807
Chernyshevskii, Nicolai Gavrilovich
  2:303–6
  partiinost' 7:239, 7:240
  Russian Hegelianism 4:305–6
  Russian Marxism 2:303
  Russian materialism 8:415, 8:418
  Russian nihilism 7:6
Cherry, C. 4:789
Chesterton, G.K. 9:224–5, 9:229,
  9:386
Chevalley, Catherine
  Bohr, N. 1:822
  Helmholtz, H. von †4:337–40
ch'i see qi
chi see qi
Chia I *see* Jia yi
chicanos (Mexican Americans)
  marginality 6:99
Chicherin, Boris 4:306, 5:607
Chico, C.A. 5:865
Chierchia, G. 7:766, 8:652
Chih *see* Zhi
Chih Tun *see* Zhi Dun
Chihara, C. 2:638, 4:115, 6:189, 8:49
Chih-i *see* Zhiyi
Chilcote, R.L. 2:170
child development
  see also cognitive development;
  developmental psychology; infant
  cognition
  child's theory of mind **6:385–90**
  false beliefs 6:385–8
  infant cognition 2:390–2
  language aquisition 9:524
  moral **6:504–5**
    Rousseau, J.-J. 8:372
  Piaget, J. 7:383–5

pretend play 6:385, 6:387
psychoanalysis
  post-Freudian 7:818–20,
  7:821–2
  Vygotskii, L.S. 9:673–4
Child, W. 1:279–80
children
  see also child development; child's
  theory of mind; family
  intergenerational sex 8:724
  mischievous
    semiotic distortions induced by
    8:676
Childress, J.F.
  bioethics 1:776
  ethics
    medical 6:263
    nursing 7:56, 7:57
    professional 7:736
child's theory of mind **6:385–90**
Chile
  analytical philosophy 1:232
  phenomenology 7:350
  positivism 7:568
Chillingworth, William **2:307–9**
  faith/reason relationship 5:677
Chin Arn-ping 2:771
China **2:315–28**
  aesthetics **1:68–75**
    calligraphy 1:68–9, 1:71–2
    ethico-aesthetics 1:68–9
    literati style 1:73–4
    order 2:317, 2:326
    painting 1:68–9, 1:71, 1:72–3
    poetry 1:68–71
  art **1:68–75**
  Buddhism 2:66, **2:80–92**, 2:315,
    2:325
    *Awakening of Faith in
      Mahāyāna* 1:603
    Confucianism 2:326
    Daoism 3:532–3, 9:866
    Fazang 3:568–9
    li 5:594
    mysticism 6:622–3
    neo-Confucianism 6:764–7
    Platform Sutra **7:398–9**
    poetry 1:68, 1:70
    self-cultivation 8:619–21
    Sengzhao 8:682–4
    xin 9:816
    Zhi Dun 9:859
    Zhiyi 9:859, 9:860–1
    Zongmi 9:870–1
  Cheng Hao **2:300–2**
  Cheng Yi **2:302–3**
  Christianity 3:192

classics **2:309–15**
Confucianism 2:319–20, **2:536–49**
Confucius **2:565–70**
correlative thinking 2:317–18
Dai Zhen **2:770–1**
dao **2:778–9**
democracy 2:327
Dong Zhongshu **3:111–13**
Fazang **3:568–9**
Han Feizi **4:219–20**
Han Yu **4:221–2**
history, philosophy of **4:446–52**
Huainanzi **4:512–14**
Hundred Schools 2:322–3
Jia Yi **5:102–3**
knowledge 2:318–19
law and ritual **5:442–54**
Legalist philosophy **5:531–8**
Linji **5:645–6**
logic **5:693–706**
Lu Xiangshan **5:851–3**
Manicheism 6:74, 6:76
May Fourth uprising 2:326
Mencius **6:302–4**
modern 2:326–7
Mohist philosophy **6:451–8**
Mozi **6:590–1**
mysticism 6:622–3
neo-Confucianism **6:764–76**
Offical Histories 4:446–7, 4:448–9
self-cultivation **8:613–26**
Sengzhao **8:682–4**
Shao Yong **8:736–7**
Sunzi **9:230–2**
Wang Chong **9:679–80**
Wang Fuzhi **9:680–2**
Wang Yangming **9:682–4**
Western philosophy comparison
  3:192–3, 3:194, 3:195
Xunzi **9:818–20**
Yang Xiong **9:821–2**
Yangzhu **9:822–3**
Yogācāra Buddhism 2:66, 9:792
Zhang Zai **9:856–7**
Zheng Xuan **9:857–8**
zhi 9:858
Zhi Dun 9:859
Zhiyi **9:859–61**
Zhou Dunyi **9:862–3**
Zhu Xi **9:863–5**
Zongmi **9:870–2**
Chinese Marxism *see* Marxism,
  Chinese
Chinese room argument **2:328–9**,
  9:395
  conceptual role semantics 8:653
  systems reply 2:328–9

Ching, J. 5:852
Chinul **2:329–32**
  post-enlightenment cultivation
    2:112
  hwadu 2:113–14
  Hwaôm synthesis 2:112–13
  Korean Buddhism assimilation
    2:111–12, 2:117
Chiodi, P. 8:479
Chisholm, Roderick Milton **2:332–5**
  a priori 1:5
  adverbial theory of mental states
    2:333, 6:317
  adverbs 1:48, 1:50
  axiology 1:611
  Brentano, F. †2:12–17
  certainty 2:266, 2:267
  commonsensism †2:453–5
  deontic logic 2:890
  dualism 3:138
  eliminativism 3:265
  empiricism 3:303
  epistemic justification 5:164, 8:130
  epistemology 3:364–5
  epistemology and ethics 3:370
  evil, problem of 3:472
  false propositions 4:58
  foundationalism 3:381, 3:723
  free will 3:751
  intellectual duty 7:36, 7:38
  intentionality 4:817–18, 4:820–1
  internalism/externalism distinction
    4:825
  knowledge
    concept of 5:275
    defeasibility theory of 5:277,
      5:279
  perception 3:381, 7:295, 7:298
  perceptual beliefs 3:301
  phenomenalism
    critique of 3:381, 7:332, 7:333
  rationalism 8:79
  religious experience 8:255
Chittick, W.C. 4:605, 6:619–20
Chiu Hungdah 5:454
Chiyông 9:442
Chizhevskii, D.I. 4:306
Cho Kwangjo 2:557
Chodkiewicz, M. 4:605, 6:620
Chodorow, Nancy 3:587, 3:613
Ch'oe Che-u 9:441
Ch'oe Han-gi 8:797
Ch'oe, Yông-Ho
  Chông Yagyong †2:341–3
  Korean Confucian philosophy
    2:565
  sirhak †8:796–8

Tonghak †9:441–2
Yi Yulgok 9:827
Chogye School of Buddhism
  2:329–31
choice
  see also autonomy; will
  existentialism 3:493
  moral
    relative/neutral agent
      distinction 6:645–6
  paternalism 7:251–2
  rational choice theory 8:64–73
  social *see* social choice
  virtuous action (Aristotle) 1:428
choice, axiom of **1:612–14**
  forcing 3:693–4
  glossary 5:797–8
  Polish logic 7:495
  proof theory 7:746
  set theory 8:700, 8:701–2
  Zermelo, E. 9:853
Chomarat, J. 4:540
Chomiak, M.B. 8:428
Chomsky, Noam **2:335–41**
  anaphora 1:239–40, 1:243
  behaviourism 1:698
  Cordemoy, G. de 2:674
  language
    animals 1:270, 1:273
    cognitive development 2:394
    conventionality of 5:370–1
    early modern philosophy of
      5:378
    I-languages 2:340–1, 5:417–18
    innateness of 2:336, 4:51–4
      empiricist response 6:674
      learning theory 5:486
      nativism 6:672, 6:673–4,
        6:675
      Skinner, B.F. 8:801
      unconscious mental states
        9:522, 9:524–5, 9:526
    knowledge of 2:338–9
  learning
    algorithmic procedures 5:486
    mental representation 4:839,
      4:842
    social nature of 5:417–18, 5:419
  learning 5:487
  ontological commitment 7:117
  syntax 5:408, 8:649, 9:246, 9:249,
    9:252–3
  tacit knowledge 5:286, 5:287
  transformational grammar
    2:336–8
  type/token distinction 9:510, 9:511
Ch'ôndogyo *see* Tonghak

Chông Sông-ch'ôl 8:797
Chông Yagyong (Tasan) **2:341–5**
  sirhak 2:558, 8:796, 8:797
Chopp, Rebecca 3:622, 3:623, 3:624
chora 5:306
Choromokos, J. 3:315
Chou Tun-i *see* Zhou Dunyi
Choueiri, Youssef
  Islamic fundamentalism †5:9–5:12
Chouillet, A.-M. 3:69
Chouillet, J. 3:69
Chrisman, L. 7:583
Christ *see* Jesus Christ
Christensen, F.M. 5:644
Christian realism (Niebuhr, R.) 6:841,
  6:843–4
Christian socialism (Barth, K.)
  1:651–2
Christian, W.A. 7:714, 9:718
Christianity
  see also Bible; Eastern Orthodox
    Christianity; Gnosticism; Gospels;
    Manicheism; Methodism; New
    Testament; patristic philosophy;
    Protestantism; Puritanism;
    Reformation; Roman Catholicism;
    Thomism
  the Absolute 1:28
  African religion relationship 1:120
  agape
    friendship relationship 3:795
  alienation 1:179
  ancient theology
    influence of 3:655–6
  anthropolatry (Leont'ev, K.N.)
    5:569–70
  anti-Semitism 1:313
  apologeticism (Bonnet, C.) 1:839
  Aristotelianism
    Aquinas, T. 6:699–700, 6:703
    Augustinianism debate 1:561–3
    Averroism conflict 1:596
    Kilwardby, R. 5:245, 5:248
    medieval
      conflict 1:398–9
      synthesis of 1:394, 1:395
    Trinity (Philoponus) 7:375–6
  asceticism 1:518, 8:455–6
  atonement 1:536–40
  Augustinianism 1:541, 1:559–64
  Averroism conflict 1:595–7
  baptism 8:455
  Bultmann, R. 2:127
  Byzantine philosophy 2:162–4
  charity 2:280–1
  China 3:192

church
  power of (Suárez, F.) 9:193
  state relationship 7:504,
    7:507–8, 7:509
clandestine literature 2:374–5
conflicts within 9:520
contextualization
  morality 8:222
conversion from Judaism 6:333
cosmology
  Platonism 7:435–6
creation 2:696–8, 5:310
critiques of
  Celsus 2:264
  Duran, P. 3:170–1
  Feuerbach, L.A. 3:635, 3:636–7,
    4:283
  Foucault, M. 3:712
  Hegelianism 4:282–3
  Ibn Shem Tov, Shem Tov ben
    Joseph 8:739
  Kireevskii, I. 8:808–9
  Porphyry 7:546
cultural crisis (Jung, C.G.) 5:134
death (Rozanov, V.V.) 8:383, 8:384
decline (Nietzsche, F.W.) 6:852
defence (More, H.) 6:576, 6:580–1
deism 2:854–5
  Butler, J. 2:154, 2:157–9
doctrinal disputes
  Carolingian 2:222
early
  see also patristic philosophy
  Graeco-Roman influence
    7:254–5, 7:256
  Origen 7:160–1
  religious legitimacy 7:259
  Tertullian, Q.S.F. 9:307–9
  Themistius 9:324–5
education
  Aquinas, T. 3:225
  Augustine 3:225
  spiritual development 8:457
emanationism 2:696–7
Epicureanism (Valla, L.) 9:569–71
eschatology 3:414–15, 3:416
eternity of the world 2:697–8
ethics (Bonhoeffer, D.) 1:835,
  1:836
Eusebius 3:456–8
evil
  Socratic influence 3:464
exclusivism 8:260–1, 8:262–3
existentialist theology 3:506–7,
  3:508
faith 3:538–43, 9:327–9

free choice (Dostoevskii, F.M.)
  3:116
Godmanhood (Solov'ëv, V.S.) 9:29
heaven 4:249–52
hell 4:329–32
hope 4:507
humanism 4:528, 4:529
Incarnation and Christology
  4:725–32
inclusivism 8:261
influence of
  African ethical systems 3:434
  Judaism
    Albo, J. 1:153
    al-Muqammas, D. 6:605
    Philo of Alexandria 7:360
    Plotinus 7:462
influenced by
  ancient philosophy 1:262, 1:265
  ancient theology 3:655–6
  Neoplatonism 8:240
  Proclus 7:730
innocence 4:797
Islam relationship
  Ibn Kammuna 4:621–2
  Liber de causis 5:596
Japan 5:658
Judaism comparison (Ibn
  Kammuna) 4:621–2
Kabbalism (Pico della
  Mirandola, G.) 7:386, 7:389,
  7:390
liberation theology 5:613–17
logos 5:819
love 5:843, 5:844–5
Marxism relationship
  African philosophy,
    Anglophone 1:99–1:100
medieval philosophy relationship
  6:269, 6:271, 6:272, 6:275–6
miracles (Campbell, G.) 2:192
morality
  emotions 6:561
  William of Ockham 9:744–5
mysteries 9:428
mysticism 6:623–5, 8:254
natural religion (Paley, W.) 7:186–8
negative theology 6:759–62
Neoplatonism
  Encyclopedists, medieval 3:305
  Marius Victorinus 6:105
  Pseudo-Dionysius 7:804–6
  'New' (Saint-Simon) 8:447
Nietzsche, F.W. reconciliation
  (Merezhkovskii, D.) 6:862–3
nihilism 7:1–2

non-religious interpretation
  (Bonhoeffer, D.) 1:836
Origen 7:161–2
original sin 8:793–5
pagan philosophy
  banning of 1:262, 1:264–5,
    8:788
pan-Africanism 7:192, 7:193
Philoponus 7:371–8
pietism 7:392–6
Platonism
  medieval 7:431–2
    Carolingian renaissance
      2:221–2
    Clement of Alexandria
      2:383–4
    Eriugena, J.S. 3:402
    William of Conches 9:730,
      9:731
  Renaissance 1:25, 7:443–4
    Council of Ferrara/Florence
      7:442–4
    critiques of Renaissance
      Platonism 7:442
    George of Trebizond 4:34,
      4:35
    Pico della Mirandola, G.
      7:388, 7:389–90
pluralism 8:263
pneuma (spirit)
  New Testament usage 7:470,
    7:471–2
  Trinity 7:472
political influence of 8:224,
  8:225–7
political philosophy
  history of
    medieval philosophy 7:508–9
    natural rights 7:511–12
    The Reformation 7:510–11
    Roman Empire 7:504,
      7:507–8
pragmatism 7:634
process theism 7:716–20
prophecy 7:769
providence 7:798–9
purgatory 7:836–9
reinterpretation of (Strauss, D.F.)
  9:164–5, 9:166
as the religion of nature
  (Tindal, M.) 9:421, 9:422
resurrection 8:38, 8:294
revelation
  Bible as 8:297–300
  Butler, J. 2:158
  denial of 8:297
  Jesus Christ 8:297

right and good
    imperative concept 8:323–4
Russian religious-philosophical
    Renaissance 8:422–5
sacraments **8:442–5**
salvation 8:450
science 8:230–1
    Boethius of Dacia 1:813, 1:814
    cosmology 8:233
    early church 8:230
    epistemology 8:231–2
    evolutionary theory 8:232
    geological history 8:232
    medieval natural philosophy
        6:694
    metaphysics 8:231
    postcolonial philosophy of
        7:576
    unity of 9:530
sexuality 8:720–2, 8:724
sin 8:791–2
slavery 8:804
social sphere (Chaadaev, P.I.)
    2:271
soul
    immortality of 9:45, 9:47
Stoicism (Blair, H.) 1:782
suffering 9:214
supererogation 9:232
symbolism (Tillich, P.) 9:411, 9:412
theism 4:96–7
theosophy 9:363–4
Tolstoian 9:439
Trinity **9:457–61**
truth
    Dostoevskii, F.M. 3:118
    Frank, S.L. 3:728
virtues 9:326–30
    Hume, D. critique 4:552
    Vysheslavtsev, B.P. 9:676
war 9:192–3, 9:688
wisdom 9:753–4
Christianson, P. 8:605
Christie, N. 2:710
Christine de Pizan **2:343–5**, 3:577,
    3:583
Christman, J. 1:591
Christmas, Simon
    intensionality †4:810–11
Christodoulidis, Emilios A.
    Dworkin, R. †3:187–9
Christoff, P.K. 8:811
Christology **4:725–32**
    see also Incarnation; Jesus Christ
    heresies 4:727–8
    liberation theology 5:615
    monophysite (Philoponus) 7:375

New Testament 4:726–7
    Nicholas of Cusa 6:835
    orthodox doctrine 4:725–8
Christopher, P. 1:558
chromosome theory 4:13–14
Chronbach, L. 7:135
Chrysippus **2:345–6**
    consequence 2:600, 2:602
    logic 5:861
    signification 8:676
    Stoicism 9:142, 9:143, 9:151
Chrysorrhoas see John of Damascus
Chrysostom, John see John
    Chrysostom
Chu Hsi see Zhu xi
Ch'ü T'ung-tsu 5:454
Chuang Tzu see Yangzhu
Chudy, W. 7:488
Chung, E.Y.J. 9:827
Chung Yung see Zhongyong
Chunqiu (Spring and Autumn
    Annals) 2:309, 2:310, 2:311, 2:312
    see also *Gongyangzhuan*;
    Guliangzhuan; *Zuozhuan*
    history, philosophy of 4:448
Chunqiufanlu (Luxuriant Dew of the
    Annals) 3:111
Church, Alonzo **2:346–9**
    see also Church numerals; Church-
    Rosser theorem; Church's
    theorem; Church's thesis; Church-
    Turing thesis
    analyticity 1:238
    computability and information
        2:482
    computer science 2:492–4, 2:495–6
    lambda calculus 5:346, 5:347,
        5:349
    logic 4:806, 4:810, 5:736
    paradoxes of set and property
        7:215, 7:220
    Post, E.L. 7:575
    predicate calculus 7:664
    property theory 7:766
    second- and higher-order logics
        8:595, 8:602, 8:603
    sense and reference 8:687
    sentences 7:788
    theory of types 9:360, 9:361–2
    verificationist theory of meaning
        1:615–16, 1:618
Church of England
    Farrer, A.M. 3:560–1
Church numerals 5:347
Church, R.W. 6:66

Churchland, Patricia Smith
    computational theories of mind
        6:394
    connectionism 2:577
    eliminativism 1:709, 3:265
    emotions 3:285
    reduction, problems of 8:148
Churchland, Paul M.
    artificial intelligence 1:492
    connectionism 2:577
    eliminativism 1:708, 1:709, 3:265
    Freud, S. 3:793
    information
        non-propositional 6:723–4,
            6:727
    introspection 4:842, 4:845
    materialism 6:177
    models 6:446
    modularity of mind 6:451
    propositional attitudes 7:786
    reductionism, philosophy of mind
        8:153
    scientific theories 9:352
    social science
        methodology of 8:867
    soul 9:48
Church-Rosser theorem 2:432, 5:347
Church's theorem
    see also Church-Turing thesis
    decision problem **2:349–51**
    glossary 5:799
    Peirce, C.S. 5:726
Church's thesis 2:347, **2:351–5**
    Church's theorem 2:349–50
    lambda calculus 5:347
    Russian constructivism 2:634
Church-Turing thesis 1:485, 2:493,
    5:799, 9:493–4
Chwistek, L. 7:495, 7:497, 8:402–3,
    9:362
Ciafardone, R. 9:321
Cicero, Marcus Tullius 1:262,
    2:355–60
    Academy 1:36
    Antiochus 1:301
    Arcesilaus 1:354
    Carneades 2:219
    Cleanthes 2:383
    doxography 3:126
    Epicureanism 3:349
    fatalism 3:564
    free will 3:751
    friendship 3:795, 3:797
    God, concepts of 4:101
    Hellenistic philosophy 4:336
    humanist ethics 2:358
    justice 5:146

natural theology 2:357–8
Panaetius 7:190
perfect-being theology 4:96
Philo of Larissa 7:363
political philosophy 7:506–8, 7:517
Ramus, P. 8:53
republicanism 2:356–7, 8:280,
    8:281, 8:282
rhetoric 8:306, 8:309
scepticism 2:357, 8:499, 8:502
Socrates 9:18
Stoicism 9:159–60
translations by 9:455
true law 5:143
universalism in ethics 9:536, 9:538
Valla, L. 9:573
Cichetti, D. 7:822
Cicourel, A.V. 3:519, 3:520
Cieszkowski, August von 2:360–2,
    4:283, 4:306
Ciliberto, M. 2:38
Cilicia
    Chrysippus 2:345–6
    Simplicius 8:788–91
cinema see film
Cioffi, F. 1:515
Cioran, E.M. 7:3, 7:4
ciphers
    Jaspers, K. 5:81
circular definition 2:847–8
circular reasoning
    fallacies 3:544–5
circumstantial implication
    as source of knowledge
        Indian thought 5:282–3
citizenship 2:362–5
    see also community; nation;
    obligation, political; society
    consent 2:598
    democratic theory 2:362–3
    'differentiated' 2:364–5
    federalism 3:572
    feminist political philosophy
        Dietz, M.G. 3:620
        Wollstonecraft, M. 3:616
    Greek political philosophy
        (Aristotle) 7:506
    identity 2:362, 2:364–5
    liberty (Tocqueville, A. de) 9:424
    responsibilities 2:363–4, 8:293
cittas (apperceptive vectors) 2:72–3
Ciudad, Mario 7:350, 7:351
Ciufolini, I. 9:68–9
civic virtue
    republicanism 8:282
civil disobedience 2:366–9
    definition 2:366–7

green political philosophy 4:163
justification 2:366, 2:367–8
transcendentalism (Thoreau, H.D.)
    9:389–90
war 9:687
civil law
    see also Roman law
    commentators 1:658
    origins of 8:343
    rationalization of (Pothier, R.J.)
        7:608
civil liberty
    republicanism (Witherspoon, J.)
        9:756
civil science
    Hobbes, T. 4:463, 4:465, 4:471–3,
        4:474–5
civil society 2:369–72
    bourgeois public sphere
        (Habermas, J.) 4:194
    citizenship 2:363
    corruption 2:675, 2:676
    critiques of 2:370–1
    Marxist analysis 6:144
    neo-Marxist revival 2:370
    polis (Aristotle) 7:506
    sovereignty (Rousseau, J.-J.)
        9:57–8
    state relationship (Oakeshott, M.J.)
        7:72
civilian tradition
    Roman law
        political philosophy
            history of 7:507
civilization
    culture 2:748
    legal idealism 5:512
Cixous, Hélène 2:372–4
    feminist literary criticism 3:612
Claeys, G. 7:186
Clagett, M.
    Blasius of Parma 1:787
    Koyré, A. 5:297
    measurement, theory of 6:249
    mechanics, Aristotelian 6:251
    natural philosophy
        medieval 6:705
    Oxford Calculators 7:182
Clair, O. 8:342–3
Clair, P. 5:332
clairvoyance
    see also mediums
    paranormal phenomena 7:221–2
    Steiner, R. 9:133
clandestine literature 2:374–6
Claparde, É. 1:840

Clapiers, L. de, Marquis de
    Vauvenargues 6:555, 6:556–8
Clarembald of Arras 2:376–8
Clarence Smith, J.A. 1:659
Claridade
    Cabral, A. 2:170
clarificatory theology 6:711–12
Clark, A. 3:108
Clark, A.J. 1:492, 2:427, 2:577
Clark, E.A. 7:163
Clark, E.G. 4:599
Clark, F. 1:772
Clark, H. 7:631
Clark, J. 3:336
Clark, J.H. 5:20
Clark, J.M. 6:288
Clark, J.P. 4:125, 9:141
Clark, K. 1:645, 3:409
Clark, M. 4:155, 4:566, 7:188
Clark, Maudemarie
    Nietzsche, F.W. †6:844–61
Clark, M.T.
    Marius Victorinus 6:106
Clark, P. 3:793, 7:844
Clark, R.C. 4:384
Clark, R.W. 8:403
Clark, S.R.L. 1:324
Clarke, A. 4:19
Clarke, B.L. 6:319
Clarke, D.M. 3:18, 8:343
Clarke, J.H. 7:194
Clarke, P.B. 2:365
Clarke, Samuel 2:378–80
    Collins, A. 2:417
    deism 2:853–4, 2:855
    God
        divine freedom 3:761
        existence of 4:87, 4:92, 8:241
        as necessary being 6:747
        omnipresence 7:107
    religion, history of philosophy of
        8:246
    Wollaston, W. 9:788
Clarke, S.G.
    examples in ethics 3:490
Clarke, S.H.
    Ricouer, P. 8:322
Clarke, T. 3:124
Clarkson, G.E. 5:469
class
    see also caste
    alienation (Marx, K.) 7:516
    conflict
        Cabral, A. 2:169
        Engels, F. 3:310–11
        Italian Marxism 5:335
        race, theories of 8:19

Confucianism, Japanese 2:553,
2:554
Confucius 5:447–8
consciousness
Lukács, G. 5:857–8
Marxism 6:141
education
Marxism 3:236
Plato 3:223–4
elites/masses relationship (Ortega
y Gasset, J.) 7:167
hegemony 4:152–3
historical materialism
Chinese Marxism 6:134–5
humanism
Chinese Marxism 6:138–9
Korea 8:796
Marxism 6:142
education 3:236
Latin America 6:160, 6:162,
6:163–4
Lukács, G. 6:143–4
partiinost' 7:239
psychological structure of (Saint-
Simon) 8:446
ruling (Marx, K.) 6:118, 6:125
sensitivity to (Camus, A.) 2:195
social theory and law 8:875–6
working
Marxism in Latin America
6:160, 6:162, 6:163
Zionism
socialist 9:869
Classen, C.J.
Anaximander 1:259
Aristippus the Elder 1:380
physis and nomos debate 7:382
Protagoras 7:790
Sophists 9:34
Thales 9:324
Xenophanes 9:810
classical conditioning see
conditioning
classical field theory see field theory,
classical
classical mechanics see mechanics,
classical
classical scepticism see Academic
scepticism
classification
see also categories; taxonomy;
typology
factors of experience
Ābhidharmika Schools 2:53,
2:54–6
Lévi-Strauss, C. 5:583
linguistic discrimination 5:641–2

Linnaeus, C. von 5:646–50
manifoldness, Jaina theory of
6:79–80
Maxwell, J.C. 6:207
natural kinds 6:682–4
situation semantics 8:670–1
species 9:78–80
structuralism in linguistics 9:179
Clauberg, J. 5:717
Clauberg, Johannes 2:380–2
Claudius Ptolemaeus see Ptolemy
Claudius Severus 6:94
Claus, D.B. 7:811
Clay, D. 3:90, 3:351, 5:854, 5:855
Clayton, G. 9:229
Clayton, J.P. 9:464
Cleanthes 2:382–3
Heraclitus 4:368–9
Cleave, J.P. 6:90
Clebsch, W. 1:205
Cleinomachus of Thurii 9:22
Clement of Alexandria 2:383–5
divine simplicity 8:787
faith 3:542
Gnosticism 4:83
influenced by
ancient philosophy 1:265
patristic philosophy 7:257–8
purgatory 7:837
Clendenning, J. 8:381
Cleomedes 2:385–6
Clerval, A. 2:291
client-centred therapy
Rogers, C. 7:828
Cliff, D. 1:492
Cliff, T. 9:466
Clifford, J. 1:65
Clifford, R.J. 2:699–700
Clifford, W.K.
epistemology
and ethics 3:369–70
justification 5:164
evidentialism
religious belief 8:212, 8:245,
9:329
God
existence of 4:92
relativity theory
philosophical significance of
8:198
religion
epistemology 8:218
history of philosophy of 8:246
theological virtues 9:330
Clifton, T. 6:612
Clines, D.J.A. 4:394
Cloeren, J.-J. 8:188

cloning
ethics 4:19, 6:260
Clooney, F.X. 8:461
closure clauses
inductive definitions and proofs
4:752, 4:753
closure principle see deductive
closure principle
Clothier, C.M. 4:19
Clouds see Aristophanes
Clowes, E. 6:866
Cloyd, E.L. 6:474
Clucas, S. 2:263
Coady, C.A.J.
Australia, philosophy in †1:574–8
moral standing 6:554
social epistemology 8:832
testimony †9:309–14
violence †9:615–17
Coakley, S. 9:464
Coase, R.H. 7:760
Coase's Theorem
economics and law 5:454–7
property 7:760
Coates, J. 5:367
Cobb, J.B. 7:714–15, 7:720
Cobos, Bernabé 5:430, 5:432
Cocchiarella, Nino B.
property theory †7:761–7
tense logic 9:307
theory of types †9:359–62
Cockburn, Catharine 2:386–7
Code, Lorraine
epistemology
feminist 3:381, †3:596–602,
5:275
virtue 9:619, 9:621
codes of practice
engineering ethics 3:313, 3:314–15
professional ethics 5:126, 7:735
social science research 9:578–9
codification
critique by Savigny, F.K. von 8:483
history of 5:466
legal hermeneutics 5:508
Coe, D.M. 5:432
coercion 2:387–90
compulsion distinction 2:387
limits of 9:432
sexuality 8:724–5
toleration contrast 9:431
coextensionality
adverbs 1:49
Coffa, J. Alberto
a priori 1:5
Bolzano, B. 1:827
Carnap, R. 2:215

explanation 3:523, 3:524
logical positivism 5:794
scientific theories 9:352
cogency of sequence
    Gurney, E. 4:188–9
cogito ergo sum
    Arnauld, A. 1:444–5
    Descartes, R. 3:1, 3:7–8
    Geulincx, A. 4:60
    Huet, P.-D. 4:515
    method of doubt 3:374
cognition
    see also infant cognition; mind;
        reasoning; thinking
    abstractive/intuitive (Blasius of
        Parma) 1:785–6
    Aquinas, T. 1:335–8
    Aristotelianism
        Renaissance 1:407–8
    art and truth 1:458–9
    Augustine 1:542, 1:546–7
    Aureol, P. 1:566
    Brahman
        Indian monism 6:477
    cognitive architecture **2:392–3**
    computational theory of
        connectionism 2:570–6
    conditional platforms of
        understanding (Oakeshott, M.J.)
        7:71
    consciousness
        Yogācāra Buddhism 2:72–4
    dialectics (Il'enkov, E.V.) 4:689
    divine illumination
        Augustinianism 1:562
    emotions 3:273–4, 3:275
    enlightenment
        Yogācāra Buddhism 2:71,
            2:73–4
    error
        Indian concepts of 3:412–13
        Yogācāra Buddhism 2:65–6
    ethology
        innate releasing mechanisms
            6:674
    Gaṅgeśa 3:843–5
    Gestalt psychology
        higher order perceptual
            processing 4:52–3
    humour 4:565
    imagination 4:707
    implicit/explicit distinction 5:287
    inaccuracy of
        Buddhism, Indian 2:97
    infant *see* infant cognition
    intellective
        scepticism 2:693

intentional objects
    Hervaeus Natalis 4:403
introspection, psychology of 4:845
intuition (Lossky, N.O.) 5:833,
    5:835
intuitive/abstractive distinction
    Aureol, P. 1:565
    Chatton/Campsall debate 2:293
    Duns Scotus, J. 1:565–6, 3:154,
        3:165–6
    John of Mirecourt 5:112
karma
    Yogācāra Buddhism 2:64, 2:66,
        2:69–70
knowledge as species of
    Indian philosophy 5:280
language of thought hypothesis
    5:404–7
learning 5:483–7
logic of (Cohen, H.) 2:399
materiality
    Yogācāra Buddhism 2:71–2
medieval attitudes to 6:274
mental constructions
    Yogācāra Buddhism critique
        2:68–9, 2:72
mental faculties (Ibn Sina)
    4:649–50
mental imagery 4:703–5
methods of
    Nyāya 3:860
    Mīmāṃsā 6:378–9
modularity of mind 6:450–1
musical expressiveness 4:189–90
Nicholas of Cusa 6:834–5
Olivi, P.J. 7:95–6
origins of 2:394
pattern matching
    reliabilism 8:207–8
perception relationship
    Yoruba epistemology 9:832
Platonic theory (Cudworth, R.)
    2:741–2
pragmatism 7:637
racial differences in
    African philosophy,
        Anglophone 1:98–9
realism/antirealism 8:117–18
representationalism (Buridan, J.)
    2:133
responsibility 6:67–8
sense perception 4:179
sensitive–intellectual opposition
    (Kant, I.) 5:182
sensory
    Yogācāra Buddhism 2:68
stages of (Tetens, J.N.) 9:320–1

Turing machines 9:494
types of (Dharmakīrti) 3:52
universals
    Indian theories of 9:546
verbal
    Indian philosophy 6:241
veridicality
    Indian epistemology 3:388,
        3:389–91
will
    role of (Locke, J.) 5:676
    William of Auvergne 9:726
cognitive anthropology 1:297
cognitive architecture **2:392–3**,
    2:575–6
cognitive certainty
    Stoic-Academic debate 7:849,
        9:142, 9:151–2
cognitive development **2:393–5**
    see also child development; infant
        cognition
    human communication
        (Mead, G.H.) 6:211
    innate predispositions 2:394–5
    nativism 6:674
    Piaget, J. 7:383–5
cognitive ethology 1:272
cognitive faculties
    logic of 5:718
    religious belief
        Freud, S. 8:215–16
        Marx, K. 8:216
cognitive pluralism **2:395–8**
    descriptive 2:395–6
    evaluative-concept 2:396, 2:397
    normative 2:396–7, 3:360
cognitive psychology
    behaviourism 1:696
    common-sense reasoning 2:451
    music 6:609
    theory of mind 7:826–7
    visual perception 9:634–7
cognitive relativism
    morality 6:540
cognitive science
    contextualism 7:629–30
    psychology
        theories of 7:827
    reliabilism 8:205
cognitive significance
    see also meaning
    sense and reference 8:684–5
cognitivism
    see also noncognitivism
    analytic ethics 1:220
    discourse ethics 4:196–7

morality
  attitudes 6:534
  judgment 6:511–12
  knowledge 6:517–18
  natural law 6:686–7
  naturalism in ethics 6:713, 6:714
  practical reason 7:613–14
Cohen, Arthur A. 4:495, 4:497–8,
  5:95
Cohen, B. 8:439
Cohen, C. 9:595
Cohen, D. 6:389
Cohen de Herrera, Abraham see
  Herrera, Abraham Cohen de
Cohen, F.S. 8:483
Cohen, G.
  Maimonides, A. 6:40
Cohen, G.A.
  analytic philosophy 1:228
  dialectical materialism 3:57
  functionalism in social science
    3:815, 3:817
  libertarianism 5:619
  Marx, K. 6:126, 6:132
  Marxism 6:146
    philosophy of science 6:150
  Pareto principle 7:228
  socialism 8:885
Cohen, H.
  analysis 1:220
Cohen, Hermann 2:398–403
  aesthetics 6:781–2
  ethics 6:781
  Jewish philosophy 5:90
    contemporary 5:91, 5:95
    early nineteenth century 5:99
  Neo-Kantianism 6:776–7, 6:780,
    6:790
  Ortega y Gasset, J. 7:166
  religion 6:782
  thought 6:781
Cohen, I. 9:870
Cohen, I.B. 3:738, 5:297, 6:828, 9:532
Cohen, J. 4:344, 4:612
Cohen, Jean L.
  civil society †2:369–72
  contractarianism 2:665
  sociology
    theories of 9:7
Cohen, L.B.
  infant cognition 2:391
Cohen, L.J.
  law
    evidence and inference 5:505
    reasoning and interpretation
      5:530

probability, interpretations of
  7:705
reasoning
  rationality of belief 8:87, 8:88,
    8:89
Cohen, M. 2:777, 3:189
Cohen, M.N. 3:108
Cohen, M.R.
  fictionalism 3:668
  legal realism 5:524
  mechanics, Aristotelian 6:251
  Savigny, F.K. von 8:483
Cohen, Paul J.
  Boolean-valued models 1:845
  continuum hypothesis 2:657
  forcing 3:693, 3:695, 3:697
  Gödel, K. 4:107
  set theory 8:706, 8:707
Cohen, Philip 7:631
Cohen, R.A. 8:361
Cohen, Richard J.
  Vallabhācārya †9:573–5
Cohen, R.S.
  Hanson, N.R. 4:225
  Mach, E. 6:16
  Naturphilosophie 6:740
  Polish logic 7:500
  quantum mechanics,
    interpretation of 7:894
  Simmel, G. 8:780
  South Slavs, philosophy of 9:54–5
Cohen, Stewart
  contextualism
    epistemological 2:649
  scepticism †8:493–8
Cohen, Ted
  aesthetic concepts 1:58
  artistic taste †1:509–13
  Cavell, S. 2:260
  humour 4:566
  Kant, I. 5:196
Cohen-Solal, A. 8:479
coherence
  conjunction distinction 5:839–40
  Yogācāra Buddhism 3:389, 3:411
coherence theory of truth see truth,
  coherence theory of
coherentism see justification,
  epistemic, coherence theory of
Cohn, Jonas 6:777, 6:787–8, 6:790
Cohn-Sherbok, D.
  Hebrew Bible †1:766–9
Coimbra, Creso 7:349, 7:351
Coimbra, University of see
  Collegium Conimbricense

coincidence
  autoinfanticide
    time travel 9:417–18
  causal theory of knowledge 5:265
  Gettier problems 5:263–5
coincidentia oppositorum in deo
  (coincidence of opposites in God)
  6:832, 6:833–4
coitus see sexuality
Coke, Sir Edward 2:442, 2:446
Colapietro, V. 7:283
Cole, G.D.H. 2:464, 8:885
Cole, T. 4:146
Coleman, Janet
  John of Paris 5:114
Coleman, J.S.
  rational choice theory 8:74
  social action 8:823
  sociology
    theories of 9:7
  systems theory in social science
    9:256
Coleman, Jules
  economics and law †5:454–7
Coleman, W. 9:643
Coleridge, Samuel Taylor 2:403–6
  distinction-in-unity 2:404
  fiction 9:481
  ideal Realism 2:403
  Ideas 2:403–4
  poetry 7:476
  social criticism
    influence on Mill, J.S. 6:372
  truthfulness 9:485
Colie, R.L. 2:743–4, 5:476, 6:582
Colish, Marcia L.
  Peter Lombard †5:821–2
  Stoicism 9:160
  Thomas à Kempis 9:374
collapse theories
  quantum mechanics 7:893
collective action
  see also joint action
  rational choice theory 8:64–73
collective knowledge
  feminist epistemology 3:599
  social epistemology 8:830–1
collective unconscious
  Jung, C.G. 5:132
collectivity
  critique by Berdiaev, N.A. 1:730
  ethnophilosophy 3:447, 3:448
  honour 4:503
  moral agents 6:499, 6:502–3
  race
    theories of 8:19–20
  self-realization 8:632–3

solidarity 9:23–4
Collegium Conimbricense **2:406–8**
Aristotelianism
seventeenth century 1:387–8
philosophy in Portugal 2:8, 2:9
Colletti, Lucio 6:146
Collie, M. 4:595
Collier, Andrew
critical realism †2:720–2
Collier, Arthur **2:408–11**
Collin, Finn
Alfred Schütz †8:559–61
Scandinavia 8:492
Collingridge, David 9:282, 9:283
Collingwood, Robin George
2:411–15
aesthetics
concepts 1:58
and ethics 1:67, 1:68
experience 2:414
and morality 1:456
anthropology 1:299
Enlightenment, Scottish 3:329–30
Hegelianism 4:292
history
metaphysics 2:411, 2:412–13
philosophy of 4:444, 4:445,
4:456–7, 4:458
Prichard, H.A. 7:682
Collingwood, S.D. 3:108
Collini, S. 3:63
Collins, A.
psychology
theories of 7:825, 7:829
Collins, Anthony **2:415–19**
Clarke, S. 2:379
deism 2:854, 2:855–6
Tindal, M. 9:423
Collins, Harry 2:629, 9:2
Collins, J. 1:128, 5:243
Collins, P.H. 3:592, 3:602
Collins, R. 9:7
Collins, S. 5:217, 6:403
Collins, V. 9:756
Collinson, D. 5:20
Colmer, J. 2:406
Colombia
phenomenology 7:349–50
colonialism
see also decolonization;
imperialism; neo-colonialism
African ethical systems 3:430
African philosophy 1:97, 1:108–9
anti-slavery arguments
(Amo, A.W.) 1:210
Brazil 2:8

economic development
Cabral, A. 2:169–70
Fanon, F. 3:553–4
ethnophilosophy 3:446, 3:447
government (Hutcheson, F.) 4:592
Indian resistance to
Ramakrishna Movement
8:39–40
international law (Vitoria, F. de)
9:644–5
Latin America **5:421–6**
liberation theology 5:613
Mexico 6:345
postcolonialism comparison
7:578–9, 7:580
psychological effects on
indigeneous population
(Fanon, F.) 3:553
racism 3:553
Renaissance philosophy 8:264
violence against (Kaunda, K.)
1:101
Colonna d'Istria, F. 2:168
colour **2:419–28, 2:428–31**
experience of
optics 7:136, 7:137
linguistic classification 9:179
objective 2:419, 2:420–1
perception 7:296, 7:297–8, 8:172
scientific–perceptual conflict
2:428–9
secondary qualities 8:595–9
subjective 2:419–20, 2:421,
2:422–3, 2:424
constancy controversy 2:420–1
dispositional explanation 2:421
identity theory 2:421–3
inverted spectrum argument
2:424, 2:425
Combes, A. 4:47
Combès, J. 2:772
combinatorial set theory
axiom of constructibility 2:623–4
combinatory logic **2:431–4**
lambda calculus 5:346
Llull, R. 5:744
possible worlds 7:571
relevance logic 8:202
set theory 8:704–5
comedy **2:434–8**
see also humour
Aristophanes 7:731, 9:9, 9:18,
9:33–4
Epicharmus 3:336
tragedy comparison 2:434–6
Comenius, John Amos **2:438–40**,
2:765, 2:769

commentaries
philosophical training
(Philoponus) 7:371–2
commentators
Bartolist school 1:658
commercial society
political philosophy
history of 7:513–14
commercialism
journalism ethics 5:126
commissurotomy *see* split brains
commitment
honour 4:502–3
social unity (Marcel, G.) 6:92
Committee of the Harvard Medical
School 5:630
commodity fetishism
see also consumerism
Derrida, J. 2:900
Lukács, G. 5:857
Marx, K. 6:128–9
common good
public interest 7:833, 7:834
threats to (Rousseau, J.-J.) 3:227
common interest games *see*
coordination games
common knowledge *see* collective
knowledge
common law **2:440–6**
change/continuity paradox 2:440,
2:441–3, 2:445
as custom 2:440, 2:441, 5:466
English
artificial reason 8:874
equity 5:150–1
hermeneutics 8:604
historical jurisprudence 2:445
history of 8:343, 8:604
methodological conservatism
2:444–5
practice/theory contrast 2:443
common nature
individuation (Duns Scotus, J.)
3:154, 3:163–5
common notions *see* koinai ennoiai
common sense
conceptual systems (James, W.)
5:64–5
defence against scepticism
(Moore, G.E.) 6:496–7
ethics 9:647
explanation 3:814
historical development (Vico, G.)
9:604
non-rational soul
Islamic philosophy 9:41

psychoanalysis
  methodological issues in
    7:815–16
theory test
  Mohism 6:454–5
common sense morality *see*
  intuitionism
common sense philosophy
  ethics **2:448–51**, 9:551–2, 9:554
Common Sense School **2:446–8**
  Aberdeen Philosophical Society
    1:15
  American philosophy, eighteenth
    and nineteenth century 1:202
  anti-sceptical realism 3:633–4
  Beattie, J. 1:677–9
  Brown, T. 2:27
  Buffier, C. 2:119–20
  Campbell, G. 2:192
  critique by Priestley, J. 7:683
  Enlightenment, Scottish 3:327
  ethics 2:448–50
  Oswald, J. 7:168–9
  Reid, T. 2:447, 8:171–9, 9:135,
    9:136
  Stewart, D. 9:135–9, 9:137–8
commonality
  of being (Nancy, J.-L.) 6:651–2
  nominalism (Buridan, J.) 2:132–3
  Zhongyong (Doctrine of the Mean)
    9:861
common-sense realism
  moral intuitionism relationship
    (Prichard, H.A.) 7:680–1
common-sense reasoning 1:488,
  2:451–3, 8:61–2
commonsensism **2:453–5**
  Australia, philosophy in 1:576
  Hamilton, W. 4:217–18
  Moore, G.E. 3:379
  Peirce, C.S. 7:275
commonwealth
  civil philosophy (Hobbes, T.)
    4:459–60, 4:471–3
  Harrington, J. 4:231, 4:232–3
communal knowledge *see* collective
  knowledge
communalism
  African philosophy 1:100–1,
    3:430–1
  African philosophy 1:98–9,
    3:447
  Feuerbach, L.A. 3:635
  Jewish (Kaplan, M.) 5:204–6
  Tillich, P. 9:411–12
communication
  see also discourse; language;

linguistics; ordinary language
  philosophy; symbolic
  interactionism
animal language and thought
  1:272
awareness
  Indian theories of 1:607
communal language
  (Dummett, M.A.E.) 5:416
conversational maxims
  (Grice, H.P.) 4:723–4
dance 2:776–7
electronic
  hyperreal culture
    (Baudrillard, J.) 1:662–3
  information technology and
    ethics 4:778–81
existential (Jaspers, K.) 5:81
intention **2:455–9**
  Grice, H.P. 4:173–4
  pragmatics 7:628, 7:629
  speech acts 2:456–8, 9:83–4
intentional-inferential model
  7:628–9
levels of
  Yoruba epistemology 9:833
Mead, G.H. 6:210–11
and meaning **6:212–14**, 6:220
mind–language connection 5:409
performatives 7:303–4
private language argument 7:695
scientific
  methodological significance
    8:580
society 8:887–8
speech acts 9:81–6
structuralism 9:186
truthfulness 9:482
verbal
  dance 2:776–7
communication theory *see*
  information theory
communicative action
  Habermas, J. 4:194, 4:195–6
communicative ethics
  Habermas, J. 4:196–7
communicative rationality **2:459–62**
  Apel, K.-O. 2:459, 2:461
  Frankfurt School 2:459–60
  Frankfurt School (Habermas, J.)
    3:735
  legal reasoning 5:527–8
  social theory and law
    (Habermas, J.) 8:878
communism **2:462–4**
  see also Marx, K.; Marxism;
  socialism; Stalinism

anarchist (Kropotkin, P.A.)
  5:313–14
collapse of
  utopianism 9:560
distribution of resources 2:463
Engels, F. 3:310–11
feminism 3:579–80
Feuerbach, L.A. 3:637–8
Gramsci, A. 4:151
Lukács, G. 5:856–7
Marx, K. 6:118–19
monastic 2:462–3
Popper, K.R. 7:536
religious perspective of 9:409
scientific socialism 3:309, 3:311
social democracy comparison
  8:827
communitarianism **2:464–71**, 7:527–8
  African ethical systems 3:430–1
  anti-liberalism 2:465–70
  criminal punishment 2:708
  definition of 2:464–5
  development ethics 3:42
  educational philosophy 3:235–6
  embeddedness 2:468
  friendship 3:796
  individual good 4:829–30
  obligations to future generations
    3:819, 3:820–1
  political neutrality 6:820
  political obligation 7:76, 7:77–8
  public interest 7:833
  republicanism 8:282
  Slavophilism 8:809
  solidarity 9:23
  Taylor, C. 9:277–8
  Watsuji Tetsurō 9:691–2
community **2:464–71**
  see also citizenship;
  communitarianism
  alterity (Blanchot, M.) 1:783
  bioethics 1:774–5
  democratic
    postmodern view of 7:591–2
  friendship (Blanchot, M.) 1:783
  'imagined' 6:658
  individual relationship
    ethnophilosophy 3:447
  Judaism
    Kaplan, M. 5:205–6
    Leibowitz, Y. 5:562, 5:564
  law interaction (Dworkin, R.)
    3:188
  lesbian 3:604
  linguistic
    expressivist theories of 9:277
  market ethics 6:109–10

moral education 6:507–8
négritude concept
    African philosophy,
        Anglophone 1:98, 1:99
political representation
    medieval philosophy 7:509
ritual 8:338, 8:341
sense of belonging
    cultural identity 2:744, 2:745
social responsibility 2:152–3
socialism 8:879, 8:885
sociological dimensions of
    (Taylor, C.) 9:277–8
theory of (Royce, J.) 8:380
trans-generational 3:820–1
utopian 9:559, 9:560
compactness
    glossary 5:799
    second-order logic 8:594
comparison
    human sentiments (Hume, D.)
        4:550
compassion
    see also sympathy
    Confucianism 6:303
    euthanasia 5:628
    Luzzatto, S.D. 5:97
    Schopenhauer, A. 8:546, 8:552
compatibilism
    see also incompatibilism
    causation (Ayer, A.J.) 1:614,
        1:617–18
    free will 2:882–3, 3:743, 3:744–5
compensation
    criminal 2:705
competence
    medical ethics 6:260, 6:262
    mental illness 6:314
competition
    sport ethics 9:111
complementarity
    Bohr, N. 1:820–1
completeness
    glossary 5:799
    ordinal logics 7:141–2
    problem
        Gödel's theorems 1:845,
            4:107–19, 5:734, 6:438–9
    quantification theory
        Löwenheim-Skolem theorem
            5:848
complex numbers 7:49
complexe significabile 9:773–4
complexity
    computational 2:471–6
        see also Turing reducibility
    information-theoretic 2:477–9

perception of
    Gestalt psychology 4:52–3
    recursion-theoretic 8:142
composition
    fallacies of
        rational choice theory 8:65
compositionality 2:476–7, 6:221
    Aristotle 5:359
    conceptual role semantics 8:655–6
    Davidson, D. 2:801–2
    proper names 7:756
    propositions 7:787
    sense and reference 8:686–7
        Frege, G. 7:772–3
compossibility
    contingency (Leibniz, G.W.) 5:550
compound terms
    Gongsun Long 5:701–2
    Mohism 5:694, 5:698–9
    Xunzi 5:704–5
comprehension see intension
comprehension principle
    property theory 7:762–3, 7:764–5
compulsion
    coercion distinction 2:387
computability theory 2:482–91
    Church's thesis 2:351–3
    computable function 5:799
    human computor 9:495–6
    and information 2:477–82
    intractability 2:494–5
    Post, E.L. 7:573, 7:574
    real numbers 2:491–4
    Turing machines 9:495–8
computation 1:236
    see also artificial intelligence;
        mind, computational theories of
    classical 1:485
    connectionist 1:485–6, 1:489–90,
        2:570–6
    human behaviour 9:493
    idealizations 4:672
intractable problems 2:473–4,
    2:494–5
    intractable problems 2:473–4,
        2:494–5
    models of
        vision 9:632, 9:634–7
    modes of 6:393
    natural-language processing 1:487
    reasoning
        language of thought hypothesis
            5:405
    research
        classical AI 1:487
computational complexity see
    complexity, computational

computational theories of mind see
    mind, computational theories of
computer science 2:491–6
    intuitionism 4:851
    lambda calculus 5:346–7, 5:349
    logic machines 5:745
    model theory 6:441–2
    Neumann, J. von 6:810–11
    proof theory 7:749
computers
    see also computer science;
        electronic technology; information
        technology
    architecture 2:392–3, 2:571, 2:573,
        2:575
    Chinese room argument 2:328–9
    computational theories of mind
        2:392–3
    dynamic logics 3:189–91
    logic
        computational theories of mind
            6:392–3
    randomness
        complexity approaches 8:56,
            8:58
        simulation of chance 8:56–7
    syntactic states
        semantic interpretation of 6:392
    Turing test 9:494–5
Comstock, Gary L.
    agricultural ethics †1:126–8
Comte, Charles 5:139, 5:141
Comte, Isidore-Auguste-Marie-
    François-Xavier 2:496–505
    anti-positivism
        Latin America 1:304
    cerebral theory 2:503–4
    consciousness 2:594
    European positivism 7:565, 7:569
    history
        philosophy of 4:455, 4:458
    introspection, psychology of 4:844,
        4:845
    Latin America
        philosophy in 1:304, 5:427,
            7:566, 7:567–8
    logic of systems 2:496, 2:501–2
    Martineau, H. 6:117
    morality
        influence on Mill, J.S. 6:368,
            6:372
    positivism 2:496–7, 2:501–2, 7:558
        Latin American 7:566, 7:567–8
        Russian 7:562
    science, nineteenth century
        philosophy of 8:566

social science
  history of philosophy of
    8:851–2, 8:857
Comtian positivism *see* Comte,
  Isidore-Auguste-Marie-
  François-Xavier
comunicative rationality
  instrumental-communicative
    contrast 2:459–60
Conant, J.B. 1:856
conception *see tasawwur*
concepts **2:505–17**
  see also ideas; intensional entities;
  language
  a priori 1:4–5
  acquisition (Aquinas, T.) 3:373–4
  aesthetic 1:59
  analysis 2:508, 5:350–1
  Aufbau (Carnap, R.) 2:209
  categorematic–syncategorematic
    distinction 2:519
  conceptual analysis **2:518–22**
  confusion elimination
    (Wittgenstein, L.) 4:401–2
  connectionist networks 2:573
  constitutive analysis 2:508
  contradictions in 4:370
  definition 2:505–6, 2:513
  educational philosophy 3:232
  empiricism (Locke, J.) 5:668
  externalism 2:510, 2:514
  family resemblances 2:512, 2:573
  formal 5:411, 5:414–15
    Fonseca, P. da 3:689
    Green, T.H. 4:167
    Renaissance theories on 5:411,
      5:414–15
  functional (Cassirer, E.) 2:224
  fuzzy logic 2:512
  German idealism 4:43
  history of
    French philosophy of science
      3:783
  images distinction 1:622
  inferential roles 2:512, 2:645
  innate 8:76–7
  intellectual (Kant, I.) 5:182, 5:183
  internalism 2:510–11, 2:513–14
  intuitions distinction (Kant, I.)
    5:182
  knowledge by acquaintance 5:261
  learning
    Bruner, J.S. 5:486
    formation of 5:485–6
  legal **5:491–6**
    feminist jurisprudence 3:609
    formation of 5:491–2

logic 5:840
  meaning
    Indian theories of 6:240
  morality (Nietzsche, F.W.) 6:853–4
  objectivity
    Hobbes, T. critique 4:467–8
  paradox of analysis 2:520–1
  philosophical/scientific contrast
    2:858–9
  possession conditions
    external versus internal
      2:510–11
  pragmatism (Peirce, C.S.) 7:273
  proper names 7:752
  properties distinction 2:509–10
  prototypes 2:512–13
  representations of representations
    (Schopenhauer, A.) 8:547–8
  saturation/unsaturation (Frege, G.)
    8:686
  scientific
    operationalism 7:133
    theories distinction
      (Canguilhem, G.) 3:781–2
  shareability of 2:506–7, 2:510
  signification, Renaissance theories
    of 5:412
  teleological theory 8:673
  as thought-elements 3:150
  transcendent philosophy
    (Tetens, J.N.) 9:320
  two-factor theories 2:514
  universal language 9:534–5
Concepts (*Begriff*) of reason
  Hegel, G.W.F. 4:260, 4:267,
    4:268–73
conceptual analysis 1:774, 2:508,
  2:518–22
  analyticity 1:236
Conceptual Analysis movement 2:518
  see also ordinary language
  philosophy
conceptual apparatus
  (Ajdukiewicz, K.) 1:136
conceptual art 1:451
conceptual conservatism
  (Strawson, P.F.) 9:173
conceptual enrichment
  cognitive development 2:395
conceptual knowledge
  Dilthey, W. 3:78
  William of Ockham 2:292, 9:736–8
conceptual role semantics **8:652–7**
  analytic-synthetic distinction 4:490
conceptual-containment
  a priori knowledge 3:376

conceptualism
  Mill, J.S. 6:363
  nominalism 7:18
  property theory 7:761–3, 7:764
  substance 9:205, 9:207–8
conceptualist theory of universals
  Aureol, P. 1:566
concomitance
  pre-established harmony
    (Leibniz, G.W.) 5:548–9
Concord Transcendentalism 1:202–3,
  9:389–90
concrete predication
  medieval logic (Wodeham, A.)
    9:774
concretism *see* reism
concretization *see determination*
concurrence
  see also justification, epistemic,
  coherence theory of
  providence 7:798
concursus doctrine 2:698
Condillac, Étienne Bonnot de
  2:522–7
  Enlightenment, continental 2:523,
    3:318
  human nature 4:526, 4:527
  language 2:523, 2:525–6
    critique by Herder, J.G. 4:380
    early modern philosophy of
      5:377
    origin of 5:376–7
  logic 5:718
  natural order 2:526
  sensation 2:523, 2:524–5, 4:345
conditional convention
  consequence 2:600
conditional excluded middle 2:687
conditional future contingents *see
  futuribilia*
conditional theory of knowledge
  contextualism 2:647–8
conditionalization
  degrees of belief 7:705, 7:706
conditionals
  see also counterfactual
  conditionals; indicative
  conditionals
  Abelard, P. 1:10–11
  consequence (Diodorus Cronus)
    3:83, 3:84–5
  deontic logic 2:888–9
  free logics 3:742
  inferential logic
    Stoicism 9:151
  Islamic philosophy 5:710
  logic 5:766

Stoicism 9:151
Stoics 5:690
vagueness 9:563–4
conditioning
  factors of experience
    Ābhidharmika Buddhism 2:56
  karmic
    potentiality 7:606–7
    Yogācāra Buddhism 2:70–1,
      2:73
  Pavlov, I.P. 8:800
  psychological theories 7:826
  scientific behaviourism 5:484
Condorcet, Marie-Jean-Antoine-
  Nicolas Caritat de **2:527–32**
  Arrow's theorem 8:69
  Enlightenment, continental 3:317
  history
    philosophy of 4:458
  human nature 2:530–1, 4:526
  probability 2:529–30
  science of man 2:530–1
  social arithmetic 2:528, 2:529–30
Condorcet paradox *see* cyclic
  majorities
Cone, E. 4:191, 6:612
Cone, James 5:616
Conee, Earl
  internalism–externalism
    distinction 4:826
  memory
    epistemic issues †6:300–2
  normative epistemology †7:35–8
confabulation
  truthfulness 9:481–2
confederalism **3:572–4**
confessional theology
  Niebuhr, H.R. 6:840
Confessiones libri tredecim
  (Confessions) *see* Augustine of
    Hippo
confidence
  moral knowledge 6:517
confirmation
  empirical
    Popperian philosophy of science
      3:218
confirmation holism
  Quine, W.V. 2:506, 2:513, 4:488,
    4:489
confirmation theory
  logical probabilities (Carnap, R.)
    2:212–13
  science **2:532–6**
    see also underdetermination
  Bayesian
    experiment 3:517

Carnap-Hintikka programme
  2:532–4
idealization 4:669–70
qualitative 2:532
theoretical/epistemic virtues 9:340,
  9:341, 9:343
truth (Hempel, C.G.) 4:348–50
conflict
  games
    rational choice theory 8:66
  social
    Latin American literature
      5:653–4
conformity
  artificial virtues (Hume, D.) 4:553,
    4:554
  postmodernism and political
    philosophy 7:591
Confucian Analects *see* Confucius
Confucianism 2:315, 2:319–20
  see also Confucius; neo-
    Confucianism
  aesthetics 1:68, 1:69–71
  art
    Japan 1:86–7
  Buddhism/Daoism harmonization
    Korea 2:114–15, 2:116
  cheng 2:300
  Cheng Hao 2:300–1
  Cheng Yi 2:302
  Chinese **2:536–49**
  Chinese classics 2:309–13
  commentaries on the canons 2:319
  contemporary 2:327
  dao
    Guanzi 4:187
  Daoism distinction 2:783–5
  de 2:809
  Dong Zhongshu 3:111–12
  East Asian Philosophy 3:194,
    3:195
  education 6:133–4
  establishment of 2:324–5
  fa 3:532
  Han Yu 4:221
  harmony 3:194
  history, theories of 4:448
  human nature 2:91
  humanism
    Chinese Marxism 6:138–40
    Daxue **2:807–9**
  Hundred Schools conflict 2:322
  Japanese **2:549–55**
    bushi philosophy 2:149
    kogaku 5:42–3, 9:440
    social order 5:68, 5:70
  Korean **2:555–65**

li 5:594
Mencius 6:302–3
Mozi 6:452, 6:456
mysticism 6:622
Nishi Amane 7:12
rulers 5:864
self-cultivation 8:617–18, 8:619
Wang Yangming 5:321–2, 9:682–4
xin (trustworthiness) 9:816
Xunzi 2:323–4, 9:818–20
Yang Xiong 9:821–2
Yijing 9:828–9
Zheng Xuan 9:857
Zongmi 9:871
Confucius 2:319–20, **2:565–70**
  see also Confucianism; neo-
    Confucianism
  Analects 2:566–7, 2:569–70
    Chinese classics 2:309, 2:312,
      2:314
    dao 2:778
    li zhi
      China 5:445
    self-cultivation 8:614, 8:615
    textual authority 2:310
    vocabulary 2:538–9
    xin (heart-and-mind) 9:815,
      9:816
  Chunqiu 9:857
  fa 3:532–3
  Five Classics 2:309
  history, theories of 4:447, 4:450–1
  law and ritual 5:445–7
  rectifying names 5:694–5
  self-cultivation 8:614–16, 8:625
  Shijing 2:309
  Shujing 2:309
  social order 4:186
  Xiaojing 2:312
Congar, Y.M.J. 5:168
Conimbricenses *see* Collegium
  Conimbricense
conjunction
  as cause of qualities 7:122–3
  coherence distinction 5:839–40
  disjunction 5:423
  epistemology 5:272
  Ibn Bajja 4:605, 4:606, 4:607
  linear logic 5:638–9
Conjunctive Principle 2:813–14
Conkey, M.W. 1:358
Conkin, P.K. 1:205
Conley, T.M. 8:309
Conley, Tom
  Certeau, M. de †2:267–9
Conley, Verena Andermatt
  Cixous, H. †2:372–4

connectibility
  Nagel reduction model 8:146
connection
  ideas (Lotze, R.H.) 5:839–40
  linguistic
    Mīmāṃsā 6:380
  unconscious mental states
    (Searle, J.) 9:525
connectionism **2:570–9**
  artificial intelligence 1:485–6
  cognitive psychology 7:827
  computation 2:570–6
    learning 2:573, 2:575
    local/global effects 2:572
    multiple soft constraint
      satisfaction 2:573–4
    patterns of connectivity 2:571–3
    unit activation 2:571
  computational models of vision
    9:637
  Fodor, J.A. critique 3:685
  language of thought hypothesis
    5:407
  learning 5:484
  pacification (Freud, S.) 3:791
  parallel processing 1:489–90
Connell, F.J. 3:121
Connell, R.W. 5:367
Connolly, W. 5:541, 7:592
Connolly, W.E. 7:612
Connor, W.R. 9:399
connotation see intension
Conradi, L.I. 4:659
conscience **2:579–81**
  Common Sense ethics (Reid, T.)
    2:449
  consciousness 2:403
  finitude 4:311
  guilt 8:139–40
    shame distinction 6:549–50
  human nature (Butler, J.) 2:155,
    2:156–7
  morality 2:876
    obligations 6:547
  Stoic concept of 5:822
consciencism
  African Marxism 1:100–1
conscientious consciousness see
  primordial awareness
consciousness **2:581–96**
  see also cognition; experience;
    mental states; mind; perception;
    unconscious mental states
  absolute (Abhinavagupta) 1:16–17
  activities (Schleiermacher, F.)
    8:534–12

aesthetic
  African culture 1:64
alienation 1:180–1
analytic behaviourism 1:691
animal 7:195–6
apperception 9:799
arising from matter (Lokāyatikas)
  6:179–80
better (Schopenhauer, A.) 8:547,
  8:551
Bloch, E.S. 1:788
Buddhism 2:583–92, 8:448
cognitive projection
  Yogācāra Buddhism 2:72
condition of (Searle, J.R.) 2:328
constitutive (Husserl, E.) 4:580–1
contemplative
  Hasidism 4:243–4
contradictions (Herbart, F.) 4:370
critique by Habermas, J. 4:198
Dennett, D.C. 2:588, 2:882,
  2:883–4
dialogic 2:125
disunity of
  split brain studies 9:107,
    9:108–9
dual-aspect approach 6:645
dualism 2:586, 3:137
duration (Bergson, H.-L.) 1:733
effective-historical
  Gadamer, H.-G. 3:828–9
eight types of
  Yogācāra Buddhism 2:72–4
eliminativism 2:582–95, 2:587–8
epiphenomenalism 3:352–3, 3:408
epistemic attitudes (Hegel, G.W.F.)
  4:266–8
false (Marx, K.) 6:124
freedom relationship (Merleau-
  Ponty, M.) 6:323
functionalism 2:425
high-level
  emergence of 7:196
historical
  Dilthey, W. 3:82
  Jaspers, K. 5:82
horizon (Husserl, E.) 4:581
imagination relationship (Sartre, J.-
  P.) 8:475–6
immortality of
  paranormal phenomena 7:222,
    7:223
intentionality 7:343, 7:345
  Husserl, E. 4:574, 4:577
  Meinong, A. 6:283
  Sartre, J.-P. 8:474–5

introspection 1:696, 4:839, 4:844
  Maine de Biran, P.-F. 6:49,
    6:51–2
Jainism 8:449
karma
  Yogācāra Buddhism 2:66
materialism 6:176
matter dualism
  Sāṅkhya-Yoga 6:197, 6:199–200
mental causation 6:308
mental operations (Brown, T.) 2:28
moral standing 6:550–1, 6:553
mysticism 6:620, 6:621
as myth (*Ausdruck*) (Cassirer, E.)
  2:224–5
mythic to rational transition
  (Vico, G.) 9:602–3
mythical (Rosenzweig, F.) 8:359
neo-spiritualism (Lachelier, A.)
  5:338–9
noema (Husserl, E.) 4:575, 4:577–8
panpsychism 7:194–7
perception 7:295
  Ābhidharmika Schools 2:57
  Leibniz, G.W. 5:542
personal identity (Butler, J.) 2:159
phenomenal character of
  colour experience 2:421
phenomenology 2:582–9
  Merleau-Ponty, M. 6:323
  Sartre, J.-P. 8:473, 8:475
production 9:198
psychology
  theories of 7:826
qualia 2:582–95, 2:588–9
racial
  négritude 1:110–11
reality relationship (Voegelin, E.)
  9:654–5
reflexive awareness 3:78
self-luminous
  Mīmāṃsā 6:378
self-reflection (Dilthey, W.) 3:78
sense certainty (Hegel, G.W.F.)
  4:266–7
sense perception
  Indian views of 8:691
social 2:270
spirituality (Santayana, G.) 8:469
stream of
  existential phenomenological
    ontology (Ingarden, R.W.)
    4:790
  James, W. 5:61–2
structuralism (Foucault, M.) 7:601

three types of
Indian philosophy of mind
6:400
transcendentalism
Fichte, J.G. 3:642, 3:646
Schelling, F.W.J. von 8:509,
8:511–12, 8:514
unconscious mental states 9:523,
9:525
unhappy (Hegel, G.W.F.) 4:267
unified (Green, T.H.) 4:167–8
universal (Royce, J.) 8:378–9
Weltalter philosophy
(Schelling, F.W.J. von) 8:515
Yogācāra Buddhism
China 2:83–4
dependent origination 9:217
consensus
applied ethics 1:322
pragmatic theory of truth 9:478,
9:479
realism 8:116–17
consensus gentium (universal consent)
Cudworth, R. 2:739–41
consent **2:596–9**
see also agreement
government 3:396, 3:398
harm principle 5:462
informed
genetic counselling 4:17
political obligation 7:78
risk 8:333
sadomasochism 8:725–6
sexuality 8:724–5
technology and ethics 9:282
consequence
conceptions of **2:599–603**
logic
medieval 5:755–6
model theory 6:438–9
multiple-conclusion logic **6:602–4**
consequentialism **2:603–6**, 3:436–7
act-consequentialism 2:603–6,
2:890–1
critiques of
Anscombe, G.E.M. 1:281
intuitionist 7:680
Ross, W.D. 8:366
Williams, B.A.O. 9:751
deontology comparison 2:890–1,
6:645–6
instrumentalism (Dewey, J.) 7:640,
7:641–2
libertarianism 5:618
life and death 5:625
moral pluralism 6:530
moral rules 6:512–13

negative duties 3:179
obligations to future generations
3:819–20
practical reason 7:614
punishment 2:704–5, 2:706–7
reductionism 6:573
right and good 4:133, 8:324
rule-consequentialism 2:606
theodicy (Bayle, P.) 1:676
virtues and vices 9:626
consequentiality
deducibility contrast (Bolzano, B.)
1:826
conservation principles **2:606–8**
Cartesian
Leibniz, G.W. rejection 5:543,
5:555
child development (Piaget, J.)
7:383–4
scientific laws (Meyerson, É.)
6:349
conservation (religious doctrine of)
2:695–700
see also creation, continuous
classical theism 4:99
deist rejection of 2:698
providence 7:798
conservatism **2:608–15**
Aristotle 2:610
assessment 2:613–14
Burke, E. 2:610–11
citizenship 2:363
economics 2:611–12
Hegel, G.W.F. 2:612–13
Hobbes, T. 2:610
law
moral limits of 5:462
logical 5:783–5
Maistre, J. de 2:610–11
market 2:611–12
moral intuitionism (Sidgwick, H.)
8:760
moral scepticism 9:357
ontological 5:783, 5:784–5
Plato 2:609
political
Burke, E. 2:136, 2:138, 2:140
Paley, W. 7:187–8
sexuality 8:724
conservativeness
theoretical/epistemic virtues 9:341,
9:342
consilience of induction 8:569–70
consistency
belief 5:160
constructible universe 2:622–4

formal systems
ordinal logics 7:139–41
glossary 5:800
principle of (Mozi) 6:454–5
proofs 4:771, 7:742–9
see also completeness, problem;
paraconsistent logic
Gentzen, G.K.E. 4:24
Herbrand's theorem 4:377
Hilbert, D. 4:426–7
conspiracy theories
Illuminati 4:697
Constable, M. 2:446
Constable, R.L. 4:852
constant
glossary 5:800
Constant, Benjamin *see* Constant de
Rebecque, Henri-Benjamin
Constant Botelho de Magalhães,
Benjamin 7:567
constant conjunction
causation (Hume, D.) 4:547
Constant de Rebecque, Henri-
Benjamin **2:615–18**
Brazil, philosophy in 2:10
citizenship 9:424
Montesquieu, C.L. 6:494
Constantine the African 9:455
Constantini, D. 2:535
Constantinople
capture of 8:264
constants
Boltzmann's 7:396
logical **5:775–81**
Planck's 7:396
constatives *see* performatives; speech
acts
constitution theory
Aufbau 2:209
constitutionalism **2:618–22**
see also sovereignty
American War of Independence
republican liberty 7:514
British
Dicey, A.V. 3:62–3
rule of law 8:388–9
utilitarian government
(Bentham, J.) 1:719, 1:724
constitutive theories of language *see*
expressivism
constraints
classical mechanics 6:255–7
constructible universe **2:622–4**
constructionalism
Goodman, N. 4:136

constructionism
  social
    sexuality 8:719–20
    Soviet Marxism 6:157
constructive existence
  constructivism in mathematics
    2:632–3
constructive nominalism
  Leśniewski, S. 7:494
constructivism **2:624–30**, 8:581
  certainty 9:601
  Church's thesis 2:352
  cognitive development
    Piaget, J. 7:384, 7:385
  Edinburgh School 2:625–6
  educational
    science learning 3:237
  epistemology 2:629
  ethical **2:630–2**
  historical knowledge (Vico, G.)
    9:604
  mathematics **2:632–9**, 5:825–8
  metaphysics (Vico, G.) 9:601
  relativism 2:627–9
  scientific realism 8:583–4
  social 2:624–5
  technology 9:283, 9:286–7
  social epistemology 8:831
  Whitehead, A.N. 9:714, 9:715,
    9:717
constructs
  theoretical
    behaviourist psychology 1:697
consubstantiation 8:444
consumerism
  see also commodity fetishism
  post-structuralism (Baudrillard, J.)
    1:662–3
containment
  inherence
    ontology in Indian philosophy
    7:119, 7:120–1, 7:124–5
Contamine, G. 9:456–7
contemplation
  Albert the Great 1:150–1
  happiness (Aristotle) 1:429–30
  Richard of St Victor 8:312–13
  spiritual growth 8:455–6
content
  see also meaning
  attributions of
    teleological theories 8:674
  behaviour
    unconscious mental states
    9:523, 9:525
  belief
    degrees of 8:46

functionalism 4:490
  mental holism 4:488–93
dreams 3:128–9
expression distinction 2:858
externalism 6:405–6
fiction 3:661–2
incommunicability of
  (Schlick, F.A.M.) 8:541–2
indexical **2:639–40**, 2:880–1, 6:405
  conceptual role semantics 8:654
  Frege, G. 2:643–4
informational semantics 8:659
intentionality 4:818–20
meaning 6:405
narrow
  holism 4:492–3
non-conceptual 2:24, **2:640–3**
  Broad, C.D. 2:24
  perception 7:291
  perceptual knowledge 7:295
object distinction
  descriptive psychology
    (Twardowski, K.) 9:508
  perception of external truths
    6:496
propositional attitudes 7:781–3,
  7:784
representational
  functionalism 3:812
social nature of language
  (Burge, T.) 5:419
thought 6:405
wide and narrow **2:643–6**
  analytic/synthetic distinction
    4:490–1
  methodological individualism
    6:341–2
contentment
  happiness relationship 4:226–7
context
  action
    praxeology 7:648
  creativity
    Zhuangzi 9:866
  hermeneutics (Heidegger, M.)
    4:388
  indexical content 2:639–40
  intensional 4:811
  pragmatics 7:623–4, 7:627
  propositional attitudes 7:626,
    7:627
  sense and reference 8:687
context-free language 3:703
contextual constructs
  aesthetic 1:55, 1:58
contextual pragmatics *see* praxeology

contextualism
  archaeology 1:357
  art works
    ontology of 1:480, 1:482–3
  basic propositions 5:269
  cognitive science 7:629–30
  conversational implicature 7:628
  epistemological **2:646–50**
  indexicals 2:648
  non-causal explanation 3:528
  ordinary language philosophy
    7:624
  propositional certainty 2:265–6
  regress argument 2:647
  relativism 2:648
  scepticism 2:646, 2:647–8
  theological
    situation ethics 8:798
Conti, Alessandro D.
  Giles of Rome 4:77
  Kilwardby, R. †5:245–9
  Paul of Venice 7:266
contiguity
  sentential meaning
    testimony in Indian philosophy
    9:316
continence *see* self-control
contingency **2:650–2**
  a priori knowledge 1:4
  absence in life (Tolstoi, L.N.)
    9:436–7
  causation (Glanvill, J.) 4:81
  continuation of motion 1:865
  divine freedom (Leibniz, G.W.)
    5:542, 5:549–51
  freedom of will (Duns Scotus, J.)
    3:166–7
  God
    relationship with 6:237
  of history 8:741, 8:744
  of human nature (Bakhtin, M.)
    1:639
  identity (Kripke, S.A.) 5:302
  indexicals 2:878–80, 2:879
  necessity distinction
    Quine, W.V. critique 1:235
  omnipotence 7:99–7:100
  one–many relationship 5:321
  Spinoza, B. de, 5:549–50
  Tolstoi, L.N. 9:436–7
continua
  classical mechanics 6:257–8
  divisibilism 2:133–4
  indivisibilism
    Bradwardine, T. 1:864–5
    Chatton, W. 2:293
    Henry of Harclay 4:360, 4:361

Nicholas of Autrecourt 6:831
problem of (Leibniz, G.W.) 5:546
sophismata (Heytesbury, W.) 4:420
continuants **2:652–4**
change 2:275–6
continuity criterion 2:652–3
events 3:462
mereology 6:318
tensed theory of time 2:653
tenseless theory of time 2:653–4,
2:653
continuity
biographical 9:244
common law 2:440, 2:441–3, 2:445
evolution 2:689–90
law of
puncta 9:50
principle of
Leibniz, G.W. 5:556
reality of
Cournot, A.A. 2:689
continuity across species (CAS)
1:269–70
continuum hypothesis **2:654–7**
Cantor, G. 2:197
forcing 3:694–5
glossary 5:800
Polish logic 7:495
set theory 8:704
Contra academicos see Augustine of
Hippo
contraception 5:629, 8:724
contractarianism **2:657–65**
see also social contract
animals and ethics 1:275
autonomy
ethical 1:587
civil society (Rousseau, J.-J.) 8:368,
8:371–2
conventionalism 2:661
critiques of
Astell, M. 1:527
Filmer, R. 3:678
deliberative ideals 4:673
democratic views 2:661–3
Kant, I. 2:662–3
Locke, J. 2:661–2
Rawls, J. 2:663
Rousseau, J.-J. 2:662–3
government
selection of (Hume, D.) 4:557–8
Hobbesian views
contemporary 2:660–1
Kantian comparison 5:201–2
human nature 3:855–6
interest-based views 2:659
moral contractualism 2:664–5

moral justification 6:516
natural right 7:512–13
obligations to future generations
3:820
political obligation 7:79
population ethics 7:541
promises (Hume, D.) 4:554
reflective equilibrium (Rawls, J.)
5:202
rights- versus interest-based
2:663–4
social choice 8:825–6
sovereignty (Rousseau, J.-J.) 7:514
contraction
glossary 5:800
contracts
Coase Theorem 5:456
promises comparison 7:741–2
rationalistic civil law (Pothier, R.J.)
7:608
trust 9:466–7
contractualism
moral (Scanlon, T.M.) 2:658,
2:664–5
slavery 8:805
contradiction
glossary 5:800
contradiction, principle of
see also non-contradiction
being
Wolff, C. 9:781
Łukasiewicz J. 5:861
contradictions
Hegel, G.W.F. 4:269, 8:515–16
law of 8:514
relations method 4:370
truth-generation 4:269
contraposition
glossary 5:800
medieval logic 5:752
contrary to duty imperative
deontic logic 2:888
control
human behaviour 7:602
responsibility 8:291–3
convention 2:667, 2:668
see also conventionalism
coordination games 8:67
coordinative definitions
(Reichenbach, H.) 8:169
critiques of
Ayer, A.J. 1:616
logical laws 5:787
morality 2:876
and nature **6:735–7**
see also naturalism, social
science

social science 8:847–9, 8:869
necessary truth **6:747–50**
a posteriori 6:748, 6:749
social
justice (Hume, D.) 4:553, 4:554
Lewis, D.K. 8:834
society
concept of 8:887
truth theory
critique by Quine, W.V. 8:10
Convention T 9:265–6
conventionalism **2:666–9**, 8:581
contructivism contrast 2:631
geometric (Poincaré, J.H.) 2:666,
7:478, 7:479–80
justice 5:142–3
language **5:368–71**
Aristotle 5:359
Carnap, R. 2:208, 2:211–12,
2:213
Chinese theories of
Confucianism 5:694, 5:704–5
Mohism 5:697
Democritus 5:357
Herder, J.G. 4:380
Hobbes, T. 5:373
Plato 5:357–8
Port-Royalists 5:373
Le Roy, É.L.E.J. 5:481–2
logical positivism 5:791
mechanics 6:252–3
natural kinds 6:684
natural laws 5:473
performatives 7:303
Putnam, H. critique 7:840
radical *see* radical conventionalism
science (Duhem, P.M.M.) 3:144–5
semantic (Poincaré, J.H.) 7:480–1
social contract 2:661
conventionality
relativity theory 8:194–6
conventions
constitutional 3:62
convergence
Bayesian epistemology 7:710
inference to the best explanation
4:768
scientific theory 3:546–7
conversation *see* discourse semantics;
pragmatics
conversational implicature *see*
implicature
conversational maxims
Grice, H.P. 4:723–4
metaphor 6:337
Conway, Anne **2:669–71**
Conway, J.H. 7:53

Conybeare, J. 9:423
Conze, E. 2:99, 6:594, 9:218
Cook, Francis H.
  Buddhism
    Chinese 2:92
    Japanese 2:105
    Fazang †3:568–9
Cook, G.A. 6:212
Cook, J.A. 3:592
Cook, N. 6:612
Cook, S.A. 2:475
Cook Wilson, J. 7:682
Cooke, D. 6:612
Cooke, M. 2:462
Cooke, R. 8:333, 8:337
Coole, D.H. 9:791
Coolidge, J. 4:32–3
Coomaraswamy, A.K. 4:256
Coomaraswamy, R. 3:43
Cooney, B. 4:61, 8:699
Cooper, Anthony Ashley see
  Shaftesbury, Third Earl of
Cooper, B. 5:291, 9:502, 9:656
Cooper, David E.
  educational philosophy 3:238
  existentialism 3:501
  existentialist ethics †3:502–5
  Marcel, G. †6:91–3
  phenomenology 7:347
Cooper, J.
  Oswald, J. 7:170
Cooper, John
  al-Dawani †2:806–7
  Mulla Sadra †6:595–9
  al-Razi, Fakhr al-Din †8:112–15
  al-Sabzawari †8:440–2
  al-Suhrawardi †9:219–24
  al-Tusi †9:504–7
Cooper, John M.
  Owen, G.E.L. †7:177–9
  Seneca, L.A. 8:682
  Socrates †9:8–9:19
Cooper, L. 1:509
Cooper, R. 8:17, 8:672
Cooper, S.A. 6:106
cooperation
  conversational implicature
    (Grice, H.P.) 4:174–5
  game theory 2:832
  social
    moral relativism 6:540, 6:541
Cooperman, D. 1:27
coordinates
  numerical
    analytical geometry 4:30–1
coordination games
  rational choice theory 8:66–7

Cope, J.I. 4:83
Copeland, J. 7:690
Copeland, R. 2:777
Copenhagen interpretation see
  quantum mechanics,
  Copenhagen interpretation
Copenhagen School 9:179–80
Copenhaver, B.P.
  Aristotelianism
    Renaissance 1:412
  Campanella, T. 2:191
  Egyptian philosophy
    ancient 3:250, 3:254
  Hermetism 4:397
  More, H. 6:582
  Platonism
    medieval 7:438
    Renaissance 7:447
Copernican astronomy
  Galilei, G. 3:836–7, 3:839–40
  Kepler, J. 5:231, 5:232
Copernicanism
  Bacon, F. 1:630
Copernicus, Nicolaus **2:671–2**
  see also Copernican astronomy;
    Copernicanism
  De Revolutionibus Orbium
    Coelestium
    sun-centred astronomy 2:671–2
  sun-centred astronomy 2:671–2
Copi, I. 8:403, 9:362, 9:595
Copleston, F.C.
  Aquinas, T. 1:347
  Frank, S.L. 3:729
  Hartmann, K.R.E. von 4:240
  John of Mirecourt 5:112
  Lavrov, P.L. 5:438
Copley, A. 7:524
Copley, S. 8:821
Copp, D. 2:871
Coppock, P. 6:749
copulation
  Chinese philosophy 2:316
  medieval position 9:748
  time contradiction 2:25
Coquart, A. 7:8
Coquilette, D.R. 1:632
Corbin, Henry
  Ibn Kammuna 4:623
  Illuminationist philosophy 4:703
  Islamic philosophy 5:9, 5:16
    mysticism 6:620
    Orientalism 7:160
  Islamic theology 5:31
  Mir Damad, Muhammad Baqir
    6:411
  neo-illuminationism 5:18, 5:20

al-Suhrawardi 9:223
Corcoran, J. 5:691, 5:692
Cordemoy, Géraud de **2:672–4**
Cordier, S. 1:661
Cordovero, Moses 4:398
co-references
  ambiguity of scope 9:251
coreferring terms,
  intersubstitutability of see
    intersubstitutability
Cornehl, P. 4:300
Corneille, Pierre 9:449–8
Cornell, D. 2:719, 2:900–1
Cornford, F.M. 4:413, 9:60, 9:64,
  9:653
Cornforth, M. 3:57
Cornman, J. 3:381, 7:293, 8:498
Cornwall, R.D. 5:469–70
corporeals
  'being' identification
    Stoicism 9:145
  incorporeals relationship
    (Porphyry) 7:547
Corpus Iuris Civilis 8:343, 8:344–5
corpuscularianism
  see also atomism; particulate
    matter
  Boyle, R. 1:853, 1:855–6
  critique by Stewart, D. 9:139
  Descartes, R. 2:295–6
  Heraclides of Pontus 4:363, 4:364
Corr, Charles
  Wolff, C. †9:776–8
Corradi Fiumara, G. 3:587
correctness definition
  discourse representation structures
    anaphora 1:242–3
correlations
  causation 2:247
  Chinese philosophy 2:317–18,
    9:831–2
correspondence
  veridicality
    Nyāya-Vaiśeṣika 3:411
correspondence principle
  quantum theory 1:821
correspondence theory
  relevance logic 8:202
correspondence theory of truth see
  truth, correspondence theory of
Corrigan, K. 7:463
corrigibility
  knowledge 3:379
corruption **2:674–7**
  investigative journalism
    ethics 5:128

political
African 3:434
Corry, L. 2:236
Corsi, M. 2:734
Corso, C. 3:559
Cortés, Hernán 5:429, 5:432
Corti, M. 1:185
Cosgrove, R.A. 3:63
cosmic city
Stoicism 9:156–7
cosmic cycle
finite beings (Pseudo-Dionysius)
7:805–6
Cosmides, L. 3:487, 8:88, 8:89
cosmogony
see also cosmology; creation;
universe
Anaximenes 1:261–2
cycle of change (Empedocles)
3:293, 3:295–6
'everything in everything'
(Anaxagoras) 1:250–2
Indian theories of 2:681–4
number (Philolaus) 7:368–9
universe
Anaxagoras 1:250
cosmological argument see God,
existence of, arguments for
cosmology 2:677–81
see also cosmogony; creation;
universe; worldview
Anaximander 1:255–9
Anaximenes 1:261–2
anthropic principle 2:679
Aristotelianism/theology
conciliation (White, T.) 9:712
Aristotle
Simplicius commentary 8:789
Ash'ariyya 1:519, 1:520
atomism (Leucippus) 5:578–9
Big-Bang theory 2:679–80
Chinese philosophy
creativity
Zhu Xi 9:863–4
Daoism 2:785–7, 2:791
genealogical 9:817
Huainanzi 4:513
myths 2:315, 2:316
qi 9:856
ren 9:864
Shao Yong 6:767–8
Western philosophy contrast
2:315, 2:316
xing 9:817
Yijing 2:311
you-wu 9:834
Confucianism, Japanese 2:550

creationism (Plato) 7:416
design argument
Hume, D. 4:559–60
Voltaire 9:659–60
determinism 3:36, 3:37
East Asian Philosophy 3:193
Epicureanism 3:345–6
esoteric
Kabbalah 5:172–3
'ever-living fire' (Heraclitus) 4:364,
4:367–8
evolutionary
objective idealism (Peirce, C.S.)
7:270, 7:280–1
al-Farabi 3:555
Fontenelle, B. de 3:691
Galilei, G. 3:835–41
genealogical
Chinese philosophy 9:817
general relativity theory
(Einstein, A.) 3:256
al-Ghazali 4:66
Greek pre-Socratic 9:530
Heraclides of Pontus 4:363
hierarchy of worlds
relation to God 4:601, 4:602–3
Ibn Massara 4:628
Indian theories of 2:681–4
infinity
Archytas 1:369
Melissus 6:293–4
Jainism 5:49
Kepler, J. 5:231–2
love
Jewish philosophy
(Abravanel, J.) 1:26
mathematics (Archytas) 1:367–8
medieval natural philosophy
6:695–8, 6:702
monads
Voltaire critique 9:660
Mu'tazalia 1:519, 1:520
myths
Chinese philosophy 2:315, 2:316
Western philosophy contrast
2:315, 2:316
qi
Zhang Zai 9:856
ren
Zhu Xi 9:864
Shao Yong 6:767–8
Native American philosophy
6:662, 6:663–4
Neoplatonism
Chaldaean Oracles 2:273
Nicholas of Cusa 6:834
nous 7:43

numbers
Pythagoreanism 7:858–60
palingenesis (Bonnet, C.) 1:838,
1:839
Philo of Alexandria 7:359–60
physicalism (Cleanthes) 2:382–3
providential (Marcus Aurelius)
6:94–5
Ptolemaic
Proclus' rejection of 7:729
rationalism 1:164, 1:166
religion and science 8:233
Renaissance
Bruno, G. 2:36
Campanella, T. 2:188
Platonism 7:439, 7:446–7
Telesio, B. 9:298
Russian Orthodox Church
(Bulgakov, S.N.) 2:124–5
steady-state theory 2:679
Stoicism 7:189, 9:142, 9:146–7
sympatheia
Stoicism 7:556
unlimiteds/limiters 7:367, 7:368
Way of Seeming (Parmenides)
7:229, 7:233
cosmopolitanism
alternative to state 9:121–2
Meinecke, F. 6:280
morality 4:830–2
cosmos
Chaos comparison
Western philosophy 2:316
Huayan Buddhism 3:569
Ibn al-'Arabi
levels 4:604
'perfect man' 4:603
relation to God 4:601, 4:602–3
Cossio, Carlos 1:378–9, 7:349
Costa, N.C.A. da 7:210
Costa Rica
phenomenology 7:350
Costabel, P. 6:330
cost–benefit analysis
green economics critique 4:164
Coste, H. de 6:330
Costello, F. 6:465
cotenability
counterfactual conditionals 2:686,
2:687
Cotterrell, Roger
Critical Legal Studies 2:719
Hart, H.L.A. 4:236
social theory and law †8:872–9
Cottingham, John
Descartes, R. 3:18
impartiality †4:714–17

Coudert, A.
  alchemy 1:158
  Conway, A. 2:670–1
  Helmont, F.M. van 4:342
  language
    Renaissance philosophy of
      5:415
  More, H. 6:582
Coughlan, N. 1:205
Couissin, P. 1:354
Coulson, W.R. 7:829
Council of Trent 1:539, 5:166
counselling
  genetics and ethics 4:17
count terms
  mass terms contrast 6:168–9
countability
  glossary 5:800
countable chain condition (CCC)
  3:695
countable infinite 5:848–50
counterfactual conditionals **2:684–8**
  action 8:47
  causation 2:249
  classification 2:685–6
  glossary 5:799–800
  metalinguistic view 2:686, 2:688
  necessitarian theories
    natural laws 5:472
  negative facts
    Indian philosophy 6:756–7
  non-monotonic reasoning 7:33–4
  phenomenalism 7:331
  possible worlds 2:686–8, 4:741,
    6:428
    Lewis, D.K. 5:591
  possible worlds semantics 8:665
  subjunctive conditionals
    phenomenalism 7:331, 7:332
counterfactuals of freedom
  see also Molinism
  providence 7:799–800
counterpart theory 6:430–1
  fiction
    semantics of 3:662
  Lewis, D.K. 5:592
Counter-Reformation
  Italy 5:34–6
  Portugal
    influence on Brazil 2:8
coup d'état
  revolution distinction 8:301–2
Couper, K. 8:20
Courbet, G. 1:449, 1:452
Courcelle, P. 1:812, 3:308
Cournot, Antoine Augustin **2:688–90**

Court of Chancery
  equity 5:150–1
Courtenay, W.J.
  Augustinianism 1:564
  Chatton, W. 2:294
  Crathorn, W. 2:693
  Gregory of Rimini 4:171
  John of Mirecourt 5:112
  natural philosophy
    medieval 6:705–6
  voluntarism 9:664
  Wodeham, A. 9:776
Courtine, J.-F. 9:195
Courtivron, I. de 3:596, 5:308, 5:479
Cousin, Victor **2:690–2**
  Common Sense School 2:447
  Desgabets, R. 3:29
  Hegelianism 4:285
Cousins, L.S.
  Buddha †2:51–3
  nirvāṇa †7:8–7:12
Couto, Sebastian de 5:412
Couturat, L. 5:561
Couture, J. 2:236
Couvalis, G. 3:642
Cova, L. 2:294, 8:311
covariance
  general
    relativity theory 8:196
Covello, V. 8:337
covenant theology
  political philosophy
    history of 7:510–11
covering-law model of explanation
  3:520, 3:521–2
Cowan, R. 5:650
Coward, H.G. 4:439–40, 5:383
Cowen, T. 4:165
Cowie, F.
  innateness of language †4:51–4
Cox, Collett
  Ābhidharmika Schools of
    Buddhism †2:53–8
Cox, Oliver Cromwell 8:19, 8:20
Coxon, A.H. 7:234
'cracking' *see* hacking
Cragg, G.R. 2:185, 2:744, 6:547
Crahay, Franz 3:448, 3:449
Craig, Edward
  concept of knowledge 5:274, 5:275
  contextualism
    epistemological 2:649
  fatalism †3:563–4
  meaning and verification 6:235
  metaphysics †6:338–41
  monism †6:474–5
  ontology †7:117–18

  pluralism †7:463–4
  private states and language
    †7:698–701
  realism/antirealism †8:115–19
  relativism †8:189–90
  social epistemology 8:830, 8:832
  solipsism †9:25–6
Craig, P.P. 3:63
Craig, W.
  see also Craig's theorem
  scientific theories 9:352
Craig, William Lane
  creation and conservation
    religious doctrine of 2:700
  eschatology 3:416
  God, existence of 4:92
  hell 4:332–3
  interpolation theorem 1:762, 1:763
  tense logic 9:307
Craig's theorem **1:760–4**
Cramér, H. 9:126
Cranbury, N.J. 2:777
Crane, Tim
  content
    non-conceptual †2:640–3
    wide and narrow 2:645
  intentionality †4:816–21
  methodological individualism
    6:344–3
  perception 7:292–3, 7:298
Cranefield, P.F. 3:131
Cranor, C. 8:286, 8:334, 8:337
Cranston, M. 8:376
Crantor 7:428
Cranz, F.E. 5:24
Crates of Thebes 2:756
Crathorn, William **2:692–4**
Cratylus **2:694–5**
Craven, W.G. 7:392
Crawford, Donald W. 5:196
created good
  classification of 7:356
Creath, Richard
  Carnap, R. †2:208–15
  logical positivism 5:794
creation **2:695–700**
  see also cosmogony; cosmology;
    decreation; emanationism;
    evolutionary theory; Genesis,
    Book of; life, origin of
  Aquinas, T. 8:310
  atheistic potentiality arguments
    Indian philosophy 7:604–5
  atomic collision
    Epicureanism 3:345–6
  atomism
    Islamic philosophy 2:243

Augustine 1:550
biblical exegesis (Philoponus)
7:374–5
Big-Bang theory 2:679–80
biological paradigm (Empedocles)
3:295
Buddhism, Indian 2:98
Byzantine philosophy 2:162
Calvinism 2:179
causality
Islamic philosophy 2:241–3,
4:66
Chinese philosophy
xing 9:817–18
common grace 3:113–14
constructivist theory of knowledge
9:601
continuous 2:698
cyclical recurrence
Stoicism 9:142, 9:146
deism 2:852–3
Demiurge 2:695–6
demythologization 9:322–3
Descartes, R. 3:3, 3:15
design argument
Hume, D. 4:559–60
Paley, W. 7:186–7
Stoicism 9:146–7
divine
Berdiaev, N.A. 1:727–8
Philo of Alexandria 7:359–60
divine freedom 3:757–61
divine infinity 3:162–3
divine perfection 6:201
as divine renunciation of ego
(Weil, S.) 9:699–700
divine simplicity 8:785
divine transcendence
Jewish philosophy 5:309–10
divine will
Jewish philosophy 4:618–19
Egyptian cosmology
ancient 3:249
emanation 2:696–7
Ibn Miskawayh 4:630
Jewish philosophy
Bar Hayya, A. 1:649
Israeli, I. 5:32–3
Judah ben Moses of Rome
5:129
eschatological cosmology 1:838,
1:839
eternity compatibility
al-Ghazali 4:64–5, 4:639–40
Ibn Rushd 4:639–40
Philoponus 7:374

eternity of the world
Averroism 1:597
Bonaventure 1:832
Maimonides, M. 6:41, 6:44–5
Matthew of Aquasparta 6:201
medieval views of 3:428
Toletus, F. 9:434
ex nihilo
Abravanel, I. 1:22
Albo, J. 1:154
Arama, I. 1:350–1
Bible 4:95–6
Crescas, H. 2:702–3
Ibn Tzaddik, J. 4:661
Nahmanides, M. 6:648–9
exemplarism 1:832
faith/reason relationship
Jewish Averroism 1:599–600
formatio mundi
Jewish philosophy (Gersonides)
4:47, 4:48–9
God
Dooyeweerd, H. 3:113
Edwards, J. 3:242
evil, problem of 3:469–70
Vital du Four 9:639
grace 4:150–1
Hebrew Bible 1:767–8
Japanese philosophy (Motoori
Norinaga) 6:589
Kabbalah
Herrera, A. Cohen de 4:397,
4:398–9
Sefirot 5:172–3
Mīmāṃsā 6:379
mind as first cause (Anaxagoras)
1:252–3
mystical structure (Bonaventure)
1:828, 1:830
myth/language relationship
Jewish philosophy
(Rosenzweig, F.) 8:359
Native American philosophy
6:663–4, 6:665
natural philosophy
medieval 6:275, 6:692
nature relationship (Eriugena, J.S.)
3:401, 3:403, 3:404
Origen 7:162
Plato 7:401, 7:416
Platonism
Bible reconciliation 2:377
medieval 7:435, 7:436
polytheism 2:695
pre-eternality (Mir Damad,
Muhammad Baqir) 6:409–10
process theism 7:717–18

quantum field theory 3:671, 3:672
reflectiveness
Jewish pietism (Ibn Paquda)
4:634
science 8:233
seminal virtues (Bernard of Tours)
1:755–6
species (Wallace, A.R.) 9:678
striving possibles account
(Leibniz, G.W.) 5:545–6
sufficient reason (Leibniz, G.W.)
5:545–6
temporal versus eternal 2:697–8
theophany
Jewish philosophy
(Maimonides, M.) 6:43
ultimate cause (Saadiah Gaon)
8:436–7
wahdat al-shuhud (unity in
conscience) (Shah Wali Allah)
8:733
wahdat al-wujud (unity of being)
(Shah Wali Allah) 8:733
William of Conches 9:731
Creative Intellect
Neoplatonism 7:727
creativity
Christian ethics of (Berdiaev, N.A.)
1:729
Daoism
Zhuangzi 9:866
discovery
logic of 3:101
educational philosophy 3:234
emotional expression 5:354–5
metaphor (Ricouer, P.) 8:320
performing art 1:469
creatures
created substance (Conway, A.)
2:670
moral standing 6:550, 6:551–2
rational (Origen) 7:162
credibility
legal evidence 5:502
credulity
Gettier problems 4:57
religious experience 8:252
Creel, H.G. 2:782
Creery, W.E. 7:89
Crenshaw, K.W. 5:644
Crescas, Hasdai **2:700–4**
creation 2:702–3
critique of Aristotle 2:700, 2:701–2
free will 2:702
Ibn Shem Tov, I. 8:738
Jewish philosophy 5:89
voluntarism 9:665

omniscience 2:702
plurality of worlds 2:703
prophecy 7:769
Cress, D. 3:168
Cresson, A. 6:53
Cresswell, Max J. 4:806, 4:810,
6:425–6, 7:778
Crete
Delmedigo, E. **2:861–3**
Crewdson, J. 7:492
Crick, Francis Harry Compton
5:635, 6:458–9
Cridos
Eudoxus **3:452–3**
crime **2:704–11**
see also criminology; punishment;
war crimes
anarchism 1:246
civil disobedience 2:366–8
freedom
Dostoevskii, F.M. 3:116
harm principle 2:705–6
male in selmale in prohibita
distinction 2:706
as public wrong 2:706
revenge (Dühring, E.K.) 3:148
sentencing 2:708–9
social injury
feminist jurisprudence 3:609
criminology
Foucault, M. 7:602
Crimmins, Mark
language †5:408–11
propositional attitude statements
7:778
semantics †8:649–52
Crippa, A. 2:11
crisis
Western civilization (Jung, C.G.)
5:134
Crisp, Roger
ethics †3:435–7
fact/value distinction †3:537–8
happiness 4:229
Mill, J.S. 6:375
moral particularism †6:528–9
utilitarianism †9:551–7
virtue ethics †9:622–6
virtues and vices 9:631
Critchley, S. 5:582, 7:592
criteria **2:711–14**
Cavell, S. 2:258
grammar 2:712–13
scepticism 2:711–12
Criterion group 3:261
La critica 4:20

critical idealism
logic (Cohen, H.) 2:398, 2:399–400
Critical Legal Studies **2:714–20**
dialectic of
Enlightenment 2:717–18
Germany 2:716–17
Great Britain 2:717
hermeneutics 5:509
United States of America 2:714,
2:715–16
critical philosophy
speculative distinction 2:24
critical rationalism
Popper, K.R. 7:533
critical realism **2:720–2**
fallacies 2:721
Kemp Smith, N. 5:227, 5:228
Lonergan, B.J.F. 5:823, 5:824
critical reasoning
role of imagery (Le Doeuff, M.)
5:476–7
critical reflection
values
ethical autonomy 1:589–90
critical theory **2:722–8**
see also Frankfurt School
Adorno, T.W. **1:41–6**, 3:732–3
communicative rationality
(Habermas, J.) 3:735
conception of 'theory' 2:723–4
critique of instrumental reason
2:724
dialectic of enlightenment 2:725–7
Frankfurt School 2:459, 3:730–1
Hegelianism 4:291
Horkheimer, M. 4:510, 4:511
internal (immanent) criticism
2:724–5
Marxism 6:144, 9:358
negative dialectics 2:727
reflexivity 8:866
social science
contemporary theories of 8:838,
8:842–3, 8:845–6
totalitarianism 9:444
critical thinking
charity principle 2:283
educational philosophy 3:233–4
criticism
art **1:460–3**
art works 1:474–5
artist's intention 1:513, 1:514
dance 2:776
Lessing, G.E. 5:576–7
textual (Bentley, R.) 1:725–6
Critique of Judgment see Kant,
Immanuel

Critique of Practical Reason see
Kant, Immanuel
Critique of Pure Reason see Kant,
Immanuel
Crittenden, C. 3:662, 3:666
Croce, Benedetto **2:728–35**
art
understanding of 1:475
Baumgarten, A.G. 1:672
Gentile, G. 2:729–30, 2:732, 4:20
Gramsci, A. 4:152
Hegelianism 4:292
historicism 4:443, 4:445
history
philosophy of 4:458
idealism 5:38, 5:40–1
intuition 2:730–1
liberalism 2:730, 2:732
Marxism
Latin America 6:163
poetry 7:476
pure concepts 2:728–9, 2:731
Vico, G. 9:606
Crocker, David
development ethics †3:39–44
Crocker, L.G. 3:69, 8:376
Crombie, A.C. 1:636, 4:182, 6:330,
6:706
Crombie, I.M. 8:259
Cromwell, R.S. 9:166
Crone, A.L. 8:385
Cronin, T. 9:195
Cronus, Diodorus 7:688
Crook, R.E. 7:684
Cropsey, J. 8:821
Crosby, Donald A.
nihilism †7:1–5
Crosby, H.L. 7:182
Crosland, C.A.R. 8:828
Crosland, M.P. 1:158
Crossan, J.D. 4:394
Crossley, J.N. 7:53
Crouse, R.D. 1:564
Crouzel, H. 7:163
Crowder, George
anarchism †1:244–9
Crowe, F.C. 5:825
Crowley, T. 1:636, 7:269
Crowther, Paul
Kant, I. 5:196
the sublime †9:201–5
crucial experiments **2:735–6**, 3:514,
3:515
Bacon, F. 3:514
Duhem, P.M.M. 3:142, 3:144

cruelty
  vices
    evil 9:629–30
Crummell, Alexander 7:192, 7:194
Crump, J. 8:886
Cruse, D.A. 1:200, 6:319
Crusius, Christian August **2:736–9**
  influence on Kant, I. 2:738, 5:179
Crutch, D. 3:109
Cruz Costa, Joao 2:11, 7:569
Cruz Hernández, M. 4:629–30, 6:620
Cruz, Sor Juana Inés de la
  colonial thought
    Mexico 6:345
  Latin America
    colonial thought in 5:421, 6:345
    feminist thought in 3:625, 3:628
    philosophy in 5:426–7
Cruz Vélez, Danilo 7:349–50, 7:351
CTM *see* mind, computational
  theories of
Cua, A.S.
  Chinese Confucianism †2:536–49
  self-cultivation
    Chinese philosophy 8:625
    Wang Yangming 9:684
    Xunzi †9:818–20
Cuba
  Latin American Marxism 6:160,
    6:162
  positivism 7:568
Cubism 1:449–50
Cudworth, Damaris *see* Masham,
  Damaris
Cudworth, Ralph **2:739–44**
  Cambridge Platonism 2:185
  Price, R. 7:679
Cuenot, C. 9:291
Cujas, Jacques 8:344
Cullen, S.P. 5:650
Culler, Jonathan
  Barthes, R. 1:658
  post-structuralism 7:600
  Saussure, F. de 8:482
  structuralism †9:174–7
Cullity, Garrett
  moral judgment †6:511–14
Cullmann, Oscar 3:416, 8:296
Culp, Sylvia 6:459–60
culpa see guilt
cultural evolution 3:483, 3:486
cultural identity *see* identity, cultural
cultural norms
  rationality and cultural relativism
    8:82, 8:85
cultural pluralism
  differentiated citizenship 2:364–5

federalism 3:573
cultural psychology
  Wundt, W. 9:799–800
cultural relativism 2:748
  African philosophy, Francophone
    1:110
  descriptive 6:539
  Herder, J.G. 4:381–2
  human nature 6:736
  moral sentiments 6:549
  normative 6:541
  Plato 7:790
  and rationality **8:80–6**
    fideism 8:85
    functionalism 8:84, 8:85
    intellectualism 8:84
    interpretation and translation
      8:83
    symbolism 8:84–5
  Todorov, T. 9:426
culture **2:746–50**
  aesthetic concepts 1:58
  aesthetic relativism 1:683
  African philosophy
    aesthetics 1:61–3
    ethical systems 3:430–4, 3:432
    nationalism 1:108–10, 1:111–12
  archaeological records 1:355–6
  common versus high 2:748–9
  consumer (Baudrillard, J.) 1:662–3
  critique of (Jung, C.G.) 5:134
  cultural imaginary
    feminist analysis of 3:586
  dance 2:777
  definition 2:746, 2:747
  diversity
    Todorov, T. 9:426
    virtues 9:627–8
  East/West comparisons of
    Ramakrishna Movement 8:40
  enforced homogeny of 9:700
  ethnophilosophical modernization
    of 3:448–9
  European influence
    postcolonial philosophy of
      science 7:575–7
  German Idealism 8:358
  guilt/shame distinction
    morality and ethics 6:567–9,
      8:139
  history of 4:623, 4:624
  hybridization
    ethnophilosophy 3:447
  ideal 5:437
  ideology 4:683–4
  individual autonomy
    (Mamardashvili, M.K.) 6:68

influence on discourse 3:446
Jewish
  reconstructionism (Kaplan, M.)
    5:205–6
language and gender 5:364–5
love 5:843–4
migration of 3:454
morality
  Christian contextualization
    8:222
multiculturalism 6:599–602
music
  function 6:607
  meanings 6:611
mythology 2:226
national liberation (Cabral, A.)
  2:170
nationalism
  African philosophy,
    Francophone 1:108–10,
    1:111–12
naturalism
  Herder, J.G. 4:378, 4:379, 4:382
  Nietzsche, F.W. 6:845–4, 6:847
neo-Confucianism 6:774
objective–subjective distinction
  (Simmel, G.) 8:779
pedagogy of (Hessen, S.I.) 4:416
popular
  consumerism (Baudrillard, J.)
    1:662–3
postmodernism 7:587, 7:588
proletarian (Bogdanov, A.A.)
  1:817–18
religious experiences 6:631
science of (*ilm al-umran*) 4:623,
  4:624
sign production
  Moscow-Tartu school 6:586
subjective-objective gap
  (Simmel, G.) 8:779
symbolic forms (Cassirer, E.)
  2:223–5
values
  philosophy of medicine 6:266
Ćulum, Jovan 9:54
Culver, C.M. 1:776
Culverwell, Nathanial **2:750–2**
Cumberland, Richard **2:752–3**, 9:725
Cummings, E.M. 7:822
Cummins, Robert
  functional explanation 3:804,
    3:805
  physical illness 6:312, 6:314
  methodological individualism
    6:343–4

Cunha de Azeredo Coutinho, José
  Joaquin 2:9
Cunliffe, C. 2:160
Cunningham, A. 6:740
Cunningham, F.A. 8:311–12
Cunningham, G.W. 1:853, 4:184,
  7:318
Cunningham, R.B. 5:590
Cuoco, Vincenzo 5:36, 5:41
Cur deus homo see Anselm of
  Canterbury
Curley, E.M. 3:18, 6:425, 6:747, 9:107
Curren, R.
  educational philosophy †3:231–40
    history of †3:222–31
Currie, Gregory
  art works
    ontology of †1:480–5
  emotion in response to art 3:280
  fiction
    semantics of 3:662
  fictional entities 3:666
  film
    aesthetics of †3:673–7
  forgery
    artistic †1:498–502
  narrative †6:654–7
  photography, aesthetics of
    †7:378–81
Curry, H.
  see also Scott-Curry theorem
  combinatory logic 2:431, 2:432,
    2:433
  lambda calculus 5:349
Curtius, E.R. 3:308
Curto, S. 3:254
curve-fitting
  simplicity 8:780–1
Curzer, H.J. 7:736
Cusanus *see* Nicholas of Cusa
Cushing, James T.
  Bell's theorem 1:716

conservation principles †2:606–8
determinism and indeterminism
  3:39
electrodynamics †3:258–60
quantum mechanics,
  interpretation of 7:894
Cussins, Adrian 2:642
custom
  see also convention
  African philosophy 3:431, 3:448
  common law 2:440–6
  legal norms 7:39
  moral relativism 6:539, 6:540
  as source of law 5:466
cut-elimination theorem
  Gentzen, G.K.E. 4:23, 4:24
  glossary 5:800–1
  Herbrand's theorem 4:376–7
  non-constructive rules of inference
    7:28–9
  proof theory 7:747
  sequent calculus 6:676, 6:679–80
  tableau systems 6:681
Cutland, N. 1:215, 2:490
Cutrofello, Andrew
  Derrida, J. †2:896–901
Cuvier, Georges 8:18
cybersex
  sexual concepts 8:718
cyclic majorities 8:69
Cynics 2:753–9
  Diogenes of Sinope 2:754–6
  Epictetus 3:339
  happiness 2:755
  human nature 2:753–4, 2:755
  Lucian 5:853–4
  politics
    Zeno of Citium 9:842
  Socratic schools 9:21
  Stoicism 1:315, 9:154
Cyprus
  Zeno of Citium 9:841–3

Cyrenaics 2:759–63
  Aristippus the Elder 1:379–80
  epistemology 2:760–1
  ethics 2:761–3
  history of school 2:760
  pleasure 3:346–7
  Socratic schools 9:21
Cyrene
  Aristippus the Elder 1:380
Czech Republic 2:763–9
  Herbartism 2:766
  Jednota Bratvská (Unity of
    Brethren) 2:765
  Marxism 2:767–8
  Prague Spring 2:768
  Reformation 2:763–4, 2:765
  Stalinism 2:768
  statehood 2:766–9
  Weyr, F. 9:707–9
Czechoslovak Republic 6:165–6
  see also Czech Republic; Slovakia
  Bolzano, B. 1:823–7
  Comenius, J.A. 2:438–40
  foundation 2:766–7
  Hus, J. 4:573–4
  Husserl, E. 4:574–88
  Mazaryk, T.G. 6:165–6
  Patočka, J. 7:252–4
  Weinberger, O. 9:701–2
  Weyr, F. 9:707–9
Czelakowski, J.
  Leśniewski, S. 5:574
  Łukasiewicz, J. 5:863
  many-valued logics 6:90
  mereology 6:320
  Polish logic 7:499
Czerkawski, Jan
  Poland †7:483–9
Czeżowski, T. 7:486, 7:493, 7:497

D

d'Abano, Pietro 1:406
Dabashi, Hamid
Mir Damad, Muhammad Baqir
†6:408–11
Dabney, R.L. 7:656
DaCosta, N.C. 9:352
daemons
Early and Middle Platonism 7:426
Plutarch of Chaeronea 7:468–9
Pythagoreanism 7:860
Xenocrates 9:807
Dahan, G. 4:51
Dahl, R.A. 2:871
Dahl, T.S. 3:610
Dahlberg, F. 3:592
Dahlhaus, C. 6:612
Dahlquist, Thorild
Hägerström, A.A.T. †4:201–4
Scandinavia
philosophy in 8:491
Dahm, H. 9:32
Dahms, H.-J. 9:612–13
Dahrendorf, R. 9:561
Dai J. 3:112
Dai Zhen 2:548, **2:770–1**, 6:774–5
Daiber, H. 7:520
Daiches, D. 1:782
Dainichi *see* Buddha Dainichi
Daktsang lodzawa *see* sTag tshang lō
tsa ba
dal Pra, M. 4:171, 7:854
Dalen, D. van 2:639, 4:853
Dales, R.C. 3:429, 4:363, 6:276, 8:317
Daley, B.E. 1:812
Dalferth, I.U. 6:5
Dalgarno, George 8:678, 8:679, 9:535
Dalgarno, M. 8:179
Dalhbom, B. 2:884
Dalibard, J. 1:716
Dalla Chiara Scabia, M. 9:352
Dallmayr, F. 4:199
Dallmeyer, D.G. 7:693
Dalton, John 2:297
d'Alverny, M.-T. 9:456
Daly, Chris
natural kinds †6:682–5
Daly, J. 3:679
Daly, Mary 3:621, 3:622–3, 3:624

Damascius **2:771–2**
Hypatia 4:596–7
Islamic philosophy 4:155–6
Damian, Peter **2:772–4**
D'Amico, R. 4:445–6
Damiens, S. 1:27
damnation
free will 4:330–1
reprobation **8:272–6**
Dan, J. 5:175
Dana, J. 4:614
dance
aesthetics of **2:774–7**
communication 2:776–7
notation 2:775–6
role of dancer 2:776
Dancy, Jonathan
deontological ethics 2:891
examples in ethics 3:490
intuitionism in ethics 4:854, 4:856
logic of ethical discourse 5:764
morality
judgment 6:514
particularism 6:528, 6:529
realism †6:534–9
perception 7:293, 7:298
Ross, W.D. 8:367
supererogation 9:235
Dancy, R.M.
Eudoxus 3:453
Speusippus 9:90
Danforth, John W. 4:561
Dani, A.H. 8:564
Daniélou, J. 7:163
Daniels, A. 6:115
Daniels, N.
epistemic relativism 3:361
medical ethics 6:264
morality
justification 6:516
knowledge 6:519
Rawls, J. 8:109
Reid, T. 8:180
Danilevskii, Nikolai Iakovlevich
cultural-historical types
(Leont'ev, K.N.) 5:569
Pan-Slavism 7:200–1, 8:811
Danneberg, L. 9:613
Dannhauer, J.C. 4:388

Danquah, J.B. 1:106, 1:139, 3:434
Dante Alighieri *see* Alighieri, Dante
Danto, A.C.
action 1:41
art, abstract 1:452
forgery
artistic 1:501
history
philosophy of 4:458
Sartre, J.-P. 8:479
style
artistic 1:508, 1:509
Danziger, K. 1:695, 4:845
dao (Way) **2:778–9**
authority of
law and ritual 5:449
Confucianism
ethics of virtue 2:538, 2:543
Guanzi 4:187
holistic nature
Xunzi 9:818, 9:819–20
li 2:540, 2:541
ren 2:540, 2:541
yi 2:540, 2:541
cosmology
East Asian Philosophy 3:193
Daodejing 2:780, 2:781
Daoism 2:785–6
Huainanzi 4:513
order 2:321
de relationship 2:320–1, 2:809
guide to rulers 5:447
history, Chinese philosophy
4:450–1
Legalism 5:531, 5:536–7
li (propriety)
Confucius 2:568
neo-Confucianism
immanence
Dai Zhen 2:770
li
Dai Zhen 2:770
sagehood
Ogyū Sorai 7:90
self-cultivation 8:616, 8:618–19,
8:622
zhi 9:858
Daodejing (*Laozi*) 2:313–14, **2:779–83**
dao 2:778

Daoism 2:789, 2:795
de 2:809
harmony 2:321
history, theories of 4:448
language 2:788
Legalism 5:536, 5:537
mysticism 6:622
self-cultivation 8:618
tilyong 9:400
wu-forms 2:789
you-wu 9:835
Daoism 2:320–2, **2:783–95**
art
Japan 1:87
Buddhism
comparison
fa 3:532–3
Confucianism harmonization
Korea 2:114–16
Chinese classics 2:313–14
Confucianism distinction 2:783
Daodejing 2:779–81
de 2:786–7, 2:809–10
East Asian Philosophy 3:195
fa 3:532–3
harmony 2:324
history, theories of 4:448
Huainanzi 4:512–13
influence of
Buddhism, China 2:81–2
language theories 5:694
Legalism 5:535, 5:536–7
mysticism 6:622
neo-Confucianism 6:765–6
poetry
Chinese 1:68, 1:70
self-cultivation 8:618–19
Lushi chunqiu 5:864
Sengzhao 8:683–4
wu 2:787–94
Zhuangzi **9:865–7**
daojia (School of the Way)
daojiao distinction 2:784
Dao'on
keyi 2:82
Dao-sheng
buddha-nature
inherence of 2:83
daotong (transmission of the Way)
Chinese Confucianism 2:540–1,
2:544–5
neo-Confucianism 6:770
daoxin (the mind of the Way)
neo-Confucianism 6:770
Daoyuan 9:870
D'Arboussier, Gabriel 1:114
D'Arcy, E. 2:581

D'Arcy, M.C. 7:69
Darden, Lindley
genetics †4:12–16
unity of science 9:532
Darley, J. 9:526
Darnton, R. 3:319
Darrigol, O. 1:822, 7:482
Dārṣṭāntika School of Buddhism
2:55, 2:56, 2:57
Darstellungsfunktion see function,
representational
Darwall, S.
analytic ethics 1:223
Cudworth, R. 2:744
deontological ethics 2:891
moral realism 6:538
moral sense theories 6:547
Nagel, T. 6:647
ontological status of value 9:581
Price, R. †7:675–9
respect for persons 8:284, 8:286
Shaftesbury, Third Earl of 8:732
Darwin, Charles Robert **2:795–9**
see also Darwinism
animals and ethics 1:274, 1:276
evolutionary theory 3:482, 9:296,
9:297
Huxley, T.H. 4:594–5
influence on Strauss, D.F. 9:165,
9:166
materialism 6:172
natural selection 8:892, 8:896
genetics 4:12
race
theories of 8:18
Wallace, A.R. 9:678
On the Origin of Species 2:795,
2:796
Huxley, T.H. 4:594
religion and science 8:235
religious opposition to 8:232
social science
history of philosophy of 8:857
theosophy 9:364
Darwin, Erasmus 4:238
Darwinism
see also Darwin, Charles;
evolutionary theory; sociobiology
Argentina, philosophy in 1:376
falsificationism 7:535
functionalism in social science
3:816–17
idealism 4:667
pragmatism 7:633, 7:636–7
self-preservation 5:314
social
Darwin, C.R. 2:795, 2:798

Spencer, H. 9:88
Dascal, M. 1:231, 1:233
Dasein (being-in-the-world)
see also existence
disclosure 4:307–8, 4:312–14
entity 4:307–8, 4:310, 4:312–13
Ereignis (disclosure-as-such) 4:315,
4:317
existentialism 3:495–7
Heidegger, M. 4:307–8, 4:310–13
hermeneutics (Heidegger, M.)
4:387–8
history of being 4:316
intentionality 1:702
phenomenology 7:337–8, 7:339
temporality 4:307, 4:309, 4:310–11
vital existence 5:80
Dasgupta, B.N. 2:6–7
Dasgupta, P. 7:542
Dasgupta, S.N.
awareness
in Indian thought 1:608
Brahman 2:4
Indian monism 6:479
matter
Indian conceptions of 6:200
mysticism, history of 6:626
Rāmānuja 8:44
self
Indian theories of 8:610
sense perception
Indian views of 8:694
Vedānta School 9:593–4
*Dasheng qixin lun see Awakening of
Faith in Mahāyāna*
Daston, L.J. 4:33, 5:720–1
Dastur, F. 4:482
databases
privacy
information technology and
ethics 4:780
Datta, D.M.
God
Indian conceptions of 4:105
knowledge
Indian views of 5:285
negative facts in classical Indian
philosophy 6:758
self
Indian theories of 8:610
Daub, K. 4:296
Dauben, J.W. 1:215, 2:198, 2:200,
2:657
Dauer, F.W. 4:566
David of Dinant **2:799–800**
Davidson, Donald **2:800–6**
action 1:41, 2:800–1

adverbs 1:48, 1:49, 1:50
akrasia 1:141–2
analytic philosophy 1:228
animal language and thought
 1:271, 1:273, 2:804
anomalous monism 1:276–9,
 1:280, 2:801
Anscombe, G.E.M. 1:282
causation 2:250
charity principle 2:283–5
coherence theory of truth 5:275,
 9:472
compositionality 2:477, 2:801–2
correspondence theory of truth
 9:474
discourse semantics 2:803, 3:98
epistemic justification 5:164
events 3:462, 3:463
holism
 belief 2:804–5, 4:487, 8:33–4
identity thesis of belief 1:707,
 1:709
indirect discourse 4:743–4, 4:745
intensionality 4:811
intention 4:813, 4:815
language
 conventionality of 5:370, 5:371
 social nature of 5:418, 5:419
logical form 5:784, 5:785
meaning
 and truth 6:225
 and understanding 6:227–9
 and verification 6:235
mental causation
 token identity theory 6:311
metaphor 6:336–7
pragmatism 7:631, 7:636–7, 7:638
propositional attitudes 7:775–6,
 7:778, 7:786
psychoanalysis
 methodological issues in 7:816
Quine, W.V. 8:14
radical interpretation 2:802,
 2:804–5, 8:25–6, 8:31–4
rationality and cultural relativism
 8:80, 8:83, 8:86
reasons and causes 8:127
reference 8:163
self-deception 8:628
semantics 8:651, 8:674
slingshot argument 3:536–7
supervenience of the mental 9:239
syntax 9:253
transcendental arguments 9:454
truth theory 8:31–4
unconscious mental states 9:526
use/mention distinction 9:551

Davidson, H.A.
 al-Baghdadi 1:638
 epistemology in Islamic
  philosophy 3:387
 eternity of the world
  medieval views of 3:429
 Hillel ben Samuel of Verona 4:433
 Ibn Sina 4:654
 Judah Halevi 4:213
 natural philosophy
  medieval 6:706
 prophecy 7:770
 Shem Tov family 8:739
Davidson, H.M. 7:246
Davie, G.
 Brown, T. 2:28
 Ferguson, A. 3:632
 Ferrier, J.F. 3:634
Davie, George
 Kemp Smith, N. †5:227–31
Davies, B. 1:347
Davies, Emily 3:583
Davies, H.E. 5:301
Davies, M.
 connectionism 2:577
 descriptions 3:23–4
 language
  conventionality of 5:371
 language of thought hypothesis
  5:407
 meaning and truth 6:225
 methodological individualism
  6:344
 unconscious mental states 9:526
Davies, P. 9:369, 9:416
Davies, S.
 presupposition 7:675
Davies, Stephen
 art
  artistic expression †1:492–8
  artist's intention 1:515
  definition of †1:463–8
  emotion in response to 3:280
 Langer, S.K.K. 5:356
 music
  aesthetics of 6:612–13
  performing art †1:468–72
Davis, C.F. 6:632
Davis, D. B. 8:806
Davis, E. 2:453
Davis, J.B. 5:235
Davis, J.K. 7:734, 7:736
Davis, M.
 Church's theorem and the decision
  problem 2:350
 Church's thesis 2:354
 computability theory 2:490

computer science 2:496
 ordinal logics 7:143
 Post, E.L. 7:575
 proof theory 7:750
 recursion-theoretic hierarchies
  8:144
 Turing machines 9:498
Davis, Michael
 engineering ethics †3:313–15
 professional ethics 7:736
Davis, Murray 8:727
Davis, N. 2:891
Davis, N.Z. 2:345
Davis, P.J. 5:345
Davis, S.
 pragmatics 7:631
Davis, Stephen T.
 eschatology †3:413–17
Davis, Wayne A.
 implicature †4:721–5
Davitt, T. 9:195
Davy, J. 9:134
Davydov, Iu.N. 6:159
al-Dawani, Jalal al-Din **2:806–7**
 Islamic moral philosophy 3:441
Dawkins, Richard
 evolutionary theory 3:482
 functionalism in social science
  3:817
 genetics 4:14, 4:15
 life, origin of 5:635
 sociobiology 8:896
Dawson, D. 2:464, 7:190
Dawson, John W. Jr.
 Gödel, K. †4:105–7
Dawson, R. 4:452
Dawson, S. 5:135
Daxue (Great Learning) 2:300,
 2:807–9, 8:617–18
Day, J.P. 4:509
Dayanand Saraswati 1:516–17
dBu ma pa 9:488
de (virtue) 2:320–1, **2:809–10**
 Confucianism 2:538–9, 2:540
 dao relationship 2:320–1, 2:778–9
 Daoism 2:786–7, 2:788
De Anima (On the soul) *see* Aristotle
de Bary, William Theodore
 Chinese philosophy 2:327
 Confucianism
  Chinese 2:548
  Japanese 2:555
 Fujiwara Seika 3:800
 Han Feizi 4:220
 Itō Jinsai 5:43
 Japanese philosophy 5:79

Korean Confucian philosophy
2:564–5
Kumazawa Banzan 5:322
Lu Xiangshan 5:852
Ogyū Sorai 7:91
Shōtoku Constitution 8:753
Tominaga Nakamoto 9:441
Yi Hwang 9:825
De Beauvoir, Simone *see* Beauvoir,
Simone de
de Biran, Pierre François *see* Maine
de Biran, Pierre-François
De Buffon, Comte Georges Louis
Leclerc *see* Buffon, Georges Louis
Leclerc, Comte de
De Civitate Dei (The City of God) *see*
Augustine of Hippo
De consolatione philosophiae (On the
Consolation of Philosophy) *see*
Boethius, Anicius Manlius
Severinus
De Cordemoy, Géraud *see*
Cordemoy, Géraud de
de dicto **2:815–17**
see also de re
descriptions 3:20–1
epistemic logic 3:358
free logics 3:743
glossary 5:801
modal logic 5:752, 5:765–6
propositional attitude statements
7:773–4
scope 8:588
tense logic 9:303–4, 9:305
De Doctrina Christiana see Augustine
of Hippo
De Duve, C. 5:635
de facto question
religious belief 8:210, 8:214, 8:217
de Finetti, B. 8:49
De Fontenelle, Bernard *see*
Fontenelle, Bernard de
De Franco, L. 9:299–300
De genesi ad litteram see Augustine of
Hippo
De Giorgi, F. 8:364
De Interpretatione see Aristotle
De Jong, J.W. 9:218
de jure question
religious belief 8:210, 8:214, 8:217
De La Forge, Louis *see* La Forge,
Louis de
De La Mettrie, Julien Offroy *see* La
Mettrie, Julien Offroy de
De libero arbitrio see Augustine of
Hippo

De Man, Paul **2:810–13**, 2:837–8,
2:839
De Marco, P. 7:392
de Menasce, J. 9:874
De Morgan, Augustus **2:813–14**
see also De Morgan's laws
logic 5:725–6, 5:727
De Morgan's laws 1:844, 2:813, 5:801
De Nicolas, A. 8:467
de Orta, Garcia 2:8
De Pauley, W.C. 2:185, 2:752
de Pizan, Christine *see* Christine de
Pizan
De processione Spiritus Sancti see
Anselm of Canterbury
de re **2:815–17**
see also de dicto
descriptions 3:20–1
epistemic logic 3:358
essentialism 3:418
free logics 3:743
glossary 5:801
modal logic 5:752, 5:765–6
omniscience 7:108
propositional attitude statements
7:773–4
scope 8:588
tense logic 9:303–4, 9:305
De Revolutionibus Orbium Coelestium
Copernicus, Nicolaus
de Roberty, Evgenii 7:563
de Sanctis, Francesco 2:730, 2:734,
4:300
de se knowledge
omniscience 7:108–9
De, S.K. 3:859
De Smet, R.V. 3:568
De Sousa, R. 3:285, 6:563
De trinitate see Augustine of Hippo
De, U.K. 9:418
De Vio, Thomas *see* Cajetan
De Vleeschauwer, H.J. 5:196
De Vooght, P. 4:574
De Wulf, M. 4:122
Deakin, Alfred 1:575–6
Dear, Peter
Aristotelianism in the seventeenth
century 1:386–93
Mersenne, M. †6:325–31
death **2:817–23**
see also eschatology; life, and
death
after-death experiences 9:48
analysis-criterion distinction
2:818–19
body/soul distinction 2:818, 2:819,
2:821

Buddhism
Shintō comparison 8:750
criteria for 5:626–7
events 3:462
'experiential blank' 2:820
fear of (Hume, D.) 4:558
heaven **4:249–53**
hell **4:329–33**
human freedom 8:38
infinity 4:777
Islamic philosophy (al-Razi, Abu
Bakr) 3:439
Jewish philosophy
Bar Hayya, A. 1:650
bioethics 1:777–8
limbo **5:635–8**
literature relationship
(Blanchot, M.) 1:783
meaning of life 2:818, 2:821–2,
5:631
mystery of 2:817–18, 2:819–20
nirvāṇa 7:9
as non-being 9:519
original sin 8:793, 8:794
public policy 2:818–19
purgatory **7:836–9**
reincarnation **8:182–6**
reprobation **8:272–6**
resurrection 3:574, 3:575, **8:294–6**
soul
immortality of the 9:44
mortality of
Epicureanism 3:340, 3:348–9
suicide 9:224–8
survival of 2:818, 2:820–1
voluntary
Jainism 5:53
death of the author 4:393
death drive
Freud, S.
Lacan, J. interpretation of 5:337
death rate
birth rate balance 7:540
Deats, P. 7:318
deautomization
mystical experiences 6:631
debate
formal 3:75
Nyāya-Vaiśeṣika 7:59–60
DeBellis, M. 6:613
Debord, G. 1:248
Deborin, A.M. 6:151
Debru, C. 3:129, 5:351
debt
gratitude relationship 8:135,
8:138–9
guilt relationship 8:139

moralization of (Nietzsche, F.W.)
6:855
Debus, A.G. 3:683–4, 7:208
Decad
  perfection of (Speusippus) 9:90
deceit *see* deception
deception
  see also self-deception
  by animals 1:272
  artistic forgery 1:499
  implicature 4:722
  truthfulness contrast 9:480–4
decidability
  see also decision problem
  Church's thesis 2:351–2
  computational complexity 2:473–4
  glossary 5:801
  Herbrand's theorem 4:377
  linear logic 5:640
  predicate calculus 7:663–4
decision problem 5:733–4
  Church's theorem 2:347, **2:349–51**
  computability theory 2:482–3,
    2:488–9
  glossary 5:802
  Post, E.L. 7:574
  Turing, A.M. 9:493
decision theory **2:823–35**
  see also expected utility theory;
    game theory; *see also* practical
    reasoning; rational choice theory
  Bayesian 7:708
    risk 8:331, 8:332
  counterfactual conditionals 2:688
  degrees of belief (Ramsey, F.P.)
    8:44, 8:45–6
  desire 3:32
  expected utility 2:824–5
  inductive inference 4:758
  maximin
    risk 8:332
  medical ethics 6:260, 6:262, 6:267
  Newcomb's problem (Nozick, R.)
    7:47
  prisoner's dilemma 2:659
  social choice 8:825, 8:826
  sociobiology 8:893
  solidarity 9:23–4
  values 1:610
decolonization
  see also colonialism
  African conceptual autonomy
    1:102, 1:105
decomposition
  see also perishability

of complex beings
  potentiality
    Indian theories of 7:605–6
deconstruction **2:835–9**
  aesthetics (Lyotard, J.-F.) 6:8
  closure of metaphysics (Nancy, J.-
    L.) 6:651–2
  Derrida, J. 2:811–12
  hermeneutics
    biblical 4:393, 4:394
  identity (Derrida, J.) 1:190
  Japanese literature 5:660
  language (Derrida, J.) 2:897–9
  literary theory (Man, P. de)
    2:810–11, 2:837–8
  ordinary language philosophy
    7:146
  postmodernism 7:588
  post-structuralism 7:598–9
  psychoanalysis (Cixous, H.) 2:372
  subject
    postmodern critique of 9:199
  theology 7:583–4
decreation
  renunciation of the ego (Weil, S.)
    9:699–700
Dedekind, Julius Wilhelm Richard
  2:839–42
  arithmetic 1:440, 1:441
  axiom of choice 1:613
  Cantor, G. 2:196–7, 2:198
  computability theory 2:483, 2:490
  foundations of mathematics 5:847
  Gödel's theorems 4:115
  Hilbert's programme and
    formalism 4:425, 4:427
  logicism 5:813, 5:815, 5:816
  mathematics
    foundations of 6:189
  numbers 1:218, 7:51, 7:53
  proof theory 7:743, 7:750
  realism
    mathematics 8:123
Dedekind, R.
  Frege, G. 3:777
deduction 3:703–4
  see also consequence; induction;
    inference; natural deduction
  archaeology 1:354
  argument (Aristotle) 1:417
  art criticism 1:460–1
  computability 2:352
  consequence contrast (Bolzano, B.)
    1:826
  demonstration (Aristotle)
    1:417–18

determination distinction
  natural law 2:444–5
  glossary 5:801
  Hume's law
    logic of ethical discourse
      5:759–60, 5:761
  legal reasoning 5:526
  metaphysical (Kant, I.) 5:185–6
  methodology of discovery 3:100
  natural (Popper, K.R.) 7:535–6
  natural theology 6:707, 6:708–9
  predicate calculus 7:663–4
  rules of inference 7:27–9
  scientific explanation (Nagel, E.)
    6:642
  scientific method
    (Tschirnhaus, E.W. von) 9:486
  second-order logic 8:592
  systems 3:703–4
  thought experiments 9:394–5
  transcendental (Kant, I.) 5:186
  underdetermination 9:528
deduction theorem
  glossary 5:801
deductive closure principle **2:842–5**,
  5:272, 8:494
  glossary 5:799
deductive-nomological model of
  explanation
  individualism/holism debate
    4:485–6
Deely, J. 5:120, 8:679
deep ecology
  environmental ethics 3:333, 3:334
  Næss, A. 3:197, 3:199–200, 6:635,
    6:636
default logic 7:31–2
Defaux, G. 8:17
defeasibility
  inference 7:32, 7:33
defeasibility theory of knowledge *see*
  knowledge, defeasibility
  theory of
Deferrari, R.J. 1:347, 7:839
definability theory
  Beth's theorem and Craig's
    interpolation theorem **1:760–4**
  Church's thesis 2:349–50
  method of forcing 3:694, 3:696–7
  ordinal logics 7:140–1
  paradoxes of 7:218
definite descriptions
  Russell, B.A.W. 8:397–8
  Strawson, P.F. 9:168, 9:169
definition **2:845–9**
  analyticity 1:234–5, 1:236, 1:237–8

Aristotle (al-Suhrawardi critique) 4:701
conceptualization
 Islamic philosophy 5:709
coordinative (Reichenbach, H.) 8:169
geometric method (Spinoza, B. de) 9:92
of God (Ibn 'Adi) 4:600
Illuminationist philosophy (al-Suhrawardi) 9:221
implicit
 concept formation (Schlick, F.A.M.) 8:540
 conventionalism 2:668
Indian concepts of **2:849–52**
inductive *see* inductive definitions
al-Kindi 5:250
nominal–real distinction
 Leibniz, G.W. 5:551
 Spinoza, B. de 9:92
operational 7:132–3, 7:134
Port-Royalists 5:373
reduction by 8:145–6
universal characteristics (Leibniz, G.W.) 5:376
definitions
 contextual 2:847
 coordinative
  conventionalism 8:169
deflationary theories
 fictional entities 3:664–6
deflationary theories of truth *see* truth, deflationary theories of
Degenaar, M. 6:468
de'Giorolami, Remigio 1:411–12
Degl'Innocenti, U. 2:201
DeGrazia, David
 suffering †9:213–15
Deguise, P. 2:618
Dehio, L. 6:282
Deichgräber, K. 4:335
deification
 of humans 7:732
Deigh, J. 3:280
deism **2:853–6**
 afterlife (Butler, J.) 2:154, 2:157–9
 conservation doctrine
  rejection of 2:698
 definition 2:852–3
 Fontenelle, B. de 3:691
 Herbert 4:373
 natural order (Condillac, É.B. de) 2:526
 Newtonian mechanics (Franklin, B.) 3:737
 polemical (Tindal, M.) 9:420–2

revelation 8:297
deities
 pre-Columbian religions 5:429, 5:430
Deitz, L. 7:428
Del Negro, W. 9:567
Del Noce, A. 4:23
Del Punta, Francesco
 Giles of Rome †4:72–8
Del Vecchio, G. 5:512, 5:513
Delafosse, Maurice 1:110
Delahunty, R.J. 9:107
Delaney, C.F.
 Sellars, W.S. 8:642
 tacit knowledge †5:286–7
Delany, Martin R. 7:192
Delaruelle, E. 4:47
Delattre, R.A. 3:245
Delbos, V. 6:53
Delbruck, Max 6:458
delegates
 political representation 8:271
Deleu, J. 6:34
Deleuze, Gilles **2:856–61**
 alterity 1:189–90, 1:191
 Dodgson, C.L. 3:108
 Foucault, M. 3:713
 Hume, D. 4:561
 Nietzsche, F.W. 6:861
 subject
  postmodern critique of 9:199, 9:200
 Whitehead, A.N. 9:718
Delft, L. van 6:558
Delgado, R. 5:644
Delhaye, P. 5:822
deliberation
 moral 6:512–13
Delius, H. 9:613
Delmedigo, Elijah **2:861–3**
 Hebrew translations of Arabic texts 5:23
 Jewish philosophy 5:89
Delmonico, N. Gorton 3:859
Delphy, C. 3:613
delta system theorem 3:695
delta-epsilon method
 nonstandard analysis 1:212, 1:213
Delvignette, Robert 1:110
Delvolvé, J. 1:677
DeMallie, R.J. 6:670
demarcation problem
 scientific discovery (Popper, K.R.) 7:534–5
 scientific-nonscientific **2:863–7**
  French philosophy of science 3:781, 3:785

Dembski, William A.
 randomness †8:56–9
Dement, W. 3:129
Demiurge 2:695–6
 Christian Platonists 7:435–6
 Gnosticism 6:75
 Paulicianism 6:76
 Plato 4:99–4:100
democracy **2:867–72**
 see also constitutionalism; majoritarianism; political representation
 China 2:327
 citizenship 2:362–3
 communicative reason (Habermas, J.) 4:197
 constitutionalism 2:620–1
  Bentham, J. 1:719, 1:724
 criterion for (Popper, K.R.) 7:537
 critiques of
  Proudhon, P.-J. 7:792
  Thucydides 9:399
 definition 2:867–8
 educational influence (Dewey, J.) 3:228
 feminist political philosophy 3:620
 freedom of speech 3:763
 human nature (Spinoza, B. de) 9:105
 India (Ambedkar, B.R.) 1:196
 journalism ethics 5:126–7
 justice
  as fairness (Rawls, J.) 8:106–8
 knowledge 2:869–70
 legitimacy 5:540
 liberalism 5:598–9, 5:602
  implicit totalitarianism 6:97
 Masaryk, T.G. 6:165, 6:166
 Mill, J.S. 6:359, 6:373–4
 multiculturalism 6:599
 noncognitivism 8:21–2
 paradox of 2:869
 positive freedom 1:268
 postmodernism 7:591–2
 rational choice theory 8:64, 8:69–70
 republicanism 8:281–2
 revolutionary (Chernyshevskii, N.G.) 2:306
 Schumpeter, J.A. 8:555–6
 social **8:827–8**
 social factors (Jefferson, T.) 5:84–5
 social intelligence (Dewey, J.) 3:49–50
 socialism 8:883
 utilitarianism 2:870
 value of 2:868–9

Democritus 1:263, **2:872–8**
  atomism 2:872–5, 6:171
  dreams 7:767
  Egyptian influence on ancient
    Greek thought 3:252
  Epicurus 3:350
  eudaimonia 3:450
  knowledge
    Pyrrhonism 7:849
  language
    philosophy of 5:357
  Leucippus 5:578
  morality 2:876–7
  plurality
    Zeno of Elea 9:844, 9:845
  psychology
    materialism 2:874–5
  theology
    naturalistic 2:875–6
demon argument
  Descartes, R. 3:7
Demonet, M.-L. 5:415
demonstration
  absolute (*demonstratio potissima*)
    (Vernia, N.) 9:596
  Cartesianism (Vico, G.) 9:599,
    9:601
  causal inference distinction
    (Hume, D.) 4:546–7
  Islamic philosophy 5:706, 5:710
  knowledge
    Zabarella, J. 9:837
  knowledge (Hume, D.) 4:546
  material logic
    John of St Thomas 5:118
  method (Wolff, C.) 9:777,
    9:778–80, 9:781
  morality
    anti-rationalism (Hume, D.)
    4:556
  science (Galilei, G.) 3:839
  scientific knowledge (*epistēmē*)
    (Aristotle) 1:417–18
  scientific methodology
    Renaissance Aristotelianism
    1:406
demonstratives **2:878–81**
  see also indexicals
  compositionality 2:477
  existential statements 3:492
  reference 8:159
Demopoulos, W. 3:777, 4:54, 8:403
DeMorgan, Augustus 8:566
Demos, R. 8:628
Demos, Raphael 6:756, 6:758
Demsetz, H. 7:760–1

demythologization
  justification by faith 2:129
  New Testament 2:126–8
Den Uyl, D. 4:229, 8:56
Dendle, B.J. 5:301
Deng Xiaoping 6:138
Dengyō Daishi *see* Saichō
Denifle, H. 2:800
Denmark 8:486–8
  Boethius of Dacia **1:813–16**
  Bohr, N. **1:820–2**
  Hegelianism 4:286
  Kierkegaard, S. **5:235–44**
  Ross, A. **8:364–5**
Dennett, Daniel Clement **2:882–4**
  behaviourism 1:698
  charity principle 2:283, 2:285
  child's theory of mind 6:389
  Chinese room argument 2:329
  computational theories of mind
    6:394
  consciousness 2:594–5
  de relde dicto belief 2:817
  dreaming 3:129
  eliminativism 2:426, 2:427, 3:265
  Fodor, J.A. 3:686
  free will 3:751
  Gödel's theorems 4:115
  information theory 4:786
  introspection, psychology of 4:845
  language of thought hypothesis
    5:407
  materialism 6:173, 6:177
    artificial intelligence 6:172
  mental imagery 4:705
  qualia 2:426, 2:588, 7:867
  reasons and causes 8:127
  reductionism, philosophy of mind
    8:153
  Skinner, B.F. 8:801
  social science
    methodology of 8:867–8
Denney, J. 8:451
Dennis, J. 9:204
denotation
  Goodman, N. 4:137
  Russell, B.A.W. 8:397–8
Dent, E. 3:254
Dent, N.J.H.
  conscience †2:579–81
  Rousseau, J.-J. †8:367–7
Denton, J. 4:377–8
D'Entrèves, A.P. 5:146, 9:122
D'Entreves, M.P. 1:372
Denyer, Nicholas
  Diodorus Cronus †3:83–6
  Philo the Dialectician †7:363–5

Denys the Carthusian **2:884–7**
Denys de Leeuwis *see* Denys the
  Carthusian
Denzen, N.K. 9:245
Denzer, H. 1:798–9
Denzinger, H. 7:286, 7:839
deontic logic **2:887–90**
  imperatives 4:719
  moral pluralism 6:530
  Wright, G.H. von 9:668
deontological ethics **2:890–2**, 3:437
  see also Kantian ethics
  consequentialism contrast
    (Nagel, T.) 6:645–6
  moral pluralism (Ross W.D.)
    8:365–7
  negative duties 3:179
  right and good 4:133, 8:324
  teleological ethics comparison
    9:294
  virtue ethics contrast 9:623
deontology
  discourse ethics (Habermas, J.)
    4:197
  virtue
    will 9:722–3
deoxyribonucleic acid (DNA)
  4:13–14, 6:458–9
dependence
  Latin American liberation
    philosophy 5:610
dependent origination, Buddhist
  doctrine of 9:215–18
depiction
  art
    aesthetics 1:60–1
    pictorial **2:892–6**
    picture interpretation 2:892,
    2:894–5
Deppert, W. 9:707
Derbolav, J. 4:300
Derham, D.P. 8:483
derivation
  glossary 5:801
  reduction by 8:145–6
DeRose, Keith 2:647–8, 2:649, 5:275
Derossi, G. 4:80
Derrett, J.D.M. 3:826
Derrida, Jacques **2:896–901**
  art
    artist's intention 1:513
    understanding of 1:475
  Bataille, G. 1:661
  being 1:702
  Cixous, H. 2:372, 2:373
  Critical Legal Studies 2:719
  deconstruction 2:836–7, 2:897–9

différance 1:190, 1:191, 2:898–9
Glas (death knell) 2:898
hermeneutics
    biblical 4:390, 4:393, 4:394
Levinas, E. 5:580, 5:582
literary deconstruction 2:810–11,
    2:812
memory 6:299
negative theology 7:584–5
Nietzsche, F.W. 6:861
phenomenological movement
    7:340
postmodern theology 7:584, 7:586
postmodernism 7:588, 7:590, 7:592
post-structuralism 7:596
    critique of logocentrism 7:598
    literary theory 7:598
social science
    history of philosophy of 8:857
subject
    postmodern critique of 9:199,
    9:200
Tel Quel school 9:293
Derveni Papyrus 7:164
Des Chene, Dennis 1:391–3, 3:18
Des Places, E. 3:458
Descartes, René **3:1–19**
    Agrippa von Nettesheim, H.C.
    1:132
    animal language and thought
    1:270
    Aristotelianism
        seventeenth century 1:387
    Arnauld, A. 1:443–5, 1:447
    Augustine 1:542, 1:544–5
    authority 2:308
    belief
        epistemic duty 8:212
        evidentialism 8:209
    bodily sensations 1:795
    bundle theory of mind 6:385
    Charleton, W. 2:286
    cogito argument 3:1, 3:7–8
    commonsensism 2:455
    concepts
        Hobbes, T. 4:467
    consciousness 2:582, 2:583, 2:595
    conservation law (Leibniz, G.W.)
    5:543, 5:555
    contingency 2:651
    Cordemoy, G. de 2:673–4
    corpuscles
        chemistry 2:295–6
    creation
        religious doctrine of 2:698,
        2:700

critiques of
    Cambridge Platonism 2:184
    Hobbes, T. 4:467
    Leibniz, G.W. 5:543, 5:553,
    5:555
    Locke, J. 5:672
    More, H. 6:579–80
    Spinoza, B. de 9:93–5, 9:97
Cudworth, R. 2:742–3
death 2:821, 2:822
Discours de la méthode (Discourse
    on Method)
    method 3:3, 3:5–6, 8:578
    Port-Royal 7:552
doubt 2:184, 3:1, 3:6–7, 3:13
dreaming 3:127–8, 3:129
dualism 3:11–12, 3:138
    argmuents for 9:45–6
    Cambridge Platonism 2:184
    eliminativism 3:265
    More, H. 6:579–80
    Spinoza, B. de 9:97
educational philosophy 3:226,
    3:229
Elisabeth of Bohemia 3:267–8
emotions 3:287, 3:289
epistemology 3:381
    advisory 7:35, 7:38
extension (Locke, J.) 5:672
external world problem 6:231,
    6:235
French philosophy of science
    3:780, 3:781
functionalism 3:813
Gassendi, P. 3:857
geometry 4:33, 9:60
    analytic 3:1, 3:2, 3:15
Glanvill, J. 4:81
God
    existence of 3:1, 3:8–9, 4:92
    infinity 4:774
    innate concept of 8:77
historical context 5:229–30
hope 4:509
ideas 8:76
illuminationism 4:699, 4:700
immaterialism (Hobbes, T.) 4:467
inductive inference 4:756, 4:758
influenced by
    Sextus Empiricus 8:717
innate knowledge 4:795, 4:797
introspection 4:837–8, 4:842
    psychology of 4:842–3, 4:845
knowledge
    concept of 5:275
La Forge, L. de 5:331, 5:332

language
    early modern philosophy of
    5:378
logic
    seventeenth and eighteenth
    century 5:717, 5:720–1
magnetism 3:259
Mamardashvili, M.K. 6:68–9
matter 6:194, 6:196
mechanism
    vitalism 9:639–40, 9:641
medicine
    philosophy of 6:265, 6:268
Meditationes de prima philosophia
    (Meditations on First
    Philosophy)
    cogito argument 3:1, 3:7–8
    doubt 3:1, 3:6–7
    dualism 3:11–12
    epistemology 3:381
    God
        existence of 3:1, 3:8–9
    immaterialism
        Hobbes, T. objections 4:467
    sensation 3:12–13
memory 6:297
mental causation 6:308
Mersenne, M. 6:326
method 1:224, 1:228, 3:1, 3:3,
    3:5–6
mind-body problem 7:824–5
morality 3:13–14
    emotions 6:560, 6:563
More, H. 6:577, 6:580, 6:582
nativism 6:675
natural theology 6:712
necessary being 6:745
occasionalism 7:87
omnipotence 7:102
particulars 7:236
Les passions de l'âme (The
    Passions of the Soul)
    morality 3:13–14
perception (Leibniz, G.W.) 5:553
personal identity 7:314
persons 7:318
pluralism (Spinoza B. de) 9:93–5
Port-Royal 7:552, 7:553
Principles of Philosophy
    wisdom 9:754
psychologism (Gioberti, V.) 4:78–9
rationalism 8:79
Regius, H. 4:353, 4:354
religious opposition to 8:230,
    8:231
revolution 8:302, 8:303

scepticism 3:374–5, 8:62, 8:63
  certainty 2:265, 2:266, 2:267
  doubt 3:123, 3:124, 3:374
  external world 3:123
  hypotheses 8:494, 8:498
  scientific method 8:578, 8:580
  sensation 3:12–13
  social science
    history of philosophy of 8:849,
      8:857
  soul 9:48
  substance 9:206, 9:210
    corporeal (Leibniz, G.W.) 5:546,
      5:555
    extension of (More, H.) 6:579
  testimony 9:310–11, 9:313
  unity of science 9:530–1
  universal language 9:534, 9:535
  vision 9:638
  voluntarism 9:663, 9:664
  wisdom 9:754
  Zar'a Ya'ecob comparison 3:443–4
Descombes, V. 1:191, 4:300–1,
  7:595–6
Descotes, D. 7:246
descriptions **3:19–24**
  see also definite descriptions;
  reference
  action 3:528–9
  ambiguity theories 3:23
  antirealism (Dummett, M.A.E.)
    3:152
  content/object distinction
    (Twardowski, K.) 9:508
  de relde dicto belief 2:816–17
  direct/indirect distinction 6:14
  disguised (Evans, G.) 3:461
  free logics 3:741–2
  interpretation distinction 1:502–3
  knowledge by **5:259–63**
  meaning
    mass and general terms 8:157
    names 7:752–3, 7:755, 8:153–4,
      8:157
    names (Kripke, S.A.) 5:303
  medieval natural philosophy 6:704
  mental imagery 4:703, 4:704, 4:705
  methodological individualism
    3:527
  normative distinction (law) 7:38–9
  ontological commitment
    (Quine, W.V.) 8:8
  ordinary language philosophy
    7:152
  quantifier account of existence
    3:491–2

realism
  Mohism 5:693–4
  reference 7:753–4, 8:159–60
  Russell, B.A.W. 1:225, 3:20–2,
    3:459, 8:392, 8:397–8
  scope 8:588–9
  semantics 8:652
descriptive psychology
  Twardowski, K. 9:508
descriptive relativism
  morality 6:539
descriptive set theory
  axiom of constructibility 2:623
  recursion-theoretic hierarchies
    8:144
descriptivism
  prescriptivism distinction 4:230–1,
    7:669–70
desert **3:24–7**
  see also blame; merit; praise
  autonomy
    ethical 6:569
  equality 3:395
  mercy 8:137–8
  moral standing 6:551
  penal
    retributive punishment 2:707
Desgabets, Robert **3:27–30**
de-Shalit, Avner
  obligations to future generations
    †3:819–22
Deshpande, Madhav M.
  interpretation
    Indian theories of †4:833–7
  language
    Indian theories of 5:383–4
  meaning
    Indian theories of †6:239–43
design
  evolutionary theory 3:481–2
  rationality of world
    Stoicism 9:142
  technology 9:285, 9:287
design argument for the existence of
  God *see* God, existence of
designators
  rigid/non-rigid distinction 7:753
  de relde dicto belief 2:815–16
desire **3:30–3**
  action (Freud, S.) 3:786–7,
    3:788–9, 3:790–1
  analytic behaviourism
    (Dennett, D.C.) 2:882
  Chinese philosophy
    Confucianism
      li 2:542
    Daoism 2:790–1

  innate knowledge (Wang
    Yangming) 9:683–4
critical assessment
  ethical autonomy 1:589
dialectics of
  postmodernism 1:188–9
emotion theory (Spinoza, B. de)
  9:101–2
  as force (Lyotard, J.-F.) 6:8
  happiness 4:228, 4:229
  heaven
    Indian concepts of 4:255–6
  hedonism
    Epicureanism 3:347
  human nature (Butler, J.) 2:155
  intention 4:812–13
  intentionality 8:864
  love relationship (Abravanel, J.)
    1:24–7
  Lyotard, J.F. 7:603
  misdirection of
    evil 3:465
  moral attitudes 6:534
  moral development
    (Wollstonecraft, M.) 9:790
  motivation
    moral 6:524
    reasons and causes 8:125–7
    Reid, T. 8:175
  psychological egoism (Butler, J.)
    2:156
  rational choice theory 8:863–4
  for reality (Weil, S.) 9:699
  rebirth
    Hindu philosophy 4:434
    Yogācāra Buddhism 2:71
  self-control 8:611, 8:612
  self-cultivation
    Chinese philosophy 8:616,
      8:617, 8:622
  self-deception 8:627–8
  sensible/intelligible beauty (Ibn
    Sina) 1:76–7
  sexual 8:717, 8:719, 8:721
  structuralist linguistics (Lacan, J.)
    5:337
  as true self 2:176
  utilitarianism 9:551, 9:553, 9:555
    Mill, J.S. 6:369–70
  voluntary action (Aristotle) 1:426
Desmond, A. 2:798, 4:595, 9:2
Desnitskii, Semën 5:606
Desrosiers-Bonin, D. 8:17
Dessauer, F. 9:287
Dessoir, M. 9:321
destiny
  see also fate

African ethical systems 3:433
evil, problem of (Voltaire) 9:661
Wang Chong 9:680
Yang Xiong 9:821
destruction
of complex beings
potentiality
Indian theories of 7:605–6
Destruktion
Derrida, J. 2:897–8
detachment
existentialism 3:496
religious 6:287
determinability
principle of 6:37
determinacy
sense (Wittgenstein, L.) 9:760
determinacy axioms
set theory 8:706–7
determination
deduction distinction
natural law 2:444–5
of the will (Reid, T.) 8:174
determination (concretization)
positive law (Aquinas, T.) 6:688
determinations
ontology (Gilbert of Poitiers)
4:69–70
determiners
constituent structure 9:247–8
determinism **3:33–9**
see also anti-determinism;
fatalism; free will; indeterminism;
predestination
agency
Alexander of Aphrodisias
critique 1:173–4
Anscombe, G.E.M. 1:281
Bakhtin, M.M. 1:639
Bernard of Tours 1:756
bivalence
many-valued logics 6:81–2
blame (Kant, I.) 7:645–6
Bradwardine, T. 1:865
Carneades 2:217–18
causal
moral psychology 6:531
causality relationship 1:281
chaos theory 2:278
classical mechanics 6:253
definition 3:36–7
desert 3:26
divination (Carneades) 2:217–18
economic
Chinese Marxism 6:134–5
Edwards, J. 3:240, 3:241
environmental 4:345

free will conflict
Anscombe, G.E.M. 2:882–3
Cicero, M.T. 2:358
Pomponazzi, P. 7:530–1
freedom 3:743, 3:744, 3:745–6
see also compatibilism
genetic
sociobiology 3:485
God 8:233–4
divine perfection 3:737
Early and Middle Platonism
7:427
Heisenberg, W. 4:328
historical (Plekhanov, G.V.) 7:454
human beings (Marcus Aurelius)
6:94
Jabriyya 5:26
Jewish philosophy (Crescas, H.)
2:702
law of universal causation 3:34
Marxism (Kautsky, K.J.) 6:142
mechanics
classical 3:34, 3:35
microdeterminism 8:147
nature–nurture debate 4:12, 4:15,
8:895
pessimistic (Voltaire) 9:657, 9:661
predictability distinction 6:254
providence 7:799
refutation
Epicureanism 3:348
relativity theory 8:193, 8:197
Russian nihilism 7:7
Schopenhauer, A. 8:552
self-formation (Mill, J.S.) 6:368
social
scientific constructivism
2:626–7
social sciences
prediction in 8:871
structuralism in 9:185, 9:188
state 3:37–9, 6:642
Stoicism 9:158–9
technological 9:283, 9:286–7
tense logic 7:688
top–down causation 8:234
universal 5:578–9
deterrent punishments
criminal law 2:707
Detlefsen, Michael
Gödel's theorems †4:107–19
Hilbert's programme and
formalism †4:422–9
mathematics
foundations of †6:181–92
proof theory 7:750
Detmold, M.J. 5:526, 5:530

Deuchler, Martina 2:565
Deústua, A. 3:513
Deutsch, E. 6:403, 9:594
Deutsch, Harry
demonstratives and indexicals
†2:878–81
proper names 7:756
Deutscher, I. 9:466
Deutscher, Max
Australia, philosophy in 1:583
Le Doeuff, M. †5:476–9
memory †6:296–300
devālaya see heaven
Devall, B. 4:165
devaloka see heaven
Devamani, B.S. 8:44
Devaney, R. 2:279
developing countries
marginality 6:99–6:100
development
see also child development;
cognitive development;
developmental psychology; infant
cognition; moral development
biological
vitalism 9:641–2
cognitive **2:393–5**
human
love 5:844
normative/descriptive distinction
3:41
development ethics **3:39–44**
see also postcolonialism
agriculture 1:126–7
environmentalism 3:335
developmental psychology
see also child development
infant cognition 2:390–1
male bias 2:281
Piaget, J. 7:383–5
Vygotskii, L.S. 9:671–5
Devereaux, M. 3:409
Devitt, Michael
concepts 2:515
constructivism 2:628, 2:629
eliminativism 3:265
holism
mental and semantic 4:493
language 5:411
proper names 7:756
propositional attitude statements
7:778
reference †8:153–64
scientific realism and antirealism
8:584
unconscious mental states 9:526
Devlin, K.J. 2:624, 8:144, 8:672

Devlin, P. 5:441, 5:442, 5:463–4
devotionalism
  Buddhism, China 2:89
Dew, K. 1:696
Dewey, A.J. 6:77
Dewey, John 3:44–51
  American philosophy
    eighteenth and nineteenth
      century 1:204–5, 1:205
  anthropology 3:45–6
  applied ethics 1:324
  certainty 2:266, 2:267
  consequentialism
    pragmatism in ethics 7:641–2,
      7:643
  contextualism 5:275
  doubt 3:124
  educational philosophy 3:228,
    3:229
  fictionalism 3:668
  habits of inquiry 3:44, 3:47–8, 3:49
  Hegelianism 4:288, 4:300
  metaphysics 3:46–7
  moral education 6:509
  moral life 3:44, 3:49–50
  naturalized philosophy of science
    6:729
  pragmatism 7:633, 7:634, 7:638–9
  symbolic interactionism 9:245
  Whitehead, A.N. 9:718
Dews, Peter
  communicative rationality
    †2:459–62
  Habermas, J. 4:199
  post-structuralism 7:600
    social sciences 7:604
dGa'-ldan-pa (Gandeba) School of
  Buddhism
  see also dGe-lugs-pa (Gelukba)
    School
  mKhas grub dge legs dpal bzang
    po 6:416–17
  rGyal tshab dar ma rin chen
    8:304–5
  Tsong kha pa Blo bzang grags pa
    9:487–90
dGe-lugs-pa (Gelukba) School of
  Buddhism
  see also dGa'-ldan-pa (Gandeba)
    School; Tsong kha pa
  Jam dbyangs bzhad pa 9:402
  Jo-nang-pa School
    rejection of 9:403
  Mādhyamika Buddhism 2:62–3
  opposition to Ultimate Reality
    (Mi bskyod rdo rje) 6:351
  Rigs-gter-ba debate 9:406–7

dhamma see dharma
Dhammapada
  duty and virtue
    Indian conceptions of 3:187
Dhammasaṅgaṇi
  Ābhidharmika Schools of
    Buddhism 2:58
Dhar, S.N. 8:41
dharma 3:183–7
  Bhartṛhari 1:765
  Buddha 2:52
  Chinese Buddhism
    fa 3:532–3
  fatalism 3:566–7
  Hinduism 4:437
  Jainism 5:49
  Mīmāṃsā 6:377, 6:381
  Sarvāstivāda Buddhism 5:214
  self
    Indian theories of 8:606–8,
      8:609–10
  ultimately real entity
    Nāgārjuna critique of 6:638–9
  wheel of
    Yogācāra Buddhism 2:64
Dharmakīrti 3:51–3
  Buddhist nominalism 7:23–6, 7:27
  causality 2:98
  epistemology 2:97
    rGyal tshab dar ma rin chen
      8:304
  Indian and Tibetan philosophy
    4:738
  inference 4:764, 4:765
  momentariness 6:472
  negative facts in classical Indian
    philosophy 6:756, 6:758
  potentiality 7:605
  sense perception 8:692
  solipsism 9:25–6
  Tibetan Buddhism 9:406–7
    Sa skya paṇḍita 8:433
  Tsong kha pa Blo bzang grags pa
    9:488
  universals 8:433
    Buddhist critique of 9:547,
      9:548
  veridicality
    Yogācāra Buddhism 3:411
Dharmarāja 3:392, 5:284, 5:285
Dharmaśāstras
  duty and virtue 3:183, 3:184–5
  interpretation 4:833, 4:836
  stages of life 4:437
Dharmottara 4:764
Dhawan, G. 7:524

Di Gregorio, Mario A.
  Huxley, T.H. †4:594–6
Di Napoli, G. 7:392, 7:532
Di Stefano, C. 3:587
diachronic analysis
  structuralism 9:176
Diaconis, P. 8:59
Diacritics (special issue)
  Lyotard, J.-F. 6:11
diadochai (successions) 3:126
diagnosis
  logics of
    philosophy of medicine 6:266–7
diairesis (Platonic division)
  logic (Speusippus) 9:90
dialectic 3:54–5, 5:750
  see also casuistry; elenchus; logic
  Advaita Vedānta 6:477–8
  Aristotelian (Owen, G.E.L.) 7:178
  Bachelard, G. 1:621
  definition (Melanchthon, P.)
    6:289–90
  Hegelian
    logic in Japan 5:714
      Tanabe Hajime 9:261
    McTaggart, J.M.E. 6:25
  history (Asmus, V.F.) 1:524–5
  knowledge (Schleiermacher, F.)
    8:533–4
  Lenin, V.I. 5:565–6
  moral reasoning
    casuistry 2:227, 2:228
  negative (Adorno, T.W.) 1:42, 1:44
  opinion 9:837
  processes 7:722
  Ramus, P. 8:51, 8:52–3
  reasoning
    Ethiopian philosophy 3:444
  rejection of (Ariston of Chios)
    1:381
  Renaissance logic 5:767–8,
    5:769–70, 8:500
  Soviet Marxism (Il'enkov, E.V.)
    4:689
  Stoicism 9:150
  theology (Barth, K.) 1:651,
    1:652–3
  topics (Agricola, R.) 1:124–5
dialectic monism see monism,
  developmental
dialectical materialism 3:53–8
  African philosophy 1:99–1:100
  Althusser, L.P. 1:193
  consciousness 3:54
  dialectical laws 3:55–6
  Engels, F. 3:309, 3:311
  Gramsci, A. 4:151

historical materialism 3:56
idealism 3:54
Lambriola, A. 5:335
Lenin, V.I. 5:565, 5:566–7
Marx, K. 6:123, 6:172
  Althusser, L.P. interpretation
    1:193
  Marxism
    Engels, F. 6:141, 6:142
    Latin America 6:161, 6:163
    philosophy of science 6:148–9
    Russian
      Deborinites 6:154–5
      empiriocriticism 6:152–4
      Lenin, V.I. 5:565, 5:566–7
      Plekhanov, G.V. 6:150–1,
        6:152
      Stalinism 6:155–6
  partisanship 3:57
  Plekhanov, G.V. 7:453, 7:454
Dialectical school **3:58–9**
see also Philo the Dialectician
  Diodorus Cronus 3:83–6
  Megarian school comparison 3:58
  Socratic stance 3:58
dialectical universal
  the world (Nishida Kitarō) 7:14
dialecticals
  Marxism (Lukács, G.) 6:141,
    6:143–4
  syllogisms
    Islamic philosophy 5:710–11
Dialecticians
  Asmus, V.F. 1:523
  Socratic schools 9:22
dialectics *see* dialectic
dialects
  linguistic discrimination 5:643–4
dialetheism
  paraconsistent logic 7:209, 7:210
dialogical logic **3:59–62**, 5:826–7
dialogue
  identity in (Cixous, H.) 2:372–3
  'I–Thou' relationship (Buber, M.)
    2:42, 2:43–4
  language as (Bakhtin, M.M.)
    1:638, 1:640
  phenomenology of self
    (Bakhtin, M.) 1:642
  revelation
    Jewish philosophy
      (Rosenzweig, F.) 8:360
dialogues
  see also Socratic dialogues
  Plato
    rationale of 7:423
Diamond, A. 2:395, 5:141

Diamond, C. 1:282
Diamond, J. 3:204–5
Diamond, S. 9:801
diaspora
  Judaism
    assimilation concerns (Ha'am,
      Ahad) 4:193
    halakhah 4:206
    Leibowitz, Y. 5:563, 5:564
    postcolonialism 7:580–1
Díaz del Castillo, Bernal 5:429, 5:432
Diaz, E. 5:301
Díaz Valcárcel, Emilio 3:510–11,
  3:513
Dicenso, J. 4:388–9
Dicey, Albert Venn **3:62–3**
  constitutionalism 2:621
  rule of law 8:388–9
dichotomies
  Western philosophy
    feminist critique of 3:601
Dichotomy Argument
  Zeno of Elea 9:843, 9:847–9
Dickey, L. 4:279
Dickie, G.
  aesthetic attitude 1:55
  Alison, A. 1:186
  art
    definition of 1:468
    Gerard, A. 4:37
    taste, artistic 1:512
Dickinson, G.L. 6:28
Dickmann, M.A. 4:771
Dickson, W.J. 3:520
dictatorship
  see also totalitarianism
  democracy contrast 2:868
Diderot, Denis **3:63–9**
  Encyclopédie 3:63–4
  Encyclopedists, eighteenth century
    3:303–4
  Enlightenment, continental 3:317
  Helvétius, C.-A. 3:66, 4:345, 4:346
  Molyneux problem 6:468
  selfish sociability 3:66–8
  theosophy 9:363, 9:365
  tradition 9:445
  unity of science 9:532
Die Grundlagen der Arithmetik (The
  Foundations of Arithmetic) Frege,
  Gottlob
Diederich, W. 3:146–7
Diels, Herman
  Aristotle commentators 1:437
  Democritus 2:877
  dissoi logoi (twofold argument)
    3:107

doxography 3:125, 3:126
  Leucippus 5:579
  Presocratics 7:671–2
  Pythagoreanism 7:861
  Sophists 9:34
Dieter of Echternach 4:431
Dietrich of Freiberg **3:69–71**
  medieval Platonism 7:437
Dietrich, Michael R.
  molecular biology †6:458–61
Dietterich, T.G. 2:577
Dietz, Mary G.
  feminist political philosophy 3:620
  Machiavelli, N. †6:17–22
Diez Macho, A. 4:614
diffeomorphisms
  spacetime symmetry
    relativity theory 8:196
différance
  Deleuze, G. 1:189–90, 2:856
  Derrida, J. 1:190, 2:898–9, 7:584
difference
  equality 3:395
  ontological significance (Madhva)
    6:31
  sexual
    Irigaray, L. 5:1–3
    Kristeva, J. 5:306–7
  universal/particular
    Buddhist nominalism 7:24
différends (disputes)
  Lyotard, J.-F. 6:9, 7:603, 8:845
differentia
  rationale/ratione uti problem
    (Gerbert of Aurillac) 4:40
differentiation (*vibhajyavāda*)
  Buddha
    Jaina theory of manifoldness
      comparison 6:78
Diffey, T.J. 1:468
Digambara Jainism *see* Jaina
  philosophy
Digby, Kenelm **3:71–4**
Diggins, J.P. 7:639
digital information *see* information
  technology
Dignāga **3:74–6**
  awareness 1:606–7, 1:608
  illusion 3:410–11
  Indian and Tibetan philosophy
    4:738
  inference 4:764, 4:765
    knowledge 5:283, 5:285
  knowledge 2:97
  sense perception 8:694
  Tibetan Buddhism 9:406–7
  Uddyotakara response to 9:514–15

dignity
see also self-respect
Camus, A. 2:194–5
Schiller, J.C.F. 8:526–7
Dihle, A. 1:558
Dijksterhuis, E.J. 6:259
Dillon, J.M.
Alcinous †1:159–60
Apuleius †1:325–6
Calcidius †2:175–6
Celsus †2:264
Damascius †2:771–2
Eusebius 3:458
logos 5:819
Neo-Pythagoreanism 6:809
Numenius †7:54–6
Philo of Alexandria 7:361
Platonism, Early and Middle
†7:421–9
Plutarch of Chaeronea †7:464–70
Speusippus †9:89–91
Xenocrates †9:806–7
Dillon, Robin 8:286, 8:637
Dilman, Ï. 3:501, 8:631
DiLorenzo, R.D. 8:314
Dilthey, Wilhelm **3:77–83**
descriptive psychology 3:77,
3:79–80
Hegelianism 3:81, 4:290, 4:296
hermeneutics 3:77, 3:81, 4:386–7,
4:389
biblical 4:392, 4:394
understanding (*verstehen*)
4:386–7
historicism 4:444, 4:446
Hölderlin, J.C.F. 4:482
human sciences
foundation of 3:77, 3:78–9
Ortega y Gasset, J. 7:166
phenomenological movement
7:340
Shpet, G.G. 8:755
social science 3:530, 6:720,
8:853–4, 8:857
South Slavs, philosophy of 9:54
worldview 3:77, 3:81–2
Dilworth, D.A. 5:716, 7:16, 9:692
al-Dimashqi, Abu 'Uthman 4:157
Dingler, Hugo 5:826, 5:828
Dini, A. 4:518
Dinnerstein, D. 3:584, 3:587
Dio Chrysostom 2:757–8, 3:91
Diodorus Cronus **3:83–6**
atomism 3:84
consequence 2:600
dialectic 1:352

possibility
definition of 3:85
master argument 3:84, 3:85–6
Diogenes of Apollonia **3:87–9**
pneuma (spirit) 7:470
Diogenes Laertius **3:86–7**
Aenesidemus 1:51
Agrippa 1:129
Anaxarchus 1:255
Antisthenes 1:317
Ariston of Chios 1:382
Carneades' rejection of 2:219
Chrysippus 2:346
Cynics 2:754, 2:755–6, 2:758
Dialectical school 3:58
Diogenes of Sinope 3:91
doxography 1:264
Epicureanism 3:349
Epicurus 3:351
Eudoxus 3:453
Hellenistic philosophy 4:336
logic 5:692
Megarian school 6:279
Plato 7:420
Pyrrho 7:848
Pyrrhonism 7:854
Pythagoras 7:856
Sextus Empiricus 8:717
Socratic schools 9:23
Stoicism 9:160
Timon 9:420
Diogenes of Oenoanda **3:89–90**
Epicureanism 3:89–90, 3:341
Diogenes of Sinope **3:90–1**
Antisthenes 1:315
Cynics 2:754–6
Socratic schools 9:21
Dionysianism
Russian Symbolism (Ivanov, V.)
6:863
Dionysius the Areopagite *see* Pseudo-
Dionysius
Dionysodorus 1:316
Diop, Cheikh Anta 1:111–12, 1:114,
3:254
Diophantine equation 2:488
Dipert, R.
music
aesthetics of 6:613
Dipert, Randall R.
logic machines and diagrams
†5:739–46
logic, nineteenth century †5:722–9
direct realism
Armstrong, D.M. 1:442
sense-data 8:697
Dirks, N. 7:524

Dirlik, A. 6:140
disagreement *see* agreement–
disagreement dichotomy
disapproval *see* blame
disciplina see mathesis
discipline
see also punishment
Foucault, M. 3:711, 7:602
disclosure
being (Beauvoir, S. de) 1:685
Heidegger, M.
Aristotle 4:309
art 4:317–19
Dasein (being-in-the-world)
4:307–8, 4:312–14
Ereignis (disclosure-as-such)
4:315, 4:317
fallenness 4:316
hiddenness 4:314–15
discontinuity *see* continuity
Discours de la méthode (Discourse on
Method) *see* Descartes, René
discourse
see also Discourse Representation
Theory; discourse semantics;
ethical discourse; legal discourse
Baumgarten, A.G. 1:670
colonialism 7:580
discourse representation structures
(DRS) 1:241–2
figurative-ambivalent (Shpet, G.G.)
8:757
genealogy (Foucault, M.) 3:711
indirect 2:803, **4:743–5**
language and gender 5:364–5
Latin American literature 5:653
particles 1:47
postmodernism 7:588, 7:589
scientific (Quine, W.V.) 8:5–6
sexual
social constructionism 8:720
spoken-written distinction
(Ricouer, P.) 8:320
Discourse Representation Theory
(DRT) 1:241–3, 3:92–7
discourse semantics 1:241–3, **3:91–9**
Discourse Representation Theory
3:92–7
Montague Grammar 3:92
segmented Discourse
Representation Theory 3:96–8
discovery
computational learning theory
5:486
logic of **3:99–103**, 4:224–5
truth
scientific responsibility 8:289

discretion
judicial 5:147, 5:152
legal realism 5:467
discrimination **3:103–6**
see also anti-Semitism; race;
racism; sexism
affirmative action **1:91–4**
anti-discrimination principle
3:103–4
caste system (Ambedkar, B.R.)
1:196
feminist jurisprudence 3:607
genetic 4:17
institutional 3:104–5
language
gender 5:361–7
linguistic **5:641–5**
merit 3:26–7
morality 3:105
speciesism 1:275
taste 1:510
disdain
guilt contrast
morality and ethics 6:567–9,
6:570
disease
see also medicine
Galen 3:833, 3:834
Hippocratic medicine 4:442–3
disinterestedness
see also gaze
aesthetics
attitude 1:53
feminist 3:595
nature 6:731–3, 6:734
disjunction *see* conjunction
Disjunctive Principle 2:813–14
Disjunctive Syllogism 7:209, 7:210
disobedience, civil *see* civil
disobedience
dispositions
causal powers 2:249–50
disputation
Albert of Saxony 1:143
Chinese philosophy
Hundred Schools era 2:322–3
dialectical form
medieval scholastic method
6:270, 6:272–3
Japanese Buddhism 2:100
legal discourse (Perelman, C.)
5:497
obligations
medieval logic 5:757–8
sophismata
Oxford Calculators 7:180–1
Dissanayake, W. 8:631

dissoi logoi (twofold argument)
3:106–7
dissolution
cosmic cycle of
Vaiśeṣika atomism 7:606
distanciation
Ricouer, P. 8:320
distinction-in-unity
Coleridge, S.T. 2:404
distinctions
Chinese theories of language
Hui Shi 5:694, 5:702–3
Mohism 5:693, 5:697–8
Mozi 5:695–6
Xunzi 5:704, 9:819
Zhuangzi 5:694
entity/attributes (Madhva) 6:31
distress
suffering 9:213
distribution
economic
development ethics 3:42
of resources
Jewish bioethics 1:778
medical ethics 6:262–3
risk 8:332–3
social
utilitarianism 9:556
distrust
trust relationship 9:467
Divanji, P.C. 3:568
diversity
moral
descriptive relativism 6:539
political (Lyotard, J.-F.) 6:9
divination
as political tool (Xenophon) 9:814
rejection of (Carneades) 2:217–18
Yijing 2:309, 2:310, 2:311
divine
see also God
divine action
atheistic potentiality argument
7:605
essence distinction
Ibn Massara 4:628
human freedom (Farrer, A.M.)
3:560–1
physics
scientific view 8:231, 8:233–4
religious predictions 8:257
top-down causation
scientific view 8:234
divine annihilation
Astell, M. 1:528
divine attributes *see* God, attributes

divine authority
morality 8:218, 8:219, 8:220–1
divine dignities
Llull, R. 5:662–3
divine election
Aquinas, T. 8:273–4
Augustine 8:273
Judaism 1:766, 1:768–9, 5:205
Reformed churches 8:274
reprobation 8:273
divine essence
as adequate object of the intellect
(Duns Scotus, J.) 3:159
non-real distinctions (Holcot, R.)
4:478
Trinity relationship (Joachim of
Fiore) 5:104
divine freedom **3:757–62**
Islamic philosophy 4:63–4
Leibniz, G.W. 5:542, 5:549–51
perfect goodness 4:142
divine goodness *see* goodness, perfect
divine ideas
theory of (Godfrey of Fontaines)
4:120
divine immutability *see* immutability
divine intervention 8:249
see also miracles; providence
classical Christian theism 7:716,
7:718
prayer 7:656
process theism 7:716
divine knowledge *see* knowledge,
divine
divine law 5:465, 5:465–6, 9:119
see also natural law
gospel distinction
(Melanchthon, P.) 6:290
Islamic philosophy 5:457–8
Judaism
Albo, J. 1:153
Arama, I. 1:350
Hebrew Bible 1:768
Saadiah Gaon 8:437
law of reputation (Locke, J.) 5:679
legal positivism (Austin, J.) 1:569
Luther, M. 6:3
Melanchthon, P. 6:290
divine middle knowledge, theory of
see Molinism
divine needs
Kabbalah 4:411–12
divine pathos
Jewish philosophy 4:411
divine power
see also omnipotence

extension of 6:579
  More, H. 6:579
  Peter of Auvergne 7:322
divine presence
  Hasidism 4:243
divine providence
  astral determinism
    Jewish philosophy 6:649
  Carneades 2:217
  Cudworth, R. 2:741
  free will
    Byzantine philosophy 2:162
    Hebrew Bible 1:768
    Maimonides, M. 6:45–6
  miracles
    Jewish philosophy
      (Nahmanides, M.) 6:649
  Molinia, L. de 6:463–4
divine revelation
  secular learning relationship
    (Damian, P.) 2:772–3
divine right
  absolutism 1:30
  political authority 1:585, 8:228
divine simplicity see simplicity, divine
divine truth
  Llull, R. 5:662–3
divine unity
  Giles of Rome 4:75
  Ṛg Veda 4:102–3
divine will
  creation
    Jewish philosophy
      Ibn Gabirol, S. 4:618–19
      Ibn Tzaddik, J. 4:661
divine wisdom
  creation (Bernard of Tours) 1:756
divinity
  causation (Cicero, M.T.) 2:358
  expression of (Tagore, R.) 9:257–8
  finitude 9:669
  principle of
    Islamic fundamentalism 5:11
  self-sufficiency
    Socrates/Cyrus comparison
      9:813–14
divisibility
  actual/potential distinction (Zeno
    of Elea) 9:848
  arguments against (Zeno of Elea)
    9:843, 9:844–51
  continuity
    Buridan, J. 2:133–4
    Henry of Harclay 4:361
  eternity 3:423
  infinite
    Anaxagoras 1:250

Aristotle 1:420–1
Buridan J. 2:133–4
Stoicism 9:145–6
minima
  Epicureanism 3:342–3
  space (Kant, I.) 5:181
division of labour
  Durkheim, É. 3:176
  Marx, K. 6:125
divorce
  feminism
    Latin America 3:627
  law 3:610
  law of unilateral
    Uruguay 3:627
Diwald, S. 4:688
Dixon, N. 2:595
Djait, Hichem 5:20
Djébar, A. 3:613
DNA see deoxyribonucleic acid
Doak, K.M. 5:660
Dobbs, B.J. 1:158, 3:74, 6:828
Dobbs-Weinstein, I.
  Abravanel, J. †1:23–7
Dobel, J.P. 2:676
Dobson, A. 4:165
Dobson, J.F. 7:557
docta ignorantia (learned ignorance)
  Nicholas of Cusa 6:832, 6:833,
    6:835
Doctrinaires group
  Tocqueville, A. de 9:423–4
doctrine
  religious
    act relationship
      Jewish Averroism 1:601
Dod, B.G. 1:403, 9:457
Dodd, V.A. 3:267
Doddridge, P. 7:684
Dodds, E.R.
  Early and Middle Platonism 7:428
  Gorgias 4:146
  Homer 4:502
  morality and ethics 6:568, 6:570
  Numenius 7:55
  Sophists 9:34
Dodge, G.H. 2:618
Dodgson, Charles Lutwidge (Lewis
  Carroll) **3:107–9**
Doeing, D. 3:263
Doering, B.E. 6:104
Doets, K. 6:442
Dōgen Kigen **3:109–11**
  buddhahood 2:102
  Buddhism 5:73–4
  enlightenment
    inherent 2:103

mujō 6:593–4
  spiritual use of language 2:100–1
dogmatism
  critiques of
    Aenesidemus 1:50–1
    Agrippa 1:129
    Pyrrhonism 7:849–50, 7:851–3,
      7:854
    idealism contrast (Fichte, J.G.)
      3:642, 3:647
    natural law 6:685–6
  scientific
    Feyerabend, P.K. critique
      3:640–2
Doig, J. 1:347
Dol bu pa Shes rab rgyal mtshan
  (Dolbuba Shayrap gyeltsen)
  9:402–3
Dolbuba Shayrap gyeltsen see Dol bu
  pa Shes rab rgyal mtshan
Dolgov, K.M. 5:570
Dolník, Peter
  Church, A. †2:346–9
Dolnikowski, E.W. 1:866
Domański, J. 7:488
Dombrowski, D. 7:549
domestic analogy
  international relations 4:829
domination
  class
    Freud/Marx synthesis 6:97
Dominicans
  Albert the Great 1:145–51
  Aquinas, T. 1:326–44
  Augustinian/Aristotelian debate
    1:561–2, 5:113
  Báñez, D. 1:647–9
  Boethius of Dacia 1:813–15
  colonial philosophy
    Latin America 5:421, 5:422
  Crathorn, W. 2:692–3
  Dietrich of Freiberg 3:69–70
  Durandus of St Pourçain 3:172–3
  Garrigou-Lagrange, R. 3:778
  Hervaeus Natalis 4:402–4
  Holcot, R. 4:477–8
  Kilwardby, R. 5:245–8
  Meister Eckhart 6:286–7
  natural philosophy
    medieval 6:691, 6:703–4
  Neo-Thomism 9:383–4
  Suso, H. 9:240–1
  Tauler, J. 9:269–70
  Thomism 9:381–2, 9:383–4
  Ulrich of Strasbourg 9:517–18
Dominicus Gundissalinus 5:22, 9:455
Dominicy, M. 1:447

Dommeyer, F.C. 3:141
Donadoni Roveri, A.M. 3:254
Donadoni, S. 3:254
Donagan, Alan
  action 1:41
  Aquinas, T. 1:347
  Australia, philosophy in 1:583
  Collingwood, R.G. 2:415
  respect for persons 8:285–6
  Spinoza, B. de 9:107
Donagan, B. 1:583
Donahue, J.R. 2:282
Donaldson, D.M. 3:442
Donati, S. 4:77
Donatus 5:389
Doncel, M. 4:402
Doner, J. 9:264, 9:264–3
Doney, W. 3:18
Dong Qichang 1:74
Dong Zhongshu 2:310, 2:312,
  3:111–13
Donington, R. 7:131
Donini, P.L. 1:175
Donnellan, Keith S.
  descriptions 3:24
  ordinary language philosophy
    7:146–7
  reference
    historical-causal theory 8:154,
      8:157–8, 8:163
  sense and reference 8:688
Donnelly, G. 9:229
Donnelly, J. 2:822, 3:434–5
Donoso, A. 7:168
Donovan, A. 2:866
Dooley, W.E. 9:543–2
Dooyeweerd, Herman 3:113–14
Döring, Frank
  counterfactual conditionals
    †2:684–8
Döring, K.
  Aristippus the Elder 1:380
  Cyrenaics 2:763
  Diodorus Cronus 3:86
  Megarian school 6:279
  Philo the Dialectician 7:365
Dörrie, H. 7:428
d'Ors, A. 5:245, 7:325
Dort, Reformed Synod of 8:274
Došen, K. 3:706, 6:682, 8:203
Dostoevskii, Fëdor Mikhailovich
  3:114–19
  emotion in response to art 3:275–6
  existentialist theology 3:507, 3:509
  freedom 3:115–19
  Hessen, S.I. 4:417
  irrationality 3:116–17

nihilism 7:1, 7:4
  polyphonics 1:642–3
  Russian materialism 8:417
  tragedy
    morality of 8:742–3
double effect, principle of 3:119–22
  Bayle, P. 1:675
  evil, problem of 3:468
  killing of innocents 4:798
  war and peace 9:687
double negation elimination (DNE)
  4:857
double predestination
  reprobation 8:272
  Roman Catholicism 8:273
Double, R. 3:751
double truth
  Averroism 1:597
doubt 3:122–5
  see also certainty; scepticism
  collective knowledge 8:830
  context-sensitivity 3:124
  Descartes, R. 3:1, 3:6–7, 3:13,
    3:374, 7:35
    Cambridge Platonism 2:184
    Peirce, C.S. 7:272
  fideism (Pascal, B.) 7:245
  inquiry (Peirce, C.S.) 7:272
  Nyāyasūtra
    knowledge
      Indian views of 5:281
  reasonable 3:122, 3:123
  universal (Descartes, R.) 8:62
Doucet, V. 1:178, 7:269, 8:317
Dougherty, J. 9:386
Douglas, M.
  atonement 1:541
  risk 8:334, 8:337
  ritual 8:341
  society
    concept of 8:889
Douglas, N. 6:352
Douie, D. 7:269
Douma, A.M.H. 8:559
Douzinas, C. 2:719, 5:497, 5:499,
  5:509–10
Dowd, J.D. 6:203
Dowe, P. 2:250
Dower, Nigel 3:43
Dowey, E.A., Jr 2:181
Dowling, W.C1:205–6
Downes, Stephen
  constructivism †2:624–30
Downie, R.S. 8:285, 8:286
Downing, F.G. 2:758
Downs, A. 8:64, 8:69–70, 8:74

Down's syndrome
  child's theory of mind 6:386
Dowty, P. 6:435
doxa see belief
doxastic conduct 7:36–7
  see also duty
doxastic practice
  religious (Alston, W.P.) 8:262
doxography 3:125–7
  ancient philosophy 1:264
  defects of 3:126
  Hippias 4:441
Doyal, L. 6:755, 9:705
Doyé, S. 3:652
Doyle, John P.
  Bonaventure 1:834
  Collegium Conimbricense
    †2:406–8
  Fonseca, P. da †3:687–90
  John of St Thomas †5:117–20
  Renaissance Aristotelianism
    †1:404–13
  Soto, D. de †9:37–40
  Suárez, F. †9:189–96
  Toletus, F. †9:433–5
dPa'bo gtsug lag phreng ba 9:408
Drabkin, I.E. 6:251
Dragišić, Juraj (Georgius Benignus
  de Salviatis) 9:49, 9:54
Dragona-Monachou, M. 9:160
Drake, S. 3:841
drama
  see also comedy; tragedy
  opera 7:128–31
Draper, J.W. 8:235
Dravid, R.R. 9:513–14, 9:548
Dray, W.H. 4:457, 4:458
dreaming 3:127–9
  Descartes, R. 3:6–7, 3:13
  film aesthetics 3:676
  moral responsibility for
    (Augustine) 1:555–6
  Native American philosophy 6:666
  prophecy 7:767–8
  psychoanalysis
    methodological issues in
      7:813–14
  sense perception
    Indian views of 8:692
  Upaniṣadic analogy of
    Brahman 2:2
  wish-fulfilment (Freud, S.)
    3:788–90
Dréano, M. 6:489
Dreben, B. 4:377–8, 7:664
Drechssler, J.G. 8:559
Drees, W.B. 2:700

Dreier, James
  Stevenson, C.L. †9:134–5
Dreier, R. 5:101
Dreiling, R. 1:566
Drengson, A. 3:201–2
Drescher, H.-G. 9:464
Dretske, Fred
  causal theory of knowledge 5:266
  concepts 2:515
  consciousness 2:595
  deductive closure principle
    2:843–4, 2:845
  information theory †4:786–9,
    4:786
  innate knowledge 4:797
  intentionality 4:821
  internalism–externalism
    distinction 4:826
  introspection
    psychology of 4:843, 4:845
  mental causation 6:311
  natural laws 5:474
  non-conceptual content 2:642
  perception 7:294, 7:295–6, 7:298
  reference 8:163
  reliabilism 5:275, 8:208
  scepticism
    fallibilist response 8:495, 8:498
  semantics
    informational 8:659, 8:660–1
    teleological 8:674–5
Drewal, H. 1:64–5
Dreyer, J.L.E. 3:453
Dreyer, M. 3:170
Dreyfus, G.
  Malebranche, N. 6:66
Dreyfus, Georges
  Buddhist nominalism 7:27
  Dharmakīrti 3:53
  rGyal tshab dar ma rin chen
    †8:304–5
  Sa skya paṇḍita †8:433–5
  Tibetan philosophy 9:408
Dreyfus, H.L.
  artificial intelligence 1:492
  Foucault, M. 3:713
  genealogy 4:4
  Heideggerian philosophy of
    science 4:327
  Husserl, E. 4:586
  intentionality 4:821
  phenomenology
    epistemic issues in 7:347
Drèze, J. 9:670
Dries, L. van den 9:264
Driesch, H. 9:640, 9:642, 9:643
Driscoll, L. 1:74

Drobisch, M. 5:728
Drobnitskii, O.G. 6:159
le droit
  natural law (Villey, M.) 9:614
Dronke, P.E.
  Bernard of Tours 1:756
  Chartres school 2:291
  Hildegard of Bingen 4:431
  medieval philosophy 6:276
  natural philosophy
    medieval 6:706
  Platonism
    medieval 7:438
  Thierry of Chartres 9:372–3
Droysen, J.G. 4:444, 4:446
drugs
  mysticism 6:631
  performance-enhancing
    sport ethics 9:111–12
Drury, Shadia B.
  Kojève, A. 5:291
  Strauss, L. †9:167–8
Dryer, Douglas P. 5:196
Du Bois, W.E.B.
  pan-Africanism 7:191, 7:193, 7:194
  postcolonialism 7:581, 7:582
Du Bois-Reymond, Emil 3:129–31
Du Châtelet-Lomont, Émilie 3:131–3
dualism 3:133–8
  aesthetic mode of living 5:320–1
  alienation
    Marcel, G. critique 6:92
  anthropological principle 2:305
  anti-positivism
    Latin America 1:305, 1:306
  artistic critique 1:514
  asceticism critique 1:518–19
  Augustine 1:547–8
  Bergson, H.-L. 1:734
  Berkeleian 1:739, 1:744
  Cambridge Platonism 2:184
  Cartesian
    alienation
      German Romanticism 8:351
    ascription problem
      (Strawson, P.F.) 9:171–2
    as category mistake (Ryle, G.)
      8:428, 8:430
  Charleton, W. 2:286
  Descartes, R. 3:11–12, 9:45–7
  Foucher, S. critique 3:713,
    3:715, 3:716–17
  La Forge, L. de 5:331–2
  Le Grand, A. 5:479–80
  mental causation 6:308
  More, H. 6:579–80

paranormal phenomena 7:222,
  7:223
  Spinoza, B. de rejection 9:97
Chinese neo-Confucianism
  li-qi 6:769
Christianity 6:76
consciousness 3:137
contingency 5:321
critiques of
  artistic 1:514
  asceticism 1:518–19
  Foucher, S. 3:713, 3:715,
    3:716–17
  Marcel, G. 6:92
  Spinoza, B. de 9:97
Daoism 2:787–8
death 2:818, 2:820, 2:821
eliminativism contrast 3:264
essentialism 3:419–20
existentialism 3:496, 3:500
Four-Seven Debate
  Korean Confucianism 2:556,
    2:559–62, 9:824
Gnosticism 4:83, 4:84–5
harmony (Leibniz, G.W.) 5:548–9
Indian
  Upaniṣads 6:400–1
introspection 4:838, 4:841
irrational world-soul (Plutarch of
  Chaeronea) 7:467
Islamic fundamentalism 5:10
Kant, I.
  critique of Maimon, S. 6:35–6,
    6:37
Manicheism 6:74, 6:75, 6:76
matter
  Sāṅkhya-Yoga 6:197, 6:199–200
mental states 3:133, 3:135, 6:395,
  6:403–4
Merleau-Ponty, M. 6:321
metaphysics 6:339
neo-Confucianism
  li-qi 6:770
Neo-Pythagoreanism
  Middle Platonism 7:425
paranormal phenomena 7:222,
  7:223
phenomenal consciousness 2:586
physical 6:95
Plato 9:44, 9:45, 9:46, 9:48
Platonism
  Numenius 7:54–5
  Plotinus 7:461–2
  Plutarch of Chaeronea 7:467
process philosophy 7:712–13
projectivism 7:739–40
qualia 3:135–6, 7:863–4

resurrection 8:295
sacraments 8:445
Sāṅkhya 4:438
sôngnihak
  Korean Confucian philosophy
  2:558–9
soul/body (Ibn Gabirol, S.) 4:618
Spinoza, B. de (Vygotskii, L.S.)
  9:673
spirit/nature (*dukh*/*priroda*)
  (Berdiaev, N.A.) 1:727
substance
  Brown, T. 2:27
  Descartes, R. 9:45–6
supervenience 9:237–8
tacit integration 7:490–1
transcendental philosophy
  Kant, I. 8:511
  Schelling, F.W.J. von 8:511,
  8:512–13, 8:514–15
Western (Cixous, H.) 2:372
Wolff, C. 9:782
Zoroastrianism 6:75
duality
  Boolean algebra 1:844
  glossary 5:802
  particle-field
    classical field theory 3:668–70
  projective geometry 4:423–4
  scientific theory (Maxwell, J.C.)
  6:208
Dobbins, J. 2:105–6
Dubin, L. 3:323
Dubois, D. 3:824
Dubs, H.H. 9:820
Ducasse, Curt John **3:138–42**
  adverbial theory of mental states
  6:317
Duchesneau, F. 5:561
Duchet, M. 2:122, 3:69
Ducret, M. 5:378
Ducrot, O. 7:631, 8:482, 9:177, 9:181
Duddington, N. 5:838
Dudley, D.R. 1:317, 2:758
Dudley, G. 3:263
Duff, R.A.
  crime and punishment †2:704–11
  double effect principle 3:121
  responsibility †8:290–4
Dufour, A. 7:836
Dufrenne, M. 4:792
Dugac, P. 2:842
Dugas, R. 6:259
Dugger, W. 3:220
Duguit, L. 5:513
Dugundji, J. 6:83
Duhem, H.-P. 3:147

Duhem, Pierre Maurice Marie
  3:142–7
  see also Duhem-thesis ('D-thesis')
  Alighieri, Dante 1:185
  Comte, A. 2:504
  concepts 2:515
  crucial experiments 2:735, 2:736,
    3:142, 3:144
  epistemological holism 3:144,
    3:145
  Eudoxus 3:452, 3:453
  Hanson, N.R. 4:225
  John of Jandun 5:109
  Le Roy, É.L.E.J. 5:482
  meaning and verification 6:233,
    6:236
  mechanics
    classical 6:259
  medieval natural philosophy
    6:703, 6:706
  models 6:446
  Ptolemy 7:831
  science
    demarcation problem 2:866
  Soto, D. de 9:39
  thought experiments 9:396
  underdetermination 3:142, 3:144,
    9:528–9
Duhem-thesis ('D-thesis') 9:528–9
Dühring, Eugen Karl **3:147–9**
Duke, A. 2:181, 2:182
Dukes, P. 3:326–7
Dulles, A. 8:300
Dülmen, R. Van 4:698
Dumas, A. 1:837–8
Dumeige, G. 8:314
Duméry, H. 5:339
Dummett, Michael Anthony Eardley
  3:149–53
  abstract objects 1:35
  analytic philosophy 1:226, 1:228
  arithmetic 1:440, 1:441
  bivalence 4:856–7
  Bolzano, B. 1:827
  Cantor's theorem 2:200
  Chomsky, N. 2:341
  conventionalism 2:668–9
  deconstruction 2:839
  Frege, G. 3:771, 3:777
  Gödel's theorems 4:113–14, 4:115
  intuitionistic logic 4:857–8,
    4:859–62
  language
    communal 5:416, 5:419
    conventionality of 5:369, 5:371
    private states 7:698, 7:701
  McTaggart, J.M.E. 6:28

many-valued logics 6:88–9, 6:90
mathematics
  antirealism 1:309, 1:310, 1:311
  constructivism 2:638
  foundations of 6:189
  intuitionism 4:851–2, 6:187
  realism 8:120, 8:123
meaning 5:410
  and truth 6:225
  and understanding 6:226–7,
    6:229
  and verification 6:230, 6:233–4,
    6:236
objectivity 7:75
quantum logic 7:886
realism/antirealism 8:119
reference 8:163, 8:685, 8:688
sacraments 8:445
testimony 9:313
understanding
  realist and antirealist models
    6:226–7
vagueness 9:566
Dumont, Stephen D.
  Duns Scotus, J. †3:153–70
  Henry of Ghent 4:359
Dumoulin, H. 5:646, 6:626
Dunbar, J. 3:330
Duncan, D. 5:854
Duncan, D.A. 6:330–1
Duncan-Jones, A. 1:708, 1:709, 2:160
Dundas, P. 6:34
Dunford, C. 4:797
Dunkel, H.D. 4:371
Dunlap, R.E. 6:720
Dunlop, D.M. 4:213
Dunlop, Francis
  Scheler, Max Ferdinand †8:504–9
Dunn, J.
  American philosophy
    eighteenth and nineteenth
      century 1:206
  political representation 8:272
  revolution 8:303
  state 9:122
Dunn, J.M.
  logical laws 5:789
  many-valued logics 6:90
  non-constructive rules of inference
    7:29
  ontological commitment 7:116
  paraconsistent logic 7:210
  relevance logic and entailment
    8:203–4
Dunn, L.C. 4:15
Dunn, R.
  intention †4:811–16

Dunne, John D.
  Buddhist nominalism †7:23–7
Dunphy, W. 7:323
Duns Scotus, John **3:153–70**
  see also Scotism
  addition theory of forms
    succession theory contrast 2:141
  Aristotelianism
    medieval 1:394, 1:401
  cognition
    intuitive/abstractive distinction
      1:565–6
  Collations 3:156
  free will 1:865
  God
    concepts of 4:101
    existence arguments 3:160–3
    as necessary being 6:745, 6:747
  Incarnation 4:150
  individuation 3:154, 3:163–5
  influence of
    Francis of Meyronnes 3:723–4
  intellectualism 9:663–4
  justification doctrine 5:166
  Lectura 3:156
  natural philosophy 6:700, 6:704
  Ordinatio 3:156
  perfect-being theology 4:97
  primary object of the intellect
    3:158–60
  Quodlibetal Questions 3:156
  Reportatio parisiensis 3:156
  reprobation 8:274
  revelation 8:300
  right and good 8:323–4
  soul 9:45, 9:48
  universals 3:163–5
  univocal concept of being 2:293
  univocity of transcendentals
    3:157–8
  will
    intellectualism 9:663
    nature of 3:166–7
Dupleix, Scipion 1:387, 1:388–9,
  1:390
Dupoux, E. 7:823
Dupré, John 1:273, 7:227, 9:532
Dupré, L. 6:626, 6:762
Dupuy, M. 8:508
Duran, Jane 3:599, 3:602
Duran, Profiat **3:170–1**, 5:89, 8:739
Duran, Simeon ben Tzemach
  3:171–2, 5:89
Durand, D.B. 7:157
Durandus of St Pourçain **3:172–4**
duration
  eternity concept 3:422, 3:423–4

unitary (Bergson, H.-L.) 1:733
Durbin, P.T. 1:347, 9:282, 9:283
Đurić, Mihailo 9:52–3, 9:54
Durkheim, Émile **3:174–7**
  behaviourism in the social sciences
    1:694
  division of labour 3:176
  God
    concepts of 4:95, 4:101
  holism and individualism in
    history and social science 4:484,
    4:487
  moral education 3:176
  religious education 3:176–7
  ritual 8:341
  Saint-Simon 8:447
  social science
    contemporary philosophy of
      8:846
    experiments in 3:518, 3:520
    functionalism 3:817
    history of philosophy of 8:855,
      8:857
    methodology of 8:862, 8:868
    naturalism in 6:720
  social socience
    value judgments in 9:576, 9:579
  social theory and law 8:876
  society
    concept of 8:888, 8:889
  sociological method 3:174–6
  solidarity 9:24–5
  suicide 1:695, 3:176, 9:224, 9:229
Dürr, K. 4:61
Düsing, K. 4:279
Dussel, Enrique 5:611, 5:612
Dussen, W.J. van der 2:415
Dutch book arguments
  criticique of 7:709
  degrees of belief 5:161–2, 7:705,
    7:706
  Jeffrey Conditionalization 7:708
  subjective probabilities 7:703–4
duties
  classification of (Kant, I.) 5:190
  of the heart
    Jewish pietism (Ibn Paquda)
      4:633–6
  of justice (Kant, I.) 5:191
  religious (Mendelssohn, M.) 6:306
  of virtue (Kant, I.) 5:190–1
Dutton, D. 1:501
Dutton, P.E. 2:291, 7:438
duty **3:178–83**
  see also dharma; supererogation
  categorical imperative (Kant, I.)
    5:201

conscience (Reid, T.) 2:449
convictions (Fries, J.F.) 3:798
deontological ethics **2:890–2**
emotions 6:559
epistemic
  religious belief 8:211–14
epistemic/intellectual 5:160, 7:36–7
happiness (Johnson, S.) 5:125
help and beneficence 4:342–3
hunger relief 1:126
ideals conflict 4:674
Indian conceptions of **3:183–7**
indirect
  animals and ethics 1:274
interest (Bentham, J.) 1:722
legal idealism 5:511
legal realist rejection of 5:522
moral intuitionism
  (Prichard, H.A.) 7:680, 7:681
moral motivation 6:526–7
moral pluralism (Ross, W.D.)
  6:529
moral scepticism (Ross, W.D.)
  6:543
morality (Bradley, F.H.) 1:858–9
perfectionism 7:300, 7:301
praise (Kant, I.) 7:645
as prediction (Holmes, O.W.) 4:494
prima facie
  conflict 3:179–80
  Ross, W.D. 8:366
renunciation
  Indian philosophy 3:183,
    3:185–7
right and good 8:322–3, 8:324
rights 3:178–9, 8:325, 8:326
  paraphrasis (Bentham, J.) 1:723
  Reid, T. 8:177–8
self-respect (Kant, I.) 8:635,
  8:636–7
Stoic ethics 9:154–5
types of 3:179–80
universalism (Kant, I.) 9:538
Duval, Edwin M.
  Rabelais, F. †8:15–18
Duval, R. 4:159
Duxbury, Neil
  Frank, J. †3:725–6
  legal realism †5:521–5
Duyvendak, J.J.L. 2:781
Dvaita Vedānta
  Brahman/individual relationship
    9:592
  Madhva 6:31–2
Dwivedi, R.C. 6:381
Dworkin, Andrea 7:543, 7:544

Dworkin, G.
  autonomy
    ethical 1:591
  economics and ethics 3:210
  educational philosophy 3:238
  freedom and liberty 3:757
  paternalism 7:252
  solidarity 9:25
Dworkin, Ronald **3:187–9**
  adjudication
    equity 5:152
  affirmative action 1:93
  contractarianism 2:665
  economics and ethics 3:210
  equality 3:395
  external preferences 5:441–2
  feminist jurisprudence 3:610
  integrity
    rule of law 8:390–1
  justice 5:146

legal norms
  as interpretation 7:40, 7:41
legal positivism 5:520
legal reasoning and interpretation
  5:530
liberalism 5:604
life and death 5:626, 5:628, 5:630
neutrality
  political 6:818–19, 6:820–1
obligation
  political 7:80
pornography 7:544–5
practical reasoning/rationality
  8:101
rights 8:327, 8:330
social norms 8:835
suicide 9:229
Dyad
  see also Indefinite Dyad

Monad
  first principles
    Xenocrates 9:806
Dyczkowski, M. 1:19
Dyer, G.J. 5:637
Dyke, C. 2:279
dynamic logics **3:189–91**, 6:420
  possible worlds semantics 8:664–5
dynamics
  Albert of Saxony 1:144
  chaos theory 2:276–7
  force/motion distinction
    (Leibniz, G.W.) 5:555
  matter (Kant, I.) 6:737
Dyson, A. 8:280
Dyson, F. 5:635
Dyzenhaus, David Ludovic
  Schmitt, C. †8:544–5
Dzielska, M. 4:597
Dzongkaba Losang dragba *see* Tsong
  kha pa Blo bzang grags pa

E

Eadmer 1:284, 1:296
Eames, C. 5:745–6
Eames, R. 5:745–6
early Christian philosophy *see*
    Christianity, early; patristic
    philosophy
Earman, J.
    chaos theory 2:279
    determinism and indeterminism
        3:39
    natural laws 5:474
    Newton, I. 6:828
    randomness 8:59
    relativity theory
        philosophical significance of
            8:198
    space 9:64
    spacetime 9:69
    thermodynamics 9:369
    time 9:416, 9:418
earth
    see also world
    age of (Buffon, G.L.L.) 2:121
    evolutionary stages of (Teilhard de
        Chardin, P.) 9:289
East Asian philosophy **3:192–6**
Eastern Learning *see* Tonghak
Eastern Orthodox Christianity
    see also Greek Orthodox
        Christianity
    atonement 1:537–8
    Eucharist 8:443, 8:444, 8:455
    grace 4:148, 4:149
    justification doctrine 5:167–8
    sacraments 8:442, 8:444
    sanctification 8:455–6
Eastern and Western Disciples
    Ramakrishna Movement 8:41
Easton, D. 9:256
Easton, L. 4:301
Easton, Patricia
    Desgabets, R. †3:27–30
    Le Grand, A. †5:479–81
    Malebranche, N. 6:66
Eaton, J.C. 3:561
Eaton, M.M. 1:58, 3:280
Eatwell, J. 8:74
Eatwell, Roger
    fascism †3:561–3

Eaves, L.J. 8:235
Ebbesen, Sten
    Averroism †1:595–8
    Boethius, A.M.S. 1:812
    Boethius of Dacia †1:813–16
    Brito, R. 2:21–3
    language, medieval theories of
        †5:389–404
Ebbinghaus, H.-D. 1:763, 4:771,
    6:442, 8:595
Ebenstein, W. 5:227
Eberhard, Johann August **3:196**
Eberle, R.A. 6:319
Ebert, T. 3:58–9
Ebner, Ferdinand 2:33, 8:360, 8:361
Eboussi-Boulaga, F. 1:112, 1:114
Ebreo, Leone *see* Abravanel, Judah
    ben Isaac
Eccles, J.C. 3:138, 3:354, 9:109
Ecclesiastes, Book of
    Neckham, A. 6:751
ecclesiology
    Nicholas of Cusa 6:835
    Slavophilism 8:809–10
Eck, J. van 2:890
Eckardt, B. von
    introspection, psychology of
        †4:842–6
Ecker, A. 7:93
Eckermann, W. 4:172
Eckert, P. 5:367
Eckhart, Meister *see* Meister Eckhart
Eckman, J. 2:204
eclectic spiritualism
    Argentina 1:376
eclecticism
    Brazil 2:10
    Cousin, V. 2:691
    Thomasius, C. 9:377
Eco, Umberto
    interpretation
        artistic 1:505
        semiotics 5:39, 5:41, 8:677, 8:679
eco-fascism 3:334
eco-feminism 3:200, 3:333–4
Ecole, J. 9:786
ecological anarchism
    Bookchin, M. 1:247
ecological optics

Gibson, J.J. 9:633–4
ecological philosophy **3:197–202**
    deep ecology
        Næss, A. 6:635, 6:636
        worldview 3:198–9
ecology **3:202–5**
    see also deep ecology;
        environment; environmental
        ethics; green political philosophy;
        social ecology
    feminist theology 3:622, 3:623–4
    relationships within (Linnaeus, C.
        von) 5:649
econometrics
    Cournot, A.A. 2:688
economic determinism
    Chinese Marxism 6:134–5
economic efficiency 5:454
'Economic Man'
    Gauthier, D. 2:660
economics **3:211–22**
    see also market economy
    alienated labour 6:121–2
    central planning 8:880, 8:881–2,
        8:883
    conservatism 2:611–12
    democracy 2:870–1
    ecology 3:204, 6:814
    efficiency 3:205, 3:208–9, 7:227–8
    entrepreneurship
        (Schumpeter, J.A.) 8:555
    equilibrium models 4:246–7
    and ethics **3:205–11**, 8:826
        business 2:150–3
        development 3:39–42
        efficiency 3:205, 3:208–9
        markets 3:213
        'moral mathematics' 3:209–10
        rationality 3:205, 3:206
        social choice theory 8:826
        sport 9:111
        welfare 3:205, 3:206–7
    family 3:550
    general (Bataille, G.) 1:659, 1:660
    gifts (Cixous, H.) 2:373
    Guanzi 4:186–7
    Hayek, F.A. 4:246–7
    human nature (Mandeville, B.)
        6:72

justice
  principle of need 6:753–4
Keynes, J.M. 5:234–5
Lassalle, F. 5:420
law **5:454–7**
Marx, K. 6:127–8
  history
    philosophy of 4:455
  political philosophy
    history of 7:516
Marxism
  Althusser, L.P. 1:193–9
  technology and ethics 9:281
monetary reform (Cieszkowski, A.)
  2:361
neoclassical 3:215
neo-liberalism (Vysheslavtsev, B.P.)
  9:676
obligations to future generations
  3:819
physiocracy (Smith, A.) 8:816
positivism (Comte, A.) 2:505
quantity theory of money
  (Bodin, J.) 1:797
rational choice theory 8:73
risk trade-off 8:333
role of theory (Schumpeter, J.A.)
  8:556
Russian Orthodoxy
  (Bulgakov, S.N.) 2:124–5
socialism 8:881–2
ecophilosophy *see* ecological
  philosophy
ecosystems
  superorganisms 3:203
écriture
  see also writing
  critical legal studies 5:509
écriture feminine (feminine writing)
  2:372–3, 3:596
ecumenism
  Chaadaev, P.I. 2:271–2
  Nicholas of Cusa 6:835
Eddington, A. 1:120
Eddy, W.C.H. 1:583
Edel, G. 2:402
Edelstein, L. 4:335, 7:555–6, 7:557
Edgar, H. 2:504
Edge, H.L. 7:227
Edgington, D. 2:688, 4:742, 6:236,
  7:214
Edgley, R. 6:675
Edict of Milan 7:259
Edie, J.M.
  Frank, S.L. 3:729
  James, W. 5:67
  Merleau-Ponty, M. 6:324

Mikhailovskii, N.K. 6:357
  Russian materialism 8:418
  Russian medieval philosophy
    6:278
  Russian nihilism 7:8
  Russian philosophy 8:427
  Russian religious-philosophical
    Renaissance 8:427
  Slavophilism 8:811
edifying philosophy 7:599–600
Edinburgh School 2:625–6
education
  see also educational philosophy;
    pedagogy
  Arya Samaj movement 1:517
  Brazil
    Portuguese reforms 2:9
  Chinese classics 2:313
  Christian
    spiritual growth 8:457
  colonial philosophy
    Latin America 5:422
  Dewey, J. 1:205
  equality (Diderot, D.) 3:63, 3:66
  ethical
    African 3:432
  habits of inquiry (Dewey, J.) 3:49
  judgment (Vico, G.) 9:601
  Marxism, Chinese 6:133–4
  medieval
    Bacon, R. 1:634
    Erasmus, D. 3:396, 3:397–8
    Gerbert of Aurillac 4:40
    natural philosophy 6:695
  Mexico 6:347–8, 7:566, 7:567
  mimēsis 6:381
  moral **6:506–9**
    China
      Confucianism 2:543–4,
        2:545, 2:546
      Jia Yi 5:102
    evil 3:464
    rules 6:506–7
    virtues 6:507–8
    Xenophon 9:812–13
  Neoplatonic curriculum 6:798,
    6:799–800
  philosophical
    ancient Greece 1:264
  rational enlightenment
    (Comenius, J.A.) 2:438, 2:439
  Renaissance logic 5:770–2
  self-cultivation
    Daxue 2:808–9
  social conditioning (Rousseau, J.-
    J.) 8:368, 8:372–3

social emancipation
  (Ambedkar, B.R.) 1:196–7
Sophism 7:789–90, 9:33–4
wisdom and prudence (Vico, G.)
  9:600–1
women
  Masham, D. 6:167
  Musonius Rufus 6:616
  Schurman, A.M. van 8:557–8
  Suchon, G. 9:211
educational philosophy **3:231–40**
  aesthetics 3:234
  ancient Greece 3:223–5
  critical thinking 3:233–4
  early Christianity 3:225
  epistemology 3:233
  ethics 3:232–3, 3:234–5
  history of **3:222–31**
  insight (Herbart, J.F.) 4:370–1
  law 3:236–7
  nineteenth century 3:227–8
  political philosophy 3:235–6
  Reformation 3:225–6
  science 3:237
Edwards, D.L. 8:51
Edwards, H. 5:312
Edwards, Jonathan 1:823, **3:240–5**
  Calvinism
    colonial America 1:201, 1:201
  ethics 3:242–3
  God
    being in general 3:242
    creation 3:242
    sovereignty 3:240, 3:241–2
  moral agents 6:503
  pietism 7:394
  redemption 3:244
  religion and epistemology 8:218
  sin 8:795
  spiritual sense 3:243–4
  theological aesthetics 3:240, 3:243
  theological determinism 3:240,
    3:241
Edwards, M.J. 7:549
Edwards, Paul
  death 2:822
  immortality 8:296
  induction 4:751
  Kierkegaard, S. 5:243
  necessary being 6:746, 6:747
  soul 9:48
  suicide †9:224–30
Edwards, R.R. 1:756, 5:454
Edwards, T. 7:177
Edwards, W.F. 9:839
Eells, E. 2:250
Eemeren, F.H. van 3:702

EFE *see* Einstein field equations
efficiency
  liberal individualism 5:461
  market ethics 6:107–8
  Pareto principle 3:205, 3:208–9,
    7:227–8
  property 7:757, 7:760
efficient causes
  action (Reid, T.) 8:174
  Duns Scotus, J. 3:160–3
  existence (Reid, T.) 8:173–4
  medieval metaphysical doctrine
    6:273–4
  William of Ockham 9:742, 9:743
efficient self
  Iqbal, M. 4:864–5
Efodi *see* Duran, Profiat
Efros, I. 1:651, 8:439
egalitarianism
  Chinese Marxism 6:134, 6:137–8
  Jewish bioethics 1:777, 1:778
  liberalism 5:600
Egan, F.
  methodological individualism
    6:344
  vision †9:631–8
Eggers, W. 2:227
Eggleston, R.E. 5:505, 5:530
ego
  see also id; super-ego
  absolute (Herbart, F.J.) 4:370
  Freud, S. 3:791–2
  idealism 4:666
  mirror identification (Lacan, J.)
    5:337
  Other (Levinas, E.) 5:580–1
  persons 7:318
  psychoanalysis
    post-Freudian 7:819–21
  renunciation of (Weil, S.) 9:698,
    9:699, 9:700
  transcendental (Sartre, J.-P.)
    8:474–5
egoism **3:245–8**
  see also self-interest; self-love
  altruism contrast (Kant, I.) 5:182
  Buddhism
    Japan 5:73
  ethical 2:604, 3:245–8
  friendship
    Epicureanism 3:348
  individual autonomy (Stirner, M.)
    9:141
  justice
    Epicureanism 3:347
  moral motivation 6:525
  moral psychology 6:531–2

perfectionism 7:301
progressive hedonism
  (Ducasse, C.J.) 3:140
psychological 2:156, 3:246, 3:247
rational
  anthropological principle
    (Chernyshevskii, N.G.) 2:305
  Russian materialism 8:416
  Russian nihilism 7:7
  Shaftesbury, Third Earl of 8:731
  sociobiology 8:892–3
  substantive 3:247
  utilitarianism conflict
    Mill, J.S. 6:369, 6:371
    Sidgwick, H. 8:760–2
Egypt
  see also Alexandria
  'Abduh, M. **1:6–8**
  Clement of Alexandria **2:383–5**
  cosmology, ancient **3:248–50**
  Hermetism 4:395–7
    ancient philosophy 4:395–7
  influence on ancient Greek
    thought 1:96, **3:250–4**
  Maimonides, A. **6:38–40**
  Maimonides, M. **6:40–9**
  Neoplatonism 6:804
  Origen **7:160–3**
  Philo of Alexandria **7:357–61**
  Plotinus **7:456–63**
  Ptolemy **7:830–2**
  Saadiah Gaon **8:435–40**
Ehlen, P. 5:832
Ehlers, B. 9:20–1
Ehlers, J. 4:33, 4:520
Ehnmark, E. 4:204
Ehrenfels, Christian von 4:51–2, 4:53
Ehrenfest, P. 9:369
Ehrenfest, T. 9:369
Ehreshefsky, M. 9:532
Ehrle, F. 7:269
Ehrlich, E. 5:513
Ehrlich, L.H. 5:83, 5:84
Ehrlich, P. 9:80–1
El-Ehwany, A.F. 1:385
Eichler, M. 3:592
Eichner, A. 3:220
Eichner, E. 8:531
eidetic method (Husserl, E.) 7:335
Eidlitz, W. 3:859
eidos (*Wesen*) 4:1, 4:575, 4:578
Eigen, M. 5:635
eigenstates 7:891–2
eigenvalues 7:891–2
Eikhenbaum, B. 8:411–12, 8:413,
  9:439
Eilenberg, S. 2:238

Einstein, Albert **3:254–8**
  see also Einstein field equations;
    Einstein-Podolsky-Rosen
    experiment
  Bell's theorem 1:716
  optics 7:138–9
  quantum theory 3:254, 3:256–7,
    7:894
  relativity theory 8:191, 8:198–9
    general 3:254, 3:255–6, 4:8–9
      positivism 4:5–6
    special 3:254, 3:255
  scientific method 3:257
  spacetime 9:66–8, 9:69
  universe-models 2:678–9
Einstein field equations (EFE) 9:68
Einstein-Podolsky-Rosen experiment
  1:713
Eisen, A.M.
  Kaplan, M. 5:206
Eisen Murphy, Claudia
  Hildegard of Bingen †4:429–31
Eisen Murphy, Sean
  Bernard of Clairvaux †1:753–5
  Joachim of Fiore †5:103–5
Eisenberg, Y. 4:636
Eisenstein, I. 5:206
Ekbom, Lennart 7:213
Ekman, R. 3:552
Ekstein, N. 3:693
élan vital (Bergson, H.-L.) 1:735
E-languages 2:340–1
Elbaz, S.W. 3:315
Elbogen, I. 4:610
Elbogen, J. 4:433
Eldridge, Niles 3:482
Elea
  Parmenides **7:229–35**
  Zeno **9:843–5**
Eleatic philosophy
  see also Parmenides; Zeno of Elea
  a priori reasoning 1:263
  Anaxagoras 1:249
  atomism, ancient 1:535
  Forms
    Plato's *Phaedo* 7:413
  influence on Megarian school
    6:279
  Melissus 6:292–5
  Presocratics 7:671
  radical monism 1:263
  Xenophanes 9:808, 9:809
election, divine *see* divine election
elections
  political representation 8:271–2
elective community
  friendship (Blanchot, M.) 1:783

electricity electrodynamics
electrodynamics **3:259–60**, 4:401
electromagnetism
  classical mechanics 6:252
  experimental anomalies 3:516
  field theory, classical 3:668–70
  Maxwell, J.C. 6:207–8
electronic technology
  ethics 4:778–81
  hyperreal culture (Baudrillard, J.)
    1:662–3
elementary logic
  extensions of
    logical constants 5:777
elements
  chemistry 2:296
    Aristotle 2:295, 2:296
  harmonization/dissolution of
    (Empedocles) 3:293, 3:294–5
  Jungius, J. 5:136
  materialism
    Indian school of 6:179–80
  natural (Ibn Tzaddik, J.) 4:660
  order of (Alighieri, Dante) 1:184
  Proclus
    rejection of Aristotle 7:729
Elena, M. 9:521–2
elenchus (refutation)
  Arcesilaus 1:352, 1:353
  Socrates 3:223, 9:11–14
Elford, E. 9:731
Elgin, Catherine Z.
  art works
    ontology of 1:484
  depiction 2:896
  Goodman, N. †4:135–40
Eliade, Mircea **3:260–3**
  alchemy 1:158
  mysticism, history of 6:626
  phenomenology of religion 7:355
  religious/non-religious distinction
    3:261
  the sacred 3:260, 3:261
Elian school 9:22
Elias del Medigo *see* Delmedigo,
  Elijah
Elias, S. 4:19
elimination, argument by 2:735–6
eliminativism **3:263–6**, 6:173
  see also materialism
  Australian materialism 1:579
  belief and knowledge 1:706,
    1:708–9
  colour 2:420, 2:426–7, 2:428–9
  dualism 3:137–8
  functionalism 6:176
  music 6:608

phenomenal consciousness 2:582,
    2:587–8
  propositional attitudes 7:785
  reductionism, philosophy of mind
    8:150, 8:152
  Rorty, R. 8:354–5
  scientific behaviourism 1:696
  social science
    methodology of 8:865
Elior, R.
  Hasidism †4:242–5
Eliot, C.W. 7:238
Eliot, George **3:266–7**
Eliot, T.S. 2:748–9, 2:750, 7:476
Elis
  Hippias 4:440–1
  Pyrrho **7:844–8**
Elisabeth of Bohemia **3:267–9**
elitism
  Strauss, L. 9:168
Elkana, Y. 2:607
Elkin, S.L. 2:621
Elkman, S. 3:859
Ellacuria, Ignacio 5:612
Ellenberger, H.F. 3:502
Ellenson, D.
  Kaplan, M. †5:204–6
Elliot, R. 3:335, 6:735
Elliot-Binns, J.E. 4:794, 7:98, 8:61,
    9:301
Elliott, G. 1:195
Elliott, R.K. 1:475, 1:498, 6:613
Ellis, B.D. 5:474
Ellis, G.F.R. 2:680, 8:235, 9:69
Ellis, J.M. 8:529
Ellis, Joseph J. 5:125–6
Ellison, J. 3:272
Ellison, R. 8:631
Ellissen, O.A. 5:354
Elliston, F. 8:727
Ellmann, M. 3:613
Ellsberg, D. 2:834, 8:101
Ellul, Jacques 9:283
Ellwood, R. 9:365
Elman, Benjamin 6:776
Elon, M. 4:207
Elorduy, E. 9:196
Elsbach, A. 4:9
Else, G.F. 5:219, 6:382
Elster, Jon
  democracy 2:871–2
  economics and ethics 3:210
  explanation in history and social
    science 3:530
  functionalism in social science
    3:815, 3:817
  Marx, K. 6:132

Marxism
  Western 6:146
practical reasoning/rationality
  8:101
  game theory 8:98
  maximization 8:97
  rational choice theory 8:74
  Scandinavia 8:492
  self-realization 8:634
  social action 8:823
  society
    concept of 8:888–9
  solidarity 9:25
  work
    philosophy of 9:796–7
Elswijk, H.C. van 4:72
emanationism
  Abhinavagupta 1:18
  Aristotelianism (Dietrich of
    Freiberg) 3:69–70
  causality
    Islamic philosophy 2:242
  Christianity 2:696–7
  creation distinction (Ibn
    Miskawayh) 4:630
  divine word (Judah Halevi) 4:208,
    4:211–12
  ex uno non fit nisi unum (al-Razi,
    Fakhr al-Din) 8:113
  hierarchical ontology (Plotinus)
    7:460
  illuminationism 4:699–700
  Islamic philosophy 2:242, 6:805–6,
    6:807
  causality 2:242
  al-Farabi 2:241, 2:244, 3:555
  al-Ghazali 4:64–5
  Ibn al-'Arabi 4:604
  Ibn Massara 4:628
  Ibn Miskawayh 4:630
  Ibn Sina 4:648–9, 4:650, 4:651
  Ibn Taymiyya 4:655, 4:656
  Ikhwan al-Safa' 4:686
  Mir Damad, Muhammad Baqir
    6:409
  al-Razi, Fakhr al-Din 8:113
  al-Tawhidi 9:271
  Jewish philosophy
  Bar Hayya, A. 1:649
  Herrera, A. Cohen de 4:397,
    4:398–9, 5:172–4
  Hillel ben Samuel of Verona
    4:432
  Ibn Gabirol, S. 4:618–19
  Israeli, I. 5:32–3
  Judah ben Moses of Rome
    5:129

Judah Halevi 4:208, 4:211–12
Kabbalah
    Herrera, A. Cohen de 4:397,
    4:398–9, 5:172–4
    Sefirot 5:172–4
Maimonides, M. 6:45
Neoplatonism
    Ibn Gabirol, S. 4:618–19
voluntarism 9:666
occasionalist opposition to 7:87
soul (Hillel ben Samuel of Verona)
    4:432
theosophy 9:364
voluntarism
    Jewish 9:666
emancipation
    social science 8:843
embarrassment
    shame distinction 3:282, 3:283
embodiment
    see also body
    omnipresence 7:103–5
    reincarnation 8:184–5
Embree, Lester
    archaeology 1:357
    phenomenological movement
    †7:333–4
    Scandinavia 8:491
Emden, A.B. 9:376
Emecheta, B. 3:613
emergentism
    consciousness
        high-level 7:196
    mental causation 6:310
    particulars 7:237
emergentism
    supervenience 7:196, 9:235
Emerson, Caryl
    Bakhtin, M.M. 1:645
    Mamardashvili, M.K. †6:66–71
Emerson, Ralph Waldo 3:269–72
    American philosophy
        eighteenth and nineteenth
        century 1:202
    influence on Thoreau, H.D. 9:389,
    9:392
    rectification and remainders 8:140
    self
        perfectionist conception of
        Cavell, S. 2:259
    Swedenborg, E. 9:243
    transcendentalism 9:137
Emerson, R.L.
    Ferguson, A. 3:632
    Home, H. †4:499–501
Emery, Kent, Jr
    Denys the Carthusian †2:884–7

Richard of St Victor †8:312–14
Thomas à Kempis †9:373–4
Emilsson, E.K.
    Scandinavia 8:493
Emilsson, Eyjolfur K.
    Plotinus †7:456–63
Emlen, S. 8:801
Emmen, A. 6:203
Emmerich, R. 5:103
Emmet, Dorothy
    Alexander, S. †1:168–9
    general will 4:11
    processes †7:720–3
    Whitehead, A.N. 9:718
emotions 3:281–5, 3:285–90
    see also morality, and emotions;
    passions; pleasure
    a priori
        values 1:609
    art 1:61, 3:273–81
        aesthetic appreciation 3:279
        expression 1:458, 1:492–8
        fiction paradox 3:274–7
        Japan 1:82, 1:83–5
        music 3:277–8
        tragedy 3:278
    blame
        moral 6:564, 6:566–7
    bodily action (Spinoza, B. de)
        9:101–2
    Confucianism (Itō Jinsai) 5:43
    conscience 2:580
    dualism (Yi Hwang) 9:824
    essentialism
        critique by Sartre, J.-P. 8:475
    family ethics 3:550–1
    Four-Seven debate
        Korean Confucianism 2:556,
        2:560–2, 9:826
    friendship 3:795–6
    good/bad 3:286
    imaginary 3:276–7, 3:278
    infant cognition 2:390
    intentionality 3:282–3
    love 5:842–3
    meaning 3:290–1
    memory 6:297–8
    and morality see morality, and
        emotions
    music 6:610
        Gurney, E. 4:190–1
        Hanslick, E. 4:222–3
        meaning 6:606
    natural imagery
        Chinese poetry 1:70
    negative 3:278–9
    négritude 1:110–11

rationality 3:284
reason relationship 3:285–6
    Clement of Alexandria 2:384
    Spinoza, B. de 9:102–3
self-cultivation
    neo-Confucianism 8:622–3
    Stoicism 9:157
of taste (Alison, A.) 1:185–6
trust 9:468
twentieth century philosophy
    3:288–9
virtues (Spinoza, B. de) 9:103
emotivism 3:291–3
    Ayer, A.J. 1:614, 1:617
    duty 3:181–2
    emotions 3:288–9
    evaluations 3:32
    expressive discourse 9:580
    fact/value distinction 3:538
    goodness 4:131
    Hägerström, A.A.T. 4:202–3
    meaning 3:290–1
    moral judgment 1:221, 6:512
    prescriptivism 7:668
    Reid, T. 2:449
    Stevenson, C.L. 9:134–5
Empedocles 1:263, 3:293–8
    atonement 1:536
    change
        cycle of 3:293, 3:294–5
    cosmogony 3:295–7
    matter 6:193
    nature 3:295, 3:297
    Pythagoreanism 3:294
    sacrifice
        sin of 3:297–8
empiricism 3:298–303
    see also logical empiricism
    a posteriori 1:1–3
    acceptance (Nietzsche, F.W.) 6:849
    analytic/synthetic distinction
        (Quine, W.V.) critique 8:3–4, 8:6
    anti-positivism
        Latin America 1:304, 1:305,
        1:306
    arithmetic 1:438
    Berkeley, G. 1:737–48
    British 8:76
    Cartesian (Desgabets, R.) 3:28
    classical
        science (Bridgman, P.W.) 2:17,
        2:18
    commonsensism (Reid, T.) 2:454
    concepts (Locke, J.) 5:668
    constructive (Fraassen, B.C. van)
        8:583

critiques of 3:302–3
   Cambridge Platonism 2:183–4
   Chomsky, N. 2:339–40
   Green, T.H. 4:167–8
   Hegel, G.W.F. 3:378
   Il'enkov, E.V. 4:689
   Lonergan, B.J.F. 5:824
   Næss, A. 6:635
   Price, R. 7:675, 7:676–7
demarcation problem 2:863–4
direct knowledge (Sergeant, J.)
   8:698–9
epistemological
   Theophrastus 9:338
epistemological (Hume, D.) 3:378
existentialist (Marcel, G.) 6:91–2
experiment 3:514–15
feminist 3:598–600
foundationalism 3:301–2
global 3:299
Hellenistic medical epistemology
   4:333–5
history
   philosophy of 4:456
Hume, D. 6:230–1
knowledge by acquaintance 5:260
language (Hobbes, T.) 5:372–3
learning 5:483
   mental representation 5:483
linguistic
   protocol statements 6:814–15
logical (Ramsey, I.T.) 8:49–50
medicine, philosophy of 6:265
nativism contrast 6:672–3, 6:674
natural laws 5:473
observation 7:84–5
observation-theory distinction
   6:724
other minds problem 6:231–2
phenomenalist 3:299–300
pleasure 7:449
pluralism (Anderson, J.) 1:267
positive freedom 3:754
pragmatism 5:60, 5:61, 5:64–5
process (Bloch, E.S.) 1:788
psychology
   foundational problems of 5:483
public 3:299
radical (James, W.) 5:60, 5:61,
   5:65–6
reason (Thomasius, C.) 9:377
religious 3:299
Russell, B.A.W. 8:392, 8:399–400,
   8:401
science
   gender distortions 3:863
scientific constructivism 2:625

social science (Neurath, O.) 6:814
speculative (Herzen, A.I.) 4:405
stratified form of 3:298–9
structuralism in social science
   9:185
syntactical logical
   natural laws 5:473
thought experiments 9:393, 9:394
truth criterion (Gassendi, P.) 3:852
underdetermination 9:529
voluntarism 9:663, 9:664
empiriocriticism
   Avenarius, R. 1:592, 1:593–4
   Russian 6:151, 6:153–4, **8:404–9**
empiriomonism
   Bogdanov, A.A. 1:818, 8:405–6
employees
   see also stakeholders; work
   business ethics 2:151–2, 2:153
employment *see* work
emptiness
   see also voidism
   Buddhism **2:76–80**
      Buddha-nature 2:79
      causation relation 2:78–9
      Fazang 3:569
      impermanence 6:592–3
      kong 2:90
      li 5:594
      Linji 5:646
      logic
         Nishida Kitarō 5:714
      Mādhyamika
         dependent origination 9:217
         Nāgārjuna 6:638–40
      Mādhyamika crtitique 2:78–9
      mKhas grub dge legs dpal
         bzang po 6:416–17
      prajñā schools 2:82
      self 2:76–7
      Ultimate Reality
         Mi bskyod rdo rje 6:351–2
      Vaibhāṣika Abhidharma 2:77–8
      Yogācāra School 2:79
      Zhi Dun 9:859
   Daoism
      China 2:90
Encompassing reason
   world order (Jaspers, K.) 5:81–2
encyclopedia
   Chinese philosophy 2:318
encyclopedia-model of science
   Neurath, O. 6:815
Encyclopedists
   eighteenth century **3:303–4**,
      3:316–17
   Isidore of Seville 1:125

medieval **3:304–9**
   learned compendia 3:305
end cause
   Aristotle
      teleology 9:295
   Duns Scotus, J. 3:160
   functional explanation 3:802
   material-efficient causes relation
      (Aristotle) 1:419–20
   medieval metaphysical doctrine
      6:273–4
end of philosophy
   Heidegger, M. 6:651
Enderton, H.B. 4:115, 7:29
Endress, G. 4:601, 5:598
ends
   intrinsic value
      good, theories of the 4:131
ends-means justification
   Camus, A. rejection of 2:195
enduring individuals
   see also actual entities
   process theism 7:716–17
energeticism
   Russian empiriocriticism 8:405–6
energy
   conservation of 2:607
   essence relation (Losev, A.F.)
      5:829–30
Enfield, W. 7:170
Engel, G. 6:266, 6:268
Engel, J.G. 3:43
Engel, J.R. 3:43
Engel, Pascal
   propositions, sentences and
      statements †7:787–8
Engelhardt, D. von 6:740
Engelhardt, H. Tristram, Jr
   bioethics 1:776
   medicine, philosophy of †6:264–9
   mental illness, concepts of 6:314
Engel-Jánosi, F. 4:446
Engels, Friedrich **3:309–13**
   communism 3:310–11
   constructivism 2:630
   dialectical materialism 3:53–7
   Dühring, E.K. 3:149
   eschatology 3:417
   feminism 3:579, 3:580–1, 3:583
      literary criticism 3:613
   historical materialism 3:56
   history
      materialist conception of 3:309,
         3:311
      philosophy of 4:458
   ideology 4:681–2, 4:685
   justice 5:146

Kautsky, K.J. 5:222
laws of dialectics 3:311
Marxism
  philosophy of science 6:149,
    6:150
  Western 6:146
  partiinost' 7:241
  religion and epistemology 8:218
  revolution 8:302–3, 8:304
  scientific socialism 3:309, 3:311,
    6:141, 6:142–3
  sexuality 8:727
  social science
    contemporary philosophy of
      8:847
    history of philosophy of
      8:854–5, 8:857, 8:858
  Trotsky, L. 9:466
  utopianism 9:557, 9:559, 9:561
Engelstein, L. 8:385
engineering ethics **3:313–15**
  see also professional ethics;
    technology, ethics
England
  see also Great Britain
  modern constitutionalism 2:619
England, Frederick Ernst 5:196
English textbook movement 5:723
Engmann, J. 1:139
enjoyment
  see also contentment; happiness;
    pleasure
  pleasure 7:448–50
  reductionist account of
    (Wodeham, A.) 9:773
enlightenment
  see also liberation; *nirvāṇa*
  Advaita Vedānta
    salvation 8:449
  Buddhism
    *Awakening of Faith in
      Mahāyāna* 1:603–4, 2:85
    as cognitive transformation
      Yogācāra 2:71, 2:72, 2:73–4
    dependent origination 9:215
    five stages of
      Yogācāra 2:74
    Great Debate of bSam-yas
      9:405–6
    introspection
      Chinul 2:330–1
  karmic conditioning
    Yogācāra 2:71
  original
    Awakening of Faith 2:85
  Pure Land
    self-power

Shinran 8:747–8
  salvation 8:448–9
  Sôn
    Chinul 2:331
    sudden/gradual
      Chinul 2:112
    Platform Sutra 7:398–9
    three gates to
  Tiantai Buddhism 2:87
  universal buddhahood 2:103
  universal capability for 2:83
  Yogācāra 3:388–9
critical theory 2:725–7
  instrumental reason
    (Adorno, T.W.) 1:43
Jainism
  salvation 8:449
Kabbalah 5:174
Linji 5:645
  rational (Comenius, J.A.) 2:438,
    2:439
reincarnation 8:183
renunciation
  Indian philosophy 3:183,
    3:185–6
salvation
  Indian monotheism 8:451
while living
  Mādhava 6:29
Zen Buddhism
  Dōgen 5:74
Enlightenment
  absolutism 1:29
  Bohemian 1:824
  Brazilian 2:9
  Cambridge Platonists (Cassirer, E.)
    2:225
  clandestine literature 2:374, 2:375
  critique by Kemp Smith, N. 5:229
  educational philosophy 3:223
    Descartes, R. 3:226–7
  Gadamer, H.-G. 3:316
  Habermas, Jürgen 3:316
  historicism 4:444, 4:445
  humanism 4:528, 4:529–30
  Italy 5:36
  liberalism 5:601, 8:224–5, 8:227–8
  Mexican 6:345
  morality 8:222
  postmodernism 7:588
    anti-postmodernism debate
      7:595
  providence 7:798–9
  religion
    transcendental critique
      (Dooyeweerd, H.) 3:113–14

Religionskritik (critique of
  religion) 8:236
'science of man' (Cabanis, P.-J.)
  2:166
slavery 8:805
Smith, A. 3:316
social theory 8:873
suicide 9:224
unity of science 9:531
Enlightenment, continental **3:315–20**
  critique by Kierkgaard, S. 3:506
  Jewish Enlightenment comparison
    3:323
  La Mettrie, J.O. de 5:334
  Montesquieu, C.L. 3:318–19,
    6:494
  philosophes 2:523
Enlightenment, French 1:164, 3:317
Enlightenment, German
  see also German Idealism
  critiques of
    Hamann, J.G. 4:213–15
    Herder, J.G. 4:381
    Thomasius, C. 9:376–80
Enlightenment, Jewish **3:320–4**, 5:87
  Krochmal, N. 5:309
Enlightenment, Russian **3:324–7**
  critique by Pan-Slavism 7:199–200
Enlightenment, Scottish **3:327–30**
  Blair, H. 1:781–2
  Campbell, G. 2:191
  Carmichael, G. 2:207
  historical jurisprudence 5:138
  Millar, J. 6:375–6
  Smith, Adam 3:328, 3:330
Ennis, R. 3:234, 3:238
Ennis, R.H. 4:769
Ensoph (the Infinite) 4:397, 4:398–9
entailment
  see also inference
  belief and knowledge 1:706–7
  preferential
    non-monotonic logic 7:33, 7:34
  relevance logic **8:200–4**
  scepticism 8:494
enterprise association
  analysis of the state
    (Oakeshott, M.J.) 7:72
enthusiasm **3:330–2**
  religious
    critique by More, H. 6:580–1
enthymemes
  consequence 2:602
  glossary 5:802
entities
  being distinction (Heidegger, M.)
    4:307

existent
Ibn al-'Arabi 4:603
extensional 4:803
momentariness of
Buddhism 6:469–72
real
Sa skya paṇḍita 8:433
scientific
reduction 8:145
spiritual (Godfrey of Fontaines)
4:120, 4:121
entitlement theory 5:144–5, 7:758,
7:759
entropy
incomplete knowledge
(Maxwell, J.C.) 6:209
information theory 4:783
thermodynamics relation
4:784–5
time asymmetry
thermodynamics 9:368–9
Entscheidungsproblem see decision
problem
enumeration theorem
Kleene, S.C. 2:487
environment
see also ecology; environmental
ethics
aesthetics 6:732, 6:735
evolutionary theory
teleology 8:673, 8:674
hazards within
risk assessment 8:334–8
nature–nurture debate 8:895
perception
computational models of vision
9:635
environmental aesthetics see nature,
aesthetic appreciation of
environmental ethics 3:333–6
see also development ethics;
ecology; green political philosophy
agricultural ethics 1:126
business ethics 2:153
liberalism conflict 7:503
moral standing 6:552–3
obligations to future generations
3:819
overpopulation 7:540–1
Passmore, J.A. 7:247
socialism 8:885
environmentalism see green political
philosophy
envy
psychoanalysis (Klein, M.) 7:818
Eötvös, József 4:569, 4:571
Epicharmus 3:336–7

Epictetus 3:337–9
Antisthenes 1:317
Cynics 2:758
educational philosophy 3:229
al-Kindi 5:251
Stoicism
Simplicius 8:789
Epicureanism 3:340–50
atomic swerve (Carneades) 2:218
atomism 1:534, 3:340, 3:342–4,
6:171
Marcus Aurelius 6:94–5
Christianized
Charleton, W. 2:286
Gassendi, P. 3:848–9, 3:850–1
Valla, L. 9:570–1
cosmology 3:345–6
critiques of
John of Salisbury 5:116
Plutarch of Chaeronea 7:465–6
death 3:340, 3:348–9
Diogenes of Oenoanda 3:89–90
Epictetus 3:339
Epicurus 3:350, 3:351
epistemology 3:372–3
free will 3:340, 3:348
god 3:340, 3:346
hedonism 3:346–7
Gassendi, P. 3:849, 3:855
language
philosophy of 5:361
Lucian 5:853
Lucretius 5:854–5
morality (Cicero, M.T.) 2:358
Philodemus 7:365–6
physics 3:340, 3:341–4
psychē (soul) 7:810
scientific method 3:345
social values 3:347–8
theology (Cicero, M.T.) 2:357–8
void 3:341, 3:342, 3:343
Epicurus 1:263, 3:350–1
see also Epicureanism
atomism 1:535
death 2:818, 2:822, 3:348–9, 5:626
friendship 3:795
God
conceptions of 3:346
Marx's view of 6:120
minima 3:342
morality
emotions 6:560
pleasure 3:346–7
substance 9:210
epieikieia (equity), paradox of
Aristotle 5:148–9
Epimenides' paradox see liar paradox

epiphenomenalism 3:351–4
identity theory of mind 6:395
materialism 6:174
mental causation 3:136, 6:308,
6:309
psychology
theories of 7:826
spiritual consciousness
Santayana, G. 8:469
epistēmē (scientific knowledge)
demonstration
Aristotle 1:417–18
epistemes
cultural force
Foucault, M. 4:3
epistemic analysis
pictorial depiction 2:895
epistemic appearances
perceptual knowledge 7:295
epistemic defeasibility see knowledge,
defeasibility theory of
epistemic duty 5:160, 7:36–7
epistemic end 5:158
epistemic holism see justification,
epistemic, coherence theory of
epistemic logic 3:354–9
possible worlds semantics 8:664
propositional 3:354–6
quantified 3:356–8
epistemic paradoxes 5:273–4,
7:211–14
epistemic paradoxes see paradoxes
epistemic paternalism
social epistemology 8:830
epistemic pessimism 3:719
epistemic priority 4:840
epistemic regress problem 5:253,
5:254–5
epistemic relativism 2:396, 2:397,
3:360–2, 8:63
see also cognitive pluralism
challenges to 3:361
ethics 3:365–6
meta-ethical relativism
comparison 6:539–40
reflective equilibrium 3:360
reliabilism 3:360–1
Yoruba epistemology 9:833
epistemic standards 7:35–6
epistemic trauma
modernism 6:447–8
epistemic virtues 9:619
see also virtues, theoretical/
epistemic
ethics 9:618–19
epistemics
Goldman, A. 7:35

epistemological break
  scientific development
    (Bachelard, G.) 1:621
epistemological contextualism
  2:646–50
epistemological obstacles
  knowledge acquisition
    (Bachelard, G.) 1:621
epistemological pluralism
  Indian 7:522–3
epistemology **3:362–5**
  see also knowledge; normative
    epistemology; religious
    epistemology; social epistemology
  advisory 7:35–6
  anti-positivism
    Latin America 1:305
  Baumgarten, A.G. 1:669–70
  Buddhism
    Indian 2:96–7
  Chinese Marxism 6:133, 6:136–7
  constructivism 2:629
  conventionalism 2:667, 2:668
  educational philosophy 3:233
  empiricism **3:298–303**, 9:338
  epistemological anarchism
    scientific method
      (Feyerabend, P.K.) 3:640–2
  ethics compared **3:365–70**
    evaluations 3:365–6
    internalism-externalism
      distinction 3:368
    justification 3:369–70
    naturalism 3:366–7
    objective-subjective distinction
      3:367–8
    'ought-implies-can' principle
      3:368
    universality 3:367–8
    virtues 3:368–9
  evaluative 3:365–6, 7:36–7
  evolutionalry
    Popper, K.R. 7:535
  evolutionary
    fitness 3:485–6
  feminist 3:380, **3:597–602**
    genealogy 3:600–1
    ideals of reason 3:598
    standpoints 3:600
  genetic *see* Piaget, Jean
  Helmholtz effect 4:337–8
  Hinduism 4:435–6
  history of **3:371–84**
  illumination theories 4:698–9
  Indian **3:388–92**
    Buddhist pragmatism 3:388–9

Mīmāṃsā self-
  certificationalism 3:390–1
  Myāya reliabilism 3:389–90
information theory **4:786–9**
internalism-externalism distinction
  4:821–6
  compared to ethical 3:368
  Islamic philosophy **3:384–8**
  justification **5:157–64**
    compared to ethical 3:369–70
  mathematical 6:186–7
    Hilbert, D. 6:185
    Platonism 8:121
    post-Kantian views 6:187–8
  memory **6:300–2**
  Native American philosophy
    6:667–9
  naturalized 3:380, **6:721–8**, 7:37
    autonomy of 6:724–5
    empiricism 5:483–4
    epistemic justification 5:157,
      5:162
    feminist critique 3:599
    Hume D. 6:721–2
    internalism/externalism 6:722–4
    normative theory 6:725–6
    Quine, W.V. 8:3, 8:5–6
    rational beliefs 8:63
    reliabilism 8:204–5
      reliable-process theories
      3:380
  Neo-Kantianism
    science 4:337–8
  Nicholas of Cusa 6:834–5
  non-naturalistic 7:37
  normative *see* normative
    epistemology
  norms
    naturalized philosophy of
      science 6:729–30
  objective/subjective distinction
    (Nagel, T.) 6:644–5
  pathē
    Cyrenaics 2:760–1
  Platonism (Plutarch of Chaeronea)
    7:469
  politics relationship
    Comte, A. 2:503
  positivism
    Habermas, J. 4:194–5
  positivism (Comte, A.) 2:497–8,
    2:500–1
  probability theory **7:705–11**
  realism (Prichard, H.A.) 7:679,
    7:680
  realism/antirealism 8:117–18

  religious *see* religious
    epistemology
  risk assessment 8:334–5, 8:336–7
  social social epistemology
  taxonomy
    phylogeny-observational reality
      conflict 9:272
  technology 9:285–6
  Tibetan philosophy 9:406–7
  virtue **9:617–22**
  Yogācāra Buddhism 2:67–9
  Yoruba *see* Yoruba philosophy
epoché
  Husserl, E. 4:575, 4:579–80
Epp, R.H. 9:160
Eppenstein, S. 6:40
Equal Freedom, Principle of
  limits of law 5:462
equal opportunity principle
  affirmative action 1:93
equality **3:392–6**
  see also inequality
  anti-slavery argument
    (Hutcheson, F.) 4:591–2
  arguments against 3:394–5
  before law (Dworkin, R.) 8:390–1
  definition 3:392–3
  democracy
    knowledge 2:869
    minorities 2:868–9
    utility 2:870
    value 2:868
  economic 3:209–10
  educational philosophy 3:236
  empiriocriticism
    Avenarius, R. 1:593
  external preferences (Dworkin, R.)
    5:441–2
  feminism 3:578, 3:579, 3:615
    jurisprudence 3:607–8
  Hayek, F.A. 4:248
  Iqbal, M.
    Islamic philosophy 4:866
  liberalism 5:600
  man as God
    Tonghak 9:441
  moral worth 3:393–4
  political institutions
    Nagel, T. 6:646
  property 7:757, 7:760
    Hume, D. 4:553–4
    Williams, B.A.O. 9:750
  sirhak
    Korean philosophy 8:796
  social contract theory
    (Rousseau, J.-J.) 8:368
  social democracy 8:827

socialism 8:884
universalism in ethics 9:536
equilibration
    cognitive development (Piaget, J.)
        7:384
equilibrium
    social sciences
        prediction in 8:872
    thermodynamics 9:367
equity **5:147–53**
    see also fairness; justice
    common law
        English 5:150–1
    discretion/legality problem 5:147,
        5:152
    feminist legal theory 5:150
    justice paradox (Aristotle) 5:148–9
    law and literature movement 5:150
    legality conflict 5:151–2
    neo-Aristotelianism 5:149–50
    positive law 5:147, 5:148–9
    principles of (Stair, J.D.) 9:119
    technological distribution 9:282
equivalence
    analogy 5:414
    fallacies 3:545
    glossary 5:802
    indicative conditionals 4:742
    Islamic philosophy 6:237–8
        religious language 4:644–5
Er Ya 2:309–10, 2:311, 2:312–13
Erasistratus 4:333
Erasmianism
    Spain, philosophy in 9:71
Erasmus, Desiderius **3:396–401**
    see also Erasmianism
    philology 4:538
    philosophia Christi 3:399
    scepticism
        Academic 8:501
        Vives, J.L. 9:650
Erb, P.C. 7:395
Erde, E. 6:268
Erdélyi, János 4:569, 4:571
Erdmann, B. 5:288–9
Erdmann, J.E. 4:296
Ereignis (disclosure-as-such)
    Heidegger, M. 4:315, 4:317
Ereshefsky, M. 9:81, 9:275
Eretrian school *see* Elian school
Erfahrung (experience)
    Gadamer, H.-G. 3:828
ergodic theorem 9:367
Ericsson, K.A.
    consciousness 2:595
    introspection, psychology of 4:843,
        4:845

unconscious mental states 9:524,
    9:526
eristic theology 2:31
Eriugena, Johannes Scottus **3:401–6**
    Aristotelianism 1:396
    Augustinianism 1:561
    Carolingian renaissance 2:220–1
    divisions of nature 3:401, 3:402–4
    influence of 3:404
    medieval Platonism 7:432,
        7:433–4, 7:438
    pantheism 7:202
    predestination controversy 2:222
    Pseudo-Dionysius 7:807
    translations by 6:692
Erkes, E. 2:782
Erlangen School 5:825
Erlebnis see experience, lived
Erler, Michael
    Diogenes of Oenoanda †3:89–90
    Lucretius †5:854–6
    Philodemus †7:365–7
Erlich, V. 1:463, 8:413
Ermarth, Elizabeth Deeds
    modernism 6:449
    postmodernism †7:586–90
Ermarth, M. 3:83
Ermatinger, C.J. 5:109
Ermichev, A.A. 1:731
Ernesti, J.A. 4:389
Ernst, G. 2:191
Ernst, P. 7:246
Ernst, W. 1:772
Erofeev, V. 8:746
eros
    see also love; sexuality
    agape distinction
        Christian love 2:280
    sexual desire 8:721
erotetic logic 8:2–3
erotic art **3:406–9**
    anti-erotic art 3:407–8
    covert 3:408
    intent 3:406–7, 3:408
    relationality 3:408
    social/political aspects 3:408–9
eroticism
    social constructionism 8:720
    transcendence
        Bataille, G. 1:660
Erpenius, Thomas 5:24
error
    beauty perception 1:683
    conceptual role semantics 8:654
    Indian philosophy **3:409–13**
        Śaṅkara 8:459
        veridicality 3:411–12

information technology and ethics
    4:780, 4:781
meaning
    Dōgen 3:110
measurement theory 6:247–9
moral scepticism 6:543, 6:544
pantheism (Spinoza, B. de) 7:204
projectivism 7:739
self-certificationalism
    Mīmāṃsā 3:391
teleological theories of meaning
    8:673–4
will
    role of (Descartes, R.) 3:9–3:10
Erskine, A. 9:160, 9:842
Erwin, E. 3:793, 7:815, 7:816
eschatology **3:413–17**
    see also afterlife; death;
    immortality; reincarnation;
    resurrection
    Christianity 3:414–15, 3:416
    cosmic 3:414–15
    feminist theology 3:623–4
    individual 3:414–15
    Jewish philosophy (Bar Hayya, A.)
        1:650
    process theism 7:718
    Russian Idea (Berdiaev, N.A.)
        8:418–19
    Sophiology (Bulgakov, S.N.) 2:125
    theology relationship
        (Bultmann, R.) 2:128–9
Eschbach, A. 8:679
Eschenbach, J.C. 2:411
Eschenbacher, W. 6:206
Escobar, A. 3:43
Escobar-Valenzuela, G. 6:348
esotericism
    Buddhist
        Japan 5:68, 5:71–2
    French
        alchemy 1:158
    Strauss, L. 9:167–8
    theosophy 9:363–4
esoterism
    Ibn Massara 4:629
ESP *see* extrasensory perception
Espinosa Medrano, Juan de 5:422,
    5:424, 5:425
Esposito, J.L. 6:740
Esquith, Stephen L.
    slavery †8:803–7
Essar, D.F. 1:167–8
Essbach, W. 8:387
esse
    Maritain, J. 6:103

esse apparens (apparent existence)
Aureol, P. 1:565–6
esse est percipi (to be is to be perceived)
Berkeley, G. 1:740, 1:743
essence
see also essence–existence relationship; essentialism; universals
abstractability of ideas
Francis of Meyronnes 3:724
Chinese philosophy *see ti*
common nature (Duns Scotus, J.) 3:154, 3:164–5
eidos (*Wesen*) (Husserl, E.) 4:575, 4:578
embodiment of (Santayana, G.) 8:468–9
energy relation (Losev, A.F.) 5:829–30
epistemic issues 7:345–6
existence relationship *see* essence–existence relationship
existence without (Nancy, J.-L.) 6:651
finite objects (Nicholas of Cusa) 6:834
of God
action distinction (Ibn Massara) 4:627–8
Ash'ariyya/Mu'tazila comparison 1:521–2, 4:63
Ibn al-'Arabi 4:601, 4:602–3
Losev, A.F. 5:829–30, 5:831
humanism 4:531–2
indefectability thesis (Desgabets, R.) 3:28
individuality of (William of Auvergne) 9:726
intellect 4:358
intensities of (al-Suhrawardi) 6:596
intentions of (Ibn Sina) 5:707
knowledge relationship (al-Razi, Fakhr al-Din) 8:113–14
logic
Islamic philosophy 3:385–6
meaning (Ibn Rushd) 6:237–8
necessary truth and convention 6:748
particulars 7:236
properties of (Ibn Sina) 5:707
reality relationship (al-Dawani) 2:807
substance distinction (Locke, J.) 5:665, 5:673–4
substantial motion (Mulla Sadra) 6:597

essence–existence relationship
Aquinas, T. 6:103
Cajetan 2:173
Denys the Carthusian 2:885
Dietrich of Freiberg 3:70
epistemic realism (Santayana, G.) 8:468–9
Fonseca, P. da 3:689
Giles of Rome 4:72, 4:73
Godfrey of Fontaines 4:119–20
Henry of Ghent 4:355–7
Ibn al-'Arabi 4:603
Ibn Rushd 4:643–4
Ibn Sina 4:648, 4:650
Illuminationist philosophy 4:701–2
Islamic philosophy 6:595–6, 6:598
Ibn al-'Arabi 4:603
Illuminationist philosophy 4:701–2
al-Suhrawardi 9:221
James of Viterbo 5:58
John of St Thomas 5:119
Mir Damad, Muhammad Baqir 6:408, 6:409
Mulla Sadra 6:595–6, 6:598
Nifo, A. 6:870
al-Razi, Fakhr al-Din 8:113
Siger of Brabant 8:765–6
universals 5:247
Vital du Four 9:638
essence-function
Wonhyo
Buddhism, Korea 2:108–9
essential properties
dualism 3:134–6
essentialism **3:417–22**
Aristotelian 7:236
Cambridge Platonism 2:183
emptiness
Nāgārjuna 6:638–9
feminism
aesthetics 3:595–6
jurisprudence 3:608
literary criticism 3:613
Henry of Ghent 4:356–7
identity 4:679
Islamic fundamentalism 5:10
modal logic 6:430
natural kinds 6:683–4
ordinary entities (Kripke, S.A.) 5:303
of self
critique by Sartre, J.-P. 8:474–5
universals (Alexander of Aphrodisias) 1:172
essentially-ordered causes
Duns Scotus, J. 3:161–2

Esser, Josef 5:527, 5:530–1
Esteban, F.D. 4:612–13
Estelrich, J. 9:650
estimation
see also wahm
social science
Bayesian approach 9:130
probability distributions 9:128–30
Estlund, D. 2:872
Estudios Lulianos 9:76
Etchemendy, J.
consequence 2:603
logical constants 5:780
logical laws 5:789
semantic paradoxes and theories of truth 8:648
situation semantics 8:672
Tarski, A. 9:264, 9:269
ETCS *see* sets, elementary theory of the category of
eternal life 2:821
see also afterlife
eternal principles
al-Razi, Abu Bakr 8:111
eternal recurrence
history (Nietzsche, F.W.) 6:858–9
eternity **3:422–7**
see also eternity of the world
atheism 7:605
divine knowledge 3:425–6
human free will 8:243
God 4:98
of the human species (Siger of Brabant) 8:765
Plotinus 7:459
pragmatism 7:637
Pure Land Buddhism (Shinran) 8:748
eternity of the world
Averroism 1:597
Bonaventure 1:831–2
creation distinction
Averroism 1:599–600
Gersonides 4:48
Maimonides, M. 6:41, 6:44–5
Nahmanides, M. critique 6:648–9
Duns Scotus, J. 3:162
al-Ghazali 4:64–5, 4:639–40
Giles of Rome 4:75
Godfrey of Fontaines 4:120
Greek paganism versus Christian creationism (Philoponus) 7:374, 7:376
Henry of Harclay 4:361
Marsilius of Inghen 6:111

Matthew of Aquasparta 6:201
medieval philosophy 2:697,
  3:427–30, 6:699
Pecham, J. 7:268
Philoponus 7:374
  Simplicius 8:789
Richard Rufus of Cornwall
  8:315–16
Siger of Brabant 8:767
substantial motion
  Mulla Sadra 6:597
ether
see also qi
scientific theories 9:344
etheric body
  Steiner, R. 9:133–4
ethic of belief
  Mīmāṃsā 3:388, 3:390–1
*Ethica Ordine Geometrico
  Demonstrata see* Spinoza,
  Benedict de
ethical autonomy *see* autonomy,
  ethical
ethical constructivism **2:630–2**
ethical discourse
  communicative rationality
    (Habermas, J.) 4:196–7
  inferences
    cognitive naturalism 6:714
  logic of **5:759–64**
  prescriptivism–descriptivism
    debate 7:669–70
ethical facts
  naturalism 6:535–6, 6:714
  supervenience 6:536
ethical individualism
  liberalism 5:602–3
ethical intuitionism **4:853–6**
  analytic ethics
    critique of 1:221
    Moore, G.E. 1:220–1
  naturalism
    Moore, G.E. 6:713, 6:715–16
  pluralism relationship 4:853
  Prichard, H.A. 7:679, 7:680–1
  utilitarianism relationship 9:552,
    9:555
ethical judgments
  value 9:580–1
ethical life
  Hegel, G.W.F. 4:264, 4:274–5
ethical maturity
  Royce, J. 8:378
ethical monism
  logic of ethical discourse 5:763
ethical naturalism *see* naturalism,
  ethics

ethical perfectionism
  pedagogics (Schleiermacher, F.)
    8:536
  political neutrality 6:818
ethical pragmatism **7:640–4**
  consequentialism (Dewey, J.)
    7:641–2
  fallibilism (James, W.) 7:640–1
  reasonableness (Peirce, C.S.) 7:641
  sociality (Mead, G.H.) 7:642–3
ethical rationalism
  Cambridge Platonism 2:184–5
ethical relativism *see* moral relativism
ethical scepticism
  natural law 6:685–6
ethical socialism
  Hess, M. 4:414
ethical subjectivism
  genetic arguments 3:474
ethical universalism **9:535–9**
  applied ethics 1:319
  Kantian ethics 5:200–1
  logic of ethical discourse 5:759,
    5:761–4
  Marxism 6:142–3
  moral motivation 6:526–7
  perfectionism 7:301
  practical reason and ethics
    7:617–18
  prescriptivism 7:668
ethicism
  individualism
    (Mikhailovskii, N.K.) 6:355–6
ethico-aesthetics
  Chinese art 1:68–9
ethics **3:435–7**
see also agricultural ethics;
  analytic ethics; economics, and
  ethics; emotivism; environmental
  ethics; ethical; good; Kantian
  ethics; meta-ethics; moral;
  morality; prescriptivism; right;
  value pluralism; virtue ethics
Abelard, P. 1:8, 1:12–13
action 6:565
aesthetics relationship **1:65–8**
  Kierkegaard, S. 5:238–9
African **3:430–5**
  contemporary trends 3:433–4
  modern society comparison
    3:432–3
  traditional cultures 3:430–2
agricultural **1:126–8**
Albert the Great 1:150–1
Alexander of Hales 1:176–7
anger (Philodemus) 7:366
animals **1:273–6**

applied **1:317–25**, 1:319–20, 3:437
Aquinas, T. 1:338–41
aretē 1:373–4
Ariston of Chios 1:381–2
Aristotle
  flourishing 8:338–9
  human good 1:427
asceticism
  Jainism 5:48–9, 5:52–3
Augustine 1:542, 1:554–6
autonomy *see* autonomy, ethical
bioethics **1:772–6**
Boethius of Dacia 1:814
Buddhism
  Confucianism similarity
    Kihwa 2:115
  Indian
    rebirth 2:94–5
  Japanese 2:105
business **2:150–4**
caste system (Radhakrishnan, S.)
  8:24
casuistical (Tolstoi, L.N.) 9:438
Chinese philosophy
  Confucianism 2:312, 2:536–47
  language standards 5:696
  li (Cheng Yi) 2:302
  neo-Confucianism 6:764–75
Christian creativity
  (Berdiaev, N.A.) 1:729
codes of conduct 9:579
common-sense **2:448–51**
communitarianism 2:470–1
conceptual scope (Aristotle) 1:414
consequentialism **2:603–6**
constructivism **2:630–2**
critical hedonism (Baumgardt, D.)
  1:668–9
definitions (Locke, J.) 5:674
demonstrative (Locke, J.) 5:678–9
deontological **2:890–2**
  consequential distinction
    6:645–6
development 1:126–7, **3:39–44**,
  3:335
doctrines of (Schleiermacher, F.)
  8:534
dogmatism
  Pyrrhonist critique of 7:851
Duns Scotus, J. 3:154–5, 3:166–7
economics *see* economics, and
  ethics
educational philosophy 3:234–5
Egyptian cosmology
  ancient 3:250
elenchus (Socrates) 9:13–14
emotions relationship 3:284

empiricism
critique by Price, R. 7:675,
7:676–7
engineering **3:313–15**
environmental *see* environmental
ethics
epistemology compared **3:365–70**
evaluations 3:365–6
internalism-externalism
distinction 3:368
justification 3:369–70
naturalism 3:366–7
objective-subjective distinction
3:367–8
'ought-implies-can' principle
3:368
universality 3:367–8
virtues 3:368–9
eudaimonia 3:450–1
Eusebius 3:456–7
evolution **3:472–6**
examples in **3:487–90**
existentialist **3:502–5**
Beauvoir, S. de 1:685
fallibilism 3:548
feminist 3:590, **3:603–6**
general good
Edwards, J. 3:242–3
genetics **4:16–19**, 8:232–3
Gerard of Odo 4:38–9
gnoseologic truth (Rosmini-
Serbati, A.) 8:362, 8:363
Godmanhood (Solov'ëv, V.S.)
9:30–1
happiness
Speusippus 9:90
Xenocrates 9:807
hedonism **4:257–9**
Eudoxus 3:453
Heraclitus 4:368
Hobbes, T. 4:469–70
human nature (Butler, J.) 2:154–7
human values shift (Socrates)
1:263
humanist (Cicero, M.T.) 2:358
humans as rational agents
(Aristotle) 1:427
idealism
opposition to Moore, G.E.
6:495
independent (Kotarbiński, T.)
5:294–5
information technology **4:778–82**
intuitionism **4:853–6**
Islamic philosophy **3:438–42**, 5:14
'Abduh, M. 1:6, 1:7

golden mean
al-Ghazali 4:66
restoration of equilibrium
al-Razi, Abu Bakr 8:111
al-Tusi 9:506
value judgments
al-Juwayni 5:170
is/ought distinction 3:474–5
Japanese philosophy
collective (Watsuji Tetsurō)
5:78, 9:691–2
individual/social interaction
(Watsuji Tetsurō) 9:691–2
practice
Japanese Buddhism 2:105
journalism **5:126–8**
Judaism
Ha'am, Ahad 4:192
Lazarus, M. 5:97–8
justice/injustice (Thrasymachus)
9:397–8
Kant, I. 5:181–2, 5:189–95
karma (Radhakrishnan, S.) 8:24
language of (Wittgenstein, L.)
9:767
law relationship
Fuller, L.L. 3:801
natural law 6:686–7
positive law 1:569
liberation
Nyāya-Vaiśeṣika 7:64
liberation theology 5:616
logic analogy (Cohen, H.)
2:399–400
loyalty (Royce, J.) 8:378
market *see* market, ethics of the
Marxism
Latin America 6:162–3
medical **6:259–64**
religion 8:223
medieval concepts of 6:274
Mexico 6:347
might is right (Callicles) 2:176–7
moderation
Peripatetics 7:305
moral psychology 6:531–3
Musonius Rufus 6:615–16
mysticism 6:632
mythology (Hesiod) 4:412–13
Native American philosophy
6:662, 6:666–7
naturalism **6:713–17**
naturalistic fallacy (Moore, G.E.)
6:494–6
Neo-Kantianism (Cohen, H.)
6:781, 6:782

Neoplatonic One
assimilation to
Porphyry 7:547–8
nomoi (laws and customs)
(Antiphon) 1:301–3
normative
critique by Price, R. 7:677–8
nursing **7:56–7**
objective/subjective distinction
(Nagel, T.) 6:645–6
objectivity 7:73–5
particularism **6:528–9**
perception
knowledge
Indian views of 5:283
perfection quest (Philo of
Alexandria) 7:360
personal identity 7:306, 7:312–14
physis and *nomos* debate 7:381–2
Plato
practical reason in 7:616
Socrates' moral choice 7:407
virtue 6:533, 7:410–11, 9:622,
9:626
Platonism
Early and Middle 7:421,
7:426–7
pleasure (Antisthenes) 1:316
Plutarch of Chaeronea 7:465,
7:466
politics
Machiavelli, N. 6:18–19
Weber, M. 9:696
population **7:540–3**
practical
Aristippus the Elder 1:380
Hierocles 4:421
pragmatism 7:633, 7:634, **7:640–4**
private judgment (Godwin, W.)
4:123
professional **7:733–7**
projectivism 7:738, 7:739
pure will (Fries, J.F.) 3:798
puritanism (Heraclides of Pontus)
4:364
recognition 8:133–4
religion 2:400, 8:223
reproduction **8:276–80**
rhetoric (Aristotle) 1:431
risk assessment 8:334–5
role of emotion in (Hume, D.)
3:287–8
Romanticism (Schlegel, F. von)
8:530
science of (Renouvier, C.B.) 8:269
self-realization
German Romanticism 8:350

Seneca, L.A. 8:680–1
sexual (Foucault, M.) 3:712
Simplicius 8:789
situation **8:798–9**
social
  Buddhism/Confucianism
    similarity
      Kihwa 2:115
  Frank, S.L. 3:728–9
social science 8:866–7
Socratic schools 9:22
speech acts 9:86
sport **9:110–12**
Stoicism 9:142, 9:144
  Epictetus 3:338–9
  indifferents 9:154–5
  oikeiōsis 9:153–4
  Panaetius 7:189–90
  Posidonius 7:556–7
sublimation
  Vysheslavtsev, B.P. 9:676
Swedish philosophy (Hedenius, I.)
  8:486
sympathy (Schopenhauer, A.)
  8:546, 8:552
technology **9:280–4**, 9:285
teleology **9:294–5**
Theophrastus 9:339
theosophy 9:365
universalism **9:535–9**
utilitarianism **9:551–7**
utility
  'famous fire cause' (Godwin, W.)
    4:123
  Mill, J.S. 6:361
value theory (Meinong, A.) 6:284
values (Scheler, M. F.) 8:504, 8:506
Veda
  materialism 6:180
virtue of (Anscombe, G.E.M.)
  1:281
vital motion (Hobbes, T.) 4:459,
  4:469–70
William of Ockham 9:743–5
Wissenschaftslehre (theory of
  science) (Fichte, J.G.) 3:649–50
Wittgensteinian **9:770–3**
Zeno of Citium 9:842
Ethics (journal) 1:325
Ethiopian philosophy **3:442–5**
ethnocentrism
  African aesthetics 1:62
  anthropological symbolism 1:117
  Enlightenment, German
    Herder, J.G. 4:381–2
  European colonialism 1:109

human diversity
  Todorov, T. 9:426
justification
  Rorty, R. 8:354
psychoanalytic feminism 3:585–6
rationality and cultural relativism
  8:83–4
ethnography *see* social anthropology
ethnophilosophy **3:446–50**
  African philosophy, Francophone
    1:111
  criticisms of 1:112, 3:447, 3:448
  feminist theology 3:622
  politics of culture 3:448–9
ethnopsychiatry
  critique by Fanon, F. 3:552, 3:553
ethology
  cognitive
    innate releasing mechanisms
      6:674
  human sciences (Mill, J.S.) 6:368
Etienne, B. 6:150
etiological necessity
  causality (Ducasse, C.J.) 3:139
etiology
  biological function 3:815–17
  selectional
    as criterion of function 3:803–4
Etkes, I. 4:245
Etruria
  Musonius Rufus **6:615–16**
etymology
  imposition 5:391
  Indian theories of 4:834, 5:380
Etzkorn, Girard J.
  Chatton, W. 2:294
  Marston, R. †6:114–15
  Pecham, J. †7:267–9
EU theory *see* expected utility theory
Euben, J.P. 2:676
Eucharist
  centrality of 8:442, 8:443–4
  consubstantiation 8:444
  memorial aspect 8:443–4
  Orthodox Churches 8:455
  transignification 8:444
  transubstantiation 8:443
Eucken, Rudolf 1:576
Euclid 4:28–9, 4:33
Euclidean geometry 4:28–9, 4:30,
  4:31
  axiomatic method 1:760
  general relativity 4:6
  spacetime (Reichenbach, H.)
    8:168–9
Euclides 6:279, 9:21–2

eudaimonia (happiness) **3:450–2**
see also good life
  conventional morality 3:450–1
    attacks on 3:451
  al-Farabi 3:557
  friendship 3:795
  happiness 4:227
  hedonism
    Cyrenaics 2:761–3
  human good (Aristotle) 1:427
  medieval ethics 6:274
  practical reason 7:616
  right and good 8:323
  Saadiah Gaon 8:438–9
  Stoicism 9:155–6
  teleological ethics 9:294
  virtue ethics 9:622, 9:623
  wisdom 9:753
Eudorus of Alexandria 6:808
Eudoxus **3:452–3**
  Egyptian influence on ancient
    Greek thought 3:252
  theory of proportions 7:48
eugenics 4:18, 8:18
Euhemerism 7:732
Euler diagrams 5:740–1
Euler, Leonhard
  see also Euler diagrams
  analysis 1:217, 1:219
  Knutzen, M. 5:289
  logic
    seventeenth and eighteenth
      century 5:721
  Newton's second law of motion
    6:254
  space 9:64
Euler, W. 6:838
Eurasian Movement **3:454–6**
Europe *see* Western philosophy
European positivism
  Latin America 7:565–6
Europeanism
  Spain, philosophy in 9:71
Eusebius **3:456–8**
  divine providence 3:457–8
  ethics 3:456–7
  Ideas 3:457
  logic 3:456
Eustachius a Sancto-Paulo 1:387–8,
  1:389, 1:390
Eustathius *see* Astat
euthanasia 1:777–8, 5:627–9, 6:260,
  8:279
Eutychus Augustinus Niphus
  Suessanus *see* Nifo, Agostino
Evagrius of Pontus 8:455, 8:458

evaluation
    art works 1:473–5, 1:476–7
    desire relationship 3:32–3
    fact/value distinction 3:538
    intention 4:813
    self-constitution (Taylor, C.) 9:277
    self-respect 8:636
evaluative hedonism 4:257–8
evanescence
    Buddhism 6:592, 6:593
Evang, M. 2:130
evangelicalism
    Llull, R. 5:662–3
    pietism 7:392, 7:393, 7:395
Evangeliou, C. 7:549
Evans, A.S. 6:268
Evans, C. Stephen
    existentialist theology †3:505–9
Evans, Colin
    Taine, H.-A. †9:258–60
Evans, D. 4:765
Evans, E. 9:309
Evans, F.J. 7:4
Evans, Gareth 3:459–61
    analytic philosophy 1:228
    anaphora 1:243
    concepts 2:515
    existence 3:492
    free logics 3:743
    Frege, G. 3:777
    indexical content of thought 2:640
    meaning and truth 6:225
    Molyneux problem 6:468–9
    non-conceptual content 2:642
    persons 7:321
    proper names 7:755, 7:756
    reference 8:161, 8:163
    scope 8:589
    sense and reference 8:688
    Strawson, P.F. 9:174
    unconscious mental states 9:526
    vagueness 9:566
Evans, G.R.
    Anselm of Canterbury 1:296
    Bernard of Clairvaux 1:755
Evans, Mark
    self-realization †8:632–5
Evans, Martyn 6:613
Evans, Mary Anne see Eliot, George
Evans, R.D. 3:76, 3:392, 9:318
Evans, R.F. 7:286
Evans-Pritchard, E.E.
    African ethical systems 3:434
    African traditional religions 1:119,
        1:120
    functionalism in social science
        3:817

Evensky, J. 8:822
event ordering
    systems of tenses
        (McTaggart, J.M.E.) 6:25–6,
        6:27
events 3:461–3
    action distinction 1:37
    adverbial modifications
        (Davidson, D.) 2:803–4
    causation
        determinism 3:35
    as concrete particulars
        (Davidson, D.) 2:801
    continuants 2:652, 2:653
    facts 3:462–3
    mental
        anomalous monism 1:276–9
        processes 7:720, 7:721–2
        sense experience (Whitehead, A.N.)
            9:715
    things 3:462
Everett, C.C. 3:652–3
Everett, H., III 7:890, 7:894
Everitt, C.W. Francis
    Maxwell, J.C. †6:206–10
Everson, S. 3:381, 5:361, 7:44
everydayness
    alienation (Lefebvre, H) 5:490
evidence
    see also confirmation theory;
        evidentialism; legal evidence;
        testimony
    archaeology 1:356–7
    conventionalism (Carnap, R.)
        2:211–12
    empirical
        sirhak 8:797
    epistemic judgments
        (Ducasse, C.J.) 3:140–1
    experimental
        sociological/political 3:517
    filling (Husserl, E.) 4:579
    intuitive/deductive distinction
        (Campbell, G.) 2:191–2
    legal 5:500–506
        admissability 5:500–1
        credibility 5:502
        direct/circumstantial distinction
            5:501–2
            probative force 5:502
            relevance 5:501–2
        moral knowledge 6:517
    negative
        language acquisition 4:53
    propositional
        evidentialism 8:211
    reasons for belief 8:128, 8:129

revelation 8:298–9
    scientific 8:573–4
    theory relationship
        underdetermination 9:527–30
    theory test for
        Mozi 6:454
    transfer principle 5:272
    types of knowledge (John of
        Mirecourt) 5:111–12
evident assent
    types of knowledge (John of
        Mirecourt) 5:111–12
evidential argument
    evil, problem of 3:471
evidentialism
    Clifford, W.K. 9:329
    critiques of 8:213–14
    Locke, J. 3:542, 8:211–13
    religious belief 8:209, 8:210–14,
        8:239, 8:245, 8:246
    trust 9:466, 9:468
evil 3:463–6
    see also evil, problem of
    the Absolute 1:28
    Aquinas, T. 1:340
    as contrast necessary for good
        3:465
    death 2:818, 2:820, 5:626
    demon argument (Descartes, R.)
        3:7
    as deviation from good 3:464–5
    divine freedom 3:759
    evolution (Teilhard de Chardin, P.)
        9:288
    evolutionary world (Aurobindo
        Ghose) 1:568
    al-Farabi 3:440
    freedom of choice (Anselm of
        Canterbury) 1:291, 1:292
    Gnosticism 4:83, 4:85
    God
        argument for the existence of
            4:92
    Holocaust (Fackenheim, E.L.)
        3:534–5
    human evolution (Teilhard de
        Chardin, P.) 9:290
    identification with matter
        (Plotinus) 7:460
    as ignorance
        Indian philosophy 7:521–2
    as illusory 3:465
    innate knowledge (Wang
        Yangming) 9:683–4
    Kabbalah 5:174
    karma
        Japanese Buddhism 2:104

knowledge relationship
  (Shestov, L.) 8:741, 8:744–5
li
  Xunzi 9:818–19
moral freedom (Kant, I.) 5:192
moral/natural distinction 3:463–4
nature of 3:463–4
necessary 8:60
  Leibniz, G.W. 5:545
neo-Confucianism
  qi (Zhu Xi) 9:864
Nietzsche, F.W. 6:854–5
non-resistance to (Tolstoi, L.N.)
  9:439
pantheism 7:204–5
perfect goodness 4:142
pessimism (Hartmann, K.R.E.
  von) 4:239
as privation of being
  Augustine 4:141
  Neoplatonism 2:696
radical (Kant, I.) 8:794–5
reincarnation 8:185
reprobation 8:274
self-control (Kant, I.) 8:611–12
Solov'ëv, V. 8:522
vices (Aristotle) 9:629–30
voluntarism 9:663, 9:664
as weakness of good (Proclus)
  7:727–8
Zoroastrianism 9:872, 9:873
evil, problem of **3:466–72**, 8:238,
  8:244–5, 8:248–9
see also theodicy
atheism justification 1:533–4
atonement 1:540
Augustine 1:542–3, 1:551–2
best of all possible worlds 3:467–8
classical theism 4:99
divine goodness 3:469–70
divine intervention 6:415
eschatology 3:415
evidential argument 3:471
free will 3:468–9
grace 4:150
hell 4:329–30
Helmont, F.M. van 4:341
Holocaust 4:495–8
Ibn Sina 4:652
Indian monism 6:478
Lossky, N.O. 5:837
Maimonides, M. 6:45
Manicheism 6:74, 6:76
natural atheology 6:711
omnipotence 7:101–2
optimism
  Voltaire 9:660–1

Origen 7:162, 7:259
perfect goodness 4:142–3
prayer 7:651–2
process theism 7:716, 7:718–19
providence 7:799, 7:800, 7:801
religious belief 8:210–11
soul-making 3:469–70
Temple, W. 9:300–1
Evlampiev, I.A. 4:695
evolution
  see also evolutionary theory
biological 3:483–4
cultural 3:486
ethics **3:472–6**
  family 3:549–50
  genetic arguments 3:474
  is-ought distinction 3:474–5
human (Prodicus) 7:732
Jewish nationhood
  Ha'am, Ahad 4:192
social
  Lavrov, P.L. 5:437–8
  Spencer, H. 8:854, 9:87–8
species
  Wallace, A.R. 9:678
voluntaristic (Lossky, N.O.)
  5:836–7
evolution theory
cosmogony (Empedocles) 3:293,
  3:296
Huxley, T.H. 4:594–6
evolutionarily stable strategy (ESS)
  2:831
evolutionary biology
ecology relationship 3:203–4
evolutionary cosmology
objective idealism (Peirce, C.S.)
  7:270, 7:280–1
evolutionary epistemology 6:724
  see also theory, choice
fitness 3:485–6
Popper, K.R. 7:535
evolutionary philosophy
anti-positivism
  Latin America 1:304
evolutionary positivism
Latin America 7:565, 7:566–7
  conflicts with social positivism
    7:567–8
evolutionary socialism
Marxism (Bernstein, E.) 6:142–3
evolutionary theory **3:476–83**
  see also natural selection;
  sociobiology
  al-Afghani 1:95
  animals and ethics 1:274

artificial intelligence
  genetic algorithms 1:491
Buffon, G.L.L. 2:120, 2:121–2
creation doctrine 2:699
criticism of (Cournot, A.A.)
  2:689–90
Darwin, C.R. 2:795–8, 6:172
design 3:481–2
élan vital (Bergson, H.-L.) 1:732,
  1:735
emotions 3:283
epiphenomenalism
  critique by Popper, K.R. 3:353
evidence 3:478–80
functional explanation 3:524,
  3:803–4
functionalism in social science
  3:815–17
genetics 4:14–15
God
  existence of 4:86, 4:89–90
Indian conceptions
  Ramakrishna Movement 8:41
individuality (Mikhailovskii, N.K.)
  6:356
language development
  (Monboddo) 6:473–4
natural selection (Wallace, A.R.)
  9:678–9
naturalized epistemology 8:63
nihilism 7:3, 7:4
optimism (Teilhard de Chardin, P.)
  9:288, 9:289–90
origins of life 5:633–4
philosophy of science 8:575–6
  naturalized 6:730, 6:731
prediction 3:481
psychoanalysis
  methodological issues in 7:814
sexuality 8:722
social science **3:483–7**
  naturalism 6:719
species 9:78–80
  Wallace, A.R. 9:678
tautology 3:480–1
taxonomy 9:273–4, 9:275
teleological argument for God,
  existence of 8:241
teleological theories of meaning
  8:673, 8:674
teleology 9:296
theological issues 8:232
theosophy 9:364–5
value theory 1:610
Evtuhov, C. 2:126
Ewald, W.B. 1:441
Ewell, J.W., Jr 6:776

Ewing, A.C. 5:196, 5:230, 6:519, 6:749
ex uno non fit nisi unum (only one can come from one) 8:113
examples in ethics **3:487–90**
excellence
  beauty (Reid, T.) 8:176–7
  ideals 4:672–4
excess
  general economy (Bataille, G.) 1:660
excluded middle, law of the
  see also conditional excluded middle
  constructive logics 2:633–4
  intuition 4:848
    logic 4:856, 4:857–8, 4:861
  Leśniewski, S. 5:571
  many-valued logics 6:84
  topos theory 2:235
  vagueness 9:565
exclusion
  Dharmakīrti
    Buddhist nominalism 7:25–6
exclusivism
  doctrinal 8:260
    Alston, W.P. 8:262–3
    Christianity 8:260–1
    transcendency 8:261
exegesis
  see also hermeneutics
  Ābhidharmika Buddhism 2:55
  allegorical
    Arama, I. 1:350
  biblical
    Hugh of St Victor 4:518–19
    Jewish philosophy
      Ibn Ezra, A. 4:611
      Immanuel ben Solomon of Rome 4:709
      midrash 6:353–4
      Nahmanides, M. 6:649–50
      Rabbinic theology 9:335
      rhetoric 6:332–3
    Luther, M. 6:3
    Nahmanides, M. 6:649–50
    Origen 7:160, 7:161
  Encyclopedists, medieval 3:305, 3:306–7
  Mīmāṃsā 6:377
  typological (Origen) 7:161
exemplarism, doctrine of
  Anselm of Canterbury 1:287
  Bonaventure 1:832
  Duns Scotus, J. 3:160, 3:163
  Henry of Ghent 4:356, 4:357
exemplars *see* ideas

exemplification
  artistic symbols (Goodman, N.) 4:137
exhaustion, method of
  infinitesimal numbers 7:49–50
exile
  Argentinian academics 1:231, 1:232, 5:611
  Spanish academics
    philosophy in Mexico 6:345–6
existence **3:490–2**
  see also being; *Dasein*; essence-existence relationship; ontological commitment
  accidentality of (Mulla Sadra) 6:595–6
  Anselm of Canterbury 1:287, 1:288–9
  apparent (*esse apparens*) (Aureol, P.) 1:565–6
  assertions of 3:491
  being in common (Nancy, J.-L.) 6:651–2
  being distinction
    Illuminationist philosophy 4:702
  Buddhism
    Indian
      ultimate parts 2:98
  categories (Anderson, J.) 1:267
  Chinese philosophy
    de 2:809
    xing 9:817
    you-wu **9:834–5**
  contingent versus necessary 6:743–4
  decomposition of complex beings
    potentiality
      Indian theories of 7:605–6
  degrees of (Anselm of Canterbury) 1:287
  denials of 3:490–1
  divine simplicity 8:785–6
  efficient cause (Reid, T.) 8:173
  emptiness
    Nāgārjuna 6:638–40
  esse est percipi (to be is to be perceived) principle (Berkeley, G.) 1:740
  essentialism 3:420
  existential quantification (Quine, W.V.) 8:7–8
  existentialism (Bultmann, R.) 2:128
  free logics 3:741
  human
    Hesiod 4:413

historical reason for (Ortega y Gasset, J.) 7:166–7
I and Thou
  Buber, M. 2:44
  Feuerbach, L.A. 3:636
immutability 4:711–12
impermanence
  Buddhism
    Dōgen 6:593–4
individual (Unamuno y Jugo, M. De) 9:519
inherence
  Navya-Nyāya theory of relations 2:850–1
intentional objects (Hervaeus Natalis) 4:403
intentionality
  Husserl, E. 4:582
  Meinong, A. 4:577
magnitude relation (Zeno of Elea) 9:846–7
Meinongian theories 3:491
mental (Mulla Sadra) 6:596
modes of
  Ābhidharmika Buddhism 2:55–6
  Jasper, K. 5:80–1
momentariness
  Buddhist doctrine of 6:469–72
necessary beings (al-'Amiri) 1:207–8
necessary (Ibn Sina) 4:650–1
nihilism 7:2–3, 7:4
objective
  intentionality (Hervaeus Natalis) 4:403
  ontology 7:117–18
  Ingarden, R.W. 4:790
perception relationship (Berkeley, G.) 1:742–3
potentiality (Misbah Yazdi, M.T.) 5:19
privacy of
  Cyrenaics 2:761
proof from concept analysis
  Kant, I. critique 5:181
quantifier account of 3:491–2
quiddity relationship
  Ibn al-'Arabi 4:603
quiddity relationship (Mulla Sadra) 6:595–6, 6:598
realism/antirealism 8:116
reality relationship (Mulla Sadra) 6:595–6
semantic epistemology (Ajdukiewicz, K.) 1:137
supra-cultural (Hessen, S.I.) 4:416

systematic ambiguity (*tashkik al-wujud*) (Mulla Sadra) 6:596, 6:597
time 9:413–14
transubstantiality (Mulla Sadra) 6:596–7
uncertainty of (Bernard of Tours) 1:756
unity of
  Sufism (Ibn Sab'in) 4:646, 4:647
universals
  Indian theories of 9:545, 9:546–7
Wolff, C. 9:781–2
existential generalization
  glossary 5:802
  intensional logics 4:807
existential graphs
  Peirce, C.S. 5:743–4
existential instantiation
  glossary 5:802
existential phenomenology
  French philosophy of science 3:779
existential quantification
  see also quantifiers
  ontological commitment 7:114–15
  Quine, W.V. 8:7–8
existentialism **3:493–502**
  Adorno, T.W. 1:42
  anti-subjectivist reaction 9:197
  Argentina 1:377
  atheistic 3:499–500
  being-in-the-world 3:495–7
  Berdiaev, N.A. 1:726, 1:727–8
  Christian theology (Bultmann, R.) 2:128
  convention 3:498
  Dostoevskii, F.M. 3:114
  ethics **3:502–5**
    authenticity 3:502, 3:504–5
    Beauvoir, S. de 1:685
    freedom 3:502–3, 3:504–5
    moral agents 6:500
    responsibility 3:503
    rules 3:503–4
    situation ethics 8:798
    values 3:503
  feminism 3:581
  Herzen, A.I. 4:404
  human condition 3:494–5
  humanism 4:530–1
  infinity 4:775
  Italy (Abbagnano, N.) 5:39
  Japanese literature 5:659–60
  Kierkegaard, S. 5:242
  Latin America **3:509–14**

'lonely man of faith' (Soloveitchik, J.B.) 9:26–7
Marcel, G. 6:91–3
Marxism synthesis 6:145
Mexico 6:346
neo-Confucianism (Wang Yangming) 6:773
oppression (Beauvoir, S. de) 1:685–6
phenomenology 7:337–9
religion (Shestov, L.) 8:741, 8:744–5
religious 3:499–500
Sartre, J.-P. 8:473–7
self-realization (Jaspers, K.) 5:80–1
social (Kaplan, M.) 5:205
existentialist theology **3:506–9**
  hermeneutics
    biblical 4:392
  phenomenology of religion 7:352, 7:353–4
  philosophical faith (Jaspers, K.) 5:81
  Tillich, P. 9:409, 9:410
Existenz (existence)
  mode of being
    Jaspers, K. 5:80–1
expansionism
  European
    postcolonial philosophy of science 7:575, 7:576–7
expectations
  influence on perception
    modularity of mind 6:450
  promising 7:741
  sentential meaning
    testimony in Indian philosophy 9:316
  social sciences
    prediction in 8:871–2
expected utility theory (EU theory)
  axioms 8:94–6
  challenges to 8:95–6
    preference formation
    psychology 8:94
  reason
    practical 8:90, 8:91–2, 8:93–6
expenditure
  general economy (Bataille, G.) 1:660
experience
  see also perception; sense-data; senses
  a posteriori knowledge 1:1–3
  the Absolute 1:28
  action 1:40

adverbial theory of mental states 2:333, 6:314–17
aesthetic
  Collingwood, R.G. 2:414
  Ingarden, R.W. 4:790–1
art works 1:514
bodily sensations 1:792–5
categories
  Sapir-Whorf Hypothesis 8:470–2
causation
  Hume, D. 2:244, 2:245
  Kant, I. 2:244, 2:246
certainty
  Yoruba epistemology 9:832–3
classification of
  Ābhidharmika Buddhism 2:53, 2:54–6
colour and qualia 2:422
common sense (Buffier, C.) 2:119–20
conscious sensory
  eliminativism 3:264
consciousness (Husserl, E.) 4:580–1
dreaming 3:127, 3:128
duration (Bergson, H.-L.) 1:733
empiricism 3:298–303
given element (Lewis, C.I.) 5:588
ideas (Locke, J.) 5:665–6, 5:669–71
identity over time 3:462
intrinsic categories (Kant, I.) 6:737–8
introspection
  phenomenal consciousness 2:587
justified belief 3:299
Kant, I.
  critique by Maimon, S. 6:35–6
lived (*Erlebnis*) (Dilthey, W.) 3:79, 3:81
medical theory (Galen) 3:834
memory (Mamardashvili, M.K.) 6:69
modes of (Oakeshott, M.J.) 7:70–1
mystical
  Kabbalah 5:171–2, 5:173
noema (Husserl, E.) 4:578
non-conceptual content 2:642
numinous (Otto, R.) 7:173–5
of the Other (Buber, M.) 2:42, 2:43–5
other minds 7:171
personal
  knowledge 1:852
persons 7:320
picture interpretation 2:894–6

pure
    James, W. 5:60, 5:66
    Nishida Kitarō 7:13
qualia
    phenomenal consciousness
      2:422, 2:588–9
    realism/antirealism 8:116
reality
    Dewey, J. 3:46–7, 3:48
    Hägerström, A.A.T. 4:202
reason
    Kant, I. 5:178, 5:183–9
reductionism 7:320
religious *see* religious experience
self-awareness
    Illuminationist philosophy (al-
      Suhrawardi) 9:220–1
self-consciousness (Kant, I.) 5:186
self-validation of
    Madhva 6:32
sense perception
    Indian views of 8:689
sensory
    concepts 2:513
Space-Time (Alexander, S.)
    1:168–9
subjective
    social science 8:841, 8:842
subjectivity of
    Vasubandhu 9:585–6
temporality 9:415–16
three types of
    Indian philosophy of mind
      6:400
transcendence (Bataille, G.) 1:660
unity of
    Nishida Kitarō 5:77
    process theism 7:717
virtue (Locke, J.) 5:679
Yogācāra Buddhism
    Indian epistemology 3:388–9
experimental logic
    Dewey, J. 3:47
experimental psychology
    cognitive development 2:394, 2:395
    logical positivism 1:696–7
experimentalism
    formal logic (Schiller, F.C.S.)
      8:523–4
    Hacking, I. 3:515–16
    moral discourse (Dewey, J.)
      3:46–7, 3:48, 3:49–50
experiments **3:514–18**
    see also verification
    Boyle, R. 1:853–5
    Bridgman, P.W. 2:17–19

Cartesian-modern comparison
    (Bachelard, G.) 3:781
critical realism 2:720–1
crucial **2:735–6**, 3:514, 3:515
    Bacon, F. 3:514
    Duhem, P.M.M. critique 3:142,
      3:144
    Galilei, G. 3:838, 3:839
    Heidegger, M. 4:325
    human
      medical ethics 6:260, 6:261–2
    medicine (Galen) 3:834
    optics 7:138–9
    paranormal phenomena 7:223–4
    parapsychology 7:225
    scientific importance (Bacon, R.)
      1:634–5
    scientific realism and antirealsim
      8:582
    in social science **3:518–20**
    theory relationship 3:514,
      3:515–17, 9:348
    thought experimentss **9:392–7**
    vitalism 9:640, 9:642
expertise
    moral **6:509–11**
      applied ethics 1:322–3
      testimony 9:311–12
explanation
    best *see* inference, to the best
      explanation
    causation
      Aristotle 1:419–20
      Galen 3:832, 3:834
      social science 3:526, 3:527–8,
        3:529, 8:869–70
    critical realism 2:721
    deductive-nomological 3:803
    functional 3:524, **3:802–5**
      historical materialism 6:126–7
      mental illness 6:313
      physical illness 6:312
      social science 8:870
    historical (Montesquieu, C.L.)
      6:492
    in history and social science
      3:525–31
      causal 3:526, 3:527–8, 3:529
      functional 3:526, 3:527
    imaginative order (Smith, A.)
      8:817–18
    individualism/holism debate
      4:485–6
    intentional action
      (Anscombe, G.E.M.) 1:280–1
    limitations of
      Pyrrhonism 7:853

moral motivation 6:524
prediction relation (Hempel, C.G.)
    4:350
reasons 8:124–5
religious
    African 1:118
scientific **3:520–5**
    Enlightenment, Scottish 3:327
    Lotze, R.H. 5:839
    Nagel, E. 6:642
scientific realism 8:582
    inference 8:582
social science **3:525–31**
    Taylor, C. 9:276
    Weber, M. 9:693, 9:694
structural 3:526, 3:527–8
synthesis (Ravaisson-Mollien, F.)
    8:104, 8:105
teleological 9:295–7
    child development 2:394
    Ravaisson-Mollien, F. 8:104
    theoretical/epistemic virtues 9:341,
      9:342
explanationist theory of justification
    theoretical/epistemic virtues 9:342
explicit definition 2:845–6
exploitation
    coercion 2:389
    market ethics 6:108–9
    natural law (Locke, J.) 5:681
    property 7:760
    socialism 8:884
expression
    aesthetic taste (Alison, A.) 1:186
    aesthetics 1:495–6
    artistic *see* art, expression
    Ausdruck (consciousnessness as
      myth) (Cassirer, E.) 2:224–5
    content distinction (Deleuze, G.)
      2:858
    dance 2:776–7
    Ducasse, C.J. 3:141
    Goodman, N. 4:138
    music 4:187, 4:189–91, 6:610
    photography 7:378–9
    poetry 7:475
    style 1:505–6, 1:507–8
    universal
      Ibn Sina 3:385–6
expressionism
    concepts 2:508
expressivism-instrumentalism
    religious statements 8:257–8
extension
    see also extensionality; intension
    consciousness (Lachelier, J.)
      5:338–9

conservative 5:800
ideas (Locke, J.) 5:671–2
individualism/holism debate 4:486
infinite intelligible
    (Malebranche, N.) 6:59, 6:60–1
intension contrast 8:663
intensional logic 4:807–10
nineteenth century 5:722–3
nonstandard analysis 1:213
Port-Royal logicians 5:718
predication 2:508–9
relativity theory 8:194
spatial
    Buddhist nominalism 7:23
spirit (More, H.) 6:579
substance
    Descartes, R. 3:1–2, 3:14
    Leibniz, G.W. 5:546, 5:555
temporal
    Buddhist nominalism 7:23–4
three valued logic 8:645
extensional entities 4:803
extensionality
see also intension; reference
adverbs 1:49

modal operators 6:434–5
set theory 8:700, 8:710, 8:714
tense operators (Prior, A.N.) 7:688
extensive abstraction
method of (Whitehead, A.N.)
    9:715
external world
denial (Collier, A.) 2:408, 2:409–10
knowledge of (Russell, B.A.W.)
    8:399–400
mind (Hobbes, T.) 4:466
necessary existence
    critique by Fardella, M. 3:559
proof of (Regius, H.) 4:353
sensation (Descartes, R.) 3:12–13
external world scepticism *see*
scepticism, external world
externalism 6:176–7
divine immutability 4:713
epistemic **4:821–6**
    see also internalism; reliabilism;
    truth-tracking theory
    causal theory of knowledge
      5:263
    concepts 2:510–11, 2:514

ethical compared 3:368
justification 5:157, 5:160–1,
    5:254
mental causation 6:309
mental content 6:405–6
naturalized epistemology 6:722
perceptual knowledge 7:296
phenomenalism contrast 7:332
practical reason 7:614
reliabilism 8:205–7
semantic reference (Putnam, H.)
    8:157
warrant 5:270–2
ethical
epistemic compared 3:368
moral motivation 6:522–3
supervenience 9:238–9
extrasensory perception (ESP)
paranormal phenomena 7:221–3
causation 7:223, 7:224
parapsychology 7:224–5, 7:226
Eysenck, H.J. 7:816
Eysteinsson, A. 6:449
Eze, E. 1:97
Ezorsky, G. 1:93, 3:104–5

F

fa (norm or standard) **3:532–3**
 Legalism 5:532–3, 5:534, 5:535
 Han Feizi 4:219
Fa yan (Model Sayings) *see* Yang
 Xiong
fa zhi (law) **5:442–54**
 Confucianism 5:450–2
 contemporary China 5:452–3
 Huang-Law School 5:449
 Xunzi 5:449–50
Fabian, B. 1:680
Fabri, H. 5:717
Fabro, C. 1:347
Fackenheim, Emil Ludwig **3:533–5**
 Holocaust 4:495, 4:496–7, 4:498
 Jewish philosophy 5:90
  contemporary 5:95
fact/value distinction **3:537–8**
 hedonism 4:257–8
 moral claims
  emotivism 3:292
 Wittgenstein, L. 9:770–1
facticity
 freedom of the self (Sartre, J.-P.)
  8:476
factionalism
 republicanism 8:280, 8:281
Factor, Regis A.
 Weber, M. †9:693–8
factorizability
 quantum mechanics 1:714–15
facts **3:535–7**
 see also ethical facts; negative facts
 analysis of (Hegel, G.W.F.) 4:260
 correspondence theory of truth
  9:472–3, 9:474
 Davidson, D. 2:805
 events 3:462–3
 institutional 4:801–2, 5:761
 knowledge by acquaintance 5:262
 legal reasoning 5:526
 negative
  Indian philosophy **6:755–9**,
   7:126–7
  Dharmakīrti 6:756
  inference 6:756–7
  Jayanta 6:757–8
  Kumārila Bhaṭṭa 6:756–7
  perception 6:757–8

 Prabhākara 6:757
 propositions 7:787–8
 qualification of
  in law 5:529
 scepticism
  Frank, J. 3:725
 scientific
  constructivism 2:626, 2:629
  Hanson, N.R. 4:224
  status of (Le Roy, É.L.E.J.)
   5:481
 social
  Durkheim, É. 3:175
  explanation in history and
   social science 3:526–7
  holism 4:483
 truth of
  Leibniz, G.W. 5:552–3
 type of knowledge 5:267
 values distinction (Weber, M.)
  6:686
La Faculté de juger (colloquium)
 Lyotard, J.-F. 6:11
faculties
 disjunction of the (Deleuze, G.)
  2:857
Faddegon, B. 7:64–5, 7:127
Faden, R.R. 8:867, 9:579
Fadner, F. 7:201
Fagin, R. 3:359
Fain, H. 9:122
Fairburn, W.R.D. 7:819, 7:822
fairness
 justice as 5:142, 5:144–5, 8:106–9
 paternalism 7:251
 sport ethics 9:111–12
faith **3:538–44**
 see also fideism; religious belief
 Aquinas, T. 9:327, 9:328
 Bonhoeffer, D. 1:835
 Bultmann, R. 2:129
 Chinese philosophy
  xin (trustworthiness) 9:816
 conquest by knowledge
  (Hegel, G.W.F.) 4:259
 demands of (Kierkegaard, S.A.)
  5:239–40
 epistemic duty (Locke, J.) 8:211–12

 ethics/religion relationship
  (Cohen, H.) 2:400
 evidentialism 9:329
 existentialist theology 3:506–7
 happiness (Bonaventure) 1:830
 Holocaust (Fackenheim, E.L.)
  3:533–4
 hope 4:507, 4:508
 infallibility of (Chillingworth, W.)
  2:307–8
 justification by (Luther, M.) 6:1,
  6:2
 Kierkegaard, S.A. 5:239–40, 9:326,
  9:329
 knowledge 8:216–17, 9:329
  Durand 3:172, 3:173
  Gerson, J. 4:46
  incompatibility of (Shestov, L.)
   8:744
 and law (Luther, M.) 6:2
 'lonely man of '
  Jewish philosophy
   (Soloveitchik, J.B.) 9:26–7
 Maimonides, M.
  Abravanel, I. 1:21
 meaning and verification 6:232
 as natural assent (Clement of
  Alexandria) 2:384
 natural theology 6:709–10
 nature of 3:538, 3:540
 New Testament 3:539–40
 obedience to God (Alexander of
  Hales) 1:177
 philosophical
  existentialist theology 5:81
 philosophy relationship
  (Maritain, J.) 6:102
 providence 7:798
 rationality of 3:538, 3:541–3,
  3:542–3
 reason relationship 2:772–3,
  8:248–9
  Augustine 1:553
  Averroism 1:595, 1:597
  Brunner, E. 2:32
  Cambridge Platonism 2:182,
   2:183
  Culverwell, N. 2:750–1
  Damian, P. 2:772–3

Jewish philosophy
    Arama, I. 1:350
    Averroism 1:598, 1:600
    Ibn Falaquera 4:616
    Le Clerc, J. 5:476
    Locke, J. 5:676–7
    religion, critique of 8:236–7
    Unamuno y Jugo, M. De 9:519
    William of Auxerre 9:728
    Wolff, C. 9:778
as relationship with God
    (Barth, K.) 1:654
religious doctrine
    Jewish Averroism 1:601
religious epistemology 8:245–6
responsibility 3:540–1
and revelation (Luther, M.) 6:3
scepticism
    Charron, P. 2:288–9
    Huet, P.-D. 4:514, 4:516–17
social commitment (Marcel, G.)
    6:92
subjectivity of (Kierkegaard, S.)
    5:236, 5:240–2
theological virtue
    Aquinas, T. 9:326, 9:327–9
    Clifford, W.K. 9:329
    epistemological reliabilism
        9:329
    Luther, M. 9:326, 9:328–9
    Tillich, P. 9:410–11
    tragedy (Shestov, L.) 8:743–4
    trust 9:468
Faivre, A. 1:158
Faivre, Antoine 9:363, 9:365–6
fakery
    see also forgery
    artistic 1:499
Fakhry, Majid
    al-Farabi 3:558
    Ibn Khaldun 4:626
    Ibn Miskawayh 4:632
    Ibn Rushd 4:646
    Ibn Sina 4:654
    Islamic philosophy
        causality and necessity 2:244
        epistemology 3:387
        ethics †3:438–42
        impact of Greek philosophy on
            †4:155–9
        Neoplatonism 6:807
        occasionalism 7:89
        science 8:564
    Mir Damad, Muhammad Baqir
        6:411
Faletto, Enzo 5:655, 5:656
Falk, W.D. 7:804

Fall, The
    Calvin, J. 2:179
    evil, problem of 3:468
    hell 4:332
    Islamic philosophy (Iqbal, M.)
        4:863, 4:864
    Origen 7:162
    original sin 8:792, 8:793–5
        Kant, I. 8:794–5
    satisfaction doctrine (Anselm of
        Canterbury) 1:293–4
fallacies 3:544–5
    ad baculum 3:544
    ad hominem 3:544
    ad ignorantiam 3:544
    ad misericordiam 3:544
    ad populum 3:544
    ad verecundiam 3:544
    'affirming the consequent' 3:545
    Aristotle 5:687–8
    circular reasoning 3:544–5
    of composition
        rational choice theory 8:65
    equivocation 3:545
    glossary 5:802
    informal logic 3:702
    modal logic 8:201
    naturalistic (Moore, G.E.) 6:494–5
    relevance logic 8:201–2
    'straw man' 3:545
    types of 3:544–5
fallenness
    disclosure (Heidegger, M.) 4:316
fallibilism 3:545–8
    a posteriori justification 1:1
    approximation 3:546–7
    Bacon, F. critique 1:628
    ethics 3:548
    Gaṅgeśa 3:845
    holistic criteria (Quine, W.V.)
        8:3–4, 8:6
    knowledge (Sidgwick, H.) 8:761–2
    modus ponens 8:494, 8:496
    Peirce, C.S. 3:378–9
    relevant alternatives 8:495–6
    scepticism relationship 8:494–5
    science
        Du Bois-Reymond, E. 3:130
        ethics (James, W.) 7:640–1
    wisdom 9:754
fallibility
    Latitudinarianism 5:433
false consciousness
    ideology (Marx, K.) 6:124
false generics
    linguistic discrimination 5:642

falsificationism
    see also verificationism
    inconclusiveness of
        Duhem-thesis 9:528–9
    Popper, K.
        history
            philosophy of 4:455–6
        scientific theories 2:863, 8:861
    Popper, K.R.
        scientific hypotheses 7:533, 7:534
falsity
    testimony
        Indian philosophy 9:317–18
family
    African conception of 1:98, 3:431
    community as (Confucius) 2:567
    ethics 3:548–52
        agricultural 1:127–8
        biological 3:549–50
        consequentialism critique 2:605
        economic approach 3:550
        impartiality 4:714, 4:715
        metaphysical approach 3:549
        narrative approach 3:551
        political 3:550
        psychological 3:550–1
        reproduction 8:279
        totalitarian (Watsuji Tetsurō)
            9:692
        vulnerability 9:670
    feminism
        Latin America 3:626, 3:627
        patriarchalism (Filmer, R.) 3:678
        privacy 7:691, 7:692
        religion (Rozanov, V.V.) 8:383
        sexual roles (Hume, D.) 4:554
        theory of (Hegel, G.W.F.) 4:274
    family resemblances
        concepts 2:512, 2:573
    famine relief
        development ethics 3:40
    famous deeds sense theories 7:753–4
    Fancher, G. 2:777
    Fancher, R.E. 7:814, 7:816
    Fang, Thomé 2:548
    Fann, K.T.
        Austin, J.L. 1:574
        Johnson, A.B. †5:120–2
    Fanon, Frantz 3:552–4
        African Anglophone philosophy
            1:106
        African philosophy 1:97
        marginality 6:100, 6:101
        négritude 1:112, 1:114–15
        postcolonialism 7:582
    Fanoudh-Siefer, L. 1:114–15

fantasies
  Freud, S. 3:790–1
al-Farabi, Abu Nasr **3:554–8**
  aesthetics 1:79
  Aristotelianism 1:383–4, 1:385,
    1:397, 3:439–40, 5:13
  beauty 1:76
  dialectic 5:711
  emanation 2:241, 2:244, 3:555
  epistemology 3:384–5, 3:387, 3:556
  ethics 3:439–40, 3:442
  Ihsa' al-'ulum (Enumeration of the
    Sciences) 1:77–8, 5:706, 5:707–8
  imagination 1:77–8
  imitation 1:78
  intellect 3:556
  just ruler 7:430
  Kitab al-burhan (Book on
    Demonstration) 5:711
  Kitab al-huruf (Book of Letters)
    1:77, 1:384
  logic 4:157, 5:706, 5:707–8, 5:709,
    5:711–12
  al-Madina al-fadila (The Virtuous
    City)
    Aristotelianism 1:383–4
    beauty 1:76
    Platonism 3:554
    political philosophy 3:556–7
  Neoplatonism 4:157, 6:805
  Platonism 3:554, 7:430
  political philosophy 3:556–7,
    7:518–19, 7:520
  prophecy 7:767, 7:768, 7:769, 7:770
  soul 9:43
  theology 5:31
Faraday, Michael 3:259, 3:260
Faral, E. 2:135
Farber, P.L. 2:122
Fardella, Michelangelo **3:558–60**
Farge, J.F. 6:56
Farias Brito, Raimundo de 2:10
Farina, P. 4:354
Farley, B.W. 7:801
Farley, J. 5:635
farming *see* agricultural ethics
Farr, J. 8:806
Farr, R. 1:695
Farrar, C. 9:399
Farrell, D. 2:710
Farrer, Austin Marsden **3:560–1**
Farrimond, Claire
  Russian medieval philosophy
    †6:277–9
Farrington, B. 1:632
Farrukh, O. 5:31
Farrukh, U. 3:558

Farthing, G.W. 4:845
Farthing, John L.
  Biel, G. †1:769–72
fascism **3:561–3**
  Croce, B. 2:730, 2:732
  ecology relationship 3:334
  Gentile, G. 4:20, 4:21, 4:22, 9:443
  Gramsci, A. 4:154
  origin of (Deleuze, G.) 2:858
  totalitarianism 9:442–3
Fast, H. 7:186
Fasting, S. 1:712
fatalism **3:563–4**
  Carneades 2:217–18
  Hinduism
    Madhva 6:31–2
  indeterminism relationship
    (Aristotle) 1:426–7
  Indian **3:564–8**
    Mahābhārata 3:565–7
fate
  see also destiny; fatalism
  African ethical systems 3:433
  anti-determinism (Alexander of
    Aphrodisias) 1:172–4
  Chinese philosophy (Wang Chong)
    9:680
  Emerson, R.W. 3:271
  Machiavelli, N. 6:19
  Stoicism 9:142, 9:157–8
Fateev, V.A. 8:385
Fatone, Vicente 3:511, 3:513
Fa-tsang *see* Fazang
Fattori, M. 5:24–5, 9:457
Faur, J. 6:354, 8:454
Fausto-Sterling, A. 3:592
Favrholdt, D. 8:492
Fay, B. 8:846, 9:358
Faye, E. de 2:385
Faye, J. 1:822
Fayol, A. 3:693
Fazang **3:568–9**, 8:620–1, 9:871
Feagin, Susan L.
  art
    emotion 3:280
    tragedy †9:447–52
Febvre, L. 5:621, 8:17
Fechner, C.
  Witherspoon, J. †9:755–7
Fechner, Gustav Theodor **3:570–2**
  see also Fechner's law
Fechner's law 3:570–1
Feckes, C. 1:772
Fedden, Henry Romilly 9:227, 9:229
federal theology
  original guilt 8:795
federalism **3:572–4**, 9:424

Fedi, Laurent
  Renouvier, C.B. †8:268–70
Fëdorov, Nikolai Fëdorovich **3:574–6**
Fedotov, G.P. 6:278
feedback loops
  social science
    functionalism 3:527, 3:815
feelings
  see also emotions; pain; pleasure
  artistic expression 1:495
  hedonism
    Epicureanism 3:345, 3:346–7
  theory of mind (Mill, J.S.) 6:367
Feenberg, A. 7:16
Feenstra, Ronald J.
  atonement 1:541
  Calvin, J. †2:177–82
  reprobation †8:272–6
Feferman, S.
  Beth's theorem and Craig's
    interpolation theorem 1:762–3
  Craig's interpolation theorem
    1:762–3
  Gödel's theorems 4:112–13, 4:115
  Hilbert's programme and
    formalism 4:427
  inference
    non-constructive rules 7:29
  logic
    early twentieth century 5:735–6
    infinitary 4:771
    second-order 8:603
  logical constants 5:780
  mathematics
    constructivism 2:638
    foundations of 6:189
  model theory 6:442
  proof theory 7:750
  quantifiers
    generalized 7:877
  Russell, B.A.W. 8:403
  semantic paradoxes and theories
    of truth 8:648
  Weyl, H. 9:707
Feferman, Solomon
  ordinal logics †7:139–43
Feffer, A. 7:643
Fehér, Ferenc 4:571
Fehige, C. 4:231
Feigenbaum, E.A. 1:492
Feigl, Herbert
  analyticity 1:238
  logical positivism 5:794, 9:608,
    9:611–12
  neutral monism 6:817
  physicalism 6:173
Feijó, Diogo Antônio 2:10

Feil, E. 1:838
Fein, A. 6:264
Feinberg, Joel
  autonomy
    ethical 1:591
  coercion †2:387–90
  community and
    communitarianism 2:471
  consent 2:598
  crime and punishment 2:710
  desert and merit 3:27
  freedom and liberty †3:753–7
  law and morality 5:442
  limits of law 5:464
  meaning of life 5:632–3
  mental illness 6:314
  moral standing 6:554
  needs and interests 6:755
  paternalism 7:252
  rectification and remainders 8:140
  reproduction ethics 8:280
  rights 8:330
  Wollaston, W. 9:788
Feingold, M. 2:38
Feld, S.L. 4:11
Feldman, D.M. 1:779
Feldman, F.
  death †2:817–23
  deontic logic 2:890
Feldman, J.A. 1:492, 2:577
Feldman, M.S. 5:499
Feldman, M.W. 3:487
Feldman, Richard
  charity, principle of †2:282–5
  epistemology and ethics †3:365–70
  Gettier problems 4:55, 4:58
  internalism/externalism distinction
    4:826
  reliabilism 3:381, 8:208
Feldman, Seymour
  Crescas, H. †2:700–4
  Gersonides †4:47–51
Feldstein, R. 7:822
felicity
  state of nature (Hobbes, T.)
    4:470–1
Fell, J. 8:479
Feller, W. 7:705
Fellows, O. 2:122
Felscher, W. 3:61, 5:828
Femia, J. 4:155
Femiano, S. 3:560
femininity
  Sophiology
    Solov'ëv, V.S. 9:29–30
feminist aesthetics 3:593–6
  see also gaze

creativity and art 3:594–5
disinterested attention 3:595
historical critiques 3:594
perception 3:595
style 3:595–6
feminist epistemology 3:380,
  3:596–602
  genealogy 3:600–1
  ideals of reason 3:598
feminist jurisprudence 3:606–11
  equity 5:150
  law as politics 5:467
  parity model 3:606–8
  subversionist critique of 3:606,
    3:609–10
  transformative model 3:606,
    3:608–9
feminist philosophy 3:576–83
  see also gender
  aesthetics 1:59–60
  Agrippa von Nettesheim, H.C.
    1:131
  anarchism (Goldman, E.) 1:247
  Australia, philosophy in 1:581
  Cartesianism (Elisabeth of
    Bohemia) 3:268
  communism 3:579–80
  consciousness
    existentialism 3:581
  critiques of
    liberalism 5:600–1, 7:502
    socialism 8:883–4
  culture 3:582
  democracy 2:871
  ecological philosophy 3:200
  écriture féminine (feminine writing)
    (Cixous, H.) 2:372–3
  education (Schurman, A.M. van)
    8:557–8
  educational philosophy 3:236
  emotions
    morality 6:558, 6:562–3
  empiricism 3:598–600
  equality 3:578, 3:579
  ethics 3:602–6
    applied 1:320
    environmental 3:333–4
    moral development 2:281, 6:506
    nursing 7:56
    professional 7:736
    religion 8:222–3
    surrogacy 8:278
  feminine writing (Cixous, H.)
    2:372–3
  friendship 3:796
  gender politics (Cavendish, M.L.)
    2:262

Irigaray, L. 5:2–3
language and gender 5:362–3
Latin America 3:625–8
  compensation 3:626–7
  cultural identity 2:745–6
  equality 3:626–7
  gender and class 3:627–8
  liberation literature 5:655
  Mexico 6:347
liberation theology 5:614
literary criticism 3:611–14
  cultural 3:612, 3:613
  essentialist/anti-essentialist
    debate 3:613
  Eurocentricity 3:613
  France 3:611–12
  Great Britain 3:611
  United States 3:612
male bias (Le Doeuff, M.) 5:477
moral stage theory
  bias claims 6:505
oppression (Beauvoir, S. de)
  1:685–6
political philosophy 3:614–21
  liberal 3:614, 3:616–17
  Marxist 3:614, 3:617–18
  postmodernism 3:619
  socialism 3:614, 3:617–18
pornography critique 7:544
practical reasoning 8:100
psychoanalysis 3:583–8
public/private distinction 7:692
radical 3:614, 3:618–19
Renaissance 3:577–8
rights 3:578–9
Russian nihilism 7:6
sadomasochism 8:726
science 3:861–8
sexual difference
  Irigaray, L. 5:1–3
  Kristeva, J. 5:306–7
sexual freedom 3:580
sexual imagery (Irigaray, L.) 5:2–3
sexual oppression 3:579–80
social practices 3:581
and social science 3:588–93
subject
  French feminist critique of
    9:199
testimony 3:601
Wollstonecraft, M. 9:788–90
writing (Cixous, H.) 2:372–3
feminist theology 3:621–5
  change/immutability 3:623
  ecology 3:623–4
  eschatology 3:623–4
  ethnicity 3:622

history of 3:621–2
immanence 3:622–3
liberation 3:623
morality 8:222–3
relation/substance 3:623
Fénelon, François de Salignac de la
    Mothe **3:629–30**
Feng Yulan (Fung You-lan)
    Cheng Hao 2:301
    Chinese Confucianism 2:548
    Chinese Legalist philosophy 5:537
    Daodejing 2:782
    Han Feizi 4:220
    logic in China 5:705
    Lu Xiangshan 5:852
    Lushi chunqiu 5:865
    mujō 6:594
    self-cultivation 8:624, 8:625
    Sengzhao 8:684
    Yangzhu 9:823
    Zhou Dunyi 9:863
    Zhu Xi 9:865
Fennell, J.L. 6:278
Fenton, Paul B.
    Ibn Ezra, M. †4:613–15
    Kabbalah 5:175
    Maimonides, A. †6:38–40
Fenton, S. 3:177
Fenves, Peter
    alterity and identity, postmodern
        theories of †1:187–92
    Nancy, J.-L. †6:651–4
Ferber, M. 3:220
Ferguson, Adam **3:630–3**
    Enlightenment, Scottish 3:330
Ferguson, J. 1:106, 7:286
Ferguson, K. 3:602
Ferguson, M. 1:529
Ferguson, W.K. 4:540
Fergusson, D. 2:130
Fermat, P. de 4:33
Fernández, P.H. 9:521
Fernández Retamar, R. 6:164
Ferrajoli, L. 5:520
Ferrariensis *see* Silvestri, Francesco
Ferrater Mora, J. 1:232
Ferreira, Alfredo 1:376
Ferreira da Silva, Vicente 1:232,
    3:512, 3:513
Ferreira Franca, Eduardo 2:10
Ferreira, M.J. 6:823, 8:180
Ferreiros, J. 2:198
Ferrell, R. 3:587
Ferriani, M. 5:758
Ferrier, James Frederick **3:633–5**
    idealism 4:668
Ferry, Luc 7:595, 7:596

Ferster, C. 8:801
Feski, R. 3:596
Fessard, G. 6:53
Festa, R. 2:533, 2:535
Festinger, L. 1:695
Festugière, A.-J. 1:158, 3:349, 4:397
fetishism, of commodities *see*
    commodity fetishism
feudalism
    Japan 2:147, 2:148, 2:149–50
Feuer, K.B. 9:439
Feuerbach, Ludwig Andreas
    3:635–40
    see also Young Hegelians
    alienation 1:179, 1:181
    communism 3:637–8
    emancipation 3:637–8
    I and Thou unity 3:636
    influence on Eliot, T.S. 3:266
    Marx, K. 6:123
    religion
        alienation 7:516
        critique of 3:635–8, 4:283,
            8:237, 8:238
    Russian materialism 8:414, 8:418
Feuerwerker, A. 4:452
Feyerabend, Paul Karl **3:640–2**
    Hanson, N.R. 4:225
    incommensurability 4:733, 4:734,
        4:735–6
    science
        demarcation problem 2:866
        philosophy of 6:727
        theories of 9:352
    theory/observation distinction
        6:724
Feys, R. 2:433, 5:349, 6:425
Fichte, Johann Gottlieb **3:642–53**
    Absolute 1:27, 1:29, 3:645, 3:648,
        9:675–6
    absolute legal idealism 5:511–12,
        5:513
    absolute liberty 1:646
    Beck, J.S. 1:689
    Chisholm, R.M. 2:335
    German idealism 4:43, 4:668
    influence on
        Schelling, F.W.J. von 8:509,
            8:510, 8:511, 8:519
    inluence on
        Bakunin, M.A. 1:646
    nation and nationalism 6:659,
        6:661
    natural right 3:650–1
    Naturphilosophie 6:738, 6:740
    pantheism 5:46, 7:202
    recognition 8:134

Wissenschaftslehre (theory of
    science) 3:642, 3:645–6, 3:647–9
Fichte-Studien (journal) 3:652
Ficino, Marsilio **3:653–9**
    critique by Pico della
        Mirandola, G. 7:386, 7:388,
        7:392
    Renaissance Platonism 7:444–5
fiction
    art and truth 1:457–8
    Baumgarten, A.G. 1:670–1
    deception 9:481
    emotion
        expression 1:496–7
    Kantian (Vaihinger, H.) 9:567
    narrative 6:654–6
    nonfiction distinction 3:663–4
    paradox of 3:274–7
    possible worlds 7:571–2
    realism/antirealism 8:118
    rights as
        Bentham, J. 1:723
    semantics of **3:659–63**
    Socratic dialogues 9:19–20
fictional entities **3:663–7**
    abstract objects 3:666
    aesthetics 1:61
    deflationary theories 3:664–6
    epistemology 3:664
    hospitable theories 3:666
    literary narrative 3:664
    logic 3:664, 3:665
    nonexistence 3:663–4
    nonfiction distinction 3:663–4
fictionalism **3:667–8**
    entities 8:145
fictum theory of concepts
    William of Ockham 2:292
fideism 3:543
    see also truth
    Bayle, P. 1:672–4
    doubt (Pascal, B.) 7:245
    Poland 7:486
fidelity
    promising (Hume, D.) 7:741
Field, Hartry
    abstract objects 1:34, 1:35
    conceptual role semantics 8:656
    incommensurability 4:736
    logic
        second- and higher-order 8:595
    mathematics
        epistemology 6:186, 6:187–8
        foundations of 6:189–90
        realism 8:121, 8:123
    methodological individualism
        6:343

Quine, W.V. 8:14
truth
deflationary theories 9:477
Tarski's definition 9:269
Field, Henry 8:163
field theory
classical 3:259, **3:668–70**
quantum **3:670–3**, 6:195
Fiering, N. 1:206, 3:245
Fierz, M. 2:204
Filangieri, G. 5:41
filiality
Confucius 2:309, 2:312
Fillmore, C.J. 2:341
film
aesthetics of **3:673–7**
anachrony 3:675–6
history 3:673–4
psychology 3:674
realism 3:673–5, 3:676
spatial properties 3:674, 3:675–6
temporal properties 3:674, 3:675–6
performing art 1:470–1
Filmer, Sir Robert **3:677–9**
patriarchalism 7:511
Locke, J. critique 5:680
religion and political philosophy 8:229
filosofstvovanie (philosophizing out loud) 6:67–9
Filthaut, E.M. 9:241
final cause *see* end cause
Finamore, J.F. 4:599
Finch, Anne *see* Conway, Anne
Findlay, J.N.
the Absolute 1:29
axiology 1:611
idealism 4:668
Meinong, A. 6:286
necessary being 6:746, 6:747
Fine, Arthur
Bell's theorem †1:712–16
Bohr, N. 1:822
constructivism 2:629
Einstein, A. †3:254–8
fictionalism †3:667–8
quantum measurement problem 7:890
quantum mechanics 7:894
scientific realism and antirealism †8:581–4
Fine, B. 7:823
Fine, G. 1:434, 3:381, 5:361
Fine, K.
analyticity 1:238
de re belief 2:817

essentialism 3:421
many-valued logics 6:90
modal logic 6:425, 6:432
quantifiers and inference 7:869
vagueness 9:566
Fine, P.M. 6:558
Finetti, B. de 7:705, 7:710
Fingarette, Herbert
Chinese Confucianism 2:548
Confucius 2:570
self-deception 8:628, 8:630–1
finiteness
Frege, G. 5:814
second-order logic 8:594–5, 8:601
set
axiom of choice 1:613
finitism
Dühring, E.K. 3:147–8
Hilbert, D. 1:439, 4:426–7
mathematics
constructivism 2:636–7
proof theory 7:744, 7:745
strict
antirealism 1:309
finitude **9:669–71**
see also mortality
Camus, A. 2:195
God
cosmological existence argument 8:240–1
Heidegger, M. 4:307, 4:311
human (Camus, A.) 2:195
postmodernism 7:589
Tillich, P. 9:410, 9:411
Fink, B. 7:822
Finkelstein, L. 8:439
Finland 8:488–9
Wright, G.H. von **9:667–9**
Finnegan, R. 1:121
Finnis, John M.
Aquinas, T. 1:347
double effect principle 3:121
law
justice and equity 5:152
legal positivism 5:520
natural †6:685–90, 8:228
legal norms 7:40–1
rule of 8:390, 8:391
religion and political philosophy 8:229
sexuality 8:724, 8:727
war and peace 9:690
Finocchiaro, M.A. 3:841
Finsen, L. 1:276
Finsen, S. 1:276
Finster, R. 2:739
Fioravanti, G. 1:598

Fiorentino, F. 7:532
Fiori, G. 4:155
fire
Cleanthes 2:382
Heraclitus 4:364, 4:367–8
Philolaus 7:368–70
Firestone, Shulamith 3:583, 3:618–19, 3:620
Firkins, O.W. 3:272
Firpo, L. 2:191
First Cause
Albert the Great 1:148–9
Boethius of Dacia 1:814
emanation
Judah ben Moses of Rome 5:129, 5:130
Kabbalah
Herrera, A. Cohen de 4:397, 4:398–9
Islamic philosophy 2:243
al-Kindi 5:251
mind as
Anaxagoras 1:249, 1:252–3
Pseudo-Dionysius 7:805–6
Siger of Brabant 8:766
First Cause argument for the existence of God *see* God, existence of
First Intellect
see also agent intellect
al-Farabi 3:555
al-Kindi 3:386
first intentions
Brito, R. 2:21–2
First Mover
see also Prime Mover
Berkeley, G. 1:747
Islamic philosophy 6:805
Siger of Brabant 8:766
first philosophy
cogito argument (Geulincx, A.) 4:60
Frank, S.L. 3:727–8
Hobbes, T. 4:459, 4:465–8
first possession theory
property 7:757, 7:759
first principles
common-sense philosophy (Reid, T.) 8:171–2, 8:173, 8:177, 8:178–9
cosmogony (Philolaus) 7:368–9
Early Platonism 7:423–4
knowledge (Aristotle) 3:598
levels of being (Speusippus) 9:89–90

127

Monad/Dyad
  Plutarch of Chaeronea 7:465,
    7:466–7
  Xenocrates 9:806
  of religion (Hume, D.) 4:560
first-order logic
  see also higher-order logic;
    predicate calculus
  Beth's theorem and Craig's
    interpolation theorem 1:760
  completeness of see Gödel's
    theorems
  decidability of 2:349–50
  early twentieth century 5:730,
    5:733–4, 5:735
  finitude 8:601
  glossary 5:802
  infinitary logic 4:769–70
  mathematics 8:600–1
  model theory 6:437–40
  property theory 7:765–6
  quantifiers 7:870, 7:871–2,
    7:874–5, 7:881
  Quine, W.V. 8:7, 8:9
  second-order comparison 8:600–1
  truth
    Quine, W.V. 8:7, 8:9
Firth, Roderick 2:267, 3:370, 4:674,
  7:333
Fisch, Menachem
  Hegelianism 4:301
  Peirce, C.S. 7:283
  Whewell, W. †9:709–11
Fischer, G. 5:609
Fischer, J.M. 2:822, 3:751, 7:112,
  8:246
Fischer, K. 6:740
Fischer, K.R. 9:613
Fischer, Kuno 4:296, 6:780
Fischer, Michael 2:260
Fischer, M.J. 3:191
Fischhoff, B. 8:89
Fish, S.E. 1:505, 1:515–16, 3:764
Fishburn, P.C. 2:834
Fisher, D. 2:577
Fisher, H.A.L. 2:42
Fisher, J. 6:613, 9:526
Fisher, R. 8:783, 9:132
Fishkin, J. 3:821
Fitch, F.B. 6:236, 7:212–13, 7:214,
  9:718
fitness 3:485–6
  natural selection (Darwin, C.R.)
    2:797
  sociobiology 3:815, 3:816, 3:817,
    8:892–4

fitness of things
  natural theology (Clarke, S.) 2:378
Fitting, M.C. 6:83, 6:682
Fitzgerald, M.J. 2:21
Fitzgerald, P. 3:426
Fitzgibbons, A. 8:821
Fitzpatrick, N.A. 2:294
Fitzpatrick, Peter 2:719
Fitzpatrick, P.J. 9:386
five elements see wuxing
Five Phases philosophy 5:864, 9:862
Fix, A. 8:891
fixed points
  computability theory 2:487–8
  Gödel, K. 4:110–11
  Kripke's theory of truth 8:645–6
  provability logic 7:794, 7:795
Flach, W. 6:792
Flage, D. 5:378
Flanagan, Owen
  consciousness 2:595
  ethics 3:490
  moral development †6:504–5
  morality and identity 6:575
  Skinner, B.F. †8:799–802
  virtues and vices 9:631
Flanders
  Henry of Ghent 4:354–60
Flashar, H. 4:336
Flaubert, Gustave 1:457–8, 8:477
Flavell, J. 7:386
Flax, J. 3:585, 3:587
Fleck, K. 6:816
Fleck, L. 6:266, 6:268, 9:2, 9:356
Fleming, R. 2:260
Fletcher, G. 2:389
Fletcher, J.C. 4:19
Fletcher, John 5:308
Fletcher, Joseph F. 2:281, 2:282,
  8:798–9
Flew, Antony
  atheism 1:534
  conceptual analysis 2:522
  creation and conservation 2:700
  eschatology 3:417
  Hume, D. 4:561
  miracles 6:415
  mysticism 6:632
  ordinary language philosophy
    7:147, 7:153
  parapsychology 7:227
  religious language 8:257, 8:259
Flew, R. 8:458
Flewelling, R.T. 7:318
Flint, R. 7:205
Flint, Thomas P.
  Molina, L. de 6:465

omnipotence 7:102
omniscience †7:107–12
providence 7:801
Flint, V.I.J. 6:706
Flintoff, E. 7:848
Fløistad, G. 1:106, 3:449
Flood, R. 9:416
Florence
  Alighieri, Dante 1:181–5
  Ficino, M. 3:653–9
  Machiavelli, N. 6:17–22
  Petrarca, F. 7:325–9
Florenskii, Pavel Aleksandrovich
  3:679–82
Floridi, Luciano
  Fardella, M. †3:558–60
  Huet, P.-D. †4:514–18
  Renaissance scepticism 8:503
Florovskii, Georgii Vasilievich
  Eurasianism 3:454–5
  Florenskii, P.A. 3:682
Florovsky, G.
  John of Damascus 5:106
Florus of Lyons 2:222, 2:223
Flottes, J.B.M. 4:518
flourishing
  Chinese philosophy 8:617–18,
    8:625
  Judaism 8:338–9, 8:341
Flower, E.
  American philosophy
    eighteenth and nineteenth
      century 1:206
  educational philosophy 3:229
  Franklin, B. 3:738
  Hegelianism 4:301
  Jefferson, T. 5:85
  Johnson, S. 5:126
  Lewis, C.I. 5:589
  Witherspoon, J. 9:756
Flower Garland Buddhism
  see also Huayan; Hwaôm; Kegon
  Úisang 9:516
Flower Garland Scripture see
  Avatamsakasūtra
Floyd, W.W. 1:838
Fludd, Robert 3:682–4
Flum, J. 4:771, 6:442, 8:595
flux 2:694, 4:364, 4:368
focalization
  narrative 6:654
Fodor, Jerry Alan 3:684–6
  behaviourism 1:698
  belief 1:706
  child's theory of mind 6:389

cognitive architecture 2:393
  classical/connectionist debate
    2:576, 2:577
computational theories of mind
  6:394
concepts 2:515
  atomistic account of 2:514
  learning
    nativism 6:394, 6:674
conceptual role semantics 8:654,
  8:655, 8:656
content
  wide and narrow 2:645–6
  Davidson, D. 2:806
  folk psychology 3:687
holism
  mental and semantic 4:492,
    4:493
innate knowledge 4:797
intentionality 4:821
language of thought hypothesis
  5:407
meaning and communication
  6:213
mental causation 6:311
methodological individualism
  6:342, 6:341–4
modularity of mind 6:405, 6:450,
  6:451
nativism 6:394, 6:674, 6:675
observation 7:86
pragmatics 7:631
propositional attitudes 7:778,
  7:786
reductionism 8:149, 8:153
reference 8:163
representation
  teleological theories 8:674,
    8:675
semantics
  informational 8:661
unconscious mental states 9:526
vision 9:638
Foerster, W. 4:85
Fogel, M. 5:137
Fogelin, Robert J. 3:124–5, 3:382,
  4:561, 9:770
Foht, Ivan 9:52, 9:54
Fois, M. 9:573
Foley, Richard
  charity principle 2:285
  epistemic justification †5:157–65,
    8:130
  epistemic relativism 3:361
  internalism/externalism distinction
    4:826

knowledge
  causal theory of 5:266
  concept of 5:275
Folina, J. 7:482
folk philosophy
  Africa 1:96
folk psychology **3:686–7**, 6:176
  child's theory of mind 6:385, 6:388
  connectionism 2:575
  functionalism 8:150–1
  mental causation 6:308, 6:309
  normativity of thought
    (Collingwood, R.G.) 2:413
  reductionism 8:149, 8:150, 8:152–3
  theory-theory 8:151
Folk theorem 2:832
Folkert, K.W. 5:56
Føllesdal, Dagfinn
  deontic logic 2:890
  Husserl, E. †4:574–88
  possible worlds semantics 8:668
  radical translation and
    interpretation 8:34
  Scandinavia, philosophy in
    †8:483–9
Folse, J.H. 1:822
Fondane, B. 8:746
Foner, E. 7:186
Fonow, M.M. 3:592
Fonseca, Pedro da **3:688–90**
  categories 2:232
  Dialectical Instructions
    Renaissance logic 5:771
  Portugal, philosophy 2:8
Fontaine, J. 3:308
Fontana, B. 2:618, 8:282–3
Fontenelle, Bernard de **3:690–3**
Foot, Philippa
  double effect principle 3:121
  ethics
    analytic 1:221–2, 1:223
    naturalism in 6:716
    virtue 9:623, 9:625
  fact/value distinction 3:538
  good, theories of the 4:135
  moral motivation 6:527
  moral relativism 6:542
Foot, Phillippa
  Anscombe, G.E.M. 1:282
Footman, D. 5:420
Forbes, D. 6:376
Forbes, Duncan 4:561
Forbes, Graeme
  essentialism 3:421
  indexical content of thought 2:640
  indexicals 2:881
  logic, philosophy †5:764–6

modal logic 6:432
  proper names †7:752–7
  tense logic 9:307
Forbes, M. 1:680
force
  collisions (Descartes, R.) 3:14
  linguistic (Dummett, M.A.E.)
    3:150–1
  meaning distinction 7:625
  measurement of (Kant, I.) 5:180
  mechanics
    Aristotelian 6:250–1
    classical 6:253–5, 6:256–7
    Newton, I. 6:825
  natural philosophy (Leibniz, G.W.)
    5:555
  probative
    legal evidence 5:502
  truth theories 6:224
forcing
  glossary 5:802–3
  method of **3:693–7**
Ford, D. 1:655
Ford, J. 2:279
Ford, John D.
  Grotius, H. †4:185–6
  Pufendorf, S. †7:835–6
  sovereignty †9:56–9
Ford, L.S. 5:48, 7:720, 9:718–19
Ford, M.P. 7:715
Forde, D. 1:106
Forde, G.O. 5:168, 8:458
foreknowledge
  divine
    Anselm of Canterbury 1:294
    Boethius, A.M.S. 1:810
    evil, problem of 3:468–9
    human free will conflict
      3:425–6, 8:238, 8:243–4
      Bradwardine, T. 1:865
      Wyclif, J. 9:803
    Joachim of Fiore 5:104
    Pomponazzi, P. 7:531
    prayer 7:649–50, 7:652
    providence 7:800, 7:801
  omniscience 7:109–11
  simple 7:800, 7:801
Foreman, D. 4:165
forensic justification
  Lutheran theology
    (Melanchthon, P.) 6:289
foreordination *see* predestination
forgery
  see also fakery
  artistic **1:499–502**, 1:508
    aesthetic significance 1:500–1
    allographic/autographic

distinction 1:483–4, 1:499, 1:500
deception 1:499
forgiveness **3:697–701**, 8:135–7
definitions 3:697–9
justification doctrine 5:166
self-respect 3:697, 3:699
form
addition theory (Duns Scotus) 2:141
alchemy 1:157
Aquinas, T. 1:335, 1:336
artistic 3:706–8
con-creation with matter (Albert the Great) 1:148
essence relationship (Santayana, G.) 8:468
God's relation to universe (Thierry of Chartres) 9:372
Ikhwan al-Safa' 4:686
intelligible (Ibn Bajja) 4:606–7
logical 3:701–2, **5:781–5**
as manner 3:706, 3:707
matter distinction
Augustinianism 1:563
Bar Hayya, A. 1:649
colonial philosophy
Latin America 5:424–5
Godfrey of Fontaines 4:120–1
Ibn Tzaddik, J. 4:660
medieval metaphysical doctrine 6:273–4
medieval natural philosophy (Marston, R.) 6:114–15
music 4:187–9
ontology (Gilbert of Poitiers) 4:69–70
ontology (Ingarden, R.W.) 4:790
perception (Aristotle) 1:425–6
plurality of
Augustinianism 1:562–3
Ibn Gabirol, S. 4:618–19
John of Jandun 5:107
Richard of Middleton 8:310–11
substance 5:248
as primary substance (Aristotle) 1:422–3
primordial matter
potentiality of 2:377
soul
Islamic philosophy 9:41, 9:42
soul/body distinction (Abravanel, J.) 1:26
as structure 3:706, 3:707
style 1:506–7
substantial
Giles of Rome 4:73–4

medieval natural philosophy 6:696–7
nature of (Aristotle) 1:422–3
Richard of Middleton 8:310–11
succession theory (Burley, W.) 2:141
theory of multiple grades (Pecham, J.) 7:268
Thomas of York 9:375
universals (Kilwardby, R.) 5:247
William of Ockham 9:736
Form of the Good 4:140, 4:698–9
formal determinations
ontology (Gilbert of Poitiers) 4:69–70
formal distinction
Trinity doctrine (Francis of Meyronnes) 3:724–5
formal languages **3:703–6**
computational theories of mind 6:392
dynamic logics 3:189–90
early twentieth century 5:730
glossary 5:803
Leibniz, G.W. 5:376
Post, E.L. 7:573–4
semantics 8:649
formal logic **3:701–3**
see also mathematical logic
application to ordinary speech (Strawson, P.F.) 9:168, 9:169–70
Aristotelian (Fonseca, P. da) 3:688
computational theories of mind 6:392
experimentalism (Schiller, F.C.S.) 8:523–4
Frege, G. 3:771–2
languages **3:703–6**
Leibniz, G.W. 5:542, 5:554
speech relationship (Strawson, P.F.) 9:168, 9:169–70
formal object
of a science (Marsilius of Inghen) 6:111
formal place (Giles of Rome) 4:74
formal systems
glossary 5:803
formalism
see also anti-formalism
arithmetic 1:437–8
art **3:706–8**
abstract 1:450
discourse ethics (Habermas, J.) 4:196
ethical see ethical universalism
Hilbert, D. **4:422–9**, 6:185, 6:186–7
intuitionistic (Leśniewski, S.) 5:572

Kantian ethics critique 5:202–3
legal
Fuller, L.L. 3:801–2
Llewellyn, K.N. 5:661
Leibniz, G.W. 5:553–4
literary
Russian **8:409–14**
mathematics
see also proof theory
Whitehead, A.N. 9:714
musical 4:189
nominalism conflict (Gerson, J.) 4:45
predicative 2:637
formality
logical consequence 2:599, 2:601
Forman, R.K.C. 6:630, 6:632
formlessness
primordial matter 2:377
Form-numbers
Early Platonism 7:424, 7:425
Forms, Platonic 7:400, 7:401
Aristotle 9:541
Aristotle harmonization 7:546
Christian Platonism (Inge, W.R.) 4:793
Eudoxus 3:452
the Good 7:414
good, theories of the 4:130
immutability 4:711
mathematical nature of 7:424
mathematicization of (Speusippus) 9:90
Middle Platonism 7:424–5
Owen, G.E.L. 7:178
Plato 7:414–15
Plutarch of Chaeronea 7:466–7
universals 9:540, 9:542
Vlastos, G. 9:652
Xenocrates 9:806–7
Formstecher, Solomon 5:98–9
Fornaro, I. 1:178
Forrest, Peter
mereology †6:317–20
quantum logic †7:882–6
Forrest, Philippe 9:293
Förster, Eckart
Beck, J.S. †1:687–9
Kant, I. 5:196
Forster, J.A. 6:229
Forster, M. 8:783
Forster, T.E. 8:715
Forsyth, M. 3:573–4, 9:690
Forsyth, P.T. 1:541
Fort, Andrew O.
Madhava 6:30
Śaṅkara †8:458–61

Fortas, A. 2:368, 2:369
Fortenbaugh, W.W. 8:806
Fortes, M. 3:434
Foster, J. 1:618, 4:668, 6:177
Foster, K. 1:347, 7:329
Foster, M.H. 9:343
Foster, R.W. 5:852
Fotion, N. 4:231
Foucault, Michel **3:708–13**
    alterity and identity 1:191
    archaeological method of
        knowledge 3:708, 3:710–11
    Blanchot, M. 1:784
    Deleuze, G. 2:860
    Enlightenment 3:316
    French philosophy of science
        3:783–5, 3:786
    genealogy 3:708–9, 3:711, 4:3–4
    postmodernism 7:590
        and political philosophy 7:592
    post-structuralism 7:597, 7:600
        social sciences 7:600, 7:601–2,
        7:604
    power 7:611, 7:612
    sexuality 3:712, 8:727
    social science
        contemporary philosophy of
            8:844–6
        philosophy of history 8:857
        post-structuralism in 7:600,
            7:601–2, 7:604
        structuralism in 9:187, 9:188
    social theory and law 8:877–8
    structuralism
        literary theory 9:183
        social science 9:187, 9:188
    style, artistic 1:509–8
    subject
        postmodern critique of 9:198,
            9:201
    totalitarianism 9:444
Foucher de Careil, L. 3:269
Foucher, L. 8:270
Foucher, Simon **3:713–18**
    Desgabets, R. 3:28
    Malebranche, N. 6:60
Foulkes, D. 3:129
foundation, axiom of 8:700
foundationalism 3:362–3, **3:718–23**
    see also justification, epistemic,
        coherence theory of
    Berkeley, G. 3:377
    Chisholm, R.M. 2:333
    commonsensism 2:453–5
    criticism of 3:379
    definition 5:157
    doubt 3:123, 3:124

epistemic supervenience 3:719–21
ethics
    intuitionism 4:854
first principles (Aristotle) 3:372
formal 3:718–19
introspection 4:840–1
justification 3:380, 5:158–60
knowledge by acquaintance/
    description 5:260, 5:261
Locke, J. 3:377
moral knowledge 6:519, 6:715–16
Peirce, C. 3:378–9
rationalism 8:78
Rorty, R. 7:599–600
scepticism 5:163
sense-data 8:695
substantive 3:718
warrant 1:2–3, 5:268–9
four Forms
    Shao Yong 6:767
Four Noble Truths 9:215–16
Four Sentence Teaching
    Wang Yangming 6:773, 9:683–4
fourfold negation
    Mādhyamika Buddhism 9:404–5
Fourier, Charles 9:557, 9:559
Fourman, M.P. 4:852
Fournier, P. 3:174
Fourny, J.-F. 1:661
Four-Seven Debate 2:556, 2:558,
    2:559–62
    Yi Hwang 9:824
    Yi Yulgok 9:826
Fowden, G. 4:397
Fowler, J.W. 6:841
Fowler, T. 8:732
Fox, C. 3:319
Fox, M. 8:553, 9:27
Fox, R. 6:844
Fox, W. 3:202
Fraassen, Bas C. van
    explanation 3:524–5
        inference to the best 4:769
        scientific realism 8:582
    identity of indiscernibles 4:680
    inductive inference 4:758
    Löwenheim-Skolem theorem and
        non-standard models 5:851
    many-valued logics 6:83
    models 6:446
    natural kinds 6:684
    natural laws 5:473, 5:474
    observation 7:86
    quantum logic 7:886
    quantum mechanics
        interpretation of 7:894
        measurement problem 7:890

reflection principle 7:707, 7:710–11
science
    demarcation problem 2:866
    theories 9:348, 9:349–50, 9:352
scientific realism
    and antirealism 8:584
    constructive empiricism 8:583
    semantic paradoxes and theories
        of truth 8:648
    theoretical/epistemic virtues 9:341,
        9:342, 9:343
Fraenkel, A.A.
    see also Zermelo-Fraenkel set
    theory
    set and property
        paradoxes 7:220
    set theory 8:715
    Zermelo, E. 9:855
Fraenkel, A.S.
    computational complexity 2:475
Fraenkel, J. 4:193
Fragata, Julio 7:349, 7:351
Frake, C. 1:299
Fraleigh, Warren 9:112
Frame, D.M. 6:489
Frampton, Kenneth 1:365, 1:366
France
    see also French Revolution
    Abelard, P. **1:8–15**
    Ailly, P. d' **1:133–5**
    Alemanno, Y. **1:161–3**
    Alembert, J. le R. d' **1:163–8**
    Althusser, L.P. **1:192–6**
    Anselm of Canterbury **1:283–97**
    anti-postmodernism **7:593–6**
    Arnauld, A. **1:443–88**
    Aureol, P. **1:565–7**
    Bachelard, G. **1:620–4**
    Barthes, R. **1:656–8**
    Bataille, G. **1:659–61**
    Baudrillard, J. **1:661–3**
    Bayle, P. **1:672–7**
    Beauvoir, S. de **1:684–7**
    Bergson, H.-L. **1:732–7**
    Bernard of Clairvaux **1:753–5**
    Bernard of Tours **1:755–6**
    Bernier, F. **1:756–8**
    Blanchot, M. **1:782–4**
    Bodin, J. **1:795–9**
    Bourdieu, P. **1:848–50**
    Boutroux, É. **1:850–2**
    Brito, R. **2:21–3**
    Brunschvicg, L. **2:39–41**
    Buffier, C. **2:118–20**
    Buffon, G.L.L. **2:120–3**
    Buridan, J. **2:131–6**
    Cabanis, P.-J. **2:166–8**

Calvin, J. **2:177–82**
Camus, A. **2:194–6**
Capreolus, J. **2:200–2**
Certeau, M. de **2:267–9**
Charron, P. **2:287–90**
Cixous, H. **2:372–4**
Clarembald of Arras **2:376–8**
Comte, A. **2:496–505**
Condillac, É.B. de **2:522–7**
Condorcet, M.J.A.N. **2:527–32**
Cordemoy, G. de **2:672–4**
Cournot, A.A. **2:688–90**
Cousin, V. **2:690–2**
David of Dinant **2:799–800**
Deleuze, G. **2:856–61**
Derrida, J. **2:896–901**
Descartes, R. **3:1–19**
Desgabets, R. **3:27–30**
Diderot, D. **3:63–9**
Du Châtelet-Lomont, É. **3:131–3**
Ducasse, C.J. **3:138–42**
Duhem, P.M.M. **3:142–7**
Durandus of St Pourçain **3:172–4**
Durkheim, É. **3:174–7**
engineering ethics 3:313
Eriugena, J.S. **3:401–6**
existential phenomenology
  7:338–9
feminism 9:199
  Cixous, Hélène **2:372–4**
  Irigaray, Luce **5:1–4**
  Kristeva, Julia **5:305–8**
feminist literary criticism 3:611–12
Fénelon, F. **3:628–30**
Fontenelle, B. de **3:690–3**
Foucault, M. **3:708–13**
Foucher, S. **3:713–18**
Francis of Meyronnes **3:723–5**
Garrigou-Lagrange, R. **3:846–8**
Gassendi, P. **3:848–57**
Gerson, J. **4:45–7**
Gersonides **4:47–51**
Gilbert of Poitiers **4:68–72**
Hegelianism 4:285–6, 4:292,
  4:294–5
Helvétius, C.-A. **4:345–8**
Hervaeus Natalis **4:402–4**
Huet, P.-D. **4:514–18**
Hugh of St Victor **4:518–20**
John of Jandun **5:106–9**
John of La Rochelle **5:109–11**
John of Mirecourt **5:111–13**
John of Paris **5:113–15**
La Forge, L. de **5:331–2**
La Mettrie, J.O. de **5:332–5**
Lacan, J. **5:336–8**

Lachelier, J. **5:338–40**
Le Doeuff, M. **5:476–9**
Le Grand, A. **5:479–81**
Le Roy, É.L.E.J. **5:481–3**
Lefebvre, H. **5:489–91**
legal institutionalism 4:800
libertins **5:619–22**
Loisy, A. **5:819–20**
Lyotard, J.-F. **6:7–6:12**
Maine de Biran, P.-F. **6:49–53**
Malebranche, N. **6:56–6**
Marcel, G. **6:91–3**
Maritain, J. **6:101–5**
Merleau-Ponty, M. **6:320–5**
Mersenne, M. **6:325–31**
Meyerson, É. **6:348–51**
modern constitutionalism
  2:619–20
Montaigne, M.E. de **6:485–9**
Montesquieu, C.L. **6:489–94**
moralistes **6:555–8**
Nancy, J.-L. **6:651–4**
Nicholas of Autrecourt **6:829–32**
Olivi, P.J. **7:95–7**
Oresme, N. **7:153–7**
Pascal, B. **7:241–7**
Peter of Auvergne **7:321–4**
Philip the Chancellor **7:355–7**
philosophe movement 7:514
Pizan, C. de **2:343–5**
Poincaré, J.H. **7:478–83**
Port-Royal **7:550–5**
post-structuralism 7:597
Pothier, R.J. **7:608–9**
Proudhon, P.-J. **7:791–3**
psychoanalysis
  post-Freudian 7:821
psychoanalytic feminism 3:585
Rabelais, F. **8:15–18**
Ramus, P. **8:51–5**
Ravaisson-Mollien, F. **8:103–6**
Régis, P.-S. **8:165–6**
Renouvier, C.B. **8:268–70**
Richard of St Victor **8:312–14**
Ricoeur, P. **8:318–22**
Rohault, J. **8:341–3**
Roscelin of Compiègne **8:356–7**
Rousseau, J.-J. **8:367–7**
Saint-Simon **8:446–7**
Sanches, F. **8:451–4**
Sartre, J.-P. **8:473–9**
Savigny, F.K. von **8:482–3**
science, philosophy of **3:779–86**
Siger of Brabant **8:764–8**
Sorel, G. **9:34–6**
Staël-Holstein, A.-L.-G. **9:116–18**

subject
  postmodern critique of
    9:196–201
Suchon, G. **9:211–13**
Taine, H.-A. **9:258–60**
Teilhard de Chardin, P. **9:288–91**
Thierry of Chartres **9:371–3**
Tocqueville, A. de **9:423–5**
Ulrich of Strasbourg **9:517–18**
Villey, M. **9:614–15**
Vital du Four **9:638–9**
Voltaire **9:657–63**
Wars of Religion 1:796
Weil, S. **9:698–701**
William of Auvergne **9:725–7**
William of Auxerre **9:727–9**
William of Champeaux **9:729–30**
William of Conches **9:730–1**
France, P. 3:69
Francis of Meyronnes 3:723–5
Francis Sylvester of Ferrara *see*
  Silvestri, Francesco
Franciscan religious order
  Alexander of Hales 1:176–7
  Augustinian/Aristotelian debate
    1:561–2, 4:355
  Aureol, P. 1:565–6
  Bacon, R. 1:632–5
  Bonaventure 1:828–34
  Brinkley, R. 2:19–20
  Chatton, W. 2:292–3
  colonial philosophy
    Latin America 5:422
  Duns Scotus, J. 3:153–67
  Francis of Meyronnes 3:723–5
  Gerard of Odo 4:38–9
  Grosseteste, R. 4:177–80
  Henry of Ghent 4:354–9
  John of La Rochelle 5:109–11
  Marston, R. 6:114–15
  Matthew of Aquasparta 6:200–2
  medieval natural philosophy
    6:691, 6:703–4
  medieval Platonism 7:436–7
  missionaries
    pre-Columbian thought 5:429
  Nahuatl thought
    Mexican philosophy 6:345
  Olivi, P.J. 7:95–6
  Pecham, J. 7:267–8
  Richard of Middleton 8:310–11
  Richard Rufus of Cornwall
    8:314–17
  Thomas of York 9:375–6
  Vital du Four 9:638–9
  William of Ockham 9:731–46

Wodeham, A. 9:773–5
Francisco de Toledo *see* Toletus, Franciscus
Franciscus Patritius *see* Patrizi da Cherso, Francesco
Francke, August Hermann 7:393–4
Franco, Eli
  Dharmakīrti 3:53
  Gautama, A. †3:859–61
  materialism, Indian school of †6:178–81
  Nyāya-Vaiśeṣika †7:57–6
Franco, P. 7:72
Frändberg, Åoke
  legal concepts †5:491–6
Franfort, H. 1:769
Frängsmyr, T. 5:650
Frank, Daniel
  Karaism †5:207–9
Frank, Daniel H.
  Albo, J. †1:152–5
  Ibn Gabirol, S. †4:617–20
  political philosophy in classical Islam †7:518–21
  ritual 8:341
Frank, F.W. 5:367
Frank, J. 1:669, 3:119, 3:668, 7:177
Frank, Jerome 3:725–6, 5:524
Frank, M. 4:371, 6:740, 8:519
Frank, Manfred 7:597, 7:600
Frank, Philipp 5:794, 9:612–11
Frank, R. 2:244, 4:67, 8:101
Frank, Semën Liudvigovich 3:726–30
  Signposts movement 8:770
Frank, V. 3:729
Frank, W.A. 3:169
Frankel, C. 2:527
Frankel, H. 4:28
Fränkel, H. 9:810
Frankena, W.
  Hutcheson, F. 4:593
  Sidgwick, H. 8:763
Frankena, W.E. 8:286
Frankena, William K.
  educational philosophy 3:238
  ethics 8:799, 9:294
  religion and morality 8:220, 8:224
  right and good 8:325
Frankenberry, N. 7:715
Frankfort, H.A. 1:769
Frankfurt, H.
  autonomy
    ethical 1:591
  coercion 2:389
  desire 3:33
  free will 3:751

Leibniz, G.W. 5:561
Frankfurt School 3:730–7
  aesthetics
    politics relationship 1:67
  art and morality 1:456
  capitalism critique (Marcuse, H.) 6:95–6, 6:97
  communicative rationality 2:459–60
  critical theory 2:459, 2:722–8, 3:730–2, 3:734–5
  instrumental reason 2:459
  Marxism
    Western 6:141–2, 6:144
  negative philosophy 3:732–3
Franklin, Albert 1:115
Franklin, Allan
  experiment 3:517
  mechanics
    Aristotelian †6:249–51
Franklin, Benjamin 3:737–8
Franklin, Julian H.
  absolutism 1:31
  Bodin, J. †1:795–9
Franklin, S. 6:278
Franks, Paul
  German idealism †4:42–5
  Maimon, S. †6:35–8
Franz, M.-L. von 5:134–5
Fraser, Lesley 3:220
Fraser, N. 9:201
Frauwallner, E.
  Ābhidharmika Schools of Buddhism 2:58
  Buddhist philosophy in India 2:99
  Dignāga 3:76
  Gautama, A. 3:861
  God
    Indian conceptions of 4:105
  Jainism 5:56
  language
    Indian theories of 5:384
  materialism
    Indian school of 6:181
  Nyāya-Vaiśeṣika Hinduism 7:59, 7:65
  suffering
    origination of
      Buddhism 9:216, 9:218
  universals
    Indian theories of 9:548
  Vasubandhu 9:584, 9:586
Frazer, Sir James
  Hägerström, A.A.T. 4:204
  phenomenology of religion 7:353, 7:355

rationality and cultural relativism 8:84, 8:85
social sciences
  functionalism 3:817
Frazier, Robert L.
  duty †3:178–83
  intuitionism in ethics †4:853–6
Freddoso, Alfred J.
  creation and conservation
    religious doctrine of 2:700
  divine middle knowledge 8:244
  Molina, L. de †6:461–5
  Molinism †6:465–7
  occasionalism 7:89
  omnipotence 7:102
  omniscience 7:112
  religion
    philosophy of history 8:246
Frede, D.
  Alexander of Aphrodisias 1:175
Frede, M.
  ancient logic 5:692–3
  categories 2:232
  Galen 3:835
  Hellenistic medical epistemology 4:335
  Hellenistic philosophy 4:336
  Numenius 7:55
  practical reason and ethics 7:619
  Pyrrhonism 7:854
  scepticism 3:382
  Stoicism 9:160
Fredegisus of Tours 2:223
Frederici Vescovini, Graziella
  Blasius of Parma †1:784–7
Frederick II, Emperor 6:694
free association
  psychoanalysis 3:788
free choice 1:648, 4:591
Free Economic Society 3:325
free logics 3:738–9, 3:739–43
free market
  conservatism 2:611–12
free mobility
  geometry 4:31–2
free rider problem
  altruism
    sociobiology 8:892–3
  applied ethics 1:319
  promising 7:741
  public interest 7:833
  rational choice theory 8:64, 8:70, 8:71
free semantics 3:738–9
free speech
  educational implications 3:236–7

free thinkers
see also libertins
Collins, A. defence 2:415–16
free will **3:743–53**
see also anti-determinism;
autonomy; determinism; freedom
'Abduh, M. 1:6, 1:7
agency 3:749–50
Anselm of Canterbury 1:290–2
Aquinas, T. 1:338–9
astrology (Ibn Ezra, A.) 4:612
benevolence (Franklin, B.) 3:737
blame (Kant, I.) 7:645–6
Boethius, A.M.S.
critique by Valla, L. 9:569,
9:571
Buridan, J. 2:134
Byzantine philosophy 2:162
compatibilism 3:743, 3:744–5
Ayer, A.J. 1:614, 1:617–18
Dennett, D.C. 2:882–3
determinism debate
Alexander of Aphrodisias
1:173–4
Cicero, M.T. 2:358
Stoicism 9:142
divine foreknowledge conflict
8:238, 8:243–4
Anselm of Canterbury 1:294
Augustine 1:541–2, 1:548–9,
1:552–3
Bradwardine, T. 1:865
Pomponazzi, P. 7:530–1
Wyclif, J. 9:803
divine justice
Ash'ariyya/Mu'tazila
comparison 1:522
divine necessity (Ibn Daud, A.)
4:609–10
divine providence
Early and Middle Platonism
7:427
environmental determinants
(Pomponazzi, P.) 7:531
Epicureanism 3:340, 3:348
ethics (Hegel, G.W.F.) 4:274
evil, problem of 3:468–9
Augustine 1:551–2
existentialism 2:128, 3:497
fatalism 3:563–4
foreknowledge 3:425–6
futuribilia (conditional future
contingents) 6:465–6, 9:189–90
Gerard of Odo 4:39
grace relationship
Augustine 1:548–9

Bernard of Clairvaux 1:754
Bradwardine, T. 1:865
Molina, L. de 6:461, 6:462–3
Molinism 6:466
hell 4:330–2
if/can distinction (Austin, J.L.)
1:572
'ilm al-kalam 5:26, 5:27–8
incompatibilism 3:743–4, 3:745–6
justification doctrine 5:166
Kant, I. 5:181
Marston, R. 6:115
mind/soul relationship
Jewish pietism (Ibn Paquda)
4:635
moral agency 6:501–2, 6:569
moral psychology 6:531
morality
James, W. 5:63
Nietzsche, F.W. 6:854–5
Nemesius 6:764
Olivi, P.J. 7:95
omniscience
Jewish philosophy 9:665
Crescas, H. 2:702
Gersonides 4:49
Kabbalah 5:173
Origen 7:258–9
Pelagianism 7:284, 7:285, 7:286
Eriugena, J.S. 3:402
pessimism 3:744, 3:746–7,
3:749–51
predestination 7:655–6
Anselm of Canterbury 1:294
psi(-phenomena) 7:225–6
randomness (Maxwell, J.C.) 6:209
rational psychology (Amo, A.W.)
1:210
al-Razi, Fakhr al-Din 8:114
reason relationship (Matthew of
Aquasparta) 6:202
relations of perfection
(Malebranche, N.) 6:63
Renaissance philosophy 8:266
Renaissance scepticism
(Erasmus, D.) 3:398
Richard of Middleton 8:311
scientific behaviourism
(Skinner, B.F.) 8:800
self-awareness (Nishida Kitarō)
7:13–14
self-determinism (Locke, J.) 5:680
self-formation (Mill, J.S.) 6:368
social predictions 8:871
unitary action (Bergson, H.-L.)
1:734

unitary function (Cudworth, R.)
2:742
voluntarism (Henry of Ghent)
4:359
will distinction 9:721–2
Freeden, Michael
ideology †4:681–5
liberalism 5:604
freedom **3:753–7**
see also anti-determinism;
autonomy; divine freedom; free
will; liberty; moral freedom
aesthetic judgment (Kant, I.)
5:178, 5:193–4
alienation 1:179
anti-subjectivism 9:197
anxiety (Kierkegaard, S.) 5:242
Aristotle's ethics (Gerard of Odo)
4:39
astrological causality (Blasius of
Parma) 1:784, 1:785
authenticity (Beauvoir, S. de)
1:685, 1:686
autonomy 3:753–4
Berlin, I. 1:752
Berdiaev, N.A. 1:727–8
categorical imperative (Kant, I.)
5:191–2
causation (Hartmann, N.) 4:241
censorship (Kant, I.) 5:195–6
of choice
Anselm of Canterbury 1:290–2
Boethius, A.M.S. 1:809–10
role of the will 2:134
classical liberalism (Spencer, H.)
9:87, 9:88
conditioning dichotomy (Sartre, J.-
P.) 8:474, 8:476, 8:477
consciousness
Merleau-Ponty, M. 6:323
Sartre, J.-P. 8:475–6
creation (Ibn Gabirol, S.) 4:619
Cynics (Diogenes of Sinope) 2:755
definition 3:753
denial of (Spinoza, B. de) 9:95
determinism
Plekhanov, G.V. 7:454
Voltaire 9:661
divine foreknowledge 7:800–1
Dostoevskii, F.M. 3:115–19
duties of justice (Kant, I.) 5:190,
5:191
duties of virtue (Kant, I.) 5:190–1
ethics (Kant, I.) 5:190
existentialism 3:497–8, 3:500
Latin America 3:511

fear of (Herzen, A.I.) 4:408
God's grace (Molina, L. de)
  6:462–3
historicism (Hegel, G.W.F.)
  7:515–16
human
  Bowne, B.P. 1:852
  determinism (Eusebius) 3:457–8
  divine action (Farrer, A.M.)
    3:560–1
  evil (Kant, I.) 8:794–5
  foreknowledge compatibility
    7:109–11
  middle knowledge 7:111–12
  moral maturity 8:220–2
  pantheism 7:204
  personalism 7:316
  providence 7:799–800
  Rahner, K. 8:37–8
human action
  Indian fatalism 3:565–7
human agency (Proudhon, P.-J.)
  7:791–2
human nature (Voltaire) 9:659
humanism
  Chinese Marxism 6:139–40
individual
  Constant de Rebecque, H.-B.
    2:615–16
  existentialist ethics 3:502–3
  German Romanticism 8:350–1
intellectual integrity
  (Bridgman, P.W.) 2:18
Islamic philosophy 2:242–3
liberalism 5:600
  Collingwood, R.G. 2:414
  Kant, I. 5:195
  Mendelssohn, M. 6:306
libertas/libentia distinction
  (Gassendi, P.) 3:855
liberty of indifference (Voltaire)
  9:660
market
  legal realism 5:523
material constraints on (Sartre, J.-
    P.) 8:477
metaphysical necessity
  (Pomponazzi, P.) 7:530
might is right (Callicles) 2:176–7
as mutual collaboration
  (Marcel, G.) 6:92
natural right (Fichte, J.G.) 3:650–1
nature relationship (Kant, I.) 5:178
necessity reconciliation
  (Fichte, J.G.) 3:645–7, 3:649

objective spirit (Hegel, G.W.F.)
  4:273–4
optionality 3:753, 3:755–6
paternalism 7:250–2
phenomenological method
  (Sartre, J.-P.) 8:475
political
  social contract theory 8:371
positive versus negative 3:754–5
property rights (Kant, I.) 5:191
providence (Molina, L. de)
  6:463–4
reciprocal
  existentialist ethics 3:504–5
through religion (Hirsch, S.) 5:99
revolution 8:301, 8:302
Schiller, J.C.F. 8:526–7
Schopenhauer, A. 8:552
'single concept' theory 3:755
socialism 8:883
of speech **3:762–5**
  see also censorship; toleration
  ethics
    information technology
      4:781
    journalism 5:127
    pornography 7:544
    privacy 7:691
  types of (Bernard of Clairvaux)
    1:754
  virtue relationship 1:833
  will (Duns Scotus, J.) 3:155,
    3:166–7
  willing (Schelling, F.W.J. von)
    8:509, 8:514
Freeman, K. 1:369, 3:337, 4:323
Freeman, Mansfield 2:771
Freeman, M.D. 8:737
Freeman, Samuel
  contractarianism †2:657–65
  moral motivation 6:527
  Rawls, J. †8:106–10
Freemantle, A. 6:626
freemasonry
  Illuminati 4:696–7
free-will theism
  divine power 7:717–18
  process theism 7:719
  providence 7:800, 7:801
Frege, Gottlob **3:765–78**
  see also Frege-Russell theory;
    Frege's theorem
  abstract objects 1:32, 1:35
  analytic philosophy 1:226, 1:228
  arithmetic 1:439–40, 1:441, 5:812,
    5:813–14

Begriffsschrift (Conceptual
  Notation) 3:766, 3:771, 3:772,
  5:725, 5:743
Church, A. 2:347–8
computability theory 2:490
concepts 2:515
  object distinction 8:686
conceptual analysis 2:518, 2:522
content
  concepts 2:643–4
  wide and narrow 2:645
conventionalism 2:669
definition 2:848–9
descriptions 3:20, 3:24
Die Grundlagen der Arithmetik
  (The Foundations of
  Arithmetic) 3:766, 3:772–4
Evans, G. 3:461
existence
  quantifier account 3:491
extension/intension 4:807
formal languages and systems
  3:706
geometry 5:732
Hempel, C.G. 4:352
identity 4:676, 4:678
imperative logic 4:720
indirect discourse 4:743, 4:745
inference
  non-constructive rules 7:29
intension 4:806, 4:811, 8:663
intersubstitutivity
  failures of 7:755, 8:687
lambda calculus 5:346, 5:349
logic
  early twentieth century 5:731,
    5:736
  mathematical 5:724–5
  nineteenth century 5:722, 5:728
  of relations 5:726–7
logicism 5:812, 5:813–15, 5:816,
  6:184
mathematics
  foundations of 5:847, 6:190
  logic 5:724–5
  realism 8:121, 8:123
meaning
  truth 6:220, 6:225
  verification 6:236
paradoxes
  set and property 7:217
predicate calculus 7:664
predication 7:666–7
presupposition 7:674, 7:675
proof theory 7:744, 7:750
proper names 7:752–3, 7:756

property theory 7:764, 7:766
propositional attitudes 7:772–3,
    7:778–9, 7:786
propositions 7:787–8
quantifiers 7:872
    and inference 7:869–70
realism
    mathematics 8:121, 8:123
    reference 8:153–4, 8:163
    and sense 8:685, 8:688
science
    philosophy of 6:729
sense and reference 8:685, 8:688
singular terms 3:459–60
universals 9:542–3
use/mention distinction 9:551
Frege-Russell theory
    existence 3:491–2
Frege's Theorem 3:774–5
Frei, Hans **3:778–9**
    Barth, K. 1:655
    Niebuhr, H.R. 6:841
Freidson, Eliot 7:733, 7:736
Freierechtslehre (free law) school
    5:513
Freigius, Johannes 8:54
Freire, P. 5:656
French Antilles
    Fanon, Frantz **3:552–4**
French moralists *see* moralistes
French, P.A. 5:304, 9:631
French, S. 9:352
French Revolution 8:301
    absolutism 1:31
    responses to 7:504, 7:514–15
    Schiller, J.C.F. 8:527
    Tocqueville, A. de 9:423–5
Freppert, L. 9:664, 9:747–8
frequency
    probability theory 7:702–3
Freud, Anna 7:817, 7:819, 7:822
Freud, Sigmund **3:786–94**
    see also Freudianism;
        psychoanalysis
    conscience 2:580, 2:581
    critique of
        Vygotskii, L.S. 9:673
    dreams 3:129, 3:788–90
    emotions 3:285
    feminist response to 3:583–4,
        3:585, 3:586
    God 4:95, 4:97
    hermeneutics 4:393
    humour 4:564, 4:566
    Jung, C.G. 5:132–3

Lacan, J.
    reinterpretation by 5:336, 5:337
Marcuse, H. 6:97
masculine/feminine orientations
    (Cavell, S.) 2:259
mind
    structure 3:791–2
moral motivation 6:524
Oedipus Complex 3:790, 3:792
pleasure 7:448, 7:450–1
political philosophy 7:504–5
psychoanalysis
    methodological issues 7:811–16
    post-Freudian 7:817
psychology
    theories of 7:828
religion and epistemology 8:210,
    8:214–16, 8:217, 8:218
Ricoeur, P. 8:319
scepticism (Cavell, S.) 2:259
self-deception 8:630, 8:632
social psychology 3:792
structuralism
    social science 9:186, 9:187
structuralism/post-structuralism
    3:585
unconscious 3:790–1
unconscious mental states 9:522,
    9:523, 9:526
women 3:582, 3:585
Freudenburg, W. 8:337
Freudenthal, H. 9:132
Freudianism
    psychoanalytic feminism 3:584
Freund, E. 8:361
Freund, J. 4:9, 5:795, 9:614–15
Frey, R.G.
    animals and ethics 1:276
    bioethics †1:772–6
    Butler, J. †2:154–60
Fricker, E. 9:313–14
Fried, A. 8:885
Fried, C. 2:891, 5:203, 7:742, 8:286
Fried, M. 1:452
Friedberg, R. 7:575, 9:502
Friedländer, M. 4:613
Friedländer, P. 7:420
Friedman, A. 9:69
Friedman, D. 5:619
Friedman, H. 7:746–7, 7:750, 8:204
Friedman, M.
    Russell, B.A.W. 8:403
    Schlick, F.A.M. 8:543
Friedman, Maurice 2:47
Friedman, Michael
    Carnap, R. 2:215

explanation 3:525
    inference to the best explanation
        4:769
    Kant, I. 5:196
    logical positivism †5:789–95
    mechanics, classical 6:259
    Poincaré, J.H. 7:482
    relativity theory
        philosophical significance 8:199
    spacetime 9:69
Friedman, Milton
    economics
        methodology 3:216
        philosophy of 3:220
    social sciences
        methodology of 8:868
        positivism 7:561
Friedmann, W. 5:513
Friedrich, Carl
    constitutionalism 2:621
    corruption 2:675, 2:676
    federalism and confederalism
        3:574
    revolution 8:303
    totalitarianism 9:443, 9:444
Friedrichs, R.W. 8:872
Friedrichsdorf, U.
    dynamic logics †3:189–91
friendship **3:794–7**
    agape relationship 3:795
    Aristotle
        good of others 1:429
        love 3:794, 5:843
        politics 1:430
    consequentialism critique 2:605
    duty 8:324
    Epicureanism 3:347, 3:348
    with God 4:147–8
    in heaven 4:251–2
    Ibn Miskawayh 4:631
    theological virtues 9:330
Fries, Jacob Friedrich **3:798–9**
Frigessi, Delia
    Cattaneo, C. †2:239–41
Frisby, David
    Simmel, G. †8:778–80
    social science
        history of philosophy of 8:857
Frisch, J.C. 4:806
Frischer, B. 3:351
Frith, U.
    child's theory of mind 6:389
Fritsch, G. 7:825, 7:829
Fritz, K. von 1:361
Fritzie, P.M. 9:561
Froebel, F. 3:229

Froehlich, C.D. 6:292
Frohlich, P. 6:7
Fröhlich, W. 1:296
Froidefond, C. 3:254, 7:470
Frolov, I.T. 6:158, 6:159
Fromm, Erich 3:731–2, 3:735, 6:144
Frondizi, R. 1:232–3
Fronto 6:95
Froude, J.A. 5:168
Frühromantik see Romanticism,
    German
Fry, F.T. 7:57
Frye, Northrop 9:182, 9:184
Fryer, B. 5:520
Fu, C. 2:547, 9:820
Fu Hualing 5:454
Fu Xi *see* Bao xi
Fuchs, E. 3:653, 4:394
Fuentes, Carlos 5:655, 5:656
Fuhrmann, André
    non-monotonic logic †7:30–5
Fuhrmann, M. 1:812
Fujiwara Seika **3:799–801**
    Confucianism, Japanese 2:552
Fujiwara Shunzei
    kokoro 5:292
Fujiwara Teika 5:292
    aesthetic ideals
        poetry 1:88
Fukuyama, F. 5:291
Fulbrook, M. 1:31
Fulda, H.F. 4:279
Fuller, G. 3:662
Fuller, Lon Louvois **3:801–2**
    legal positivism 5:520
    rule of law 8:389, 8:391
Fuller, T. 3:238
Fullilove, M.T. 9:526
Fullinwider, R. 3:238
Fulton, J. 1:856
Fumagalli Beonio-Brocchieri,
    Mariateresa
    Durandus of St Pourçain †3:172–4
Fumerton, Richard
    charity principle 2:285
    internalism/externalism 3:382
    knowledge by acquaintance and
        description †5:259–63
    phenomenalism †7:330–3
function
    representational
        (*Darsetellungsfunktion*)
        (Cassirer, E.) 2:224–5
    significative (*Bedeutungsfunktion*)
        (Cassirer, E.) 2:225

function theory
    Poincaré, J.H. 7:478
functional explanation **3:802–5**
    biology 3:524
    effect/function distinction 3:802–4
    historical materialism (Marx, K.)
        6:126–7
    informational semantics 8:660–1
    mental illness 6:313
    physical illness 6:312
    teleology 9:295, 9:296–7
functionalism **3:805–13**, 6:404,
    8:150–1
    art 1:464, 1:465–6
    colour and qualia 2:423–6
    computational theories of mind
        6:390–4, 6:404–5
    conceptual role semantics 8:653
    consciousness 6:174–5
    Fodor, J.A. 3:684
    folk psychology 8:150–1
    goodness 4:130
    identity theory of mind 6:394,
        6:397–9
    ideology 4:683
    intentionality 6:176
    inverted spectra argument
        3:808–11
    knowledge argument 6:174–5
    language
        Prague School 9:179
    matter 6:175
    mental causation 6:406
    mental/semantic holism 4:489–90
    morality 6:565–6
    Nagel, E. 6:642
    other minds 7:171
    propositional attitudes 7:780–1
    psychoanalysis (Freud, S.) 3:791–2
    Putnam, H. 7:842
    qualia 3:806, 3:811–12, 6:406,
        7:866
    reasons and causes 8:126
    representational content 3:812
    Sellars, W.S. 8:639
    social science 3:526, 3:527,
        3:813–18
        critical theory 3:732
    critiques of 3:815
        Durkheim, É. 8:855
        methodological individualism
            8:861–3
        rational choice explanation
            3:813–14
        rationality
            cultural diversity 8:84

social versus biological
    functions 3:815–16
structuralism relationship
    3:814–15
substantialism 5:495
teleological 3:806, 3:812
token identity 6:174
Turing machines 9:494
functions
    see also reucursion theory,
    recursive functions
    Church, A. 2:347
    computable
        Church's thesis 2:351–2
        Turing machines 2:472, 9:496–8
    glossary 5:803
    lambda calculus 5:346
    mathematical analysis 1:216, 1:219
functors
    category theory 2:237–8
fundamental theorem of the calculus
    1:216–17, 1:218
fundamentalism
    Christian
        heaven 4:250
    Islamic **5:9–12**
    Jewish 5:92
Funes, Gregorio 1:375
Funk, V.A. 9:276
Funkenstein, A. 6:650, 6:706
Furbank, P.N. 3:69
Furley, D.J.
    Anaximander 1:259
    Antiphon 1:303
    Aristotle 1:434
    atomism, ancient 1:535
    Democritus 2:877
    Epicureanism 3:349
    Parmenides 7:234
    Presocratics 7:672
    Strato 9:163
    Zeno of Elea 9:852
Furman, N. 5:367
Furniss, T. 2:140
Furth, M. 1:253–4, 1:434, 7:234,
    8:688
furu' al-fiqh (branches of
    jurisprudence) 5:457, 5:459
Fuschian functions
    Poincaré, J.H. 7:478
Futabatei Shimei
    Japanese philosophy in modern
        literature 5:658
future
    contingency (Diodorus Cronus)
        3:85

divine knowledge of (Gersonides)
4:49
eternity of the world (Gersonides)
4:48
fatalism 3:564
knowledge of 4:755, 4:838
suffering 9:213–14

future generations
obligations to **3:819–22**
agricultural ethics 1:126
germline therapy 4:18
risk 8:332
futuribilia (conditional future
contingents) 6:465–6, 9:189–90

Futurism 6:865–6
Futuyama, D.J. 3:482
fuzzy logic **3:822–4**
see also vagueness
concepts 2:512
legal inference 5:504–5

G

Gabbay, D.M.
  common-sense reasoning 2:453
  logic in the early twentieth century
    5:736
  modal logic 6:425
  non-monotonic logic 7:34
Gabbey, A. 2:671, 6:582
Gabel, M. 8:508
Gabel, P. 2:719
Gabler, G.A. 4:296–7
Gabriel 2:769
Gächter, O. 4:837
Gács, P. 2:482
Gadādhara 3:825–7, 4:738
Gadamer, Hans-Georg 3:827–31
  Enlightenment 3:316
  Hegelianism 4:294
  hermeneutics 4:388, 4:389
    art 3:828, 3:829–30
    biblical 4:390, 4:392–3, 4:394
    legal 5:508–9, 5:510
    phenomenology 7:339, 7:341
    Rabbinic theology 9:335
    understanding 3:827, 3:828–9
  historicism 4:444
  phenomenology of religion 7:353
  social science
    contemporary philosophy of
      8:846
Gadow, S. 7:56, 7:57
Gaetano of Thienne see Cajetan of
  Thienne
Gaetano, Chiurazzi
  Italy
    philosophy in †5:34–42
Gaia
  feminist theology 3:622
Gaidenko, P.P. 1:731
Gaiger, Jason
  Lebensphilosophie †5:487–9
Gaius 3:831–2
  Roman law 8:345, 8:346, 8:347
Gaj, Ljudevit 7:198
Gál, Gedeon
  Alexander of Hales †1:176–8
  Brinkley, R. 2:21
  Gregory of Rimini 4:172
  Kilwardby, R. 5:249
  Richard Rufus of Cornwall 8:317

Wodeham, A. 9:776
Galarowicz, J. 4:792
Galasso, G. 2:734
Galavotti, M.C. 2:535
Gale, Richard 9:307
Gale, R.M.
  atheism 1:534
  Bergson, H.-L. 1:736–7
  immutability 4:713
  mysticism, nature of 6:633
  religion and epistemology 8:218
Galeffi, Romano 2:11
Galen 3:832–5
  ancient philosophy 1:265
  Aristotelianism 1:406
  Chrysippus 2:346
  conventionalism v naturalism
    5:361
  medicine, philosophy of 4:333–4,
    4:335, 6:265
  unconscious mental states 9:522
Galiani, F. 5:41
Galicia
  Krochmal, N. 5:308–11
Galilei, Galileo 3:836–41
  Church opposition to 8:230–1
  colour, theories of 2:431
  Descartes, R. 3:18
  dualism 3:138
  mathematics 3:837–8
  mechanics 3:836, 3:837–9
  natural science 3:837–8
  scientific method 5:35, 5:41
  theology 3:839–40
Galipeau, C.J. 1:753
Galison, P. 3:517, 8:584, 9:532–3
Gallagher, K.T. 6:93
Gallardo, Helio 7:350, 7:351–0
Gallegos, Rómulo 5:654–5, 5:656
Gallie, Roger
  Reid, T. †8:171–80
Gallie, W.B.
  civil society 2:371
  democracy 2:872
  ideology 4:684–5
  linguistic discrimination 5:644
  political philosophy
    nature of 7:528
Gallin, D. 4:810, 6:435

Gallistel, C.R.
  behaviourism
    methodological and scientific
      †1:696–9
  cognitive development 2:395
  learning 5:487
  Skinner, B.F. 8:801
Gallois, André
  de re/de dicto †2:815–17
  sense-data †8:694–8
Gallop, D. 6:475, 7:234
Galluppi, Pasquale 5:37, 5:41
Gallus, T. 7:807–8
Galston, M. 3:558, 5:712, 7:520
Galston, William A. 2:365, 5:196,
  7:528
Gal'tseva, R.A. 8:746
Galtung, Johan 9:615–16, 9:617
Gambetta, D. 9:467, 9:469
Gamboba see sGam-po-pa
game theory 2:823–35
  see also decision theory; games;
    rational choice theory
  counterfactual conditionals 2:688
  determinacy axioms 8:706
  epistemic logic 3:355–7
  Folk theorem 2:832
  Minimax theorem 2:825
  Nash equilibrium 2:826–5
  Neumannn, J. von 6:810
  practical reasoning 8:90, 8:98–9
  promising 7:741
  society
    concept of 8:887
games
  see also game theory
  bargaining 2:832–3
  cooperative 2:833–4
  evolutionary 2:831
  extensive form 2:829–31
  normal form 2:825–9
  play contrast 6:211
  repeated 2:831–2
game-theoretic semantics *see*
  semantics, game-theoretic
Gamut, L.T.F. 1:243
gandhabba, Pāli theory of 9:216–17
Gandhi, Mahatma *see* Gandhi,
  Mohandas Karamchand

Gandhi, Mohandas Karamchand
3:841–3
  Ambedkar, B.R. 1:196
  non-violence 7:523
  self-reliance 7:523
  work
    philosophy of 9:796, 9:797
Gandillac, M. de 9:270
Gandy, Robin
  Church's thesis 2:354
  computability theory 2:489, 2:490
  Turing machines 9:498–9
Ganeri, Jonardon
  Gadādhara †3:825–7
Gaṅgeśa **3:843–6**
  awareness 1:607–8
  cognition 3:844–5
  dialectics 6:478
  error and illusion 3:413
  Indian and Tibetan philosophy
    4:738
  inference 4:765
  knowledge 5:285
  language 8:694
  ontology 3:845–6
Gangopadhyaya, M.K. 6:180–1
Ganoczy, A. 2:181
Gans, C. 7:80
Gans, Eduard 4:281, 4:297
ganzfield studies 7:225
Gaos, José 1:230, 9:74
Garasse, F. 5:621
Garber, Daniel
  Aristotelianism in the seventeenth
    century 1:391–3
  Clauberg, J. †2:380–2
  Descartes, R. †3:1–3:19
  Digby, K. 3:74
  Keckermann, B. 5:225
  Leibniz, G.W. †5:541–62
  Regius, H. †4:352–4
Garcia, J. 6:533
Garcia, L.L. 3:761
García Bacca, Juan David 9:74–5
Garcia-Carpentera, M. 9:551
García Márquez, Gabriel 5:655
Garcia Mateo, R. 5:301
García Morente, M. 9:76
Garciadiego, A. 7:220
Garcías Palou, S. 5:664
Gardell, Mary Ann 8:727
Garden, R.W. 7:886
Gärdenfors, Peter 7:34, 8:101
Gardet, L. 2:244, 5:31, 5:170
Gardin, J-C. 1:357–8
Gardiner, A. 7:631

Gardiner, Patrick
  explanation in history and social
    science 3:530
  history
    philosophy of 4:458
    Kierkegaard, S. †5:235–44
    Schopenhauer, A. 8:553
Gardiner, W. 5:635
Gardner, D.K. 6:776, 9:865
Gardner, M. 5:721, 5:746
Gardner, Martin 3:108–9
Gardner, S. 3:793
Garey, M.R. 2:475, 2:496, 7:664, 8:59
Garfield, J.L. 2:257, 6:451
Garfinkel, A. 4:487
Garfinkel, Harold 1:694, 1:695,
    8:857, 9:7
Garforth, F.W. 3:229
Garibay, A.M. 5:432
Garin, E.
  Aristotelianism
    Renaissance 1:412
  Fardella, M. 3:560
  Italy
    philosophy in 5:41
  Pico della Mirandola, G. 7:392
  Platonism
    medieval 7:438
'Garland' 8:356
Garnett, W. 6:210
Garola, C. 7:886
Garon, J. 2:578
Garrett, Brian
  personal identity †7:305–14
  persons †7:318–21
Garrett, M. 2:595
Garrigou-Lagrange, Réginald
3:847–8
  heaven 4:252–3
  justification doctrine 5:168
  Molina, L. de 6:465
  Molinism 6:466
  purgatory 7:839
  reprobation 8:275
Garson, James W.
  intensional logics †4:807–10
Garver, Eugene
  rhetoric †8:305–10
  slavery 8:806
Garver, N. 9:617
Garvey, Marcus 3:253, 7:193, 7:194
Gasché, R. 2:812, 2:901, 4:301
Gaskell, I. 6:735
Gaskill, Thomas E.
  al-'Amiri †1:207–8
Gaskin, J.C.A. 4:561
Gaskin, R. 4:502

Gasman, D. 4:201
Gasparov, B. 6:588
Gasparski, W. 5:295
Gasper, D. 3:43
Gassendi, Pierre **3:848–57**
  atomism 3:848–9, 3:850–1, 3:852–3
  Christianized Epicureanism
    3:848–9, 3:850–1
  civil society 3:855–6
  critique of
    Bernier, F. 1:757
  ethics 3:855
  logic 3:851–2
  materialism 6:171, 6:173
  natural philosophy 2:286, 3:852–5
Gassmann, E. 4:431
Gatens, M. 5:478–9
Gates, G. 8:661
Gates, H.L. 3:613, 7:582
Gāthās 9:872–3
Gätje, H. 8:791
Gatzemeier, M. 9:163
Gauchet, M. 7:596
Gaudapāda 4:438, 8:465, 8:466
Gauḍīya Vaiṣṇavism **3:857–9**
Gaukroger, Stephen
  Clarke, S. †2:378–80
  Descartes, R. 3:18
  Fludd, R. †3:682–4
  logic in the seventeenth and
    eighteenth centuries 5:721
Gaunilo 1:288, 4:88, 4:92, 8:242
Gaurinath Sastri 5:384
Gaus, G.F. 1:848, 7:693
Gauss, Karl Friedrich 4:115, 6:190,
    7:49
Gaut, B. 6:514, 8:367
Gautama, Akṣapāda **3:859–61**, 4:738
Gauthier, David P.
  contractarianism 2:665
  duty 3:182
  economics and ethics 3:210
  egoism and altruism 3:248
  ideals 4:675
  justice 5:146
  morality
    will 9:723, 9:725
  obligations to future generations
    3:821
  political philosophy
    history of 7:517
  practical reasoning/rationality
    8:101–2
    contractarian reasoning 8:100
    resoluteness 8:97
  prudence 7:804
  rational choice theory 8:74

rights 8:330
  social contract 2:660–1
Gauthier, R.-A. 1:347, 1:598
Gavison, R. 4:781, 5:520
Gawlick, G. 2:360, 9:423
Gawron, J.M. 8:672
Gay, J. 4:238
Gay, P.
  Bernstein, E. 1:759
  Enlightenment, continental 3:319
  Freud, S. 3:793
  human nature, science of in the
    eighteenth century 4:527
  humanism 4:532
  Rousseau, J.-J. 8:376
  social democracy 8:828
gay-lesbian studies 3:611, 3:612
  see also homosexuality
  feminist literary criticism 3:611,
    3:612
Gazdar, G. 4:725, 7:631
gaze
  feminist aesthetics 3:595
Gbadegesin, S. 1:102, 1:106
Geach, Peter T.
  analytic behaviourism 1:692
  analytic ethics 1:221, 1:223
  anaphora 1:243
  art
    understanding of 1:475
  change 2:274, 2:276
  continuants 2:654
  discourse semantics 3:98, 4:745
  facts 3:537
  historical chain theory of reference
    7:752, 7:754
  identity
    Trinity 9:459–60
  immortality 8:296
  Incarnation and Christology 4:732
  intentionality 4:820
  McTaggart, J.M.E. 6:28
  many-valued logics 6:90
  moral scepticism 6:545
  predication 7:667
  proper names 7:756
  reference 8:164
  religion and morality 8:219, 8:224
  statements 7:788
  Stevenson, C.L. 9:135
  Trinity 9:459–60, 9:461
  use/mention distinction 9:551
Geary, D. 5:224
Gebhardt, E. 3:735
Gedankenexperimente see thought
  experiments
Gedatsukai 2:104

Geertz, C. 1:299, 9:7
Geertz, Clifford 4:684, 4:685
Geffen, D. 2:863
Geffriaud-Rosso, J. 9:212
Geier, M. 9:613
Geiss, I. 7:194
Geist (spirit) 1:179, 5:310
Geistesgeschichte (history of thought)
  4:570
Gelasius I, Pope 7:508
Gelber, H.G. 2:693, 4:479, 9:776
Gelder, B. de 9:321
Gelenius see Řehoř Hrubý of Jelení
Gellner, E.
  African philosophy, Francophone
    1:115
  nation and nationalism 6:661
  ordinary language philosophy
    7:153
  Popper, K.R. 7:539
  social science 8:857
Gelman, C.R. 2:395, 6:675
Gelwick, R. 7:492
Gemeinschaft/Gesellschaft distinction
  8:874
Gemistos see Pletho
gender
  see also androcentrism; feminist
    philosophy
  aesthetics 3:593–6
  coding 3:864–5
  egalitarianism 6:357
  ethics 3:603–5
  feminism 3:582
  jurisprudence
    feminist 3:608
  language 5:361–8, 5:642, 5:643
  moral stage theory 6:505
  neutrality
    French feminist critique 9:199
  personhood 9:212
  privacy 7:692–3
  and science 3:861–8
  social construction of
    (Wollstonecraft, M.) 9:788,
    9:789–90
  social sciences
    feminist critiques of 3:588–90
gene theory
  functionalism in social science
    3:817
genealogy 4:1–5
  feminist epistemology 3:600–1
  Foucault, M. 3:708–9, 3:711, 9:198
Genequand, Charles
  al-Tawhidi †9:271–2
general covariance 8:196

general economy 1:659, 1:660
general ontology (ontologia generalis)
  Chinese philosophy 2:316
general relativity theory see relativity
  theory, general
general terms
  free logics 3:742–3
general will 4:9–12
  see also social choice
  ethical autonomy 1:587
  Rousseau, J.-J.
    public interest 7:832
    social contract theory 2:658,
      2:662–3, 8:368, 8:371, 9:424
    sovereignty relationship 9:58
generalization
  art criticism 1:461–2
  belief states
    holism problems 4:488
  laws of nature 8:45
  natural law distinction 3:522
  reliabilism 9:620
  substitutive schemes
    (Whitehead, A.N.) 9:714
  universal
    genetics 4:14
    Hintikka, J. 2:534
generalized quantifiers see
  quantifiers, generalized
generation, spontaneous see
  spontaneous generation
generative grammars 4:52–3,
  9:248–52, 9:249, 9:250–2
Genesis, Book of
  Augustine 1:546, 1:550, 1:553–4
  Clarembald of Arras 2:377, 7:435
  Thierry of Chartres 9:371
Genest, J.-F. 1:564, 1:866
genetic determinism
  sociobiology 3:485
genetic engineering 1:127, 6:260
genetic epistemology 6:724
genetic fallacy 1:472, 3:474
geneticism see discrimination, genetic
genetics 3:477, 4:12–16
  see also eugenics; evolutionary
    theory; genetic; Mendel, G.;
    species; transgenics
  ethics 1:772–3, 4:16–19, 8:276–7
  evolutionary synthesis 3:478
  genetic drift 3:476, 3:477
  Mendelian 4:12–13, 4:14
  molecular 4:12, 4:13–14
  nature–nurture debate 4:12, 4:15
  population 3:478, 4:12
  sociobiology 8:893, 8:894–5
  theological issues 8:232–3

Genette, Gérard 6:657
genitalia 8:718–19
genius
  artistic 3:594–5
Genovesi, A. 5:41
Gentile, Giovanni **4:20–23**
  Croce, B. 2:729–30, 2:732, 4:20
  Gioberti, V. 4:80
  Gramsci, A. 4:152
  Hegelianism 4:292
  idealism 5:38, 5:41
  Rosmini-Serbati, A. 8:364
  totalitarianism 9:442–3
Gentili, Alberico 5:41
Gentzen, Gerhard Karl Erich **4:23–5**
  formal languages and systems
    3:706
  natural deduction 4:859, 4:862,
    6:678–80, 6:682
  non-constructive rules of inference
    7:29–30
  proof theory 7:747, 7:750
Gentzen's normal form theorem
  6:677–8, 6:679
genus
  see also species
  God (Ibn 'Adi) 4:600
  logic of (Tanabe Hajime) 5:715
Gény, F. 5:512–13
Geoghegan, Vincent
  Bloch, E.S. †1:787–90
geography
  Posidonius 7:557
geology **4:25–8**
geometrodynamics
  relativity theory 8:198
geometry **4:28–34**
  see also Euclidean geometry
  a priori truth of 4:6, 5:791–2
  analytic
    Descartes, R. 3:1, 3:2, 3:15, 9:92
    genetic definition (Spinoza, B.
      de) 9:92
  ancient Greek (Thales) 9:323–4
  arithmetic distinction 6:181–3,
    6:184
  atomism
    Epicureanism 3:342
  certainty (Vico, G.) 9:601
  conventionalism 2:666, 5:791,
    7:479–81
  elementary 4:29
  empiricism (Mill, J.S.) 6:363
  epistemological break
    (Bachelard, G.) 1:621
  formalism (Hilbert, D.) 4:423–4
  Hilbert, D. 4:30, 5:732–3

Hobbes, T. 4:459, 4:468
  ideas
    structure of (Locke, J.) 5:671
  logical positivism 5:790, 5:791–2
  logicism 5:814–15
  natural science (Hobbes, T.) 4:468
  Oresme, N. 7:153, 7:154
  Pascal, B. 7:241, 7:243–4
  Riemannian (Weyl, H.) 9:706
  space 4:31–2
    Greek philosophy 9:60
    Kant, I. 5:184–5
    Reichenbach, H. 8:168–9
  spirit of (Pascal, B.) 7:244
George of Trebizond **4:34–6**
  humanist critique of Plato 7:441,
    7:444, 7:447
George, Alexander
  antirealism
    mathematics 1:311
  Frege, G. †3:765–78
  unconscious mental states 9:526
George, Rolf 1:827
George, R.P. 5:442
George, W. 9:679
Gera, D.L. 9:814
Gerard, Alexander 3:330, **4:36–7**
Gerard of Cremona **4:37–8**
  translations by 1:397, 5:22,
    9:455–6
Gerard of Odo **4:38–40**
Geras, N. 1:195, 6:7, 6:146, 8:355
Gerbert of Aurillac **4:40–1**, 5:747,
  6:692
Gerbi, A. 2:122
Gerdil, Giancinto Sigismondo **4:41–2**
Gergonne, José Díez 1:761, 1:763
Gerlach, H.-M. 9:786
German, T.J. 4:217
German, T.P. 6:389
German Enlightenment *see*
  Enlightenment, German
German Historical School 3:214
German idealism 3:54–5, **4:42–5**
  anti-Semitism
    Hegel, G.W.F. 1:311, 1:312,
      1:313
    Kant, I. 1:311–12, 1:313
  Carlyle, T. 2:205
  dialectical materialism 3:54–5
  Hegel, G.W.F. (Rosenzweig, F.)
    8:357, 8:358
  influence on Russian philosophy
    8:419
  Jewish Enlightenment
    (Krochmal, N.) 3:321–2,
    5:308–9, 5:310

German Romanticism **8:348–52**
Germany
  see also Enlightenment, German;
  German idealism
  the Absolute 1:27–8, 4:665–7
  Adorno, T.W. **1:41–6**
  Agrippa von Nettesheim, H.C.
    1:129–33
  Albert the Great **1:145–52**
  Albert of Saxony **1:143–5**
  Arendt, H. **1:369–73**
  Avenarius, R. **1:592–5**
  Barth, K. **1:651–6**
  Bauer, B. **1:663–7**
  Baumgardt, D. **1:667–9**
  Beck, J.S. **1:687–9**
  Benjamin, W. **1:716–18**
  Bernstein, E. **1:758–60**
  Biel, G. **1:769–72**
  Bloch, E.S. **1:787–90**
  Bonhoeffer, D. **1:835–8**
  Büchner, L. **2:48–51**
  Bultmann, R. **2:126–31**
  Cantor, G. **2:196–9**
  Carnap, R. **2:208–15**
  Cassirer, E. **2:223–7**
  Clauberg, J. **2:380–2**
  Cohen, H. **2:398–403**
  Critical Legal Studies 2:716–17
  Crusius, C.A. **2:736–9**
  Dedekind, J.W.R. **2:839–42**
  Dietrich of Freiberg **3:69–71**
  Dilthey, W. **3:77–83**
  Du Bois-Reymond, E. **3:129–31**
  Dühring, E.K. **3:147–9**
  Eberhard, J.A. **3:196**
  Einstein, A. **3:254–8**
  Elisabeth of Bohemia **3:267–9**
  Engels, F. **3:309–13**
  Fackenheim, E.L. **3:533–5**
  Fechner, G.T. **3:570–2**
  Feuerbach, L.A. **3:635–40**
  Fichte, J.G. **3:642–53**
  Frankfurt School 2:722–8, **3:730–7**
  Frege, G. **3:765–78**
  Fries, J.F. **3:797–9**
  Gadamer, H.-G. **3:827–31**
  Gentzen, G.K.E. **4:23–5**
  Gödel, K. **4:105–7**
  Goethe, J.W. von **4:125–9**
  Habermas, J. **4:193–200**
  Haeckel, E.H. **4:200–1**
  Hamann, J.G. **4:213–17**
  Hartmann, K.R.E. von **4:238–40**
  Hartmann, N. **4:240–2**
  Hegel, G.W.F. **4:259–80**

Hegelianism 4:281–2, 4:290–2, 4:294–5
Heidegger, M. **4:307–23**
Heisenberg, W. **4:327–9**
Helmholtz, H. von **4:337–40**
Hempel, C.G. **4:348–52**
Herbart, J.F. **4:369–71**
Herder, J.G. **4:378–84**
Hertz, H.R. **4:400–2**
Hess, M. **4:413–15**
Hildegard of Bingen **4:429–31**
Hölderlin, J.C.F. **4:479–82**
Horkheimer, M. **4:510–12**
Humboldt, W. von **4:541–3**
idealism *see* German idealism
Jacobi, F.H. **5:45–8**
Jaspers, K. **5:80–4**
Jhering, R. von **5:100–2**
Jungius, J. **5:135–8**
Kant, I. **5:177–96**
Kautsky, K.J. **5:222–4**
Kepler, J. **5:231–3**
Knutzen, M. **5:287–9**
Krause, K. **5:298–301**
Kronecker, L. **5:311–13**
Lambert, J.H. **5:350–2**
Lange, F. **5:352–4**
Lassalle, F. **5:419–21**
Lebensphilosophie **5:487–9**
Leibniz, G.W. **5:541–62**
Lessing, G.E. **5:574–8**
Lichtenberg, G.C. **5:622–5**
logic 5:719–20, 5:723–4
Lorenzen, P. **5:825–8**
Lotze, R.H. **5:838–42**
Luther, M. **6:1–5**
Luxemburg, R. **6:5–7**
Maimon, S. **6:35–8**
Marcuse, H. **6:95–9**
Marsilius of Inghen **6:110–12**
Marx, K. **6:117–33**
Mauthner, F. **6:203–6**
Meinecke, F. **6:280–2**
Meister Eckhart **6:286–8**
Melanchthon, P. **6:288–92**
Mendelssohn, M. **6:304–7**
Neo-Kantianism **6:776–92**
Nicholas of Cusa **6:832–8**
Nietzsche, F.W. **6:844–61**
Oken, L. **7:92–3**
Otto, R. **7:173–5**
pietism 5:173, 7:393–4, 7:395
Planck, M.K.E.L. **7:396–8**
Platonism, Renaissance 7:445–6
Pufendorf, S. **7:835–6**
Radbruch, G. **8:21–3**
Rahner, K. **8:35–9**

Reichenbach, H. **8:166–71**
Reinach, A. **8:180–2**
Reinhold, K.L. **8:186–9**
Romanticism **8:348–52**
Rosenzweig, F. **8:357–62**
Ruge, A. **8:385–7**
Scheler, M. F. **8:504–9**
Schelling, F.W.J. von **8:509–20**
Schiller, J.C.F. **8:524–9**
Schlegel, F. von **8:529–31**
Schleiermacher, F.D.E. **8:531–9**
Schmitt, C. **8:544–5**
Schopenhauer, A. **8:545–54**
Simmel, G. **8:778–80**
Steiner, R. **9:133–4**
Stirner, M. **9:140–1**
Strauss, D.F. **9:164–7**
Strauss, L. **9:167–8**
Suso, H. **9:240–1**
Tauler, J. **9:269–71**
Tetens, J.N. **9:319–22**
Thielicke, H. **9:370–1**
Thomas à Kempis **9:373–4**
Thomasius, C. **9:376–80**
Troeltsch, E.P.W. **9:461–4**
Tschirnhaus, E.W. von **9:485–7**
Ulrich of Strasbourg **9:517–18**
Vaihinger, H. **9:566–8**
Voegelin, E. **9:654–7**
Weber, M. **9:693–8**
Weyl, H. **9:706–7**
Wolff, C. **9:776–8**
Wundt, W. **9:798–802**
Zermelo, E. **9:853–5**
germline therapy 4:18
Gernet, Jaques 2:327, 3:192, 3:195
Gernet, J.W.F. 9:682
Gero, J.M. 1:358
Gersh, S.
    Calcidius 2:176
    Damascius 2:772
    Eriugena, J.S. 3:405
    Iamblichus 4:599
    Neoplatonism 6:803
    Platonism
        Early and Middle 7:428
        medieval 7:438
    Proclus 7:731
    Pseudo-Dionysius 7:808
    Thierry of Chartres 9:373
Gershenzon, Mikhail O. 2:272, 5:609, 8:771
Gerson, Jean **4:45–7**
Gerson, L.P. 4:336, 7:463, 9:160

Gersonides **4:47–51**
    Averroism
        Messer Leon opposition to 6:332
    creation 2:703, 4:47, 4:48–9
    divine knowledge 2:702, 4:49
    immortality
        active intellect 4:49–50
    Jewish philosophy 5:89
    translation by 5:23
Gert, B. 1:776
Gerth, H.H. 9:698
Gesellschaft/Gemeinschaft distinction 8:874
Gestalt psychology **4:51–4**, 7:827
    Austro-Italian production theory 4:52–3
    Berlin school 4:53
    essence 7:346
    Gestalt-switch phenomenon 4:52–3
    perceptual integration 5:286
    visual perception 9:633
Gettier, Edmund
    see also Gettier problems
    concepts 2:515, 5:275
    deductive closure principle 2:845
    epistemology 3:365
    internalism/externalism distinction 4:826
    justified belief 3:379, 3:382
    sufficiency claim 1:617, 1:618
Gettier problems **4:54–9**
    causal theory of knowledge 5:263–4
    deductive closure principle 2:843
    defeasibility theory of knowledge 5:276–7
    epistemology 3:363
        paradoxes 7:211–12
    internal justification 3:722
    Nozick, R. 7:46
Geulincx, Arnold **4:59–61**
    causation principle 7:87
    seventeenth-century logic 5:717
Geurts, A.J. 9:374
Geuss, Raymond
    alienation 1:181
    critical theory †2:722–8
    social science
        methodology of 8:868
Gewesenheit (alreadiness) 4:310
Gewirth, A.
    Kantian ethics 5:203
    Marsilius of Padua 6:114
    political philosophy 7:528
    risk 8:334

universalism in ethics 9:538–9
Geworfenheit see thrownness
Geyer, D.L. 9:477
Geymonat, L. 4:42, 5:41
Ghaffar Khan, Hafiz A.
Shah Wali Allah †8:732–5
Ghana
Akan philosophical psychology
1:138–9
Amo, Anton Wilhelm **1:210–11**
al-Ghazali, Abu Hamid **4:61–8**
Aristotelianism 1:384–5, 4:158
causality 4:640
cosmology 4:66
creation 4:639–40
divine agency 2:243
emanation 2:242, 2:244
existence/essence relationship
4:644
God's knowledge of the world
4:640–1
Ibn Miskawayh 4:632
Ibn Rushd 4:639–41
Islamic theology 5:31
Jewish Averroism 1:599
Maimonides, A. 6:40
Maqasid al-falasifah (The
Intentions of the Philosophers)
4:64, 5:22, 5:23
meaning 6:237–8
moral philosophy 3:441–2
mystical philosophy 6:619
necessity 2:241
Neoplatonism 6:806, 6:807
occasionalism 7:87, 7:89
philosophy
attack on 4:61–2, 4:64–5,
4:639–41, 5:8, 5:13–14
prophecy 7:767, 7:768, 7:770–1
soul 4:641
Sufism 4:61–3, 4:65, 4:66
Tahafut al-falasifa (The
Incoherence of the
Philosophers)
Aristotelianism 1:384–5
emanation 2:242, 2:244
Ibn Rushd 4:639–41
Neoplatonism 6:806
philosophy critique 5:8, 5:9
translations of 5:22, 5:23
Ghert, P.G. van 4:286
Ghio, M. 6:53
Ghirardi, G.C. 7:890, 7:894
Ghiselin, M. 2:798, 9:81
Ghost in the Machine *see* dualism,
Cartesian

ghosts
see also spirits
fear of as social control 6:454
Giacon, C. 3:690, 8:777
Giannantoni, G.
Antisthenes 1:317
Aristippus the Elder 1:380
Cynics 2:758
Cyrenaics 2:763
Dialectical school 3:59
Diodorus Cronus 3:86
Diogenes of Sinope 3:91
Megarian school 6:279–80
Philo the Dialectician 7:365
Pyrrho 7:848
Socrates 9:18
Socratic dialogues 9:21
Socratic schools 9:23
Giarrizzo, G. 9:606
Gibb, H. 5:16
Gibbard, Allan 6:570
analytic ethics 1:223
emotions 3:285
emotive meaning 3:291
morality
judgment 6:512, 6:514
realism 6:538
sentiments 6:550
naturalism 6:716
objectivity 7:75
ontological status of value 9:581
practical reasoning/rationality
8:102
projectivism 7:740
reciprocity 8:131–2
Gibbins, John
Grote, J. †4:183–5
Gibbins, P. 7:886
Gibbon, G. 1:358
Gibbs, B. 7:451
Gibbs, F.W. 7:684
Gibbs, R. 2:47, 7:631
Gibson, James J.
perception 7:293
direct realist theory 4:53
visual 9:633–4, 9:638
psychology 7:825, 7:829
Gibson, M.T. 1:812, 3:308, 7:438
Gibson, Roger F.
analytic philosophy 1:228
Quine, W.V. 8:13–14
radical translation and radical
interpretation †8:25–3
Gibson-Wood, C. 9:504
Giddens, Anthony 8:857, 9:7, 9:188
Gieben, G.R. 4:182
Gieben, S. 7:96

Giedymin, J. 5:482, 7:482
Giere, Ronald N.
models 6:446
risk assessment 8:337
science
naturalized philosophy of
†6:728–31
nineteenth-century philosophy
of 8:571
theories 9:352–3
social science
contemporary philosophy of
8:846
statistics 9:126
Vienna Circle 9:613
Gierulanka, D. 4:792
Giesen, B. 9:256
Giesey, R.E. 1:31
gifts
economics 2:373
Gigante, M. 7:367
Gikatilla, J. 5:175
Gil, Didier
Boutroux, É. †1:850–2
Gilbert of Poitiers **4:68–72**
Bernard of Clairvaux 1:754
Boethius, A.M.S. 1:811
Chartres school 2:290, 2:291
the individual 4:69–70
language theories 5:395, 5:396
multiformity of being 4:69
natural science 4:70
theological discourse 4:70–1
Gilbert de la Porrée *see* Gilbert of
Poitiers
Gilbert, Margaret
social epistemology 8:832
social norms †8:834–6
society 8:889
Gilbert, N. 5:225, 7:182
Gilbert, S.M. 3:613
Gilbert, William 3:259, 3:260
Gilby, T. 1:347
Giles, J. 6:385
Giles of Rome **4:72–8**
essence–existence debate 4:72, 4:73
Liber de causis 5:598
natural philosophy 4:72, 4:74–5
unity of God 4:75
Gilkey, L. 9:412
Gill, C. 7:190
Gill, J. 2:475
Gill, M. 3:793
Gill, N.S. 1:505
Gilleman, Gérard 2:282
Gillespie, Ch.C. 5:297–8
Gillet, G. 7:829, 9:109

Gillette Sturm, Fred
  Brazil
    philosophy in †2:7–2:12
Gilligan, Carol
  applied ethics 1:324
  care ethic 2:281, 2:282
  feminism
    ethics 3:603, 3:605
    and social science 3:592
  justice, equity and law 5:152
  moral development 6:506, 6:509
  moral stage theory 6:505
  nursing ethics 7:56, 7:57
  virtue ethics 9:625
Gillispie, C.C. 2:607–8
Gillon, Brendan S.
  inference
    Indian theories of †4:759–66
  negative facts in classical Indian
    philosophy †6:755–9
Gillon, R. 1:776, 6:264
Gilmore, M. 1:31
Gilson, Étienne
  Alighieri, Dante 1:185
  Aquinas, T. 1:347, 4:73
  Aristotelianism in the seventeenth
    century 1:391–3
  Augustine 1:558–9
  Bernard of Clairvaux 1:755
  Bonaventure 1:834
  Cajetan 2:174
  Descartes, R. 3:18
  Dietrich of Freiberg 3:70–1
  Duns Scotus, J. 3:169
  Garrigou-Lagrange, R. 3:848
  Maritain, J. 6:102, 6:103
  Marston, R. 6:115
  medieval philosophy 6:276–7
  Neo-Thomism 9:381, 9:385
  Peter Lombard 5:822
  Suárez, F. 9:195
  Thomas of York 9:376
  Thomism 9:381, 9:386–7
Gimaret, D. 1:523, 2:244, 5:252
Gimelfarb-Brack, M. 7:177
Gimello, R. 2:92
Ginet, C. 1:41, 4:826, 6:302
Ginzberg, Asher Hirsch see Ha'am,
  Ahad
Gioberti, Vincenzo 4:78–80
  Hegelianism in Italy 5:37, 5:41
Gioia, M. 5:41
Gioja, A.L. 1:231
Giovanni, George di
  German idealism 4:44
  Jacobi, F.H. †5:45–8
  Naturphilosophie 6:740–1

Reinhold, K.L. †8:186–9
Gipper, H. 8:473
Girard, J.-Y. 5:640, 6:678, 6:682,
  8:204
Girard, René 1:536, 1:541
Girardot, N. 2:782
Girgerenzer, G. 8:88, 8:89
Girotto 8:90
Giseke, P.D. 5:650
Givant, S. 9:264
given element
  experience (Lewis, C.I.) 5:588
Given, Myth of the 8:638, 8:640
Gjertsen, D. 1:120, 6:828
Glanvill, Joseph 4:80–3
  supernatural phenomena 6:580,
    6:582
Glas see Derrida, Jacques
Glasenapp, H. von 5:217, 6:34
Glasser, H. 6:637
Glatzer, N.N. 8:361
Glausser, W. 8:806
Gleason, A. 8:811
Gleason's theorem 7:884
Gleitman, H. 2:514, 8:801
Gleitman, L. 2:514
Glennon, R.J. 3:726
Glimm, J. 6:812
global politics
  development ethics 3:39–42
global scepticism see scepticism,
  global
globalism
  Islamic philosophy
    modern 5:17–18
Glockner, H. 4:297, 4:301
Glorieux, P. 5:111, 6:115
glossary of logical and mathematical
  terms 5:795–811
glossematics 9:179–80
Glouberman, E. 8:385
Glover, Jonathan
  applied ethics 1:324
  development ethics 3:43
  happiness 4:229
  life and death 5:630
  medical ethics 6:264
  utilitarianism 9:556
Gloy, K. 6:741
Gluck, Christoph von 7:129
Glucker, J. 1:36, 1:301, 2:360, 7:428
Glucksmann, A. 1:195
Glymour, Clark
  causation 2:251
  crucial experiments 2:736
  Freud, S. 3:793
  learning †5:483–7

psychoanalysis
  methodological issues in 7:815,
    7:816
relativity theory
  philosophical significance of
    8:198
spacetime 9:69
statistics and social science 9:133
theoretical/epistemic virtues 9:343
underdetermination 9:529
gnosis
  Gnosticism 4:83, 6:75
  Hermetism 4:396
Gnosticism 4:83–5
  see also mysticism
  creation doctrine 2:695–6
  definitions 4:83–4
  first principle 7:256–7
  Florenskii, P.A. 3:681
  hermeneutics 4:390
  Ibn al-'Arabi 4:602
  Jung, C.G. 5:134
  Manicheism 6:75
  Mir Damad, Muhammad Baqir
    6:408–10
  Origen 7:162
  origins of 4:83–4
  Voegelin, E. 9:654, 9:655–6
gNubs chen Sangs rgyas ye shes 9:408
Go ram pa bSod nams seng ge
  (Goramba Sönam segge) 9:402
  Jo-nang-pa School 9:403
  Mādhyamika free from extremes
    position 9:404
  Tsong kha pa Blo bzang grags pa
    9:490
  universals 9:406–7
goals
  epistemic
    naturalized philosophy of
      science 6:730
  teleological 9:295–6
Gobineau, Arthur de 1:109, 1:115
Gockel, H. 5:624
God
  see also Brahman; creation; deism;
    divine; goodness, perfect;
    necessary being; occasionalism;
    omnipotence; omnipresence;
    omniscience; the One; providence;
    religious belief; religious
    epistemology; religious experience;
    religious knowledge; revelation;
    theism; Ticci Viracocha; Trinity
  the Absolute 1:28
  absolute being (Scheler, M.F.)
    8:507

active principle
  divine causal force 9:144
agency
  Islamic philosophy 2:242–3
  Jewish philosophy
    early nineteenth century 5:96
    Stenheim, S.L. 5:98
    voluntarism 9:665–6
agent intellect (William of
  Auvergne) 9:726
anthropomorphism
  Kabbalah 5:173
  Maimonides, M. 6:46
apocatastasis 9:520
art as language of 4:216
atonement 1:536–40
attributes of 8:238, 8:243–4
  Aquinas, T. 4:142
  Ash'ariyya/Mu'tazila
    comparison 1:521–2, 4:63
  Augustine 1:549–50
  Christian Platonism 4:793
  classical theism 4:98
  Cohen, H. 6:782
  Ibn al-Arabi 4:601, 4:602–3
  Ibn Daud, A. 4:609
  Ibn Massara 4:628
  Ibn Taymiyya 4:655–6
  identities 8:784, 8:786–7
  'ilm al-kalam 5:28
  impartiality 9:492
  infinite 9:94
  Islamic fundamentalism 5:11
  Islamic philosophy 6:237–8
  Jabriyya 5:26
  al-Kindi 5:251, 6:805
  Paley, W. 7:187
  pantheism 7:203–4
  Price, R. 7:677
  providence 9:492
  Qur'anic description of 6:805
  Saadiah Gaon 8:437
  al-Sijistani 8:774, 8:775
  Sufi 4:656
  uniqueness 8:785
  Wolff, C. 9:783
autonomy of 4:621
awe of 8:339
beatific vision 4:251
beauty of 3:240
  Edwards, J. 3:243–4
  al-Farabi 1:76
being
  Duns Scotus, J. 3:157–8
  Edwards, J. 3:242
  Henry of Ghent 4:358–9
  Meister Eckhart 6:287

Rahner, K. 8:37
Being
  values (Niebuhr, H.R.) 6:840
Being simpliciter (Geulincx, A.)
  4:59–60
Brahman as
  Indian theism 2:4
as causal agent
  Cordemoy, G. de 2:673
  La Forge, L. de 5:332
causality
  Islamic philosophy 6:237–8
  fundamentalism 5:12
  occasionalist view 7:86–7,
    7:88–9
concepts of 4:93–102, 8:248
  Abyss 1:799–800
  African sage philosophers 1:104
  analogy doctrine (Browne, P.)
    2:29
  anti-Iconoclast view (John of
    Damascus) 5:105–6
  Aristotle 1:424
  Aztec civilization 5:430
  being
    Conway, A. 2:670
    as Being/Mind simpliciter
      (Geulincx, A.) 4:60
  Bowne, B.P. 1:852
  Brentano, F. 2:16
  Celsus 2:264
  Chinese philosophy see tian
  classical theism 4:98–4:100
  constructivism (Vico, G.) 9:601
  David of Dinant 2:799
  Epicureanism 3:340, 3:346
  Eriugena, J.S. 3:401, 3:403–4
  Eusebius 3:457
  Gilbert of Poitiers 4:70–1
  Giles of Rome 4:75
  Hegelian 9:164
  Hinduism 4:434–5, 8:609
  immutability 7:109
  Indian 4:102–5
    Advaita Vedānta/theistic
      Vedānta disputes 9:590,
      9:591–2
    Gaudīya Vaisnavism 3:858
    Mīmāmsā 4:103
    monism 6:476, 6:478
    Nyāya 4:104–5
    Rg Veda 4:102–3
    Vedānta 4:103–4
    Yoga 4:104
  Islamic philosophy
    Ibn Hazm 4:620–1

Ikhwan al-Safa' 4:685,
  4:686–7
'ilm al-kalam 5:26, 5:28
Islamic fundamentalism
  5:9–5:10, 5:11
Mu'tazila 4:620
Jewish philosophy
  Hebrew Bible 1:766–9
  Hellenistic Judaism 7:255–7
  Judah Halevi 4:210
  Kabbalah 6:623
  Kaplan, M. 5:204, 5:205
  Leibowitz, Y. 5:563
  Maimonides, M. 6:41, 6:43
  Rabbinic theology 9:333,
    9:334
Manicheism 6:74, 6:75
as mathematical mind
  (Maimon, S.) 6:36–7
Matthew of Aquasparta 6:201
monotheism 6:480–1
Old Academy
  Middle Platonism 7:425–6
Origen 7:161–2
otherness of (Barth, K.) 1:652–3
pantheism 7:202–5
perfect-being theology 4:95–8,
  4:99
perfection 6:760, 6:761
  negative theology 6:760,
    6:761
Platonism
  Early and Middle 7:424–6
  medieval 7:432–3, 7:437
  Plutarch of Chaeronea 7:466
Pseudo-Dionysius 7:805
simplicity 8:784–8
Thierry of Chartres 9:371–2
William of Ockham 9:742–3
contingency 2:650, 2:651
  Leibniz, G.W. 2:651
  Spinoza, B. de 2:650–1
correlation with man
  Jewish philosophy 2:400
creation 2:695–9
  Bar Hayya, A. 1:649
  Crescas, H. 2:703
  design argument 1:531
    Hume, D. 4:559–60
    Kant, I. 5:194–5
  Eriugena, J.S. 3:402
  Gersonides 4:48–9
  Lossky, N.O. 5:836
  Maimonides, M. 6:43, 6:44–5
  Mīmāmsā 6:379
  Neoplatonism 7:727
  Origen 7:162

potentiality
  Indian theories of 7:604–5
Siger of Brabant 8:766–7
death of
  Camus, A. 2:194
  Nietzsche, F.W. 6:852–3
  Tillich, P. 3:508
definition of 4:94–5, 4:600
design
  Gettier problems 4:57
divine knowledge *see* knowledge,
  divine
divine renunciation of ego
  (Weil, S.) 9:699–700
divine sustenance (La Forge, L. de)
  5:332
divine wisdom (Cudworth, R.)
  2:741–2
Divine–human–world relationship
  (Tagore, R.) 9:257–8
duality of natures
  (Boethius A.M.S.) 1:807–8
duty 3:180–1
emanationism
  Bonaventure 1:830
  al-Farabi 3:555
  Israeli, I. 5:32–3
  Judah Halevi 4:208, 4:211–12
essence
  action distinction (Ibn
    Massara) 1:522, 4:628
  Ash'ariyya/Mu'tazila
    comparison 1:521–2, 4:63
  energy relation (Losev, A.F.)
    5:829–30, 5:831
  existence relationship
    Philo of Alexandria 7:359
    al-Razi, Fakhr al-Din 8:113
  Ibn al-'Arabi 4:601, 4:602–3
  'ilm al-kalam 5:28
  negative theology 6:759
as Essence
  Nicholas of Cusa 6:834
eternity 3:422, 3:423, 3:424, 4:98
eternity (Whitehead, A.N.) 9:717
eternity of the world
  medieval views of 3:427, 3:428
evil demon argument
  (Descartes, R.) 3:7
evil, problem of 3:466–71,
  4:329–30, 8:244–5
  hell 4:330–2
  Holocaust 4:495–8
  Ibn Sina 4:652
  perfect goodness 8:238
  Temple, W. 9:300–1
exemplarism 1:832

existence
  Ash'ariyya/Mu'tazila
    comparison 1:521
  essence relationship
    Philo of Alexandria 7:359
    al-Razi, Fakhr al-Din 8:113
  Ibn al-'Arabi 4:603
existence of 4:665
  agnostic view of 1:121–3
  arguments for **4:85–93**, 4:89–91,
    8:248
    a posteriori 9:782–3
    a priori 4:358–9, 9:783
    Abelard, P. 1:13
    Augustine 1:549
    Bonaventure 1:831
    Cartesian 2:743
    causal 3:375
    from conscience 6:822
    consensus gentium (universal
      consent) (Cudworth, R.)
      2:739–41
    cosmological 4:86–7, 4:95–6,
      8:238
      Aquinas, T. 4:85–6, 4:87
      atheist view of 1:532
      Berkeley, G. 1:747
      Clarke, S. 2:378
      Hindu philosophy 4:435
      history of 8:239–41
      immutability 4:711
      Leibniz, G.W. 5:545
      necessary existence (Ibn
        Sina) 4:650–1
    critique of
      Kant, I. 5:181, 5:189
    Descartes, R. 1:445, 3:1,
      3:8–9
    design 1:531
      atheist view of 1:532
      Kant, I. 5:194–5
      Paley, W. 7:186–7
      Voltaire 9:659–60
    design argument
      atheist view of 1:532
    divine simplicity 8:785–6
    Duns Scotus, J. 3:154,
      3:160–3
    efficient causality
      Duns Scotus, J. 3:160–1
      William of Ockham 9:743
    evidentialism 8:210
    evil
      problem of 8:248–9
    fine-tuning of universe
      scientific view 8:233
    first cause *see* cosmological

    first truths 2:119
    Holcot, R. 4:477
    Hume, D. 4:559–60
    independent beings 8:316
    James, W. 5:63–4
    John of St Thomas 5:119–20
    Matthew of Aquasparta
      6:201
    mental proof (Lewis, C.S.)
      5:589
    moral 1:532–3, 8:238,
      8:242–3
    natural theology 6:709, 6:710
    ontological 4:87–9, 7:117,
      8:238
      Anselm of Canterbury
        1:283, 1:286–9, 1:831,
        4:86
      atheist view of 1:532
      history of 8:242
      Leibniz, G.W. 5:544–5
      More, H. 6:579
      necessary being 6:743,
        6:743–6, 6:745–6
      Spinoza, B. de 9:95
    Peter Lombard 5:821
    religious experience
      atheist view of 1:533
    Siger of Brabant 8:765
    Stoicism 9:146–7
    Suárez, F. 9:191
    teleological 4:83, 4:89–91,
      8:238, 8:241–2, 9:296
      history of 8:241–2
      More, H. 6:579
      Shaftesbury, Third Earl of
        8:731
      Tennant, F.R. 9:301, 9:302
    theology **4:93–102**
    Toletus, F. 9:434
    Tucker, A. 9:492
    universal theism 1:532
    Voltaire 9:658
  atheist view of 1:530–4, 6:711
  Kant, I. 1:700, 6:305
existentialism 3:494
experience of
  Ficino, M. 3:656
fitness doctrine (Clarke, S.) 2:378
foreknowledge
  Anselm of Canterbury 1:294
  Boethius, A.M.S. 1:810
  free will conflict
    Bradwardine, T. 1:865
    Wyclif, J. 9:803
  Joachim of Fiore 5:104
  Pomponazzi, P. 7:531

free will of
al-Razi, Fakhr al-Din 8:114
Wyclif, J. 9:803
freedom
divine **3:757–62**
perfect goodness 4:142
futuribilia (conditional future
contingents) (Suárez, F.)
9:189–90
genus (Ibn 'Adi) 4:600
goodness of
Origen 7:162
Thomasius, C. 9:377–8
Vital du Four 9:639
governance of nature
(Maimonides, M.) 6:45–6
grace **4:146–51**
happiness 9:492
history
spiritual progression of 2:691
hope
Bloch, E. 4:508
Kant, I. 4:507–8
Leibniz, G.W. 4:507
human freedom
Báñez, D. 1:648
Ibn Daud, 4:609–10
Ibn Paquda 4:635
Islamic philosophy 2:242–3,
4:63–4
human knowledge of 8:60
see also religious epistemology;
religious knowledge
Barth 3:507
Brunner, E. 2:30–1
Calvin, J. 2:177, 2:178–9
Clement of Alexandria 7:258
divine illumination 4:699
Duns Scotus, J. 3:154, 3:157–8
Fontenelle, B. de 3:691
Godfrey of Fontaines 4:120
Hermetism 4:396
Ibn Falaquera 4:616
Ibn Massara 4:627
Ibn Tufayl 4:657–9
Ibn Tzaddik, J. 4:661
Johnson, S. 5:124–5
Kabbalah 5:171
More, H. 6:576
natural theology 6:707, 6:709
Norris, J. 7:41–2
Richard of Middleton 8:311
Siger of Brabant 8:766
Spinoza, B. de 9:103
Ulrich of Strasbourg 9:517–18
univocity of being 3:154,
3:157–8

human mind as image of 9:600
as a human projection 3:635, 3:637
human relationship with 4:146–9,
8:37–8
anti-Semitism 1:312
Barth, K. 1:654
Maimonides, M. 6:45, 6:47
Philo of Alexandria 7:360
Rahner, K. 8:35
Rāmānuja 8:43
Thielicke, H. 9:370
Tonghak 9:441
hypostasis of
Byzantine philosophy 2:162
ideal formula 4:78, 4:79
idealism (Berkeley, G.) 1:740,
1:741, 1:743–4, 4:663, 4:664
ideas in the mind of
Francis of Meyronnes 3:724
illumination 1:828, 1:833
Matthew of Aquasparta 6:201
Peter of Spain 7:324
immanence
sacramentality of the universe
8:444–5
immutability **4:710–14**
imperfections
Jewish Averroism 1:601–2
Incarnation **4:725–32**
indefectibility thesis 3:28
as infinite space (More, H.) 6:576,
6:580
infinity
Descartes, R. 4:774
Duns Scotus, J. 3:154, 3:157,
3:160, 3:162–3
innate idea of 1:832–3, 6:578
intellect
Duns Scotus, J. 3:159
Ibn Sina 4:650, 4:651
intellectual ascent to
(Bonaventure) 1:829
justice
Ash'ariyya/Mu'tazila
comparison 1:519, 1:520,
1:522, 4:61–4
forgiveness and mercy 3:700
justification by faith (Luther, M.)
6:1, 6:2
language
origins of 5:413
religious 8:248, **8:255–60**
Augustinian-Boethian
doctrine 5:390, 5:393,
5:395–6
Islamic philosophy 6:238
Nicholas of Autrecourt 6:831

Rabbinic theology 9:336
Ramsey, I.T. 8:49–50
symbolism (Tillich, P.) 9:409,
9:410, 9:411
likeness to
as ethical aim 7:466
love
agape 2:280, 3:795
love of 5:843
Indian theism
Brahman 2:4
Spinoza, B. de 6:560
love towards
Abravanel, J. 1:26–7
Fénelon, F. 3:629–30
Ibn Paquda 4:635–6
Masham, D. 6:167
Norris, J. 7:42
Spinoza, B. de 9:103–4
man as God (Tonghak) 9:441
matter
Aristotelianism 1:388–9
meaning
Islamic philosophy 6:237–8
meonic freedom 1:727–8
metaphysical hierarchy
James of Viterbo 5:58–9
Paul of Venice 7:265
monotheistic view of 6:479–83
moral authority of 8:218, 8:219–21
moral perfectionism
(Wollstonecraft, M.) 9:790
moral sense (Hutcheson, F.) 4:591
moral values (al-Razi, Fakhr al-
Din) 8:114
mystical experience 6:630–2,
8:250–5
Kabbalah 5:172
Meister Eckhart 6:624–5
natural law 8:226
natural motion (Malebranche, N.)
6:63
natural philosophy
Cudworth, R. 2:740–1
medieval
absolute/ordained powers
6:700–1, 6:702
cosmology 6:700
John of Jandun 5:107
naturalism
Cambridge Platonism 2:184
nature
identification with (Spinoza, B.
de) 9:91, 9:95–7
Jewish pietism 4:634
Schelling, F.W.J. von 8:509,
8:514

needs of
  Kabbalah 4:411–12
negative theology 3:402
Neostoicism 5:651
obedience towards
  Jewish pietism 4:634–5
objective morality 8:60
obligations to
  Jewish philosophy
    Ibn Paquda 4:633–6
    Saadiah Gaon 8:437
omnipotence of *see* omnipotence
omnipresence *see* omnipresence
omniscience of *see* omniscience
ownership of man
  suicide 9:225–6
pathos of
  Jewish philosophy 4:411
perfect goodness **4:140–4**
perfection
  Duns Scotus, J. 3:158
  omnipotence 7:99
philosophical faith (Jaspers, K.)
  5:81
plastic nature (Cudworth, R.)
  2:741
Platonic Forms 7:466–7
possible worlds (Leibniz, G.W.)
  5:542, 5:544, 5:545
power *see* divine power;
  omnipotence
praxis 2:361
predestination
  Eriugena, J.S. 3:402
  Gassendi, P. 3:855
pre-eternality (Mir Damad,
  Muhammad Baqir) 6:408–9
principle of intelligibility 2:862
projectivism 7:738
prophecy 7:768, 7:769, 7:770
providence *see* providence
punishment 7:162
Pythagoreanism
  Platonism 6:808
religious alienation 1:179
reprobation **8:272–6**
salvation 7:162
scepticism 4:516–17
Sefirot
  Kabbalah 5:172–3
self relationship 7:14–15
selfhood 4:864
self-revelation
  through Jesus Christ
    Barth, K. 1:653, 1:654
    Brunner, E. 2:31, 2:32
    Luther, M. 6:3

postmodern theology 7:586
soul
  difference from
    Madhva 6:31
  immortality of 9:47
  relationship with
    Jewish philosophy 8:438
sovereignty of
  Edwards, J. 3:240, 3:241–2
  Niebuhr, H.R. 6:839
Spinozism (Herder, J.G.) 4:382–3
spirit
  Jewish philosophy 5:310
spiritualistic metaphysics 8:362–3
substance-monism (Spinoza, B.
  de) 9:93
supremacy of (Madhva) 6:31–2
theodicy
  Bayle/Leibniz debate 1:675–6
  Bayle/Malebranche debate
    1:672, 1:674–5
  Helmont, F.M. van 4:341
  Huet, P.-D. opposition 4:515
  Leibniz G.W.
    Malebranche, N. critique
      6:64
  Malebranche, N. 1:446–7,
    6:56–7, 6:63–4
theologia (Geulincx, A.) 4:60
theological contextualism
  situation ethics 8:798
theology of humility (Luther, M.)
  6:1–2
theosophy 9:363
three levels of being (Numenius)
  7:54–5
time
  atemporality
    omniscience 8:243
  creation of 4:712
    Augustine 1:550–1
    al-Ghazali 4:64–5
  as transcendent spirit
    Judaism 1:312
  as truth (Gandhi, M.K.) 3:842
  ultimacy of 4:94–5
  unimaginability of
    negative theology 6:759
union with 6:274
  Bonaventure 1:830–1
  Pseudo-Dionysius 7:806
  Richard of St Victor 8:312–13
unity of
  Islamic philosophy
    Ash'ariyya/Mu'tazila
      comparison 1:519,
      1:521–2

Ibn 'Adi 4:599–601
al-Kindi 5:251
Jewish philosophy
  Ibn Paquda 4:634
  Ibn Tzaddik, J. 4:661
  Nahmanides, M. 6:649
  Saadiah Gaon 8:437
  Shah Wali Allah 8:733
Sufism
  Ibn Sab'in 4:647
unity in conscience
  Shah Wali Allah 8:733
as universal cause (Molina, L. de)
  6:462–3
vision in
  critiques of
    Arnauld, A. 1:446
    Leibniz, G.W. 5:552
    Malebranche, N. 6:56, 6:58–61
    Norris, J. 7:42
voluntarism 9:663–4, 9:665–6
will of
  Fénelon, F. 3:629
  Gerdil, G.S. 4:41
  Ibn Gabirol, S. 4:618–19
  'ilm al-kalam 5:28
  as moral good (Cumberland, R.)
    2:752–3
Word of
  Brunner, E. 2:31
  Jewish scripture
    logos 5:819
  as world consciousness 2:270
Godard de Donville, L. 5:621
god-building (*Bogostroitel'stvo*)
  5:565, 6:865, 8:407
Goddu, A. 6:706, 9:748
Gödel, Kurt **4:105–7**
  see also Gödel-numbering; Gödel's
    axiom; Gödel's theorems
  arithmetics 7:52
  Church's theorem and the decision
    problem 2:350
  completeness problem 4:108–12,
    4:114, 4:115–16
  computability 2:482, 2:490
  constructible universe 2:622, 2:624
  continuum hypothesis 2:656–7
  finite computations 2:484–5
  general relativity 4:9
  incompletness theorem
    computational theories of mind
      6:393
  intuitionism 4:850, 4:851, 4:852
  logic
    early twentieth century 5:736
    many-valued 6:90

modal 6:425
ordinal 7:143
provability 7:796
logicism 5:816
mathematics
foundations of 6:188, 6:190
Neumann, John von 6:810
predicate calculus 7:664
proof theory 7:745, 7:747, 7:750–1
quantifiers 7:872–3
realism
mathematics 8:121, 8:123
Russell, B.A.W. 8:403
semantic paradoxes and theories
of truth 8:643, 8:648
set theory 8:706, 8:707, 8:715
spacetime 9:69
theory of types 9:362
time 9:416, 9:417, 9:418
universals 9:543
Gödel-numbering 2:486, 4:110
Gödel's axiom 6:234–5
Gödel's theorems 4:107–19, 5:734
completeness 4:109–10
Hilbert, D. 4:422, 4:426–7
incompleteness 4:107, 4:110–13,
5:730, 5:734
computability 2:352, 2:478
paradoxes 7:220
proof theory 7:745
second-order logic 8:592
logicism 5:815
modal operators 6:435
second-order logic 8:600, 8:602
Godet, P. 3:174
Gode-von Aesch, A. 6:741
Godfrey of Fontaines 4:119–22
being 4:119
essence 4:119–20, 4:356
Peter of Auvergne 7:322
Godfrey, E. 3:269
Godfrey, J.J. 4:509
Godfrey, M. 6:812
Godfrey-Smith, Peter
Fodor, J.A. †3:684–6
functional explanation 3:805
semantics
teleological †8:672–5
Godlovitch, Stan 1:470, 1:472, 6:613
Godmanhood
Frank, S.L. 3:728
Solov'ëv, V.S. 9:29, 9:30–1
gods
see also Brahman; God; Kṛṣṇa;
Osiris; Zeus
anthropomorphism critique 9:809

Buㅏhism
Shintō comparison 8:750–1
creation of
Brahman 2:1
duality of
pre-Columbian religions 5:430
etymological explanation
Indian philosophy 5:380
existence of
arguments against 2:217
fate
Hinduism 3:564–6
Greek
allegorical interpretation 7:732
human deification 7:732
knowledge of 9:810
Shintō 2:103–4, 8:748–9, 8:750–1
God-seekers see Russia, religious-
philosophical Renaissance
Godwin, J. 9:366
Godwin, William 4:122–5
anarchism 1:244–5, 1:248, 4:122,
4:124
authority 1:585, 1:586
'famous fire cause' 4:123
Hartley, D. 4:238
impartiality 4:714–15, 4:717
utilitarianism 9:556
Godzich, W. 2:812
Goehr, L. 6:613
Goekoop, C. 3:846
Goethe, Johann Wolfgang von
4:125–9
Cassirer, E. 2:225
the daemonic (das Dämonische)
4:128
metamorphosis 4:127–8
Naturphilosophie 6:739
primal phenomena (Urphänomene)
4:128
renunciation (Ent sagung) 4:128
Steiner, R. 9:133
tragedy 9:450
Goethe-Jarbuch 4:129
Goetzmann, W. 4:300
Goffhelf, A. 1:434
Goffman, E. 9:245
Gogacz, Mieczysław 7:488
Goguen, J. 9:566
Goicoechea, D. 4:532
Goitein, S.D. 4:213, 6:40
Golb, M. 1:602
Gold, E. Mark 5:486
Goldbach's conjecture
computability 2:480
intuitionism 1:437, 1:439, 1:440
number theory 2:353

realism 1:309, 1:310
Goldberg, A. 6:354–5
Goldberg, D.T. 5:644
Goldberg, M. 1:314
Goldberg, Stephen J.
aesthetics
Chinese †1:68–75
Goldblatt, R. 3:191, 6:425
Golden, L. 5:219–20, 6:382
Golden Age
Chinese philosophy of history
4:447–8, 4:449–50
colonial philosophy
Latin America 5:421, 5:422,
5:423–4
Portugal
influence on Brazilian
philosophy 2:7–8
golden mean
al-Ghazali 4:66
Golden Rule
Hare, R.M. 4:230–1
universalism in ethics 9:537–8
Golden Section 1:461
Goldfarb, W. 2:215, 7:873
Goldfarb, W.D. 4:378, 7:664
Goldie, Mark
Harrington, J. †4:231–4
political philosophy
history of 7:517
Golding, D. 8:337
Goldman, Alan
art
value of 1:480
interpretation
artistic †1:502–5
music
aesthetics of 6:613
opera, aesthetics of 7:131
sexuality 8:724, 8:727
Goldman, Alvin I.
action 1:41
child's theory of mind 6:389
deductive closure principle 2:845
discrimination 3:105
epistemics 7:35, 7:38
epistemology
a posteriori knowledge 1:3
causal theory of knowledge
5:263–4, 5:265, 5:266
concept of knowledge 5:275–6
defeasibility theory of
knowledge 5:278, 5:279
and ethics 3:370
justification 5:164, 8:130
naturalized 6:727
paternalism 8:830, 8:832

virtue 9:618, 9:621
internalism/externalism distinction
4:826
memory 6:302
perception 7:295, 7:298
power 7:612
practical reasoning/rationality
8:102
professional ethics 7:736–7
rationality of belief 8:89
reliabilism 3:361, 3:382, †8:204–9
social science
prediction in 8:872
Stevenson, C.L. 9:135
Goldman, E. 1:248, 3:580, 3:583
Goldmann, L. 7:246, 7:553
Goldsmith, H.H. 7:822
Goldsmith, M.M.
Mandeville, B. †6:71–4
Goldstein, B. 3:453, 4:51, 7:135
Goldstein, D. 4:613, 4:710
Goldstein, H. 2:608
Goldstein, K. 6:324
Goldstine, H. 5:746, 6:812
Goldziher, I. 4:621, 5:31
Golla, S. 6:670
Gollerbakh, E.V. 8:385
Golomb, J. 3:501
Gombocz, W. 1:296
Gombrich, E.H.
art
artistic expression 1:498
depiction 2:896
forgery 1:501–2
style 1:507, 1:509
and truth 1:459
Gombrich, R. 2:53, 2:684
Gomes, M. 9:366
Gomez, L.O. 9:408
Gómez Caffarena, J. 4:359
Gómez-Lobo, A. 1:232–3
Gómez-Martínez, José Luis
Latin America literature,
philosophy in †5:653–7
Gonçalves de Magalhães, Domingo
José 2:10, 2:11
Gonda, J. 4:256
Gondeshapur 6:804
Gongsun Long 5:697, 5:700–2
Gongyangzhuan (Gongyang Annals)
2:309, 2:312, 2:314
Gonsalvez de Burgos, Juan 5:22
Gonsalvus of Spain 3:155
Gonzaga, Tomáz Antônio 2:9, 2:11
Gonzales, A. 1:144
González, Juliana 6:346–7

González Maldonado, Edelmira
3:510, 3:513
Good, D. 9:469
Good, P. 8:508–9
good 4:130–5
see also consequentialism;
eudaimonia; evil; goodness;
hedonism; intuitionism;
perfectionism; summum bonum;
utilitarianism; virtue ethics
absolute 2:741
Aristotelian concept of 9:753
as beautiful
German Romanticism 8:349–50
common
Cumberland, R. 2:752
public interest 7:833, 7:834
Confucianism 9:821
construction of (Dewey, J.) 3:49
created (Philip the Chancellor)
7:356
egoism 3:245–8
happiness 7:466
highest
Kant, I. 5:192
human 5:248
Ibn Sina 4:652
indefinability of
naturalistic fallacy 6:495
individual
relativity of 8:469
innate knowledge 9:683–4
inner harmony 8:730–1
karma
Japanese Buddhism 2:104
li 9:818–19
medieval conceptions of 6:274
metaphysics 4:130–1
moral character 4:132–3
moral (Nietzsche, F.W.) 6:854
multivocity 1:417
necessary evil 8:60, 9:300
objective
Anderson, J. 1:266
practical reason 7:615–16
values 9:582
personal 8:108
pleasure
hedonism 4:257–8
public 7:833
right relationship 4:133, 8:322–5
deontological ethics 2:890
political neutrality 6:820
Ross, W.D. 8:366
teleological ethics 9:294
theories of the 3:436
Aquinas, T. 1:333–4

Boethius, A.M.S. 1:809
perfection 9:783
Saadiah Gaon 8:438–9
ultimate 8:759
usefulness of 6:454
value distinctions 4:131–2
virtues 9:728
Good, the
good people distinction 3:337
identity with the One 7:726
Platonic Form 9:753
Platonic Forms 7:414
rationality 8:681
good life 4:133–4, 9:753, 9:754
see also eudaimonia
green political philosophy 4:162,
4:163
intellectual thought (Ibn Rushd)
4:642–3
Jewish philosophy
Rabbinic theology 9:334
Saadiah Gaon 8:438–9
nature of
Aristotle 1:427
Stoicism 9:156
Good Samaritan paradox
deontic logic 2:889
good works
salvation 5:167
Goodchild, P. 2:860
Goode, P 6:146
Goodfield, J. 6:196
Goodin, R.E. 3:395, 4:165, 6:821,
7:503
Gooding, David
experiment 3:517
thought experiments †9:392–7
Gooding, J. 5:609
Goodman, Lenn E.
causality and necessity in Islamic
philosophy 2:244
Ibn Bajja 4:608
Ibn Gabirol, S. 4:620
Ibn Massara 4:630
Ibn Miskawayh 4:632
Ibn Paquda †4:633–6
Ibn Sina 4:654
Ibn Tufayl 4:659
Ikhwan al-Safa' 4:688
Jewish philosophy †5:85–90
contemporary 5:95
voluntarism 9:666
Judah Halevi †4:207–13
Maimonides, M. †6:40–9
Neoplatonism in Islamic
philosophy 6:807
al-Razi, Abu Bakr 8:112

Saadiah Gaon †8:435–40
Goodman, Madeleine J. 6:807
Goodman, Nelson **4:135–40**
  abstract objects 1:35
  adverbs 1:48, 1:50
  aesthetics 4:137–8
  architecture
    aesthetics of 1:366
  art
    ontology of art works 1:480,
      1:483–4
    and truth 1:459–60
  Carnap, R. 2:215
  concepts 2:515–16
  confirmation theory 2:532, 2:535
  counterfactual conditionals 2:686,
    2:687, 2:688
  dance
    aesthetics of 2:777
  depiction 2:896
  epistemic relativism 3:360, 3:362
  explanation 3:522, 3:525
  fictional entities 3:665, 3:667
  forgery
    artistic 1:499, 1:500, 1:502
  Grue Paradox 9:341–2, 9:343
  induction 4:138–9, 4:746, 4:751
  knowledge 5:276
  mereology 6:319
  metaphor 6:337
  metaphysics 4:136–7
  music
    aesthetics of 6:613
  natural kinds 6:684
  nominalism 7:22
  particulars 7:237, 7:238
  realism/antirealism 8:119
  resemblance 2:893–4
  style, artistic 1:507, 1:509
  type/token distinction 9:511
  underdetermination 9:528, 9:530
Goodman, Russell B.
  American philosophy in the
    eighteenth and nineteenth
    centuries †1:201–7
  Emerson, R.W. †3:269–72
goodness
  see also aretē; good
  Aquinas, T. 1:333–4
  divine
    Hebrew Bible 1:768
    Thomasius, C. 9:377–8
    divine creation (Vital du Four)
      9:639
    happiness (Hobbes, T.) 4:470
    metaphysics of 7:356

moral
  natural goodness relationship
    4:131
moral standards 8:220
natural
  source of pleasure 4:131
original nature
  Confucianism 2:551
perfect **4:140–4**
  Aristotle 4:140–1
  Augustine 4:141
  divine freedom 3:759–60, 4:142
  evil, problem of 3:466–71,
    4:142–3, 8:238
  hell, problem of 4:329–30
  omnipotence compatibility
    4:141–2, 7:101–2
  Plato 4:140
persons
  moral virtue 4:132–3
self-realization 8:634
Stoicism 9:155
Tolstoian Christianity 9:439
Goodpaster, K. 6:554
Goodrich, Peter
  Critical Legal Studies 2:716, 2:717,
    2:719–20
  legal discourse 5:497, 5:498–9
  legal hermeneutics †5:506–10
  Selden, J. †8:604–5
goodwill
  friendship 3:794
  trust 9:467
Goodwin, B. 9:561
Goodwin, M.H. 5:367
Goody, Jack 1:119, 1:120
Goonatilake, S. 7:577
Gopnik, Alison
  child's theory of mind 6:389
  infant cognition †2:390–2
  introspection 4:842
  Piaget, J. †7:383–6
Goramba Sönam segge *see* Go ram
    pa bSod nams seng ge
Gorbachev, Mikhail 7:240
Gorce, M.M. 1:598
Gordan's problem 5:311
Gordon, A.D. 9:869
Gordon, C. 8:290
Gordon, R. 3:687, 4:495, 6:563
Gordon, S. 7:561
Gordon, William M.
  Bartolus of Sassoferrato †1:658–9
  Roman law/civilian tradition 8:347
Goré, J.-L. 3:630

Gorgias **4:144–6**
  language
    philosophy of 5:357
  Sophists 9:33
  tragedy 9:448
Goris, W. 6:288
Gor'kii, Maksim (Gorky, Maxim)
  6:862, 6:864–5, 6:866
Görler, W. 2:360
Gorman, D. 8:413
Górski, Jakub 7:485
Gortari, Eli de 6:346
Gośāla 6:78
Gosling, J.C.B.
  akrasia 1:142
  Eudoxus 3:453
  hedonism †4:257–9
  pleasure 7:451
Gospels
  Bauer, B. critique 1:664
  divine law distinction
    (Melanchthon, P.) 6:290
  interpretation of (Loisy, A.) 5:820
  St John 7:256
Gosse, E. 2:387
Gosselin, E.A. 2:38–9
Gössmann, E. 1:178
Gosvāmins of Vṛndān 3:858
Goswami, H. 3:859
Gotama *see* Gautama, Akṣapāda
Gottdiener, M. 5:491
Gottfried of St Disibod 4:431
Gottlieb, D. 7:881
Gottlieb, E. 8:739
Gottschalk of Orbais 2:222, 2:223,
  8:273
Gottschalk, H.B.
  Heraclides of Pontus †4:363–4
  Peripatetics 7:305
  Strato 9:163
Gottsched, Johann Christoph 9:450
Goudge, T. 7:283
Gouges, O. de 3:578, 3:583
Gough, I. 6:755, 9:705
Gough, J. 2:665
Gouhier, Henri
  Comte, A. 2:504
  Fénelon, F. 3:630
  Foucher, S. 3:717
  Maine de Biran, P.-F. 6:53
  Malebranche, N. 6:66
  Rohault, J. 8:343
Gouinlock, James
  Dewey, John †3:44–51
Gouinlock, John
  pragmatism in ethics 7:643
Gould, J.B. 2:346

Gould, J.L. 4:797, 5:487, 6:390
Gould, Steven Jay 3:482, 7:93
Gould, Timothy
  Thoreau, H.D. †9:388–92
Gouldner, A. 8:132
Goulet, Denis 3:40, 3:43
Goulet, R. 1:255, 2:758, 3:90
Goulet-Cazé, M.-O. 2:758
Gourevitch, V. 5:291
Gournay, M. le J. de 3:583, 8:559
Gove, A. 2:578
governance
  providence 7:798
government
  see also constitutionalism;
  parliament; political
  representation; state
  absolutism 1:29–31
  authority (Locke, J.) 5:665–6,
    5:680–2
  church/state relationship
    (Calvin, J.) 2:180–1
  civil science (Hobbes, T.) 4:463,
    4:465
  commercial society (Smith, A.)
    8:820
  commonwealth
    Harrington, J. 4:232–3
    Hobbes, T. 4:459–60, 4:471–3
  Confucianism
    Zhouli 2:312
  Confucianism, Japanese 2:550
  constitutional
    rule of law 8:388–9
  contractarianism 2:657–8
  Daoism
    Huainanzi 4:512–13
  democratic 2:867–71
    freedom of speech 3:763
  Filmer, R. 3:677
  function of (Hume, D.) 4:556–7
  interests 6:754
  Jia Yi 5:102–3
  Kauṭilya 5:220–1
  Legalism 5:532, 5:533–5, 5:536–7
  liberalism 5:195, 5:603–4
  limits to (Hutcheson, F.) 4:592
  local 4:384
  mixed
    republicanism 8:281
  monarchy (Abravanel, I.) 1:20,
    1:21–2
  morality
    enforcement of 5:438–42
  public virtues (Smith, A.) 8:820
  representative democracy (Mill, J.)
    6:359

rights (Bentham, J.) 1:719
selection of
  Hume, D. 4:557–8
  Marsilius of Padua 6:112–13
Shōtoku Constitution 8:752–4
social contract theory 8:371
sovereignty 9:57, 9:58
state relationship 9:120
trust 9:469
as unifying ethical agent
  (Confucius) 5:447
utilitarianism
  Bentham, J. 1:719, 1:721–2,
    1:723–4
Government Binding (GB) 2:337–8
Govier, T. 2:285, 9:469
Gowans, C. 3:182
Gower, Barry
  Naturphilosophie 6:741
  Oken, Lorenz †7:92–3
Goy, R. 4:520
Goyard-Fabre, S. 1:799
Grabit example 4:55–6, 5:270
Grabmann, M. 2:201, 9:376, 9:518
grace 4:146–51
  creation 4:148, 4:150–1
  economy of 4:149
  election 8:273
  Eucharist 8:443
  and free will
    Augustine 1:548–9
    Bernard of Clairvaux 1:754
    Bradwradine, T. 1:865
    Molina, L. de 6:461, 6:462–3
    Molinism 6:466
    Wyclif, J. 9:803
  Joachim of Fiore 5:104
  justification doctrine 5:165
    Augustine 5:166
    medieval theology 5:166
    Roman Catholicism 5:167
  as love without desire 9:700
  nature 4:147–8
  Pelagianism 7:284, 7:285–6
  personal relationship with God
    4:146–9
  prophetic religion 7:97–8
  Protestantism 4:148, 5:166–7
  Roman Catholicism 4:148, 4:149,
    5:167, 8:456
  salvation 4:149–50
  sanctification 8:456
  Schiller, J.C.F. 8:526–7
  theodicy 6:64
  uncreated 4:148

Gracia, J.J.E.
  analytical philosophy
    Latin America 1:230–1, 1:232–3
  Argentina, philosophy in 1:379
  Gilbert of Poitiers 4:72
  literature
    Latin America 5:656
  Suárez, F. 9:196
  Wolff, C. 9:786
Gracyk, T. 8:180
Gradualists 9:405–6
Graeco-Roman culture
  influence on early Christianity
    7:254–5, 7:256
Graeco-Roman philosophy see Greek
  philosophy, ancient; Roman
  philosophy
Graeser, A. 9:842–3
Graf, F.W. 9:166, 9:464
Graf, O. 5:177
Gräfrath, B. 9:579
Grafton, A. 4:397
Graham, Angus C.
  categories 2:229, 2:232
  cheng 2:300
  Cheng Hao 2:301
  Cheng Yi 2:303
  Chinese philosophy 2:327
    Legalist 5:537
  Confucianism 2:548
  dao 2:779
  Daodejing 2:782
  Daoist philosophy 2:795
  Han Feizi 4:220
  Huainanzi 4:514
  li 5:595
  linguistic relativism 2:232
  Lushi chunqiu 5:865
  Mencius 6:303–4
  Mohist Canons 5:697, 5:705
  Mohist philosophy 6:457
  Mozi 6:591
  neo-Confucianism 6:776
  ti/yong 9:400
  xing 9:817, 9:818
  Yangzhu 9:823
  yin-yang 9:832
  you-wu 9:835
  zhi 9:858
Graham, Daniel W.
  Vlastos, G. †9:650–4
Graham, Gordon
  history
    philosophy of †4:453–9
Graham, K. 2:872
Graham, W.F. 2:181–2
Grahek, Nikola 9:53, 9:54

grammar
  see also grammarians; phrase structure grammars; syntax; Universal Grammar
  acquisition
    Chomsky, N. 2:336–8
  Bhartṛhari 1:764, 1:765
  generative 4:52–3, 9:248–52
  Indian theories of 4:834–5, 5:380–1, 5:383
  innateness of language 4:52–3, 9:522, 9:524
  liberation (Bhartṛhari) 1:764, 1:765
  logic relationship
    Islamic philosophy 5:707–8
  Minimalism (Chomsky, N.) 2:338
  Protagoras 7:789–90
  Theophrastus 9:338
  transformational (Chomsky, N.) 2:336–8
  universals
    Indian theories of 9:544
grammarians
  Bhartṛhari 1:764–5
  heaven 4:256
  interpretation 4:834–5
  meaning 6:240, 6:241, 6:242–3
  semantic analysis 5:380–1
  sphoṭa theory 5:382–3
grammatical categories
  criteria
    Wittgenstein, L. 2:712–13
  Port-Royalists 5:373–4
  structuralism 9:178
grammaticism
  structuralism in social science 9:185
Gramsci, Antonio **4:151–5**
  civil society 2:370, 2:371
  educational philosophy 3:238
  Hegelianism 4:292
  hegemony 6:144–5
  ideology 4:682, 4:685
  Labriola, A. 5:336
  Marxism 6:142
    Italy 5:38–9, 5:41
    Latin America 6:162
  totalitarianism 9:443
grand narrative
  history
    philosophy of 4:455, 4:457–8
grandeur
  beauty 8:176–7
Grandy, R. 2:477, 4:177
Granet, M. 2:327
Granger, G.-G. 2:531–2

Granger, G.G. 1:231, 1:233
Granovskii, Timofei 5:607
Grant, D. 2:263
Grant, E. 2:135, 6:706, 7:157, 9:64
Grant, P. 5:470
Grant, R.A.D. 2:614
Grant, R.M. 4:85
Grant, Roger 7:72
Grapard, A.G. 8:751
Grassi, O. 9:776
Grassmann, H. 4:33, 5:728, 9:64
Gratieux, A. 8:811
gratitude 8:135, 8:138–9
Grattan-Guinness, I.
  analysis †1:216–20
  logic in the early twentieth century 5:736
  Post, E.L. 7:575
  Russell, B.A.W. 8:403
gratuity thesis 9:475, 9:476–7
Graumann, C.F. 9:801
Grave, S.A.
  Australia, philosophy in 1:583
  Beattie, J. 1:680
  Common Sense School 2:448
  common-sense ethics 2:450
  Hamilton, W. 4:219
gravity
  Bentley, R. 1:725
  Kepler, J. 5:231
  Newton, I. 3:669, 5:557, 6:826
  Strato 9:162
Gray, Asa 1:276
Gray, J.G. 9:690
Gray, J.N.
  Berlin, I. 1:753
  freedom and liberty 3:757
  Hayek, F.A. 4:249
  Mill, J.S. 6:375
  socialism 8:885
  Spencer, H. 9:88–9
  toleration 9:432
Gray, R. 8:727
Gray, Tim S.
  Spencer, Herbert †9:87–9
Graycar, R. 3:608–9, 3:610
Grayling, A.C. 1:749, 8:403, 9:454
Grazia, S. de 6:22
Gṛdharpiccha *see* Kundakunda
Grean, S. 8:732
Great Britain
  see also Scotland; Wales
  Aberdeen Philosophical Society **1:15**
  absolute idealism 4:667
  Alexander of Hales **1:176–8**
  Alexander, S. **1:168–9**

Alison, A. **1:185–7**
Anscombe, G.E.M. **1:280–3**
Anselm of Canterbury **1:283–97**
Astell, M. **1:527–30**
Austin, J. **1:569–70**
Austin, J.L. **1:571–4**
axiology 1:609–10
Ayer, A.J. **1:614–19**
Bacon, F. **1:624–32**
Bacon, R. **1:632–6**
Beattie, J. **1:677–80**
Bentham, J. **1:718–25**
Bentley, R. **1:725–6**
Berlin, I. **1:750–3**
Blackstone, W. **1:780–1**
Blair, H. **1:781–2**
Bold, S. **1:822–3**
Boole, G. **1:841–3**
Bosanquet, B. **1:846–8**
Boyle, R. **1:853–7**
Bradley, F.H. **1:857–63**
Bradwardine, T. **1:863–7**
Brinkley, R. **2:19–21**
Broad, C.D. **2:23–6**
Brown, T. **2:26–9**
Bryce, J. **2:41–2**
Burke, E. **2:136–40**
Burley, W. **2:140–4**
Burthogge, R. **2:144–6**
Butler, J. **2:154–60**
Cambridge Platonism **2:182–5**
Campbell, G. **2:191–3**
Campbell, N.R. **2:193–4**
Carlyle, T. **2:204–6**
Carmichael, G. **2:206–8**
Cavendish, M.L. **2:260–4**
Charleton, W. **2:285–7**
Chatton, W. **2:292–4**
Chillingworth, W. **2:307–9**
Clarke, S. **2:378–80**
Cockburn, C. **2:386–7**
Coleridge, S.T. **2:403–6**
Collier, A. **2:408–11**
Collingwood, R.G. **2:411–15**
Collins, A. **2:415–19**
common law 5:150–1, 8:874
Conway, A. **2:669–71**
Crathorn, W. **2:692–4**
Critical Legal Studies 2:717
Cudworth, R. **2:739–44**
Culverwell, N. **2:750–2**
Cumberland, R. **2:752–3**
Darwin, C.R. **2:795–8**
De Morgan, A. **2:813–14**
Dicey, A.V. **3:62–3**
Digby, K. **3:71–4**
Dodgson, C.L. **3:107–9**

Dummett, M.A.E. **3:149–53**
Duns Scotus, J. **3:153–70**
Eliot, G. **3:266–7**
empiricism 8:75–6
Engels, F. **3:309–13**
English common law 5:150–1, 8:874
Evans, G. **3:459–61**
Farrer, A.M. **3:560–1**
feminist literary criticism 3:611
Ferguson, A. **3:630–3**
Ferrier, J.F. **3:633–5**
Filmer, R. **3:677–9**
Fludd, R. **3:682–4**
Gerard, A. **4:36–7**
Glanvill, J. **4:80–3**
Godwin, W. **4:122–5**
Green, T.H. **4:166–70**
Grice, H.P. **4:172–7**
Grosseteste, R. **4:177–83**
Grote, J. **4:183–5**
Gurney, E. **4:187–91**
Hamilton, W. **4:217–19**
Hare, R.M. **4:229–31**
Hart, H.L.A. **4:234–6**
Hartley, D. **4:236–8**
Hayek, F.A. **4:245–9**
Hegelianism 4:288–90, 4:292, 4:295–6
Henry of Harclay **4:360–3**
Herbert, E. **4:371–5**
Heytesbury, W. **4:419–21**
Hobbes, T. **4:459–76**
Holcot, R. **4:477–9**
Home, H. **4:499–501**
Hooker, R. **4:504–7**
Hume, D. **4:543–62**
Hutcheson, F. **4:588–94**
Huxley, T.H. **4:594–6**
Inge, W.R. **4:793–4**
Isaac of Stella **5:4–5**
John of Salisbury **5:115–17**
Johnson, A.B. **5:120–2**
Johnson, S. **5:122–3**
Kemp Smith, N. **5:227–31**
Keynes, J.M. **5:233–5**
Kilvington, R. **5:244–5**
Kilwardby, R. **5:245–9**
Latitudinarianism 5:432–5
Law, W. **5:468–70**
Lewis, C.S. **5:589–90**
Locke, J. **5:665–87**
McTaggart, J.M.E. **6:24–8**
Major, J. **6:54–6**
Mandeville, B. **6:71–4**
Marston, R. **6:114–15**
Martineau, H. **6:116–17**

Marx, K. **6:118–33**
Masham, D. **6:166–8**
Maxwell, J.C. **6:206–10**
Mill, J. **6:359–60**
Mill, J.S. **6:360–75**
Monboddo, Lord (James Burnett) **6:473–4**
Moore, G.E. **6:494–9**
moral realism 6:536–7
More, H. **6:576–83**
Neckham, A. **6:750–2**
Newman, J.H. **6:821–3**
Newton, I. **6:823–8**
Norris, J. **7:41–3**
Oakeshott, M.J. **7:70–3**
Oman, J.W. **7:97–8**
ordinary language philosophy **7:147–53**
Ordinary Language School **7:147–53**
Oswald, J. **7:168–70**
Overton, R. **7:175–7**
Owen, G.E.L. **7:177–9**
Paine, T. **7:184–6**
Paley, W. **7:186–8**
Pecham, J. **7:267–9**
personal idealism 4:668
Popper, K.R. **7:533–40**
Price, R. **7:675–9**
Prichard, H.A. **7:679–82**
Priestley, J. **7:682–4**
Pseudo-Grosseteste **7:808–9**
psychoanalysis
    post-Freudian 7:817–19
Race Relations Act (1965) 7:692
Ramsey, F.P. **8:44–9**
Ramsey, I.T. **8:49–51**
Rashdall, H. **8:59–61**
Reid, T. **8:171–80**
Richard of Middleton **8:310–12**
Richard Rufus of Cornwall **8:314–18**
Ross, W.D. **8:365–7**
Russell, B.A.W. **8:391–404**
Ryle, G. **8:428–32**
Schiller, F.C.S. **8:522–4**
Selden, J. **8:604–5**
Sergeant, J. **8:698–9**
Shaftesbury, Third Earl of **8:730–2**
Sidgwick, H. **8:758–64**
Smith, A. **8:815–22**
Spencer, H. **9:87–9**
Stewart, D. **9:135–40**
Strawson, P.F. **9:168–74**
Taylor, H. **9:279–80**
Temple, W. **9:300–1**
Tennant, F.R. **9:301–3**

Thomas of York **9:375–6**
Tindal, M. **9:420–3**
Tucker, A. **9:490–3**
Turing, A.M. **9:493–5**
Turnbull, G. **9:502–4**
Venn, J. **9:594–5**
Wallace, A.R. **9:678–9**
Whewell, W. **9:709–11**
White, T. **9:712–13**
Whitehead, A.N. **9:713–20**
William of Ockham **9:731–48**
William of Sherwood **9:748–9**
Williams, B.A.O. **9:749–52**
Witherspoon, J. **9:755–7**
Wittgenstein, L. **9:757–70**
Wodeham, A. **9:773–6**
Wollaston, W. **9:786–8**
Wollstonecraft, M. **9:788–92**
Wyclif, J. **9:802–5**
Great Chain of Being *see scala natura*
Great Debate of bSam-yas (Samyay) 9:405–6
Great Soul
    Ibn Massara 4:628
El Greco 1:683
Greco, John 9:619, 9:621
Greece
    see also Greek philosophy, ancient
    Aenesidemus **1:50–36**
    Alcmaeon **1:160–1**
    Alexander of Aphrodisias **1:169–76**
    Ammonius **1:208–10**
    Anaxarchus **1:254–5**
    Anaximander **1:255–9**
    Anaximenes **1:259–62**
    Antiochus **1:299–301**
    Antiphon **1:301–3**
    Antisthenes **1:314–17**
    Aristippus the Elder **1:379–80**
    Ariston of Chios **1:380–2**
    Aristotle **1:413–35**
    Callicles **2:176–7**
    Carneades **2:215–20**
    Celsus of Alexandria **2:264**
    Cleomedes **2:385–6**
    Cratylus **2:694–5**
    culture
        Plato's critique of 7:414
    Delmedigo, E. **2:861–3**
    Democritus **2:872–8**
    Diodorus Cronus **3:83–6**
    Diogenes of Apollonia **3:87–9**
    Epictetus **3:337–9**
    Epicurus **3:350–1**
    Eudoxus **3:452–3**
    Galen **3:832–5**

Heraclitus **4:364–9**
Hesiod **4:412–13**
Hippias of Elis **4:440–1**
Homer **4:501–2**
Leucippus **5:578–9**
Melissus **6:292–6**
Panaetius **7:188–90**
Parmenides of Elea **7:228–35**
Philo the Dialectician **7:363–5**
Philo of Larissa **7:361–3**
Philodemus **7:365–7**
Plato **7:399–421**
Plutarch of Chaeronea **7:464–70**
Prodicus **7:731–3**
Protagoras **7:788–91**
Pseudo-Dionysius **7:804–8**
Pyrrho **7:844–8**
Pythagoras **7:854–7**
Socrates **9:8–9:19**
Speusippus **9:89–91**
Thales **9:322–4**
Theophrastus **9:337–40**
Thrasymachus **9:397–8**
Thucydides **9:398–9**
Timon of Philius **9:419–20**
Xenocrates **9:806–7**
Xenophanes **9:807–10**
Xenophon **9:810–15**
Zeno of Elea **9:843–5**
Greef, W. de 2:182
Greek
    syllogisms 9:572
Greek mythology *see* myth, Greek
Greek Orthodox Christianity
    limbo 5:636
    purgatory 7:838
Greek philosophy, ancient **1:262–5**
    see also Aristotelianism;
    Neoplatonism; Platonism
    love 5:843
    Academy **1:36**
    Aenesidemus **1:50–1**
    Agrippa **1:129**
    Alcinous **1:159–60**
    Alcmaeon **1:160–1**
    Alexander of Aphrodisias
        1:169–76
    Ammonius **1:208–10**
    analytic interpretation of
        (Vlastos, G.) 9:650–2
    Anaxagoras **1:249–54**
    Anaxarchus **1:254–5**
    Anaximander **1:255–9**
    Anaximenes **1:259–62**
    Antiochus **1:299–301**
    Antiphon **1:301–3**
    Antisthenes **1:314–17**

Apuleius **1:325–6**
Arcesilaus **1:351–4**
archē **1:359–61**
Archytas **1:366–9**
aretē **1:373–4**
Aristippus the Elder **1:379–80**
Ariston of Chios **1:380–2**
Aristotle **1:413–35**
Aristotle commentators **1:435–7**
atomism **1:534–5**, 6:171
atonement 1:536
Byzantine affinity with 2:161,
    2:162, 2:164
Calcidius **2:175–6**
Callicles **2:176–7**
Carneades **2:215–20**
Celsus **2:264**
Chaldaean Oracles **2:273–4**
Chrysippus **2:345–6**
Cleanthes **2:382–3**
Cleomedes **2:385–6**
Cratylus **2:694–5**
Cynics **2:753–9**
Cyrenaics **2:759–63**
Damascius **2:771–2**
Democritus **2:872–8**
Dialectical school **3:58–9**
Diodorus Cronus **3:83–6**
Diogenes of Apollonia **3:87–9**
Diogenes Laertius **3:86–7**
Diogenes of Oenoanda **3:89–90**
Diogenes of Sinope **3:90–1**
dissoi logoi (twofold argument)
    3:106–7
doxography **3:125–7**
dualism 9:44
educational philosophy 3:223–5
Egyptian influence upon 3:250–3
Empedocles **3:293–8**
Epicharmus **3:336–7**
Epictetus **3:337–9**
Epicurus **3:350–1**
eudaimonia **3:450–2**
Eudoxus **3:452–3**
faith 3:541
Galen **3:832–5**
Gorgias **4:144–6**
hedonism 4:257–8
Hellenistic philosophy **4:335–7**
    medical epistemology **4:333–5**
Heraclides of Pontus **4:363–4**
Heraclitus **4:364–9**
hermeneutics 4:390
Hermetism **4:395–7**
Hesiod **4:412–13**
Hierocles **4:421–2**
Hippias **4:440–1**

Hippocratic medicine **4:441–3**
Homer **4:501–2**
Hypatia **4:596–7**
Iamblichus **4:598–9**
influence on
    Abelard, P. 1:9–1:10
    Eriugena, J.S. 3:402
    Islamic philosophy **4:155–9**,
        5:6–8, 5:13–14, 7:159–60
        al-'Amiri 1:208
        al-Kindi 5:250
        Liber de causis 5:596
    medieval ethics 6:274
katharsis **5:218–20**
language **5:356–61**
Leucippus **5:578–9**
logic **5:687–93**
logos **5:817–19**
Lucian **5:853–4**
medicine 6:264, 6:265
Megarian school **6:279–80**
Melissus **6:292–6**
mimēsis **6:381–2**
Neoplatonism **6:797–803**
Neo-Pythagoreanism **6:808–9**
nous **7:43–4**
Numenius **7:54–6**
optics 7:136
Orphism **7:163–5**
Panaetius **7:188–90**
Parmenides **7:228–35**
perfect goodness concept 4:140–1
Peripatetics **7:304–5**
Philo of Alexandria **7:357–61**
Philo the Dialectician **7:363–5**
Philo of Larissa **7:361–3**
Philodemus **7:365–7**
Philolaus **7:367–71**
Philoponus **7:371–8**
physis and *nomos* debate **7:381–2**
plagiarism 2:384
Plato **7:399–421**
Platonism
    Early and Middle **7:421–9**
Plutarch of Chaeronea **7:464–70**
pneuma (spirit) **7:470–2**
poetry 7:472
political 7:503–4, 7:505–6
    Aristotle 7:506
    Hellenistic schools 7:506
    Plato 7:506
    presocratics and Sophists
        7:505–6
    Socrates 7:506
Posidonius **7:555–8**
Presocratics **7:671–2**
Proclus **7:723–31**

Prodicus **7:731–3**
Protagoras **7:788–91**
providence 7:797
psychē (soul) **7:809–11**
Ptolemy **7:830–2**
Pyrrho **7:844–8**
Pyrrhonism **7:848–54**
Pythagoras **7:854–7**
Pythagoreanism **7:857–61**
rhetoric
    style 1:506
Sextus Empiricus **8:716–17**
Simplicius **8:788–91**
slavery 8:804
Socrates **9:8–19**
Socratic dialogues **9:19–21**
Socratic schools **9:21–3**
Sophists **9:33–4**
Speusippus **9:89–91**
Stoicism **9:141–60**
Strato **9:161–4**
Strauss, L. 9:167–8
texts
    Carolingian renaissance
      2:220–1
    medieval philosophy 6:271–2
    Renaissance humanism 4:533,
      4:537
Thales **9:322–4**
Theophrastus **9:337–40**
Thrasymachus **9:397–8**
Thucydides **9:398–9**
Timon **9:419–20**
translations of
    Arabic 9:455
Vaiśeṣika atomism contrast 7:606
wisdom 9:752–4
Xenocrates **9:806–7**
Xenophanes **9:807–10**
Xenophon **9:810–15**
Zeno of Citium **9:841–3**
Zeno of Elea **9:843–5**
Greek tragedy 9:447–8
Green, A. 4:245
Green, E. 5:505–6
Green, G. 3:779, 7:631
Green, L.C. 6:292
Green, Leslie
    authority †1:584–6
    consent 2:598
    obligation
      political 7:80
    power †7:610–13
    state 9:122
Green, Mitchell S.
    imperative logic †4:717–21
Green, O.H. 8:286–7

Green, R.L. 3:109
Green, R.M. 1:779, 5:243
Green, T.F. 3:238
Green, Thomas Hill **4:166–70**
    empiricism 4:167–8
    freedom 3:754–5, 3:757
    Hegelianism 4:289
    idealism 4:668
    legitimacy 5:541
    liberalism 4:168–9, 5:599, 5:604
    obligation
      political 7:80
    positive liberty 4:168, 4:169
green anarchism 3:333–4
green ethics *see* environmental ethics
green political philosophy **4:159–66**
    see also ecology; environment;
      environmental ethics
    business ethics 2:153
    economic thought 4:164–5
    political agency 4:162–3
    political institutions 4:163
    public policies 4:162
    value theory 4:161–2
Greenawalt, Kent
    civil disobedience †2:366–9
Greenbaum, S. 6:170
Greenberg, C. 1:452
Greenberg, D. 2:621
Greenberg, J.H. 3:434
Greenberger, D.M. 1:716
Green-Pedersen, N.J. 1:126, 5:758,
    9:730
Greene, M. 3:234, 3:238–9
Greene, R.A. 2:752, 6:582
Greenfeld, L. 6:661
Greenfield, S. 9:521
Greenleaf, W.H. 7:72
Greeno, J.G. 2:251
Greenspan, L. 3:535
Greenspan, P. 3:285, 6:533
Greffe, J.L. 7:482
Gregg, J. 1:784
Grégoire, F. 3:693
Gregor, A.J. 3:563, 9:444
Gregor, Mary 5:196
Gregor, M.J. 1:672
Gregory I, the Great, Pope 4:391
Gregory IX, Pope 1:398–9
Gregory of Nazianzus 4:727, 4:732,
    7:259
Gregory of Nyssa 1:538, 1:541, 5:636,
    7:259
Gregory of Rimini **4:170–2**
    Augustinianism 1:564, 4:170
    propositions 5:401
    William of Ockham 4:171

Gregory, F. 2:51
Gregory, Peter N.
    Awakening of Faith in Mahāyāna
      †1:603–4
    Buddhism
      Chinese 2:92
      Zongmi †9:870–2
Gregory, T. 2:376, 2:744, 7:438, 9:731
Greimas, A.J. 9:184
Grelling, Kurt 7:217–18, 7:220
Grey, T.C. 2:621, 4:495
Griaule, Marcel 1:104, 1:106, 1:110,
    1:115
Grice, Herbert Paul **4:172–7**
    ambiguity 1:200
    analyticity 1:238, 1:239
    axiology 1:611
    belief and knowledge 1:709
    communication and intention
      2:455–8
    concepts 2:516
      analysis 2:522
    descriptions 3:24
    discourse semantics 3:98
    formal and informal logic 3:702
    implicature 4:174–5, 4:721–4,
      4:725
      conventional/conversational
        distinction 4:722–3, 7:622–3
      pragmatics 7:622, 7:624, 7:627,
        7:631
    indicative conditionals 4:742
    meaning and communication
      4:173–4, 6:213
    metaphor 6:337
    ordinary language philosophy
      7:147
    perception 7:293, 7:298
    pragmatics 5:409
    propositional attitudes 7:786
    rationality of belief 8:89
    reference 8:164
    semantics
      informational 8:662
    society
      concept of 8:887, 8:889
    speech acts 9:86
    value 4:175–6, 9:583
Grice-Hutchison, M. 9:76
Grieder, J.B. 4:452
Grier, Philip T.
    Il'in, I.A. †4:692–6
Griffin, David Ray
    evil, problem of 3:472
    process philosophy †7:711–16
    process theism 7:720
    providence 7:801

Griffin, James P.
  economics and ethics 3:210
  good, theories of the 4:135
  happiness †4:226–9
  logical atomism 5:775
  utilitarianism 9:556
  value 9:583
  welfare 9:705
Griffin, M. 2:360, 4:336, 8:682
Griffin, Nicholas
  neutral monism †6:816–18
  Russell, B.A.W. †8:391–404
Griffin, R. 3:563
Griffin-Collart, E. 9:139
Griffith, E. 3:583
Griffith, R.T.H. 8:611
Griffiths, G. 7:578–9, 7:581
Griffiths, J. Gwyn 3:250
Griffiths, M. 5:479
Griffiths, Paul 3:805
Griffiths, P.J. 2:75, 2:99, 6:403
Grignaschi, M. 5:109
Grigor'ev, Apollon 8:521, 8:522
Grille, D. 1:820
Grimal, P. 8:682
Grimes, T.R. 9:238
Grimm, D. 2:621
Grimm, R. 6:344
Grimshaw, S. 5:479
Grimsley, R. 1:168, 8:376–7
Grisez, G. 3:121–2, 6:690, 9:690
Groenendijk, J. 1:243, 3:98, 8:3
Grofman, B. 4:11
Grondin, J. 3:831, 4:389
Groner, P. 2:105
Grootendorst, R. 3:702
Grosholz, E. 3:18
Gross, G.S. 5:123
Gross, H. 2:389
Grosseteste, Robert 4:177–83
  Aristotelian commentaries 1:399
  Augustinianism 4:179
  Greek-Latin translations 9:456
  indivisibilism
    Bradwardine critique of 1:864
  light 1:634, 4:179–80
  Platonism
    medieval 7:436
  translation of John of Damascus
    5:105
Grossmann, R. 6:286
Grosz, B. 3:98, 7:631
Grosz, E. 3:587, 5:479
Grot, Nikolai 7:563
Grote, G. 7:420, 9:18
Grote, John 4:183–5
Grothendiek, A. 2:237, 2:238

Grotiana 4:186
Grotius, Hugo 4:185–6
  applied ethics 1:324
  deception 9:483
  historical theory of law 9:601
  human rights 5:465
  influence of
    Pufendorf, S. 7:835–6
    Stair, J.D. 9:119
  natural law 7:504, 7:512
  Roman law/civil tradition 8:347
  Socinianism 8:891
  truthfulness 9:485
grounds for belief see reasons,
  epistemological belief
group conciousness
  cultural identity 2:745–6
group knowledge see collective
  knowledge
group theory 5:846–7
grouping
  negative
    Buddhist nominalism 7:25–6
groups
  collective self-deception 8:631
  interests
    African ethical systems 3:430–1,
      3:432–3
  natural selection
    sociobiology 8:892–3
  power 7:611
  psychology of (Freud, S.) 3:792
  rational choice theory 8:64, 8:70–1
  social 4:623, 4:625
    Ibn Khaldun 4:623, 4:625
  solidarity 9:23–4
Grover, Dorothy L. 7:690, 7:881,
  9:477
Grube, G. 7:420
Gruber, H.E. 7:829
Gruber, J. 1:812
Grue Paradox 4:746, 5:273–4,
  9:341–2
Gruenbaum, J. 2:146
Gruenler, R. 7:720
Grünbaum, Adolf
  Freud, S. 3:793
  Poincaré, J.H. 7:482
  psychoanalysis
    methodological issues in 7:811,
      7:812, 7:816
  Reichenbach, H. 8:171
  relativity theory
    philosophical significance of
      8:199
  spacetime 9:69
  time 9:416

unconscious mental states 9:526
underdetermination 9:530
Zeno of Elea 9:852
Gründer, K. 7:5
Grundnorm 5:226–7
Grundy, K.W. 9:617
Grzegorczyk hierarchy 8:144
gSang-phu Ne'u-thog monastery
  9:406–7
Guadarrama González, P. 6:164
Guamán Poma de Ayala, F. 5:432
Guan Zhong see Guanzi
Guanding 9:860–1
Guanzi (Book of the Master Guan)
  4:186–7
  Legalist philosophy 5:532, 5:537
  qi 7:862, 7:863
Guattari, Félix 1:191, 2:858–9, 9:200
Gubar, S. 3:613
Gudorf, Christine 8:722, 8:727
Guehenno, J. 8:377
Guellouz, S. 4:518
Guelzo, Allen C.
  American philosophy
    eighteenth and nineteenth
      century 1:206
  pietism †7:392–6
Guenthner, F. 5:736, 6:425
Guerlac, Rita
  Vives, J.L. †9:645–50
Gueroult, M.
  Descartes, R. 3:18
  Fichte, J.G. 3:652
  Leibniz, G.W. 5:561
  Malebranche, N. 6:66
  Spinoza, B. de 9:107
Guerrero, Juan Luis 7:349
Guest, S. 3:189
Guha, D.C. 7:65
Guha, R. 7:524, 7:582
Guhrauer, G.E. 5:137
Guifeng Zongmi see Zongmi
Guignon, Charles
  existentialism †3:492–50
guild socialism
  Hessen, S.I. 4:417–18
Guiliano, E. 3:109
Guillelmi de Militona see William of
  Militona
Guillelmus Altissiodorensis see
  William of Auxerre
guilt 8:135, 8:139–40
  actual sin 8:792–3
  existential 3:499
  intent 1:13
  Nietzsche, F.W. 6:855
  original sin 8:792, 8:793–5

punishment 2:707
purgatory 7:838
relevance to moral judgments
  6:532
self-deception 8:629
self-punishment
  conscience 2:580
  shame contrast 6:567–9, 6:570,
    8:139
  moral sentiments 6:548,
    6:549–50
Güiraldes, Ricardo 5:654, 5:656
Guliangzhuan (Guliang Annals)
  2:309, 2:312, 2:314
Gulley, N. 1:460
Gullvåg, Ingemund
  Næss, A. †6:635–8
Gumley, J.E. 4:446
Gumperz, J.J. 8:473
Gunatilleke, G. 3:43
Gunten, A.F. 2:174
Gunter, P.A.Y. 1:737, 7:715
Gunther, H. 6:866
Gunton, Colin E.
  atonement †1:536–41
Guo Xiang 5:594
Gupta, Anil
  definition 2:849
  revision theory
    semantic paradoxes and
      theories of truth 8:646–7,
      8:648
  Tarski's definition of truth
    †9:265–9
Gupta, M. 8:41–2
Gupta, R. 9:218
Gurney, Edmund **4:187–91**
  cogency of sequence ('organicity')
    4:188–9
  'Ideal Motion' 4:188, 4:189
  music
    aesthetics of 6:609, 6:613
Gurock, J.S. 5:206
Gurvitch, Georges 4:800, 4:802

Gurwitsch, Aron 4:587, 7:337, 7:341
Guseinov, A.A. 6:159
Gustafson, R.F. 2:126, 9:439–40
Gustafsson, B. 1:759–60
Gustavson, P. 8:427
Gutas, D. 1:385, 4:654
Gutheil, G.
  cognitive development †2:393–5
Guthrie, K.S. 6:809
Guthrie, W. 8:483
Guthrie, W.K.C. 4:146
  Alcmaeon 1:161
  Anaxagoras 1:254
  Anaximander 1:259
  Anaximenes 1:262
  ancient philosophy 1:265
  Antiphon 1:303
  Antisthenes 1:317
  Callicles 2:177
  Democritus 2:877
  Diogenes of Apollonia 3:89
  dissoi logoi (twofold argument)
    3:107
  Empedocles 3:298
  Eudoxus 3:453
  Heraclitus 4:369
  Hippias 4:441
  Leucippus 5:579
  matter 6:196
  Melissus 6:295
  Parmenides 7:234
  physis and *nomos* debate 7:382
  Plato 7:420
  Presocratics 7:672
  Prodicus 7:732
  Protagoras 7:790
  Pythagoras 7:856
  Pythagoreanism 7:861
  Sophists 9:34
  Thales 9:324
  Thrasymachus 9:398
  Xenophanes 9:810
  Zeno of Elea 9:852

Gutiérrez, Gustavo 5:613, 5:615,
  5:616, 5:656
Gutiérrez Vega, L. 1:648–9
Guttenplan, S. 6:407
Guttentag, Otto 6:264–5
Gutting, Gary
  Foucault, M. †3:708–13
  French philosophy of science
    †3:779–86
  incommensurability 4:736
  Kuhn, T.S. 5:318
  post-structuralism †7:596–600
  social sciences †7:600–4
Guttmann, A. 3:235–6, 3:239, 6:602,
  9:278–9
Guttmann, J.
  Albo, J. 1:154
  Ibn Ezra, A. 4:613
  Ibn Gabirol, S. 4:620
  Ibn Tzaddik, J. 4:662
  Jewish philosophy
    voluntarism 9:666
  Jewish philosophy, early
    nineteenth century 5:99
  Krochmal, N. 5:311
  Shem Tov family 8:739
Gutwirth, M. 2:437–8, 9:118
Guy, A. 9:76, 9:650
Guyer, M. 8:74
Guyer, Paul
  Cavell, S. 2:260
  Kant, I. 5:196
  language
    early modern philosophy of
      5:378
  taste, artistic 1:512
Gwynne, G.E. 9:118
Gyekye, D. 5:712
Gyekye, K. 1:102, 1:103, 1:106, 1:139
Gyeltsap darma rinchen *see* rGyal
  tshab dar ma rin chen
gZhan-stong-pa School of Buddhism
  6:351–2, 9:402–3, 9:488

H

Haack, S. 6:90, 7:664, 9:307, 9:719
Haag, E. 5:476
Haag's theorem 3:672
Haakonssen, Knudd
    Cumberland, R. †2:752–3
    Hutcheson, F. 4:593
    Millar, J. 6:376
    Smith, A. †8:815–22
    Thomasius, C. †9:376–80
Ha'am, Ahad 4:192–3
    Jewish philosophy 5:90
    Zionism 9:868
Haaparanta, L. 4:587
Haardt, Alexander
    Losev, A.F. 5:832
    Shpet, G.G. †8:754–8
Haas, A. 9:241, 9:270
Haas, F.A.J. 7:377
Haas, G. 3:61
Habermas, Jürgen 4:193–200
    African Francophone philosophy
        1:115
    alterity and identity 1:191
    architecture
        aesthetics of 1:366
    Bataille, G. 1:661
    civil society 2:371
    communicative action 4:194,
        4:195–6
    communicative rationality
        2:459–61, 2:462
        social theory and law 8:878
    Critical Legal Studies, Germany
        2:716, 2:720
    critical theory 2:727
    critiques of
        Apel, K.-O. 2:461
    Enlightenment 3:316
    ethics
        discourse ethics 4:196–7
        Kantian 5:202, 5:203
        practical reason and 7:619
    Frankfurt School 3:730, 3:733–6
    Gadamer, H.-G. 3:831
    Hegelianism 4:295
    hermeneutics
        biblical 4:390, 4:393–4, 4:395
    ideals 4:675
    legitimacy 5:541

Marcuse, H. 6:98
Marx, K. 6:145–6
meaning and communication
    6:213
moral justification 6:516
political philosophy 4:197–8, 7:528
rational discourse
    legal reasoning 5:527
    recognition 8:134
social science 8:846, 9:256
society
    concept of 8:888, 8:889
sociology 9:7
technology 9:287
theology, political 9:332
habit
    desire distinction 3:30–1
    human nature (Dewey, J.) 3:45–6
    karma
        Indian philosophy 7:606–7
    nature (Ravaisson-Mollien, F.)
        8:104
habitus (dispositions)
    Bourdieu, P. 1:849
Haboush, Jahyun Kim 2:564–5, 9:825
Hacker, P.M.S.
    legal positivism 5:520
    Madhava 6:30
    private language argument 7:698
    Wittgenstein, L. 9:769–70
Hackett, J.M.G. 1:636
Hackforth, R. 9:163
hacking
    information technology and ethics
        4:781
Hacking, Ian
    analytic philosophy 1:228
    constructivism 2:629
    experiment 3:515–16, 3:517
    incommensurability 4:736
    Kuhn, T.S. 5:318
    Lakatos, I. 5:345
    linguistic discrimination 5:644
    logic
        seventeenth and eighteenth
            century 5:721
    logical constants 5:779, 5:780
    observation 7:86
    Pascal, B. 7:246

pragmatic virtues 9:343
randomness 8:59
scientific realism and antirealism
    8:582–3, 8:584
statistics 9:126
unity of science 9:533
Hacohen, M.H. 7:539
Hadamard, J.S. 7:217, 7:482
Hadassi, Judah 5:207–8
Haddon, A.C. 8:18, 8:20
Haden, C. 6:812
Hadi, A. 6:411
Hadot, I. 3:308, 8:791
Hadot, P. 6:106–7, 7:261, 7:549–50
Hadreas, P. 6:324
haecceity
    see also individual difference
    particulars 7:236
Haeckel, Ernst Heinrich 4:200–1
    Huxley, T.H. 4:595
Haegeman, L. 2:341
Haering, T. 4:297
Häfner, Ralph
    Jungius, J. †5:135–8
Hagameister, M. 3:576
Hagberg, G. 5:356
Hagemann, L. 6:838
Hagen, J.B. 3:205
Hager, L. 3:592
Hägerström, Axel Anders Theodor
    4:202–4
    legal norms 7:41
    legal realism 5:521, 5:522, 5:524
    theology critique 7:68
    Uppsala school 8:485
Hahm, D.E. 3:126
Hahn, Hans 6:190, 9:609–11
Hahn, L.E. 7:715, 8:14, 9:669
Haight, G.S. 3:267
Haight, M.R. 8:628, 8:632
Haight, Roger
    liberation theology †5:613–17
Hailperin, Theodore
    Boole, G. †1:841–3
    Boolean algebra 1:846
    De Morgan, A. 2:814
    logic in the nineteenth century
        5:728
Hainthaler, T. 7:377

hairgrease, Gothic 1:801
Ha'iri Yazdi, Mahdi
  Illuminationist philosophy 4:703
  knowledge by presence 5:19, 5:20
  mysticism
    Islam 6:620
    al-Suhrawardi 9:223
al-Hakam, Hisham 5:28
Hakamaya, N. 2:75
Hakeda Yoshito 1:604
Haksar, Vinit
  moral agents †6:499–504
halakhah **4:204–7**
  aggadah relationship
    (Heschel, A.J.) 4:411
  biblical law 4:205
  halakhic man
    Soloveitchik, J.B. 9:26–7
  Jewish bioethics 1:776–9
  Leibowitz, Y. 5:562–4
  post-Talmudic Judaism 4:206
Halbertal, M. 5:95
Halbfass, Wilhelm
  heaven
    Indian concepts of 4:256
  Hindu philosophy 4:440
  Jainism 5:56
  karma and rebirth
    Indian concepts of †5:209–18
  Nyāya-Vaiśeṣika 7:65
  ontology in Indian philosophy
    7:127
  Ramakrishna Movement 8:42
  universals
    Indian theories of 9:548
Halbronn, J. 4:613
Haldane, E. 3:634
Haldane, J.
  Reid, T. 8:180
Haldane, J.B.S.
  life, origin of 5:635
Haldane, John
  Thomism †9:380–8
Haldane, John J.
  aesthetics of architecture †1:361–6
  Ferrier, J.F. †3:633–5
Hale, B. 7:844
Hale, Sir M. 2:442, 2:446
Hale, R.L. 5:524
Hale, Robert J.
  abstract objects †1:32–5
  materialism 6:177
  objectivity 7:75
  type/token distinction 9:511
Halevi, Judah **4:207–13**
  Jewish philosophy 5:88
  Kuzari 4:208–12

prophecy 7:769
Halévy, E. 4:238
half-intuitionism 4:857
Halfpenny, P. 9:356
Halkin, A. 5:24
Hall, A.R. 6:582, 6:828, 9:64
Hall, David L.
  aesthetics
    Chinese 1:74
  Chinese philosophy †2:315–28
    law and ritual 5:454
  Confucianism, Chinese 2:548
  Confucius 2:570
  dao †2:778–9
  Daoist philosophy †2:783–95
  de †2:809–10
  East Asian philosophy 3:195
  qi †7:862–3
  Rorty, R. 8:355
  tian †9:400–2
  xin (heart-and-mind) †9:815–16
  xing †9:817–18
  yin-yang 9:832
  you-wu †9:834–5
  zhi †9:858
  Zhuangzi 9:866
Hall, G.S. 4:240
Hall, H. 4:821
Hall, J.W. 2:555
Hall, K. 5:367
Hall, M.B. 1:856
Hall, Robert T. 3:177
Hall, Roland 4:562
Hall, T. 7:69
Hallam, N. 7:886
Hallaq, W. 4:656, 5:31, 5:460
Hallauer, H. 6:838
Halldén, Sören 8:486, 8:491
Halle, M. 9:184
Hallen, Barry
  African aesthetics †1:61–5
  African traditional religions 1:119,
    1:120
  Yoruba epistemology 1:103–4,
    1:106, †9:832–4
Haller, R.
  Brentano, F. 2:17
  logical positivism 5:794
  Mach, E. 6:16
  Vienna Circle 9:613
Hallet, M. 2:198, 2:657, 4:427, 8:715
Halleux, R. 1:158
Hallie, P.C. 6:489
Hallie, P.P. 6:53
Halliwell, S. 5:220, 6:382
Hallman, J. 4:713

hallucinations
  see also illusion
  bodily sensations 1:794
  perception 7:288–9, 7:291–2
  religious experiences 8:252
  sense-data 8:696
Halmos, P.R. 1:846, 8:708
Halonen, Ilpo
  epistemic logic †3:354–9
Haloun, G. 4:187
Halperin, David 8:727
Halpern, B. 9:870
Halpern, J.Y. 3:359
Halting problem
  computability theory 2:488–9,
    2:494
  glossary 5:803
  Turing machines 9:497–8
Halyburton, T. 4:375
Hamacher, W. 2:812
Hamann, Johann Georg **4:213–17**
  Enlightenment, German 4:213–15
  God
    art as language of 4:216
  influence on Herder, J.G. 4:379
  language 4:215–16
  Sturm und Drang 4:214
Hamblin, C.L. 3:545, 4:720
Hamburg, C.H. 2:227
Hamburg, G.M.
  liberalism
    Russian †5:605–10
Hamburger, J. 1:570
Hamburger, L. 1:570
Hamelin, O. 8:270
Hamesse, J. 5:24–5, 9:457
Hamhô Tûkt'ong *see* Kihwa
Hamilton, A. 2:872, 3:574
Hamilton, Alexander 1:206
Hamilton, Andy
  Mach, E. †6:13–16
Hamilton, B. 9:39, 9:645
Hamilton, G. 3:593
Hamilton, K. 4:402
Hamilton, W.D. 8:893, 8:896
Hamilton, William **4:217–19**
  Australia, philosophy in 1:576
  complex numbers 7:49
  critique by Mill, J.S. 6:366
  logic in the seventeenth and
    eighteenth centuries 5:721
Hamlin, Alan
  social choice †8:824–6
Hamlyn, D.W. 8:553
Hammacher, K. 5:48
Hammer, W. 6:292
Hammerstein, N. 9:380

Hamming nets 2:571–2
Hamming, R.W. 4:786
Hamminga, B. 3:219
Hammond, Guyton B.
  Tillich, P. †9:409–13
Hammond, M. 7:347
Hammond, P. 8:96, 8:102
Hamori, A. 4:213
Hamowy, R. 3:632
Hampe, M. 9:719
Hampsher-Monk, Iain
  Burke, E. †2:136–40
  political philosophy 7:503,
    †7:503–18
Hampshire, Stuart 1:68, 1:463, 4:815,
  9:107
Hampson, N. 3:319
Hampton, Jean
  contractarianism 2:665
  crime and punishment 2:710
  democracy 2:871
  forgiveness and mercy 3:701
  practical reasoning †8:90–103
  rectification and remainders 8:141
Han Fei/Han Fei-tqu see Han Feizi
Han Feizi 4:219–20
  Daodejing 2:782
  history, theories of 4:448
  language 5:694, 5:705
  Legalism 5:537–8
    Daoism 5:536–7
    fa 5:532–3
    historical relativism 5:535–6
    rulers 5:448
    shi 5:533–4
    shu 5:534–5
Han Wônjin 4:220–1
  Horak controversy 2:563–4, 9:825
Han Yu 4:221–2, 6:766
Hanafi, Hasan 5:17
Hanák, T. 4:571–2
Hand, Michael
  game-theoretic semantics †8:657–8
Handelman, S.A. 6:355, 9:336
Hands, D. 3:220
Handy, R. 9:567
Hanen, M. 1:356, 1:358
Hanf, W. 4:771
Hanfeizi see Han Feizi
Hanfling, O. 9:613
Hanke, L. 5:425
Hankins, James
  Ficino, M. †3:653–9
  humanism, Renaissance 4:540
  Pico della Mirandola, G.
    †7:386–92

Platonism
  medieval 7:438
  Renaissance †7:439–47
Hankins, T. 1:168
Hankinson, R.J.
  Aenesidemus †1:50–1
  Agrippa †1:129
  Galen †3:832–5
  Hellenistic medical epistemology
    †4:333–5
  Hippocratic medicine †4:441–3
  Pyrrho 7:848
  Pyrrhonism †7:848–54
  Sextus Empiricus †8:716–17
  Timon 9:420
Hanna, Robert
  conceptual analysis †2:517–22
Hanna, T. 2:196
Hannan, B. 3:265
Hannay, Alastair 2:548–9, 5:243,
  8:492
Hansen, Chad
  dao 2:779
  Daodejing 2:782
  fa 3:533
  logic in China †5:693–706
Hansen, F. 5:356
Hansen-Love, A. 8:413
Hanshu see Ban gu
Hanslick, Eduard 4:222–4
  art, formalism in 3:708
  Gurney, E. 4:187
  intentionality 4:222
  music
    aesthetics of 6:609, 6:613
    and emotion 4:223
Hanson, Norwood Russell 4:224–6
  materialism 6:172
  modularity of mind 6:450, 6:451
  observation 7:86
  science
    method 8:580
    theories 9:353
  theory-observation distinction
    6:724, 6:727
Hanson, Russell L.
  republicanism †8:280–3
Hao, B.-L. 2:279–80
happiness 4:226–9
  see also eudaimonia; pleasure
  agent intellect 4:607
  Aquinas, T. 1:339–40
  Aristippus the Elder 1:380
  Aristotelianism/Augustinianism
    synthesis (Kilwardby, R.) 5:248
  Averroism 1:597
  capacity for 2:437

contemplation (Aristotle)
  1:429–30
Cynics 2:755
definitions of 7:426, 9:90
Diogenes of Sinope 3:91
as divine union (Bonaventure)
  1:828, 1:830
duty (Johnson, S.) 5:125
good 4:131
  Aristotle 1:427, 1:429
  Plutarch of Chaeronea 7:466
heaven 4:251–2
Ibn Miskawayh 3:441
Ibn Rushd 4:641–3
Ibn Shem Tov, J. 8:739
through knowledge
  Islamic philosophy 3:384, 3:385,
    4:642–3
life goal 4:134
life meaning 5:631
maximization of
  critical hedonism 1:668–9
medieval ethics 6:274
Mill, J. 6:359
morality relationship
  (Wollaston, W.) 9:787
motivation (Tucker, A.) 9:490–2
mystical (Ibn Miskawayh) 4:631
natural good (Johnson, S.) 5:125
perfect life (Plotinus) 7:462
pessimism (Hartmann, K.R.E.
  von) 4:239
politics (Aristotle) 1:430
principles of (Xenocrates) 9:807
pursuit of (Hobbes, T.) 4:470
Pyrrho 7:846–7
reason
  Ibn Bajja 4:606–7
  al-Sijistani 8:774, 8:775
rebirth
  Buddhism 2:94–5
self-love distinction (Butler, J.)
  2:156
society (al-Farabi) 3:557
Stoicism 9:155–6
utilitarianism
  Bentham, J. 1:718–19, 1:720–4
  Mill, J.S. 6:360, 6:361, 6:369–70,
    6:372
  practical reason 7:615
  Sidgwick, H. 8:759
virtue relationship 1:833–4
  Buddhism 2:95
  Early and Middle Platonism
    7:426–7
  Kant, I. 5:192
through wisdom (Confucius) 2:568

Haq, M. 3:44
Harada, S. 2:63
al-Haramayn, Imam (al-)Juwayni
Haraway, Donna 3:602, 3:867
Hardcastle, G. 7:135
Hardenberg, F. von (Novalis) 8:349
Hardie, C.D. 3:239
Hardie, W.F.R. 1:434
Hardimon, Michael O. 4:279, 8:134
Hardin, C.L.
    colour
        and qualia 2:421, 2:427
        theories of 2:428, 2:431
    optics 7:139
    secondary qualities 8:599
Hardin, Garrett 3:43, 7:542
Hardin, R.
    rational choice theory †8:64–75
    trust 9:469
Harding, Sandra
    feminism 3:589, 3:592, 3:602
    gender and science †3:861–8
    science
        postcolonial philosophy of
            †7:575–8
    social science 3:589, 3:592, 8:857
Harding, W. 9:392
Hardman, O. 1:519
Hardt, M. 2:860
Hardwig, J. 9:314
Hardy, G.H. 1:220
Hardy, L. 1:716
Hare, E.M. 7:11
Hare, P.H. 3:141–2, 3:466
Hare, Richard Mervyn 4:229–31
    educational philosophy 3:235,
        3:239
    emotive meaning 3:291
    ethics 6:570
        analytic 1:223
        applied 1:324
        naturalism in 6:717
        universalism in 5:762, 5:764,
            9:539
    fact/value distinction 3:538
    ideals 4:675
    impartiality 4:717
    imperative logic 4:720
    morality 6:570
        education 3:235, 6:509
        judgment 6:514
        justification 6:516
    obligation
        political 7:80
    prescriptivism †7:667–71
    akrasia 1:142

utilitarianism relationship
    9:555, 9:556
slavery 8:806
Stevenson, C.L. 9:135
supervenience 9:238
truth
    moral scepticism 6:544, 6:545
Hare, T.B. 9:841
Harel, D. 2:496, 3:191
Haren, M. 7:438
Hargreaves Heap, S. 7:834, 9:705
Haribhadra 2:62, 5:55, 5:56
Häring, Bernard 2:282
Häring, N.M. 2:292, 2:378, 9:372,
    9:373
Harker, R. 1:850
Harl, M. 7:163
Harland, G. 6:844
Harland, R. 9:177
harm 5:460
    crime 2:705–6
    definition of 5:440–1
    justification of 3:463
    law
        limits of 5:462–3
        and morality (Mill, J.S.) 5:439,
            5:440–1
    paternalism (Mill, J.S.) 7:250
    sexuality 8:725
Harman, Gilbert
    cognitivist naturalism 6:715, 6:717
    coherence theory of justification
        5:259
    concepts 2:516
    conceptual role semantics 8:654,
        8:656
    consciousness 2:588–9, 2:595
    contractarianism 2:665
    doubt 3:125
    holism
        mental and semantic 4:491,
            4:493
    inference to the best explanation
        4:769
    intention 4:815
    knowledge
        defeasibility theory of 5:278,
            5:279
    language of thought hypothesis
        5:407
    logic 5:780, 5:785
    memory 6:302
    morality
        knowledge 6:519
        realism 6:538
        relativism 6:542
        scepticism 6:545

naturalized epistemology 6:727
    perception 7:293
    propositional attitudes 7:786
    rationality of belief 8:89
Harman, P.M. 6:259
harmonia see Philolaus;
    Pythagoreanism
harmony
    anarchism (Kropotkin, P.A.)
        5:313–14
    cosmic
        human influence on (Dong
            Zhongshu) 3:111–12
    cosmogony (Philolaus) 7:368–9
    integration
        Slavophilism 7:199
    music 6:329, 7:370, 7:858
    nature 5:314, 8:730–1
    pre-established
        Leibniz, G.W. 5:288, 5:542,
            5:548–9
        Wolff, C. 9:782
    Pythagoreanism (Archytas) 1:368
    radial
        East Asian Philosophy 3:194–5
    self-cultivation
        Chinese philosophy 8:619
    society
        Daoism 2:321, 4:513
Harnish, R.M. 4:725, 7:304, 7:630–1,
    9:86
Harootunian, H.D. 5:660, 6:590
Harper, C. 1:789–90
Harper, W.L.
    counterfactual conditionals 2:688
    Newton, I. †6:823–8
    practical reasoning/rationality
        8:102
Harpocration 7:429
Harrah, David
    questions †8:1–3
Harré, Rom
    Bentley, R. †1:725–6
    causation 2:250
    natural laws 5:474
    psychology 7:829
    scientific theories 9:353
    social science
        behaviourism in †1:693–6
        philosophy history 8:857–8
        scientific realism and 8:587
Harries, K. 6:838
Harrington, James 4:231–4
    republicanism 8:281, 8:283
Harrington, L. 4:117–18
Harris, C.E. 3:315
Harris, E.E. 9:719

Harris, Horton
  Hegel, G.W.F. 4:279
  Strauss, David Friedrich †9:164–7
Harris, H.S. 4:23, 4:44, 9:444
Harris, Jay M.
  Ibn Ezra, A. 4:613
  Jewish Enlightenment †3:320–4
  Krochmal, N. †5:308–11
Harris, John
  bioethics 1:776
  life and death †5:625–30
  reproduction ethics 8:280
Harris, J.W. 5:468, 5:520, 7:761, 8:365
Harris, K.M. 2:206
Harris, Marvin 3:816, 3:817–18,
  8:868
Harris, Olivia
  Lévi-Strauss, C. †5:582–5
Harris, P.L. 6:389
Harris, R. 8:482
Harris, S.E. 8:556
Harris, William Torrey 4:287, 4:300
Harris, W.V. 8:679
Harris, Z.S. 9:180–1
Harrison, B. 2:427
Harrison, E.R. 2:680
Harrison, F. 2:504
Harrison, J. 6:828
Harrison, M.A. 3:706
Harrison, P. 4:375
Harrison, Ross
  Bentham, J. †1:718–25
  democracy †2:867–72
  transcendental arguments
    †9:452–4
  Williams, B.A.O. †9:749–752
Harrisville, R. 2:130
Harrold, C.F. 2:206
Harsanyi, J.
  decision and game theory 2:834
  economics and ethics 3:210
  practical reasoning/rationality
    8:102
  Rawls, J. 8:109
  risk 8:334
Hart, Herbert Lionel Adolphus
  4:234–6
  Austin, J. 1:570
  authority 1:584, 1:586
  Bentham, J. 1:724
  crime and punishment 2:710
  equality 3:395
  homosexuality
    legalization of 5:463
  law
    limits of 5:464

and morality (Devlin, P.) 5:441,
    5:442
  legal concepts 5:495
  legal norms 7:39, 7:41
  legal positivism 5:514, 5:516, 5:520
  obligation
    political 7:80
  practical reasoning/rationality
    8:102
  public interest 7:834
  responsibility 8:293–4
  rights 8:330
  social norms 8:834–5
Hart, K. 7:585, 7:586
Hart, W.D.
  Löwenheim-Skolem theorems and
    non-standard models †5:846–51
  meaning and verification †6:230–6
  realism
    mathematics 8:123
Hartfelder, K. 6:292
Harth, E. 1:31, 3:269
Hartley, David 4:236–8
  human nature, science of 4:527
  Priestley, J. 7:684
Hartley, R.V.L. 4:782
Hartman, Charles
  Han Yu †4:221–2
Hartman, David
  Jewish philosophy, contemporary
    5:95
  Leibowitz, Y. †5:562–4
  Maimonides, M. 6:48
  Soloveitchik, J.B. †9:26–8
Hartmanis, J. 2:475
Hartmann, A. von 4:240
Hartmann, B. 7:542
Hartmann, Heinz 7:819, 7:822
Hartmann, Karl Robert Eduard von
  4:238–40, 9:165–6
Hartmann, Nicolai 4:240–2
  Hegelianism 4:297
  Latin America
    existentialism 3:511, 3:512
    phenomenology 7:348, 7:349,
      7:350
  phenomenological movement
    7:341
  values 1:609, 1:611
Hartmann, W. 8:509
Hartnack, Justus 8:492
Hartshorne, Charles
  God
    concepts of 4:101
    existence arguments 4:88–9,
      4:92, 8:242
  idealism 4:668

immutability 4:713
  omnipresence 7:107
  panentheism 4:100–1
  panpsychism 7:197
  process philosophy 7:714, 7:715
  process theism 7:720
  process theology 8:245
  religion, philosophy history 8:246
Hartsock, Nancy 3:602, 8:720, 8:727
Hartwell, R.M. 4:452
Hartz, G. 4:566
Hartz, L. 1:206
Harvey, D. 7:590
Harvey, E. 3:602
Harvey, I. 1:492, 2:901
Harvey, P. 2:53, 7:11
Harvey, S. 4:617
Harvey, Van A. 3:639
Harvey, W. 2:704
Harwood, J. 9:2
Harzer Clear, Edeltraud
  cosmology and cosmogony, Indian
    theories of †2:681–4
  Hindu philosophy †4:433–40
  Mādhava †6:28–31
Hasenjäger, G. 4:116, 7:664–5
Hasidism 4:242–5
  Kabbalah (Heschel, A.J.) 4:411
  mysticism 6:623
  spiritual content (Buber, M.) 2:43
Haskalah see Enlightenment, Jewish
Hasker, William
  creation and conservation
    †2:695–700
  Molina, L. de 6:465
  occasionalism †7:86–90
  omniscience 7:112
  prayer 7:653
  providence †7:797–802
  religion, philosophy history 8:246
Haskins, C.H. 9:457
Hasler, L. 6:741
Hasnawi, A. 1:175
Hassan, Riffat
  Iqbal, M. †4:863–8
Hastie, R. 5:505
Hatfield, Gary
  science
    naturalized philosophy of 6:731
    scientific method †8:576–81
Hattiangadi, J.N. 7:539
Hattori, M. 3:76, 7:65
Haubst, R. 6:838
Hauerwas, Stanley 8:222, 8:224
Haugeland, J. 4:821
'hauntology'
  Derrida, J. 2:900

Hauriou, Maurice 4:800, 4:802
Hause, Jeffrey
   Francis of Meyronnes †3:723–5
   Origen †7:160–3
Hauser, C. 9:321
Hausheer, Roger
   Meinecke, F. †6:280–2
Hausman, C. 7:283
Hausman, Daniel M.
   economics
      and ethics †3:205–11
      philosophy of †3:211–22
   social science
      methodology of 8:868
      positivism 7:561
Havel, Vaclav 8:290
Havens, G.R. 3:319
Havens, T.R.H. 7:12–13
Hawi, S. 4:659
Hawking, S. 4:93
Hawkins, G. 7:545
Hawkins, T.W. 1:220
Hawksworth, M.E. 3:592
Hawthorn, G. 8:834
Hawthorne Effect 3:518, 3:519
Hay, J. 1:74
Hayami, Y. 1:128
Hayashi Razan 2:552, 3:800–1
Hayek, Friedrich August von 4:245–9
   authority 1:586
   conservatism 2:614
   desert and merit 3:27
   Enlightenment, Scottish 3:330
   holism and individualism in
      history and social science
      4:487–8
   justice
      international 5:156
   law 5:468
   legal norms 7:39, 7:41
   liberalism 5:604
   Mandeville, B. 6:74
   market
      ethics of the 6:107, 6:110
   political authority 1:585
   rule of law 8:388, 8:391
   socialism 8:885
   tradition and traditionalism 9:446,
      9:447
Hayes, P. 2:452, 2:453
Hayes, Richard P.
   Buddhist nominalism 7:27
   Buddhist philosophy in India
      †2:92–9
   Dignāga †3:74–6
   Indian philosophy
      awareness 1:608

epistemology 3:392
   inference 4:765
   testimony 9:318
   Indian and Tibetan philosophy
      †4:736–40
   potentiality †7:604–8
   Vasubandhu †9:583–7
   Yogācāra Buddhism 2:75
Hayes, Z. 6:203
Haym, R.
   Hegel, G.W.F. 4:279
   Hegelianism 4:297
   Herder, J.G. 4:384
   Humboldt, W. von 4:543
   Romanticism, German 8:351
   Schlegel, F. von 8:531
Hayman, D. 9:293
Hayoun, M.-R. 1:602, 4:646
Hayry, H. 7:737
Hayry, M. 7:737
Hayy Ibn Yaqzan (The Living Son of
   the Vigilant) see Ibn Tufayl
Hazard, P. 3:319
Hazen, Allen
   constructivism in mathematics
      2:638
   non-constructive rules of inference
      †7:27–30
   quantifiers and inference 7:870
He Xiu 9:857
Headley, John M.
   Campanella, T. †2:186–91
Heal, Jane
   Wittgenstein, L. †9:757–70
Healey, R. 7:894
health
   see also medical ethics
   medicine
      Hippocratic 4:441–3
      philosophy of 6:264–9
   nursing ethics 7:56–7
   risk assessment 8:334–8
   Tschirnhaus, E.W. von 9:486
heart
   Chinese philosophy see xin
Heart Sutra
   emptiness 6:592–3
heart-and-mind, learning of the see
   learning of the heart-and-mind
Heath, A.C. 8:235
Heath, P. 1:79, 2:814
Heath, Peter
   Dodgson, C.L. †3:107–9
Heath, Stephen
   Tel Quel school †9:291–4
Heath, T.L. 1:369, 9:324

heaven 4:249–53
   beatific vision 4:249, 4:251
   Bible 4:250
   Chinese philosophy see tian
   Indian concepts of 4:253–7
      classical religious systems
      4:254–5
      philosophical schools 4:255–6
      Veda 4:253–4
   Jewish philosophy 8:438
   purgatory 7:838
   resurrection 4:250–1
   salvation 4:250–1
   society in 4:251–3
Hebb, D. 2:573, 2:577
Hebblethwaite, B. 3:561
Hebrew
   translation of Arabic texts to
      5:23–4
Hebrew Bible see Bible, Hebrew
Hebrew Humanism
   Zionism 9:869
Hecht, E. 7:139
Heck, P. von 5:513
Heck, Richard G.
   Dummett, M.A.E. 3:153
   Frege, G. †3:765–78
Hecker, J.F. 5:438, 6:357, 7:564
Heckmann, R. 6:741
Hedenius, Ingemar 4:204, 5:495,
   8:486
hedonism 4:257–9
   see also evaluative hedonism;
     psychological hedonism; reflective
     hedonism
   Aristippus the Elder 1:380
   Charleton, W. 2:286
   cheerfulness (Democritus) 2:876
   consequentialism 2:604
   critical (Baumgardt, D.) 1:668–9
   egoism 3:246
   Epicureanism 3:346–7
   eudaimonism
      Cyrenaics 2:761–3
   Eudoxus 3:453
   folly of
      Islam 3:439
   Gassendi, P. 3:855
   good, theories of the 4:132
   Helvétius, C.-A. 4:345–6
   Lokāyata 6:180
   progressive (Ducasse, C.J.) 3:140
   quality/quantity distinction
      (Mill, J.S.) 6:370, 6:371
   utilitarianism 9:551, 9:552–3
      Bradley, F.H. 1:858
      happiness 4:227

Hedwig, K. 4:404
Heehs, P. 1:568–9
Heelan, P. 7:341
Hefner, P. 8:235
Hegel, Georg Wilhelm Friedrich
  4:259–80
  see also German Idealism
  the Absolute 1:27–8, 1:29
  absolute legal idealism 5:512,
    5:513
  aesthetics 2:304
  alienation 1:178–9, 1:180, 1:181
  anti-Semitism 1:311, 1:312, 1:313,
    1:314
  anti-subjectivist reaction to 9:197
  art
    and morality 1:453, 1:455, 1:456
    value of 1:480
  Belinskii, V.G. 1:710–12
  civil society 2:369, 2:371
  commentary by Il'in, I.A. 4:692–3
  Concept (Begriff) of reason 4:260,
    4:267, 4:268–73
  consciousness 2:584, 4:261,
    4:266–8
  conservatism 2:608, 2:612–13,
    2:614
  contractarianism 2:665
  critiques of
    Chernyshevskii, N.G. 2:304
    Irigaray, L. 5:2, 5:3
    Kierkegaard, S. 3:507
    Marx, K. 6:118, 6:120–1, 6:123
    Schelling, F.W.J. von 8:509,
      8:515–16
    Young Hegelians 6:118, 6:120
  dialectic
    Irigaray, L. 5:2, 5:3
    Japan 5:714
    McTaggart, J.M.E. 6:25, 6:26,
      6:27
    Unamuno y Jugo, M. de 9:519
  dialectical materialism 3:55, 3:57
  emotions 3:289
  empiricism 3:378, 3:382
  Enlightenment, continental 3:316
  ethical life 4:264, 4:274–5, 7:617
  ethnocentrism 1:109
  existentialism 4:284–5
  general will 4:11
  German idealism 4:43, 4:44, 8:357,
    8:358
  Hegelianism 4:280–1
  historicism 4:443, 4:446
  history
    philosophy of 4:454, 4:458
  human nature 4:524, 4:525

  idealism 4:668
    influence on Russian Marxism
      6:152
    political philosophy 7:504,
      7:515–16
  Ideas 4:271
  infinity 4:775, 4:777
  influence of
    Marxism
      Latin America 6:161, 6:163
      Russian Marxism 6:152
      Strauss, D.F. 9:164
  Jena period 4:263–4
  Jewish Enlightenment 3:322
  Krochmal, N. 5:309–10, 5:311
  Lassalle, F. 5:420
  legitimacy 5:541
  life (Leben) 4:262–3
  logic
    nineteenth century 5:723, 5:728
    reason 4:266, 4:268–72
  Marx, K. contrast (Althusser, L.P.)
    1:193
  Marxism (Lukács, G.) 5:857, 5:858
  metaphysics 6:338
  monism of reason 4:265
  morality
    and art 1:453, 1:455, 1:456
    and ethics 6:568, 6:569–70
  nature
    aesthetic appreciation of 6:733
    philosophy of 4:263–4, 4:272–3
  Naturphilosophie 6:738–9, 6:741
  panlogicism
    critique by Schelling, F.W.J.
      4:284
  pantheism 4:100
  period styles 1:506
  Phenomenology of Spirit
    consciousness 4:261, 4:266–8
  philosophy
    criticism of 4:269–70
    task of 4:268
  Philosophy of Nature
    system of reason 4:260
  Philosophy of Right
    morality and ethics 6:569–70
  pluralism 7:463
  poetry 7:476–7
  political philosophy 4:260, 4:273–4
  processes 7:722, 7:723
  property 7:759
  punishment
    deterrence 2:707
  Rawls, J. 8:109
  reality
    unified theory of 4:259, 4:262–3

  reason
    as reality 4:259–60, 4:264–6,
      4:277
  recognition 8:132–3, 8:134
  religion
    critique of 4:262, 8:236, 8:237,
      8:238
    philosophy history 8:239, 8:246
  Science of Logic
    system of reason 4:260, 4:267,
      4:268–72
  sense certainty 4:266–7
  slavery 8:805, 8:806
  social contract
    critique of 2:663
  social theory (Taylor, C.) 9:276–7
  Socrates 9:18
  soul
    immortality of 4:273
  spirit 4:263–4, 4:273–7
  subject/object unity (Marcuse, H.)
    6:97–8
  thought/life relationship
    (Fackenheim, E.L.) 3:534
  totalitarianism 9:443
  tragedy 9:447, 9:450, 9:451
  transcendence (Gentile, G.) 4:21
  war and peace 9:689, 9:690
Hegelian idealism
  see also Hegelianism
  critiques of 4:282–5
    Kierkegaard, S. 5:236, 5:237–8
    Croce, B. 2:728–9
    materialism (Engels, F.) 3:309
Hegelian Marxism
  post-Stalin (Il'enkov, E.V.) 4:688–9
Hegelian monism 4:265
Hegelianism **4:280–302**
  see also anti-Hegelianism;
    Hegelian idealism; neo-
    Hegelianism; Young Hegelians
  Bohemia 2:766
  critiques by
    Lambriola, A. 5:335
    Solov'ëv, V.S. 9:29
  Denmark 4:286
  Fascism (Gentile, G.) 4:22
  France 4:285–6, 4:292, 4:294–5
  Germany 4:281–2, 4:290–2,
    4:294–5
  Great Britain 4:288–90, 4:292,
    4:295–6
  Hegel, G.W.F. 4:280–1
  history, end of (Kojève, A.)
    5:289–90
  identity
    postmodernism 1:187–8

ideological divisions 4:282, 4:283
influence of
  Marx, K. 3:309, 3:311
  Russian philosophy 8:419
Islamic philosophy 5:20
Italy 4:287, 4:292, 4:294, 5:37
Netherlands 4:286–7
Old Hegelians 4:281
religion
  Bauer, B. 1:664
  critique of 8:236, 8:237
  Russian **4:302–7**
    Belinskii, V.G. 1:710–11
    critique by Slavophiles 8:808
    Herzen, A.I. 4:405, 4:406–7
    liberalism 5:607
  Scandinavia 8:484
United States of America 1:203–4,
  4:287–8, 4:292, 4:295–6
Hegemonious 6:77
hegemony
  Marxism (Gramsci, A.) 4:152–3,
    6:144–5
Hegenberg, L. 1:233
Hegesians
  hedonism
    Cyrenaics 2:760, 2:762
Hegyi, J. 8:777
Heiberg, Johan Ludwig 4:286, 4:299
Heidegger, Martin **4:307–23**
  architecture
    aesthetics 1:366
  art 4:317–19
  authenticity 4:311
  being 1:701–2
    intentionality 1:702
  Being and Time
    Destruktion 2:897–8, 2:901
    Bultmann, R. 2:130
  critiques of
    Gadamer, H.-G. 3:829, 3:831
    Habermas, J. 4:198
  Dasein 4:307–8, 4:311–13
    intentionality 1:702
  deconstruction 2:838–9
  Destruktion 2:897–8
  disclosure 4:307–8, 4:312–14,
    4:316
  emotions 3:289
  environmental ethics 3:334, 3:335
  Ereignis (disclosure-as-such) 4:315
  essence 7:346
  existentialism 3:501
    Bultmann, R. 2:128
    ethics 3:505
    Latin America 3:511, 3:512, 3:513

Geworfenheit (thrownness)
  2:225–6, 2:227, 4:308–9, 4:312
Hartmann, N. 4:242
Hegelianism 4:294
hermeneutics 4:384, 4:387–8,
  4:389, 4:392
hiddenness 4:314–15
historicism 4:444
Hölderlin, J.C.F. 4:482
humanism 4:531–2
Husserl, E. 4:587
infinity 4:777
influence on Levinas, E. 5:579
die Kehre (The Turn) 4:315–16
Lacoue-Labarthe, P. 5:340–1
language 2:373, 2:897
Lyotard, J.-F. 6:9
Nietzsche, F.W. 6:861
nihilism 7:3, 7:4
ontology 7:118, 9:410
Parmenides 7:234
phenomenology 7:341, 7:347–8
  existential 7:337–8
  hermaneutical 7:339
  Husserl, E. 4:574
  religion 7:353
poetry 7:477
postmodern theology 7:583–4,
  7:586
praxeology 7:648
Schelling, F.W.J. von 8:519
science
  philosophy of **4:323–7**
subjectivity
  postmodern critique 9:197–8
technology 9:281–2, 9:283, 9:287
Thoreau, H.D. 9:392
time 9:415–16
vulnerability and finitude 9:670
Heideggerian philosophy of science
  4:323–7
Heidel, A. 2:700
Heidelberger, Michael
  Büchner, L. †2:48–51
  Naturphilosophie †6:737–43
Heidenheimer, A.J. 2:676
Heidingsfelder, G. 1:144
Heidsieck, F. 1:737
Heijenoort, J. van
  computability theory 2:490
  constructivism in mathematics
    2:638
  Gödel's theorems 4:116
  Hempel, C.G. 4:352
  Herbrand's theorem 4:378
  intuitionism 4:852

logic
  early twentieth century 5:736
  second-order 8:603
logicism 5:816
mathematics, foundations of 6:190
paradoxes of set and property
  7:220
set theory 8:715
Zermelo, E. 9:855
Heil, J. 1:280
Heilbron, J.L. 7:397
Heilbroner, R.L. 4:165
Heim, Irene
  anaphora 1:240–2, 1:243
  discourse semantics 3:92–3, 3:98
  dynamic semantics 1:240–2, 1:243
  pragmatics 7:631
Heims, S. 6:812–13
Heimsoeth, H. 2:739, 4:242
Hein, H. 3:596
Heinämaa, S.S. 8:437
Heine, H. 8:351
Heine, Steve
  Dōgen 3:111
  Kumazawa Banzan †5:321–2
Heinekamp, A. 5:378
Heinimann, F. 7:382
Heinzmann, G. 7:482
Heisenberg, Werner **4:327–9**
  uncertainty principle 7:841
Heisig, James W.
  Kyoto School †5:323–30
  logic in Japan 5:716
  Miki Kiyoshi †6:358–9
  Nichiren †6:828–9
  Tanabe Hajime 9:262
Heiss, H. 4:242
Heitsch, E. 9:810
Hejdánek, Ladislav 2:768
Hekhalot (palace) mysticism 5:171–2
Hekman, S. 3:602
Held, D. 2:728, 3:736, 4:199
Held, Virginia 3:605, 6:563, 8:330
hell **4:329–33**
  evil, problem of 3:469
  free-will defences of 4:330–2
  pragmatism 4:332
  problem of 4:329–30
  Vasubandhu 9:585
Hellenistic philosophy **4:335–7**
  see also Epicureanism; Stoicism
  characteristics of 1:263–4
  educational philosophy 3:224–5
  Egyptian influence on 3:250–3
  epistemology 3:372–3
  influence on
    Aristotle 1:431

medical epistemology **4:333–5**
political philosophy 7:506
Stoicism **9:141–60**
Themistius 9:324–5
Heller, Ágnes 4:571
Heller, E. 4:129
Heller, J. 9:870
Heller Wilensky, S.O. 1:351
Hellin, J. 9:196
Hellman, G.
　Gödel's theorems 4:113, 4:116
　Goodman, N. 4:140
　mathematics
　　foundations of 6:190
　reduction, problems of 8:149
　supervenience 9:238
Helm, P.
　Cambridge change 2:276
　duty 3:182
　immutability 4:713–14
　providence 7:801
　religion and morality 8:224
Helmholtz, Hermann von **4:337–40**
　epistemology 4:337–8
　geometry 4:32, 4:33
　intuition 4:338, 4:339
　logical positivism 5:790
　naturalized epistemology 5:483–4
　Naturphilosophie 6:739, 6:741
　science
　　nineteenth century philosophy
　　8:565
　vision 9:633, 9:638
Helmont, Franciscus Mercurius van
　4:340–2
Helms, H.G. 9:141
Heloise 1:8–9
help **4:342–4**
　impartiality 4:715
　responsibility 8:290
Helvétius, Claude-Adrien **4:345–8**
　art
　　sociopolitical analysis 4:347–8
　education (Diderot, D.) 3:66, 4:345
　hedonism 4:345–6
　philosophes 4:345, 4:346, 4:348
　politics
　　culture relationship 4:346–8
　utilitarianism 9:556
Hemacandra 5:55, 5:56
Hemerken, Thomas *see* Thomas à
　Kempis
Hempel, Carl Gustav **4:348–52**
　causation 2:247
　coherentism 5:254, 5:259
　conceptual analysis 2:522
　confirmation theory 2:532, 2:535

evolution 3:482
explanation 3:525
　functional 3:805
　history and social science 3:530
history
　philosophy of 4:456, 4:458
legal concepts 5:495
logical positivism 5:794, 9:531–2
operationalism 7:135
rationality of belief 8:88
reasons and causes 8:127
　scientific behaviourism 8:800–1
scientific theories 9:353
Skinner, B.F. 8:801
social science
　contemporary philosophy of
　8:846
　functionalism 3:817–18
　methodology of 8:868
thought experiments 9:396
underdetermination 9:528, 9:530
verificationism 6:233, 6:236
Vienna Circle 9:611, 9:613
vitalism 9:643
Hempel, J. 3:843
Hendel, Charles 4:561
Henderson, E. 3:561
Henderson, G. 2:343
Henderson, J.B. 2:328
Henderson, W.O. 3:312
Hendry, D. 6:812
Hendry, J.M. 6:210
Hendry, John 2:153–4
Hengehold, Laura
　subject
　　postmodern critique of
　　†9:196–201
Henkin, Leon A.
　see also Henkin semantics
　Gödel's theorems 4:116
　logic
　　early twentieth century 5:736
　　infinitary 4:771
　　provability 7:793–4, 7:796
　　second-order 8:600, 8:603
　non-constructive rules of inference
　　7:30
　predicate calculus 7:665
　quantifiers 7:873
　scientific theories 9:353
Henkin semantics 8:592–5
Henle, R.J. 1:347, 7:438
Hennelly, A.T. 5:616
Henning, L. von 4:297
Henninger, M.G. 1:566, 4:363, 8:312
henotheism 2:1, 4:102

Henrich, Dieter
　Fichte, J.G. 3:653
　German idealism 4:45
　Hegel, G.W.F. 4:279
　Hölderlin, J.C.F. 4:482
　Kant, I. 5:196
　Schelling, F.W.J. von 8:519
Henrichs, A. 7:732
Henrick, D. 4:593
Henricks, R.G. 2:781
Henricus Aristippus
　Greek-Latin translations 9:456
　medieval Platonism 7:436
Henricus Regius **4:352–4**
　Descartes, R. 3:3–4, 3:19
Henry of Ghent **4:354–60**
　Aristotelianism 1:401, 4:357–8
　Duns Scotus, J. 3:154, 3:156,
　　3:162–3
　essence-existence relationship
　　4:356–7
　　Giles of Rome 4:72, 4:73
　　Godfrey of Fontaines 4:120–1
　God
　　existence proofs 3:160, 4:358–9
　　infinity 3:162–3
　　illuminationism 3:154, 4:699–700
　　Liber de causis 5:598
　　Platonism 4:356, 7:437
　　primary object of the intellect
　　　3:159
　　reprobation 8:274
　　theory of mind 4:357–8
　　thing (*res*) 4:355–6
　truth
　　knowledge of 4:357
　universals 3:164
　univocity of being (Duns Scotus, J.)
　　3:157–8
Henry of Harclay **4:360–3**
　eternity of the world 3:429
　indivisibilism 1:864
Henry I, King of England 1:284
Henry, C. 4:518
Henry, D.P. 1:296, 6:319
Henry, J. 3:74, 7:264, 9:713
Henry, M. 6:53
Henry, P. 6:807, 9:662
Henschel, R.L. 8:872
Henschen-Dahlquist, Ann-Mari
　Hägerström, A.A.T. †4:201–4
　Scandinavia 8:491
Henson, C.W. 1:215
Hentschel, K. 4:9
Hepburn, R.W. 6:633, 6:733, 6:735
Heppe, H. 7:395
Heraclides of Pontus **4:363–4**

Heraclitus 1:263, **4:364–9**
  becoming (Derrida, J.) 2:899
  cosmology 4:364, 4:367–8
  Cratylus 2:694
  ethics 4:368
  logos 5:817, 5:818
  Presocratics 7:671
  processes 7:722
  psychē (soul) 7:810
  unity of opposites 4:366–7
Herbart, Johann Friedrich **4:369–71**
  educational philosophy 3:227–8,
    3:229
  Lotze, R.H. 5:841
Herbartism
  Bohemia 2:766
Herberger, Hans 8:646–7, 8:648
Herbert, Edward (Baron Herbert of
    Cherbury) **4:371–5**
  deism 2:854, 2:856
Herbert, R.T. 4:731, 4:732
Herbrand, J. 5:736–7
Herbrand's theorem **4:375–8**, 7:745
herd morality
  Nietzsche, F.W. 6:853, 6:856
Herder, Johann Gottfried **4:378–84**
  culture 2:746–8, 2:750
  genetic method 4:381
  historicism 4:443, 4:446
  history 4:458
  Humanität (humanity) 4:382
  language 4:379–80
  nation and nationalism 6:659,
    6:661
  naturalism 4:378, 4:379, 4:381–2
  social science 8:852, 8:858
heredity *see* genetics
heresy
  Augustine 1:541, 1:543
  David of Dinant 2:799
  Duran, S. 3:172
Herken, R. 2:350–1, 2:490, 9:499
Herman, A.L. 3:843
Herman, Barbara
  ethics
    practical reason and 7:619
    teleological 9:294
    universalism in 9:539
  Kant, I. 5:196
  Kantian ethics 5:203
  moral motivation 6:527
  moral rules 6:513, 6:514
  sexuality 8:727
Herman, Louis 1:272
Hermann of Carinthia 9:455
Hermann the German 5:22–3
Hermann, A. 4:329, 7:397

Hermann, I. 4:572
Hermansen, M. 8:735
Hermarchus 3:350, 3:351
hermeneutic circle 4:384–6
hermeneutics **4:384–9**
  see also exegesis; interpretation;
    legal hermeneutics
  action (Ricouer, P.) 8:320
  African Anglophone philosophy
    1:103–4
  ancient philosophy 4:390
  art (Gadamer, H.-G.) 3:828,
    3:829–30
  biblical 4:385, **4:389–95**, 5:819–20
    Collins, A. 2:417–18
    Frei, H. 3:778–9
    Gadamer, H.G. 4:392–3
    Jewish philosophy
      Buber, M. 2:45
      Immanuel ben Solomon of
        Rome 4:709
      Mendelssohn, M. 3:321
      midrash 6:353–4
      Nahmanides, M. 6:649–50
      Rabbinic theology 9:335
    medieval philosophy 4:390–1
    Reformation 4:391
    revelation 8:299–300
  Buddhism 2:55
  Copernican debate (Galilei, G.)
    3:839–40
  critical realism 2:721
  genealogy 4:1
  ideology 4:684–5
  Islamic philosophy 5:169, 5:170,
    6:237, 6:238–9
  Italy (Vattimo, G.) 5:39
  Latin American culture 6:347
  liberation theology 5:615
  objective spirit
    Dilthey, W. 3:77, 3:81
  phenomenology 7:339–40, 8:756–7
  psychoanalysis (Ricoeur, P.) 8:319
  sociological theories 9:3, 9:4
  structuralism 8:319–20, 9:176
  textual analysis (Ricouer, P.) 8:320
  theosophy 9:363
  understanding
    Gadamer, H.-G. 3:827, 3:828–9
    Heidegger, M. 4:312
    Schleiermacher, F. 8:535–6
Hermes Trismegistus (pseud.) 1:132,
    3:252–3
  see also Hermetism
Hermetism **4:395–7**
  Agrippa von Nettesheim, H.C.
    1:131

  alchemy 1:157, 1:158
  Islamic philosophy 6:617
  knowledge
    Fludd, R. 3:683
    Paracelsus 7:206
    Patrizi, F. 7:263
    Renaissance 8:265
    Steiner, R. 9:133
    theosophy 9:363
Hermodorus 7:429
Hernández de Ragoña, Carmen
    Cecilia 7:350, 7:351–0
Hernandez-Galiano, M. 4:502
heroes 2:436, 2:437
Herold, J.C. 9:118
Herophilus 4:333, 4:335
Herr, Lucien 4:286, 4:299
Herre, Heinrich
  formal languages and systems
    †3:703–6
Herrera, Abraham Cohen de
    4:397–400, 5:89
Herrigel, E. 9:115, 9:116
Hersch, J. 5:83
Herschel, Sir J.
  Bacon, F. 1:632
  chemistry 2:299
  science, nineteenth century 8:567,
    8:568–9, 8:571
Herscher, I. 1:178
Hersh, R. 5:345
Hershbell, J.P. 3:339
Hershey, Alfred 6:458
Hertz, Heinrich Rudolf **4:400–2**
  electrodynamics 3:259
  experiment 3:516
  Maxwell, J.C. 6:210
  mechanics, classical 6:257, 6:259
Hertzberg, A. 9:870
Hervaeus Natalis (Hervé Nédellec)
    3:174, **4:402–4**
Hervé Nédellec (Nédélec) *see*
    Hervaeus Natalis
Herz, Marcus 3:321
Herzberger, R. 3:76
Herzen, Aleksandr Ivanovich
    4:404–10
  Hegelianism
    Russian 4:303–4, 4:306, 4:405,
      4:406–7
  liberalism
    Russian 4:409, 5:607
    Russian philosophy 8:421
Herzl, Theodor 9:868, 9:870
Heschel, Abraham Joshua **4:410–12**
  Hasidism 4:245
  Jewish philosophy 5:90

prophecy 7:771
Rabbinic theology 9:336
ritual 8:339, 8:341
Saadiah Gaon 8:440
Hesiod **4:412–13**
pantheism 7:202
providence 7:797
Theogony 4:412–13
Works and Days 4:413
Hess, D. 7:577
Hess, Moses **4:413–15**
Hegelianism 4:283
Zionism 9:867, 9:870
Hess, R. 5:491, 9:526
Hess, T. 3:409
Hesse, Benedykt 7:484
Hesse, Mary B.
field theory, classical 3:670
Maxwell, J.C. 6:210
models 6:446
natural laws 5:474
scientific theories 8:783, 9:353
sociology of knowledge 9:2
Hesselink, J. 2:34
Hessen, Sergei Iosifovich **4:415–19**
Neo-Kantianism 4:415, 6:797
rule of law socialism 4:415,
4:417–18
Hessenberg, Gerhard 7:217, 7:220
Hessing, J. 4:286–7
hesychasm 6:278, 6:624
'heterodox Aristotelianism' *see*
Averroism
heterogeneity
postmodernism 6:9
heteroglossia
Bakhtin, M.M. 1:640–1
heterology
alterity (Certeau, M. de) 2:268
anti-systematicity (Bataille, G.)
1:659–60
heterophenomenology
Dennett, D.C. 2:883
heterosexuality 8:719, 8:720, 8:726
Hetherington, N.S. 2:680
Hett, W.S. 6:296
Heubeck, A. 4:502
Heuser-Keßler, M.-L. 6:741, 8:519
Heussi, Karl 4:443–4, 4:446
Hewitt, D. 1:680
Hewitt, E. 1:214, 1:215
Hewitt, J.N.B. 6:670
hexagrams *see Yijing*
Heyd, David
population ethics †7:540–3
supererogation 9:235
toleration 9:432

Heygi, J. 2:174, 2:201
Heytesbury, William **4:419–21**
modal logic 5:752–3
sophismata 5:245, 7:181
supposition theory 5:754
Heyting, Arend
see also Heyting's semantics
constructivism in mathematics
2:638
intuitionism 4:848, 4:849–50, 4:852
intuitionistic logic 4:857, 4:862
mathematics
foundations of 6:187, 6:190
Heyting's semantics 3:152
Heyward, Carter 3:622, 3:624
Heze School of Buddhism 2:111–12
Hibbat-Zion movement 9:867–8
Hick, J.
Gandhi, M.K. 3:843
Newman, J.H. 6:823
Hick, John
eschatology 3:415, 3:417
evil, problem of 3:472, 8:244–5
heaven 4:253
hell 4:333
limbo 5:637
prayer 7:653
purgatory 7:838, 7:839
religion, history of philosophy of
8:246
religious pluralism 8:261–2,
8:263–4
Tennant, F.R. 9:302, 9:303
Hicks, E. 2:345
Hicks, J.R. 3:210, 8:68, 8:74
Hicks, N. 3:44
hiddenness
Heidegger, M. 4:307–8, 4:314–15
Hierapolis
Epictetus **3:337–9**
hierarchies
ecological 3:202–3
metaphysical
Renaissance Aristotelianism
1:410–11
recursion theoretic *see* recursion-
theoretic hierarchies
taxonomic
classification problems 9:274–5
Hierocles **4:421–2**
Aristotle commentators 1:435–6
Foundations of Ethics 4:421–2
hieroglyphics 5:428–9
Hieronymus Cardanus *see* Cardano,
Girolamo
hierophanies 3:260, 3:261–2
Hierro, G. 3:628

Higginbotham, James
adverbs †1:46–50
indirect discourse 4:744, 4:745
meaning and truth 6:225
propositional attitude 7:776–9
scope 8:589
Higgins, K.M. 4:45, 6:613, 8:554
higher-order logics **8:591–5**
glossary 5:802
Higton, Michel
Luther, M. †6:1–5
Hijmans, B.L. 1:326, 3:339
hikma
falsafa contrast 5:7–8
Hilbert, David
see also Hilbert space; Hilbert's
programme
arithmetic 1:439, 1:441
Cantor, G. 2:198
computability theory 2:482–3,
2:490
critique by Ramsey, F.P. 8:45
decision problem 2:349
formalism 1:438, 6:185, 6:186–7
geometry 4:30, 4:33, 5:731
Gödel's theorems 4:107, 4:108,
4:116
Herbrand's theorem 4:378
inference 7:30
infinity 4:777
Kronecker, L. 5:311, 5:312–13
logic
early twentieth century 5:732,
5:737
first-order 5:729–30, 5:733–4
higher-order 8:595
infinitary 5:734
second-order 8:595, 8:603
mathematics
constructivism in 2:636, 2:638
foundations of 6:190–1
Neumann, J. von 6:810
paradoxes
set and property 7:215–16,
7:217
perception 7:298
predicate calculus 7:665
proof theory 7:743–4, 7:751
quantifiers 7:873
Zermelo, E. 9:855
Hilbert, David R.
colour
and qualia 2:421, 2:427
colour, theories of †2:428–31
Hilbert space 7:883–5

Hilbert's programme **4:422–9**,
5:847–8
  Gentzen, G.K.E. 4:23–4
  Gödel's theorems 4:113
  proof theory 7:742, 7:744–6
Hild, H. 2:577
Hildegard of Bingen **4:429–31**
  natural philosophy 6:690, 6:694
Hiley, D.R. 4:11
Hilferding, Rudolf 6:143
Hilgard, E. 9:526
Hill, C.S. 4:845–6, 7:173, 7:844, 7:867
Hill, D. 8:564
Hill, E. 9:461
Hill, E., Jr 1:93–4
Hill, E.L. 2:608
Hill, J. 1:782
Hill, K.R. 8:746
Hill, P.J. 5:637
Hill, R. Kevin
  genealogy †4:1–5
Hill, Thomas E., jr
  ethics
    autonomy 1:591
    constructivism in 2:632
    Kantian 5:203
    practical reason 7:619
   forgiveness and mercy 3:701
   Kant, I. 5:196
   paternalism 7:252
   respect for persons †8:283–7
   self-respect 8:637
Hill, W.S. 4:506
Hillel ben Samuel of Verona 4:390,
4:431–3, 5:88
Hillery, G.A. 2:464
Hillgarth, J.N. 5:664
al-Hilli, Hasan b. Yusuf b. al-
Mutahhar 9:505
Hilpinen, R. 2:535, 2:890
Himi Kiyoshi
  Nishi Amane †7:12–13
  Tanabe Hajime †9:261–2
Himmelfarb, G. 9:280
Hīnayāna School of Buddhism *see*
  Sarvāstivāda; Sautrāntika;
  Theravāda; Vaibhāṣika
Hincmar of Rheims 2:222, 2:223
Hindemith, P. 6:613
Hindley, J. 2:433, 5:349
Hindu philosophy **4:433–40**
  see also Advaita Vedānta;
  Brahmanism; Cārvāka;
  Dharmaśāstras; Mīmāṃsā; Neo-
  Hinduism; Nyāya; Śaivism;
  Sāṅkhya; Vaiśeṣika; Veda;
  Vedānta; Yoga

Arya Samaj movement 1:516–17
  asceticism 1:518
  ātman 4:434
  Brahmo Samaj movement 2:5–6
  consciousness 2:583
  cosmology and cosmogony
   2:681–3
  critiques of (Ambedkar, B.R.)
   1:196, 1:197
  duty 3:183–7
  epistemology 3:390–1
  heaven 4:254–5
  Indian and Tibetan 4:737–8
  karma 5:210–11, 5:212–13
   ethics 4:437, 8:24
   liberation 4:434
   modern philosophy 5:215–16
   origins of doctrine 5:211–12
   reincarnation 8:182–5
    evidence for 9:47–8
   self
    theories of 8:606–8
   texts 5:210–11
  knowledge 4:435–6
  language 4:436–7
  law
   interpretation 4:836
  liberation 4:434
  Madhva 6:31–2
  morality 4:437
  mysticism 6:621–2, 8:254
  nationalism 7:522–3
  Ramakrishna Movement **8:39–42**
  reincarnation 8:183–4, 8:185
  renunciation 3:183, 3:184, 3:185–7
  Śaṅkara 8:458–61
  schools of 4:437–9
  self
   theories of 8:605–10
  universals 9:544
Hine, E.M. 2:527
Hine, W.L. 6:331
Hinman, P. 8:144
Hinnebusch, W.A. 3:174
Hinrichs, C. 9:380
Hinshelwood, R.D. 7:822
Hinske, N. 5:351–2
Hinsley, F.H. 9:59
Hintikka, Jaakko
  Carnap, R. 2:215
  confirmation theory 2:532, 2:534,
   2:535
  Descartes, R. 3:18
  Gödel's theorems 4:116
  logic
   epistemic †3:354–9
   modal 6:425

Lorenzen, P. 5:828
  model theory 6:442
  Montague, R.M. 6:485
  probabilism 7:711
  quantifiers †7:870–3
  questions 8:3
  Quine, W.V. 8:14
  semantics
   game-theoretic 8:658
   possible worlds 8:488, 8:492,
    8:668
  Wright, G.H. von 9:669
Hintikka, M.B. 3:359, 3:867–8, 8:857
Hinton, G.E. 2:573–4, 2:577, 4:705,
  9:638
Hintzman, Douglas 7:630, 7:631
Hinz, H. 7:488
Hipparchia of Maronea 2:756
Hippias **4:440–1**
Hipple, W. 1:186
Hippocrates 3:833, 4:441–3, 6:265
Hippocratic medicine **4:441–3**
Hirakawa, Akira 2:58, 4:256
Hiriyanna, M. 3:568, 8:610–11
Hirnheim, Hieronymus 2:765
Hiroko Odagiri 1:90
Hirota, D. 8:748
Hirsch, A. von 2:710, 5:146
Hirsch, E. 5:3
Hirsch, E.D. 1:505, 3:831
Hirsch, H. 5:48
Hirsch, Samuel 5:99
Hirschfeld, J. 1:214, 1:215
Hirschmann, N. 7:80
Hirshliefer, J. 3:487
Hirst, P. 8:885
Hirst, P.H. 3:239
Hisamatsu Sen'ichi 5:292
Hissette, R. 1:598, 6:115, 8:768
historical chain theory 7:752, 7:754–5
historical consciousness 3:82, 5:82
historical determinism 7:454
historical jurisprudence **5:138–41**,
  8:874
historical materialism 3:56
  Chinese Marxism 6:133, 6:134–5,
   6:140
  class consciousness (Lukács, G.)
   5:858
  functional explanation 6:126–7
  Marx, K. 6:126–7
  Marxism 6:141, 8:879
   Engels, F. 6:142
   Gramsci, A. 4:152
   Latin America 6:161–2, 6:163
   Lukács, G. 6:144
   Russian 1:817, 6:357, 7:451

Millar, J. 6:376
structuralism 6:145
historical method 4:408
historical optimism
  providence 7:798–9
historical relativism
  Chinese philosophy
    Legalism 5:531, 5:535–6
historical subject
  postmodernism 9:197, 9:198
historicism **4:443–6**
  see also historical subject
  absolute (Croce, B.) 2:728, 2:730,
    2:731–2
  African Francophone philosophy
    1:112
  art 1:466–8
  critiques of
    Popper, K.R. 4:456, 7:536,
      9:443
  Dilthey, W. 8:853–4
  Enlightenment, German
    (Herder, J.G.) 4:381
  epistemic reliabilism 3:361
  ethical life (Hegel, G.W.F.) 4:275
  genealogy 4:1
  Jewish philosophy 5:86–7, 5:92
  knowledge 4:443–4
  liberation philosophy 5:611, 5:612
  Meinecke, F. 6:281
  metaphysics (Collingwood, R.G.)
    2:411, 2:412–13
  postmodernism 7:589
  revolution 8:302–3
  social science
    methodology of 8:866
  totality 4:445
historiography
  colonialism 7:580
  Posidonius 7:557
  prehistoric Greece
    Thucydides' account of 9:399
  religion 2:128
  Talmudic 9:335
history
  see also historical subject
  aesthetics 1:67
  Axial Period (Jaspers, K.) 5:82
  Chinese philosophy of **4:446–52**
  Confucianism 2:546–7, 2:550–1
  contingency of
    Shestov, L. 8:741, 8:744
    Tolstoi, L.N. 9:437–8
  critical theory 3:731
  cultural-historical types
    (Leont'ev, K.N) 5:569

cycle of
  Indian philosophy 7:522, 7:523
development of (Saint-Simon)
  8:446
dialectic method (Asmus, V.F.)
  1:524–5
end of
  Hegelianism 5:289–90
epistemological understanding
  (Oakeshott, M.J.) 7:71
evolutionary stages of (Teilhard de
  Chardin, P.) 9:289
explanation in **3:525–31**
  causal 3:526, 3:527–8, 3:529
  functional 3:526, 3:527
  holistic 3:525–7
  individual action 3:526–7,
    3:528–9
  non-causal 3:528, 3:529
  structural 3:526, 3:527–8
irrationality of
  Dostoevskii, F.M. 3:117
Jewish
  root experiences 4:496–7
knowledge
  constructivism 9:604
law (Vico, G.) 9:601–2
literary and cultural
  (Schiller, J.C.F.) 8:528
meaning within (Voegelin, E.)
  9:655
mystical language (Certeau, M.
  de) 2:268
as myth
  German Romanticism 8:349
naturalism (Herder, J.G.) 4:381–2
negative
  Adorno, T.W. 3:732
objectification of (Berdiaev, N.A.)
  1:728
objective spirit (Hegel, G.W.F.)
  4:275
patterns of
  Chinese philosophy 4:449–50,
    8:736
  Joachim of Fiore 5:103–4
  Vico, G. 9:599–600, 9:602–4
recurrent (Bachelard, G.) 1:621
religion
  reason conflict 9:604–5
  science relationship 9:461–2
  timescales 8:232
Roman (Montesquieu, C.L.)
  6:491–2
sacred 4:454
  alternatives 4:454–5

science
  religion relationship 9:461–2
spiritual progression of
  (Cousin, V.) 2:691
theory of (Benjamin, W.) 1:718
three ages (Kang Youwei) 4:451
tripartite development of
  (Stirner, M.) 9:140
vital reason relationship (Ortega y
  Gasset, J.) 7:165, 7:166–7
history, philosophy of **4:453–9**
  see also historicism
  'absolute present' (Nishida Kitarō)
    7:14
  al-Afghani 1:94–5
  All-Unity (Solov'ëv, V.S.) 9:28–9
  analytical 4:455–6
  anti-universalism (Herzen, A.I.)
    4:406–8
  Augustine 1:542, 1:556–7
  contextualism 7:505
  dialectic of enlightenment 2:725–7
  eschatology 3:413–16
  evolutionism (Ramakrishna
    Movement) 8:41
  French anti-postmodernism 7:593,
    7:594
  genetic method (Herder, J.G.)
    4:381
  grand theory 4:457–8
  Hegelianism
    Kojève, A. 5:289–90
    political philosophy 7:515–16
  holism 4:482–7
  Ibn Khaldun 4:623, 4:624–5
  individualism 4:482–7
  Judaism
    Abravanel, I. 1:22
    Krochmal, N. 5:310
    Rabbinic theology 9:334
  law of motion (Engels, F.) 3:311
  methodology 4:453, 4:456
  narrative 6:655–6
  origins 4:453–4
  postmodernist/anti-postmodernist
    debate 7:594–5
  progress (Condorcet, M.J.A.N.)
    2:530–1
  Russian Hegelianism 8:419
    Belinskii, V. 4:304
    Kavelin, K. 4:304–5
  Russian Schellingianism 8:521–2
  Russian-Western contrast
    (Chaadaev, P.I.) 2:270, 2:271
  scientific analogy 4:456
  Slavophilism 8:808–9

sobornost (conciliarity)
(Losev, A.F.) 5:830
social sphere (Chaadaev, P.I.)
2:270–1
socialism (Mikhailovskii, N.K.)
6:356–7
sociopolitical (Montesquieu, C.L.)
6:492–3
subjectivism (Lavrov, P.L.) 5:437
Young Hegelians 2:360–1
Hitler, Adolf 4:497
Hitzig, E. 7:825, 7:829
Hjelmslev, J. 9:179–80, 9:181
Hjort, M. 3:280
Hoagland, Sarah Lucia 3:604, 3:605
Hobart, R.E. 3:751
Hobbes, Thomas **4:459–76**
absolutism 1:31
authority 1:584, 1:586
Chillingworth, W. 2:308
conservatism 2:608, 2:610, 2:614
contractarianism 2:657, 2:665
critiques of
Cambridge Platonism 2:184–5
Cumberland, R. 2:752
Hutcheson, F. 4:589–90
duty 3:182
educational philosophy 3:226,
3:229
egoism and altruism 3:248
empiricism
language 5:372–3
enthusiasm 3:332
equality 3:393, 3:395
eternity 3:424, 3:426
ethics 4:459, 4:469–70
first philosophy 4:459, 4:465–8
free will 3:751–2
geometry 4:459, 4:468
gratitude 8:139, 8:140
happiness 4:229
honour 4:504
hope 4:509
human nature 4:522, 4:525
science 4:463–5, 4:474
war 4:470–1, 4:475
humour 4:563
international relations 4:832
justice 5:146
international 5:154
language 5:372–3, 5:378
legitimacy 5:541
Leviathan
interpretation by Schmitt, C.
8:544
language 5:372
politics 4:472–3

power of sovereign 8:227
rational choice theory 8:65
liberalism 5:601, 5:602, 5:603–4,
5:605
materialism 6:171, 6:173
moral sense theories 6:545, 6:547
nominalism 7:20, 7:22
optics 4:468–9
partiinost' 7:238–9, 7:240
physics 4:469
political philosophy
commonwealth 4:459–60,
4:471–3
history of 7:517
realism 4:827–8
and religion 8:229
scientific basis 4:461, 4:474–5
Spinoza, B. de comparison
9:105–6
state of nature 4:470–1
power 7:610, 7:612
prophecy 7:769–70
public interest 7:833, 7:834
rational choice theory 8:64, 8:65,
8:74
religious authority 8:224, 8:227
revelation 7:771
'ship of Theseus' puzzle 7:237
slavery 8:804, 8:806
social contract
interest-based 2:659
political philosophy
history of 7:512–13
social science
history of philosophy of 8:850,
8:858
sovereignty 9:56–7, 9:59
state of nature 4:470–1
substance 9:206, 9:210
thought experiments 9:395
tragedy 9:449
trust 9:467, 9:469
voluntarism 2:184–5
war and peace 9:685, 9:689, 9:690
White, T. 9:713
will 9:724, 9:725
Hobbs, Angela
Antiphon †1:301–3
Callicles †2:176–7
physis and *nomos* debate †7:381–2
Thrasymachus †9:397–8
Hobbs, J. 2:280, 3:98
Hobek, F. 1:595
Hobhouse, L.T. 1:848, 5:599, 5:605
Hocedez, E. 7:323, 8:312
Hodder, I. 1:358

Hodes, Harold
mathematics
foundations of 6:186, 6:190–1
recursion-theoretic hierarchies
†8:141–5
Turing reducibility and Turing
degrees †9:499–502
Hodges, A. 9:495
Hodges, D.C. 6:164
Hodges, J.L. 9:126
Hodges, Wilfrid
mathematics
foundations of 6:191
model theory †6:436–42
Tarski, A. 9:264
Hodgson, G. 9:89
Hodgson, L. 9:461
Hodgson, P.C. 4:301
Hodgson, P.E. 8:199
Hodgson, Shadworth 3:352, 3:354
Hödl, L. 4:359–60
Hoecker-Drysdale, S. 6:117
Hoekema, D. 3:239
Hoenen, M.J.F.M. 1:152, 3:429,
6:111–12
Hoene-Wroński, Józef Maria 7:486
Hoeres, W. 9:196
Hoernlé, R.F.A. 1:848
Hoesterey, I. 1:191
Hofer, W. 6:282
Höffding, Harald 8:487
Höffe, Ottfried 5:196
Hoffman, Frank J.
Gandhi, M.K. †3:841–3
Hoffman, John 9:122
Hoffman, Joshua
omnipotence †7:98–7:103
religion, philosophy history 8:247
Hoffman, P. 9:212
Hoffman, R.L. 7:793
Hoffman, W.M. 2:153
Hoffmann, F. 4:479
Hoffmann, M. 3:401
Hoffmann, P. 8:791
Hofstadter, A. 4:720
Hofstadter, D. 2:329
Hogarth, R.M. 8:88, 8:89
Hogenson, George B.
Jung, C.G. †5:131–5
Hogger, C.J. 2:453, 7:34
Hoggett, B. 3:607, 3:610
Hogrebe, W. 8:514, 8:519
hoguk pulgyo (state-protection)
Buddhism 2:116–17
Hohenheim, Phillippus Aureolus
Theophrastus Bombastus von *see*
Paracelsus

Hohfeld, Wesley Newcomb **4:476–7**
  Austin, J. 1:570
  legal concepts 5:495
  property 7:761
  rights 8:326, 8:330
Höistad, R. 2:758
Holbach, Paul H.D. de 6:171, 6:173
Holcot, Robert **4:477–9**
Holdcroft, David
  Saussure, F. de †8:479–82
  structuralism in linguistics
    †9:177–81
Hölderlin, Johann Christian
  Friedrich **4:479–82**
  German idealism 4:44
  subject-object relation 8:511
Hölderlin-Jahrbruch 4:482
Holdsworth, D. 7:737
Holdsworth, D.G. 7:886
holiness *see* sanctification
holism
  see also confirmation holism
  analytic philosophy 1:227
  belief
    animal language and thought
      1:271
    Davidson, D. 2:804–5, 8:33–4
  Davidson, D. 1:278–9, 2:804–5,
    6:228, 8:33–4
  empiricism
    critique by Quine, W.V. 8:6
  epistemic *see* justification,
    epistemic, coherence theory of
  epistemological
    scientific theories 3:144, 3:145
  functionalism 8:863
  in history and social science
    4:482–8
    explanation 4:485–6
    ontology 4:484–5
  individualism debate 4:482–3,
    4:486–7
  intentional states (Searle, J.) 8:589
  Marxist philosophy of science
    6:148
  meaning (Davidson, D.) 6:228,
    8:33–4
  mental and semantic **4:488–93**
    analytic/synthetic distinction
      4:490–1
    conceptual role semantics 8:655
    Davidson, D. 1:278–9
    motivations for 4:489
    narrow content 4:490–1,
      4:492–3
  methodological 3:486

perception
  Gestalt theory 9:633
reasons
  moral particularism 5:763
social analysis 9:253–4
Holland, G.J. 5:721
Holland, Guy 7:177
Holland, J.H. 1:492
Holland, P. 2:250
Holland, R.F. 6:415
Hollander, S. 8:821
Hollier, D. 1:661
Hollis, Martin
  anthropology
    philosophy of 1:299
  cognitive pluralism 2:397
  epistemic relativism 3:362
  honour 4:504
  public interest 7:834
  rationality and cultural relativism
    8:86
  relativism 8:190
  social relativism 8:838
  social science
    contemporary philosophy of
      8:846–7
  sociology of knowledge 9:2
  welfare 9:705
Holloway, J. 2:720
Holmes, Janet 5:367
Holmes, Oliver Wendell, Jr **4:493–5**,
  5:524
Holmes, R.L. 1:559
Holmes, R.W. 4:23
Holmes, S. 2:618, 2:621, 5:605
Holocaust **4:495–9**
  atheism (Rubenstein, R.L.)
    4:495–6
  Biblical reflection (Buber, M.) 2:45
  faith response (Fackenheim, E.L.)
    3:534, 4:495, 4:496–7
  forgiveness (Wiesenthal, S.)
    8:136–7
  Jewish philosophy
    (Fackenheim, E.L.) 5:90
  process theology (Cohen, A.A.)
    4:495, 4:497–8
  thought/life relationship
    (Fackenheim, E.L.) 3:534–5
  totalitarianism (Blanchot, M.)
    1:783
  war crimes (Arendt, H.) 1:371
Holquist, M. 1:645
Hölscher, L. 9:561
Hölscher, U. 1:259
Holstroem-Hintikka, G. 8:823–4
Holt, N.R. 4:201

Holton, G. 3:258, 6:16, 7:482
Holton, R.J. 9:8
Holy Communion *see* Eucharist
Holyoak, K.J. 1:492
Holz, H. 7:723, 9:719
Holzhey, H. 2:402, 6:792
Homans, G.C. 8:858, 9:7
Homans, P. 5:135
Home, D. 4:329
Home, Henry (Lord Kames)
  4:499–501
  common law 2:444
  Enlightenment, Scottish 3:330
  human nature
    knowledge relationship 4:499
  moral sense theories 4:500
Homer 1:262, **4:501–2**, 7:809–10
homology 2:238, 9:273–5
homomorphism 6:246
  glossary 5:803
homonyms 1:198, 1:199, 5:358–9
homophobia *see* discrimination
homosexuality
  see also gay-lesbian studies
  ascetics (Rozanov, V.V.) 8:383
  condemnation by Kant, I. 8:723
  cultural identity 2:745–6
  evolutionary justification 8:722
  legalization debate 5:463
  lesbian ethics 3:604
  sadomasochism 8:726
  Thomism 8:722
Honderich, Ted
  anomalous monism 1:280
  Ayer, A.J. 1:618
  conservatism 2:614
  crime and punishment 2:710
  desert and merit 3:27
  free will 3:751–2
  justice
    international 5:156
  violence 9:617
Hōnen 8:747
honesty 9:482
Hong, Chang-hwa 9:442
honji- suijaku (true nature-trace
  manifestations) 2:103–4
Honnefelder, L. 3:169, 3:170
Honner, J. 1:822
Honneth, Axel
  Frankfurt School †3:730–7
  Habermas, J. 4:199
  recognition †8:132–4
Honoré, A.M. 3:832, 7:761
Honoré, T. 5:169, 8:347
Honorton, C. 7:227

honour **4:502–4**
  African ethical systems 3:433
  shame cultures 6:568
Hont, I. 3:330, 3:632
Hood, L. 4:15
Hook, Sidney 3:229–30, 6:675, 9:615
Hooke, Robert 6:580, 6:582
Hooker, Brad
  moral expertise †6:509–11
  utilitarianism 9:556
Hooker, C.A.
  Bohr, N. 1:822
  laws, natural †5:470–5
  quantum logic 7:886
  reduction, problems of 8:149
  scientific theories 9:352, 9:353
Hooker, C.W. 6:446
Hooker, J.R. 7:194
Hooker, R.
  Chillingworth, W. 2:308
Hooker, Richard **4:504–7**
Hookham, S.K. 2:80
hooks, bell 3:612, 3:613
Hookway, Christopher
  Peirce, C.S. 3:382, †7:269–84
Hoorman, C.F.A., Jr 5:721
Hoose, Bernard
  charity †2:280–2
  innocence †4:797–8
Hoover, K. 3:220
Hooykaas, R. 8:54
Hopcroft, J.E. 2:475, 3:706
Hope, V.M. 4:593, 6:547
hope **4:507–10**
  faith 3:539
  theological virtue 9:326, 9:327,
    9:329–30
Hopfield networks 2:572
Höpfl, H.M.
  Voegelin, E. †9:654–7
Hopkins, A.J. 1:158
Hopkins, E.W. 3:187, 3:568
Hopkins, G.M. 8:445
Hopkins, J. 6:417
Hopkins, James
  dreaming 3:129
  Freud, Sigmund †3:786–94
  psychoanalysis
    post-Freudian †7:817–24
Hopkins, Jasper
  Anselm of Canterbury †1:283–97
  Nicholas of Cusa †6:832–8
Hopkins, N.H. 4:16
Hopkins, R.D.
  pictorial depiction †2:892–6
Hopkinson, A.W. 5:470
Hopper, D. 9:412

Horace 9:449
Horak, P. 7:253–4
Horak controversy 2:556–7, 2:558,
  2:562–4, 4:220–1, 9:825
Horgan, T. 2:577–8, 5:764, 6:311,
  9:566
Horigan, S. 6:736
horizon
  experience (Husserl, E.) 4:581
Horkheimer, Max **4:510–12**
  Adorno, T.W. 3:732–3
  capitalism 6:97, 6:98
  communicative rationality 2:461
  critical theory 2:722–8
  Frankfurt School 3:730, 3:731,
    3:736
  Marxism
    Western 6:144
  social science
    contemporary philosophy of
      8:846
  theology, political 9:332
  totalitarianism 9:444
Horn, B. 9:638
Horn, L.R. 4:725
Hornblower, S. 9:399
Horne, M.A. 1:716
Horne, T.A. 6:74
Horner, I.B. 7:238
Hornsby, Jennifer
  action †1:36–41
  Prichard, H.A. 7:682
Hornstein, D.T. 8:337
Hornstein, Norbert
  Chomsky, N. †2:335–41
  innateness of language 4:54
Hornung, E. 3:250
Horowitz, M.C. 2:289
Horowitz, T. 9:396
horror vacui
  Strato 9:162
Horsch, P. 5:217
Horstmann, Rolf-Peter
  Bradley, F.H. 1:862
  Hegel, G.W.F. †4:259–80
  Naturphilosophie 6:741
  transcendental arguments 9:454
Horton, John
  obligation
    political 7:80
  toleration †9:429–33
Horton, Robin
  African Francophone philosophy
    1:115
  African traditional religions
    1:117–21

  ethnophilosophy, African 3:448,
    3:449
  MacIntyre, A. 6:24
  rationality and cultural relativism
    8:84, 8:86
Horton, W.M. 4:794, 7:98, 9:301
Horty, J.F.
  common-sense reasoning †2:451–3
Horwich, Paul
  conceptual role semantics 8:656
  conventionalism †2:666–9
  deflationary theories of truth
    9:476, 9:477
  Hempel, C.G. 4:352
  Kuhn, T.S. 5:318
  Tarski's definition of truth 9:269
  thermodynamics 9:369
  time 9:416
  time travel †9:417–19
Horwitz, R. 2:48
Hosiasson, J. 4:352
Hoskin, M. 7:182
Hoskyns, Sir E. 5:820
Hospers, J. 4:191
hospitable theories
  fictional entities 3:666
Hossō school of Buddhism 2:101
Hotman, François 8:344
Houben, J.E.M. 1:766, 5:384, 7:65
Houlgate, L. 3:552
Hountondji, Paulin J.
  African philosophy 1:97
    Anglophone 1:106
    Francophone 1:115
  Amo, A.W. 1:211
  ethnophilosophy, African 1:102,
    1:112–13, 3:448, 3:449
Hourani, A. 1:7–8
Hourani, G.
  Ash'ariyya and Mu'tazila 1:523
  ethics in Islamic philosophy 3:442
  Ibn Hazm 4:621
  Ibn Tufayl 4:659
  al-Juwayni 5:170
  al-Razi, Abu Bakr 8:112
  science in Islamic philosophy 8:564
House, D.K. 8:717
Houston, J. 6:415
Howard, Don
  Duhem, P.M.M. †3:142–7
  Einstein, A. †3:254–8
  Le Roy, É.L.E.J. †5:481–3
  Planck, M.K.E.L. †7:396–8
Howard, R. 3:434–5
Howard, W. 5:349

Howarth, Jane
  phenomenology
    epistemic issues †7:343–8
Howe, A. 3:609, 3:610
Howe, R.B.K. 4:846
Howell, Robert
  fiction, semantics of †3:659–63
  fictional entities 3:667
  Kant, I. 5:196
Howell, W.S. 2:193, 5:721
Howells, Christina
  Sartre, J.-P. †8:473–9
Howells, R. 3:693
Howison, George Holmes 4:668,
  7:317, 7:318
Howson, C. 5:345, 8:783, 9:126
Hoy, D. 3:713, 3:831, 4:200
Hoyningen-Huene, Paul
  incommensurability 4:736
  Kuhn, T.S. †5:315–18
Hraban Maur 2:222, 2:223
Hrushovski, 6:439
Hrušovský, Igor 8:812, 8:813
Hsiao, Kung-ch'üan 5:103, 5:865
hsin (heart and mind) see xin (heart-
  and-mind)
hsin (trustworthiness) see xin
  (trustworthiness)
hsing see xing
Hsu, Cho-yun 2:782
Hsün Tzu see Xunzi
Hu Qiaomu 6:140
Huai-Nan Tzu see Huainanzi
Huainanzi 4:512–14
  knowledge 2:788–9
  ritual 2:324
  syncretic Daoism 2:321–2
Huang Siu-chi 5:852, 6:776, 9:856–7,
  9:863
Huang Tingjian 9:863
Huangbo 5:645, 8:621
Huang-Lao School 4:512–13, 5:449
Huayan (Flower Garland) Buddhism
  2:85, 2:87–8, 2:91
  see also Hwaôm
  Fazang 3:568–9
  'ten ages' 6:593
  Zongmi 9:870, 9:871
Hübner, K. 9:707
Huby, Pamela M.
  prophecy 7:771
  Theophrastus †9:337–40
Huch, R. 8:351
al-Hudhayl, Abu 1:520
Hudson, A. 9:804
Hudson, D. 3:109
Hudson, D.W. 9:387

Hudson, S.D. 8:287
Hudson, Wayne 1:790
Hudson, W.D. 5:764, 6:519, 7:679
Huet, Pierre-Daniel 4:514–18
  anti-Cartesianism 4:515
  scepticism 4:515–17
Huffman, C.A. 1:361, 7:371, 7:861
Hügel, F. von 6:633
Hugh of St Victor 4:518–20
  Augustinianism 1:561
  Bernard of Clairvaux 1:754
  hermeneutics
    biblical 4:391
    mysticism 1:830
    Pseudo-Dionysius 7:808
Hugh of Santalla 9:455
Hughes, C. 8:787
Hughes, G. 9:656
Hughes, G.E. 6:425–6
Hughes, Gerard J.
  prudence †7:802–4
Hughes, John A.
  experiments in social science
    †3:518–20
Hughes, P. 7:220
Hughes, R.I.G. 5:766, 6:828, 7:886,
  7:894
Hughes, R.P. 8:427
Hughes, T.P. 9:283, 9:287
Hugly, P. 4:771
Huguenots 2:375
Hui Shi 5:694, 5:702–3
Huineng
  enlightenment 2:88
  Platform Sutra 7:398–9
  self-cultivation 8:620, 8:621
Huisi 8:619
Huisman, G.C. 1:126
Huiyuan 2:86
Huizinga, J. 9:113, 9:116
Hull, Clark L.
  learning 5:487
  operationalism 7:135
  psychology
    theories of 7:826, 7:829
  scientific behaviourism 1:697
Hull, David L.
  evolution, theory of 3:482
  evolutionary theory and social
    science 3:487
  science
    naturalized philosophy of 6:731
    unity of 9:533
  species 9:81
  taxonomy †9:272–6
Hull, Monte
  mujō †6:591–4

Hulliung, M.
  Helvétius, C.-A. †4:345–8
  Montesquieu, C.L. †6:489–94
Hülser, K. 9:160
Hulsewe, A.F.P. 5:454
human condition
  existentialism 3:494–5
  suffering
    Jainism 5:50
    theology (Pascal, B.) 7:241,
    7:244–5
human dignity
  Camus, A. 2:194–5
human exceptionalism (HE) 1:269–71
human genome project 4:19
human interaction see social
  interaction
human nature 4:520–6, 7:525–6
  see also Dasein; humanity; nature-
    nurture debate
  alienation 1:181
  altruism
    socialist conception of 8:882
  animal distinction
    eighteenth century views
    4:526–7
  anthropodicy (Florenskii, P.A.)
    3:681
  Berlin, I. 1:751
  Bernard of Tours 1:756
  Buddhism 2:89–90, 2:93–4
  capitalist traits
    socialist critique of 8:882
  caring 3:603–4
  Chinese philosophy
    see also xing
    Confucianism (Cheng Hao)
    2:301
    good and evil (Dong Zhongshu)
    3:112
    Legalism 5:531, 5:532–3
    li (Cheng Yi) 2:302
    long life
      spontaneous tendency for
      9:822–3
    qi (Zhu Xi) 9:864
    value neutral (Xunzi) 9:818–19
  civil society
    Ferguson, A. 3:631
    Gassendi, P. 3:855–6
  cognitive/religious typology 9:26
  communal
    alienated labour 6:122
  Confucianism (Cheng Hao) 2:301
  cultural identity 2:744, 2:745
  Cynics 2:753–4, 2:755
  evil 3:463, 3:464, 3:465–6

evolutionary theory
  (Darwin, C.R.) 2:797–8
families 3:550–1
friendship 3:604
good and evil (Dong Zhongshu)
  3:112
goodness of
  Mencius 2:309, 2:313, 2:560,
    2:561, 6:303
  morality 6:561–2
  Rousseau, J.-J. 8:372
happiness (Johnson, S.) 5:125
harmonious development
  (Comenius, J.A.) 2:438, 2:439
Hierocles 4:422
historical development (Vico, G.)
  9:604
historical product
  (Plekhanov, G.V.) 7:454
human genome project 4:19
humour (Bergson, H.-L.) 1:735
ideal Realism (Coleridge, S.T.)
  2:403
ideal state
  Aristotle 1:430
imagination to reason transition
  (Vico, G.) 9:603
incompleteness (Lacoue-
  Labarthe, P.) 5:341
individuality 5:463, 9:822–3
innocence (Rousseau, J-J.) 4:798
interdependence (Beauvoir, S. de)
  1:685
'I-Thou' mode (Buber, M.) 2:42,
  2:43–5
knowledge relationship (Home, H.)
  4:499
Latin American Marxism
  (Mariátegui, J.C.) 6:162–3
levels of (Steiner, R.) 9:133–4
li (Cheng Yi) 2:302
liberal view 5:601–2
linguistic structuralism 9:186
long life
  spontaneous tendency for
    (Yangzhu) 9:822–3
love 5:842–3, 5:844
Mandeville, B. 6:71–2
Marcus Aurelius 6:94, 6:95
moral sense
  Hume, D. 4:544
  Hutcheson, F. 4:588, 4:589–91
moralistes 6:555–7
morality
  development 6:506
  Nietzsche, F.W. 6:845, 6:853
  sentiments 6:548

thought (Mead, G.H.) 7:640,
  7:642–3
Williams, B. 6:574
mother-child paradigm 3:604
natural order (Condillac, É.B. de)
  2:526
naturalist versus anti-naturalist
  view 4:521
neo-Confucianism 6:767
'new man'
  Russian philosophy 8:420
Niebuhr, R. 6:842–3
nomoi (laws and customs)
  (Antiphon) 1:302–3
passions
  Hume, D. 4:543
  Thomasius, C. 9:377
perfectionism 4:521–2, 7:299–300
pessimistic view of (Thucydides)
  9:398–9
plasticity (Herder, J.G.) 4:382
political philosophy 4:524–5,
  7:501, 7:526
political philosophy (Spinoza, B.
  de) 9:105
progress (Condorcet, M.J.A.N.)
  2:530–1
psychological egoism 3:246, 3:247
qi (Zhu Xi) 9:864
rationality
  Hume, D. 4:543
  Musonius Rufus 6:615–16
  Philo of Alexandria 7:360
reason/emotion conflict
  Spinoza, B. de 9:102–3
reciprocal freedom
  existentialism 3:504
religion
  belief (Hume, D.) 4:558, 4:560
  Islamic fundamentalism 5:10
  sentiments (Hume, D.) 4:558,
    4:560
  universal (Calvin, J.) 2:178
Renaissance philosophy 7:389,
  8:267
respect for persons (Kant, I.)
  8:283, 8:285
science
  eighteenth century **4:526–7**
  Hobbes, T. 4:463–5, 4:474
science of man
  Hume, D. 4:526
self-cultivation
  Chinese philosophy
    cheng 2:300
self-discovery
  antipaternalism 7:251

self-interest
  Chinese law 5:443, 5:449–50
selfish sociability (Diderot, D.)
  3:65–8
self-preservation (Spinoza, B. de)
  9:91–2
self-realization 8:632–4
self-referential versus other-
  referential 4:523–4
sexuality (Aquinas, T.) 8:722
social theory
  Enlightenment, Scottish
    3:327–9
  morality
    Voltaire 9:659
    Smith, A. 8:819–20
  soul (Isaac of Stella) 5:4
  state of nature 2:659
  values
    Mozi 6:453
  suffering 9:213–14
  system of parts (Butler, J.) 2:154–7
  teleological ethics 9:294
  total unity (Frank, S.L.) 3:728
  unfinalizability (Bakhtin, M.M.)
    1:639
  universal
    Chinese Marxist rejection of
      6:138–9
  value neutral (Xunzi) 9:818–19
  virtue (Aristotle) 9:627
  vita activa (Arendt, H.) 1:370–1
  war (Hobbes, T.) 4:470–1, 4:475
  Wittgensteinian ethics 9:771
human relationships
  East Asian Philosophy 3:194
  friendship (Ibn Miskawayh) 4:631
  harmonious
    Chinese philosophy 2:318
  self-cultivation
    Chinese philosophy 8:615
  social (Hierocles) 4:422
human rights see rights
humaneness, Chinese philosophy see
  ren
humanism **4:528–32**
  see also anti-humanism
  anti-postmodernist 7:595
  Byzantine 2:161
  Chinese Marxism 6:134, 6:138–40
  Christian 4:529
  Confucian
    Daxue 2:807–9
  critical (Todorov, T.) 9:426
  Dai Zhen 2:770
  Enlightenment 4:528, 4:529–30
  existentialism 3:500

Hebrew
  Zionism 9:869
Heideggerian 4:531–2
history (Vico, G.) 5:35–6
I and Thou unity
  (Feuerbach, L.A.) 3:636
Islamic philosophy (Ibn
  Miskawayh) 4:632
Marxist 4:531
Masaryk, T.G. 6:165
modern 4:530–2
neo-Confucianism
  self-cultivation 8:613, 8:624–5
pragmatic 4:528, 4:530–1
radical
  Russian philosophy 8:420–1
religion of (Ruge, A.) 8:386–7
Renaissance **4:533–41**
  see also Platonism, Renaissance
  Aristotelian texts 1:405
  Christian 3:396, 4:540
  classical texts
    rediscovery of 8:265
  empirical approach (Vives, J.L.)
    9:648
  Florentine Platonism 7:444–5
  George of Trebizond 4:34–6
  Jewish philosophy 1:161–2,
    6:333
  language 4:536–7, 5:411, 5:415
  legal hermeneutics 5:507
  logic 5:767, 5:768, 5:769–71
  medieval philosophy 6:270
  Niethammer, F.J. 4:533
  Petrarca, F. 4:535, 7:325–8
  philology 4:537–9
  Platonism 7:440–2, 7:445–6
  Rabelais, F. 8:15–17
  Ramus, P. 8:51–4
  rhetoric 4:533–5
  scepticism 8:498, 8:500
sixteenth century
  Portugal
    influence on Brazil,
      philosophy in 2:8
  utopianism debate
    Signposts movement 8:770
humanism ethics (Cicero, M.T.) 2:358
Humanismus 4:529
humanista 4:529
humanity
  distinctiveness of
    nature and convention 6:735–6
  Divine expression
    Tagore, R. 9:258
  end of history (Kojève, A.)
    5:289–90

evolution
  Prodicus 7:732
  Teilhard de Chardin, P. 9:288
existence (Hesiod) 4:413
human-animal distinction
  Schopenhauer, A. 8:549
Humanität 4:382
league of (Krause, K.) 5:299
mutability of (Epicharmus) 3:337
principle of
  cultural interpretation 8:83
religious/non-religious distinction
  3:261
Humber, J. 8:337
Humberstone, I.
  deontic logic 2:890
Humberstone, Lloyd
  many-valued logics †6:81–4
Humbert, H. 3:818
Humboldt, Wilhelm von **4:541–3**
Hume, David **4:543–62**
  see also Humean projection;
  Hume's law
  abstract ideas 7:22
  aesthetic concepts 1:55–6, 1:58
  agnosticism 1:122, 1:123
  anti-rationalism 4:556
  art 1:463, 1:477–8, 1:480, 1:510–11
  associationism
    critique by Kemp Smith, N.
      5:230–29
  Bayle, P. 1:677
  beauty 1:682, 1:684
  belief 1:706
  bundle theory of mind 4:548–9,
    6:231, 6:382, 6:383, 6:385
  Butler, J. 2:160
  Campbell, G. 2:192, 2:193
  causal inference 4:546–8, 4:547–8
  causation 2:244, 2:245–6, 2:250
    Brown, T. 2:27
    Ducasse, C.J. 3:139, 3:142
    Glanvill, J. comparison 4:81
    inference 4:544, 4:546–8
  commercial society 7:513–14
  concepts 2:516
  contractarianism 2:661, 2:665
  critiques of
    Aberdeen Philosophical Society
      1:15
    Beattie, J. 1:679
    Kemp Smith, N. 5:230–29
    Lewis, C.S. 5:589–90
    Reid, T. 8:172
  desire 3:33
  doubt 3:123–4, 3:125
  duty 3:182

egoism and altruism 3:248
empiricism
  learning 5:483
Enlightenment, Scottish 3:330
*An Enquiry Concerning Human
  Understanding* 4:547–8, 4:551,
  4:558
enthusiasm 3:331, 3:332
equality 3:395
ethics 1:319–20, 4:551–6
  common-sense 2:449, 2:450
fact/value distinction 3:538
Foucher, S. 3:717
free will 3:752
God
  teleological argument for the
    existence of 8:241
Hamann, J.G. 4:214
honour 4:504
Hutcheson, F. 4:593
imagination 4:707, 4:708
induction 4:751
infinity 4:774
influence on Smith, A. 8:816–17
innate ideas 8:77
internalism
  moral motivation 6:522–3,
    6:527
introspection 4:838, 4:842
is-ought distinction 3:474–5
  applied ethics 1:319–20
  logic of ethical discourse
    5:759–61, 5:764
  moral knowledge 6:517, 6:518,
    6:520
justice 5:143, 5:146
knowledge 4:545–9
law as convention 5:466
liberalism 5:605
libertarianism 5:618
love 5:845
Malebranche, N. 6:65
meaning and verification 6:230–1
memory 6:299, 6:302, 6:572, 6:575
merit 3:26, 3:27
miracles 6:415, 6:710
  critique by Lewis, C.S. 5:589–90
  prophecy 7:770, 7:771
  testimony 8:245
monotheism 6:483
morality 4:544
  obligations
    sympathy 6:546–7
  scepticism 6:545
  sentiments 6:550, 6:566, 6:570
  standing 6:552, 6:554
natural law critique 6:686, 6:690

natural theology 6:712
naturalized epistemology 6:721–2,
  6:727
naturalized philosophy of science
  6:728
obligation
  political 7:80
'Of Tragedy' 9:449–50
Oswald, J. 7:169
Paley, W. 7:188
passions 3:286, 3:287–8, 3:289,
  4:543, 4:549–51
perception
  Reid, T. critique 8:172
personal identity 6:572, 6:575,
  7:314
persons 7:320, 7:321
physical bodies 4:548
pleasure 7:451
political philosophy 4:556–8,
  7:513–14
practical reason 7:615, 7:619,
  8:101, 8:102
prayer 7:653
prescriptivism 7:668, 7:670
projectivism 7:740, 9:580
promising 7:741, 7:742
property 7:758–9
rational choice theory 8:74
reason 4:543, 8:91
relations
  Deleuze, G. 2:857
religion
  critique 4:543, 4:548, 4:558–60
  philosophy history 8:246
religious sentiments 4:558, 4:560
rhetoric 8:308, 8:309
right and good 8:324, 8:325
scepticism 3:378, 3:382
  enumerative induction 6:360
  Maimon, S. 6:35–6
science of man 4:526, 4:527
sexuality 8:727
social philosophy 4:558
  moral agents 6:502–3
subjectivism 7:75
substance 9:207, 9:210
suicide 9:224, 9:226, 9:229
sympathy
  moral motivation 6:561, 6:563
taste, artistic 1:512
testimony 8:829, 8:832, 9:311–12,
  9:314
tragedy 3:278, 9:451
A Treatise of Human Nature
  anti-rationalism 4:556
  causal inference 4:546–8

human nature 4:543
ideas 6:230, 6:236
mind 4:548–9
passions 4:550
physical bodies 4:548
political philosophy 4:556–7
will 4:551
underdetermination 9:528
utilitarianism 9:556
virtues and vices 9:631
will 4:551, 9:724, 9:725
Wollaston, W. 9:788
Hume, R.E. 8:610–11
Humean projection
objective value
  Grice, H.P. 4:175–6
Hume's law
  see also is-ought distinction
  logic of ethical discourse 5:759–61
Hume's principle
  Frege, G. 3:774, 3:775–6
humility
  Judaism 1:650, 4:635
humour **4:562–6**
  see also comedy
  analysis 4:564–5
  Bergson, H.-L. 1:735
  incongruity 4:562, 4:563, 4:564–6
  objectivity 4:563
  perception 4:562, 4:563
  physiological explanations 4:564
  release theory 4:564
  relief theory 4:564
  superiority theory 4:563–4
Humphrey, G. 7:829
Humphreys, Paul
  explanation 3:525
  probablitiy
    interpretations of †7:701–5
Humphreys, W.C. 4:225
Hundert, E.J. 6:74
Hundred Schools 2:315, 2:322–3
Hungary **4:567–73**
  Budapest School 4:570
  Communism 4:570–1
  institutional philosophy 4:569
  Lakatos, I. **5:342–5**
  Lukács, G. **5:856–9**
  Neumann, J. von **6:809–13**
  Polanyi, M. **7:489–92**
  'reconciliation' school 4:569
Hunger, H. 2:165
hunger relief
  agricultural ethics 1:126, 1:127
Hungerland, Isabel 1:57, 1:58–9,
  5:378
Hunsinger, G. 1:655

Hunt, Alan
  Critical Legal Studies 2:720
  Dworkin, R. 3:189
  legal positivism 5:520
  social theory and law 8:878
Hunt, B.J. 6:210
Hunt, Geoffrey
  Lambriola, A. †5:335–6
  nursing ethics †7:56–7
Hunt, R.W. 6:752
Hunter, M. 1:856–7
Hunter, W.B. 2:744
Hunting, C. 8:806
Huntington, E.V. 1:846, 4:116–17,
  5:733
Huntley, M. 4:720
Hurka, Thomas
  perfectionism †7:299–302
Hurley, S. 1:611
Hursthouse, Rosalind
  applied ethics 1:324
  moral psychology 6:533
  reproduction ethics †8:276–80
Hurvitz, L. 2:92, 9:861
Hus, Jan 2:763–4, **4:573–4**
Husbands, P. 1:492
Husik, I. 1:154, 1:651, 4:620, 5:208
Húska, Martin 2:764–5
Husserl, Edmund **4:574–88**
  a priori 1:5
  being 1:702
    intentionality 1:701–2
  consciousness 2:593, 2:595
  critiques of
    Sartre, J.-P. 8:474–5
  Dilthey, W. 3:83
  directedness 4:577, 4:578
  ego
    critique by Sartre, J.-P. 8:474–5
  existence 4:582
  Heidegger, M. 4:308–9, 4:323
  idealism 4:668
  influence on Latin American
    phenomenology 7:348–9,
    7:350–1
  influence on Shpet, G.G. 8:754–8
  intentionality (Reinach, A.) 8:181,
    8:182
  intuition (*Anschauung*) 4:579,
    7:166
  memory 6:297, 6:299
  Merleau-Ponty, M. 6:321–2,
    6:324–5
  noema 4:574–5, 4:577–8
  noeme 4:817
  paradoxes of set and property
    7:217

Patočka, J. 7:252–3
phenomenology 7:341–2
    constitutive 7:336–7
    Derrida, J. 2:897
    eidetic method 7:335
    Heidegger, M. 4:324
    lifeworld 4:582–4
    method 7:343–4, 7:348
    reductions 4:580
    religion 7:353
    transcendental 7:336, 7:346
    transcendental idealism 4:577
predication 7:666
presence/absence 7:598
psychology
    theories of 7:827–8, 7:829
reference 8:164
time 9:415, 9:416
Twardowski, K. 9:508
Yogācāra Buddhism comparison
    2:69
Hussey, E. 4:369, 7:234, 7:672
Husson, L. 1:737
Hutcheon, L. 7:590
Hutcheson, Francis **4:588–94**
    beauty 1:682, 1:684
    Carmichael, G. 2:207
    egoism and altruism 3:248
    Enlightenment, Scottish 3:330
    human nature, eighteenth-century
        science of 4:526, 4:527
    influence on Witherspoon, J.
        9:755–6
    moral sense 4:588, 4:589–91,
        6:546, 6:547
        critique by Price, R. 7:676,
            7:679
    politics 4:592
    utilitarianism 9:556
Hutcheson, J.C. 5:524
Hutchings, S. 8:385
Hutchins, E. 2:397
Hutchison, Terence 3:220, 8:872
Hutin, S. 3:684
Hutton, C. 9:511
Hutton, Sarah
    Cockburn, C. †2:386–7

Conway, A. †2:669–71
Cudworth, R. †2:739–44
Masham, D. †6:166–8
More, H. 6:582–3
Norris, J. †7:41–3
Huusman, Roeloff *see* Agricola,
    Rudolph
Huxley, Sir Julian 8:18, 8:20
Huxley, L. 4:595
Huxley, Thomas Henry **4:594–6**
    agnosticism 1:121, 1:122, 1:123
    consciousness 2:595
    epiphenomenalism 3:354
    evolution and ethics 3:475
    Hume, D. 4:561
    science, nineteenth century
        philosophy of 8:568
Huygens, Christian 7:136, 8:559
Hva-shang Mahāyāna 9:405–6
hwajaeng (harmonization) 9:793
Hwaôm (Flower Garland) Buddhism
    2:109–10, 9:793
hybridization
    cultural 3:447, 7:579, 7:581
Hyland, Drew A.
    sport †9:112–16
    sport ethics †9:110–12
Hyland, J.M.E. 5:640
hyle 4:574–5, 4:578–9
hylomorphism
    Aristotelian (William of Ockham)
        9:736
    Jewish philosophy (Ibn Gabirol, S.)
        4:618–19
    rejection of (Campanella, T.)
        2:186, 2:187–8
    universal
        angelic intelligences 5:247–8
        Bonaventure 1:832
Hylton, P. 1:228, 4:170, 8:403
Hyman, A. 1:154
Hymes, D. 8:473
Hymes, R. 5:852
Hypatia **4:596–7**
hyperarithmetical hierarchy 8:144
hyperelementary set 4:754

hyperreality
    postmodern culture
        (Baudrillard, J.) 1:662–3
hypnosis 6:298
hypostases
    see also Intellect; the One; Soul
    hierarchy of
        Plotinus 7:457–8
    Plotinus 7:457–9, 7:460
    ultimate causes
        Liber de causis 5:596
hypostasis
    Enlightenment, German 4:213–15
hypostatic union
    Alexander of Hales 1:177
hypotheses
    evaluation
        inductive inference
            archaeology 1:356
    formation
        Schlick, F.A.M. 8:541
    logic of discovery
        Hanson, N.R. 4:225
    pragmatism 7:274–5
    scientific
        appraisal of
            underdetermination
                9:527–30
        falsificationism (Popper, K.R.)
            7:533, 7:534
        Poincaré, J.H. 7:479
        testing 2:865
            confirmation theory 2:532–6
    scientific inductivism
        Stewart, D. critique 9:138–9
hypothetico-deductivism
    inductive inference 4:756–7
    scientific method
        demarcation problem 2:864
Hyppolite, Jean 4:293, 4:299
Hyslop, A.
    other minds †7:170–3
hysteria 3:787, 3:788
Hyujông *see* Sôsan Hyujông
Hyun, Sang-yun 9:827

I

I li (Ceremony and Rites) *see Yili*
i (principle)
　see also li; ri
　ki relationship 2:558–64
Iakovenko, Boris 6:796
Iakubinskii, L. 8:410, 8:413
Iamblichus **4:598–9**
　Aristotle commentators 1:435–6
　Neoplatonism
　　founding of 6:798–9
　Pythagoras 7:856
　Speusippus 9:90
Iaroshevskii, M. 9:675
Ibn 'Adi, Yahya **4:599–601**
　al-Farabi 3:557
　logic 5:707, 5:708, 5:712
　translations by 4:156, 4:157
Ibn Anas, Malik 5:27
Ibn al-'Arabi, Muhyi al-Din **4:601–5**
　epistemology 4:601–2
　Hermetism 6:617
　Ibn Massara 4:629
　imagination 4:603–4, 6:598
　Mulla Sadra 6:598
　mystical philosophy 4:603–4, 6:619
　ontology 4:603
　theology 4:602–3
　wahdat al-wujud (unity of being)
　　6:806, 8:733
Ibn ar-Rawandi **4:636–8**
Ibn Bajja, Abu Bakr Muhammad ibn
　Yahya ibn as-Say'igh **4:605–8**
　Aristotelianism 1:384
　Ibn Tufayl 4:657
　mystical philosophy 6:618
　political philosophy 7:519
Ibn al-Bitriq, Yahya 4:156
Ibn Caspi, Joseph 1:600
Ibn Crescas, Hasdai *see* Crescas,
　Hasdai
Ibn Daud, Abraham (Avendauth/
　Avendaugh) **4:608–11**
　Jewish philosophy 5:88
　translations from Arabic by 5:22
Ibn Ezra, Abraham **4:611–13**
　Ibn Shem Tov, Shem Tov 8:737–8
　Jewish philosophy 5:87–8
　Karaism 5:208

Ibn Ezra, Moses ben Jacob **4:613–15**,
　5:87
Ibn Falaquera, Shem Tov **4:615–17**,
　5:88
Ibn Gabirol, Solomon **4:617–20**
　Latin translations of 5:22
　voluntarism 5:87, 5:88, 9:665
Ibn al-Haytham 8:563
Ibn Hayyan, Jabir 6:617
Ibn Hazm, Abu Muhammad 'Ali
　4:620–1
Ibn Ishaq, Hunayn 4:156
Ibn al-Jawzi 4:638
Ibn Kammuna **4:621–3**, 5:88
Ibn Khaldun, 'Abd al-Rahman
　2:676–7, **4:623–7**
Ibn al-Khammar 4:157, 4:600
Ibn Luqa, Qusta 4:157
Ibn Maimon, Musa *see* Maimonides,
　Moses
Ibn Massara, Muhammad ibn 'Abd
　Allah **4:627–30**
Ibn Miskawayh, Ahmad ibn
　Muhammad **4:630–3**
　ethics 3:440–1, 3:442, 4:157
　Platonism 7:430
Ibn al-Nadim 1:383, 1:385
Ibn Na'imah al-Himsi 4:156–7
Ibn Paquda, Bahya **4:633–6**
　Jewish philosophy 5:88
　Sufism
　　Kabbalah 5:174
Ibn Qurra, Thabit 1:436, 4:157
Ibn Rushd, Abu'l Walid Muhammad
　4:638–46
　see also Averroism
　acquired intellect 1:150–1
　aesthetics 1:79
　Aristotelianism 1:384, 1:385–6,
　　1:407, 6:869
　Aristotle
　　commentaries on 4:158, 4:639
　　Categories 5:709
　　condemnations of 1:400–1
　　influence on medieval
　　　philosophy 6:272
　　John of Jandun 5:106–8
　　Latin versions of 1:399–400,
　　　5:22–4

　rehabilitation of 1:402
　causality and necessity 2:244
　Delmedigo, E. 2:861, 2:862
　epistemology 3:384, 3:387
　eternity of the world 7:322
　existence/essence relationship
　　4:643–4
　al-Ghazali 4:67, 4:639–41
　God's knowledge of the world
　　4:640–1
　Hillel ben Samuel of Verona 4:433
　Ibn al-'Arabi 4:602
　Ibn Bajja 4:608
　imitation 1:78
　intelligible species
　　Renaissance Aristotelianism
　　　1:408–9
　Latin scholasticism 1:595
　logic 5:712
　meaning 6:237–8, 6:239
　morality 3:440, 4:641–2
　Neoplatonism 6:806, 6:807
　philosophy/theology relationship
　　4:642, 4:643
　political philosophy 7:519–20
　religion
　　use of reason 5:14
　Siger of Brabant 8:764, 8:765
　soul 9:43
　　union with intellect 1:147–8
　Tahafut al-tahafut (Incoherence of
　　the Incoherence) 4:639
　translations of 5:22–4, 9:456
　universal soul 4:432
Ibn Sab'in, Muhammad Ibn 'Abd al-
　Haqq **4:646–7**, 5:14, 6:618
Ibn Safwan, Jahm 5:26
Ibn Shem Tov, Isaac 8:738
Ibn Shem Tov, Joseph 8:738, 8:739,
　8:740
Ibn Shem Tov, Shem Tov 8:737–8,
　8:739
Ibn Shem Tov, Shem Tov ben Joseph
　8:738, 8:740
Ibn al-Sid 6:618
Ibn Sina, Abu 'Ali al-Husayn
　4:647–54
　aesthetics 1:77, 1:79

181

Aristotelianism 1:383, 1:384,
  1:386, 1:397, 1:407
  Albert the Great 1:148
beauty 1:76–7
being 2:242, 3:160
common nature 3:154
emanation 8:113
epistemology 3:384, 3:385, 3:386,
  3:387
evil, problem of 4:652
existence
  accidentality 6:595
  essence relationship 4:643–4
al-Farabi 3:557
God
  existence arguments 4:650–1
happiness 3:387
Ibn Kammuna 5:88
Illuminationist philosophy 4:701
imagination 1:77–9, 6:598
immutability 4:713
Kitab al-shifa (Book of Healing)
  4:648
  God
    existence arguments 4:650
  logic 5:706–7, 5:708
  translations of 4:653, 5:22
logic 5:706–7, 5:708, 5:712
love and beauty 1:76–7
meaning 6:237
medieval philosophy 6:272
moral philosophy 3:440
necessary being 6:743, 6:744, 6:747
Neoplatonism 6:805
oriental philosophy 5:7
poetics 1:77, 1:78–9
prophecy 7:768, 7:771
al-Razi, Fakhr al-Din 8:115
resurrection 4:65
science 4:622, 8:562–3
Siger of Brabant 8:765
soul 4:651–2, 9:43–4
al-Suhrawardi 8:220
translations of 4:653, 5:22
al-Tusi 9:505, 9:507
Ibn Taymiyya, Taqi al-Din 1:385,
  1:386, 4:655–6
Ibn Tibbon, Moses 5:23
Ibn Tufayl, Abu Bakr Muhammad
  4:657–9
  epistemology 3:387, 4:657–8
  mystical philosophy 6:618
  political philosophy 7:519, 7:520
  science 8:562, 8:564
Ibn Turkah Isfahani 6:618
Ibn Tzaddik, Joseph ben Jacob
  4:659–62, 5:88

Ibn Zur'ah 4:157
Ibsen, Henrik 8:632, 9:451
Icaza, Jorge 5:655, 5:656
Iceland 8:491
I-Ching see Yijing
Iconoclasts
  John of Damascus 5:105–6
icons 7:278–9, 7:585–6
id 3:791–2, 9:523
  see also ego; super-ego
ideal
  Dionysian
    Nietzsche, F.W.W. 6:855–6
ideal elements
  method of
    Hilbert's formalism 4:424–6
ideal formula
  Gioberti, V. 4:79
ideal language philosophy 7:620–1
'Ideal Motion'
  Gurney, E. 4:188, 4:189
Ideal Observer theory 8:220
Ideal Person
  Iqbal, M. 4:865
ideal Realism
  Coleridge, S.T. 2:403
ideal realism
  Lossky, N.O. 5:833
idealism 4:662–9
  see also absolute idealism;
    actualism; German idealism;
    Hegelian idealism; immaterialism;
    legal idealism; personalism
  the Absolute 1:28
  absolute liberty 1:646, 1:647
  art and morality 1:455
  Australia 1:576
  awareness
    Yogācāra Buddhism 1:606–7
  Berkeley, G. 1:737, 1:740–5, 2:625,
    2:629
  Burthogge, R. 2:144, 2:145–6
  coherence theory of truth 9:470
  common-sense philosophy
    conciliation 9:136
  Confucianism 5:322
  critical (Cohen, H.) 2:398,
    2:399–400
  critiques of
    Ajdukiewicz, K. 1:136–7
    Jacobi, F.H. 5:46
    Kant, I. 5:187
    Lonergan, B.J.F. 5:824
    Lotze, R.H. 5:839
    Marx, K. 6:123, 8:853
    Moore, G.E. 6:495, 6:496
  dialectical materialism 3:54

Edwards, J. 3:241
epistemological 2:67
  Yogācāra Buddhism 2:69
essence of God 7:42
ethical
  Moore, G.E. critique 6:495
  Gramsci, A. 4:152
humanistic
  Signposts movement 8:769
Johnson, S. 5:124
McTaggart, J.M.E. 6:24–7
materialism contrast 2:66–7, 7:451,
  7:454
Mazzini, G. 5:37
metaphysics 6:339, 8:769
neo-Hegelianism
  Croce, B. 5:38
  Gentile, G. 5:38
objective
  Peirce, C.S. 7:270, 7:280
partiinost' 7:239
  Lenin, V.I. 5:565
personal 4:667–8
pluralistic
  Neo-Leibnizianism 5:834
political philosophy
  history of 7:504, 7:515–16
Rashdall, H. 8:60
as rationalized rage (Adorno, T.W.)
  1:43–4
Russian religious-philosophical
  Renaissance 8:423, 8:426–7
Śaṅkara 7:605
scepticism 1:744, 1:747–8
scientific 9:707
social relativism 8:837–8
social science/epistemology
  distinction 8:586
theosophy 9:364
transcendental 4:664–5, 9:454
  Fichte, J.G. 3:642, 3:646–7
  Husserl, E. 4:577
  Kant, I.
    autonomy 5:196
    certainty 5:182
    free will 5:192
    space and time 5:184–5
  Russian positivism 7:564
  Schelling, F.W.J. von 8:509,
    8:511
  Schopenhauer, A. 8:548–9,
    8:550
  self 2:67
  Strawson, P.F. 9:172
universal consciousness 8:378–9
Yogācāra Buddhism contrast with
  2:66–7

ideality
    social process
        Il'enkov, E.V. 4:688–92,
        4:689–90
idealizations 4:669–72
    economics 3:213
    models
        classical mechanics 6:255
        natural laws 5:471
    scientific
        fictionalism 3:668
        thermodynamics 9:367, 9:368
    thought experiments 9:394–5
ideals 4:672–5
    morality conflict 4:674
    substantive/deliberative distinction
        4:672–4
ideas
    see also concepts
    Abelard, P. 1:12
    abstract (Hume, D.) 4:546
    adequate (Spinoza, B. de)
        9:99–9:100
    archetypes 5:124, 5:125
    Aristotelianism 1:390
    association
        Alison, A. 1:186
        human nature 4:526
        Hume, D. 4:543–4
        Tucker, A. 9:491
    Berkeley, G. 1:740, 1:742–4, 1:743,
        1:745, 3:377, 4:663
    Cartesian
        Foucher, S. critique 3:715–16
    classification (Locke, J.) 5:671–3
    esse est percipi (to be is to be
        perceived) principle 1:740, 1:743
    experience (Locke, J.) 5:665,
        5:669–71
    geometrical (More, H.) 6:578
    God
        source of (Berkeley, G.) 1:737,
            1:740, 1:741, 1:743–4
    Hume, D. 4:543–4, 4:546, 4:556,
        6:230, 6:236
    impressions (Hume, D.) 4:546,
        4:556
    innateness of 8:76–7, 8:362
        Buffier, C. 2:119
        Leibniz, G.W. 5:551–2
        Locke, J. 5:668
        More, H. 6:578
        Rosmini-Serbati, A. 8:362
    justification
        intellectual responsibility
            8:288–9

knowledge
    Berkeley, G. 3:377
    Bold, S. 1:822–3
    Locke, J. 3:376
    language 6:51
    Locke, J. 2:29, 3:376, 5:665, 5:668,
        5:669–73
    in the mind of God
        Francis of Meyronnes 3:724–5
        Godfrey of Fontaines 4:120
    natural selection of (al-Afghani)
        1:95
    perception (Berkeley, G.) 1:742–4,
        1:745
    reason relationship (Price, R.)
        7:676–7
    representations
        Desgabets, R. 3:28
        Le Grand, A. 5:479
    sensations
        Johnson, S. 5:124
        Leibniz, G.W. 5:552
        Locke, J.
            Browne, P. critique 2:29
        Malebranche, N. 6:58–9
    spiritual substance (Foucher, S.)
        6:60
    thinking (Spinoza, B. de) 9:97
    vision in God (Malebranche, N.)
        1:445–6, 5:552, 6:58–60, 8:165
ideas, simple see simples
Ideas
    Hegelian 4:271
    Platonist
        Coleridge, S.T. 2:403–4
        Eusebius 3:457
        Schopenhauer, A. 8:546, 8:550,
            8:551
Idel, M. 1:163, 5:175, 6:650, 8:361
identicals, indiscernibility of see
    Leibniz's Law
identification
    groups (Freud, S.) 3:792
    psychoanalysis (Lacan, J.) 5:337
identifying reference
    Strawson, P.F. 9:169
identity
    see also personal identity
    cultural 2:744–6
        African 1:109, 1:110–11, 1:112
        Africans in Brazil 2:8–9
        art
            Japan 1:89–90
        citizenship 2:362, 2:364–5
        communitarianism 9:278
        diaspora
            postcolonialism 7:581

    existentialism 3:495, 3:500
    Florenskii, P.A. 3:680–1
    Latin America 5:653–5, 5:656,
        7:348–9, 7:350
        literature 5:653–5, 5:656
    Mexican philosophy 6:344,
        6:346
    and morality 6:571–6
    multiculturalism 6:600, 6:601
    national 6:658, 6:660
        Zionism 9:867–9
    Other
        ethical relation to the
            (Levinas, E.) 5:580
    phenomenology
        Latin America 7:348–9,
            7:350
    politics of 7:502–3
    population ethics 7:541
    post-colonialism
        India 7:524
    postmodern theories of
        1:187–92
    sexual 2:372–3
    symbolic interactionism 9:244
    Western philosophy
        influence on Latin American
            philosophy 2:744–5
    Zionism 9:867–9
logical 4:675–8
    absolute (Schelling, F.W.J. von)
        8:509, 8:513
    aggregate particulars 7:237
    conditions for (Leibniz, G.W.)
        5:551
    criteria 4:676–7
    divine attributes 8:784
    essentialism 3:417–21
    events 3:462
    free logics 3:742
    of indiscernibles 3:418, 4:676,
        4:678–81
        counterpart theory 6:430–1
        criticism of 4:677
        glossary 5:803
        McTaggart, J.M.E. 6:26–7
    intensional entities 4:804
    logical predication
        (Wodeham, A.) 9:774
    necessity of (Kripke, S.A.)
        5:302–3
    numerical 4:676, 4:678–9, 5:803
    philosophy of (Schelling, F.W.J.
        von) 8:509, 8:512–14
    possible worlds 7:570–1
        counterpart theory 6:430–1
        Lewis, D.K. 5:591, 5:592

psychophysical 1:276–7
qualitative 4:676, 4:678–9, 5:803
Sāṅkhya-Yoga 2:251, 2:252,
  2:253–4
sense and reference 8:684–5
spatio-temporal continuity
  2:652–3
subject-object unity
  (Hegel, G.W.F.) 4:263–4
Trinity 9:458, 9:459–61
vagueness 9:564
identity of indiscernibles *see* identity,
  logical
identity theory of mind **6:394–9**,
  6:404
Armstrong, D.M. 1:442
central state identity theory
  colour and qualia 2:421–3
materialism 6:174
mental causation 6:308–10
neutral monism 6:817
phenomenal states 2:586
reductionism 8:150
Smart, J.J.C. 8:814
identity theory of truth
Bradley, F.H. 1:860
identity thesis
belief and knowledge 1:706, 1:707
identity thinking
negative dialectics (Adorno, T.W.
  1:42, 1:44
identity-reduction
social laws 4:485
ideograms
religious experience 7:174
ideology **4:681–5**, 7:502
aesthetics 2:838
artistic value 1:476
class
  partiinost' 7:239
critique by Dostoevskii, F.M.
  3:117
culture 4:683–4
French
  Argentinian philosophy 1:375
French philosophy of science 3:782
hegemony 6:144–5
hermeneutics 4:684–5
knowledge problem 4:682–3
Marx, K. 6:123–6
Marxist 4:681–2, 6:142, 6:143
political science 4:683
as social cohesion 1:194
Soviet Marxism
  Asmus, V.F./Var'iash, A. debate
    1:524
totalitarianism 1:369–70

utopianism 9:558
Western
  comedy 2:436
Idinopulos, T.A. 3:263
idiolects
Chomsky, N. 2:340–1, 5:370
as social phenomenon 5:417,
  5:418–19
idols 7:585–6
Idowu, E.B. 1:106
ìgbàgbó
Yoruba epistemology 9:832–3
Iggers, George G. 4:444, 4:446,
  8:853–4, 8:858
Ignatieff, M. 3:330, 3:632, 6:376
ignorance
  Awakening of Faith in Mahāyāna
    1:603, 1:604
  vagueness as a kind of 9:566
  weakness of will 9:15–16
Ihde, D. 4:327, 7:342, 8:322
Ihsa' al-'ulum see al-Farabi, Abu
  Nasr
Iida, Shotaro
  Wônch'ūk †9:792–3
al-Iji 5:31
Ijsewijn, J. 4:540
ijtihad (independent judgment)
  5:458–60
Ikeda, Sadao 4:562
Ikhwan Al-Safa' (Brethren of Purity)
  4:685–8
  knowledge 7:159
  Orientalism 7:160
  Pythagoreanism 6:617
iktisab see kasb
I-languages *see* idiolect
Ilarion 6:278
Il'enkov, Eval'd Vasil'evich **4:688–92**
  dialectics 4:689
  Marxist philosophy, Russian and
    Soviet 6:159
  problem of the ideal 4:689–90
Ilgauds, H.J. 7:751
Ilie, H. 6:56
Il'in, Ivan Aleksandrovich **4:692–6**
  ethics 4:694
  Hegel, G.W.F. 4:692–3
  political theory 4:693–4
illative sense 6:822
illegality
  see also crime
  revolution 8:301, 8:302
Illich, I. 4:520
Illich, Ivan 7:734, 7:737, 9:283
illness
  see also health

mental **6:311–14**
physical
  concepts of 3:833, 6:311,
    6:312–13
illocutionary acts 9:82–3
  Austin, J.L. 7:621
  fiction 3:661
  intention 9:83–4
  types of 9:84–5
Illuminati **4:696–8**
illumination **4:698–700**
  Buddhism
    Chinul 2:330–1
  epistemological 4:698–9
  metaphysical 4:699–700
  Neoplatonism 4:698–9
illuminationism **4:698–700**
  Augustinianism 1:562
  Bonaventure 1:828, 1:833
  Duns Scotus, J. 3:154, 3:159, 3:165
  Henry of Ghent 4:357
  Peter of Spain 7:324
  Ulrich of Strasbourg 9:517–18
  Vital du Four 9:639
Illuminationist philosophy, Islamic
  4:700–3, 5:16–17, 5:18–19
  Aristotelianism 1:385
  al-Dawani 2:807
  existence-quiddity relationship
    4:701–2, 6:595–6
  Jewish philosophy comparison
    1:637
  Mir Damad, Muhammad Baqir
    6:409
  mystical philosophy 6:617–19
  Neoplatonism 6:806
  al-Suhrawardi 4:622, 6:806, 9:219,
    9:220–3
illusion
  see also hallucinations
  film aesthetics 3:676
  Indian concepts of **3:409–13**
    monism 6:476, 6:477
    sense perception 8:692–3
    veridicality 3:411–12
  metaphysical (Kant, I.) 5:188–9
  optical
    modularity of mind 6:450
  perception 7:288
  sensory 7:294, 7:295, 7:296–7,
    7:298
  Wodeham, A. 9:773
Illyricus, Mattias Flacius *see* Vlačić,
  Matija
'ilm al-kalam 5:25–30
  argument for the existence of God
    4:86–7

atomism
    matter 6:194
falsafa
    al-Muqammas, D. 6:605
    Ibn Tzaddik, J. 4:660
    Karaism 5:207, 5:208
'ilm al-'umran see culture, science of
image
    concept distinction 1:622
imagery
    Chinese aesthetics
        natural 1:69–70, 1:71–2
        physiological 1:71, 1:72
    media 1:662
    memory 6:297
    mental **4:703–5**, 4:705–8
        descriptionalism 4:703, 4:704,
            4:705
        pictorial conception of 4:703,
            4:704–5
    natural
        Japanese aesthetics 1:82
    role in reasoning
        male bias 5:476, 5:477
imaginal world
    Illuminationist philosophy 4:702
    Mulla Sadra 6:598
    al-Suhrawardi 9:222
imaginary
    feminine 5:2–3
imagination **4:705–8**
    see also fantasies
    aesthetics
        Islamic philosophy 1:77–9
        judgment (Kant, I.) 5:193, 5:194
    association
        aesthetic (Alison, A.) 1:185–6
    Baumgarten, A.G. 1:670–1
    beauty
        perception of 1:682–3
    expression of
        as religion (Tagore, R.) 9:258
    fiction 3:661–2
    freedom of consciousness
        (Sartre, J.-P.) 8:475–6
    historical transition to reason
        (Vico, G.) 9:603, 9:604–5
    Ibn al-'Arabi 4:603–4
    Ibn Sina 4:649–50, 4:652
    Illuminationist philosophy
        (Corbin, H.) 5:18
    logical behaviourism (Ryle, G.)
        8:430
    non-rational soul
        Islamic philosophy 9:41–2
    phenomenological method
        (Sartre, J.-P.) 8:475

picture interpretation 2:895
poetic language (Ibn Sina) 4:652
prophecy 7:768–9, 7:770
    Abravanel, I. 1:21
    Maimonides 6:46–7
reality relationship (Weil, S.) 9:699
Smith, A. 8:817–18
taste (Gerard, A.) 4:36
Imam 3:441, 5:26, 6:617, 7:518
Imanaka, Kanshi 3:800, 7:91
Imbach, R. 1:185, 6:832
Imbelli, R. 8:458
imitation
    art
        Japanese aesthetics 1:84
    comedy 2:435–6
    doctrine of (Hamann, J.G.) 4:216
    Ibn Rushd, Abu'l Walid
        Muhammad 1:78
    Islamic philosophy 1:77–9
    Lessing, G.E. 5:575, 5:577
    poetry defined as 7:473–4
immanentism
    see also pantheism
    absolute
        epistemology (Lossky, N.O.)
            5:833, 5:834–5
    absolute (Gentile, G.) 4:21
    feminist theology 3:622–3
    Hebrew Bible 1:767
    history (Chaadaev, P.I.) 2:270–1
    spiritual
        Japanese philosophy 5:69
Immanuel ben Solomon of Rome
    4:708–10, 5:88
immaterialism
    see also Cartesianism; dualism;
    idealism
    Berkeley, G. 1:737
    Collier, A. 2:408, 2:409–10
    divine 4:98
    Hobbes, T. objections 4:467–8
    occasionalism 7:88–9
    simplicity
        divine 8:785
    soul
        Clarke, S. 2:378–9
        Collins, A. 2:417
        Digby, K. 3:71
        Overton, R. denial 7:176
immigrants
    marginality 6:99
immoralism
    Nietzsche, F.W. 6:853–5
immortality
    see also mortality; soul,
    immortality of

Active Intellect
    Jewish philosophy (Gersonides)
        4:49–50
    Cajetan 2:172–3
    criticism of
        Feuerbach, L.A. 3:635–6
    desire for (Unamuno y Jugo, M.
        De) 9:519, 9:520–1
    infinity 4:777
    pantheism 7:204
    Renaissance Aristotelianism
        (Pomponazzi, P.) 7:529–30
    of the soul *see* soul, immortality of
    theory of social control (Ibn
        Rushd) 4:641
    through personal effort (Iqbal, M.)
        4:865
immutability **4:710–14**
    see also change
    divine (Augustine) 1:549
    eternality of God 3:425
    feminist theology 3:623
    Ibn al-'Arabi 4:603
    impassibility 4:711
    natural order 6:736
    omniscience 7:109
    simplicity
        divine 8:785
Impagliazzo, J. 6:812
impartial care *see jian'ai*
impartiality **4:714–17**
    consequentialism 8:324
    egoism 3:247
    friendship 3:796
    journalism ethics 5:127
    love 5:844
    moral motivation 6:525–6
    nursing ethics 7:56
    obligations to future generations
        3:820
    personal identity
        reductionism (Parfit, D.) 6:573,
            6:574
    utilitarianism 6:371, 9:552, 9:555
impassibility
    immutability 4:711
impeccability
    divine simplicity 8:786
imperative *see* categorical imperative;
    moral judgment; prescriptivism
imperative logic **4:717–21**
    Jörgensen's dilemma 4:718, 4:719
    reductionism 4:718–19
    Ross's 'paradox' 4:718
    satisfaction-preservation 4:717,
        4:719–20
    sentence radicals 4:718

truth theories 6:224
truth-preservation 4:717, 4:718–19
imperatives
  hypothetical
    practical reasoning 8:91
imperialism
  see also colonialism
  in Africa 2:169–70
  capitalism 6:6–7
  cultural relativity 9:426
  decline of
    cultural identity 2:745, 2:746
  Eurasian Movement 3:455
  Marxism
    Latin America 6:160, 6:163–4
  Orientalism 7:158–9
impermanence
  see also momentariness
  Ābhidharmika Schools 2:56
  Buddhism
    Japan 6:591–4
  emptiness 6:639
  heaven, Indian concepts of 4:255
  law of
    momentariness, Buddhist
      doctrine of 6:471
impersonalism
  population ethics 7:541
impetus, theory of
  Buridan, J. 2:133
  Marsilius of Inghen 6:111
  Paul of Venice 7:266
  Philoponus 7:373, 7:375, 7:376
implication
  see also consequence; implicature;
    inference
  circumstantial
    as source of knowledge
      Indian thought 5:282–3
  logic
    linear 5:638–9
    multiple-conclusion 6:602–4
    relevance 8:200–3
implicature 4:721–5
  contextual
    pragmatics 7:621–2
  conventional (Grice, H.P.)
    4:722–3, 7:622–3
  conversational (Grice, H.P.)
    4:174–5, 4:721–4, 7:622, 7:624,
    7:627–8
  language and gender 5:366
  logic
    linear 5:638–9
    multiple-conclusion 6:602–4
    relevance 8:200–3
  speech acts 9:85–6

utterances (Grice, H.P.) 4:173–5
implicit definition 1:761–2, 2:845,
  2:847
imposition
  medieval theories of 5:389, 5:391–2
impossibility theorems 8:824
  Arrow, K.J. 8:64, 8:68, 8:824, 8:826
  conditions of aggregation 8:824
  orderings 8:824, 8:825
impossible objects
  Meinong, A. 6:283
impossible things
  Ibn al-'Arabi 4:603
Impressionist art
  phenomenology (Merleau-
    Ponty, M.) 6:323–4
impressions
  ideas (Hume, D.) 4:546, 4:556,
    6:230
  inner life (Epictetus) 3:339
impressiveness
  music 4:188, 4:189–90
improvisation
  performing art 1:468–9, 1:471
impulsions
  psychology of law (Petrażycki, L.)
    7:329–30
impurity
  Brahmanism (Vallabhācārya)
    9:574–5
In nae ch'ôn (Man is God) 9:441
in vitro fertilization (IVF) 8:276,
  8:277–9
Inada, K. 6:594
Inati, Shams C.
  Ibn 'Adi †4:599–601
  Ibn Bajja †4:605–8
  Ibn ar-Rawandi †4:636–8
  Ibn Sina 4:654
  Ibn Tufayl †4:657–9
  Islamic philosophy
    epistemology †3:384–8
    soul †9:40–4
Inayatullah, Sohail
  political philosophy
    Indian †7:521–5
Inca de la Vega, G. 5:430, 5:432
Inca (Quechua) civilization
  colonial thought 5:422
  culture 5:429
  Marxism 6:162
  religion 5:430
  thought 5:428–9, 5:430, 5:431
Incarnation 4:725–32
  see also Christology
  attributive solutions 4:728–30
  faith 3:507

grace 4:150
identity 4:731–2
immutability 4:712–13
kenoticism 4:729–30
logical problems of 4:728
necessity for (Anselm of
  Canterbury) 1:283–4, 1:293–4
orthodox doctrine 4:725–7
predictive solutions 4:730
salvation 8:450
Trinity (Anselm of Canterbury)
  1:292–4
incentives
  rational choice theory 8:71
  work 3:394–5
incest
  taboo (Lévi-Strauss, C.) 5:583
inclusivism
  doctrinal 8:260–1
The Incoherence of the Incoherence
  see Ibn Rushd, Tahafut al-tahafut
The Incoherence of the Philosophers
  see (al-)Ghazali, Tahafut al-
    falasifa
incommensurability 4:732–6
  art works 1:477
  Ramsey sentences 8:47–8
  science
    demarcation problem 2:865
    scientific revolutions (Kuhn, T.S.)
      5:316
    scientific theory (Feyerabend, P.K.)
      3:640
incompatibilism
  see also libertarianism; pessimism
  belief and knowledge 1:706,
    1:707–8
  blame (Kant, I.) 7:645–6
  causation (Aristotle) 1:420
  evil, problem of 3:468–9
  freedom 3:743–4, 3:745–6
incomplete objects
  Meinong, A. 6:283–4
incompleteness theorems
  glossary 5:803–4
  Gödel, K. 4:107, 4:110–13, 5:734
    computability 2:352, 2:478
    computational theories of mind
      6:393
    ordinal logics 7:139–40
    paradoxes 7:220
    proof theory 7:745
    second-order logic 8:592
incongruity
  humour 4:562, 4:563, 4:564–5

inconsistency
  inference
    Indian theories of 4:761–2
  rational belief 8:61
inconsistent numbers 7:53
incontinent action (*akrasia*) *see*
  akrasia
incorporeals
  Stoicism 9:148
indecision
  semantic
    vagueness 9:565–6
indefeasibility *see* knowledge,
  defeasibility theory of
indefectibility
  essence-existence (Desgabets, R.)
  3:28
indefinability theorem
  Tarski, A. 7:220, 9:266
Indefinite Dyad
  attributes of
    Early Platonism 7:423–4
  creative role (Speusippus) 9:89–90
  disorderly principle (Plutarch of
    Chaeronea) 7:466
  Pythagoreanism (Numenius) 7:54,
    7:55
  relationship to the One
    Early Platonism 7:423–4
indemonstrables
  Stoicism 5:690–1, 9:150–1
Inden, R. 7:524
independence
  effect on Brazil 2:9–2:10
  international law 9:58
  social relationship 7:792
independence, set theory
  glossary 5:804
  proofs of
    set theory 1:845–6, 2:654,
      2:656–7
    forcing 3:693–7
independent assortment
  law of
    Mendelian genetics 4:13
independent ethics
  Kotarbiński, T. 5:294–5
indestructibility
  of real universals 9:802, 9:803
indeterminacy
  Critical Legal Studies 2:714, 2:718
  learning (Chomsky, N.) 2:339
  legal realism 5:523–4
  rational choice theory 8:73
  of reference (Quine, W.V.) 1:226,
    1:227, 8:9–8:10

indeterminism 3:33–9
  see also determinism
  Chisholm, R.M. 2:333–4
  vs fatalism
    Aristotle 1:426–7
index theory
  possible worlds semantics 8:666
indexical content *see* content,
  indexical
indexicals 2:878–81
  see also demonstratives
  ambiguity 1:199
  belief 2:879–81
  character 2:880–1
  contextualism 2:648
  descriptions 3:22
  direct reference thesis 2:881
  hidden 7:777–8
  indexical content 2:880–1
  ineliminability 2:879–80
  informational semantics 8:660–1
  Kaplan-Perry theory (KPT)
    2:880–1
  possible worlds semantics 8:667
  pragmatics 7:623
  reference 8:158–9
  representation
    semantics 8:673–4
  signs
    interpretation of 7:278–9
India
  see also Indian philosophy
  Abhinavagupta 1:15–19
  Ambedkar, B.R. 1:196–7
  Arya Samaj movement 1:516–17
  Aurobindo Ghose 1:567–9
  Bhartṛhari 1:764–6
  Brahmo Samaj movement 2:5–7
  Buddha 2:51–3
  Buddhism *see* Buddhist
    philosophy, Indian
  Dharmakīrti 3:51–3
  Dignāga 3:74–6
  Gadādhara 3:825–7
  Gandhi, M.K. 3:841–3
  Gaṅgeśa 3:843–6
  Hindu philosophy 4:433–40
  Iqbal, M. 4:863–8
  Islam
    mystical philosophy 6:619
  Kauṭilya 5:220–2
  Mādhava 6:28–31
  Madhva 6:31–3
  Mādhyamika Buddhism 2:58–64
  Mahāvīra 6:33–5
  mysticism 6:621–2
  Nāgārjuna 6:638–41

Patañjali 7:248–50
Radhakrishnan, S. 8:23–5
Ramakrishna Movement 8:39–42
Rāmānuja 8:42–4
Śaṅkara 8:458–61
Shah Wali Allah 8:732–5
Tagore, R. 9:257–8
Udayana 9:512–14
Uddyotakara 9:514–16
Vallabhācārya 9:573–5
Vasubandhu 9:583–7
Vātsyāyana 9:587–8
Indian philosophy 4:736–40
  see also Tibetan philosophy
  Ābhidharmika Schools of
    Buddhism 2:53–8
  awareness 1:604–8
  Brahman 2:1–5
  Buddhism *see* Buddhist
    philosophy, Indian
  causation 2:251–7
  classical
    negative facts in 6:755–9
  cosmology and cosmogony
    2:681–4
  definition 2:849–52
  duty and virtue 3:183–7
  emptiness, Buddhist concept of
    2:76–80
  epistemology 3:388–92
  error and illusion 3:409–13
  fatalism 3:564–8
  Gauḍīya Vaiṣṇavism 3:857–9
  God
    conceptions of 4:102–5
  heaven
    concepts of 4:253–7
  inference 4:759–66
  interpretation 4:833–7
  Islamic *see* Iqbal, Muhammad;
    Shah Wali Allah
  Jainism 5:48–5
  karma and rebirth 5:209–18
  knowledge 5:280–5
  language 5:379–84
  Mādhyamika School of Buddhism
    2:58–64
  manifoldness, Jaina theory of
    6:77–81
  materialism 6:178–81
  matter 6:196–200
  meaning 6:239–43
  Mīmāṃsā 6:376–81
  mind 6:399–403
  momentariness 6:469–73
  monism 6:475–9
  nirvāṇa 7:8–7:12

nominalism
  Buddhist doctrine of **7:23–7**
Nyāya-Vaiśeṣika **7:57–6**
ontology **7:118–12**
political **7:521–5**
potentiality **7:604–8**
Sāṅkhya **8:461–7**
self
  theories of **8:605–11**
suffering
  Buddhist views of origination of
  9:215–19
testimony **9:314–19**
Vedānta **9:588–94**
Yogācāra School of Buddhism
  2:64–76
indicative conditionals **4:740–3**
  assertion conditions 4:741–2
  counterfactual conditionals
    distinction 2:685
  material conditionals 4:740–1
  possible worlds 4:741
  supplemented equivalence theory
    4:742
indifference
  Bayesian epistemology 7:710
  Keynes, J.M. 5:234
  Scepticism (Pyrrho) 7:846
  Stoicism (Ariston of Chios)
    1:381–2
indigenous peoples
  see also Mestizo people
  Latin America **5:428–32**
    Brazil 2:8
    colonial philosophy 5:421
    literature 5:654, 5:655
    marginality 6:99–6:101
    Marxism 6:162, 6:163
    'nature' mysticism 6:621
indignation
  moral blame 6:564, 6:568
indirect discourse **4:743–5**
indirect quotations
  Davidson, D. 2:803
indiscernibility of identicals see
  Leibniz's Law
indiscernibles, identity of 3:418,
  4:676, **4:678–81**
  counterpart theory 6:430–1
  criticism of 4:677
  glossary 5:803
  McTaggart, J.M.E. 6:26–7
indiscerpibility
  More, H. 6:578–9
individual
  society interaction (Watsuji
    Tetsurō) 9:691–2

individual contract
  agreement 2:658
individual difference
  Duns Scotus, J. 3:164–5
individual essences 6:429
individualism
  see also anti-individualism
  anarchism 1:245
  China 2:327, 9:822–3
  communalism contrast
    ethnophilosophy 3:447, 3:448
  communitarianism relationship
    (Taylor, C.) 9:277–8
  critique by Berdiaev, N.A. 1:730
  dialectic of liberty (Lachelier, J.)
    5:339
  efficiency argument 5:461
  ethical 5:602–3
  harm principle 5:463
  in history and social science
    4:482–8
    explanation 4:485–6
    ontology 4:484–5
  holism debate 4:482–3, 4:486–7
  homosexuality
    legalization of 5:463
  human nature
    liberty 5:463
  illusion of (Schopenhauer, A.)
    8:552
  intentionality 4:486
  Japan
    Nishi Amane 7:12
    Nishida Kitarō 7:14
    Tanabe Hajime 5:715
  liberalism 5:600–3
    communitarian critique of
      2:466, 2:467
  limits of law 5:461
  methodological 6:405–6
    Anderson, J. critique 1:268
    explanation 3:526–7
    and functionalism 8:861–3
    Popper, K.R. 7:536
    positivism 7:559
  methodological (MI) **6:341–4**
  ontological categories
    Indian philosophy 7:121–2
  organicism (Mikhailovskii, N.K.)
    6:356
  paternalism 7:251
  political neutrality 6:818, 6:820
  political obligation 7:78–9
    nonvoluntarism 7:76, 7:77,
      7:78–9
    voluntarism 7:76, 7:77, 7:78
  possessive 7:175–6

postmodernism 7:589
psychic nexus (Dilthey, W.) 3:80
public interest 7:834
responsibility 8:293
Russian communalism
  (Mikhailovskii, N.K.) 6:355,
  6:356
self-realization 8:633–4
testimony 8:828–9, 9:310–11
individuals
  autonomy
    rule of law relationship
      8:389–90
  morality
    state intervention 5:438–42
  panlogic reality 3:635
  particulars 7:235
  Scheler, M.F. 8:506–7
  state relationship 9:121
    Slavophilism 8:809
individuation
  Aquinas' treatment of (Richard of
    Middleton) 8:310
  Cajetan 2:172
  Capreolus, J. 2:200–1
  continuous consciousness
    (Locke, J.) 5:665
  Duns Scotus, J. 3:154, 3:163–5
  Giles of Rome 4:74
  ontological concept of (Gilbert of
    Poitiers) 4:69–70
  Richard Rufus of Cornwall 8:316
  universals
    Indian theories of 9:545–6
    Kilwardby, R. 5:247
indivisibility
  see also divisibility
  atomism, ancient 1:535
    Democritus 2:873–4
  continua
    Bradwardine, T. 1:864–5
    Chatton, W. 2:293
    Gerard of Odo 4:39
    Henry of Harclay 4:360, 4:361
    Wodeham, A. 9:775
Indohispanic socialism 6:162, 6:163
induction **4:745–52**
  see also inductive inference
  analogy
    confirmation theory 2:533–4
  art criticism 1:460–1
  belief 6:723
  discovery
    logic of 3:100
  eliminative (Bacon, F.) 1:624,
    1:628, 1:629–30

empiricism
  criticism of 3:302–3
Goodman, N. 4:136, 4:138–9,
  9:341–2
Grue Paradox
  epistemic principles 5:273–4,
    9:341–2
  Goodman, N. 9:341–2
hypothesis evaluation
  archaeology 1:356
inference to the best explanation
  4:767–8
infinite
  rule of 7:27–9
inverse theory (Łukasiewicz, J.)
  5:860
justification 4:748, 8:570
logic of 8:568–70, 9:528
  mathematical 1:437, 5:804, 5:814
    proof theory 7:748
meaning claim 4:750
natural (Popper, K.R.) 7:534
naturalism 4:750
optimum
  Carnap, R. 2:533
  Festa, R. 2:533
ordinary-language 4:750–1
Peirce, C.S. 7:274–5
pragmatism 4:747–8
presupposition 4:746–52
probabilism 4:748–9
probability
  Broad, C.D. 2:23, 2:25
  Keynes, J.M. 5:233–4
  Reichenbach, H. 8:167, 8:168
problem of (Hume, D.) 4:544
psychologism (Mill, J.S.) 6:360–1,
  6:364–5
qualitative (Peirce, C.S.) 7:274–5
reflective-equilibrium 4:749–50
sceptical critique of (Nicholas of
  Autrecourt) 6:830
science
  demarcation problem 2:863
  seventeenth century 8:578
scientific (Mill, J.S.) 6:365–6
second-order logic 8:601–2
testimony 8:829
transfinite 8:702–3
truth
  Russell, B.A.W. 8:401
  Wright, G.H. von 9:667
'induction'
  Whewell, W. 9:709, 9:710
  Wittgensteinian doctrine 4:751
inductive definitions and proofs
  4:752–5

inductive inference **4:755–9**, 8:495,
  8:496
  see also inference
  fallibility of
    examples 4:756, 4:758
  hypothetico-deductive model
    4:756–7
  medicine, philosophy of 6:265–7
  natural theology 6:707, 6:708–9
  premise-conclusion relationship
    4:757–8
  Reichenbach H. 5:486
  reliability of 4:756–8
  science
    philosophy of
      epistemology 6:728, 6:729
      naturalized 6:728, 6:729
      nineteenth-century 8:567,
        8:568–70
  structures of 4:755
  types of 4:756
inductive probability
  arguments for the existence of God
    9:302
inductive-statistical explanation (I-S
  explanation)
  covering-law model 3:521–2, 3:523
inductivism
  science 2:864, 9:138–9
industrialization
  farming
    developing countries 1:126–7
  technological 9:281
industry
  capitalism 8:879
  production 4:153–4
  risk
    government regulation 8:333
    trade-off 8:333
inequality
  see also equality
  global
    development ethics 3:39–42
  origins of 8:370
  risk distribution 8:332–3
inertia
  collisions (Descartes, R.) 3:14
inevitable progress
  providence 7:798–9
infallibility
  belief 5:159
  certainty compared to 2:265
  divine illumination 1:833
  introspection 4:837–8, 4:839–40,
    4:841
    Descartes, R. 4:843, 4:844

phenomenal consciousness
  2:591–2
qualia 7:865–6
infancy
  ego development
    post-Freudian psychoanalysis
      7:819–20
infant cognition **2:390–2**
  see also child development;
    developmental psychology
  concepts of knowledge
    nativism 6:674
  infant 9:673
  Piaget, J. (Vygotskii, L.S.) 9:673
  psychoanalysis (Klein, M.)
    7:818–20, 7:821–2
infanticide 5:629, 8:276, 8:279
inference
  see also inductive inference; logical
    consequence; syllogism
  analogical
    other minds 7:171–2, 7:173
  archaeology 1:356
  belief
    reasons for 8:127, 8:129
  categories
    Mohism 6:456–7
  causal (Hume, D.) 4:544, 4:546–8
  causality
    Hanson, N.R. 4:224
    risk assessment 8:337
  conceptual (Sa skya paṇḍita) 8:434
  consequence 2:600
  criticism of
    Bradley, F.H. 1:860
    Lokāyatikas 6:180
  deductive
    Frege, G. 3:765
    Galilei, G. 3:838
  deductive closure principle **2:842–5**
  distortion (rGyal tshab dar ma rin
    chen) 8:305
  epistemic validity
    Indian philosophy 2:68
  fallible (Ajdukiewicz, K.) 1:137
  habits of
    desire distinction 3:30–1
  hypothetic
    other minds 7:172
  imperative logic 4:718, 4:719
  Indian theories of **4:759–66**
    canonical inference 4:762–4
    Dharmakīrti 3:52–3
    Dignāga 3:75
    Gaṅgeśa 3:845
    momentariness 6:472

Navya-Nyāya theory of
definition 2:851
rational inquiry 4:759–62
indicative conditionals 4:740
indirect theories of perception
9:633
inductive-statistical explanation
3:521–2
infant cognition 2:390–1
infinitary rule of 5:735
instantial terms **7:867–70**
Jainism 5:48, 5:51
knowledge
Hindu philosophy 4:435–6
Hume, D. 4:546
Indian views of 5:280–1,
5:283–4
Sāṅkhya 8:464–5
legal evidence **5:499–506**
linguistic rules (Sellars, W.S.)
8:640–1
logical
probability (Keynes, J.M.)
5:233–4
logical constants 5:779
logical laws 5:786, 5:787–8
meaning-constitutive
analytic-synthetic distinction
4:490–1
multiple-conclusion logic 6:602–4
naturalized philosophy of science
6:728, 6:729–30
negative facts
Indian philosophy 6:756–7
non-constructive rules of **7:27–30**
non-monotonic 7:30–4
Nyāya (Uddyotakara) 9:514
perception distinction
Yogācāra Buddhism 2:68
as *pramā*
Nyāya-Vaiśeṣika 7:63
prepositions (Mill, J.S.) 6:362–3
reflective equilibrium 3:360
rules of (Ackermann, W.) 8:200–1
scientific behaviourism 1:697
scientific method (Newton, I.)
6:825–6
to the best explanation **4:766–9**
abduction 9:478
enumerative induction 4:767–8
epistemology 3:362–3
Galilei, G. 3:839
inductive 4:757
legitimacy 4:766–7, 4:768–9
scientific realism 8:582
inferential logic
Stoicism 9:150–1

infertility 1:779, 8:278–9
infinitary logic **4:769–72**, 5:734–5,
6:440
infinite
see also countable infinite;
Ensoph; infinity
argument for impossibility of
kalam argument 4:86–7
mathematics
foundations of 5:847
infinite being
Duns Scotus, J. 3:154, 3:160,
3:162–3
infinite numbers 7:47, 7:50
see also transfinite numbers
antinomy of 7:216
paradoxes of set and property
7:215–16
Renaissance logic 9:434–5
infinitesimals 7:47–50
limit
notion of 7:51
mathematical analysis 1:219
nonstandard analysis 1:211–16,
7:52
infinitism
warrant theory
knowledge 5:268
infinity **4:772–8**
see also finitude
actual-potential distinction
4:773–4, 4:775–6
Aristotle 4:773–4, 4:775, 4:777
axiom of choice 1:613
Cantor, G. 2:197–8, 2:199, 4:776
categorematic-syncategorematic
distinction 4:773–4, 4:776
and continuity (Henry of Harclay)
4:360, 4:361
denial of (Dühring, E.K.) 3:147–8
divine existence arguments
(Crescas, H.) 2:701–2
divisibilism
Aristotle 1:420–1
Buridan, J. 2:133–4
equinumerosity paradox 4:776
eternity of the world
Jewish philosophy (Gersonides)
4:48
medieval theories of 1:832,
3:428–9
existentialism 4:775
God 4:774
human finitude 4:775, 4:776–7
irrational (Vysheslavtsev, B.P.)
9:675–6
Kronecker, L. 5:312

medieval natural philosophy
(Wodeham, A.) 9:775
modern mathematics 4:775–6
past time incompatibility (Richard
Rufus of Cornwall) 8:315–16
rationalist/empiricist debate 4:774
Scope Distinction 4:774, 4:775,
4:776–7
spatial (Melissus) 6:294
temporal (Melissus) 6:293, 6:294
universe
Epicureanism 3:342
infinity, axiom of 5:798
informal logic **3:701–3**
information
see also cognitive science
channels 4:783–4
computability **2:477–82**
epistemic value
observation 7:80–1, 7:82, 7:86
mutual 4:786–7, 4:788
objective 4:786–7
philosophical interpretations 4:785
processing
connectionism 2:570–6
psychophysical 2:883
visual perception 9:632, 9:634–7
semantic 4:786–7, 4:788
technical concept of 4:782–3
withholding of
truthfulness and deception
9:482
information technology
see also artificial intelligence;
computer science; computers
ethics **4:778–82**, 9:282–3
information theory **4:782–6**
and epistemology **4:786–9**
informational independence
epistemic logic 3:356–7
informational semantics *see*
semantics, informational
informational states
non-conceptual content 2:641
informational-theoretic semantics *see*
semantics, informational
Ingalls, D.H.H.
Gadādhara 3:826–7
Gaṅgeśa 3:846
Indian philosophy
ontology 7:127
potentiality 7:607
Jainism 5:56
Ingarden, Roman Witold **4:789–93**
aesthetics 4:790–1
Husserl, E. 4:587
instrumental reason 2:459

music
  aesthetics of 6:613
  ontology 4:790
  phenomenology 7:342, 7:487
Ingardia, R. 1:347, 1:862, 9:387
Inge, William Ralph **4:793–4**, 6:633
Ingegno, A. 2:204
Ingenieros, José 1:376, 1:379,
  7:566–7, 7:569
Ingham, M.E. 3:169
Ingram, D. 4:199
inherence
  causation
    Nyāya-Vaiśeṣika 2:255
  ontological categories
    Nyāya-Vaiśeṣika 4:439, 7:62,
      7:119, 7:120
      Aristotle comparison
        7:125–6
  qualities
    ontology in Indian philosophy
      7:122
  relations
    Navya-Nyāya theory of 2:850–1
  substance
    ontology in Indian philosophy
      7:120–1, 7:124–5
  universals
    ontology in Indian philosophy
      7:124
iniquity
  injustice distinction (Hobbes, T.)
    4:472
injustice
  iniquity distinction (Hobbes, T.)
    4:472
  Plato 9:397–8
  vices (Aristotle) 9:629
innateness 4:794–5
  see also nativism
  acquired/innate distinction 4:795
  ethology
    innate releasing mechanisms
      6:674–5
  of ideas 8:362
    Buffier, C. 2:119
    Leibniz, G.W. 5:551–2
    Locke, J. 5:668
    More, H. 6:578
    Rosmini-Serbati, A. 8:362
  of knowledge **4:794–7**, 5:286
    cognitive development 2:390,
      2:391
    infant cognition 2:390, 2:391
    James of Viterbo 5:58
    nativist/empiricist debate
      6:672–4

Plato 6:673
  special-purpose structures
    nativism 6:674
  Spinoza, B. de 9:100
  unconscious mental states 9:524
  Wang Yangming 9:683–4
  Zhu Xi 9:683
  of language **4:51–4**
    Chomsky, N. 2:336, 4:51–4
    empiricist response 6:674
    learning theory 5:486
    nativism 6:672, 6:673–4
    Skinner, B.F. 8:801
    unconscious mental states
      9:522, 9:526
    universal grammar 9:524–5
  learning
    behaviourism 1:697–8
    cognitive development 2:394–5
    rationalism 5:483
  of object relations
    psychoanalysis 7:818
inner life
  ethics (Epictetus) 3:338–9
Innewerden see reflexive awareness
innocence **4:797–8**
  redemption
    German Romanticism 8:349
innovation
  conceptual
    scientific theory 3:547
Inoue, Tadashi 5:177
Inoue, Y. 2:555, 3:201–2
I-novel
  Japanese philosophy 5:658–9
inquiry
  appearances (*phainomena*)
    (Aristotle) 1:416
  habits of (Dewey, J.) 3:44, 3:47–8,
    3:49
  method of (Peirce, C.S.) 7:272,
    7:280–1
Inquiry (Symposium)
  Quine, W.V. 8:14
Inquisition
  French (Siger of Brabant) 8:764
insanity
  masturbatory 8:720
inscrutability of reference *see*
  reference, indeterminacy of
Insler, S.H. 9:874
insolubles
  see also paradoxes
  medieval logic 5:756–7
inspiration
  divine
    enthusiasm 3:330–2

instantaneous descriptions
  computability theory 2:485, 9:497
instantial terms
  inferential role 7:868–9
instants
  first and last
    medieval natural philosophy 2:141
instinct
  see also appetite
  reason distinction
    will 9:720–1
Institute for Social Research *see*
  Frankfurt School
institutional theory
  art
    definition of 1:466
institutionalism
  see also neo-institutionalism
  legal **4:799–803**
  Weinberger, O. 9:701–2
institutions
  deliberative politics (Habermas, J.)
    4:197–8
  discrimination 3:104–5
  subjectivity (Foucault, M.) 9:198
  trust 9:468–9
instrumental rationality
  see also identity thinking;
  rationality
  critical theory
    Frankfurt School 2:723
instrumental reason
  critical theory
    Frankfurt School 2:722
instrumentalism 8:581
  see also antirealism; scientific
  antirealism
  Dewey, J. 3:47–8
  fictionalism 3:667
  functional explanation
    (Cummins, R.) 3:804
  Hilbert, D. 7:744
  moral thought (Dewey, J.) 7:641–2
  Poincaré, J.H. 7:479
  Popper, K.R. critique 8:582
  pragmatic theory of truth 9:478,
    9:479–80
  propositional attitudes
    (Dennett, D.C.) 2:882
  religious language 8:257–8
  science 3:452, 8:568, 9:346–7
instrumentation
  experimentalism 3:515–16
  scientific method 8:579
integral calculus
  Leibniz, G.W. 5:554

integral personality
  Signposts movement 8:769
integrity
  Chinese philosophy see cheng
  intellectual 2:18
  judicial reasoning 3:188, 8:390–1
  personal
    conscience 2:579–80
intellect
  see also acquired intellect; Active
  Intellect; agent intellect; Intellect;
  material intellect; productive
  intellect
  Aquinas, T. 1:333–4, 1:336–7
  Aristotle
    Albert the Great 1:147–8
    Themistius' interpretation 9:325
  Averroist concept of the soul (Paul
    of Venice) 7:266
  conceptualization/assent
    dichotomy
    Islamic philosophy 5:708–9
  divine 4:99
    Abravanel, J. 1:26–7
    Ibn Sab'in 4:647
  divine relationship (Peter of Spain)
    7:324
  emanationism
    Ibn Sina 4:648–9, 4:650, 4:651
    al-Tawhidi 9:271
  happiness
    Averroism 1:597
  Henry of Ghent 4:357–8
  imagination (Ibn Sina) 1:77–9
  immortality of
    al-'Amiri 1:207, 1:208
    Gersonides 4:49–50
    al-Kindi 5:251
    Telesio, B. 9:299
  indivisibility of (Ibn Sina) 4:651
  intellective perception (Rosmini-
    Serbati, A.) 8:362
  intelligibles (Mulla Sadra) 6:597
  intuitive/abstractive cognition
    (Duns Scotus, J.) 3:154, 3:165–6
  knowledge
    of the singular (Pecham, J.)
      7:267
  matter distinction (Theophrastus)
    9:338
  non-eternal (al-Razi, Abu Bakr)
    8:111
  perception distinction (Ptolemy)
    7:830
  philosophy of the (Meyerson, É.)
    6:349

potential
  al-Farabi 3:556
  Ibn Bajja 4:606
practical
  Islamic philosophy 9:40, 9:42
  primary object of (Duns Scotus, J.)
    3:158–60
  rational power (Duns Scotus, J.)
    3:167
role in perception
  Vital du Four 9:638–9
  William of Auvergne 9:726
sense/mind distinction
  Campanella, T. 2:187
  Kant, I. 5:182
shared
  Averroism 1:596
theoretical
  Islamic philosophy 3:386–7,
    9:40, 9:42–3
unicity/plurality of (Siger of
  Brabant) 8:765, 8:767
unity of
  Giles of Rome 4:74
  Vernia, N. 9:596
will relationship
  Descartes, R. 3:9–3:10
  Matthew of Aquasparta 6:202
  Richard of Middleton 8:311
  Schopenhauer, A. 8:545,
    8:549–50
Intellect
  see also Active Intellect; Creative
  Intellect; First Intellect; Universal
  Intellect
  hierarchy of principles (Plotinus)
    7:457
  nature of (Plotinus) 7:458–9
  Neoplatonism (Proclus) 7:727
  Platonic Forms (Plotinus) 7:458
intellectio theory of concepts
  Chatton, W. 2:292
intellection
  Judah ben Moses of Rome 5:129,
    5:130
  nature of
    Neoplatonism 6:800
  soul
    Kabbalah (Herrera, A. Cohen
      de) 4:399
intellective soul
  body relationship (John of
    Jandun) 5:107
intellectual disorder
  MacIntyre, A. 6:23

intellectualism
  Descartes, R.
    Huet, P.-D. critique 4:515
  Eurasian Movement 3:454, 3:455
  in mathematics 2:40
  Roman law 8:345–7
  voluntarism 9:663
intellectuals
  definition 8:288
  responsibilities of 8:287–90
intelligence
  see also artificial intelligence
  air (Diogenes of Apollonia) 3:88
  artificial 1:485–92
    anti-Cartesian critique 1:491–2
    dynamical systems theory
      1:491–2
  human
    evolution of (Darwin, C.R.)
      2:798
    innate (Ibn Sina) 5:706–7
    truth inference (Vives, J.L.) 9:647
intelligibilia (intelligibles)
  rational soul (Judah ben Moses of
    Rome) 5:129, 5:130
intelligible species
  Renaissance Aristotelianism 1:408
intelligibles
  al-Farabi 5:707–8
  Ibn Bajja 4:606–7
  Ibn Sina 4:648–9
  Mulla Sadra 6:597
  Plotinus 7:457
  Proclus 7:726–7
intension 4:810–11
  see also extensionality;
  intersubstitutability; non-
  extensionality; sense and reference
  algebra 4:806
  doctrine history 4:803–4
  extension contrast 8:663
  as function 2:509, 2:510–11
  hyper-intensionality
    unconscious mental states 9:525
  individualism/holism debate 4:486
  intensional logics 4:807–10
  intentionality distinction 4:819
  logical laws 5:786
  meaning
    Lewis, C.I. 5:586–7
  medieval natural philosophy
    Oxford Calculators 7:179–80
  ontological commitment 7:115
  Port-Royal logicians 5:718
  possible worlds semantics 6:484,
    8:662–8
  vagueness 9:563

intensional entities **4:803–7**
intensional algebra 4:806
possible worlds 4:804
propositional attitudes 7:783
questions 8:1, 8:2
Quine, W.V. 2:520, 2:521, 8:9, 8:10
intensional logics **4:807–10**
see also conditionals; modal logic;
temporal logic
Church, A. 2:347–8
nineteenth century 5:722–3
structured complexes
propositional attitude
statements 7:776–7
synonymy (Carnap, R.) 2:212
intensity
difference (Deleuze, G.) 1:190
intention **4:811–16**
action 1:37, 1:38, 1:41
artist's 1:473, 1:503–4, **1:513–16**
authorial
hermeneutics 4:386
behaviour
sociobiology 8:894
blame 6:567
communication **2:455–9**
pragmatics 7:628, 7:629
speech acts 9:83–4
double effect principle 3:120–1
hope 4:507
individualism/holism debate 4:483,
4:486, 4:487
joint 8:822–3
karma
Yogācāra Buddhism 2:69–70
processualism (Dostoevskii, F.M.)
3:116, 3:117
purity of
Jewish pietism 4:635
rape 8:719
religious obligations
Rabbinic theology 9:334–5
responsibility 8:291
self-deception 8:626–7
sexual 8:719
truthfulness and deception
9:481–2
war 9:687
Weber, M. 9:696
intentional community *see*
community, utopian
The Intentional Fallacy 1:513
intentionality **4:816–21**
action (Anscombe, G.E.M.)
1:280–1
agency (Heidegger, M.) 4:324
Augustine 1:542

bodily 7:346–7
Brentano, F. 2:13–14, 4:574,
4:576–7, 4:817, 4:819–20
causal interactive relations 2:329
Chisholm, R.M. 2:332–3
cognition (Hervaeus Natalis)
4:403–4
collective (Searle, J.) 8:590
concepts 2:506
of consciousness 7:343, 7:345
consciousness (Sartre, J.-P.)
8:474–5
descriptive psychology
(Twardowski, K.) 9:508
directedness (Husserl, E.) 4:577,
4:578
double (Polanyi, M.) 7:490
eliminativism 3:264
emotions 3:282–3, 4:222
existence (Husserl, E.) 4:582
functionalism 6:176
God
existence of 4:91
Heidegger, M. 1:702, 4:324
imagination 4:705–6
intensionality distinction 4:819
intrinsic
consciousness requirement
Chinese room argument
2:328
language relationship (Searle, J.)
8:589
materialism 6:176
meaning and communication
6:213
mental acts (Meinong, A.) 6:283
mental causation 6:308
mental holism (Searle, J.) 8:589
Native American philosophy
6:664–5
noema (Husserl, E.) 4:574–5,
4:577–8
non-conceptual content 2:641
non-existent objects (Meinong, A.)
4:577
objectifying acts (Husserl, E.)
8:181
perception 6:59, 7:291–2
phenomenology of perception
(Merleau-Ponty, M.) 6:322
propositional attitudes 7:783–4
Prior, A.N. 7:689
qualia 7:866
radical empiricism (James, W.)
5:65–6
rational choice theory 8:71–2
representation (Arnauld, A.) 1:446

sentential meaning
testimony in Indian philosophy
9:316
social acts (Reinach, A.) 8:181
social science
methodology of 8:863–5
teleology 9:295–7
utterances (Grice, H.P.) 4:173–4
intentions
Islamic logic
quiddities (Ibn Sina) 5:707
interaction
aesthetic attitude 1:53
quantum field theory 3:672
social relations 8:779
interactionism *see* parallelism;
symbolic interactionism
intercultural philosophy
Latin American literature
(Jácome, G.A.) 5:655–6
Interessenjurisprudenz 5:513
interest theory
sociology of science 2:626
interests **6:752–5**
see also needs; public interest;
welfare
democracy 2:870
economic distribution 6:754
green political philosophy 4:162
group
African ethical systems 3:430–1,
3:432–3
ideology (Marx, K.) 6:124–6
moral powers 6:754–5
moral standing 6:551, 6:552
in politics 6:754
power 7:610–11
rational choice theory 8:64–73
social contract (Rousseau, J.-J.)
2:662
sociological jurisprudence
(Pound, R.) 7:609
theory choice 8:831
intermodal mapping
infant cognition 2:390
internal relations
Japanese logic 5:713–14
internalism
see also conceptual role semantics;
externalism
concepts
possession conditions 2:510–11
epistemic **4:821–6**
accessibility 4:821, 4:822
causal theory of knowledge
5:263

justification 5:157, 5:160–1,
  5:254, 8:206
naturalized epistemology
  6:723–4
perceptual knowledge 7:296
ethical
  epistemic comparison 3:368
  moral motivation 1:610–11,
  6:522–4, 6:536–7
  practical reason 7:614
internalist externalism
  Alston, W. 4:825
international justice *see* justice,
  international
international law 3:573
  see also international relations;
  justice, international
  Austin, J. 1:569
  Grotius, H. 4:185
  positive morality
  Austin, J. 1:569
  Pufendorf, S. 7:835
  sovereignty 9:58
  Suárez, F. 9:192
  Vitoria, F. de 9:644–5
international relations **4:826–33**,
  7:502
  see also federalism; international
  law; justice, international
  cosmopolitanism 4:830–2
  human rights 4:832
  law of nations 4:827
  political realism 4:827–8
  state morality 4:828–30
  Vitoria, F. de 9:644–5
  war and peace 9:689–90
interpretation
  see also exegesis; hermeneutics;
  translation
  anticipation contrast (Bacon, F.)
  1:628
  archaeological observation
  1:356–7
  artistic **1:502–5**, 1:513–15
  charity principle **2:282–5**
  complete statements (al-Farabi)
  5:709
  cultural relativism 8:80, 8:83
  dance 2:776
  fusion of horizons (Gadamer, H.-
  G.) 3:829
  glossary 5:804
  Indian theories of **4:833–7**
  etymologists 4:834
  grammarians 4:834–5
  Hindu law 4:836
  Mīmāṃsā 4:835

inflationary
  genealogy critique 4:2
legal hermeneutics 5:506–9
legal idealism (Gény, F.) 5:512–13
legal positivism 5:518–19
legal reasoning **5:525–31**
literature
  meaning 1:513–14, 1:515
  narratives
  social science 8:841–2
  pictures 2:894–5
  propositional attitudes
  (Dennett, D.C.) 2:882
  radical **8:25–3**
  Davidson, D. 2:802, 2:804–5,
  6:227–8
  structuralist literary theory
  (Todorov, T.) 9:425, 9:426
  textual analysis (Ricouer, P.) 8:320
interpretativism
  language of thought hypothesis
  5:407
interpreted logical forms (ILFs)
  7:776–7
interpretive school
  social science
  contemporary theories of 8:839,
  8:841–2
interrogatives *see* questions
inter-subjectivity 4:581–2, 8:117
intersubstitutability 4:743–5, 8:686–7
  context-dependence 8:687
  indirect discourse 4:743–5
  intensional entities 4:803–4
  proper names 7:755–6
interval scales
  measurement theory 6:244–5
intervention, divine *see* divine
  intervention
intimacy
  sexual relationships 8:726
intransitive particularity
  aesthetic attitude 1:54
intransitivity paradox
  economic efficiency 5:455
intrinsic properties
  beauty 1:681–2
intrinsic validity
  Mīmāṃsā 6:378, 6:379
intrinsicality
  perception
  phenomenal consciousness
  2:589
introjection
  elimination of (Avenarius, R.)
  1:594

psychoanalysis (Klein, M.) 7:818,
  7:819
introspection
  attentive-inattentive distinction
  2:590
  consciousness 2:581–94
  eliminativistic account of 3:264
  epistemology of **4:837–42**
  dualism 4:838, 4:841
  empiricism 3:299
  epistemic priority 4:840
  transparency 1:708, 4:838–9
  experiential
  phenomenal consciousness
  2:587
  folk psychology 3:686–7
  as inner perception
  phenomenal consciousness
  2:592–3
  knowledge by (Cousin, V.) 2:691
  Korean Buddhism (Chinul)
  2:330–1
  logical behaviourism (Ryle, G.)
  8:430
  Maine de Biran, P.-F. 6:49, 6:51–2
  mental content (Wundt, W.)
  7:825–6, 7:830
  mental imagery
  pictorial conception of 4:703,
  4:704
  methodological behaviourism
  1:696
  perception 7:290–1, 7:296
  phenomenal consciousness 2:582,
  2:589–90
  private language argument
  (Wittgenstein, L.) 7:696–7
  private states
  language 7:698–701
  psychoanalysis
  methodological issues in 7:815
  psychology of 4:839–40, **4:842–6**
  nature 4:843–4
  reliability 4:844–5
  qualia 2:588
  reliability of
  phenomenal consciousness
  2:591–2
  unconscious mental states
  castration complex 9:522
  connection principle 9:525
  informational pathways 9:523–4
  universal grammar 9:522, 9:524
intuition
  adequate knowledge (Spinoza, B.
  de) 9:100–1
  Anschauung (Husserl, E.) 4:579

art
Croce, B. 2:730–1
perception of 5:355
Bergson, H.-L. 1:732, 1:735
concepts (Helmholtz, H. von)
4:338, 4:339
of essence (Santayana, G.) 8:469
as a form of knowledge (al-
Sijistani) 8:775
intellectual
Fichte, J.G. 3:648
perceptual distinction 4:854–5
justification relationship 4:853,
4:854–5
Kant, I. 5:182
knowledge
rationalism 8:77–9
real-apparent distinction 8:79
veridicality of 8:79
Lessing, G.E. 5:576
mathematics (Poincaré, J.H.) 7:481
method (Descartes, R.) 3:5–6
moral (Mencius) 5:696
ontological commitment 7:113
perfection
divine 4:97–8
picture interpretation 2:893
rationality of belief 8:88–9
reason distinction (Iqbal, M.)
4:865–6
scepticism 8:496–7, 9:773
self analysis (Krause, K.) 5:299
of sensa (Kemp Smith, N.) 5:229
of space and time (Kant, I.)
5:184–5
vital reason (Ortega y Gasset, J.)
7:166
intuitionism
antirealism 4:856–63
Dummett, M.A.E. 3:152–3
Ariston of Chios 1:382
critiques of
Locke, J. 5:668
Ramsey, F.P. 8:45
ethical 4:853–6
Broad, C.D. 2:25–6
challenges to 1:221
Moore, G.E. 1:220–1, 6:713,
6:715–16
pluralism relationship 4:853
Prichard, H.A. 7:679, 7:680–1
utilitarianism relationship
9:552, 9:555
Golden Rule (Hare, R.M.) 4:230
infinity 4:776
legal reasoning 5:526, 5:528

logic 4:856–63
bivalence 4:856, 4:858–9
classical logic comparison
5:788–9
definition 4:857
many-valued logics 6:89–90
logical laws 5:788
mathematics 4:846–53, 6:183–4,
6:187
arithmetic 1:438–9
Brouwerian 2:635–6
category theory 2:235
geometry 4:31, 4:32
Kronecker, L. 5:311
logicism distinction 6:184
mathematical objects 8:120
meaning (Dummett, M.A.E.)
6:230, 6:233–4
truth
Dummett, M.A.E. 6:234
natural law 6:687
utilitarianism reconciliation
(Sidgwick, H.) 8:759–60
intuitive cognition
abstractive distinction
Chatton/Campsall debate 2:293
Duns Scotus, J. 1:565, 3:154,
3:165–6
existence of objects (John of
Mirecourt) 5:112
intuitive insight
Chinese philosophy (Sengzhao)
8:683
intuitivism
cognition (Lossky, N.O.) 5:833,
5:834–5
invariance
conservation principles 2:607
logical constants 5:777–9
measurement theory 6:246–7
invention
dialectic (Melanchthon, P.)
6:289–90
discursive knowledge as (Le Roy,
É.L.E.J.) 5:481
rhetoric (Melanchthon, P.) 6:289
subversion (Certeau, M. de)
2:268–9
inverted spectrum argument 2:420,
2:424, 2:425
investigative journalism
ethics of 5:128
Inwood, Brad
Epictetus †3:337–9
Hellenistic philosophy 4:336
Hierocles †4:421–2
Marcus Aurelius †6:93–5

Musonius Rufus †6:615–16
Seneca, L.A. †8:679–82
Stoicism 9:160
Inwood, Michael
Hartmann, N. †4:240–2
Hegel, G.W.F. 4:279
hermeneutics †4:384–9
Ionescu, Nae 3:260
Ioppolo, A.M. 1:382
Iqbal, Muhammad 4:863–8
knowledge 4:865–6
politics 4:866
Self 4:863, 4:864–5
Iran
see also Persia
al-'Amiri 1:207–8
al-Dawani 2:806–7
Ibn Miskawayh 4:630–3
al-Juwayni 5:169–70
Mir Damad, Muhammad Baqir
6:408–11
Mulla Sadra 6:595–9
al-Razi, Abu Bakr 8:110–12
al-Razi, Fakhr al-Din 8:112–15
al-Sabzawari 8:440–2
al-Sijistani 8:774–6
al-Suhrawardi 9:219–24
al-Tawhidi 9:271–2
al-Tusi 9:504–7
Iraq
al-Baghdadi 1:636–8
al-Ghazali 4:61–8
Ibn 'Adi 4:599–601
Ibn Kammuna 4:621–3
Ibn ar-Rawandi 4:636–8
al-Kindi 5:249–53
al-Sijistani 8:774–6
Ireland
Berkeley, G. 1:737–50
Boyle, R. 1:853–7
Browne, P. 2:29–30
Burke, E. 2:136–40
Eriugena, J.S. 3:401–6
Hutcheson, F. 4:588–94
Richard of St Victor 8:312–14
Toland, J. 9:427–9
Irele, F. Abiola
African philosophy
aesthetics 1:65
Francophone †1:108–17
Iremonger, F. 9:301
Irenaeus
divine simplicity 8:787
Gnosticism 4:84, 4:85
providence 7:798, 7:801
irenicism 6:326, 7:393
Iriarte, J. 9:196

Irigaray, Luce **5:1–4**
  language and gender 5:367
  psychoanalytic feminism 3:584,
    3:587
  subject
    postmodern critique of 9:201
Irish, J.A. 6:841
Iriya, Y. 5:646
Irizawa, Sōju 5:177
ironism
  epistemological justification
    (Rorty, R.) 8:353–4
irony
  meaning of life 5:631
irrational numbers 1:218, 7:48–9, 7:51
irrationalism
  paradox of fiction 3:276
  scepticism (Feyerabend, P.K.)
    3:641–2
irrationality
  see also rationality
  charity (Dennett, D.) 2:283
  Dostoevskii, F.M. 3:116–17
  naturalized epistemology 6:725
irrationals
  thermodynamics (Meyerson, É.)
    6:349–50
irreflexivity
  belief basis 3:721, 3:722
Irvine, M. 3:308
Irving, L. 5:425
Irwin, A.C. 9:412
Irwin, J.L. 8:559
Irwin, T.
  Aristotle 3:382
  language
    ancient philosophy of 5:361
Irwin, Terence H.
  Aquinas, T. 1:347
  Aristotle †1:413–35
  Cyrenaics 2:763
  eudaimonia 3:451
  Plato 7:420
Isaac ben Moses Levi *see* Duran,
  Profiat
Isaac Israeli *see* Israeli, Isaac ben
  Solomon
Isaac, J.C. 2:196
Isaac of Stella **5:4–5**
Isaacson, H. 7:65
Isbell, J.C. 9:118
Isenberg, A. 3:708
Isfahan, School of 6:408, 6:618–19
Isham, C.J. 2:680
Ishida, Ichirō 5:43
Ishiguro, H. 5:378, 5:561
Ishikawa, Matsutaro 5:177

ishraq see Illuminationist philosophy
Isidore of Seville
  Encyclopedists, medieval 3:305,
    3:307
  logic 5:747
  natural philosophy
    medieval 6:692
Islam
  see also Ash'ariyya; Islamic
  philosophy; Mu'tazila; Qur'an;
  Shi'a; Sufism
  African ethical systems 3:434
  attributes of
    fundamentalism 5:11–12
  Christianity comparison (Ibn
    Kammuna) 4:621–2
  creation 2:241–2, 2:243, 4:630
  divine simplicity 8:784–5
  early disputes 5:26
  emanationism
    objections to 2:696–7
  equality 4:866
  eternity of the world
    medieval view 2:697–8
  exclusivism 8:260
  fundamentalism 5:9–5:12
  human freedom 2:242–3
  immortality 4:641
  inclusivism 8:261
  influence of
    Jewish philosophy 6:38–9,
      6:604–5
    Proclus 7:730
  Judaism comparison (Ibn
    Kammuna) 4:621–2
  just ruler
    Platonism 7:429–30
  mysticism **6:616–20**, 6:625–6
    influence on Jewish philosophy
      (Maimonides, A.) 6:38–9
  Orientalism 7:158–9
  philosophy relationship 5:5–9,
    5:14–15, **5:25–31**
    al-'Amiri 1:207
    Aristotelianism 1:384–5
    al-Ghazali 4:639–41
    Ibn al-'Arabi 4:602–3
    Ibn Rushd 4:643
    al-Kindi 5:250
    Mulla Sadra 6:598
    Platonism 7:429–30
    al-Razi, Fakhr al-Din 8:112–13
    al-Sijistani 8:774, 8:775
  political philosophy in **7:518–21**
  providence 7:798
  resurrection 8:294

  revelation 8:298–300
    Qur'an 8:297
  science **8:561–5**
  sin 8:791–2
  state
    divinity of 7:518
  theology **5:25–31**
    Ibn al-'Arabi 4:602–3
    al-Razi, Fakhr al-Din 8:112–13
  unity of 5:10–11
Islamic fundamentalism *see*
  fundamentalism
Islamic medicine *see* (al-)Razi, Abu
  Bakr Muhammad ibn
  Zakariyya'
Islamic philosophy **5:5–9, 5:13–16**
  'Abduh, M. **1:6–8**
  aesthetics **1:75–9**, 5:15
  al-Afghani **1:94–5**
  al-'Amiri **1:207–8**
  Aristotelianism *see*
    Aristotelianism, Islamic
    philosophy
  Ash'ariyya **1:519–23**
  beauty 1:75–7
  causality **2:241–4**
  Christianity relationship
    Liber de causis 5:596
    Nicholas of Cusa 6:835
  al-Dawani **2:806–7**
  definition of 5:5–6
  early history 5:6–7, 5:13–14
  epistemology **3:384–8**
  ethics **3:438–42**
  al-Farabi **3:554–8**
  al-Ghazali **4:61–8**, 4:639–41
  God
    existence of
      kalam argument 4:86–7
  Ibn al-'Arabi **4:601–5**
  Ibn Hazm **4:620–1**
  Ibn Khaldun **4:623–7**
  Ibn Massara **4:627–30**
  Ibn Miskawayh **4:630–3**
  Ibn ar-Rawandi **4:636–8**
  Ibn Rushd **4:638–46**
  Ibn Sab'in **4:646–7**
  Ibn Sina **4:647–54**
  Ibn Taymiyya **4:655–6**
  Ibn Tufayl **4:657–9**
  Ikhwan al-Safa' **4:685–8**
  Illuminationist philosophy **4:700–3**
    Jewish philosophy comparison
      (al-Baghdadi) 1:637
  imagination 1:77–9
  imitation 1:77–9

influence of
  medieval philosophy 6:271–2,
    6:275
influenced by
  Greek philosophy **4:155–9**
  Plotinus 7:462
  Simplicius 8:790
Iqbal, M. **4:863–8**
al-Juwayni **5:169–70**
al-Kindi **5:249–53**
law **5:457–60**
logic 5:15, **5:706–13**
meaning 5:15, **6:236–9**
Mir Damad, Muhammad Baqir
  6:408–11
modern **1:6–8**, **5:16–21**, 5:30
Mulla Sadra **6:595–9**
Mu'tazila **1:519–23**
mystical philosophy 5:14, **6:616–20**
natural philosophy 2:243
necessity **2:241–4**, 4:640
Neoplatonism 3:554, 3:555–6,
  5:13, 5:13–14, **6:803–8**
occasionalism 7:87
Orientalism **7:158–60**
Platonism 5:13–14, **7:429–30**
poetics 1:75, 1:77
political philosophy 5:14–15
prophecy 7:768
al-Razi, Fakhr al-Din **8:112–15**
al-Sabzawari **8:440–2**
science and religion 8:230
scientific
  influence on medieval natural
    philosophy 6:275
Shah Wali Allah **8:732–5**
al-Sijistani **8:774–6**
soul **9:40–4**
al-Suhrawardi **9:219–24**
al-Tawhidi **9:271–2**
theology relationship 1:77, **5:5–9**,
  5:6–7, 5:14–15, **5:25–31**
  al-'Amiri 1:207
  Aristotelianism 1:384–5
  al-Ghazali 4:639–41
  Ibn al-'Arabi 4:602–3
  Ibn Rushd 4:643
  al-Kindi 5:250
  Mulla Sadra 6:598
  Platonism 7:429–30
  al-Razi, Fakhr al-Din 8:112–13
  al-Sijistani 8:774, 8:775
translations
  of Aristotle 1:394, 1:397,
    1:398–9
  by Gerard of Cremona 4:37–8
  to Latin 9:455

medieval natural philosophy
  6:692–3, 6:698
transmission into Western Europe
  5:21–5
al-Tusi **9:504–7**
Isma'ilism
  mystical philosophy 6:617
  Neoplatonism 6:804–5, 6:806–7
  al-Tusi 9:504, 9:505
Isnardi Parente, M. 4:422, 9:163
isomorphism
  category theory 2:233
  glossary 5:804
  invariance under
    logical constants 5:778
    type quantifiers 7:874, 7:876
  measurement theory 6:244
    ordinal scales 6:245–6
is/ought distinction
  applied ethics 1:320
  evolution 3:474–5
  legal positivism 5:515
  logic of ethical discourse 5:759–61
  moral action
    utilitarianism (Bentham, J.)
      1:718–19, 1:721, 1:722
  moral knowledge 6:517, 6:518
  morality
    Humean challenge 4:556
  natural law 6:685–6
  non-derivability of (Weinberger, O.)
    9:702
  political philosophy 7:526
  practical reason and ethics
    (Hegel, G.W.F.) 7:617
  scientific explanation (Lotze, R.H.)
    5:839
Israel
  divine election
    Hebrew Bible 1:766, 1:768–9
    Holocaust relationship 4:497
  Jewish eschatology (Bar Hayya, A.)
    1:650
  Leibowitz, Yeshayahu **5:562–4**
  providence (Nahmanides, M.)
    6:649
  reconstructionism (Kaplan, M.)
    5:205
  state/religion relationship
    (Leibowitz, Y.) 5:562, 5:563–4
  world Jewry relations (Ha'am,
    Ahad) 4:193
  Zionism **9:867–70**
Israel Ben Eliezer, Rabbi 4:243, 5:87
Israel, D. 8:672
Israel, H. 7:135

Israeli, Isaac Ben Solomon **5:31–4**,
  5:87
Issawi, Charles
  Ibn Khaldun †4:623–7
Isupov, K.G. 3:682
Īśvarakṛṣṇa 2:257, 6:200, 8:462
IT *see* information technology
Italy **5:34–42**
  Alemanno, Y. **1:161–3**
  Alighieri, Dante **1:181–5**
  Aquinas, T. **1:326–50**
  Archytas **1:366–9**
  Bartolus of Sassoferrato **1:658–9**
  Blasius of Parma **1:784–7**
  Bobbio, N. **1:790–2**
  Boethius, A.M.S. **1:801–13**
  Bonaventure **1:828–35**
  Bruno, G. **2:34–9**
  Cajetan **2:171–5**
  Campanella, T. **2:186–91**
  Cardano, G. **2:202–4**
  Cattaneo, C. **2:239–41**
  Cicero, M.T. **2:355–60**
  Counter-Reformation 5:34–6
  Croce, B. **2:728–35**
  Damian, P. **2:772–4**
  Delmedigo, E. **2:861–3**
  Empedocles **3:293–8**
  Enlightenment 5:36
  Fardella, M. **3:558–60**
  Ficino, M. **3:653–9**
  Galilei, G. **3:835–41**
  Gentile, G. **4:19–23**
  George of Trebizond **4:34–6**
  Gerard of Cremona **4:37–8**
  Gerdil, G.S. **4:41–2**
  Giles of Rome **4:72–8**
  Gioberti, V. **4:78–80**
  Gorgias **4:144–6**
  Gramsci, A. **4:151–5**
  Gregory of Rimini **4:170–2**
  Hegelianism 4:287, 4:292, 4:294
  Herrera, A. Cohen de **4:397–400**
  Hillel ben Samuel of Verona
    4:431–3
  humanism 4:529
  Immanuel ben Solomon of Rome
    4:708–10
  James of Viterbo **5:58–60**
  Joachim of Fiore **5:103–5**
  Judah ben Moses of Rome
    5:128–31
  Labriola, A. **5:335–6**
  legal institutionalism 4:800–1
  Machiavelli, N. **6:17–22**
  Marcus Aurelius **6:93–5**
  Marius Victorinus **6:105–7**

Marsilius of Padua **6:112–14**
Matthew of Aquasparta **6:200–3**
Messer Leon **6:331–5**
Musonius Rufus **6:615–16**
Nifo, A. **6:867–72**
Parmenides **7:228–35**
Patrizi, F. **7:261–5**
Paul of Venice **7:265–6**
Peter Lombard **5:821–2**
Petrarca, F. **7:325–9**
Philolaus **7:367–71**
Pico della Mirandola, G. **7:386–92**
Pomponazzi, P. **7:529–33**
Rosmini-Serbati, A. **8:362–4**
Silvestri, F. **8:776–8**
Telesio, B. **9:297–300**
Tertullian, Quintus Septimus
    Florens **9:307–9**
Valla, L. **9:568–73**
Vernia, N. **9:596–9**
Vico, G. **9:599–606**
Zabarella, J. **9:836–9**

iteration operation
    dynamic logics 3:190–1
iterative conception
    set theory 8:709, 8:713
I–Thou relationship
    Buber, M. 2:42, 2:43–5
    Feuerbach, L.A. 3:636
Itinerarium mentis in Deum (Journey
    of the Mind to God) *see*
    Bonaventure
Itō Jinsai **5:42–4**, 7:90
al-ittisal see conjunction
Iturrioz, J. 9:196
Iudin, P.F. 1:526, 6:158
iusnaturalists *see* natural law
Ivanhoe, Philip J.
    cheng †2:300
    Chinese philosophy of history
        †4:446–52
    li †5:594–5
    Mencius 6:304
    Mohist philosophy †6:451–8

neo-Confucianism †6:764–76
self-cultivation
    Chinese philosophy 8:625–6
ti/yong †9:399–400
xin †9:816–17
Ivan'o, I. 8:803
Ivanov, Viacheslav 6:863, 6:866
Ivanov, V.V. 6:588
Iversen, E. 3:254
IVF *see* in vitro fertilization
Ivry, A.L. 6:334
Iyer, K.A.S. 1:766, 4:837
Iyer Raghavan, N. 3:843
Izenberg, G. German 8:351–2
Izutsu Toshihiko
    Ibn al-'Arabi 4:605
    Ibn Taymiyya 4:656
    Illuminationist philosophy 4:703
    Mulla Sadra 6:599
    al-Sabzawari 8:441
    Zeami 9:841

J

Jaanus, M. 7:822
al-Jabiri, Muhammad 'Abid 5:17
Jabre, F. 4:67–8
Jabriyya 5:26, 5:27–8
Jack, H.A. 3:843
Jack, M. 3:632
Jackendoff, R. 2:516, 5:407
Jackson, B.S. 5:497, 5:499, 5:531
Jackson, C.T. 8:42
Jackson, D.P. 8:434, 9:408
Jackson, Frank
  adverbial theory of mental states
    6:317
  Armstrong, D.M. †1:441–3
  Australia, philosophy in 1:579,
    1:583
  belief †1:702–6
  bodily sensations 1:795
  colour 2:427, 2:431
  concepts 2:516
  consciousness 2:595
  counterfactual conditionals 2:688
  desire 3:33
  dualism 3:138
  epiphenomenalism 3:354
  identity theory of mind †6:394–9
  indicative conditionals †4:740–3
  materialism 6:177
  mental causation 6:311
  mind, philosophy of †6:403–7
  Passmore, J.A. †7:247–8
  perception 7:293, 7:298–9
  phenomenal consciousness
    2:584–5
  propositional attitudes 7:786
  qualia 2:427, 7:867
  reasons and causes 8:127
  sense-data 8:698
  Smart, J.J.C. †8:813–15
Jackson, J.D. 3:260
Jackson, R. 7:607, 8:434–5
Jackson, R.L. 3:119
Jacob, J.R. 1:857
Jacob, M. 9:429
Jacob, Margaret C.
  Bentley, R. 1:726
  Illuminati †4:696–8
Jacob, W. 4:207
Jacobelli, J. 4:23

Jacobi, Friedrich Heinrich 5:45–8
  German idealism 4:42, 4:44
  Herder, J.G. 4:382–3
  pantheism controversy
    (Schelling, F.W.J. von) 8:510
Jacobi, H. 6:34
Jacobi, Klaus
  Gilbert of Poitiers †4:68–72
  medieval logic 5:758
  Nicholas of Cusa 6:838
Jacobitti, E.E. 2:734, 4:301
Jacobovits, I. 1:779
Jacobs, C. 2:812
Jacobs, L. 1:769
Jacobs, W.G. 3:652, 6:741
Jacobsen, T. 1:769
Jacobson, K. 2:391–2, 2:395
Jacobus de Voragine 6:624
Jácome, Gustavo Alfredo 5:655–7
Jacquette, D. 8:554
Jadaane, Fehmi 5:252, 8:775
Jaeger, W. 1:434, 6:764, 9:653–4
Jaeschke, W. 3:639
Jaffa, H.V. 1:347
Jäger, G. 7:748, 7:751
Jager, R. 8:403
Jaggar, Alison M. 3:604–5
al-Jahiz 4:637
Jähnig, D. 8:519
Jahoda, G. 9:801
Jain, A.K. 2:579
Jain, H. 6:34
Jaina philosophy 5:48–5
  cosmology 2:681, 2:684
  epistemology 5:50–2
  ethics 5:52–3
  heaven 4:255
  Indian and Tibetan 4:737, 4:738
  influence of (Gandhi, M.K.)
    3:842–3
  karma 5:211, 5:215, 8:449
  Kundakunda 5:53–4
  logic 5:50–2
  Mahāvīra 6:33–4
  manifoldness 6:77–81
    seven standpoints 6:78–81
    syāt 6:78
  metaphysics 5:50
  mysticism 6:622

nonabsolutism
  causation 2:252–3, 2:256–7
  ontology 5:49–50, 7:119
  reincarnation 8:183, 8:184–5
  renunciation 3:183, 3:185
  salvation 8:447–8, 8:449
  Siddharsena Divākara 5:54–5
  Umāsvāti 5:54
  universals 9:546
  virtue 3:185–6
Jaini, P.S. 5:56, 5:217, 9:586–7
Jaki, S.L. 3:147
Jakobson, E. 7:822
Jakobson, R.
  Russian literary formalism 8:413
Jakobson, Roman
  influence on Lévi-Strauss, C.
    5:582–3
  structuralism 9:175
    in literary theory 9:183–4
Jakovenko, B. 2:769, 4:306, 5:838
Jalal al-Azm, S. 7:160
'Jam dbyangs bzhad pa (Jamyang
  shayba) 9:402
'Jam mgon kong sprul (Jamgön
  gongtrul) 9:403
James of Venice 1:397, 9:455–6
James of Viterbo 5:58–60
James, E.D. 3:693, 9:662–3
James, F.A. III 1:564
James, G.G.M. 3:254
James, H. 5:67
James, Susan
  feminism †3:576–83
  holism and individualism in
    history and social science 4:488
James, William 5:60–8
  agnosticism 1:123
  American philosophy
    eighteenth and nineteenth
      century 1:204, 1:206
  consciousness 2:595
  Dewey, J. 3:45, 3:51
  Ducasse, C.J. 3:142
  emotions 3:281–2, 3:285, 3:288,
    3:289
  epiphenomenalism 3:354

fallibilism
    pragmatism in ethics 7:640–1,
        7:643
Fechner, G.T. 3:572
Hegelianism 4:287–8
Husserl, E. 4:582, 4:587
inner life
    moral agents 6:502, 6:503
instrumentalism 9:478, 9:479–80
introspection, psychology of 2:593,
    4:844, 4:846
mysticism, nature of 6:627–8,
    6:629, 6:633
neutral monism 6:816, 6:817
panpsychism 7:197
phenomenology 7:342
of religion 7:353, 7:355
pluralism 7:463–4
pragmatism 5:60, 5:64–5, 7:633–4,
    7:639
psychology 5:61–2
radical empiricism 5:60, 5:61,
    5:65–6
realism/antirealism 8:119
religious experience 5:63–4,
    8:250–2, 8:255
Royce, J. 8:379
symbolic interactionism 9:245
theological virtues 9:330
Jameson, Fredric
    alterity and identity
        postmodern theories of 1:191
    Derrida, J. 2:901
    Lefebvre, H 5:491
    Lukács, G. 5:859
    Lyotard, J.-F. 6:11
    post-structuralism/postmodernism
        distinction 9:200, 9:201
    Russian literary formalism 8:413
Jamgön gongtrul see 'Jam mgon kong
    sprul
Jami, C. 7:577–8
Jamieson, D.
    animal language and thought
        †1:269–73
Jammer, M. 4:329, 6:196, 7:894
Jamyang shayba see 'Jam dbyangs
    bzhad pa
Jan Marcus Marci of Kronland 2:765
Jan, Yün-hua 9:872
Jana 8:813
Janáček, K. 8:717
Janaway, Christopher
    Schopenhauer, A. †8:545–54
Jancel, R. 9:369
Janet, P. 2:51
Janich, P. 5:826, 5:828

Janik, L.G. 3:133
Janke, W. 3:653
Jansen, B. 7:96
Jansen, C.O. 7:286
Jansenism
    clandestine literature 2:375
    Pascal, B.
        anti-casuistry 2:228
        conversion to 7:241, 7:242–3
        Jesuit attack 7:243
    Port-Royal 7:551–2
Jansenius, C.
    see also Jansenism
    Arnauld, A. 1:447
    Port-Royal 7:553–4
Janssens, J.L. 4:654
Jantzen, G. 7:107
Janz, C.P. 6:861
Japan 5:68–79
    aesthetics 1:79–91
    Buddhist philosophy 2:99–2:106
    bushi philosophy 2:146–50
    Confucian philosophy 2:549–55
    Dōgen 3:109–11
    existential phenomenology 7:338
    Fujiwara Seika 3:799–801
    Itō Jinsai 5:42–4
    Kaibara Ekken 5:176–7
    kokoro 5:291–3
    Kūkai 5:318–20
    Kuki Shūzō 5:320–1
    Kumazawa Banzan 5:321–2
    Kyoto School 5:323–30
    logic 5:713–16
    Miki Kiyoshi 6:358–9
    modern literature 5:657–60
    Motoori Norinaga 6:588–90
    mysticism 6:622–3
    Nichiren 6:828–9
    Nishi Amane 7:12–13
    Nishida Kitarō 7:13–16
    Nishitani Keiji 7:16–17
    Ogyū Sorai 7:90–2
    senguku age 2:148
    Shinran 8:746–8
    Shintō 8:748–51
    Shōtoku Constitution 8:752–4
    Tanabe Hajime 9:261–2
    Tominaga Nakamoto 9:440–1
    Watsuji Tetsurō 9:691–3
    Zeami 9:839–41
Jaquelot, Isaac 1:676, 1:677
Jardin, A. 9:425
Jardine, L.
    Bacon, F. 1:632
    Erasmus, D. 3:401

language
    Renaissance philosophy of
        5:415
logic
    Renaissance 5:772
scepticism
    Renaissance 8:503
Jardine, N. 6:740, 8:580
Jarka-Sellers, Hannes
    Liber de causis †5:595–8
    Pseudo-Dionysius †7:804–8
Jarrett, J. 1:716
Jarvie, I.C.
    Popper, K.R. †7:533–40
Jarvis, S. 1:46, 4:301
Jarvis Thompson, Judith 8:277, 8:280
Jasanoff, S. 9:283
Jaśkowski, S. 7:210, 7:497
Jasper, D. 2:406
Jaspers, Karl 5:80–4
    existentialism 3:505, 5:80–1
    reason 5:81–2
    Schelling, F.W.J. von 8:519–20
    technology and ethics 9:283
    Transcendence 5:81
Jaspert, B. 2:130
Jay, J. 2:872, 3:574
Jay, M.
    Adorno, T.W. 1:46
    critical theory 2:728
    Frankfurt School 3:736–7
    Hegelianism 4:301
    Lefebvre, H 5:491
    Marcuse, H. 6:98
Jayanta (Bhaṭṭa) 6:757–8, 7:65, 9:548
Jayarāśi 5:56, 6:180, 6:181
Jayatilleke, K.N. 4:765, 6:181
Jaynes, E.T. 7:710, 7:711, 9:369
Jeanrond, W.G. 4:395
Jeanson, F. 8:479
Jeauneau, Edouard 2:292, 9:373,
    9:731
Jech, T.J. 1:614, 3:697, 8:708
Jednota Bratvská (Unity of Brethren)
    2:765
Jefferson, Thomas 5:84–5
    religious liberty 8:227
Jeffery, G.B. 8:199
Jeffner, A. 2:160
Jeffrey conditionalization (JC) 7:707,
    7:708
Jeffrey, J.C. 3:702–3
Jeffrey, Richard
    see also Jeffrey conditionalization
        (JC)
    causation 2:251
    computer science 2:495

explanation 3:523, 3:525
Gödel's theorems 4:114
Hempel, C.G. †4:348–52
inductive inference 4:758
models 6:446
probability
    and epistemology 7:707, 7:711
    interpretations of 7:705
Ramsey, F.P. 8:49
Jeffreys, Harold 8:783
Jehuda ben Becalel Liva (Rabbi Löw)
    2:765, 2:769
Jenkins, I. 5:101
Jenkins, R. 1:850
Jennings, Jeremy
    Sorel, Georges †9:34–6
Jennings, W.I. 4:802
Jensen, H. 4:593
Jensen, J.V. 4:595–6
Jenson, K. 1:820
Jenson, R.W. 3:245
Jenyns, Soame 5:122–3
Jerome 7:285, 7:837
Jeroslow, R. 4:112, 4:117
Jesuits (Society of Jesus)
    Brazilian philosophy
        Portuguese influence 2:8, 2:9
    casuistry 2:228
    Collegium Conimbricense 2:406–7
    colonial philosophy
        Latin America 5:422, 5:424
        Mexico 6:345
    Fonseca, P. da 3:687–90
    Illuminati 4:697
    Jansenism dispute (Pascal, B.)
        7:243
    Latin America
        modernity in 5:427
    Teilhard de Chardin, P. 9:288–91
    Thomism 9:382–3
Jesus Christ
    see also Christology; Incarnation;
        Trinity
    Adam comparison 8:793
    atonement 1:536, 1:537–40
    concepts of
        Gnosticism 6:75
        Manicheism 6:75, 6:76
        Niebuhr, H.R. 6:839–40
        Niebuhr, R. 6:842
    divinity of (Brunner, E.) 2:31
    Eucharist 8:443, 8:444
    exemplar of virtue (Bonaventure)
        1:833
    faith 3:539
    Gospels
        literal interpretation of 3:778–9

representation in (Loisy, A.)
    5:819, 5:820
heaven 4:250
human/divine nature
    Boethius, A.M.S. 1:807
    Hellenistic Judaism 7:256
    Nicholas of Cusa 6:835
justification by faith (Luther, M.)
    6:1, 6:2
Lewis trilemma 5:590
liberation theology 5:614, 5:615
middle nature (Conway, A.) 2:670
Muhammad comparison
    Orientalism 7:158–9
mysticism 6:623
mythology of
    Bultmann, R. 2:126, 2:127–8,
        2:129
    Strauss, D.F. 9:164–5, 9:166
reality of (Bonhoeffer, D.) 1:836
redemption (Calvin, J.) 2:180
religious symbolism (Tillich, P.)
    9:411
reprobation 8:275
resurrection 8:38, 8:294
salvation 8:249
sanctification 8:455–6
Scriptures (Origen) 7:161
suffering of (Bonhoeffer, D.)
    1:835–6
theology of the word (Barth, K.)
    1:653
two natures controversy
    monophysitism (Philoponus)
        7:375
unification of humanity (Teilhard
    de Chardin, P.) 9:288, 9:290
Jevons, William Stanley
    Boole, G. 1:843
    logic
        logic machines 5:744
        nineteenth century 5:728
    science, nineteenth century
        philosophy of 8:566, 8:570,
            8:571
Jewish bioethics 1:776–80
    abortion 1:778–9
    euthanasia 1:777–8
    medicine 1:777
    organ donation 1:779
    triage 1:778
Jewish philosophy 5:85–90
    see also Judaism
    Abravanel, I. 1:19–23
    Abravanel, J. 1:23–7
    Albo, J. 1:152–5
    Alemanno, Y. 1:161–3

Arama, I. 1:350–1
Averroism 1:598–602
al-Baghdadi 1:636–8
Bar Hayya, A. 1:649–51
Baumgardt, D. 1:667–9
Buber, M. 2:42–8
Christian philosophy
    medieval 6:271–2
Cohen, H. 2:398–403
contemporary 5:90–6
Crescas, H. 2:700–4
Delmedigo, E. 2:861–3
Duran, P. 3:170–1
Duran, S. 3:171–2
early nineteenth century
    5:96–5:100
Enlightenment 3:320–4
Fackenheim, E.L. 3:533–5
Gersonides 4:47–51
Ha'am, Ahad 4:192–3
halakhah 4:204–7
Herrera, A. Cohen de 4:397–400
Heschel, A.J. 4:410–12
Hillel ben Samuel of Verona
    4:431–3
Holocaust 4:495–9
Ibn Daud, A. 4:608–11
Ibn Ezra, A. 4:611–13
Ibn Ezra, M. 4:613–15
Ibn Falaquera 4:615–17
Ibn Gabirol, S. 4:617–20
Ibn Kammuna 4:621–3
Ibn Paquda, B. 4:633–6
Ibn Tzaddik, J. 4:659–62
Immanuel ben Solomon of Rome
    4:708–10
Islamic philosophy
    influence on 5:21, 5:23–4
Israeli, I. 5:31–4
Judah ben Moses of Rome
    5:128–31
Judah Halevi 4:207–13
Kaplan, M. 5:204–6
Krochmal, N. 5:308–11
Leibowitz, Y. 5:562–4
logos
    Philo of Alexandria 5:819
Maimon, S. 6:35–8
Maimonides, A. 6:38–40
Maimonides, M. 6:40–9
Mendelssohn, M. 6:304–7
Messer Leon 6:331–5
midrash 6:353–5
al-Muqammas, D. 6:604–6
Nahmanides, M. 6:647–51
Philo of Alexandria 7:357–61
pneuma (spirit) 7:470, 7:471

prophecy 7:768–9
Rosenzweig, F. **8:357–62**
Saadiah Gaon **8:435–40**
Shem Tov family **8:737–40**
Soloveitchik, J.B. **9:26–8**
strengths 5:87
traditionalism
    contemporary 5:92–4
voluntarism **9:664–7**
weaknesses 5:86–7
Zionism **9:867–70**
Jha, G. 4:256, 6:381
Jhering, Rudolf von **5:100–2**
Ji 9:792
Jia Yi **5:102–3**
jian'ai (impartial care) 6:452, 6:453–4,
    6:457
jihad 5:10, 5:17–18, 5:19
Jiménez Garcia, A. 9:521
jin (humaneness) 7:90
Jinas (Fordmakers) 5:52–3
jing (classics)
    Chinese Confucianism
        tradition 2:545
jing (stillness)
    neo-Confucianism (Zhou Dunyi)
        6:768
jing (vital essence)
    Yangzhu 9:822
Jing Hao 1:72–3
Jinsai *see* Itō Jinsai
Jiří-Novy 2:769
Jiuyuan *see* Lu Xiangshan
Jñānagarbha 2:61
Jñānaśrīmitra 9:512–13
Joachim of Fiore 1:828, **5:103–5**
Joachim, H.H. 9:107
Joas, Hans
    Frankfurt School 3:736
    Habermas, J. 4:199
    Mead, G.H. †6:210–12
    pragmatism in ethics 7:643
Job, Book of
    Aquinas' commentaries on
        1:329–30
Jōdo School *see* Pure Land
    Buddhism
Joel, K. 9:814
Joerges, C. 2:720
Johansson, I. 7:539
John of Alexandria *see* Philoponus
John Chrysostom 4:94, 4:101, 4:391
John of the Cross 6:625, 6:762
John of Damascus **5:105–6**
John of Fidanza *see* Bonaventure
John the Grammarian *see* Philoponus

John of Jandun **5:106–9**
    agent sense 1:407–8
    Ibn Rushd 1:402, 1:408
John of La Rochelle 1:176, 1:177,
    5:109–11
John of Mirecourt **5:111–13**
John of Paris **5:113–15**
John of St Thomas **5:117–20**
John of Salisbury **5:115–17**
    Chartres school 2:292
John of Scythopolis 7:808
John of Seville 9:455
John of Spain *see* Ibn Daud,
    Abraham
John XXII, Pope 9:732, 9:733–4
John Paul II, Pope 9:384–5, 9:388
Johnson, Alexander Bryan **5:120–2**
Johnson, B. 8:337
Johnson, C. 9:256
Johnson, D. 2:496
Johnson, D.G. 3:315, 4:781
Johnson, D.S. 2:475, 7:664, 8:59
Johnson, E. 6:554
Johnson, Elizabeth 3:622, 3:624
Johnson, F. 5:692, 5:693
Johnson, F.E. 8:260
Johnson, L.E. 4:165
Johnson, M. 4:708, 6:338, 7:299
Johnson, M.H. 6:675
Johnson, P.F.
    Alembert, J. le R. d' †1:163–8
    Condillac, É.B. de †2:522–7
Johnson, R.A. 2:130
Johnson, Samuel **5:124–6**
Johnson, Dr Samuel **5:122–3**
    art and morality 1:456
    poetry 7:477
Johnson, W.E. 7:721, 7:723
Johnson-Laird, P.N.
    behaviourism in the social sciences
        1:695
    reasoning
        rationality of belief 8:86–7,
            8:88, 8:89, 8:90
Johnston, D. 4:476
Johnston, E.H. 8:467
Johnston, G.A. 1:749–50, 2:411
Johnston, Mark 2:431, 2:654, 6:575,
    8:599
Johnston, Mark D.
    Llull, R. †5:662–4
Johnston, P. 9:770, 9:772
Johnstone, P. 2:236
joint action
    social action 8:822–3
joint commitment
    social rules 8:835

joint intention
    social action 8:822–3
Jōjitsu (Establishment of Truth)
    school 2:101
Jolivet, J. 1:14, 5:25, 5:252
Jolivet, R. 5:339
Jolley, N. 5:561–2, 6:66, 8:891
Jolowicz, H.F. 3:832
Joly, B. 1:158
Jomier, J. 1:8
Jo-nang-pa School of Buddhism
    9:402–3
Jonas, H. 3:501, 4:85
Jonas, Hans 3:335–6, 9:280, 9:281,
    9:283, 9:287
Jones, C.P. 5:854
Jones, D.H. 2:581
Jones, G. 2:130
Jones, G.H. 3:857, 9:713
Jones, H. 3:349
Jones, J. 8:470
Jones, J.M. 1:790
Jones, K. 2:263
Jones, Karen
    trust †9:466–70
Jones, O.R. 6:407, 7:698
Jones, Peter
    freedom of speech †3:762–5
    Hume, D. 4:561
    Smith, A. 8:821
Jones, R. 5:474
Jones, R.A. 3:177
Jones, R.M. 7:470
Jones, Roger
    optics †7:136–9
Jones, W. Gareth
    Russian Enlightenment †3:324–7
Jones myth
    folk psychology (Sellars, W.)
        3:686–7
Jonsen, A.R. 2:228, 3:490
Joos, M. 9:181
Joost, U. 5:624
Joravsky, David
    Bogdanov, A.A. †1:816–20
    partiinost' †7:238–41
    Russian empiriocriticism †8:404–9
    Vygotskii, L.S. †9:671–5
Jordan, C. 1:132
Jordan, G. 6:5
Jordan, J. 5:644
Jordan, Mark D.
    Aquinas, T. 1:347–8
    Aristotelianism
        medieval †1:393–404
    Augustinianism †1:559–65
    Gerard of Cremona †4:37–8

Hugh of St Victor †4:518–20
John of La Rochelle †5:109–11
John of Paris †5:113–15
John of Salisbury †5:115–17
Neckham, A. †6:750–2
Pseudo-Grosseteste †7:808–9
Jordan, Z.J. 7:488, 7:493, 7:497
Jörgensen, J. 4:720
    see also Jörgensen's dilemma
Jørgensen, Jørgen 8:487, 8:492
Jörgensen's dilemma 4:718, 4:719
Jori, Mario
    Bobbio, N. 1:792
    legal positivism †5:514–21
Joseph, H.W.B. 7:682
Joshi, L.V. 7:65
Joshi, S.D. 7:250
Jospe, Raphael
    Ibn Ezra, A. †4:611–13
    Ibn Falaquera †4:615–17
Jouffroy, T. 2:447–8
journalism
    ethics of 5:126–8
Jouvenel, B. de 9:59
Jouvet, M. 3:129
Joy, L.S. 3:857
Joyce, James 5:845
Joynton, O. 9:788
Jubien, Michael
    Kripke, S.A. †5:301–5
    ontological commitment
        †7:112–17
    proper names 7:756
    property theory 7:766
Judaeo-Christian thought
    Philo of Alexandria 7:357–60
Judah ben Moses of Rome 5:88–9,
    5:128–31
Judah ben Yehiel Messer Leon see
    Messer Leon
Judah Halevi see Halevi, Judah
Judah Romano see Judah ben Moses
    of Rome
Judaism
    see also Hasidism; Jewish
        philosophy; Kabbalah
    anti-Semitism 1:311–14
    beliefs
        Albo, J. 1:153, 1:154
        Maimonides, M. 1:153
    Christianity
        comparison with (Ibn
            Kammuna) 4:621–2
        early Church 7:254, 7:255–6
        influence of scholasticism
            (Albo, J.) 1:153

community definition
    halakhah 4:206–7
contemplation/observance debate
    (Nahmanides, M.) 6:648
credal structure of (Crescas, H.)
    2:701
critiques of
    Hegel, G.W.F. 1:311, 1:312
    Kant, I. 1:311–12
    Spinoza, B. de 5:93
dogma (Duran, S.) 3:171–2
ethics
    Ha'am, Ahad 4:192
    Lazarus 5:97–8
exclusivism 8:260
explication of (Judah Halevi)
    4:209–10
faith 3:539–40
family (Rozanov, V.V.) 8:381,
    8:383–4
Gnosticism 4:83, 4:84
Hasidism 4:242–5
heaven 4:250
Hebrew Bible 1:766–9
Hegelianism 4:282, 4:298
Hellenistic
    influence on New Testament
        7:256
intellectual tradition
    (Soloveitchik, J.B.) 9:26
Islam comparison (Ibn
    Kammuna) 4:621–2
Kabbalah 5:171–6
Karaism 5:206–9
liturgy 8:340
Manicheism 6:75
modern decline of (Kaplan, M.)
    5:204–5
monotheism 6:480
    ethical (Formstecher, S.) 5:98–9
mysticism 5:171–6, 6:623
nature of (Duran, S.) 3:171–2
phenomenology (Levinas, E.)
    5:580
philosophy relationship 5:86, 5:87
    Abravanel, I. 1:22–3
    Delmedigo, E. 2:861–2
pietism (Ibn Paquda) 4:633–6
pluralism 8:260
providence 7:797–8
Rabbinic theology 9:333–7
rationality of (Messer Leon) 6:332
reconstructionism (Kaplan, M.)
    5:204–6
resurrection 8:294
revelation 8:297
    Bible 8:298

ritual 8:338–41
sacred history 4:454
sin 8:791–2
socialism (Hess, M.) 4:414
state relationship (Leibowitz, Y.)
    5:562–4
truth (Mendelssohn, M.) 5:96
Judaistic philosophy see Jewish
    philosophy
judges
    common law 2:443
judgment
    see also analyticity; equity; moral
        judgment
    aesthetic 1:57, 1:460–3, 1:477–8,
        1:683
        Kant, I. 1:60, 5:193–4
    categories of (Kant, I.) 5:185–6
    common-sense philosophy
        (Reid, T.) 8:171
    conformity of
        realism/antirealism 8:117
    critical
        postmodernist discourse
            (Lyotard, J.-F.) 6:9
    criticism of (Bradley, F.H.)
        1:859–60
    desire 3:32–3
    empirical knowledge (Lewis, C.I.)
        5:585, 5:587–8
    epistemic
        will to believe (Ducasse, C.J.)
            3:140–1
    ethical
        Chinese Confucianism 2:545–7
    historical (Croce, B.) 2:731, 2:732
    identity philosophy
        (Schelling, F.W.J. von) 8:512,
        8:513
    linguistic discrimination 5:643
    logic of place (Nishida Kitarō)
        5:77–8
    mathematical (Kant, I.) 6:182,
        6:185
    multiple relations theory
        (Russell, B.A.W.) 8:398–9
    normative
        rationality and cultural
            relativism 8:81–3
    principles of (Kant, I.) 5:186–8
    private (Godwin, W.) 4:123
    projectivism 7:740
    reflective (Kant, I.) 5:193, 5:195
    strength-of-evidence 9:578
    synthetic a priori (Kant, I.)
        5:183–4
    taste 1:510–11

teleological
    autonomy (Kant, I.) 5:194–5
    temporal (Kant, I.) 5:187
value
    social science **9:575–80**
judgmentalism
    paradox of fiction 3:275–6
Judson, H.F. 4:15, 6:460
Judson, L. 1:434
Juergensmeyer, M. 3:843
Juhasz, S. 5:367
Juhos, B. 9:611
Julian 2:758
Juliard, P. 5:378–9
Julien, S. 2:782
Julius Caesar problem 1:439–40
Jullien, François 9:682, 9:866–7
July, R. 1:109, 1:115
jump function 9:501–2
Junankar, N.S. 3:861
Jung, Carl Gustav **5:131–5**
    alchemy 1:157–8, 5:133–4
    culture 5:134
    personality theory 5:133
Jung, Patricia 8:728
Jung, R. 5:624
Jüngel, E. 1:655, 4:297
Jungius, Joachim **5:135–8**, 5:717
Jungnickel, C. 4:402
Jung-Palczewska, E. 2:143, 5:109
junzi (paradigmatic individuals)
    2:538, 2:543, 2:544, 2:545
Jürgensen, H. 2:481
juridification
    autopoietic theory 2:716–17
jurisprudence
    see also law; legal theory
    Cicero, M.T. 2:357
    feminist **3:606–11**
        equity 5:150
    historical **5:138–41**
        Bryce, J. 2:41
        Savigny, F.K. von 8:483
    Islamic law
        furu' al-fiqh 5:457, 5:459
        scripture (Ibn Hazm) 4:620
        usul al-fiqh 5:457, 5:458–9
    legal hermeneutics 5:507–8
    legal realism 5:468
    liberal 3:606, 3:607, 3:610
    meta-jurisprudence distinction
        (Bobbio, N.) 1:791
    property (Gadādhara) 3:826
    Roman law/civilian tradition
        8:343–7
    sociological (Pound, R.) 7:609

jury
    evidence 5:500
Jüssen, G. 9:727
justice **5:141–7**
    see also fairness; injustice; law;
    mercy; natural justice
    agreement 2:658
    autonomy relationship (Rawls, J.)
        1:590
    Buddhism 8:449
    charity as (Leibniz, G.W.) 5:557–8
    civil
        natural justice distinction
            (Carneades) 2:217
    civilized life
        Enlightenment, Scottish 3:329
    compensatory
        racial discrimination 1:91,
            1:92–3
    constructivism (Rawls, J.) 2:631
    contractarianism (Hume, D.) 4:554
    conventionalism 5:142–3
    corrective 5:141–2
    crime and punishment 2:704–10
    critiques of 5:146
    deconstruction (Derrida, J.) 2:899
    desert 3:26–7
    distributive 5:141
        agricultural ethics 1:126–7
        information technology and
            ethics 4:779, 4:781
        international relations 4:831
        medical ethics 6:262–3
        Nozick, R. 7:45
        risk 8:332–3
        socialism 8:884
        technological goods 9:282
        utilitarianism 9:556
    divine (Ash'ariyya/Mu'tazila)
        1:519, 1:520, 1:522, 4:63–4, 5:27
    duties of (Kant, I.) 5:191
    eidos versus genealogy 4:1
    Epicureanism 3:347–8
    equity and law **5:147–53**
        Aristotle 5:148–9
        Roman 5:150
    as fairness 5:142, 5:144–5
        Rawls, J. 8:106–9
            social contract 2:663
    faith
        Christian political philosophy
            7:507–8
    al-Farabi 3:440–1
    feminism
        Latin American 3:626
    formal/substantive conflict 5:151

friendship relationship 3:794–5,
    3:796
government (Hume, D.) 4:556–7
human rights (Mill, J.S.) 6:361,
    6:371–3
as implicit concept in law
    (Villey, M.) 9:614
informal
    crime and punishment 2:709
interests 6:754–5
international **5:153–7**
    cosmopolitan 5:154–6
    definition 5:153
    distributive 4:831
    principle of need 6:754
    scepticism 5:154
Jainism 8:449
Jewish pietism (Ibn Paquda) 4:636
legal idealism
    Del Vecchio, G. 5:512
    Kant, I. 5:511
    Stammler, R. 5:512
liberation theology 5:613, 5:615
market ethics 6:108–9
mercy 3:697, 3:699–700
might is right (Calicles) 2:176–7
morality
    Marx, K. 6:130
    moral standing
        Hume, D. 6:552
        Rawls, J. 6:500–1
mutual advantage 5:142, 5:143–4
natural law 6:687
nomoi (laws and customs)
    (Antiphon) 1:302
normative legal adjudication 5:148
Other
    ethical relation to the
        (Levinas, E.) 5:580
physis and *nomos* debate 7:381
Plato 7:407–8, 7:413–14
    Republic 9:397–8
population issues 7:540, 7:542
positive law 5:147–8
praise and blame 7:644–5
principle of need 6:753–4
property 7:760
public interest 7:834
Rawlsian account 8:106–9
    autonomy relationship 1:590
    beneficence 4:343
    constructivism 2:631
    moral standing 6:500–1
    self-respect 8:635, 8:637
reciprocity 8:130
republicanism 8:280–1
rights (Smith, A.) 8:819

Roman law 8:345
rule of law 8:388, 8:390
self-interest (Thucydides) 9:399
social
    agricultural ethics 1:126–7
    feminist jurisprudence 3:607–8
    liberalism 7:502
    violence 9:615–16
stability 8:108
teleology 5:142, 5:143
truth conflict (Lyotard, J.-F.) 7:603
as virtue
    Hume, D. 4:553–4
    prudence contrast 7:802
    Shi'ism (al-Tusi) 9:506
    Smith, A. 8:815, 8:819, 8:821
war and peace 9:685–6
will (Anselm of Canterbury) 1:292
justification
    see also moral justification
    deflationary theories of truth 9:476
    duty 3:178
    epistemic 5:157–65
        see also certainty;
            foundationalism
        a posteriori 1:1–3
        a priori 1:3–5
        by acquaintance/description
            5:259–62
        anti-foundationalism (Rorty, R.)
            8:353–4
        Buridan, J. 2:133
        cognitive spontaneity 5:256
        coherence theory 5:253–9, 8:206
        coherence theory of 3:380,
            5:159–60, 5:253–9
            a posteriori knowledge 1:1–2
            access problem 5:258
            alternative coherent systems
                5:257
            coherence theory of truth
                distinction 5:253–6,
                5:257–8
            commonsensism 2:454–5
        definition 5:157

foundationalism contrast
    3:719–20, 3:721–3, 5:253
global scepticism 6:727
inferential relation of beliefs
    5:255
introspection 4:840–1
isolation problem 5:257
justified belief 8:206
logical consistency 5:255
mental states 2:333
observation 5:253, 5:256–7
paradoxes 7:212
regress problem 5:254–5
warrant 5:268, 5:269–70
deductive closure principle
    2:843
defeasibility 5:277
experience 3:299
Gettier problems 5:263–4
group 8:830–1
gynocentric 3:599
history of 3:379–80
Indian philosophy 2:67–8
infinite regress 3:720
innate beliefs 4:796
internalist-externalist debate
    5:160–1
introspection 4:840–1
Lotze, R.H. 5:840–1
mediate-immediate distinction
    3:721
memory 6:301
moral justification contrast
    3:369–70
mutual support 5:255
naturalized epistemology 5:157,
    5:162
non-epistemic distinction 5:158
non-linear 5:254–5
observation 5:256
'ought-implies-can' principle
    3:368
relevant alternatives 2:843–4
scepticism 2:333, 5:162–3
social epistemology 5:163–4
testimony 5:164, 8:828–30

virtue epistemology 9:621
warrant distinction 5:268
Yoruba epistemology 9:833
forensic (Melanchthon, P.) 6:289
imagination 4:707–8
lifeworld (Husserl, E.) 4:584–5
propositional evidence 8:214
religious belief
    agnosticism 1:121–3
    trust 9:466, 9:468
    truthfulness 9:482–3
    vindications (Sellars, W.S.) 8:641
justification, religious doctrine of
    5:165–8
    see also atonement; salvation
    atonement 1:537
    Augustine 5:166
    belief 8:209–10, 8:211–14
    Bible 5:165–6
    Calvin, J. 1:538–9, 2:177, 2:180
    by faith 3:540–1
        Bultmann, R. 2:129
        Luther, M. 6:1, 6:2
    grace 4:148
        Luther, M. 5:165, 5:166–7, 6:1,
            6:2
        by faith 6:1, 6:2
    medieval theology 5:166
    Pelagianism
        Biel, G. 1:770–1
    pietism 7:395
    Protestantism 5:167
    religious knowledge 8:245–6
    Roman Catholicism 5:165, 5:167
    sanctification 8:447–8
Justin Martyr 7:257, 9:754
Justinian 5:168–9
    Corpus Iuris Civilis 8:343, 8:344–5
    Gaius 3:832
    pagan philosophy ban 1:262
    philological reinterpretation of
        Renaissance humanism 4:538
    Roman law/civilian tradition 8:347
Justman, S. 8:821–2
al-Juwayni, Abu'l Ma'ali 5:169–70

K

ka 3:249–50
Kabbalah 5:87, 5:89, **5:171–6**
  Abraham Abulafia 5:174
  cosmology 5:172–3
  critique of (Delmedigo, E.) 2:861
  divine needs 4:411–12
  halakhah 4:207
  Hasidism 4:242–3, 4:244, 4:411
  Helmont, F.M. van 4:341
  Herrera, A. Cohen de 4:397–9
  Heschel, A.J. 4:411–12
  mysticism 6:623
    Merkavah/Hekhalot 5:171–2
  Neoplatonic influence (Ibn
    Ezra, M.) 4:614
  Pico della Mirandola, G. 7:389,
    7:390
  Platonism
    opposition of Messer Leon
      6:331, 6:333
  Renaissance scepticism 8:500
  Shem Tov family 8:738
  Sufism 5:174–5
  theosophy (Nahmanides, M.)
    6:648
  Torah (Duran, P.) 3:170
Kabeš, Jaroslav 2:767
Kabīr 1:196
Kaczmarek, L. 1:135
Kadane, J. 3:211
Kadarkay, A. 5:859
Kaddushin, M. 9:336
Kadler, A. 7:488
Kaehler, S.A. 4:543
Kaelber, W.O. 1:519
Kaeppeli, T. 2:201–2, 5:114
Kaern, M. 8:780
Kafker, F.A. 3:304
Kafker, S.L. 3:304
Kagamé, Alexis 1:111, 1:115, 3:449
Kagan, J. 6:505
Kagan, S. 4:344, 4:717, 6:533
Kahan, A.S. 6:375
Kahn, C.H.
  Anaximander 1:259
  Anaximenes 1:262
  Empedocles 3:298
  Gorgias †4:144–6
  Heraclitus 4:369

Hippias †4:440–1
  logos 5:819
  Parmenides 7:234
  Philolaus 7:371
  Plato 7:420
  Prodicus †7:731–3
  Protagoras †7:788–91
  Pythagoreanism 7:861
  Socratic dialogues †9:19–21
  Sophists †9:33–4
  Thales 9:324
  will 9:725
Kahneman, D. 7:705
  decision and game theory 2:834
  reasoning
    inductive 8:64
    practical
      expected utility theory 8:95,
        8:102
      probabilistic 7:711
      rationality of belief 8:87, 8:88,
        8:89, 8:90
    risk 8:334, 8:337
Kahrs, E. 7:250
Kaibara Ekken **5:176–7**
  ki/ri relationship 5:75
Kaibel, G. 3:337
Kaila, Eino 8:488, 8:492
Kajiyama, Y. 2:63
kalam see 'ilm al-kalam
Kaldor, N. 3:210
Kaldor-Hicks criterion 5:455
Kalman, L. 5:524
Kalsbeek, L. 3:114
Kaltenmark, M. 2:782
Kalton, Michael C.
  Korean Confucian philosophy
    †2:555–6
  sirhak 8:797
  Yi Yulgok 9:827
Kalupahana, D.J.
  Buddhist philosophy in India 2:99
  causation
    Indian theories of 2:257
  Mādhyamika Buddhism in India
    and Tibet 2:63
  mujō 6:594
  suffering
    Buddhist views of 9:218

Kaluza, Z. 1:152, 2:21
Kamalaśīla 2:61, 2:62, 9:405–6
Kamen, H. 9:433
Kamenka, E. 3:639, 6:661
Kamenskii, Z.A. 2:272
Kames, Lord *see* Home, Henry
kami (gods) 5:69, 5:71–2, 8:749
kami no michi (way of the *kami*) *see*
  Shintō
Kamin, L.J. 6:721
Kaminsky, H. 4:574
Kaminsky, J.S. 3:239
Kamitz, R. 9:613
Kamlah, A. 9:613
Kamm, F.M. 2:822, 6:264
Kamp, Hans
  anaphora 1:240–2, 1:243
  discourse semantics 3:92–5, 3:98–9
  dynamic semantics 1:240–2, 1:243
  indexicals 2:881
  possible worlds semantics 8:668
  pragmatics 7:631
Kamp, J.A.W. 9:307
Kamuf, P. 6:653
Kaṇāda 7:606
Kandinsky, W. 1:449, 1:452
Kane, P.V. 3:187, 4:837
Kane, R. 3:752
Kang, Hugh H. 2:565, 9:827
Kang, Man'gil 2:343
Kang Youwei 4:451, 4:452
Kanger, Stig 6:426, 8:486, 8:491,
  8:668
Kangjie *see* Shao Yong
Kangrga, Milan 9:54
Kangro, H. 5:137, 7:397
Kanizsa, G. 4:53–4
Kann, C. 1:144–5
Kant, Immanuel **5:177–96**
  see also Kantian ethics; Kantian
    fiction; Kantianism; Neo-
    Kantianism
  a posteriori 1:1, 1:3
  a priori 1:3, 1:5–6
  aesthetics
    architecture 1:362, 1:364, 1:366
    art
      formalism 3:708
      value of 1:477–8, 1:480

art criticism 1:463
artistic taste 1:511
concepts 1:55, 1:56, 1:58, 1:59
ethics relationship 1:65, 1:66,
    1:68
experience 3:828
judgments 1:60
moral freedom 5:178
agnosticism 1:122, 1:123
Alison, A. 1:186
analytic philosophy 1:228, 1:234,
    1:238
analytic/synthetic distinction
    3:378, 3:382
anti-Semitism 1:311–12, 1:313,
    1:314
atonement 1:539, 1:541
autonomy 5:178, 5:189, 5:193–5
    ethical 1:586, 1:587–8, 1:591–2,
        6:569, 6:570
beauty 1:682–3, 1:684
being 1:702
    necessary conditions of 1:701
    property 1:700
bundle theory of mind 6:385
categorical imperative
    duty 5:201
    ethical autonomy 1:588
    impartiality 4:716
    moral development 6:504
    moral reasoning 5:201
    practical reason 7:617–18,
        8:100, 8:102
    respect for persons 8:285
    universalism 9:538, 9:539
categories 2:229, 2:231–2, 5:185–6,
    6:338
    schemata 5:186
    of thought
        Heidegger, M. comparison
            2:897
causation 2:244, 2:246, 2:250
commentary by Asmus, V.F. 1:525
common-sense ethics 2:450
completeness problem 4:108
concepts 2:507, 2:516
    analysis of 2:518, 2:522
consciousness 2:583
contractarianism 2:665
correspondence theory of truth
    9:475
critical idealism (Cohen, H.) 2:398
critical judgment
    postmodernist interpretation
        (Lyotard, J.-F.) 6:9
Critique of Judgment 5:178,
    5:193–5

Critique of Practical Reason
    hope 4:508
    moral law/laws of nature
        distinction 5:178
    moral sentiments 6:549, 6:550
    practical reason 5:192–3
    reason
        morality 5:178
Critique of Pure Reason
    a priori 1:3, 1:5–6
    analyticity 1:234
    categories 5:185–6
        schemata 5:186
    consciousness 2:583
    experience 5:183–9
    introspection 4:840, 4:842
    Kemp Smith, N. 5:227, 5:228
    metaphysical illusions 5:188–9
    principles of judgment
        natural science 5:186–8
    reason
        experience 5:178
        metaphysical illusions
            5:188–9
        uses of 5:189
    synthetic a priori judgments
        5:183–4
    transcendental idealism 5:184–5
critiques of
    Deleuze, G. 2:857
    Eberhard, J.A. 3:196
    Hamann, J.G. 4:214, 4:215
    Jacobi, F.H. 5:46
    Maimon, S. 6:35–6, 6:37
    Marx, K. 6:125–6
    Moore, G.E. 6:496
    Rahner, K. 8:36
    Romantics 8:350
    Troeltsch, E.P.W. 9:462
deduction
    metaphysical 5:185–6
    transcendental 5:186
democratic contract 2:662–3
duty 3:180, 3:182
    moral motivation 6:527
educational philosophy 3:227,
    3:230
egoism and altruism 3:248
emotions 3:288, 3:289
    morality 6:559, 6:560–1, 6:563
Enlightenment 3:316, 3:317–18
ethical universalism
    influence on Western Marxism
        6:143
ethics 5:189–95, 5:200–1, 5:203
    animals and 1:276
    applied 1:324

deontological 2:891
environmental 3:333, 3:336
examples in 3:488, 3:490
Euclidean geometry
    (Reichenbach, H.) 8:168–9
evil 3:466
experience 5:183–9
Fichte, J.G. 3:643
forgiveness and mercy 3:700, 3:701
free will 3:752
freedom
    nature relationship 5:178
friendship 3:795–6, 3:797
general will 4:11
geometry 4:31, 4:33
German idealism 4:42–3, 4:44
God
    existence of 4:93
        moral argument 4:91, 8:242,
            8:245
        natural theology 6:710
        ontological argument 4:88–9,
            8:242
        teleological argument 4:89,
            4:91
good, theories of the 4:131, 4:132,
    4:133, 4:135
help and beneficence 4:344
Herder, J.G. 4:379, 4:382
history
    philosophy of 4:454, 4:458
honour 4:504
hope 4:507–8, 4:509
humanism 4:529, 4:532
humour 4:563, 4:564, 4:566–7
Hutcheson, F. 4:593
idealism 4:668
    Moore, G.E. critique 6:496
    political philosophy
        history of 7:504, 7:515
ideals 4:675
imagination 4:707, 4:708
impartiality 4:714, 4:717
infinity 4:774–5, 4:777
influence of
    Jewish philosophy, early
        nineteenth century 5:96–7
    Lichtenberg, G.C. 5:623–4
influenced by
    Beck, J.S. 1:687–8, 1:689
    Crusius, C.A. influence 2:738
intellective perception (Rosmini-
    Serbati, A.) 8:362
international law 3:573
international relations 4:827, 4:832
introspection 4:840, 4:842

intuitionism
  mathematics 1:438–9, 4:847,
    4:852
Jewish Enlightenment 3:321
judgment
  natural science 5:186–8
justice as fairness 5:145
Kemp Smith, N. 5:227, 5:228,
  5:230
Knutzen, M. 5:289
legal idealism 5:511, 5:513
liberalism 5:600, 5:601, 5:605
libertarianism 5:619
logic
  eighteenth century 5:720, 5:721
  imperative 4:720
  interpretation by
    Hägerström, A.A.T. 4:202
  nineteenth century 5:723, 5:728
love 5:843, 5:845
mathematics
  foundations of 5:812–13,
    6:181–4, 6:185, 6:191
  intuitionism 1:438–9, 4:847,
    4:852
meaning and verification 6:236
metaphysical deduction 5:185–6
metaphysical illusions 5:188–9
moral agents 6:504
moral justification 6:516, 8:220
moral knowledge 6:520
moral law/laws of nature
  distinction 5:178
moral sentiments 6:548–9, 6:550
moral standing 6:554
moral virtue 5:461
morality
  Marx, K. critique 6:129
natural theology 6:712
nature 6:732–3
  aesthetic appreciation of 6:731
  freedom relationship 5:178
Naturphilosophie 6:737–8, 6:741
ontology 7:117, 7:118
personalism 7:315
phenomenology of religion 7:353,
  7:354
pluralism 7:463
practical reason 5:189–95
  categorical imperative 7:617–18,
    7:619
practical reasoning 8:102
  hypothetical imperatives 8:91
  moral law 8:100, 8:101
praise and blame 7:646
  determinism 7:645–6
  motivation 7:645

prescriptivism 7:670
projectivism 7:740
property 7:759
radical evil 8:794–5
Rahner, K. 8:39
rationality 8:63
reason
  autonomy 5:178, 5:189
  experience 5:178, 5:183–9
  Horkheimer, M. 4:511
  metaphysical illusions 5:188–9
  morality 5:178, 5:183
  uses of 5:189
rectification and remainders 8:135,
  8:140
Reid, T. comparison (Stewart, D.)
  9:137
Reinhold, K.L. 8:186
religion
  critique of 8:236–7, 8:238
  experience 7:173–4
  history of philosophy of 8:246–7
  pluralism 8:263
  and reason 8:239, 8:245
  and science 8:230
respect for persons 8:283, 8:285,
  8:287
rhetoric 8:308, 8:309
Schiller, J.C.F. 8:525, 8:526, 8:527
science
  demarcation problem 2:866
  naturalized philosophy of
    4:338–40, 6:728–9
self-control 8:611–12, 8:613
self-deception 8:629, 8:632
self-respect 8:635, 8:636–8
sexuality 8:721, 8:722–3, 8:728
sin 8:795
soul 9:48
  immortality of 9:46–7
space 9:61–2, 9:65
the sublime 6:9, 9:203, 9:204
substance 9:207, 9:210
suicide 9:225, 9:226, 9:227–8, 9:229
Swedenborg, E. 9:243
synthetic a priori
  Lewis, C.I. critique 5:587
synthetic a priori judgments 1:4,
  5:183–4
synthetic a priori knowledge
  logical positivism 5:790, 5:791
taste, artistic 1:512
teleology 5:309, 9:296, 9:297
theory and practice 9:358
things-in-themselves 4:663
Thoreau, H.D. 9:389, 9:392
time 9:415, 9:416

transcendental arguments
  (Strawson, P.F.) 9:172
transcendental deduction 5:186
transcendental idealism 2:231,
  4:664–5, 5:184–5, 8:37, 9:454
transcendental logic
  Cohen, H. comparison 2:399
transcendental subject
  (Schelling, F.W.J. von) 8:510
truth metaphor
  Le Doeuff, M. critique 5:477
truthfulness 9:485
  absolutism 9:483, 9:484
unity of science 9:531
universals 9:541–2
virtue ethics 9:625
vulnerablity and finitude 9:670
war and peace 9:689–90
Yogācāra Buddhism comparison
  2:69
Kantian ethics 5:200–4
  see also practical reasoning
  aesthetic judgments 1:66
  business ethics 2:151, 2:152
  constructivism 2:631–2
  contractarianism (Rawls, J.) 5:202
  critiques of 5:202–3
    Moore, G.E. 6:495
    Williams, B.A.O. 9:750–1
  discourse ethics comparison
    (Habermas, J.) 4:196–7
  duty 5:201
  eudaimonia 3:451
  impartiality 4:716
  moral agents 6:499, 6:501–2, 6:503
  moral education 6:507
  moral imperatives 6:536
  moral motivation 6:524, 6:526–7
  moral rules 6:513
  moral sentiments 6:548–9
  moral standing 6:553
  prudence 7:803
  psychological egoism 3:247
  self-determination (Price, R.)
    7:678
  self-respect 8:635–6
  sexuality 8:723–4
  utilitarianism synthesis
    (Baumgardt, D.) 1:668
  virtue ethics contrast 9:623
Kantian fiction
  Vaihinger, H. 9:567
Kantianism
  see also Kantian ethics
  child development
    moral 6:504–5
  influence of Thomism 9:384

in Italy
    Galluppi, P. 5:37
    Rosmini-Serbati, A. 5:37
Jewish Enlightenment 3:322
moral psychology 6:532
representation theory
    (Reinhold, K.L.) 8:186
in Scandinavia 8:484
Kantorovich, A. 3:102
Kantorowicz, H. 5:514
Kanz, K.T. 6:741–2
Kanze Motoyoshi *see* Zeami
Kao, Ming 2:548
Kaplan, David
    compositionality 2:477
    concepts 2:516
    contextualism
        epistemological 2:649
    descriptions 3:24
    epistemic paradoxes 7:214
    indexicals 2:879, 2:880–1
    modal logic 6:432
    possible worlds 6:429, 8:667, 8:668
    pragmatics 7:631
    proper names 7:757
    reference 8:158–9, 8:164
    sense and reference 8:685, 8:688
    substitutional/objectual
        quantifiers 7:881
Kaplan, F. 2:206
Kaplan, L. 6:48
Kaplan, Mark
    Bayesian epistemology
        acceptance in 7:711
    epistemic paradoxes 7:214
    induction †4:745–52
Kaplan, Mordecai **5:204–6**
    Jewish philosophy 5:90
Kaplan-Perry theory (KPT) 2:880–1
Kapoor, O.B.L. 3:859
Käppeli, T. 4:404
Karađorđević, Petar 9:50
Karaism **5:206–9**
    halakhah 4:207
    Jewish philosophy 5:87
    Judah Halevi 4:211
Karaki Junzō 6:359, 6:594
Karatani, Kōjin 5:660
Kareev, Nikolai 5:438, 7:564
Kargon, R.H. 2:263, 2:287
Kariamu, W.A. 3:449
Karl, F. 3:267
Karlgren, B. 2:781
Karlsson, M.M. 8:493

karma
    Buddhism
        Awakening of Faith in
            Mahāyāna 1:604
        Buddha 2:52
        dependent origination 9:216
        human nature 2:94–1:9
        Indian conceptions of 5:211,
            5:213–15
        Japanese 2:104–5
        Linji 5:646
        potentiality
            habits 7:606–7
        Yogācāra 2:69–71
            cognition 2:64
            consciousness 2:72–4
            seed metaphor 2:70–1, 2:73
    duty and virtue 3:185
    fatalism 3:565
    heaven 4:253, 4:254
    Hinduism 5:210–11, 5:212–13
        as ethical principle
            (Radhakrishnan, S.) 8:24
        ethics 4:437
        liberation 4:434–5
        reincarnation 8:182–5
            evidence for 9:47–8
        self
            theories of 8:606–8
    Indian conceptions of **5:209–18**
        early developments 5:211–12
        modern philosophy 5:215–16
        terminology 5:210
        texts 5:210–11
    Jainism 5:211, 5:215
        classification 6:79
        Mahāvīra 6:33–4
    salvation 8:448
    theosophy 9:365
Karma bKa'-brgyud (Kagyü) School
    of Buddhism 6:351–2
karma yoga 3:842
Karmay, Samten Gyaltsen 9:408
Karp, C. 4:772
Karp, Ivan
    ethnophilosophy, African
        †3:445–50
Karpovich, M. 5:609
Karttunen, L. 4:725, 7:631
kasb 2:242–3
Kaschewsky, R. 9:490
Kashani, Bata Afdal 4:702
Kasoff, Ira E. 6:776, 9:856
Kasper, G. 2:621–2
Kastil, A. 2:17
Kasulis, Thomas P.
    Dōgen †3:109–11

fa †3:532–3
Japanese philosophy †5:68–79
Kūkai †5:318–20
logic
    Japanese philosophy †5:713–16
Motoori Norinaga †6:588–90
Sengzhao †8:682–4
Kateb, G. 1:372, 3:272, 9:561
katharsis (purgation) **5:218–20**
Kathāvatthu (Points of Controversy)
    2:58
    see also Tissa Moggalīputta
kathēkonta (proper duty) 9:154–5
Katō, Nihei 5:43–4
Kato, S. 9:840
Katsura Shoryu 4:765
Kātyāyana 4:835
Katz, B. 6:98
Katz, D.S. 9:535
Katz, J.J.
    analyticity 1:238
    concepts 2:516
    innateness of language 4:54
    pragmatics 7:631
    type/token distinction 9:511
Katz, J.N. 5:644
Katz, S. 4:54
Katz, S.N. 2:621
Katz, Steven T.
    Holocaust †4:495–9
    Jewish voluntarism 9:666–7
    Maimonides, M. 6:48
    mysticism 6:628, 6:629–30, 6:633
    Saadiah Gaon 8:440
Katznelson, Berl 9:869
Kauffman, S.A. 5:635
Kauffman, W. 1:314
Kaufmann, Felix 3:220
Kaufmann, W. 6:861
Kaunda, Kenneth 1:97, 1:101, 1:106
Kauppi, N. 9:293
Kauther, R. 5:624
Kauṭilya 4:738, **5:220–2**
    Arthaśāstra 5:220–1
    inference 4:765
    political philosophy 7:521, 7:524
Kautsky, Karl Johann **5:222–4**
    dialectics
        Lenin, V.I. 5:566
    Marxism
        Western 6:142, 6:143
Kavelin, Konstantin 4:304–5, 5:607,
    7:563
Kavka, G. 8:74, 8:97, 8:102
Kawahara Hiroshi 6:359

Kawamura, Leslie S.
 Mādhyamika Buddhism in India
  and Tibet †2:58–64
Kaydrup gelek belsangbo *see* mKhas
  grub dge legs dpal bzang po
Keane, J. 2:371
Keaney, J.J. 4:502
Keat, Russell
 phenomenology 7:347
 social science
  history of philosophy of 8:858
  scientific realism †8:584–7
  theory and observation 9:356
  value judgments 9:579
 socialism †8:879–86
Keckermann, Bartholomew **5:224–5**,
  5:717
Keddie, N. 1:95
Kedourie, E. 1:95, 6:661
Keefer, Michael H.
 Agrippa von Nettesheim, H.C.
  †1:129–33
Keel, Hee Sung 2:332, 2:118
Keen, R. 6:292
Keenan, E.L. 7:877
Keenan, J. 2:75
Keenan, J.F. 2:228–9, 2:282
Keene, Donald
 Japanese philosophy 5:79
  aesthetics 1:89, 1:90
  modern literature 5:660
  Kumazawa Banzan 5:322
  Tominaga Nakamoto 9:441
  Zeami 9:841
Keer, D. 1:197
Kegley, C.W.
 Brunner, E. 2:33
 Bultmann, R. 2:130
 Niebuhr, R. 6:844
 Nygren, A. 7:69
 Tillich, P. 9:412
Kegon (Flower Garland) Buddhism
  2:101, 2:102, 5:319
Keil, F.C.
 cognitive development †2:393–5
Keimatsu Mitsuo 3:112
Keisler, H.J.
 Beth's theorem and Craig's
  interpolation theorem 1:763
 infinitary logic 4:772
 logical constants 5:780
 many-valued logics 6:83
 nonstandard analysis 1:215
Keith, Sir Arthur 8:18
Kekes, John
 evil †3:463–6
 wisdom 9:754

Keller, Evelyn Fox
 ecology 3:205
 evolution, theory of 3:482
 feminist epistemology 3:602
 gender and science 3:866, 3:868
 psychoanalytic feminism 3:587
Kellert, Stephen H.
 chaos theory †2:276–80
Kelley, D.R.
 common law 2:446
 legal hermeneutics 5:510
 political philosophy
  history of 7:517
 Selden, J. 8:605
 social theory and law 8:878
Kelley, F.E. 4:404
Kelley, J. 1:356, 1:358
Kelley, J.L. 8:715
Kellner, D. 1:663, 6:98–9
Kellner, Menahem
 Abravanel, I. 1:23
 Albo, J. 1:154
 Arama, I. 1:351
 Crescas, H. 2:704
 Duran, P. †3:170–1
 Duran, S. †3:171–2
 Gersonides 4:51
 Maimonides, M. 6:48
Kelly, Aileen
 Bakunin, M.A. †1:645–7
 Herzen, A.I. †4:404–10
 Marxist philosophy, Russian and
  Soviet 6:159
 Russian philosophy †8:418–22
  empiriocriticism 8:409
 Signposts movement †8:768–74
Kelly, G.A. 2:692, 9:425
Kelly, G.B. 1:838
Kelly, J.N.D. 4:732
Kelly, K. 3:102, 5:486–7
Kelly, M. 4:301
Kelly, P.J. 1:724
Kelly, T. 6:350
Kelly-Gadol, J. 3:592
Kel'man, E. 7:240
Kelman, H. 9:579
Kelman, M. 2:720, 5:467–8
Kelman, P.J. 6:675
Kelsen, Hans **5:226–7**
 legal concepts 5:495
 legal norms
  as interpretation 7:39–40, 7:41
 legal positivism
  rules as judgments 5:516, 5:520
 pure theory of law 8:389, 8:391
Kemal, R. 8:735

Kemal, Salim
 aesthetics in Islamic philosophy
  1:79
 Ibn Sina †4:647–54
 nature 6:735
 Shah Wali Allah 8:735
Kemeny, J.
 see also Kemeny-Oppenheim
  reduction model
 reduction, problems of 8:149
Kemeny-Oppenheim reduction
  model 8:146–7
Kemp Smith, Norman **5:227–31**
 Hume, D. 4:561
 Kant, I. 5:196
Kemp, T.P. 8:322
Kempe, A.B. 8:381
Kempis, Thomas à *see* Thomas à
  Kempis
Kempson, R. 7:631
Kendler, H.H. 1:699
Kendrew, John 6:459
Kendrick, I. 9:663
Kendzierski, L.H. 3:429, 6:705
Ken'en School of Confucianism
  2:553
Kennan, George 4:832
Kennedy, D. 7:582
Kennedy, Duncan
 Critical Legal Studies 2:719, 2:720
 legal discourse 5:499
 legal realism 5:524
Kennedy, G. 8:309, 1:509
Kennedy, L.A. 4:479, 9:387, 9:664
Kennedy-Day, Kiki
 Aristotelianism in Islamic
  philosophy †1:382–6
 al-Kindi †5:249–53
Kenney, John Peter
 Marius Victorinus †6:105–7
 patristic philosophy †7:254–61
 Tertullian, Q.S.F. †9:307–9
Kenny, Anthony
 Aquinas, T. 1:348
 Descartes, R. 3:18
 emotions 3:285
 eudaimonia 3:451
 faith 3:543
 Gregory of Rimini 4:172
 intentionality 4:821
 language
  medieval theories of 5:404
 logic
  medieval 5:758
  natural philosophy 6:706
 medieval philosophy 6:277
 moral luck 6:521

morality and emotions 6:563
Newman, J.H. 6:823
Prior, A.N. 7:690
private language argument 7:698
rationalism 8:79–80
theological virtues 9:330
war and peace 9:690
Wittgenstein, L. 9:770
Wyclif, J. 9:804
kenoticism 4:729–30
Kent, B. 9:725
Kent, Bonnie
Bonaventure †1:828–35
Duns Scotus, J. 3:169
Gerard of Odo †4:38–40
Kenyon, T. 2:464
Keohane, N 1:31
Keown, J. 5:630
Kepler, Johannes **5:231–3**
Ailly, P. d' 1:134
planetary motions 2:678
scientific hypotheses (Stewart, D.)
9:138
Kepnes, S. 2:48
Ker, Ian
Newman, J.H. †6:821–3
Kerferd, G.B.
Antiphon 1:303
Callicles 2:177
Gorgias 4:146
Hippias 4:441
physis and *nomos* debate 7:382
Prodicus 7:732
Protagoras 7:790
social science
history of philosophy of 8:858
Sophists 9:34
Thrasymachus 9:398
Kerman, J. 7:131
Kern, I. 4:586, 4:587
Kern, O. 7:165
Kern, S.J. 6:449
Kernan, J. 6:104–5
Kernberg, O. 7:819, 7:822–3
Kernohan, A. 7:612
Kerr, J. 5:135
Kerr-Lawson, A. 8:470
Kerruish, V. 3:189
Kersting, Wolfgang 5:196
kerygma 2:127, 2:129
Kessel, B.A. 5:24
Kessler, Eckhard
Alexander of Aphrodisias 1:175
Cardano, G. †2:202–4
Renaissance Aristotelianism 1:412
Telesio, B. †9:297–300
Vernia, N. 9:598

Zabarella, J. †9:836–9
Kesteloot, L. 1:115
Kettler, David
Ferguson, A. †3:630–3
Kevles, D.J. 4:15
Keynes, John Maynard **5:233–5**
critique of (Hayek, F.A.) 4:246
economics
philosophy of 3:212, 3:220
Moore, G.E. 6:498
Ramsey, F.P. 8:49
social democracy 8:827
Venn, J. 9:595
Keynes, John Neville 3:214, 3:220
Keyt, D. 1:434
Khadduri, M. 3:442
Khai-dub *see* Mkhas grub dge legs
dpal bzang po
Khawarij 5:26, 5:27–8
Kheraskov, Mikhail 3:325–6
Khin Zaw, Susan
Wollstonecraft, M. †9:788–92
Kholeif, F. 8:115
Khomeini, Ruhollah (al-)Khumayni
Khomiakov, Aleksei 8:809–10
Khoruzhii, S. 5:832, 8:427
Khrushchev, Nikita Sergeevich 7:240
al-Khumayni, Imam Ruhollah 5:9,
5:12, 5:19, 5:21
ki (material force)
see also qi
i relationship
Korean Confucianism 2:559–64
Korean neo-Confucianism (Yi
Hwang) 9:824
li relationship
Han Wônjin 4:220–1
Horak controversy (Yi Kan)
9:825
Yi Yulgok 9:826
ri relationship
Confucianism, Japan 2:551
neo-Confucianism 5:75
Ki no Tsurayuki
Japanese aesthetics 1:83, 1:89, 1:91
kokoro 5:291–3
poetry
nature 1:81
Ki Taesûng 2:558, 2:560–1
Kidd, I.G. 2:386, 7:555–6, 7:557
Kidder, J. 8:806
Kieckhefer, R. 9:241
Kiefer, F. 8:3
Kieffer, G.H. 8:290
Kielhorn, F. 4:837
Kielmeyer, C.F. 6:739, 6:742
Kiener, R. 4:613

Kierkegaard, Søren Aabye **5:235–44**
aestheticism 5:238–9
existentialism 3:501
ethics 3:505
faith 5:236, 5:239–42, 8:245–6,
9:326, 9:329
reason 8:239
freedom 5:242
friendship 3:797
Hegelianism critique 4:286
hope 4:509
humour 4:567
influence on existentialist theology
3:506–7, 3:508, 3:509
natural theology 6:711, 6:712
religion
existential phenomenology
7:353–4
history of philosophy of 8:247
sexuality 8:723, 8:728
Socrates 9:18
stages of life (Shinran) 8:747–8
theological contextualism
situation ethics 8:798, 8:799
theological virtues 9:330–1
Kihwa 2:114–15, 2:116
killing
ethics of (Augustine) 1:556
of innocents
Roman Catholicism 4:798
justice of (John of Salisbury) 5:116
Kilvington, Richard **5:244–5**, 7:180
Kilwardby, Robert **5:245–9**
form 5:247, 5:248
language 5:246–7
logic 5:246–7
Kim Han-kyo 2:565, 9:827
Kim Hee-jin 3:111
Kim, Jaegwon
anomalous monism 1:280
causal relevance
mental causation 6:310, 6:311
Chisholm, R.M. 2:335
epistemology and ethics 3:370
events 3:463
metaphysics 6:341
naturalized epistemology 3:382
reduction, problems of †8:145–9
Stevenson, C.L. 9:135
supervenience 9:238, 9:239
Kim, Kyung Tak 9:827
Kim Oaksook 9:827
Kim, O.C. 5:852
Kim, Yong Choon 9:442
Kim, Young-tae 9:37, 9:794
Kimelman, R. 1:23

Kimon School of Confucianism
2:552
Kimura, Eiichi 5:44
kin selection
sociobiology 8:893
Kincaid, Harold
positivism in the social sciences
†7:558–61
Kincaid, J. 3:109
Kindersley, R. 8:773
al-Kindi, Abu Yusuf Ya'qub ibn
Ishaq **5:249–53**
Aristotelianism 1:383, 1:386, 4:157
ethics 3:438–9, 3:442
God
attributes of 6:805
intellect 3:386
Neoplatonism 6:804
philosophy/religion relationship
5:6
soul in Islamic philosophy 9:44
Trinity
unity of God 4:600
kinds
criteria of identity for 4:676–7
natural **6:682–5**
Kindstrand, J.F. 2:759
kinēsis 7:722
kinetic theory 9:366–7
King, E.B. 1:564
King, E.H. 1:680
King, Jeffrey C.
quantifiers and inference
†7:867–70
King, Lester 6:266, 6:268
King, Martin Luther 3:105, 5:616
King, P. 3:169, 9:59, 9:433
King, William 2:417, 2:419
Kingdom, Elizabeth F.
feminist jurisprudence †3:606–11
law 5:468
Kingsbury, B. 4:186
kingship
see also monarchy; rulers
Germanic 7:508
Kingsland, S.E. 3:205
Kingsley, C. 4:596–7
Kingsley, P.
Empedocles 3:298
Hermetism 4:397
Neo-Pythagoreanism 6:809
Philolaus 7:371
Pythagoras 7:856
Pythagoreanism 7:861
Kinnaird, J. 1:529
Kinsey, Richard
Renner, K. †8:267–8

kinship
African ethical systems 3:431–3
classical structuralism 9:186
Lévi-Strauss, C. 5:583
Kipnis, K. 3:552
Kirby, W.R.T. 4:506
Kirchheimer, Otto 3:733–4, 3:737
Kireevskii, Ivan 8:807–9
Kirfel, W. 4:256
Kirk, G.S.
Anaxagoras 1:254
Anaximander 1:259
Anaximenes 1:262
chemistry
philosophical aspects of 2:299
colour, theories of 2:431
Diogenes of Apollonia 3:89
Empedocles 3:298
Heraclitus 4:369
Hesiod 4:413
Homer 4:502
Melissus 6:296
nous 7:44
Parmenides 7:234
Presocratics 7:672
Thales 9:324
Vlastos, G. 9:653–4
Xenophanes 9:810
Zeno of Elea 9:852
Kirk, L. 2:753
Kirk, Robert 2:585–6, 2:595
Kirkham, Richard L.
truth
coherence theory †9:470–2
correspondence theory
†9:472–5
deflationary theories †9:475–8
pragmatic theory †9:478–80
al-Kirmani, Hamid al-Din 6:805
Kirmani, Z. 8:564
Kirwan, Christopher
Augustine 1:559
Manicheism †6:74–7
Pelagianism †7:284–7
Kis, János 4:571
Kisch, B. 6:249
Kisiel, T. 4:323
Kiss, E. 4:572
Kistiakovskii, Bogdan 5:608, 5:609,
6:795, 6:797
Kitab al-burhan see al-Farabi, Abu
Nasr
Kitab al-shifa see Ibn Sina
Kitabatake Chikafusa 8:751
Kitagawa, J.M. 2:105, 8:753
Kitchel, M.J. 2:143
Kitchener, R.F. 6:727

Kitcher, Patricia S.
Freud, S. 3:793
Kant, I. 5:196
psychoanalysis
methodological issues in
†7:811–17
Kitcher, Philip
causal theory of knowledge 5:266
constructivism 2:629
evolution
and ethics 3:475
and social science 3:487
explanation
functional 3:805
scientific †3:520–5
genetics 4:15, 4:16
Gödel's theorems 4:117
incommensurability 4:736
induction 4:752
mathematics 6:188
foundations of 6:191
molecular biology 6:459–60
naturalized philosophy of science
6:731
science, philosophy of 8:576
scientific method 8:580
social epistemology 8:832
sociobiology 8:896
species 9:81
Kittay, E. 6:505
Kittel, G.F. 5:819, 7:472
Kitts, D. 4:28
Kivy, Peter
aesthetic concepts 1:57, 1:59
Alison, A. 1:187
art
artistic expression 1:498
artistic taste 1:512–13
emotion in response to 3:280
ontology of art works 1:484
Gerard, A. 4:37
Hanslick, E. †4:222–3
Hutcheson, F. 4:593
music
aesthetics of 6:613
opera, aesthetics of 7:131
Reid, T. 8:180
Kiyota, Minoru 2:105, 5:320
Ki-zerbo, J. 1:115
Klagge, J.C. 9:238
Klaidman, S. 5:128
Klamer, A. 3:220–1
Klatzkin, Jacob 9:868, 9:870
Kleene matrices 6:85–7
Kleene, Stephen C.
see also Kleene matrices

Beth's theorem and Craig's
  interpolation theorem 1:763
Church's thesis 2:354–5
combinatory logic 2:433–4
computability theory 2:487–8
formal languages and systems
  3:706
intuitionism 4:850, 4:851, 4:852
lambda calculus 5:349
many-valued logics 6:83
natural deduction, tableau and
  sequent systems 6:682
ordinal logics 7:141, 7:143
predicate calculus 7:665
recursion-theoretic hierarchies
  8:144
semantic paradoxes and theories
  of truth 8:645, 8:648
Turing machines 9:499
Klein, E. 1:243
Klein, F.
  geometry 4:33, 9:63
  logical constants 5:778, 5:780
  space 9:65
Klein, G. 6:389, 7:816
Klein, L. 8:732
Klein, Martha
  love 5:845
  morality and emotions 6:563
  praise and blame †7:644–7
Klein, Melanie 7:817–19, 7:822
Klein, M.J. 7:397–8
Klein, Peter D.
  certainty †2:264–7
  charity principle 2:285
  deductive closure principle 2:845
  epistemology †3:362–5
  knowledge
    causal theory of 5:266
    concept of †5:266–7
    defeasibility theory of 3:382,
      4:55–6, 4:58, 5:278, 5:279
  modus ponens fallibilism 8:498
Klein, S.B. 5:487
Kleiner, S. 3:102
Klein-Franke, F. 5:252
Kleinig, J. 2:598, 3:239, 5:630
Kleitmann, N. 3:129
Klemke, E.D. 5:633
Klemm, D.E. 8:322
Klemmt, A. 8:188
Klépinine, T. 1:731
Kleutgen, Joseph 9:384, 9:387
Klibansky, R. 7:438, 8:491
Klim Smoliatich 6:277
Klima, G. 2:135
Klíma, Ladislav 2:767

Kline, George L.
  Frank, S.L. 3:729
  Leont'ev, K.N. †5:567–70
  Losev, A.F. †5:828–33
  Nietzsche, F.W.: impact on
    Russian thought 6:866–7
  process philosophy 7:715
  Rozanov, V.V. 8:385
  Russian empiriocriticism 8:409
  Shestov, L. 8:746
  Vysheslavtsev, B.P. 9:677
  Whitehead, A.N. 9:718–19
Kline, P. 3:793
Kloetzli, R. 2:684
Klooster, F.H. 8:275
Klosko, G. 7:80
Kloth, K. 1:680
Klubertanz, G. 2:174
Kluckhohn, P. 8:352
Kluge, E.-H. 8:357
Knapp, V.J. 5:420–1
Knasas, J.F.X. 9:387
Kneale, M.
  Boethius, A.M.S. 1:812
  consequence 2:603
  logic
    ancient 5:693
    machines and diagrams 5:746
    nineteenth century 5:728
    seventeenth and eighteenth
      centuries 5:721
  Philo the Dialectician 7:365
  Stoicism 9:160
Kneale, W.C.
  Boethius, A.M.S. 1:812
  consequence 2:603–1:15
  de re/de dicto belief 2:817
  logic
    ancient 5:693
    machines and diagrams 5:746
    multiple-conclusion 6:604
    nineteenth century 5:728
    seventeenth and eighteenth
      centuries 5:721
  necessary truth and convention
    6:749–50
  Philo the Dialectician 7:365
  Stoicism 9:160
Knechtges, D. 9:822
Kneepkens, C.H. 5:404
Kneese, A.V. 8:334, 8:337, 8:338
Knei-Paz, B. 9:466
Kneser, A. 5:313
Kneževic, Božidar 9:50, 9:54
Knigge, A.F. Von 4:697
Knight, Frank 3:221
Knight, I.F. 2:527, 4:527

Knight, K. 1:492
Knight, W.S.M. 4:186
Knittermeyer, H. 6:742
Knoblock, J. 2:548, 9:823
Knoepfler, D. 3:87
Knorr, W.R. 8:791
Knorr-Cetina, K. 2:629–30
Knott, Edward 2:307–8
knowability paradox 7:211, 7:212–13
knowability principle
  bivalence 4:859, 4:860
knowing
  understanding distinction
    testimony in Indian philosophy
      9:317
knowledge 5:266–7
  see also belief; epistemology;
  gnōsis; justification, epistemic;
  moral knowledge; religious
  knowledge
  a posteriori 1:1–3
  a priori 1:3–6, 3:302
    concepts 2:508
    naturalized philosophy of
      science 6:728, 6:729, 6:730
    science, demarcation problem
      2:863–4
    synthetic (Kant, I.) 5:790, 5:791
  absolute (Hegel, G.W.F.) 4:267
  acquaintance (Russell, B.A.W.)
    8:399
  by acquaintance/description
    5:259–63
  acquisition
    see also learning
    Dignāga 3:75
    epistemic appearances 7:295
    perceptual recognition 7:294,
      7:295
    Zabarella, J. 9:837
  action
    Confucianism 2:537
    neo-Confucianism 6:772–3
  adequate (Spinoza, B. de) 9:91,
    9:99–9:100
  African modes of 1:98–9
  analyticity 1:237–8
  anomalous
    paranormal phenomena
      7:221–2
  anthropological account of (Lévi-
    Strauss, C.) 5:584
  anti-positivism
    Latin America 1:306–7
  anti-scepticism (Saadiah Gaon)
    8:435, 8:436

antithetical (Whewell, W.)
9:709–10
apprehensive appearance
(Carneades) 2:218
Aquinas, T. 1:335–8
archaeology of (Foucault, M.)
3:708, 3:710–11
archetype/ectype (form/copy)
(Cudworth, R.) 2:741–2
assimilation
Islam 7:159
Baumgarten, A.G. 1:671
belief relationship **1:706–9**
eliminativism thesis 1:706,
1:708–9
entailment thesis 1:706–7
identity thesis 1:706, 1:707
incompatibility thesis 1:706,
1:707–8
Locke, J. 5:674–5
Ramsey, F.P. 8:46
realist position 7:680
separability thesis 1:706, 1:708
true belief/knowledge
distinction 5:267–8
Yoruba epistemology 1:103–4
Buddhism
Indian 2:96–7
Nyāya debate (Vātsyāyana)
9:587–8
categories of judgment (Kant, I.)
5:185–6
causa sui (self-caused) (Spinoza, B.
de) 9:92–3
causal theory of **5:263–6**, 5:270–1
see also reliabilism
Gettier problems 4:57–8
warrant 5:270–1
causal (Vernia, N.) 9:596
certainty
antisceptical arguments
(White, T.) 9:712
demonstration (Vico, G.) 9:601
Descartes, R. 3:374–5
elenctic distinction (Vlastos, G.)
9:652
Nicholas of Autrecourt 6:829,
6:830
Chinese Marxism 6:136–7
classical theism
divine 4:99
classification of
al-Farabi 3:556
al-Sijistani 8:775
cogito argument (Descartes, R.)
3:5

cognition
intuitive/abstractive (Duns
Scotus, J.) 3:165–6
cognition-truth relationship
(Hegel, G.W.F.) 4:266
coherence (Descartes, R.) 3:4
coherence theory of *see*
justification, epistemic,
coherence theory of
collective 8:830–1
feminist epistemology 3:599
collective consciousness
(Chaadaev, P.I.) 2:270
concepts 2:511
intuitions distinction (Kant, I.)
5:182
concepts of
Plato 3:371
Rickert, H. 6:785
conceptual
Schlick, F.A.M. 8:541–2
self-reflection 3:78
William of Ockham 9:736–8
conceptualization/assent
dichotomy
Islamic philosophy 5:708–9
conditional theory (DeRose, K.)
2:647–8
connaissance-savoir distinction
French philosophy of science
3:783–4
constructivism (Vico, G.) 9:601
contemplative sciences
(Zabarella, J.) 9:837–8
contingent (al-Juwayni) 5:169
of contingent particulars (Vital du
Four) 9:638
corrigibility 3:379
criteria
Ayer, A.J. 1:617
Philo of Larissa 7:362–3
critical realism 2:721
critical theory 2:726
dao 2:778
Daoism 2:787, 2:788–9
Zhuangzi 9:866
deductive closure principle **2:842–5**
defeasibility theory of 3:379,
5:276–80
a posteriori justification 1:1
Barn Facsimile example 5:278
common-sense reasoning 2:452
Gettier problems 4:55–6,
5:276–7
memory retention 6:301
ultimate defeat 5:278–9
warrant 5:270

definition theory (al-Suhrawardi)
9:221
degrees of
Locke, J. 5:675
Yoruba epistemology 9:832–3
democracy 2:869–70
demonstrative
doubt 3:122
Locke, J. 3:376
rationalism 8:77–9
desire
neo-Confucianism 6:769, 6:770
development
French philosophy of science
3:784
Dharmakīrti 3:52
dialectics (Schleiermacher, F.)
8:533–4
direct
Berkeley, G. 3:377
Sergeant, J. 8:698–9
discovery
logic of 3:99–3:103
divine
see also omniscience
de re 7:108
de se 7:108–9
eternality 3:425–6
al-Ghazali 4:65, 4:640–1
Jewish philosophy
Gersonides 4:49
middle knowledge 4:331,
7:111–12
omnipresence 7:106
of particulars
al-Ghazali 4:65
propositional analysis 7:108–9
providence 7:799–801
al-Razi, Fakhr al-Din 8:113–14
religious language 8:258–9
al-Tusi 9:505
of the world
Islamic philosophy 4:640–1
divine illumination
Bonaventure 1:828, 1:832–3
Marston, R. 6:114
Matthew of Aquasparta 6:201
division of (Wolff, C.) 9:778
educational philosophy (Locke, J.)
3:226
empirical
Ibn al-'Arabi 4:602
Maimon, S. 6:36–7
empirical evidence
sirhak 8:797
empirical statements (Lewis, C.I.)
5:587–8

epistemic empiricism 3:299
epistemic paradoxes 7:212–13
epistemic principles 5:272–5
essence relationship (al-Razi,
    Fakhr al-Din) 8:113–14
evil relationship (Shestov, L.)
    8:741, 8:744–5
of existence (Anselm of
    Canterbury) 1:287
experience
    Alembert, J. le R. d' 1:166
    doubt 3:123, 3:124
    Kant, I. 5:183–4
    Locke, J. 5:665, 5:668–9, 5:673,
        5:675
external world
    Descartes, R. 3:12
    Russell, B.A.W. 8:399–400
externalism 5:270–2, 8:206
faculties (Ibn Sina) 4:648,
    4:649–50
faith
    incompatibility with
        (Shestov, L.) 8:744
faith as 9:329
fallibility
    Latitudinarianism 5:433
farming
    virtue of 1:127–8
fiducial
    theology of the word (Barth, K.)
        1:653
first principles
    Aristotle 3:372
    Fichte, J.G. 3:646–7
forms of (Scheler, M.F.) 8:505–6
foundation of (Natorp, P.) 6:782–3
foundationalism 5:268–9
    sense-data 8:695
functionalism 6:174–5
genealogies (Foucault, M.)
    3:708–9, 3:711
general theory of (Schlick, F.A.M.)
    8:540
geometrical method (Spinoza, B.
    de) 9:91
Gettier problems 3:379, 4:54–5,
    5:263–4
Giles of Rome 4:74
of God 8:60
    Barth, K. 3:507
    Brunner, E. 2:30–1
    Calvin, J. 2:177, 2:178–9
    Clement of Alexandria 7:258
    divine illumination 4:699
    Duns Scotus, J. 3:154, 3:157–8
    Fontenelle, B. de 3:691

Godfrey of Fontaines 4:120
Hermetism 4:396
Ibn Falaquera 4:616
Ibn Massara 4:627
Ibn Tufayl 4:657–9
Ibn Tzaddik, J. 4:661
Johnson, S. 5:124–5
Kabbalah 5:171
More, H. 6:576
natural theology 6:707, 6:709
Norris, J. 7:41–2
Richard of Middleton 8:311
Siger of Brabant 8:766
Spinoza, B. de 9:103
Ulrich of Strasbourg 9:517–18
univocity of being 3:154,
    3:157–8
good and evil (Wang Yangming)
    9:683–4
grounding 8:548
happiness (Confucius) 2:568
hermetism (Fludd, R.) 3:683
hierarchical organization
    (Descartes, R.) 3:5, 3:6
Hindu philosophy 4:435–6
historical
    constructivism (Vico, G.) 9:604
historicism 4:443–4
human nature (Home, H.) 4:499
Hume, D. 4:545–9
idealism (Burthogge, R.) 2:144,
    2:145
ideas
    Bold, S. 1:822–3
    Johnson, S. 5:124
immortality of the soul (Denys the
    Carthusian) 2:885
implicit-explicit distinction 5:286
incorrigibility 3:379
Indian philosophy 3:388–91,
    4:737, **5:280–5**
infant cognition 2:390–1
innateness of **4:794–7**, 5:286
    infant cognition 2:390, 2:391
    James of Viterbo 5:58
    nativist/empiricist debate
        6:672–4
    Plato 6:673
    special-purpose structures 6:674
    Spinoza, B. de 9:100
    unconscious mental states 9:524
    Wang Yangming 9:683–4
    Zhu Xi 9:683
inquiry (Dewey, J.) 3:48
integral
    Kireevskii, I. 8:807–8
    Solov'ëv, V.S. 9:31

intellective perception (Rosmini-
    Serbati, A.) 8:362–3
intentional action
    (Anscombe, G.E.M.) 1:281
internalism-externalism distinction
    4:822, 4:825
introspection 1:708, 3:299, 4:56,
    4:837–41
intuition
    Descartes, R. 3:6
    rationalism 8:77–9
    real-apparent distinction 8:79
intuitions
    concepts distinction (Kant, I.)
        5:182
intuitive 8:77–9
    Illuminationist philosophy
        4:700–1
    Locke, J. 3:376
    Spinoza, B. de 9:100–1
justification see justification,
    epistemic
language
    Chinese
        propositional belief 5:695
    Chomsky, N. 2:338–9
    Condillac, É.B. de 2:523,
        2:525–6
    Mohism 5:697
    truth conditions 6:222–3
levels of
    Ibn al-'Arabi 4:602
    Neoplatonism 6:798, 6:800
    Proclus 7:729
    Spinoza, B. 3:375–6
    Steiner, R. 9:133–4
limits of
    Dilthey, W. 3:80
    Johnson, A.B. 5:121
    Plato 3:371–2
    Xenophanes 9:809–10
linguistic
    compositionality 2:477
    Indian philosophy 9:315–18
logic
    inference
        Jainism 5:51–2
    mathematical
        empirical evidence 3:302
        Mersenne, M. 6:325, 6:327–8
memory 6:296–9, **6:300–2**
mind/matter relationship
    (Lichtenberg, G.C.) 5:623
misperception 7:287
modes of (Frank, S.L.) 3:727–8
moral luck 6:521

morality relationship
  Daxue 2:808
More, H. 6:577–8
mystical
  Vedānta 9:590–1
  Vysheslavtsev, B.P. 9:676
nativism
  common-sense principles 9:136
  Locke, J. 6:673
naturalistic account 4:786
naturalized philosophy of science
  6:728
nature of
  Lonergan, B.J.F. 5:823
  Schelling, F.W.J. von 8:515
  of necessary truths (Vital du Four)
    9:639
negative facts
  Indian philosophy 6:755–8
neo-Confucianism 6:769, 6:770,
  6:772–3
Nietzsche, F.W. 6:849–50
objective theory 4:787
objective/subjective distinction
  (Nagel, T.) 6:644–5
objects of
  Chinese philosophy 5:697
observation 6:724
observation sentences
  (Quine, W.V.) 8:3–4, 8:5–6
omniscience
  Jainism 5:48, 5:51
operationalism (Lorenzen, P.)
  5:825–6, 5:827
as organic unity (Alembert, J. le R.
  d') 1:166–7
organism-environment interplay
  (Piaget, J.) 7:383, 7:385
organization of
  Chinese philosophy 2:318
other minds 7:171
  children 6:385–8
perception 7:296–8
  Aristotle 3:372
  information theory 4:786
  intellect distinction (Ptolemy)
    7:830
  Lenin, V.I. 5:566
perceptual 7:293–9
perspectival
  epistemic logic 3:358–9
phenomenalist 3:299–300
plausibility (Carneades) 2:219
pluralism
  political philosophy
    Indian 7:522
poetic (Maritain, J.) 6:103

popular opinion (Taylor, H.) 9:279
postmodernism 1:187
power relationship (Foucault, M.)
  7:602
praxeology 7:648
predicate-in-notion principle 3:376
by presence
  Ha'iri Yazdi, M. 5:19
  Illuminationist philosophy
    4:701, 6:618
preservation
  memory **6:300–2**
privacy 7:699
probability
  Leibniz, G.W. 5:552–3
  Reichenbach, H. 8:167–8
projectivism 7:739
  Fëdorov, N.F. 3:575
propositional 3:357, 5:267–8
  phenomenology 7:343, 7:345,
    7:347
propositional (Locke, J.) 5:675–6
public 3:300–1
  epistemic logic 3:358–9
pure theories 4:787–8
qualia 7:864, 7:865–6
  colour vision 2:422
questions 8:2
rational realism (Krause, K.) 5:299
rational soul
  Jewish philosophy (Ibn
    Tzaddik, J.) 4:661
real/ordinary distinction
  neo-Confucianism 6:769
realism/antirealism 8:117–18
reason
  Cambridge Platonism 2:182,
    2:183–4
  intuition distinction (Iqbal, M.)
    4:865–6
  and reality (Hegel, G.W.F.)
    4:259–60
  revelation reconciliation
    (Witherspoon, J.) 9:755–6
reflection (Suchon, G.) 9:211
reflective
  phenomenal consciousness
    2:589–90
relativity of
  Cournot, A.A. 2:689
  Mill, J.S. 6:360, 6:366–7
  Scheler, M.F. 8:506
relevant alternatives 2:843–4
reliabilism 4:788, 5:271, 8:204,
  8:205
  Armstrong, D.M. 1:442

deductive closure principle
  2:844
pattern matching 8:207–8
religious *see* religous knowledge
resemblance theory (Broad, C.D.)
  2:24
revelation (Rāmānuja) 8:43
risk assessment 8:335, 8:336,
  8:336–7, 8:337
Sāṅkhya 8:464–5
scale of forms (Collingwood, R.G.)
  2:414
scepticism
  Academic (Cicero, M.T.) 2:357
  apologetic function (Huet, P.-
    D.) 4:515–17
  Austin, J.L. critique 1:572
  Pyrrhonism 7:848–54
  Renaissance 8:451–3, 8:498–503
scientific
  Aquinas, T. 3:373–4
  Aristotle 1:417–18, 3:372
  Buridan, J. 2:133
  Epicureanism 3:345
  fallibilism **3:545–8**
  feminist epistemology 3:597,
    3:600
  Galen 3:835
  investigation of 6:721
  Islamic fundamentalism 5:12
  naturalized epistemology
    6:721–2
  Peter of Spain 7:324
  social constitution 2:624–5
of self
  Boehme, J. 1:799
  Hermetism 4:396
  Ibn Tzaddik, J. 4:660
self-awareness
  Illuminationist philosophy (al-
    Suhrawardi) 9:220–1
self-consciousness (Fichte, J.G.)
  6:738
self-cultivation
  Chinese philosophy 8:618,
    8:623–4
Selfhood
  Iqbal, M. 4:864
senses 3:379
  Campanella, T. 5:35
  Condillac, É.B. de 2:523,
    2:524–5
  Epicureanism 3:340
  Helvétius, C.-A. 4:345
  Indian views of 8:689, 8:691–2
sensitive (Locke, J.) 3:376–7
of the singular (Pecham, J.) 7:267

social epistemology 5:163–4
social factors 8:829–30
sociology **9:1–2**
  Chinese philosophy 2:322–3
  constructivism 2:625
sociology of science
  Edinburgh School 2:625–6
of the soul prior to God
  Jewish philosophy (Ibn
    Falaquera) 4:616
sources of
  Gauḍīya Vaiṣṇavism 3:858
  inference
    Indian theories of 4:761
  Islamic philosophy 3:385
  Nyāya 3:860
of space and time (Kant, I.)
  5:184–5
spheres of being (Scheler, M.F.)
  8:507
subjectivity of (Bridgman, P.W.)
  2:18
substantial motion (Mulla Sadra)
  6:597
Sufism
  Ibn Sab'in 4:646–7
synthetic a priori judgments
  (Kant, I.) 5:183–4
system of (Keckermann, B.) 5:225
tacit **5:286–7**
  mental imagery 4:705
  Polanyi, M. 7:489, 7:490–1
technology 9:285–6
testimony **9:309–14**
theoretical
  Boethius of Dacia 1:814
  demonstrative science 6:708
  Gilbert of Poitiers 4:70
  tacit distinction (Hayek, F.A.)
    4:247
Thomas of York 9:375–6
thought experiments 9:394, 9:396
Tibetan philosophy 4:737
tracking analysis 2:844
transcendental apperception
  (Kant, I.) 5:186
transcendental (Gentile, G.) 4:21
transcendental subject
  (Schelling, F.W.J. von) 8:510
transmission of
  Chinese philosophy 2:318–19
true belief distinguished from
  5:267–8
of truth
  Henry of Ghent 4:357
  William of Auvergne 9:726

truth-tracking theory (Nozick, R.)
  7:46
types of
  Jainism 5:51
  John of Mirecourt 5:111–12
understanding
  Crusius, C.A. 2:737–8
  private states 7:700
universal (Comenius, J.A.) 2:439
values (Alexander, S.) 1:168
virtues
  Socrates 7:408, 9:14–15
  Spinoza, B. de 9:91–2, 9:102
vision in God (Malebranche, N.)
  6:58–60
warrant theory 5:268–72
will (Locke, J.) 5:676
zhi **9:858**
Knowles, D. 7:438
Knowlson, J. 9:535
Knox, R.A. 3:332
Knudsen, A. 4:821
Knudsen, C. 2:294
Knuth, D.E. 8:59
Knutzen, Martin **5:287–9**
Knuuttila, S.
  Bradwardine, T. 1:866
  Buridan, J. 2:135–6
  divine simplicity 8:787
  logic
    medieval 5:758
    modal 6:426
  necessary being 6:747
Knysh, A. 6:620
Kobayashi Hideo 5:659
Kōbō Daishi *see* Kūkai
Kobong *see* Ki Taesûng
Koch, A. 5:85
Koch, H. 9:309
Koch, J. 3:174, 7:808
Koch, Robert 6:267
Koch, S. 7:135, 7:826, 7:829
Kochen, S. 1:716, 7:884, 7:886
Kochumuttom, T.A. 2:75, 9:218,
  9:587
Kockelmans, J.J. 7:342
Kodalle, K. 5:301
Kodera, T.J. 9:692
Koehler, L. 3:576
Koehn, Darryl 7:734, 7:735, 7:737
Koehne, R. 5:624
Koenen, L. 6:77
Koenigsberger, L. 4:340
Koerner, E.F.K. 8:473
Koerner, K. 5:404
Koerner, L. 5:650

Koertge, Noretta
  chemistry
    philosophical aspects of
      †2:294–300
Koester, H. 4:85
Koestler, A. 4:563, 4:567
Koffka, Kurt 4:54, 7:829
Kofman, S. 2:901, 3:588
kogaku (Ancient Learning)
  Itō Jinsai 5:42–3
  morality 5:76
  Ogyū Sorai 7:90
  Tominaga Nakamoto 9:440
Kogan, B. 4:646
Koh, Ikchim 9:794
Kohak, E. 7:254
Kohanski, A.S. 2:48, 5:838
Kohlberg, E. 2:834
Kohlberg, Lawrence
  feminist ethics 3:603, 3:605
  moral development 2:281, 6:509
  moral stage theory 6:504–5
Kohlenbach, U. 7:751
Kohler, J. 5:512, 5:514
Köhler, L. 5:83
Köhler, Wolfgang 4:53, 4:54, 9:633
Kohn, E. 5:206
Kohn, H. 6:661, 7:201
Köhnke, K.C. 2:402, 6:792, 8:780
Kohut, Heinz 7:820–1, 7:823
koinai ennoiai (common notions)
  2:742
Kojève, Alexandre **5:289–91**
  Hegelianism 4:293–4
  master-slave dialectic
    postmodernism 1:188, 1:191
  subject
    postmodern critique of 9:201
Kojiki (Record of Ancient Matters)
  5:76, 6:589
kokoro ('heart') **5:291–3**
  Motoori Norinaga 5:76, 6:589
kokugaku (Native Studies School)
  5:76
  Motoori Norinaga 6:588, 6:589
  Ogyū Sorai 7:90
Kolakowski, L.
  Bergson, H.-L. 1:737
  Bogdanov, A.A. 1:820
  Lenin, V.I. 5:567
  Marx, K. 6:133
  Marxism
    Russian and Soviet 6:159
    Western 6:146
  Plekhanov, G.V. 7:455
  Russian empiriocriticism 8:409
  socialism 8:885

Kolenda, K. 8:355
Kollár, Jan 7:198, 8:812
Koller, P. 9:702
Kollontai, A. 3:579–80, 3:583
Kolm, S.-C. 3:210
Kölmel, W. 4:172
Kolmogorov, A.N. 2:482, 2:490, 2:496
Kolmogorov Machines 2:485, 2:489
Kolnai, A. 3:701, 8:140
Kologriwof, I. von 5:570
Komensky, Jan Amos see Comenius, John Amos
Komoguchi, Isao 5:177
Kong Yingda 9:831
König, A. 8:188–9
König, Julius 2:654, 7:218
Konishi Jin'ichi 1:83, 1:89, 1:90, 9:840
Koons, R.C. 1:50
Koopmans, T. 3:221
Kopf, D. 2:7
Koran see Qur'an
Korcik, A. 7:497
Korea
    Buddhist philosophy 2:106–18
    Chinul 2:329–32
    Chŏng Yagyong 2:341–3
    Confucianism 2:555–6
    Han Wŏnjin 4:220–1
    sirhak movement 8:796–8
    Sôsan Hyujông 9:36–7
    Tonghak 9:441–2
    Ûisang 9:516–17
    Wŏnch'ūk 9:792–3
    Wŏnhyo 9:793–4
    Yi Hwang 9:823–5
    Yi Kan 9:825–6
    Yi Yulgok 9:826–8
The Korean Buddhist Research Institute 9:37
Kormondy, E.J. 3:205
Korn, Alejandro 1:305, 1:307, 1:376, 1:379
Kornblatt, J.D. 2:126, 8:385, 8:427
Kornblith, Hilary
    epistemic justification 5:164
    introspection †4:837–42
    natural kinds 6:684
    naturalized epistemology 6:727
    naturalized philosophy of science 6:731
    normative epistemology 7:36, 7:38
Körner, S. 9:454, 9:478
Kornis, Gy. 4:572
Korol'kov, A. 5:570
Korovikov, V.I. 4:692
Kors, A.C. 2:376
Korsch, K. 4:297

Korsgaard, Christine M.
    autonomy
        ethical 1:592
        axiology 1:611
        duty 3:182
        good, theories of the †4:130–5
        Kantian ethics 5:203
        moral motivation 6:527
        moral standing 6:554
        practical reason and ethics 7:619
        teleological ethics †9:294–5
        value 9:583
Korsmeyer, Carolyn
    aesthetic concepts 1:58
    feminist aesthetics †3:593–6
Kortian, G. 4:301
Kōsai, T. 9:841
Kosaka Masaaki see Kyoto School
Koshelev, A.D. 6:588
Koshelëv, Aleksandr 8:810
Kosko, B. 3:824
Koslow, A. 7:665
kosmos (world)
    Anaximander 1:256–9
Kosslyn, S. 4:704, 4:705
Kosso, Peter
    archaeology 1:358
    observation †7:80–6
Kosulin, A. 9:675
Kotarbińska, J. 5:295
Kotarbiński, Tadeusz 5:293–6
    Polish logic 7:494, 7:497
    praxeology 7:648
Kotatko, P. 8:14
Kothari, R. 7:524
kotodama (spiritual power of words) 2:100–1, 5:69
Kovalevskii, Maksim 7:563–4
Kovesi, J. 4:572
Kovtun, J.G. 6:166
Kowalski, J. 4:792
Koyama Iwao see Kyoto School
Koyasu, Nobukuni 5:44
Koyré, Alexandre 5:296–8
    Boehme, J. 1:801
    Chaadaev, P.I. 2:272
    Galilei, G. 3:841
    Hegelianism 4:299
        Russian 4:306–7
    historiography of science 5:315–16
    Kepler, J. 5:232
    matter 6:196
    More, H. 6:583
    Newton, I. 6:828
    omnipresence 7:107
    space 9:65
Kozen, D. 3:191

Kozlov, Aleksei Aleksandrovich 5:834, 5:838
Kozyrev, A. 5:570
Krabbe, Erik C.W.
    dialogical logic †3:59–62
Krabbenhoft, K. 4:400
Kracauer, S. 8:780
Kraemer, J.L. 4:632–3, 6:48, 7:430, 8:775–6
Kraft, Viktor 5:794, 9:611–12
Kragh, H. 2:680
Krailsheimer, A. 7:246
Král, Josef 2:769, 8:813
Krämer, H.-J. 7:429, 9:807
Kramer, Matthew H.
    Holmes, O.W. †4:493–5
Kramers, R.P. 9:858
Kramnick, Isaac 2:140
Kranakis, E. 8:59
Krantz, D.H. 6:249
Kranz, W.
    Democritus 2:877
    dissoi logoi (twofold argument) 3:107
    Leucippus 5:579
    Presocratics 7:671–2
    Pythagoreanism 7:861
    Sophists 9:34
Kraus, Paul 8:115
Kraus, S. 5:479, 7:34
Krause, Karl Christian Friedrich 5:298–301, 9:519
Krausism 1:376
Krausopositivism 9:72–3, 9:519
Krauss, L. 6:196
Krausz, M. 6:613
Kraut, R. 2:817, 3:230, 7:420
Kraut, Richard
    Aristotle 1:434
    egoism and altruism †3:245–8
    happiness 4:229
Kraye, J. 1:412, 4:540, 7:447
Kreeft, P. 5:590
Kreisel, Georg
    Gödel's theorems 4:117
    Herbrand's theorem 4:378
    Hilbert's programme and formalism 4:428
    intuitionism 4:850, 4:852
    mathematics
        foundations of 6:191
    ordinal logics 7:142, 7:143
    proof theory 7:748, 7:749, 7:751
    provability logic 7:793–4, 7:796
    second-order logic 8:604
Kreisler, H.J. 5:851
Krell, D. 6:299

Kremer, E.J. 1:447–8, 5:379
Kremer, K. 1:348
Kremer-Marietti, Angèle
    Comte, A. †2:496–505
Kren, C. 1:158
Kreps, D. 2:834–5
Kretschmann, E. 8:199
Kretzmann, B.E. 5:245, 7:182
Kretzmann, Norman
    Aquinas, T. †1:326–50
    atomism, ancient 1:535
    Boethius, A.M.S. 1:812, 1:813
    creation and conservation
        religious doctrine of 2:700
    divine freedom 3:761
    divine simplicity 8:787
    eternity †3:422–7
    eternity of the world
        medieval views of 3:429
    Gregory of Rimini 4:172
    immutability 4:714
    Kilvington, R. †5:244–5
    language
        ancient philosophy of 5:361
        early modern philosophy of
            5:379
        medieval theories of 5:404
    logic
        medieval 5:758
    medieval philosophy 6:277
    natural philosophy
        medieval 6:706
    natural theology 6:712–13
    omniscience 7:112
    Oxford Calculators 7:182
    perfect goodness 4:143, 4:144
    prophecy 7:771
    religion
        history of philosophy of 8:247
        and morality 8:224
    syncategorematic words 1:50
    Wodeham, A. 9:776
Kretzschmar, H. 7:398
Krieger, L. 7:836
Krieger, M. 2:739
Krikorian, Y. 1:123
Krimsky, S. 8:337
Krings, H. 6:741
Kripacharyulu, M. 6:30
Kripal, J.J. 8:42
Kripke models
    modal logic 6:419, 6:423–5
Kripke, Saul Aaron 5:301–5
    a posteriori knowledge 1:1, 1:3
    a priori knowledge 1:4, 1:6
    ambiguity 1:200

causal theory of reference
    (Putnam, H.) 7:841
colour and qualia 2:427
concepts 2:516
conceptual role semantics 8:654,
    8:656
descriptions 3:24
dualism 3:138
essentialism 3:421
Evans, G. 3:461
fiction
    semantics of 3:662
historical chain theory 7:754–5
identity 4:678
intuitionism 4:850–1, 4:852
meaning
    and communication 6:213
    and rule-following 6:216,
        6:217–18, 6:219
modal logic 5:765, 6:419–20, 6:426,
    6:432
modal operators 6:435
natural kinds 6:684
necessary truth
    convention 6:749, 6:750
ontological commitment 7:116
possible worlds 6:427–8, 6:430,
    8:663–4, 8:668
private language argument 7:694,
    7:697, 7:698
private states and language 7:701
proper names 7:752, 7:757
propositional attitudes 7:786
qualia 7:867
quantifiers 7:873
reference
    description theory critique
        8:155, 8:157
    historical-causal theory 8:154,
        8:157–8, 8:164
semantic paradoxes and theories
    of truth 8:642–3, 8:644–6, 8:648
sense theories 7:753–4
substance 9:208, 9:210
substitutional/objectual
    quantifiers 7:881
Wittgenstein, L. 6:216, 6:217–18,
    6:219, 9:765, 9:770
Krishan, Y. 5:217–18
Krishna see Kṛṣṇa
Krishna Rao, M.V. 5:221
Kristeller, Paul O.
    Aristotelianism
        Renaissance 1:412–13
    Bruno, G. 2:39
    dance
        aesthetics of 2:777

    Ficino, M. 3:659
    humanism 4:529, 4:532
        Renaissance 4:541
    libertins 5:621
    Patrizi, F. 7:264
    Petrarca, F. 7:329
    Platonism
        Renaissance 7:447
    Pomponazzi, P. 7:532
    Telesio, B. 9:300
Kristeva, Julia 5:305–8
    alterity
        dialectics of desire 1:188–9,
            1:191
    feminist literary criticism 3:612
    psychoanalytic feminism 3:588
    revolution 8:303
    Tel Quel school 9:293
Krochmal, Nachman 5:308–11
    Jewish Enlightenment 3:321–2
    Jewish philosophy 5:90
    Poland 7:486
Kroes, Peter
    technology, philosophy of
        †9:284–8
    time 9:416
Krois, J.M. 2:227
Kronecker, Leopold 4:117, 4:847,
    5:311–13
Kroner, R. 4:45, 4:297
Krönert, G. 5:562
Kronhausen, P. 3:409
Kronman, A.T. 5:152
Krook, D. 3:74, 8:699
Kroon, F. 3:662–3
Kropotkin, Pëtr Alekseevich
    5:313–14
    anarchism 1:245, 1:246, 1:248
Kṛṣṇa 3:186–7, 3:566–7, 9:574–5
Krüger, L. 9:454
Kruglikov, V. 6:70
Kruks, S. 1:687, 3:501
Krutch, Joseph Wood 9:451
Krygier, Martin
    common law/custom †2:440–6
Krynicki, M. 7:877
Kuan Tzu see Guanzi
Kubes, V. 9:708
Kuehn, M. 7:170, 9:321
Kuflik, Arthur
    moral standing †6:550–5
Kühn, J. 6:206
Kuhn, Steven T.
    modal logic †6:417–26
Kuhn, Thomas Samuel 5:315–18
    concepts 2:516

conceptual role semantics 8:653, 8:656
Copernicus, N. 2:672
discovery
  logic of 3:102
economics
  philosophy of 3:221
educational philosophy
  relativism 3:237
experiment 3:515
fallibilism 3:545–6, 3:548
foundationalism 3:723
  French philosophy of science 3:785
geology 4:27
Hempel, C.G. 4:352
incommensurability 4:732–5, 4:736
Koyré, A. 5:298
Lakatos, I. comparison 5:343, 5:344, 5:345
logical positivism 5:794, 9:347
modularity of mind 6:450, 6:451
naturalism in social science 6:720
naturalized philosophy of science 6:729
Naturphilosophie 6:742
observation 7:86
paradigms 8:63
Planck, M.K.E.L. 7:398
pragmatism 7:639
reference 8:164
revolution 8:303–4
science
  demarcation problem 2:866
scientific method 8:580
  demarcation problem 2:864
  Feyerabend, P.K. 3:641
scientific theories 9:353
  simplicity 8:783
social science
  history of philosophy of 8:858
  theory and observation in 9:356
The Structure of Scientific Revolutions 5:315–17
  experiment 3:515
  French philosophy of science 3:785
  incommensurability 4:733, 4:734
tacit knowledge 5:287
theory change
  justification of 8:354
thought experiments 9:396
Kühne-Bertram, G. 5:488
Kuhse, H. 7:57
Kuijp, L.W.J. van der 6:417, 8:435, 9:408

Kuipers, Theo A.F.
  confirmation theory †2:532–6
Kūkai 2:100, 2:104, 5:71, **5:318–20**
Kukathas, Chandran
  Hayek, F.A. †4:245–9
  multiculturalism 6:602
  Rand, A. †8:55–6
Kuki Shūzō **5:320–1**
  aesthetics 1:84–5, 1:90
  philosophy in modern literature 5:659
Kuklick, Bruce
  American philosophy
    eighteenth and nineteenth century 1:206
  Lewis, C.I. 5:589
  Paine, T. †7:184–6
  Royce, J. 8:381
Kuksiewicz, Z. 1:598, 5:109, 7:488
Kulas, J. 7:873, 8:658
Kulka, T. 4:567
Kulke, E. 9:874
Kûm Changt'ae 2:343, 8:797
Kumar, R. 4:256
Kumar, Shikha
  Arya Samaj †1:516–17
  Brahmo Samaj †2:5–7
  knowledge 5:285
Kumārajīva 2:82–3, 8:683
Kumārila (Bhaṭṭa)
  atheism 4:439
  Buddhist nominalism 7:26, 7:27
  language
    Indian theories of 5:384
    sphoṭa theory 5:382
  meaning 4:436
  Mīmāṃsā 6:379, 6:380, 6:381
    intrinsic validity 6:378, 6:379
    knowledge
      Indian views of 5:282–3, 5:285
    realism 6:378
    unchanging self 6:379
  negative facts in classical Indian philosophy 6:756–7, 6:758
  self-certificationalism
    Indian epistemology 3:391, 3:392
  universals
    Indian theories of 9:546, 9:547, 9:548
Kumazawa Banzan **5:321–2**
Kumin, I. 7:823
Kummel, W.G. 5:820
Kundakunda 5:53–4, 5:56
Kunen, K. 8:708–9

Küng, Hans 3:417, 4:148, 4:151, 5:168
Kunjunni Raja, K.
  Hindu philosophy 4:439–40
Künne, Wolfgang
  Bernard Bolzano †1:823–7
  Husserl, E. 4:587
Kuper, Leo 8:19
Kuratowski, C. 1:763, 8:711, 8:715
Kurtz, P. 7:227
Kurz, G. 4:482, 8:519
Kusch, Gunther Rodolfo 5:610–12
Kutter, H. 2:33–4
Kuvakin, V. 8:427–8
Kuyper, Abraham 3:113, 3:114
Kvanvig, Jonathan L.
  creation and conservation
    religious doctrine of 2:700
  epistemic paradoxes †7:211–14
  epistemology
    and ethics 3:370
    virtue 9:618, 9:621
  limbo 5:637
  occasionalism 7:89
Kwahagwôn Ch'ôrhak Yônguso 2:343
Kwiatkowski, T. 5:863
Kybal, V. 4:574
Kyburg, H.E.
  Campbell, N.R. 2:194
  deductive closure principle 2:845
  Lottery Paradox 7:211, 7:214
  non-monotonic logic 7:34
  statistics 9:126
Kymlicka, Will
  citizenship †2:362–5
  community and communitarianism 2:471
  equality 3:395
  justice 5:146
  morality and identity 6:575
  multiculturalism 6:600–1, 6:602
  political philosophy 7:503, 7:528
  public interest 7:834
Kyo Buddhism 2:115–16, 2:329, 2:330, 9:36
Kyoto School **5:323–30**
  East Asian Philosophy 3:195
  Japanese philosophy 5:77–8
  logic 5:714
  Miki Kiyoshi 6:358
  Nishida Kitarō
    Japan 7:13
  Nishitani Keiji 7:16–17
  Tanabe Hajime 9:261–2
  Watsuji Tetsurō 9:691–2

L

La Bruyère, Jean de 6:555, 6:556
La Caze, M. 5:479
La Fontaine, J. de 7:554
La Forge, Louis de **5:331–2**
La Loubère, Simon de 7:10
La Mettrie, Julien Offroy de **5:332–5**
　human nature
　　eighteenth century science of
　　　4:527
　materialism 6:171, 6:173
La Mothe Le Vayer, François 5:620–1
La Torre, Massimo
　Fuller, L.L. †3:801–2
　Radbruch, G. †8:21–3
La Valette Monbrun, A. de 6:53
La Vallée Poussin, L. de 2:58, 4:256,
　9:218
labour
　see also work
　alienated 1:178–9, 1:180, 9:795
　division of 9:795
　　Durkheim, É. 3:176
　　Marx, K. 6:125
　　retrogression
　　　(Mikhailovskii, N.K.) 6:356
　equality 3:394–5
　exploitation
　　market ethics 6:108–9
　feminism 3:579–80
　market economy (Smith, A.) 8:820
　Marx, K.
　　alienation 6:118, 6:122
　　social relations 6:127–9, 6:131
　property 7:757, 7:758, 7:759–60
　slavery 8:805
　socialism 8:884
　unalienated 9:794, 9:795–6
Labriola, Antonio **5:335–6**
　Croce, B. 2:729
　Hegelianism 4:287, 5:335
　Marxism
　　Italy 5:38
　　Western 6:143
Labrousse, E. 1:677
Labry, R. 4:410
Lacan, Jacques **5:336–8**
　see also Lacanian theory
　desire
　　Lyotard, J.-F. critique 6:8

dialectics of desire 1:188, 1:191
Freudian psychoanalysis 7:602–3
Kristeva, J. 5:308
language and gender 5:363
psychoanalysis
　post-Freudian 7:823
　symbolism/language
　　post-Freudian 7:821
social science
　history of philosophy of 8:858
　structuralism 9:185, 9:186–7,
　　9:188
subject
　postmodern critique of 9:198–9,
　　9:201
Lacanian theory
　psychoanalytic feminism 3:584,
　　3:585
LaCapra, D. 3:177
Lacey, A.R.
　Bergson, H.-L. †1:732–7
Lacey, N. 2:710, 7:693
Lachelier, Jules **5:338–40**
Lachenaud, G. 3:126
Lachs, John
　epiphenomenalism 3:354
　Santayana, G. †8:467–70
Lackey, D.P. 9:690–1
Lackner, J. 2:595
Laclau, E. 2:901, 8:304
Lacohe, H. 6:389
Lacombe, O. 8:44, 9:594
Lacoue-Labarthe, Philippe **5:340–2**,
　7:477
Lacroze, R. 6:53
Lacy, D.M. 1:358
Ladd, J. 6:670
Ladd, R.E. 3:552
Laddaga, R. 7:711
Ladenson, R.F. 3:315
Ladner, R.E. 3:191
Ladokha, G. 5:438
LaFargue, Michael
　Daodejing †2:779–83
　Daoist philosophy 2:795
　Zhuangzi 9:867
Laffranque, M. 7:557
Lafitau, J.F. 6:670

LaFleur, W.R.
　Buddhism
　　Japanese 2:105–6
　　Dōgen 3:111
　Japanese aesthetics 1:90
　mujō 6:594
　Watsuji Tetsurō 9:692
LaFollette, H.
　ethics
　　agricultural 1:128
　　development 3:43
　　family 3:552
　help and beneficence 4:344
　humour 4:567
Lafond, J. 7:554
Lafont, Y. 5:640
Lagarrigue, Jorge 7:568
Lagarrigue, Juan Enrique 7:568
Lagerspetz, Eerik
　social sciences
　　prediction in †8:871–2
Lagrange, Joseph Louis 1:217, 4:30,
　6:256
Lagrée, J. 5:479, 5:652
Laguna, Andrés 9:71, 9:76
Lahbabi, M. 5:21
Laine, Joy
　mind
　　Indian philosophy of
　　　†6:399–403
　　Udayana †9:512–14
　　Uddyotakara †9:514–16
　　Vātsyāyana †9:587–8
Laird, John 4:561
laissez-faire theory 9:87, 9:88
Lajpat Rai, L. 1:517
Lakatos, Imre **5:342–5**
　economics
　　philosophy of 3:217–18, 3:221
　incommensurability 4:736
　Kuhn, T.S. 5:318
　numbers 7:53
　scientific theories 9:353
Lake, P. 4:506
Lakhsassi, A. 4:626
Lakoff, Robin 5:362–3, 5:367
Laks, A.
　Cicero, M.T. 2:360
　Diogenes of Apollonia 3:89

Hellenistic philosophy 4:336
hermeneutics 4:389
Orphism 7:165
Lamarque, P.
emotion in response to art 3:280
fictional entities †3:663–7
Lamb, D. 5:630
Lamb, M.E. 7:822
Lamb, S. 6:505
Lambalgem, M. van 4:117, 8:59
lambda calculus **5:345–50**
Church, A. 2:347
property theory 7:762
relevance logic 8:202
Lambek, J. 2:236, 2:238, 4:853
Lambert, Johann Heinrich **5:350–2**
see also Lambert's Law
Hilbert's programme and
formalism 4:428
logic machines and diagrams
5:741–2, 5:746
logical calculus 5:719–20
Lambert, Karel
free logics †3:739–43, 3:739
Meinong, A. 6:286
scientific theories 9:353
Lambert, M.J. 7:813, 7:816
Lamberti, J.-C. 9:425
Lambertini, R. 4:77
Lamberton, R. 4:502, 6:803, 7:550
Lambert's Law 3:742
Lameer, J. 5:712
Lammers, W. 4:543
Lamotte, É.
Ābhidharmika Schools of
Buddhism 2:58
Buddha 2:53
karma and rebirth 5:218
suffering
Buddhist views of origination of
9:216, 9:218
Lampen, W. 8:312
Lampert, E. 4:410, 8:418
Lamphere, L. 3:593
Lancaster, L.R. 2:118, 9:793
Lancelot, C. 5:373, 5:377, 7:553
Land, J.P.N. 4:61
Land, S. 5:379
Land and Liberty movement 7:451–2
Landa, Diego de 5:429, 5:432
Landau, E. 2:842
Landau, L. 1:220
Landdley, D. 9:132
Landini, G. 8:403
Landino, C. 7:447
Landmarks movement see Signposts
movement

Landry, D. 3:613
Landsberg, P. 9:416
Landsman, N. 9:756–7
Lanford, M.J. 7:801
Lanfranchi, E. 1:792
Lang, A. 6:53
Lang, B.
Bosanquet, B. 1:848
heaven 4:251–2, 4:253
Langer, S.K.K. 5:356
style, artistic 1:509
Lang, H.S. 6:251
Langacker, R. 7:631
Langan, J. 7:737–6
Langdell, Christopher Columbus
5:522–3
Lange, Friedrich Albert **5:352–4**
Büchner, L. 2:51
materialism 6:172, 6:173
Neo-Kantianism 6:790
Nietzsche, F.W. 6:861
Lange, J. 5:457
Lange, M. 5:474
Lange, O. 7:648
Langer, M.M. 7:348
Langer, Susan Katherina Knauth
5:354–6
Cassirer, E. 2:227
music
aesthetics of 6:609, 6:613
Langermann, Y. Tzvi
al-Baghdadi †1:636–8
Ibn Kammuna †4:621–3
Langewand, A.
Herbart, J.F. †4:369–71
Langford, C.H. 2:520–1, 2:522, 6:426,
8:668
Langford, T.
Inge, W.R. 4:794
Oman, J.W. 7:98
Polanyi, M. 7:492
Rashdall, H. 8:61
Temple, W. 9:301
Langholm, O. 4:39
Langley, P. 3:102, 3:103
Langton, Stephen 5:393
language **5:408–11**
see also communication; discourse;
grammar; grammarians; ideal
language philosophy; language of
thought; legal discourse;
linguistics; moral language;
ordinary language philosophy;
philology; private language
argument; reference; scientific
language; semantics; sense;
utterances

accents (Rousseau, J.-J.) 8:370
acquisition
innate predispositions 2:394
African Francophone philosophy
1:111
agreement (*Verständigung*) 2:459
analytical
sophismata 7:181–2
ancient philosophy of **5:356–61**
animal **1:269–73**
anthropodicy (Florenskii, P.A.)
3:681
anthropology (Monboddo)
6:473–4
Aristotle 5:358–60
Aristotle-Plato agreement
(Porphyry) 7:546–7
artist's intention 1:513, 1:515
author relationship (Barthes, R.)
1:656–7
automatized
Russian literary formalism
8:410, 8:411
behavioural (*moralis*) 5:396
behaviourism
Bloomfield, L. 9:178
Quine, W.V. 8:12–13
biblical rhetoric
Jewish philosophy (Messer
Leon) 6:332–3
Buddhist nominalism 7:23–6
canonical notation (Quine, W.V.)
8:7–8
categorical sentences (William of
Champeaux) 9:729
child development (Piaget, J.)
7:383, 7:385
Chinese philosophy **5:693–706**
Confucius 5:694–5, 5:704–5
Daoism 2:788
effect of Chinese language on
2:316, 2:323
Gongsun Long 5:700–2
Hui Shi 5:702–4
Mohism 5:696–700, 6:456–7
Mozi 5:695–6
Sengzhao 8:683
closed/connected distinction
(Ajdukiewicz, K.) 1:136
compositional meaning theory
(Davidson, D.) 2:801–2
compositionality **2:476–7**
conception (Reid, T.) 8:175–6
conceptual role semantics 8:653
consensus (Ibn Rushd) 4:645
consumer culture (Baudrillard, J.)
1:662, 1:663

context (Tominaga Nakamoto)
9:440
contingent images (Mauthner, F.)
6:203
conventionality of **5:368–71**
Ajdukiewicz, K. 1:136–7
Aristotle 5:359
Carnap, R. 2:208
Chinese philosophy 5:694, 5:697
Democritus 5:357
Plato 5:357–8
conversational implicature
(Grice, H.P.) 4:172–5
correspondence theory of truth
9:473, 9:474
criteria 2:711–14
critiques of
Bacon, F. 1:628
Locke, J. 5:673
Mauthner, F. 6:204
cultural dimension (Humboldt, W.
von) 4:542
dance 2:776–7
deconstruction 2:836
deflationary theories of truth 9:475
descriptive psychology
(Twardowski, K.) 9:508, 9:509
dialects
linguistic discrimination
5:643–4
dialogic (Bakhtin, M.M.) 1:640
discrimination **5:641–5**
doubt 3:124
essential/crude distinction
(Blanchot, M.) 1:783
eternality of
Mīmāṃsā 6:377, 6:379–80
universals 9:544–5
Eurasianism 3:454–5
expressivist theories of (Taylor, C.)
9:277
fallibility of (Dignāga) 3:75
family resemblences
(Wittgenstein, L.) 9:762–3
fine distinctions in (Prodicus)
7:731
formal
logical positivism 5:793–4
second-order logic **8:599–604**
syntactic engines
computational theories of
mind 6:392
Frege, G. 3:765, 3:766–9, 3:770–1
function (Shpet, G.G.) 8:756–7
gender **5:361–8**
heteroglossia (Bakhtin, M.)
1:640–1

hierarchical structure
logic of truth 8:644–5, 9:266–7
theory of types 9:359–60, 9:361
Hindu philosophy 4:436–7
Hobbes, T. 5:372–3
hybridity
postcolonialism 7:579
idealism (Burthogge, R.) 2:145
ideas
Locke, J. 5:672
Maine de Biran, P.-F. 6:51
implicit meanings
African Anglophone
philosophy 1:103–4
Indian theories of **5:379–84**
Gadādhara 3:825–6
linguistic units 5:379, 5:380–2
Patañjali 7:248–9
sphoṭa theory 5:379, 5:382–3
inference
Mill, J.S. 6:361–3
perception distinction
Yogācāra Buddhism 2:68
innateness of **4:51–4**, 5:286–7
Chomsky, N. 2:335, 2:336,
4:51–2
empiricist response 6:674
learning theory 5:486
nativism 6:672, 6:673–4,
6:675
Skinner, B.F. 8:801
unconscious mental states
9:522, 9:524–5, 9:526
conventions contrasted 5:370
poverty of the stimulus 4:52–3
intention **2:455–9**
intentionality
Reinach, A. 8:181
Searle, J. 8:589
interpretation
context 6:222
Indian theories of 4:833–7
introspection 4:839
Japanese
Buddhism 2:100–1
Kyoto School 5:325
knowledge of (Chomsky, N.)
2:338–9
knowledge relationship
(Condillac, É.B. de) 2:523,
2:525–6
langue-parole distinction
(Saussure, F. de) 8:480
learning
computer science 5:486
lekton
Stoicism 9:148–9

Locke, J. 5:374–5
logic and 5:765–6
Aristotle 1:416–17
artificial intelligence
common-sense reasoning
2:452
Islamic philosophy 4:649, 5:706,
5:707–8, 6:237
logical analysis of 1:32
analytic philosophy 1:224,
1:225–6
logical atomism (Wittgenstein, L.)
9:757
Logos (Coleridge, S.T.) 2:404
Marxist theory of 6:155–6
meaning
Indian theories of 6:239–43
potentiality
Indian theories of 7:607
medieval theories of **5:389–404**,
6:274–5
Abelard, P. 1:8, 1:10–11
Augustine 1:542, 1:545–6
Bacon, R. 1:635
Boethius of Dacia 1:814–15
Brinkley, R. 2:20
Brito, R. 2:22
Encyclopedists 3:306
Heytesbury, W. 4:419–20
James of Viterbo 5:58
Kilwardby, R. 5:246–7
Marsilius of Inghen 6:110–11
Paul of Venice 7:265
Peter of Auvergne 7:321
Peter of Spain 7:324–5
William of Ockham 9:739–41
William of Sherwood 9:748,
9:748–9
Wodeham, A. 9:773–4
Wyclif, J. 9:802
mental
Ailly, P. d' 1:134
speech in the mind (*verbum
mentis*) 5:390
William of Ockham 5:392
metalanguages (Carnap, R.)
2:210–11
modern philosophy of
early **5:371–9**
Moscow-Tartu school 6:583, 6:585
myth relationship
creation (Rosenzweig, F.) 8:359
names
Chinese theories of 5:693,
5:694–5, 5:696, 5:697–8
Wittgenstein, L. 9:762

nationalism
Japanese philosophy 5:77
natural
identity 4:676
Leibniz, G.W. 5:554
logical form **5:781–5**
parsing of
connectionist networks 2:573
predicate calculus 7:659
quantifiers 7:875–7, 7:880–1
semantics 8:649, 8:650
syntax **9:246–53**
Tarski's definition of truth
9:268
naturalism
Barthes, R. rejection of 1:656–7
Plato 2:694
Neoplatonism (Simplicius) 8:790
noematic meaning (Husserl, E.)
4:574, 4:578
nominalism
Sellars, W.S. 8:639, 8:640
universals (Stewart, D.) 9:138
numbers (Frege, G.) 3:773–4
observational
incommensurability
(Feyerabend, P.K.) 3:640
ontology of 1:32
origin of
Bible 5:372
Condillac, É.B. de 5:376–7
Hamann, J.G. 4:216
Herder, J.G. 4:379–80
Locke, J. 5:372
Rousseau, J.-J. 5:377
ortholanguage (Lorenzen, P.)
5:826–7
paternal laws (Irigaray, L.) 5:1–2
perception
Merleau-Ponty, M. 6:323
Vātsyāyana 9:588
philosophic
Greek origins 1:262–3
phonology
Prague School 9:179
pictorial depiction 2:892, 2:893–4
Plato 2:694, 5:357–8
Port-Royalists 5:373–4
positive logic (Comte, A.) 2:501–2
postmodernism 7:588–9
practical/poetic comparison
Russian literary formalism
8:409, 8:410
pragmatics **7:620–33**, 7:634–5,
7:636
prescriptive role (Confucius)
5:694–5

private states **7:698–701**
programming
classical AI 1:487
proper names 7:752–7
psychoanalysis 7:602–3
Lacan, J. 7:821
purpose of
Berkeley, G. 5:375
Locke, J. 5:374
radical physicalism (Neurath, O.)
6:814–15
reality
Nietzsche, F.W. critique 6:850–1
ontological categories
Indian philosophy 7:120
reason
Reinhold, K.L. 8:187
Thomasius, C. 9:378
relations with world 1:33
religious see religious language
Renaissance philosophy of
5:411–15, 8:266
analogy 5:414–15
beings of reason 5:413–14
Collegium Conimbricense 2:407
Erasmus, D. 3:398–9
humanism 4:536–7, 5:415
Latin usage (Valla, L.) 9:569,
9:571–2
magic (Agrippa von
Nettesheim, H.C.) 1:131
mental 5:412–13, 6:54–5
signification 5:411–12
Soto, D. de 9:38
theories of origins of 5:413
rhetoric 2:810–11, 8:306, 8:307,
8:308–9
rule-following (Wittgenstein, L.)
9:763–4
sacred
Vedas 4:833–4
Sanskrit 4:738–9
self-presence (Derrida, J.) 2:896,
2:898
semantic reism (Kotarbiński, T.)
5:294
semiotic-symbolic dialectic
(Kristeva, J.) 5:305–6
sense perception
Indian views of 8:689, 8:693–4
signs
Bacon, R. 1:635
Berkeley, G. 1:742, 1:746
Kristeva, J. 5:305
similarity classes (Hui Shi) 5:702–3
social conduct (Dewey, J.) 3:46

social nature of **5:415–19**
gender 5:363–4
Mauthner, F. 6:204
socialization
Chinese philosophy 5:696
spiritual power of
Buddhism
Japanese 2:100–1
Japanese philosophy 2:100–1,
5:69
standards
Chinese philosophy 5:696
structuralism
Barthes, R. 1:656–7
Lacan, J. 5:337
literary theory 9:181, 9:182
social science 7:600–1, 9:184–6
testimony 9:312
Indian philosophy 9:315–18
theological roots (Losev, A.F.)
5:829–30
and thought
Aristotle 5:359
Condillac, É.B. de 5:376–7
Hamann, J.G. 4:215–16
Heidegger, M. 2:897
Sapir-Whorf Hypothesis
8:470–3
unity of 4:542
thought-vehicle paradigm
(Dummett, M.A.E.) 3:149–50
Tibetan 4:739–40
transposition of (Gilbert of
Poitiers) 4:70–1
truth theories 6:221–2
typology (Humboldt, W. von)
4:542
understanding 4:861
universal 9:533–5
Leibniz, G.W. 5:553–4
usage (Theophrastus) 9:338
use/mention distinction **9:548–51**
utterances (Bakhtin, M.M.) 1:640,
1:641
vernaculars (Alighieri, Dante)
5:403
Weltalter philosophy
(Schelling, F.W.J. von) 8:515
worldview
Chinese philosophy 2:778
written
Derrida, J.
deconstruction 2:898–9
phonetic/non-phonetic
contrast 2:898–9
language games 2:712–13
see also private language argument

heterogeneity (Lyotard, J.-F.) 6:9
Wittgenstein, L. 9:757, 9:762–3
Wittgensteinian ethics 9:770, 9:771
language matrix
symbolic interactionism 9:243–4
language of thought **5:404–8**
belief 1:703–5
common-sense reasoning 2:451
Fodor, J.A. 3:684
informational semantics 8:660
propositional attitudes 7:782
Fodor, J.A. 1:486
la langue 8:479, 8:480–1, 9:178
Laṅkāvatāvasūtra 2:75
Lannay, M. 5:378
Lanning, J.T. 5:425
Lanson, G. 2:376
Lanza, D. 1:254
Laocoon group 5:574–5
Laoism 2:779–81
Laoust, H. 4:68
Laozi 4:448, 5:696
see also Daodejing; Huang-lao
LaPiana, W.P. 5:524
Lapidge, M. 1:361
Laplace, Pierre 3:34, 3:39, 6:172
Laplanche, J. 3:588, 3:793, 7:823
Lapointe, F.H. 4:587
Laporte, J. 1:448
Lappe, F.M. 1:128
Lappe, J. 6:832
Lappo-Danilevskii, Aleksandr 6:795, 6:797
Lapshin, Ivan 6:794, 6:797
Larain, J. 4:685
'large and small' argument 9:846–7
Largeault, J. 6:350–1
largest cardinal, paradox of 7:51, 7:214, 7:216
largest ordinal, paradox of 7:215–16, 7:219–20
Largier, N. 6:288
Larizza-Lolli, M. 2:504
Larmer, R.A.H. 6:415–16
Larmore, Charles E.
Bayle, P. †1:672–7
examples in ethics 3:490
MacIntyre, A. 6:24
moral judgment 6:514
moral pluralism 6:531
neutrality
political 6:821
right and good †8:322–5
Laroui, A. 5:21
Larrabee, M.J. 2:282
Larre, C. 4:514
Larsen, B.D. 4:599

Larson, G. 4:440, 8:467
Larson, J.L. 5:650
Larson, R. 6:225, 6:344, 7:779, 8:652
Lascarides, A. 1:243, 3:98, 3:99
Lasch, C. 8:634
Lashley, K. 9:522, 9:526
Lask, Emil 6:777, 6:786–7, 6:790
Lasker, Daniel J.
Duran, P. 3:171
Israeli, I. †5:31–4
Jewish Averroism 1:602
Karaism 5:208
Shem Tov family 8:740
Laski, Harold 1:586
Laslett, P. 3:679, 3:821, 6:168
Lasota, A. 8:59
Lassalle, Ferdinand **5:419–21**
Lasserre, F. 3:453
Lasson, Georg 4:184, 4:290, 4:297
Lastarria, José Victorino 7:568, 7:569
Latané, B. 9:526
Latham, J.D. 8:565
Latham, W. 1:492
Latin
influence of
medieval philosophy 6:271
intellectual culture 6:692
neoclassical
Renaissance humanism 4:536–7
Renaissance logic 5:767
usage
Renaissance 9:569, 9:571–2
Latin America
see also Argentina; Brazil; Chile; Mexico; Peru
analytical philosophy **1:229–34**
anti-positivist thought **1:303–7**
colonial philosophy **5:421–6**, 5:426
existentialism **3:509–14**
feminist philosophy **3:625–8**
liberation philosophy **5:610–13**
liberation theology 5:613–15
literature
phenomenology 7:348–9
philosophy in **5:653–7**
marginality **6:99–101**
Marxism **6:160–5**
phenomenology **7:348–52**
philosophy in **5:426–8**
positivism **7:565–70**
pre-Columbian and indigenous thought **5:428–32**
Spanish colonization 5:429, 5:430, 6:345
Latin Averroism *see* Averroism
Latitudinarianism **5:432–5**
see also Cambridge Platonism

Newtonian world picture (Bentley, R.) 1:725
Latour, Bruno
constructivism 2:626–7, 2:628, 2:630
experiment 3:517
social epistemology 8:832
Latsis, S. 3:221
Latter Day Saints (Mormons) 4:250–1
Lattre, A. de 4:61
Lau, D.C.
aesthetics
Chinese 1:75
Chinese Confucianism 2:541, 2:548–9
Daodejing 2:781, 2:782
Mencius 6:304
Sunzi 9:231–2
Laube, J. 9:262
Lauchert, F. 8:777
Laudan, Larry
Comte, A. 2:504–5
constructivism 2:627, 2:630
incommensurability 4:736
logic of discovery 3:102
Mach, E. 6:16
naturalized philosophy of science 6:730, 6:731
positivism in the social sciences 7:561
science, demarcation problem 2:866
underdetermination †9:527–30
Laudan, Rachel
geology
philosophy of †4:25–8
science, demarcation problem 2:866
laughter 2:434–5
Laugwitz, D. 1:216
Laukāyatikas *see* Lokāyata
Laurent, M.-H. 8:777
Laurenti, R. 6:616
Lauria, D. 3:560
Laurie, H. 2:28–9, 7:170
Laursen, J.C. 6:489
Lauth, R. 3:653, 8:189
Lavenda, R.H. 6:670
Laver, S. 3:280
Lavers, A. 1:658
Lavine, Shaughan
predicate calculus †7:657–65
second- and higher-order logics †8:591–5
Zermelo, E. 9:855

Lavoisier, Antoine Laurent 2:296,
    2:296–7, 2:299, 6:195
Lavretskii, A. 2:306
Lavrov, Pëtr Lavrovich **5:435–8**
    partiinost' 7:239, 7:240
    Plekhanov, G.V. 7:452
Law, B.C. 9:218
Law, D.R. 5:243
Law, William **5:468–70**
    Tindal, M. 9:423
law **5:464–8**
    see also civil law; common law;
        Critical Legal Studies; divine law;
        halakhah; international law;
        jurisprudence; laws; legal;
        legislation; natural law; *nomos*;
        positive law; rule of law
    administrative law
        critique by Dicey, A.V. 8:389
    African ethical systems 3:432–3
    ancient
        historical jurisprudence
            (Maine, H.S.) 5:139
    change
        jural postulates 5:512
    Chinese Legalism 5:533–4
    Chinese philosophy **5:442–54**
    civil disobedience 2:366–8
    classical texts interpretation
        Renaissance humanism 4:538
    colonial philosophy
        Latin America 5:421
    Confucianism 2:542
    consent 2:598
    crime and punishment **2:704–11**
    as custom *see* common law
    decisional model (Wróblewski, J.)
        9:797
    as discourse 5:496, 5:498–9
    divine *see* divine law
    economic approach to **5:454–7**
    educational philosophy
        relation to 3:236–7
    equity **5:147–53**
    eternal (Suárez, F.) 9:192
    ethics of (Berdiaev, N.A.) 1:729
    as evolution
        historical jurisprudence 5:138
        Petrażycki, L. 7:330
    externality of (Holmes, O.W.)
        4:494
    fa 3:532
    freedom of speech 3:764
    Hegelian theory of 4:274
    Hindu
        interpretation 4:836

historical jurisprudence 5:138–9,
    8:482, 8:483
historical theory of (Vico, G.)
    9:599, 9:601–2
human existence (Hessen, S.I.)
    4:418
implicit (Fuller, L.L.) 3:801
as independent imperatives
    (Olivecrona, K.) 7:94
innocence 4:797–8
as interpretation (Dworkin, R.)
    3:187–8
Islamic **5:457–60**
    see also shari'a
    Shah Wali Allah 8:734
justice **5:147–53**
justification doctrine 5:167, 8:457
Latin American phenomenology
    7:349, 7:350
limits of **5:460–4**
    Hart, H.L.A. 4:235
    moral 5:460, 5:461–2
    practical 5:460, 5:461
    principles 5:462–3
and literature movement
    (Nussbaum, M.) 5:150
as male bias 3:606, 3:607
medieval
    Roman law influence 8:344
as a medium of control
    (Habermas, J.) 2:716
mercy 8:137–8
minimum morality (Solov'ëv, V.S.)
    9:31
moral
    Kant, I.
        hope 4:507–8
        respect for persons 8:285
        self-control 8:612
morality **5:438–42**
    Aristotelian versus liberal
        traditions 5:439–40
    harm principle 5:440–1
    Hart/Devlin debate 5:441
    legal positivism 5:514–15
    limits of 5:460–3
    moral sense theories (Home, H.)
        4:500
    rule of law 8:389–90
    separation (Austin, J.) 1:569–70
necessity for (Thucydides) 9:399
philosophical (Locke, J.) 5:679
politics 5:467–8
    Critical Legal Studies 2:715–16
    religion conflict 8:225–6
pornography 7:544
postmodernism 8:873, 8:878

practical (Kauṭilya) 5:220–1
predictive theory of (Holmes, O.W.)
    4:494
private
    public distinction (Kant, I.)
        5:191
    public law relationship 8:388–9
    Roman 8:346–7
professional ethics 7:734
public
    absolutism 1:796–7
    private distinction (Kant, I.)
        5:191
    sovereignty 1:796
pure theory of
    Brno School 9:708
    criticisms of 8:389
Rabbinic *see* halakhah
Radbruch formula 8:22
as reason 5:464–5, 9:119
and religion (Hooker, R.) 4:504–5
Renaissance (Soto, D. de) 9:38–9
    responsibility 8:291
as rhetoric 5:496–7
religious
    Jewish philosophy
        Leibowitz, Y. 5:562, 5:563–4
        Saadiah Gaon 8:437
Roman **8:343–8**
    political philosophy
        history of 7:507, 7:509
    science of (Austin, J.) 8:874–5
    as social rules (Hart, H.L.A.)
        4:235
    social theory **8:872–9**
    social utility (Jhering, R. von)
        5:100–1
    socialism (Hessen, S.I.) 4:417–18
    sovereignty 9:57, 9:58
    systematization of (Blackstone, W.)
        1:780
    terminology
        paraphrasis (Bentham, J.) 1:719,
            1:722–3
    tripartite division of (Gaius) 3:832
    values relationship 3:801, 5:466–7
    voluntary nature of
        political theology 9:331
    war and peace 9:685–6, 9:688–9,
        9:690
    as will 5:465–6
    written *see* legal hermeneutics
Law of Effect 1:697, 8:800
law of excluded middle (LEM)
    intuitionistic logic 4:856, 4:857–8,
        4:861
    many-valued logics 6:84

vagueness 9:565
law of motion in history
  Engels, F. 3:311
law of nations
  see also international relations
  rights of conquest (Vitoria, F. de)
    9:644–5
Lawal, B. 1:65
law-jobs theory
  Llewellyn, K.N. 5:661
Lawler, E.G. 9:166–7
Lawrence, C.R. III 5:644
Lawrence, F. 9:656
Lawrence, N. 7:715, 9:719
Lawrence, S. 2:516
laws
  causal 2:247–8
    intentionality 8:863–5
    Mill, J.S. 2:246
  classification of (Mill, J.S.) 8:852
  covering *see* covering-law model of
    explanation
  of logic 5:785–9
  natural
    causal generalizations
      (Ramsey, F.P.) 8:45, 8:47
    common sense (Oswald, J.)
      7:169
    conservation of motion
      (Leibniz, G.W.) 5:555–6
    Davidson, D. 1:277
    deism (Condillac, É.B. de) 2:526
    empirical physics (Kant, I.)
      5:187–8
    geology 4:25–6
    God, existence arguments 7:187
    Helmholtz, H. von 4:339
    knowledge (Cournot, A.A.)
      2:689
    limitations of modern science
      7:576–7
    miracles 6:411, 6:412–13, 6:414
    moral law distinction (Kant, I.)
      5:178
    necessitarian theories 5:472
    parapsychology 7:226
    perception (Kant, I.) 5:186–7
    Poincaré, J.H. 7:479
    reduction 8:145–8
    scientific explanation 3:520,
      3:521–2, 5:180
    systematic account
      (Ramsey, F.P.) 8:47
    universals (Armstrong, D.M.)
      1:443
    variational principles 6:256

psychological 8:833
  holism 4:492
scientific
  covering-model of explanation
    4:350
  nineteenth century science
    8:565, 8:566–8
  theories distinction
    (Campbell, N.R.) 2:193–4
social 8:832–4
  antecedents/consequents 8:833
  causal laws 8:832–3
  definition 8:832–3
  psychological laws 8:833
  reduction 4:485
  social properties 8:833
laws of thought
  Boole, G. 1:841–2
  Cohen, H. 6:781
  glossary 5:804
Lawson, B.E. 8:806
Lawson, F.H. 3:63
Lawson, P. 1:94
Lawson, T. 2:722
Lawvere, F.W. 2:235, 2:236, 4:851
Laymon, Ronald
  idealizations †4:669–72
  scientific theories 9:353
Layton, B. 4:85
Laywine, A.
  Knutzen, M. †5:287–9
  Swedenborg, E. †9:241–3
Lazaroff, A.
  Jewish voluntarism †9:664–7
Lazarsfeld, P.F. 3:518, 3:520
Lazarus, Moritz 5:97–8, 5:99–100
Lazarus, Richard 6:563
Lazarus, S. 1:195
Lazarus-Yafeh, H. 4:68
Lazere, D. 2:196
Lazerowitz, M. 6:498
Lazović, Živan
  South Slavs, philosophy of
    †9:48–56
Le Blanc, A. 6:319
Le Clerc, Jean 5:475–6
Le Corbusier 1:365, 1:366
Le Doeuff, Michèle 5:476–9
  Beauvoir, S. de 8:437
  psychoanalytic feminism 3:586,
    3:588
  Suchon, G. †9:211–13
Le Goff, J. 7:839
Le Grand, Antoine 5:479–81
Le Poidevin, Robin
  change †2:274–6
  continuants †2:652–4

tense logic 9:307
time 9:416
Le Quesne, A.L.
  Carlyle, T. †2:204–6
Le Roy, Édouard Louis Emmanuel
  Julien 5:481–3
Le Roy, G. 6:53
Leach, E. 5:585
leadership
  Indian philosophy 7:523–4
  moral obligations 4:828
Leahy, M.P.T. 1:273
Leal, Francisco Luís 2:9
Leaman, Oliver
  Abravanel, I. †1:19–23
  al-Afghani †1:94–5
  anti-Semitism †1:311–14
  Ash'ariyya and Mu'tazila 1:523
  Duran, P. †3:170–1
  al-Ghazali 4:68
  Ibn Hazm †4:620–1
  Ibn Khaldun †4:623–7
  Ibn Miskawayh †4:630–3
  Ibn Rushd †4:638–46
  Ibn Sab'in 4:647
  Islam
    concept of philosophy in †5:5–9
  Islamic philosophy †5:13–16
    Aristotelianism of 1:386
    ethics 3:442
    Illuminationist †4:700–3
    meaning †6:236–9
    modern †5:16–21
    mystical philosophy 6:620
    Neoplatonism in 6:807
    Orientalism in 7:160
    political philosophy in classical
      7:520
    science in 8:564
    transmission into Western
      Europe 5:25
  Jewish Averroism †1:598–602
  al-Juwayni †5:169–70
  Kabbalah †5:171–6
  Mir Damad, Muhammad Baqir
    6:411
  al-Sijistani 8:776
  Soloveitchik, J.B. 9:27
  al-Tawhidi 9:272
Lear, J.
  ancient logic 5:693
  antirealism
    mathematics 1:311
  Aristotle 1:435
  Freud, S. 3:793
  infinity 4:777
  Zeno of Elea 9:852

learning **5:483–7**
see also developmental
psychology; education;
educational philosophy
animal behaviour 1:697–8
'dead reckoning' 1:698
biological adaptation
teleology 8:673
computation
derived knowledge 1:698
solvable problems 5:486
connectionism 2:570–1
connectionist networks 2:572–3
division of (Bacon, F.) 1:626–7
educational concepts 3:232
from experience
probability systems (Carnap, R.)
2:532–3
holism
mental/semantic 4:488
implicit 5:287
infant cognition 2:391
innateness of 1:697–8
learned/innate distinction 4:795
nativism (Fodor, J.A.) 3:685
passive
animal behaviour 1:697–8
scientific behaviourism
blank-slate assumption 1:697–8
empiricism 1:696
law of effect 1:697
theoretical constructs 1:697
stimulus-reponse (S-R)
behaviourism 1:697, 1:698
Turing machine 5:486–7
learning of the heart-and-mind
Lu Xiangshan 5:851–2
learning of the Way see neo-
Confucianism
Leary, J.E., Jr 1:632
least indefinable ordinal, paradox of
7:218
Leatherbarrow, W.J. 8:811
Leavis, F.R. 2:749, 2:750
Lebanon
Porphyry **7:545–50**
Lebedev, A.A. 8:409
Leben see life
Lebenskraft (vital force) 5:839
lebenskunst (art of living) see
Lebensphilosophie
Lebensphilosophie **5:487–9**
lebensweisheit (wisdom of life) see
Lebensphilosophie
Lebenswelt (lifeworld)
justification (Husserl, E.) 4:584–5
Patočka, J. 7:252

phenomenology (Husserl, E.)
4:582–4
social life (Habermas, J.) 4:196
Lebesgue measure 8:705
LeBlanc, C. 4:514
Leblanc, H. 1:232, 7:539
LeBlanc, S.A. 1:359
Lecaldano, Eugenio 4:561
Lecercle, J.-J. 3:109
Lechte, J. 5:308
Lecky, W.E.H. 9:229
Leclerc, I. 7:715
Leclerq, J. 5:114
Lecourt, D. 1:624, 3:786
Lectura see Duns Scotus, John
Ledderose, Lother 1:71, 1:75
Ledley, R.S. 6:268
Lee, E.N. 9:653–4
Lee, H.D.P. 9:852
Lee, P.
Sapir-Whorf Hypothesis 8:473
Lee, Peter H.
Buddhist philosophy, Korean
2:118
Korean Confucian philosophy
2:565
Sôsan Hyujông 9:37
Wônhyo 9:794
Yi Yulgok 9:827
Lee, S. 5:128, 9:617
Lee, T.-S. 7:377
Lee, W. 8:797–8
Leech, G. 4:725, 6:170
Leekam, S.R. 6:386, 6:389
Leeuw, G. van der 7:354–5, 8:247
Leeuwen, J. van 2:475–6
Leeuwis, Denys de see Denys the
Carthusian
Lefebvre, Henri **5:489–91**
Leff, G. 4:172, 7:286
Lefkowitz, Mary R.
Egyptian philosophy, influence on
Greek thought †3:250–4
postcolonialism 7:582
Left Hegelians see Young Hegelians
Leftow, Brian
divine simplicity †8:783–8
eternity 3:426
God, concepts of †4:93–4:102
immutability †4:710–14
necessary being †6:743–7
omnipresence †7:103–7
religion, philosophy history 8:247
voluntarism †9:663–4
legal categories
feminist jurisprudence 3:608–9

legal concepts **5:491–6**
absolutism 5:495
feminist jurisprudence 3:609
juridical 5:492, 5:494
metaphysical framework
Hägerström, A.A.T. 4:203
legal consciousness
Critical Legal Studies 2:715
legal discourse **5:496–9**
courtroom studies 5:496, 5:497–8
linguistic formalism 5:498
New Rhetoric movement 5:496–7
reasoning 5:527–8
legal evidence **5:499–506**
see also proof
admissability 5:500–1
credibility 5:502
direct/circumstantial distinction
5:501–2
probative force 5:502
relevance 5:501–2
legal formalism
rule-scepticism
Llewellyn, K.N. 5:661
legal hermeneutics **5:506–10**
common law
philological analysis 8:604
critical movement 5:509
Hart, H.L.A. 4:235
legal humanism
Roman law 5:507
legal idealism **5:510–14**
see also legal norms; legal realism
absolute 5:511–12
historical/social 5:511, 5:512–13
transcendental 5:511, 5:512
legal institutionalism **4:799–803**
see also neo-institutionalism
classical 4:799
idée directrice (directing idea)
4:800
transpersonalism 4:800
legal Marxists see Marxism, legal
legal norms **7:38–41**
see also legal idealism
formalism (Fuller, L.L.) 3:801–2
Grundnorm (Kelsen, H.) 5:226–7
interpretive theory 7:38, 7:39–41
Kelsen, H. 5:226–7
legal reasoning 5:525
logic (Weinberger, O.) 9:701, 9:702
phrastic/neustic distinction
(Ross, A.) 8:365
practice theory 7:39
Wróblewski, J. 9:797
legal obligations
legal norms (Hart, H.L.A.) 7:39

moral obligation distinction
  (Hart, H.L.A.) 4:234–5
Roman law/civilian tradition 8:346
rule of law 8:388, 8:390–1
legal positivism **5:514–21**
  analytical 1:790, 5:516
  common law critique 2:443, 2:444,
    2:445
  constitutional law (Dicey, A.V.)
    3:62
  Critical Legal Studies 2:717, 2:718
  critiques of
    Dworkin, R. 3:187
    Fuller, L.L. 3:801
    Radbruch, G. 8:22
  institutionalist (Weinberger, O.)
    9:701–2
  Kelsen, H. 5:226–7
  law as custom 5:466
  legal realism conflict 5:515,
    5:516–17
  legal rules 5:515–16, 5:517–18
  linguistic-analytical (Hart, H.L.A.)
    4:234
  natural law conflict 5:514–15
  prescriptive approach (Bobbio, N.)
    1:791
  verifiability (Ross, A.) 8:364–5
legal realism **5:521–5**
  see also legal idealism
  Critical Legal Studies 2:715, 5:509
  critique of (Fuller, L.L.) 3:801
  discretion 5:467
  fact scepticism (Frank, J.) 3:725–6
  formalism (Llewellyn, K.N.) 5:661
  Hägerström, A.A.T. 4:203
  institutionalism 4:799–800
  legal concepts 5:492
  legal positivism conflict 5:515,
    5:516–17
  Ross, A. 8:364
  Scandinavian 5:521–2
  United States 5:521, 5:522–4
legal reasoning **5:525–31**
  chains of (Venn, J.) 5:502
  deductive
    confusion with law 5:526
  deontological/teleological
    distinction 5:529–30
legal representation
  hermeneutics 5:507
legal rules
  appropriateness 5:526–7
  exclusionary reasons 5:528–9
  Hart, H.L.A. 4:235, 7:39
  legal positivism 5:515–16,
    5:517–18

legal systems distinction
  (Bobbio, N.) 1:790–1
  principles distinction
    (Dworkin, R.) 3:187, 3:188
  as reasons 5:526
legal standing
  moral standing comparison 6:551
legal systems
  legal rules distinction (Bobbio, N.)
    1:790–1
  logical positivism 5:517–18
legal theory
  see also Critical Legal Studies;
  jurisprudence; social theory, law
  a priori (Reinach, A.) 8:180–1
  democratic-socialist (Renner, K.)
    8:267
  norms (Wróblewski, J.) 9:797
  public reason (Habermas, J.) 4:198
  Soviet Marxist (Pashukanis, E.B.)
    8:267
  structure (Weyr, F.) 9:708
legalism
  Judaism
    anti-Semitism 1:311–12
Legalist philosophy
  Chinese **5:531–8**
    fa 3:532
    Guanzi 4:186
    Han Feizi 4:219–20
    history 4:448
    Hundred Schools era 2:322
    law and ritual 5:448–9
    Lushi chunqiu 5:864
legality
  equity 5:147, 5:152
Legendre, G. 2:579
Léger, F. 9:260
legislation
  common law distinction 2:444
  judicial (Austin, J.) 1:570
  popular authorization of
    (Marsilius of Padua) 6:112–13
legitimacy **5:538–41**
  see also authority
  authority model 9:4
  liberal democracy 5:540
  performance criteria 5:539–40
  social contract theories 5:539
  social science accounts 5:540–1
  violence 9:615
  Weber, M. 9:695
'legitimate murder'
  Camus, A. 2:194–5
LeGrand, H. 4:28
Lehman, W. 3:633
Lehmann, D. 7:34

Lehmann, E.L. 9:126
Lehmann, J. 8:522
Lehmann, W.C. 6:376
Lehnerer, T. 8:538
Lehrer, Keith
  causal theory of knowledge 5:266
  coherence theory of justification
    5:256, 5:259
  Common Sense School 2:448
  defeasibility analysis 4:58–9
  epistemology 3:365
  Gettier problems 4:55, 4:57, 5:277,
    5:279
  introspection 4:842
  justification
    epistemic 5:164
    personal 5:258
  knowledge 1:707, 1:709, 3:382,
    5:276
  probabilism 7:711
  Reid, T. 8:180
  reliabilism 5:271
  social epistemology 8:832
lei 1:68, 1:69, 1:72
Leibniz, Gottfried Wilhelm **5:541–62**
  see also Leibniz's Law; Neo-
  Leibnizianism
  Bayle, P. 1:677
  calculus 1:217
  contingency 2:651
  continuity 2:655
  critiques of
    Arnauld, A. 1:447
    Locke, J. 5:375, 5:376
    Malebranche, N. 6:63, 6:64
    Masham, D. 6:167
    Voltaire 9:659, 9:660
  Crusius, C.A. 2:737
  divine freedom 3:758, 3:761
  Du Châtelet-Lomont, É. 3:132
  Eberhard, J.A. 3:196
  essentialism 3:418
  evil, problem of 3:465, 3:466,
    3:467–8, 8:244
  Foucher, S. 3:716–17
  free will 3:752
  God
    existence of 4:87, 4:93, 8:242
    harmony 5:548–9
  Helmont, F.M. van collaboration
    4:341
  hope 4:507, 4:509–10
  ideas 5:551–2
  identity 4:678
  indiscernibles
    identity of 4:678–81
  individual essences 7:235

infinitesimals 7:50
knowledge 4:797, 5:552–3
Knutzen, M. 5:287–8
language
    early modern philosophy of
        5:378
logic
    calculus 5:542, 5:554, 5:718–19
    logic machines 5:744
    seventeenth and eighteenth
        century 5:721
matter 6:194–5, 6:196
Mendelssohn, M. 6:304–5
metaphysics
    critique by Arnauld, A. 1:447
Molyneux problem 6:467–8, 6:469
Monadology
    harmony 5:548–9
    knowledge 5:552–3
    monads 5:547
monads 3:559, 5:542, 5:547–8, 8:77
nativism 6:675
natural philosophy 5:542, 5:554–7
necessary being 6:743, 6:745, 6:747
Newton debate 2:379, 5:556–7
nonstandard analysis 1:212
omnipresence 7:107
Ortega y Gasset, J. 7:167
perfect-being theology 4:97
philosophical optimism 5:542,
    5:544, 5:545, 5:550, 9:660–1
pluralism 7:463
predicate-in-notion principle 3:376
Principle of Sufficient Reason
    8:241
psycho-physical parallelism 7:824,
    7:825
rationalism 3:376, 3:382, 8:80
relations 5:554
religion
    critique of 8:238
    history of philosophy of 8:247
space 9:61, 9:65
substance 9:206–7, 9:210
unconscious mental states 9:522
universal language 9:534–5
will 9:725
Leibniz's Law 4:678
    glossary 5:804
    identity theory of mind 6:396
    propositional attitude statements
        7:771–2
    relative identity 9:460
    Trinity 9:458
Leibowitz, Yeshayahu **5:562–4**
    Jewish philosophy 5:90
        contemporary 5:95

Maimonides, M. 6:48
Leidhold, W. 4:593
Leighton, L.G. 8:522
Leijonhufvud, A. 3:221
Leinfellner, E. 6:206
Leisenring, A.C. 7:870
Leiss, W. 4:165
leisure
    work contrast 9:794–5
Leiter, B. 7:75
Leites, E. 2:229
Leitz, R.C. 8:470
Lejeune, A. 7:831
Lejewski, C. 5:693, 6:319–20
lekton ('sayable') 9:148–9
Lektorskii, V.A. 6:159
Leland, J. 4:375
LeMahieu, D. 7:188
Lemaire, P. 3:29
Lemay, P. 6:53
Lemay, R. 4:38
Lemerle, P. 2:165
Lemmon, E.J. 1:142, 4:720, 6:426,
    7:665
Lemos, Miguel 7:567
Lendvai, L.F. 4:572
Leng Shao-chuan 5:454
Lenin, Vladimir Il'ich **5:564–7**
    see also Leninism; Marxism-
        Leninism
    Avenarius, R. 1:594
    Bogdanov, A.A. 1:816–17
    critique of
        Luxemburg, R. 6:7
    dialectical materialism 3:54, 3:57
    Kautsky, K.J. 5:224
    Marxism
        Chinese 6:140
        philosophy of science 6:149,
            6:150
        Western 6:143
    partiinost' 5:565, 7:239, 7:240–1
    partisanship 3:57
    Russian empiriocriticism 8:409
        materialism 5:565–7
        realism 6:153–4, 6:159
Leninism
    political philosophy, history of
        7:516–17
Lennon, K. 3:602
Lennon, Thomas M.
    Bernier, F. †1:756–8
    Burthogge, R. 2:146
    Malebranche, N. 6:66
    Régis, P.-S. †8:165–6
Lennox, J. 1:434
Lenoble, R. 6:331

Lenoir, T. 5:635
Lenzen, W. 3:359
Lenzer, G. 8:858
Leo XIII, Pope (Pecci, Gioacchino)
    3:848, 6:104–5, 9:384
Leocata, F. 1:379
Léon de Portilla, M. 6:348
Léon, X. 3:653
Leonard, Henry 3:738, 3:739, 3:743
Leonardi, P. 8:14
Leonardo, M. di 3:592
Leone Ebreo *see* Abravanel, Judah
    ben Isaac
Leone, M.P. 1:358
León-Portilla, Miguel 5:430–1, 5:432
Leont'ev, Konstantin Nikolaevich
    5:567–70
    history (Losev, A.F.) 5:830
    Rozanov, V.V. relationship 8:382–3
Leontief, W. 3:221
Leontowitsch, V. 5:609
Leopardi, G. 9:227, 9:229
Leopold, Aldo 3:333, 4:160, 4:165,
    6:554
Leopold, David
    Cousin, V. †2:690–2
    Saint-Simon †8:446–7
    Staël-Holstein, A.-L.-G. †9:116–18
    Stirner, M. †9:140–1
Leplin, J. 8:584, 9:353, 9:530
LePore, Ernest
    anomalous monism 1:280
    conceptual role semantics 8:655,
        8:656
    Davidson, D. 1:709, †2:800–6
    holism
        mental and semantic 4:492,
            4:493
    meaning and truth 6:225
    mental causation 6:311
    radical translation and radical
        interpretation 8:35
    Searle, J. †8:589–91
Lerclerc, I. 9:719
Lerman, M. 9:502
Lerner, M.-P. 2:191
Lerner, R. 7:520–1
Leroux, R. 4:543
Lesaulnier, J. 7:554
lesbianism *see* gay-lesbian studies;
    homosexuality
Lesbos
    Theophrastus **9:337–40**
Lescoe, F.J. 9:518
Lesevich, Vladimir 7:562
Lesher, J.H.
    Xenophanes †9:807–10

Lesley, A.M. 6:334
Leslie, A.M.
child's theory of mind †6:385–90
Leslie, J. 2:651–2, 2:680, 8:235, 8:247
Leśniewski, Stanisław **5:571–4**
definition 2:849
mereology 5:573, 6:320
ontology 5:572–3
Polish logic 7:493–4, 7:497
prototothetic 5:572
Lessing, Gotthold Ephraim **5:574–8**
Burke, E. 2:140
Eberhard, J.A. 3:196
Illuminati 4:697
painting/poetry comparison 5:575
rationalist aesthetics 5:576–7
signs 5:575–6
Spinozism (Jacobi, F.H.) 5:45–6
tragedy 9:450
Lessing, H.-U. 3:83
Letelier, Valentín 7:568
letters, science of (Ibn Massara) 4:629
La Lettre clandestine 2:376
Leucippus **5:578–9**
Levenson, J.R. 4:452, 9:400
Levi ben Gershom, Rabbi *see*
Gersonides
Levi, E.H. 5:531
Levi, Isaac
inductive inference 4:758
Nagel, E. †6:641–3
non-monotonic logic 7:34
practical reasoning/rationality
8:96–7, 8:102
probabilism 7:711
Levi, M. 8:74
Levin, D.M. 7:4–5
Levin, J.
qualia †7:863–7
Levin, L.A. 2:482
Levin, Michael 8:722, 8:728
Levinas, Emmanuel **5:579–82**
alterity 1:189, 1:191
Blanchot, M. 1:784
Buber, M. 2:44–5, 2:48
Jewish philosophy, contemporary
5:95
Rosenzweig, F. 8:361
vulnerability and finitude 9:670
Levine, A. 4:11, 8:828, 8:885
Levine, D.N. 9:7
Levine, Joseph
colour and qualia †2:419–27
explanatory gap problem 3:265
phenomenal consciousness 2:585,
2:595
qualia 7:867

Levine, M. 4:101
Levins, R. 9:466
Levinson, H.S.
James, W. 5:67
Jewish philosophy, contemporary
†5:90–6
Santayana, G. 8:470
Levinson, Jerrold
aesthetic concepts 1:59
art
definition of 1:468
emotion in response to
†3:272–81
erotic †3:406–9
ontology of art works 1:484
and truth 1:460
Gurney, E. †4:187–91
humour †4:562–6
music †6:606–15
performing 1:472
Levinson, P. 7:539
Levinson, S. 5:510
Levinson, S.C.
discourse particles 1:50
Grice, H.P. 4:177
implicature 4:725
pragmatics 7:631–2
Sapir-Whorf Hypothesis 8:473
Lévi-Strauss, Claude **5:582–5**
critique of (Ricoeur, P.) 8:319
cultural anthropology 7:600–1
epistemology 5:584
ideology 4:684
kinship systems 5:583
mythology 5:583–4
Native American philosophy
6:667–8, 6:670
postmodernism 7:587
post-structuralism 7:598
social science
contemporary philosophy of
8:847
history of philosophy of 8:858
structural linguistics 5:583
structuralism
in literary theory 9:183, 9:184
in social science 9:184–5, 9:186,
9:188–9
totemism 5:583
Levitas, R. 9:561
Levitskii, S.A. 1:731
Levy, A. 7:220, 8:715, 9:264
Levy, P. 6:498
Levy, Z.
Baumgardt, D. †1:667–9
Ha'am, Ahad †4:192–3
Zionism †9:867–70

Lévy-Bruhl, Lucien
African Francophone philosophy
1:109, 1:115–16
cognitive pluralism 2:397
Jacobi, F.H. 5:48
Lewin, R. 1:273
Lewis, A.D.E. 5:169
Lewis, C.
Oxford Calculators 7:182
Lewis, Clarence Irving **5:585–9**
a posteriori knowledge 1:2, 1:3
a priori knowledge 1:5
analyticity 1:238
conceptual analysis 2:522
consequence 2:600
foundationalism 3:723
good, theories of the 4:135
knowledge 3:379, 3:382
logic
early twentieth century 5:737
modal 6:419, 6:426, 8:663
nineteenth century 5:728
seventeenth and eighteenth
century 5:721
phenomenalism 7:332, 7:333
empiricism 3:300, 3:303
possible worlds semantics 8:668
pragmatism 7:639
relevance logic and entailment
8:200, 8:204
Lewis, Clive Staples **5:589–90**
conscience 2:581
prayer 7:653
Lewis, David Kellogg **5:590–4**
abstract objects 1:35
adverbs 1:50
analyticity 1:238
Australian materialism 1:580
Ayer, A.J. 1:618
being 1:702
belief 1:706
causation 2:249, 2:250
communication and intention
2:458
computational theories of mind
6:394
concepts 2:516
contextualism
epistemological 2:649
conventionalism 2:669
counterfactual conditionals
2:686–8
decision and game theory 2:835
essentialism 3:421
fiction
semantics of 3:663
functionalism 3:810, 3:813

holism
    mental and semantic 4:493
identity theory of mind 6:399
indicative conditionals 4:741–3
intensional entities 4:806
Kripke, S.A. 5:304
language
    conventionality of 5:368–9,
      5:371
logic
    deontic 2:890
    imperative 4:720
    modal 6:432
    non-monotonic 7:34
meaning
    and communication 6:213
    and understanding 6:229
mereology 6:318–19, 6:320
natural laws 5:475
nominalism 7:22, 7:23
objective probability 7:707–8,
    7:711
particulars 7:238
perception 7:299
personal identity 7:314
possible worlds 7:572
    counterparts 6:430–1
    semantics 8:667–8
practical reasoning/rationality
    8:102
pragmatics 7:632
probability, interpretations of
    7:705
propositional attitudes 7:786
propositional certainty
    contextualist account 2:266,
      2:267
qualia 7:867
Ramsey, F.P. 8:49
rational choice theory 8:74
semantics 8:651
set theory 8:715
social norms 8:834, 8:835
society
    concept of 8:887, 8:889
syntax 9:253
time travel 9:418
universals 9:543
vagueness 9:566
value
    ontological status of 9:581
Lewis, F.A. 1:435
Lewis, G. 2:181, 2:182
Lewis, George Cornewall 1:584, 1:586
Lewis, I.M. 6:626
Lewis, J. 8:543
Lewis, J.U. 7:94

Lewis, L. 2:118
Lewis, P.M. II 2:475
Lewis, R.W.B. 5:67
Lewis trilemma 5:590
Lewontin, R.C. 4:16, 6:721, 9:466
Lewry, P.O. 5:249, 5:758
Lewy, H. 2:274
lex mercatoria 4:801
Leyh, G. 5:510
Li Dazhao 6:135–6
Li Disheng 2:548–9
Li Gou 2:541
Li Guangdi 9:831
Li, M. 2:482, 2:496
Li Tong 9:863, 9:864
Li, V.H. 5:454
Li Zehou 6:140
li (mourning)
    Xunzi 9:819
li (pattern or principle) **5:594–5**
    see also i; ri
    Cheng Hao 2:301
    Cheng Yi 2:302
    Confucianism 2:541–4
    Confucius 3:532
    cosmic creativity (Zhu Xi) 9:863–4
    dao (Dai Zhen) 2:770
    Huainanzi 4:513
    ki relationship
      Horak controversy (Yi Kan)
        9:825
      neo-Confucianism (Han
        Wŏnjin) 4:220–1
      Yi Yulgok 9:826
    Legalism 5:536
    neo-Confucianism 6:769
      China 6:767, 6:769, 6:774
      Korean (Yi Hwang) 9:824
    shi relationship
      Chinese Buddhism 2:87
    you-wu 9:834–5
li (propriety)
    Confucius 2:320, 2:568
    Xunzi 9:818–19
li zhi (ritual) **5:442–54**
    Chinese Legalism 5:448–9
    Confucianism 5:450–2
    Confucius 5:445–8
    contemporary China 5:452–3
    Huang-Lau 5:449
    Xunxi 5:449–50
Liang Congjie 8:626
Liang Qichao 4:451
liar paradox 7:214, 8:642–4, 8:645
    glossary 5:804
    Łukasiewicz, J. 5:860–1
    medieval logic 5:756–7

Stoicism 9:151
Tarski, A. 9:266–7
Liber de causis **5:595–8**
    Islamic philosophy 6:804
    translations of
      Gerard of Cremona 4:37
    translations of Proclus 1:397
Libera, Alain de
    Albert the Great †1:145–52
    Averroism 1:598
    Ibn Rushd 4:646
    language
      medieval theories of 5:404
    medieval logic 5:758
    Peter of Spain 7:325
    Richard Rufus of Cornwall 8:317
    William of Sherwood 9:749
liberal democracy
    Bobbio, N. 1:791
    implicit totalitarianism
      Frankfurt School 6:97
    Rawlsian (Cavell, S.) 2:259
Liberal Protestantism
    Unamuno y Jugo, M. de 9:519,
      9:520
liberal theology
    epistemology 8:232
liberal virtue theory 2:363–4
liberalism **5:598–605**
    see also individualism
    antipaternalism (Mill, J.S.) 7:250–1
    autonomy
      ethical 1:590
    civil society 2:369
    classical (Spencer, H.) 9:87, 9:88
    communicative reason
      (Habermas, J.) 4:197
    consent 2:597
    conservatism conflict 2:611–12,
      2:613
    criminal punishment 2:708
    critiques of
      communitarianism 2:465–70
      Dostoevskii, F.M. 3:117–18
      Hessen, S.I. 4:418
      MacIntyre, A. 6:23
      Schmitt, C. 8:544
      socialist 8:880, 8:883
    definitions 5:598–9
    democracy relationship
      (Bobbio, N.) 1:791
    economic view 5:601–3
    educational philosophy 3:235
    freedom
      Constant de Rebecque, H.-B.
        2:615–16
      Kant, I. 5:195

freedom of contract (Green, T.H.)
4:168–9
freedom of speech
  journalism ethics 5:127
  German (Humboldt, W. von)
    4:541–2
  Hayek, F.A. 4:245, 4:248–9
  invisible hand argument 7:45
  Judaism conciliation
    (Mendelssohn, M.) 6:306
  justice
    as fairness 8:106, 8:108–9
  law limiting principles 5:462–3
  metapolitical (Croce, B.) 2:729,
    2:730, 2:732
  moral judgment 5:439–40
  moral relativism 6:541
  multiculturalism 6:600–2
  mutual recognition
    (Collingwood, R.G.) 2:414
  neutrality 8:882
  organicist theories of society
    9:253–4
  political philosophy 7:502–3
  pornography 7:544
  postmodernism 7:592
  privacy 7:691
  professional ethics 7:736
  proponents 5:599–600
  religion 8:224–5, 8:228–9, 8:230
  Russian **5:605–10**
    Herzen, A.I. critique 4:409
  sexuality 8:721
  social contract theories 5:603–4
  toleration 9:429, 9:430
  value pluralism (Berlin, I.) 1:751–2
  vulnerability 9:670
liberation
  see also enlightenment; *nirvāṇa*
  Hinduism 4:434–5, 6:400
    Advaita Vedānta School
      monism 6:475, 6:477
    Brahman
      Śaṅkara 8:459
    causation 2:251, 2:252
    ethics
      Nyāya-Vaiśeṣika 7:64
      Mīmāṃsā School 8:609–10
      Nyāya School 3:860
      Nyāya-Vaiśeṣika School 8:608
    qualifications for (Śaṅkara)
      8:460
    rejection of action (Śaṅkara)
      8:460
    Sāṅkhya School 8:461, 8:466,
      8:609
    Yoga School 8:609

while-still-alive 8:609
Liberation of Labour 7:452, 7:453
liberation philosophy **5:610–13**
  anti-colonial revolution
    (Cabral, A.) 2:170
  Argentina 1:377–8
  Latin America 5:428, 5:611, 5:612
    cultural identity 2:745
    debate topics 5:611–12
    literature 5:653, 5:655–6
liberation theology **5:613–17**
  ethics 5:616
  feminist theology 3:621, 3:623
  Marxism
    Latin America 6:163
libertarianism **5:617–19**
  critique of
    social democracy 8:828
  equality 3:394
  freedom 3:743–4
  history 5:618
  individual contract view
    (Nozick, R.) 2:658
  justice 8:884
  market ethics 6:108
  Molinism 7:111–12
  Nozick, R. 2:658, 7:44, 7:45–6
  property 7:759
  sexuality 8:723–4
  vulnerability 9:670
liberties
  basic (Rawls, J.) 8:107, 8:328
  difference principle 8:107–8
libertins **5:619–22**
liberty **3:753–7**
  see also autonomy; freedom
  British constitutional law
    (Dicey, A.V.) 3:62
  certainty relation (Renouvier, C.B.)
    8:268
  citizenship (Tocqueville, A. de)
    9:424
  civil (Hutcheson, F.) 4:591–2
  definition 3:753
  educational philosophy 3:235
  equality of
    democracy 2:867–72
  feminism
    jurisprudence 3:606–7
    Suchon, G. 9:211
  freedom of speech 3:763
  individual
    law and morality 5:438–42
  individuality 5:463
  Jewish philosophy
    (Mendelssohn, M.) 6:304, 6:306
  of labour (Smith, A.) 8:820

liberalism 5:600
  limits of law 5:461, 5:462–3
  Machiavelli, N. 6:20–1
  natural (Gauthier, D.) 2:660
  necessity debate (Collins, A.)
    2:416–17
  paternalism 7:250–2
  perfectionism 7:301–2
  political (Montesquieu, C.L.)
    6:493
  positive
    Green, T.H. 4:168, 4:169
    negative distinction (Berlin, I.)
      1:750, 1:752
  poverty 5:617–18, 5:619
  privacy
    information technology and
      ethics 4:780
  of religion (More, H.) 6:576, 6:581
  republicanism
    political philosophy
      history of 7:504
    Witherspoon, J. 9:756
  rights 8:178, 8:326–7, 8:328
  rule of law 5:151, 8:390
  self-determination (Price, R.)
    7:675, 7:678
  self-determinism (Locke, J.) 5:680
  state authority 4:829–30
  state of nature (Locke, J.) 5:681
  technology and ethics 9:282–3
  Tocqueville, A. de 9:424
  types of (Price, R.) 7:678
  utility principle (Mill, J.S.) 6:361,
    6:373–4
Libet, B. 3:138
Lichtenberg, Georg Christoph
  5:622–5
Lichtenstein, A. 2:185, 6:583
Lichtenstein, D. 2:475
Lichtheim, G. 8:885–6
Lichtheim, M. 3:250
Lidin, O. 7:91
Lieber, H.-J. 5:488–9
Lieberman, D. 2:446
Lieberson, S. 3:519, 3:520
Lieberwirth, R. 9:380
Liebeschütz, H. 5:117
Liebich, A. 2:362
Liebig, Justas 9:640–1, 9:643
Liebknecht, Karl 6:7
Liebman, C. 5:206
Liebmann, O. 6:779, 6:790
Lienhardt, G. 1:106
Lierse, C. 5:474
lies *see* deception
Lieu, S.N.C. 6:77

Lievers, Menno
  Molyneux problem †6:467–9
life
  see also vitalism
  and death 5:625–30
    contraception 5:629
    criteria for death 5:626–7
    euthanasia 5:628–9
    infanticide 5:629
    persistent vegetative state
      5:627–8
  meaning of 5:630–3
  mind relationship (Spinoza, B. de)
    9:98–9
  as narrative 6:656
  origin of 5:633–5
    Anaximander 1:258
    God
      design argument 4:90–1
    Islamic fundamentalism 5:12
  predestination (Schurman, A.M.
    van) 8:558
  psychic
    Frank, S.L. 3:728
    Shpet, G.G. 8:755
  reality as state of unity
    (Hegel, G.W.F.) 4:262–3
  reason relationship (Ortega y
    Gasset, J.) 7:166–7
  resurrection (Fëdorov, N.F.) 3:574,
    3:575
  thought relationship
    (Fackenheim, E.L.) 3:533,
    3:534–5
  value of 5:625–6
  will to power (Nietzsche, F.W.)
    6:857–8
life support
  death criteria 5:626–8
lifeboat ethics 3:40
lifestyles
  choice 1:458
lifeworld *see Lebenswelt*
Light, A. 6:638
Light, S. 5:321
light
  see also illumination;
    illuminationism
  Christian mysticism 6:624
  corporeal reality (Grosseteste, R.)
    4:177, 4:179–80
  Descartes, R. 3:3
  Illuminationist philosophy 4:702,
    9:219, 9:220–3
  medieval theories 6:698
  metaphysical principle of
    (Patrizi, F.) 7:261–2, 7:263

Newton, I. 6:824–5
  optics 7:136–9
  theories of
    Latin America
      colonial philosophy 5:425
light invariance principle
  relativity theory 8:192–3, 8:194–5
Light of Lights 4:702, 6:806, 9:219,
  9:220
Lightfoot, D.W. 2:341, 4:54
Liji (Book of Rites) 2:309, 2:311–12,
  2:314
  see also Daxue; *Zhongyong*
  history, Chinese theories of 4:452
  ritual rites 2:541–2
  Zheng Xuan 9:857–8
Lijing (Classic of Rites) 2:309,
  2:311–12, 2:560
  see also Liji; *Yili*; *Zhouli*
likeness thesis
  photography 7:379
Lilla, M. 7:596, 9:606
Lilla, S. 2:385
Lilly, Reginald
  French anti-postmodernism
    †7:593–6
limbo 5:635–8
  of the children 5:635–7
  of the fathers 5:635–7
  grace 4:150
  original sin 8:793
  of the sages 5:637
Limbrick, E. 8:454
limbus infantium see limbo
limbus patrum see limbo
limit theory
  Cantor, G. 2:197–8, 2:655
  mathematical analysis 1:217–18,
    1:219
limitation of size theory 7:218, 8:709
Lin Chao'en 8:624
Lin-chi *see* Linji
Lincoln, J.S. 6:670
Lindahl, B.I.B. 6:268–9
Lindberg, D.C. 1:787, 6:803, 7:269,
  8:235
Lindemann, H. 1:230, 1:233
Linden, R.R. 8:728
Lindenbaum, A. 7:495
Lindenbaum-Tarski algebras 1:844–5
Lindgren, U. 4:41
Lindley, D.V. 9:126
Lindström, P. 4:772, 5:780, 6:440,
  7:877
Lindstrøm, T. 1:215
Lindström's theorem 5:735
Lindtner, C. 2:63, 6:640

Lindzey, G. 1:695
linear logic 5:638–41
line-drawing
  truthfulness 9:483–4
Lingis, A. 6:11
linguistic analysis *see* ordinary
  language philosophy
linguistic discrimination 5:641–5
linguistic formalism
  legal discourse 5:498
linguistic relativity hypothesis *see*
  Sapir-Whorf Hypothesis
linguistic structuralism *see*
  structuralism, linguistic
linguistic theory of necessity 6:748–9
linguistic units
  see also sphoṭa theory
  Indian theories of 5:379, 5:380–2
linguisticism
  a priori 1:5
linguistics 5:408–9, 5:410–11
  see also language; phonology;
    semantics; semiotics;
    structuralism, linguistics
  bodies relations (Deleuze, G.)
    2:858–9
  cognitive development 2:394
  conceptual role semantics 8:653
  Humboldt, W. von 4:542
  meaning
    concepts 2:507–8
  nativism
    Chomsky, N. 6:672, 6:673–4
  post-structuralism 7:596, 7:600
  pragmatism 7:634–5
  psychoanalysis 7:814
  rationalist (Cordemoy, G. de)
    2:673–4
  structuralism *see* structuralism,
    linguistic
  structure
    slovo ('the word') (Shpet, G.G.)
    8:756
  synchronic-diachronic distinction
    (Saussure, F. de) 8:480–1
  testimony in Indian philosophy
    9:315–18
  theoretical 5:286–7
  type/token distinction 9:509–11
  typology (Humboldt, W. von)
    4:542
Linji 5:645–6
Linji School of Chan Buddhism
  2:88–9
Linklater, A. 9:122
Linnaeus, Carl von 5:646–50
  medicine, philosophy of 6:268

taxonomy 9:275
Linsky, L. 6:432
Lionnet, Françoise
  Todorov, T. †9:425–7
Lipman, M. 3:239
Lipner, J.J. 8:44
Lipp, S. 5:301
Lippens, H. 8:312
Lippman, E. 6:614
Lips, Joest see Lipsius, Justus
Lipset, S.M. 5:541
Lipsius, Justus **5:650–2**
Lipton, P. 4:769
LiPuma, E. 1:850
liquidationism 6:154
Lisitsa, Iu.T. 4:695–6
Liss, S.B. 6:164
List, E. 8:561
listening
  modes of 4:189
litera mortua 5:507
literacy
  influence on belief
    African traditional religions
      1:119–20
  influence on moral discourse
    African ethical systems 3:433–4
literariness
  Russian literary formalism
    8:410–11
literary theory
  Barthes, R. 1:656–7
  Belinskii, V.G. **1:709–12**, 4:304,
    8:521
  characterization (Schlegel, F. von)
    8:530
  civic criticism
    Russian materialism 8:417
  Hebrew Bible (Ibn Ezra, M.)
    4:613–14
  interpretaton 1:503
  Judaic/Hellenic distinction
    midrash 6:354
  katharsis 5:218–19
  moral disagreement comparison
    (Hume, D.) 4:555–6
  Moscow-Tartu School 6:584
  novels (Bakhtin, M.M.) 1:638–9,
    1:643–4
  polyphony (Bakhtin, M.M.)
    1:642–3
  Porphyry 7:548
  postcolonialism 7:578–9
  rhetoricity (Man, P. de) 2:810–12
  Russian Hegelianism
    (Belinskii, V.G.) 4:304

Russian literary formalism
  8:409–13
Schellingianism 8:521
structuralism 9:181–4
  Todorov, T. 9:425–6
taste (Blair, H.) 1:782
literati aesthetics
  Chinese 1:73–4
literature
  see also art; art works; comedy;
    deconstruction; fiction; fictional
    entities; literary theory; narrative;
    poetry; tragedy
  alchemy 1:156
  art and truth 1:459
  clandestine 2:374–6
  colonial novels 1:109
  criticism
    see also feminist philosophy,
      literary criticism
    Barthes, R. 1:656–7
    psychoanalytic feminism 3:584
  death relationship (Blanchot, M.)
    1:783
  devaluation (Lacoue-Labarthe, P.)
    5:340
  genres
    revelation 8:299–300
  interpretation of 1:503
  Latin America **5:653–7**
    phenomenology 7:348–9
  mimēsis 6:381–2
  modern
    Japanese philosophy **5:657–60**
  moral insight 1:458
  parody
    Cynics 2:754, 2:755, 2:756–7
  philosophy assimilation (Man, P.
    de) 2:810, 2:811–12
  post-structuralism 7:598–9
  scriptor (Barthes, R.) 1:656–7
  Socratic dialogues 9:19–20
  structuralism 9:175
  Tel Quel school 9:291, 9:292–3
Lithuania
  Levinas, E. **5:579–82**
  Maimon, S. **6:35–8**
Litt, T. 4:297
Little, A. 7:438
Little, D. 3:221, 8:847
Little, I.M.D. 3:210, 7:228
Little, M. 6:538
Littmann, E. 3:445
Liu An see Huainanzi
Liu, J.J.Y. 1:75
Liu Ming-wood 2:92, 3:570
Liu Xiang 4:186

Liu Zhiji 4:450
Liu Zhongzhou 8:624
Lively, A. 8:272
Lively, J. 8:272, 9:425
living force see vis viva
Livingston, P. 1:516
Livingstone, Donald 4:561
lixue (learning of principle) 6:771
Llambías de Azevedo, Juan 7:350,
  7:351
Llewellyn, Karl Nickerson 5:524–5,
  5:661–2
Llewelyn, J. 5:582
Lloyd, A. 6:264
Lloyd, A.C. 1:175, 6:803, 7:463, 7:731
Lloyd, E. 8:102
Lloyd, Elisabeth A.
  ecology 3:205
  evolution, theory of †3:476–83
  explanation 3:525
  feminism and social science 3:592
  models †6:442–7
  scientific theories 9:353
Lloyd, Genevieve
  feminism 3:583
    Australian philosophy 1:581,
      1:583
  epistemology 3:602
  Le Doeuff, M. 5:479
Lloyd, G.E.R.
  Alcmaeon 1:161
  Archytas 1:369
  Eudoxus 3:453
  Hippocratic medicine 4:443
  Ptolemy 7:832
Lloyd, S.A. 3:230
Lloyd-Jones, H. 9:420
Llull, Ramon **5:662–4**, 9:70
  see also Llullism
  Averroism 1:595, 1:598
  logic machines 5:744
Llullism 9:70
Loades, A. 3:561
Loar, Barry
  content
    wide and narrow
      twin earth thought
        experiments 2:645, 2:646
  Grice, H.P. 4:177
  holism
    mental and semantic 4:493
  language
    conventionality of 5:371
  methodological individualism
    6:344
  propositional attitudes 7:786
  qualia 7:867

Löb, M.H.
  Gödel's theorems 4:112, 4:117
  provability logic 7:794, 7:795–6
Lobachevskii, N.I. 4:29
Lobban, M. 1:781, 2:446
Lobkowicz, Nikolaus 2:362, 2:769,
  8:813
locality
  Bell inequalities
    quantum mechanics 1:714–15
Lochner, N. 1:211
Lockard, J.S. 8:628, 8:632
Locke, D. 4:125
Locke, John **5:665–87**
  analytic philosophy 1:224, 1:228
  arithmetica 1:441
  authority 1:584, 1:586
  Bacon, F. 1:632
  Berkeley, G. 1:739, 1:741–2, 1:750,
    3:377
  Bold, S. 1:822–3
  Butler, J. 2:160
  Cockburn, C. 2:386–7
  coherence theory of truth 9:470,
    9:472
  colour, theories of 2:429, 2:431
  concepts 2:516, 2:518, 2:522
  Condillac, É.B. de 2:523, 2:524
  consciousness 2:583, 2:595
  consent theory 2:598
  contractarianism 2:657–8, 2:665
  conventionalism 6:748, 6:750
  critiques of
    Astell, M. 1:528–9
    Berkeley, G. 5:375–6
    Browne, P. 2:29
    Clarke, S. 2:379
    Condillac, É.B. de 5:376
    Hutcheson, F. 4:588, 4:589
    Leibniz, G.W. 5:375, 5:376
    Reid, T. 2:447
  deism 2:854
  democratic contract 2:661–2
  educational philosophy 3:223,
    3:226–7, 3:230
  Edwards, J. 3:245
  empiricism 4:795, 4:797
  enthusiasm 3:331, 3:332
  An Essay Concerning Human
    Understanding
    ethics 5:679–80
    language 5:374–5
  eternity 3:424–5, 3:426
  ethics 3:551, 5:678–80
    applied 1:324
    autonomy 1:587, 1:592
  evaluative epistemology 7:36, 7:38

faith 3:538, 3:542–3
  reason 3:543
Filmer, R. 3:679
foundationalism 5:276
free will 3:752
help and beneficence 4:344
human nature 4:525
ideas 5:665, 5:668–73
  innate
    sensory experience 8:77
interests 6:753
introspection, psychology of 2:590,
  4:846
Johnson, S. 5:126
knowledge 3:376–7, 3:382
land 4:161, 4:165
language 5:374–5
  early modern philosophy of
    5:378
  origins of 5:372
law
  limits of 5:461, 5:464
  and morality 5:439
  rule of 8:388, 8:391
legitimacy 5:541
liberalism 5:600, 5:602, 5:603–4,
  5:605
libertarianism 5:618
logic of cognitive faculties 5:718
Masham, D. 6:167
matter
  Astell, M. critique 1:528–9
memory 6:299
mental science (Maine de Biran, P.-
  F.) 6:51
mind
  Latitudinarianism 5:434
Molyneux problem 6:467, 6:469
nativism 6:673, 6:675
natural kinds 6:684
natural theology 6:709, 6:713
needs and interests 6:755
neutrality
  political 6:818–19, 6:821
nominalism 7:20–1, 7:23
obligation
  political 7:78, 7:80
original sin 8:794, 8:795–6
personal identity 5:665, 5:677–8,
  7:314
  morality 6:572, 6:575
persons 7:319, 7:321
political theory 5:680–2
primary-secondary distinction
  7:74, 7:75, 7:684–5, 7:687
property 7:758, 8:850–1
prophecy 7:769–70, 7:771

religion
  belief 8:211–12
    evidentialism 8:209
  and epistemology 8:218
  liberalism 8:224–5
  and political philosophy 8:229
  toleration 8:227
representative realism
  Reid, T. critique 2:447
secondary qualities 8:599
slavery 8:805, 8:806
social epistemology 8:832
social science
  history of philosophy of 8:858
Socinianism 8:891
state
  political philosophy 7:513
substance 9:207, 9:210
suicide 9:225, 9:229
testimony 9:314
theology (Chillingworth, W.) 2:308
Toland, J. 9:427
toleration 9:430, 9:433
trust 9:469
Voltaire 9:658
Wollstonecraft, M. 9:791
work
  philosophy of 9:796, 9:797
Lockwood, M. 6:177, 9:416
locutionary acts 9:82–3
Loeb, L. 8:80
Loeb, P.A. 1:214, 1:215
Loemaker, L. 4:240
Loewe, M. 9:680
Loewe, R. 1:23
Loewenberg, J. 6:351
Loewenthal, N. 4:245
Loewer, Barry
  content
    wide and narrow 2:646
  Davidson, D. 2:806
  deontic logic 2:890
  Fodor, J.A. 3:686
  language of thought hypothesis
    5:407
  mental causation †6:307–11
  probability theory and
    epistemology †7:705–11
  semantics
    informational 8:662
  supervenience of the mental
    †9:238–40
Loftus, E. 9:526
logic **5:764–6**
  see also Boolean algebra;
    combinatory logic; dialectic; first-
    order logic; formal logic; fuzzy

logic; imperative logic; logicism; many-valued logics; mathematical logic; modal logic; predicate calculus; predicate logic; second-order logic; temporal logic; tense logic
Abelard, P. 1:8, 1:9, 1:10–11
Albert the Great 1:146–7
algebra of see Boolean algebra
analytic/synthetic character
   mathematical knowledge 5:812
analytical philosophy
   Latin America 1:230, 1:231–2
ancient 5:687–93, 7:493
anti-Aristotelian
   Middle Platonism 7:428
anti-positivism
   Latin America 1:306
argument
   deduction (Aristotle) 1:417
Aristotelian 5:687–9
   Boethius, A.M.S. 1:396, 1:805, 1:806–7
   conceptual scope 1:414
   empirical judgment
     Jungius, J. reform 5:135, 5:136
   essentialism 3:419
   language 1:416–17
   logical form in 5:781–2, 5:783–4
   new twelfth century texts 1:398
   Philoponus 7:372
   Plato harmonization (Porphyry) 7:546–7
   Plutarch of Chaeronea 7:469
assent
   Locke, J. critique 5:668–9
beauty 1:681
branching
   medicine 6:267
Buddhism
   Dharmakīrti 3:51–3
   Tibet 9:407
   Yogācāra 3:389
Carolingian renaissance 2:221
Cartesian (Clauberg, J.) 2:380
chains of reason (Hobbes, T.) 4:465
China 5:693–706
   dialectical 2:779
   Mohist philosophy 6:456–7
classical
   intuitionistic logic comparison 5:788–9
colonial philosophy
   Latin America 5:421, 5:422, 5:423–4

conditional
   possible worlds semantics 8:665
conditions of existence (Anderson, J.) 1:267
of continua (Heytesbury, W.) 4:420
critical idealism (Cohen, H.) 2:399
De Morgan, A. 2:813–14
deductive
   methodology of discovery 3:100
definition
   Indian concepts of 2:849–52
definition of 5:750
demonstrative method
   Wolff, C. 9:781
deontic 2:887–90
   critique of moral pluralism 6:530
   Wright, G.H. von 9:668
diagrams 5:724–5, 5:726–7, 5:739–46
diairesis (Platonic division) (Speusippus) 9:90
Dialectical school 3:58
dialogical 3:59–62, 5:826–7
of discovery 3:99–3:103
educational philosophy 3:233–4
eighteenth century 5:716–22
epistemic 3:354–9
erotetic 8:2–3
of ethical discourse 5:759–64
   is/ought question 5:759–61
   particularism 5:763–4
   universalism 5:759, 5:761–3
ethics
   Cohen, H. 2:399–400
Epictetus 3:338
Eusebius 3:456
existential quantification (Quine, W.V.) 8:7–8
experimental (Dewey, J.) 3:47
extensions of
   logical constants 5:777
fictional entities 3:664, 3:665
first-order see first-order logic
formal see formal logic
free 3:738–9, 3:739–43
glossary 5:795–811
grammar distinction (Kilwardby, R.) 5:246–7
Hellenistic (Philo the Dialectician) 7:363–4
higher-order 8:591–5
history of (Łukasiewicz, J.) 5:862
history relationship (Croce, B.) 2:731

hypothesis testing
   computational theories of mind 6:392–3
inference
   momentariness
     Buddhist doctrine of 6:472
inferential
   Stoicism 9:142, 9:144, 9:150–1
infinitary 4:769–72, 5:734–5, 6:440
informal 3:701–3
intensional 2:212, 4:807–10
intuitionistic 4:856, 4:856–63, 4:857, 4:858–9, 5:788–9, 6:89–90
Islamic philosophy 3:385–6, 5:15, 5:706–13
   language relationship 4:649, 5:706, 5:707–8, 6:237
Jainism 5:48, 5:50–1
Japanese philosophy 5:713–16
Jewish philosophy
   Messer Leon 6:331, 6:332
language relationship
   Islamic philosophy 4:649, 5:706, 5:707–8, 6:237
laws of 5:785–9
laws of thought (Mill, J.S.) 6:360, 6:361–3, 6:364–5
lekton
   Stoicism 9:149
linear 5:638–41
many-valued see many-valued logic
master argument (Cleanthes) 2:383
mathematico-deductive (Amo, A.W.) 1:210
medieval 5:746–59, 6:274–5
   Buridan, J. 2:131, 2:132
   intentionality 4:816–17
   Kilvington, R. 5:244–5
   Llull, R. 5:663
   natural philosophy 6:701–2
   Oxford Calculators 7:181
   Peter of Auvergne 7:321
   Peter of Spain 7:324–5
   Richard Rufus of Cornwall 8:316
   Roscelin of Compiègne 8:356–7
   William of Ockham 9:739–41
   Wodeham, A. 9:774
   Wyclif, J. 9:802
methodology (Lambert, J.H.) 5:350
modal see modal logic
multiple-conclusion 6:602–4
naturalized epistemology (Quine, W.V.) 8:4, 8:7
new (Bacon, F.) 1:627–8

New Logic School
    Indian philosophy (Gaṅgeśa)
      3:843–6
nineteenth century **5:722–9**
non-monotonic **7:30–5**
    common-sense reasoning 2:451,
      2:452–3
Nyāya (Uddyotakara) 9:514
ontology of (Łukasiewicz, J.) 5:862
paraconsistent **7:208–11**
Paul of Venice 7:265
Peripatetic
    Encyclopedists, medieval 3:306
Platonism
    Early and Middle 7:427–8
Polish 5:862, **7:492–500**
Port-Royal (Arnauld, A.) 1:444
pragmatic a priori (Lewis, C.I.)
    5:585, 5:586
primacy of (Wolff, C.) 9:780
proof of reality (Owen, G.E.L.)
    7:178
propositional
    consequence (Geulincx, A.)
      4:59–60
    epistemic 3:354–6
    terminist (Buridan, J.) 2:132
propositional (Geulincx, A.)
    4:59–60
provability **7:793–7**
psychology relationship
    (Twardowski, K.) 9:509
psychology theory 7:828
quantum **7:882–6**, 7:893
questions
    effective systems 8:1–2
reality relationship
    Islamic philosophy 3:385
reism (Kotarbiński, T.) 5:293–4
relations (Leibniz, G.W.) 5:554
relative identity 9:459–61
relevance **8:200–4**
Renaissance **5:766–72**, 8:266, 8:500
    Aristotelianism
      Fonseca, P. da 3:688
      Toletus, F. 9:434
    divisions of 5:768
    George of Trebizond 4:34
    infinite numbers (Toletus, F.)
      9:434–5
    John of St Thomas 5:118–19
    linguistic usage (Valla, L.)
      9:571–2
    medieval influence 5:767
    medieval logic contrast 5:768–9
    method 5:771–2
    Ramus, P. 8:52–3

Soto, D. de 9:38
Zabarella, J. 9:836–7
second-order *see* second-order
    logic
semantics (Marsilius of Inghen)
    6:110–11
set theory (Quine, W.V.) 8:7
seventeenth century **5:716–22**
social relativism 8:838
social theory (Bourdieu, P.) 1:849
soku
    Kyoto School 5:326–7
Stoicism 5:690–1, 7:556
suppositions (William of
    Sherwood) 9:748–9
syllogistic
    Encyclopedists, medieval 3:306
    Holcot's application 4:478
    Philoponus 7:372
    Theophrastus 9:337–8
syntactic categories
    (Ajdukiewicz, K.) 1:137
System Sigma (Royce, J.) 8:380
temporal *see* temporal logic
tense 7:687, 7:688, **9:303–7**
theology relevance (Bonaventure)
    1:830–1
tolerance (Carnap, R.) 2:211
truth constants (Quine, W.V.) 8:10
truth theories
    language 6:221–2
twentieth century, early **5:729–38**
validity
    logical laws 5:786–7, 5:788
verificationism (Ayer, A.J.)
    1:615–16
Logic
    reason (Hegel, G.W.F.) 4:266,
      4:268–72
logic machines **5:739–46**
logic of place
    Nishida Kitarō 5:77–8, 5:714–15,
      7:14
logic of signs *see* semiotics
logic of species
    Tanabe Hajime 9:261, 9:262
logic of systems
    Comte, A. 2:496, 2:501–2
Logica vetus (Old Logic) 5:747, 5:748
logical atomism **5:772–5**
    facts 3:536
    Russell, B.A.W. 5:774–5, 8:399
    Wittgenstein, L. 1:225, 5:773–4,
      9:757, 9:760–2
logical behaviourism *see*
    behaviourism, analytic

logical closure
    glossary 5:799
logical consequence 2:601
    see also entailment
    formal systems 3:704–6
    logical constants 5:775–7
    model theory 2:354, 6:441
    predicate calculus 7:661–4
logical conservatism
    logical form 5:783–5
logical constants **5:775–81**
    bivalence
      intuitionistic logic 4:858–9
    logical truth 5:775–7
logical empiricism
    see also logical positivism
    chemistry 2:295
    Einstein, A. 3:257
    explanation
      covering-law model 3:520,
      3:521–3
    postmodernism (Hempel, C.G.)
      4:348–9, 4:350–1
    Ramsey, I.T. 8:49–50
    Reichenbach, H. 8:167
    synthetic a priori judgments
      Vienna Circle rejection 9:608–9
logical form **5:781–5**
    ambiguity 1:200
logical identity *see* identity, logical
logical implication
    glossary 5:804–5
logical operations
    child development (Piaget, J.)
      7:383–4
logical positivism **5:789–95**
    see also logical empiricism; Vienna
    Circle
    agnosticism 1:122, 1:123
    analytic method (Hanson, N.R.)
      4:224
    analytical philosophy
      Latin America 1:230, 1:231–2
    atheism 1:530
    Ayer, A.J. 1:614, 1:615
    causation 2:246–7
    critiques of 9:347–8
      Feyerabend, P.K. 3:640
      Popper, K.R. 7:534
      Schlick, F.A.M. 8:541
    Du Bois-Reymond, E. 3:130
    economics 3:215
    empiriocriticism 1:592, 1:593–4
    expected utility theory 8:94
    experiment 3:515
    experimental psychology 1:696–7
    legal discourse 5:498

logic of discovery 3:99
mathematics 5:791–2
meaning and verification 6:230,
  6:231–2
metaphysics 6:340
moral judgments
  analytic ethics 1:221
  necessary truth 6:748
observational concepts 7:558–9
operationalism 7:132–4
ordinary language philosophy
  7:144, 7:148, 7:149–50
philosophical analysis 1:223–4,
  1:225
political philosophy 7:526
practical reasoning/rationality
  expected utility theory 8:94
pragmatism 7:635
probability
  Reichenbach, H. critique
    8:167–8
Putnam, H. 7:840
Ramsey, I.T. 8:50
relativity
  general 4:7–8, 5:791
science 8:572–3
  demarcation problem 2:865
  French philosophy of 3:779–80
  Mach, E. 6:13–14
  scientific theories 9:344–6
semantic holism 4:489
semantics 8:649
Tarski's definition of truth 9:268
top-down causation
  divine action 8:234
unity of science 9:531–2
logical realism
  Brinkley, R. 2:20
  property theory 7:761, 7:764
  William of Champeaux 9:729
logical sentences
  possible worlds 7:572
logical terms
  glossary of 5:795–811
logical truth
  see also tautologies
  conventions (Prior, A.N.) 7:689
  indexicals 2:880
  logical constants 5:775–7
  necessity 6:429
  negation (Wittgenstein, L.)
    9:759–60
  objective harmony (Burthogge, R.)
    2:145
  reference (Quine, W.V.) 8:7
  tautologies (Wittgenstein, L.)
    9:759–60

logic-gates 1:486, 6:391
logicism 5:811–17
  arithmetic 1:439–40
  Gödel's theorems 4:113
  logical positivism 5:792
  mathematics 6:184–5, 6:186
    Poincaré, J.H. critique 7:481
    Russell, B.A.W. 8:391–2, 8:394
  semantic paradoxes (Ramsey, F.P.)
    8:45
logocentrism 5:477, 7:598
logos 5:817–19
  see also Jesus Christ
  Antisthenes 1:316–17
  Christianity 5:819
  conformity-nonconformity to
    5:818–19
  creation (Rosenzweig, F.) 8:359
  of God
    Philo of Alexandria 5:819
  Gorgias 4:144–5
  Hellanistic Judaism
    Clement of Alexandria 7:258
    St Paul 7:256
    Philo of Alexandria 7:255–6
  Heraclitus 5:818
  Jewish Scripture 5:819
  language (Coleridge, S.T.) 2:404
  Philo of Alexandria 7:359
  Platonism (Plutarch of Chaeronea)
    7:466
  pneuma (spirit) 7:471, 7:472
  Stoicism 5:817, 5:818, 5:819
  theosophy 9:364
  understanding of (Heraclitus)
    4:365–6, 4:368
Løgstrup, Knud Ejler 8:492
Lohr, Charles
  Aristotelianism
    medieval 1:404
    Renaissance 1:413
    seventeenth century 1:391–3
  Collegium Conimbricense 2:408
  Fonseca, P. da 3:690
  John of St Thomas 5:120
  logic
    Renaissance 5:772
  Nifo, A. 6:871
  Peter of Auvergne 7:323
  Silvestri, F. 8:777
  Soto, D. de 9:39–40
  Toletus, F. 9:435
  Zabarella, J. 9:839
Lohse, B. 6:5
Loi, Maurice
  Brunschvicg, L. †2:39–41
Loisy, Alfred 5:819–20

Lokāyata 6:178–81
Lombard, Peter 5:821–2
  challenge to (Joachim of Fiore)
    5:104
  creation doctrine 7:436
  free choice (Duns Scotus, J.)
    3:166–7
  influence of
    medieval philosophy 6:272
  limbo 5:636, 5:637
  Sentences 5:821, 5:822
    Alexander of Hales 1:177
    Aureol, P. 1:565
    creation doctrine 7:436
    Duns Scotus, J. 3:156, 3:166–7
    influence on medieval
      philosophy 6:272
    Olivi, P.J. 7:95
    Richard of Middleton 8:310,
      8:311
    Richard Rufus of Cornwall
      8:314
    William of Ockham 9:733
  William of Auxerre comparison
    9:728
Lombardo, P. 1:658
Lombardo, S. 2:781
Loménie de Brienne, H. de 7:554
Lomonosov, M.V. 3:324
London, F. 7:890
loneliness
  aesthetic ideals
    Japanese 1:88
Lonergan, Bernard Joseph Francis
  1:348, 5:822–5
Long, A.A.
  Arcesilaus 1:354
  Ariston of Chios 1:382
  Cleanthes 2:383
  Cratylus †2:694–5
  Diodorus Cronus 3:86
  Epictetus 3:339
  Epicureanism 3:349–50
  epistemology 3:382
  eudaimonia 3:451
  free will 3:752
  Hellenistic philosophy 4:336
  Heraclitus †4:364–9
  language
    ancient philosophy of 5:361
  Lucretius 5:856
  morality and emotions 6:563
  nous †7:43–4
  Parmenides 7:234
  Philo the Dialectician 7:365
  Presocratics 7:672
  psychē (soul) †7:809–11

Ptolemy 7:831–2
Pyrrho 7:848
Stoicism 9:160
Timon 9:420
Long, D. 1:724–5
Longeway, John
  Heytesbury, W. †4:419–21
  John of Damascus †5:105–6
  William of Sherwood †9:748–9
Longeway, John L.
  Oxford Calculators 7:182–3
  Peter of Spain †7:324–5
Longino, Helen
  feminism
    epistemology 3:599, 3:602
    social science 3:592
    gender and science 3:866, 3:868
    social epistemology 8:832
    value judgments in social science
      9:579
Longinus 7:477, 9:202, 9:204
Longpré, E. 9:376
Longrigg, J. 4:443
long-term memory (LTM) 4:845
Lønning, J.-T. 6:170
Loomes, G. 8:102
Lopatin, L.M. 5:838
Lopez Morillas, J. 5:301
Lopez-Escobar, E.G.K. 4:772
Lorber, J. 5:644
Lorentz, H.A. 3:258, 3:669, 8:199
Lorentz transformations 8:191–3
Lorenz, Kuno 3:61
Lorenzen, Paul 5:825–8
  dialogical logic 3:60
Lormand, Eric
  concepts 2:516
  consciousness †2:581–96
Los, J. 7:496
Losano, M.G. 5:101
Losee, J. 8:580
Losev, Aleksei Fëdorovich 5:828–33
  religion 5:831
  sobornost' 5:830
  Solov'ëv, V.S. 9:32
Lossky, B. 5:838
Lossky, N. 5:838
Lossky, Nicholas Onufrievich
  5:833–8
  absolutism 5:833, 5:837
  Florenskii, P.A. 3:682
  Frank, S.L. 3:729
  ideal realism 5:833
  intuitivism 5:833, 5:834–5
  Russian religious-philosophical
    renaissance 8:428
  Supracosmic Principle 5:836

Lossky, V. 6:626, 6:762
Loti, Pierre 1:109, 1:116
Lotman, Iu.M. 6:585–7
Lott, E.J. 8:44, 8:451
Lottery paradox 7:211–12, 7:708
  epistemic principles 5:273
  inductive inference 4:758
Lottin, O. 5:111, 9:728
Lottman, H. 2:196
Lotus Sutra 2:103, 6:829, 9:860–1
Lotze, Rudolph Hermann 5:838–42
  personalism 7:315
Louden, Robert B.
  examples in ethics †3:487–90
Lough, J. 1:168, 3:69, 3:304
Loughlin, Martin
  Dicey, A.V. †3:62–3
  Millar, J. †6:375–6
  rule of law 8:391
Loughney, John A.
  cultural identity †2:744–6
Louton, J. 5:865
Louvain School 7:487
Loux, Michael J.
  Aristotle 1:435
  nominalism †7:17–23
  possible worlds 7:572
Love, H. 2:376
Love, M.L. 4:765
love 5:842–6
  see also agape; eros
  Alcibiades
    Socratic dialogues 9:19, 9:20
  amour-propre/amour de nous-
    mêmes (self-love/love of self)
    distinction
    moralistes 6:557
  androgynous unity (Solov'ëv, V.S.)
    9:29–30
  Bayle/Malebranche debate 1:675
  of beauty (Ibn Sina) 1:76
  beauty (Plato) 7:411–12
  Chinese Confucianism
    ren 2:302, 2:539, 2:540
  Christian
    charity 2:280–1
    desire/benevolence distinction
      (Norris, J.) 7:42
  ethic of
    German Romanticism 8:350
    familial relationships 3:550–1
    friendship 3:794, 3:795–6
  of God
    faith 3:542
    Fénelon, F. 3:629–30
    grace relationship (Weil, S.) 9:700
    Ibn Hazm 4:620

moral emotion of (Hegel, G.W.F.)
  4:262–3
morality
  Christian view 6:561
  nature of (Abravanel, J.) 1:23,
    1:24–7
  Platonic
    Ficino, M. 3:657–8
    Pico della Mirandola, G. 7:386,
      7:388
  pragmatism 7:638
  Scheler, M.F. 8:507
  sexuality 8:724, 8:726
  theological virtue 9:326, 9:327,
    9:329–30
  unity (Tillich, P.) 9:411
love mysticism
  Catherine of Siena 6:625
  Sufism 6:625–6
  Zaehner, R.C. 6:630
Lovejoy, A.O. 2:122, 2:411, 6:736,
  8:377
Lovelace, R.F. 7:395
Lovell, Stephen
  Russian nihilism †7:5–8
Lovelock, J.E. 3:202, 6:554
Lovers of Wisdom see
  Schellingianism
Lovibond, Sabina
  Wittgensteinian ethics †9:770–3
Löw, Rabbi see Jehuda ben Becalel
  Liva
Lowe, E.J. 6:385
Lowe, S. 6:457, 6:591
Lowe, V. 7:715, 9:719
Lowe, W. 7:586
Löwenheim, Leopold
  see also Löwenheim-Skolem
    theorems
  Church's theorem and the decision
    problem 2:351
  first/second-order logic 5:731,
    5:733
  Gödel's theorems 4:117
  Herbrand's theorem 4:378
  infinitary logic 5:734
  logic
    early twentieth century 5:731,
      5:737
  logical constants 5:780
  logicism 5:817
  Löwenheim-Skolem theorem and
    non-standard models 5:846,
    5:848
Löwenheim-Skolem theorems 5:777,
  5:780, 5:846–51
  axiom of choice 1:614

glossary 5:805
logicism 5:815
model theory 6:438
non-standard models 5:846,
  5:848–50, 5:851
second-order logic 8:600–1,
  8:602–3
Lowenstein, T. 6:670
Lowinger, A. 3:147
Löwith, Karl
  Feuerbach, L.A. 3:639
  Hegelianism 4:297, 4:301
  historicism 4:445, 4:446
  Rosenzweig, F. 8:361
  Ruge, A. 8:387
Lowood, H. 7:398
Lowrie, D.A. 1:732
Löwy, M. 5:859, 6:164, 9:466
loyalty
  ethics (Royce, J.) 8:378
  trust comparison 9:468
Loyola, Ignatius 8:455–6, 8:458
Lu Hsiang-shan see Lu Xiangshan
Lu Ji 1:69–70
Lu Xiangshan 5:595, 5:851–3,
  6:770–1
Lu Zuqian 2:301
Lubac, Henri de
  Garrigou-Lagrange, R. 3:848
  grace 4:151
  Pico della Mirandola, G. 7:392
  Richard of St Victor 8:314
  Teilhard de Chardin, P. 9:291
Luban, David 4:832
Lübbe, H. 2:51, 3:639, 4:297
Lublin school 9:384–5
Lubomír 2:769
Lucas, D.W. 5:220, 6:382
Lucas, J.
  computational theories of mind
    6:394
  justice, equity and law 5:152
  rule of law 8:391
Lucas, J.A.
  desert and merit 3:27
  responsibility 8:294
Lucas, J.R.
  Gödel's theorems 4:114, 4:117
  relativity theory
    philosophical significance of
      8:199
Luce, A.A. 1:747, 1:750
Luce, R.D. 6:249, 8:74, 8:103
Lucey, K. 3:365, 5:276
Lucian 2:757, 2:759, 5:853–4
Lucid, D.P. 6:587
Lucie-Smith, E. 3:409

luck
  circumstantial 6:520
  constitutive 6:520
  deterministic 6:521
  moral 6:520–2
    Aristotelian/Platonic contrast
      6:521
    will 9:722–3
    Williams, B.A.O. 9:750–1
  resultant 6:521
Luckhardt, H. 7:751
Luckmann, T. 9:356
Lucretius 1:262, 5:854–6
  atomism 6:171, 6:173
  body-void distinction 3:341–2
  death 2:820, 3:349
  Epicureanism 3:349–50
  free will 3:752
  language
    early modern philosophy of
      5:372, 5:378
  minima 3:343
Lucy, John A.
  Sapir-Whorf Hypothesis †8:470–3
Lüders, H. 4:256
Ludlow, P. 7:779
Ludwig, G. 7:886
Ludwig, K. 6:311
Luft, E. von der 8:554
Lugon, C. 2:464
Lugones, M. 3:605
Luhmann, Niklas
  social theory and law 8:878
  systems theory in social science
    9:255, 9:256
  trust 9:469
Luig, K. 8:347
Luik, John C.
  humanism †4:528–32
Lukács, Georg 5:856–9
  critique of capitalism 6:96–7, 6:99
  Hegelianism 4:297
  influenced by Plekhanov, G.V.
    7:454
  Marx, K. 6:133
  Marxism
    science, philosophy of 6:149–50
    Western 6:141, 6:143–4, 6:146
  Sunday Circle 4:569–70
Lukashevich, S. 3:576
Łukasiewicz, Jan 5:859–63
  ancient logic 5:691, 5:693
  fuzzy set theory 3:823–4
  many-valued logics 6:84–6, 6:90,
    6:91
  paraconsistent logic 7:210
  Polish logic 7:492–3, 7:497–8

Lukes, S.
  anthropology
    philosophy of 1:299
  authority 1:586
  cognitive pluralism 2:397
  Durkheim, É. 3:177
  epistemic relativism 3:362
  holism and individualism in
    history and social science 4:488
  power 7:610, 7:612
  rationality and cultural relativism
    8:86
  social relativism 8:838
  social theory and law 8:878–9
  sociology of knowledge 9:2
Lull, Ramon see Llull, Ramon
Luna, C. 4:77–8
Lunacharskii, Anatolii
  Nietzsche, F.W.: impact on
    Russian thought 6:862, 6:864,
    6:865, 6:867
  Russian empiriocriticism 8:407–8
El Lunarejo see Espinosa Medrano,
  Juan de
Lundgren-Gothlin, Eva
  Beauvoir, S. de †1:684–7
Lundstedt, Vilhelm 5:522, 5:525
Lunheng see Wang Chong
Lunyu see Confucius Analects
Luo Qinshun 5:43
Luper, Steven
  belief and knowledge †1:706–9
  naturalized epistemology †6:721–8
Luper-Foy, S. 1:709, 4:826, 6:727,
  7:47
Luppé, R. 2:196
Luria, A.R. 9:672, 9:675
Luria, S. 2:877
Luria, Salvador 6:458
Luschei, E.C. 5:574, 7:498
Luscombe, D.E. 1:14
Lushi chunqiu 5:863–5
Lü-shih Ch'un-ch'iu see Lushi chunqiu
lust 8:721
Lusted, L.B. 6:268
Lusthaus, Dan
  Buddhism
    Chinese †2:80–92
    Sāṅkhya †8:461–7
    Yogācāra School of Buddhism
      †2:64–76
Luther, Martin 6:1–5, 8:249
  see also Lutheran Reformation;
    Lutheran theology
  Biel, G. 1:771
  consubstantiation 8:444
  educational contribution 3:225–6

Erasmus, D. debate 3:397, 8:501
ethics 6:2–3
Eucharist 1:133
faith 9:326, 9:328–9
friendship 3:795
grace 4:148
hermeneutics
    biblical 4:391, 6:3
justification 5:165, 5:166–7, 5:168
    by faith 6:1, 6:2
law 6:2–3
love 9:330
political obedience 7:510
reprobation 8:274, 8:275
revelation 6:3
sacraments 8:445
sanctification 8:456–7, 8:458
theology of humility 6:1–2
virtues
    theological 9:331
Lutheran Reformation 8:301
Lutheran theology
    forensic justification
        (Melanchthon, P.) 6:289
Lutosławski, Wincenty 7:486, 7:488
Lutz, C. 6:563
Lutz-Bachmann, Matthias
    religion, critique of †8:236–8
    theology, political †9:331–3
Lu-Wang Learning 2:325
    see also xinxue
Luxemburg, Rosa **6:5–7**
Luxemburg, W.A.J. 1:214, 1:215
Luzzatto, S.D. 5:97, 5:100

Lvóv-Warsaw School 5:293, 7:486,
    9:507, 9:508
Lyas, Colin
    art
        art criticism †1:460–3
        artist's intention 1:516
        understanding of †1:472–6
Lycan, William G.
    computational theories of mind
        6:394
    consciousness 2:427, 2:585, 2:595
    Dennett, D.C. †2:882–4
    eliminativism 3:265–6
    holism: mental and semantic 4:493
    introspection, psychology of 4:846
    language of thought hypothesis
        5:407
    reductionism, philosophy of mind
        8:153
    theoretical/epistemic virtues
        †9:340–3
Lyceum
    see also Theophrastus
    Aristotle 1:263, 1:415
    Strato 9:161
Lycia
    Diogenes of Oenoanda **3:89–90**
Lyell, C.
    geology, philosophy of 4:28
    uniformitarianism 4:25–7
Lyman, J.R. 3:458
Lynch, H.R. 7:194
Lynch, J.E. 9:639
Lynn, Richard John
    Yijing †**9:828–31**

Lyons, B. 7:834, 9:705
Lyons, D. 1:725, 3:285, 6:375, 9:556–7
Lyons, J. 8:482, 9:181
Lyons, William
    consciousness 2:595
    introspection 4:842, 4:846
    morality and emotions 6:563
    Ryle, G. †8:428–32
    unconscious mental states 9:526
Lyotard, Jean-François **6:7–6:12**
    African Francophone philosophy
        1:116
    alterity and identity
        postmodern theories of 1:187,
            1:191
    anti-postmodernism 7:596
    environmental ethics 3:334–5
    postmodernism 7:590
        political philosophy 7:592
        post-structuralism distinction
            9:200–1
    post-structuralism
        postmodernism distinction
            9:200–1
    post-structuralism
        in the social sciences 7:600,
            7:602–4, 7:603, 7:604
    social science
        contemporary philosophy of
            postmodernism 8:844,
                8:845–6, 8:847
    social theory and law 8:877, 8:879
    the sublime 9:205

M

Maassen, H. 9:719
Mabbott, J.D. 7:682, 8:140
Mac Lane, S. 2:236, 2:238–9
Macadam, Jim
  Prichard, H.A. †7:679–82
McAlister, L.L. 2:17
McAllester, M. 1:624
McAllister, J. 1:509
Macaulay, C. 9:791
Macaulay, T. 1:632
McAuliffe, J.D. 8:115
McAuliffe, P. 5:616
McBarnet, D. 5:520
McBride, W.L. 3:502
McCall, S. 5:693, 6:83, 7:498
MacCallum, G.C. 3:755, 3:757, 9:122
McCann, H. 4:816
McCann, H.J. 2:700, 7:89
McCarthy, J. 2:452, 2:453
McCarthy, P. 2:196
McCarthy, T.
  constructivism in ethics 2:632
  Habermas, J. 4:199–200
  hope 4:510
  postmodernism and political
    philosophy 7:592
  practical reason and ethics 7:619
  systems theory in social science
    9:256
McCarthy, Timothy
  logical constants †5:775–81
McCartney, J. 6:314
McCarty, C.
  Church's thesis 2:355
McCarty, David Charles
  combinatory logic †2:431–4
  constructivism in mathematics
    †2:632–9
  intuitionism †4:846–53
  lambda calculus †5:345–50
McClain, J. 5:577
McClary, S. 6:614
McClellan, J.E. 7:577
McClelland, J.L. 2:578, 2:579, 5:487
McClennen, E. 3:210, 8:97, 8:103
McClintock, Anne 7:579, 7:582
MacClintock, S. 5:109
McCloskey, D. 3:220–1, 7:561
McCloskey, H.J. 8:330

McCole, J. 4:511–12
McConica, J.K. 3:401
McConnell, A. 3:327
McConnell, F.J. 1:853
McConnell, T. 8:141
McConnell-Ginet, Sally
  language and gender †5:361–8
  semantics 8:652
McCool, G. 8:39, 9:387
McCormack, B. 1:655
MacCormack, G. 5:141, 5:454
MacCormack, G.D. 7:94, 8:365
McCormack, J. 8:470
McCormick, J. 8:545
MacCormick, Neil
  Critical Legal Studies 2:720
  Frank, J. †3:725–6
  Hart, H.L.A. †4:234–6
  Hohfeld, W.N. †4:476–7
  law †5:464–8
    legal concepts 5:495
    legal discourse 5:499
    legal positivism 5:520–1
    legal reasoning and
      interpretation †5:525–31
  Llewellyn, K.N. †5:661–2
  neo-institutionalism 4:801–2
  Pothier, R.J. †7:608–9
  Pound, R. †7:609–10
  promising 7:742
  Renner, K. †8:267–8
  rights 8:330
  Savigny, F.K. von †8:482–3
  Stair, J.D. 9:119
  Villey, M. †9:614–15
  Weinberger, O. †9:701–2
  Wróblewski, J. 9:798
McCormick, R.A. 4:798
McCormmach, R. 4:402, 7:482
MacCorquodale, K. 7:134, 7:135,
  8:801–2
McCosh, J.
  Alison, A. 1:187
  Brown, T. 2:29
  Common Sense School 2:448
  Gerard, A. 4:37
  Stewart, D. 9:139
McCown, J. 6:93
McCoy, D. 1:206

McCoy, E.D. 3:205
McCracken, Charles J.
  Collier, A. 2:411
  Fardella, M. 3:560
  Johnson, S. †5:124–6
  Malebranche, N. 6:66
  Norris, J. 7:43
McCulloch, Gregory 8:479
McCulloch, J. 3:554
McCulloch, W.S. 1:486, 6:813
McCulloch-Pitts neurones 1:486
McDannell, C. 4:251–2, 4:253
McDermott, J.P. 5:218
MacDonald, C. 3:793–4
MacDonald, D. 3:793–4
Macdonald, D.B. 4:68, 5:31
Macdonald, Graham
  Ayer, A.J. †1:614–19
MacDonald, L. 4:184
MacDonald, Scott
  Aquinas, T. 1:348
  epistemology 3:382
  Grosseteste, Robert †4:177–83
  illumination †4:698–700
  medieval philosophy †6:269–77
  natural theology †6:707–13
  perfect goodness 4:143–4
  Philip the Chancellor †7:355–7
  William of Auxerre †9:727–9
Macdonell, Sir J. 5:101
MacDowell, D. 8:806
McDowell, John
  analytic ethics 1:222, 1:223
  antirealism
    mathematics 1:311
  criteria 2:713
  de re belief 2:817
  Evans, G. †3:459–61
  intuitionist logic 4:862
  justice
    equity and law 5:152
  language
    communal 5:416–17, 5:419
  meaning
    and rule-following
      sceptical paradox 6:216–17,
      6:219
    and truth 6:225
  moral judgment 6:512, 6:514

moral particularism 6:529
moral realism 6:538
non-conceptual content 2:643
objectivity 7:75
other minds 7:173
perception 7:299
persons 7:321
quietism 6:218
theory and practice 9:358
universalism in ethics 9:539
value
  ontological status of 9:581
virtue ethics 9:625
Wittgenstein, L. 9:770
Wittgensteinian ethics 9:772
Macedo, S. 2:365, 3:239
Macedon
  Aristotle **1:413–35**
Macer, D.R.J. 4:19
McEvoy, J. 4:182, 7:438–9
McEvoy, J.G. 7:684
McEwan, J. 7:91
Macey, D. 3:713
McFague, S. 3:624, 7:107, 8:259
McFarlane, J. 6:449
MacFarlane, L.J. 1:32
McFee, Graham
  dance
    aesthetics of †2:774–7
    performing art 1:472
McGary, H. 1:94, 8:806
McGary, Howard 8:141
McGee, Vann
  inductive definitions and proofs
    †4:752–5
  semantic paradoxes and theories
    of truth †8:642–8
McGhee, P. 4:567
MacGillivray, C. 2:374
McGinn, Bernard 5:5, 5:104, 6:628,
  6:633
McGinn, Colin
  charity principle 2:285
  consciousness 2:595
  dualism 3:138
  Dummett, M.A.E. 3:153
  materialism 6:177
  meaning and rule-following 6:219
  methodological individualism
    6:344
  mind, philosophy of 6:407
  Nagel, T. 6:647
  other minds 7:173
  phenomenal consciousness 2:585
  primary-secondary distinction
    7:687
  secondary qualities †8:595–9

value
  ontological status of 9:581
McGinn, Marie
  criteria †2:711–14
  Wittgenstein, L. 9:770
McGovern, A.F. 5:616
McGrade, A.S.
  Hooker, R. †4:504–7
  Marsilius of Padua †6:112–14
  William of Ockham 9:748
  Wodeham, A. 9:776
McGrath, A.E.
  Biel, G. 1:772
  Christology 4:732
  justification doctrine 5:168
  Luther, M. 6:5
  Melanchthon, P. 6:292
  salvation 8:451
  Thielicke, H. 9:371
  Trinity 9:461
McGuinness, A.F. 4:501
McGuinness, B. 3:153, 8:543–4, 9:770
Mach, Ernst **6:13–16**
  antimetaphysical analysis of
    science (Neurath, O.) 6:814
  Avenarius, R. 1:594
  economy of thought 6:14
  general relativity 4:9
  Hempel, C.G. 4:352
  logical positivism 5:790–1
  mechanics, classical 6:259
  neutral monism 6:13, 6:14–16,
    6:816, 6:817
  Planck, M.K.E.L. 7:396–7, 7:398
  relativity theory
    philosophical significance of
      8:197–8, 8:199
  science
    nineteenth century philosophy
      of 8:566, 8:568, 8:569–70,
      8:571
    scientific methodology 6:13,
      6:14
    unity of 9:531
  sensory atomism
    Gestalt psychology 4:52, 4:54
  space 9:65
Mácha, Karel 2:769
MacHale, D. 5:728
Machamer, P. 3:841
Machan, T.R. 4:229
Machiavelli, Niccolò **6:17–22**
  deception 9:483
  Gramsci, A. 4:154
  political philosophy
    history of 7:510, 7:517
  rational choice theory 8:64, 8:65

republicanism 6:17, 6:19–21, 8:283
social science
  history of philosophy of 8:850,
    8:858
truthfulness 9:485
virtù 6:17, 6:18–19
Machina, M. 2:835, 8:103
machines
  mentality of
    Turing test 9:494–5
Machlup, F. 3:221
Machover, Moshé
  nonstandard analysis †1:211–16
  numbers 7:53
Mach's principle
  relativity theory 8:197–8
McIlwain, C.H. 2:622
McInerney, P. 9:416
McInerny, Ralph
  Aquinas, T. 1:348
  Garrigou-Lagrange, R. †3:846–8
  Maritain, J. †6:101–5
  Silvestri, F. 8:777
  Thomism 9:388
McIntire, C.T. 3:114
MacIntosh, J.J. 3:429
McIntosh, R.P. 3:205
MacIntyre, A. 6:191
McIntyre, A. 9:526
MacIntyre, Alasdair C. **6:22–4**
  analytic ethics 1:222
  architecture
    aesthetics of 1:366
  community and
    communitarianism 2:471
  critiques of 6:23–4
  desert and merit 3:27
  educational philosophy 3:239
  history
    philosophy of 4:457, 4:458
  honour 4:504
  human nature 4:524, 4:525
  Kantian ethics 5:203
  modernity
    moral pluralism 6:529, 6:531
  moral philosophy
    history of 6:23
  moral relativism 6:542
  morality and religion 8:223
  nation and nationalism 6:661
  Neo-Thomism 9:385, 9:387
  practical reason and ethics 7:619
  religion and morality 8:224
  Sidgwick, H. 8:763
  social sciences
    prediction in 8:872

virtue ethics 6:22, 6:23, 9:624, 9:625
virtues and vices 9:631
MacIntyre, Alasdair C. C.
  justice
    equity and law 5:152–3
MacIntyre, Alasdair C. C. C.
  narrative 6:657
McIntyre, J. 1:296, 1:541
McIntyre, L. 8:868, 8:870–1
McIntyre, R. 4:587
Mack, Peter
  Agricola, R. †1:123–6
  logic
    Renaissance 5:772
  Melanchthon, P. †6:288–92
  Ramus, P. †8:51–5
  Valla, L. 9:573
MacKay, D.M. 4:786, 8:296, 9:109
Mackay, J.H. 9:141
Mckay, N.Y. 7:582
McKay, Thomas J.
  modal logic †6:426–33
Macken, R. 2:886, 4:360
McKenna, Antony
  clandestine literature †2:374–6
  Huet, P.-D. 4:518
  Pascal, B. 7:246
  Port-Royal †7:550–5
Mackenzie, C. 5:479
MacKenzie, J.M. 7:582
Mackenzie, M.M. 7:234
McKeon, C.G. 7:809
McKeon, R. 8:309
Mackey, G. 7:886
Mackey, L. 5:243
Mackey, M.C. 8:59
Mackie, John L.
  Anderson, J. 1:269
  atheism 1:534
  Australia, philosophy in 1:583
  causation 2:249, 2:250
  contingency 2:652
  duty 3:182
  evil, problem of 3:472
  fact/value distinction 3:537, 3:538
  Hume, D. 4:561
  Mill, J.S. 6:375
  moral knowledge 6:520
  moral realism critique 6:538
  moral relativism 6:542
  moral scepticism 6:545
  morality and ethics 6:570
  natural theology 6:713
  naturalism in ethics 6:717
  realism/antirealism 8:119
  religion and epistemology 8:218

religious experience 8:255
testimony 9:314
value
  ontological status of 9:580, 9:581
  Wollaston, W. 9:788
Mackie, Penelope
  existence †3:490–2
McKim, D.K. 2:182
McKinney, H. 9:679
McKinnon, A. 6:416
MacKinnon, Catharine
  Critical Legal Studies 2:720
  feminist jurisprudence 3:608, 3:610
  freedom of speech 3:764
  linguistic discrimination 5:644
  morality
    emotions 6:562, 8:611–6563
  pornography 7:543, 7:544, 7:545
  sexuality 8:728
MacKinnon, D.M. 2:700
MacKinnon, Edward
  Hanson, N.R. †4:224–6
MacKinnon, F.I. 7:43
MacKinnon, K.A.B. 9:504
McKinsey, J.C.C. 4:720, 9:353
McKirahan, Richard D.
  Anaximander †1:255–9
  Anaximenes †1:259–62
  archē †1:359–61
  Democritus 2:877–8
  Heraclitus 4:369
  physis and nomos debate 7:382
  Presocratics 7:672
  Thales †9:322–4
McKitterick, R. 2:223
McKusick, J.C. 2:406
McKusick, K.B. 2:577
McLachlan, H. 8:891
McLarty, Colin
  category theory †2:237–9
  foundations of mathematics †2:233–7
McLaughlin, Brian P.
  anomalous monism †1:276–80
  connectionism †2:570–9
  Davidson, D. 2:806
  mental causation 6:311
  perception †7:293–9
  radical translation and radical interpretation 8:35
  self-deception 8:628
  semantics
    informational †8:658–62
Maclean, A. 6:511
MacLean, D. 8:334, 8:337, 8:338
McLean, G. 3:613

Maclean, I. 3:583, 5:510
MacLean, I. 8:290
Maclean, Ian
  libertins †5:619–22
  moralistes †6:555–8
  Pascal, B. †7:241–7
McLellan, D. 4:415, 8:886, 9:701
McLelland, J.L. 7:829
McLeod, Grant
  Gaius †3:831–2
  Justinian †5:168–9
McMahon, C. 1:586
McMorran, C.I. 9:682
McMullen, J. 5:322
McMullen, T. 1:269
McMullin, Ernan
  Bell's theorem 1:716
  Copernicus, N. †2:671–2
  cosmology †2:677–81
  creation and conservation
    religious doctrine of 2:700
  Galilei, G. †3:835–41
  Kepler, J. †5:231–3
  matter 6:196
  quantum mechanics 7:894
McNair, T.
  Tucker, A. †9:490–3
McNally, R.T. 2:272
McNaughton, David
  consequentialism †2:603–6
  deontological ethics †2:890–2
  Ross, W.D. †8:365–7
  Shaftesbury, Third Earl of †8:730–2
McNay, D. 3:713
McNeill, J.T. 2:182
McNeley, J.K. 6:670–1
McNulty, G.F. 9:264
Macomber, J. 2:395
Maconi, H. 1:354
McPeck, J. 3:234, 3:239
Macpherson, C.B. 7:177, 7:761
McPherson, Michael
  economics and ethics †3:205–11
  economics, philosophy of 3:220
Macquarrie, J. 3:502, 3:505
MacQueen, G. 6:181
McRae, John R.
  Platform Sutra †7:398–9
  Zhi Dun †9:859
McRae, R. 9:533
McRobbie, M.A 8:204
Macrobius 3:305–6, 7:433, 7:438
McSorely, H.J. 6:5
McTaggart, John McTaggart Ellis
  6:24–8
  the Absolute 1:28, 1:29, 4:668

Broad, C.D. 2:26
change 2:275–6
correspondence theory of truth
  9:475
Hegel, G.W.F. 4:279
Hegelianism 4:289
time
  unreality of 9:413, 9:416
McTighe, T. 6:838
McVeigh, S. 5:499, 5:509–10
Macy, J. 7:771
Madame de Staël see Staël-Holstein,
  Anne Louise Germaine, Mme de
Madan, F. 3:109
Madariaga, I. de 5:609
Madaura
  Apuleius 1:325–6
Madden, Edward H.
  Common Sense School †2:446–8
  Ducasse, C.J. †3:138–42
  evil 3:466
  natural laws 5:474
  Stewart, D. †9:135–40
Madden, T.E. 2:250
Maddi, S.R. 7:829
Maddison, R.E.W. 1:857
Maddy, P. 6:188, 6:191, 8:709
Madelung, Wilferd 5:31, 9:507
Mader, J. 4:301
Mader, W. 8:509
Mādhava 6:28–31
  Hindu schools 4:437
  Indian and Tibetan philosophy
    4:738
Madhva 6:31–3
  Brahman 4:438
  God
    concepts of 9:592
  Indian and Tibetan philosophy
    4:738
  mysticism 6:622
Mādhvaism see Madhva
Mādhyamika (Madhyamaka) School
  of Buddhism 2:58–64
  see also Prāsaṅgika; Svātantrika
  causation
    Indian theories of 2:256
  dependent origination
    (Nāgārjuna) 9:217
  emptiness 2:78–9
  'free from extremes' 9:404–5
  illusion 3:410
  Indian philosophy –4:738
  karma and rebirth 5:214
  Nāgārjuna 6:638–40, 9:217
  nirvāṇa 7:11

Prāsaṅgika/Svātantrika distinction
  9:403–4
Sengzhao 8:683–4
Tibetan philosophy 4:738, 9:402–5
  Mi bskyod rdo rje 6:351–2
Yogācāra Buddhism
  China 9:792
  Korea 2:109
Madigan, T. 4:532
Madile, J.A. 7:349
al-Madina al-fadila (The Virtuous
  City) see (al-)Farabi
Madison, G. 6:325
Madison, G.B. 8:322
Madison, James
  American philosophy
    eighteenth and nineteenth
      century 1:202, 1:206
  Church disestablishment 8:227
  democracy 2:868, 2:872
  federalism and confederalism
    3:574
  religion and political philosophy
    8:229
Madkour, I.
  Islamic philosophy
    Greek philosophy influence on
      4:159
    logic 5:712
madness see mental illness
Madrid, School of 9:73–4
Maes, P. 1:492
Magee, B. 7:153, 7:539, 8:432
Magee, J. 1:812
Magendie, François 9:640, 9:643
magic
  see also alchemy; mysticism;
    occultism; witchcraft
  Bruno, G. 2:35–6
  empiricist notion of (William of
    Auvergne) 9:726–7
  Hermetism 4:396–7
  Kabbalah 5:171
  language
    Renaissance philosophy of
      5:413, 5:415
  legal concepts
    (Hägerström, A.A.T.) 4:203
  opposition to (Oresme, N.)
    7:155–6
  psychic health (Ficino, M.) 3:655
  religion distinction 7:355
  Renaissance 8:265
  verbal (Agrippa von
    Nettesheim, H.C.) 1:131
Magidor, M. 7:34
Maginot, N. 2:886–7

Magnin, F. 2:505
magnitude
  existence relation (Zeno of Elea)
    9:846–7
  infinite (Anaxagoras) 1:250, 1:251
Mah, H. 1:667
Mahābhārata
  see also Bhagavad Gītā
  fatalism 3:565–7, 3:568
  karma and rebirth 5:212
  Nyāya-Vaiśeṣika 7:59
  Sāṅkhya 8:462
Mahadevan, T.M.P.
  Mādhava 6:30
  Ramakrishna Movement 8:42
  Vedānta
    Neo-Vedānta movement 9:593,
      9:594
Mahan, A. 2:448
Mahar, C. 1:850
Mahāvīra 6:33–5
  Jainism
    Indian and Tibetan philosophy
      4:738
  manifoldness, Jaina theory of 6:77,
    6:78
Mahāyāna School of Buddhism
  see also Mādhyamika
    (Madhyamaka) School of
    Buddhism; Pure Land Buddhism;
    Yogācāra
  Awakening of Faith in Mahāyāna
    1:603–4
  China (Fazang) 3:569
  India
    nirvāṇa 7:10–11
    reincarnation 8:184
    salvation 8:448–9
    virtue 3:186
  Japan 2:99
    art 1:80, 1:85
    emptiness 6:592
    Shōtoku Constitution
      influenced by 8:753
    Tominaga Nakamoto 9:440
Mahdi, M.
  Ibn Khaldun 4:626
  Islamic philosophy
    Aristotelianism 1:386
    logic 5:712–13
    meaning 6:239
    political 7:520–1
Maher, Patrick
  inductive inference †4:755–9
  statistics 9:126
Mahler, Margaret S. 7:820, 7:823

Mahoney, Edward P.
  Cajetan †2:171–5
  James of Viterbo †5:58–60
  John of Jandun †5:106–9
  Nifo, A. †6:867–72
  Renaissance Aristotelianism
    †1:404–13
  Vernia, N. †9:596–9
Mahoney, J. 8:799
Mahoney, T.S. 1:636
Maia Neto, J. 8:746
Maidenbaum, A. 5:135
Maienschein, J. 9:643
Maier, A.
  Blasius of Parma 1:787
  Burley, W. 2:143
  Henry of Harclay 4:363
  natural philosophy
    medieval 6:706
  Oxford Calculators 7:183
Maier, H. 9:18, 9:332
Maierù, A.
  language
    medieval theories of 5:404
  logic
    medieval 5:758
  Wodeham, A. 9:776
Maigron, L. 3:693
Mailloux, S. 5:510
Maimon, Abraham ben Moses see
    Maimonides, Abraham ben
    Moses
Maimon, Moses ben see
    Maimonides, Moses
Maimon, Salomon 6:35–8
  German idealism 4:42, 4:44
  Jewish Enlightenment 3:321
  Jewish philosophy 5:90
Maimonidean controversy
  philosophical study
    (Nahmanides, M.) 6:648
Maimonides, Abraham ben Moses
  6:38–40
  Jewish philosophy 5:88
  Sufism
    Kabbalah 5:175
Maimonides, Moses 6:40–9
  see also Maimonism
  Abravanel, I. 1:19, 1:20, 1:21
  Albo, J. 1:152, 1:153
  anthropomorphism
    of God 6:42–3, 6:46
  Aristotelianism
    Crescas, H. critique 2:701
  Averroism
    Jewish 1:599–600

bioethics
  Jewish 1:777
creation
  eternity of the world
    (Gersonides) 4:48, 4:49
  critiques of
    Crescas, H. 2:701
    Delmedigo, E. 2:861
Dalalat al-ha'irin (Guide to the
    Perplexed) 6:41, 6:42–4
  anthropomorphism 6:42–3, 6:46
  creation
    eternity of the world 6:41,
      6:44–5
  God
    human relationship 6:45,
      6:47
  Jewish philosophy 5:88
  nature 6:45–6
  translation to Latin 5:23
divine simplicity 8:787
dogma
  Judaism (Duran, S.) 3:171–2
Duran, P. commentary 3:170–1
eternity of the world 2:697, 6:41,
  6:44–5
God
  human relationship 6:45, 6:47
halakhah 4:206
Ibn Daud, A. 4:608–9, 4:610–11
influence of (Nahmanides, M.)
  6:648, 6:649–50
influenced by (Ibn Paquda) 4:633
Jewish philosophy 5:88
Karaism 5:208
natural philosophy 6:693, 6:699,
  6:700, 6:705
natural providence
  Nahmanides, M. comparison
    6:649
nature
  God's governance of 6:45–6
negative theology 6:760
omnipotence 7:102
prophecy 7:767, 7:768–9, 7:771
religious language 8:248
resurrection 8:294
Shem Tov family 8:737–9
Maimonides, O.
  Maimonides, A. 6:40
Maimonism
  allegorical exegesis (Arama, I.)
    1:350
Maine de Biran, Pierre-François
  6:49–53
  introspection 6:49, 6:51–2

Maine, H.S. 5:138, 5:139–40, 5:141,
  5:153
Mainkar, T.G. 8:467
Maio, M.C. di 2:535
Maiocchi, R. 3:147
Maioli, B. 4:72
Maiorca, B. 1:792
Mair, John see Major, John
Mairan, Dortous de 3:132
Mairena, Juan de 9:72, 9:76
Maisonneuve, John 1:402
Maistre, Comte Joseph de 2:608,
  2:610–11, 2:614
Maitra, S.K. 1:569, 3:187
Maitreya 2:65
Maitzen, Stephen
  Tennant, F.R. †9:301–3
Majer, Ulrich
  Cantor, G. †2:196–9
  Kronecker, L. †5:311–13
Major, John 6:54–6, 7:511–12
Major, J.S. 4:514, 7:863
major term
  glossary 5:805
majoritarianism
  see also democracy
  law and morality 5:441
  republicanism 8:281–2
Mäki, U. 3:221
Makin, Stephen
  atomism, ancient 1:535
  Democritus 2:877
  Megarian school 6:280
  Zeno of Elea †9:843–5
Makinson, D.C. 7:34, 7:214
Makkreel, Rodolf
  Dilthey, W. †3:77–83
Makkreel, Rudolf
  social science
    history of philosophy of 8:858
Malachowski, A. 8:355–6
malakut (invisible world)
  al-Ghazali 4:66
Malament, D. 8:171, 8:199, 9:69,
  9:418
Malantschuk, G. 5:243–4
Malbreil, G. 4:61, 4:518
Malcolm, Norman
  animal language and thought
    1:270–1, 1:273
  Anselm of Canterbury 1:296
  Augustine 1:559
  criteria 2:711–12, 2:713
  dreaming 3:128, 3:129
  God
    ontological argument for the
      existence of 8:242, 8:247

moral agents 6:504
natural theology 6:713
private language argument 7:698
Malcolm X 5:17
Malcomber, J. 2:391–2
Malebranche, Nicolas **6:56–6**
    Arnauld, A. 1:444, 1:445–7, 1:448,
        7:553, 7:554
    Bayle, P. 1:674–5, 1:677
    Berkeley, G. 1:739, 1:742
    critique of (Foucher, S.) 3:715,
        3:717
    Descartes, R. 3:16
    Fénelon, F. 3:629, 3:630
    free will 6:63
    Gerdil, G.S. 4:41
    God
        vision in 6:56, 6:58–61
    ideas
        Desgabets, R. 3:28
        Leibniz, G.W. 5:552
    Norris, J. 7:41–2
    occasionalism 6:56, 6:61–3, 7:87–8,
        7:89
    rationalism 8:80
    theodicy 1:674–5, 6:56–7, 6:63–4
malfunction
    shift to practical-theoretical
        (Heidegger, M.) 4:324
Malherbe, A.J. 2:759
Malherbe, Michel 4:561
Malia, M. 4:410
Malik, H. 8:735
Malino, J.W.
    Jewish philosophy, contemporary
        †5:90–6
Malinovskii, Aleksandr
    Aleksandrovich *see* Bogdanov,
        Aleksandr Aleksandrovich
Malinowski, B. 3:813, 3:814, 3:818,
    7:632
Malinowski, G. 5:863
Malkhos *see* Porphyry
Mallard, W. 9:804
Mallea, Eduardo 5:655, 5:656–7
Mallet, M. 2:901
Mallin, S. 6:325
Malliṣeṇa 6:81
Malloy, R.P. 8:822
Maloney, J. 5:407
Malotki, E. 6:670
Malter, H. 4:617, 8:440
Malthus, Thomas 7:540
Maltsev, A.I. 4:117, 5:737
Malvezin, T. 6:489

Mamardashvili, Merab
    Konstantinovich **6:66–71**
    Marxist philosophy, Russian and
        Soviet 6:159
Mamura, M.E. 4:654
Man is God
    Tonghak 9:441–2
manas (mind)
    Nyāya 3:860
    sense perception
        Indian philosophy 8:690
Mānavadharmaśāstra
    duty and virtue
        Indian conceptions of 3:187
Manchester, P. 6:107
Mancini, G. 9:573
Mandaeism 4:84
Maṇḍana Miśra 5:382, 5:384
Mandelbaum, M.
    Mach, E. 6:16
    science, nineteenth century
        philosophy of 8:571
    social laws 4:485, 4:488
    social science
        history of philosophy of 8:858
Mandelker, A. 1:645
Mander, W. 1:862
Mandeville, Bernard **6:71–4**
    critiques of
        Hutcheson, F. 4:589–90, 4:593
    egoism and altruism 3:248
    political philosophy
        history of 7:513
    rational choice theory 8:65–6
    virtues and vices 9:631
Mandonnet, P. 1:598, 3:174, 8:768
Manekin, C. 1:154, 4:51
Manes *see* Mani
Mangan, J. 3:122
Mani 6:74, 6:75–6
Manicas, Peter T.
    critical realism 2:722
    social science
        history of philosophy of
        †8:847–59
Manichaeus *see* Mani
Manicheism **6:74–7**
    Augustine 1:541, 1:543, 1:544,
        1:551, 7:259
    Gnosticism 4:84
    virtues and vices 9:630
manifestation
    matter
        Sāṅkhya-Yoga dualism
        6:199–200

manifoldness (*anekāntavāda*)
    Jaina theory of **6:77–81**
        seven standpoints 6:78–81
        syāt 6:78
Māṇikyanandīn 5:56
Mann, N. 7:329
Mann, T. 8:529
Mann, William E.
    Damian, P. †2:772–4
    David of Dinant †2:799–800
    divine simplicity 8:787
    immutability 4:714
    theological virtues †9:326–31
    Vital du Four †9:638–9
manner adverbials 1:46–9
Mannheim, Karl
    anti-positivism
        Latin America 1:306–7
    constructivism 2:625
    ideology 4:682–3, 4:685
    utopianism 9:558, 9:561
Manninen, J. 4:488
Manning, D. 5:605
Manning, Richard N.
    functional explanation †3:802–5
Mannoni, O. 3:553, 3:554
Manns, James W.
    Buffier, C. †2:118–20
    Common Sense School 2:448
Manschreck, C.L. 6:292
Mansel, H.L. 2:814, 4:219
Manser, A. 1:862
Mansfeld, J.
    Anaxagoras 1:254
    ancient philosophy 1:265
    Diogenes Laertius 3:87
    doxography 3:126
    Philo of Alexandria 7:361
Mansfield, B. 3:401
Manson, E. 5:101
Mansur, John *see* John of Damascus
Mantinus, Jacob 5:23–4
al-Mantiqi (the Logician) *see*
    (al-)Sijistani
mantras
    linguistic power of 7:607
Manuel, F.E. 3:319, 4:532, 8:447,
    9:561
Manuscrito (Journal)
    analytical philosophy in Latin
        America 1:233
many-valued logics **6:81–4**, **6:84–91**
    evaluation 6:87, 6:88–90
    frameworks 6:86
    intuitionistic 6:89–90
    Kleene matrices 6:85
    Łukasiewicz, J. 5:861–2

narrow/broad sense distinction
    6:86–7
non-tabular 6:87–8
valuation 6:87, 6:88–90
Mao Zedong
    humanism 6:134, 6:138–9
    knowledge 6:136–7
    Marxism
        Chinese 2:326, 6:140–1
    permanent revolution 6:135–6
Maoism see Mao Zedong; Marxism,
    Chinese
Maqasid al-falasifah (The Intentions
    of the Philosophers) see
        (al-)Ghazali, Abu Hamid
al-Maqtul see (al-)Suhrawardi
Maraldo, John C.
    Japanese Buddhism †2:99–2:106
    Kyoto School 5:329
    Nishida Kitarō †7:13–16
Marbach, E. 4:586, 4:587
Marburg School of Neo-Kantianism
    2:398, 6:776–7, 6:781–4
Marc, A. 2:175
Marcel, Gabriel 6:91–3
    ethics
        existentialist 3:505
    hope 4:508–9, 4:510
    phenomenology
        existentialist 7:338
Marcel, R. 3:659
March, J.G. 8:847
Marchant, J. 9:679
Marchi, N. de 3:221
Marcil-Lacoste, L. 2:120
Marcovich, M. 4:369
Marcucci, S. 9:711
Marcus Aurelius 1:264, 6:93–5
Marcus Cornelius Fronto 6:94
Marcus, L.
    Benjamin, W. 1:718
Marcus, Ruth Barcan
    Kripke, S.A. 5:304
    ontological commitment 7:116
    possible worlds semantics 8:665–6,
        8:668
    proper names 7:757
    reference 8:164
    substitutional/objectual
        quantifiers 7:881
Marcuse, Herbert 6:95–9
    critical theory 2:722–8
    Frankfurt School 3:731, 3:737
    Hegelianism 4:291–2
    Marxism
        Western 6:144, 6:146
    technology and ethics 9:283

toleration 9:433
totalitarianism 9:444
Marc-Wogau, Konrad 4:204, 8:485,
    8:491
Maréchal, Joseph
    Aquinas, T. 8:36
    mysticism, nature of 6:633
    Rahner, K. 8:39
    Transcendental Thomism 9:381
Marek, W. 7:498
Marenbon, John
    Boethius, A.M.S. 1:812
    Carolingian renaissance †2:220–3
    Chartres school †2:290–2
    Duns Scotus, J. 3:169
    Eriugena, J.S. 3:405
    Gerbert of Aurillac 4:41
    Islamic philosophy, transmission
        into Western Europe 5:25
    medieval philosophy 6:277
    Thierry of Chartres †9:371–3
    William of Conches †9:730–1
Marfatia, M.I. 9:575
Margain, H. 1:233
Margalit, A. 1:753, 5:95, 6:661
Margalit, E. 1:753
marginal philosophy 6:99, 6:100–1
marginality 6:99–101
    Latin America 5:610, 5:611
Margolin, J.-C. 2:204
Margoliouth, D.S. 5:713
Margolis, E. 2:516
Margolis, Joseph
    structuralism in literary theory
        †9:181–4
Margulis, L. 5:635
Marheinecke, P.K. 4:297
Marías, Julián 9:76
Mariátegui, José Carlos 5:428, 6:161,
    6:162–4
Marin, L. 7:246
Marinov, M.S. 2:578
Marion, Jean-Luc 3:19, 7:585–6
Maritain, Jacques 6:101–5, 8:249
    aesthetics 6:103
    Aquinas, T. 1:348
    connatural knowledge 6:687
    educational philosophy 3:230
    Garrigou-Lagrange, R. 3:848
    John of St Thomas 5:120
    metaphysics 6:103
    moral philosophy 6:103
    mysticism 6:630, 6:633
    natural law 8:228
    negative theology 6:762
    Neo-Thomism 9:381, 9:385, 9:387
    science 6:103

Universal Declaration of Human
    Rights 6:103–4
Maritain, Raissa 6:101–2, 6:104
Marius Victorinus 6:105–7
    logic 5:747
    patristic philosophy 7:259
    Porphyry 1:805
Mark, T. 6:614
Mark, Thomas Carson 1:470, 1:472
market
    anarchism 1:246
    contract
        critical social theory 9:358
    dominance of
        impact on society
            Marxist philosophy of
                science 6:149–50
    ethics of the 3:213, 6:107–10
        business 2:150, 2:153
        Coase Theorem 5:455–7
        community 6:109–10
        efficiency 6:107–8
        justice 6:108–9
        responsibility 8:292
    journalism ethics 5:126
    libertarianism 5:618
    socialism 8:881–3, 8:884–5
    tradition 9:446
market economy
    governmental role (Smith, A.)
        8:820
    liberty of labour (Smith, A.) 8:820
    self-interest (Smith, A.) 8:815
    work
        philosophy of 9:795
market socialism 8:881, 8:884–5
Markie, Peter J.
    Descartes, R. 3:19
    rationalism †8:75–80
    subjective certainty 2:267
Markov, A.A. 2:638
    see also Markov's principle
Marković, Franjo 9:54
Marković, Mihailo 9:54–5
Marković, Svetozar 9:50
Markov's principle 2:634
Marks, C.E.
    split brains †9:107–10
Marks, E. 3:596, 5:308, 5:479
Marks, J. 3:33
Márkus, György 4:571
Markus, R.A. 1:559, 6:107, 7:69
Marler, P. 4:797, 5:487
Marmo, C. 1:815–16, 2:23, 4:172,
    5:404
Marmura, M.E. 4:68, 5:713

Marpriest, Martin *see* Overton, Richard
Marquand, Allan 5:745
Marques Pereira, Nino 2:11–2:9
Marques, V.S. 3:639
Marquet, Y. 4:688
Marquis, J.-P. 2:236
Marr, David
  computational models of vision 9:634–6, 9:638
  methodological individualism 6:342, 6:344
  non-conceptual content 2:643
  perception 7:293
  psychology
    theories of 7:829
marriage
  contractarianism (Astell, M.) 1:527
  female modesty (Hume, D.) 4:554
  feminism (Suchon, G.) 9:212
  monogamy
    Latin America 5:431
  Rousseau, J.-J.
    feminist critique of 8:372–3
  sacramental nature of (Peter Lombard) 5:821
  sexuality 8:722–3
Marrone, Steven P.
  Duns Scotus, J. 3:169
  Henry of Ghent †4:354–60
  Matthew of Aquasparta 6:203
  William of Auvergne †9:725–7
Marrou, H. 1:564, 3:230, 3:309
Marsh, C. 1:838
Marsh, J. 1:206
Marshall, G. 8:365
Marshall, Graeme
  pleasure †7:447–51
Marshall, John
  Latitudinarianism †5:432–5
  Socinianism †8:889–92
Marshall, P. 2:759, 5:314
Marshall, R., Jr 8:803
Marshall, T.H. 2:363, 2:365
Marsilio Ficino 1:185
Marsilius of Inghen **6:110–12**
  'imaginable tense' 5:399
  obligations 5:757–6
Marsilius of Padua **6:112–14**, 8:849
  papal authority
    political authority conflict 8:226
  political philosophy
    history of 7:509
Marston, Roger **6:114–15**
Martensen, Hans L. 4:286, 4:299–300

Marti, Genoveva
  sense and reference †8:684–8
Martí, José 5:653, 5:654, 5:656–7, 7:568
Martí, Oscar R.
  analytical philosophy
    Latin America †1:229–34
  Mexican philosophy 6:348
  positivism
    Latin America †7:565–70
Martianus Capella 3:306, 5:747, 7:438
Martin, A. 3:298, 7:554
Martin, C. 2:143–4, 6:299
Martin, C.B. 1:583, 6:633, 8:255
Martin, C.J. 8:204
Martin, D.A. 3:696, 3:697, 8:709
Martin, J.-C. 2:860
Martín, J.I. 9:196
Martin, J.R. 3:239
Martin, M.
  atheism 1:534
  Hart, H.L.A. 4:236
  limits of law 5:464
  social science
    methodology of 8:868
    philosophy of 8:870–1
Martin, M.G.F.
  bodily sensations †1:792–5
  non-conceptual content 2:643
  perception †7:287–93
  self-deception 8:628
Martin, Mike W.
  engineering ethics 3:315
  self-deception, ethics of †8:629–32
Martin, M.L. 9:343
Martin, M.N. 7:575
Martin, M.W. 4:567
Martin, N.G. 8:235
Martin, Rex
  Rawls, J. 8:109
  rights †8:325–31
Martin, R.L. 6:83, 8:648
  see also Martin's axiom
Martin, R.M. 2:215, 2:814, 3:174
Martin, R.N.D. 3:147
Martin, S. 5:135
Martineau, Harriet **6:116–17**
Martineau, James 6:533
Martinet, M. 8:343
Martínez Estrada, Ezequiel 5:655, 5:657
Martinich, A.P.
  implicature 4:725
  language 5:411
  metaphor †6:335–8

  ordinary language philosophy †7:143–7
Trinity 9:461
Martin-Löf, P. 2:482, 4:853, 5:349
Martin's axiom 3:696
Martins, J.V. de Pina 1:27
Martins, M. 5:491
Martucelli, D. 8:20
Marty, Martin E.
  Niebuhr, H.R. †6:838–41
  Niebuhr, R. †6:841–4
Maruyama, Masao
  Confucianism, Japanese 2:555
  Japanese philosophy 5:79
  Motoori Norinaga 6:590
  Ogyū Sorai 7:91–2
Ibn-Marwan, Daud *see* (al-)Muqammas, Daud
Marx, J. 1:840
Marx, Karl **6:117–33**
  see also communism; Marxism; socialism
  alienation 1:179–81, 6:118, 6:121–2
    labour 9:795
    market ethics 6:109
  Althusser, L.P. 1:192, 1:193–4
  capitalism 6:118, 6:127–9, 6:131
  Chinese Marxism 6:141
  civil society 2:369, 2:371
  class consciousness (Lukács, G.) 5:857–8
  communism 2:462, 2:463–4, 6:118–19
  constructivism 2:625, 2:630
  cosmic eschatology 3:414, 3:417
  critique of (Popper, K.R.) 7:537
  Das Kapital (Capital)
    capitalism 6:118, 6:127–8
  dialectical materialism 3:53–7, 6:123
  economics 3:221, 6:127–8
  Engels, F. 3:309–13
  The German Ideology
    ideology 6:123–6
  Hegelianism 4:297
    Lukács, G. 5:856
  historical materialism 3:56, 6:126–7, 6:134
  history
    philosophy of 4:454–5, 4:458
  human nature 4:525
  humanism 4:528, 4:531
  ideology 4:681–2, 4:685, 6:123–6
    influence on educational theory 3:228, 3:230

influence of
  Adorno, T.W. 1:42–3
  Gentile, G. 4:20
  Mikhailovskii, N.K. 6:357
  Miki Kiyoshi
    Kyoto School 5:328
  Neurath, O. 6:814
justice 5:146
Kautsky, K.J. 5:222
morality 6:129–30
nature 4:161
Paris Manuscripts
  alienation 6:121–2
partiinost' 7:239, 7:241
philosophy
  critique of 6:122–3
political philosophy
  history of 7:516
privacy 7:692
processes 7:722
property 7:759
Proudhon, P.-J. 7:793
rational choice theory 8:74
religion 6:118, 6:121, 6:123
  cognitive malfunction 8:216
  critique of 8:217, 8:236, 8:237,
    8:238
  and epistemology 8:218
  ideology 8:228
republicanism 8:282
revolution 8:302–3, 8:304
self-realization 6:139
slavery 8:805, 8:806
social science
  contemporary philosophy of
    8:847
  history of philosophy of
    8:852–3, 8:858
socialism 6:118, 6:130–1, 8:879,
  8:883
spectrality (Derrida, J.) 2:900
technology and ethics 9:281, 9:283
theory and practice 9:358
utopianism 9:557, 9:559
Weber, M. comparison 9:697
work
  philosophy of 9:797
Young Hegelians 6:120–1
Marx, M.W. 4:225
Marx, W. 8:520
Marxism
see also communism; historical
  materialism; Marx, K.; Marxism-
  Leninism; neo-Marxism; post-
  Marxism; socialism
adaptation of (Cabral, A.) 2:168,
  2:169

aesthetics and ethics 1:65, 1:67
African philosophy relationship
  Nkrumah, K. 1:99–1:101
  Senghor, L. 1:99
alternative interpretations 8:853
anti-humanism (Althusser, L.)
  7:594
art 1:717
  and morality 1:455–6
  understanding of 1:473–4
Bloch, E.S. 1:787–9
Chinese 2:316, 2:326, **6:133–41**
  history, theories of 4:447,
    4:451–2
  humanism 6:138–40
  self-cultivation 8:624
class consciousness (Lukács, G.)
  5:857–8
colonialism
  Fanon's rejection of 3:553
consumerism (Baudrillard, J.)
  1:662
Critical Legal Studies
  Germany 2:716, 2:717
critical social theory 9:358
critiques of
  Croce, B. 2:729
  libertarianism 5:618
  Lyotard, J.-F. 6:8
Czech Republic, philosophy in
  2:767–8
dogmatism
  Lyotard, J.-F. critique 6:8
education
  class stratification 3:236
Engels, F. 3:309–13
existentialism (Sartre, J.-P.) 7:593,
  8:474, 8:477
feminism 3:581–2, 3:614, 3:617–18
  literary criticism 3:611, 3:612
Frankfurt School **3:730–7**
functionalist explanation 3:815
God
  concepts of 4:95
Gramsci, A. 4:151–4
Hegelian
  Il'enkov, E.V. 4:688–9
  Lukács, G. 5:856
Hegelian (Il'enkov, E.V.) 4:688–9
historicity
  Japan 5:328
Horkheimer, M. 4:510
humanism 4:528, 4:531
influence of
  African ethical systems 3:434
  Frankfurt School 6:96–7
  Marcuse, H. 6:97

Italy
  Gramsci, A. 5:38–9
  Labriola, A. 5:38
Japan
  Miki Kiyoshi 6:358
  modern literature 5:659
Kautsky, K.J. 5:222–3
Labriola, A. 5:335–6
Latin America 5:428, **6:160–5**
  liberation philosophy 5:612
  Mexico 6:346
legal
  Signposts movement 6:152–3
liberation theology 5:613, 5:615
Lukács, G. 5:856, 5:857–8, 5:857
Luxemburg, R. 6:5–7
Masaryk, T.G. 6:165
method (Lukács, G.) 5:857
naturalist perfectionism 4:521
négritude interpretation 1:110
neo-structuralism 9:187
orthodox (Kautsky, K.J.) 5:222–3
philosophy of science **6:147–50**
pluralist interpretation
  (Anderson, J.) 1:268
Poland 7:488
political philosophy
  history of 7:516–17
psychology (Vygotskii, L.S.)
  9:671–2, 9:674
realism
  social science 8:586
reinterpretation of (Sorel, G.) 9:35
religious policy 8:224, 8:228
revisionist debate (Bernstein, E.)
  1:758, 1:759
Russian/Soviet **6:150–6**
  Chernyshevskii, N.G. 2:303
  critiques of
    Berdiaev, N.A. 1:730
    Mikhailovskii, N.K. 6:357
    Novgorodtsev, P. 5:608
  dialectical materialism
    (Chernyshevskii, N.G.) 2:303
  ideology
    Asmus, V.F./Var'iash, A.
      debate 1:524
  legal theory (Pashukanis, E.B.)
    8:267
  Lenin, V.I. 5:564–7
  Nietzsche, F.W. influence
    6:864–5, 6:866
  partiinost' 7:238–40
  Plekhanov, G.V. 7:451–5
  Russian materialism influence
    8:417
  Signposts movement 6:152–3

Western Marxism distinction
civil society 2:370
scientific socialism
Russian positivism 7:564
self-realization
collectivist 8:633
Slovakia 8:812, 8:813
social theory and law 8:875–6,
8:877
socialism 8:884
Spain 9:75
structuralism 9:176
Tel Quel school 9:292
totalitarianism 9:443
Trotsky, L. 9:464–5
utopianism 9:559
Western **6:141–7**
Althusser, L.P. 1:192–4
analytic 6:142, 6:146
Critical Legal Studies 2:716,
2:717
disintegration of 6:145–6
Hegelianism 4:291
Latin American Marxism
contrast 6:162
Lefebvre, H 5:490
main concerns 6:141–2
Second International Marxism
6:142–3
social theory and law 8:875–6
Soviet Marxism distinction
civil society 2:370
Zionism 9:869
Marxism-Leninism 6:151, 6:153–4,
6:155–6, 6:157
totalitarianism 9:443
Masaoka Shiki 1:81
Masarriya *see* Ibn Massara
Masaryk, Tomáš Garrigue **6:165–6**
Czechoslovak Republic 2:764,
2:766
Russian philosophy 8:422
materialism 8:418
nihilism 7:8
masculinism
Le Doeuff, M. critique 5:477
Masham, Damaris **6:166–8**, 6:578
Masi, M. 1:813
Masing-Delic, I. 3:576
maskilim
Jewish Enlightenment 3:320,
3:322–3
Maskit, Jonathan
Bataille, G. †1:659–61
Masnovo, A. 9:727
Masolo, Dismas
African philosophy 1:97, 1:116

ethnophilosophy, African
†3:445–50
Mason, Andrew
solidarity †9:23–5
Mason, D. 8:21
Mason, H.E. 2:646
Mason, J.H.
Encyclopedists, eighteenth century
†3:303–4
Maspero, H. 2:328
mass
classical mechanics 6:252, 6:255
Mass *see* Eucharist
mass terms **6:168–70**
count terms distinction 6:168–9
description theory of meaning
8:157
semantics 6:169
mass-density
cosmology
universe-models 2:679–80
Massey, G.J. 9:396
Massey, S. 8:638
Massilianism *see* Pelagianism
Massimi, J.-R. 4:518
Masson, J.L. 1:19, 3:793, 3:859
Massumi, B. 2:860
Masters, R.D. 3:230, 8:377
master-slave dialectic
historical development (Kojève, A.)
5:289–90
political philosophy
history of 7:504
postmodernism (Kojève, A.) 1:188
Mastroianni, G. 5:336
masturbation
conservative view 8:724
insanity 8:720
Masud, M.K. 5:460
matching phrases *see* phrase
matching
Matczak, S.A. 3:543
Matejka, L. 6:587
material conditionals 4:740–1
glossary 5:800
material implication, paradoxes of
see indicative conditionals
material intellect
Alexander of Aphrodisias 1:171
material place
Giles of Rome 4:74
materialism **6:170–3**, **6:173–8**
see also immaterialism;
physicalism
abstract objects 6:177
analytical behaviourism 6:174
anthropocentric

(Chernyshevskii, N.G.) 2:304,
2:305
Aristotelianism 9:44
Australian philosophy 1:574,
1:578–80
Cartesianism 2:883, 8:640
Cārvāka 6:197
critiques of
Brown, T. 2:28
Cohen, H. 2:399
Marx, K. 6:123
Signposts movement 8:769
death 2:818, 2:819, 2:820–1
deterministic
human freedom 1:852
Signposts movement critique
8:769
dialectical *see* dialectical
materialism
eliminativism 6:173, 6:176
epiphenomenalism 6:174
Gramsci, A. 4:152
historical
Bogdanov, A.A. 1:817
Chinese Marxism 6:133,
6:134–5, 6:140
critique by Mikhailovskii, N.K.
6:357
functional explanation 6:126–7
Marx, K. 6:126–7
Russian Marxism
(Plekhanov, G.V.) 7:451
history (Engels, F.) 3:309, 3:311
human nature (Cabanis, P.-J.)
2:166, 2:167
idealism 2:66–7
Lange, F. 5:352–3
Plekhanov, G.V. 7:451, 7:454
Schopenhauer, A. 8:548
identity theory of mind 6:174
Indian school of **6:178–81**
epistemology 6:180
ethics 6:180
ontology 6:179–80
intentionality 6:176
'man machine' (La Mettrie, J.O.
de) 5:333–4
metaphysics 6:339
mind, philosophy of **6:173–8**
mind-body problem 3:134, 6:177
Armstrong, D.M. 1:442
Gödel's theorems 4:114
monads (Helmont, F.M. van)
4:341
Naturphilosophie 6:739
organicist (Cavendish, M.L.) 2:261
paranormal phenomena 7:222–3

physiological psychology
(Hartley, D.) 4:237
Priestley, J. 7:683
radical (Bloch, E.S.) 1:788
reductionism 6:173
resurrection 8:295–6
Russian **1:680–4**
nihilism 7:5–8
scientific *see* scientific materialism
secondary qualities 8:599
social science 8:853
Socinianism 8:890
soft versus hard 6:173
soul (Overton, R.) 7:176
Stoicism 9:145
Strato 9:161–2
theistic atomism (Cudworth, R.)
2:741
vitalist (Diderot, D.) 3:66–7
materiality
karma
Yogācāra Buddhism 2:70
substance
ontology in Indian philosophy
7:121
maternal ethics 3:604
Mates, B. 4:681, 5:693, 7:665, 9:160
mathematical logic
early twentieth century 5:729–30,
5:735
Frege, G. 5:725, 5:727
Neumann, J. von 6:810
numbers 7:52
proof theory 7:744–5
Royce, J. 8:379–80
scientific theories 9:344, 9:346
seventeenth and eighteenth
century 5:718
mathematical objects
Aristotle 1:423–4
Platonism and intuitionism
8:120–2
mathematical terms
glossary of 5:795–811
mathematicization
Aristotle's objections to
(Speusippus) 9:89, 9:90
Platonic theory of Forms
(Speusippus) 9:90
mathematics
see also arithmetic; geometry;
mathematical logic; mathematical
objects; mathematicization;
metamathematics
abstract objects 1:32, 1:34
aetiological unsuitability of
(Posidonius) 7:557

analysis **1:216–20**
archē 1:360
astronomy (Eudoxus) 3:452–3
Boethius, A.M.S. 1:805
calculus (Leibniz, G.W.) 5:542,
5:554
certainty
Neoplatonism 6:801
Vico, G. 9:601
chaos theory **2:276–80**
constructivism **2:632–9**
constructivism (Lorenzen, P.)
5:826
dialectical reasoning
(Bachelard, G.) 1:621, 1:622
Entscheidungsproblem
(Turing, A.M.) 9:493
Eudoxus 3:452–3
evident truths (Foucher, S.)
3:714–15
foundations of **6:181–92**
category theory **2:233–7**
Leśniewski, S. 7:493–4
logical positivism 5:791–2
non-standard models 5:846–8
geometric spirit (Pascal, B.) 7:241,
7:243–4
geometry
Oresme, N. 7:153, 7:154
Thales 9:323–4
Gibert of Poitiers 4:70
glossary 5:795–811
Heyting's semantics
(Dummett, M.A.E.) 3:152
history of (Brunschvicg, L.)
2:39–40
infinity 4:772, 4:773, 4:774,
4:775–6
intuitionistic logic 4:856, 4:857–9
Jewish philosophy (Maimon, S.)
6:36–7
knowledge
Locke, J. critique 5:668–9
Mersenne, M. 6:325, 6:327–8,
6:329
logic reduction (Ramsey, F.P.) 8:45
logicism
Russell, B.A.W. 8:391–2, 8:394
Whitehead, A.N. 9:714–15
medieval
Aristotelianism
Oresme, N. 1:402
Oxford Calculators 1:401–2
Gerbert of Aurillac 4:40
natural philosophy 6:702–3
Platonism 7:432
metaphysics (Xenocrates) 9:806–7

method
Fardella, M. 3:558–9
philosophy comparison
(Wolff, C.) 9:781
motion (Galilei, G.) 3:836, 3:837–9
music
Archytas 1:367, 1:368
Mersenne, M. 6:329
nature (Alembert, J. le R. d')
1:164, 1:166
necessary truth (Putnam, H.)
7:842
Neoplatonism
Proclus 7:729–30
Simplicius 8:790
Newton, I. 6:826
Newtonian calculus
Berkeley, G. critique 1:746–7
Nicholas of Cusa 6:835
non-naturalistic epistemology 7:37
numerology
Pythagoreanism 7:858–60
physical world description
(Proclus) 7:729
physics (Descartes, R.) 3:15
Plato 7:410
in Platonism (Wittgenstein, L.)
9:766–7
Poincaré, J.H. 7:481
primacy of
Galilei, G. 3:837–8
science, nineteenth century
philosophy of 8:566
proofs
Frege, G. 3:765, 3:772–3, 5:725
intuitionism 4:849–50
intuitionistic logic 4:858
Lakatos, I. 5:342–3
propositions (Mill, J.S.) 6:360,
6:363–4
Pythagoreanism
Archytas 1:367–9
Plato 7:423
Ramus, P. 8:53–4
ratios (Oresme, N.) 7:153, 7:154–5
realism
bivalence 4:856
Ptolemy 7:831
reason-giving (Schopenhauer, A.)
8:547–8
scientific importance (Bacon, R.)
1:634
scientific method 8:579, 9:486
second-order logic 8:600, 8:601–3
set theory (Quine, W.V.) 8:7, 8:10

social analysis
  (Condorcet, M.J.A.N.) 2:528,
    2:529–30, 2:531
sophismata (Heytesbury, W.) 4:420
the sublime 9:203
substitutive schemes
  (Whitehead, A.N.) 9:714–15
mathesis
  theoretical knowledge (Gilbert of
    Poitiers) 4:70
mathesis universalis
  Llull, R. 9:70
Matijasevic, Y.V. 2:488, 2:490
Matilal, Bimal K.
  awareness
    in Indian thought 1:608
  Dignāga 3:76
  error and illusion
    Indian concepts of 3:413
  Gaṅgeśa 3:846
  Indian epistemology 3:392
  inference
    Indian theories of 4:765
  Jainism 5:56–7
  knowledge
    Indian views of 5:281, 5:285
  language
    Indian theories of 5:384
  manifoldness, Jaina theory of 6:78,
    6:81
  meaning
    Indian theories of 6:243
  mind
    Indian philosophy of 6:403
  Nyāya-Vaiśeṣika 7:65
  ontology in Indian philosophy
    7:127
  sense perception
    Indian views of 8:694
  testimony 9:314, 9:318
  Udayana 9:514
  Uddyotakara 9:515
  universals
    Indian theories of 9:548
  Vātsyāyana 9:588
Matravers, D. 3:280
Matravers, Matt
  justice 5:141–7
    international †5:153–7
Matsuda, Michio 5:177
Matsuda, M.J. 5:644
Matsumoto, Shigeru 2:63, 6:590,
  9:408
Matsunaga, A. 2:106, 5:79, 6:829
Matsunaga, Daigan 2:106, 5:79,
  6:829

Matta, Abu Bishr 4:156, 4:157, 5:707,
  6:237
matter **6:192–6**
see also divisibility; indivisibility
  active powers in (Kilwardby, R.)
    5:248
  activity/passivity of 6:194–5
  addition of thought (Bold, S.)
    1:822, 1:823
  alchemy 1:155, 1:156–7
  ancient concepts of 2:295, 6:192–4
  atomism 6:193, 6:194
    Jainism 5:49
  body distinction (Cordemoy, G.
    de) 2:673
  con-creation with form (Albert the
    Great) 1:148
  consciousness relations
    (Lokāyatas) 6:179–80
  corpuscularianism
    Boyle, R. 1:853, 1:855–6
    Descartes, R. 2:295–6
    Heraclides of Pontus 4:363
  creation
    Gersonides 4:49
    Philo of Alexandria 7:359–60
  difference within (Madhva) 6:31
  dualism (Numenius) 7:54–5
  dynamism (Kant, I.) 6:737
  emanation
    Jewish philosophy (Israeli, I.)
      5:32–3
  epistemological idealism 2:67
  eternal principle of (al-Razi, Abu
    Bakr) 8:111
  existence debate
    Aristotelianism 1:388–9
  field theory
    classical 3:668–70
    quantum 3:670–3, 6:195
  form
    Aristotle 1:422
    colonial philosophy
      Latin America 5:424–5
    creation (Bar Hayya, A.) 1:649
    ontology (Ibn Tzaddik, J.) 4:660
    Pecham, J. 7:268
  four elements (Aristotle) 2:295
  God's relation to universe (Thierry
    of Chartres) 9:372
  human vulnerability
    (Maimonides, M.) 6:41, 6:45
  Indian conceptions of **6:196–200**
    Sāṅkhya dualism 6:199–200
    Vaiśeṣika atomism 6:198–9
  indiscerpibility (More, H.) 6:578–9

individuation
  Giles of Rome 4:74
  Kilwardby, R. 5:247
intellect distinction
  (Theophrastus) 9:338
intelligible (Ibn Gabirol, S.) 4:618
karmic
  Jainism 5:215
medieval concepts of 6:194,
  6:273–4
mind relationship
  Astell, M. 1:528–9
  Lichtenberg, G.C. 5:623–4
  Plutarch of Chaeronea 7:469
nature of
  Neoplatonism (Proclus) 7:727
  Plotinus 7:459–60
  Stoicism 9:144–5
neutral monism (Russell, B.A.W.)
  8:400
permeation by god
  Stoicism 9:145
potentiality of (Bonaventure)
  1:832
prime
  nature of (Simplicius) 8:789
primordial
  formlessness of 2:377
priority of (Ibn Gabirol, S.) 4:619
privation (Thomas of York) 9:375
Scientific Revolution 6:192,
  6:194–5
spirit relationship (More, H.)
  6:579
structure of (Voltaire) 9:660
twentieth-century concepts of
  2:298–9, 6:192, 6:195–6
William of Ockham 9:736
Yogācāra Buddhism 2:71–2
Matthew of Aquasparta **6:200–3**
Matthews, E. 8:179
Matthews, Freya
  Australia, philosophy in 1:583
  ecological philosophy †3:197–202
Matthews, Gareth B.
  Augustine of Hippo †1:541–59
Matthews, M.R. 3:239
Matthews, R.J. 4:54, 6:344
Maturana, H. 3:202
Maturo, Graciela 7:348–9, 7:352
Maudlin, T. 8:576
Maull, N. 4:15, 9:532
Maurer, A. 2:175, 2:294, 5:109
Maurer, W. 6:292
Maus, F. 6:614
Mauss, M. 2:374, 3:818, 8:132,
  8:140–1

Mauthner, Fritz **6:203–6**
Mautner, F.H. 5:624
Mautner, T. 4:204
Mauzi, R. 3:69
Mavrodes, George I.
  God, existence of 4:93
  monotheism †6:479–83
  prayer †7:649–53
  predestination †7:653–7
al-Mawdudi, Abu al-'Ala 5:9, 5:12
maxima/minima
  as analytical language
    Oxford Calculators 7:181–2
maximal consistent set
  glossary 5:805
Maximos Planudes 1:803
Maxwell, G. 7:86
Maxwell, James Clerk **6:206–10**
  electrodynamics 3:259, 3:260,
    6:207–8
  field theory, classical 3:669, 3:670
  Hertz, H.R. 4:400–1
  light propagation
    optics 7:136–7
  thermodynamics 9:367
May, R. 1:200, 3:502, 9:253
May, T. 1:248
māyā (illusion)
  Vallabhācārya critique 9:574–5
Mayan (Quiché) civilization
  culture 5:429
  religion 5:430
  thought 5:428–9, 5:430, 5:431
Mayberry, J. 2:236
Mayer, G. 3:312
Mayer, S. 2:227
Maynard-Smith, J. 2:835, 3:482,
    8:896
Mayo, B. 3:634, 8:330
Mayo, D. 9:126
Mayo, D.J. 8:728, 9:229
Mayor, J.B. 4:184
Mayr, Ernst
  evolution, theory of 3:477–8, 3:482
  species 9:81
  taxonomy 9:275
  unity of science 9:533
  vitalism 9:643
Mayr, E.W. 2:476
Mays, W. 9:719
Mayz Valenzillà, Ernesto 3:512,
    7:351, 7:352
Mazlow, I. 9:115
Mazrui, Ali 1:107, 5:17–18
Mazzarella, P. 6:203
Mazzini, Giuseppe 5:37
Mbembe, Achille 1:113, 1:116

Mbiti, J. 1:107, 3:435, 3:449
Mead, George Herbert **6:210–12**
  sociality
    pragmatism in ethics 7:642–3
  society
    concept of 8:888, 8:889
  symbolic interactionism 9:245
meaning
  see also cognitive significance;
    content; intension; interpretation;
    reference; semantics
  action/product distinction
    (Twardowski, K.) 9:509
  ambiguity 1:197–201
  antirealism (Dummett, M.A.E.)
    3:149, 3:152–3
  appropriateness (Kripke, S.) 9:765
  Aristotle 5:359–60
  artist's intention 1:513–14, 1:515
  assertability (Wittgenstein, L.)
    9:765
  assymetric dependence theory
    (Fodor, J.A.) 3:684, 3:685
  atomism/holism 4:489
  Bible
    allegory 4:390–1
  biblical hermeneutics
    Frei, H. 3:778–9
    midrash 6:353–4
  biological theories of **8:672–5**
  bivalence
    realism 4:860–2
  Buddhist theory of
    Uddyotakara critique 9:514–15
  causal theory
    epiphenomenalism 3:353–4
  and communication **6:212–14**
  compositionality 2:476–7, 2:801–2
  concepts 2:507–8
  conceptual role semantics 8:653–5
  content
    Deleuze, G. 2:858
    representational 7:625
  context
    Dōgen 5:74
    Tominaga Nakamoto 9:440
  conventionalism 2:667, 2:668,
    7:480–1
  conventionality **5:368–71**
  critiques of (Quine, W.V.) 1:226,
    8:10–12
  emotive **3:290–1**
    Stevenson, C.L. 9:134–5
  eternality of words
    universals 9:544–5
  ethical discourse 5:759
  externalism (Putnam, H.) 8:157

extrusion of (Dummett, M.A.E.)
    6:233
  force distinction 7:625
  holism 4:486–7, 4:488, 4:489
    agreement-disagreement
      dichotomy 4:491–2
    analytic-synthetic distinction
      4:490–1
    narrow content 4:492–3
  ideas (Locke, J.) 5:674
  implicature **4:721–5**
  indexicals **2:878–81**
  Indian theories of **6:239–43**
    Patañjali 7:248–9
  induction 4:750
  intention
    Diodorus Cronus 3:84
    Grice, H.P. 2:456–8
  inviolability
    common sense principles
      (Stewart, D.) 9:136–7
  Islamic philosophy 5:15, **6:236–9**
    ambiguity (Ibn Rushd) 4:644
    language/logic debate 5:707–8,
      6:236–7
  language-mind-world connections
    5:409–10
  legal (Bentham, J.) 1:722–3
  levels of 7:623–4
  of life
    death 2:818, 2:821–2
    nihilism 7:1, 7:2–3, 7:4
    realism/antirealism 8:115–19
  linguistic
    analyticity (Lewis, C.I.) 5:586–7
    concepts 2:507–8
    Mīmāṃsā 6:377, 6:380
    nominalism (Sellars, W.S.)
      8:638, 8:639
    pictorial distinction 6:8
    potentiality
      Indian theories of 7:607
  linguistic units
    Indian philosophy 5:380–2
  literary texts 1:503
  logical atomism 5:773
  logical positivism (Carnap, R.)
    5:793–4
  logical versus expressive
    (Vygotskii, L.S.) 9:674
  mental content 6:405
  methodological individualism
    Burge, T. critique 8:157
  naming (Wittgenstein, L.) 9:762
  noema (Husserl, E.) 4:574, 4:578
  nominalism
    Buddhism 7:25–6

non-natural 2:456
non-truth-conditional theories of
 7:622–3
objectivity 7:75
ordinary language philosophy
 7:621
performatives 7:303
picture theory of (Wittgenstein, L.)
 4:401, 9:758–9, 9:761
pluralism
 French anti-postmodernism
  7:594
polyvalency of
 biblical hermeneutics 4:393,
  4:394
Port-Royalists 5:373
pragmatism 5:60, 5:64–5
predication 7:666
prescriptive/descriptive distinction
 7:668–9
 Hare, R.M. 4:230
presence (Dōgen) 3:110
private states 5:416–17, 7:699–700
propositional attitudes 7:780
Putnam, H. 7:839, 7:840–1
radical interpretation
 (Davidson, D.) 2:802, 8:25–6,
  8:31
relational theory of 8:670
religious statements 8:257
rule-following **6:214–19**
 private states 7:700–1
 Wittgenstein, L. 9:763–4, 9:766
scientific terms
 incommensurability 4:734
sense and reference distinction
 8:685
sentences
 Hindu philosophy 4:436–7
 testimony in Indian philosophy
  9:315–17
shifts of
 scientific revolutions
  (Kuhn, T.S.) 5:317
signification (Kilwardby, R.) 5:247
situation semantics 8:670–1
speech acts
 ordinary language philosophy
  7:621
Stoics 5:360
syntax 9:246–7
teleological 8:672–4
textual
 Barthes, R. 1:657
 Man, P. de 2:811
theological discourse (Gilbert of
 Poitiers) 4:70–1

as translation 6:213
and truth **6:219–26**
 conceptual role semantics
  8:654–5
 conditions of 6:221–3, 7:625
 Dummett, M.A.E. 3:149,
  3:150–2
 Strawson, P.F. 9:170
 knowledge 6:222–3
 language 6:219–25
 pragmatics 6:224
 proper names 6:220, 6:221,
  6:223
 satisfaction (Davidson, D.)
  8:31–4
underdetermination
 Rabbinic theology 9:335–6
understanding 6:222, **6:226–9**
use/mention distinction 9:549
utterances (Grice, H.P.) 4:172–4
verification 4:860, 4:861–2,
 6:230–6
 phenomenalism 7:332
 words (Patañjali) 7:248–9
meaning of life **5:630–3**
 subjective/objective distinction
  5:632
means-ends analysis
 classical AI 1:487
means-justification
 Camus, A. rejection of 2:195
measurement **6:243–9**
 Campbell, N.R. 2:193–4
 error 6:247–9
 as evidence
  inductive inference 4:756–7
 ordinal scales 6:243–4, 6:245–6
 physics (Bridgman, P.W.) 2:18
 problem
  quantum mechanics **7:890–4**
  Putnam, H. 7:841
 relativity theory 8:194
 scales of 6:243–4, 6:245
 scientific
  operationalism 7:131–4
 uncertainty principle
  (Heisenberg, W.) 4:327–8
measures on sets of points
 geometry of physical space 4:31–2
 point sets theory 8:705–6
mechanical philosophy
 Aristotelianism (Digby, K.) 3:72
 body
  Descartes, R. 3:1–2, 3:16
  Regius, H. 4:353
 Conway, A. critique 2:670

Epicurean atomism (Gassendi, P.)
 3:853
Newtonian world picture
 (Bentley, R.) 1:725
soul
 Digby, K. 3:72
 Elisabeth of Bohemia 3:267–8
mechanicity thesis
 photography 7:379–80
mechanics
 Aristotelian **6:249–51**
 classical **6:251–9**
  conservation laws 2:607
  constraints 6:255–7
  continua 6:257–8
  determinism 3:34, 3:35, 6:253
  field theory 3:668–70
  Hertz, H.R. 4:401
  point mass approach 6:255
  universe states 7:887
 medieval science (Hugh of St
  Victor) 4:519
 motion
  Galilei, G. 3:836, 3:837–9
  Newton, I. 6:252–5
 nature (Hegel, G.W.F.) 4:272
 Newtonian
  electrodynamics 3:259–60
  laws of motion 6:252–5
 Newtonian-Einsteinian
  incommensurability 4:732–3
 optics (Hobbes, T.) 4:468–9
 Oresme, N. 7:154–5
 perception (Digby, K.) 3:72–3
 quantum see quantum mechanics
mechanism
 anomalies
  spirit of nature (More, H.) 6:580
 mixed mathematical sciences
  (Mersenne, M.) 6:329
 natural philosophy
  Charleton, W. 2:286
  Leibniz, G.W. 5:542, 5:554–7
  Nyāya-Vaiśeṣika 7:58
 philosophy of mind
  Gödel's theorems 4:114
 science
  nineteenth-century philosophy
   of 8:570
 selective Aristotelianism (Strato)
  9:161–2
 Soviet Marxism 6:154
 vitalism 9:639–40, 9:641–2
Meckenstock, Günter
 Schleiermacher, F. †8:531–9
media
 see also journalism

hyperreality (Baudrillard, J.)
1:662–3
privacy 7:691
medical ethics **6:259–64**
see also bioethics; genetics; Jewish
bioethics; medicine; nursing ethics
abortion 4:798
consent 2:598
doctor/patient relationship 6:260,
6:261, 6:262
euthanasia 5:627–8
experimentation 6:260, 6:261–2
Jewish 1:777
killing of innocents
Roman Catholicism 4:798
professional/client relationship
7:734
religion 8:223
suicide 9:224, 9:228
technology and ethics 9:282
Tuskegee project 1:321
medicine **6:264–9**
see also medical ethics
Chinese 1:72
qi 7:862
Galen 3:832–3, 3:834
health and disease concepts 6:266
Hellenistic methodology 4:333–5
Hippocratic **4:441–3**
Islam
Ibn Sina 8:562–3
pharmacology 8:563
al-Razi, Abu Bakr 8:563
Jewish bioethics 1:777
logics of diagnosis 6:266–7
models of 6:266
philosophy parallel (Philo of
Larissa) 7:362
Renaissance (Paracelsus) 7:205,
7:207
sympathetic (Digby, K.) 3:73
system of opposites (Alcmaeon)
1:160
medieval law
Roman law influence 8:344
medieval philosophy **6:269–77**
see also Aristotelianism, medieval
ancient philosophy influence 1:265
epistemology 3:373–4, 6:274
eternity 3:424
ethics 6:274
heaven 4:249–50
hermeneutics
biblical 4:391
historical development 6:270–3
intentionality 4:816–17

language theories **5:389–404**,
6:274–5
logic **5:746–59**, 6:274–5
metaphysics 6:273–4
natural philosophy 6:275,
6:690–707
perfect goodness concept 4:140–1
political 7:504, 7:508–9
realism (Baumgarten, A.G.) 1:670
Russian **6:277–9**
slavery 8:804
theology relationship 6:275–6
translators **9:455–7**
medieval Platonism *see* Platonism,
medieval
Medin, D. 2:394–5, 2:517
Meding, W. von 8:538
meditation
see also asceticism
bodhi (awakening)
Buddha 2:52
Chan Buddhism (Linji) 5:646
Chogye Buddhism (Chinul) 2:330
Confucianism
Korean
i 2:562
ki 2:562, 9:825
emptiness
Buddhist concept of 2:79
enlightenment
Japanese Buddhism 2:103
mahāmudrā (Mi bskyod rdo rje)
6:351, 6:352
neo-Confucianism
Korean
self-cultivation 9:823–4
seiza (quiet-sitting) (Fujiwara
Seika) 3:799, 3:800
purpose of 6:401–2
self-cultivation
Chinese Buddhism 8:620
Sufism
Kabbalah 5:175
Tiantai Buddhism (Zhiyi) 9:860
Yogācāra Buddhism 3:388–9
Zen Buddhism (Dōgen) 3:110, 5:74
Meditationes de prima philosophia
(Meditations on First Philosophy)
see Descartes, René
mediums 7:222, 9:47–8
see also clairvoyance
Meehl, Paul E.
medicine, philosophy of 6:266,
6:268
operationalism 7:134, 7:135
Meek, R. 3:633
Meerhoff, K. 6:292, 8:54

Megarian school **6:279–80**
Dialectical school comparison
3:58
Socratic schools 9:21–2
Meggle, G. 4:231
Megill, R. 9:201
Mehler, J. 7:823
Mehlman, J. 1:784
Meier, H.C. 8:357
Meier, K.V. 9:116
Meijers, A. 2:458
Meiklejohn, A. 3:764
Meilaender, G. 7:737
Meinecke, Friedrich **6:280–2**
historicism 4:446
morality 6:281
Rosenzweig, F. 8:358, 8:361
Meinel, C. 5:137–8
Meinong, Alexius **6:282–6**
axiology 1:611
Chisholm, R.M. 2:335
existence 3:491, 3:492
fictional entities 3:666, 3:667
Gestalt psychology 4:52
intentionality 4:577, 4:587
objects 6:283–4
semantics of fiction 3:659–61
value theory 6:284
meiosis
conversational cooperation 6:337
metaphor comparison 6:336
Meisner, M. 6:141
Meissner, W. 6:141
Meister Eckhart **6:286–8**
Christian mysticism 6:624–5
negative theology 7:584–5
Platonism, medieval 7:437
Suso, H. 9:240
Tauler, J. 9:269–70
Mejer, J. 3:87
Mejía Vallejo, Manuel 5:655, 5:657–4
Mejor, Marek
suffering
Buddhist views of origination of
†9:215–19
Vasubandhu †9:583–7
Melamed, A.
Alemanno, Y. †1:161–3
Ibn Falaquera 4:617
Messer Leon 6:334–5
Melamed, Douglas 7:758, 7:760
Melanchthon, Philipp **6:288–92**
logic
textbooks 5:770
Melden, A.I. 8:127, 8:330
Mele, Alfred R.
anomalous monism 1:280

artist's intention 1:516
free will 3:752
intention 4:814, 4:816
self-deception †8:626–9, 8:632
Melhuish, K.J. 5:604
Melia, Joseph
  possible worlds †7:570–3
Melissus 1:263, **6:292–6**
  changeless unity 6:294–5
  cosmology 6:293–4
  Eleatic monism 6:292–5
  infinity
      temporal and spatial 6:293–4
  Parmenides 6:292–5
Mella, Julio Antonio 6:161
Mellema, G. 9:235
Mellor, D.H.
  Campbell, N.R. †2:193–4
  causation 2:250
  change 2:276
  continuants 2:654
  events †3:461–3
  facts 3:537
  McTaggart, J.M.E. 6:28
  natural laws 5:475
  Ramsey, F.P. †8:44–9
  Tennant, F.R. 9:302, 9:303
  time 9:416
Melnick, Arthur 5:199
melody 4:188–9
Meløe, Jakob 7:647, 7:648–9
Meltzer, B. 7:214
Meltzoff, A.N.
  infant cognition †2:390–2
Melzack, R. 9:215
memorial
  Eucharist 8:443–4
memories
  persons 7:320
memory **6:296–300**
  see also long-term memory (LTM);
    short-term memory (STM)
  artificial neural networks
    connectionism 2:570
  causal analysis 6:298–9
  contingency (Tolstoi, L.N.) 9:437
  dreaming 3:127
  epistemology of **6:300–2**
    loss 6:302
    retention 6:301–2
  false belief acquisition
    children 6:387–8
  hysteria (Freud, S.) 3:787, 3:788
  ideas (Locke, J.) 5:670
  implicit 5:287
  introspection 4:839, 4:844, 4:845
  justification for 5:259

language
  sphoṭa theory 5:382
mind, philosophy of (Augustine)
  1:547–8
personal identity
  Hume, D. 6:572
  Locke, J. 6:572
Plato 6:296–7
Proustian experience
  (Mamardashvili, M.K.) 6:69
sense perception
  Indian views of 8:690
sexual abuse (Freud, S.) 3:787–8
techniques (Bruno, G.) 2:35–6
testimony 9:312
Memphite Theology
  Egyptian cosmology
    ancient 3:249
Menchú, R. 3:628
Mencius **6:302–4**
  categories 6:457
  cheng 2:300
  history, theories of 4:448
  human nature 2:91, 2:560, 2:561
  humanism
    Chinese Marxist critique
      6:138–9
  inference
    Mohist philosophy 6:457
  li 2:543–4, 5:594
  Mengzi 6:302, 6:303
    Chinese classics 2:309, 2:311,
      2:313, 2:314
    qi 7:863
    self-cultivation 8:616
    xin (heart-and-mind) 9:816
  moral intuition 5:696
  qi 7:862–3
  ritual 8:339
  self-cultivation 8:616, 8:617
  xin (heart-and-mind) 9:816
Mendel, A.P. 1:647, 8:773
Mendel, Gregor 4:12
  see also Mendelian genetics
Mendelian genetics 4:12–13, 4:14
Mendelson, E. 2:355
Mendelssohn, Moses **6:304–7**
  Enlightenment
    German 3:317
    Jewish 3:320–1, 3:323–4
  Jewish philosophy 5:89–90
    contemporary 5:91, 5:95
    early nineteenth century 5:96,
      5:100
  Lessing, G.E. 5:577
Mendes-Flohr, P. 5:95

Mendus, Susan
  feminist political philosophy
    †3:614–21
  MacIntyre, A. 6:24
  medical ethics 6:263
  pornography †7:543–5
  toleration 9:432–3
Menedemus of Eretria 9:22
Menéndez y Samara, Adolfo 3:512,
  3:513
Menezes, Djacir 2:11
Meng Ke *see* Mencius
Meng Tzu *see* Mencius
Menger, C. 3:221
Menger, Karl 9:611–12
Mengzi see Mencius
Menippus 2:756
Menk, G. 2:382
Menshivism
  Plekhanov, G.V. 7:453
mental activity
  brain death 5:627
mental causation **6:307–11**
  action 1:39–40, 6:407
  Brown, T. 2:26, 2:28
  content
    wide and narrow 2:643
  dualism 3:133, 3:136–7
  emotions 3:283
  epiphenomenalism 3:136, 3:352–3
  functionalism 6:406
  identity theory of mind 6:308–10,
    6:394–6
  memory 6:298–9
  methodological individualism
    Fodor, J.A. 6:342
  other minds 7:172
  propositional attitudes 7:783–4
  reasons as causes 8:124–5
    logical connections 8:125–6
mental concepts
  acquisition
    autism 3:686, 3:687
    folk psychology 3:686
  conceptualist theory of universals
    (Aureol, P.) 1:566
mental construction
  Yogācāra Buddhism critique
    2:68–9, 2:72
mental development
  Lamarckian explanation
    (Spencer, H.) 9:87
mental events
  Abelard, P. 1:12
  anomalous monism 1:276–9
  objects (Meinong, A.) 6:283
  predication 7:666

privacy of (Frege, G.) 3:770–1
taxonomy of (Brentano, F.) 2:13
William of Ockham 9:736–8
mental health
    positive thinking (Spinoza, B. de)
        9:104
    Tschirnhaus, E.W. von 9:486
mental holism *see* holism, mental and
        semantic
mental illness
    concepts of **6:311–14**
    Foucault, M. 3:709–10
mental imagery **4:703–5**
    descriptionalism 4:703, 4:704,
        4:705
    imagination 4:705–8
    pictorial conception 4:703, 4:704–5
mental language
    Ailly, P. d' 1:134
    Major, J. 6:54–5
    speech in the mind (*verbum mentis*)
        (Augustine) 5:390
    theories of
        Renaissance 5:411, 5:412–13
    William of Ockham 5:392
mental phenomena
    eliminativism 3:263, 3:264
mental processes
    computational model simulation
        computational theories of mind
            2:392–3
    mechanical explanation of
        (Turing, A.M.) 9:494
    rational choice theory 8:71–2
mental properties
    causal relations 6:309–10
    colour experience
        intrinsic/relational 2:419–20,
            2:421
    neurophysiological relation
        6:309–10
    physical properties relation
        supervenience 9:238–9
mental representations
    computational theory of vision
        (Burge, T.) 6:342, 6:343
    concepts distinction 2:506–7
    content
        indexical 2:639
        wide and narrow 2:643
    criticism of functionalism 3:806,
        3:812
    learning
        empiricism 5:483
mental states
    see also bodily sensations;
        consciousness; sensation; sense-

data; unconscious mental states,
    adverbial theory of **6:314–17**
    Ducasse, C.J. 3:139–40
    perception 7:290
    phenomenalism 7:331
    propositional attitudes 7:785–6
    Sellars, W.S. 8:639–40
    sense experience (Chisholm, R.)
        2:333, 3:300, 3:301–7
analytic behaviourism 1:689–90,
    1:691–2, 6:395–6, 6:404
artificial intelligence limitations
    Chinese room argument 2:328
autism 6:386
brain states identity (Smart, J.J.C.)
    8:814
central state theory
    (Armstrong, D.M.) 1:442
child's theory of mind 6:385,
    6:386–7, 6:388
Chisholm, R.M. 2:333
colour experience 2:423
consciousness 2:581–94
content
    informational semantics 8:659
    non-conceptual 2:640–3
    wide and narrow 2:643–5
dualism 3:133, 3:135, 6:395,
    6:403–4
epiphenomenalism 3:351–4
folk psychology 3:686
functionalism **3:805–13**
happiness **4:226–9**
identity theory of mind 6:395,
    6:397–9
intentionality 4:816–20
introspection 4:838–9
    Maine de Biran, P.-F. 6:49,
        6:51–2
    phenomenal consciousness
        2:589
    psychology of 4:842–5
karmic consciousness
    Yogācāra Buddhism 2:72–3
music 6:610
non-conceptual content 2:641–2
other minds 7:170–3
    infant cognition 2:391
persons 7:318–19, 7:320
phenomenal consciousness
    introspection 2:589
    Shoemaker, S. 2:593–4
phenomenalism 7:331
pleasure
    utilitarianism 9:552–3
Price, H.H. 3:415–16
propositional attitudes 7:780–1

qualia 7:863, 7:865–6
sensations (Bonnet, C.) 1:839
Twardowski, K. 9:509
unconscious **9:522–7**
mental terms
    meaning of
        folk psychology 3:686
mentalese *see* language of thought
mentalism
    Quine, W.V. critique 8:10–11
    scientific behaviourism
        (Skinner, B.F.) 8:800–1
mentality
    evidence for
        eliminativistic account 3:265
    machines
        Turing test 9:494–5
mention/use distinction **9:548–51**
Menut, A.D. 7:157
Menzel, Christopher 6:747
    intensional entities 4:806–7
    logical form †5:781–5
Menzies, P. 2:250
meonic freedom
    divine creation (Berdiaev, N.A.)
        1:727–8
Mepham, T.B. 1:776
Mera, Juan León 5:654, 5:657
Mercado, Tomás de 5:422, 9:72, 9:76
Mercer, Christia
    Digby, K. †3:71–4
    Keckermann, B. †5:224–5
    Leibniz, G.W. 5:562
Mercer, R. 2:555
Merchant, C. 2:263, 2:671, 3:868
Mercier, A. 5:644–5
mercy **3:697–701**, 8:135, 8:137–8
    definitions 3:697–9
    equity 5:149
    justice 3:697, 3:699–700
mercy killing *see* euthanasia
mereology **6:317–20**
    Goodman, N. 4:136
    historical explanation 3:526
    Leśniewski, S. 5:571, 5:573
    mass terms 6:169–70
    particulars as aggregates 7:237
Merezhkovskii, Dmitrii
    Nietzsche/Christianity
        reconciliation 6:862–3, 6:867
    Russian religious-philosophical
        renaissance 8:424–5, 8:427
    symbolism
        Signposts movement 8:770
merit **3:24–7**
    equality 3:395

neutrality distinction
  art works 1:461–2
merkavah (chariot) mysticism
  5:171–2, 6:623
Merki, H. 7:429
Merkle, J.C. 4:412
Merlan, P. 1:175–6, 1:209–10, 6:626,
  9:90–1
Merleau-Ponty, Maurice **6:320–5**
  bodily intentionality 7:346–7
  consciousness 6:323
  essence 7:346
  existentialist ethics 3:505
  freedom 6:323
  language 6:323
  Marxism 6:145
  memory 6:299
  phenomenology 7:342
    existential 7:338
    perception 6:321–3, 7:348
  physiological psychology 6:321
  Sartre, J.-P. 8:479
  structuralism 9:176, 9:177
Mermin, N.D. 1:716
Merquior, J.G. 5:585, 6:146–7
Merriam, C.E. 9:59
Merrill, Daniel D.
  De Morgan, A. †2:813–14
  logic in the nineteenth century
    5:728
  methodological individualism
    6:344
  Venn, J. †9:594–5
Merrill, R.E. 8:56
Mersch, É. 4:149, 4:151
Mersenne, Marin **6:325–31**
  Descartes, R. 3:2–3
  libertins 5:621
  universal language 9:535
Mertens, J.-F. 2:834
Merton, Robert
  constructivism 2:630
  functionalism in social science
    3:818
  religion and science 8:235
  sociology
    of science 2:625–6
    theories of 9:7
Merz, J.T. 5:231
Merzbach, U.C. 5:727, 7:53
Mesch, B. 1:602
Meschini, F.A. 3:560
Mesnard, J. 7:246, 7:554
Mesnard, P. 1:799
Mesopotamia
  creation myths 2:695
  Manicheism 6:74–5, 6:76

Mesquita, R. 7:65
Messer Leon, Judah **6:331–5**
  Jewish philosophy 5:89
Messiah
  Hebrew Bible 1:766, 1:769
Messianism
  Poland 7:486
Messick, B. 5:460
Mestizo people 5:654, 7:350
Meszaros, I. 1:181
meta-archaeology
  scientific research 1:354–5
meta-ethics 3:435
  see also analytic ethics
  applied/theoretical distinction
    1:319
  rationalism (Price, R.) 7:675,
    7:676–7
  relativism 6:539–41
metalanguage
  logic in the early twentieth-century
    5:733
  Tarski, A. 8:642, 8:643, 8:644
metallurgy
  archaic
    alchemy 1:155
metamathematics
  intuitionism 4:850–1
  models 6:443–4
  proof theory 7:743–4
  second-order logic 8:594–5
  Tarski, A. 7:494, 9:263
metamorphosis
  Goethe, J.W. von 4:125, 4:127–8
metaphilosophy
  Mulla Sadra 6:595
metaphor **6:335–8**
  art
    deception 9:481
    expression 1:497
  comparison theory 6:335–6
  conversational implicature 4:723
  creativity (Ricouer, P.) 8:320
  gender coding
    androcentrism in science 3:865
  imagery
    Chinese aesthetics 1:71–2
  interaction theory 6:335, 6:336–7
  medieval language theory 5:389,
    5:396–7
  poetic language (Ibn Sina) 4:652
  religious statements 8:259
  speech act theory 6:335, 6:337
metaphysical deduction
  categories of judgment (Kant, I.)
    5:185–6

metaphysical hierarchy
  James of Viterbo 5:58–9
  Paul of Venice 7:265
metaphysical transubstantiation
  value attribution
    Grice, H.P. 4:175–6
Metaphysics see Aristotle
metaphysics **6:338–41**
  see also categories; existence;
    experience; first philosophy;
    realism; speculative metaphysics;
    time
  the Absolute **1:27–9**
  absolutist
    theosophy 9:363, 9:364
  Aristotle
    conceptual scope 1:421–2
  Bachelard, G.
    French philosophy of science
      3:780–1
  being **1:699–702**
  bivalence 4:859–60
  closure of *see* deconstruction
  conceptual role semantics 8:652–3
  critiques of
    Dewey, J. 3:46–7
    Kant, I. 5:182, 5:188–9
    Swedenborg, E. 9:242
    Theophrastus 9:338–9
  descriptive 6:340
  epistemic (Lonergan, B.J.F.) 5:824
  essential properties 3:417
  eternity 7:637
  Goodman, N. 4:136–7
  history relationship
    (Collingwood, R.G.) 2:411,
    2:412–13
  idealism **4:662–9**
    McTaggart, J.M.E. 6:25, 6:26–7
  infinity **4:772–8**
  introspection 4:838, 4:841
  Jewish philosophy
    (Mendelssohn, M.) 6:304–5
  logical laws 5:787
  materialism **6:173–8**
  mereology 7:237
  monism **6:474–5**
  Native American philosophy
    6:664–5
  Neoplatonism 6:799
  object of (Suárez, F.) 9:190
  ontology 6:338, 6:340, **7:117–18**
    Ingarden, R.W. 4:790
  Platonism
    Early 7:423–4
    Middle 7:424–5
  pluralism **7:463–4**

quantum mechanics 8:575
religion
    religious statements 8:256–7
    and science 8:231
science 6:340, 8:573, 8:574–5
    Popper K.R. 7:534–5
    and religion 8:231
supervenience **9:235–8**
Thomism (Maritain, J.) 6:103
transcendence
    dimension of being
        Jaspers, K. 5:81
    truth (Nietzsche, F.W.) 6:848–9
universals **9:539–44**
world pictures (Heidegger, M.)
    4:325
metatheorems
    logic, early twentieth century 5:733
Metatron
    Kabbalah 5:172
method
    see also scientific method
    Aristotelianism 1:388
    demonstrative (Wolff, C.) 9:777,
        9:781
    Descartes, R. 3:1, 3:3, 3:5–6
    dialectical
        Aristotle 7:178
        Buddhism
            Wŏnhyo 9:793
        Hegel, G.W.F. 4:269
        Hessen, S.I. 4:416
        post-Stalinist philosophy
            6:156–7
    dialectical theology (Barth, K.)
        1:653
    eliminative induction (Bacon, F.)
        1:624, 1:628, 1:629–30
    genetic (Lambriola, A.) 5:335
    geometrical (Spinoza, B. de) 9:91,
        9:92–3
    historical (Herzen, A.I.) 4:408
    mathematics/metaphysics
        distinction (Kant, I.) 5:181
    new logic (Bacon, F.) 1:627–8
    Popper, K.R. 7:534–5
    scholastic (Meister Eckhart)
        6:286–7
    scientific *see* scientific method
    systems theory (Keckermann, B.)
        5:225
method of doubt *see* doubt
Methodism
    pietism 7:392–3, 7:394, 7:395
    salvation 4:150
    sanctification 8:457

Methodism (first century AD)
    Hellenistic medical epistemology
        4:334–5
methodological behaviourism *see*
    behaviourism, methodological
methodological holism *see* holism,
    methodological
methodological individualism (MI)
    6:341–4
    Anderson, J. critique 1:268
    politics (Popper, K.R.) 7:536
    public interest 7:834
methodological solipsism 9:25
methodology
    history
        philosophy of 4:453, 4:456
    legal science
        multi-dimensional model 9:797
    logic (Zabarella, J.) 5:772
    medical
        Greek philosophy, ancient
            4:333–5
    natural reasoning (William of
        Auxerre) 9:728
    ordo doctrinae/methodus
        distinction (Zabarella, J.) 9:836,
        9:837
    psychoanalysis
        issues in 7:811–16
    of *regressus* (Zabarella, J.) 9:836,
        9:837–8
    scientific
        application to social sciences
            8:860
        empiricism (Strato) 9:163
        Islam 8:563–4
        positivism 7:558, 7:560
        Renaissance
            Aristotelianism 1:406
            scepticism 8:452, 8:453–4
    social science **8:859–68**
        comparative method 6:718
        statistical analysis 6:718
    three laws of (Ramus, P.) 8:53
Metrodorus 3:350, 3:351
Mette, H.-J. 1:301, 1:354, 2:220, 7:363
Metz, C. 3:677
Metz, Johann Baptist 9:332–3
Metz, R. 5:231
Metzer, S.E. 7:246–7
Metzger, Thomas A. 6:776
Metzler, N. 4:704–5
Meuthen, E. 6:838
Meuthrath, A. 3:861
Mews, C.J. 1:14, 8:357
Mexico
    analytical philosophy 1:230–1

    colonial philosophy 5:421, 5:422
    existentialism 3:512
    marginality 6:99–100
    phenomenology 7:350
    philosophy in **6:344–8**
    positivism 7:567
Meyendorff, J. 2:165
Meyenn, K.V. 4:329
Meyer, A.R. 2:476, 5:348, 5:349
Meyer, D.H. 9:139, 9:757
Meyer, G.D. 2:263
Meyer, J.B. 6:780, 6:790
Meyer, K. 5:491
Meyer, Leonard 1:508, 1:509, 6:609,
    6:614
Meyer, R.K. 7:210, 8:204
Meyer, R.W. 5:138–7, 6:741, 8:166
Meyer, T.L. 1:689, 1:760
Meyers, D. 6:505
Meyers, D.T. 3:552
Meyerson, Émile **6:348–51**
    general relativity, philosophical
        responses to 4:9
    Le Roy, É.L.E.J. 5:482–3
Meyerstein, F.W. 2:481
Meynell, Hugo
    Lonergan, B.J.F. †5:822–5
Mezei, B. 4:573
MI *see* methodological individualism
Mi bskyod rdo rje (Mikyö Dorje)
    6:351–3
Miami Theory Collective
    Nancy, J.-L. 6:653–4
Miccolo, L. 4:172
Michael, B. 2:136
Michael, Fred 3:857
Michalson, G.E. 5:244
Michaud-Quantin, P. 5:111
Michel, P.-H. 2:39
Michelet, K.L. 4:297–8
Michelfelder, D. 3:831
Michotte, Albert 4:53, 4:54
micro-reduction *see* identity-
    reduction
microvoids
    Strato 9:162
Middle Ages *see* medieval philosophy
middle knowledge *see* knowledge,
    divine
Middle Platonism *see* Platonism,
    Middle
Middle Stoicism
    Panaetius 7:188–90
middle term
    glossary 5:805
Middle Way
    Buddha 2:52

San-lun Buddhism
  Korea 2:107–8
Midelfort, C.E. 3:818
Midgley, Mary 1:324
midrash **6:353–5**
  Barcelona disputation
    (Nahmanides, M.) 6:648
Mies, M. 3:592–3
Miethe, T.L.
  Thomism 9:388
Mieville, D. 5:574
Mignucci, M. 4:336
Míguez Bonino, José 5:615, 5:616
Mikhailov, F.T. 4:692, 6:159
Mikhailovskii, Nikolai
  Konstantinovich **6:355–7**
  individuality 6:356–7
  Nietzsche, F.W., impact on
    Russian thought 6:864
  progress 6:356
  subjective sociology 6:355–6
Miki Kiyoshi **6:358–9**
Mikkeli, H. 9:839
Mikuláš, T. 3:319
Mikyö Dorje see Mi bskyod rdo rje
Milchman, Alan
  Blanchot, M. †1:782–4
Miles, R. 8:21
Milesian philosophy
  matter 6:193
  Presocratics 7:671
  rational criticism (Anaximenes)
    1:260
Milet, J. 1:737
Miletus
  Thales **9:322–4**
Milgate, M. 8:74
Milgram, S. 1:695, 3:519, 3:520
Milgrom, P. 2:835
Miliband, R. 7:612
Milindapañha
  mind
    Indian philosophy of 6:403
  philosophy of mind 6:401
Milindapañho
  inference
    Indian theories of 4:765–6
military philosophy
  China
    Sunzi 9:230–1
Mill, Harriet see Taylor, Harriet
Mill, James **6:359–60**
  democracy 2:870, 2:872
  legitimacy 5:541
Mill, John Stuart **6:360–75**
  action 1:41
  agnosticism 1:122, 1:123

applied ethics 1:324
arithmetic
  empiricism in 1:438
autonomy
  ethical 1:590, 1:592
Berkeley, G. 1:747, 1:750
categorical imperative
  critique of Kant, I. 9:538
causation 2:246
common-sense ethics 2:450
Comte, A. 2:503, 2:505
critique of (Stephen, J.F.)
  5:439–40, 5:441
democracy 2:868–9, 2:872
economics
  philosophy of 3:214–15, 3:221
educational philosophy 3:230
empiricism 3:302
environmental ethics 3:336
European positivism
  Latin America 7:565, 7:569
experiments in social science 3:520
explanation in history and social
  science 3:530
externalism
  moral motivation 6:523, 6:527
federalism and confederalism
  3:573–4
feminism 3:579, 3:583, 3:620
foundationalism 3:723
freedom 6:367–9
freedom of speech 3:762, 3:764
  journalism ethics 5:127
Godwin, W. 4:125
good, theories of the 4:134, 4:135
Hamilton, W. 4:219
happiness 4:228, 4:229, 6:369–70
harm principle 5:462
  law and morality 5:439,
    5:440–1, 5:442
hedonism 9:551, 9:553
history
  philosophy of 4:458
imagination 4:708
impartiality 4:717
induction 6:365–6
inductive inference 4:756, 4:758
international relations 4:832
introspection, psychology of 4:846
justice 5:143, 5:147, 6:372–3
legitimacy 5:541
liberal nationalism 6:659
liberalism 5:604, 5:605
liberty 6:373–4
limits of law 5:464
logic 5:728–9
mind 6:366–7

moral sentiments 6:566, 6:570
morality
  emotion 6:563
  and religion 8:220
multiculturalism 6:600
nation and nationalism 6:661
nature and convention 6:736
neutrality
  political 6:819, 6:821
omnipotence critique 8:245
On Liberty
  paternalism 7:250–1, 7:252
other minds 6:231–2
paternalism 7:250–1, 7:252
phenomenalism 7:331, 7:333
pleasure 6:370–1, 7:449, 7:451
pluralism 7:464
poetry 7:477
political representation 8:272
prescriptivism 7:668, 7:670
privacy 7:693
proper names 8:154–5, 8:164
psychologism 6:364–5
public interest 7:834
religion
  history of philosophy of 8:247
  and morality 8:224
rhetoric 8:306, 8:309
science
  demarcation problem 2:866
  nineteenth-century philosophy
    of 8:566, 8:567–9, 8:572
scientific method 8:578, 8:580
sexuality 8:725
slavery 8:805, 8:806
social science
  contemporary philosophy of
    8:847
  history of philosophy of 8:851,
    8:852, 8:858
supererogation 9:233, 9:235
teleological ethics 9:294–5
Thoreau, H.D. 9:392
Tocqueville, A. de 9:425
toleration 9:430, 9:433
truthfulness 9:481, 9:483, 9:484,
  9:485
utilitarianism
  golden rule 9:537, 9:539
  hedonistic 4:259
  political philosophy
    history of 7:515
  proof arguments 9:555, 9:557
Utilitarianism
  justice 6:372, 6:373
  pleasure 6:370
  utility principle 6:371

utility principle 6:371–3
welfare 9:703
women 3:616
Millar, J.
    Enlightenment, Scottish 3:330
Millar, John **6:375–6**
Millas, Jorge 7:352
Millenarianism 4:250–1
Miller, A.I. 7:482
Miller, Alexander
    objectivity †7:73–6
Miller, B. 8:787
Miller, C. 5:367
Miller, D. 7:539
Miller, David
    anarchism 1:248
    desert and merit †3:24–7
    freedom and liberty 3:757
    Hume, D. 4:561–2
    market
        ethics of the †6:107–10
    nationalism †6:657–62
    needs and interests 6:755
    Pareto principle †7:227–8
    political philosophy †7:500–3
    social democracy †8:827–8
    socialism 8:886
    state 9:122
Miller, Dickenson 3:140–1, 3:142
Miller, D.L. 6:212
Miller, F.D. 1:434, 1:435, 4:344
Miller, G. 8:656
Miller, G.A. 1:695
Miller, H.B. 9:557
Miller, I. 4:587
Miller, M.A. 5:314
Miller, Perry 1:206, 3:245, 7:385–6, 9:392
Miller, Richard W.
    Marxist philosophy of science †6:147–50
    scientific realism and antirealism 8:584
Miller, S. 7:385–6, 8:823–4
Miller, Samuel 9:224, 9:229
Miller, T.P. 1:782
Millet, K. 3:583
Millet, L. 5:339–40
Millikan, Ruth Garrett
    concepts 2:516
    functionalism 3:804, 3:805, 3:813
    methodological individualism 6:344
    reference
        teleological theory 8:162, 8:164
    teleological theories of meaning 8:673, 8:675

teleology 9:297
Milliken, S.F. 2:122
Mills, C.W. 8:858–9, 9:698
Mills, D.E. 2:150
Milton, John 3:765
Milton, J.R.
    Bacon, F. †1:624–32
    Chillingworth, W. †2:307–9
    inductive inference 4:759
Mimaki, K. 2:63, 6:473, 9:408
Mīmāṃsā 4:439, **6:376–81**
    see also Bhāṭṭa; Prābhākara; Seśvara
    analogy
        knowledge 5:282
    circumstantial implication 5:282
    duty and virtue 3:184–5
    epistemology 6:378–9
    heaven 4:255
    history of 6:377–8
    Indian and Tibetan philosophy 4:737
    intrinsic validity 6:378, 6:379
    karma and rebirth 5:213
    language philosophy 4:436
    meaning 6:240, 6:241, 6:243
    sacrifice
        God concepts 4:103
    scriptural language 6:379–81
    self
        theories of 8:609–10
    self-certificationalism
        epistemic 3:388, 3:390–1
    sense perception 8:691
    universals 9:544–5, 9:546
    Veda interpretation 4:102, 4:835
    Vedānta School differentiation 9:590–1
    veridicality 3:411
Mīmāṃsāsūtra 5:283, 5:285
mimēsis (imitation) **6:381–2**
    feminist textual criticism (Irigaray, L.) 5:2
    Heidegger, Martin 5:340–1
    Islamic philosophy (Ibn Rushd) 1:78
    verisimulitude (Lacoue-Labarthe, P.) 5:340, 5:341
    Western poetry 1:69
Minamoto, Ryōen 9:440–1
mind
    see also consciousness; mental; mind-body problem; nous; other minds; psyche; psychology; xin
    actuality of (Wundt, W.) 9:799
    adverbial theory of mental states **6:314–17**

Akan philosophy 1:103, 1:138
    analytic behaviourism **1:689–93**, 6:174
    analytic philosophy 1:226
    anomalous monism **1:276–80**
    Aquinas, T. 1:334–5
    Aristotle
        conceptual scope 1:414
    artificial intelligence debate 2:393
    artistic intention 1:514–15
    associationism (Tucker, A.) 9:491
    Augustine 1:542, 1:547–9
    Awakening of Faith in Mahāyāna 1:603–4
    belief **1:702–6**
    bodily sensations **1:792–5**
    brain relationship
        Dennett, D.C. 2:883
        Hartley, D. 4:236, 4:237
    bundle theory of **6:382–5**, 7:331
    Cartesian concept of
        Sellars, W.S. critique 8:639, 8:640
    causality (Wundt, W.) 9:799–800
    Chan Buddhism
        Linji 5:646
    child's theory of **6:385–90**
    cognition
        computational theories 2:392–3
        Tetens, J.N. 9:319, 9:320–1
    computational theories of **6:390–4**, 6:404–5
        cognitive architecture 2:392–3
        critique 1:491–2
        descriptionalism 4:704
        Fodor, J.A. 3:684
        learning 5:486
        scientific behaviourism 8:800
        Turing, A.M. 9:493
        vision 6:342–3
    concepts 2:505–14
    dualism **3:133–8**
    eliminativism 6:173, 6:176
    emotions (Spinoza, B. de) 9:101
    post-enlightenment cultivation of Buddhism
        Korean 2:112
    epiphenomenalism **3:351–4**, 6:174
    evolutionary theory (Darwin, C.R.) 2:797–8
    existence in the (Mulla Sadra) 6:596
    external world (Hobbes, T.) 4:466
    externalism 6:176–7
    faculty theory (Herbert, E.) 4:372–3

as first cause (Anaxagoras) 1:249,
  1:252–3
formal causes of
  Buddhism
    Chinese 2:89–90
functionalism **3:805–13**, 6:174–5,
  8:150–1
German idealism 4:43
Henry of Ghent 4:357–8
holism 4:488–93
idealism 4:662–9
ideas
  innate
    Leibniz, G.W. 5:551–2
    Locke, J. 5:668
    More, H. 6:578
  Malebranche, N. 6:58–9
  Spinoza, B. de 9:99–100
identity theory of **6:394–9**, 6:404
  Armstrong, D.M. 1:442
  colour and qualia 2:421–3
  materialism 6:174
  neutral monism 6:817
  phenomenal states 2:586
  reductionism 8:150
  Smart, J.J.C. 8:814
idols (Bacon, F.) 1:628–9
imagination **4:705–8**
immortality (Astell, M.) 1:528
Indian philosophy of **6:399–403**
  Buddhism 6:401–2
  personal identity 6:402
  Upaniṣads 6:400–1
inner harmony (Shaftesbury, Third
  Earl of) 8:730–1
intention **4:811–16**
introspection **4:837–42**
  Maine de Biran, P.-F. 6:49,
    6:51–2
irrelevance to scientific
  explanation (Skinner, B.F.)
  8:800
language relationship
  meaning 5:409–10
  Searle, J. 8:589
logical behaviourism (Ryle, G.)
  8:428, 8:430
materialism 3:134, **6:173–7**
  ontology in Indian philosophy
    7:121
mathematical point (Fardella, M.)
  3:559
matter
  Astell, M. 1:528–9
  Lichtenberg, G.C. 5:623–4
  Plutarch of Chaeronea 7:469
  Sāṅkhya-Yoga dualism 6:200

memory **6:296–300**
mental content 6:405–6
as mental habits (Tolstoi, L.N.)
  9:438
mentalistic explanation (Piaget, J.)
  7:384
Mill, J.S. 6:366–7
modularity of **6:450–1**
  computational models of vision
    9:635–6
  Fodor, J.A. 6:405
monism (Spinoza, B. de) 9:97–9
motions (Hobbes, T.) 4:469–70
multiplication of
  split brain studies 9:107,
    9:108–9
Native American philosophy
  6:665–6
naturalism 6:406
neo-Confucianism
  China 6:770, 6:773
neutral monism **6:816–17**
partitioning of
  self-deception 8:626–7
perception **7:287–93**
personal identity (Hume, D.)
  4:548–9
persons 7:318–19
philosophy of **6:403–7**
  computer model
    Neumann, J. von 6:810–11
  materialism
    Gödel's theorems 4:114
Platonic theory (Cudworth, R.)
  2:741–2
pluralist determinism
  (Anderson, J.) 1:267–8
privacy 1:514
property supervenience 9:238–9
propositional attitudes **7:779–87**
psychological nominalism
  (Sellars, W.S.) 8:639–40
reductionism **8:149–53**
representational modes (Le
  Grand, A.) 5:479
science of (Vygotskii, L.S.) 9:674
self-consciousness
  (Anscombe, G.E.M.) 1:281
self-cultivation
  Chinese philosophy 8:617,
    8:622, 8:623
  Buddhism 8:619–21
self-determination (Johnson, S.)
  5:124
sensation (Condillac, É.B. de)
  2:524–5

soul distinction (Plutarch of
  Chaeronea) 7:467–8
structure (Freud, S.) 3:791–2
study of
  introspection 4:844–5
subconscious (James, W.) 5:62
substance dualism (Brown, T.)
  2:26, 2:28
supervenience 6:175–6, 9:236
transcendent principles
  (Tetens, J.N.) 9:320
type/token distinction 9:510
vita contemplativa (Arendt, H.)
  1:371–2
William of Auvergne 9:726
world connection
  meaning 5:409
Yogācāra Buddhism (Wônch'ūk)
  9:792
Mind simpliciter
  God (Geulincx, A.) 4:60
mind-body problem
  anomalous monism (Davidson, D.)
    2:801
  Augustine 1:547–8
  Cambridge Platonism 2:184
  Clauberg, J. 2:381
  consciousness (Searle, J.) 8:589–90
  Cordemoy, G. de 2:673
  Descartes, R. 3:11–12
  dialectical concept of behaviour
    (Merleau-Ponty, M.) 6:321
  Du Bois-Reymond, E. 3:130
  dual-aspect approach (Nagel, T.)
    6:645
  Elisabeth of Bohemia 3:267–8
  Foucher, S. 3:716
  Indian philosophy 6:402–3
  Kant, I.
    Maimon, S. 6:36
  Leibniz, G.W. 5:549
    Marcel, G. critique 6:92
  materialism 6:177
  occasionalism 7:87–8
  organic theory (Herder, J.G.)
    4:378, 4:380–1
  panpsychism 7:197
    Burthogge, R. 2:145–6
  process philosophy 7:713
  psychophysical parallelism
    (Wundt, W.) 9:799
  Regius, H. 4:353
  self-cultivation
    Chinese philosophy 8:622
  split brains 9:109
  sport 9:112–13, 9:116
  Tolstoi, L.N. 9:438

Vives, J.L. 9:648
minds, other *see* other minds
Miner, E. 1:90
Minerva, N. 9:561
minima 1:535
 Epicureanism 3:340, 3:342–3
minimal entities
 mass terms 6:169
minimalism
 art 1:451
 Chomsky, N. 2:338
minimality lemma
 method of forcing 3:694, 3:696–7
Minimax theorem
 game theory 2:825
Mink, L.O. 2:415
Minkowski, Hermann
 Baumgardt, D. 1:669
 Einstein, A. 3:258
 relativity theory
  philosophical significance of
   8:192–3, 8:199
 spacetime 9:66–7, 9:69
Minnis, A.J. 1:813
Minogue, Kenneth
 Oakeshott, M.J. †7:70–3
Minor, Robert N.
 Radhakrishnan, S. †8:23–5
 Tagore, R. †9:257–8
minor term
 glossary 5:805
Minor, V.H. 1:509
minorities
 cultural identity 2:745–6
 democracy 2:868–9
 marginality **6:99–101**
 social
  oppression of 8:637
Minowitz, P. 8:822
Minsky, Marvin 1:492, 2:496, 2:578
Minsky, R. 3:588
Mints, G. 6:426, 7:751
Mintz, Grafton 2:118
Mintz, S. 4:476
Mir Damad, Muhammad Baqir
 6:408–11
 emanationism 6:409
 time 6:408, 6:409–10
miracles **6:411–16**
 as acts of God 6:414–15
 counterfactual conditionals
  2:687–8
 credibility
  Latitudinarianism 5:434
 definition 6:412
 divine intervention 8:249
 Enlightenment 7:798

evidence for (Campbell, G.) 2:191,
 2:192
Jewish philosophy
 Arama, I. 1:350–1
 Averroism 1:600, 1:602
 Nahmanides, M. 6:648–9
 prophecy
  Abravanel, I. 1:20–1
  Judah ben Moses of Rome
   5:129–30
mythological explanation of
 (Strauss, D.F.) 9:164–5
natural causes 6:413–14
natural explanation
 (Pomponazzi, P.) 7:529, 7:530
natural religion (Paley, W.) 7:187
polemical deism (Tindal, M.)
 9:422
possibility of 6:412–13
prayer
 response to 7:652
prophecy 7:768, 7:769–70
religious belief 8:245
revelation 8:298–9
scientific realism 8:581, 8:582
testimony
 Hume, D. 4:548
 personal 6:413
uniform experience (Lewis, C.S.)
 5:589–90
world of images (Ibn al-'Arabi)
 4:604
Miranda, M. do C.T. de 5:483
Mirimanoff, Dmitrii 9:855
Miró Quesada, Francisco
 analytical philosophy
  Latin America 1:229, 1:231–2,
   1:233
 phenomenology
  Latin America 7:350, 7:352
Mironenko, S.V. 5:609
Mirowski, P. 3:221
mirth 4:562
Misak, C. 7:283–4
Misbah Yazdi, Muhammad Taqi 5:19
Miščevic, Nenad 9:55
Misch, G. 5:489
misery
 aesthetic experience
  (Schopenhauer, A.) 8:550–1
Mises, Dr *see* Fechner, Gustav
 Theodor
Mises, Ludwig von
 economics 3:221, 4:246
 Hayek, F.A. 4:246
 praxeology 7:649
 socialism 4:247

Mises, Richard von 2:482, 7:705,
 8:59, 9:612–11
Mishnah
 Rabbinic Judaism
  halakhah 4:205–6
Mishra, G. 6:30
misperception
 knowledge 7:287
 objects 7:288
Misra, U. 6:200
misrepresentation
 informational semantics 8:659–61
missionaries
 pre-Columbian thought
  Latin America 5:429, 5:430,
   5:431
Mitarai, Masaru 9:822
Mitcham, Carl
 information technology and ethics
  4:781
 technology and ethics †9:280–4
Mitchell, Basil
 negative theology 6:762
 Newman, J.H. 6:823
 religion
  history of philosophy of 8:247
  morality 8:220, 8:224
 Tennant, F.R. 9:303
Mitchell, J. 3:584, 3:588, 3:613
Mitchell, P. 6:389
Mitchell, Sir William 1:575, 1:576,
 1:583
mitigated scepticism *see* scepticism
Mitin, M.B. 1:526, 6:158
Mito tradition
 Confucianism, Japanese 2:554
Mitsis, P. 3:350, 3:797
Mittelstadt, P. 7:886
Miura Baien 5:75–6
mixed motive games
 prisoner's dilemma 8:67–8
 rational choice theory 8:66, 8:67–8
Miyagawa, T. 7:13
Miyake, Masahiko 5:44
Miyamoto Kenji 5:659
Miyata, Y. 2:579
Miyoshi, Masao 5:660
Mizuta, H. 8:822
mKhas grub dge legs dpal bzang po
 6:416–17
mKhas grub rje *see* mKhas grub dge
 legs dpal bzang po
mnemonics, syllogistic
 glossary 5:805
Mo Ti *see* Mozi
Mo Tzu *see* Mozi
Mochulský, K. 9:32

modal logic **6:417–26, 6:426–33**
  see also deontic logic; modal
  operators; quantified modal logic
  ability
    logic of 6:431–2
  adverbs 1:49
  Alexander of Aphrodisias 1:170
  compounded/divided 5:752–3
  impact on philosophy of logic
    5:764–5
  Kanger, S. 8:486
  Kripke, S.A. 5:302–3
  many-valued logic (Łukasiewicz, J.)
    5:861–2
  meaning and verification 6:234–5
  medieval 5:752–3
  modal operators **6:433–6**
  possible worlds 6:427–9, 6:430–2,
    8:663–4
  possible worlds semantics 8:663–4
  property theory 7:764
  provability logic 7:793–6
  quantified 6:429–30
  Segerberg, K. 8:486
modal operators **6:433–6**
  monadic connective accounts
    6:433–4
  predicate accounts 6:434–5
  quantifier accounts 6:434
modality
  Carnap, R. 2:212
  de re/de dicto belief 2:815–17
  essence (Henry of Ghent) 4:356–7
  fallacies of
    relevance logic 8:201–2
  free logics 3:742
  possible worlds (Lewis, D.K.)
    5:591–3
  second-order logic 8:603
model theory 5:735, **6:436–42**
  decidability (Tarski, A.) 9:263
  definability 1:762
  epistemic logic 3:355
  logical laws 5:786
  Löwenheim-Skolem theorems and
    non-standard models 5:846
  scientific theories 9:350
    logical positivism 9:346
  Tarski's definition of truth 9:268
models **6:442–7**
  see also model theory
  computer
    architecture 2:392
    cognitive/non-cognitive 2:392
  non-standard **5:846–51**
    mathematics 1:212

scientific
  determinism 3:37
  Duhem, P.M.M. critique of
    3:144
  fictionalism 3:668
model-theoretic approach
  social science
    naturalism 8:839–41
Moderatus of Gades 6:808
modern logic *see* mathematical logic
modernism **6:447–9**
  see also postmodernism
  anti-positivism
    Latin America 1:304–5
  artistic (Adorno, T.W.) 1:44–5
  critiques of
    Habermas, J. 4:198
    Lukács, G. 5:856, 5:858–9
  Cubism 6:448
  epistemic trauma 6:447–8
  ethnophilosophy relationship
    3:448–9
  observation 6:448–9
  postmodernism
    revolution 8:303
  reflexivity 6:449
  Relativity Theory 6:447–8
  religion 6:447
  representation 6:448
modernity
  critiques of
    Leont'ev, K.N. 5:568–9
    Losev, A.F. 5:830–1
  gnosticism (Voegelin, E.) 9:655–6
  Heideggerian philosophy of
    science 4:326
  Islamic philosophy (al-Afghani)
    1:95
  Judaism (Kaplan, M.) 5:204–5
  moral pluralism (MacIntyre, A.)
    6:529
  nationalism
    political philosophy
      Indian 7:522–3
  postmodernism 6:449, 7:587–8,
    7:589, 7:590–1
  revolution 8:301
  technological transformation
    9:281
  thought (Stirner, M.) 9:140
  totalitarianism 9:444
  tragedy of
    German Romanticism 8:349
  transition to
    social theory 8:874
  Western
    Latin American literature 5:655

modes
  eternal-infinite distinction
    (Spinoza, B. de) 9:95–6
  God relationship (Spinoza, B. de)
    9:95–7
  ideas (Locke, J.) 5:671–2
Modi *see* Mozi
Modiano, R. 2:406
modism 5:389, 5:393–4, 5:402–3
  grammar 5:393, 5:397, 5:402
  medieval logic 5:749
    Peter of Auvergne 7:321
  modes of signifying 5:393–4, 5:400
Modrzewski, Andrzej Frycz 7:485,
  7:488
modularity
  mind **6:450–1**
    computational models of vision
      9:635–6
    Fodor, J.A. 6:405
    self-deception 8:626–7
    pragmatics 7:629
modus ponens
  glossary 5:805
  indicative conditionals 4:740,
    4:742
modus tollens
  glossary 5:805
  indicative conditionals 4:740
Moerdijk, I. 2:236–7, 2:239
Moggach, D. 1:667
Moggalīputta Tissa
  inference
    Indian theories of 4:766
  nirvāṇa 7:11
Moggridge, D.E. 5:235
Mohaghegh, M. 8:441
Mohanty, C.T. 3:593
Mohanty, J.N.
  epistemology, Indian 3:392
  error and illusion
    Indian concepts of 3:413
  Gaṅgeśa 3:846
  Hindu philosophy 4:440
  Husserl, E. 4:587
  Indian and Tibetan philosophy
    4:740
  phenomenological movement
    7:342
  testimony in Indian philosophy
    9:318–19
  Vātsyāyana 9:588
Mohe Zhiguan see Zhiyi
Mohist philosophy **6:451–8**
  see also Mozi
  assertibility 5:698, 5:703
  Canons 5:696–7

Heaven 5:697
history
    Golden Age 4:447–8
human nature 6:453
Hundred Schools conflict 2:322
jian'ai (impartial care) 6:453–4
language theories 5:693–4, 5:697,
    5:699–700, 6:456–7
li 5:594
Lushi chunqiu 5:864
rationalism 2:323
Mohr, R. 8:638
Moi, T. 1:687, 2:374, 3:613, 5:479
Mojsisch, B. 6:288
mokṣa
    see also enlightenment; liberation;
    nirvāṇa
    causation
        Indian theories of 2:251, 2:252
    fate 3:567
    Hindu philosophy (Śaṅkara) 8:459
    self
        Indian theories of 8:608
Mokṣākaragupta 4:766
Molander, Bengt
    praxeology †7:647–9
molecular biology 6:458–61
molecular genetics 4:12, 4:13–14
    reduction 4:14
molecularism
    semantic/mental 4:488, 4:489,
        4:490
Moles, Robert N.
    Austin, J. †1:569–71
Moleschott, Jacob 2:51, 6:173
Molesworth, W. 7:238
Molière, J-B.P. 8:632
Molina Flores, C. 1:230, 1:233
Molina, Luis de 6:461–5
    see also Molinism
    Báñez, D. 1:648
    de auxiliis 9:72, 9:76–7
    divine foreknowledge 8:244
    futuribilia (conditional future
        contingents) 6:465–6, 9:189–90
    Jesuits
        Thomism 9:383
    Pelagianism 7:286–7
    providence 7:799, 7:801
    religion, history of philosophy of
        8:247
Molinism 6:465–7
    divine foreknowledge 7:110
    middle knowledge 7:111–12,
        7:799–800
    providence 7:799–801

Molland, A. George
    Bradwardine, T. 1:866
    Henry of Harclay 4:360–3
    natural philosophy, medieval 6:706
    Oresme, Nicole 7:153–7
    Oxford Calculators 7:182, 7:183
Molnár, G. von 4:129
Molnar, T. 9:561
Moltmann, J. 4:298, 4:510
Molyneux problem 6:467–9
    infant cognition 2:390
Molyneux, William 6:467, 6:469
momentariness
    see also impermanence
    Buddhist doctrine of 6:469–73
        Dharmakīrti 7:23–4
        exposition 6:469–70
        Japan 6:591–4
        matter 6:198
        potentiality 7:605–6
        proofs 6:471–2
        Sarvāstivāda School 2:56
        Udayana 9:512–13
moments
    modes of being (Ingarden, R.W.)
        4:790
Momigliano, A. 9:21, 9:814
Mommsen, W. 9:698
Monad
    see also Indefinite Dyad
    dualism (Numenius) 7:54–5
    first principle (Xenocrates) 9:806
    Indefinite Dyad opposition
        (Plutarch of Chaeronea) 7:465,
        7:466–7
monadic connectives
    modal operators as 6:433–4
monads 8:77
    interaction (Knutzen, M.) 5:288
    Leibniz, G.W. 5:542, 5:547
        Voltaire critique 9:660
        Wolff, C. comparison 9:782
    materialism problem
        (Helmont, F.M. van) 4:341
    Russian Neo-Leibnizianism
        (Lossky, N.O.) 5:833, 5:834,
        5:836
monarchy
    see also kingship
    Alighieri, Dante 1:183
    Aquinas, T. 1:341
    constitutional (Schleiermacher, F.)
        8:537
    critique of (Helvétius, C.-A.)
        4:346–7
    Judaism (Abravanel, I.) 1:20,
        1:21–2

republicanism 8:281
al-Tusi 3:441
monasticism
    Rabelais, F. critique 8:16
Monboddo, Lord (James Burnett)
    6:473–4
Monchamp, G. 4:61
Mondolfo, R. 4:369
money
    philosophy of (Simmel, G.) 8:778
    professionalism conflict
        medical ethics 6:261
    quantity theory (Bodin, J.) 1:797
    scientific responsibility 8:289
Monfasani, John
    George of Trebizond †4:34–6
    Petrarca, F. †7:325–9
    Renaissance humanism †4:533–41
    Valla, L. †9:568–73
monism 6:474–5
    see also atomism; dualism;
    Hegelian monism; materialism;
    pluralism
    anomalous 1:276–80, 1:278–9,
        2:801
    anomalous (Davidson, D.) 2:801
    Buddha's rejection of 2:52
    descriptive
        pluralism contrast 2:396
    developmental 4:43
    Diogenes of Apollonia 3:88
    Eleatic (Melissus) 6:292–5
    eliminative (Parmenides) 7:232
    Engels, F. 8:854–5
    ethical
        logic of ethical discourse 5:763
    evolutionary (Haeckel, E.H.)
        4:200–1
    field theory, classical
        electromagnetic particles 3:669
    Indian 6:475–9
        Advaita Vedānta
            dialectical 6:477–8
            self 6:476
        Radhakrishnan, S. 8:23–5
        sublatability 6:476–7
        theological 6:478–9
    material
        Anaximenes 1:259, 1:260
        Thales 9:322
    metaphysics 6:339
    Milesian philosophy
        matter 6:193
        Presocratics 7:671
    mind-body (Spinoza, B. de) 9:97–9
    neutral 6:475, 6:816–18
        Mach, E. 6:13, 6:14–16

paranormal phenomena 7:222
normative
  pluralism contrast 2:397
  the One (Plotinus) 7:458
Parmenides 5:356–7
  Zeno of Elea 9:844–5
psychological
  Advaita Vedānta 2:3–4
radical
  Eleatic philosophy 1:263
self
  Indian theories of 8:610
Spencer, H. 8:854
substance (Spinoza, B. de) 9:93–5
theosophy 9:364
transitivity (Schelling, F.W.J. von)
  8:512–13
Vedānta 4:438
monistic idealism
  the One (Radhakrishnan, S.)
    8:23–4
Monk, J.D. 1:846, 8:595, 9:264
Monk, Ray 8:403, 9:770
Mönnich, M. 2:191
Mönnich, U. 7:766
Monod, Jacques 7:2, 7:5
monodualism
  Grot, N.
    Russian positivism 7:563
Monologion see Anselm of
  Canterbury
monologism
  Bakhtin, M. critique 1:641–2
monophyly
  classification problems
    taxonomy 9:273–5
monophysitism
  Christology 4:727
    Philoponus 7:375
monopsychism
  Averroism 1:596
monotheism 6:479–83
  see also God; polytheism
  cultic 6:480, 6:481
  descriptive 6:480, 6:482
  divine simplicity 8:785
  Hinduism
    Brahmo Samaj movement 2:5,
      2:6
  Judaism
    ethical (Formstecher, S.) 5:98–9
    pietism (Ibn Paquda) 4:634
    Rabbinic theology 9:333–6
  Latin American
    pre-Columbian religions 5:430

metaphysics
  adaptation of Platonism to
    7:806
  moral critique of (Hume, D.) 4:559
  normative 6:480
  putative (Xenophanes) 9:809
  radical (Niebuhr, H.R.) 6:839
Rashdall, H. 8:60
reincarnation 8:182–3, 8:185
Rg Veda
  Brahman 2:1
salvation 8:447, 8:449–50
supernatural 7:97
Monro, D.H. 4:567
Monro, H.D. 6:74
Montagnes, B. 2:175
Montague Grammar 1:240–2, 3:92,
  6:484–5, 8:666–7
Montague, Richard Merett 6:483–5
  see also Montague Grammar;
    Montague's theorem
  adverbs 1:50
  compositionality 2:477
  concepts 2:516
  determinism and indeterminism
    3:39
  epistemic paradoxes 7:214
  intensional logics 4:810
  modal logic 6:426
  modal operators 6:435
  possible worlds 6:432, 8:666–7,
    8:668–9
  pragmatics 7:632
  property theory 7:765, 7:766
  second-order logic 8:604
  semantic paradoxes and theories
    of truth 8:648
  theory of types 9:361, 9:362
Montague's theorem 8:647
Montaigne, Michel Eyquem de
  6:485–9
  Agrippa von Nettesheim, H.C.
    1:133
  influenced by
    Sextus Empiricus 8:717
  scepticism 3:374, 3:382
    Renaissance 8:498, 8:499, 8:503
  truthfulness 9:482, 9:485
Montebello, R. 6:53
Montefiore, Alan
  analytic philosophy 1:228
  neutrality
    political 6:821
  responsibilities of scientists and
    intellectuals †8:287–90
Monteiro, J.P. 1:231

Montesquieu, Charles Louis de
  Secondat, Baron de 6:489–94
  constitutionalism 2:619
  democracy 2:872
  Enlightenment, continental
    3:318–19
  federalism and confederalism
    3:574
  historical explanation 6:491–2
  law and society
    historical jurisprudence 5:138,
      5:141
    Russian Enlightenment 3:327
  slavery 8:805, 8:806
  social criticism 6:490–1
  social theory and law 8:873–4,
    8:879
  sociopolitical forms 6:492–3
    Helvétius, C.-A. 4:346
Monteverdi, Claudio 7:129
Montgomery, F.K. 2:120
Montgomery Watt, W. 5:31
Montmarquet, James A. 9:619, 9:621
mood
  glossary 5:805
Moody, E.A. 4:479, 6:706, 9:727,
  9:748
Mooij, J.J.A. 7:482
Mook, D. 6:449
Mookerjee, S. 2:99, 3:76, 6:81
Mooney, M. 9:606
Mooney, R. 2:578, 2:579
Moor, James
  information technology and ethics
    4:781
  Turing, A.M. †9:493–5
Moore, A.W.
  antirealism
    mathematics †1:307–11
  infinity †4:772–8
  Zeno of Elea 9:852
Moore, B. 7:823, 9:433
Moore, C. 2:596, 9:229
Moore, C.A.
  causation
    Indian theories of 2:257
  Chinese Confucianism 2:548
  Japanese Philosophy 5:79
  reincarnation 8:186
  truthfulness 9:485
Moore, C.N. 8:559
Moore, F.C.T.
  Bergson, H.-L. 1:737
  Bonnet, C. †1:838–40
  Cabanis, P.-J. †2:166–8
  Maine de Biran, P.-F. †6:49–53

Moore, George Edward **6:494–9**
analytic ethics 1:220–1, 1:223
analytical philosophy
    Latin America 1:230, 1:233
axiology 1:609–10, 1:611–12
beauty 1:682, 1:684
certainty 2:265, 2:267
commonsensism 2:455, 3:379,
    3:382
conceptual analysis 2:518, 2:522
consciousness 2:595
critique of (Austin, J.L.) 1:574
doubt 3:125
egoism and altruism 3:248
epistemology and ethics 3:370
essentialism 3:421
ethics 6:495–6
    normative 3:720, 3:723
fact/value distinction 3:538
good
    non-natural property 9:580,
      9:581
    theories of the 4:131–2, 4:135
hedonism 4:259
honour 4:504
ideal utilitarianism 2:606
idealism rejection 6:496
ideals 4:675
intuitionism in ethics 4:856
knowledge
    concept of 5:276
McTaggart, J.M.E. 6:28
method of analysis 1:224, 1:228
modus ponens fallibilism 8:498
monism 6:475
moral scepticism 6:543, 6:545
naturalistic fallacy 6:713, 6:714,
    6:717
    applied ethics 1:319–20
    logic of ethical discourse 5:761,
      5:764
    'open-question' argument
      moral knowledge 6:517, 6:520,
        6:714–15
perception 7:299
perfectionism 7:302
phenomenal consciousness 2:588
philosophical analysis 6:497–8
Principa Ethica
    normative ethics 3:720, 3:723
Ross, W.D. 8:367
scepticism 8:497
    common sense defence 6:496–7
    Wittgenstein, L. critique 9:768
sense-data 3:300–1, 8:695
Sidgwick, H. 8:763
supervenience 9:238, 9:239–40

utilitarianism 9:557
value 9:582
Moore, Gregory H.
axiom of choice †1:612–14
infinitary logic 4:772
logic, early twentieth century
    †5:729–38
paradoxes of set and property
    †7:214–21
second- and higher-order logics
    8:595
Zermelo, E. 9:855
Moore, J.
Carmichael, G. †2:206–8
Darwin, C.R. 2:798
Hutcheson, F. 4:593
Moore, K.D. 3:701, 8:141
Moore, M.H. 2:690
Moore, Peter 6:629
Moore, R.C. 7:34
Moore, U. 5:525
Moorhouse, B. 5:520
Moosa, M. 5:252
Mora, José María Luis 7:567, 7:569
Morais, H.M. 2:856
Morais Valle, José María de 2:10
moral action
    abstract/practical distinction
      (Price, R.) 7:678
    Jewish philosophy (Saadiah Gaon)
      8:437–8
moral agents 2:890–1, **6:499–504**
see also moral luck; moral
    standing
autonomy 6:569
collectivity 6:502–3
deontology 2:890–1
duty relationship 3:179, 3:181
free will 3:749–50
Kantian view 6:501–2
mental illness 6:313–14
recipients distinction 6:499
relativity 2:890–1
responsibility 8:287–90, 8:291
self (Taylor, C.) 9:277
Soviet Marxism 6:158
universalism in ethics 9:536
utilitarianism 9:553
virtue ethics 9:623
will 9:722–3
moral certainty
    Latitudinarianism 5:433
moral character
    as beauty
      African aesthetics 1:63–4
moral codes
    sociobiology 8:895

moral consciousness
    development (Berdaev, N.A.)
      1:729
moral contractualism
    Scanlon, T.M. 2:658, 2:664–5
moral development **6:504–5**, 6:506
see also moral education
care ethic 2:281
education (Rousseau, J.-J.) 8:372
feminist ethics 3:603
Panaetius 7:189–90
universal role taking (Mead, G.H.)
    6:211
Xunzi 9:819
moral dilemmas *see* moral pluralism
moral discourse
    aesthetic discourse relationship
      African culture 1:63
    halakhah
      Jewish bioethics 1:777
moral education **6:505–9**
see also moral development
African ethical systems 3:432
childhood (Rousseau, J.-J.) 8:372
Durkheim, É. 3:176
emotions 6:559
family hierarchies 3:551
particularism 6:528
role of examples 3:487, 3:488
moral expertise **6:509–11**
    medical ethics 6:261, 6:263
moral facts *see* ethical facts
moral faith
    Kant, I. 4:507–8
moral feeling *see* moral sentiments
moral freedom
    Herzen, A.I. 4:408
    Kant, I.
      categorical imperative 5:191–2
      evil 5:192
      transcendental idealism 5:192
    Mill, J.S. 6:367–9
    Saadiah Gaon 8:437
moral health
    Ibn Miskawayh 4:630, 4:631–2
moral ideal
    independent ethics
      (Kotarbiński, T.) 5:294
moral judgment **6:511–14**
see also moral reasoning
analytic ethics **1:220–3**
    emotivism 1:221
    intuitionism 1:220–1
    noncognitivism 1:221–2
Chinese Confucianism 2:545–7
Chinese neo-Confucianism 6:772,
    6:775

convergence
  objectivity 9:582–3
disagreement
  bioethics 1:775–6
  Hume, D. 4:555–6
emotions 6:532
emotivism **3:291–3**
  Stevenson, C.L. 9:134–5
examples 3:488
first principles (Reid, T.) 8:171,
  8:177
liberalism 5:439–40
moral relativism 6:539–40
moral sentiment (Hume, D.) 4:555
natural law 6:686
passions (Hume, D.) 4:551
practical reason 7:613, 7:618
private (Godwin, W.) 4:123
realism 6:535, 6:536
reasons holism
  logic of ethical discourse 5:763
rightness of actions (Ross, W.D.)
  8:366–7
scepticism 6:543, 6:544
social theory of (Smith, A.) 8:818,
  8:819
subjectivity of 7:526
theory and practice 9:357
universalism
  logic of ethical discourse 5:759,
    5:762
  particularism contrast 9:537
virtue ethics 9:625
voluntary/involuntary (Hume, D.)
  4:552–3
moral justification **6:514–16**
see also moral reasoning
applied ethics 1:319
  Confucianism
    moral judgment 2:545–6
constructivism 2:630–1
epistemic justification contrast
  3:369–70
intuitionism in ethics 4:853–5
moral knowledge 6:519
moral luck 6:520
moral motivation 6:524–5
moral rules 6:513–14
moral scepticism 6:543, 6:544
praise and blame 7:644–5
reflective equilibrium (Rawls, J.)
  5:202
moral knowledge **6:516–20**
see also moral scepticism
autonomy
  ethical 1:587
cognitive naturalism 6:715–16

conscience 2:580
moral agents 6:499–500
prescriptivism/descriptivism
  debate 7:669–70
Prichard, H.A. 7:680–1
reason (Hutcheson, F.) 6:546
Wang Fuzhi 9:681
moral language
Ash'arites 4:641
emotivism (Stevenson, C.L.)
  9:134–5
meaning 3:290–1
moral relativism 6:540
usage 1:221–2
moral law
Kant, I.
  hope 4:507–8
  respect for persons 8:285
  self-control 8:612
moral laxism
casuistry 2:227–8
moral life
Dewey, J. 3:44, 3:49–50
moral luck **6:520–2**
see also blame; praise
Aristotelian/Platonic contrast
  6:521
circumstantial 6:520
constitutive 6:520
deterministic 6:521
moral agents 6:501
responsibility relationship 8:292–3
resultant 6:521
will 9:722–3
Williams, B.A.O. 9:750–1
moral motivation **6:522–8**
see also moral psychology
artificial virtues (Hume, D.)
  4:554–5
autonomy
  ethical 1:587, 1:591
cognitive naturalism 6:715
duty 3:181
emotion 6:507
emotivism 3:292
help and beneficence 4:342–3
human nature
  Butler, J. 2:157
  Hutcheson, F. 4:589–90
internalism/externalism debate
  6:522–3
  practical reason 7:614
  virtue theory 1:610–11
knowledge relationship (Price, R.)
  7:677
Locke, J. 5:678–80
moral judgment 6:512

moral knowledge 6:517
moral sense theories 6:545–6
praise and blame (Kant, I.)
  7:644–5
prescriptivism 7:669
realism 6:535–7
right and good 8:323
Sidgwick, H. 8:759
sympathy (Hume, D.) 6:561
trust 9:467
virtue ethics 9:623–4
virtues and vices 9:626, 9:629
moral norms
see also moral rules
development ethics 3:42
individual autonomy
  (Mamardashvili, M.K.) 6:69
motivation 6:525
practical reason 7:614–15,
  7:616–17
moral order
Socratic explanation of evil
  3:464–5
moral particularism **6:528–9**
development ethics 3:42
logic of ethical discourse 5:763–4
monologism (Bakhtin, M.)
  1:641–2
theory and practice 9:357
universalism contrast 9:537
moral personality
inner life (Epictetus) 3:339
social theory of (Smith, A.) 8:818
moral philosophy
Australia 1:580
James, W. 5:60, 5:62–3
Thomism (Maritain, J.) 6:101,
  6:103
moral pluralism **6:529–31**
see also value pluralism
act-consequentialism 2:604
Common Sense ethics (Reid, T.)
  2:450
deliberative ideals 4:673
development ethics 3:42
intuitionism relationship 4:853
Jewish philosophy (Saadiah Gaon)
  8:438–9
logic of ethical discourse 5:763
perfectionism 7:302
respect for persons 8:286
Ross, W.D. 8:365–7
self-deception 8:630
Williams, B.A.O. 9:751
moral principles
particularism 6:528
pluralism (Reid, T.) 2:449–50

sentiments (Kant, I.) 6:549
moral psychology **6:531–4**
see also moral motivation
free will 3:749
reason/passion relationship
(Wollstonecraft, M.) 9:789,
9:790
will (Seneca, L.A.) 8:680
moral realism **6:534–9**
cognitivism 6:534
consequentialist/deontologic
division (Nagel, T.) 6:645–6
constructivism contrast 2:631
externalism 6:535–7
fact/value distinction 3:538
God
existence of 1:532–3
good, theories of the 4:131
Hutcheson, F. 4:589
internalism 6:523, 6:536–7
intuitionism 4:853–4, 4:855
knowledge 6:518
naturalism 6:535–6
non-naturalism 6:536–7
objectivism 6:534
subjective/objective distinction
(Nagel, T.) 6:645–6
value theory 1:610
Williams, B.A.O. critique 9:751
moral reasoning
see also moral judgment; practical
reasoning
casuistry 2:227–8
emotivism 3:292–3
logic of ethical discourse 5:759–64
subsumptive model 5:762–3,
5:764
rules 6:512–13
Spencer, H. 8:759–60
moral reasons
see also moral justification
action 6:565, 6:566
obligation/supererogation
distinction 9:232, 9:233
moral recipients see moral standing
moral relativism **6:539–42**
see also social relativism
Cockburn, C. critique 2:386
cognitive 6:540
constructivism contrast 2:631
descriptive 6:539
expertise 6:509–10
fallibility of law 5:148
knowledge
scepticism 6:518
language games
Wittgensteinian ethics 9:771

meta-ethical 6:539–41
cognitive 6:540
moral pluralism comparison 6:530
moral sentiments 6:549–50
normative 6:541
prescriptivism 7:668
Signposts movement critique 8:771
virtue ethics 9:624
moral rules
see also moral norms
action (Wollaston, W.) 9:787–8
judgment 9:357
deliberation 6:512–13
justification 6:513–14
moral scepticism **6:542–5**
see also moral knowledge
education 6:507
emotivism (Hume, D.) 2:449
political realism 4:828
theory and practice 9:357–8
toleration 9:432
values 1:610
moral science
Cumberland, R. 2:753
psychology relationship
Mill, J.S. 6:368
moral sense **6:545–8**
see also moral sentiments;
sentimentalism
American philosophy, eighteenth
and nineteenth century 1:202
evolutionary psychology 1:610
human nature (Hutcheson, F.)
4:588, 4:589–91
instincts (Home, H.) 4:500
knowledge 6:519
neo-Confucianism
China 6:772
Price, R. critique 7:676
reason/revelation reconciliation
(Witherspoon, J.) 9:756
moral sentiments **6:548–50**
blame 6:564, 6:565, 6:566–9
sympathy (Hume, D.) 4:550–1,
4:555
moral stage theory
moral development 6:504–5
moral standing **6:550–5**
agent/recipient distinction 6:499
bioethics 1:774–5
environmental ethics 3:333
moral truth
contractualism 2:664–5
moral universalism see ethical
universalism

moral values
God's determinism of (al-Razi,
Fakhr al-Din) 8:114
innate nature of
evolutionary theory
(Darwin, C.R.) 2:798
moral worth 9:582–3
equality 3:393–4
Morales, C. 6:348
moralistes **6:555–8**
morality 3:435
see also ethical; ethics; good; herd
morality; moral; positive morality;
right
aesthetic values (Leont'ev, K.N.)
5:568
akrasia 1:142
Albert the Great 1:150–1
anarchism (Tolstoi, L.N.) 9:439
anti-rationalism (Hume, D.) 4:556
art relationship **1:452–6**, 1:474
Tolstoi, L.N. 9:439
atheism (Bayle, P.) 1:673
attractive conception 8:322, 8:323,
8:324
autonomy of
Bayle, P. 1:675
categorical imperative (Kant, I.)
5:189–90
duty 5:201
ethical autonomy 1:588
impartiality 4:716
moral reasoning 5:201,
7:617–18, 8:100
respect for persons 8:285
Christianity (Frank, S.L.) 3:728–9
civil disobedience 2:366
comedy 2:435–6
compassion (Schopenhauer, A.)
8:546, 8:552
concrete identity 6:571, 6:574–5
cosmopolitan 4:830–2
critiques of 6:564–5, 6:569–70
Hegel, G.W.F. 6:569–70
Williams, B. 6:564–5, 6:569
death of God (Camus, A.) 2:194
divine authority 8:219–20
sin 8:792–3
divine justice (Mu'tazilites) 1:522
divine sanctions (Democritus)
2:876–7
double effect principle **3:119–22**
Bayle, P. 1:675
killing of innocents 4:798
war and peace 9:687
education 3:235
Xenophon 9:812–13

egoism (Stirner, M.) 9:141
and emotions **6:558–64**
    ancient Graeco-Roman theories
      6:559–60
    anti-Stoicism 6:561–2
    development
      (Wollstonecraft, M.) 9:790
    feminist views 6:562–3
    Hägerström, A.A.T. 4:202–3
    Itō Jinsai 5:43
    moral judgment 9:134–5
    moral judgments 6:532
    motivation 6:507
    sentiments 6:548, 6:549
    Spinoza, B. de 9:102
    Stoicism 6:560–1
    twentieth century views 6:562
    Williams, B.A.O. 9:750
empirical science
    Cumberland, R. 2:753
ethical life (Hegel, G.W.F.) 4:274–5
and ethics **6:564–71**
eudaimonia 3:450–1
evil, problem of 3:468
experimental methodology
    (Turnbull, G.) 9:503
fa 3:532–3
feelings
    self-cultivation (Xunzi) 8:622–3
first principles
    common-sense philosophy
      (Reid, T.) 8:171–2, 8:177–8
freedom
    Herzen, A.I. 4:408
    Mill, J.S. 6:361, 6:367–9,
      6:371–3
as functional term 6:564, 6:565–6,
    6:567
God
    existence argument 4:91
    will of (Geulincx, A.) 4:60
happiness relationship
    (Wollaston, W.) 9:787
hedonism 4:257, 4:258
hell 4:332
Hindu philosophy 4:437
historical perspective of (Smith, A.)
    8:818–19
hope 4:507, 4:508
human nature
    exceptionalism 1:270
    Hume, D. 4:544
    Mandeville, B. 6:71–2
    moral psychology 6:531–2
ideals conflict 4:674
and identity **6:571–6**
impartiality 4:715

imperative conception 8:322,
    8:323–4
innate (Mencius) 5:696
innocence 4:797–8
internal/external reason distinction
    (Williams, B.A.O.) 9:751
international 4:826–7, 4:828–30
introspection 4:841–2
Islamic philosophy
    'Abduh, M. 1:6, 1:7
    Ibn Rushd 4:641–2
justification **6:514–16**, 8:219–20
knowledge relationship
    Daxue 2:808
law **5:438–42**
    Aristotelian versus liberal
      traditions 5:439–40
    harm principle 5:440–1
    Hart/Devlin debate 5:441
    legal positivism 5:514–15
    limits of 5:460–3
    moral sense theories (Home, H.)
      4:500
    rule of 8:389–90
    separation (Austin, J.) 1:569–70
libertarianism 5:619
Marx, K. 6:129–30
materialism (La Mettrie, J.O. de)
    5:334
maturity 8:220–1
minimum (Solov'ëv, V.S.) 9:31
motion (Hobbes, T.) 4:459,
    4:469–70
mutual aid (Kropotkin, P.A.)
    5:314
natural law (Thomasius, C.) 9:376,
    9:378
natural religion (Paley, W.) 7:187
nature/convention debate
    Sophists 6:713–14
neo-Confucianism (Dai Zhen)
    2:770
Nietzsche, F.W. 6:845, 6:853–6
nomos/physics (law/nature)
    contrast (Democritus) 2:877
objective basis (Cumberland, R.)
    2:752
obligations
    incompatibility of 9:751
open/closed distinction
    (Bergson, H.-L.) 1:735
origin of (Hutcheson, F.) 4:589
perfection
    Mendelssohn, M. 6:306
    Wolff, C. 9:783
personal/public distinction
    applied ethics 1:318

philosophy as moral good
    Alighieri, Dante 1:183
    John of Salisbury 5:116
pleasure 7:449–50
politics
    Croce, B. 2:732
    Latin America 1:306
power of the will (Gerard of Odo)
    4:38, 4:39
practical (Beattie, J.) 1:678–9
predestination 7:655–6
Prodicus 7:731
provisional (Descartes, R.) 3:13–14
psychology of (Williams, B.A.O.)
    9:750–1
public-mindedness (Lu
    Xiangshan) 5:852
purgatory 7:838
qi 9:856
radical evil doctrine (Kant, I.)
    8:794
Rand, A. 8:55
reason
    Kant, I. 5:178, 5:189–95
    Wollaston, W. 9:787
relativism 8:189, 8:190
religion **8:218–24**
    compatibilist approach
      8:219–20
    James, W. 7:641
    Masham, D. 6:167
    narrative 8:222
    worldviews 8:219
responsibility 8:291–2
    Stoicism 9:158–9
rightness
    Confucian philosophy 2:320
rights 8:328–9
Russian philosophy
    Neo-Kantianism 6:793–4
    nihilism 7:7
sceptical defence (Charron, P.)
    2:289
Schiller, J.C.F. 8:527
science relationship (Rousseau, J.-
    J.) 8:368, 8:370
self-deception 8:629, 8:631
social
    obligation/supererogation
      distinction 9:232, 9:233
as social function 6:565–6
sociality
    Mead, G.H. 7:642–3
    Voltaire 9:659
soul
    immortality of 9:46–7
Spinoza, B. de 9:102–3

suffering 9:213, 9:214
suicide 9:227–8
supremacy of 6:564, 6:566, 6:567
violence 9:615
virtue (William of Auxerre) 9:728
virtues (Hume, D.) 4:551–5
wish fulfilment (Dostoevskii, F.M.)
    3:118
Moran, Dermot
    Eriugena, J.S. †3:401–6
    medieval Platonism †7:431–9
    Thomism 9:387
Moran, R. 3:280
Moraux, P. 1:176, 7:305, 7:429
Moravcsik, J. 6:485
Moravia, S. 2:168
More, Henry **6:576–83**
    Cambridge Platonism 2:184, 2:185
    Descartes, R. 6:577, 6:580
    enthusiasm 3:332, 6:580–1
    knowledge 6:577–8
    moral sense 6:547
    spirit 6:578–80
More, Thomas
    communism 2:462–3, 2:464
    influence of
        Latin American colonial
            philosophy 5:421
    Le Doeuff, M. analysis 5:477
    pre-existence (Glanvill, J.) 4:81–2
    Utopia
        Le Doeuff, M. analysis 5:477
    utopianism 9:557, 9:558, 9:561
Moreno Rodríguez, F. 5:664
Morenz, S. 3:254
Moreschini, C. 1:326
Morewedge, Parviz
    Ibn Sina 4:654
    Islamic philosophy
        modern †5:16–21
    Islamic theology 5:31
    al-Tusi 9:507
Morford, M. 5:652
Morgan, Charles G.
    archaeology 1:358
    fuzzy logic †3:822–4
    many-valued logics †6:81–4,
        6:83–4
Morgan, J. 3:608–9, 3:610
Morgan, J.L. 7:631
Morgan, M. 3:221
Morgan, M.J. 5:842
Morgan, M.L.
    Fackenheim, E.L. †3:533–5
Morgan, R. 2:130
Morgan, Robin 8:724–5, 8:728
Morgan, T.H. 4:13, 4:15–16

Morgan, W. 9:116
Morganbesser, S. 6:643
Morgen, C.L. 8:149, 9:238
Morgen, G. 6:861
Morgenstern, O. 2:835, 8:74, 8:93–5,
    8:103
Morgenthau, Hans 4:832
Mori Ōgai 5:658
Morison, W.L. 1:570
Moritz, K.P. 7:477
Morley, S. 5:432
Mormann, T. 5:475
Mormons *see* Latter Day Saints
morphology
    post-Bloomfieldian linguistics
        9:180
Morraga, C. 3:613–14
Morreall, John
    comedy †2:434–8
    emotion in response to art 3:280
    humour 4:567
Morrell, R.E. 1:90
Morris, C. 5:454
Morris, Charles
    pragmatics 7:624–5, 7:632
    semiotics 8:677
    unity of science 9:532
    Vienna Circle 9:612
Morris, Herbert 2:710, 3:701, 8:139,
    8:141
Morris, M. 2:710, 5:479
Morris, P. 7:613
Morris, Phyllis 8:479
Morris, R.L. 7:227
Morris, Thomas
    divine freedom 3:761
    divine simplicity 8:787
    God, concepts of 4:101
    Incarnation and Christology
        4:730, 4:732
    natural theology 6:713
    necessary being 6:747
    perfect goodness 4:144
Morrison, D. 9:814
Morrison, J.C. 9:786
Morrison, Margaret
    experiment †3:514–18
Morrison, Toni 7:582
Morriston, W. 3:761
Morrow, J. 2:406
Morrow, P.C. 2:464
Morscher, E. 1:827
Morse, A. 8:715
Morse-Kelley schema
    set theory 8:712
Morson, Gary Saul
    Bakhtin, M.M. †1:638–45

Dostoevskii, F.M. †3:114–19
    Signposts movement 8:774
    Tolstoi, L.N. †9:435–40
mortality
    see also finitude; immortality
    doctrine of (Pomponazzi, P.) 7:529
    Fall 8:794
    Heidegger, M. 4:307, 4:310, 4:312
    meaning of life 5:630, 5:631
    Socinianism 8:890
Mortensen, C. 6:320, 7:53, 7:210
Mortier, A. 8:777
Morton, A. 8:190
Morton, Adam 7:816
Morton, J. 6:675
Morton, S. 3:593, 3:868
Moschovakis, A. 7:30
Moschovakis, Y.N. 4:755
Moscovici, S. 1:695
Moscow-Tartu School **6:583–8**
Moser, C. 7:8
Moser, Paul K.
    a posteriori †1:1–3
    a priori †1:3–6
    empiricism 3:303
    epistemology 3:365
    evidence 8:130
    foundationalism 3:383, 3:723,
        5:276
    Gettier problems 4:59
    rationality of belief 8:89
Moses
    patristic philosophy 7:255
    Philo of Alexandria commentary
        7:358–9
Moses ben Maimon, Rabbi *see*
    Maimonides, Moses
Moses ben Nahman *see* Nahmanides,
    Moses
Moses ibn Ezra *see* Ibn Ezra, Moses
    ben
Moses of Narbonne 5:23
Moses, W. 7:194
Moses, Y. 3:359
Moss, Lenny
    life, origin of †5:633–5
Mosse, G. 3:563
Mossner, Ernest Campbell 2:160,
    4:562
Most, Glenn W.
    Epicharmus †3:336–7
    Hesiod †4:412–13
    Homer †4:501–2
    katharsis †5:218–20
    mimēsis †6:381–2
    Orphism 7:165

Mostowski, A.
  logic, early twentieth century 5:737
  non-constructive rules of inference
    7:30
  Polish logic 7:495, 7:496, 7:498
  quantifiers
    generalized 7:877
  recursion-theoretic hierarchies
    8:144–5
  Tarski, A. 9:264
Mothersill, Mary
  aesthetics
    beauty 1:683, 1:684
    concepts 1:57, 1:59
    and ethics 1:68
Mothu, A. 2:376
Motilal Banarsidass 3:76
motion
  Aristotelian physics (Philoponus)
    7:373
  atomism
    Democritus 2:873, 2:874
    Diodorus Cronus 3:84
    Epicureanism 3:340, 3:343,
      3:348
  Averroism (Vernia, N.) 9:597
  bodies (Hobbes, T.) 4:469
  causation
    Cavendish, M.L. 2:261
    Malebranche, N. 6:62–3
  concomitance (Cavendish, M.L.)
    2:261–2
  conservation of
    Descartes, R. 3:14
    Leibniz, G.W. rejection 5:543,
      5:555
  continuation of (Bradwardine, T.)
    1:865
  falling bodies (Soto, D. de) 9:38
  first philosophy (Hobbes, T.) 4:459
  immobility (Parmenides) 7:231–2
  impetus (Buridan, J.) 2:133
  Jewish philosophy (al-Baghdadi)
    1:637
  law of (Oresme, N.) 7:155
  mechanics
    Aristotelian 6:249–51
    classical
      Galilei, G. 3:836, 3:837–9
      Newton, I. 6:252–4, 6:825
  mind (Hobbes, T.) 4:469–70
  minima
    Epicureanism 3:342–3
  modal system (Spinoza, B. de) 9:96
  Moving Rows (Zeno of Elea)
    9:843, 9:851
  nominalism (Burley, W.) 2:141–2

nonexistence of
  arguments for (Zeno of Elea)
    9:843, 9:847–51
ontological categories
  Indian philosophy 7:61, 7:123
Oresme, N. 7:154, 7:155
paradox (Bergson, H.-L.) 1:732,
  1:733–4
phenomenal
  Gestalt psychology 4:53
phi-phenomenon
  Gestalt psychology 4:53
planetary (Eudoxus) 3:452–3
projectile
  Philoponus 7:373
  Richard Rufus of Cornwall
    8:315
quantification of
  Oxford Calculators 7:180,
    7:181, 7:182
ratios of velocity (Bradwardine, T.)
  1:863–4
soul/heaviness analogy (Alexander
  of Aphrodisias) 1:170–1
Space-Time (Alexander, S.) 1:168
substantial (Mulla Sadra) 6:596–7
time
  Hellenistic philosophy 5:251
void
  Epicureanism 3:341
  as necessary condition for
    (Melissus) 6:295
motivation
  see also action; intention; moral
    motivation
  agency (Stewart, D.) 9:137
  desire 3:30
  free will (al-Razi, Fakhr al-Din)
    8:114
  Freud, S. 3:786, 3:789
  happiness (Tucker, A.) 9:490–2
  hedonistic theory (Locke, J.) 5:680
  law of (Schopenhauer, A.) 8:548
  moral intuitionism
    (Prichard, H.A.) 7:680
  passions (Hume, D.) 4:551
  reason
    Burke, E. critique 2:139–40
  reasons and causes 8:125–7
  Reid, T. 8:174–5
  self-deception 8:627–8
  sin (Anselm of Canterbury) 1:291
  symbolic interactionism 9:244
  virtue (Locke, J.) 5:679–80
Motoori Norinaga 6:588–90
  kami
    Shintō 8:749

kokoro 5:292
Native Studies School 5:76–7
Motzkin, A. 4:213
Mouchel, C. 5:652
Mouffe, C. 2:365, 8:304
Moulier Boutang, Y. 1:195
Moulin, A.M. 7:577–8
Moulines, C.U. 1:230–1, 1:233, 4:672,
  9:353
Mounce, H.O.
  Cournot, A.A. †2:688–90
  Hamilton, W. †4:217–19
  Wittgensteinian ethics 9:772
Mouraviev, S.N. 2:695
Mourelatos, A. 6:170
Mourelatos, A.P.D. 7:234, 7:672,
  9:653–4
Mourgues, O. de 6:558
Mouw, Richard J.
  religion and morality †8:218–24
Mouy, P. 2:674, 8:343
Mouzelis, N. 9:7
movement
  bodily
    will relationship (Reid, T.) 8:174
  dance 2:775–6
  pres-abs-ence (Heidegger, M.)
    4:310
  trajectory distinction (Bergson, H.-
    L.) 1:732, 1:733–4
Mowrer, R.R. 5:487
Moxter, M. 8:538
Moyer, A.E. 2:19, 7:135
Moylan, Tom 9:561
Moyle, W. 4:234
Mozart, Wolfgang Amadeus
  7:129–30
Mozi 6:590–1
  knowing 5:697
  language utilitarianism 5:695–6
  Mohist philosophy 6:451–6,
    6:457–8
Mozley, J.K. 4:794, 7:98, 8:61, 9:301
al-Mu'ayyad fi al-Din 4:638
Much, M.T. 3:53
Muchnik, A.A. 7:575
Mudarris Radawi, Muhammad Taqi
  9:507
Mudimbe, Valentin Y.
  African philosophy 1:113, 1:116
    ethnophilosophy 3:449
    postcolonialism 7:582
Muehlenhard, C.L. 8:725, 8:728
Muehlmann, R.G. 1:750
Muelder Eton, Marcia
  aesthetic concepts †1:55–9
Mueller, D. 8:74

Mueller-Lauter, W. 6:861
Mueller-Volmer, K. 4:389
Mues de Schrenk, Laura
  pre-Columbian and indigenous
    thought †5:428–32
Muhajarani, A. 5:31
Muhammad 4:603, 7:158–9, 7:518,
  8:297
Muhammad 'Abduh see 'Abduh,
  Muhammad
Muhammad Iqbal see Iqbal, M.
Muir, J. 6:733
Muirhead, J.H. 2:406, 4:301, 9:295
mujō (impermanence) 6:591–4
  art
    Japanese aesthetics 1:85
  Buddhism 6:592–3
Mukhejee, M. 3:614
Mukhopadhyay, P.K. 8:694
Mul Shankar see Dayanand
  Saraswati
Mulhall, S.
  Cavell, S. †2:257–60
  community and
    communitarianism 2:471
Mulkay, M. 2:629–30, 4:567
Mulla Sadra (Sadr al-Din
  Muhammad al-Shirazi) 6:595–9
  Asfar 6:597–8
  epistemology 6:597
  Islamic philosophy
    modern 5:16, 5:19
  Mir Damad, Muhammad Baqir
    6:410, 6:411
  mystical philosophy 6:618–19
  quiddity 6:596, 9:221
  al-Sabzawari 8:440–1
  substantial motion 6:596–7
  systematic ambiguity of existence
    6:596, 6:597
Mullarkey, J. 1:737
Mullen, P.C. 7:93
Müller, E. 3:174, 8:811
Müller, G.H. 1:840
Muller, H.J. 4:15, 5:635
Müller, I. 4:33
Muller, J.-P. 7:323
Muller, J.Z. 8:822
Müller, K. 5:562
Müller, Max 4:102, 8:42
Muller, R.A. 2:182, 8:275
Muller-Ortega, Paul E.
  Abhinavagupta †1:15–19
Mullett, Sheila 3:605
Mulligan, J. 4:402

Mulligan, Kevin
  phenomenological movement
    7:342
  predication †7:665–7
  Reinach, A. 8:182
Mullins, W.A. 4:685
Multhauf, R.P. 1:158
multiculturalism 6:599–602
  see also race; toleration
  communitarianism (Taylor, C.)
    9:278
  cosmopolitan view 6:600–1
  education
    ethics 3:235
    science 3:237
  expressivist view 6:600–1
  identity view 6:600, 6:601
multiformity of being
  ontology (Gilbert of Poitiers) 4:69
multiple realization argument
  reduction theory 8:147–8
multiple worlds
  Goodman, N. 4:135–6
multiple-conclusion logic 6:602–4
  formal systems 3:705
multiplicity
  Deleuze, G.
    fascism 2:858
    subject, postmodern critique of
      9:199
    time 2:857
multivocity
  Aristotle 1:417, 1:418
Mulvey, L. 3:409, 3:596, 3:614, 3:677
Munakata, K. 1:75
Münch, R. 9:7, 9:256
Mundici, Daniele
  primitive recursive functions
    †2:482–91
Munevar, G. 3:642
Mungello, D.E. 3:195
Munis 4:103
Munitz, M.K. 2:680
Munk, S. 4:617
Muñoz, B. 5:657
Muñoz Delgado, V. 1:649, 9:40
Munro, C.R.
  Bryce, J. †2:41–2
Munro, Donald
  Confucianism, Chinese 2:548
  Marxism
    Chinese †6:133–41
Munsat, S. 7:723
Munz, P. 7:539
Munzer, Stephen R. †7:757–61
al-Muqammas, Daud 5:87, 6:604–6
Muralt, A. de 4:171–2

Muratori, L.A. 5:41–2
Murawski, Roman
  Tarski, A. †9:262–5
Murchland, B. 6:71
murder
  see also infanticide
  euthanasia distinction
    Jewish bioethics 1:778
  Hume, D. 4:552
  legitimate (Camus, A.) 2:194–5
Murdoch, D. 1:822
Murdoch, Iris 5:845, 9:481, 9:485,
  9:625
Murdoch, J.E.
  Blasius of Parma 1:787
  Bradwardine, T. 1:866
  Burley, W. 2:144
  Chatton, W. 2:294
  Gerard of Odo 4:39
  Henry of Harclay 4:363
  John of Mirecourt 5:112–13
  natural philosophy, medieval
    6:706–7
  Oxford Calculators 7:183
Muroji, Y. 9:218
Murphey, M.G.
  American philosophy, eighteenth
    and nineteenth century 1:206
  educational philosophy 3:229
  Franklin, B. †3:737–8
  Hegelianism 4:301
  Jefferson, T. †5:84–5
  Johnson, S. 5:126
  Lewis, C.I. 5:589
  Peirce, C.S. 7:284
  Witherspoon, J. 9:756
Murphy, A.W. 9:719
Murphy, C., Jr. 3:552
Murphy, Jeffrie G.
  crime and punishment 2:711
  forgiveness and mercy †3:697–701
  moral agents 6:500, 6:504
  rectification and remainders 8:141
Murphy, J.P. 7:639
Murphy, Liam B.
  help and beneficence †4:342–4
Murphy, Nancey
  religion and science †8:230–6
Murphy, T.F. 8:728
Murphy, W.F. 2:622
Murphy, W.T. 2:720
Murr, S. 1:758
Murray, John Courtney 8:228, 8:229
Murray, M. 8:250
Murti, T.R.V. 6:640, 9:218–19
Murty, K.S. 7:524

Museum of Modern Art, New York
1:452
Musgrave, Alan
  incommensurability 4:736
  Kuhn, T.S. 5:318
  Lakatos, I. 5:345
  social relativism †8:836–8
music **6:606–15**
  see also art; art works; dance;
    harmony; opera
  audiences 6:610
  autonomous faculty 4:189
  beauty 4:189–90, 6:611–12
  Boethius, A.M.S. 1:805
  Chinese aesthetics 1:71
  context 6:608
  culture 6:611
  dance 2:774–5
  'definable expression' 4:190
  definition 6:606–7
  emotions
    expression 3:277–8, 4:190–1,
      6:606, 6:610
    Hanslick, E. 4:222–3
    truth 1:458
  expressiveness 4:189–91, 6:610,
    6:612
    arousalism 4:189–90
    cognitivism 4:189–90
    Gurney, E. 4:187
  form 6:608–9
    beauty and expression 4:189
    definitive listening mode 4:189
    understanding of 4:187–9
    variety 4:190
  formalism 3:707, 4:189
  Gurney, E. 4:187–91
  harmony (Confucius) 2:567
  impressiveness 4:188, 4:189–90
  intentionality 6:607, 6:608, 6:611
  interpretation 1:504
  mathematics
    Archytas 1:367, 1:368
    Mersenne, M. 6:329
  meaning 6:609–11
    metaphysical 6:611
  modes of listening 4:189
  number relationship
    Pythagoreanism 7:858
  ontology of 6:607–8
  opera 7:128–31
  perception 4:187–8, 6:608–9
  performance 6:608
  popular 1:471
  psychological states 6:610
  representation 6:611

response to
  emotional 3:277–8
  structure 6:608
  understanding 6:609
  value 4:190, 6:606, 6:611–12
  will-less calm (Schopenhauer, A.)
    8:551
Muslim philosophy *see* Islam; Islamic
  philosophy
Musonius Rufus **6:615–16**
Mussen, P. 7:823
Mussolini, Benito 3:562, 9:442–3
Musto, R. 6:740
al-Muta'allihin, Sadr *see* Mulla Sadra
mutability
  of humans
    'growing argument'
      (Epicharmus) 3:337
Mutanen, A. 3:359
Mu'tazila **1:519–23**
  see also Mu'tazilites
  freedom of will 5:27–8
  Ibn Ezra, M. 4:614
  'ilm al-kalam 5:25, 5:26–7, 5:28,
    5:29
  Karaism 5:207–8
  al-Kindi 5:250, 5:251
  moral truths (al-Juwayni) 5:170
  religious belief 5:29
  science 8:562, 8:563
Mu'tazilites
  freedom of will 2:242
  al-Ghazali comparison 4:63–4
  God
    concepts of 4:620
    Ibn ar-Rawandi 4:636–7
  influenced by
    Greek philosophy 4:155
    moral philosophy 3:438
Mutiso, G.-C.M. 1:107
Mutschler, H.-D. 6:742
mutual aid
  survival (Kropotkin, P.A.) 5:314
mutual awareness 8:887
Myers, G. 2:777
Myers, G.E. 5:67, 7:643–4
Myers, W. 3:267
Myerson, J. 9:392
Myerson, R. 2:835
Myhill, J.R.
  Church's thesis 2:355
  Gödel's theorems 4:113, 4:117
  Russell, B.A.W. 8:403
  theory of types 9:362
Myrdal, G. 9:579
mystery
  being (Marcel, G.) 6:92

Mystical Anarchism
  Ivanov, V.
    Nietzscheanism 6:863
mysticism
  see also Rosicrucianism;
    spirituality; Sufism
  Augustine 1:546, 1:553–4
  Brahman
    awareness of
      Vedānta 9:589, 9:590
  Byzantine philosophy 2:163
  Chinese 6:622–3
    Daodejing 2:780, 2:781
  Christian 6:623–5
    Gospel of John 5:820
    negative theology 6:759
    Pseudo-Dionysius 7:806
  cognitive value 6:630–2
  definition of 6:628–9
  divine creation (Bonaventure)
    1:828, 1:830
  drugs 6:631
  emotions (Hägerström, A.A.T.)
    4:203
  exclusivism 8:262–3
  experiences **8:250–5**
    interpretation 6:629–32
    'extrovertive' 6:621
  God 6:630–2
    Indian conceptions of 4:102
  Hildegard of Bingen 4:429–30
  history of **6:620–7**
  Indian 6:621–2
    illusion 3:409, 3:410
  Islamic 5:14, **6:616–20**, 6:625–6
    Ibn al-'Arabi 4:603–4
    Ibn Khaldun 4:625
    Ibn Massara 4:628–9
    Ibn Taymiyya 4:655–6
    Illuminationist philosophy
      4:700, 4:702
    influence on Jewish pietism
      (Maimonides, A.) 6:38–9
    modern philosophy 5:16, 5:20
    Mulla Sadra 6:597
    quest for God 3:441–2
    science 8:564
    al-Suhrawardi 9:219–23
  Japanese 6:622–3
  Jewish 6:623
    halakhah 4:207
    Hasidism 4:242–5
    Kabbalah **5:171–6**
      Hekhalot (palace) 5:171–2
      Herrera, A. Cohen de
        4:397–9
      Heschel, A.J. 4:411–12

Merkavah (chariot) 5:171–2
Nahmanides, M. 6:648, 6:649
Saadiah Gaon 8:436
union (Buber, M.) 2:42, 2:43
Native Americans 6:621
nature of **6:627–34**
Neo-Vedānta movement 9:592–3
pluralism 8:263
prophecy 7:768, 7:770
Rhineland school 9:240, 9:269–70
Śaivism (Abhinavagupta) 1:18
salvation (Tonghak) 9:441–2
science relationship (Certeau, M. de) 2:268
Spanish
    Renaissance scepticism 8:500
Suso, H. 9:240–1
Swedenborg, E. 9:241–3
Tauler, J. 9:269–70
theology
    Law, W. 5:469
theosophy 9:363, 9:365
Vedānta 9:590–1

Yogācāra Buddhism 3:388–9
mystics
    Certeau, M. de 2:268
myth
    see also gods
    Bible (Frei, H.) 3:778
    demythologization (Bultmann, R.) 2:127–8
    enlightenment
        critical theory 2:725–7
        Horkheimer, M. 4:511
    etymology
        Indian philosophy 5:380
    geneaology 4:2
    gnosticism 4:84–5
        Voegelin, E. 9:654
    Greek
        creation (Thales) 9:322–3
        Hesiod 4:412–13
        Homer 4:501–2
        Orphism 7:163–4
        rationalization of (Empedocles) 3:296–7

    Hinduism
        Arya Samaj rejection of 1:516
        cosmology and cosmogony 2:681–2
    historical development (Vico, G.) 9:602–3
    language relationship
        creation (Rosenzweig, F.) 8:359
    Lévi-Strauss, C. 5:583–4
    Native American philosophy (Lévi-Strauss, C.) 6:667–8
    practice relationship 3:448
    religious language 8:257
    semiological analysis (Barthes, R.) 1:656–7
    state (Cassirer, E.) 2:225–6
    symbolic forms (Cassirer, E.) 2:223–5
    theophany (Voegelin, E.) 9:655
    transformation (Cohen, H.) 2:400
    truth (Losev, A.F.) 5:830

N

Nader, A.N. 1:523
Nadler, Steven
  Arnauld, A. †1:443–88
  Cordemoy, G. de †2:672–4
  Foucher, S. †3:713–18
  La Forge, L. de †5:331–2
  Malebranche, N. †6:56–6
  occasionalism 7:90
  Port-Royal 7:554
Næss, Arne **6:635–8**
  Chinese Confucianism 2:548–9
  deep ecology 3:197, 3:199–200
  environmental ethics 3:333
  moral standing 6:554
  self-realization 8:634–5
Naffah Neto, Alfredo 7:349, 7:352
Naffine, N. 3:610
Nagai Kafū 5:659
Nagami, Isamu 9:692
Nagamoto Shigenori
  Linji †5:645–6
Nagao, Gadjin 2:75, 2:80, 9:587
Nāgārjuna **6:638–41**
  Buddhist philosophy in India 2:99
  causation 2:256, 2:257
  emptiness 2:78–9
  illusion 3:410
  Indian philosophy 4:738
  justified belief 2:96–7
  Mādhyamika Buddhism in India
    and Tibet 2:58, 2:59, 2:63
  reality
    consensual v. ultimate 2:98
  scepticism
    knowledge 5:280, 5:284, 5:285
  Sengzhao 8:683
  suffering 9:217, 9:218–19
  Tibetan philosophy 4:738, 9:402–3
  Vātsyāyana conflict 9:587–8
  void doctrine 6:78
Nagatomo Shigenori
  Dōgen 3:111
  Kuki Shūzō †5:320–1
Nagel, Ernest **6:641–3**
  Campbell, N.R. 2:194
  explanation 3:525
  functional explanation 3:803,
    3:805
  geometry 4:33

Gödel, K. 4:107
  logic, early twentieth century 5:737
  proof theory 7:751
  reduction
    problems of 8:146, 8:147, 8:149
  relativity theory
    philosophical significance of
    8:199
  teleology 9:297
  unity of science 9:531–2, 9:533
Nagel, Thomas **6:643–7**
  consciousness 2:584, 2:595
  contractarianism 2:665
  cosmopolitan justice 5:155–6
  death 2:820, 2:822
  deontological ethics 2:892
  doubt 3:125
  dualism 3:138
  egoism and altruism 3:248
  equality 3:395
  ethics
    analytic 1:223
    autonomy 1:592
    practical reasoning 7:619
  functionalism 3:813
  good, theories of the 4:135
  help and beneficence 4:344
  impartiality 4:717
  introspection 4:842
  justice 5:147
  materialism 6:177
  meaning of life 5:631, 5:633
  mental causation 6:311
  morality
    luck 6:520–1, 6:522
    motivation 6:524, 6:527
    pluralism 6:531
    relativism 6:542
  neutrality
    political 6:821
  panpsychism 7:197
  practical reasoning 7:619, 8:103
  prudence 7:804
  qualia 7:867
  responsibility 8:294
  sexuality 8:728
  split brains
    multiplication of minds
    9:109–10

  will 9:722, 9:725
Nāgeśa (Bhaṭṭa) 4:256, 5:383
Nag-Hammadi texts 4:84, 4:85
Nagy, P. 7:395
Nahda 5:17
Nahmanides, Moses 5:88, **6:647–51**
Nahuatl thought *see* Aztec
  civilization
Naipaul, V.S. 6:100
naïve philosophy 3:575
naïve realism
  perception 7:292
naïvity
  innocence 4:798
Najib, Zaki Mahmud 5:17
Najita, Tetsuo
  Kaibara Ekken 5:177
  Tominaga Nakamoto 9:441
Nakae Tōju 5:322
Nakamura, Hajime 2:106, 5:79
Nakamura Kojiro
  al-Ghazali †4:61–8
Nakhimovsky, A.D. 6:587
Nakhimovsky, A.S. 6:587
Namai, M. 6:181
Namdang *see* Han Wôn-jin
names
  see also proper names
  Aristotle 1:416–17
  Chinese theory of language 5:693
  co-referring 9:251
  descriptive psychology
    (Twardowski, K.) 9:508
  ethics
    Chinese philosophy 5:696
  Hobbes, T. 5:372–3
  linguistic naturalism (Cratylus)
    2:694
  Locke, J. 5:374–5
  masculine/feminine differences
    (Irigaray, L.) 5:1–2
  Mohism 5:697–8
  naturalism versus conventionalism
    5:357
    Aristotle 5:359
    Democritus 5:357
    Plato 5:357–8
  possible worlds semantics 8:667
  rectifying (Confucius) 5:694–5

theological roots (Losev, A.F.)
5:829–30
Wittgenstein, L. 9:762
Names, School of 5:693, 5:697–700
Ñāṇamoli, B. 2:53
Nancy, Jean-Luc **6:651–4**
poetry 7:477
Nandy, Ashis 7:524, 7:582
Nanji, A. 6:620, 6:807
Nanyue Hsuisi 9:860
Naples
James of Viterbo **5:58–60**
Napper, E. 2:80, 9:490
Nara, Six Schools of 2:101–2, 5:70–1
Narain, H. 7:65–6
Narain, K. 9:594
Naravane, V. 9:258
Narboni, Moses 1:600–1, 6:48
Nardi, B.
Alighieri, Dante 1:185
Nifo, A. 6:872
Renaissance Aristotelianism 1:413
Silvestri, F. 8:777–8
Vernia, N. 9:599
Nardin, Terry
international relations 4:832
war and peace †9:684–91
Narodism 7:451–3, 7:455
Narodniki see Narodism
narrative **6:654–7**
aesthetics 1:61
Bible 3:778–9
expression of emotion 1:494
fictional 1:496
Kataribe
Japanese aesthetics 1:85
mimetic function 8:320–1
morality 8:222
social science
interpretive school 8:841–2
structure
film aesthetics 3:675–6
narrator
author distinction 6:654–5
Narveson, J. 7:542
Nash equilibrium 2:826–5
Nash, J.F. 2:835, 8:103
see also Nash equilibrium
Nash, P.W. 4:78
al-Nashshar, A. 5:31
Nasr, Seyyed Hossein
Ibn Sina 4:654
Ikhwan al-Safa' 4:688
Illuminationist philosophy 4:703
Islamic philosophy 5:16
concept of 5:9
modern 5:18–19, 5:21

mystical †6:616–20
science in 8:564
Mir Damad, Muhammad Baqir
6:411
Mulla Sadra 6:599
al-Sabzawari 8:442
al-Suhrawardi 9:223
theosophy 9:366
Natanson, M. 8:561, 8:859
Nathan, A. 5:454
Nathan, O. 3:258
Nathanson, S. 6:661
nation **6:657–62**
see also community; international
relations; nationalism; state
definition 6:657–8
evolution of 6:658–9
state relationship 9:120–1
state/church unity (Coleridge, S.T.)
2:405
National Bolshevism 8:772
national identity
Latin America
existentialism 3:510–11
Marxism 6:161, 6:162
National Research Council (USA)
8:334
National Socialism *see* Nazism
National Studies School *see*
kokugaku
nationalism **6:657–62**
see also fascism; nation;
patriotism; Zionism
African philosophy, Francophone
1:108–10, 1:111–12
authoritarian 6:657, 6:659
black 7:191
cultural 6:659
ethnophilosophy relationship
3:448
fascism 3:562–3
Fries, J.F. 3:798–9
Herder, J.G. 4:383–4
Indian 7:522–3, 7:524
Aurobindo Ghose 1:567
international justice 5:154
Japan 5:77
literature 5:659
Nishida Kitarō 7:14
Judaism
Ha'am, Ahad 4:192–3
negative effect on (Kaplan, M.)
5:204
Zionism 9:867–9
liberal 6:657, 6:659
Meinecke, F. 6:280
multiculturalism 6:600

Pan-Slavism 7:198, 7:201
problems 6:659–61
race theories 8:20
're-Africanization' (Cabral, A.)
2:169, 2:170
Russian religious-philosophical
renaissance 8:426
self-conciousness
Russian medieval philosophy
6:277, 6:278
Nationalist Socialist German
Workers Party *see* Nazism
nationality *see* nation
nationhood
Jewish (Ha'am, Ahad) 4:192–3
Native American philosophy **6:662–7**
cosmology 6:663–5
dreams 6:665
early colonization
Christian view 8:226
ethics 6:666–7
mysticism 6:621
soul 6:665
Native Studies School *see kokugaku*
nativism **6:672–6**
see also innateness; language,
innateness
concepts (Fodor, J.A.) 2:514
innate representations
infant cognition 2:391
language acquisition 4:51–3
linguistic (Chomsky, N.) 6:672,
6:673–4
Soviet Marxism 6:157
Natorp, P. 6:777, 6:782–3, 6:790–1
natural atheology 6:711
natural deduction **6:676–82**
intuitionistic logic 4:859
multiple-conclusion logic 6:604
natural history
evolutionary theory
(Buffon, G.L.L.) 2:120, 2:121–2
Jungius, J. 5:136
theology (Neckham, A.) 6:750,
6:751
natural indication
informational semantics 8:659
natural justice
Cicero, M.T. 2:357
critique of (Carneades) 2:217
might is right (Callicles) 2:176–7
natural kinds 5:625–6, **6:682–5**
natural language *see* language,
natural
natural law **6:685–90**
see also divine law
anarchism 1:245

Aquinas, T. 1:340–1
  political-religious authority
    conflict 8:224, 8:226
Cicero, M.T. 2:357, 5:143
in common law 2:444–5
contemporary political philosophy
  8:228
conventional law relationship
  Greek political philosophy
    7:505–6
critiques of
  Hamann, J.G. 4:217
  Hegel, G.W.F. 4:260
Crusius, C.A. 2:738
Cumberland, R. 2:752, 2:753
English law (Blackstone, W.) 1:780
Enlightenment, German
  Hamann, J.G. critique 4:217
eternal law (Suárez, F.) 9:192
good, theories of the 4:131
Huang-Lao school
  China 5:449
human rights
  Hart, H.L.A. 4:235
  Pufendorf, S. 7:835, 7:836
  Stair, J.D. 9:119
individuals
  Carmichael, G. 2:206–7
  morality 5:438–9
Jewish philosophy 1:351
  Arama, I. 1:351
justice as charity (Leibniz, G.W.)
  5:557–8
law of nations distinction
  (Toletus, F.) 9:434
le droit (Villey, M.) 9:614
legal idealism 5:510
legal positivism conflict 5:514–15
monarchy bound by (Bodin, J.)
  1:797
morality
  Hobbes, T. 4:469, 4:471
  Thomasius, C. 9:376, 9:378
obligations (Locke, J.) 5:678–9
political philosophy
  history of 7:512
procedural (Fuller, L.L.) 3:801–2
rationalism 5:464–5
reason-faith relationship
  (Culverwell, N.) 2:750–1
rights (Smith, A.) 8:819
Soto, D. de 9:38–9
sovereignty (Hobbes, T.) 4:471–2
Suárez, F. 9:192
suum (Olivecrona, K.) 7:94
voluntarism 5:465
war 9:686, 9:687–8

natural laws see laws, natural
natural philosophy
  atomism
    Charleton, W. 2:286
    Cudworth, R. 2:741
    Gassendi, P. 3:852–5
    Cambridge Platonism critique
      2:184
    certainty (Mersenne, M.) 6:327–8
    Islamic philosophy 2:243
    Latin America
      colonial thought in 5:421,
        5:422, 5:424–5
    mathematical science contrast
      (Mersenne, M.) 6:325, 6:329
  mechanism
    Fontenelle, B. de 3:691
    Leibniz, G.W. 5:542, 5:554–7
  medieval 6:275, **6:690–707**
    Albert of Saxony 1:143–4
    Alighieri, Dante 1:182, 1:184
    Bacon, R. 6:704, 6:705
    Buridan, J. 2:133–4
    Burley, W. 2:141–2
    Dietrich of Freiberg 3:69
    Giles of Rome 4:72, 4:74–5
    Gregory of Rimini 4:171
    Grosseteste, R. 4:178, 4:179–80
    happiness in this life 1:597
    indivisibilism (Wodeham, A.)
      9:775
    John of Jandun 5:107
    Marsilius of Inghen 6:111
    Marston, R. 6:114–15
    Neckham, A. 6:750, 6:751
    Oresme, N. 6:705
    Paul of Venice 7:266
    Pecham, J. 7:268
    quantification
      Oxford Calculators
        7:179–80, 7:182
      William of Ockham 9:741–2
  methodology (Bacon, F.) 1:627–8
  organicist materialism
    (Cavendish, M.L.) 2:261
  physics (Bacon, F.) 1:630–1
  Renaissance
    Aristotelianism 1:406–7
    Cajetan 2:172
    Cardano, G. 2:203–4
    John of St Thomas 5:119
    motion (Soto, D. de) 9:38
    Nifo, A. 6:868–9
    Oxford Calculators 1:407
    Paracelsus 7:206–7
    Patrizi, F. 7:262, 7:263–4
    Telesio, B. 9:297, 9:298

Vernia, N. 9:596–7
    Zabarella, J. 9:838
  Rohault, J. critique 8:342
  scientific method
    (Tschirnhaus, E.W. von) 9:486
  theology synthesis (White, T.)
    9:712
  translations 6:692–4, 6:698
natural reasoning see reasoning,
  natural
natural religion see religion, natural
natural rights see rights, natural
natural science
  Aristotle
    twelfth century texts 1:398
  concepts 2:508
  empirical approach (Buridan, J.)
    2:131, 2:133–4
  ethics comparison
    pragmatism 7:641
  first philosophy (Hobbes, T.)
    4:459, 4:465–8
  geometry (Hobbes, T.) 4:468
  human nature 4:463–5, **4:526–7**
  laws of nature (Kant, I.) 5:187–8
  mathematics relation 6:187–8
  mathematization of (Galilei, G.)
    3:837–8
  miracles 6:411–12, 6:414
  optics (Hobbes, T.) 4:468–9
  physics (Hobbes, T.) 4:469
  principles of judgment (Kant, I.)
    5:186–8
  social science comparison
    6:718–19, 8:870
  theology synthesis (Teilhard de
    Chardin, P.) 9:288–9
  Theophrastus 9:339–40
  theoretical knowledge (Gilbert of
    Poitiers) 4:70
  Xenophanes 9:809
natural selection 3:479–80
  see also evolutionary theory;
    sociobiology
  biological norms
    physical illness 6:312–13
  Darwin, C.R. 2:795, 2:797, 4:12
  ecology 3:203–4
  ethics/evolution relationship 3:475
  evolutionary theory 3:476–8
  functional explanation 3:524,
    3:803–4, 3:817
  Huxley, T.H. 4:594
  of ideas (al-Afghani) 1:95
  Lamarckian principles
    (Spencer, H.) 9:87–8
  naturalized epistemology 6:722

race theories 8:18
social science 3:484
sociobiology 8:892–5
teleology 8:673, 8:674, 8:862–3
units of 4:14–15, 8:894
Wallace, A.R. 9:678–9
natural theology **6:707–13**
Aquinas, T. 1:341–4
atheology 6:711
Brunner, E. 2:31
Cicero, M.T. 2:357–8
Clarke, S. 2:378
critiques of 6:707, 6:710–11
Barth, K. 1:654
Inge, W.R. 4:793
Democritus 2:875–6
dialectical 6:708–9
faith 3:541–2
Llull, R. 5:663
moral action (Wollaston, W.) 9:787
Wolff, C. 9:782
naturalism
see also anti-naturalism; European
positivism; naturalized philosophy
of science; non-naturalism
action (Sellars, W.S.) 8:639
agnosticism 1:122–3
anti-religious (Hume, D.) 4:543
contextual (Nagel, E.) 6:641, 6:642
critiques of
Kemp Smith, N. 5:228
Nietzsche, F.W. 6:851–2
culture
Herder, J.G. 4:378, 4:379, 4:382
Nietzsche, F.W. 6:845, 6:847
design argument (Tennant, F.R.)
9:302
Dewey, J. 3:228
epistemology 3:366–7
see also naturalized
epistemology
ethics 3:366–7, **6:713–17**
critique by Moore, G.E. 6:495–6
epistemology 6:715–16
fact/value distinction 3:538
logic of ethical discourse
5:760–1, 5:764
metaphysics 6:714–15
Moore, G.E.
applied ethics 1:319–20
moral knowledge 6:518, 6:519
moral realism 6:535
sexuality 8:721
history (Herder, J.G.) 4:381–2
human nature 4:521
induction 4:750

language
Aristotle 5:359
Barthes, R. rejection of 1:656–7
Cratylus 2:694
Democritus 5:357
Herder, J.G. 4:379–80
Plato 5:357–8
magic (Campanella, T.) 2:186–7
mind 6:406
mind (Mill, J.S.) 6:364–5, 6:367
moral philosophy (Dühring, E.K.)
3:148
moral theory
Scottish Enlightenment 3:328
mystical experiences 8:253
negative effect on Judaism 5:204
physical illness
concepts of 6:312–13
Platonism (Thierry of Chartres)
9:372
Pomponazzi, P.
Mersenne, M. refutation 6:326
Presocratic concepts of 9:651
reductive 8:260
social science **6:717–21**, 8:584–5
contemporary theories of 8:838,
8:840–1
economics 3:213
epistemological 6:718
individualism/holism debate
4:485
methodological 6:718–19
non-reductionist 6:719–20
ontological 6:719–20
positivism 7:558, 7:559, 7:560–1
varieties 6:717–18
spiritual
African ethical systems 3:431
naturalistic fallacy
critical hedonism (Baumgardt, D.)
1:668
logic of ethical discourse 5:761
Moore, G.E. 4:131, 6:494–5
political philosophy 7:526
naturalized epistemology **6:721–8**
autonomy of 6:724–5
Hume D. 6:721–2
internalism/externalism 6:722–4
normative theory 6:725–6
rational beliefs 8:63
reasoning
rationality of belief 8:88
scepticism 6:722
naturalized philosophy of science
6:728–31
Heidegger, M. 4:326

nature
see also human nature;
Naturphilosophie; pantheism;
physis; xing
active-passive (naturans-naturata)
distinction (Spinoza, B. de) 9:95
aesthetic appreciation of 1:52,
1:59, **6:731–5**
objectivity 6:732, 6:734
science 6:732, 6:734
subjectivity 6:732, 6:734
anarchist communism
(Kropotkin, P.A.) 5:313–14
architecture 1:365
art
Japanese aesthetics 1:80–3
beauty
Alison, A. 1:186
Fechner, G.T. 3:571
Kant, I. 5:193–4
biology (Empedocles) 3:295, 3:297
classification of (Linnaeus, C. von)
5:646–50
conservation laws (Knutzen, M.)
5:288
and convention **6:735–7**
see also naturalism, in social
science
social science 8:847–9, 8:869
'correspondence' theory
spiritual influx (Swedenborg, E.)
9:242–3
cosmogony (Empedocles) 3:296
creation (Bernard of Tours)
1:755–6
critical realism 2:721
cycle of change (Empedocles)
3:293, 3:294–5
definition of (Boethius, A.M.S.)
1:807–8
design argument
autonomy (Kant, I.) 5:194–5
developmental aspects of
Naturphilosophie 6:739–40
dialectic of (Trotsky, L.) 9:465
as divine text (Boyle, R.) 1:855
divisions of (Eriugena, J.S.) 3:401,
3:402–4
Emerson, R.W. 3:270, 3:271
environmentalism 6:732, 6:735
aesthetics 6:732, 6:735
ethics 3:333–5
experimentation (Heidegger, M.)
4:325
explanation
Naturphilosophie 6:739

first principles of (Telesio, B.)
9:297, 9:298
force
classification (Leibniz, G.W.)
5:555
forms (Bacon, F.) 1:630
freedom relationship (Kant, I.)
5:178
functional/ecological relationships
(Linnaeus, C. von) 5:649
God
governance of
Jewish philosophy
(Maimonides, M.) 6:45–6
identification with (Spinoza, B.
de) 9:91, 9:95–7
grace 4:147–8
habit (Ravaisson-Mollien, F.)
8:104
harmony
Kropotkin, P.A. 5:314
Shaftesbury, Third Earl of
8:730–1
Hegel, G.W.F. 4:263–4, 4:272–3
horror vacui (Strato) 9:162
human *see* human nature
human interference
agricultural ethics 1:126
human relationship to
Daoism 2:321
as subject/object unity
(Marcuse, H.) 6:97–8
humanized (Il'enkov, E.V.) 4:690
imagery
Chinese aesthetics 1:68,
1:69–70, 1:71–2
laws of *see* laws, natural
mathematical principles
(Alembert, J. le R. d') 1:164,
1:166
mechanistic explanation
Boyle, R. 1:855
Strato 9:161–2
metamorphosis (Goethe, J.W. von)
4:125, 4:127–9
might is right (Callicles) 2:176–7
moral insight (Diogenes of Sinope)
3:91
multiple relations theory
(Whitehead, A.N.) 9:715
natural/supernatural distinction
Jewish philosophy (Arama, I.)
1:351
necessitarian theories 5:470–1
Newtonian account of
Whitehead, A.N. critique 9:715
nomoi (Antiphon) 1:302–3

objectification of (Berdiaev, N.A.)
1:728
order
Aristotelianism 6:44
imagination (Smith, A.)
8:817–18
original
Han Wôn-jin 2:563–4
Horak controversy 2:556–7,
2:562–3
perfection of
alchemy 1:156–7
philosophy of
see also Naturphilosophie
Nyāya-Vaiśeṣika 7:59, 7:60–1
physical explanation (Anaxagoras)
1:253
purposefulness of (Paley, W.)
7:186–7
rationality of (Epictetus) 3:338
reality
Kemp Smith, N. 5:228–9
Skovoroda, H.S. 8:802–3
reflectiveness towards
Jewish pietism (Ibn Paquda)
4:634
representations of science
postcolonial philosophy of
7:575, 7:576
self-cultivation
Chinese philosophy 8:618
Shintō 8:749
sociobiology 8:892–5
Sophiology (Bulgakov, S.N.) 2:124
Spinoza, B. de 7:203–4
spirit of (More, H.) 6:580
spirit of
Cambridge Platonism 2:184
spirit relationship (Berdiaev, N.A.)
1:727
state of
Hobbes, T. 4:470–1
liberty (Locke, J.) 5:681
study of
Islamic philosophy of science
8:562
the sublime 9:202–3
superiority to culture
Cynics 2:754, 2:755
al-Tawhidi 9:271
technology relationship 9:280
teleology
Galen 3:833
Kant, I. 6:737
theodicy (Malebranche, N.) 6:63–4
tian 9:401
time 9:415–16

transcendental philosophy
(Schelling, F.W.J. von) 8:509,
8:511–12
unity of
Bruno, G. 5:34–5
Lichtenberg, G.C. 5:623
Naturphilosophie 6:739
will (Schopenhauer, A.) 8:549–50
Wissenschaftslehre (theory of
science) (Fichte, J.G.) 3:649
nature-nurture debate 4:522–3
genetic determinism 4:12, 4:15
human nature 4:522–3
sociobiology 8:895
sport 9:114
Naturphilosophie **6:737–43**
see also German idealism
Fichte, J.G. 6:738
German Romanticism 8:351
Kant, I. 6:737–8
major doctrines of 6:739–40
Oken, L. 7:92
Schelling, F.W.J. von 6:738–9,
8:509, 8:511–12
Nauern, F.-G. 4:45
Nauert, C.G., Jr 1:133
Navarro, B. 5:425
Navia, L.E. 7:856, 7:861
Navya-Nyāya (New Logic) 4:738
see also Nyāya
Gadādhara 3:825
Gaṅgeśa 3:843–6, 4:765
God
omnipotence 4:105
nonexistence
ontological categories 7:126–7
Nyāya-Vaiśeṣika School 7:58
relations
ontological categories 7:126
theory of definition 2:850, 2:851–2
relations 2:850–1
Udayana 9:512
Nazism
see also Holocaust
ecology relationship 3:334
fascism 3:562–3
green political philosophy 4:163
Heidegger, M. support for 4:309
mythical nature (Lacoue-
Labarthe, P.) 5:340–1
Tillich, P. 9:409
totalitarianism
Arendt, H. 1:369–70, 1:371
Blanchot, M. 1:783
n-body problem 7:478–9
Ndaw, A. 1:116
Ndiaye, A.R. 1:448

Nead, L. 1:718, 3:409
Neale, Stephen
  Davidson, D. 2:806
  descriptions †3:19–24
  Grice, H.P. 4:177
  reference 8:164
  scope 8:589
  Strawson, P.F. 9:174
  syntax †9:246–53
Neander, Karen
  language of thought hypothesis
    5:407
  mental illness
    concepts of †6:311–14
  semantics
    teleological 8:675
Nebraska Feminist Collective 3:593
nebular hypothesis 5:179
necessarianism 6:116
necessary being 1:701, **6:743–7**
  see also existence
  al-'Amiri 1:207–8
  Aquinas, T. 6:744–5
  classical theism 4:98
  contingency 6:744
  divine simplicity
    God, attributes of 8:785–6
  Ibn al-'Arabi 4:603
  Ibn Sina 2:242, 4:650–1
  objections to 6:746
  ontological argument 6:743,
    6:745–6
necessary truth
  see also a priori; necessity
  a posteriori 6:748, 6:749
  cogito ergo sum (Geulincx, A.) 4:60
  conceptual-containment 3:376
  conventionalism **6:747–50**
  first principles 3:373
  as knowledge of God (Norris, J.)
    7:41, 7:42
  logical/mathematical (Putnam, H.)
    7:842
  medieval epistemology 6:274
necessitarianism
  natural laws 5:472
  nature 5:470
  Spinoza, B. de 9:96–7
necessity
  see also necessary truth
  a posteriori 1:1
  a priori 1:4
  a prioricity distinction
    (Kripke, S.A.) 5:302–3
  absolute 2:377
  analyticity distinction
    (Kripke, S.A.) 5:303

Asmus, V.F. 1:525
causal (Hume, D.) 4:547
contingency
  Quine, W.V. 1:235
  Spinoza, B. de 5:549–50
divine freedom (Leibniz, G.W.)
  5:542
etiological
  causality (Ducasse, C.J.) 3:139
evil (Leibniz, G.W.) 5:545
free will
  Early and Middle Platonism
    7:427
freedom reconciliation
  (Fichte, J.G.) 3:645–7, 3:649
Ibn Rushd 4:643–4
Islamic philosophy **2:241–4**, 4:640,
  6:237–8
liberty debate (Collins, A.)
  2:416–17
linguistic theory of 6:748–9
logical
  consequence 2:599, 2:602
  Duns Scotus 6:745
  Wittgenstein, L. 9:760
materialism (Weil, S.) 9:698, 9:699
mathematical arguments 6:182,
  6:185
meaning
  Islamic philosophy 6:237–8
modal logic 6:417–18, 6:419,
  6:421–2, 6:427–8, 8:664
modal operators 6:433–6
Mohist philosophy 2:323
occasionalist view 7:87
possibility
  interdefinability with 6:427
  Quine, W.V. 6:429
transcendence (Bataille, G.) 1:660
Trinity 9:458–9
will contrast
  Jewish voluntarism 9:666
Nechaev, I.V. 7:53
Neckam, Alexander *see* Neckham,
  Alexander
Necker Cube 6:450
Neckham, Alexander **6:750–2**
Nédellec, Hervé *see* Hervaeus Natalis
Nederman, C.J. 5:117, 6:114
Needham, Joseph
  Daodejing 2:782
  Daoist philosophy 2:795
  history, Chinese theories of 4:452
  Lushi chunqiu 5:865
  Mohist philosophy 6:458
  Mozi 6:591

science
  postcolonial philosophy of
    7:576, 7:577
  Zhou Dunyi 9:863
  Zhu Xi 9:865
Needham, M. 4:234
Needleman, J. 9:365–6
needs **6:752–5**
  see also interests
negation
  see also double negation
  elimination
  descriptions 3:21
  logic 5:788
  truth (Wittgenstein, L.)
    9:759–60
negative facts
  Indian philosophy **6:755–9**,
    7:126–7
  Dharmakīrti 6:756
  inference 6:756–7
  Jayanta 6:757–8
  Kumārila Bhaṭṭa 6:756–7
  perception 6:757–8
  Prabhākara 6:757
negative philosophy
  Schelling, F.W.J. von 8:509, 8:514,
    8:515–16
negative theology **6:759–63**
  agnosticism 6:761–2
  Aquinas, T. 6:759–61
  atheism 6:761–2
  deconstruction
    Derrida, J. 2:899
  God, concepts of
    Eriugena, J.S. 3:402
  patristic philosophy 7:256–7, 7:258
  postmodern 7:584–5
  Rabbinic theology 9:333
  Tauler, J. 9:270
negative utilitarianism
  progressive hedonism comparison
    (Ducasse, C.J.) 3:140
negotiatio intellectus 9:596, 9:838
negotiation
  symbolic interactionism 9:244–5
Negri, A. 2:51
négritude 1:108–9, 1:110–11, 1:114
  African aesthetics 1:62
  critiques of
    Cabral, A. 2:170
    Fanon, F. 1:112, 3:552–3
    Hountondji, P.J. 1:112–13
    Towa, M. 1:112
  Sartre, J.-P. 1:110
  Senghor, L.S. 1:98–9, 1:110–11

Nehamas, A. 1:434, 3:230, 6:657,
    6:861
Neher, W. 8:387
neighbourhood models 6:424
Neihardt, J.G. 6:671
Neill, A. 3:280
Neimann, S. 7:619
Nell, Onora 5:199
    see also O'Neill, Onora
Nelson, A. 2:630
Nelson, E. 1:214, 1:215
Nelson, H. 3:426, 3:552
Nelson, J. 3:220
Nelson, L. 7:220
Nelson, Leonard 3:799
Nelson, Lynn 3:599, 3:602
Nelson, Mark T.
    moral scepticism †6:542–5
Nelson, W.N. 2:872
Nemesius **6:763–4**
Nemeth, E. 6:815
Nemeth, Thomas
    Neo-Kantianism
        Russian †6:792–7
Nemoy, Leon 4:623, 5:208
Nenninger, C. 7:66
Neo-Aristotelianism
    legal reasoning
        equity 5:149–50
neo-Catholicism
    Chaadaev, P.I. 2:272
neo-colonialism
    Cixous, H. 2:373
neo-Confucianism
    cheng 2:300
    Cheng-Zhu school 2:325–6
    China **6:764–76**
        Dai Zhen 2:770
        humanism
            self-cultivation 8:624–5
        learning of the heart and mind
            (Lu Xiangshan) 5:851–2
        Lu-Wang school 2:325
        morality (Dai Zhen) 2:770
        Shao Yong 8:736
        ti/yong 9:400
        Wang Fuzhi 9:680–1
        Zhang Zai 9:856
        Zhou Dunyi 9:862–3
        Zhu Xi 9:863–4
    Japan 5:68, 5:75–6
        Fujiwara Seika 3:799–801
        Kaibara Ekken 5:176–7
        Ogyū Sorai 7:90–1
        Zhu Xi 2:551–2

Korea 2:114
    Four-Seven Debate 2:556,
        2:558, 2:559–62, 9:824, 9:826
    Horak controversy 4:220–1,
        9:825
    Marxism comparison 2:557
    Yi Hwang 9:823–4
    Yi Yulgok 9:826–7
    Zhu Xi 9:823–4
landscape painting (Jing Hao) 1:73
li 5:594–5
self-cultivation 2:325–6, 8:622–4
neo-criticism
    Renouvier, C.B. 8:268
neo-Hegelianism 4:290–1, 5:38
Neo-Hinduism
    karma and rebirth 5:216
neo-institutionalism 4:799, 4:801–2
Neo-Kantianism **6:776–92**
    critical theory (Habermas, J.) 2:727
    epistemology
        science 4:337–8
    Fischer, K. 6:780
    general relativity 4:6–7
    logical positivism 5:790
    logistic interpretation by
        (Hägerström, A.A.T.) 4:202
    Marburg School 2:398, 6:776–7,
        6:781–4
    materialism
        Lange, F.A. 6:172
    origins 6:779–81
    practical reason
        value 9:582
    Renouvier, C.B. **8:268–70**
    Russian **6:792–7**, 8:418
        Hessen, S.I. 4:415
        social sciences 6:794–5
        Vvedenskii, A. 6:793–4
    Southwest School 4:290, 6:776–7,
        6:784–8
    Tetens, J.N. 9:321
Neo-Leibnizianism
    Russia (Lossky, N.O.) 5:834
neo-liberalism
    socioeconomics
        (Vysheslavtsev, B.P.) 9:676
Neo-Marxism
    civil society 2:370
    South Slavs, philosophy of 9:49,
        9:52
neo-modernism *see* anti-
    postmodernism
Neoplatonism **6:797–803**
    see also Cambridge Platonism;
        Neo-Pythagoreanism; Platonism
    Albert the Great 1:146, 1:147

Alexandrian
    Ammonius, son of Hermeas
        1:208–10
    Aristotle commentators 1:436
Anselm of Canterbury 1:287
Aristotelian-Platonic
    reconciliation 1:431
Aristotle commentators 1:435–6
Augustine 1:541, 1:543
Averroism (Narboni, M.) 1:600–1
Boethius A.M.S. 1:802, 1:805
Bonaventure 1:829
Byzantine philosophy 2:163
Chaldaean Oracles 2:273
Christian mysticism 6:624
Christianity
    Encyclopedists, medieval 3:305
    Marius Victorinus 6:105
    Pseudo-Dionysius 7:804–6
    commentaries (Philoponus)
        7:371–2
critique of (Judah Halevi) 4:208
Damascius 2:771–2
Dietrich of Freiberg 3:69–70
emanation
    Christian views on 2:696–7
    al-Farabi 3:555
    Ibn Ezra, M. 4:614
    Kabbalah 5:173–4
    al-Tawhidi 9:271
Encyclopedists, medieval 3:305–6,
    3:307
God
    existence of 8:240
    nature of 7:432
Hypatia 4:596
Iamblichus 4:598–9
illuminationism 4:698–9
Islamic philosophy 4:155–6, 5:6,
    5:13, **6:803–8**
    afterlife (al-Amiri) 1:207, 1:208
    causality 2:242
    emanation 3:555, 6:807, 9:271
    al-Farabi 3:554, 3:555–6
    Ibn Miskawayh 4:630–1
    Ikhwan al-Safa' 4:686–8
    morality 3:438, 3:440
    al-Tawhidi 9:271
Jewish philosophy
    Herrera, A. Cohen de 4:397,
        4:398, 4:399
    Ibn Ezra, M. 4:614
    Ibn Gabirol, S. 4:618–19
    Ibn Tzaddik, J. 4:659–62
    Israeli, I. 5:32–3
    Judah Halevi 4:208
    Narboni, M. 1:600–1

voluntarism (Maimonides, M.)
6:45
Kabbalah
emanation 5:173–4
Herrera, A. Cohen de 4:397,
4:398, 4:399
Ibn Ezra, M. 4:614
scepticism 8:500
knowledge
levels of 6:798, 6:800
Liber de causis 5:595–7
Llull, R. 5:663
Patrizi, F. 7:262–3
Peter Lombard 5:821
Plato-Aristotle concord (Pico della
Mirandola, G.) 7:390–1
Plotinus **7:456–63**
psychē (soul) 7:810–11
poetry 7:474
Porphyry 7:545–9
Proclus **7:723–31**
Renaissance Platonism 7:440–1
science 6:801–2
self-enriching alienation
(Solov'ëv, V.S.) 9:28–9
Simplicius 8:788–90
soul 6:800–1, 7:810–11
Tauler, J. 9:270
theistic (Bodin, J.) 1:797–8
theosophy 9:363
Trinity conceptions
Marius Victorinus 6:105–6
universal knowledge
(Comenius, J.A.) 2:439
virtue 6:799–800
voluntarism (Maimonides, M.)
6:45
neopositivism
see also logical positivism
existentialism
Latin America 3:512
Neo-Pythagoreanism **6:808–9**
Iamblichus 4:598
influenced by
Middle Platonism 7:422
Rome 6:809
nature of god
Middle Platonism 7:425
Numenius 7:54
Speusippus 9:89
neo-spiritualism
Lachelier, J. 5:338–9
Neostoicism
Lipsius, J. 5:650, 5:651
neo-structuralism 9:187
Dodgson, C.L. 3:107–8

structuralism in social science
9:187
Neostrukturalismus see post-
structuralism
Neo-Thomism 7:512, 9:381, 9:383–6
Nequam, Alexander *see* Neckham,
Alexander
Nerlich, G. 6:320
Nerode, A. 9:502
Neschke, A. 4:389
Nestor 6:278
Nestorianism 4:727, 6:804
Nestorius 4:727
see also Nestorianism
Netanyahu, B. 1:23
Netherlands
Agricola, R. **1:123–6**
Dooyeweerd, H. **3:113–14**
Erasmus, D. **3:396–401**
Grotius, H. **4:185–6**
Hegelianism 4:286–7
intuitionism 4:847–8
Regius, H. **4:352–4**
Schurman, A.M. van **8:556–9**
Spinoza, B. de **9:91–107**
Thomas à Kempis **9:373–4**
Neto, J.R.M. 4:518
Nettl, J.P. 6:7
Netton, Ian Richard
al-Farabi †3:554–8
Ikhwan al-Safa' †4:685–8
Illuminationist philosophy 4:703
mystical philosophy in Islam 6:620
Neoplatonism in Islamic
philosophy †6:803–8
networks
see also neural networks
brain structure
associationist psychology 5:484
connectionist
computation 2:570–6
information technology and ethics
4:779, 4:781
Netzahualcoyotl, King of Texcoco
5:431
Neu, J. 3:285, 3:794
Neufeldt, R.W. 5:218
Neugebauer, O. 2:672
Neugebauer-Wölk, M. 4:697–8
Neuhouser, F. 3:653
Neuman, A.A. 8:440
Neumann, Franz 3:733–4, 3:737
Neumann, John von **6:809–13**
axiom of choice 1:614
computability theory 2:490–1
decision and game theory 2:824–5,
2:835

measurement
quantum 7:889, 7:890
theory of 6:249
paradoxes of set and property
7:219–20
practical reasoning/rationality
8:103
expected utility theory 8:93–5
game theory 8:98
quantum logic 7:886
quantum mechanics,
interpretation of 7:894
rational choice theory 8:66, 8:74
scientific theories 9:351, 9:353
set theory 8:715–16
Neumark, D. 4:213
neural networks 1:486, 2:570, 2:575
Neurath, Otto **6:813–16**
coherence theory of justification
5:254, 5:259
Hempel, C.G. 4:352
logical positivism 5:792–3, 5:794–5
social science
methodology of 8:868
unity of science 9:532
Vienna Circle 9:609–12
neurobiology
see also neurophysiology
psychological theory constructs
1:697, 1:698
neurology
emotions 3:282
neurones
McCulloch-Pitts 1:486
neurophilosophy
emotions 3:282
neurophysiology 1:486
see also neurobiology
artificial intelligence 1:486
central state identity theory
2:421–3
computation
connectionist networks 2:570,
2:575
dialectical development of
(Merleau-Ponty, M.) 6:321
Gestalt psychology
Berlin school 4:53
subjective colour perception
2:422–3
supervenience of the mental
9:238–9
Neusner, J. 6:355, 9:336
neutral monism 6:475, **6:816–18**
definition 6:816
identity theory 6:817
James, W. 6:816

Mach, E. 6:13, 6:14–16
paranormal phenomena 7:222
Russell, B.A.W. 6:816–17, 8:400
neutrality
merit distinction
art works 1:461–2
political **6:818–21**
human nature 4:524
liberalism 5:462, 8:882
multiculturalism 6:600
postmodernism 7:592
Neville, H. 4:234
Neville, R. 7:720
New Academy *see* Academic
scepticism
New, C. 2:722
new constructivism 2:635
New England transcendentalism *see*
Concord Transcendentalism
New Jerusalem 4:414
New Left Movement 1:247, 6:145
New Liberals 5:599
New Logic *see* Navya-Nyāya
New Rhetoric movement 5:496–7
New Testament
see also Gospels
atonement 1:537–8
Christology 4:726–7
demythologization (Bultmann, R.)
2:126–8
faith 3:538, 3:539–40
heaven 4:250
hell 4:330
hermeneutics
Bultmann, R. 4:392
interpretation of Old Testament
4:390
Loisy, A. 5:820
Incarnation 4:729
influenced by Hellenistic Judaism
7:256
Latin translation
Valla, L. critique 9:569
logos 5:819
original sin 8:793
pneuma (spirit)
usage 7:470, 7:471–2
providence 7:798
purgatory 7:837
sin 8:792
New Text school 9:680
New Thinking
Jewish philosophy (Rosenzweig, F.)
8:357, 8:358–60
New Zealand
Prior, A.N. **7:687–90**

Newcomb, A. 6:614
see also Newcomb's problem
Newcomb's problem 7:47
Newell, A.
cognitive architecture 2:393
computational theories of mind
6:394
language of thought hypothesis
5:407
logic of discovery 3:102–3
Turing machines 9:499
Newman, A.J. 2:807
Newman, B. 4:431
Newman, John Henry **6:821–3**
religion, history of philosophy of
8:247
religious belief 8:246
revelation 8:300
toleration 9:433
tradition and traditionalism
9:446–7
Newman, J.R. 4:107
Newman, L.A. 1:779
Newman, L.E. 3:701
Newman, M.H.A. 8:403, 9:707
Newman, P. 8:74
Newman, R.A. 5:153
Newman, W.R. 1:158
Newmeyer, O. 4:54
Newsome, D. 2:406
Newton, Isaac **6:823–8**
see also Newtonian physics
absolute time 9:414
analysis 1:217, 1:220
Bentley, R. 1:725–6
continuity 2:655
geometry 4:29–31, 4:33
human nature, eighteenth century
science of 4:526, 4:527
idealizations
thought experiments 9:394–5
infinites 2:678
infinitesimals 7:50
Leibniz, G.W. debate 5:544,
5:556–7
Leibniz/Clarke debate 2:379
light 6:824–5, 7:136
mathematics 6:826
matter 6:194, 6:195, 6:196
mechanics, classical 6:259
More, H. 6:578–9, 6:583
motion 2:296, 6:252–5, 6:825
Opticks
motion 2:296
*Philosophia naturalis principia
mathematica* (*Mathematical*

*Principles of Natural
Philosophy*)
scientific method 6:823,
6:825–6, 8:578
principle of true causes
geology 4:26
prophecy 7:770
science
method 8:578, 8:580–1
scientific hypotheses
(Stewart, D.) 9:138
science, demarcation problem
2:864, 2:866
space 9:59, 9:60–1, 9:65
Newton, K.M. 3:267
Newtonian physics
divine action 8:230, 8:231, 8:233
worldview 3:197
Newton-Smith, W.H. 5:345, 9:416
Neyman, J. 9:127
Ngok lodzawa loden shayrap *see*
rNgog lō tsa ba Blo ldan shes
rab
Ni Can 1:73–4
Nicaea, First Council of 7:259
Nicaea, Second Council of 2:222
Nicaragua 6:160, 6:162
Nicene Creed 4:726, 9:459
see also Athanasian Creed
Nichiren 2:100, **6:828–9**
Nicholas of Autrecourt **6:829–32**
Nicholas of Chuguet 7:49
Nicholas of Cusa **6:832–8**
calendar 1:134
Christology 6:835
cosmology 6:834
ecclesiology 6:835
ecumenism 6:835
epistemology 6:834–5
God, nature of 7:437
Platonism
medieval 7:439
Renaissance 7:443, 7:447
Nichols, B. 3:832, 8:347
Nichols, B. 3:677
Nichols, S. 3:687, 6:389
Nicholson, G. 3:535, 7:342
Nicholson, P.
Egyptian cosmology
ancient 3:250
Nicholson, P.P.
Bosanquet, B. †1:846–8
Bradley, F.H. 1:862
general will †4:9–4:12
Green, T.H. 4:170
state †9:120–3
toleration 9:433

Nichtweiß, B. 9:333
Nickel, James W.
　affirmative action 1:94
　discrimination †3:103–6
　international relations 4:832
　rights 8:330
Nickles, T. 1:358
Nickles, Thomas
　discovery
　　logic of †3:99–3:103
Nicod criterion 9:528, 9:529
Nicol, Eduardo 6:346–7
Nicolai, H. 5:48
Nicole, P. 5:373, 5:377, 7:553
Nicolini, F. 9:606
Nicomachean Ethics see Aristotle
Nicomachus of Gerasa 6:808
Niderst, A. 3:693
Niebuhr, Helmut Richard 6:838–41
　confessional theology 6:840
　God
　　sovereignty 6:839
　Troeltsch, E.P.W. 9:464
Niebuhr, Reinhold 6:841–4
　Christian realism 6:841, 6:843–4
　feminist theology 3:624
　human nature 6:842–3
　public theology 6:841, 6:842
　situation ethics 8:799
Niehues-Pröbsting, H. 2:759, 5:854
Nielsen, J.M. 3:593
Nielsen, L.O. 4:72
Nielsen, R. 4:300
Niesel, W. 2:182
Nietzsche, Friedrich Wilhelm
　6:844–61
　Also Sprach Zarathustra (Thus
　　Spoke Zarathustra)
　　Übermensch 6:856–7
　art 1:717
　　and morality 1:453
　ascetic ideal
　　critique of 1:518, 1:519, 6:845,
　　　6:851–2
　Berdiaev, N.A.
　　Signposts movement 8:770
　Christianity reconciliation
　　(Merezhkovskii, D.) 6:862–3
　cultural identity
　　Latin American 2:744
　deconstruction (Derrida, J.) 2:899
　educational philosophy 3:228,
　　3:230
　emotions 3:285, 3:288, 3:289
　　morality 6:561, 6:563
　eternal recurrence 6:858–9

existentialism 3:502
　ethics 3:505
fascism 3:562
forgiveness and mercy 3:701
free will 3:747, 3:752
genealogy 4:2–3, 4:4
God
　death of 6:852–3
　guilt 8:139, 8:141
Herzen, A.I. comparison 4:407
historicism 4:445, 4:446
honour 4:503
ideals 4:675
influence of
　existentialist theology 3:507
　Leont'ev, K.N. 5:568
　Marxism
　　Latin America 6:163
　　Russia 6:861–7, 8:418, 8:420
knowledge 6:849–50
memory (Deleuze, G.) 2:857
metaphysics 6:848–9
morality 6:845, 6:853–6
　and ethics 6:565, 6:571
　motivation 6:524
music
　aesthetics of 6:614
Nachlaß 6:847–8
nihilism 3:494, 7:1–2, 7:5
　French anti-postmodernism
　　7:594
　Nishitani Keiji 7:17
perfectionism 7:302
pluralism 7:463–4
poetry 7:477
postmodern theology 7:585
religious belief
　irrationality of 8:210
　rationality 8:214
revenge
　critique of Dühring, E.K. 3:148
role of philosophy 6:850–1
self-deception 8:630, 8:632
slavery 8:805, 8:806
Socrates 9:18
sport 9:113
Strauss, D.F. 9:166
suicide 9:224, 9:229
tragedy 9:450, 9:451
　critique by Shestov, L. 8:742,
　　8:743
Übermensch (the overhuman)
　6:856–7, 6:858
utilitarianism 9:557
virtues and vices 9:631
vulnerability and finitude 9:670
will to power 6:857–8, 7:516

Nifo, Agostino 6:867–72
　Aristotelianism 6:867–70
　　Renaissance 1:406, 1:407, 1:409
　metaphysics 6:869–70
　soul, nature and origin of 6:869
nightwatchman theory 9:87
nihilation
　negation by consciousness
　　(Sartre, J.-P.) 8:475
nihilism 7:1–5
　see also moral scepticism
　assumptions 7:3–4
　cosmic 7:1, 7:2, 7:3–4
　emptiness distinction (Nāgārjuna)
　　6:639
　epistemological 7:1
　ethical naturalism 6:714
　existential 3:500, 7:1, 7:2–3, 7:4
　Indian philosophy 6:179
　language
　　ancient philosophy of 5:357
　metaphysics (Heidegger, M.)
　　4:307, 4:317
　moral 7:1
　Nietzsche, F.W. 3:494, 6:853, 7:594
　Nishitani, Keiji 5:328, 7:16–7
　Parmenidian ontology (Gorgias)
　　4:144, 4:145
　political 7:1
　rationalization of culture
　　(Adorno, T.W.) 1:42–3
　Russian 7:5–8
　　progress 8:421
　scientific understanding 7:2, 7:4
　values 7:2, 7:4
Niiniluoto, Ilkka
　confirmation theory 2:535
　Finland 8:488, 8:492
　idealizations 4:672
　Wright, G.H. von †9:667–9
Niklaus, R. 9:663
Nikoliukin, A.N. 8:385
Nilsson, M.P. 7:165
Nine Mountain Schools of Sôn
　Buddhism 2:110–11
Niphus, Augustinus see Nifo,
　Agostino
nirvāṇa 7:8–7:12
　see also enlightenment; liberation
　awareness
　　Vasubandhu 9:585–6
　Buddhism 8:184
　　China 2:82
　definitions 7:8–7:10
　Jainism 8:184
　Mahāyāna Buddhism 7:10–11
　salvation 8:448

self
  emptiness 2:76–7
Nisbet, H.B. 4:129
Nisbett, R.E.
  artificial intelligence 1:492
  consciousness 2:595–6
  folk psychology 3:687
  introspection 4:842
  introspection, psychology of 4:843,
    4:844–5, 4:846
  naturalized epistemology 6:727
  psychoanalysis
    methodological issues in 7:817
  rationality of belief 8:89
  unconscious mental states 9:523–4,
    9:527
Nishi Amane **7:12–13**
Nishida 7:91–2
Nishida Kitarō **7:13–16**
  influence of (Miki Kiyoshi) 6:358
  Japanese philosophy in modern
    literature 5:659, 5:660
  Kyoto School 5:77–8, 5:79,
    5:323–9
  logic 5:713–15, 5:716
Nishitani Keiji **7:16–17**
  Kyoto School 5:323–9
  mujō 6:594
  Nishida Kitarō 7:16
Nissenbaum, Helen
  information technology and ethics
    †4:778–82
  technology and ethics †9:280–4
Nissus, Vitalis 5:23
nisus 1:168
Nivedita 8:42
Nivison, David S. 4:452, 6:304, 6:458,
  6:776
Njegoš, Petar Petrović 9:50, 9:55
Nkrumah, Kwame 1:97, 1:99–1:101,
  1:107
Nō 9:839–40
Noble, Margaret *see* Nivedita
'noble savage'
  pre-political society (Rousseau, J.-
    J.) 8:370
Nobo, J.L. 9:719
Nóbrega, Manuel da 2:8, 2:11
Nochlin, L. 3:408, 3:409
Nock, A.D. 4:397
Noddings, Nel
  feminist ethics 3:603–4, 3:605
  justice 5:147
  morality and emotions 6:563
  nursing ethics 7:57
  virtue ethics 9:625–6
Nöel, G. 4:299

noema
  Husserl, E. 4:574–5, 4:577–8
noemata
  Husserl, E. 4:817
noesis *see* noema
no-freedom theory *see* pessimism
Nogarola, Isotta 4:540
Nogot example 4:55–8
Noland, A. 7:793
Nolhac, P. de 7:329
Noll, M. 9:757
nominal essence
  natural kinds 6:683–4
nominalism **7:17–23**
  see also conventionalism;
    Platonism; realism
  abstract objects 1:32, 1:33–4
  Buddhist doctrine of **7:23–7**
    Dharmakīrti 3:52
      meaning 7:25–6
      ontology 7:23–4
      universals 7:24–5, 9:544, 9:547
    Chinese
      Mohist philosophy 2:323
      Xunzi 2:323
    classical empiricism 7:18, 7:20–1
      eighteenth century
        universals (Stewart, D.) 9:138
      mathematics (Mill, J.S.) 6:363–4
      semantics (Hobbes, T.) 5:373
    Goodman, N. 4:136
    Indian philosophy 7:123–4
    linguistic
      see also psychological
        nominalism
      Platonism debate (Quine, W.V.)
        8:8–9
      Ramsey sentences 8:47–8
      reism (Kotarbiński, T.) 5:293–4
    medieval
      realism/antirealism 8:116
      Roscelin of Compiege 7:18–19
    psychological (Sellars, W.S.)
      8:639–40
    twentieth century 7:21–2
      critical theory 2:725
      substitutional quantification
        7:880–1
      type/token distinction 9:510
    universals 9:540, 9:541–2
      metaphysics 6:338–9
  nominalism, scholastic
    Abelard, P. 7:19
    Báñez, D. 1:647–8
    colonial philosophy
      Latin America 5:424

formalism conflict (Gerson, J.)
  4:45–6
Gregory of Rimini 4:170
imposition 5:391
logic (Major, J.) 6:54
motion (Burley, W.) 2:141–2
natural philosophy
  medieval 6:701–2, 6:701
omnipotence (Peter Lombard)
  5:821
propositional logic (Buridan, J.)
  2:131, 2:132
realism conflict
  medieval Platonism 7:434–5
refutations of
  Brinkley, R. 2:20
  Duns Scotus, J. 3:163–5
signification 5:392–3
universals 5:389
  Buridan, J. 2:132–3
  Crathorn, W. 2:693
  William of Champeaux 7:18
  William of Ockham 7:18,
    7:19–20
William of Ockham 9:732, 9:734–6
nomos
  justice (Antiphon) 1:302
  nature (Antiphon) 1:302–3
  physis relationship
    Callicles 2:176, 2:177
    Greek philosophy **7:381–2**
    political philosophy
      history of 7:505–6
    social science 8:848–9
    Sophists 9:33–4
nonabsolutism (*anekāntavadā*)
  Jainism 2:252–3, 2:256–7
non-Aristotelian logic *see* many-
  valued logics
non-being
  and being
    Eriugena's division of nature
      3:403
  pluralism
    matter 6:193
nonbeing, Chinese philosophy *see* wu;
  wuji
noncognitivism 1:221–2, 3:366–7,
  6:511–12, 7:73
  see also cognitivism
  democracy (Radbruch, G.) 8:21–2
  internalism
    moral motivation 6:523
  language theories (Taylor, C.)
    9:277

morality
  attitudes
    direction of fit 6:534
    knowledge 6:517–18
    scepticism 6:543–4
    sentiments 6:548, 6:549
  naturalism in ethics 6:713, 6:714
  verificationism (Reichenbach, H.)
    8:170
non-conceptual content see content,
  non-conceptual
non-conscious phenomena 9:522
nonconsequentialism 3:120–1
non-constructive rules of inference
  7:27–30
non-contradiction, principle of
  Aristotle 1:421
  Kant, I. critique 5:180–1
  Nicholas of Autrecourt 6:830
  paraconsistent logic 7:209, 7:210
  William of Ockham 9:734–5
non-directive therapy 7:828
non-Euclidean geometry
  foundations of mathematics
    4:31–2, 6:181–2, 6:183
nonexistence
  'as a harm' 2:820
  ontological categories
    Indian philosophy 7:126–7
non-extensionality
  see also intension
  adverbs 1:49
nonfigurative art see art, abstract
non-identity
  Nyāya-Vaiśiṣika
    causation 2:251, 2:252, 2:255
non-monotonic logic 2:451, 2:452–3,
  7:30–5
non-naturalism
  see also naturalism
  ethics 3:366
non-reductionism 4:484
non-rigid designators 2:815–16
non-sentience, principle of
  Jainism 5:49–50
nonstandard analysis 1:211–16
  infinitesimal numbers 7:52
  non-standard models
    mathematics 1:212
nonuniversalism
  ethical 4:503–4
nonviolence see pacifism
Noonan, H.W. 1:35, 2:654, 4:678,
  7:314
Noonan, J.T. 8:728
Noone, T. 8:317

Nooruddin, Ubai
  Orientalism in Islamic philosophy
    †7:158–60
Noppen, J.P. van 6:338
Nora, P. 7:596
Norberg-Schulz, C. 3:334, 3:336
Norden, H. 3:258
Nordenfelt, L. 6:266, 6:269
Nordenstam, T. 7:648
normal form (conjunctive)
  glossary 5:805–6
normal form (disjuntive)
  glossary 5:806
normal form (prenex)
  glossary 5:806
normal forms
  computability theory 2:487
  Gentzen, G. 6:677–8, 6:679
  lambda calculus 5:347
Norman, J. 5:789, 7:211, 8:204
Norman, K.R. 7:11
Norman, R. 9:691
Norman, Wayne
  citizenship 2:365
  federalism and confederalism
    †3:572–4
normative concepts
  deontic logic 2:887–9
normative epistemology 7:35–8
  challenges 5:274–5
  epistemic advice 7:35
  evaluative concepts 7:35
  historical epistemology 7:35
  non-naturalistic 7:35
normative nature
  differentiated
    Han Wŏnjin 4:221
    Yi Kan 9:825
normative relativism
  morality 6:539, 6:541
normative theory of law see pure
  theory of law
normativity
  legal 7:38–41
    Bobbio, N. 1:790
    descriptive laws distinction
      7:38–9
  physical illness
    concepts of 6:312–13
norm-logic 9:702
Normore, C. 1:566, 1:866, 2:136
norms
  see also legal norms; social norms
  biological
    French philosophy of science
      3:782–3
    physical illness 6:312–13

cultural
  relativism 8:82, 8:85
epistemic
  science, naturalized philosophy
    of 6:729–30
human rights 8:328–9
moral
  development ethics 3:42
  practical reason 7:614–15,
    7:616–17
Næss, A. 6:635
scientific
  objectivity of (Foucault, M.)
    3:784–5
social 8:834–6
  convention
    Lewis, D.K. 8:834
    definition 8:834
    French philosophy of science
      3:782, 3:783
    rules 8:834–5
  society
    concept of 8:887, 8:888
Norrie, Alan
  Critical Legal Studies †2:714–20
Norris, Christopher
  alterity and identity
    postmodern theories of 1:192
  deconstruction †2:835–9
Norris, John 7:41–3
  Masham, D. 6:168
  More, H. 6:583
  occasionalism
    Astell, M. critique 1:527–8
Norris, S. 3:239
North Africa
  Apuleius 1:325–6
  Islamic philosophy 5:14
North, J. 3:453, 6:706–7
Nortmann, U. 5:693
Norton, David Fate
  Home, H. 4:501
  Hume, D. 4:562
  Hutcheson, F. †4:588–94
  Turnbull, G. 9:504
Norton, John D.
  Einstein, A. †3:254–8
Norton, R.E. 4:384
Norway 8:489–91
  Næss, A. 6:635–8
Nosco, Peter
  Confucianism, Japanese †2:549–55
  Motoori Norinaga 6:590
Nose, A. 9:841
no-self theory
  Buddhism 1:606, 6:401–2

notation
  canonical (Quine, W.V.) 8:7–8
  Polish 7:496
not-being
  impossibility of (Parmenides)
    7:229, 7:230
nothingness
  absolute
    Kyoto School 5:327–8
    Nishida Kitarō 7:14
    Tanabe Hajime 9:261
  and being (Eriugena) 3:403, 3:404
  Gorgias 4:144, 4:145
  Japanese Buddhism (Nishitani
    Keiji) 7:16–17
  prajñā schools of Buddhism
    China 2:82
notions
  common *see koinai ennoiai*
noumenal Real
  religious pluralism (Hick, J.)
    8:261–2
nouns
  see also names; proper names
  copula (Abelard, P.) 1:10
  descriptions **3:19–24**
  mass terms **6:168–70**
  paronymy
    Anselm of Canterbury 1:289–90
  phrases
    constituent structure 9:247–8
  predicates as common nouns 7:666
nous (intellect) **7:43–4**
  see also Intellect
  nature of
    Neoplatonism (Proclus) 7:727
  wisdom 9:753
Novack, G. 9:466
Novak, B.C. 1:163
Novak, David 5:95, 6:650
Novak, J.
  Heschel, A.J. †4:410–12
  Masaryk, T.G. 6:166
Novaković, Staniša 9:55
Novalis *see* Hardenberg, F. von
novels
  theories of (Bakhtin, M.M.)
    1:638–9, 1:643–4
Novgorodtsev, Pavel
  critique of Russian liberalism
    5:608
  Il'in, I.A. 4:692
  Neo-Kantianism
    Russian 6:794–5, 6:797
  Signposts movement 8:773
  Solov'ëv, V.S. 9:32
Novikov, Nikolai 3:326

Novokhat'ko, A.G. 4:692
Novotný, V. 4:574
Nowak, L. 6:150
Nowell-Smith, P.H. 8:224
Nowicki, Andrzej 7:487–8
Noxon, James 4:562
Nozick, M. 9:521
Nozick, Robert **7:44–7**
  axiology 1:612
  coercion 2:389
  contractarianism 2:665
  epistemic paradoxes 7:214
  equality 3:395–6
  Gettier problems
    conditional approach 4:57, 4:59
  internalism-externalism distinction
    4:826
  justice 5:147
    entitlement theory 5:144–5
  liberalism 5:604, 5:605
  libertarianism 2:658, 5:618, 5:619
  meaning of life 5:633
  ontology 7:118
  paternalism 7:252
  personal identity 7:314
  practical reasoning/rationality
    8:103
  property 7:759, 7:761
  reliabilism 5:276, 8:209
  scepticism 8:498
  statistics 9:127
  tracking analysis 2:844, 2:845
  value 9:583
  work
    philosophy of 9:797
Nuchelmans, G.
  Ailly, P. d' 1:135
  Burthogge, R. 2:146
  Crathorn, W. 2:693
  Geulincx, A. 4:61
  language
    ancient philosophy of 5:361
    early modern philosophy of
      5:379
    medieval theories of 5:404
    Renaissance philosophy of
      5:415
  logic, seventeenth and eighteenth
    century 5:721
  propositions 7:788
  Wodeham, A. 9:776
Nucho, F. 1:732
nuclear deterrence 9:688
numbers **7:47–54**
  see also arithmetic; cardinal;
    infinite; numerology; ordinal
  epistemology (Frege, G.) 3:773–4

  infinite (Toletus, F.) 9:434–5
  natural 2:841, 7:48, 7:51
    axiom of constructibility 2:623
    compositeness 2:495
    second-order logic 8:601–2
  negative 7:49
  patterns of change (Shao Yong)
    8:736
  Pythagoreanism
    cosmogony (Philolaus) 7:368–9
    cosmology 7:858–60
    music 7:858
  real
    computability of 2:491–4
    continuum of 8:704
      Cantor, G. 2:196–7,
        2:199–200
      paradoxes 7:218
    Dedekind, J.W.R. 2:841
    nonstandard analysis 1:212–13,
      5:847
    Russian constructivism 2:634–5
    second-order logic 8:601
  science of
    geometry distinction 4:30–1,
      4:32
  significance
    Gnosticism 4:84
  use/mention confusions 9:550–1
Numbers, R.L. 8:235
Numenius of Apamea 6:808–9,
  7:54–6
numerology
  neo-Confucianism (Shao Yong)
    6:767, 8:736
numinous experience
  Otto, R. 7:173–5
Nunes, Esther Vas 4:287
Nunes, Pedro 2:8
Nuño, J.A. 1:230, 1:232, 1:233
nuraniya (mysterious letters of the
  Qur'an)
  Ibn Massara 4:629
nursing ethics **7:56–7**, 7:733
  see also bioethics; medical ethics
Nuseibeh, S. 3:387–8
Nussbaum, Martha C.
  Aquinas, T. 1:348
  Aristotle 1:435
  art and truth 1:460
  development ethics 3:43
  educational philosophy 3:234,
    3:239
  equality 3:396
  examples in ethics 3:490
  forgiveness and mercy 3:701
  Hellenistic philosophy 4:336–7

justice, equity and law 5:149–50, 5:153
love †5:842–6
moral luck 6:522
morality and emotions †6:558–64
nature and convention 6:736–7
Owen, G.E.L. 7:179
Philodemus 7:367
sexuality 8:727, 8:728
Stoicism 9:160
vulnerability and finitude 9:670–1
welfare 9:705
Nuyoricans (Puerto Rican Americans) 6:99
Nya dbon Kun dga' dpal (Nyawön Güngapel) 9:407
Nyawön Güngapel *see* Nya dbon Kun dga' dpal
Nyāya 4:439
    see also Navya-Nyāya; *Nyāyasūtra*; Nyāya-Vaiśeṣika
    Akṣapāda Gautama 3:859–60
    awareness
        realist view 1:607
    Buddhism debate (Vātsyāyana) 9:587–8
    cognition
        error and illusion 3:412
    duty and virtue 3:184–5
    God
        concept of 4:102, 4:104–5
    Indian and Tibetan philosophy 4:738
    karma and rebirth 5:212–13
    knowledge 4:435
    language 4:437
    logic
        Jainism 5:48, 5:50
    realism
        Vātsyāyana 9:587–8
    reliabilism
        epistemic 3:388, 3:389–90, 3:391

self
    theories of 8:608
    sense perception 8:691–3
    substance-pluralism 6:197
    testimony 9:315, 9:317, 9:318
    Udayana 9:512–13
    Uddyotakara 9:514–15
        inference 4:764–5
    universals 9:545, 9:546
    Vedānta School relationship 9:591
nyāya (colloquial wisdom)
    interpretation
        Indian theories of 4:836
nyāya (method of proof) *see* Nyāya-Vaiśeṣika
Nyāyasūtra 3:859–60
    awareness 1:608
    inference 4:766
    knowledge 5:281, 5:284, 5:285
    Nyāya-Vaiśeṣika 7:62, 7:64, 7:66
    ontology 7:127
    sense perception 8:694
    Uddyotakara 9:515
    Vātsyāyana commentary on 9:587–8
Nyāya-Vaiśeṣika **7:57–6**
    see also Nyāya; *Nyāyasūtra*; Vaiśeṣika
    analogy
        knowledge 5:282
    Buddhism agreement
        causality 7:121
    circumstantial implication
        knowledge 5:283
    epistemology 7:62–4
        inference 5:283, 5:284–5, 7:63
        perception 7:62–3
    Indian and Tibetan philosophy 4:737
    inference
        knowledge 5:283, 5:284–5
    Mahābhārata 7:59

meaning 6:240
    monism 6:477–8
    nonidentity
        causation 2:251, 2:252, 2:255
    ontology 7:60–2
        categories 7:118–27
        origin of 7:59–60
    sense perception 8:690, 8:691
    soteriology 7:64
    Uddyotakara
        heaven 4:255
        universals 9:547
    Vaiśeṣikasūtra 7:58, 7:60–1, 7:64, 7:67
    veridicality
        error and illusion 3:411–12
Nye, J.S. 2:675, 2:677
Nye, M.J. 7:482
Nyerere, Julius K.
    African philosophy 1:97
    African socialist society 1:101, 1:107
    ethnophilosophy, African 3:449
    Marxism
        metaphysics relationship 1:101
Nygren, Anders **7:67–9**
    agape
        charity as Christian love 2:280, 2:282
    Thielicke, H. 9:371
Nyíri, J.C. 4:572
Nyíri, K. 4:572
Nylan, Michael
    Dong Zhongshu †3:111–13
    Jia Yi †5:102–3
    Yang Xiong †9:821–2
    Zheng Xuan †9:857–8
Nyman, C.
    anti-Semitism †1:311–14
nymphomania 8:720
Nyquist, Harry 4:782
Nys, T.V. 4:360

O

O raznoglasii na filosofskom fronte
(On a Disagreement on the
Philosophical Front) 6:159
Oakes, G. 6:792, 9:698
Oakeshott, Michael Joseph **7:70–3**
   conservatism 2:612, 2:614
   limits of law 5:464
   theory and practice 9:358
Oaklander, L.N. 9:307
Oakley, A. 3:583
Oakley, F. 6:56, 7:517, 9:664
Oatley, K. 3:280, 6:564
Obbink, D. 7:367
obedience
   Christianity (Bonhoeffer, D.) 1:835
   Jewish pietism (Ibn Paquda)
     4:634–5
Obenga, T. 1:116
Oberdan, T.
   Carnap, R. 2:215
   Schlick, F.A.M. †8:539–44
Oberg, B.B. 4:238
Oberhammer, G. 7:66
Oberländer, E. 8:774
Oberman, H.A.
   Augustinianism 1:564
   Biel, G. 1:772
   Bradwardine, T. 1:866–7
   Gregory of Rimini 4:172
   Holcot, R. 4:479
   Luther, M. 6:5
   voluntarism 9:664
Obertello, L. 1:210, 1:813
object
   adequate (Duns Scotus, J.)
     3:159–60
   content distinction
     descriptive psychology
       (Twardowski, K.) 9:508
     perception of external truths
       (Moore, G.E.) 6:496
   identity philosophy
     (Schelling, F.W.J. von)
     8:511–13, 8:515, 8:516
   intuitive cognition (Duns
     Scotus, J.) 3:154, 3:165–6
   objectivity contrast
     Daoism 2:790–1

religion
   phenomenology 7:354–5
subject unity
   human/nature harmonization
     (Marcuse, H.) 6:97–8
object permanence
   child development 2:390–1, 7:383,
     7:385
object recognition
   computational models of vision
     9:636–7
   film aesthetics 3:674
object (syntax)
   word order 9:246
object-consciousness
   self-consciousness distinction
     (Schleiermacher, F.) 8:535
object-dependence
   de re belief 2:816, 2:817
   indexicals 2:879
objectification
   of sex (Kant, I.) 8:722–3, 8:724
objectivism
   critical theory 2:725
   moral realism 6:534
   participant 1:849
   phenomenology (Ingarden, R.W.)
     4:789, 4:790
   values 9:582
objectivity **7:73–6**
   see also intersubjectivity
   aesthetics
     concepts 1:55, 1:56
     nature 6:732, 6:734
   anthropology 1:298
   anti-foundationalism 8:354
   anti-realism 7:73, 7:74–5
   archaeology 1:357
   beauty 1:511–12
   best judgments 7:74
   critical judgments 1:460, 1:462,
     1:463
   East Asian philosophy 3:193
   epistemic
     sceptical doubt 6:644–5
   ethics
     epistemology 3:367–8
     Rosmini-Serbati, A. 8:363
   faith (Kierkegaard, S.A.) 9:329

feminism
   empiricism 3:599
   science 3:866–7
   and social science 3:588, 3:591
   French philosophy of science
     3:782, 3:783, 3:784–5
   goodness 4:132
   Hegelian concepts 4:271
   humour 4:563
   ideal 3:597
   knowledge (Rosmini-Serbati, A.)
     8:362
   meaning 7:75
   modernism 6:448–9
   non-cognitivism 7:73
   object contrast
     Daoism 2:790–1
   phenomenology of perception
     (Merleau-Ponty, M.) 6:322–3
   physics
     operationalism
       (Bridgman, P.W.) 2:18
   postcolonial philosophy of science
     7:577
   prescriptivism (Hare, R.M.)
     4:230–1
   primary-secondary distinction
     7:74, 7:75
   pure (Fichte, J.G.) 3:642
   quietism 7:73, 7:75
   rule-following considerations
     (RFC) 7:75
   science
     feminism 3:866–7
   semantic function 7:73
   social factors (Hegel, G.W.F.)
     4:260
   social science 8:867
     Weber, M. 9:694
   subjectivism 7:73–4
   subjectivity distinction
     Hegel, G.W.F. 4:263–4
     Nagel, T. 6:643–6
   theory-laden observation 7:81,
     7:83–4
   of thought (Frege, G.) 3:770–1
   truth 7:74, 7:75

object-relations
　　psychoanalysis
　　　Klein, M. 7:817–19
　　　post-Freudian 7:819–20,
　　　　7:821–2
objects
　　abstract **1:32–5**
　　　Kotarbiński, T. 5:293–4
　　continuants **2:652–4**
　　eternal (Whitehead, A.N.)
　　　9:716–17
　　impossible (Meinong, A.) 6:283
　　incomplete (Meinong, A.) 6:283
　　Indian concepts of 2:849–52
　　intentional (Hervaeus Natalis)
　　　4:403–4
　　paradoxical (Meinong, A.) 6:283
　　perception 7:288–9
　　　Kant, I. 5:187
　　physical
　　　understanding of
　　　　cognitive development
　　　　　2:390–1, 2:394
　　properties
　　　essentialism **3:417–22**
　　representation
　　　awareness
　　　　Indian theories of 1:606
　　　Schopenhauer, A. 8:547,
　　　　8:548–9
　　sense-experience
　　　(Whitehead, A.N.) 9:715
　　simple *see* simples
　　theory of (Meinong, A.) 6:282,
　　　6:283–4
objectual quantification 7:878–80
obligation
　　see also duty; responsibility
　　animals and ethics 1:274
　　duty relationship 3:178
　　engineering ethics 3:313, 3:314–15
　　epistemic justification 3:368
　　ethics
　　　'ought-implies-can' principle
　　　　3:368
　　ethics (Panaetius) 7:189, 7:190
　　to future generations **3:819–22**
　　genetic enhancement 4:18
　　gratitude relationship 8:138–9
　　help and beneficence 4:342–3
　　judicial
　　　rule of law 8:390–1
　　kinship
　　　African ethical systems 3:431
　　legal
　　　moral obligation distinction
　　　　4:234–5

norms (Hart, H.L.A.) 7:39
　　rule of law 8:388, 8:390–1
　　legal authority (Locke, J.) 5:679
　　medieval logic 5:757–8, 5:768
　　moral
　　　Cockburn, C. 2:386
　　　Cumberland, R. 2:752
　　　incompatibility of 9:751
　　　legal obligation distinction
　　　　(Hart, H.L.A.) 4:234–5
　　Nietzsche, F.W. 6:855
　　to the Other (Levinas, E.) 5:579–81
　　political **7:76–80**
　　　see also authority; legitimacy
　　　anarchist theories 7:76, 7:79–80
　　　communitarian theories 7:76,
　　　　7:77–8
　　　Locke, J. 5:681–2
　　　nonvoluntarist theories 7:76,
　　　　7:77, 7:78–9
　　　voluntarist theories 7:76, 7:77,
　　　　7:78
　　promises 7:740–1
　　　Hume, D. 4:554
　　Roman law/civilian tradition 8:346
　　supererogation distinction 9:232,
　　　9:233
　　sympathy (Hume, D.) 6:546–7
Obradović, Dositej 9:50
O'Brien, C.C. 2:140, 2:196
Obrist, B. 1:158
obscenity 7:544
observation **7:80–6**
　　coherence theory of justification
　　　5:253, 5:256–7
　　conventionalism (Carnap, R.)
　　　2:211–12
　　empiricism 7:84–5, 7:86
　　experiment 3:515
　　Galilei, G. 3:838–9
　　incommensurability
　　　(Feyerabend, P.K.) 3:640
　　indirect 7:81, 7:84
　　information 7:80–1, 7:82, 7:86
　　introspection 4:843–4
　　　scientific behaviourism
　　　　(Skinner, B.F.) 8:800
　　naturalized epistemology 6:724
　　　Quine, W.V. 8:5–6
　　operationalism 7:131–4
　　reliability of
　　　inductive inference 4:756
　　sentences
　　　naturalized epistemology 8:3–4,
　　　　8:5–6
　　social sciences **9:355–6**
　　testimony 9:312

theoretical claims
　　Sellars, W.S. 8:640–1
　　theory distinction 6:724
　　　social science 8:870
　　theory-ladenness 7:82–4
　　　archaeology 1:356–7
　　　experiment 3:515
　　　Hanson, N.R. 4:224
obsession
　　self-cultivation
　　　Chinese philosophy 8:617
obstacles
　　epistemological
　　　French philosophy of science
　　　　3:780, 3:782, 3:783
Occam, William of *see* William of
　　Ockham
Occam's razor *see* Ockham's razor
occasionalism **7:86–90**
　　Clauberg, J. 2:381
　　continuous creation 2:698
　　Cordemoy, G. de 2:673
　　critiques of
　　　Astell, M. 1:527–8
　　　Cudworth, R. 2:741
　　　Leibniz, G.W. 5:549
　　Descartes, R. 3:16
　　Edwards, J. 3:241
　　al-Ghazali 4:644, 7:87
　　immaterialism 7:88–9
　　Islamic philosophy 2:243
　　　al-Ghazali 4:644
　　Jewish pietism 4:635
　　　Ibn Paquda 4:635
　　La Forge, L. de 5:331–2
　　Malebranche, N. 6:56, 6:61–3
　　Régis, P.-S. 8:166
occasions
　　actual (Whitehead, A.N.) 9:714,
　　　9:716
occultism
　　Agrippa von Nettesheim, H.C.
　　　1:130, 1:132
　　alchemy 1:156
　　Hermetism 4:396–7
　　Jung, C.G. 5:133
　　science (Paracelsus) 7:207
occurrence
　　type/token distinction 9:510
The Ocean Seal Buddhism, Korea
　　2:109–10
Ochorowicz, Julian 7:486
Ochs, P. 7:715
Ockham, William of *see* William of
　　Ockham
Ockhamism
　　foreknowledge and freedom 7:110

Ockham's Razor
    abstract objects 1:33
    Chatton, W. 2:292
    Durandus of St Pourçain 3:172,
        3:173
    fictional entities 3:664
    Gregory of Rimini 4:171
    ontological commitment 7:113,
        7:114
    pluralism 7:463
    universals 9:540, 9:541
    William of Ockham 9:735
O'Cleirigh, P. 7:463
O'Connell, J. 9:258
O'Connor, David K.
    Xenophon †9:810–15
O'Connor, D.J. 7:214
O'Connor, T. 3:752
O'Daly, G.P.D. 1:559, 1:813, 7:808
Odifreddi, P. 2:491, 8:145, 9:502
Odin, Steve
    Buddhist philosophy, Korean
        2:118
    Ûisang 9:516–17
    Watsuji Tetsurō †9:691–3
Odoevskii, V. 8:522
O'Donnell, J.J. 3:309
O'Donnell, M. 1:699
O'Donnell, R.M. 5:235
Ody, H.J. 2:692
Oedipus Complex 3:790, 3:792
Oehler, K. 2:165
Oelkers, J. 6:792
Oelmüller, W. 4:301
Oenomaus of Gadera 2:757
Oenopides of Chios 3:252
Oesterreich, T.K. 6:777–8
Oestreich, G. 5:652
Oetke, C. 3:861, 5:218, 6:473
Offermanns, W. 4:696
Offner, M. 1:840
Offord, D.C. 5:609, 8:811
O'Flaherty, J.C. 4:217
O'Flaherty, W.D. 3:568, 5:218,
        8:185–6
Ofstad, H. 8:491
Ogden, C.K. 3:667, 7:284
Ogg, D. 8:605
Ogle, P. 3:677
Ogonowski, Z. 7:488, 7:489
Oguah, B.E. 1:139
Ogyū Sorai **7:90–2**
    Ancient Studies
        Confucianism, Japanese 2:549,
            2:553
    Itō Jinsai 5:43
O'Hanlon, R. 7:582

O'Hara, R.J. 9:81
Ohashi Ryosuke 5:329–30
O'Hear, Anthony
    conservatism †2:608–15
    culture †2:746–50
    Popper, K.R. 7:539
    tradition and traditionalism
        †9:445–7
O'Higgins, J. 2:419
Ohira, S. 5:57, 6:34
oikeiōsis (affiliation) 4:421–2, 9:153–4
Oizerman, T. 3:57
Okada, Takehiko 5:177
Okakura Kakuzō 1:90
Oken, Lorenz **7:92–3**
    Naturphilosophie 6:742
Okere, T. 1:107
Okin, S.M. 3:551, 3:607, 3:610, 3:620
Okrent, Mark
    being †1:699–702
    pragmatism 7:639
Okruhlik, K. 3:593, 3:602, 3:868
Oladipo, O. 1:116
Olafson, F. 3:505, 6:325, 8:479
Olbrecht-Tyteca, Lucy 5:496, 8:309
Olby, R. 6:460
Olcott, Henry Steel 9:364
Old Academy 1:300, 7:422
Old Hegelians see Hegelianism
Old Testament see Bible, Hebrew
Old Text school 9:680
Oldfield, A. 2:365
Oldrini, G. 4:301
O'Leary-Hawthorne, J.
    imagination †4:705–8
Olivé, L. 1:233
Olivecrona, Karl **7:93–5**
    legal positivism 5:521
    legal realism 5:522, 5:525
    Petrażycki, L. 7:330
Oliver, A.
    Llull, R. 5:664
Oliver, Alex
    facts †3:535–7
    logical atomism †5:772–5
    ontological status of value
        †9:580–1
Oliver, Amy A.
    Latin America
        feminist thought †3:625–8
        literature in 5:657
        philosophy in †5:426–8
        marginality †6:99–101
Oliver, K. 5:308
Oliveri, G. 3:153
Olivero, M.B. 2:621
Olivi, Peter John **7:95–7**

Olivieri, L. 1:413, 7:266
Olkowski, Dorothea
    Deleuze, G. †2:856–61
Ollig, Hans-Ludwig
    Neo-Kantianism †6:776–92
Olsen, Frances
    privacy †7:690–3
Olsen, J.P. 8:847
Olsen, M., Jr 8:70–1, 8:74
Olsen, S.H. 3:667
Olson, A.M. 5:83
Olson, C. 3:263
Olson, G.A. 5:3
Olson, K.R. 3:537
Olson, R.E. 8:491
Olson, Richard 9:139–40
O'Malley, J. 3:401
Oman, J.C. 1:519
Oman, John Wood **7:97–8**
    grace 4:148, 4:151
O'Meara, D.J. 4:599, 6:803, 6:809,
        7:463
O'Meara, J.J. 3:405–6
O'Meara, T.A. 9:412
Omega number 2:480
Omega rule 7:27–9
omega-completeness
    glossary 5:806
omega-consistency
    glossary 5:806
Omi, M. 8:21
omnipotence **7:98–7:103**, 8:238, 8:243
    Abelard, P. 1:13–14
    analysis 7:100–1
    Augustine 1:549
    classical theology 4:99
    contingency 7:99–7:100
    creation (Ibn Rushd) 4:639–40
    Damian, P. 2:773
    definition of 7:99–100
    divine freedom 3:759, 3:761
    divine power
        classical Christian theism 7:717
        free-will theism 7:717
        process theism 7:717, 7:719
        providence 7:798, 7:799, 7:800
    evil, problem of 3:466–7, 8:245
    God
        attributes of 8:243
        goodness compatibility 7:101–2
        Hebrew Bible 1:767
        human acts
            al-Ghazali 4:63
        immutability 4:713
        Incarnation 4:729
        nominalist defence of 5:821
        occasionalism 7:87

paradox of 7:100
perfect goodness
    compatibility 4:141–2
polytheism 6:482–3
revelation 8:298
William of Ockham 9:734
omnipresence **7:103–7**
classical theology 4:98–9
divine simplicity 8:786
divine spatiality 7:103, 7:105
embodiment 7:103–5
Hebrew Bible 1:767
Incarnation 4:729
Jewish philosophy
    Hasidism 4:243, 4:244
omniscience **7:107–12**, 8:238, 8:243–4
see also knowledge, divine
atheism 1:533
divine knowledge
Jewish philosophy (Gersonides)
    4:49
eternality 3:425–6
evil, problem of 3:466–7
foreknowledge 7:109–11
free will 1:865
    Kabbalah 5:173
God
    attributes of 8:243–4
hell, problem of 4:329–30
immutability 4:713, 7:109
Incarnation 4:729
Jewish philosophy
    Crescas, H. 2:702
    Gersonides 4:49
    Hebrew Bible 1:767
knowledge
    Jainism 5:48
middle knowledge 7:111–12
Mīmāṃsā 6:380–1
paradox of
    epistemic logic 3:359
perfect being theology 4:97
perfection 7:108
prayer 7:649–50
process theism 7:718
al-Razi, Fakhr al-Din 8:113–14
theological determinism
    Edwards, J. 3:241
Thomism 9:383
timelessness of (Pomponazzi, P.)
    7:531
Omote, A. 9:840
Omran, Elsayed
    al-Afghani †1:94–5
    Ibn Sab'in †4:646–7
On the Origin of Species see Darwin,
    Charles Robert

One, the
    Ammonius, son of Hermeas 1:209
ethics
    Porphyry 7:547–8
Form-numbers generation
    Early Platonism 7:424
foundation of all existence
    (Porphyry) 7:547
Iamblichean Neoplatonism
    (Porphyry) 7:547
identified with the Good
    hierarchical ontology (Plotinus)
        7:457–8
    Neoplatonism (Proclus) 7:726
    Neo-Pythagoreanism 6:808
identity with the Good (Proclus)
    7:726
nature of
    Neoplatonism (Proclus) 7:726
    Neo-Pythagoreanism 6:808–9
    Speusippus 9:89
Neoplatonism 6:800–1
Parmenides (Zeno of Elea)
    9:844–5
relationship to Indefinite Dyad
    Early Platonism 7:423–4
that-which-is (Melissus) 6:292–5
union with (Plotinus) 7:458
O'Neil, Edward N. 2:759
O'Neill, Eileen
    Astell, M. †1:527–30
    Cavendish, M.L. †2:260–4
    Elisabeth of Bohemia †3:267–9
    Schurman, A.M. van †8:556–9
O'Neill, Eugene 8:632
O'Neill, John
    environmental ethics 3:336
    green political philosophy 4:165
    holism and individualism in
        history and social science 4:488
    Merleau-Ponty, M. 6:325
    socialism †8:879–86
    theory and practice †9:356–9
O'Neill, Onora
    see also Nell, Onora
    ethics
        applied 1:324
        constructivism in †2:630–2
        development 3:43
        examples in 3:490
        family 3:551, 3:552
        Kantian ethics †5:200–4
        practical reason and †7:613–20
        universalism in †9:535–9
    help and beneficence 4:344
    justice
        international 5:156

Kant, I. 5:199
MacIntyre, A. 6:24
moral standing 6:554
practical reasoning/rationality
    principle-based 8:100, 8:103
reproduction ethics 8:280
sexuality 8:726, 8:728
vulnerability and finitude
    †9:669–71
One-Mind
    Buddhism, Korea 2:108–9
one-one correspondence
    glossary 5:806
Ong, W. 5:721, 8:54
Ono, Sokyo 8:751
Onoda, S. 9:408
onto function
    glossary 5:806
ontological arguments for the
    existence of God *see* God,
    existence of
ontological commitment **7:112–17**,
    7:118
    adverbs (Davidson, D.) 2:803–4
    as a binary relation 7:113
    criterion of 7:112–14, 7:116
    logical form 5:784–5
    quantifiers 7:880–1
    Quine, W.V. 8:4, 8:7–8
    second-order logic 8:602
ontological conservatism
    logical form 5:783, 5:784–5
ontological determinacy
    McTaggart, J.M.E. 6:26–7
ontological difference
    entity-being distinction
        (Heidegger, M.) 4:307
ontological reism
    Kotarbiński, T. 5:293–4
ontological relativity *see* reference,
    indeterminacy of
ontology **7:117–18**
see also being; metaphysics
abstract objects 1:32–3
art works **1:480–5**
    aesthetics 1:60
deep ecology (Næss, A.) 6:636
as epistemological construction
    Yogācāra Buddhism 2:69
existentialism
    Latin America 3:511–12
Hartmann, N. 4:241–2
hierarchical
    Neoplatonism (Plotinus)
        7:457–8
history of (Heidegger, M.) 7:583
ideal formula (Gioberti, V.) 4:79

Indian philosophy **7:118–128**
  action 7:123
  categories 7:119–20
  inherence 7:124–6
  nonexistence 7:126–7
  qualities 7:122–3
  relation 7:120, 7:126
  self 7:127
  substance 7:120–2
  universality and particularity
    7:123–4
language (Frege, G.) 3:766–7
metaphysics dualism
  (Ingarden, R.W.) 4:790
music 6:607–8
naturalism 6:719–20
  hierarchies 6:720
  human uniqueness 6:719
Parmenidean (Gorgias) 4:145–6
persons 7:319–21
primacy of
  Western idealism 2:66–7
protothetic (Leśniewski, S.)
  5:572–3
Quine, W.V. 1:701
realism 3:845–6, 8:116–17
reduction 7:117–18
scientific inquiry
  Marcel, G. critique 6:92
subordination to epistemology
  Yogācāra Buddhism 2:68
subservience to ethics (Levinas, E.)
  5:579–80, 5:581
things-in-themselves 7:117, 7:118
William of Ockham 9:735–6
Wolff, C. 9:781–2
onto-theo-logy 7:583–4, 7:585–6
onto-typo-logy 5:340
Onuma, Y. 4:186
opacity *see* indirect discourse;
  intensional logics; modal logic;
  possible worlds semantics;
  propositional attitude
  statements
Oparin, A.I. 5:635
opera
  aesthetics of **7:128–31**
  art and morality 1:454–5
  history 7:129
  interpretation 1:504
operant conditioning
  see also conditioning
  scientific behaviourism
    (Skinner, B.F.) 8:799, 8:800
operationalism **7:131–6**
  experiment 3:515
  knowledge (Lorenzen, P.) 5:825–6

mathematics (Mersenne, M.) 6:328
science (Bridgman, P.W.) 2:18,
  7:131–2, 7:134
social science
  Bridgman, P.W. 2:17–18
  positivism 7:559
testability
  scientific theories 8:861
operators *see* modal operators;
  predicate operators
Ophuls, W. 4:165–6
opinion
  dialectics (Zabarella, J.) 9:837
Opitz, P.J. 9:656–7
Opoku, K.A. 1:139
Oppenheim, F.M. 8:381
Oppenheim, P.
  see also Kemeny-Oppenheim
  reduction model
  reduction
    problems of 8:149
  unity of science 9:533
opportunism
  coercion 2:389
opposites
  Japanese logic
    internal relations 5:713–14
  Sengzhao 8:683
  unity of
    logos (Heraclitus) 4:364,
      4:366–7
opposition
  glossary 5:806
oppositions
  metaphysical (Kant, I.) 5:181
  Prague School 9:179
oppression
  feminism
    Beauvoir, S. de 1:685–6
    and social science 3:590
  indigenous peoples
    Latin American literature 5:655
  liberation theology 5:614, 5:615
  ontological naturalism 6:719
  rebellion (Camus, A.) 2:194
  self-respect 8:637
Oppy, G.
  propositional attitudes †7:779–87
optatives 6:224
optical illusions 6:450
optics **7:136–9**
  see also light
  classical 7:137
  ecological (Gibson, J.J.) 9:633–4
  mechanical model (Hobbes, T.)
    4:468–9
  Newton, I. 6:824–5

Pomponazzi, P.
  Mersenne, M. refutation 6:326
refraction
  law of (Descartes, R.) 3:2
sense perception (Blasius of
  Parma) 1:786
optimism
  evil, problem of (Voltaire) 9:660–1
  evolutionary
    scientific critique of 9:290
    Teilhard de Chardin, P. 9:288,
      9:289–90
  hope 4:507
  Leibniz, G.W. 5:542, 5:544, 5:545
  Leibnizian
    Voltaire 9:657
optionality
  see also freedom
  freedom as 3:753, 3:755–6
oracle machine
  Turing machines 2:475, 9:498,
    9:499–501
Oratorian religious order 2:9, 5:422
oratory
  Cicero, M.T. 2:356
  Gorgias 4:144–5
Orcibal, J. 7:554
order
  aesthetics (Baumgarten, A.G.)
    1:671
  Aristotelianism, seventeenth
    century 1:388
  cosmological
    Chinese philosophy 2:316–17
    dao 2:321
    Daoism 2:783–4, 2:785, 2:791–2
    design argument (Hume, D.)
      4:558–9
    East Asian Philosophy 3:193
    li 5:594
    tian 2:325, 9:400, 9:401
    warfare 9:231
    Zhuangzi 2:321
  harmony
    East Asian Philosophy 3:195
  moral
    imagination (Smith, A.) 8:818
    Socratic explanation of evil
      3:464–5
  scientific
    imagination (Smith, A.)
      8:817–18
  Voegelin, E. 9:654
order types
  combinatorial set theory 8:704–5
  well-ordered set 8:702
    number theory 7:52

paradoxes 7:215
   Zermelo, E. 1:613, 9:853
ordering
   glossary 5:806
orderings
   social choice 8:824, 8:825
ordinal logics **7:139–43**
   Feferman, S. 7:142, 7:143
   incompleteness 7:139–41
   Turing, A. 7:141–2
ordinal numbers 7:51–2
   see also largest ordinal
   glossary 5:806
   set theory 8:701–3
   transfinite (Cantor, G.) 2:197,
      2:656, 8:702
ordinal theory
   measurement 6:243–4, 6:245–6
   rational choice theory 8:64, 8:66,
      8:68
ordinary language philosophy
   7:143–7, 7:147–53
   analytic philosophy 1:224,
      1:225–6, 1:225
   Austin, J.L. 1:571–3
   contextualism 7:624
   conversational implicature
      Grice, H.P. 4:174–5
   description (Wittgenstein, L.)
      7:150
   paradigm case arguments 7:145
   pragmatics 7:620–1
   systematic restatement (Ryle, G.)
      8:429
Ordinatio see Duns Scotus, John
Orenstein, Alex
   Quine, W.V. †8:3–8:14
Oresme, Nicole **7:153–7**
   mathematics 1:402, 7:154–5
   natural philosophy, medieval 6:705
   ratios (Bradwardine, T.) 1:864
   space 9:65
Orey, S. 7:28, 7:30
organ donation 1:779
Organ, T.W. 1:435
organicism 9:253–4
'organicity' *see* cogency of sequence
organics
   philosophy of nature
      (Hegel, G.W.F.) 4:272–3
organisms
   explanatory models
      Naturphilosophie 6:739
   species 9:78–80
Organization of African Unity 7:191,
   7:194

organizations
   responsibility 8:293
Organon see Aristotle
orginal logics
   incompleteness 7:139–41
oriental philosophy
   Ibn Sina 5:7
Orientalism
   Islamic philosophy **7:158–60**
   postcolonialism (Said, E.W.) 7:578
   Ramakrishna Movement 8:40
Origen **7:160–3**
   biblical interpretation 4:390–1,
      8:300
   Celsus 2:264
   influenced by
      ancient philosophy 1:265
   mysticism 6:624
   patristic philosophy 7:258–9
origin
   philosophy of (Brunner, E.) 2:32
original sin 8:792, 8:793–5
   Anselm of Canterbury 1:294
   grace 4:149
   knowledge (Suchon, G.) 9:211
   limbo 5:636
   Niebuhr, R. 6:841, 6:842–3
   Pelagianism 7:284, 7:285
   Socinianism denial 8:890
   Suchon, G. 9:211
origination
   dependent
      Buddhism
         Indian 2:252, 9:215–18
         Tsong kha pa Blo bzang grags
            pa 9:488
Orlik, F. 2:402
Ormsby, E.L. 4:68
Ornato, E. 2:345
O'Rourke Boyle, M. 3:401
O'Rourke, F. 7:808
Orphism **7:163–5**
Orr, J. 7:205
Orr, R.R. 2:308–9
Orringer, Nelson R.
   Ortega y Gasset, J. †7:165–8
   Unamuno y Jugo, M. De
      †9:519–22
Orrú, Marco
   Durkheim, É. †3:174–7
Ors, Eugenio d' 9:75
Orsini, G.N.G. 2:734
Ørsted, Hans Christian 6:742
Ortega y Gasset, José **7:165–8**
   cultural identity 2:744–5
   existentialism 3:509–10, 3:511,
      3:512

Latin America
   philosophy in 5:427
   marginality 6:100
   modernism 6:449
   phenomenology 7:348, 7:350,
      7:352
   Spain, philosophy in 9:73–4, 9:77
   technology and ethics 9:281, 9:284
Orth, E.-W. 3:83, 5:842, 6:792
orthogonality relation 7:882–4
orthomodular property 7:883–4
Ortiz, A. 6:671
Ortner, S.B. 7:582
Ortony, A. 6:337
Oruka, Odera 1:102–3, 1:104, 1:107
Orwell, George 8:632
Orwin, C. 9:399
Orzechowski, Stanislaw 7:485
Osborn, E.F. 2:385, 7:261
Osborne, H. 1:452, 1:498
Osborne, M. 2:835
O'Shaughnessy, Brian
   action 1:41
   Australia, philosophy in 1:583
   bodily sensations 1:795
   dualism 3:138
   perception 7:293
Osherson, D.N. 2:516, 5:487
Osiris 7:466
Osler, Margaret J.
   Charleton, W. 2:287
   Gassendi, P. †3:848–57
Oslo School 6:635
Osman, F. 4:802
Osorio, I. 6:348
Ostrom, E. 4:166, 8:847
Ostwald, M. 9:399
Oswald, James **7:168–70**
Ota, Seikyū 3:800–1
Other
   see also alterity; wholly other
   Derrida, J. 1:190
   ethical obligation to (Levinas, E.)
      5:579–81
   'I–Thou' relationship (Buber, M.)
      2:42, 2:43–5
   Kristeva, J. 1:188–9
   Lacan, J. 1:188
   Levinas, E. 1:189, 5:579–81
   woman as (Irigaray, L.) 5:1, 5:2
other minds 6:231–2, **7:170–3**
   argument from analogy (Mill, J.S.)
      6:231–2
   child's theory of mind 6:385–8
   communal language (McDowell, J.)
      5:416–17
   consciousness 2:586–7

criteria 2:711–14
folk psychology 3:686
introspection 4:838
mental states
  infant cognition 2:391
private language argument 7:695
Russian Neo-Kantianism
  Lapshin, I. 6:794
Scheler, M.F. 8:507
solipsism 9:25
verificationist solution 6:232
Other Power
Pure Land Buddhism 8:747–8
otherness
postmodernism
  political philosophy 7:591
Ott, H. 1:838
Otto, Rudolf **7:173–5**
Fries, J.F. 3:799
mysticism, nature of 6:633
  negative theology 6:762
phenomenology of religion 7:355
Ought Suicide to be a Crime (report)
  9:229
'ought'/'can' question
Augustine 1:555
Ouimette, V. 7:168

Outhwaite, William
social science
  history of philosophy of 8:859
  scientific realism 8:587
  theory and observation
  †9:355–6
Outka, Gene
charity 2:282
situation ethics †8:798–9
out-of-body experiences (OBE's)
  7:223
Outram, D. 3:319
Ouy, G. 1:135
overdetermination
causal theory of knowledge 5:264
Overton, Richard **7:175–7**
Owen, Gwilym Ellis Lane **7:177–9**
Aristotle 1:435
infinity 4:778
Parmenides 7:234
Plato 7:420
pleasure 7:449, 7:451
Zeno of Elea 9:852
Owen, H.P. 6:823
Owen, Robert 9:557, 9:559
Owens, C. 7:590
Owens, J. 1:348–9, 3:169
Owens, S. 1:75

Owensby, J. 3:83
ownership
see also property
Buddhism
  Indian 2:93
genetics and ethics 4:17, 4:19
information technology and ethics
  4:779
property rights
  Hume, D. 4:553
socialism 8:879, 8:880, 8:881
Oxford Calculators **7:179–83**
see also ratios
Aristotelianism, medieval 1:401–2
natural philosophy 1:407
Oresme, N. 7:154
sophismata 7:180–1
Swineshead, Richard 7:179–80
Oxford Philosophy *see* Conceptual
  Analysis movement; ordinary
  language philosophy
Oxtoby, J. 6:813
Ozawa, B. 9:858
Ozment, S.E. 9:270–1
Oznovy marksistko-leninskoi filosofii
  (Fundamentals of Marxist-
  Leninist Philosophy) 6:159

P

Pa tshab Nyi ma grags (Batsap
  Nyimadrak) 9:404
Pacchi, A. 5:109
Pace, D. 5:585
Pacetti, D. 7:96–7
Pachmuss, T. 8:428
Paci, Enzo 5:39
pacification
  see also wish-fulfilment
  mental function (Freud, S.)
    3:786–7, 3:789, 3:790–1
pacifism 9:688
  see also peace; war
  Erasmus, D. 3:396, 3:398
  Jainism 5:49, 5:52
  war and peace dichotomy 9:688
Packe, M. 9:280
Packer, B.L. 3:272, 9:392
Packer, M. 3:280
Padgug, R. 8:728
Padley, G.A. 5:415
Padmanandi *see* Kundakunda
Padmarajiah, Y.J. 6:81
Padmore, George 7:193, 7:194
Padoa, Alessandro
  Beth's theorem and Craig's
    interpolation theorem 1:763
  definability of concepts 1:760–1,
    2:847
  logic, early twentieth century
    5:732, 5:737
Padoux, A. 1:19, 5:384
Padovani, U. 4:80
Pae, C. 9:827
Paesi, King 6:179
Pagallo, G.F. 9:599
Paganini, G. 2:376
paganism
  see also Greek philosophy, ancient;
  Hermetism; Orphism; Roman
  philosophy
  assimilation into Christianity
    Abelard, P. 1:9–10
  banning of 1:262, 1:264–5
    Encyclopedists, medieval 3:306
      John of Salisbury 5:116
  banning of
    Simplicius 8:788, 8:789
  Buddhism comparison 7:10

Christianity and
  Foucault, M. 3:712
  influence on Greek philosophy
    (Clement of Alexandria) 2:384
  Islamic fundamentalism 5:10
  nature/spirit duality 5:98
Pagano, D. 8:728
Pagano, Mario 5:36, 5:42
Pagden, Anthony
  absolutism †1:29–32
  Vitoria, F. de †9:643–5
Pagel, W. 7:208
Pagels, E.H. 4:85, 8:796
Pagin, Peter
  intuitionistic logic †4:856–63
Pahuus, M. 7:649
Pailin, David A.
  Herbert, Edward †4:371–5
Paim, Antônio 2:11–12
pain
  see also bodily sensations
  aesthetic concept 1:56
  asceticism 1:518
  emotion theory (Spinoza, B. de)
    9:101–2
  Epicureanism 3:340, 3:345,
    3:346–7
  functionalism
    holism 4:490
  multiple realization argument
    reduction theory 8:147–8
  pathē
    Cyrenaics 2:759, 2:760, 2:763
  pleasure relationship (Ryle, G.)
    7:450
  punishment (Bentham, J.) 1:723
  suffering 9:213
  utilitarianism (Bentham, J.)
    1:718–19, 1:721–2
Paine, Thomas 7:184–6
  American Revolution 7:184, 7:185
  deism 2:855, 2:856
  French Revolution 7:185
  republicanism 8:281–2, 8:283
Painter, F. 3:230–1
Painter, J. 2:130–1
painting
  Chinese 1:68–9, 1:71, 1:72–3
    literati style 1:73–4

interpretation of 1:503
Japanese
  nature 1:81
  photography comparison 7:378–9
  poetry comparison (Lessing, G.E.)
    5:575
Pais, A. 1:822, 3:258
Pak, C. 9:827
Pakistan
  Vasubandhu 9:583–7
Pakṣilasvāmin *see* Vātsyāyana
Palacký, František 2:764, 2:766
Palais, J.B. 8:797
Palestine
  Eusebius 3:456–8
  Zionism 9:867–9
Paley, William 7:186–8
  God, teleological argument for the
    existence of 4:89, 4:93
  influence of (Tucker, A.) 9:492,
    9:493
  natural religion 7:186–8
  organic design 8:241
  religion, history of philosophy of
    8:247
  utilitarianism 9:557
Paliard, J. 6:53
Palin, D.A. 7:720
palingenesis 1:839
Palmer, J. 7:227
Palmer, Richard E. 3:831, 4:389,
  8:322
Palter, R. 3:254, 6:828, 9:719
Pamiati filosofa (special forum) 6:71
Panaccio, Claude
  language
    medieval theories of 5:404
  William of Ockham †9:731–48
Panaetius 7:188–90
  influence on Roman thought
    7:189, 7:190
pan-Africanism 7:190–4
  DuBois, W.E.B. 7:191
  Garvey movement 7:193
  nineteenth century 7:191–3
Pande, G.C. 8:461
Pandektenrecht 8:482
Pandey, K.C. 1:19

panentheism 4:100–1
  definition 4:94
  Krause, K. 5:299
  omnipresence 7:103–4
  pantheism comparison 4:100
Paneth, F. 2:299
panexperientialism 7:713, 7:714
Pangle, T. 9:691
Pāṇini
  Aṣṭādhyāyī
    Patañjali's commentary 7:248–9
  grammar
    interpretation
      Indian theories of 4:834–5
    universals 9:544
  language
    Indian theories of 5:379,
      5:380–1, 5:384
  Patañjali 7:250
Pankenier, D. 3:112
panlogicism 4:284
Pannenberg, W. 4:298, 8:300
Panofsky, Erwin 1:363, 1:366–, 1:507,
  1:509
panpsychism **7:195–7**
  see also process philosophy
  consciousness 7:195–7
  Fechner, G.T. 3:571
  idealism 4:667
  materialism (Cavendish, M.L.)
    2:261
  metaphysics 6:339
  Neo-Leibnizianism (Kozlov, A.A.)
    5:834
  Schelling, F.W.J. 8:351
Pan-Slavism **7:197–201**
  Central and Eastern Europe
    7:198–9
  Eurasian Movement 3:455
  Russia 7:199–201
  Slavophilism 8:811
pansophy 9:363
pantheism 4:100, **7:202–5**
  see also monotheism;
    panentheism; polytheism
  definition 4:93–4, 6:479, 7:201–2
  error 7:204
  Florenskii, P.A. 3:681
  freedom 7:204
  God
    ultimacy of 4:94
  immortality 7:204
  omnipresence 7:103
  panentheism comparison 4:100
  Russian Orthodox cosmology
    (Bulgakov, S.N.) 2:125

the supernatural 7:97
  Oman, J.W. 7:97
varieties 7:202–3
vitalist (Herder, J.G.) 4:378,
  4:382–3
Pap, A. 1:6, 1:238, 6:750, 7:482
papal authority
  Bellarmine, R. 8:226–7
  Marsilius of Padua 6:113
  resistance to (Marsilius of Padua)
    6:112–13
  secular authority conflict
    Bellarmine, R. 8:226–7
    John of Paris 5:113–14
    William of Ockham 9:732, 9:734,
      9:745
Papanicolaou, A.C. 1:737
Paperno, I. 6:587, 7:8, 8:427
Papert, S. 1:492, 2:578
Papillon 9:212
Papineau, David
  causation 2:250
  concepts 2:516
  functionalism †3:805–13
  materialism 6:177
  reference 8:164
  science, philosophy of 8:576
  teleological theories of meaning
    8:673, 8:674, 8:675
Pappas, George S.
  epistemology
    history of †3:370–84
Pappas, J.N. 1:168
Paqué, R. 4:172
Paquet, L. 2:759, 3:91
Paracelsus (Philippus Aureolus
  Theophrastus Bombastus von
  Hohenheim) **7:205–8**
  alchemy 1:157
  sympathetic medicine (Digby, K.)
    3:73
  theosophy 9:363
paraconsistent logic 5:788–9,
  7:208–11, 8:203
paradigm case arguments 7:145,
  7:151
paradigms
  linguistic discrimination 5:642
  scientific
    Kuhn, T.S. 5:316, 5:317
    incommensurability 4:732–4
Paradis, J.G. 4:596
paradise
  al-Ghazali 4:65
paradoxes
  see also liar paradox
  Diodorus Cronus 3:83, 3:84

epistemic **7:211–14**
  knowability 7:211, 7:212–13
  Lottery Paradox 2:843, 5:273,
    7:211–12
  surprise examination 7:211,
    7:213
of fiction
  emotional response to art
    3:274–7
fuzzy logic 3:822
Grue Paradox 4:746, 5:273–4,
  9:341–2
  Goodman, N. 4:746, 9:341–2
incompleteness theorem 4:110
inductive inference 4:758
logical
  semantic distinction 9:361
  theory of types 9:361
Mahāyāna Buddhism 6:640
of material implication 4:740–1
medieval logic 5:755–7
motion (Bergson, H.-L.) 1:732,
  1:733–4
names (Xunzi) 5:705
omniscience
  epistemic logic 3:359
Parmenidean
  Plato 7:401
rational beliefs 8:61–2
Russell, B.A.W. 5:808, 8:394–7
self-referential (Russell, B.A.W.)
  8:394–5
semantic 7:214, **8:642–8**
  Chinese theories of 5:698–9
  logical distinction 9:361
  logicism
    Ramsey, F.P. 8:45
  many-valued logics 6:82
  medieval logic 5:756–7
  theory of types 9:361
  William of Sherwood 9:749
set and property **7:214–21**
  nonstandard models 5:847
set theory **7:214–21**
sophismata (Kilvington, R.) 5:244
Sorites 5:809
Stoics 5:690
of strict implication
  medieval logic 5:755–6
substitutional theory
  (Russell, B.A.W.) 8:395
temporal
  relativity theory 8:193–4
theory of types (Russell, B.A.W.)
  8:395–7

time
  Aristotle
    Simplicius discussion of
      8:790
time travel 9:417–18
of tragedy
  emotional response to art
    3:278–9
underdetermination 9:529
vagueness 9:564
  sorites 9:564, 9:566
Zeno 9:843–52
zig-zag theory (Russell, B.A.W.)
  8:395
paradoxical objects
  Meinong, A. 6:283
paradoxical sleep (PS) 3:127
parallel distributed processing (PDP)
  1:489–90
parallel processing 1:486, 1:489
parallelism 3:136, 4:513
Paramārtha 2:84, 9:584
parameter theorem 2:487
paranormal phenomena **7:221–4**
  psychokinesis 7:221, 7:222–3
    causation 7:223–4
paraphrasis 1:722–3
parapsychology **7:224–7**
Parekh, B. 6:602
Parekh, Bhai Manilal C. 9:575
Parekh, Bhikhu
  Arendt, H. †1:369–73
Pareto principle **7:228**
  economic approach to law 5:454–5
  efficiency 6:107, 6:108, 7:228
  social choice 8:824
  welfare economics 3:205, 3:208–9
Pareto, Vilfredo
  human nature 4:525
  Pareto principle 7:228
  rational choice theory 8:64, 8:68–9
  social science
    history of philosophy of 8:855,
      8:859
Pareyson, L. 3:653, 5:42
Parfit, Derek
  bundle theory of mind 6:385
  consequentialism 2:606
  economics and ethics 3:210
  green political philosophy 4:165
  happiness 4:229
  life and death 5:630
  obligations to future generations
    3:821
  particulars 7:238
  paternalism 7:252

personal identity 6:572–4, 6:575,
  7:314
population and ethics 7:542
practical reasoning/rationality
  8:103
risk 8:332, 8:334, 8:338
Sidgwick, H. 8:763
utilitarianism 9:554, 9:557
welfare 9:705
Pargetter, R.
  functional explanation 3:805
  identity theory of mind 6:399
  mental illness
    concepts of 6:314
  other minds 7:173
  universals 9:543
Paribhāṣā ('Maxims of
  Interpretation') 4:836
Parijs, P. van 3:818, 9:797
Parikh, Rohit
  Church's theorem and the decision
    problem †2:349–51
Paris, B. 3:267
Paris, J. 4:117–18
Paris, University of 5:749, 8:52
Parish, R. 7:247
Park, Chong-hong 9:794
Park, Robert E. 8:19
Park Sung Bae
  Buddhist philosophy, Korean
    2:118
  Chinul 2:332
  Sôsan Hyujông †9:36–7
  Wônhyo †9:793–4
  Yi Yulgok 9:827
Parker, E. 2:196
Parker, Theodore 9:137
Parker, T.H.L. 2:182
Parkes, Graham
  Nishitani Keiji †7:16–17
Parkin, F. 3:177
Parkinson, G.H.R. 3:383
Parliament
  sovereignty of (Dicey, A.V.) 3:62
Parmenides 1:263, **7:229–35**
  atomism 1:535
  being 1:700, 1:702, 7:230–3
  cosmology 7:229, 7:233
  eternity 3:424
  God 4:98
  influence of (Melissus) 6:292–5
  language
    philosophy of 5:356–7
  matter 6:193
  monism 6:474
  nous 7:43
  ontology (Gorgias) 4:145–6

processes 7:722
reality (Owen, G.E.L.) 7:178
Way of Seeming
  cosmology 7:229, 7:233
Way of Truth
  being/not-being 7:229–33
Zeno of Elea 9:844–5
Parodi, M. 5:113
parody
  Cynics 2:754, 2:755, 2:756–7
  Epicharmus 3:336
  Lucian 5:853–4
  Timon 9:419
le parole 8:480, 9:178
paronymy 1:289–90
Parousia (Second Coming) 4:250–1
Parra, Teresa de la 3:625
Parrinder, Geoffrey 1:139, 6:626
Parrott, S. 3:670
Parry, B. 7:582
parsimony see simplicity
Parsons, Charles
  analyticity 1:238
  Frege, G. 3:777
  hierarchy theory 9:266–7
  mathematics
    epistemology 6:191
    foundations of 6:187
  property theory 7:766–7
  realism
    mathematics 8:123
  semantic paradoxes and theories
    of truth 8:648
  substitutional/objectual
    quantifiers 7:881
Parsons, P. 9:420
Parsons, Talcott
  civil society 2:371
  Habermas, J. 4:199
  power 7:611, 7:613
  social science
    functionalism in 3:818
    systems theory in 9:256
  sociology
    theories of 9:5, 9:7
Parsons, Terence
  adverbs 1:50
  essential properties 6:430
  existence 3:492
  fiction
    fictional entities 3:666, 3:667
    semantics of 3:663
  intensional entities 4:807
  modal logic 6:432–3
  Montague, R.M. †6:483–5
  predication 7:667
  property theory 7:767

sense and reference 8:688
Partee, Barbara
  compositionality 2:477
  discourse semantics 3:99
  Montague, R.M. 6:485
  possible worlds semantics 8:669
  property theory 7:766
partial recursive function 7:141
partiality
  see also impartiality
  value judgments in social science
    9:577
participant objectivism 1:849
particularism
  moral **6:528–9**
    see also value pluralism
    act-consequentialism 2:604
    Common Sense ethics (Reid, T.)
      2:450
    deliberative ideals 4:673
    intuitionism relationship 4:853
    Jewish philosophy (Saadiah
      Gaon) 8:438–9
    logic of ethical discourse 5:763
    perfectionism 7:302
    respect for persons 8:286
    Ross, W.D. 8:365–7
    self-deception 8:630
    Williams, B.A.O. 9:751
particularity
  see also individualism
  environment assimilation
    Chinese philosophy 2:809
  ontological categories
    Indian philosophy 7:62, 7:123
  transitive/intransitive
    aesthetic attitude 1:54
particulars **7:235–8**
  see also universals
  bare 7:236
  Boethius, A.M.S. 1:806
  as bundles of properties 7:236
  eliminative induction (Bacon, F.)
    1:629–30
  events 3:462–3
  haeccities 7:236
  impermanency of 7:235
  metaphysics 6:338–9
  Strawson, P.F. 9:171
  type/token distinction 9:510
  universals
    Stoicism 9:142, 9:149–50
particulate matter
  see also atomism;
    corpuscularianism
  field/particle duality 3:669–70
  quantum field theory 3:670–3

partiinost' (party spirit) 5:565,
  7:238–41
partisanship 3:57
  see also partiinost'
Partridge, E. 3:821, 4:166
part–whole relation, theory of *see*
  mereology
Pascal, Blaise **7:241–7**
  see also Pascal's wager
  Butler, J. 2:160
  casuistry 2:228, 2:229
  geometry 4:33
  historical testimony
    Port-Royal 7:551, 7:553, 7:554
  Jansenism 7:242–3
  legal evidence
    probabilistic analysis 5:504
  logic machines 5:744
  vacuum, existence of 7:242
Pascal (journal) 7:554
Pascal's wager 7:241, 7:245
Pasch, M. 4:30, 4:428–9
Paschal II, Pope 1:284
Pasewark, K.A. 9:412
Pasnau, Robert
  Aureol, P. †1:565–7
  Crathorn, W. †2:692–4
  Holcot, R. †4:477–9
  Olivi, P.J. †7:95–7
Passeron, C. 8:857
passion
  human error (Thomasius, C.)
    9:377
  moral autonomy
    moralistes 6:557
  moral development
    (Wollstonecraft, M.) 9:790
  morality
    Descartes, R. 3:13–14
    Stoicism 6:560–1
  nature of (Descartes, R.) 3:13
  reason conflict (Spinoza, B. de)
    9:102–3
  Seneca, L.A. (Le Grand, A.) 5:479
passions
  see also emotions 4:543
  Hume, D. 4:543, 4:549–51
    action 4:551
    human nature 4:543
    will 4:551
  irrational faculties of the soul
    (Posidonius) 7:556
  language development
    (Rousseau, J.-J.) 5:377
  particular (Butler, J.) 2:155
  primitive (Descartes, R.) 3:287

reason relationship (Seneca, L.A.)
  8:680
sentiments (Hume, D.) 4:549–50
Stoicism 9:157
sympathy (Hume, D.) 4:550–1
violent (Hume, D.) 4:550
Passmore, John A. **7:247–8**
  analytic philosophy 1:228–9
  applied ethics 1:324–5
  Bradley, F.H. 1:862–3
  Cambridge Platonism 2:185
  Cudworth, R. 2:744
  Culverwell, N. 2:752
  educational philosophy 3:239
  green political philosophy 4:166
  Hägerström, A.A.T. 4:204
  humanism 4:532
  Hume, D. 4:562
  Kemp Smith, N. 5:231
  logic, early twentieth century
    5:737–8
  obligations to future generations
    3:821
  ordinary language philosophy
    7:153
  Pelagianism 7:287
  positivism in the social sciences
    7:561
  Prichard, H.A. 7:682
  Ryle, G. 8:432
  social science
    history of philosophy of 8:859
  Venn, J. 9:595
past
  see also temporality; time
  eternity of the world
    Jewish philosophy (Gersonides)
      4:48
  interpretation of
    geology 4:26–7
  knowledge of 4:838
  time travel 9:417
    self-defeating causal chains
      9:417–18
Pasteur, Louis
  vitalism 9:641, 9:643
Pastine, D. 2:376
Patai, D. 3:628
Patañjali **7:248–50**
  God
    conceptions of 4:104
  grammar
    interpretation 4:835
  Indian and Tibetan philosophy
    4:738
  karma and rebirth 5:218
  language 5:379, 5:382, 5:384

matter 6:200
phonemes 5:380, 5:381
universals 9:544, 9:548
Patch, H.R. 1:813
Pateman, Carole
consent 2:598
Critical Legal Studies 2:720
feminism 3:583
feminist political philosophy 3:620
Filmer, R. 3:679
obligation
political 7:80
privacy 7:692, 7:693
sexual contract
feminist jurisprudence 3:607,
3:610
social science
history of philosophy of 8:859
state 9:122
vulnerability and finitude 9:671
Pateman, T. 2:722
Pater, W. 1:456
paternalism **7:250–2**
critiques of
Brown, W.B. 9:112
Kant, I. 5:195
Mill, J.S. 5:440
drugs in sport 9:111–12
epistemic 8:830
government
public interest 6:754
harm principle 5:463
law and ritual, China 5:444
medical ethics 6:261
pornography 7:544
risk assessment 8:331–2
Paterson, R.W.K. 9:141
pathē (subjectivism)
Aristippus the Elder 1:379–80
Cyrenaics 2:759
epistemology 2:759–61
ethics 2:759–60, 2:761–3
pathetic fallacy 1:82
pathology 1:779
pathos
divine
Jewish philosophy
(Heschel, A.J.) 4:411
Patočka, Jan **7:252–4**
Paton, G.W. 4:477, 8:483
Paton, H.J. 5:199
patriachy
political philosophy
history of (Filmer, R.) 7:511
patriarchy
comedy 2:436
family ethics 3:550

feminism 3:579, 3:582
theology 3:621–2
political analogy (Filmer, R.) 3:678
Patricius, Franciscus *see* Petrić,
Franjo
Patrides, C.A. 2:185
Patrik, L.E. 1:358
patriotism
see also nationalism
ancient Greece 6:658
patristic philosophy **7:254–61**
see also Christianity, early
ancient philosophy distinction
1:265
Carolingian renaissance
textual sources 2:221
Hellenistic
Judaism influences 7:254,
7:255–6
Origen 7:258–9
Platonism 7:257–8
Tertullian 9:307–8
Patrizi da Cherso, Francesco **7:261–5**,
7:447
Pattaro, Enrico
Ross, A. †8:364–5
Patte, D. 4:395
pattern, Chinese philosophy *see li*
pattern matching
reliabilism 8:207–8
pattern-breaking
randomness as 8:58–9
pattern-recognition
computation
connectionist networks 2:570,
2:574
patterns
natural *see* regularities
Patterson, R. 5:693
Patterson, S. 2:645, 2:646, 6:344
Patterson, T.C. 1:358
Pattin, A. 5:597
Patwardhan, M.V. 1:19, 3:859
Paty, M. 3:258
Patzer, A. 4:441
Patzig, G. 5:624, 5:693
Pauck, M. 9:412–13
Pauck, W. 9:412–13
Paul the Apostle
atonement 1:537
faith 3:539–41
Gnosticism 4:83
heaven 4:251
hermeneutics
Hebrew Bible 4:390
justification doctrine 5:165–6

New Testament
Hellenistic Judaism 7:256
original sin 8:792, 8:793, 8:794
resurrection 3:416
salvation 4:150
Paul VI, Pope 6:102, 8:724, 8:726,
8:728
Paul of Venice **7:265–6**
Aristotelianism
Renaissance 1:406, 1:409
liar paradox 5:756–7
sophismata 5:749
supposition theory 5:754
Paul, A.M. 8:491
Paul, D.V. 9:793
Paul, E.F. 4:344
Paul, G.A. 1:578, 1:583
Paul, J. 4:344, 7:47
Paul, R.W. 3:234, 3:239
Paul, S. 9:392
Pauler, ákos 4:570, 4:572
Paulhus, D.L. 8:628, 8:632
Paulicianism
Manicheism influence 6:76
Pauling, Linus 6:458
Paulsen, F. 6:173, 6:780, 7:197
Paulson, S.L. 5:521
Paulus, Israelita 5:23
Paulus, J. 4:360
Paulus Venetus *see* Paul of Venice
Pavel, T.G. 5:585, 7:596
Pavković, Aleksander
South Slavs, philosophy of
†9:48–56
Pavlin, James
Ibn Hazm 4:621
Ibn Taymiyya †4:655–6
Islamic theology 5:31
Pavlov, Ivan Petrovich
classical conditioning 8:800
learning 5:487
psychological reductionism
(Vygotskii, L.S.) 9:671, 9:672
psychology
theories of 7:826
scientific behaviourism 1:697
Skinner, B.F. 8:802
Paxson, T. 4:59, 5:279
Payne, G.R. 6:203
Payne, M. 2:260
Payne, Stanley 3:563
Payne, Steven
mysticism †6:627–34
history of †6:620–7
Payne, T.R. 7:829
Paz, Octavio 5:655, 5:657, 6:100,
6:101

P'Bitek, Okot 1:102, 1:107
peace **9:684–91**
  see also pacifism
  conception of 9:685
  as an institution 9:688–90
  international 9:690
Peacocke, A.R. 8:234, 8:235–6
Peacocke, Christopher
  colour, theories of 2:431
  concepts 2:516
  conceptual role semantics 8:656
  depiction 2:896
  Dummett, M.A.E. 3:153
  intention 4:816
  logical constants 5:780
  meaning and truth 6:225
  Nagel, T. 6:647
  non-conceptual content 2:643
  perception 7:293, 7:295, 7:299
  transcendental arguments 9:454
  unconscious mental states 9:527
peak experiences
  in sport 9:115
Peano axioms 5:806–7, 7:52
Peano, Giuseppe
  see also Peano axioms
  logic
    early twentieth century 5:738
    machines and diagrams 5:740,
      5:746
    mathematical 1:218, 5:731–2
    nineteenth century 5:729
Pearce, C. 3:449
Pearce, D. 7:498
Pearce, D.G. 2:835
Pearce, G. 2:688
Pearce, Zachary 9:225, 9:229
Pearl, C. 1:351
Pearl, J. 7:34, 9:132
Pearl, Judea 2:250
Pears, David F.
  Hume, D. 4:562
  logical atomism 5:775
  moral psychology 6:533
  ordinary language philosophy
    7:153
  Russell, B.A.W. 8:403
  Scandinavia, philosophy in 8:491
  self-deception 8:629, 8:632
  Wittgenstein, L. 9:770
Pearson, E.S. 9:127
Pearson, K. 8:567, 8:572
Pecci, Gioacchino *see* Leo XIII, Pope
Pecham, John 1:562–3, 3:429,
  7:267–9
Pecheco Pereira, Duarte 2:8
Pêcheux, M. 5:499

Peck, W.J. 1:838
Peckham, John *see* Pecham, John
Peckhaus, Volker
  Gentzen, G.K.E. †4:23–5
  paradoxes of set and property
    7:220
  Zermelo, E. †9:853–5
Peczenik, Aleksander
  legal reasoning and interpretation
    5:531
  Olivecrona, K. †7:93–5
  Petrażycki, L. †7:329–30
pedagogy
  Agricola, R. 1:125
  ethical perfection
    (Schleiermacher, F.) 8:536
  humanist (Vives, J.L.) 9:646, 9:648
  Krause, K. 5:300
Pederson, O. 6:707
Peebles, C.S. 1:357–8
Peel, J.D.Y. 7:569, 9:89
Peerenboom, R.P.
  law and ritual in Chinese
    philosophy †5:442–54
Pefanis, J. 1:192
Pegis, A.C. 1:349, 6:465
Peirce, Charles Sanders **7:269–84**
  abduction 7:274–5
  American philosophy, eighteenth
    and nineteenth century 1:203–4
  belief 7:271–3
  Bolzano, B. 1:827
  Boole, G. 1:843
  categories 7:270, 7:276–8
  commonsensism 2:454–5, 8:62,
    8:63
  Comte, A. 2:505
  doubt 8:830, 8:832
  fallibilism 3:545, 3:548
  foundationalism
    criticism of 3:378–9, 3:383
  Hegelianist influence 4:288
  induction 7:274–5
  inference to the best explanation
    4:769
  logic
    algebra of 5:726, 5:727
    infinitary 5:734
    machines and diagrams 5:740,
      5:743–4, 5:746
    nineteenth century 5:723,
      5:724–5, 5:729
    of relation 5:726
  models 6:446
  pragmaticism *see* pragmatism

  pragmatism 7:273–4, 7:279,
    7:633–4, 7:639
  truth 7:270, 9:478–9, 9:480
  use of signs 7:634
  predicate calculus 7:665
  realism 7:279–80
  reasonableness
    pragmatism in ethics 7:641,
      7:644
  Royce, J. 8:381
  scientific metaphysics 7:270,
    7:280–1
  semantics
    informational 8:662
  semiotics 8:676–8
  space 9:65
  symbolic interactionism 9:245
  type/token distinction 9:510, 9:511
Pelacani da Parma, Biagio *see* Blasius
  of Parma
Pelaez, J. 6:48
Pelagianism **7:284–7**
  Augustinian opposition to
    (Bradwardine, T.) 1:563–4,
    1:865
  Biel, G. 1:770–1
  Eriugena, J.S. 3:402
  free will 7:285, 7:286
  justification doctrine (Augustine)
    5:166
  limbo 5:636
  Massilians 7:285
  Ockhamism 7:285–6
  original sin 8:792, 8:793
  'ought'/'can' question (Augustine)
    1:555
Pelagius 4:147, 7:284
  see also Pelagianism
Peleczynski, Z.A. 3:757
Pelikan, J. 2:548–9, 7:261
Pellegrino, E.D. 7:737
Pellegrino, Edmund
  medicine, philosophy of 6:264–5,
    6:268, 6:269
Pelletier, Francis Jeffry
  compositionality 2:477
  fuzzy logic 3:824
  many-valued logics 6:84
  mass terms †6:168–70
  Post, E.L. 7:575
Pelster, F. 4:363, 6:115, 8:317–18
Pemberton, J. 1:64–5
Pembrey, M.E. 4:19
penal desert 2:707
penal institutions 2:709

penal law
  Chinese
    Legalism 5:531, 5:532
penal theory
  see also punishment
  panopticon prison (Bentham, J.)
    1:720
  sentencing 2:708–9
Pence, G. 1:776
Penelhum, Terence
  Butler, J. 2:160
  eschatology 3:417
  Hume, D. 4:562
  necessary being 6:747
  paranormal phenomena 7:224
  theological virtues 9:331
penitence 4:635
Penn, J. 8:473
Penn, W. 3:269
Penner, J.E. 7:761
Pennington, A. 7:135
Pennington, N. 5:505
Pennock, J.R. 7:693
penology 7:602
Penrod, S. 5:505
Penrose, R. 1:492, 4:118, 6:394
Pentateuch 4:205, 7:358
Pentonen, M. 1:632
Penzo, G. 5:83
Pepe, L. 3:560
Peperzak, A. 5:582
Pépin, J. 7:731
Pepis, J. 7:495, 7:498
Peralta Barnuevo, Pedro 5:422–3
Peralva, A. 8:20
perception 7:287–93
  see also experience; misperception;
    sensation; sense perception; senses
  Ābhidharmika Buddhism 2:56–7
  adverbial theory
    Ducasse, C.J. 3:139–40
    Sellars, W.N. 8:639–40
    Whitehead, A.N. 9:717
  aesthetic (Alison, A.) 1:185–6
  analysis (Moore, G.E.) 6:497
  apparent existence (Aureol, P.)
    1:565–6
  Aristotle 3:372
  art
    criticism 1:462
    and truth 1:458–9
  artificial neural networks
    connectionism 2:570
  atomism (Democritus) 2:874–5
  autonony from cognitive inference
    6:450–1
  Baumgarten, A.G. 1:670
belief
  interaction 7:295–6
  reasons for 5:269, 8:129–30
bodily sensations 1:792, 1:793,
  1:794–5
cognitive contamination of 6:450
cognitive development 2:394
colour
  phenomenalism 2:428
  physical sciences conflict
    2:428–9
  relational theories 2:428,
    2:429–30
common-sense realism
  Prichard, H.A. 7:680
  Reid, T. 8:171
  rGyal tshab dar ma rin chen
    8:305
commonsensism 2:454
concomitance (Cavendish, M.L.)
  2:261–2
conscious/unconscious distinction
  (Leibniz, G.W.) 5:542
consciousness (Husserl, E.) 4:580
definition of (Aristotle) 1:425–6
Dharmakīrti 3:52
direct realism
  Armstrong, D.M. 1:442
  sense-data 8:697
distinct (Descartes, R.) 3:10
dreaming 3:127–8
educational philosophy 3:234
epistemic appearance 7:295
epistemic issues 7:293–9
epistemic validity
  Indian philosophy 2:68
epistemology (Sellars, W.S.) 8:640
error
  and illusion
    Indian concepts of 3:410,
      3:412–13
  McTaggart, J.M.E. 6:27
esse est percipi (to be is to be
  perceived) principle
  Berkeley, G. 1:740, 1:743
existence relationship
  (Berkeley, G.) 1:742–3
fallibility 7:296–8
feminist aesthetics 3:595
Gaṅgeśa 3:844–5
Gestalt psychology 4:51–3, 7:827
Hinduism 4:435
  Mīmāṃsā 6:378–9
idealism 4:664
ideas
  Arnauld, A. 1:445–6
  Berkeley, G. 1:742–4, 1:745
Johnson, S. 5:124, 5:125
imagination comparison 4:706–7
indirect realism
  sense-data 8:697
inference distinction
  Yogācāra Buddhism 2:68
intellect
  Ptolemy 7:830
  Vital du Four 9:638–9
intellective (Rosmini-Serbati, A.)
  8:362
intentionality 7:291–2
introspection 4:838, 4:841, 4:843,
  4:844
  consciousness 2:592–3
  observation 4:843–4
intuitive knowledge 3:376
judgment (Nishida Kitarō) 5:714
knowledge
  Indian views of 5:280, 5:283–4
  intuitive 3:376
  Lenin, V.I. 5:566
  Sāṅkhya 8:464–5
language
  Merleau-Ponty, M. 6:323
  Vātsyāyana 9:588
mechanical physics (Digby, K.)
  3:72–3
modularity of mind 6:450–1
  pathologies 6:451
  post-perceptual effects 6:450
Molyneux problem 6:467–8
monads (Leibniz, G.W.) 5:547
music 4:187–8, 6:608–9
naïve realism 7:292
negative facts
  Indian philosophy 6:755–6,
    6:757–8
noema (Husserl, E.) 4:574–5,
  4:578–9
non-conceptual
  Sa skya paṇḍita 8:433–4
non-conceptual content 2:642
optics
  mechanical model (Hobbes, T.)
    4:468–9
perceiving-that 7:294–6
persons 7:320
petites (Leibniz, G.W.) 5:552
phenomenology 7:330–1, 7:332
  epistemic issues 7:344–5, 7:346
  Merleau-Ponty, M. 6:320,
    6:321–3
philosophical terminology
  (Austin, J.L.) 1:572
pragmatic theory of truth 9:478–9

as *prama*
  Nyāya-Vaiśeṣika 7:62–3
process philosophy 7:713–14
propensity relationship
  (Ducasse, C.J.) 3:139
psychology
  theories of 7:825
psychology of vision (Berkeley, G.)
  1:740–1
psychophysics (Fechner, G.T.)
  3:570–1
radical empiricism (James, W.)
  5:65–6
realism
  Ockham, W. of 3:374
  Uddyotakara/Dignāga debate
    9:515
reliabilism
  Nyāya 3:390
religious knowledge (Durandus of
  St Pourçain) 3:173
representationalism (Buridan, J.)
  2:133
secondary qualities **8:595–9**
self-certificationalism
  Mīmāṃsā 3:390–1
self-consciousness (Merleau-
  Ponty, M.) 6:323
sensation
  Bergson, H.-L. 1:732, 1:734–5
  Reid, T. 8:172–3
sense-data 7:289–91, **8:694–8**
  Broad, C.D. 2:23, 2:24
sensibilia (Russell, B.A.W.)
  8:399–400
spectator problem (Marcel, G.)
  6:92
spiritual
  Isaac of Stella 5:4
  Santayana, G. 8:469
subjective/objective contrast
  (Kant, I.) 4:338
substance 9:205, 9:209
  successive states of (Kant, I.)
    5:187
universals
  Indian philosophy 9:546
valid cognition (Lokāyata) 6:180
verificationism (Ayer, A.J.)
  1:616–17
vision 2:896, 9:631–7
  Blasius of Parma 1:785–6
  data-driven models 9:634–5
  direct versus indirect 9:632–3
  optics 7:137
vision in God (Malebranche, N.)
  6:58–61

will relationship (Maine de
  Biran, P.-F.) 6:51
will-less
  aesthetic experience 8:546,
    8:550–1
perceptual beliefs
  empiricism 3:299–300
perceptual integration
  Gestalt psychology 5:286
perceptual knowledge 7:293–9
perceptual recognition
  knowledge acquisition 7:294, 7:295
Percival, W.K. 5:415
perdurability 6:366
Pereboom, D. 3:501
Perecz, László
  Hungary, philosophy in †4:567–73
Pereira Barreto, Luís 2:10, 2:12,
  7:567, 7:569–70
Pereira de Graça Aranha, José 2:10
Pereira, José Elias del Carmen 5:422,
  5:424–5
Pereira, Michela
  alchemy †1:155–9
Pereira, N.G.O. 2:306
Perelman, C. 8:309
Perelman, Chaim 5:496–7, 5:499,
  5:527, 5:531
perennial philosophy *see philosophia
  perennis*
perestroika 6:157
Pérez-Ramos, A. 1:632
'perfect man'
  Ibn al-ʿArabi 4:603, 4:604
perfect-being theology 4:95–8, 4:99,
  4:711–12
perfection
  see also goodness, perfect; perfect-
    being theology
  concepts of 4:97–8
  divine
    Anselm of Canterbury 1:288
    Jewish philosophy
      (Maimonides, M.) 6:46
    Matthew of Aquasparta 6:201
  efficient causality (Duns Scotus, J.)
    3:161–2
  feminist theology 3:623
  Jewish philosophy
    Alemanno, Y. 1:162
    Mendelssohn, M. 6:306
  moral (Wolff, C.) 9:783
  omnipotence 7:99
  omnipresence 7:103
  omniscience 7:108
  pure (Duns Scotus, J.) 3:158

soul
  Islamic philosophy 9:41
univocity 3:158
perfectionism **7:299–302**
  anarchism 1:245
  human nature 4:521–2
  private judgment (Godwin, W.)
    4:122, 4:123
  rational beliefs 8:62
  self-concept (Cavell, S.) 2:259
  socialism 8:882–3
  teleological ethics 9:294
performance 2:774, 2:775, 6:608
performative theory of truth 9:475,
  9:476–7
performatives 5:389, 5:402, **7:302–4**,
  9:81–2
  Austin, J.L. 1:571, 1:572–3, 9:82,
    9:83–4
  imperative inference 4:719
  speech acts 7:302–4
performing arts **1:468–72**
  aesthetics 1:61
  creativity 1:469
  improvisation 1:468–9, 1:471
  Japanese aesthetics 1:83
  performer's role 1:470
Perinbanayagam, R.S. 9:245
Peripateticism
  see also Aristotelianism;
    Peripatetics
  Islamic philosophy 5:5, 5:7–8,
    5:13–14, 5:15–16
    definition theory (al-
      Suhrawardi) 9:221
    Illuminationist philosophy
      4:701
    knowledge (al-Suhrawardi)
      9:220
    mystical philosophy 5:14, 6:617
    substantial motion (Mulla
      Sadra) 6:596
Peripatetics **7:304–5**
  see also Peripateticism
  Alcinous 1:159
  Alexander of Aphrodisias
    1:169–76
  Aristotle commentators 1:435
  Carneades **2:215–20**
  colonial philosophy
    Latin America 5:424
  Diogenes Laertius **3:86–7**
  doxography 3:126
  ethics (Plutarch of Chaeronea)
    7:466
  influence of
    Middle Platonism 7:424

methodical (Keckermann, B.)
5:225
Strato **9:161–4**
textual commentaries 7:304–5
Theophrastus 9:337–40
perishability
inference from
Buddhist doctrine of
momentariness 6:472
Perkins Gilman, C. 3:583
Perkins, M. 7:293, 7:299
Perkins, Mary Anne
Coleridge, S.T. †2:403–6
Perler, Dominik
Alighieri, Dante †1:181–5
Aureol, P. 1:566
Hervaeus Natalis †4:402–4
Nicholas of Autrecourt †6:829–32
Perlin, S. 9:229
perlocutionary acts 7:628, 9:82–3
permanence
see also impermanence;
momentariness
human desire for
Yogācāra Buddhism 2:70
permanent revolution
Chinese Marxism 6:133, 6:135–6,
6:137
Perner, J. 6:386, 6:389, 6:390
Perrault, Claude 1:363, 1:366
Perreiah, A.R. 7:266
Perrett, Roy W.
causation
Indian theories of †2:251–7
Perrett, W. 8:199
Perry, B.M. 7:66
Perry, Sir E. 8:483
Perry, John
see also Kaplan-Perry Theory
Butler, J. 2:160
facts 3:537
indexical content of thought
2:639–40
indexicals 2:879, 2:880–1
intensional entities 4:807
intensional logics 4:810
morality and identity 6:575
possible worlds semantics
†8:662–9
pragmatics 7:631
propositional attitude statements
7:778
semantic paradoxes and theories
of truth 8:648
sense and reference 8:688
situation semantics †8:669–72

Perry, R.B.
American philosophy, eighteenth
and nineteenth century 1:206
good, theories of the 4:135
James, W. 5:67–8
neutral monism 6:817
Perry, Ruth
Astell, M. 1:529
Persia
see also Iran
al-'Amiri **1:207–8**
al-Baghdadi **1:636–8**
al-Dawani **2:806–7**
al-Ghazali **4:61–8**
Ibn Miskawayh **4:630–3**
Illuminationist philosophy 4:700–1
al-Juwayni **5:169–70**
Mir Damad, Muhammad Baqir
6:408–11
modern Islamic philosophy
5:18–20
Mulla Sadra **6:595–9**
mysticism in Islamic philosophy
6:618–19
al-Razi, Abu Bakr **8:110–12**
al-Razi, Fakhr al-Din **8:112–15**
al-Sabzawari **8:440–2**
al-Sijistani **8:774–6**
al-Suhrawardi **9:219–24**
al-Tawhidi **9:271–2**
al-Tusi **9:504–7**
Zoroastrianism 6:75
persistent vegetative state (PVS)
5:627–8
personal identity **7:305–14**, 8:61
see also identity; self
afterlife (Butler, J.) 2:159
autonomy
ethical 1:590–1
bodily identity (Williams, B.A.O.)
9:750–1
bundle theory of mind 6:383
concrete 6:571, 6:574–5
continuous consciousness
(Locke, J.) 5:665, 5:677–8
criteria
mixed 7:309
physical 7:307–8
psychological 7:307, 7:308–9
cultural identity 2:746
ethics 7:306, 7:312–14
fission of persons thought
experiment 7:306, 7:309–12
human mutability
'growing argument'
(Epicharmus) 3:337
Indian philosophy 6:402

Locke, J. 5:665, 5:677–8
mind (Hume, D.) 4:548–9
morality **6:571–6**
impartiality 4:715
reductionism (Parfit, D.)
6:572–3
non-existence of
Buddhism
Indian 2:93–4
personal experience 1:852
personalism 7:315–16
persons 7:319, 7:320
practical reasoning 8:97
reincarnation 8:183, 8:184–5
resurrection 8:295–6
rights (Reid, T.) 8:178
salvation
Advaita Vedānta 8:449
Jainism 8:449
monotheism 8:450
survival after death 3:415
Williams, B.A.O. 9:750
personalism **7:315–18**
Bowne, B.P. 1:852–3
definition 7:314–15
hierarchical
Neo-Leibnizianism
(Lossky, N.O.) 5:833, 5:836
Renouvier, C.B. 8:269
personalistic socialism
Berdiaev, N.A. 1:730
personality
Akan philosophical psychology
1:138
'inner quality' (Hessen, S.I.) 4:416
integral
Kireevskii, I. 8:808
Signposts movement 8:769
Jung, C.G. 5:133
property 7:757, 7:760
psychology in social science
7:828–9
sexual 8:720
style 1:508–9
persons **7:318–21**
see also agents; personal identity
Akan philosophical psychology
1:138–9
animalism 7:319
Buddhism 8:448, 8:449
Chinese philosophy
Daoism 2:787–91
criteria 7:306–9
definition of (Boethius, A.M.S.)
1:807–8
East Asian Philosophy 3:194
fission problem 7:306, 7:309–12

gender (Suchon, G.) 9:212
God 4:98
individual/social dichotomy
    (Watsuji Tetsurō) 9:691–2
intentions (Sellars, W.S.) 8:641
Jainism 8:449
monotheistic traditions 8:449–50
necessarily embodied 7:320
ontology of (Capreolus, J.) 2:200–1
other minds 7:171
personeity 2:404
as primitive concept
    (Strawson, P.F.) 9:171–2
reductionism 7:314, 7:319–21
respect for **8:283–7**
self-respect 8:635–7
social development (Smith, A.)
    8:819
sociality (Il'enkov, E.V.) 4:688,
    4:690
value of life 5:625
perspective
    imagination-perception
        comparison 4:706
perspectivism
    Nietzsche, F.W. 6:849–50, 7:463
    quantum mechanics (Putnam, H.)
        7:841–2
    ratio-vitalism 9:74
    reality (Bhartṛhari) 1:765
    sceptical (Zhuangzi) 5:703–4
persuasion
    scientific method (Pascal, B.) 7:244
persuasiveness
    legal reasoning 5:527
Peru
    see also Inca civilization
    analytical philosophy 1:231–2
    colonial philosophy 5:421, 5:422
    existentialism 3:512
    Marxism 6:161, 6:162–4
    phenomenology 7:350
    pre-Columbian culture 5:429
Peshkov, Aleksei see Gor'kii, M.
Pesiqta de Rav Kahana (homiletic
    commentary) 6:355
Pešková, J. 2:440
pessimism
    epistemic 3:719
    freedom 3:744, 3:746–7, 3:749–51
    Hartmann, K.R.E. von 4:239
    Schopenhauer, A. 8:546, 8:552
Pessin, A. 7:786
Pestalozzi, J.H. 3:227–8, 3:231
Peter of Ailly see Ailly, Pierre d'
Peter of Auvergne **7:321–4**
Peter of Corbeil 1:398

Peter Lombard see Lombard, Peter
Peter of Spain **7:324–5**
    influence of
        Latin American colonial
            thought 5:422
    logic 5:768
        logical terminism 2:132
    supposition theory 5:753
Peters, F. 1:386, 4:159
Peters, R.H. 3:205
Peters, R.S. 3:233, 3:239, 4:476, 6:509
Peters, S. 4:725, 6:435, 8:672
Peters, W.S. 5:352
Petersen, P. 6:292
Peterson, Erik 9:331–2, 9:333
Petersson, B. 4:204
Petersson, R.T. 3:74
Petit, A. 2:505
Petit, P. 1:59
Petitjean, P. 7:577–8
Petrarca, Francesco **7:325–9**
    humanism 4:535–4
    Renaissance Platonism 7:440,
        7:447
Petrarch see Petrarca, Francesco
Petrażycki, Leon **7:329–30**
Petrement, S. 9:701
Petrić, Franjo (Franciscus Patricius)
    9:49–50, 9:55
Petronijević, Branislav 9:51, 9:55
Petrosyan, M. 4:532
Petrović, G. 9:55
Petrovich, M.H. 7:201
Petry, M.J. 6:741, 6:742
Pettegree, A. 2:181, 2:182
Pettis, B. 6:813
Pettit, Philip
    concepts 2:516–17
    consequentialism 2:606
    crime and punishment 2:710
    desire †3:30–3
    moral realism 6:538
    political philosophy 7:503
    reasons and causes 8:127
    Smart, J.J.C. 8:815
    social laws †8:832–4
Petzoldt, J. 4:9
Peuckert, W.E. 1:801, 9:366
Peukert, H. 4:508, 4:510
Pfänder, Alexander 7:335, 7:342,
    8:182
Phaedo of Elis 9:22
Phalén, Adolf 8:485, 8:491
phallocentrism 3:585
phantasms 2:885
Pharisees 4:205

pharmacology
    Islamic medicine 8:563
Phelps, M. 5:59
Phemister, P. 8:699
phenomena
    paranormal **7:221–4**
phenomenal consciousness 2:581–94
    see also qualia
    dualism 2:586–7
    eliminativism 2:587–9
    introspection 2:582, 2:589–91
    physicalism 2:582
    subjectivity 2:584–6
phenomenal Real
    religious pluralism (Hick, J.)
        8:261–2
phenomenalism **7:330–3**
    see also antirealism
    Berkeley, G. 3:377
    colour, theories of 2:428
    critique of (Chisholm, R.M.) 2:332
    empiricism 3:299–300, 3:301, 3:379
    Goodman, N. 4:137
    idealism 4:664
    illusion
        Yogācāra Buddhism 3:410
    Japanese Buddhism 2:102–3
    matter (Mill, J.S.) 6:360–1, 6:366,
        6:367
    mental (Edwards, J.) 3:241–2
    physical object statements 7:330,
        7:331, 7:333
phenomenology **7:333–43**
    see also heterophenomenology
    a priorism (Reinach, A.) 8:180
    Austro-German movement
        axiology 1:609
    categories (Peirce, C.S.) 7:277–8
    consciousness (Dennett, D.C.)
        2:883–4
    constitutive 7:336–7
    dialectical (Losev, A.F.) 5:830
    epistemic issues in **7:343–8**
        essence 7:345–6
        ontology 7:346–7
        presuppositionless description
            7:344–5
        reduction 7:343–4
    existential 7:337–9
        French philosophy of science
            7:779
    expression (Cassirer, E.) 2:224–5
    Heidegger, M.
        Husserl, E. influence 4:308
    hermeneutical 7:339–40
    historicism (Lyotard, J.-F.) 6:8
    imagination (Sartre, J.-P.) 8:475

intentionality (Husserl, E.)
4:576–7
in Italy (Paci, E.) 5:39
Latin America **7:348–52**
analytical philosophy 1:230
existentialism 3:510
lifeworld (Husserl, E.) 4:582–4
methods (Ingarden, R.W.)
4:789–91
Mexico 6:346
moral realism 6:535
opposition to (Weyl, H.) 9:707
Other *see* alterity; Other
perception (Merleau-Ponty, M.)
6:320–4
psychology
theories of 7:827–8
realistic 7:335–6
reductions (Husserl, E.) 4:580
of religion **7:352–5**
descriptive 7:352–3
existential 7:352, 7:353–4
the sacred 7:354–5
scientific 7:352, 7:353, 7:354
the Sacred (Bataille, G.) 1:660
of self
dialogues (Bakhtin, M.M.)
1:642
sense-data (Ayer, A.J.) 1:616
Shpet, G.G. 8:754–7
structuralism 9:176
subjective spirit (Hegel, G.W.F.)
4:273
Teilhard de Chardin, P. 9:289
time 9:415–16
transcendental idealism
(Husserl, E.) 4:577
transcendental (Schütz, A.) 8:560
will (Ricoeur, P.) 8:319
Yogācāra Buddhism comparison
2:69
philanthropy 2:152–3
philia see friendship; love
Philibert, M. 8:322
Philinus 4:333–4
Philip the Chancellor **7:356–7**
Philip, J.A. 7:861
Philippo-Ramist school of logic 5:717
Phillips, A. 2:872, 3:620, 8:272
Phillips, B. 8:780
Phillips, David
emotive meaning †3:290–1
Phillips, D.C. 3:239
Phillips, Derek L. 9:279
Phillips, D.Z. 3:417, 3:543, 8:631,
9:772
Phillips Griffiths, A. 8:272

Phillips, Robert 3:109
Phillips, R.P. 9:388
Phillips, Stephen H.
African philosophy, Anglophone
1:106
Aurobindo Ghose †1:567–9
awareness
in Indian thought †1:604–8
Brahman †2:1–5
epistemology
Indian schools of †3:388–92
error and illusion
Indian concepts of †3:409–13
Gaṅgeśa †3:843–6
Hindu philosophy 4:440
knowledge
Indian views of †5:280–5
monism, Indian †6:475–9
sense perception
Indian views of †8:688–94
Uddyotakara 9:515–16
Vatsyayana 9:588
Vedānta School †9:588–94
Phillipson, Nicholas 1:680, 4:562
Phillipus Cancellarius *see* Philip the
Chancellor
Philo of Alexandria **7:357–61**
cosmology 7:359–60
ethics 7:360
God 7:359, 7:360
Hellenistic Judaism 7:255–6
immutability 4:712, 4:714
Jewish philosophy 1:265, 5:87
logos 5:819
mysticism 6:623
Old Testament
hermeneutics 4:390
Pentateuch commentaries 7:358
pneuma (spirit) 7:471
Philo the Dialectician **7:363–5**
Philo of Larissa **7:361–3**
Philo of Megara 2:600, 2:602
Philodemus **7:365–7**
Academy 1:36
Arcesilaus 1:354
Carneades 2:220
Epicureanism 3:341, 3:350
Philolaus **7:367–71**
astronomy 7:369–70
cosmogony 7:368–9
cosmology 7:367, 7:368
first principles 7:368
philology
Chinese philosophy
neo-Confucianism 6:774–5
classical Latin
Renaissance humanism 4:537–9

legal hermeneutics 5:507, 5:508
philosophy relationship (Vico, G.)
9:604
Philonenko, A. 3:653
Philoponus **7:371–8**
Aristotelian physics 7:373–4
Aristotle commentators 1:436
Christian theology 7:374–6
creation 7:374–5
eternity (Richard Rufus of
Cornwall) 8:315–16
eternity of the world critique
7:374, 7:376, 8:789
influenced by
ancient philosophy 1:265
monophysite Christology 7:375
patristic philosophy 7:261
Zeno of Elea 9:844
philosopher-rulers
Plato 7:400–1, 7:414, 7:518, 7:519
philosophers
imperfect society
Ibn Bajja 7:519
philosophes
Condillac, É.B. de 2:523–4
Helvétius, C.-A. 4:345, 4:346,
4:348
influence on Russian
Enlightenment 3:324, 3:325
public opinion
sovereignty 7:514
philosophia Christi 3:399
philosophia perennis (perennial
philosophy) 2:740–1
philosophical analysis
see also conceptual analysis
Moore, G.E. 6:497–8
'philosophy of life' *see*
Lebensphilosophie
Philp, Mark
corruption †2:674–7
Godwin, W. †4:345–6
phi-phenomena 4:53
phonology
Indian philosophy of language
5:381–2, 7:249
influence on Lévi-Strauss, C. 5:583
Prague School 9:179
Photios, Patriarch of Constantinople
2:161
photography
aesthetics of **7:378–81**
film aesthetics 3:673–4
painting comparison 7:378–9
phrase matching
Mohism 5:699–700

phrase structure grammars 9:247, 9:248, 9:250–2
phronēsis (practical wisdom)
　see also prudence
　educational philosophy 3:223, 3:224
　law
　　Aristotle 5:148
Phule, Jyotib 1:196
Phya pa Chos kyi seng ge (Chaba Chögyi sengge) 8:433, 9:406–7
phylogeny
　classification problems
　　taxonomy 9:272, 9:275–6
　evolutionary theory 3:483
　species concepts 9:78, 9:79–80
Physical Soul 4:628
physical world
　idealism 4:662–9
　knowledge of 4:837–8, 4:840–1
　panpsychism 7:195, 7:196
physicalism
　see also materialism
　colour
　　objective 2:420–1
　　and qualia 2:419–20
　　theories of 2:430
　connectionism (Freud, S.) 3:791
　Feigl, H. 6:172
　fire (Cleanthes) 2:382–3
　intentionality 4:818
　non-reductive
　　supervenience 9:239
　parapsychology relationship 7:225–7
　phenomenal consciousness 2:587
　qualia 7:864–5, 7:866
　radical
　　scientific language (Neurath, O.) 6:815
　Skinner, B.F. 8:800
　Stoicism (Marcus Aurelius) 6:95
　Vienna Circle (Schlick, F.A.M.) 8:542
physicality
　dance 2:774–5
physician–patient relationship
　medicine, philosophy of 6:266
physics
　see also mechanics; quantum mechanics; relativity theory
　Albert of Saxony 1:143–4
　Aristotelian
　　Boethius of Dacia 6:699, 6:701
　　critique of
　　　Philoponus 7:373–4
　　　Proclus 7:729

　　Simplicius 8:789–91
　　White, T. 9:712–13
　　Bradwardine, T. 1:863–4
　causal completeness of
　　mental causation 6:308
　chemistry
　　reducibility of 2:299
　classical
　　indispensibility of (Bohr, N.) 1:821
　colonial philosophy
　　Latin America 5:424
　computability and information 2:478, 2:480–1
　conservation of energy
　　critique of dualism 3:136
　contemporary
　　French philosophy of science 3:780–1
　　goals of 2:865–6
　Descartes, R. 3:14–15
　determinism and indeterminism **3:33–9**
　divine action theories 8:230, 8:231, 8:233–4
　Eusebius 3:457
　experimental
　　Bridgman, P.W. **2:17–19**
　　Rohault, J. 8:342
　falling bodies (Soto, D. de) 9:38
　field theory
　　classical 3:668–70
　　quantum **3:670–3**
　identity of indiscernibles 4:680
　John of Jandun 5:107
　laws of
　　parapsychology 7:226
　Marsilius of Inghen 6:111
　mathematical
　　dualism 3:134–5
　　Oresme, N. 7:154–5
　microvoids (Strato) 9:162
　modal system (Spinoza, B. de) 9:96
　motion
　　Descartes, R. 3:14–15
　　Hobbes, T. 4:469
　natural philosophy (Gassendi, P.) 3:852–3
　nature (Hegel, G.W.F.) 4:272
　Newtonian
　　determinism 3:33–4, 3:35
　　space 9:62
　non-mechanistic (Bacon, F.) 1:630–1
　objective (Planck, M.K.E.L.) 7:397
　optics **7:136–9**

　paradigms of
　　operationalism 7:132
　Paul of Venice 7:266
　probability (Ramsey, F.P.) 8:46
　Ramus, P. 8:54
　reduction 8:148
　relativistic
　　logical positivism 5:791
　Sceptical
　　Pyrrhonism 7:853
　scientific realism (Smart, J.J.C.) 8:814
　speculative nature of
　　ancient philosophy 1:263
　Stoicism 9:142, 9:144–5
　　Epictetus 3:338
　　Posidonius 7:556
　symmetries
　　conservation laws 2:607
　William of Ockham 9:741–2
Physics see Aristotle
physiocracy
　economics (Smith, A.) 8:816
physiology
　see also neurophysiology
　chemistry
　　vitalism 9:640–1
　Diogenes of Apollonia 3:88–9
　emotions 3:281–2
　experimental
　　vitalism 9:640
　Hippocratic medicine 4:442
　　Galen 3:833
　imagery
　　Chinese 1:71, 1:72
　materialism
　　Cabanis, P.-J. 2:167
　　La Mettrie, J.O. de 5:333–4
　mental states (Bonnet, C.) 1:839
　mind–brain relationship (Hartley, D.) 1:136, 4:236
　Nemesius 6:763, 6:764
pneuma (spirit)
　early Greek philosophy 7:470–1
physis (nature)
　see also nature
　body relationship
　　Neoplatonism (Proclus) 7:727
　change in
　　Aristotle 1:418–19
　nomos debate
　　Callicles 2:176
　　Greek philosophy **7:381–2**
　　political philosophy
　　　history of 7:505–6
　　social science 8:848–9
　　Sophists 9:33–4

science of
Aristotle 1:414
study of
Stoicism 9:144–5
unlimiteds/limiters
Philolaus 7:368
Piaget, Jean **7:383–6**
cognitive development
experimental study 2:394
developmental stages 7:383–4
genetic epistemology 6:724
infant cognition 2:391
moral development 6:504, 6:505,
6:506
psychology
theories of 7:827
structuralism in social science
9:187, 9:189
Vygotskii, L.S. 9:672, 9:673, 9:675
Piattelli-Palmarini, M. 4:54, 6:675,
8:89–90
Picard, E. 3:147
Picasso, Pablo 2:892
Picavet, F. 8:357
Piccinini, Mario
Gioberti, V. †4:78–80
Picciotto, S. 2:720
Piccolomini, Francesco 1:412
Pichler, T.G. 8:813
Pickard-Cambridge, Sir A. 3:337
Pickering, A. 2:630, 3:517–18, 9:2
Pickering, M. 2:505
Pickering, W.S.F. 3:177
Piclin, Michel
Lachelier, J. †5:338–40
Pico della Mirandola, Gianfrancesco
scepticism, Renaissance 8:501
Pico della Mirandola, Giovanni
7:386–92
Aristotelianism 7:390
love 7:387–8
Platonism, Renaissance 7:388,
7:441
theology
concordist project 7:386, 7:387,
7:388–90
picture theory of meaning
see also types, theory of
Wittgenstein, L. 9:758–9, 9:761
pictures
depiction **2:892–6**
picturesque, the 6:731, 6:732
Pieper, J. 9:331
Piers, G. 8:141
Pierson, G. 9:425
Pietarinen, J. 2:535

pietism **7:392–6**
Crusius, C.A. 2:737
German
Kabbalah 5:173
Jewish
Hasidism 4:242–5
Ibn Paquda 4:633–6
Sufism inspired
(Maimonides, A.) 6:38–9
Protestant
influence on Russian
Enlightenment 3:324
Pietroski, P. 8:675
Pigou, A.C. 3:210
Pigozzi, D. 9:264
Pike, Nelson
eternity 3:426
evil, problem of 3:472
mysticism 6:630, 6:633
omnipotence 7:102
omniscience 7:112
perfect goodness 4:144
religion, history of philosophy of
8:247
Pikulik, L. 8:352
Pimsler, M. 3:315
Pinborg, J.
Bacon, R. 1:636
Boethius of Dacia 1:816
Brito, R. 2:23
Buridan, J. 2:136
Gregory of Rimini 4:172
language
medieval theories of 5:404
logic, medieval 5:758
medieval philosophy 6:277
natural philosophy, medieval 6:706
Pinch, T.J.
constructivism 2:629
experiment 3:517
science, demarcation problem
2:866
technology 9:287
and ethics 9:283
Pinchard, B. 2:175
Pincoffs, E. 3:239
Pine, F. 7:823
Pine, Martin L.
Pomponazzi, P. †7:529–33
Pineau, L. 8:728
Pines, C.L. 8:632
Pines, S.
Alexander of Aphrodisias 1:176
al-Baghdadi 1:638
Crescas, H. 2:704
Damascius 2:772

Greek philosophy, impact on
Islamic philosophy 4:159
Ibn Ezra, M. 4:614
Jewish philosophy, contemporary
5:95
Judah Halevi 4:213
Maimonides, M. 6:48
science in Islamic philosophy 8:564
Pinheiro Ferreira, Silvestre 2:9–10
Pink, Thomas
will †9:720–5
Pinkard, T. 4:279
Pinker, S.
Chomsky, N. 2:341
connectionism 2:578
innateness of language 4:54
learning 5:487
nativism 6:675
Skinner, B.F. 8:802
unconscious mental states 9:527
Pinnock, C. 7:719, 7:720
Pinsker, Leopold 9:867–8, 9:870
Pinsky, V. 1:358–9
Pintard, R. 5:621
Pintore, Anna
institutionalism in law †4:799–803
Piovani, P. 9:606
Piovesana, G.K. 5:79, 5:716
Pipes, R. 5:609
Pippin, R.B. 4:279, 6:99
Pisarev, Dmitrii I.
materialism
Russian 8:416
nihilism
Russian
aesthetics 7:7
education 7:7–8
youth 7:6
Pitassi, M.C. 5:476
Pitcher, G.
Berkeley, G. 1:750
bodily sensations 1:795
correspondence theory of truth
9:475
epistemology 3:383
perception 7:299
Ryle, G. 8:432
suffering 9:215
Pitkin, H.F.
consent 2:598
Machiavelli, N. 6:22
obligation
political 7:80
political representation 8:272
Wittgensteinian ethics 9:772
Pitt, J.C. 3:525, 3:841, 8:642
Pitts, W. 1:486, 6:813

place
  concept of
    Aristotelianism, seventeenth
      century 1:389–90
    formal/material distinction (Giles
      of Rome) 4:74
  logic of *see* logic of place
  space
    Neoplatonism 6:801–2
    Philoponus 7:373
    Proclus 7:729
    Stoicism 9:148
    Strato 9:162
Placita (views) 3:125
plagiarism 2:384
Plamenatz, J.P.
  alienation 1:181
  consent 2:598
  hedonism 4:259
  Mill, J. 6:360
  political philosophy
    history of 7:517
  Rousseau, J.-J. 8:377
Planck, Max Karl Ernst Ludwig
  7:396–8
  see also Planck's constant
  optics 7:138
  unity of science 9:531
Planck's constant 7:396
planning
  practical reasoning 8:98
Plant, Raymond
  community and
    communitarianism 2:471
  market
    ethics of the 6:110
  needs and interests 6:755
  political philosophy †7:525–8
  welfare 9:705
Plantinga, Alvin
  agnosticism 1:123
  being 1:702
  Calvin, J. 2:182
  de re/de dicto belief 2:817
  divine simplicity 8:787
  epistemic justification 5:164
  eternity 3:426
  evil, problem of 3:472
  faith 3:543
  Gettier problems 4:55, 4:57–8
  God
    arguments for the existence of
      †4:85–93
    ontological argument 8:242
  knowledge
    analysis 4:59
    causal theory 5:266

Kripke, S.A. 5:304
Lewis, D.K. 5:593
modal logic 6:433
monotheism 6:483
natural theology 6:713
necessary being 6:747
omnipotence 7:102
omniscience 7:112
possible worlds 7:572
prayer 7:653
Reformed epistemology 6:709,
  8:246
reliabilism
  design 9:620–1
religion
  and epistemology †8:209–18
  history of philosophy of 8:247
  language 8:259
  pluralism 8:264
virtues
  theological 9:331
warrant theory 5:276, 8:130
  intellectual duty 7:36, 7:37, 7:38
  virtue epistemology 9:619, 9:622
Plantinga, C. 1:541
plants
  classification of (Linnaeus, C. von)
    5:647–8
Planty-Bonjour, G. 4:307
Plass, P.C. 4:599
plastic nature
  see also nature, spirit of
  divine providence (Cudworth, R.)
    2:741
plate tectonic theory 4:27
Platform Sutra **7:398–9**
  enlightenment
    sudden
      China 2:88
  ti/yong 9:400
Plato **7:399–421**
  see also anti-Platonism;
    Neoplatonism; Platonic love;
    Platonism
  abstraction of ideas (Francis of
    Meyronnes) 3:724–5
  Academy 1:36
  akrasia 1:139–40, 1:142
  analytic interpretation (Vlastos, G.)
    9:650, 9:651–2
  animal language and thought
    1:269
  Apology
    Socrates' defence 9:8, 9:9,
      9:10–11
    Socrates' moral choice 7:406,
      7:407

applied ethics 1:320
archē 1:360, 1:361
Archytas 1:368, 1:369
Aristotle
  harmonization with (Porphyry)
    7:546–7
Aristotlelianism
  reconciliation with
    (Boethius, A.M.S.) 1:396
art
  and morality 1:456
  value 1:476, 1:478–9, 1:480
beauty 1:681–2, 1:684
being
  property/entity debate 1:700
Callicles 2:176–7
Carolingian renaissance 2:221
cave analogy 7:400–1, 7:414
  moral development 6:504
Charmides
  sōphrosynē (moderation) 7:408
chora (Kristeva, J.) 5:306, 5:308
comedy 2:434–5, 2:438
commentaries on (Calcidius) 2:175
communism 2:464
concepts 2:516–17
conservatism 2:608, 2:609, 2:614
correspondence theory of truth
  9:475
corruption 2:675, 2:677
cosmology 2:677–8
courage 7:408
Cratylus 2:694
Cratylus
  language 5:357–8
  object of knowledge 3:372
  semiotics 8:677–8
creation 2:695–6, 7:401
  Gersonides 4:49
  religious doctrine of 2:700
Crito
  Socrates, death sentence 7:406,
    7:407
daemons 7:426
death 2:817, 2:819, 2:822–3
defence of
  colonial philosophy
    Latin America 5:422, 5:424
democracy 2:872
  equality 2:869
  truth 2:870
dialogues *see* Plato, Socratic
  dialogues
dualism 9:44, 9:45
educational philosophy 3:222,
  3:223–4, 3:231
egoism and altruism 3:248

emotions 3:286, 3:289
   morality 6:558, 6:559, 6:564
epiphenomenalism 3:354
eros
   sexuality 8:721, 8:728
eschatology 3:417
esotericism (Strauss, L.) 9:167–8
eternity 3:424, 3:426
ethics
   applied 1:320
   Islamic philosophy 3:439, 3:440
   practical reason in 7:616
   universalism 9:539
   virtue 6:533, 7:410–11, 9:622,
     9:626
     moral psychology 6:533
eudaimonia 3:452
evil 3:466
faith 3:541
fallibility 1:708
Form of the Good 4:140
Forms
   see also Forms, Platonic
   immutability 4:711
   theory of 7:409–10
     self-critique 7:401, 7:414–15
friendship 3:794, 3:797
geometry 4:28, 4:29, 4:33
God
   concepts of 4:101
   existence of
     cosmological arguments
       4:93, 8:240
good, theories of the 4:130, 4:135
Gorgias 4:146
Gorgias
   Callicles 2:176–7, 2:176, 2:177
   Socrates' defence 7:404, 7:408
happiness 4:229
hedonism 4:259
Heraclides of Pontus 4:364
hermeneutics 4:390
Hippias 4:441
illumination 4:698–9, 4:700
imitation
   Islamic philosophy 1:78
immutability 4:710, 4:711, 4:714
Indefinite Dyad 7:423–4
infinity 4:773
influence of 7:423
   Augustine 1:541–2, 1:546–7
   scientific theories (Heraclides of
     Pontus) 4:363
   Western philosophy 7:417
influenced by
   Egyptian philosophy 3:251,
     3:252–3

Pythagoreanism 7:857–8, 7:860,
   7:861
intellect (Gersonides) 4:50
Islamic political philosophy 7:518–
   7:520
just ruler (al-Farabi) 7:430
justice 5:142, 5:144, 5:147,
   5:148–53, 7:413–14
   eidos
     genealogy 4:1, 4:4
     normative 5:464–5
katharsis 5:218, 5:220
knowledge
   concept of 3:371–2, 3:383, 5:276
   innate 2:390, 2:391
   objects of 3:372, 8:577
   and truth 7:401
Laches
   courage 7:408
language 5:357–8, 5:361
Laws
   politics 7:401, 7:417
logic
   categories 7:427
logos 5:818
   Antisthenes 1:316–17
love 5:843, 5:844, 5:845, 7:411–12
matter 6:193, 6:196
memory 6:296–7, 6:299–300
Meno
   ethics
     virtue 7:410–11
   knowledge
     concept of 3:371
     innate 2:391
   nativism 6:673
mimēsis 6:381–2
morality
   divine 8:219
   education 6:507, 6:508, 6:509
   expertise 6:511
   luck 6:521
   relativism 6:542
nativism 6:673
natural philosophy
   medieval 6:691
naturalism in ethics 6:717
nous 7:43, 7:44
obligation
   political 7:77, 7:80
omnipresence 7:107
ownership
   collective 2:462–3
Parmenidean paradox 7:401
Parmenides 7:229, 7:234
Parmenides
   language 5:358

theory of Forms
   self-critique of 7:401,
     7:414–15
particulars 7:235
perfect goodness 4:140, 4:141,
   4:144
perfect-being theology 4:96
personal identity
   morality 6:571
persons 7:318
Phaedo
   immortality of the soul 7:400,
     7:412–13
   indestructability of the soul
     3:371
   nativism 6:673
   Socrates' philosophy
     Platonism as development of
       7:410
   suicide 9:225
Phaedrus
   rhetoric 7:414–15
philosopher-rulers 7:400–1, 7:414
physical theory 7:416–17
physis/nomos debate 7:381–2
Platonism
   Early and Middle 7:429
pleasure 7:448, 7:449, 7:451
Plutarch of Chaeronea 7:470
pneuma (spirit) 7:471
poetry 7:472, 7:473, 7:477
politics 7:401–2, 7:413–14, 7:417
   history of 7:506
   ideal state 7:417
prescriptivism 7:670–1
property 7:758
Protagoras
   akrasia 1:139–40, 1:142
   Socratic dialogue 7:408–9
providence 7:797, 7:802
psychē (soul)
   tripartation of 7:810, 7:811
Pythagoreanism 6:808, 7:857–8,
   7:860, 7:861
rational choice theory 8:74
religion, history of philosophy of
   8:247
Republic 7:413–14
   cave analogy 7:400–1
   esotericism (Strauss, L.)
     9:167–8
   geometry 4:29, 4:30
   illumination 4:698–9
   immutability 4:711
   just ruler 7:430
   justice 5:142, 5:144, 7:413–14
     normative 5:464–5

katharsis 5:218, 5:220
knowledge 3:371–2
mimēsis 6:381–2
philosopher-rulers 7:400
politics 7:413–14, 7:506
psychē 7:810
Thrasymachus 9:397–8
virtue ethics 6:533
republicanism 8:280, 8:282, 8:283
rhetoric 7:415–16, 8:305, 8:306–7,
8:309
scientific method 8:581
scope of works 1:263
self-control 8:611, 8:612, 8:613
semiotics 8:676, 8:677–8, 8:679
slavery 8:804, 8:806–7
social science
history of philosophy of 8:849
Socrates
death sentence 7:406, 7:407
defence 7:404–5, 9:9, 9:10–11
moral choice 7:407
philosophy
Platonism as development of
7:400, 7:410
relationship with (Vlastos, G.)
9:652
rhetoric 7:408
soul's reincarnation 2:582
Socratic dialogues 9:8, 9:18,
9:19–20
apologetic works 7:407–8
aretē 1:373–4
critiques 7:414–15
early 7:406–7
elenchus 7:404–5, 7:407
historical Socrates 9:20
of inquiry 7:408–9
interpretation of 7:405–6,
9:9–9:10
later works 7:415–17
nature of 7:399–400, 7:406–7
Owen, G.E.L. 7:177–8
Platonism
introduction of 7:400,
7:409–10
Prodicus 7:731, 7:732
Protagoras 7:789, 7:790–1
rationale of 7:423
Socrates
portrayal of 7:405
Vlastos, G. 9:650, 9:652
Sophist
language 5:358
Parmenidean paradox 7:401
Sophists 9:33, 9:34
sōphrosynē (moderation) 7:408

soul 9:48
Early and Middle Platonism
7:425
immortality of 3:414, 7:400,
7:412–13, 8:294–5, 9:46
indestructability 3:371
sport 9:113
state
substantive ideals 4:675
substance 9:205, 9:210
suicide 9:225, 9:230
Symposium
love 7:411–12
theory of Forms 7:409–10
testimony 9:314
Theaetetus
analytic philosophy 1:224, 1:229
knowledge
concept of 3:371
and truth 7:401
Third Man Argument (Vlastos, G.)
9:651, 9:652
thought experiments 9:395
Timaeus
analytic interpretation
(Vlastos, G.) 9:650
Carolingian renaissance 2:221
chora (Kristeva, J.) 5:306, 5:308
commentaries on (Calcidius)
2:175
cosmology 2:677–8
creation 2:695–6, 7:401
eternity 3:424
matter 6:193, 6:196
medieval natural philosophy
6:691
physical theory 7:416–17
Pythagoreanism 6:808
totalitarianism (Popper, K.R.)
7:536–7
tragedy 9:447–8, 9:451–2
translations into Arabic 4:156
truthfulness 9:485
unconscious mental states 9:522
universals 9:540, 9:541, 9:542
unwritten doctrines 7:406
utilitarianism 9:552, 9:557
virtue ethics 9:622, 9:626
moral psychology 6:533
virtues 9:627, 9:631
vocabulary 1:262–3
war and peace 9:691
wisdom 9:752–3, 9:754
writings
authenticity of 7:403
chronology of 7:402–4
stylistic analysis 7:403–4

Zeno of Elea 9:852
Plato of Tivoli 5:88
Plato, J. von 8:492
Platonic Forms *see* Forms, Platonic
Platonic love
Ficino, M. 3:657–8, 7:386, 7:388
Platonism
see also anti-Platonism;
Neoplatonism
Academy 1:36
Alcinous 1:159
Apuleius 1:325–6
Aquinas, T. 1:327, 1:330
Arcesilaus 1:352
Aristotelianism synthesis
Abravanel, J. 1:23, 1:25–6
Augustine
patristic philosophy 7:259–60
Byzantine philosophy 2:163
Cambridge Platonism **2:182–5**
see also Latitudinarianism
Conway, A. 2:669–70
Cudworth, R. 2:739–44
Culverwell, N. 2:751
Chartrian 2:291
Christianity
Carolingian renaissance
2:221–2
Clement of Alexandria 2:383–4
Clement of Alexandria
2:383–4
early 7:254, 7:257–8
Eriugena, J.S. 3:402
Eusabius 3:456–8
Inge, W.R. 4:793–4
medieval 7:431–2
Peter Lombard 5:821, 5:822
political philosophy
history of 7:508
Tertullian 9:308
William of Auvergne 9:726
William of Conches 9:730,
9:731
Early **7:421–9**
epistemology
Ikhwan al-Safa' 4:687
problems for 1:34–5
Gnosticism 4:84
Henry of Ghent 4:356
influence on
Western philosophy 1:263
Islamic philosophy **7:429–30**
Ikhwan al-Safa' 4:685, 4:687
Kabbalah
Messer Leon opposition 6:331,
6:333
linguistics 5:416

Lotze, R.H. 5:840
love
  Abravanel, J. 1:23, 1:25–6
  mathematical 8:119, 8:120–1
  see also realism, mathematics
  epistemology 8:121
  Wittgenstein, L. rejection
    9:766–7
  medieval **7:431–9**
    Christianity 7:431–2
    texts 7:432–4
    universals 7:434–5
  Middle **7:421–9**
    see also Neo-Pythagoreanism
    Academy 7:421–2, 7:423
    Calcidius 2:175–6
    Celsus 2:264
    ethics 7:421, 7:426–7
    happiness 7:426–7
    influence of
      Plotinus 7:456
    logic 7:427–8
    metaphysics 7:424–5
    Plotinus 7:456
    Plutarch of Chaeronea 7:464–9
    theology 7:425–6
  moral philosophy
    Islamic 3:440, 3:441
  naturalism (Thierry of Chartres)
    9:372
  Neo-Pythagoreanism 6:808–9
  nominalism debate (Quine, W.V.)
    8:8–9
  Numenius 7:54–5
  patristic philosophy 7:259, 7:260–1
  Renaissance **7:439–47**
    Christian Council of Ferrara/
      Florence 7:442–3
    Christian Florentine school
      7:444–5
    Christianity 7:439, 7:442–5
    Ficino, M. 3:655
    Pico della Mirandola, G.
      7:388
    classical texts 4:537
    concord with Aristotle (Pico
      della Mirandola, G.) 7:390–1
    George of Trebizond 4:34, 4:35
    humanism 4:539, 7:440–2,
      7:445–6
    Jewish philosophy
      Abravanel, J. 1:23, 1:25
      Alemanno, Y. 1:162
    Latin translations (Ficino, M.)
      3:653, 3:654
    revival 7:439–41
      cosmology 7:446–7

    Council of Ferrara/Florence
      7:442–4
    Germany 7:445–6
    translations 7:440
    scepticism (Sanches, F.) 8:453
    scholastic criticism 7:441
  revival of
    ancient philosophy imperial
      phase 1:264
  Speusippus 9:89, 9:90
  teleology (Galen) 3:833
  Themistius 9:325
  universals (William of Ockham)
    9:734
Platti, E. 4:601
Platts, M. 6:225
Platzeck, E.-W. 5:664
plausibility 2:215–16, 2:217, 2:218–19
play
  art
    Japanese aesthetics 1:89
  child's theory of mind 6:385, 6:387
  games contrast (Mead, G.H.)
    6:211
  hermeneutics (Gadamer, H.-G.)
    3:829, 3:830
Plé, B. 2:505
pleasure **7:448–51**
  aesthetic concept 1:56
  altruism
    Epicureanism 3:347–8
  beauty 1:682–3
  critical hedonism (Baumgardt, D.)
    1:668–9
  emotion theory (Spinoza, B. de)
    9:101–2
  Epicureanism 3:340, 3:345,
    3:346–8
  eudaimonia
    Cyrenaics 2:761–3
  in God's beauty (al-Farabi) 1:76
  good relationship 4:132
  happiness relationship 4:226, 4:228
    Wollaston, W. 9:787
  hedonism **4:257–9**
    Christian (Gassendi, P.) 3:855
  Lokāyata 6:180
  moral sense (Hutcheson, F.) 4:590
  moral theory (Spinoza, B. de)
    9:103
  pathē
    Cyrenaics 2:759, 2:760, 2:763
  pursuit of (Hobbes, T.) 4:470
  quality of (Mill, J.S.) 6:369–71
  restoration of equilibrium (al-
    Razi, Abu Bakr) 8:111

  sexual 8:717, 8:719, 8:721
    Antisthenes 1:316
    objectification 8:722
  utilitarianism 9:551, 9:552–3
    Bentham, J. 1:718–19, 1:721–2
  virtuous action (Aristotle) 1:428–9
Pleger, W. 8:538
Plekhanov, Georgii Valentinovich
  7:451–6
  Chernyshevskii, N.G. 2:306
  dialectical materialism 3:53,
    3:57–8
  Hegelianism, Russian 4:306
  Lenin, V.I. 5:565
  Marxism, Russian 6:150, 6:152,
    6:159–60
  Narodism 7:451–3, 7:455
  Russian empiriocriticism 8:409
plenitude, principle of 5:556
  Leibniz, G.W. 5:556
plenum (full physical world) 2:753
Pletho 7:443, 7:447
Plevano, R. 8:318
Pliny 3:305
Plotinus **7:456–63**
  Alexandria 6:804
  ancient philosophy 1:262, 1:264
  aretē 1:374
  beauty 1:681–2, 1:684
  causation 7:460–1
  creation doctrine 2:696
  divine simplicity 8:784
  emanation
    hierarchical ontology 7:460
  eternity 3:426–7
  God
    concepts of 4:101
    existence of 8:240
  Iamblichus 4:598
  illuminationism 4:699, 4:700
  infinity 4:774
  influence of
    Christian mysticism 6:624
    Ikhwan al-Safa' 4:686
    Liber de causis 5:595, 5:596
    Marius Victorinus 6:105–6
  influenced by (Alexander of
    Aphrodisias) 1:174
  Intellect 7:458–9
  monism 6:474, 6:475
  necessary being 6:743, 6:744, 6:747
  Neoplatonism
    founding of 6:799
  nous 7:44
  omnipresence 7:105, 7:107
  the One 7:457–8
  perfect-being theology 4:97

poetry 7:477
psychē (soul) 7:810–11
religion, history of philosophy of
8:247
Soul 7:457, 7:458–60
teachings of
Porphyry 7:545–6, 7:548
ultimate reality 4:99
unconscious mental states 9:522
Ploucquet, G. 5:719
Plucknett, T. 5:505
Plumwood, Val 3:202, 3:336, 8:204
pluralism **7:463–4**
see also cognitive pluralism;
epistemological pluralism; moral
pluralism; multiculturalism;
religious pluralism; substance-
pluralism; value pluralism
aesthetic 7:131
cognitive **2:395–8**
descriptive 2:395–6
evaluative-concept 2:396, 2:397
normative 2:396–7
culture 7:463, 7:464
knowledge (Anderson, J.) 1:267,
1:268
liberation theology 5:614
matter 6:193
methodological 7:464, 9:35
monotheism and 7:463
property theories 7:760
relativism 7:463, 7:464
religious *see* religious pluralism
scientific method
(Feyerabend, P.K.) 3:640–2
toleration 7:464
plurality
Zeno of Elea 9:843, 9:844–7, 9:846
Pluta, Olaf
Ailly, P. d' †1:133–5
Plutarch of Chaeronea **7:464–70**
daemonology 7:468–9
dualism 7:467
Early and Middle Platonism 7:422
ethics 7:465, 7:466
first principles 7:465, 7:466–7
geometry 4:33–4
mind 7:467–8, 7:469
pneuma (spirit) **7:470–2**
soul
Strato 9:162–3
vital power of
Stoicism 9:145
pneumatology *see* rational
psychology

Pocock, J.G.A.
American philosophy, eighteenth
and nineteenth century 1:206
Burke, E. 2:140
common law 2:441–2, 2:446
Harrington, J. 4:233, 4:234
Machiavelli, N. 6:22
political philosophy
history of 7:517
public interest 7:834
republicanism 8:283
Pococke, Edward 5:24
Podolsky, B. 1:716, 7:894
see also Einstein-Podolsky-Rosen
experiment
Podro, M. 1:509, 8:529
Podskalsky, G. 2:165
Poe, Edgar Allen 7:477
poena see punishment
Poetics see Aristotle
poetry **7:472–8**
art and truth 1:459
artefacts
theories of 7:474–5
Baumgarten, A.G. 1:670
Chinese 1:68–71
literati style 1:73
Shijing 2:311
expression theory 7:475
formalism 3:707
Hesiod 4:412–13
Homer 4:501
interpretation of 1:503
Islamic philosophy 1:75, 1:77, 5:15
imagination 1:77–9
syllogisms 4:652, 5:710
Japanese 1:84, 1:88, 1:89
kokoro 5:291–2
nature 1:80–2
religion 1:85, 1:86
language (Shpet, G.G.) 8:757
Lucretius 5:854–6
mimēsis 6:381–2
opera relationship 7:130
painting comparison
(Lessing, G.E.) 5:575, 5:576
Parmenides 7:228–35
Philodemus 7:365–7
philosophy relationship 5:855,
6:103, 7:473
Plato's dismissal of 1:479
politics (Zabarella, J.) 9:837
prosaics comparison
literary theory (Bakhtin, M.M.)
1:638–9
as religion
Brahman 2:1

Tagore, R. 9:257, 9:258
rhetoric 8:307, 8:308–9
Sanskrit
interpretation 4:836–7
structuralist literary theory
(Todorov, T.) 9:425–6
Timon of Philius 9:419–20
tragedy 1:431, 9:447–8, 9:449
Urdu (Iqbal, M.) 4:864
use theories 7:475
Vedic
power of 7:607
Xenophanes 9:807–10
Pogge, R. 8:109–10
Pogge, T.W. 5:156, 9:705
Poggi, G. 8:780
Poggi, S. 6:742
Pöggler, O. 4:323
Poguelin, Jean-Baptiste *see* Molière
Pohle, J. 6:466
Pohlenz, M. 9:160
Pohlers, W. 4:772, 7:30, 7:750
Pohribny, A. 1:452
Poincaré, Jules Henri **7:478–83**
conventionalism 2:669, 6:252–3,
9:62
Cournot, A.A. 2:690
empiricism (Reichenbach, H.)
8:169, 8:171
geometry 4:34
convention 2:666, 7:479–80
Schlick, F.A.M. 8:540
intuitionism 4:847
Le Roy, É.L.E.J. 5:481–2, 5:483
logical positivism 5:790–1
mathematics 7:481, 8:566
foundations of 6:191
mechanics
classical 6:259
paradoxes of set and property
7:218, 7:219
relativity theory
philosophical significance of
8:199
science
demarcation problem 2:866
space 9:65
Poinsot, John *see* John of St Thomas
point sets theory 8:705–6
points of view
language (Ibn Rushd) 4:644–5
Poirier, R. 3:272
Pois, R.A. 3:336, 4:166
Pojman, L. 1:223
Pokora, T. 9:680
Polak, F.L. 9:560, 9:561

Poland **7:483–9**
Ajdukiewicz, K. **1:135–8**
Boehme, J. **1:799–801**
Cieszkowski, A. **2:360–2**
contemporary philosophy 7:487–8
Copernicus, N. **2:671–2**
Heschel, A.J. **4:410–12**
humanism 7:484–5
Ingarden, R.W. **4:789–93**
Keckermann, B. **5:224–5**
Kotarbiński, T. **5:293–6**
Krochmal, N. **5:308–11**
Leśniewski, S. **5:571–4**
logic **7:492–500**
    analytic philosophy 1:226
Łukasiewicz, J. **5:859–63**
Luxemburg, R. **6:5–7**
Marxism 7:488
medieval period 7:483–4
Messianism 7:486
Meyerson, É. **6:348–51**
Petrażycki, L. **7:329–30**
Post, E.L. **7:573–5**
Tarski, A. **9:262–5**
Thomism 7:485, 7:487
Twardowski, K. **9:507–9**
Wróblewski, J. **9:797–8**
Polanyi, K. 8:886
Polanyi, L. 3:99
Polanyi, Michael **7:489–92**
    tacit knowledge 5:286, 5:287
    unconscious mental states 9:524,
        9:527
polemic
    anti-Christian (Celsus) 2:264
    Scepticism (Arcesilaus) 1:353
polemical deism
    Tindal, M. 9:421, 9:422
Polemo 1:381, 7:429
polis
    Greek political philosophy
        (Aristotle) 7:506
political action
    Machiavelli, N. 7:510
political authority **1:584–6**
    Enlightenment 8:227–8
    ethical autonomy 1:587
    Herder, J.G. 4:384
    Hume, D. 4:556–7
    'ilm al-kalam 5:27
    Marsilius of Padua 6:112–13
    Molina, L. de 6:464
    religious authority conflict 8:224,
        8:225–6
    secular
        Marsilius of Padua 6:112–13

political economy
    capitalism
        Marx, K. critique 6:127–8
political neutrality *see* neutrality,
    political
political obedience
    The Reformation 7:510–11
political obligation *see* obligation,
    political
political philosophy **7:500–3**
    see also government; law; politics;
        state
    Alighieri, Dante 1:181–2, 1:183–4
    anarchism **1:244–9**
        (Godwin, W.) 4:122, 4:124
    anti-positivism
        Latin America 1:306
    Aquinas, T. 1:341
    Aristotle
        conceptual scope 1:414
    Australia 1:580
    autonomy
        ethical 1:587
    Chinese
        de 2:809–10
        fa 3:532–3
        Guanzi 4:186–7
        Han Feizi 4:219–20
        Huainanzi 4:512–13
        Jia Yi 5:102
        Legalism 5:531, 5:533–5,
            5:536–7
        Marxism **6:133–41**
        Sunzi 9:230–1
    civic theology (Toland, J.) 9:428
    commonwealth (Hobbes, T.)
        4:459–60, 4:471–3
    communism **2:462–4**
    communitarianism **2:464–71**
    confederalism **3:572–4**
    Confucianism
        order 2:538
    conservatism **2:608–15**
    constitutionalism **2:618–22**
    contractarianism **2:657–65**
        Gassendi, P. 3:855–6
        Rousseau, J.-J. 8:368, 8:371–2
    critique of 7:526–7
    cultural identity 2:745
    culture
        Helvétius, C.-A. 4:346–8
        Schleiermacher, F. 8:536–7
    Daoism 2:789
    deconstruction (Derrida, J.) 2:899
    democracy **2:867–72**
        Jefferson, T. 5:84–5

Diderot, D.
    Rousseau, J.-J. contrast 3:65
différends (disputes) (Lyotard, J.-
    F.) 6:9
education 3:235–6
fascism **3:561–3**
    Gentile, G. 4:22
federalism **3:572–4**
feminist **3:614–21**
government (Kauṭilya) 5:220–1
green **4:159–66**
historicism
    Popper, K.R. critique 7:536
history of **7:503–18**
    ancient
        Greek 7:505–6
        Roman 7:506–8
    contemporary commercial
        society 7:513–14
    French Revolution
        responses to 7:514–15
    idealism 7:515–16
    Marxism 7:516–17
    medieval 7:508–9
    natural rights theory 7:511–13
    The Reformation 7:510–11
    Renaissance 7:509–10
    toleration 7:511
Hobbes, T.
    Spinoza, B. de comparison
        9:105–6
human nature (Arendt, H.) 1:370,
    1:371, 1:372
ideal states (Aristotle) 1:430
imperfect states (Aristotle) 1:430–1
Indian **7:521–5**
    structure 7:523–4
    varṇa 7:523
individual/society relationship
    (Nagel, T.) 6:646
interference with individual
    morality 5:438–42
Islam 5:14–15, **7:518–21**
Jewish state, modern
    (Leibowitz, Y.) 5:563–4
John of Salisbury 5:116
justice
    Smith, A. 8:819
    Thrasymachus 9:397–8
law
    cultural specificity (Diderot, D.)
        3:64–5, 3:68
legitimacy
    Weil, S. critique 9:700
liberalism **5:598–605**
    Croce, B. 2:730, 2:732
libertarianism **5:617–19**

Luther, M. 6:2–3
market economy (Smith, A.)
  8:815, 8:820
Marsilius of Padua 6:112–13
Marxism
  Chinese **6:133–41**
  Frankfurt School **3:730–7**
  Latin American **6:160–5**
  Russian **6:150–6**
  Soviet **6:150–6**
  Western **6:141–7**
methodological individualism
  (Popper, K.R.) 7:536
Mexico 6:347
Mohism 6:452
monistic idealism
  (Radhakrishnan, S.) 8:24–5
Montesquieu, C.L. 6:490, 6:492–3
moral pluralism 6:529, 6:530
nationalism **6:657–62**
  Herder, J.G. 4:383–4
natural law
  Hamann, J.G. critique 4:217
natural right (Fichte, J.G.) 3:650–1
natural rights (Paine, T.) 7:184–5
nature of **7:525–8**
objective spirit (Hegel, G.W.F.)
  4:273–4
objectivist assumption
  (Polanyi, M.) 7:491
perfectionism 7:301–2
physis-nomos debate 7:382
Plato
  Republic 7:413–14
    philosopher-ruler 7:400–1,
    7:414
pluralism
  German Romanticism 8:350
positivism (Comte, A.) 2:498
pragmatism 7:638
public virtues (Smith, A.) 8:820
Rawls, J. **8:106–10**
religion **8:224–30**
Renaissance 8:267
  Molina, L. de 6:464
republicanism **8:280–3**
  Cicero, M.T. 2:356–7
revolution **8:301–4**
self-respect 8:637
social democracy **8:827–8**
socialism **8:879–86**
state, the **9:120–3**
state of nature (Hobbes, T.)
  4:470–1
technology and ethics 9:283
theological principles
  (Cieszkowski, A.) 2:361

totalitarianism **9:442–4**
  environmental ethics 3:334
  Popper, K.R. 7:536–7
traditionalism
  German Romanticism 8:350
utopianism (Zeno of Citium) 9:842
value pluralism (Berlin, I.) 1:750,
  1:751–2
values
  social science 8:843
William of Ockham 9:732–3,
  9:734, 9:745–6
Zionism (Leibowitz, Y.) 5:563
political realism
  international relations 4:826,
  4:827–8
  war and peace 9:685–6, 9:688
political representation **8:270–2**
  see also democracy; government;
  state
political science
  ideology 4:683
political theology **9:331–3**
politics
  see also government; political
  philosophy; state
  aesthetics relationship
    Frankfurt School 1:67
  art relationship (Belinskii, V.G.)
    1:709, 1:711, 1:712
  artificial distinctions
    (Wollstonecraft, M.) 9:789–90
  comparative (Bryce, J.) 2:41
  deliberative (Habermas, J.) 4:197–8
  downgrading of
    Stoicism 9:156–7
  economics
    Keynes, J.M. 5:234–5
  social science
    history of philosophy of
    8:851
  epistemology relationship
    (Comte, A.) 2:500–1
  ethics
    Aristotle 1:427
    Weber, M. 9:696
  global
    development ethics 3:39–42
  historical context 7:505
  journalism ethics 5:127
  law relationship 5:464, 5:467–8
    Critical Legal Studies 2:715–16
  liberalism
    Kant, I. 5:195
  libidinal (Lyotard, J.-F.) 6:8
  mathematical calculation
    (Archytas) 1:368–9

participation in
  communitarian critique of
    liberalism 2:466, 2:467
party (Burke, E.) 2:136, 2:138
philosophy relationship
  Heidegger, M. 4:326
  Xenophon 9:813–14
Plato
  involvement in 7:401–2
political reform
  Shōtoku Constitution 8:753
pravosoznanie (right-
  consciousness) (Il'in, I.A.)
  4:693–4
reason relationship (Jaspers, K.)
  5:81–2
revolution
  Kant, I. critique 5:195
rhetoric (Aristotle) 1:431
rule of law 5:467
  separation of powers 8:388–9,
  8:390
safety of the people
  (Hutcheson, F.) 4:592
scientific basis (Hobbes, T.) 4:461,
  4:474–5
self-government (Price, R.) 7:676,
  7:678–9
stability
  corruption 2:675
  federations 3:573
  justice as fairness 8:108
  state law (Austin, J.) 1:569
  systems theory 9:254–5
women's rights
  see also feminist philosophy
  Latin America 3:626–7
Politics see Aristotle
Politische Rechtstheorie see Critical
  Legal Studies
Polkinghorne, J.C. 8:296
Pollack, M. 7:631
Pollock, G. 3:409, 3:596
Pollock, John L.
  concept of knowledge 5:276
  defeasibility theory of knowledge
    4:56, 4:59, 5:279
  empiricism 3:303
  epistemic paradoxes 7:214
  internalism–externalism
    distinction 4:826
  practical reasoning/rationality
    8:103
pollution 3:335
Polonsky, S. 9:526
Polotsky, H.J. 6:77
Póltawski, A. 4:792

Poltoratzskii, N. 4:696, 8:428
Polyaenus 3:350, 3:351
polyphony 1:642–3
polytheism
    see also monotheism; Orphism
    creation doctrine 2:695
    descriptive 6:480, 6:481, 6:482–3
    pre-Columbian religions 5:429,
        5:430
    Stoicism 9:146
    the supernatural 7:97
polyvalency of meaning 4:393, 4:394
Poma, A. 2:402
Pomeau, Y. 2:279
Pomedli, M.M. 6:671
Pomian, K. 7:596
Pompa, L.
    Vico, G. †9:599–606
Pompeo Faracovi, O. 2:376
Pomper, P. 5:438
Pomponatius, Petrus *see*
        Pomponazzi, Pietro
Pomponazzi, Pietro **7:529–33**
    Aristotelianism 1:405, 7:529–31
    immortality 1:409–10
    naturalism
        Mersenne, M. refutation 6:326
    Overton, R. 7:177
Ponce, Anibal 6:161
Poncelet, J.V. 4:34, 9:65
Poniatowska, Elena 5:655, 5:657
Pontalis, J.B. 3:588, 3:793, 7:823
Poole, D. 7:34
Pope, W. 3:177
popes *see* individual names
Popkin, Richard H.
    Charron, P. †2:287–90
    clandestine literature 2:376
    Condorcet, M.J.A.N. 2:532
    Conway, A. 2:671
    Cudworth, R. 2:744
    Erasmus, D. 3:401
    faith 3:543
    Foucher, S. 3:717–18
    Gassendi, P. 3:857
    Glanvill, J. 4:83
    Huet, P.-D. 4:518
    libertins 5:621
    Mersenne, M. 6:331
    Montaigne, M.E. de †6:485–9
    prophecy 7:771
    Sanches, F. †8:451–4
    scepticism, Renaissance
        †8:498–504
Popper, Karl Raimund **7:533–40**
    anti-Semitism 1:314

critical rationalism
    Kuhn, T.S. critique 5:317
critiques of
    Kuhn, T.S. 5:317
    Lakatos, I. 5:343
dualism 3:138
economics
    philosophy of 3:217–18, 3:221
epiphenomenalism 3:354
evolutionary theory and social
    science 3:487
explanation 3:525
fallibilism 3:548
falsificationism 7:533, 7:534
    economics 3:217–18
fascism 3:563
historicism 4:445, 4:446
history
    philosophy of 4:455–6, 4:458–9
holism and individualism in
    history and social science 4:488
induction/demarcation problems
    7:534–5
instrumentalism critique 8:582
Kuhn, T.S. 5:318
logic of discovery 3:99, 3:101,
    3:103
Marx, K. 6:133
natural laws 5:475
open–closed distinction
    application to African cultures
        1:118, 1:119, 1:121
Parmenides 7:235
Plato 7:420
politics 7:536–7
positivism in the social sciences
    7:561
Presocratics 7:672
probability, interpretations of
    7:705
processes 7:722, 7:723
psychoanalysis
    methodological issues in 7:811,
        7:812, 7:817
science
    demarcation problem 2:863,
        2:864, 2:866
        falsifiability 2:863
    realism and antirealism 8:584
    simplicity 8:782, 8:783
social science
    contemporary philosophy of
        8:847
    evolutionary theory 3:487
    methodology of 8:868
    positivism in 7:559
testimony 9:314

The Logic of Scientific Discovery
    induction/demarcation
        problems 7:534–5
    totalitarianism 7:536–7, 9:443,
        9:444
    tradition and traditionalism 9:445,
        9:447
    underdetermination 9:528
    utopianism 9:559, 9:561
    World 3 7:535
Poppi, A. 1:413, 2:175, 6:872
population
    ethics **7:540–3**
    genetics 4:12
    policy
        obligations to future
            generations 3:819
populism
    Critical Legal Studies 2:715
    Russian (Mikhailovskii, N.K.)
        6:355
Porchat Pereira, O. 1:231
Pörn, I. 8:492
pornography **7:543–5**
    erotic art relationship 3:406,
        3:408–9
    freedom of speech 3:763
    harm principle
        law and morality 5:441
Porphyry **7:545–50**
    Aristotle commentators 1:435
    Boethius 1:805, 1:806
    colonial philosophy
        Latin America 5:422, 5:425
    Enneads
        editorship 7:548
        ethics 7:547–8
    individuation (Kilwardby, R.)
        5:247
    influence on Islamic philosophy
        5:709
    Isagōgē
        Boethius 1:805, 1:806
        colonial philosophy
            Latin America 5:422, 5:425
        influence on Islamic philosophy
            5:709
    literary theory 7:548
    metaphysics
        language 7:546–7
    Neoplatonism
        founding of 6:799
    Pythagoras 7:856
    rationale/ratione uti problem
        (Gerbert of Aurillac) 4:40
    universals
        Albert the Great 1:146–7

319

medieval Platonism 7:434
Porrit, J. 4:166
Porro, P. 4:360
Porset, C. 5:379
Port, R. 1:492
Portale, V. 4:80
Portalie, E. 1:559
Porter, R.
    Enlightenment, continental 3:319,
        3:320
    Hartley, D. †4:236–8
    Johnson, S. †5:122–3
Portnoy, J. 1:369
Port-Royal **7:550–5**
    see also Arnauld, A.; Jansenism
    intensional entities 4:803
    language 5:373–4
    logic
        Arnauld, A. 1:444
        seventeenth century 5:717–18
    Pascal, B. 7:242–3
    religious toleration 7:552
Portugal
    Abravanel, I. **1:19–23**
    Abravanel, J. **1:23–7**
    Brazil, philosophy in 2:7–8
    Collegium Conimbricense **2:406–8**
    Fonseca, P. da **3:687–90**
    John of St Thomas **5:117–20**
    Molina, L. de **6:461–5**
    Peter of Spain **7:324–5**
Porzio, Simone 1:410
Posidonius **7:555–8**
    Cleomedes 2:385, 2:386
positive aesthetics 6:734
positive law
    a priorism (Reinach, A.) 8:180–1
    Aquinas, T. 6:688
    equity principles (Stair, J.D.) 9:119
    Legalism
        China 5:448–9
    medieval philosophy
        political (Aquinas, T.) 7:508–9
    sovereignty (Austin, J.) 1:569, 9:57
    value-relevance 5:466–7
positive morality
    Austin, J. 1:569
    Hart, H.L.A. 4:235
positive philosophy
    Schelling, F.W.J. von 8:509, 8:514,
        8:515–16
positive philosophy *see* positivism
positive reals
    relations
        Navya-Nyāya theory of 2:850–1
positive religion
    Hegel, G.W.F. 4:262

positivism
    see also anti-positivism;
    empiricism; European positivism;
    evolutionary positivism; legal
    positivism; social positivism
    anthropologism (Lavrov, P.L.)
        5:436
    Argentina, philosophy in 1:376
    autochthonous 7:565, 7:566
    challenges to
        Latin American
            phenomenology 7:348, 7:350
    Comte, A. 2:496–7, 2:501, 2:502–3
    Comtean
        Brazil 2:10
    Condorcet, M.J.A.N. 2:528
    critical theory 2:724, 2:725
        Habermas, J. 4:194–5
    critiques of
        Planck, M.K.E.L. 7:396–7
        scientific realism 8:584–5
    epistemological naturalism 6:718
    evolutionary
        Latin America 7:565, 7:566–7
    experimentation 3:515
    general relativity 4:5–6
    hermeneutics conflict 2:721
    historicism
        Jewish philosophy 5:86
    history
        philosophy of 4:455
    Italian Enlightenment 5:37
    Latin America 1:304, 1:306–7,
        5:427, **7:565–70**
    Marxism
        Russian 8:405
    Mexico 6:345
    nihilist movement
        Russian 7:5–8
    Poland 7:486
    Russian **7:561–4**
    science 7:565
        archaeology 1:354–5
    in the social sciences **7:558–61**
        criticisms of 7:560–1
        doctrines 7:558–9
        history of philosophy of 8:848,
            8:851–2, 8:855
        influence on practice 7:559–60
        logical positivism 7:558–9
    technology
        Il'enkov, E.V. critique 4:690–1
    Victorian 8:566
Posner, R. 8:679
possession *see* ownership

possibility
    definitions
        Diodorus Cronus 3:85
        Philo the Dialectician 7:364–5
    imagination 4:707–8
    interdefinability with necessity
        6:427
    master argument (Diodorus
        Cronus) 3:83, 3:84, 3:85–6
    modal logic 6:417–18, 6:419,
        6:427–9
        ability 6:431–2
        counterparts 6:430–1
    modal operators 6:433–6
    realism
        Armstrong, D.M. 1:443
possible things
    Ibn al-'Arabi 4:603
possible worlds **7:570–3**
    see also possible worlds semantics
    ability 6:431–2
    anti-essentialism 3:418
    best of all 3:467–8, 3:470
        evil, problem of 3:467–8, 3:470
        philosophical optimism
            (Leibniz, G.W.) 5:542, 5:544,
            5:545, 5:550
    closeness of (Lewis, D.K.) 5:591
    counterfactual conditionals
        2:685–8
        Lewis, D.K. 5:591–2
    deontic logic 2:888–9
    divine will (Wolff, C.) 9:783
    epistemic logic 3:355–7
    evil, problem of 3:468–9
    existence 6:428–9, 6:430
    as fictions 7:571–2
    identity
        Lewis, D.K. 5:591, 5:592
        transworld 4:677, 6:430
            counterparts 6:430–1
    indicative conditionals 4:741
    intensional entities 4:804
    intensional logics 4:807, 4:808–10
    Lewis, D.K.
        Kripke, S.A. critique 5:302–3
        modal logic 5:765, 6:418, 6:419–21,
            6:422–4
            semantics of 6:426, 6:427–8
        modal operators 6:434, 6:435
        model theory 6:441
    natural place doctrine (Crescas, H.)
        2:703
    nominalism 7:22
    propositional attitudes 7:781–2

possible worlds semantics (PWS)
8:650–1, **8:662–9**
conditional logic 8:665–6
Hintikka, J. 8:488
modal logic 8:663–4
Montague, R.M. 6:484, 8:666–7
temporal logic 8:665
possiblism
Næss, A. 6:635
Post, Emil Leon **7:573–5**
completeness problem 4:118
computability 2:353
logic
early twentieth century 5:738
predicate calculus 7:665
proof theory 7:751
Post, H.R. 2:299
Post, R.R. 9:374
Post, W. 8:238
postcolonialism **7:578–83**
see also development ethics
philosophy of science **7:575–8**
political philosophy
Indian 7:524
Postel, Guillaume 5:24
Postema, G.J. 1:725, 2:446, 5:521
post-empiricism
science
androcentricism 3:863–4
Poster, Mark
Baudrillard, J. †1:661–3
Lefebvre, H 5:491
Posterior Analytics see Aristotle
postglossators *see* commentators
post-Marxism
civil society 2:370
postmodern theology **7:583–6**
negative theology 7:584–5
postmodernism **7:586–90**
alterity and identity **1:187–92**
anarchism 1:247
anti-postmodernism **7:593–6**
architecture 1:365
assumptions 7:587
consumer culture (Baudrillard, J.)
1:662–3
critique
Habermas, J. 4:198
critiques of
French **7:593–6**
episteme 7:588
existentialism 3:500, 3:501
feminism 3:619
functionalism contrast 3:813
historical context 7:587–8
language and gender 5:363

logical empiricism (Hempel, C.G.)
4:348–9, 4:350–1
Lyotard, J.-F. 6:8–9
midrash analogy 6:354
modernism 6:449, 7:587–8, 7:589
moral relativism 8:222
political philosophy **7:590–3**
post-structuralism distinction
9:200
reflexiveness 7:587, 7:588,
7:589–90
relativism 8:190
revolution 8:301, 8:303
social science
contemporary theories of 8:839,
8:840, 8:843–5, 8:846
social theory and law 8:873, 8:878
subject
critique of **9:196–201**
the sublime 9:204
truth 7:589
Postone, M. 1:850
post-structuralism **7:596–600**
consumer culture (Baudrillard, J.)
1:662–3
linguistics (Man, P. de) 2:811
literary studies 7:598–9
Barthes, R. 1:656, 1:657
postmodernism 7:587, 9:200
psychoanalytic feminism 3:584,
3:585
in the social sciences **7:600–4**
Lyotard 7:602–4
structuralism 9:175, 9:176
Poteat, W. 7:492
potential intellect
al-Farabi 3:556
potentiality
change (Aristotle) 1:420–1
eternal objects (Whitehead, A.N.)
9:716
Indian theories of **7:604–8**
decomposition of complex
beings 7:605–6
God 7:604–5
language 7:607
matter
Sāṅkhya-Yoga dualism 6:199
virtue 7:606–7
Pothier, Robert Joseph **7:608–9**
Potrč, Matijaž 9:55
Potter, E. 3:592, 3:601, 8:223
Potter, J. 1:695
Potter, Karl H.
Brahman 2:4
causation
Indian theories of 2:257

definition
Indian concepts of 2:852
Gaṅgeśa 3:846
God
Indian conceptions of 4:105
heaven
Indian concepts of 4:256
Hinduism 4:440
inference
Indian theories of 4:759, 4:766
monism
Indian 6:479
Nyāya-Vaiśeṣika 7:66
ontology in Indian philosophy
7:127–8
Śaṅkara 8:461
Udayana 9:514
Uddyotakara 9:516
Vātsyāyana 9:588
Vedānta 9:594
Potter, M.E. 3:625
Potter, Michael D.
arithmetic †1:437–41
set theory †8:709–16
Potter, N. 9:539
Potter, V.R. 1:773, 1:776, 6:264
Potts, T.C. 2:581
Poulain, A. 8:255
Poulain de la Barre, F. 3:578, 3:583,
9:212
Poulantzas, N. 7:611, 7:613
Pound, Roscoe **7:609–10**
justice, equity and law 5:151, 5:153
legal realism 5:522, 5:525
Poundstone, W. 6:813
poverty
see also liberation theology
developing countries
agricultural ethics 1:126–7
development ethics 3:39–42
libertarianism 5:617–18, 5:619
poverty of stimulus (POS) 4:52–3
Powell, G.B. 9:256
Powell, J.G.F. 2:360
power **7:610–13**
see also authority
absolute
sovereignty 9:56–7, 9:58
agency 7:611
divine *see* divine power
equality of
democracy 2:867
human
divine omnipotence
Islamic philosophy 4:63
relation to God 6:842
inner life (Epictetus) 3:338, 3:339

interests 7:610–11
judicial
    independence of 8:388, 8:390
knowledge relationship
    (Foucault, M.) 3:711
normative 7:611
patriarchalism (Filmer, R.) 3:678
post-structuralism (Foucault, M.)
    7:602
republicanism 8:280, 8:281
sacred
    phenomenology of religion
        7:354–5
secondary qualities (Locke, J.)
    5:671
separation of
    British constitutional law
        3:62–3
    rule of law 8:388–9, 8:390
social
    scientific responsibility 8:289
sovereign (Spinoza, B. de) 9:105
spiritual-temporal distinction
    Giles of Rome 4:75
    John of Paris 5:113–14
state of nature (Hobbes, T.) 4:470
temporal (Giles of Rome) 4:75
types of
    political philosophy
        Indian 7:523–4
values 7:611–12
power set algebra 1:844, 1:845, 2:234
power set algebra 5:807
Powers, D. 5:460
Powers, J. 2:75, 4:740
Poyer, G. 2:168
Pozzo, R. 1:840
Prābhākara 6:377, 6:378, 6:379
    atheism 4:439
    meaning 4:436, 6:242, 6:380
    Mīmāṃsā 6:378, 6:381
    negative facts
        Indian philosophy 6:757
    self-certificationalism 3:391
    universals 6:379
    veridicality 3:411
practical ethics see applied ethics
practical intellect
    non-rational soul
        Islamic philosophy 9:40, 9:42,
            9:43
practical learning school see sirhak
practical morality
    Beattie, J. 1:678–9
practical philosophy
    Wolff, C. 9:780, 9:783

practical postulates
    morality (Kant, I.) 5:193
practical reason
    will 9:721, 9:723–4
practical reasoning 8:90–8:103, 8:90,
    8:100–1
    ethics 7:613–20
        act-oriented 7:614–15, 7:616–18
        categorical imperative (Kant, I.)
            5:200–1
        end-oriented 7:614, 7:615–16
        instrumentality 7:613, 7:615
        moral motivation 6:523–4
        sentiments (Kant, I.) 6:548–9
        theoretical reason distinction
            7:613, 7:618
        values 9:582
    expected utility theory 8:90
    Game theory 8:90
    instrumental/non-instrumental
        distinction 8:93
    Kant, I. 5:178, 5:183, 5:189–95,
        5:200–1, 6:548–9
    maximization/anti-maximization
        8:96–8
    morality 8:100–1
    motivational power 8:90–1
    planning 8:98
    principle-based 8:99–8:100
    rational action 8:90, 8:93
    theoretical reason contrast 8:90,
        8:91
    theories of 8:90, 8:92–3,
        8:99–8:100
    uncertainty situations 8:98
    value conflict 8:96–7
practice
    see also codes of practice; praxis
    belief relationship
        Torah (Duran, P.) 3:170
    definition 9:357
    ethics
        Chinese Confucianism 2:537
        Japanese Buddhism 2:105
    scientific
        naturalized philosophy of
            science 6:728
    theory relationship 9:356–9
    truth
        criterion of (Bogdanov, A.A.)
            1:818
Prade, H. 3:824
pradhāna (primal matter) 6:197, 6:199
Praechter, K. 4:422
pragmatic a priori
    Lewis, C.I. 5:585, 5:586, 5:587
pragmatic presupposition 7:674–5

pragmatic theory of truth 7:635–7,
    9:478–80
pragmatic virtues see virtues,
    theoretical/epistemic
pragmaticism see pragmatism
pragmatics 5:408–9, 7:620–33
    see also implicature; semantics
    communicative intentions 7:628
    context 7:621–2, 7:623–4, 7:627
    indexicals 7:623
    intentional-inferential model
        7:628–9
    modularity 7:629
    paradoxes 7:622
    possible worlds semantics
        (Montague, R.M.) 6:484
    presupposition 7:626–7
    semantics distinction 7:624–6
pragmatism 7:633–40
    see also instrumentalism
    a priori 1:5
    African philosophy, Francophone
        (Hountondji, P.) 1:112–13
    American (Mead, G.H.) 6:210–12
    conversational implicature
        (Grice, H.P.) 4:172–3, 4:174–5
    Dewey, J. 1:205
    epistemic
        Yogācāra Buddhism 3:388–9
    ethical see ethical pragmatism
    Hegelianism 4:287–8
    humanism 4:528, 4:530–1
    induction 4:747–8
    James, W. 1:204–5, 5:60, 5:61,
        5:64–5, 8:379
    naturalized philosophy of science
        6:730
    Peirce, C.S. 7:270, 7:273–4, 7:279
    rational beliefs 8:62
    reality (Schiller, F.C.S) 8:523
    science, nineteenth century
        philosophy of 8:566
    toleration 9:431
    transcendental (Lorenzen, P.)
        5:827–8
    truth 9:478–9
    veridicality
        error and illusion
            Indian concepts of 3:411–12
Prague School 9:178–9
praise 7:644–7
    see also merit; moral luck;
        rectification; remainders
    desert 7:645
    perfect goodness 4:142
    supererogation 9:234
Prajñā Schools of Buddhism 2:82

Prajñākaramati
  Mādhyamika Buddhism 2:60
Prajñāpāramitā (Perfection of
  Wisdom) 2:78
Prajñāpāramitā-sūtras
  Chinese Mādhyamika Buddhism
    9:792
Prakash, B. 7:524
Prakash, G. 7:582
prakṛti
  Sāṅkhya 8:461, 8:462–4, 8:466
    causation 8:465
    existence proofs 8:465
  Sāṅkhya-Yoga dualism 6:199–200
pramāṇa (instruments of knowledge)
  5:51, 5:280–5, 7:62–4, 9:587–8
Prandstetter, J. 7:66
Prang, H. 8:352
Prasad, R. 5:218
Prāsaṅgika School of Buddhism 2:60,
  2:61, 9:403–4, 9:489
Praśastapāda
  Nyāya-Vaiśeṣika 7:66
  ontology 7:122, 7:123, 7:128
  qualities 7:122, 7:123
  universals 9:548
  Vaiśeṣika
    inference 4:764
pratītyasamutpā see suffering,
  Buddhism
Pratt, Vernon 1:118, 1:121
Pratt, V.R. 3:189, 3:191, 8:669
Prauss, Gerold 5:199
pravosoznanie (right-consciousness)
  4:693–4
Prawer, S. 8:352
Prawitz, Dag
  antirealism
    mathematics 1:311
  Gentzen, G.K.E. 4:25
  Gödel's theorems 4:118
  Hilbert's programme and
    formalism 4:429
  intuitionistic logic 4:862–3
  logical laws 5:789
  natural deduction 4:859, 8:486,
    8:491
  natural deduction, tableau and
    sequent systems 6:682
  proofs 4:858
praxeology 7:647–9
  language games
    heterogeneity (Lyotard, J.-F.)
      6:9
    Kotarbiński, T. 5:295
praxis
  Cieszkowski, A. 2:360, 2:361

idealist theory of (Gentile, G.) 4:22
Lambriola, A. 5:335
Marx, K. 6:121, 6:123
South Slavs, philosophy of 9:52
Young Hegelians 2:361
prayer 7:649–53
  communal (Ibn Miskawayh) 4:632
  for the dead 7:836, 7:837, 7:838
  eternality of God 3:424
  evil, problem of 7:651–2
  Jewish philosophy (Judah ben
    Moses of Rome) 5:130
  omniscience
    implications for 7:649–50
  petitionary 7:650–1, 7:652
  process theology 7:718
  ritual 8:338, 8:340–1
  spiritual growth
    Christianity 8:455–6
precalabrian civilization 2:7
precognition
  paranormal phenomena 7:222
pre-Columbian thought 5:428–32
  Mexican philosophy 6:344, 6:345,
    6:347
Predaval Magrini, M.V. 3:560
predestination 7:653–7
  see also divine election;
  reprobation
  'Abduh, M. 1:7
  Anselm of Canterbury 1:294
  Aquinas, T. 8:273–4
  Augustine 8:273
  Calvin, J. 2:177, 2:180
  Carolingian renaissance 2:222
  divine
    Eriugena's denial of 3:402
  divine foreknowledge
    (Gassendi, P.) 3:855
  Farrer, A.M. 3:561
  foreknowledge distinction
    (Joachim of Fiore) 5:104
  free will, reconciliation with
    (Augustine) 1:549, 1:553
  'ilm al-kalam 5:28
  limits of life (Schurman, A.M.
    van) 8:558
  Luther, M. 8:274
  material constraints on freedom
    (Sartre, J.-P.) 8:477
  Molinism 6:466
  necessary beings (al-'Amiri)
    1:207–8
  Pelagianism 7:285
  reprobation 8:273
predetermination
  Islamic moral philosophy 3:438

predisposition distinction
  genetic discrimination 4:17
predicables
  Aristotle 5:687, 9:206
  Islamic philosophy 5:709
predicate calculus 7:657–65
  arguments 7:658–9
  completeness 7:660–1
  deduction 7:663–4
  notation 7:657–8
  ontological commitment
    (Quine, W.V.) 8:7–8
  sentential logic 7:659–60
  truth 7:661–3
predicate logic
  see also first-order logic; second-
  order logic
  Aristotelian logic contrast 5:783
  dynamic 3:190–1
  free logics 3:739–40
  singular identity 4:678–9
predicate operators
  adverbs 1:46, 1:47, 1:48–9
predicate-in-notion principle 3:376
predicates
  see also predicate logic; predicate
  operators; predication
  adverbs 1:46, 1:47, 1:48–9
  determinacy of meaning 4:860
  Frege, G. 3:766–7
  modal operators as 6:433, 6:434–5
  religious language 8:256, 8:258–9
  truth conditional semantics 6:220,
    6:221, 6:223
  verb phrases 9:247
predication 7:665–7
  see also predicates
  analogical (Collins, A.) 2:417
  Aristotle 1:418, 5:687
  concrete (Wodeham, A.) 9:774
  explanation (Strawson, P.F.)
    9:170–1
  external representation
    (Crathorn, W.) 2:693
  lekton
    Stoicism 9:148–9
  manifoldness, Jaina theory of 6:77,
    6:79–81
  Plato
    analytic study by Vlastos, G.
      9:652
  property theory 7:761–6
  slovo ('the word') (Shpet, G.G.)
    8:756
  transposition (Gilbert of Poitiers)
    4:70–1
  Trinity (Wodeham, A.) 9:774

universals (Wyclif, J.) 9:802–3
predicativism
  constructivism in mathematics
    2:637–8
prediction
  chaos theory 2:277–8
  determinism distinction 6:254
  evolutionary theory 3:481
  explanation relation
    (Hempel, C.G.) 4:350
  physics
    determinism and indeterminism
    3:35
  in the social sciences **8:871–2**
    reflexivity 8:865–6
    self-modifying effect 8:871–2
predisposition
  predetermination distinction
    genetic discrimination 4:17
  Sāṅkhya 8:466
pre-established harmony
  Leibniz, G.W. 5:288
  Wolff, C. 9:782
pre-eternality
  Mir Damad, Muhammad Baqir
    6:409–10
pre-existence
  soul 9:46, 9:47–8
preface paradox 7:211–12
preference
  desire distinction 3:31–2
  economics 3:215
  rational choice theory 8:64, 8:69
  revealed
    utility as 9:553
preference-affecting proposals
  coercion 2:388
preferential models
  non-monotonic logic 7:32–4
preferential treatment *see* affirmative
  action
preformation 5:633
  Bonnet, C. 1:839
  vitalism 9:641–2
pregiveness
  lifeworld (Husserl, E.) 4:583–4
Preisendanz, Karin
  Gautama, A. †3:859–61
  materialism, Indian school of
    †6:178–81
  Nyāya-Vaiśeṣika †7:57–6
prejudice
  see also discrimination; race;
  racism
  hermeneutics (Gadamer, H.-G.)
    3:829
Premack, David 6:386, 6:389–90

Prentice, R. 3:169
Preobrazhenskii, V.P. 6:863–4
pres-abs-ence 4:310
Presbyterianism 4:505–6
prescriptivism **7:667–71**
  see also descriptivism
  akrasia (Hare, R.M.) 1:142
  fact/value distinction 3:538
  Hare, R.M. 1:142, 4:229–31,
    9:537–8
  universalism in ethics (Hare, R.M.)
    9:537–8
  utilitarianism relationship 9:555
presence
  divine immutability 4:711–12
  logocentricity (Derrida, J.) 2:896,
    2:898
  metaphysics of (Derrida, J.) 7:584
  mortal becoming (Heidegger, M.)
    4:310
Présence Africaine 2:170–1
present
  experience (Mamardashvili, M.K.)
    6:69
presentations
  content/object distinction
    (Twardowski, K.) 9:508
Preserved Tablet
  al-Ghazali 4:66
  Ibn Massara 4:628, 4:629
Presocratics **7:671–2**
  Alcmaeon 1:160–1
  analytic interpretation (Vlastos, G.)
    9:651
  Anaxagoras 1:249–53
  Anaximander 1:255–9
  Anaximenes 1:259–62
  Archytas 1:366–9
  atonement 1:536
  chemistry 2:295
  Cratylus 2:694
  Democritus 2:872–7
  Diogenes of Apollonia 3:87–9
  dominant concerns of 1:262, 1:263
  Empedocles 3:293–8
  Gorgias 4:144–6
  Heraclitus 4:364–9
  Hesiod 4:412–13
  influence of
    Islamic philosophy 4:158
  Leucippus 5:578–9
  matter 6:193
  Melissus 6:292–5
  naturalism/religion relationship
    9:651
  Parmenides 7:229–34
  Philolaus 7:367–70

political philosophy
  history of 7:505–6
  Pythagoras 7:854–7
  Thales 9:322–4
  Thucydides 9:398–9
  Xenophanes 9:807–10
  Zeno of Elea 9:843–5
Prestwich, M. 2:182
presumption
  role in interpretation
    hermeneutics 4:387–8
  as source of knowledge
    Indian thought 5:282–3
presupposition **7:672–5**
  descriptions 3:23
  implicature 4:724–5
  induction 4:746–7
  inheritance of 7:673
  logical constants (Strawson, P.F.)
    9:169–70
  pragmatics 7:626–7, 7:672, 7:674–5
  semantic 7:672, 7:674
  sociological theories 9:3–4
  Strawsonian 7:672, 7:673–4,
    9:169–70
presuppositionless description
  epistemic issues in phenomenology
    7:344–5
pretence
  fiction 3:661
  metarepresentational theory of
    child's theory of mind 6:387,
    6:388
preterition *see* reprobation
preternatural 4:147
Prets, E. 7:66
Preuß, Ulrich K.
  constitutionalism †2:618–22
Preucel, R.W. 1:359
'pre-understanding'
  hermeneutics 4:391
Prevost, R. 2:652
Prezelecki, M. 9:353–4
Prezioso, F. 6:115, 6:203
Pribram, K. 3:793
Price, A.W.
  Hare, R.M. †4:229–31
  love 5:845
  Plato 7:420
  sexuality 8:728–9
Price, G. 6:813
Price, H.H.
  eschatology 3:417
  Hume, D. 4:562
  mental world 3:415–16
  Newman, J.H. 6:823
  perception 7:299

Prichard, H.A. 7:682
  sense-data 3:300–1, 3:303, 8:698
  testimony 9:314
Price, Huw 9:478
Price, K. 3:231, 5:356
Price, Richard **7:675–9**
  ethical rationalism 7:675, 7:676–7
  Hutcheson, F. 4:594, 7:676
  moral agency 7:677–8
  self-government 7:676, 7:678–9
Prichard, Harold Arthur **7:679–82**
  intuitionism in ethics 4:856
  knowledge 5:276
  moral justification 6:516
  psychological certainty 1:708,
    1:709
Priest, Graham
  logical laws 5:789
  numbers †7:47–54
  paraconsistent logic †7:208–11
Priestley, Joseph **7:682–4**
  Oswald, J. 7:170
  utilitarianism 9:557
Priestly, F.E.L. 2:380
Prigogine, I. 9:369
prima facie duties
  conflict 3:179–80
  moral action (Ross, W.D.) 8:366
'primary goods'
  welfare (Rawls, J.) 9:704
primary linguistic data (PLD) 2:335,
  2:336
primary object of the intellect
  3:158–60
primary process
  unconscious fantasies (Freud, S.)
    3:790
Primas, H. 2:299–300
primates
  language experiments 1:269,
    1:271–2
Primavesi, O. 3:59, 3:298
prime matter
  Aristotelianism
    seventeenth century 1:388–9
    Simplicius 8:789
prime mover 3:160–1, 3:162–3
  see also First Mover
Primer, I. 6:74
primitive peoples
  Lévi-Strauss, C. 5:583, 5:584
primitivism
  Diderot, D. 3:65–6
Primorac, Igor 9:55
Primoratz, I. 1:848, 2:711, 8:729
primordial awareness
  Chinese philosophy 8:623–5

primordial matter
  formless
    potentiality of 2:377
Prince, A. 2:578
Prince, S. 2:578
Principe, W.H. 1:178
Principia Mathematica see
  Russell, B.A.W.;
  Whitehead, A.N.
principle of charity *see* charity,
  principle of
principles
  see also arché
  Chinese philosophy (Zhu Xi) 9:683
  policies distinction (Dworkin, R.)
    3:187
principles, eternal
  al-Razi, Abu Bakr 8:111
Pringle Pattison, A.S. 1:576
Pring-Mill, R.D.F. 5:664
printing 8:264
Prior Analytics see Aristotle
Prior, Arthur Norman **7:687–90**
  analyticity 1:238
  conventionalism 2:669
  Diodorus Cronus 3:86
  logic of ethical discourse 5:764
  logical constants 5:780
  many-valued logics 6:91
  Polish logic 7:498–9
  Prichard, H.A. 7:682
  tense logic 9:307
  time 9:416
Prior, E. 6:399
Prior, W.J. 1:374
Priscian 5:389
prison
  panopticon (Bentham, J.) 1:720
prisoner's dilemma
  game theory 2:831
  Hobbes, T. 4:473–4
  rational choice theory 8:67–8
  sociobiology 8:893
  solidarity 9:24
  state of nature 2:659
Pritchard, M.S. 3:315
privacy **7:690–3**
  see also private language argument
  adverbial theory of mental states
    6:314–15
  epistemic 7:699
  information technology and ethics
    4:779–80
  journalism ethics 5:126, 5:128
  mental events (Frege, G.) 3:770–1
  mind 1:514

private language argument 2:711,
  7:693–8
  see also language games
  critique of (Gentile, G.) 4:21
  language acquisition 7:699, 7:700
  language manifestation 7:699,
    7:700
  other minds 7:173, 7:695
  private states 7:698, 7:699
  sensations 7:694–6
  sense-data 8:697
  transcendental arguments 9:452–3
  Wittgenstein, L. 9:765–6
private law
  government subservience
    rule of law 8:388–9
  Roman law/civilian tradition
    8:346–7
privation
  Thomas of York 9:375
pro-attitudes
  moral judgment 6:534
probabilism 5:157–8, 5:161–2,
  7:705–11
  see also Bayesian epistemology;
  confirmation theory
  degrees of belief 7:706
  doubt 3:122
  induction 4:748–9
  inference to the best explanation
    4:769
probability 5:503–5
  see also Bayesian epistemology;
  confirmation theory; probabilism
  causal laws 2:248
  classical statistics 9:123–4
  conditional 7:707–8
  confirmation theory
    Carnap, R. 2:212–13, 2:532–4
    C-systems 2:533
    Hempel, C.G. 4:349–50
    H-systems 2:534
  degrees of belief 7:707–8
  degrees of (Locke, J.) 5:676
  distributions
    causal models 9:130–2
    thermodynamics 9:367–8
  eliminative induction
    (Wright, G.H. von) 9:667
  expected utility 2:824–5
  frequency
    Reichenbach, H. 8:168
    Venn, J. 9:595
  God
    existence arguments
      (Tennant, F.R.) 9:302
  inductive inference 4:757, 4:758

inductive-statistical explanation
3:521–2, 3:523
influence on learning theories
5:485
interpretations of **7:701–5**
law 5:503–5
Baconian 5:504
Bayes' rule 5:504
proof 5:526
logic 7:710
De Morgan, A. 2:814
Leibniz, G.W. 5:553
Łukasiewicz, J. 5:860
logical positivism
(Reichenbach, H.) 8:167
medical diagnostic logic 6:266–7
objective 7:707–8
partial entailment (Ramsey, F.P.)
8:45
Peirce, C.S. 7:273–4
physics (Ramsey, F.P.) 8:46
projectivism 7:738
propensities (Popper, K.R.)
7:535–6
quantum field theory 3:670, 3:671,
3:672
randomness 8:56–7, 8:58
reasoning
rationality of belief 8:87, 8:88
St Petersburg paradox 2:823
science of man
(Condorcet, M.J.A.N.) 2:528,
2:529–30
scientific reasoning (Keynes, J.M.)
5:233–4
subjective 7:706
probability calculus
degrees of belief 7:706
probability induction
Broad, C.D. 2:24–5
probability theory
epistemology **7:705–11**
probative force
legal evidence 5:502
problem of evil *see* evil, problem of
problematics of philosophy
Latin American liberation
philosophy 5:611
problem-solving
classical AI 1:487
computation
connectionist networks 2:573–4
science
androcentric bias 3:864
logic of discovery 3:100
procedural natural law
Fuller, L.L. 3:801–2

proceduralism
art
definition of 1:464, 1:466
process empiricism
Bloch, E.S. 1:788
process philosophy **7:711–16**
Bergson, H.-L. 1:734
central task 7:711–12
'concrescence'/'transition'
7:712–13
mind–body problem 7:713
panexperientialism 7:713, 7:714
panpsychism 7:713
perception/prehension 7:713–14
science/religion reconciliation
7:714
process reliabilism
see also reliabilism
foundationalism 1:2
process theism **7:716–20**
classical theism comparison 7:716,
7:717–19
evil 8:245
miracles 6:412–13
providence 7:797, 7:799, 7:800,
7:801
process theology
Holocaust 4:495, 4:497–8
processes **7:720–3**
see also change
causation 7:721
events 7:720, 7:721–2
metaphysics 7:722–3
nature and types of 7:720–1
primitive
computational theories of mind
6:391
processing
parallel
connectionist AI 1:489–90
statistical 1:486
symbolic
connectionist AI 1:489
processualism
intention (Dostoevskii, F.M.)
3:116, 3:117
Procházka, Jiří 2:766, 2:769
Proclus **7:723–31**
Aristotle commentators 1:436
body–soul relationship 7:728–9
Chaldaean Oracles 2:274
eternity of the world defence 7:374
evil 7:727–8
God, concepts of 4:102
intelligibles 7:726–7
Liber de causis 5:595, 5:596
the One 7:726, 7:727

science 7:729–30
ultimate reality 4:95
Procopé, John
Hermetism †4:395–7
Seneca, L.A. 8:682
procreation
see also reproduction
evolutionary theory
(Buffon, G.L.L.) 2:122
Jewish bioethics 1:778–9
sexual concepts 8:719, 8:720
Proctor, R. 9:579
Prodicus **7:731–3**
productive intellect
universals grasp (Aristotle) 1:426
productivity
equality 3:394–5
nature (Schelling, F.W.J. von)
8:511
professional ethics **7:733–7**
see also business ethics;
engineering ethics; medical ethics;
nursing ethics
applied ethics 1:322
archaeology 1:357
information technology and ethics
4:780–1
journalism comparison 5:126
responsibilities of scientists and
intellectuals 8:287–8
Profiat Duran *see* Duran, Profiat
prognosis
logics of
philosophy of medicine 6:266–7
programming
see also computer science
artificial intelligence
evolutionary 1:491
high-level languages 1:487
toy example 1:486–7
genetic algorithms (GAs) 1:491
sequential 1:486–7
progress
empirical (Lakatos, I.) 3:217–18
evolutionary theory 3:482
historical
Berdiaev, N.A. 1:728
Bulgakov, S.N. 8:770
human nature
(Condorcet, M.J.A.N.) 2:528,
2:530–1
Russian communalism
(Mikhailovskii, N.K.) 6:356
scientific (Kuhn, T.S.) 5:316
subjective ethics (Lavrov, P.L.)
5:436

progressive hedonism
    moral theory (Ducasse, C.J.) 3:140
progressivism
    Indian philosophy
        Ramakrishna Movement 8:41
Prohászka, Lajos 4:570, 4:572
projection
    cognitive
        Yogācāra Buddhism critique
            2:68–9, 2:72
    induction 4:746–7
    psychic functioning (Jung, C.G.)
        5:133–4
    psychoanalysis (Klein, M.) 7:818,
        7:819, 7:821
projective geometry
    French school of 4:31
projectivism 7:737–40
prolēpsis (anticipation) 2:742
prolēpsis (preconception) 3:338,
    3:345, 3:346
Proletarian Culture (*Proletcult*) 1:818
Promies, W. 5:624
promising 7:740–2
    see also honour; trust
    a priori laws (Reinach, A.) 8:180
    artificial virtues (Hume, D.) 4:554
    intentional social acts
        (Reinach, A.) 8:181
    moral intuitionism
        (Prichard, H.A.) 7:681
pronominal anaphora
    Discourse Representation Theory
        3:93–4, 3:96–7
    Montague Grammar 3:92
    scope 8:588
pronouns
    see also anaphora; pronominal
    anaphora
    ambiguity 1:200
    descriptions 3:21
    reference 8:154, 8:161
    scope 8:588
proof
    see also proof theory
    burden of 5:500
        legal reasoning 5:525–6
        risk evaluation 5:500, 5:525–6,
            8:332
    conditional 5:800
    Lakatos, I. 5:342–3
    law 5:500, 5:501, 5:504
        see also legal evidence
        admissability 5:500–1
    probability 5:526
    procedures
        art criticism 1:460–1

propositions (Wyclif, J.) 9:802
proof theory 7:742–5
    formal systems 3:705
    Gödel's theorems 4:113–14
    intuitionistic logic 4:858
    many-valued logics 6:83
    monotonicity
        common-sense reasoning
            2:452–3
    sequent calculus 6:679–80
proofs of terms 5:754–5
propensity
    perception relationship
        (Ducasse, C.J.) 3:139
    probability theory 7:703
proper names 7:752–7
    see also names; nouns
    Church, A. 2:347–8
    conceptual notation (Frege, G.)
        3:766
    de relde dicto belief 2:815–16
    descriptions 8:153–7
        Russell, B.A.W. 3:21
        Strawson, P.F. 9:169
    existential statements 3:492
    famous deeds sense theories
        7:753–4
    fictional characters 3:659–62
    free logics 3:741
    'God' 4:94
    historical-causal theory 7:752,
        8:154, 8:157–8, 8:161–2
    identity (Kripke, S.A.) 5:302–3
    indexicals 2:880
    meanings 6:220
    Mill, J.S. 6:362
    modal logic 5:765
    predication 7:666
    reference (Russell, B.A.W.)
        3:459–60
    scope 8:589
    sense and reference distinction
        8:685
    sense of (Searle, J.) 8:685, 8:688
    stable essences (Ibn Rushd) 4:640
    truth theories 6:221, 6:223
properties
    see also colour; mental properties;
    property theory; qualities;
    universals
    accidental
        essentialism 3:417–22
    aesthetic 1:59
    atomism
        Epicureanism 3:340, 3:343–4
    bundles of
        particulars 7:236

Cartesian doubt 2:266
    causal powers 2:249
    concepts distinction 2:509–10
    definition
        Indian concepts of 2:849–52
    dependence on substance
        Islamic fundamentalism 5:10
    essential
        dualism 3:134–6
        Kripke, S.A. 5:303
    essentialism 3:417–22, 6:430
    indiscernibility of identicals
        4:678–81
    inference (Dignāga) 3:75
    intensional entities 4:804
    momentariness
        Buddhist doctrine of 6:471
    non-existence of (Kotarbiński, T.)
        5:293–4
    numbers 7:235, 9:542–3
    particulars 7:236–7
    perception 7:344, 7:347
    possible worlds 4:804
    propositional-function theory
        4:805
    referent of predicates 2:508–9
    social 8:833
    Śrīharsa
        Indian monism 6:478
    universals 9:539, 9:540–1
    values 9:580–1
    vital
        living tissues 9:640
property 7:757–61
    see also ownership
    anarchism 1:244
    authority relationship (Locke, J.)
        5:680–1
    communism 2:462–3
    contract theory 8:850–1
    information technology and ethics
        4:779
    labour 9:796
    libertarianism 5:617, 5:618, 5:619
    morality relationship (Franklin, B.)
        3:737
    rights
        Hume, D. 4:553–5
        Kant, I. 5:191
        liberalism 5:604
        political philosophy
            history of 7:513
        Proudhon, P.-J. 7:791
        Reid, T. 8:178
    unhappiness (al-Kindi) 5:251–2
    utilitarian government
        (Bentham, J.) 1:723–4

property theory **7:761–7**
see also properties
prophecy **7:767–71**
  Christianity 7:769
  comparative religions (Ibn
    Kammuna) 4:622
  dreams 7:767–8
  Islam 7:768
  Jewish philosophy 7:768–9
    Abravanel, I. 1:20–1
    Averroism 1:600
    Ibn Kammuna 4:622
    Ibn Tzaddik, J. 4:661–2
    Israeli, I. 5:33
    Judah ben Moses of Rome
      5:129–30
    Kabbalah 5:174
    Maimonides, M. 6:46–7
    Kabbalah 5:174
  naturalistic 7:767, 7:768, 7:769
  philosophy relationship
    (Maimonides, M.) 6:46–7
  psychological account of
    (Israeli, I.) 5:33
  supernatural 7:767, 7:768, 7:769
  Swedenborg, E. 9:242
  types of (Philo of Alexandria)
    7:358–9
prophets
  functions of 7:767
  Ibn Sina 4:651
  knowledge of 3:386–7
  mysteries (Ibn al-'Arabi) 4:602
  'perfect man' (Ibn al-'Arabi) 4:603
  philosopher-king
    Platonic 7:518, 7:519
  al-Razi, Abu Bakr 8:110
proportion
  architecture 1:363–4
  punishment 2:705, 2:708–9
  reciprocity 8:130, 8:131
propositional analysis
  divine knowledge 7:108–9
propositional attitude statements
  7:771–9
  see also propositional attitudes
  Frege, G. 7:772–3
  hidden indexicals 7:777–8
  intensional logics 4:807, 4:809–10
  intensionality 4:811
  referential opacity 7:773–5
  structured complexes 7:776–7
propositional attitudes 5:267–8,
  5:405–6, **7:779–87**
  see also belief; desire; intention;
  pro-attitudes; propositional
  attitude statements

analytic behaviourism
  (Dennett, D.C.) 2:882
content 7:781–3, 7:784
context 7:626, 7:627
eliminativism 3:265
functionalism 7:780–1
identity theory of mind 6:396–7
inner-cause thesis (Dennett, D.C.)
  2:882
intentionality 4:818–19, 7:783–4
logical constructions (Prior, A.N.)
  7:689
mental holism (Davidson, D.)
  1:278–9
phenomenology 7:343, 7:345,
  7:347
philosophical analysis
  (Moore, G.E.) 6:497
possible worlds semantics 8:667
psychology
  eliminativism 3:265
  recursion 9:249–50
  theoretical terms 7:784–5
propositional belief *see* belief,
  propositional
propositional calculus *see* sentential
  logic
propositional certainty 2:265–7
propositional dynamic logic 3:189–90
propositional functions
  ramified type theory 9:359–60
propositional logic
  consequence (Geulincx, A.)
    4:59–60
  epistemic 3:354–6
  terminist (Buridan, J.) 2:132
propositional operator/connective
  glossary 5:807
propositional s5
  modal logic 6:418, 6:420–4
propositions **7:787–8**
  see also intensional entities;
  propositional attitude statements;
  propositional attitudes
  a priori–a posteriori distinction
    (Kant, I.) 5:183–4
  analysis of (Moore, G.E.) 6:497–8
  analyticity (Bolzano, B.) 1:826
  antiscepticism (White, T.) 9:712
  categorical (Theophrastus) 9:337
  concepts 2:506
  false
    Gettier problems 4:58
  glossary 5:807
  inferences (Mill, J.S.) 6:360,
    6:362–3

judgment
  Port-Royalists 5:374
language of thought hypothesis
  1:703–4
logic (Philo the Dialectician)
  7:363–4
mathematical
  tautologies (Ramsey, F.P.) 8:45
medieval language 5:401–2
nominalism (Hobbes, T.) 5:373
possible worlds 7:781–2
pragmatism (Peirce, C.S.) 7:273
predicates of 6:435
probability (Keynes, J.M.) 5:233–4
propositional-complex reduction
  theory 4:804–5
propositional-function theory
  4:805
self-evidence (Reid, T.) 8:178
semantics 8:650
set-theoretic structures 7:782–3
singular 5:809
synthetic (Kant, I.) 5:183
Propp, V. 9:184
prosaics
  poetics comparison
    (Bakhtin, M.M.) 1:638–9
Prosch, H. 7:492
prosentential theory of truth 9:475,
  9:477
Proslogion see Anselm of Canterbury
Prosper of Aquitaine 7:287
Prost, J. 2:674, 5:332, 6:66
prostitution 8:724–5
Protagoras **7:788–91**
  educational philosophy 3:223
  nature and convention 8:848–9
  physis and *nomos* debate 7:381–2
  relativism 8:189
  Sophists 9:33
protection
  rights 8:328
Protestant Reformation *see*
  Reformation
Protestantism
  see also Calvinism; Liberal
  Protestantism; Methodism;
  Reformation
  Barth, K. 1:652
  Calvin, J. 2:177–81
  Catholicism debates
    (Chillingworth, W.) 2:307–8
  enthusiasm 3:330–2
  grace 4:148
  influence of
    Russian Enlightenment 3:324
  justification doctrine 5:167

Liberal (Unamuno y Jugo, M. De)
9:519, 9:520
limbo 5:637
mysticism 6:625
pietism 7:392–5, 7:394, 7:395
purgatory 7:837, 7:838
reprobation 8:274
Romanticism comparison
(Ruge, A.) 8:386
sacraments 8:442, 8:444
sanctification 8:455, 8:456–7
science 8:231
spiritual growth
education 8:457
protocol statements
scientific language (Neurath, O.)
6:814–15
protophysics
constructivism (Lorenzen, P.)
5:826
protothetic
Leśniewski, S. 5:572
prototypes 2:512–13
Proudfoot, W. 6:633
Proudhon, Pierre-Joseph **7:791–3**
anarchism 1:246, 1:248
influence of
Herzen, A.I. 4:405, 4:406–7
Proust, J. 3:69, 3:304
Proust, M. 5:844, 5:845–6
provability logic **7:793–7**
proverbs
African ethical systems 3:432
providence **7:797–802**
see also predestination
Aristotelianism (Alexander of
Aphrodisias) 1:172–4
astral determinism
(Nahmanides, M.) 6:649
Boethius, A.M.S. 1:809–11
Calvin, J. 2:179–80
Eusebius 3:457–8
free will
Early and Middle Platonism
7:427
Hebrew Bible 1:768
historical development (Vico, G.)
9:603–4
immutability 4:712
Maimonides, M. 6:45–6
miracles (Nahmanides, M.) 6:649
Molina, L. de 6:463–4
Molinism 6:465–6
prayer response 7:652
salvation 8:450
theodicy problem (Voltaire)
9:659–61

providentialism
deistic (Voltaire) 9:657, 9:658,
9:659–60, 9:661
prudence **7:802–4**
cultivation of (Vico, G.) 9:599,
9:600–1
virtuous action (Aristotle) 1:428
Prudentius of Troyes 2:222, 2:223
Prudhommeaux, J. 2:464
Prust, J.
discourse semantics 3:99
pseudepigrapha 6:808
Pseudo-Dionysius **7:804–8**
Aquinas, T. 1:330
Carolingian renaissance 2:221
God
natural knowledge of (Duns
Scotus, J.) 3:158
influence of
Christianity 8:240
mysticism 6:624
natural philosophy
medieval 6:692
negative theology 7:584–5
Eriugena, J.S. 3:402
patristic philosophy 7:260–1
Platonism
medieval 7:433–4
sanctification 8:455, 8:458
Pseudo-Empedocles 4:627, 4:628
Pseudo-Grosseteste 7:808–9
Pseudo-Quintilian 9:573
psi(-phenomena)
see also extrasensory perception;
psychokinesis
physicalism 7:224–6
Rhine, J.B. 7:225–6
psychē (soul) **7:809–11**
knowledge
Neoplatonism 6:800
logos (Heraclitus) 4:368
nature of (Proclus) 7:728
tripartition of (Plato) 7:810, 7:811
psychiatry
experience of madness
(Foucault, M.) 3:709–10
psychic ability 7:225
psychic essentialism doctrine
Augustinianism 1:562
psychic life
Frank, S.L. 3:728
psychic nexus
individuality (Dilthey, W.) 3:80
psychical causality
Wundt, W. 9:799–800
psychoanalysis
colonial discourse analysis 7:580

conscience 2:580
deconstruction (Cixous, H.) 2:372
development of (Jung, C.G.) 5:132
dynamic objectivity
feminism 3:866
feminism 3:580–2, **3:583–8**
continental 3:585
dynamic objectivity 3:866
limits of philosophy 3:586
literary criticism 3:611–13
methodological issues 3:585–7
object-relations theory 3:584–5
Freud, S. **3:786–94**, 7:828
Lacan, J. 7:602–3
functionalism analogy 3:814
hermeneutics (Ricoeur, P.) 8:319
introspection 2:590
Kantian synthesis
post-Freudian 7:819
language
Kristeva, J. 5:305, 5:306, 5:307
Lacan, J. 5:336–7
methodological issues in **7:811–17**
probative value 7:815
of non-Europeans
Fanon, F. critique 3:552, 3:553
post-Freudian **7:817–24**
language 7:821
object-relation 7:817–19
self-psychology 7:819–21
scepticism (Cavell, S.) 2:259
sport 9:115
subject
postmodern critique of 9:198–9
the sublime 9:204
textual criticism (Barthes, R.)
1:657
the unconscious
introspection problems 4:843
psychokinesis 7:223–5, 7:226
paranormal phenomena 7:221,
7:222–3
psycholinguistics
introspection 4:839
psychological anomalism
Davidson, D. 1:277–8
psychological certainty
epistemic 2:264–5
psychological egoism
ethics
Russian materialism 8:416
psychological hedonism 4:257–8
psychological laws 4:492, 8:833
psychological monism
Advaita Vedānta 2:3–4
psychological nominalism
Sellars, W.S. 8:639–40

psychological types
    Jung, C.G. 5:133
psychological verbs *see* verbs,
    sentential
psychologism
    a priori 1:5
    Descartes, R.
        Gioberti, V. critique 4:78–9
    Frege, G. 3:765, 3:769, 3:770–1
    Fries, J.F. 3:798
    logic (Mill, J.S.) 6:364–5
    Russian positivism 7:562–3
psychology
    see also cognitive psychology;
        developmental psychology;
        Gestalt psychology; mind; moral
        psychology
    analytical (Jung, C.G.) 5:131–3
    artificial intelligence **1:485–92**
    associationist (Tucker, A.) 9:491
    atomism
        mental and semantic 4:488,
            4:489, 4:492
    behaviourism **1:696–9**
    child's theory of mind **6:385–90**
    classical AI relationship 1:488–9
    cognitive development (Piaget, J.)
        7:383–5
    cognitive stages (Tetens, J.N.)
        9:320–1
    common-sense reasoning **2:451–3**
    connectionism **2:570–9**
    consciousness **2:581–96**
    critique of (Collingwood, R.G.)
        2:413
    cultural
        Marxism 6:155, 6:157
    cultural (Wundt, W.) 9:799–800
    descriptive
        Dilthey, W. 3:77, 3:79–80
        Shpet, G.G. 8:755
        Twardowski, K. 9:508
    dialectical concept of behaviour
        (Merleau-Ponty, M.) 6:321
    Diogenes of Apollonia 3:88–9
    dreaming 3:128
    economics 3:213
    educational philosophy influence
        3:237–8
    eliminativism **3:263–6**
    emotions 3:282
        morality 6:562
    empirical
        soul (Wolff, C.) 9:782
    evolutionary
        axiology 1:610

expected utility theory
    preference formation 8:94
folk **3:686–7**
    child's theory of mind 6:385,
        6:388
    connectionism 2:575
    mental causation 6:308, 6:309
Gestalt *see* Gestalt psychology
God
    concepts of 4:95
holism
    mental and semantic **4:488–93**
ideology
    Dostoevskii, F.M. critique
        3:117
idols of the mind (Bacon, F.)
    1:628–9
indexical content of thought
    2:639–40
infant cognition **2:390–2**
influence on philosophy of mind
    6:406–7
intentionality 8:864–5
interpersonal relationships
    families 3:550–1
introspection 4:839–40, **4:842–6**
    Maine de Biran, P.-F. 6:49,
        6:51–2
James, W.
    American philosophy
        eighteenth and nineteenth
            century 1:204
    learning 5:483–7
    logic relationship (Twardowski, K.)
        9:509
    materialism (Democritus) 2:875
    mental causation **6:307–11**
    mental imagery **4:703–5**
    mental phenomena (Brentano, F.)
        2:13
    mental states
        content, wide and narrow
            2:643–6
    metaphysics distinction (James, W.)
        5:61–2
    methodological individualism
        (MI) **6:341–4**
    modularity of mind **6:450–1**
    moral development **6:504–5**
    moral sciences
        Mill, J.S. 6:368
    nativism **6:672–6**
    naturalized philosophy of science
        6:728, 6:729
    non-conceptual content 2:641–2
    parapsychology **7:224–7**

pastoral
    spirituality 8:457
physiological (Hartley, D.) 4:237
Platonism
    Early and Middle 7:425
preference formation 8:94
propositional attitudes
    eliminativism 3:265
psychophysics
    Fechner, G.T. 3:570–1
    Wundt, W. 9:799
rational
    Amo, A.W. 1:210
    empirical distinction (Wolff, C.)
        9:782
realism (Herbart, J.F.) 4:370
scientific behaviourism
    operationalism 7:133–4
semantics
    analogy with (Twardowski, K.)
        9:508
    teleological **8:672–5**
sense perception
    Indian views of 8:689–91
split brains **9:107–10**
subjective spirit (Hegel, G.W.F.)
    4:273
Theophrastus 9:338
theories of **7:824–30**
    cognitive 7:826–7
    personality 7:828–9
    phenomenological 7:827–8
    scientific 7:824, 7:826
vision **9:631–8**
Vygotskii, L.S. **9:671–5**
psychology, sensationalist *see*
    sensationalist psychology
psychopathology
    moral agents 6:500
    psychoanalysis
        post-Freudian 7:819, 7:820–1
    psychophysical anomalism
        Davidson, D. 1:278–9
    psycho-physical parallelism 7:824,
        7:825
    see also mind-body problem
psychophysics
    Fechner, G.T. 3:570–1
    Gestalt psychology (Köhler, W.)
        4:53
    introspection 4:843, 4:844
Pszczołowski, T. 5:295
Ptolemaic astronomy
    attack on
        Islamic science 8:563
Ptolemy **7:830–2**
    ancient philosophy 1:265

knowledge 7:830
mathematical astronomy
  (Copernicus, N.) 2:671–2
Ptolemy of Lucca
  Renaissance Aristotelianism 1:411
public
  see also society
  obligations to
    engineering ethics 3:314
  private distinction 7:690–3
  journalism ethics 5:128
public interest **7:832–5**
  see also general will
  corruption 2:675–6
  democracy 2:870
  Rousseau, J.-J. 4:10–11
public law
  Bodin, J.
    absolutism 1:796–7
    sovereignty 1:796
public morality
  African ethical systems 3:433
public order
  republicanism 8:280–1
public policy
  definition of death 2:818–19
public sphere
  social theory (Habermas, J.) 4:194
public theology
  Niebuhr, R. 6:841, 6:842
publicity
  utilitarianism (Bentham, J.) 1:722
public-mindedness
  Lu Xiangshan 5:852
Puccetti, R. 9:110
Pucciarelli, Eugenio 1:233, 3:511
Puccio, U. 2:241
Pucelle, J. 4:170
Puech, B. 3:90
Puerto Rico
  existentialism 3:510–11
    cultural tensions 3:510
    marginality 6:99
    phenomenology 7:350
    positivism 7:568
Pufendorf, Samuel **7:835–6**
  federalism and confederalism
    3:574
  Thomasius, C. 9:377–8
Pugliese Carratelli, G. 7:165
Pūjyapāda 5:57
Pulleyblank, E.G. 4:452
Pulliam, H. 4:797
puncta 9:50
punishment
  see also capital punishment; crime;
    discipline; penal theory;

rectification; rehabilitation;
  remainders
  Abelard, P. 1:13
  abolitionism 2:705, 2:709–10
  actual sin 8:792–3
  blame 6:564, 6:566, 6:568
  censure 2:705, 2:707–8
  Chinese Legalism 5:532
  civil disobedience 2:367–8
  communication of 2:707–8
  consequentialism 2:704–5, 2:706–7
  crime **2:704–10**
  desert 3:25
  deterrent
    criminal law 2:707
  divine justice
    Ashʿariyya/Muʿtazila
      comparison 1:522
    al-Razi, Fakhr al-Din 8:114
  forgiveness 8:136
    and mercy 3:697, 3:698,
      3:699–700
  al-Ghazali 4:63–4
  God (Origen) 7:162
  guilt 8:139
  hell 4:331, 4:332
  Ibn Sina 4:652
  justification 2:705–6, 2:709
  karma
    Japanese Buddhism 2:104–5
  limbo 5:636
  mercy 8:137–8
  original sin 8:793–5, 8:794
  providence (Nahmanides, M.)
    6:649
  purgatorial 7:837, 7:838
  reciprocity 8:131
  retributivism 2:705, 2:707–8
    Hart, H.L.A. 4:235
  scientific behaviourism
    (Skinner, B.F.) 8:800
  self
    conscience 2:580
  social control (Mozi) 6:452, 6:453,
    6:454, 6:456
  soul (al-ʿAmiri) 1:207, 1:208
  utilitarianism (Bentham, J.) 1:719,
    1:721–2
  war and peace 9:686
Punyavijaya, Muni 6:34
Pupi, A. 8:189
Purāṇas 1:516
Purandara 6:180, 6:181
Purcell, E.A. 5:525
Purdy, L. 3:239

pure concepts
  Hegelian idealism
    Croce, B. 2:728–9, 2:731
Pure Land Buddhism
  China 2:89
  eternity (Shinran) 8:747–8
  Japanese philosophy 5:73
  liberation 2:102, 2:103
  Shinran 8:746–8
  spiritual power of language
    Japan 2:100
  Zhi Dun 9:859
pure theory of law
  Weyr, F. 9:708
purgatory **7:836–9**
  atonement 1:539
purification
  purgatory 7:836–8
  Shintō 8:749–50
Puritanism
  authority (Hooker, R.) 4:505
  critique of (Hume, D.) 4:552
  pietism 7:392, 7:394
purity
  morality
    Zoroastrianism 9:873, 9:874
Purkert, W. 7:751
Purkyně, Jan Evangelista 2:766
Purnell, F., Jr 7:264–5
purpose
  see also meaning of life
  desire distinction (Mill, J.S.)
    6:369–70
purpose in nature see teleology
Purtill, Richard L.
  Lewis, C.S. †5:589–90
puruṣa
  Sāṅkhya 8:461, 8:462–4, 8:466
    existence proofs 8:465
  Sāṅkhya-Yoga 8:608–9
Pūrva Mīmāṃsā see Mīmāṃsā
Putallaz, F.-X. 6:203
Putnam, C. 9:518
Putnam, G. 6:797, 8:385, 8:428
Putnam, Hilary **7:839–44**
  abstract objects 1:35
  analytic behaviourism 1:692
  analytic ethics 1:223
  analyticity 1:238
  anti-individualism
    content 6:341, 6:344
  antirealism
    mathematics 1:310, 1:311
  arithmetic 1:440
  art and truth 1:460
  Cavell, S. 2:260

computational theories of mind
  5:486, 6:394
concepts 2:513–14, 2:517
conceptual analysis 2:521, 2:522
conceptual role semantics 8:653–4,
  8:656–7
dreaming 3:129
epistemic justification 5:164
externalism
  supervenience 9:239
holism
  mental and semantic 4:493
holism and individualism in
  history and social science
  4:486–7, 4:488
indexicals 2:881
indispensability argument 1:34
internal realism 7:843, 8:581, 8:583
language
  conventionality of 5:369, 5:371
  social nature of 5:418, 5:419
many-valued logics 6:84
mathematics
  antirealism 1:310, 1:311
  constructivism 2:638
  foundations of 6:186, 6:189,
    6:191
meaning 7:839, 7:840–1
mental causation 6:309, 6:311
nativism 6:675
  Chomsky, N. 6:674
natural kinds 6:684
necessary truth and convention
  6:750
pragmatism 7:635–6, 7:639
proper names 7:757
quantum logic 7:885, 7:886
quantum mechanics,
  interpretation of 7:894
realism
  antirealism 8:119
  mathematics 8:121, 8:123
recursion-theoretic hierarchies
  8:145
reduction
  problems of 8:149

reference 8:157, 8:164
scientific realism and antirealism
  8:584
scientific theories 9:354
substance 9:208, 9:210
taste, artistic 1:512
transcendental arguments 9:454
Twin Earth thought experiments
  7:840–1
  content
    holism 4:491
    wide and narrow 2:644, 2:646
unity of science 9:533
Putnam, R.D. 2:371–2, 2:677
Putnam, Ruth Anna
  James, W. †5:60–8
Pybus, C. 1:583
Pye, J. 8:51
Pye, M. 2:53
Pylyshyn, Zenon
  cognitive architecture †2:392–3,
    2:576, 2:577
  language of thought hypothesis
    5:407
  mental imagery 4:705
  modularity of mind †6:450–1
  vision 9:638
Pyman, A. 8:428
Pyrrho of Elis **7:844–8**
  see also Pyrrhonian scepticism
  scepticism 8:499
  Timon 9:419, 9:420
Pyrrhonian Scepticism 1:263–4,
  3:373, **7:848–54**
  see also Pyrrho of Elis
  Aenesidemus 1:50–1
  Agrippa 1:129
  Arcesilaus 1:352–4
  dissoi logoi (twofold argument)
    3:106–7
  doubt 3:122–3
  Hellenistic philosophy 4:335
  Lucian 5:853–4
  Mersenne, M. 6:326–8
  Montaigne, M.E. de 6:487
  moral scepticism 6:543

Næss, A. 6:635–6
  physics 7:853
  Renaissance 8:499
  Sextus Empiricus 8:716–17
  slogans 7:851
  Ten Modes of 7:850–1
  Timon 9:419, 9:420
Pythagoras **7:854–7**
  see also Neo-Pythagoreanism;
    Pythagoras' theorem;
    Pythagoreanism
  architecture 1:363
  Egyptian influence on ancient
    Greek thought 3:251–2
  geometry 4:28
  psychē (soul)
    transmigration of 7:810
  school of 1:264
Pythagoras' theorem 4:28, 4:773
Pythagoreanism **7:857–61**
  see also Neo-Pythagoreanism;
    Orphism
  Alcmaeon 1:160
  Archytas 1:366–9
  cosmology 7:858–60
  geometry 4:28, 4:30
  Gnosticism 4:84
  indivisibilism
    Bradwardine, T., critique 1:864
  infinity 4:773
  Islamic philosophy 6:617
  mathematics 7:423, 7:858–60
  music–number relationship 7:858
  numbers 7:48
  Philolaus 7:367–70
  Platonism
    Speusippus 9:89, 9:90
  Presocratics 7:671
  reincarnation
    Empedocles 3:293, 3:294
  school of 1:263, 1:264
  soul
    immortality of 7:857, 7:860

Q

Qadariyya school
  Islamic theology 5:26
al-Qadi, W. 8:776
qi (material force) **7:862–3**
  see also ki
  aesthetics 1:72
  cosmic creativity (Zhu Xi) 9:863–4
  Huainanzi 4:513
  human nature (Zhu Xi) 9:864
  Kaibara Ekken 5:176
  li 5:595
    neo-Confucianism 6:767, 6:770
  sensory stimulation (Yangzhu)
    9:822
  taiji
    Zhou Dunyi 6:768
    Wang Fuzhi 9:681
    Zhang Zai 9:856
Qi, Y. 5:103
al-Qifti, A. 4:608, 5:250
al-Qirqisani 5:207
Qom, School of 5:19–20
Quadarite theology 3:438
quadruples 9:497
qualia 6:406, **7:863–7**
  see also phenomenal
    consciousness; sense-data
  colour **2:419–27**, 2:428
  consciousness 2:582, 2:588–9
  dualism 3:135–6, 7:863–4
  eliminativism 2:426–7
  functionalism 3:806, 3:811–12,
    6:174–5
    inverted spectra argument
      3:808–11
  identity theory of mind 6:397
  perceptual judgment (Ayer, A.J.)
    1:616–17
  primary–secondary distinction
    7:686
qualities
  abstraction
    Berkeley, G. 1:741–2
  action distinction
    ontology in Indian philosophy
      7:123
  category of
    Nyāya-Vaiśeṣika ontology 7:61
  perceptual knowledge 7:297

primary
  colour, theories of 2:429
  secondary qualities distinction
    7:684–7, 8:595
    colour, theories of 2:429
    Locke, J. 5:671
    Reid, T. 8:172
  quantification of
    Oxford Calculators 7:179–80
secondary **8:595–9**
  Berkeley, G. 1:743
  colour, theories of 2:429
  observer-dependence
    (Democritus) 2:873, 2:874–5
soul relationship
  ontology in Indian philosophy
    7:127
substance
  ontology in Indian philosophy
    7:121, 7:122–3
    Aristotle comparison
      7:125–6
substance (Madhva) 6:31
unitary nature (Digby, K.) 3:72–3
universals
  Vaiśeṣika 9:545
quan
  Chinese Confucianism 2:545
Quandt, G. 7:165
quantification
  adverbs of 1:47, 1:48
  De Morgan, A. 2:813
  existential *see* existential
    quantification
  Frege, G. 5:725
  game-theoretic semantics 8:658
  Herbrand's theorem 4:375–7
  human nature 4:526
  inference **7:867–70**
    adequacy condition 7:867–8
    non-constructive rules of 7:27,
      7:28
    universal generalization rule
      7:868
  modal logic 6:422–3
  Oxford Calculators 7:180
  tense logic 9:304
quantified modal logic (QML)
  8:665–6, 8:667

quantifiers **7:870–3**
  count nouns 6:168
  descriptions 3:20, 3:21–2, 3:23
  free logics 3:741
  Frege, G. 3:771
  generalized **7:873–7**
  glossary 5:807
  infinitary logic 5:734
  interpretation of 7:870–1
  Lindström's theorem 7:875
  logical constants 5:777–8
  logical laws 5:788
  mass terms 6:168, 6:169
  modal logic 6:429–30
  modal operators 6:434–3
  numerically definite
    logicism 1:439
  reference 8:160–1
  substitutional/objectual **7:877–82**
  symbolic logic (Russell, B.A.W.)
    5:732
  of type 7:873–4
quantitative risk assessment (QRA)
  8:331
quantum logic **7:882–6**
quantum mechanics
  Bell's theorem 1:712–15
  Bohr, N. 1:820
  causal laws (Kant, I.) 5:187
  chaos theory 2:278
  chemistry applications 2:298–9
  Copenhagen interpretation 7:892
  Bohr, N. 1:820
  Heisenberg, W. 4:328
  Planck, M.K.E.L. 7:396
  Putnam, H. 7:839, 7:841
  determinism 3:34–5, 3:36
  Einstein, A. 3:254, 3:256–7
  electrodynamics 3:260
  field theory 3:670, **3:670–3**
  interpretation of **7:890–5**
  irrationals (Meyerson, É.)
    6:349–50
  light
    optics 7:136, 7:138–9
  logic (Putnam, H.) 7:841
  many-worlds interpretation 7:893
  matter 6:195

measurement problem 6:248,
7:886–90
Heisenberg, W. 4:328
Putnam, H. 7:841
metaphysics 8:575
Neumann, J. von 6:810
parapsychology comparison 7:226
Planck formula 7:396
religion 8:230, 8:233–4
superposition 7:891–2
uncertainty principle
(Heisenberg, W.) 4:327–8
universe states 7:887–9
Weyl, H. 9:706
quarks 3:516
quasi-memory 7:320
quasi-quotation 9:550
see also quotation
quaternions 7:49
Quayson, Ato
postcolonialism †7:578–83
al-Qudat Hamadani, 'Ayn 6:619
Quechua *see* Inca civilization
Queen, S. 3:112–13
Quénet, C.H. 2:272
Quesnay, Francois 8:848
Quesnel, P. 7:554
questions **8:1–3**
Quetzalcoatl, King of Tula 5:431
Queyrel, F. 1:255
Quiché thought *see* Mayan
civilization
quiddity *see* essence
Quidot, John *see* John of Paris
quietism
Fénelon, F. 3:629–30
neo-Confucianism (Yi Hwang)
9:823–4
objectivity 7:73, 7:75
rule-following (McDowell, J.)
6:218
Quiles, Ismael 3:511
Quillet, J. 6:114, 7:157
Quine, Willard Van Orman **8:3–14**
a priori 1:6
abstract objects 1:35
analytic philosophy 1:224,
1:226–7, 1:229
Latin America 1:230, 1:231,
1:233
analyticity 1:235–6, 1:238–9, 2:520
animal language and thought
1:273
Ayer, A.J. 1:619
belief 1:706
Bolzano, B. 1:827
Carnap, R. 2:213, 2:215

Cartesian doubt 8:62, 8:63–4
charity principle 2:283, 2:285
Chomsky, N. 2:339, 2:341
cognitive pluralism 2:398
coherence theory of justification
5:254, 5:276
concepts 2:517
conceptual analysis 2:522, 7:635,
7:639
conceptual role semantics 8:657
confirmation holism
externalism 2:506
semantic holism 2:513, 4:488,
4:489, 4:493
consequence 2:601
continuants 2:653, 2:654
conventionalism 2:669
critique 2:667
web of belief 2:667
de re/de dicto 2:816, 2:817
eliminativism 3:266
epistemic holism 1:2, 1:3
epistemology
autonomy of 6:724, 6:725
justification 5:165
observation 6:724
paradoxes 7:213, 7:214
essentialism 3:421, 7:114–15, 7:238
existence 1:702, 3:492
necessary conditions 1:701
fictional entities 3:664, 3:665,
3:667
holism
mental and semantic 4:493
indeterminacy
of reference 8:29–31
of translation 8:26–9
indirect discourse 4:745
indispensability argument 1:34
intensional entities 2:520, 2:521
intensionality 4:811
intentionality 4:818, 4:821
Kripke, S.A. 5:304
logical laws 5:789
logical positivism 5:794
Löwenheim-Skolem theorem and
non-standard models 5:851
mass terms 6:169, 6:170
mathematics
empiricism 6:186, 6:187
foundations of 6:191
meaning
Strawson, P.F. 9:170
and understanding 6:229
mereology 6:319
modal logic 6:429, 6:433
modal operators 6:433, 6:436

nativism 6:675
naturalized epistemology 3:383,
6:721, 6:727–8
empiricism 6:722, 8:3, 8:5–6
ethics 3:367, 3:370
natural selection 6:722
naturalized philosophy of science
6:729
necessary truth and convention
6:750
nominalism 7:22, 7:23
ontological commitment 7:113–14,
7:116–17, 7:118, 8:4
being 1:700–1
canonical notation 8:7–8
translation 7:115–16
particulars
time slices 7:237
positivism
social sciences 7:561
pragmatic virtues 9:343
propositional attitudes 7:773–5,
7:779, 7:786
propositions 7:788
provability logic 7:796–7
quantifiers 6:429–30, 7:870, 7:879,
7:882
radical translation 5:410, 8:12–13,
8:25, 8:26, 8:35
radical interpretation 8:31
rationalism 8:80
realism
mathematics 8:121, 8:123
reduction
problems of 8:149
reference 8:164
referential opacity 7:773–5, 7:779
Russell, B.A.W. 8:403–4
science
demarcation problem 2:866
second-order logic 8:604
Sellars, W.S. 8:639
semantic paradoxes and theories
of truth 8:643, 8:648
semantics
informational 8:662
set theory 8:709, 8:714–15, 8:716
substance 9:207, 9:210
truth
Tarski's definition of 9:269
type/token distinction 9:511
types
theory of 9:362
underdetermination 9:528–9, 9:530
universals 9:543
use/mention distinction 9:549,
9:550, 9:551

verificationism 6:230, 6:233, 6:236
Vienna Circle 9:613
Whitehead, A.N. 9:719
Quinlan, J.R. 2:578
Quinn, Daniel 1:128
Quinn, J.F. 1:834–5
Quinn, Philip L.
  agnosticism 1:123
  asceticism †1:517–19
  creation doctrine 2:700
  divine freedom 3:761
  forgiveness and mercy 3:701
  religion and morality 8:224
  religion, philosophy of 8:250
  religious pluralism †8:260–4
  self-control †8:611–13
  sin †8:791–6
Quinn, W. 3:122
Quintilian 3:225, 3:231, 8:53
  see also Pseudo-Quintilian
Quinton, A.M.
  Bacon, F. 1:632
  bundle theory of mind 6:385
  conservatism 2:614
  Grote, J. 4:184–5
  Ryle, G. 8:432
Quirk, R. 6:170
Quodlibetal Questions see Duns
  Scotus, John
quotation
  quasi-quotation 9:550
  use/mention distinction **9:548–51**
Qur'an
  allegory (Ibn Rushd) 4:643
  atheistic view of (Ibn ar-Rawandi)
    4:637
  creation of 2:241, 5:27, 5:28
  divine law 5:457, 5:458
  The Fall (Iqbal, M.) 4:864
  God
    attributes of 1:520–3, 6:805
  Ikhwan al-Safa' 4:687
  interpretation of
    exoteric/esoteric 6:237, 6:238–9
  Islamic fundamentalism
    (Qutb, S.) 5:11–12
  al-Juwayni 5:169, 5:170
  methodology
    Islamic fundamentalism 5:11
  nuraniya (mysterious letters) (Ibn
    Massara) 4:629
  Persian translation (Shah Wali
    Allah) 8:733
  providence 7:798
  reason–revelation conflict 5:8–9
  revelation 8:297, 8:298–300
  sciences of (Ibn Massara) 4:628
  scientific enquiry 8:562
  sin 8:792
Qutb, Sayyid
  attributes of Islam 5:11–12
  causation 5:12
  divinity of God 5:11
  origin of life 5:12
  paganism 5:9–10, 5:12

R

Raab, F. 1:594
Rabad *see* Ibn Daud, Abraham
Rabbe, F. 3:718
Rabbinic law *see halakhah*
Rabbinic theology **9:333–7**
  action 9:334–5
  halakhah 4:204, 4:205–6
  intention 9:334–5
  Karaism 5:206, 5:207, 5:208
  meaning 9:335–6
  underdetermination 9:335–6
Rabel, G. 4:129
Rabelais, François **8:15–18**
  Renaissance scepticism 8:640
Rabil, A., Jr 4:541
Rabinow, Paul 3:713, 4:4
Rabins, M.J. 3:315
Rabossi, E. 1:230, 1:233
race **8:18–21**
  see also discrimination;
  multiculturalism; racism
  cognitive differences
    African philosophy,
      Anglophone 1:98–9
  definition of (Crummell, A.) 7:192
  European 8:18, 8:20
  Latin American literature 5:654
  linguistic discrimination 5:641–2
  postcolonialism 7:581
  racial discrimination problematic
    8:19, 8:20
  racism problematic 8:19–20
  unequal development 8:18
Rachels, James
  animals and ethics †1:273–6
  applied ethics 1:325
  ethics 3:437
  life and death 5:630
racism
  see also anti-Semitism;
  discrimination; race
  affirmative action **1:91–4**
  colonial ideology 1:109, 3:553
  explanation of (Sartre, J.-P.)
    1:312–13
  fascism 3:562
  freedom of speech 3:764
  imperialism
    Latin America 6:163–4

liberation theology 5:614
pan-Africanism 7:190–4
positivism
  Latin America 7:566
privacy 7:691–2
psychological effects of (Fanon, F.)
  3:553
'scientific' 8:18
sport 9:112, 9:114
Raciti, G. 5:5
Rack, H.D. 7:395
Raconis, Charles d'Abra de 1:388,
  1:389
Rácz, L. 4:572
Radbruch, Gustav **8:21–3**
Radcliffe-Browne, A.R. 3:818
Radford, Colin
  concept of knowledge 5:276
  emotion in response to art 3:280–1
  music
    aesthetics of 6:614
  separability thesis of belief and
    knowledge 1:708, 1:709
Radhakrishna, C. 5:221–2
Radhakrishnan, Sarvepalli **8:23–5**
  causation 2:257
  consciousness 2:596
  God 4:105
  matter 6:200
  Rāmānuja 8:44
  reincarnation 8:186
  self 8:611
  truthfulness 9:485
  Vedānta
    Neo-Vedānta movement 9:593,
      9:594
radical Aristotelianism *see* Averroism
radical behaviourism *see*
  behaviourism, scientific
radical conventionalism
  Ajdukiewicz, K. 1:135, 1:136
radical empiricism
  James, W. 5:60, 5:61, 5:65–6
radical evil
  original sin doctrine 8:794–5
radical feminism *see* feminist
  philosophy, radical

radical interpretation **8:25–35**
  Davidson, D. 2:802, 2:804–5,
    8:25–6, 8:31–4
    conceptual schemes 2:804–5
    meaning 6:227–8
radical materialism *see* materialism,
  radical
radical novelty
  revolution 8:301, 8:302
radical physicalism
  scientific language (Neurath, O.)
    6:815
radical reality
  vital reason (Ortega y Gasset, J.)
    7:166–7
radical translation **8:25–35**
  cultural relativism (Davidson, D.)
    8:80, 8:83
  indeterminacy of reference 8:29–30
    criticsms 8:30–1
  indeterminacy of translation
    8:26–7
    criticisms 8:27–9
  Quine, W.V. 8:12–13, 8:25, 8:26,
    8:31
  truth theory 8:31–4
    criticisms 8:34
Radice, R. 7:361
Radin, M.J. 7:760, 7:761
Radin, P. 6:671
Radishchev, Aleksandr A. 3:326,
  5:606, 5:609
Radner, D. 6:66
Radnitzky, G. 7:539
Radrizzani, I. 3:653
Rae, J. 8:822
Raedts, P. 8:318
Raeff, M. 3:327, 5:609, 8:811
Raffman, D. 2:596, 6:614
Raghavachar, S.S. 8:44
Raghunātha Śiromaṇi
  jurisprudence (Gadādhara) 3:826
  Nyāya-Vaiśeṣika 7:62, 7:67
Ragionieri, E. 5:336
Ragnisco, P. 9:599
Rahe, P. 8:283
al-Rahim, Qutb al-Din Ahmad *see*
  Shah Wali Allah

Rahman, Fazlur
  Ibn Sina 4:654
  Illuminationist philosophy 4:703
  Islamic philosophy
    modern 5:17, 5:21
  Mulla Sadra 6:599
  prophecy 7:771
al-Rahman, Nasir al-Din 9:506
Rahner, Karl **8:35–9**
  freedom 8:37–8
  grace 4:148–9, 4:151
  heaven 4:253
  knowledge
    religious 8:36–7
  mysticism, nature of 6:633
  transcendental hope 8:38
Rahula, W. 2:75, 7:11, 9:215
Rāhulabhadra 2:59
Raiffa, H. 8:74, 8:103
Railton, Peter
  analytic ethics †1:220–3
  explanation 3:525
  friendship 3:797
  ideals 4:675
  inference to the best explanation
    4:769
  metaphysics of value 9:581
  moral realism 6:538
  naturalism in ethics 6:717
  utilitarianism 9:557
rainbows 3:69
Rainsborough, Colonel 5:600
Raja, K.K.
  interpretation
    Indian theories of 4:837
  language
    Indian theories of 5:383, 5:384
  meaning
    Indian theories of 6:243
  Sāṅkhya 8:467
Rajchman, J. 3:713
Raju, P.T. 4:740, 6:200, 9:594
Ralbag see Gersonides
Raley, H.C. 7:168
Ram Shanker, B. 8:467
Ramakrishna 6:622, 8:39, 8:41
Ramakrishna Movement **8:39–42**
Ramanan, K.V. 2:63
Rāmānuja **8:42–4**
  Brahman
    qualified monism 4:438
    souls distinction 2:4
  fatalism 3:567, 3:568
  God
    concepts of 9:592
    self-surrender to 4:102, 4:104

Indian and Tibetan philosophy
    4:738
  mysticism 6:622
  panentheism 4:100–1
Ramanujam, P.S. 7:67
Rambachan, A. 8:42
Rambam see Maimonides, Moses
Ramban see Nahmanides, Moses
Ramée, Pierre de la see Ramus,
    Petrus
Ramee, Pierre de la see Ramus,
    Petrus
ramified type theory 9:359–60, 9:361
ramified-analytical hierarchy 8:143–4
Ramirez, J.M. 5:120
Ramm, T. 5:421
Rammohun Roy, Raja see Brahmo
    Samaj
Ramos, Samuel
  anti-positivism
    Latin America 1:306–7
  phenomenology
    Latin America 7:350, 7:352
  problem of identity
    Latin American philosophy
      5:654, 5:655, 5:657
Ramseier, Y. 1:766
Ramsey, Frank Plumpton **8:44–9**
  see also Ramsey sentences
  belief
    degrees of 8:46
    map theory 1:705–6
  causation
    generalizations 8:47
  conditionalization 7:706, 7:711
  decision theory 8:44, 8:45–6
  deflationary theories of truth
    9:475, 9:478
  generalizations 8:47
  Hempel, C.G. 4:352
  logicism 5:817
  natural law 7:738
  possible worlds semantics 8:669
  practical reasoning/rationality
    8:103
  predication 7:667
  probability
    projectivist theory of 7:738,
      7:740
  rational choice theory 8:74
  scientific theories 9:354
  semantic paradoxes
    Russell, B.A.W. 8:45, 8:397,
      8:404
  and theories of truth 8:648

theories
    unobservable entities 3:806–7,
      3:813
  types
    theory of 9:362
Ramsey, Ian Thomas **8:49–51**
Ramsey, P. 6:841, 8:799
Ramsey sentences 8:45, 8:47–8
Ramsey, W. 2:578
Ramus, Petrus **8:51–5**
  dialectic/logic debate 5:767–8,
    5:770
  logic
    Renaissance 5:771
  martyrdom 8:52
  method 5:772
  rhetoric 8:308, 8:309–10
  topics 5:770
Ranade, R.D. 8:610
Rand, Ayn **8:55–6**
Randall, J.H. 8:859, 9:839
Randawa Shönnu lodrö see Red
    mda'ba gZhon nu blo gros
Randle, H.N. 3:861
randomized clinical trials (RCTs)
    6:262
randomness **8:56–9**
  see also chaos theory
  chance 8:56, 8:59
    simulation of 8:56–7
  computability and information
    2:471–5
  Maxwell, J.C. 6:209
  paradox of 2:478–9
  physics 2:480–1
  random number generators
    (RNGs) 8:57
Rang, B. 7:220
Ranggyuba see Svātantrika
Rang-rgyud-pa see Svātantrika
Rani, A. 3:843
Ranke, Leopold von 4:443
Ransel, D. 5:609–10
Rantala, V. 3:359, 6:614
rape 8:719, 8:724–5, 9:357
Raphael, D.D. 4:594, 6:547, 7:188,
    8:822
Raphals, Lisa
  Chinese classics †2:309–15
Raphelengius, Franciscus 5:24
rapid eye movement (REM) 3:127
Rapoport, A. 8:74
Rapoport-Albert, A. 4:245
Rapp, F. 9:287, 9:719
al-Raqqi see al-Muqammas, Daud
Rashdall, Hastings **8:59–61**
  axiology 1:610, 1:612

metaphysics 8:60
Nicholas of Autrecourt 6:832
rectification and remainders 8:141
religion 8:60
Rasiowa, H. 1:846, 4:853, 7:498–9
Raskin, V. 4:567
Rasmussen, D. 8:56, 8:322
Rasmussen, L. 6:844
Rathjen, M. 7:748–9, 7:751
ratio scales
measurement theory 6:243, 6:244
rational agents
autonomy 1:587–8
rational argument
Anselm of Canterbury 1:284,
1:285–6, 1:294–5
syllogisms (Ibn Sina) 4:649
rational beliefs 8:61–4
see also justification
rational choice theory 8:64–75
see also decision theory; game
theory
Arrow problem 8:65, 8:68–9
democracy 8:64, 8:69–70
economics 3:213
game theory 8:64–5, 8:66–8
intentional behaviour 8:71–2
limitations 8:813–14
logic of collective action 8:65,
8:70–1
mixed-motive games 8:66, 8:67–8
naturalism 8:863–4
prisoner's dilemma
solidarity 9:24
prudence 7:803
race theories 8:19
reciprocity 8:131
value theory 8:72–3
rational creatures
Origen 7:162
rational egoism
anthropological principle
(Chernyshevskii, N.G.) 2:305
moral agents 6:501
rational expectations theory
predictions 8:865–6
rational inference
principles of
naturalized philosophy of
science 6:729–30
rational justification
Frege, G. 3:765
rational numbers 7:48, 7:51
rational psychology
Amo, A.W. 1:210
rational realism
Krause, K. 5:299

rational soul
Active Intellect
Jewish philosophy (Judah ben
Moses of Rome) 5:129
rational theology
critique of (Kant, I.) 5:189
rationalism 8:75–80
see also anti-rationalism
Abelard, P. 1:8
applied
Bachelard, G. 3:780–1
French philosophy of science
3:780–1
Baumgarten, A.G. 1:669–70, 1:671
certainty 8:79
continental 8:75–6
British empiricism comparison
8:75–6
critical (Popper, K.R.) 7:533
critiques of
Dostoevskii, F.M. 3:116–17
Kant, I. 5:181
divine existence arguments
Kant, I. critique 5:181
ethics
see also practical reason
Cambridge Platonism 2:184–5
Hutcheson, F. critique 6:546
moral education 6:507, 6:508
Neo-Kantianism
values 9:581, 9:582
Price, R. 7:675, 7:676–7
Hellenistic medical epistemology
4:334–5
historical (Xunzi) 2:323, 2:324
history
philosophy of 4:455
language
Chomsky, N. 2:339–40
Port-Royalists 5:373–4
Leibniz, G. 3:376
methodology 8:78
Zar'a Ya'ecob 3:443–4
Mu'tazila 5:25
nativism 6:672, 6:673
natural law (Culverwell, N.)
2:750–1
Popperian
Kuhn, T.S. critique 5:317
religion relationship
Judaism
Delmedigo, E. 2:861
Nahmanides, M. 6:647–8
religious (Zar'a Ya'ecob) 3:443
Spinoza, B. de 3:375–6, 9:91

theory choice
contrast with sociology of
science 8:831
thought experiments 9:393, 9:394
rationality
see also communicative rationality;
irrationality; rational beliefs;
rational choice theory;
rationalism; reason; reasoning
action
legal reasoning 5:525
Bayesian decision theory 7:708
of belief 8:86–90
charity principle 2:282–3
coherence standards
(Davidson, D.) 1:278–9
common sense
French anti-postmodernism
7:595
and cultural relativism 8:80–6
fideism 8:85
functionalism 8:84, 8:85
intellectualism 8:84
interpretation and translation
8:83
symbolism 8:84–5
degrees of belief 7:706
doctrinal exclusivism 8:262–3
economics 3:205
emotions 3:284
ethical scepticism
natural law 6:686
feminist political philosophy
(Wollstonecraft, M.) 3:615–16
game theory 2:827–8
genealogy of (Adorno, T.W.) 1:43
human nature 4:524
ideal
probabilistic epistemology 7:705
instrumental
action 3:529
critical theory 2:723
Horkheimer, M. 4:511
interactive choice 8:68
internal divinity (Marcus Aurelius)
6:94, 6:95
justification of religious belief
(Locke, J.) 8:211–12
law as reason 5:465
legal evidence 5:501
MacIntyre, A. 6:23
as material faculty (Overton, R.)
7:176
Meyerson, É. 6:350
motivation (Reid, T.) 8:175
Nozick, R. 7:46–7
panlogic (Feuerbach, L.A.) 3:635

passions
  Stoicism 9:157
  practical **8:90–103**
  probability 2:824–5
    Condorcet, M.J.A.N. 2:529–30
  psychoanalytic feminism 3:585
  purposive (*Zweckrationalität*)
    2:459
  reasoning problem (Gerbert of
    Aurillac) 4:40
  religious belief 8:217
    de facto/de jure question 8:214,
      8:217
    de jure objections 8:210
    Freud, S. 8:214–16
  religious pluralism 8:263
  resoluteness
    practical reasoning 8:97
  revealed-preference theory 3:206
  right conduct
    principles 8:100–1
  risk assessment 8:332, 8:336
  ritual law
    halakhah 4:207
  social relativism 8:838
  synchronic/diachronic 5:162
  tradition 9:445, 9:446
  utility theory 2:660, 3:206
  vulnerability and finitude 9:670
  Western society (Weber, M.)
    9:696–7
  will 9:720–1, 9:723
  of world
    Stoicism 9:141–2
rationalization
  as causal explanation
    (Davidson, D.) 2:800–1
  humour 4:566
  reasons as causes 8:124–5
    logical connections 8:125–6
ratione uti 4:40
ratios
  see also Oxford Calculators
  language of (Oresme, N.) 7:153,
    7:154–5
  quantification of motions
    Oxford Calculators 7:181
  velocity (Bradwardine, T.) 1:863–4
ratio-vitalism 9:74
ratiovitalism *see* vital reason
Ratnagotravibhāga (Differentiation of
  the Lineage of the [Three] Jewels)
  9:402–3
Ratnākaraśānti 6:472
Ratnakīrti 2:96
Ratnamati 2:83
Ratramnus of Corbie 2:223

Rattigan, W.H. 8:483
Rattner Gelbart, N. 2:287
Rattray, R.S. 3:435
Ravaisson-Mollien, Jean-Gaspard
  Félix Lacher **8:103–6**
Raven, J.E.
  Anaxagoras 1:254
  Anaximander 1:259
  Anaximenes 1:262
  chemistry
    philosophical aspects of 2:299
  colour, theories of 2:431
  Diogenes of Apollonia 3:89
  Empedocles 3:298
  Heraclitus 4:369
  Hesiod 4:413
  Homer 4:502
  Melissus 6:296
  nous 7:44
  Parmenides 7:234
  Presocratics 7:672
  Thales 9:324
  Vlastos, G. 9:653–4
  Xenophanes 9:810
  Zeno of Elea 9:852
Raven, P. 9:80–1
Ravenscroft, I. 3:687
Ravier, E. 5:562
Ravitzky, A. 2:704, 4:710
ar-Rawandi *see* Ibn ar-Rawandi
Rawidowitz, S. 3:639
Rawling, P. 2:891
Rawls, John **8:106–10**
  Berlin, I. 1:753
  civil disobedience 2:367, 2:368,
    2:369
  community and
    communitarianism 2:471
  consent 2:599
  contractarianism 2:658, 2:663,
    2:665
  democracy 2:872, 8:107–8
  desert and merit 3:27
  duty 3:182
  equality 3:394–5, 3:396
  ethics
    analytic 1:223
    applied 1:325
    autonomy 1:590, 1:592
    common-sense 2:450
    constructivism in 2:631, 2:632
    economics and 3:210–11
    medical 6:264
    naturalism in 6:717
    population and 7:541, 7:542
    practical reason and 7:619
  feminist jurisprudence 3:610

freedom and liberty 3:757
good, theories of the 4:130–1,
  4:135
happiness 4:229
help and beneficence 4:343, 4:344
higher-order interests 6:754–5
human nature 4:523, 4:524–5
international relations 4:833
justice 5:147, 5:148, 5:153
  as fairness 5:145, 8:106–7
  international 5:156
  self-respect 8:637, 8:638
Kantian contractualism 5:202,
  5:204
legitimacy 5:541
liberal democracy
  religion 8:225, 8:228–9
liberalism 5:605, 8:108–9
moral agents 6:500–1, 6:504
moral pluralism 6:531
moral sentiments 6:550
needs and interests 6:755
neutrality
  political 6:821
obligation
  political 7:78, 7:80
obligations to future generations
  3:821
'original position'
  deliberative ideals 4:673, 4:675
Pareto principle 7:228
perfectionism 7:302
pluralism 7:464
practical reasoning/rationality
  contractarian reasoning 8:100,
    8:103
promising
  practice-based account 7:741,
    7:742
property 7:760
rational choice theory 8:74
reciprocity 8:132
rectification and remainders 8:141
reflective equilibrium 3:360, 3:362,
  9:343
  moral justification 6:515, 6:516
  theory and practice 9:358–9
religion and political philosophy
  8:229
respect for persons 8:287
rights 8:328, 8:329, 8:330–1
risk 8:334
rule of law
  justice relationship 8:390, 8:391
slavery 8:807
solidarity 9:24, 9:25
stability 8:108

toleration 9:433
'veil of ignorance'
  impartiality 4:716, 4:717
war and peace 9:690, 9:691
welfare 9:704, 9:705
Rawson, E. 2:360
Ray, C. 2:380
Ray, John
  Egyptian cosmology
    ancient †3:248–50
Raychaudhuri, T. 8:42
Raz, Joseph
  authority 1:584, 1:585, 1:586
  economics and ethics 3:211
  legal concepts 5:495
  legal norms 7:40, 7:41
  legal positivism 5:520, 5:521
  legal reasoning and interpretation
    5:531
  liberalism 5:602, 5:605
  Nagel, T. 6:647
  nation and nationalism 6:661
  neutrality
    political 6:821
  perfectionism 7:302
  practical reason and ethics 7:619
  promising 7:742
  public interest 7:835
  rights 8:327, 8:331
  rule of law 8:391
  social norms 8:835
al-Razi, Abu Bakr Muhammad ibn
  Zakariyya' 8:110–12
  ethics 3:439, 3:442, 8:111
  Plato 4:157
al-Razi, Fakhr al-Din 8:112–15
  al-Tusi 9:505
al-Raziq, Mustafa 'Abd 5:17
Razran, G. 7:829
reactive effects
  experiments in social science 3:519
Read, C.
  empiriocriticism
    Russian 8:409
  Lenin, V.I. 5:567
  liberalism
    Russian 5:610
  Russian religious-philosophical
    Renaissance 8:428
  Signposts movement 8:774
Read, H. 1:248
Read, Stephen
  medieval logic 5:758
  relevance logic and entailment
    †8:200–4
reader/textual unity
  Barthes, R. 1:657

Readings, B. 7:604
Reagan, C.E. 8:322
Real, L.A. 3:205
real numbers
  computability of 2:491–4
  continuum of 8:704
    Cantor, G. 2:196–7, 2:199–200
    paradoxes 7:218
  Dedekind, J.W.R. 2:841
  nonstandard analysis 1:212–13,
    5:847
  Russian constructivism 2:634–5
  second-order logic 8:601
Real, the
  noumenal
    religious pluralism 8:261–2
  phenomenal
    religious pluralism 8:261–2
Reale, G. 6:296, 6:809, 7:848
Reale, Miguel 2:11
realism 8:115–19
  see also antirealism; critical
  realism; legal realism; logical
  realism; moral realism;
  nominalism; political realism;
  scientific antirealism; scientific
  realism; systematic realism
  absolute
    Russell, B.A.W. 8:394–5
  adverbial 3:139–40, 8:639–40,
    9:717
  Aurobindo Ghose 1:567
  beauty 1:680, 1:681–3
  bivalence 4:856–7, 4:859–62
  Christian see Christian realism
  colour, theories of 2:428, 2:430–1
  common-sense
    moral intuitionism assimilation
      7:680–1
  Daoism 2:790
  Dharmakīrti nominalism debate
    7:24–5
  direct
    Armstrong, D.M. 1:442
    Moore, G. 3:379
    sense-data 8:697
  doubt 3:124
  epistemic (Lotze, R.H.) 5:840
  extreme
    possible worlds 7:571
  Frege, G. 3:770
  ideal (Lossky, N.O.) 5:833
  Indian logic (Dharmakīrti) 3:52–3
  indirect
    sense-data 8:697
  individuality of essence (William
    of Auvergne) 9:726

internal 8:116
  Putnam, H. 7:843
  Kantian 4:665
  language
    medieval theories of 5:393
    Mohism 5:693–4
  Marxism, Russian (Lenin, V.I.)
    6:153
  mathematics 1:308, 4:857,
    4:859–60, 8:119–23
  meaning (Dummett, M.A.E.)
    6:226–7
  meta-ethics (Price, R.) 7:677
  metaphysical
    Nagel, T. 6:644
    Putnam, H. 7:839–40, 7:841–3
  Mill, J.S. 6:363
  Mīmāṃsā 6:378
    veridicality 3:411
  moderate
    possible worlds 7:572
    rGyal tshab dar ma rin chen
      8:304–5
    William of Ockham 9:734–5
  mournful
    situation ethics 8:798, 8:799
  naïve
    perception 7:292
  natural
    property theory 7:761, 7:763
  Neoplatonism (Proclus) 7:724–5
  nominalism conflict
    Gerson, J. 4:45–6
    medieval Platonism 7:434–5
  Nyāya (Vātsyāyana) 9:587–8
  Nyāya-Vaiśeṣika
    awareness 1:606, 1:607
    veridicality 3:411
  Peirce, C.S. 7:279–80
  perception (William of Ockham)
    3:374
  Peripatetics 7:305
  phenomenology 7:335–6
  pluralistic
    ontology in Indian philosophy
      7:118–27
  Prichard, H.A. 7:679, 7:680
  Putnam, H. 8:116
  rational (Krause, K.) 5:299
  reality of knowledge
    (Hamilton, W.) 4:218
  representative
    phenomenalism 7:331
    Reid, T. critique 2:447
  Santayana, G. 8:467, 8:468–9
  sense perception
    Indian views of 8:692–3

sense-data 6:496, 7:296, 7:297
socialist (Lunacharskii, A.)
    8:407–8
sophisticated (Ayer, A.J.) 1:614,
    1:616–17
structural (Russell, B.A.W.) 8:400
substance 9:208–9
transcendental *see* dogmatism
universals 9:540, 9:541
    Armstrong, D.M. 1:442–3
    Brinkley, R. 2:20
    Duns Scotus, J. 3:163–5
    Kilwardby, R. 5:247
    Peter of Spain 7:324
    Reid, T.
        Stewart, D. critique 9:138
    transcendent/immanent 9:540
    William of Champeaux 9:729
    Whitehead, A.N. 9:716–17
    William of Champeaux 7:18–19
reality
    absolute (Bradley, F.H.) 1:860–1
    aesthetics
        Russian nihilism 7:7
    anti-metaphysical stance
        (Hägerström, A.A.T.) 4:202
    appearance distinction
        emptiness
            Buddhist concept of 2:76,
                2:77–8
    categories
        ontology in Indian philosophy
            7:120
    classification of
        ontology in Indian philosophy
            7:119
    consciousness relationship
        (Voegelin, E.) 9:654–5
    consensual/ultimate distinction
        Buddhism
            Indian 2:98
    criterion of (Bradley, F.H.) 1:861
reality
    degrees of
        Plato
            analytic interpretation
                9:651–2
            Proclus 7:726
    Divine manifestation (Tagore, R.)
        9:257
    existence relationship (Mulla
        Sadra) 6:595–6
    existentialism 3:497
    flux (Cratylus) 2:694
    Hasidism 4:243

human experience
    Japanese philosophy
        modern literature 5:660
    imagination relationship (Weil, S.)
        9:699
    intuition of (Kemp Smith, N.)
        5:228–9
language relationship
    Buddhist theory of meaning
        6:240
levels of (Bhartṛhari) 1:764–5
Meyerson, É. 6:350
monistic idealism
    (Radhakrishnan, S.) 8:23–4
mystical experiences 8:253–5
nature of
    Ābhidharmika Buddhism
        2:55–6
    process theism 7:716
objective–subjective relationship
    (Nagel, T.) 6:644
organic model
    Chinese Buddhism (Sengzhao)
        8:683–4
Parmenides' conception of
    (Owen, G.E.L.) 7:178
physical
    panpsychism 7:196
physics (Heisenberg, W.) 4:328
pragmatic theory of truth 9:478–80
pragmatism
    Peirce, C.S. 7:273, 7:279–80
    Schiller, F.C.S. 8:523
process theism 7:717
quiddity relationship (al-Dawani)
    2:807
representation of (Dilthey, W.)
    3:78–9
science, philosophy of 8:574–5
self-expression
    Japanese philosophy 5:71, 5:72
self-representation of reason
    (Hegel, G.W.F.) 4:259–60,
    4:264–6
sentience/non-sentience
    Jainism 5:48
suprasensible
    Socratic explanation of evil
        3:464–5
time 9:413–14
triadic division of (Xenocrates)
    9:807
ultimate
    emptiness 6:351–2
    God's role 4:94–5
    Nāgārjuna 6:638–40
    religious pluralism 8:260–2

unity of
    Cohn, J. 6:787
    Hegel, G.W.F. 4:259, 4:262–3,
        4:267–8
    virtues (Aristotle) 9:628–9
reality thesis
    photography 7:379, 7:381
realizability interpretation
    intuitionism 4:851
reason
    see also practical reason;
        rationality; reasoning; unreason
    a priori knowledge (Kant, I.)
        5:178–9
    adequate knowledge (Spinoza, B.
        de) 9:100, 9:103
    autonomy (Kant, I.) 5:177–8,
        5:189
    Baumgarten, A.G. 1:671
    categories of (al-Farabi) 3:556
    certain knowledge
        Neoplatonism 6:800
    Chinese philosophy
        li 9:834–5
    Christianity
        Porphyry critique 7:545
    church authority
        Socinianism 8:890
    critical theory (Horkheimer, M.)
        4:511
    critiques of
        Burke, E. 2:138–40
        Fries, J.F. 3:798
        Vasubandhu 9:585
    desire
        conflict
            self-control 8:611
    development of (Ibn Tufayl)
        4:657–9
    divine freedom 3:758–9
    educational philosophy
        Augustine 3:225
        Bacon, R. 1:634
        Descartes, R. 3:226
    emotions and
        Clement of Alexandria 2:384
        Hume, D. 3:287–8
        Kant, I. 3:288
    Enlightenment, German
        Hamann, J.G. critique 4:213–15
    ethics–religion relationship
        Cohen, H. 2:400
        Maimon, S. 6:37
    Ethiopian philosophy (Zar'a
        Ya'ecob) 1:104–5
    experience (Kant, I.) 5:178,
        5:183–9

explanatory principles
(Schopenhauer, A.) 8:547–8,
8:549
faith and 2:772–3, 3:538, 3:541–3,
8:248
Arama, I. 1:350
Astell, M. 1:528
Augustine 1:553
Averroism 1:595, 1:597, 1:598,
1:600
Brunner, E. 2:32
Cambridge Platonism 2:182,
2:183
Culverwell, N. 2:750–1
Damian, P. 2:772–3
Gerson, J. 4:46
Ibn Falaquera 4:616
Kierkegaard, S. 5:241
Le Clerc, J. 5:476
Locke, J. 5:676–7
Unamuno y Jugo, M. De 9:519
William of Auxerre 9:728
Wolff, C. 9:778
Zar'a Ya'ecob 3:443
free thinkers
Collins, A. defence 2:415–16
free will 3:750–1
Matthew of Aquasparta 6:202
God
belief in 1:121–3
happiness
Ibn Bajja 4:606–7
al-Sijistani 8:774, 8:775
historical
radical reality of humans
(Ortega y Gasset, J.) 7:166–7
hope relationship 4:508
ideals of
feminist epistemology 3:598
ideas relationship (Price, R.)
7:676–7
inference
Indian theories of 4:760
instinct distinction
will 9:720–1
instrumental 2:459
Adorno, T.W. 1:43
critical theory 2:724
instrumental role
Hume, D.
Common Sense ethics
response 2:449
intuition distinction (Iqbal, M.)
4:865–6
language
Herder, J.G. 4:380
Reinhold, K.L. 8:187

Thomasius, C. 9:378
law 5:464–5
common law 2:443, 2:444–5
formal cause (Stair, J.D.) 9:119
life relationship (Ortega y
Gasset, J.) 7:166–7
limits of
Desgabets, R. 3:28
Vives, J.L. 9:647–8
linguistic (Mauthner, F.) 6:203–4
logocentrism (Le Doeuff, M.)
5:477
masculinism (Le Doeuff, M.) 5:477
metaphysical illusions (Kant, I.)
5:188–9
monism of (Hegel, G.W.F.) 4:265
moral development
(Wollstonecraft, M.) 9:790
moral distinctions
Hume, D. critique 4:556
morality and
African ethical systems 3:431
Kant, I. 5:178, 5:183
Wollaston, W. 9:787
Native American philosophy
6:662, 6:667–9
negative dialectics (Adorno, T.W.)
1:43–4
passion and
Seneca, L.A. 8:680
Spinoza, B. de 9:102–3
persons 7:319
pneuma (spirit)
early Greek philosophy 7:471
politics (Jaspers, K.) 5:81–2
positive philosophy
(Schelling, F.W.J. von) 8:516
public (Bentham, J.) 1:722
rational consideration (Ibn al-
'Arabi) 4:602
as reality (Hegel, G.W.F.)
4:259–60, 4:264–6, 4:277
religious belief
'ilm al-kalam 5:28–9
Vico, G. 9:603, 9:604–5
revelation and
Ash'ariyya 1:522
Fackenheim, E.L. 3:534
Ibn Ezra, A. 4:611, 4:612
Ibn Massara 4:627–8
Ibn Taymiyya 4:655
Islamic philosophy 5:6, 5:8–9
Witherspoon, J. 9:755–6
ritual commandments
Jewish philosophy (Saadiah
Gaon) 8:437

scepticism
mitigated (Bayle, P.) 1:673–4
science of
Nyāya-Vaiśeṣika 7:60
scripture (Ibn Hazm) 4:620, 4:621
self-knowledge of (Hegel, G.W.F.)
4:265–6
self-realization
Hegel, G.W.F. 4:264, 4:265
Schleiermacher, F. 8:533
social organization (Hayek, F.A.)
4:248
sociality
Enlightenment, Scottish 3:328
substantive 2:727
critical theory 2:727
sufficient (Leibniz, G.W.) 5:545–6
system of (Schleiermacher, F.)
8:533
theoretical-practical integration
(Fichte, J.G.) 3:642, 3:646, 3:648
traditionalism 9:445, 9:446
truth
Herbert, E. 4:372
Leibniz, G.W. 5:552–3
understanding distinction
Coleridge, S.T. 2:404
Jacobi, F.H. 5:46
uses of (Kant, I.) 5:189
validation (Descartes, R.) 3:1,
3:9–3:11
Young Hegelians 6:118
reasonableness
constructivism (Rawls, J.) 2:631
ethical inquiry (Peirce, C.S.) 7:640,
7:641
moral contractualism 2:664
reasoning
see also legal reasoning; moral
reasoning; practical reasoning;
rationality; reason
art criticism 1:461
belief acquisition 8:86–9
child development (Piaget, J.)
7:383–4
circular
fallacies 3:544–5
common-sense
classical AI 1:488
theories of **2:451–3**
non-monotonic logic 2:451,
2:452–3
computer programs
computational theories of mind
6:390–3

counterfactual
    negative facts
        Indian philosophy 6:757
defeasible (Thucydides) 9:399
dialectical (Bachelard, G.) 1:621
endogenous preference formation
    8:97–8
epistemic relativism 3:360–1
Golden Rule (Hare, R.M.) 4:230
holism 4:488
inductive (Broad, C.D.) 2:23, 2:25
intelligibles (Ibn Sina) 4:648–9,
    4:650
medical 6:264, 6:265–6
natural
    faith relationship (William of
        Auxerre) 9:728
    religious knowledge (Gerson, J.)
        4:46
principles of (Peirce, C.S.) 7:272,
    7:274–5
probability (Condorcet, M.J.A.N.)
    2:529
public (Habermas, J.) 4:194
rational 8:61–4
rationality problem (Gerbert of
    Aurillac) 4:40
religious belief (Newman, J.H.)
    6:822
role of imagery (Le Doeuff, M.)
    5:476–7
truth-generating capacity 3:360–1
reasons
see also justification; moral
    reasons
and causes 8:124–7
as causes (Davidson, D.) 2:800–1
epistemological belief 5:158,
    8:127–30
    explanatory 8:127–8, 8:129
    grounding 8:127–8, 8:129
    normative 8:127–8, 8:129
    possessed 8:127–8, 8:129
    pragmatic 8:128
exclusionary 5:528–9
intention 4:815
of principle 5:529–30
rules 5:526
universality
    legal discourse 5:527–8
reasons holism
moral particularism
    logic of ethical discourse 5:763
Reath, Andrews
autonomy
    ethical †1:586–92

rebellion
see also civil disobedience;
    revolution
oppression (Camus, A.) 2:194–5
revolution distinction 8:301–2
Reber, A 5:287
rebirth
see also reincarnation
Indian conceptions of 5:209–18
    Buddhism 5:211, 5:213–15
        Buddha 2:52
        ethics 2:94–5
        human nature 2:94
    early developments 5:211–12
    Hinduism 5:210–11, 5:212–13
        liberation 4:434
    Jainism 5:211, 5:215
    modern philosophy 5:215–16
    terminology 5:210
    texts 5:210–11
Recanati, François
indexical content of thought 2:640
performatives 7:304
pragmatics †7:620–33
proper names 7:757
propositional attitude statements
    7:779
receptivity
senses (Schleiermacher, F.) 8:534–5
Rechtsstaat see rule of law
Recife, School of 2:10
reciprocity 8:130–2
altruism
    sociobiology 8:893
egoism 3:246
freedom
    existentialist ethics 3:504
sexual relationships (Kant, I.)
    8:722–3
recognition 8:132–4
see also respect
absolute consciousness
    (Abhinavagupta) 1:17
Buddhism
    momentariness 6:472
    nominalism (Dharmakīrti) 7:25
communication (Grice, H.P.)
    2:455, 2:456
Hegelian historical development
    (Kojève, A.) 5:289–90
moral punishment 6:564, 6:568
politics of
    communitarianism 9:278
self-respect 8:635–6
recollection
memory 6:297
reconciliation see atonement

reconstructionism
Judaism in the modern world
    (Kaplan, M.) 5:204–6
rectification 8:134–41
see also blame; praise;
    punishment; remainders
forgiveness 8:135–7
gratitude 8:135, 8:138–9
mercy 8:135, 8:137–8
recursion theory
generative grammar 9:249–50
Kleene, S.C.
    computability theory 2:487–8
    ordinal logics 7:140
Post, E.L. 7:574
recursive functions
    Church's thesis 2:351, 2:352,
        2:353
    general 2:484–5
    glossary 5:807
    partial 2:486, 9:500–1
    primitive 2:483–4, 2:636
    proof theory 7:745
recursively enumerable 4:112–13,
    7:28
transfinite 8:702–3, 8:708
recursion-theoretic hierarchies
    8:141–5
recursive set
glossary 5:807
recursively enumerable set
glossary 5:807–8
Red mda'ba gZhon nu blo gros
    (Rendawa Shönnu lodrö) 6:416,
    9:488
Reddaway, W.F. 5:610
Reddick, A. 5:123
redemption
grace 4:150
Gregory of Nyssa 1:538
history of (Edwards, J.) 3:244
Jewish philosophy (Saadiah Gaon)
    8:438
partial
    Rabbinic theology 9:334
religious doctrine of
    alchemy 1:155
Redhead, Michael L.G.
Bell's theorem 7:716
field theory, quantum 3:673
quantum logic 7:886
relativity theory
    philosophical significance of
        †8:191–200
Reding, J.-P. 2:232
Redman, C.L. 1:359
Redman, D. 3:221

Redmond, Walter
  Latin America, colonial thought in
    †5:421–6
Redondi, Pietro
  Koyré, A. †5:296–8
reducibility
  see also Turing reducibility
  axiom of
    theory of types 9:360–1
    combinatory logic 2:432
    computational complexity 2:473
    lambda calculus 5:347
reductio
  as 'retracing'
    divine union 1:830–1
reductio ad absurdum
  glossary 5:808
reductio ad Hitlerium
  legal positivism 5:515
reduction 8:145–9
reduction
  see also reductionism
  biological selection 4:14–15, 8:894
  bridge laws 8:146–7
  chaos theory 2:279
  chemistry to physics 2:299
  eidetic (Husserl, E.) 4:575, 4:579
  Hegelian
    Rosenzweig, F. critique 8:359
  Kemeny-Oppenheim model
    8:146–7
  method (Descartes, R.) 3:5–6
  microreduction 8:147
  molecular biology 4:14, 6:459,
    6:460
  naturalized philosophy of science
    6:728
  ontology 7:117–18
  phenomenological 7:343–4
    Husserl, E. 4:575, 4:580
  realism/antirealism 8:117
  scientific (Kuhn, T.S.) 5:316–17
  transcendental (Husserl, E.) 4:575,
    4:579–80
  unity of science 9:531–2
reduction property
  inductive sets 4:754
reduction sentences
  operationalism 7:133, 7:134
reductionism
  see also anti-reductionism;
    reduction
  antirealism (Dummett, M.A.E.)
    3:152
  Australian materialism 1:579
  Buddhism 6:638
  critical social theory 8:842–3

critique of substantialism 5:494–5
critiques of
  Chomsky, N. 2:339–40
  Quine, W.V. 8:6
eliminativism relationship 3:264
ethical 3:366–7
  Moore, G.E. 6:496
imperative logic 4:718–19
individualism–holism debate 4:485
of intensional entities 4:804–5
knowledge
  testimony 9:310–12
personal identity (Parfit, D.)
  6:572–4
persons 7:319–21
philosophy of mind 8:149–53
projective
  Yogācāra Buddhism critique
    2:69
psychological (Vygotskii, L.S.)
  9:671, 9:673
realism relationship (Nagel, T.)
  6:644, 6:645
Russian materialism 8:416
scientific explanation
  (Anaximenes) 1:260
social science 3:486
supervenience 9:237–8
reductive naturalism
  religious pluralism 8:260
reductive programme
  proof theory 7:743, 7:746–9
redundancy theory of truth 6:225,
  9:475, 9:476
Rée, J. 8:432
Reece, W. 4:101
Reed, P. 6:638
Reed, T.J.
  Goethe, J.W. von 4:129
  Schiller, J.C.F. †8:524–9
Rees, B.R. 7:287
Rees, J. 9:466
Reesink, H.J. 5:476
Reeve, Andrew
  neutrality
    political 6:821
  political representation †8:270
Reeve, C.D.C. 3:231, 9:18
Reeves, M. 5:104–5
reference 8:153–64
  see also denotation; descriptions;
    extensionality; sense; sense and
    reference; signification;
    supposition
  beings of reason 5:413–14
  causal theory of
    epiphenomenalism 3:353–4

incommensurability 4:735
Chinese theories of language
  Gongsun Long 5:702
  Mohism 5:697, 5:699–700
  Zhuangzi 5:703
cognitive significance 8:684–5
count/mass terms 6:168
descriptions 3:23, 8:153–7
  Frege, G. 3:19–20
  Russell, B. 3:20–1
  Strawson, P.F. 3:22–3
Evans, G. 3:459–61
famous deeds sense theories 7:754
fictional characters 3:659–62
figurative (Goodman, N.) 4:138
free logics 3:741, 3:742
general terms 8:685–6
historical chains 7:754–5
human nature 4:523–4
Ibn Rushd 4:644–5
improper terms 3:20
indeterminacy of 8:29–31
  Quine, W.V. 8:9–10
indexicals 2:878–9, 2:880, 2:881
indirect discourse 4:743, 4:744
intensionality 4:810–11
Kripke, S.A. 5:303
logical truth (Quine, W.V.) 8:7
modal logic 5:765
nominalism 5:413
paronymy (Anselm of Canterbury)
  1:289
Peirce, C.S. 7:280
proper names 7:752–7, 8:685
  Quine, W.V. 8:4, 8:7, 8:9–11
reliabilism
  naturalism 8:162
semantics 8:651
sentences
  Frege, G. 7:772
  testimony in Indian philosophy
    9:316
  Strawson, P.F. 9:169
teleological theory (Millikan, R.)
  8:162
truth conditions
  context 6:224
referential opacity
  Prior, A.N. 7:689
  propositional attitude statements
    (Quine, W.V.) 7:773–5
referents
  abstract art 1:451
  concepts 2:508–9
reflection
  see also introspection
  accessibility internalism 4:823

critical *see* critical reflection
finiteness of (Hegel, G.W.F.) 4:266
identity philosophy
(Schelling, F.W.J. von) 8:513,
8:516
internal sense (Locke, J.) 5:665,
5:670
knowledge (Suchon, G.) 9:211
moral consciousness (Ross, W.D.)
8:366
moral intuitionism (Sidgwick, H.)
8:759–60
Ryle, G. 8:428, 8:431
self-awareness (Nishida Kitarō)
7:13–14
Reflection condition
degrees of belief 7:707
reflection principles
ordinal logics 7:140–1, 7:142
reflective equilibrium
epistemic relativism 3:360
induction 4:749–50
moral justification (Rawls, J.)
5:202, 6:515
theoretical/epistemic virtues
9:342–3
theory and practice 9:358
reflective hedonism 4:257, 4:258
reflective philosophy
judgments (Hegel, G.W.F.) 4:263,
4:270
reflectiveness
divine creation
Jewish pietism (Ibn Paquda)
4:634
reflexive awareness (*Innewerden*)
Dilthey, W. 3:78
reflexivity
identity 4:676
modernism 6:449
scientific constructivism 2:626
social science 8:865–6
prediction in 8:871–2
symbolic interactionism 9:244
Reformation
see also Calvinism; Counter-
Reformation; Luther, Martin;
Protestantism
Augustinianism 1:564
Calvin, J. 2:177–81
critique of (Troeltsch, E.P.W.)
9:461–2
educational philosophy 3:223,
3:225–6
Erasmus, D. 3:396, 3:397, 3:399
hermeneutics
biblical 4:391

justification doctrine 5:165
original guilt 8:795
Platonism 7:441
political philosophy
history of 7:504, 7:510–11
Renaissance
humanism
philology 4:538–9
philosophy
effect on 8:264–5
scepticism 8:501–2
reprobation 8:274
supererogation 9:232
voluntarism 9:664
reformation
revolution distinction 8:301
Reformed epistemology 8:239, 8:246
natural theology 6:709
reformism
liberalism 5:603
refutations
Socratic method 9:652
Regan, P. 4:781
Regan, T.
agricultural ethics 1:128
animals and ethics 1:276
bioethics 1:776
Moore, G.E. 6:498
moral standing 6:554
Regev, S. 8:740
Régis, Pierre-Sylvain **8:165–6**
register machine
glossary 5:808
Regnier, L. 5:640
Regoliosi, M. 9:573
regress argument
coherence theory of justification
5:254–5
contextualism 2:647
regression
causal inferences 5:485
regret 8:136, 8:139–40
regularities
laws of nature 5:470, 5:471,
5:472–3
pattern-breaking
randomness as 7:889–90
rehabilitation 2:708–9
Rehg, W. 4:199–200
Řehoř Hrubý of Jelení (Gelenius)
2:765
Reich, C. 7:761
Reich, Klaus 5:199–200
Reich, W.T. 1:776, 6:264
Reichenbach, B.R. 3:417, 4:144,
5:218, 8:186

Reichenbach, Hans **8:166–71**
causation 2:250
conventionalism 2:669
conventionality thesis 8:194–5,
8:199
explanation 3:525
general relativity 4:7, 4:9
geometry 4:34
Hempel, C.G. 4:352
inductive inference
learning theory 5:486
inference to the best explanation
4:769
many-valued logics 6:84
Poincaré, J.H. 7:482
reference 8:164
relativity
logical positivism 5:791, 5:793,
5:795
spatiotemporal conventions 2:666
thermodynamics 9:369
time 9:416
Reichert, E.O. 6:5
Reichling, M.J. 5:356
Reichner, W. 8:189
Reid, Thomas **8:171–80**
Aberdeen Philosophical Society
1:15
action 8:174–5
anti-Aristotelian theory of
language 8:181
beauty 8:176–7
bodily sensations 1:795
Carmichael, G. 2:208
causality 8:173–4
common sense philosophy 9:135,
9:136
Beattie, J. comparison 1:677,
1:679
Stewart, D. critique 9:137–8
Common Sense School 1:576,
2:447, 2:448
common-sense ethics 2:448,
2:449–51
commonsensism 2:454, 2:455
conception 8:175–6
consciousness 2:596
Enlightenment, Scottish 3:330
first principles 8:171–2, 8:173,
8:177, 8:178–9
foundationalism 3:723
inductivism
Stewart, D. critique 9:138
Kant, I. comparison (Stewart, D.)
9:137
language 8:175–6
moral judgment 8:177

perception 8:172–3
rights 8:177–8
scepticism 3:378, 3:383
social epistemology 8:828,
    8:829–30, 8:832
substance (Brown, T.) 2:27
testimony 9:314
universals 8:175–6
    Stewart, D. critique 9:138
Reidel, M. 2:372
Reif, Patricia 1:391–3
Reill, P.H. 3:319, 4:446
Reilly, J. 9:376
Reimarus, H.S. 8:238
Reimer, B. 5:356
Reina, M.E. 9:776
Reinach, Adolf **8:180–2**
    legal a priori 8:180–1
    phenomenological movement
        7:342
    promises 8:181
    social acts theory 8:181–2
reincarnation **8:182–6**
    see also rebirth
    Buddhism
        salvation 8:448
    enlightenment 8:182, 8:183, 8:184
    escape from
        importance of 8:183–4
    evidence for 9:47–8
    evil 8:185
    karma
        Indian fatalism 3:565
    paranormal phenomena 7:222
    personal identity 8:295–6
    Plato 8:294–5
    Pythagoreanism (Empedocles)
        3:293, 3:294
    theosophy 9:363, 9:365
    Vedantic Hinduism 3:414
Reiner, H. 4:504, 8:529, 9:539
Reines, A. 7:771
reinforcement
    scientific behaviourism
        (Skinner, B.F.) 8:800, 8:801
Reinhardt, H. 7:392
Reinhardt, K. 7:235, 7:557
Reinhardt, L. 1:443
Reinhardt, W. 4:113, 4:118
Reinharz, S. 3:593
Reinhold, Karl Leonhard **8:186–9**
    influence of (Fichte, J.G.) 3:646
reism
    Kotarbiński, T. 5:293–4
Reiss, E. 1:813
Reiss, H. 3:574
Reiter, R. 7:34

Reiter, Raymond 2:453
relation
    feminist theology 3:623
    inherence
        ontology in Indian philosophy
            7:120, 7:124–6
    'I–Thou' mode (Buber, M.) 2:42,
        2:43–5
    monism
        Advaita Vedanta 6:478
    mystical union as aim of
        (Buber, M.) 2:42, 2:43
    Navya-Nyaya theory of 2:850–1
relational properties
    identity of indiscernibles 4:680
relational structure
    model theory 5:735
relational theories
    colour, perception of 2:428,
        2:429–30
    meaning
        situation semantics 8:670
relationalism
    space 9:61–2
        Poincaré, J.H. 7:480
    time 9:414
relationism
    ideology 4:683
relations
    converse of 5:800
    discourse semantics 3:95–7
    existence of (Bradley, F.H.)
        1:860–1
    glossary 5:808
    ideas
        Hume, D. 3:378
        Kant, I. 3:378
    ideas of (Locke, J.) 5:672–3
    identity 4:676, 4:677
    intensional entities 4:804
    logic of
        converse relations
            Latin America 5:423–4
        De Morgan, A. 2:814
        nineteenth century 5:725–7
    ontological commitment 7:112–16
    particulars 7:235
    properties of 5:808
    property theory 7:761–6
    propositional (Locke, J.) 5:675–6
    qualitative mental states as 2:423
    reduction (Leibniz, G.W.) 5:554
    social see human relationships
    speculative metaphysics
        (Whitehead, A.N.) 9:715, 9:717
    transcendental/predicamental
        distinction (Suárez, F.) 9:191

unity (Deleuze, G.) 2:857
yin-yang 9:831–2
relationships see human relationships
relative identity logic
    Trinity 9:459–61
relativism **8:189–90**
    see also cognitive relativism;
        cultural relativism; epistemic
        relativism; meta-ethics; moral
        relativism; normative relativism;
        social relativism
    antirationalist 2:627
    antirealist 2:627
    beauty 1:683
    Berlin, I. 1:751
    contextualism 2:648
    credibility of 8:190
    critical thinking 3:234
    critique of (Anderson, J.) 1:266–7
    Daoism 2:793
    descriptive 6:539
    descriptivism (Hare, R.M.)
        4:230–1
    educational theory (Kuhn, T.S.)
        3:237
    epistemological
        underdetermination 9:527–9
    ethnocentrist alternative
        (Rorty, R.) 8:354
    hermeneutical meanings
        African philosophy,
            Anglophone 1:103
    ideology 4:683
    incommensurability 4:734
    individuality (Mikhailovskii, N.K.)
        6:355
    judgmental 2:627–8
    knowledge (Mill, J.S.) 6:366, 6:367
    law and ethics 5:148
    linguistic (Zhuangzi) 5:694, 5:703
    meaning
        Dogen 3:110
        Wittgenstein, L. 9:765
    Meinecke, F. 6:281
    metaphysical (Goodman, N.)
        4:136–7
    money (Simmel, G.) 8:778
    morality 8:189, 8:190
    pluralism 7:463, 7:464
    political
        universalism debate 7:501
    postmodernism
        revolution 8:303
    Protagoras 7:790
    Pyrrhonism 7:850, 7:851
    scientific constructivism 2:624
    subjectivism 2:627

truth 8:189, 8:190
of truth
Ramakrishna Movement 8:40
relativity
ambiguity 1:199
relativity theory
conventionalism (Schlick, F.A.M.)
8:539–40
critique of (Whitehead, A.N.)
9:715–16
determinism and indeterminism
8:193
extension 8:194
general 4:5–9, 8:191, 8:196–8
Bridgman, P.W. 2:18
determinism 8:197
Einstein, A. 3:254, 3:255–6,
4:8–9
logical positivism 4:7–8, 5:791
Mach's principle 8:197–8
Neo-Kantianism 4:6–7
philosophical responses to
4:5–9, 8:191, 8:196–8
positivism 4:5–6
Weyl, H. 9:706
general
Weyl, H. 9:706
Hamilton, Sir W. 6:207
logical positivism 5:791
Lorentz transformations 8:191–3
matter 6:195
Maxwell, J.C. 6:209
measurement 8:194
modernism 6:447–8
operationalism (Bridgman, P.W.)
7:132
optics 7:137–8
philosophical significance of
8:191–200, 8:575
Planck, M.K.E.L. 7:396
simultaneity 8:193
conventionality thesis 8:194–6
spacetime 9:67–8
special 8:191, 8:192–6
Bridgman, P.W. 2:18
determinism and indeterminism
3:34
Einstein, A. 3:254, 3:255
positivism 4:5
twin paradox 8:193–4
successive states of affairs
(Kant, I.) 5:187
supersubstantivalism 8:198
time 8:193–4, 9:414–15
time travel 9:417
relevance logic 2:599, 2:600, 8:200–4
relevant alternatives see scepticism

reliabilism 8:204–9
abstract objects
knowledge of 1:35
causal theory of knowledge 5:265,
8:205
cognition (Wodeham, A.) 9:773
consequences 9:618
deductive closure principle 2:844
defeasibility theory of knowledge
5:277
epistemic relativism 3:360–1
epistemological
faith 9:329
externalism 8:205–7
Gaṅgeśa 3:843, 3:844–5
information theory 4:787
innate belief 4:796
justification 4:824–5, 5:160–1
learning theories 5:485
naturalism 8:162
Nozick, R. 7:46
Nyāya 3:388, 3:389–90, 3:391
pattern matching 8:207–8
process reliabilism 1:2
reliable-process theory 3:380
virtue epistemology 9:618, 9:620
warrant theory 5:271
reliance
trust distinction 9:467
religion
see also positive religion; religious;
theology
alienation 1:179
political philosophy
history of 7:516
ancient philosophy relationship
1:264–5
apocatastasis (Unamuno y
Jugo, M. De) 9:520–1
asceticism 1:517–18
Augustine 1:553–4
authority (Hooker, R.) 4:505–6
causes of (Hume, D.) 4:544,
4:558–9
certainty (Sergeant, J.) 8:698, 8:699
'civil' (Harrington, J.) 4:233
common notions (Herbert, E.)
4:373–4
Comtean logics (Comte, A.)
2:502–3, 2:504–5
contribution to civilization (al-
Afghani) 1:94–5
critical realism (Lonergan, B.J.F.)
5:824–5
critiques of 8:236–8
Diderot, D. 3:63
Feuerbach, L.A. 3:635–8, 4:283

Hegel, G.W.F. 4:262
Hume, D. 4:543, 4:558–60
causes of 4:544, 4:558–9
cosmic design 4:558–9
human nature 4:559–60
miracles 4:548
Marx, K. 6:121, 8:217, 8:236,
8:237, 8:238
cognitive malfunction 8:216
ideology 8:228
Young Hegelians 6:118
culture 2:747, 2:749
deism (Butler, J.) 2:154, 2:157–9
emotions (Hägerström, A.A.T.)
4:203
enforcement of (Locke, J.) 5:461
enthusiasm 3:330–2
and epistemology 8:209–18
de facto and de jure 8:214, 8:217
evidentialism 8:210–13
criticism 8:213–14
Freud, S. 8:214–16
Marx, K. 8:216
ethics
distinctivist approach 8:220
Judaism
Cohen, H. 2:400
Ha'am, Ahad 4:192
existentialism 3:494, 3:499–500
experiential awareness
Ahndung (inkling) 3:798
free thinkers (Collins, A.) 2:415–16
hope (Bloch, E.) 4:508
inclusivism (Radhakrishnan, S.)
8:24
influenced by Neoplatonism 6:802
language see religious language
Le Roy, É.L.E.J. 5:481
liberation theories
cultural identity 2:745
liberty (Constant de Rebeque)
2:616–17
Marxism
African philosophy,
Anglophone 1:99–1:100
Latin America 6:161, 6:163
meaning of life 5:630, 5:631
modernism 6:447
morality 8:218–24
descriptive relativism 6:539
James, W. 7:641
Masham, D. 6:167
motivation
Latitudinarianism 5:434
natural
critique of 8:236–7
Ficino, M. 3:655–6

Hegel, G.W.F. 4:262
Paley, W. 7:186–8
Tindal, M. 9:420, 9:421–2
naturalism
  Presocratic philosophy 9:651
Neoplatonism
  Bodin, J. 1:797–8
non-reductionist understanding of
  (Cohen, H.) 6:782
obligation
  Jewish pietism (Ibn Paquda)
    4:633–6
origin of (Prodicus) 7:732
pagan (Theophrastus) 9:339
phenomenology of 7:352–5
  Latin America 7:349
philosophical faith (Jaspers, K.)
  5:81
philosophy of 8:248–50
philosophy relationship
  Fichte, J.G. 3:651
  Islam 1:77, 3:386–7, 5:14–15,
    6:238–9
    al-'Amiri 1:207
    al-Ghazali 4:639–41
    Ibn Rushd 4:638, 4:642,
      4:643
  Judaism
    Abravanel, I. 1:22–3
    Averroism 1:598, 1:599–600,
      1:601–2
    Gersonides 4:49
    Ibn Falaquera 4:616
    Ibn Shem Tov, J. 8:739
    Jewish Enlightenment
      3:321–2
    Maimonides, M. 6:41, 6:43
    Mendelssohn, M. 6:306
    Messer Leon 6:332
  Marx, K. 6:123
  al-Sijistani 8:774, 8:775
poetry conflict
  Japanese Buddhism
    kokoro 5:292
political authority conflict
  (Marsilius of Padua) 6:113
political neutrality 6:818–19
political philosophy 8:224–30
Porphyry 7:547
pre-Columbian America 5:429,
  5:430
primitive
  supernatural 7:97
public duties of (Hooker, R.) 4:505
reason and
  Astell, M. 1:528
  Hegel, G.W.F. 4:259, 4:276–7

historical transition to (Vico, G.)
  9:602–3, 9:604–5
Le Clerc, J. 5:476
Witherspoon, J. 9:755–6
Renaissance humanism 4:538–9
revelation (Butler, J.) 2:158
Russian Hegelianism conciliation
  4:306
sacred history 4:454
science and 8:230–6
  Ibn Daud, A. 4:610
  Spencer, H. 9:87
  Unamuno y Jugo, M. De 9:519
  as social control (Ibn Tufayl) 4:659
social sphere (Chaadaev, P.I.)
  2:270
spiritual arts (Scheler, M.F.) 8:506,
  8:507
spiritual transformation
  Russian philosophy 8:420, 8:421
state relationship
  Hobbes, T. 4:462, 4:472–3
  Leibowitz, Y. 5:562–4
  political philosophy
    Indian 7:521, 7:522–3
static/dynamic distinction
  (Bergson, H.-L.) 1:735
suffering 9:214
supernaturalism
  Judaism
    modernity 5:204
symbolic representation of truth
  (Ibn Tufayl) 4:657, 4:658–9
toleration 9:430, 9:432
  Gandhi, M.K. 3:842–3
  Latitudinarianism 5:433
  Locke, J. 5:677
  More, H. 6:576, 6:581
  political philosophy
    history of 7:511
tradition 9:446
traditional African 1:117–21
truthfulness 9:482
typology 7:352, 7:353
universality of (Calvin, J.) 2:178
utopianism (Bloch, E.S.) 1:789
Xenophanes 9:809
Religion of the Heavenly Way see
  Tonghak
Religionskritik see religion,
  critiques of
religious belief
  see also faith; religious
  epistemology; theism
  African 1:117–20, 3:431–2
  African ethical systems 3:431–2
  agnosticism 1:121–3

certainty 8:209
cognitive
  Freud, S. 8:215–16
  Marx, K. 8:216
critique of (Marx, K.) 8:216
de facto/de jure question 8:210,
  8:214, 8:217
epistemic duty 8:213–14
  Locke, J. 8:211–13
evidentialism 8:209, 8:210–14
Freud, S. 8:214–16
Judaism
  Albo, J. 1:153, 1:154
  Maimonides, M. 1:153
justification 4:95, 8:209–10,
  8:213–14
  Locke, J. 8:211–12
knowledge 8:211
  Locke, J. 3:542–3, 8:211–12
mysticism 6:630–2, 8:251–2
natural 8:216–17
propositional evidence 8:211,
  8:214
rationality of 8:217
reason conflict (Vico, G.) 9:603,
  9:604–5
reasoning (Newman, J.H.) 6:821,
  6:822
reliability
  miracles 6:413
religious language 8:256
Rousseau, J.-J. 8:372, 8:373
religious epistemology 8:209–18,
  8:238–9
  biological sciences 8:232–3
  Calvin, J. 2:177, 2:178–9
  cosmology 8:233
  de facto and de jure 8:214, 8:217
  evidentialism 8:210–13
    criticism 8:213–14
  Freud, S. 8:214–16
  geological history 8:232
  illumination theories 4:698–9
  justification 8:245–6
  language 8:234–5
  Marx, K. 8:216
  physics 8:230, 8:233–4
  religious statements 8:257
  science and 8:231–2
  statements 8:257
religious existentialism
  Shestov, L. 8:741, 8:744–5
religious experience 8:250–5
  African 1:120
  as a basis for belief 8:251–2
  belief about God 3:299

doxastic practice
  exclusivism 8:262–3
God
  atheist view of 1:533
  awareness of 8:250–1
  James, W. 5:63–4
  miracles
    Lewis, C.S. 5:589–90
  models of (Ramsey, I.T.) 8:49–50
  mysticism **6:627–32**
  naturalism 8:253
  numinous (Otto, R.) 7:173–5
  revelation 8:297, 8:298
  supernatural (Oman, J.W.) 7:97
  visions (Hildegard of Bingen)
    4:429–30
religious hero
  halakhic man (Soloveitchik, J.B.)
    9:26
religious knowledge
  see also religious epistemology
  Calvin, J. 2:177, 2:178–9
  Clement of Alexandria 2:384
  Durandus of St Pourçain 3:173
  evidentialism 8:211
  Gerson, J. 4:46
  Gnosticism 6:75
  Holcot, R. 4:477–8
  illumination theories 4:698–9
  justification of 8:245–6
  mysticism 6:628
  natural 8:216–17
  personal experience (Bowne, B.P.)
    1:852
  Rahner, K. 8:36–7
  religious experiences as basis for
    8:251–2, 8:254
  science 8:231–2
religious language 8:248, **8:255–60**
  Augustinian-Boethian doctrine
    5:390, 5:393, 5:395–6
  epistemology 8:234–5
  Ibn Rushd 4:644–5
  Islamic philosophy 4:644–5,
    6:238–9
  Judaism (Leibowitz, Y.) 5:563
  natural theology 6:710–11
  negative theology 6:761–2
    Aquinas, T. 6:760–1
  Nygren, A. 7:68
  predicates 8:258–9
  Ramsey, I.T. 8:49–50
  terminology 8:258–9
  Wittgenstein, L. 9:767–8
religious obligations
  intention
    Rabbinic theology 9:334–5

religious orders
  see also Augustinian religious
    orders; Dominicans; Franciscan
    religious order; Jesuits; Oratorian
    religious order
  Latin America
    pre-Columbian thought 5:430
religious philosophy
  history of **8:238–4**
    definitions 8:239
    divine attributes 8:243–4
    epistemology 8:245–6
    evil 8:244–5
    God, arguments for the
      existence of 8:239–43
religious pluralism **8:260–4**
  exclusivism 8:262–3
  Hick, J. 8:261–2
  history of 8:260–1
  Jewish philosophy, contemporary
    5:93
  mystical experience 8:254
  rationality of 8:263
religious scepticism
  toleration 9:432
'religious socialism'
  Tillich, P. 9:409
Relihan, J.C. 2:759, 5:854
REM *see* rapid eye movement
remainders **8:134–41**
  see also rectification; regret; shame
  guilt 8:135, 8:139–40
Remigius of Auxerre 2:223
Remonstrants 8:274
remorse 8:139–40
Remusat, C.F.M. de 4:375
ren (becoming a person)
  Confucius 2:567–8
ren (humaneness or benevolence)
  see also jin
  Cheng Hao 2:301
  Confucianism 2:539, 2:540
  love (Cheng Yi) 2:302
  neo-Confucianism 6:769
ren (ideal of humanity)
  cosmic creativity (Zhu Xi) 9:864
Renaissance
  alchemy 1:157
  ancient philosophy influence 1:265
  Aristotelianism **1:404–13**
  educational philosophy 3:225–6
  feminism 3:577–8
  historical study (Cassirer, E.) 2:225
  humanism 4:528, 4:529, **4:533–41**
    view of medieval philosophy
      6:270
  language **5:411–15**

logic **5:766–72**
philosophy **8:264–7**
  Platonism **7:439–47**
  political philosophy
    history of 7:509–10
  postmodernism 7:587
  rhetoric 8:306
  scepticism **8:498–504**
  social science
    history of philosophy of 8:849
renaissance, Carolingian **2:220–3**
Renan, E. 1:598, 4:299, 6:661
Renard, Georges 4:800, 4:802
Renaudet, A. 6:56
Renaut, A. 3:653, 7:596
Rencho *see* Nichiren
Rendawa Shönnu lodrö *see* Red
  mda'ba gZhon nu blo gros
Renner, Karl 6:143, **8:267–8**
Rennie, Bryan Stephenson
  Eliade, M. †3:260–3
Renou, L. 2:4
Renouvier, Charles Bernard **8:268–70**
renunciation
  duty
    Indian philosophy 3:183,
      3:185–7
  Jainism 6:33
Reny, P. 2:835
Repellini, Ferruccio Franco
  Ptolemy †7:830–2
repentance
  forgiveness 3:699, 8:136
  free will (Anselm of Canterbury)
    1:291
  guilt comparison 8:139
Repici, L. 9:163
Reportatio parisiensis see Duns
  Scotus, John
reported speech *see* indirect discourse
representation
  see also representationalism
  artistic
    Cubism 6:448
    pictorial 2:892–6
    Wollheim 1:473
  biological function
    teleological theories 8:673–4
  computation
    connectionist networks 2:572–3
  logical
    common-sense reasoning 2:452
  measurement theory 6:244
  mental
    causal (Locke, J.) 5:665, 5:669
    cognitive stages (Tetens, J.N.)
      9:320–1

colour experience 2:423–4
computational theory of vision
    (Burge, T.) 6:342, 6:343
concepts 2:513
content
    wide and narrow 2:643
criticism of functionalism 3:806,
    3:812
explanatory principle
    (Schopenhauer, A.) 8:547–8
imagery 4:704
indexical content of thought
    2:639
innate/learned
    infant cognition 2:391
introspective awareness 4:843
language of thought hypothesis
    2:451, 5:405
perceptual–conceptual
    distinction 8:549
referents
    concepts 2:508
Reinhold, K.L. 8:186
self
    psychoanalysis 7:817
    vision in God (Malebranche, N.)
    6:58–61
political **8:270–2**
    see also democracy;
    government; state
saying/showing (Wittgenstein, L.)
    9:757, 9:761
symbolic (Piaget, J.) 7:383
representational art
    emotional response to 3:274–7
    truth 1:456–7
representational power
    non-rational soul 9:41
representationalism
    awareness
        Indian theories of 1:606
    cognition
        Buridan, J. 2:131, 2:133
    pragmatism as anti 7:635–7
    science
        Heidegger, M. 4:326
repression
    Freudian
        Jung, C.G. 5:132
        social revolution (Marcuse, H.)
        6:97
    political
        Latin American academics
        1:231, 5:611
reprobation **8:272–6**
    Augustine of Hippo 8:273
    Calvin, J. 2:180

negative 8:273, 8:274
predestination 7:656
Reformation 8:274
reproduction
    see also procreation
    ethics **8:276–80**
        contraception 5:629
        gene therapy 4:18
        genetic screening 4:16–17
        sexuality 8:720
    species classification
        biological concept 9:78–9
republicanism **8:280–3**
    Aristotle 7:506
    Cicero, M.T. 2:356–7
    citizenship 2:364
    civic 2:364, 7:832
    communicative reason
        (Habermas, J.) 4:197
    confederation 3:573
    corruption 2:676
    Harrington, J. 4:231–3
    historical change
        political philosophy
        history of 7:513
    Kant, I. 5:195
    liberty
        political philosophy
        history of 7:504
    Machiavelli, N. 6:17, 6:19–21
    peace 9:689
    political realism (Witherspoon, J.)
        9:756
    public interest 7:832
    Renaissance philosophy
        political 7:509–10
    Roman
        political philosophy
        history of 7:506–8
    social contract theory
        (Rousseau, J.-J.) 8:368, 8:370–2
    sovereignty relationship 9:57–8
    United States of America 2:868
        Paine, T. 7:185
        War of Independence 7:514
reputation
    African ethical systems 3:433
res ('thing')
    Henry of Ghent 4:355–6
Rescher, Nicholas
    Chinese Confucianism 2:548–9
    coherence theory of justification
        5:255–6, 5:258, 5:259
    fallibilism †3:545–8
    imperative logic 4:720–1
    logic, Islamic philosophy 5:713
    Łukasiewicz, J. 5:863

many-valued logics 6:84, 6:91
Peirce, C.S. 7:284
risk 8:334, 8:338
research
    see also experiments; scientific
    method
    applied ethics 1:323
    computational
        classical AI 1:487
    economics 3:213–14
    embryonic and foetal 8:276–7
    human experimentation
        medical ethics 6:260, 6:261–2
    interdisciplinary (Horkheimer, M.)
        4:510–11
    scientific
        androcentrism 3:861–2, 3:864
        archaeology 1:354–7
        experiment **3:514–18**
        Heidegger, M. 4:325
        logic of discovery **3:99–103**
        research groups 8:580
        women's role 3:864
    scientific responsibility 8:289
    social sciences 8:860
        feminism 3:588, 3:589–91
        operationalism 7:134
resemblance
    abstract ideas (Hume, D.) 4:546
    artistic expression 1:497
    pictorial depiction 2:892–3,
        2:895–6
    primary–secondary distinction
        (Locke, J.) 7:685
resentment
    moral sentiments 6:549
Resnik, M. 4:118, 8:123–4
resolution
    humour 4:566
resources
    health care
        medical ethics 6:262–3
    scientific responsibility 8:289
    shared (Proudhon, P.-J.) 7:791
respect
    see also self-respect
    African ethical systems 3:433
    appraisal–recognition distinction
        (Darwall, S.) 8:284
    Kant, I. 8:132
    living things
        agricultural ethics 1:126
        for persons 4:133, **8:283–7**
        sexuality (Kant, I.) 8:722–3
responsibilities of scientists and
    intellectuals **8:287–90**
    see also bioethics; engineering

ethics; genetics, ethics; technology,
ethics
responsibility **8:290–4**
action 1:40–1
causa sui 3:744, 3:747
desert 3:25–6
extent of (Levinas, E.) 5:581
faith 3:538, 3:540–1, 3:542–3
free will 3:747–9
incompatibilism 3:743–4, 3:746,
3:749–50
individual
beneficence 4:343
existentialist ethics 3:503
information technology and ethics
4:780–1
mental illness 6:313–14
moral
atonement 1:540
moral agents 6:499–501
moral expertise 6:510
moral luck 6:521
notion of
continuants 2:652
power relationship 7:612
praise and blame 7:644
predestination 7:655–6
self-deception 8:630–1
social
business ethics 2:152–3
Stoicism 9:158–9
technology and ethics 9:282
universalism in ethics 9:536
Restall, Greg
logical laws †5:785–9
restoration (*apocatastasis*)
Origen 7:162
restoration of equilibrium
al-Razi, Abu Bakr 8:111
restriction
medieval language 5:399
resurrection **8:294–6**
see also palingenesis
Bultmann, R. 2:129
Christianity 3:414–15, 3:416
Fëdorov, N.F. 3:574, 3:575
al-Ghazali 4:64, 4:65
heaven 4:249, 4:250–1
Ibn Sina 4:65
interpretation of meaning
Islamic philosophy 6:238–9
Jesus 8:38
Rahner, K. 8:38
Jewish philosophy (Saadiah Gaon)
8:438
al-Razi, Fakhr al-Din 8:114
soul, immortality of 3:416

retention
Ibn Sina 4:649–50
retributivism
punishment 2:705, 2:707–8
Hart, H.L.A. 4:235
retrospection
introspection (James, W.) 4:844
Reusch, J.P.
logical calculus 5:719
revelation 8:249, **8:296–300**
see also religious experience
Barth, K. 1:652–3, 1:654
Brunner, E. 2:31, 2:32
Christian
Butler, J.
credibility 2:158
moral motivation 2:157
denial of
deism 2:852–4, 3:113–14
divine law 8:226
divine/human action 3:560, 3:561
faith 8:245
historical evidence for 8:298–9
interpretation 8:299, 8:300
Islamic philosophy
al-'Amiri 1:207
Ash'ariyya 1:522
al-Ghazali 4:66
Ibn Massara 4:627–8
Ibn Taymiyya 4:655
law 5:457–8, 5:459–60
modern philosophy 5:17
mystical philosophy 6:618
Jewish philosophy
anti-Semitism (Kant, I.)
1:311–12
Buber, M. 4:496
Heschel, A.J. 4:411
Ibn Shem Tov, Shem Tov 8:738
Mendelssohn, M. 6:306
myth–language relationship
(Rosenzweig, F.) 8:357,
8:359–60
prophetic (Judah ben Moses of
Rome) 5:129–30
Stenheim, S.L. 5:98
as knowledge (Rāmānuja) 8:43
Locke, J. critique 5:677
Luther, M. 6:3
natural theology 6:707, 6:709–10
philosophy incompatibility
(Shestov, L.) 8:741, 8:744
propositional 8:297, 8:298–300
reason and
Ash'ariyya 1:522
Ibn Massara 4:627–8
Ibn Taymiyya 4:655

Islamic philosophy 5:6, 5:8–9
Jewish philosophy
Fackenheim, E.L. 3:534
Ibn Ezra, A. 4:611, 4:612
Le Clerc, J. 5:476
Witherspoon, J. 9:755–6
Scripture (Calvin, J.) 2:179
secular learning relationship
2:772–3
symbolic language (Tillich, P.)
9:410
transcendent (Thielicke, H.) 9:370
revenge 3:148, 3:286–7
Reventlow, H.G. 2:380
revisionism
hermeneutics 4:388
Russian empiriocriticism 8:404–5
revolution **8:301–4**
see also communism; Marxism;
rebellion; socialism
anarchism 1:246–7
anti-colonialism
Cabral, A. 2:170
Fanon, F. 3:553–4
Arendt, H. 1:371
critique of (Kant, I.) 5:195
Kautsky, K.J. 5:223
Luxemburg, R. 6:5, 6:6, 6:7
Marx, K.
political philosophy
history of 7:516
Marxism
Latin America 6:161–2, 6:163
Lukács, G. 5:857
moral evolution
(Wollstonecraft, M.) 9:790
Paine, T. 7:185
permanent
Chinese Marxism 6:133,
6:135–6, 6:137
Trotsky, L. 9:464
Plekhanov, G.V. 7:451–3
political philosophy
history of 7:504
rebellion contrast (Camus, A.)
2:194–5
Russian materialism 8:416, 8:417
sensualism (Feuerbach, L.A.)
3:637–8
social (Marcuse, H.) 6:96, 6:97
Sorel, G. 9:34–5
revolutionary democracy
Chernyshevskii, N.G. 2:306
revolutions, scientific
chemistry 2:294
effect on epistemology (Taylor, C.)
9:276

experiment 3:514–15
Kuhn, T.S 4:732–3, 5:316, 5:317
matter 6:192, 6:194–5
reward
   divine
      providence (Nahmanides, M.)
         6:649
      divine justice
         Ash'ariyya 1:522
         al-Ghazali 4:63–4
         Mu'tazila 1:522, 4:63–4
         al-Razi, Fakhr al-Din 8:114
      social control (Mozi) 6:452, 6:453,
         6:454, 6:456
      of the soul (al-'Amiri) 1:207, 1:208
Rex, J. 8:21
Rey, A. 7:482
Rey, Georges
   colour and qualia 2:427
   computational theories of mind
      †6:390–4
   concepts †2:505–17
   connectionism 2:578–9
   consciousness 2:596
   content
      wide and narrow 2:646
   eliminativism †3:263–6
   Fodor, J.A. 3:686
   folk psychology †3:686–7
   holism
      mental and semantic 4:493
   language of thought hypothesis
      †5:404–8
   mind, philosophy of †6:403–7
   semantics
      informational †8:658–62
   Skinner, B.F. †8:799–802
   unconscious mental states
      †9:522–7
Reyes, Alfonso 6:100
Reyes, G. 2:236–7
Reyle, U. 1:243, 3:98–9
Reymer Baer, Nicolas 9:138
Reymond, B. 8:538
Rg Veda
   Brahman 2:1, 2:4
   cosmology and cosmogony
      2:681–2, 2:684
   duty 3:183–4
   fate 3:565
   God
      concepts of 4:102–3, 4:105
   interpretation 4:834
   self 8:606, 8:611
rGyal tshab dar ma rin chen
   (Gyeltsap darma rinchen) 8:304–5
Rhazes (al-)Razi, Abu Bakr

Rhees, R. 1:269, 9:772
Rhetoric see Aristotle
rhetoric 8:305–10
   applied ethics 8:308–9
   biblical
      Jewish philosophy (Messer
         Leon) 6:331, 6:332–3
      Chinese philosophy (Sengzhao)
         8:683
   concept of style 1:506
   education
      Erasmus, D. 3:398–9
      Melanchthon, P. 6:289
   Gorgias 4:144–5
   human nature (Campbell, G.)
      2:191–2
   of inquiry
      logic of discovery 3:102
   Islamic philosophy 1:75, 1:77
   isssues (staseis) 8:308
   John of Salisbury 5:115–16
   legal discourse 5:496–7
   legal reasoning 5:527
   literary theory (Man, P. de) 2:811
   logic 8:308
   moral and political theory
      (Aristotle) 1:431
   oratory (Cicero, M.T.) 2:356
   persuasion 8:307
   poetics 8:307, 8:308–9
   politics (Zabarella, J.) 9:837
   Ramus, P. 8:53
   Renaissance humanism 4:533–5,
      5:769, 5:770
   Tertullian, Q.S.F. 9:308
   tropes 8:308–9
Rhine, J.B. 7:225–6, 7:227
Rhineland school of mysticism 9:240,
   9:269–70
rhizome
   Deleuze, G. 2:856, 2:858
Rhodes
   Panaetius 7:188–90
Rhomeyer-Dherbey, G. 6:53
Rhook, G. 2:680–1
Rhul, Charles 1:200–1
rhythm
   Kristeva, J. 5:306
ri (principle)
   see also i; li
   ki relationship
      Confucianism
         Japanese 2:551, 5:75
Riasanovsky, Nicholas V.
   Eurasian Movement †3:453–6
   Pan-Slavism †7:197–201
Ribaillier, J. 9:728

Ricci, S. 2:175
Rice, E.F. 2:289–90
   see also Rice's theorem
Rice's theorem 2:488
Rich, Adrienne 6:100, 8:729
Rich, E. 1:492
Richard of Middleton 8:310–12
Richard of St Victor 8:312–14
Richard Rufus of Cornwall 8:314–18
   Aristotelian commentaries 1:399
Richard, Jules 7:218
   see also Richard's paradox
Richard, Mark
   compositionality †2:476–7
   propositional attitude statements
      7:779
   scope †8:587–9
   substitutional/objectual quantifers
      †7:877–82
Richards, D.J. 9:433
Richards, G. 3:843
Richards, I.A. 1:460, 7:284, 7:477,
   8:310
Richards, P. 6:844
Richards, R. 2:798
Richard's paradox 7:218
Richardson, A.W. 2:215, 9:612
Richardson, H. 1:612, 6:352
Richardson, J. 6:861
Richardson, M. 1:661
Richardson, R.D., Jr 3:272, 9:392
Richardson, Robert C.
   vitalism †9:639–43
Richardson, W.J. 4:323
Richarson, P. 8:896
Richer 4:41
Richerson, P. 3:487
Richir, M. 7:254
Richman, F. 2:638
Richman, M. 1:661
Richter, M. 4:170
Richter, V. 2:693
Rickard, M. 7:57
Ricken, U. 5:379
Rickert, Heinrich
   Ajdukiewicz, K. 1:136–7
   historicism 4:445, 4:446
   Lebensphilosophie 5:489
   Neo-Kantianism 6:777, 6:785–6,
      6:791
Ricketts, M.L. 3:263
Ricketts, T. 2:215, 3:777–8
Rickey, V.F. 5:574, 6:320, 7:499
Rico, F. 7:329
Ricoeur, Paul 8:318–22
   emotions 3:289–90

hermeneutics
    biblical 4:390, 4:393, 4:394,
        4:395
    hope 4:510
    ideology 4:684
    metaphor 8:320
    narrative 8:320–1
    phenomenology
        hermeneutical 7:339, 7:342
        of religion 7:355
    psychoanalysis 8:319
    rhetoric 8:310
    sin 8:796
    structuralism 8:319–20, 9:177
    textual interpretation 8:320
Rida, A. 3:388–7
ridicule
    comedy 2:435
Ridington, R. 6:671
Ridley, A. 3:281, 6:614
Ridley, M. 9:81, 9:275
Riedel, M. 4:301
Riedweg, C. 7:165
Riegel, J. 9:823
Rieger, R. 8:538
Riehl, Alois 5:230, 6:780–1, 6:791
Riemann, B. 4:31–2, 9:63–4, 9:65–6
Riffaterre, Michael 9:183, 9:184
Rigaldi, Odo 1:177
Riggs, P. 6:684
right
    Anselm of Canterbury 1:290
    good relationship 4:133, **8:322–5**
        consequentialism 2:603–4
        deontological ethics 2:890
        Fuller, L.L. 3:801
        political neutrality 6:820
        Ross, W.D. 8:366
    natural (Fichte, J.G.) 3:650–1
    well-being of the group (Mozi)
        6:453
the right (le droit)
    Thomism
        Villey, M. 9:614
righteousness
    Chinese philosophy (Mencius)
        6:303
rightness
    Chinese philosophy see yi
rights **8:325–31**
    absolutism 1:30
    animals
        agricultural ethics 1:127
    artificial fertilization
        reproduction ethics 8:276, 8:278
    autonomy
        ethical 1:590

characterization of 8:325–6
children
    educational philosophy
        3:234–5, 3:236–7
constitutionalism 2:620
critique of Kantian ethics 5:203
duty relationship 3:178–9
external preferences (Dworkin, R.)
    5:441–2
family
    reproduction ethics 8:279
feminism
    Latin America 3:626–7, 5:655
feminist jurisprudence 3:606,
    3:607–8, 3:609
foetal
    reproduction ethics 8:276
freedom of speech 3:762, 3:763
functions 8:328
individual
    communitarian critique of
        liberalism 2:466–7, 2:469–70
    families 3:550
international relations 4:832
justice
    Mill, J.S. 6:361, 6:371–3
    Smith, A. 8:819
justification 8:325, 8:327, 8:328–9
law and ritual, China 5:444–5,
    5:453
legal
    Stair, J.D. 9:119
    utilitarianism (Bentham, J.)
        1:719, 1:722–3
legal positivism 5:519
legal realist rejection of 5:522
as legal relations (Hohfeld, W.N.)
    4:476–7
libertarianism 5:617, 5:618
maternal
    abortion 8:277–8
moral standing 6:551
morality (Marx, K.) 6:130
multiculturalism 6:601
natural
    anarchism 1:245
    Burke, E. critique 2:139
    divine law (Carmichael, G.)
        2:206–7
    Fichte, J.G. 3:650–1
    French Revolution
        Burke, E. critique 7:514–15
    political philosophy
        history of 7:504, 7:511–13,
            7:514–15
    Suchon, G. 9:211–12

    utilitarianism (Bentham, J.)
        1:719, 1:723
    Vitoria, F. de 9:643–4
    William of Ockham 9:745–6
natural jurisprudence (Reid, T.)
    8:177–8
natural law 6:685, 6:688–9
    Hart, H.L.A. 4:235
normative direction 8:326–7, 8:328
Nozick, R. 7:45
as predictions (Holmes, O.W.)
    4:494
privacy 7:691
    information technology and
        ethics 4:780
property 7:757–8, 7:759–60
    Hume, D. 4:553–5
    information technology and
        ethics 4:779
    Kant, I. 5:191
    liberalism 5:604
    political philosophy
        history of 7:513
Roman private law 8:346
security of
    government (Hume, D.) 4:556–7
social choice 8:824, 8:825
social development (Smith, A.)
    8:819–20
social recognition 8:327–8
socialism 8:883
    Hessen, S.I. 4:418
socialism (Hessen, S.I.) 4:418
women's 3:578–9
workers 8:827
Rights of Women 3:610–11
rigid body
    geometry of physical space 4:32
rigid designators
    de relde dicto belief 2:815–16
    rigid–non-rigid distinction 1:639
    singular terms (Kripke, S.A.)
        5:302–3
Riginos, A.S. 3:254
Rigo, Caterina
    Hillel ben Samuel of Verona
        †4:431–3
    Immanuel ben Solomon of Rome
        †4:708–10
    Judah ben Moses of Rome
        †5:128–31
rigour
    mathematical
        geometry 4:29–30, 4:31
        Hilbert, D. 4:423
Rigs-gter-ba 9:406–7

Rijk, L.M. de
  Boethius, A.M.S. 1:813
  Buridan, J. 2:135
  Gilbert of Poitiers 4:72
  language
    medieval theories of 5:404
  logic, medieval 5:758–9
riken no ken 9:839–40
Riker, W.H. 2:872, 3:574
Riley, Patrick
  Fénelon, F. †3:628–30
  general will 4:11–12
  Gerdil, G.S. †4:41–2
  human nature 4:525
Rimer, J.T. 1:90, 5:660, 9:841
Rimini, A. 7:890, 7:894
ar-Rindi *see* Ibn ar-Rawandi
Ringer, F.K. 4:240
Ringleben, J. 8:538
Rinzai Zen Buddhism 3:799–800
Río, Julian Sanz del 9:72–3
Ríos, Fernando Giner de los 9:75,
  9:77
Rios Urruti, F. de los 5:301
Rips, L. 2:517, 8:90
Ripstein, Arthur
  multiculturalism †6:599–602
risk 8:331–4
  assessment of 8:331, 8:334–8
    quantitative 8:334–7
    trust 9:467
  gene therapy 4:18
  information technology and ethics
    4:780
  technology and ethics 9:282
  trust relationship 9:466
Riska, Augustin
  Avenarius, R. †1:592–5
risk-benefit analysis (RBA) 8:331
Risse, W.
  Collegium Conimbricense 2:408
  Fonseca, P. da 3:690
  logic
    Renaissance 5:772
    seventeenth and eighteenth
      century 5:721
  Melanchthon, P. 6:292
  Ramus, P. 8:54–5
  Soto, D. de 9:40
  Toletus, F. 9:435
Risser, James
  Barthes, R. †1:656–8
Rist, J.M. 7:261, 7:463, 9:160
Ristau, Carolyn 1:273
Ritchie, D.G. 4:300, 8:763
Ritschl, A. 9:520, 9:521
  see also Ritschlianism

Ritschlianism 9:520
  see also Liberal Protestantism
Ritsu (Precept) Buddhism 2:101
Ritter, A. 1:248, 7:793
Ritter, C. 7:420
Ritter, Gerhard 4:46, 4:47
Ritter, J.
  nihilism 7:5
Ritter, Johann Wilhelm
  Naturphilosophie 6:738
ritual 8:338–41
  see also sacraments
  awe 8:339
  Chinese philosophy 2:541
  Christian (Augustine) 1:554
  dance 2:777
  developed religious character
    8:339–40
  duty
    Indian concepts of 3:183–4
  ethical value 8:338–9
  as 'folkways'
    Judaism (Kaplan, M.) 5:205
  karma and rebirth
    Indian conceptions of 5:211–12,
      5:213
  Mīmāṃsā
    Vedānta School differentiation
      9:590–1
  nonlinguistic 8:340–1
  purification
    Shintō 8:749–50
  Ṛg Veda
    God 4:103
  sacraments 8:442–5
  self-expression (Kūkai) 5:319
  socialization (Xunzi) 2:324
  theistic
    Lokāyata opposition to 6:180
Ritzer, G. 9:7
Rivas Saínz, Arturo 7:350, 7:352
ar-Riwindi *see* Ibn ar-Rawandi
Rizvi, S. 8:735
rNgog lō tsa ba Blo ldan shes rab
  (Ngok lodzawa Loden shayrap)
  8:433, 9:406
Ro Youngchan
  Korean Confucian philosophy
    2:565
  Yi Yulgok †9:826–8, 9:827
Robands, J. 9:132–3
Robb, C. 7:318
Robbe-Grillet, A. 7:590
Robbins, C. 4:594
Robbins, D. 1:850
Robbins, Lionel 3:208, 3:211, 3:221,
  4:247

Robel, G. 3:327
Robert of Courçon 1:398
Roberts, A. 1:65, 4:186
Roberts, D.D. 2:734, 5:746
Roberts, H. 3:593
Roberts, J. 2:835
Roberts, Julian
  Benjamin, W. †1:716–18
  honour †4:502–4
  Lorenzen, P. †5:825–8
Roberts, J.W. 4:16
Roberts, M. 1:65
Roberts, R.H. 1:790
Roberts, S. 8:385
Robertson, J.G. 5:577
Robertson, William 3:330
Robey, D. 9:189
Robilliard, J.A. 8:314
Robin, L. 7:848
Robin, R. 7:284
Robinet, A. 3:29, 6:66, 9:196
Robinet, Isabelle
  Guanzi †4:186–7
  Huainanzi 4:514
Robinson, Abraham
  mathematics
    foundations of 6:186, 6:191–2
  models 6:446
  nonstandard analysis 1:213, 1:214,
    1:215–16, 7:52
Robinson, C. 5:854
Robinson, Daniel N.
  Du Bois-Reymond, E. †3:129–31
  Fechner, G.T. †3:570–2
  Stewart, D. 9:140
  Wundt, W. 9:801
Robinson, D.S. 2:29–8
Robinson, Howard
  Alexander of Aphrodisias 1:176
  dualism 3:138
  materialism †6:173–8
Robinson, I. 6:48
Robinson, J.A. 2:453, 7:34
Robinson, Jenefer
  art
    artistic expression 1:498
    artistic style †1:505–9
    emotion in response to 3:281
  music
    aesthetics of 6:614
Robinson, J.M. 4:85
Robinson, Neal
  'Abduh, M. †1:6–8
  Ash'ariyya and Mu'tazila
    †1:519–23
  Ibn al-'Arabi †4:601–5
Robinson, O.F. 8:347

Robinson, R.H. 2:92, 8:684
Robinson, Richard G.F. 2:849
Robinson, T.M. 3:107, 4:369
Roblin, R. 1:512
robot reply
    Chinese room argument 2:329
robotics
    situated
        artificial intelligence 1:490–1
robots
    persons 7:319
Robson, J.A. 9:804
Robson, P. 8:268
Rocci, G. 1:840
Rochat de la Vallée, E. 4:514
Roche, K.F. 4:798
Rochefoucauld, François, Duc de la
    6:555, 6:556, 6:558
Rochot, B. 3:857
Rock, Irvin 9:633, 9:638
Rock, P. 9:245
Rockefeller, S. 1:206, 3:51
Rocker, R. 1:248
Rockmore, T. 3:563, 3:652, 3:653
Rodi, F. 3:83
Rodis-Lewis, G.
    Descartes, R. 3:19
    Desgabets, R. 3:29–30
    Huet, P.-D. 4:518
    Malebranche, N. 6:66
    Port-Royal 7:554
    Régis, P.-S. 8:166
Rodó, José Enrique 5:654
Rodriguez de Lecea, Teresa
    Krause, K. †5:298–301
Roe, S.A. 5:635, 9:643
Roemer, John E.
    democracy 2:871
    economics and ethics 3:210, 3:211
    market
        ethics of the 6:110
    Marx, K. 6:133
    property 7:761
    socialism 8:886
Roensch, F.J. 4:404, 5:114–15, 7:323,
    9:388
Roethlisberger, F.J. 3:520
Roger Bacon see Bacon, Roger
Roger, G. 1:716
Roger, J. 1:840, 2:122
Rogers, Carl 7:828, 7:829
Rogers, G.A.J.
    Bold, S. †1:822–3
    Charleton, W. †2:285–7
    Cudworth, R. 2:744
    Glanvill, J. †4:80–3
    Hobbes, T. 4:476

Rogers, H.
    Church's thesis 2:355
    computability theory 2:491
    recursion-theoretic hierarchies
        8:145
    Turing machines 9:499
    Turing reducibility and Turing
        degrees 9:502
Rogers, J. 2:263
Rogers, P. 3:320, 5:157
Rogers, R. 3:320
Rogers, T.B. 7:135
Rohault, Jacques **8:341–3**
Rohio, S.W. 1:107
Rohls, J. 9:727
Rohr, Michael David
    Rorty, R. †8:352–6
Rohrer, C. 1:243
Roig, Arturo Andrés
    Argentina, philosophy in 1:379
    liberation philosophy 5:611, 5:612
    marginality
        Latin America 6:100, 6:101
roles
    human interaction (Mead, G.H.)
        6:210–11
    social
        responsibility 8:287–8, 8:289–90
Rolland, R. 8:42
Roll-Hansen, N. 8:492
Rollins, C.D. 1:583, 7:248
Rollins, P. 8:473
Rolston, H. 3:202, 3:821, 6:554, 8:236
Roman, C. 5:367
Roman Catholicism
    see also Counter-Reformation;
        neo-Catholicism; papal authority;
        transubstantiation
    Aristotelianism conciliation
        (White, T.) 9:712–13
    capital punishment 4:798
    casuistry 2:228
    charity
        as Christian love 2:280–1
    defence of (Charron, P.) 2:288
    Eucharist 8:443–4
    evolutionary theory (Teilhard de
        Chardin, P.) 9:288–9
    freedom of conscience 8:228
    Galilei, G. 3:836–7, 3:839–40
    grace 4:148, 4:149
    heaven 4:250, 4:252
    justification doctrine 5:165, 5:167
    killing of innocents 4:797, 4:798
    liberation theology 5:613–14,
        5:616
    limbo **5:635–7**, 5:637

Manicheism comparison 6:76
    morality 8:222
    natural law
        political philosophy
            history of 7:511–12
    Poland 7:486
    Protestantism debates
        (Chillingworth, W.) 2:307–8
    purgatory 7:836–8
    Rahner, K. 8:36
    reprobation 8:273–5
    role of
        liberation theology 5:615–16
    Russia (Solov'ëv, V.S.) 9:28, 9:30
    sacraments 8:442–5
    sanctification 8:454–5, 8:456
    science
        suppression of 8:230–1
    sexuality 8:724
    Thomism 6:101–4, 9:380–6
    Trinity
        Swedenborg, E. critique 9:242
Roman Empire
    collapse of
        effect on medieval philosophy
            6:270–1
    Manicheism 6:74–5, 6:76
    political philosophy
        history of 7:504, 7:506–8
Roman law **8:343–8**
    absolutism 1:30
    civilian tradition 8:343
    Corpus Iuris Civilis 8:344–5
    equity/law (*ius/aequitas*)
        distinction 5:150
    Gaius 3:831–2
    historical jurisprudence 5:138
    history of 8:343–4
    Justinian 5:168–9
    legal hermeneutics 5:507
    medieval 5:506, 5:507
    political philosophy
        history of 7:507, 7:509
    written reason 5:465
Roman philosophy
    see also Greek philosophy, ancient
    Alexander of Aphrodisias
        1:169–76
    Ammonius **1:208–10**
    Carneades 2:216
    Celsus of Alexandria **2:264**
    Cicero, M.T. **2:355–60**
    Galen **3:832–5**
    Lucretius **5:854–6**
    Marcus Aurelius **6:93–5**
    Musonius Rufus **6:615–16**
    Neoplatonism **6:797–803**

Plotinus **7:456–63**
Porphyry **7:545–50**
Pythagoreanism 6:809
rhetoric
　style 1:506
Seneca, L.A. **8:679–82**
Stoicism 9:143, 9:159
Roman stoicism *see* Epictetus;
　Marcus Aurelius; Musonius
　Rufus; Seneca; Stoicism
Roman tragedy 9:448–9
Romania
　Eliade, M. **3:260–3**
Romano, F. 7:550
Romano, Judah *see* Judah ben Moses
　of Rome
Romano Muñoz, José 3:512–14
Romano, Santi 4:800–1, 4:802
Romanoff, J. 8:385
Romanticism
　aesthetics (Schlegel, F. von)
　　8:529–31
　Cavell, S. 2:258
　existentialism 3:493
　German **8:348–52**
　hermeneutics
　　biblical 4:391–2
　individual style 1:506
　poetry 7:473, 7:474–6
　Protestantism comparison
　　(Ruge, A.) 8:386
　self-realization 8:633
Rombach, H. 6:838
Rome
　Augustine of Hippo **1:541–59**
　Boethius, A.M.S. **1:801–13**
　Carneades 2:216
　Cicero, M.T. **2:355–60**
　Gaius **3:831–2**
　Galen **3:832–5**
　Immanuel ben Solomon of
　　4:708–10
　Judah ben Moses of **5:128–31**
　Justinian **5:168–9**
　Lucretius **5:854–6**
　Marcus Aurelius **6:93–5**
　Marius Victorinus **6:105–7**
　Musonius Rufus **6:615–16**
　republicanism (Machiavelli, N.)
　　6:19–21
　Tertullian, Q.S.F. **9:307–9**
　Themistius **9:324–6**
Römer, C. 6:77
Romero, Francisco
　Argentina, philosophy in 1:377,
　　1:379

Latin America
　analytic philosophy 1:230, 1:233
　existentialism 3:511
Romero, Silvio 2:10, 2:12
Rommen, H. 5:468, 6:690, 9:196
Roncaglia, G. 5:415, 5:721–2
Ronchi, V. 7:139
rōnin, the forty-seven 2:149–50, 7:90
Ronzeaud, P. 9:212–13
Root, M. 5:645, 8:870–1
Roques, R. 3:406, 7:808
Rorem, P. 7:808
Rorty, A.O.
　Aristotle 1:435
　Descartes, R. 3:19
　emotions 3:285
　katharsis 5:220
　mimēsis 6:382
　morality and identity 6:575
　multiculturalism 6:602
　self-control 8:613
　self-deception 8:628
Rorty, Richard **8:352–6**
　African philosophy, Francophone
　　1:116
　alterity and identity
　　postmodern theories of 1:192
　analytic philosophy 1:229
　eliminativism 3:266
　epistemological behaviourism
　　8:353–4
　fictional entities 3:666, 3:667
　hermeneutics
　　biblical 4:393–4
　history
　　philosophy of 4:457, 4:459
　Lyotard, J.-F. 6:11–12
　metaphilosophy 8:353
　mind, philosophy of 8:354–5
　poetry 7:477
　political philosophy
　　nature of 7:528
　post-structuralism 7:596,
　　7:599–600
　pragmatism †7:633–40
　rationalism 8:80
　social philosophy 8:354
　solidarity 9:24, 9:25
　substance 9:210
　Vlastos, G. 9:653–4
Rosa, R. 2:535
Rosaldo, M.Z. 3:593
Rosario, Charles 7:350, 7:352
Rosati, Connie S.
　ideals †4:672–5
Roscelin of Compiègne **8:356–7**
　Platonism, medieval 7:434

Trinity
　Anselm of Canterbury critique
　　1:292–3
　universals 7:18–19
Rosch, E. 1:492, 2:517
Roscher, W. 3:221–2
Rose, G. 1:46
Rose, H. 3:602, 3:868
Rose, J. 3:409
Rose, M. 9:215
Rose, Paul L. 1:314, 1:799, 4:541
Rose, S. 6:720–1
Rosen, E. 2:672
Rosen, F. 1:725
Rosen, G. 7:572, 8:584, 9:230
Rosen, H. 3:315
Rosen, Michael
　Hegel, G.W.F. 4:279
　Marx, K. †6:117–33
Rosen, N. 1:716, 7:894
　see also Einstein-Podolsky-Rosen
　experiment
Rosen, S. 7:5
Rosen, Z. 1:667
Rosenau, P.M. 8:847
Rosenbaum, Alyssa *see* Rand, Ayn
Rosenberg, Alan
　Blanchot, M. †1:782–4
Rosenberg, Alex
　economics
　　philosophy of 3:222
　Hume, D. 4:561
　social science
　　methodology of †8:859–68
　　prediction in 8:872
　sociobiology †8:892–6
Rosenberg, C. 2:579
Rosenberg, C.M. 1:452
Rosenberg, Jay F.
　Sellars, W.S. †8:638–42
Rosenberg, M. 3:520
Rosenberg, S. 6:335
Rosenblatt, R. 4:495
Rosencreutz, Christian 9:363
Rosenfeld, B.A. 9:66
Rosenfield, L.C. 5:481
Rosenkrantz, Gary
　omnipotence †7:98–7:103
　religion, history of philosophy of
　　8:247
Rosenkrantz, Karl 4:279, 4:282, 4:298
Rosenkrantz, R. 7:711, 8:783, 9:127
Rosenstock-Huessy, Eugen 8:360,
　8:361
Rosenthal, Bernice Glatzer
　Bulgakov, S.N. †2:123–6
　empiriocriticism, Russian 8:409

Nietzsche, F.W.
    impact on Russian thought
        †6:861–7
Rozanov, V.V. †8:381–5
Russian religious-philosophical
    Renaissance †8:422–8
Shestov, L. †8:740–6
Rosenthal, David M.
    consciousness 2:596
    dualism †3:133–8
    functionalism 3:813
    higher-order thought
        phenomenal consciousness
        2:593
    identity theory of mind 6:399
    introspection, psychology of 4:843,
        4:846
    qualia 7:867
Rosenthal, E.I.J. 2:807, 4:626–7,
    7:521, 8:440
Rosenthal, F.
    epistemology in Islamic
        philosophy 3:388
    al-Kindi 5:252–3
    Orientalism in Islamic philosophy
        7:160
    Platonism in Islamic philosophy
        7:430
    Saadiah Gaon 8:440
Rosenthal, R. 3:520
Rosenthal, Sandra B.
    Lewis, C.I. †5:585–9
Rosenzweig, Franz 8:357–62
    Buber, M. 2:44–5
    German Idealism 8:357, 8:358
    Jewish philosophy 5:90
        contemporary 5:90, 5:91,
        5:92–3, 5:95
    New Thinking 8:357, 8:358–60
Rosicrucianism 3:682–3, 9:363
Rosier, I. 5:404
Rosmaita, Brian
    Neumann, J. von †6:809–13
Rosmini-Serbati, Antonio 8:362–4
    Kantianism in Italy 5:37, 5:42
Rosner, F. 1:779
Rosnow, R.L. 3:520
Rospatt, Alexander von
    momentariness
        Buddhist doctrine of †6:469–73
Ross, A.
    see also Ross's paradox
    imperative logic 4:721
    Overton, R. 7:177
Ross, Alf 8:364–5
    legal concepts 5:495–6
    legal norms 7:41

legal positivism 5:521
legal realism 5:525
Ross, Angus
    society
        concept of †8:886–9
Ross, D. 6:196, 8:859
Ross, I.S. 4:501, 8:822
Ross, J.F. 1:349, 9:314
Ross, J.J. 3:551
Ross, K. 5:491
Ross, L. 6:727, 8:89
Ross, William David 8:365–7
    Aristotle 1:435
    axiology 1:610, 1:612
    deontological ethics 2:892
    duty 3:178, 3:182
        moral pluralism 6:529, 6:531
        moral scepticism 6:543, 6:545
    foundationalism 3:723
    help and beneficence 4:344
    intuitionism in ethics 4:856
    logic of ethical discourse 5:764
    moral knowledge 6:520
    moral particularism 6:529
    Plato 7:420–1
    Prichard, H.A. 7:682
    right and good 8:323, 8:325
    semiotics 8:679
    truthfulness 9:485
Rosser, J.B.
    combinatory logic 2:433–4
    Gödel's theorems 4:118
    lambda calculus 5:349
    many-valued logics 6:84
    non-constructive rules of inference
        7:30
Rossetti, L. 9:21
Rossi, Alejandro 6:346
Rossi, Leandro 2:280, 2:282
Rossi, M.M. 4:375
Rossi, P. 1:632, 2:735, 5:42, 5:722
Rossiiskaia Akademiia Nauk 1:820
Ross's 'paradox'
    imperative logic 4:718
Rostand, J. 1:840
Roszak, T. 3:202
Rotenstreich, N. 1:314, 3:323, 5:100,
    5:311
Roth, A. 3:222
Roth, B. 3:725
Roth, D. 6:388, 6:390
Roth, G. 9:7
Roth, H.D.
    Daodejing 2:782
    Huainanzi †4:512–14
    Yangzhu †9:822–3
    Zhuangzi 9:867

Roth, J. 4:207
Roth, Michael S.
    Hegelianism 4:301
    Kojève, A. †5:289–91
Roth, P.A. 2:630
Rothbard, M. 1:245, 1:248
Rothenberg, D. 3:202, 6:638
Rotman, B. 1:311
Roudinesco, E. 3:588
Rougès, Alberto 1:376–7, 1:379
Rougier, L.A.P. 7:482
Roulier, F. 7:392
Rouse, Joseph
    Heideggerian philosophy of
        science †4:323–7
    scientific realism and antirealism
        8:584
    social epistemology 8:832
Rousseau, Jean-Jacques 8:367–77
    civil society 8:368, 8:371–2
    Constant de Rebecque, H.-B.
        2:615
    contractarianism 2:657–8, 2:662–3,
        2:665
    critiques of
        Gerdil, G.S. 4:41–2
        Herder, J.G. 4:380
    deconstruction (Derrida, J.) 2:836
    deism 2:855
    democracy 2:872
    education 3:223, 3:227, 3:231,
        8:368, 8:372–3
        Diderot, D. contrast 3:66
    egoism and altruism 3:248
    Émile 8:372–3
    Enlightenment 3:317
    environmental ethics 3:333, 3:336
    ethical autonomy 1:587, 1:592
    federalism and confederalism
        3:574
    general will 4:10–11, 4:12, 9:424
        sovereignty 9:57–8, 9:59
    human nature 4:525
    innocence 4:798
    justice 5:147
    language 4:380, 5:377, 5:378
    legitimacy 5:539, 5:541
    liberalism 5:601, 5:603–4, 5:605
    morality
        moral education 6:509
        sympathy 6:561, 6:564
    nation and nationalism 6:658–9,
        6:661
    nature/nurture controversy 4:522
    personal independence 7:792
    politics
        Diderot, D. contrast 3:65

public interest 7:832
rationality
    Wollstonecraft, M. critique
        3:616
slavery 8:805, 8:807
The Social Contract
    civil society 8:368, 8:371–2
social contract
    genealogy 4:2, 4:4–5
    political philosophy
        history of 7:514
social science 8:851, 8:859
Tocqueville, A. de 9:425
Wollstonecraft, M. 9:791–2
Rousseau, N. 5:379
Routley, Richard 3:663, 5:789, 6:286,
    7:211
Rouvray, Claude-Henri de *see* Saint-
    Simon
Roux, Wilhelm 9:642, 9:643
Rovatti, P.A. 5:42
Rovee-Collier, C. 2:391
Rowbotham, S. 3:614
Rowe, C.J. 4:413
Rowe, William L.
    agnosticism †1:121–3
    Anselm of Canterbury 1:296
    atheism †1:530–4
    Collins, A. 2:419
    Common Sense School 2:448
    deism †2:852–6
    divine freedom †3:757–62
    evil, problem of 3:472
    God
        existence of 4:93, 8:241
    Reid, T. 8:180
    religion
        history of philosophy of 8:247
        religious experience 8:255
    Tillich, P. 9:413
Rowell, L. 6:614
Rowley, C.K. 8:826
Rowson, E.
    Liber de causis 5:598
Rowson, E.K.
    al-'Amiri 1:208
    al-Tawhidi 9:272
Roy, J.-P. 1:624
Roy, Raja Rammohun 2:5–6, 2:7,
    9:593, 9:594
Royalty
    emanationism (Ibn Massara) 4:628
Royce, Josiah **8:377–81**
    the Absolute 1:28, 1:29
    American philosophy, eighteenth
        and nineteenth century 1:204
    Australia, philosophy in 1:575

ethics 8:377–8
German idealism 4:45
Hegelianism 4:288
idealism 4:669
mathematical logic 8:379–80
panpsychism 7:197
universal consciousness 8:378–9
Rozanov, Vasilii Vasil'evich **8:381–5**
    Signposts movement 8:772
Rozeboom, W.W. 7:829
Rozenberg, G. 2:482
Rubanowice, R.J. 9:464
Rubel, M. 3:312–13, 8:886
Ruben, David-Hillel
    dialectical materialism 3:58
    explanation in history and social
        science †3:525–31
    holism and individualism in
        history and social science 4:488
    social laws 8:834
    social sciences
        philosophy of †8:868–71
Rubenstein, Richard L. 4:495–6,
    4:499
Rubin, D.-H. 3:525
Rubin, G. 3:614
Rubin, H. 1:614
Rubin, J.E. 1:614
Rubinstein, A. 2:835
Rubio, Antonio de la Rueda
    Logica mexicana
        colonial philosophy
            Latin America 5:422,
                5:423–4, 5:426
Ruby, J.E. 5:475
Ruch, C. 1:772
Rucker, R. 4:778
Rudavsky, T.M.
    Crescas, H. 2:704
    Gersonides 4:51
    Ibn Gabirol, S. 4:620
    Ibn Tzaddik, J. †4:659–62
Rudd, A. 5:244
Ruddick, C.T. 2:690
Ruddick, Sara
    feminism
        ethics 3:605
        political philosophy 3:619,
            3:620
    morality and emotions 6:564
    practical reasoning/rationality
        8:103
Ruddick, William
    ethics
        family †3:548–52
        reproduction 8:280
Ruderman, D. 1:27, 6:335

Rüdiger, A. 5:719
Rudner, Richard 9:580
Rudnick, H.H. 4:792
Rudolf, E.P. 5:470
Rudolph, K. 4:85
Rudowski, V.A. 5:577–8
Rue, L.D. 7:3, 7:5
Ruegg, D. Seyfort
    emptiness, Buddhist concept of
        2:80
    Mādhyamika Buddhism in India
        and Tibet 2:63–4
    Mi bskyod rdo rje 6:352–3
    mKhas grub dge legs dpal bzang
        po 6:417
    Nāgārjuna 6:640
    Tibetan philosophy 9:408
Ruello, F. 5:59
Ruether, Rosemary Radford 3:621–2,
    3:624, 5:616
Rufus, Richard *see* Richard Rufus of
    Cornwall
Ruge, Arnold **8:385–7**
Ruhism *see* Confucianism
Ruiter, D.W.P. 7:94
Ruiz Moreno, I. 9:196
Ruiz-Miguel, A. 1:792
Rukmani, T.S.
    self
        Indian theories of †8:605–11
rule of law **8:387–91**
    British constitutional law
        (Dicey, A.V.) 3:62
    civil law (Pothier, R.J.) 7:608
    constitutionalism 2:618, 8:388–9
    judicial obligation 8:390–1
    justice 8:388, 8:390
    legal positivism 5:518
    legality principle 5:151
    morality 8:389–90
    necessity of (Chernyshevskii, N.G.)
        2:306
    principle–policy distinction 8:390
    social theory (Weber, M.) 8:876
    socialism (Hessen, S.I.) 4:415,
        4:417–18
rule-consequentialism *see*
    consequentialism
rule-following
    extension (Wright, C.) 6:218–19
    language (Wittgenstein, L.)
        9:763–4, 9:766
    meaning **6:214–19**
        private states 7:700–1
        quietism (McDowell, J.) 6:218
        sceptical paradox
            dispositional response 6:217

Kripke, S.A. 6:216, 6:217–18
  linguistic community 6:217
  McDowell, J. 6:216–17
objectivity 7:75
Wittgensteinian ethics 9:771–2
rulers
  see also leadership; monarchy;
  sages
  Chinese philosophy
    Daodejing 2:779–80
    de 2:809–10
    fa 3:532
    Guanzi 4:186
    Jia Yi 5:102
    Legalism 4:219, 5:531–2,
      5:533–5, 5:536–7
    self-cultivation 5:864
  dao
    Huainanzi 4:513
  duties (Kauṭilya) 5:220–1
  education of
    Kauṭilya 5:221
    Plato 7:400–1
  feudalism
    Japan 2:147, 2:148, 2:149–50
  Islamic philosophy
    authority 5:27
    al-Farabi 3:556–7, 7:518
    Platonism 7:429–30
    Shi'a 5:26
  just
    Islamic philosophy 7:429–30
  philosopher-rulers (Plato) 7:400–1,
    7:414
  social harmony (Confucius) 5:447
rules
  see also legal rules; rule-following
  Chinese philosophy
    li 2:541–3
  constitutive (Searle, J.) 5:761
  corruption 2:675–6
  epistemic
    naturalized philosophy of
      science 6:730
  inadequacy of (Tolstoi, L.N.) 9:436
  indifference (Ariston of Chios)
    1:381–2
  limitations
    existentialist ethics 3:503–4
  moral
    Confucianism 2:542–3
    deliberation 6:512–13
    justification 6:513–14
    moral education 6:506–7
    theory and practice 9:357
    Wollaston, W. 9:787–8

rule-following regress
  computational theories of mind
    2:393
  social
    see also social norms
    anthropology 8:864–5
    interpretive school 8:841, 8:842
    joint acceptance account 8:835
    nature-convention dualism
      6:736
    postmodernism 8:845
    practice theory 8:834–5
    promising 7:740–1
  sport ethics 9:110–11
  utilitarianism 9:554–5
rule-scepticism
  Llewellyn, K.N. 5:661
rule-utilitarianism *see* utilitarianism,
  rule
Rumble, W.E. 1:570–1
Rumelhart, D.E.
  connectionism 2:578, 2:579
  learning 5:487
  meaning 7:630, 7:632
  psychology
    theories of 7:829
Rumfitt, Ian
  meaning and understanding
    †6:226–9
  presupposition †7:672–5
Rummel, Erika
  Erasmus, D. †3:396–401
Runciman, S. 6:77
Runciman, W.G. 4:12, 8:847
Runde, J. 5:235
Runia, David T.
  Diogenes Laertius †3:86–7
  doxography †3:125–7
  Philo of Alexandria †7:357–61
Runkle, G. 1:248
Rüping, H. 9:380
Rupp, E.G. 7:287, 9:423
Ruse, Michael
  evolution
    and ethics 3:475–6
    theory of 3:482
  naturalized philosophy of science
    6:731
  sexuality 8:729
Rush, J.H. 7:227
Russell 8:404
Russell, Bertrand Arthur William
  8:391–404
  see also Russell's paradox

analytical philosophy 1:224, 1:225,
  1:229
  Latin America 1:230, 1:231,
    1:233
  Augustine 1:559
  axiom of choice 1:612, 1:614
  being 1:702
  Bosanquet, B. 1:848
  Carnap, R. 2:215
  change 2:274, 2:275–6
  concepts 2:517
  consequence 2:600, 2:603
  descriptions 3:19–23, 3:24
    definite 8:392, 8:397–8, 9:168,
      9:169
  empiricism 3:303
  Evans, G. 3:461
  existence
    quantifier account 3:491–2
  external world 8:399–400
  facts 3:537
    negative
      Indian philosophy 6:758
  fiction
    fictional entities 3:664, 3:665,
      3:667
    semantics of 3:660, 3:663
  foundationalism
    a posteriori 1:2
  Frege, G. 3:765, 3:774
  Hempel, C.G. 4:352
  infinity 4:778
  intensional entities 4:803, 4:807
  knowledge
    by acquaintance/description
      5:259–60, 5:262–3
    sense-data 3:379, 3:383
  Leibniz, G.W. 5:562
  Lewis, C.I. 5:589
  logic
    early twentieth century 5:729,
      5:738
    modal 6:419
  logical atomism 5:774–5, 8:399
  logical form 5:782–3, 5:785
  logical positivism 5:792, 5:795
  logicism 5:814, 5:817, 6:184–5,
    8:394
  McTaggart, J.M.E. 6:26, 6:28
  mathematics
    constructivism 2:638
    foundations of 6:192
  meaning and verification 6:236
  Meinong, A. 6:286
  memory 6:302
  motion 7:722, 7:723
  neutral monism 6:816–18, 8:400

nonstandard analysis 1:216
ordinary language philosophy
7:148, 7:152, 7:153
paradoxes of set and property
7:215, 7:216–17, 7:218–19,
7:220–1, 8:394–7
Post, E.L. 7:575
power 7:611, 7:613
presupposition 7:673–4
Principia Mathematica
consequence 2:603
constructivism 2:639
definition 2:846, 2:849
descriptions 3:21–2, 3:24
Gödel's theorems 4:108, 4:119
intensional entities 4:807
lambda calculus 5:349
logic
early twentieth century
5:733, 5:738
modal 6:419
logical form 5:782, 5:785
logical positivism 5:792, 5:795
logicism 5:817, 8:394
mathematics
foundations of 6:192
Post, E.L. 7:573, 7:575
predicate calculus 7:665
scientific theories 9:346
semantic paradoxes 8:643–4,
8:648
truth
theories of 8:643–4, 8:648
types
theory of 9:362
Principles of Mathematics 7:218,
7:221
proper names 7:754–5, 7:757
property theory 7:764–5, 7:767
propositions 7:788
Quine, W.V. 8:14
Ramsey, F.P. 8:49
realism
absolute 8:394–5
reference
description theory 8:153–4,
8:164
scientific theories 9:355
scope 8:589
sexuality 8:724, 8:729
solipsism 9:26
space 9:62, 9:66
suicide 9:230
symbolic logic 5:732
syntax 9:253
testimony 9:314

truth
correspondence theory of 9:473,
9:475
theories of 8:643–4, 8:648
types
theory of 1:763, 8:395–7,
9:359–60, 9:362
universals 9:543
use/mention distinction 9:551
Whitehead, A.N. 9:719
Wittgenstein, L. (:757–60
Russell, D.E.H. 8:728
Russell, G.A. 5:25
Russell, Letty 3:622, 3:624
Russell, R.J. 8:236
Russell Smith, H.F. 4:234
Russell's paradox 7:214, 7:216–17,
7:219–20, 7:765
glossary 5:808
Russia 8:418–22
see also Soviet Union; Ukraine
Bakhtin, M.M. **1:638–45**
Bakunin, M.A. **1:645–7**
Belinskii, V.G. **1:709–12**
Bogdanov, A.A. **1:816–20**
Bulgakov, S.N. **2:123–6**
Chaadaev, P.I. **2:269–73**
Chernyshevskii, N.G. **2:303–6**
Dostoevskii, F.M. **3:114–19**
Eurasian movement **3:453–6**
Fëdorov, N.F. **3:574–6**
Florenskii, P.A. **3:679–82**
Frank, S.L. **3:726–30**
Hegelianism **4:302–7**
Herzen, A.I. **4:404–10**
Hessen, S.I. **4:415–19**
Il'in, I.A. **4:692–6**
Kojève, Alexandre **5:289–91**
Koyré, A. **5:296–8**
Kropotkin, P.A. **5:313–14**
Lavrov, P.L. **5:435–8**
Lenin, V.I. **5:564–7**
Leont'ev, K.N. **5:567–70**
liberalism **5:605–10**
Russian philosophy 8:419
literary formalism **8:409–14**
Shpet, G.G. 8:756
Losev, A.F. **5:828–33**
Lossky, N.O. **5:833–8**
mathematical constructivism
2:634–5
medieval philosophy **6:277–9**
Mikhailovskii, N.K. **6:355–7**
Neo-Kantianism **6:792–7**
Nietzsche: impact on Russian
thought **6:861–7**
Pan-Slavism 7:199–201

Plekhanov, G.V. **7:451–6**
populism (Lavrov, P.L.) 5:435–8
positivism **7:561–4**
religious-philosophical renaissance
8:422–8
Rozanov, V.V. **8:381–5**
Schellingianism **8:520–2**
Signposts movement **8:768–74**
Slavophilism 7:199–200, **8:807–11**
Solov'ëv, V.S. **9:28–33**
Tolstoi, L. N. **9:435–40**
Trotsky, L. **9:464–6**
Russian empiriocriticism **8:404–9**
Bogdanov, A.A. 1:817, **8:405–7**
Lunacharski 8:407–8
Marxism 6:151, 6:153, 8:420, 8:421
materialism (Lenin, V.I.) 5:565–7
politics–philosophy relationship
8:404–5
'Russian Idea'
Berdiaev, N.A. 8:418–19
Russian Marxism *see* Marxism,
Russian/Soviet
Russian Materialism **8:414–18**
Russian Orthodox Church
community
Slavophilism 8:809
Russian Revolution (1917) 5:223,
9:464
Russian Symbolism
Nietzscheanism 6:862–3
religious-philosophical
Renaissance 8:422, 8:423,
8:425–6
Russo, A. 3:593
Russo, J. 4:502
Russow, L. 4:708
Rüstow, A. 7:221
Rutherford, Donald
language
early modern philosophy of
5:379
Leibniz, G.W. 5:562
universal language †9:533–5
Rutherford, R.B. 3:254, 6:95
Ruttan, V. 1:128
Ryan, Alan
Berlin, I. 1:753
history and social science
explanation in 3:531
holism and individualism in 4:488
Hobbes, T. 4:476
Mill, J.S. 6:375
property 7:761
Russell, B.A.W. 8:404
systems theory in social science
†9:253–6

Ryan, J.A. 8:737
Ryan, J.K. 3:169, 5:481
Ryan, L. 4:482
Rybak, J. 1:269
Ryckman, T.A.
   general relativity, philosophical
     responses to †4:5–9
   geometry †4:28–34
   Weyl, H. †9:706–7
Ryle, Gilbert **8:428–32**
   analytic behaviourism 1:692
   analytic philosophy 1:229
   Anderson, J. 1:269
   belief 1:706

   categories 2:229, 2:230–1, 2:232
   causation 2:250–1
   conceptual analysis 2:522
   consciousness 2:596
   deconstruction 2:839
   dissoi logoi (twofold argument)
     3:107
   educational philosophy 3:239
   emotions 3:285
   folk psychology 3:686, 3:687
   imagination 4:706, 4:708
   introspection 4:842
   memory 6:300

   ordinary language philosophy
     7:147, 7:150, 7:153
   pleasure 7:450, 7:451
   reductionism, philosophy of mind
     8:153
   tacit knowledge 5:286, 5:287
   unconscious mental states 9:527
   volition
     action 1:39, 1:41
Ryle, M. 8:886
Ryll-Nardzewski, C. 7:496
Rymer, Thomas 9:449, 9:452
Rynin, C. 5:122
Ryusaku, Tsunoda 2:150

S

Sa skya paṇḍita Kun dga' rgyal
    mtshan (Sakya Paṇḍita) **8:433–5**
    epistemology
        gSang-phu Ne'u-thog
            monastery debate 9:406–7
        Great Debate of bSam-yas 9:405–6
        Tibetan philosophy 9:408
Saadawi, N. 3:614
Saadiah Gaon **8:435–40**
    creation 8:436–7
    eudaimonia 8:438–9
    good life 8:438–9
    Jewish philosophy 5:87
    Nahmanides, M. 6:650
Saarinen, E. 8:658
Saarinen, R. 2:136, 4:39
Saatkamp, H.J. 7:639–40, 8:356,
    8:470
Śabarasvāmin 5:382, 6:381, 9:548
Sabbadini, R. 9:573
al-Sabbah, Hasan 6:617
Sabbath
    Jewish philosophy
        Heschel, A.J. 4:411
śābdapramāṇa (knowledge through
    words) 9:315–18
Sablayrolles, P. 3:98
Sabra, A.I. 3:19, 5:713, 8:564–5
Sabrié, J.B. 2:290
al-Sabzawari, al-Hajj Mulla Hadi
    8:440–2
Saccaro Battisti, G. 4:400
Saccheri, G. 5:717
Sachs, A. 3:607, 3:611
Sachs, D. 8:287
Sacks, G.E. 4:755
Sacks, M. 1:46
sacramentality
    of the universe 8:442, 8:444–5
sacraments **8:442–5**
    see also baptism; Eucharist;
    marriage
    Cartesianism
        Rohault, J. 8:342
    the sacred
        awe 8:339
        Eliade, M. 3:260, 3:261
        phenomenology of religion
            7:354–5

transcendence
    Bataille, G. 1:659–60
sacred language
    Vedas
        interpretation
            Indian theories of 4:833–4
sacrifice
    atonement 1:537–8
    Brahmanic emanation 2:4
    God
        Indian conceptions of 4:103
    Hinduism 3:184
    human
        pre-Columbian thought 5:431
    inference
        Indian theories of 4:760
    killing prohibition (Empedocles)
        3:293, 3:297–8
    the sacred
        Bataille, G. 1:660
    utilitarianism
        beneficence 4:343–4
Saddhātissa, H. 7:11
Sadhāran Brahma Samāj 2:6
sadness
    artistic expression 1:494–5
Sadock, J.M. 1:201, 4:725
sadomasochism 8:725–6
Sadovskii, V.N. 1:526–7
Saffrey, H.D.
    Chaldaean Oracles 2:274
    Iamblichus 4:599
    Neoplatonism 6:803
    Proclus 7:731
    Pseudo-Dionysius 7:808
Safouan, M. 9:177
sages
    see also philosopher-rulers
    Chinese philosophy
        tian 2:325
    Confucianism
        Han Yu 4:221
    Daoism
        desire 2:794
        mirror-like knowing 2:788–
            2:790, 2:792
        wu-forms 2:790–1
    ideal observer
        Mohism 6:457

individuality
    traditional African philosophy
        1:104
    intuitive insight
        Chinese Buddhism (Sengzhao)
            8:683
    Ogyū Sorai 7:90
    self-cultivation
        neo-Confucianism 8:622
        Xunzi 9:818, 9:819
        Zhi Dun 9:859
        Zhou Dunyi 9:862–3
Sagie, A. 5:564
Sagoff, M. 4:166, 8:334
Sagres, School of (Portugal) 2:8
Sagya Paṇḍita *see* Sa skya paṇḍita
Sagyaba *see* Sa-skya-pa
Saha, S. 3:861
Sahagún, Bernard de 5:429, 5:431,
    5:432
Sahlin, N.-E. 8:49, 8:101, 8:491–2
Sahlins, M. 8:132
Saichō 5:71
Said, Edward W.
    marginality 6:100
    Orientalism
        Islamic philosophy 7:160
    political philosophy
        Indian 7:525
    postcolonialism 7:578, 7:582
Said, H.M. 8:565
Saigyō 5:292
Sailor, D.B. 2:744
Sainati, V. 2:735
Sainsbury, R.M. 3:24, 6:818, 9:852
St Pierre, J.A. 9:728–9
saints
    see also sanctification
    knowledge of mysteries (Ibn al-
        'Arabi) 4:602
    'perfect man' (Ibn al-'Arabi) 4:603
Saint-Sernin, B. 3:786
Saint-Simon, Claude-Henri de
    Rouvroy, Comte de **8:446–7**
    positivism 7:558
    utopianism 9:557, 9:559
Śaiving, Valerie 3:621, 3:624–5
Śaivism 1:15–18, 7:58
Sakai, Naoki 5:44, 7:91

Sakharov, Andrei 5:608–9, 5:610
sākṣin (witnessing subject) 6:32
Śākya mchog ldan 9:406–7
Sala, G.B. 5:825
Salamucha, J. 7:493, 7:499
Salamun, Kurt
  Jaspers, K. †5:80–4
Salamun-Hybasek, E. 5:83
Salaquarda, J. 5:354
Salazar Bondy, A. 1:231–2, 1:234
Salem, J. 2:878
Saliba, G. 8:565
Salleras i Carolà, M. 5:664
Sallis, J. 4:323
Salman, H.D. 5:111
Salmerón, Fernando 1:230, 1:234,
  6:346
Salmon, J.H.M. 7:517
Salmon, Merrilee H.
  anthropology
    philosophy of †1:297–9
  archaeology 1:356, 1:359
  science, philosophy of 8:576
Salmon, Nathan
  concepts 2:517
  direct reference theory 7:755–6,
    7:757
  intensional entities 4:807
  intentionality 4:821
  propositional attitudes 7:786
  propositions 7:788
  sense and reference 8:688
Salmon, Norman 7:777, 7:779
Salmon, V. 9:535
Salmon, W. 4:752
Salmon, Wesley C.
  Carnap, R. 2:215
  causation 2:251
  explanation 3:523, 3:525
  infinity 4:778
  Reichenbach, H. †8:166–71
  relativity theory 8:199
  Zeno of Elea 9:852
Salomaa, A. 2:481, 2:482, 3:706
Salter, J. 8:807
Saltz, D. 1:472
Salutati, Coluccio 4:535
salva veritate intersubstitution see
  intersubstitutability
Salvadori, M. 5:224
Salvadori, R. 5:298
salvation 8:447–51
  see also justification, religious
    doctrine of; predestination
  Advaita Vedānta 8:447–8, 8:449
  baptism 5:637
  beliefs comparison 8:450–1

Buddhism
  Indian 8:447–9
Calvin, J. 2:180
Christian exclusivism 8:260
creativity
  Berdiaev, N.A. 1:729
faith 9:327
  Luther, M. 9:328
feminist theology 3:623
Gnosticism 4:83
good works (Luther, M.) 5:167
grace 4:149–50
happiness (al-Farabi) 3:557
heaven 4:250–1
hope 9:329, 9:330
Ibn Massara 4:629
Ikhwan al-Safa' 4:685–6, 4:687–8
inclusivism 8:261
Jainism 8:447–8, 8:449
through Jesus Christ 8:249
Jewish philosophy (Abravanel, I.)
  1:22
knowledge for (Heilswissen)
  (Scheler, M.F.) 8:506
limbo 5:635–6
monotheism 8:447, 8:449–50
mysticism (Tonghak) 9:441–2
Origen 7:162
philosophic life (al-Razi, Abu
  Bakr) 8:111
pluralism 8:260, 8:261
predestination 7:653, 7:654
purgatory 7:836–8
Rāmānuja 8:43
suffering (Shestov, L.) 8:743–4
theology of humility (Luther, M.)
  6:1–2
tragedy (Schopenhauer, A.) 8:546,
  8:551
Salviatis, Georgius Benignus de see
  Dragišić, Juraj
Samarin, Iurii 8:810–11
Samay, S. 5:83
Sambin, G. 7:796
Sambursky, S.
  conservation principles 2:608
  Damascius 2:772
  matter 6:196
  Philoponus 7:377
  Stoicism 9:160
Saṃdhinirmocanasūtra 2:64, 9:792
Samely, A. 6:355
samesayers (Davidson, D.) 4:743–4
Samet, J. 6:675
Śaṃkara see Śaṅkara
Sāṃkhya see Sāṅkhya

Samos
  Melissus 6:292–6
  Pythagoras 7:854–7
Samour, H. 5:612–13
Sampford, C. 5:521
sampling 7:82
saṃsāra (cycles of existence)
  Jainism
    Mahāvīra 6:33–4
  origin of doctrine 5:211, 5:212
  Pure Land Buddhism
    Shinran 8:747–8
  scope of 5:209, 5:210
  transmigration
    Japanese Buddhism 2:104–5
  yoga 5:212
  Yogācāra Buddhism 2:70
saṃskāra see saṃsāra
Samuel, A. 6:450, 6:451
Samuels, A. 5:135
Samuels, W. 3:222
Samuelson, Norbert M.
  Gersonides 4:51
  Ibn Daud, A. †4:608–11
Samuelson, Paul A. 3:211, 3:222, 8:74
samurai see bushi philosophy
Samyay, Great Debate of see bSam-
  yas
Sanari, K. 9:841
Sanches, Francisco 8:451–4
  Renaissance scepticism 8:502–3
  School of Sagres 2:8
Sánchez Reulet, Anibal 1:379, 3:511,
  3:512–14
Sánchez Vázquez, Adolfo 6:164,
  6:346, 9:77
Sánchez Villaseñor, J. 3:514
sanctification 8:454–8
  see also justification, religious
    doctrine of
  awe 8:339
  Eastern Orthodoxy 8:455–6
  pastoral psychology 8:457
  Protestantism 4:148, 8:455,
    8:456–7
  Roman Catholicism 8:454–5, 8:456
sanctions
  motivation (Bentham, J.) 1:721–2
Sand, S. 9:36
Sandbach, F.H. 5:819, 7:472, 9:160
Sandberger, J. 9:167
Sandel, Michael
  community and
    communitarianism 2:471
  contractarianism 2:665
  educational philosophy 3:239
  justice 5:147

political neutrality 6:820, 6:821
Rawls, J. 8:110
Sandelin, K. 8:492
Sanders, A.F. 7:492
Sanders, R. 8:885
Sanders, V. 6:117
Sanderson, A. 1:19
Sanderson, Robert 5:771, 5:772
Sandin, R.T. 4:204
Sandkaulen-Bock, B. 8:520
Sandkühler, H.J. 6:742, 8:520
Sandmann, J. 4:201
Sándor, P. 4:572
Sandoz, E. 9:657
Sandu, Gabriel
  epistemic logic 3:359
  quantifiers †7:870–3
  semantics, game-theoretic 8:658
Saner, H. 5:83
Sanford, D.H. 2:688, 7:297
Sangharakshita 1:197
Śaṅkara **8:458–61**
  appearance theory
    causation 2:254
  Brahman 4:438
    ātaman relationship 6:622
    pure existence 8:43
  Brahmasūtra commentary 9:591
  critique of Vaiśeṣika atomism
    6:198–9
  error and illusion 3:410
  fatalism 3:567, 3:568
  God
    concepts of 4:102, 4:103–4
  heaven
    Indian concepts of 4:256
  idealism 6:197
  Indian and Tibetan philosophy
    4:738
  knowledge 5:283–4, 5:285
  pantheism 7:202
  superimposition 4:435
Śaṅkarasvāmin 4:764, 4:766
Sankey, H. 4:736
Sāṅkhya (Sāṃkhya) **8:461–7**
  see also Sāṅkhya-Yoga
  Buddhi 8:463–4, 8:466
  causality 8:460, 8:465–6
  cosmology and cosmogony 2:682
  dualism 4:438
  epistemology 8:464–5
  identity theory
    causation 2:251, 2:252, 2:253–4
  Indian and Tibetan philosophy
    4:737
  karma and rebirth 5:212
  knowledge 4:435

perception
  awareness 1:605–6
  puruṣa/prakṛti 8:461, 8:462–4,
    8:466
  causation 8:465
  existence proofs 8:465
self
  theories of 8:608–9
  soteriology 8:466
  Vedānta School comparison 9:591
  Yoga relationship 4:439
Sāṅkhyakārikā of Īśvara-kṛṣṇa (text)
  8:462, 8:611
Sāṅkhya-Yoga
  sense perception 8:691
  substance-pluralism 6:197,
    6:199–200
San-lun School of Buddhism 2:107–8
Sanlun (Three Treatises) School of
  Buddhism
  China 2:82–3
Sanron (Three Treatises) School of
  Buddhism
  Japan 2:101
Sanskrit
  poetics 4:836–7
  pronunciation 4:738–9
Sansom, G. 8:753
Santamaria, J.A.F. 9:650
Santambroggia, M. 8:14
Śāntarakṣita 2:61, 2:62, 6:197, 6:200
Santas, G. 1:142
Santayana, George **8:467–70**, 9:75,
  9:77
  epiphenomenalism 3:354
  humour 4:567
  Lotze, R.H. 5:842
  religious language 8:257–8,
    8:259–60
Śāntideva 2:60
Santillana, G. de 8:572
Santos Moray, M. 6:164
Sa-Pan *see* Sa skya paṇḍita
Saperstein, M. 8:740
Sapir, Edward 8:471–2
Sapiro, V. 9:791
Sapir-Whorf Hypothesis **8:470–3**
  linguistic discrimination 5:641
  metaphysics 6:339
Sarachek, J. 6:48
Sarasohn, L.T. 2:263, 3:857
Saraswati, Swami Dayanand *see*
  Arya Samaj
Saravia, H. 3:678, 3:679
Šarčević, Abdullah 9:52, 9:55

Sardar, Ziauddin
  political philosophy
    Indian 7:525
  science
    Islamic philosophy †8:561–5
Sargent, Lyman Tower
  communism †2:462–4
  utopianism †9:557–62
Sargent, Rose-Mary
  Boyle, R. †1:853–7
Śāriputra 9:216
Śārīrakamīmāṃsāsūtra see
  Bādarāyaṇa
Sarkar, P.R. 7:523–4, 7:525
Sarkar, S. 2:215
Sarmiento, Domingo Faustino
  Latin America
    literature 5:653–4, 5:657
    positivism 7:566, 7:570
Sarnowsky, J. 1:145
Sarot, M. 7:107
Sartori, G. 4:683, 4:685
Sartre, Jean-Paul **8:473–9**
  anti-Semitism 1:311, 1:312–13,
    1:314
  anti-subjectivist reaction to 9:197
  Beauvoir, S. de 1:685
  consciousness 3:581, 3:583
  Derrida, J. 2:901
  emotions 3:285, 3:289, 3:290
  essence 7:346
  existentialism 3:494, 3:502
    ethics 3:502–5
    Marxist
      anti-postmodernism 7:593
    phenomenology 7:338, 7:342
  family ethics 3:551–2
  free will 3:752
  human essence
    denial of 4:531, 4:532
  Husserl, E. 4:587
  imagery
    Le Doeuff, M. critique 5:477
  imagination 4:707, 4:708, 8:475
  Lefebvre, H 5:491
  L'Etre et le Néant (*Being and
    Nothingness*) 8:473–4, 8:475–6
  literary studies
    Barthes, R. comparison 1:656
  Marxism
    anti-postmodernism 7:593
    existentialism reconciliation
      6:145, 8:474, 8:477
  Merleau-Ponty, M. 6:323, 6:325
  négritude 1:110, 1:116, 3:553,
    3:554
  nihilism 7:2–3, 7:5

phenomenal consciousness 2:593, 2:596
phenomenology 7:348
poetry 7:477
responsibility 3:497
self 3:496
self-deception 8:629–30, 8:632
Taine, H.-A. 9:260
Sarvāstivāda School of Buddhism
   see also Vaibhāṣika
   Abhidharma 2:54, 2:55, 2:56, 2:57
   causation
      Indian theories of 2:256
   impermanence 6:592
   karma and rebirth 5:214
   linguistic units 5:381
   momentariness 6:470–1
   Vasubandhu 9:217, 9:583
Sasaki, R.F. 5:646
Sa-skya-pa (Sagyaba) School
   Go ram pa 9:402
Sass, Hans-Martin
   Feuerbach, L.A. †3:635–40
   Hegelianism 4:301
   Heidegger, M. 4:323
   Ruge, A. †8:385–7
Sasso, G. 2:735
Sasso, R. 3:560
Sastri, D.N. 9:514, 9:516, 9:588
Satan
   foreknowledge of his fall 1:285–6
   free will (Anselm of Canterbury) 1:292
   Jewish philosophy (Maimonides, M.) 6:45
satire
   see also parody
   Lucian 5:853–4
satisfaction
   atonement 1:538
   glossary 5:808
   Incarnation (Anselm of Canterbury) 1:284, 1:293–4
   Jesus Christ
      Socinianism denial 8:890
   model theory (Tarski, A.) 6:437
   sentential function (Tarski, A.) 2:601
   truth definitions (Tarski, A.) 9:267–8
satisfaction-preservation
   imperative logic 4:717, 4:719–20
satisfiability
   computational complexity 2:474
   Herbrand's theorem 4:377
   quantificational theory 4:109
Satō, Akira 5:103

Sattelmeyer, R. 9:392
satyāgraha (holding fast to the truth) 3:842
Saunders, J.L. 5:652
Saussure, Ferdinand de **8:479–82**
   ideology 4:685
   influence on Lévi-Strauss, C. 5:583
   langue–parole distinction 8:480
   postmodernism 7:588, 7:590
   post-structuralism 7:596–8
   signs 8:481–2
   structuralism 9:174–5, 9:176, 9:177
      linguistic
         influence on Barthes, R. 1:656
      linguistics 7:600, 9:177–8
      literary theory 9:181, 9:184
      social science 9:184–5, 9:186, 9:189
Sautrāntika School of Buddhism
   causation
      Indian theories of 2:256
   existent–real distinction
      awareness 1:606
   impermanence 6:592
   karma and rebirth 5:214
Sauvages de la Croix, F.B. de 6:269
Savage, C.W. 8:404
Savage, L.
   decision and game theory 2:835
   practical reasoning/rationality
      expected utility theory 8:94–5, 8:103
   probabilism 7:711
Savage-Rumbaugh, E.S. 1:271, 1:273
Savalskii, V. 6:797
Savigny, Friedrich Karl von **8:482–3**
   historical jurisprudence 5:138–9, 5:141
Savile, Anthony 3:793
Savioz, R. 1:840
Savitskii, Pëtr Nikolaevich 3:454, 3:455
Savory, R. 6:411
Savoy
   Gerdil, G.S. **4:41–2**
Sawyer, H. 1:107
Saxony
   Crusius, C.A. **2:736–9**
Saydah, J.R. 5:589
Sayer, A. 8:587, 8:859
Sayer, D. 8:857
Sayers, J. 3:586, 3:588
saying
   see also showing
   Strawson, P.F. 9:170
Sayre, F. 2:759

Sayre, Kenneth M.
   information theory †4:782–6, 4:789
Sayre-McCord, Geoffrey
   analytic ethics 1:223
   duty 3:182
   moral knowledge †6:516–20
   value
      ontological status of 9:581
Sayward, C. 4:771
Sayyid al-Afadil *see* Mir Damad, Muhammad Baqir
Sbrozi, M. 1:867
scala natura (ladder of nature) 2:37
Scalabrini, Pedro 7:566
Scandinavia **8:483–9**
   see also Denmark; Finland; Norway; Sweden
   legal realism 5:521–2
      Hägerström, A.A.T. 4:203
   praxeology **7:647–9**
Scanlan, James P.
   Berdiaev, N.A. †1:726–32
   Frank, S.L. 3:729
   Lenin, V.I. 5:567
   Losev, A.F. 5:833
   Lossky, N.O. †5:833–8
   Marxist philosophy, Russian and Soviet 6:160
   Mikhailovskii, N.K. 6:357
   Russian materialism: 'The 1860s' †8:414–18
   Russian philosophy 8:422
   Russian religious-philosophical Renaissance 8:427, 8:428
   Slavophilism 8:811
   Vysheslavtsev, B.P. †9:675–7
Scanlan, Michael J.
   Beth's theorem and Craig's interpolation theorem 1:763
   logic
      early twentieth century 5:738
   Post, E.L. †7:573–5
Scanlon, J. 3:83
Scanlon, Thomas M.
   contractarianism 2:658, 2:665, 8:100, 8:103
   ethics
      autonomy 1:592
      constructivism 2:632
      economics 3:211
      freedom of speech 3:765
      Herbrand's theorem 4:378
      ideals 4:675
      justice 5:147, 5:157
      moral standing 6:554

morality
  contractualism 2:664–5
  justification †6:514–16
  motivation 6:526, 6:527
  promising †7:740–2
Scannone, Juan Carlos 5:611, 5:613
Scarpelli, U. 5:521
Scarpellini, B. 3:824, 6:84
Scarre, G. 3:552, 6:375, 9:557
sceptical perspectism see
  perspectivism
scepticism **8:493–8**
  see also Academic scepticism;
  certainty; doubt; fideism; moral
  scepticism; Pyrrhonian Scepticism;
  religious scepticism
  Academic-Stoic debate 7:849,
    9:142, 9:151–2
  Anaxarchus 1:255
  ancient philosophy 3:373–4
  anti-essentialism 3:417–18
  anti-religious
    Hume, D. 4:543
  apologetic function
    Huet, P.-D. 4:514, 4:515–17
  Augustine 3:373
  Berkeley, G. 3:377
  Buddhism
    Indian
      Nāgārjuna 2:96–7
  Cartesian
    Cambridge Platonism critique
      2:184
    relevant alternatives 2:843–4
  Cārvāka materialism
    Indian theories of causation
      2:251, 2:253
  causal inference (Hume, D.)
    4:547–8
  certain knowledge (Nicholas of
    Autrecourt) 6:830
  charity principle 2:283–5
  coherence theory of truth 9:471–2
  common-sense defence
    (Moore, G.E.) 6:496–7
  contextualism 2:646, 2:647–8
  criteria (Cavell, S.) 2:258
  critiques of
    fallibilist 8:494–5
    Ferrier, J.F. 3:634
    Gaṅgeśa 3:845
    phenomenalist 7:330–1
    Santayana, G. 8:468
    White, T. 9:712
  Cyrenaic 2:761
  deductive closure principle 2:842
  Descartes, R. 3:6

dreaming–perception distinction
  3:127–8
epistemology 3:363–4
  justification 5:157, 5:162–3
  objectivity (Nagel, T.) 6:644–5
  pragmatism 7:636
ethical
  natural law 6:685–6
experience
  modes of experience
    (Oakeshott, M.J.) 7:71
external world 3:123, 3:124
  see also physical world,
  knowledge of; solipsism
  Descartes, R. 3:123, 6:231
  Hobbes, T. 4:466
  Hume, D. 3:123–4, 6:230–1
  verificationalism 6:232
fact (Frank, J.) 3:725
Feyerabend, P.K. 3:641–2
first principles (Reid, T.) 8:179
global 5:272–3, 6:726–7
Greek 1:263–4, 7:849
Holcot, R. 4:477–8
Hume, D. 3:378
idealism (Berkeley, G.) 1:744,
  1:747–8
innateness of ideas (Rosmini-
  Serbati, A.) 8:362
internalism 4:823
intuitive cognition (Wodeham, A.)
  9:773
knowledge
  direct (Sergeant, J.) 8:698
  Indian views of 5:284–5
  pure 4:788
  sources of (More, H.) 6:577
language games
  Wittgenstein, L. 9:768
memory
  epistemic role 6:300–1
method of doubt (Descartes, R.)
  3:374, 7:35
mitigated
  Bayle, P. 1:672–4
  Gassendi, P. 3:850, 3:851–2
  Mersenne, M. 6:325, 6:328
natural science (Hobbes, T.) 4:463
naturalism (Mill, J.S.) 6:365
Ockham, W. of 3:374
Oresme, N. 7:153, 7:155–6
other minds 2:711–12
phenomenology 7:344
psychoanalysis (Cavell, S.) 2:259
Putnam, H. 7:843
rational beliefs 8:61, 8:62, 8:63
reliabilist alternative 8:204

Renaissance **8:498–504**
  Agrippa von Nettesheim, H.C.
    1:131
  anti-scholasticism 8:502–88
  Charron, P. 2:287, 2:288–9
  Erasmus, D. 3:396, 3:398, 8:501
  Montaigne, M.E. de 6:485,
    6:486–8, 8:502–3
  Reformation 8:501–2
  Sanches, F. 8:451–4, 8:452,
    8:453–4
Romanticism (Cavell, S.) 2:258–9
rule (Llewellyn, K.N.) 5:661
sceptical alternative 8:493–4
science, nineteenth century
  philosophy of 8:570–1
self-fulfilling (Hegel, G.W.F.)
  4:267–8
sensory impressions (Crathorn, W.)
  2:693
solipsism 9:25
transcendental arguments 9:452–4
  Strawson, P.F. 9:168–9, 9:172–3
universal 3:123, 3:124
William of Ockham 9:738–9
wisdom 9:753
Scerri, E. 2:300
Scha, R. 3:99
Schabas, Margaret
  Keynes, J.M. †5:233–5
Schacht, J. 5:460
Schacht, R. 4:5, 6:861
Schachter, J.J. 5:206
Schachter, S. 3:285
Schaefer, D.L. 6:489
Schaefer, J.T. 1:564
Schaefer, O. 3:169
Schäfer, L. 9:612
Schafer, P. 5:175
Schaff, P. 7:287, 8:275
Schaffer, J. 6:267
Schaffer, S. 1:857, 3:517, 9:2, 9:711
Schaffner, Kenneth F.
  medicine, philosophy of †6:264–9
  models 6:446
  molecular genetics 6:459, 6:460–1
  reduction
    problems of 8:149
  scientific theories 9:354
  unity of science 9:533
Schajowicz, L. 1:230, 1:234
Schaper, E. 3:281, 3:668, 8:529, 9:454
Schapiro, L. 5:610, 8:774
Schapiro, Meyer 1:452, 1:507, 1:509
Scharfe, H. 5:384
Scharff, R. 2:505
Scharlemann, R.P. 9:413

Schatzki, Theodore R.
structuralism in social science
†9:184–9
Schatz-Uffenheimer, R. 4:245
Schauer, F. 3:765, 5:531, 7:41, 7:619
Schaupp, Z. 2:527
Scheandes, P. 9:133
Schechterman, D. 4:710
Schecter, D. 4:154
Scheffler, I.
educational philosophy 3:233,
3:234, 3:240
fictionalism 3:668
indirect discourse 4:745
Kuhn, T.S. 5:318
ontological commitment 7:117
pragmatism 7:640
Scheffler, S. 2:606, 4:344, 4:675, 6:527
Scheindlin, R. 4:213
Scheines, R. 2:251
Scheler, Max Ferdinand **8:504–9**
axiology 1:609, 1:612
emotions 3:290
gratitude 8:141
Hartmann, N. 4:242
Latin American phenomenology
7:348, 7:349–50
Lebensphilosophie 5:489
phenomenological movement
7:342
sympathy 8:504, 8:507
technology and ethics 9:281, 9:284
values 8:504, 8:506
Schelling, Friedrich Wilhelm Joseph
von **8:509–20**
see also Schellingianism
the Absolute 1:27, 1:29
art
influence on Belinskii, V.G.
1:710
German idealism 4:44
Goethe, J.W. von 4:126, 4:127
Hegelian critique 8:515–16
idealism 4:669
identity philosophy 8:509,
8:512–14
Naturphilosophie 6:738, 6:742–3,
8:509, 8:511–12
panlogicism (Hegel, G.W.F.) 4:284
panpsychism
German Romanticism 8:351,
8:352
poetry 7:477
Rosenzweig, F. 8:358, 8:359, 8:362
theosophy 9:366
transcendental philosophy
8:510–12

Weltalter philosophy 8:514–15
Schelling, T. 2:835, 8:74–5, 8:835–6
Schellingianism **8:520–2**
Belinskii, V.G. 1:710
Scheman, Naomi
linguistic discrimination †5:641–5
psychoanalytic feminism 3:584,
3:588
schemata
categories (Kant, I.) 5:186
schematism
Hilbert's formalism 4:423
'schematizing abstraction'
art 1:449–50, 1:451–2
Schenk, G. 9:786
Schepers, H. 2:693–4, 4:479, 5:722
Scherer, E. 4:299, 9:801
Scherrer, J. 8:409, 8:428
Schervish, M. 3:211
Scheuerman, W. 8:545
Schevill, F. 6:22
Schiappa, E. 7:791
Schibli, Hermann S.
Archytas †1:367–9
Neo-Pythagoreanism †6:808–9
Philolaus †7:367–71
Pythagoras †7:854–7
Pythagoreanism †7:857–60
Schick, F. 8:90
Schiebinger, L. 2:263
Schier, Flint 2:895, 2:896
Schiffer, Stephen
Grice, H.P. 4:177
language
conventionality of 5:368,
5:369–70, 5:371
pragmatics 7:632
propositional attitude statements
7:779
propositional attitudes 7:786–7
Schiffman, Z.S. 6:489
Schillebeekx, E. 8:445
Schiller, Ferdinand Canning Scott
8:522–4
Schiller, Johann Christoph Friedrich
8:524–9
aesthetics 1:480, 8:349, 8:524
educational philosophy 3:231
Herzen, A.I. 4:408
myth
German Romanticism 8:349
the sublime 8:523–4
tragedy 9:450
Schilpp, P.A.
Broad, C.D. 2:26
Carnap, R. 2:215
Cassirer, E. 2:227

Einstein, A. 3:258
Jaspers, K. 5:83–4
Lewis, C.I. 5:589
Moore, G.E. 6:498–9
process philosophy 7:715
Quine, W.V. 8:14
Radhakrishnan, S. 8:25
Russell, B.A.W. 8:404
Wright, G.H. von 9:669
Schimmel, A.M. 4:867, 6:626
Schinzinger, R. 3:315
Schirach, G.B. von 5:488, 5:489
Schirokauer, C. 9:865
Schlag, P. 5:510
Schlanger, J. 4:620
Schlatter, R. 9:399
Schlegel, August 9:450
Schlegel, Friedrich von **8:529–31**
art
German Romanticism 8:349
poetry 7:477
Schlegel, J.H. 5:525
Schleichert, H. 6:206
Schleiermacher, Friedrich Daniel
Ernst **8:531–9**
aesthetics 8:535
dialectics 8:533–4
divine atemporality 8:243
ethics 8:532–3, 8:534
hermeneutics 4:385–6, 4:389,
8:535–6
biblical 4:390, 4:391–2, 4:395
Neo-Kantianism 6:791
pedagogics 8:536
phenomenology of religion 7:355
politics 8:536–7
psychology 8:534–5
religion 8:535–6
Schleifer, J. 9:425
Schlesinger, G. 9:303, 9:416
Schlick, Friedrich Albert Moritz
8:539–44
analyticity 1:239
Avenarius, R. 1:594–5
coherence theory of justification
5:255, 5:259
general relativity 4:7–8, 4:9
knowledge
conceptual form 8:541–2
general theory of 8:540
logical positivism 5:795
relativity 5:791, 5:795
Mach, E. 6:16
necessary truth and convention
6:750
operationalism 7:135

Vienna Circle 8:539, 8:540–1, 9:608–9, 9:612
Schlingloff, D. 9:219
Schlodder, H. 1:669
Schlossberger, E. 3:315
Schmaus, W. 2:505
Schmerl, U. 7:30
Schmidheiny, S. 2:153
Schmidt, A. 4:301
Schmidt, J. 3:319
Schmidt, Johann Kaspar *see* Stirner, Max
Schmidt, M.A. 4:72
Schmidt, P.F. 9:719
Schmidt, W. 9:380
Schmieden, C. 1:216
Schmied-Kowarzik, W. 6:743, 8:362
Schmithausen, L. 2:63–4, 5:218, 7:67
Schmitt, Carl **8:544–5**
  German Romanticism 8:352
  legal institutionalism 4:801, 4:802
  theology, political 9:331–2, 9:333
Schmitt, C.B.
  Campanella, T. 2:191
  Keckermann, B. 5:225
  libertins 5:621
  medieval Aristotelianism 1:404
  medieval natural philosophy 6:707
  medieval Platonism 7:438
  Patrizi, F. 7:265
  Renaissance Aristotelianism 1:412, 1:413
  Renaissance humanism 4:541
  Renaissance Platonism 7:447
  Renaissance scepticism 8:504
  Zabarella, J. 9:839
Schmitt, Frederick
  epistemic justification 5:165
  reliabilism 8:209
  social epistemology 3:383, †8:828–32
  testimony 9:314
Schmitt, F.S. 1:286–7, 1:296
Schmitz, R.M. 1:782
Schmucker, J. 2:739
Schmucker-Hartmann, J. 1:689
Schmugge, L. 5:109
Schnädelbach, H.
  Büchner, L. 2:51
  communicative rationality objections to Habermas, J. 2:460, 2:462
  historicism 4:446
  Lebensphilosophie 5:489
  Lotze, R.H. 5:842
Schneeberger, G. 8:520

Schneewind, J.B.
  Cumberland, R. 2:753
  ethics
    autonomy 1:592
    common-sense 2:451
    intuitionism in 4:856
  Grote, J. 4:185
  MacIntyre, A. 6:24
  moral sense theories 6:547–8
  Paley, W. 7:188
  Sidgwick, H. 8:763
Schneider, H.W. 1:206, 5:125–6
Schneider, I. 4:9
Schneider, M. 3:585, 3:588
Schneiders, S.M. 4:395
Schneiders, W. 9:380, 9:786
Schnoor, C.P. 2:482
Schochet, G.J. 3:679, 7:517
Schock, R. 7:767
Schoeman, F. 3:552, 7:693
Schoenberg, A. 6:614
Schoenmetzer, A. 7:286, 7:839
Schofield, M.
  colour, theories of 2:431
Schofield, Malcolm
  Alcmaeon †1:160–1
  Anaxagoras †1:249–54
  Anaximander 1:259
  Anaximenes 1:262
  ancient philosophy 1:265
  Antisthenes †1:314–17
  Ariston of Chios 1:382
  Aristotle 1:434
  Cicero, M.T. 2:360
  Diogenes of Apollonia †3:87–9
  Empedocles †3:293–8
  Hellenistic philosophy 4:336, 4:337
  Heraclitus 4:369
  Hesiod 4:413
  Homer 4:502
  Melissus 6:296
  nous 7:44
  Owen, G.E.L. 7:179
  Parmenides 7:234
  Plato †7:399–421
  Presocratics 7:672
  Thales 9:324
  Xenophanes 9:810
  Zeno of Citium 9:843
  Zeno of Elea 9:852
Schofield, Robert E.
  Priestley, J. †7:682–4
scholarship
  medieval
    high standards of 6:694
scholastic nominalism *see* nominalism, scholastic

scholasticism
  see also anti-scholasticism; Aristotelianism, medieval; medieval philosophy
  Alexander of Hales 1:176
  Anselm of Canterbury 1:285–6
  Argentina, philosophy in 1:375
  colonial philosophy
    Latin America 5:421, 5:422, 5:424
    Mexico 6:345
  critique by Digby, K. 3:72–3
  Duns Scotus, J. 3:156–7
  historical development of 6:272–3
  Iberian (Molina, L. de) 6:461–4
  identity of indiscernibles 4:678
  influence of
    Renaissance philosophy 8:265–6
  influenced by
    Suarezian metaphysics 9:193
  logic
    Jewish philosophy (Messer Leon) 6:331, 6:332
  methods
    disputation 6:270, 6:272–3
    Meister Eckhart 6:286–7
    textual commentary 6:269–70, 6:272
  Olivi, P.J. 7:95–6
  Portuguese
    influence on Brazilian philosophy 2:8
  Spain, philosophy in 9:71, 9:72
Scholem, G.
  Hasidism 4:245
  Herrera, A. Cohen de 4:400
  Kabbalah 5:175
  mysticism 6:626
  Rosenzweig, F. 8:362
Schöllgen, W. 4:404
Scholten, C. 7:377
Scholtz, G. 8:538
Scholz, H. 4:279, 5:722, 7:499, 8:520
Schöne, A. 5:624
Schönfeld, Martin
  Fontenelle, B. de †3:690–3
  Tschirnhaus, E.W. von †9:485–7
Schönfinkel, M. 2:431–2, 2:433–4
School of Names *see* Names, School of
School of Translators of Toledo 9:70
schools *see* education
Schopenhauer, Arthur **8:545–54**
  aesthetic experience 8:546, 8:550–1
  critiques of
    Herzen, A.I. 4:407

death 2:822
humour 4:563, 4:564, 4:567
idealism 4:666–7, 4:668–9
intuitionism 4:847, 4:853
meaning of life 5:633
moral motivation 6:527–8
music
    aesthetics of 6:609, 6:614
Nietzsche, F.W. 6:861
nihilism 7:2, 7:5
right and good 8:325
sexuality 8:721, 8:729
suicide 9:230
sympathy 8:546, 8:552
    morality 6:562, 6:564
tragedy 9:450, 9:452
world as will 8:545–6, 8:549–53
Schotch, P.K. 8:846
Schotel, G.D.J. 8:559
Schouls, Peter A.
educational philosophy 3:231
revolution †8:301–4
Schrader-Frechette, Kristin
risk assessment †8:334–8
Schrag, C.O. 3:502, 7:342
Schrag, J.L. 8:725, 8:728
Schrag, O.O. 5:84
Schram, S. 6:141
Schreiner, K. 2:51
Schreiner, S.E. 2:182
Schröder, Ernst
logic
    algebra of 5:724–5, 5:727
    early twentieth century 5:731,
        5:738
    infinitary 5:734
    machines and diagrams 5:746
    nineteenth century 5:729
    notation 5:724
    relations 5:726
paradoxes of set and property
    7:217
Schrodinger, E. 7:890
Schrödinger's Cat 7:888
Schroeder, F.M. 7:463, 9:326
Schroeder-Heister, Peter
formal languages and systems
    †3:703–6
Popper, K.R. 7:539
relevance logic and entailment
    8:203
Schubeck, T.L. 5:617
Schubert, L.K. 6:170
Schubring, W. 2:684, 6:34
Schuffenhauer, W. 3:639
Schuhmann, K. 4:587, 8:182, 9:300
Schulthess, D. 8:180

Schultz, Bart
Grote, J. †4:183–5
Sidgwick, H. †8:758–64
Schultz, D.P. 1:699
Schultz, S.E. 1:699
Schultze, W. 8:338
Schulz, W.K. 6:792, 8:520
Schulze, G.E. 8:189
Schulze, W.D. 8:334, 8:337
Schum, David A.
legal evidence and inference
    †5:499–506
Schumpeter, Joseph Alois 8:554–6
democracy 2:872
public choice incentives 8:71
social science 8:859, 9:580
Schurman, Anna Maria van 4:540,
    8:556–9
Schürmann, R. 4:323
Schurr, V. 1:813
Schüssler-Fiorenza, F. 8:39
Schuster, P. 5:635
Schutrumpf, E. 8:807
Schütte, Kurt
inference
    non-constructive rules of 7:28,
        7:29, 7:30
ordinal logics 7:142
proof theory 7:747–8
Schutte, Ofelia
cultural identity 2:746
Latin America
    feminism 3:628
    literature 5:657
    Marxism †6:160–5
liberation philosophy 5:613
Schütz, Alfred 8:559–61
constitutive phenomenology 7:337,
    7:342
ideal types 8:560
social reality (lebenswelt) 8:560
social science 8:859
society
    concept of 8:886–7, 8:889
Schutz, B.F. 9:66
Schwab, B. 8:545
Schwab, R.N. 3:304
Schwabhäuser, W. 9:264
Schwann, Theodor 9:641
Schwartz, B.I.
Chinese Confucianism 2:549
Chinese Legalist philosophy 5:538
Chinese philosophy 2:328
Daodejing 2:782
Daxue 2:809
Han Feizi 4:220

Marxism
    Chinese 6:141
Mohist philosophy 6:458
Zhongyong 9:862
Schwartz, H. 2:175
Schwartz, M. 2:244
Schwartz, R. 4:140, 7:117, 9:638
Schwartz, S.P. 6:684
Schwartzmann, J. 8:740
Schwarz, Karl 9:165–6, 9:167
Schwarz, R.B. 5:123
Schwarzschild, S.S. 2:402, 5:100
Schweickart, D. 6:110
Schweid, E. 2:704
Schweizer, Paul
matter
    Indian conceptions of
        †6:196–200
modal operators †6:433–6
Schwemmer, O. 3:61
Schwichtenberg, H. 3:706, 4:378,
    6:682, 7:751
Schwoerer, L.G. 7:517
Schwyzer, H.R. 6:807
Sciacca, G.M. 4:518
Scibilia, Giovanni
Lacoue-Labarthe, P. †5:340–2
science
see also archaeology; biology;
    chemistry; genetics; information
    technology; natural history;
    natural philosophy; natural
    science; physics; psychology;
    revolutions, scientific; science,
    philosophy of; scientific language;
    scientific method; scientific
    realism; scientists; technology;
    universal science
African traditional religion
    analogy 1:117–18, 1:119–20
Alighieri, Dante 1:181, 1:182–3
antirealism 2:865, 8:581–4
archaeology 1:354–9
archē 1:360–1
atheism 1:531
Bacon, R. 1:634–5
Bohr, N. 1:820–2
Campbell, N.R. 2:193–4
chaos theory 2:276–80
chemistry 2:294–300
Chinese-European comparison
    studies (Needham, J.) 7:576
Christianity see Christianity,
    science
civil (Hobbes, T.) 4:463, 4:465,
    4:474–5
classification of (al-Farabi) 3:556

colour
  theories of **2:428–31**
colour-perception conflict 2:428–9
computer **2:491–6**
conservation principles **2:606–8**
constructivism **2:624–30**
Copernicus, N. **2:671–2**
cosmology **2:677–81**
Cournot, A.A. 2:689
creation doctrine 2:699
critical realism 2:721
critiques (Nietzsche, F.W.) 6:845,
  6:849, 6:851–2
Darwin, C.R. **2:795–8**
demarcation problem **2:863–7**
demonstrative
  natural theology 6:708
determinism and indeterminism
  3:33–9
development of
  Brunschvicg, L. 2:40
  disciplines 5:316
  Pascal, B. 7:244
discovery
  logic of **3:99–103**
Duhem, P.M.M. **3:142–7**
ecology **3:202–5**
economic theory 3:213–14
Einstein, A. **3:254–8**
electrodynamics **3:258–60**
empiricism (Neurath, O.) 6:813–15
encyclopedia-model (Neurath, O.)
  6:815
ethics
  embryonic and foetal research
    8:276–7
  engineering **3:313–15**
  expertise 6:509, 6:510
  human experimentation 6:260,
    6:261–2
  human genome project 4:19
  meta-ethical relativism
    6:539–40
  pragmatism 7:641
  risk definition 8:331–2
experiments **3:514–18**
  Bacon, R. 1:634–5
  crucial **2:735–6**
fallibilism **3:545–8**
fallible inferences
  (Ajdukiewicz, K.) 1:137
Feyerabend, P.K. **3:640–2**
fictionalism **3:667–8**
field theory
  classical **3:668–70**
  quantum **3:670–3**

foundationalist model (William of
  Auvergne) 9:726
functional explanation **3:802–5**
Galilei, G. **3:835–41**
gender **3:861–8**
general relativity **4:5–9**
genetics **4:12–16**
geology **4:25–8**
God
  existence of 8:241–2
Gregory of Rimini 4:171
Heideggerian philosophy of
  4:323–7
Heisenberg, W. **4:327–9**
Helmholtz, H. von **4:337–40**
Hertz, H.R. **4:400–2**
hierarchy of (Comte, A.) 2:496–7
historical nature of
  French philosophy of science
    3:779–80, 3:785
history (Bachelard, G.) 1:621
history of
  alchemy as error 1:157
  Bachelard, G. 3:780
  contrasting historiographies
    5:315–16
  Duhem, P.M.M. 3:143–4
  Koyré, A. 5:296
  Kuhn, T.S. 5:315–16
  Lakatos, I. 5:344
  logic of discovery 3:100–1
  medieval natural philosophy
    6:703–4
  sociology of knowledge 9:1–2
Hobbes, T. 4:465
human
  foundation of 3:77, 3:78–9
  Mill, J.S. 6:367–9
Huxley, T.H. **4:594–6**
hypotheses
  inductivism (Stewart, D.)
    9:138–9
ideology
  French philosophy of science
    3:782
imagination (Smith, A.) 8:817–18
incommensurability **4:732–6**
induction problem (Popper K.R.)
  7:534
inductive (Mill, J.S.) 6:365–6
information theory **4:782–6**
inquiry (Dewey, J.) 3:47–8
instrumental rationality
  critical theory 2:723
instrumentalism (Eudoxus) 3:452
intuition (Iqbal, M.) 4:865–6

irrationalism (Feyerabend, P.K.)
  3:641–2
Islam 3:556, 4:865–6, 5:12, **8:561–5**
  modern philosophy 5:18–19,
    8:564
John of Mirecourt 5:112
Kepler, J. **5:231–3**
knowledge
  achievement (*Leistungswissen*)
    (Scheler, M.F.) 8:506
  Aristotle 1:417–18
  collective 8:831
  divine illumination (Peter of
    Spain) 7:324
  Galen 3:835
  limits of (Du Bois-Reymond, E.)
    3:130
  mathematical 6:325, 6:327–8,
    6:329
  moral distinction
    (Williams, B.A.O.) 9:751–2
  objective (Bachelard, G.)
    1:620–1
  objectivity of 6:814–15
  sociology of 9:1–2
  tacit 5:286
Krause, K. 5:299
Kuhn, T.S. **5:315–18**, 5:316
Le Roy, É.L.E.J. **5:481–3**
life
  origin of **5:633–5**
lifeworld (Husserl, E.) 4:584
Linnaeus, C. von **5:646–50**
logic
  relation to
    Latin America 5:423–4
logic of discovery (Hanson, N.R.)
  4:224–5
logic of (Nagel, E.) 6:641–2
logical positivism (Mach, E.)
  6:13–14
Marxist philosophy of **6:147–50**
mathematics
  Bacon, R. 1:634
  Galilei, G. 3:838–9
  Mersenne, M. 6:325, 6:327–8,
    6:329
matter **6:192–6**
Maxwell, J.C. **6:206–10**
measurement
  theory of **6:243–9**
mechanics
  Aristotelian **6:249–51**
  classical **6:251–9**
medicine, philosophy of **6:264–9**
medieval *see* natural philosophy,
  medieval

medieval Aristotelianism 1:398
metaphysics
    Peirce, C.S. 7:270, 7:280–1
metaphysics relationship 6:340,
    7:534–5
method *see* scientific method
models 6:444–5
    Ramsey, I.T. 8:50
    theories distinction 6:445
model-theoretic view
    social science 8:840–1
molecular biology **6:458–61**
morality relationship
    Rousseau, J.-J. 8:368, 8:370
mysticism relationship
    (Certeau, M. de) 2:268
natural bodies (Hobbes, T.) 4:465
natural laws **5:470–5**
naturalistic explanation (Kant, I.)
    5:180
naturalized philosophy of
    6:728–31
nature
    aesthetic appreciation of 6:732,
    6:734, 6:735
Neoplatonism 6:801–2, 7:729–30
Newton, I. **6:823–8**
nineteenth century philosophy of
    8:565–72
normative
    Peirce, C.S. 7:278
observation **7:80–6**
    Carnap, R. 2:210, 2:211–12
occultism (Paracelsus) 7:207
ontological inquiry (Marcel, G.)
    6:92
operationalism **7:131–6**, 7:131–4
optics **7:136–8**
personalism (Bowne, B.P.) 7:316
philosophy relationship
    Arendt, H. 1:372
    Deleuze, G.) 2:858–9
    Galilei, G. 3:838
    Islamic fundamentalism 5:12
    Kemp Smith, N. 5:230
Planck, M.K.E.L. **7:396–8**
pluralist methodology
    Feyerabend, P.K. 3:640–1
Poincaré, J.H. **7:478–83**
Portugal
    influence on Brazilian
        philosophy 2:8
positive heuristics
    Lakatos, I. 5:343–4
practice
    Oakeshott, M.J. 7:71
    social nature of 2:624–5

quantum measurement problem
    7:886–90
randomness **8:56–9**
rationalism (Alembert, J. le R. d')
    1:164–5, 1:166
ratios (Bradwardine, T.) 1:863–5
realism *see* scientific realism
reasoning
    probability (Keynes, J.M.)
    5:233–4
reduction
    problems of **8:145–9**
religion and **8:230–6**
    early modern 8:230–1
    Judaism (Ibn Daud, A.)
        4:609–610
    Presocratic philosophy 9:651
    Spencer, H. 9:87
    Unamuno y Jugo, M. De 9:519
Renaissance Aristotelianism 1:406,
    8:266–7
Renaissance scepticism
    Sanches, F. 8:452, 8:453–4
semantics (Næss, A.) 6:635
sense experience (Whitehead, A.N.)
    9:715–16
society relationship (Neurath, O.)
    6:814
sociobiology **8:892–6**
space **9:59–66**
species **9:78–81**
systematization of
    (Schleiermacher, F.) 8:533
taxonomy **9:272–6**
theology
    Galilei, G. 3:839–40
    Troeltsch, E.P.W. 9:461–2
theories **9:343–55**
    holism 4:489
    incommensurability
        Feyerabend, P.K. 3:640
    proliferation
        Feyerabend, P.K. 3:641
    Whewell, W. 9:709–10
theosophy 9:364
thermodynamics **9:366–9**
Thomism (Maritain, J.) 6:103
thought experiments **9:392–7**
time **9:413–17**
time travel **9:417–19**
unity of **9:530–3**
    Heidegger, M. 4:326
    Neurath, O. 9:610–11
vitalism **9:639–43**
Wallace, A.R. **9:678–9**
Weyl, H. **9:706–7**
William of Auvergne 9:726–7

science of lights *see* Illuminationist
    philosophy
science, philosophy of **8:572–6**
    Argentinian
        colonial period 1:375
    educational theory 3:237
    French **3:779–86**
    green political 4:161
    Mexico 6:347
    Poincaré, J.H. 7:479
    postcolonial philosophy **7:575–8**
    Vienna Circle 9:607–11
science, social *see* social science
scientia
    faith 3:541, 3:542
    medieval epistemology 8:231
scientific antirealism **8:581–4**
    constructivism 2:625
    demarcation problem 2:865
    entities 8:145
    fictionalism **3:667–8**
    scientific theories 9:348–50
scientific behaviourism *see*
    behaviourism, scientific
scientific determinism
    contingent laws (Boutroux, É.)
        1:850, 1:851
scientific humanism
    Enlightenment 4:529–30
    modern 4:530–1
scientific knowledge *see* knowledge,
    scientific
scientific language
    radical physicalism (Neurath, O.)
        6:814–15
scientific materialism
    Büchner, L. 2:48, 2:49
    process philosophy 7:712
scientific method **8:576–81**
    analysis–synthesis distinctions
        8:577–8
    Aristotle 8:577
    chemical research 2:299
    critiques of
        demarcation problem 2:864,
            2:864–5
        Feyerabend, P.K. 3:640–2
        Kuhn, T.S. 5:317
        psychoanalysis 7:811–16
        Rorty, R. 8:353
        theory-ladenness
            Nagel, E. 6:642
    dogmatism
        Pyrrhonist critique 7:853
    empiricism (Strato) 9:163
    Epicureanism 3:345
    experiment (Boyle, R.) 1:853–5

French philosophy of science 3:780
Galilei, G. 5:35
gender bias 3:588, 3:589–90
indirect description (Mach, E.)
6:14
induction (Peirce, C.S.) 7:269–70,
7:274–5, 7:278, 7:280–1
Islamic philosophy 8:563–4
logic of discovery 3:99–103
Mill, J.S. 8:578
model-theory distinction 6:445
natural philosophy
(Tschirnhaus, E.W. von) 9:486
naturalized philosophy of science
6:728, 6:730
Pascal, B. 7:242, 7:244
philosophical application
(Twardowski, K.) 9:508
Plato 8:577
Popper, K.R. 8:578–9
principle-constructive theories
distinction (Einstein, A.) 3:257
protocol statements (Neurath, O.)
6:815
statistics 9:125
tacit integration (Polanyi, M.)
7:491
theories 8:573–4
Whewell, W. 8:578
scientific philosophy
feminism 3:861–8
scientific realism 2:865, 8:581–4
challenges to (Heidegger, M.)
4:326
Copernicus, N. 2:672
determinism 3:36, 5:823–4
Einstein, A. 3:257
entities 8:145
fictionalism 3:668
inquiry (Dewey, J.) 3:48
Kuhn, T.S. 5:316
Maxwell, J.C. 6:209
mental states (Sellars, W.S.) 8:639
physics (Smart, J.J.C.) 8:814
Planck, M.K.E.L. 7:396–7
probability (Reichenbach, H.)
8:168
Putnam, H. 7:839, 7:840
scientific theories 9:346–7,
9:348–50
social science 8:584–7
anti-naturalism 8:586–7
critique of positivism 8:585
observation
theory-choice 9:355–6
scientific revolutions see revolutions,
scientific

scientific socialism see dialectical
materialism
scientific theories see theories,
scientific
scientism
see also European positivism;
positivism
human diversity (Todorov, T.)
9:426
nihilism
Russian 7:6, 7:7–8
philosophical response
Japan 5:77
refutation of (Sorel, G.) 9:35
social studies 8:446–7
Soviet Marxism
critique by Il'enkov, E.V. 4:689
scientists
definition 8:288
responsibilities of 8:287–90
Scipionic circle 7:189
Scitovsky, Tibor 5:455
Sclafani, R. 1:512
scope 8:587–9
adverbs 1:48–9
ambiguity of 1:200, 9:246–7,
9:250–2
de relde dicto belief 2:815
descriptions 3:21, 3:22
distinction 4:774
the infinite 4:775, 4:776–7
Scorraille, R. de 9:196
Scot, Michael 1:399, 5:22, 9:456
Scotism
see also Duns Scotus
Franciscans
Latin America 5:422, 5:424
matter 1:388–9
place 1:389
Scotland
Aberdeen Philosophical Society
1:15
Alison, A. 1:185–7
Beattie, J. 1:677–80
Blair, H. 1:781–2
Brown, T. 2:26–9
Campbell, G. 2:191–3
Carmichael, G. 2:206–8
Common Sense School 2:446–8
Duns Scotus, J. 3:153–70
Enlightenment see Enlightenment,
Scottish
Eriugena, J.S. 3:401–6
Ferguson, A. 3:630–3
Gerard, A. 4:36–7
Home, H. 4:499–501
Hume, D. 4:543–62

Kemp Smith, Norman 5:227–31
Major, J. 6:54–6
Millar, J. 6:375–6
Monboddo, Lord (James Burnett)
6:473–4
Oswald, J. 7:168–70
Reid, T. 8:171–80
Richard of St Victor 8:312–14
Smith, A. 8:815–22
Stair, J.D. 9:118–20
Stewart, D. 9:135–40
Turnbull, G. 9:502–4
Witherspoon, J. 9:755–7
Scott, D.
Cudworth, R. 2:744
Hellenistic philosophy 4:337
nativism 6:675
Plato 7:420–1
Polanyi, M. 7:492
possible worlds semantics 8:669
Scott, D.S.
intuitionism 4:850, 4:852, 4:853
lambda calculus 5:345, 5:348,
5:349
logic
combinatory 2:431, 2:433
infinitary 4:772
many-valued 6:84, 6:91
set theory 8:713, 8:716
Scott, F.R. 4:594
Scott, H.M. 3:319
Scott, J.C. 2:677
Scott, P. 4:853
Scott, Sir Walter 8:21
Scott, W.R. 8:822
Scott-Curry theorem 5:347–8
Scotus, John Duns see Duns Scotus,
John
Scotus, Michael see Scot, Michael
Screech, M.A. 8:17–18
scriptor
intransitive writing (Barthes, R.)
1:657
Scripture
see also Bible; Bible, Hebrew; New
Testament; Qur'an
church authority (Wyclif, J.) 9:802,
9:803
commentaries on (Origen) 7:160,
7:161
Copernican theses (Galilei, G.)
3:840
interpretation of
apparent meaning (Ibn Hazm)
4:620, 4:621
esoteric meaning (Ibn Hazm)
4:620

Hugh of St Victor 4:519
  humanist philology influence
    4:538–9
  midrash 6:353–4
Jewish Averroism (Albalag, L.)
    1:599
Mīmāṃsā 6:380–1
  as revelation 8:297–300
Calvin, J. 2:179
  superiority over natural
    philosophy (Boyle, R.) 1:855
theological exposition of (Bernard
    of Clairvaux) 1:754
theology of the word (Barth, K.)
    1:653
Scriven, Michael 3:522, 3:525, 7:224
Scruton, Roger
  architecture
    aesthetics of 1:362, 1:364–5,
      1:366
  art
    erotic 3:409
    understanding of 1:475
  artistic expression 1:498
  conservatism 2:614–15
  culture 2:750
  humour 4:567
  intentionality 4:821
  music
    aesthetics of 6:614
  nation and nationalism 6:661
  photography, aesthetics of 7:380–1
  sexual desire 8:721, 8:729
Scudder, D.L. 9:303
Scull, A. 8:878–9
sculpture 5:574–5
Scult, M. 5:206
Séailles, G. 5:340, 8:270
Seanor, D. 4:231
Searle, John Rogers **8:589–91**
  action 1:41
  Austin, J.L. 1:574
  Chinese room argument **2:328–9**
    language of thought hypothesis
      5:405–6, 5:407
    thought experiments 9:395
  classical ai
    critique of 1:488
  communication and intention
    2:458
  computational theories of mind
    6:394
  conceptual role semantics 8:653,
    8:657
  deconstruction 2:839
  imperative logic 4:721
  institutionalism in law 4:802–3

intensionality 4:811
intention 4:814, 4:816
intentionality 4:821
is–ought distinction
  constitutive rules 5:761, 5:764
materialism 6:178
meaning and communication
    6:213
metaphor 6:337
methodological individualism
    6:344
perception 7:293
performatives 7:304
pragmatics 7:632
promising 7:742
proper names 7:753, 7:757
  sense 7:753, 8:685, 8:688
qualia 7:867
reference 8:164
speech acts 9:86
transcendental arguments 9:454
Turing, A.M. 9:495
unconscious mental states 9:525,
    9:527
Seban, Jean-Loup
  Barth, K. †1:651–6
  Boehme, J. †1:799–801
  Bonhoeffer, D. †1:835–8
  Brunner, E. †2:30–4
  Bultmann, R. †2:126–31
  Tindal, M. †9:420–3
  Troeltsch, E.P.W. †9:461–4
Sebba, G. 3:19, 6:66, 9:656–7
Sebeok, Thomas A. 8:677, 8:679
Sechenov, Ivan 8:418
Second Being *see* first intellect
Second Coming *see Parousia*
second intentions
  medieval logic 5:750–1
Second International Marxism
    6:142–3
Second Order 1:107
Second World War
  new anarchism 1:247
secondary qualities *see* qualities,
    secondary
second-order arithmetic
  proof theory 7:746
second-order logic **8:591–5,
    8:599–604**
  early twentieth century 5:730
  first-order comparison 8:600–1
  mathematics 8:600, 8:601–3
  non-standard models 8:601
  property theory 7:762–3, 7:765
  singular identity 4:678–9
Secord, P.F. 1:695, 8:858

secular humanism
  Enlightenment 4:529–31
secularism
  political authority (Marsilius of
    Padua) 6:112–13
secularization
  pastoral psychology 8:457
  salvation concept 8:448
Seddon, F.A. 5:863
Sedivy, Sonia
  Nagel, T. †6:643–7
Sedley, David N.
  ancient philosophy †1:262–5
  aretē †1:373–4
  Ariston of Chios †1:380–2
  atomism, ancient †1:534–5
  Chrysippus †2:345–6
  Cleanthes †2:382–3
  Dialectical school †3:58–9
  Diodorus Cronus 3:86
  Empedocles 3:298
  Epicharmus 3:337
  Epicureanism †3:339–50
  Epicurus †3:350–1
  eudaimonia 3:451
  Eudoxus 3:453
  free will 3:752
  Hellenistic philosophy 3:382,
    †4:335–7
  language
    ancient philosophy of 5:361
  Lucretius 5:856
  Megarian school †6:279–80
  Melissus 6:292–6
  morality and emotions 6:563
  Parmenides †7:228–35
  Philo the Dialectician 7:365
  Philodemus 7:367
  Presocratics †7:671–2
  psychē (soul) 7:811
  Pyrrho 7:848
  Stoicism †9:141–60
  Timon 9:420
  Zeno of Citium †9:841–3
Seeberg, R. 5:168
Seebohm, T. 7:342
Seeff, A.F. 6:828
Seeger, R. 6:16
Seelig, C. 3:258
Seeskin, Kenneth
  Jewish philosophy
    contemporary 5:95
    early nineteenth century
      †5:96–5:100
Seeskin, K.R. 6:91
Sefer Yetzirah (text) 5:175–6

Sefirot
  Kabbalah 5:171, 5:172–3, 5:174
    Herrera, A. Cohen de 4:398–9
Segal, C. 5:856
Segal, Gabriel
  indirect discourse †4:743–5
  meaning and truth 6:225
  methodological individualism
    †6:341–4
  propositional attitude statements
    7:779
  semantics 8:652
Segal, H. 7:823
Segal, Jerome M. 3:43–4
Segal, L. 3:614
Segerberg, Krister
  dynamic logics 3:189, 3:191
  modal logic 8:486, 8:491–2
  possible worlds semantics 8:669
segmented Discourse Representation
  Theory (SDRT) 3:96–8
Segner, J.A. 5:719
Segoloni, D. 1:659
Segonds, A.P. 7:157
segregation, law of
  Mendelian genetics 4:13, 4:14
Segundo, Juan Luis 5:615, 5:617
Seibt, J. 8:642
Seidel, A. 9:567–8
Seidel, G.J. 3:653
Seidel, G.S. 7:234
Seidenfeld, T. 3:211, 9:127
Seidler, M.J.
  Crusius, C.A. †2:736–9
  Pufendorf, S. 7:836
Seidman, S. 9:7
Seigel, J.E. 4:541
Seigfried, C.H. 1:687, 3:602
seiza (quiet-sitting) 3:799, 3:800
Sejnowski, T.J. 2:579, 6:394
Sekuler, R. 4:846
Sekyi-Otu, A. 7:582
Selden, John 8:604–5
Seldin, J. 2:433, 2:434, 5:349
selection, evolutionary see natural
  selection
self
  see also ātman; consciousness; ego;
    identity; personal identity; puruṣa
  absence of
    emptiness
      Buddhist concept of 2:76–8
  absolute 1:27
  alienation of (Berdiaev, N.A.)
    1:728
  alterity
    postmodernism 1:187–8

autonomy
  axiology 1:611
bundle theory of mind (Hume, D.)
  6:231, 6:383
cogito argument (Descartes, R.)
  3:1, 3:7–8
community relationship
  (Taylor, C.) 9:278
composite nature of
  Buddhist philosophy 6:401
  Hindu philosophy 6:400–1
concept of (James, W.) 5:62
construction of (Sartre, J.-P.) 8:476
continuity of 8:605, 8:607–8
culture of (Mill, J.S.) 6:373–4
Daoism 2:787–8, 2:791
  Zhuangzi 9:866
discovery of
  antipaternalism 7:251
disordered (Kant, I.) 8:611–12
distinction-in-unity
  (Coleridge, S.T.) 2:404
divine creation of
  Sufism (Ibn Sab'in) 4:647
efficient/appreciative aspects
  (Iqbal, M.) 4:863, 4:864–5
enduring 4:838
essential (Krause, K.) 5:299
ethical (Foucault, M.) 3:711–12
existence of (Emerson, R.W.) 3:270
finitude (Fichte, J.G.) 3:642,
  3:648–9
formation of
  Mead, G.H. 6:211
  Mill, J.S. 6:368
  post-Freudian psychoanalysis
    7:821
  psychoanalysis (Lacan, J.)
    9:198–9
freedom of
  Indian fatalism 3:566, 3:567
God relationship (Nishida Kitarō)
  7:14–15
impermanence
  Ābhidharmika Buddhism 2:56
  Yogācāra Buddhism 2:70, 2:72
indexicals 2:878
Indian theories of 8:605–11
individualism (Nishida Kitarō)
  7:14
inner life
  moral agents 6:499, 6:501–2
Japan
  modern literature 5:658–9
Kierkegaard, S.A. 3:495
knowledge of
  Boehme, J. 1:799

gnosis
  Hermetism 4:396
  Indian views of 5:282
liberalism
  communitarian critique of
    2:466, 2:467–9
liberation of
  Indian political philosophy
    7:521, 7:522–3
nature of
  Taylor, C. 9:277
non-existence of
  Indian Buddhism 2:93–4,
    8:689–90
ontological categories
  Indian philosophy 7:127
Other
  Buber, M. 2:42, 2:43–5
  Derrida, J. 1:190
  Kristeva, J. 1:188–9
  Lacan, J. 1:188
  Levinas, E. 1:189, 5:580–1
pathology
  post-Freudian psychoanalysis
    7:820–1
phenomenology of
  Bakhtin, M.M. 1:642
postmodern critique of subject
  9:196–201
pragmatism 7:633
'principle of the three Ks'
  Mamardashvili, M.K. 6:69–70
representations of
  post-Freudian psychoanalysis
    7:817
Sartre, J.-P. 3:496
self-control 8:611, 8:612
sense of
  Indian philosophy 6:402
social theory of the
  Fichte, J.G. 3:642–3
  Smith, A. 8:818
symbolic interactionism 9:243,
  9:244
thought distinction
  (Wittgenstein, L.) 9:761
transcendental idealism 2:67
unchanging
  Mīmāṃsā 6:379
unity
  Tathandlung (fact/act)
    (Fichte, J.G.) 3:647–8, 3:649
universe relationship
  Hindu philosophy 8:606, 8:607
  Yogācāra Buddhism doctrines 2:66
self-awareness
  Avaita Vedānta 9:589

existentialism 3:494–5
free will (Nishida Kitarō) 7:13–14
Hindu philosophy 8:607
Illuminationist philosophy 9:220–1
impossibility of complete 3:585
Indian theories of 1:607–8
Jewish philosophy (al-Baghdadi) 1:637
Kyoto School 5:325–6
monism
    Indian 6:475, 6:476–7
recognition 8:133
will
    Schopenhauer, A. 8:549–50
self-certificationalism
    Mīmāṃsā 3:388, 3:390–1
self-consciousness
alienation 1:179
communalist concept of
    African philosophy,
      Anglophone 1:98–9
existentialism (Sartre, J.-P.) 8:474–5
experience (Kant, I.) 5:186
idealism (Schelling, F.W.J. von) 8:511–12
mind (Anscombe, G.E.M.) 1:281
object–consciousness distinction (Schleiermacher, F.) 8:535
persons 7:318–19
phenomenology of perception (Merleau-Ponty, M.) 6:323
recognition 8:132–3
self-control **8:611–13**
see also akrasia
emotions
    morality 6:559
moral education 6:507
rationality
    Musonius Rufus 6:615, 6:616
    Peirce, C.S. 7:275–6
self-cultivation
Chinese philosophy **8:613–26**
    aesthetics 1:68, 1:71, 1:72
    body 8:621–2
    Buddhism 8:619–21
    cheng 2:300
    Confucianism
      de 2:538
    Confucius 2:319–20, 8:614–16
    Daodejing 2:779, 2:780–1
    Daoism 2:788, 8:618–19
    Daxue 2:808–9
    human flourishing 8:617–18, 8:625
    Lushi chunqiu 5:864
    Mencius 8:616, 8:617

neo-Confucianism 2:325–6, 6:769, 6:770–3, 8:622–5
    sages 8:622
    Wang Yangming 9:683
    Xunzi 8:616–17
    Zhongyong 9:861–2
    Zhu Xi 9:683, 9:864
East Asian Philosophy 3:195
Japanese philosophy
    Kaibara Ekken 5:176
Korean philosophy
    Horak controversy 2:562–3
    neo-Confucianism 9:823–4, 9:826–7
    sôngnihak 2:558–9
self-deception **8:626–9**
ethics of **8:629–32**
moral psychology 6:532–3
self-defence
Camus, A. 2:195
double effect principle 3:120
self-determination
see also autonomy
medical ethics 6:262
mind
    Johnson, S. 5:124
multiculturalism 6:600
national 6:660
self-esteem
self-respect distinction 8:636
self-evident belief
a priori 1:5
propositions (Reid, T.) 8:178
self-expression
art 1:493, 3:141
self-fulfilment
existentialism 1:686, 3:493
self-governance
autonomy
    ethical 1:586–7, 1:588–9
self-illumination
Advaita Vedānta 6:476–7
self-image
construction of (Sartre, J.-P.) 8:476
cultural identity 2:745
self-improvement
introspection 4:838, 4:841–2
self-interest
see also egoism; self-love
Chinese
    Legalism 5:533
hope (Marcel, G.) 4:509
justice relationship 6:754–5
morality
    moral motivation 6:525
    will 9:723

rational choice theory 8:64, 8:65, 8:66
supererogation conflict 9:233
self-knowledge
friendship 3:796
introspection 4:838, 4:840–2
Jewish philosophy
    Ibn Falaquera 4:616
    Ibn Paquda 4:635
    Ibn Tzaddik, J. 4:660
    Ramsey, I.T. 8:50
sport 9:112, 9:115–16
self-locating beliefs
indexicals 2:879
self-love
see also egoism; self-interest
human nature (Butler, J.) 2:155–6
love of self distinction
    moralistes 6:557
self-nature
three types of
    Yogācāra Buddhism 2:74
self-observation
sociality (Smith, A.) 8:818
self-ownership
libertarianism 5:618
self-power
Pure Land Buddhism
    Shinran 8:747–8
self-predication
Plato
    analytic study by Vlastos, G. 9:652
self-presence
language (Derrida, J.) 2:898
self-preservation
mutual aid (Kropotkin, P.A.) 5:314
the sublime 9:202
self-psychology
psychoanalysis
    post-Freudian 7:819–21, 7:820–1
self-realization **8:632–5**
Chinese Marxism 6:139–40
Daoism
    Huainanzi 4:512–13
existentialism (Jaspers, K.) 5:80–1
humanism
    Chinese Marxism 6:134
love (Zhu Xi) 9:864
qi 7:862
reason (Hegel, G.W.F.) 4:264, 4:265
self-cultivation (Zhu Xi) 9:864
social organisms (Bradley, F.H.) 1:858–9

xin (heart-and-mind) 9:815
self-reference
  intention 4:813–14
  paradoxes of
    Ailly, P. d' 1:134
    Albert of Saxony 1:143
self-reflection
  conceptual knowledge
    (Dilthey, W.) 3:78
  human sciences (Dilthey, W.) 3:78
self-respect **8:635–8**
  see also dignity; self-esteem
  forgiveness 3:697, 3:699
  respect for persons 8:286
self-revelation
  postmodern theology 7:586
self-sacrifice
  moral psychology 6:531–2
self-sufficiency
  divinity
    Socrates–Cyrus comparison
      (Xenophon) 9:813–14
self-transcendence
  the sublime 9:202
Selge, K.-V. 8:538
Selin, H. 7:578
Sellars, Wilfrid Stalker **8:638–42**
  adverbial theory of mental states
    6:317
  correspondence theory of truth
    9:475
  descriptions 3:24
  foundationalism 3:383
  inference to the best explanation
    4:769
  Jones myth
    folk psychology 3:686–7
  justification 5:159, 5:165, 5:259
  knowledge by acquaintance/
    description 5:261, 5:263
  nominalism 7:21–2, 7:23
  non-conceptual content 2:643
  perception 7:296, 7:299
  pragmatism 7:640
  primary–secondary distinction
    7:687
  processes 7:723
  theoretical/epistemic virtues 9:343
Sellers, M. 3:240
Sellers, S. 2:374
Sellien, E. 4:9
Sellier, P. 7:247, 7:554–5
Sellmann, James D.
  Lushi chunqiu †5:863–5
Sells, Peter 4:54, 9:253
Selten, R. 2:835

selves, community of
  McTaggart, J.M.E. 6:24–5, 6:26–7
semantic holism *see* holism, mental
  and semantic
semantic indecision
  game-theoretic quantifiers 7:871–2
  vagueness 9:565–6
semantic materialism 9:293
semantic paradoxes *see* paradoxes
semantic reism
  Kotarbiński, T. 5:294
semantic value
  imperative logic 4:719–20
semantics 5:408, **8:649–52**
  see also discourse semantics;
  meaning; possible worlds; possible
  worlds semantics; pragmatics;
  reference; truth-conditions
  adverbs 1:46–50
  anaphora **1:239–44**
  Aristotle 5:688
  assertibility
    Mohism 5:698
  bivalence 4:856–7, 4:859–62
  Buridan, J. 2:132
  Carnap, R.
    logical positivism 5:793–4
  Chinese room argument 2:328
  classical AI 1:488–9
  cognitive 5:409
  compositionality 2:476–7
  compound terms
    Chinese theories of language
      (Xunzi) 5:704–5
    Gongsun Long 5:701–2
    Mohism 5:698–9
  concepts 2:505–14
  conceptual role **8:652–7**
    analytic–synthetic distinction
      4:490
  constructivism
    see also dialogical logic
  conventionalism 2:667, 2:668
  descriptions **3:19–24**
  descriptive psychology
    (Twardowski, K.) 9:508, 9:509
  discourse **3:91–9**
  dynamic 1:240–3
  empirical (Næss, A.) 6:635
  epistemology (Ajdukiewicz, K.)
    1:136–7
  fiction **3:659–63**
  free *see* free semantics
  game-theoretic **8:657–8**
    dialogical logic 3:61
    quantifiers 7:871–2
  holism **4:488–93**

ideal language philosophy 7:620–1
indexicals **2:878–81**
Indian philosophy 5:379–83,
  6:239–43
  'fitness' 9:316–17
  potentiality 7:607
informational 3:684, **8:658–62**
language of thought hypothesis
  5:405–6
linguistic nominalism
  (Sellars, W.S.) 8:639
logical constants 5:779
logical laws 5:786–7
Marsilius of Inghen 6:110–11
mass terms 6:168, 6:169
matching phrases
  Mohism 5:699–700
meaning 6:220
modal logic **6:426–33**
Nicholas of Autrecourt 6:831
nominalism
  Buddhism 7:23–6
paradoxes
  medieval theories on 2:132
  Poincaré, J.H. 7:480–1
possible worlds 6:484, **8:662–9**
pragmatics distinction 7:624–6
predication **7:665–7**
presupposition 7:626, 7:673–4
quantifiers
  inferential adequacy 7:868
  instantial terms 7:868–9
  natural language 7:875–7
religious statements 8:257
signs
  Renaissance theories of
    5:411–12
situation **8:669–72**
static
  anaphora 1:239–40
Stoics 5:690
structuralist literary theory
  (Todorov, T.) 9:425–6
supervaluational *see*
  supervaluational semantics
syntax distinction 6:390, 6:391–2
teleological **8:672–5**
truth theories 6:221
Wodeham, A. 9:773–4
Semenova, S.G. 3:576
seminal reasons
  doctrine of 1:562, 5:58
semiology *see* semiotics
semiotics 5:409, **8:675–9**
  see also signification; signs
  chora (Kristeva, J.) 5:306, 5:307
  Comte, A. 2:501–3

consumer culture (Baudrillard, J.)
1:662
in Italy (Eco, U.) 5:39
Kristeva, J. 9:293
linguistic structuralism 9:186
literary theory (Barthes, R.)
1:656–7
Moscow-Tartu school 6:583–7
Peirce, C.S. 7:270, 7:278–9
psychoanalysis (Lacan, J.) 5:337
rhythms (Kristeva, J.) 5:305–6
Saussure, F. de 8:481–2, 9:181
structuralism 9:175
Sen, Amartya K.
equality 3:396
ethics
development 3:40, 3:43, 3:44
economics 3:211
market 6:110
general will 4:12
impossibility theorems 8:824–5
obligations to future generations
3:822
Pareto principle 7:228
prudence 7:804
rational choice theory 8:75
social choice 8:826
social sciences
prediction in 8:872
utilitarianism 9:557
vulnerability and finitude 9:670
welfare 9:705
wellbeing 3:207–8
Sen, Keshub Chunder 2:6, 2:7
Sen, N.B. 1:517
Sen, P.B. 9:174
Sendlinger, A. 5:489
Seneca, Lucius Annaeus 1:262,
8:679–82
Ariston of Chios 1:382
Cynics 2:759
emotions 3:290
Letters to Lucilius
moral philosophy 8:681
moral philosophy 8:680–1
morality and emotions 6:564
passion (Le Grand, A.) 5:479
Roman philosophy overview 8:681
suicide 9:230
tragedy 9:448–9
Seng-chao *see* Sengzhao
Senghor, Leopold S.
ethnophilosophy, African 3:449
Marxism 1:99–100
Nkrumah, K. contrast 1:99–100
négritude 1:98–9, 1:107, 1:110–11,
1:116

Sengzhao 2:83, **8:682–4**
Senior, Nassau 3:214, 3:222
Senko, W. 4:404
sensa
intuition of (Kemp Smith, N.)
5:229
sensation
see also bodily sensations;
experience; perception; sense
perception; sense-data; senses
adverbial theory
Ducasse, C.J. 3:139–40
mental states 6:314–17
Sellars, W.N. 8:639–40
Whitehead, A.N. 9:717
appearances (Gassendi, P.) 3:852
Aristotle (Theophrastus) 9:338
bodily **1:792–5**
brain as seat of (Alcmaeon)
1:160–1
categories dualism (Maimon, S.)
6:36
cognition
Yogācāra Buddhism 2:68
common sense (Reid, T.) 2:447
consciousness (Brown, T.) 2:28
constructed experience
(Helmholtz, H. von) 4:338
dualism 3:137
emotions (James, W.) 3:281–2
emptiness (Nāgārjuna) 6:638–9
external world (Descartes, R.)
3:12–13
Fechner's law 3:570–1
human nature (Cabanis, P.-J.)
2:167
ideas
Berkeley, G. 1:740, 1:741, 1:745
Johnson, S. 5:124
Leibniz, G.W. 5:551–2
Malebranche, N. 6:58–9
intellect relationship (Vital du
Four) 9:638–9
knowledge
Condillac, É.B. de 2:523,
2:524–5
Helvétius, C.-A. 4:345
Hume, D. 4:546
Jainism 5:51
Locke, J. 5:669, 5:670
materiality as
Yogācāra Buddhism 2:71
mind-brain identity (Smart, J.J.C.)
8:814
occasionalism (Astell, M.) 1:527–8
pain–pleasure relationship
(Ryle, G.) 7:450

perception distinction
(Bergson, H.-L.) 1:732, 1:734–5
phenomenalism 7:330–3
phenomenology 7:344–5
physiological account
Bonnet, C. 1:839
Hartley, D. 4:237
pleasure 7:450
private language argument 7:694–6
Wittgenstein, L. 9:765–6
qualia 7:863
qualities (Reid, T.) 8:172
thought (Strato) 9:163
unreliability of (Proclus) 7:729
sensationalist psychology
Locke, J.
influence on
Condorcet, M.J.A.N. 2:530
Mach, E. 6:15
neutral monism 6:816
sense
see also intension; meaning; sense
perception; sense and reference;
sense-data; senses; sensibility
meaning
concepts 2:510–11
denotation (Church, A.)
2:347–8
determinancy (Wittgenstein, L.)
9:760
force distinction 7:625
Lewis, C.I. 5:586–7
semantic theory
(Dummett, M.A.E.)
3:149–51
testimony in Indian philosophy
9:316
moral *see* moral sense
sense and force *see* pragmatics
sense impressions
Berkeley, G. 4:663
sense perception
see also sense-data; senses
abstraction (Ibn Sina) 4:649–50
aesthetics (Baumgarten, A.G.)
1:669–70, 1:671
Augustine 1:542, 1:546
Blasius of Parma 1:786
causal model
Dharamakīrti
Buddhist nominalism 7:24,
7:25
consciousness (Hegel, G.W.F.)
4:266–7
fallibility of 6:829, 6:830
Indian views of 6:403, **8:688–94**
epistemology 8:689, 8:691–2

language 8:689, 8:693–4
negative facts 6:755–6, 6:757–8
object relationship 8:690–1
psychology 8:689–91
Sāṅkhya 8:464
knowledge
of God (Bonaventure) 1:832–3
Hindu philosophy 4:435
Nyāya 3:860
logic (Cohen, H.) 2:399
Reid, T. 8:171, 8:172–3
scepticism (Crathorn, W.) 2:693
soul
Plotinus 7:461
Proclus 7:728
transience
Neoplatonism 6:800
truth
Epicureanism 3:340, 3:344–5
unreliability of
Democritus 2:873, 2:875
Melissus 6:295
Yogācāra Buddhism
Indian epistemology 3:389
sense and reference **8:684–8**
see also meaning; sense
cognitive significance 8:684–5
Frege, G. 3:767–9
general terms 8:685–6
improper terms 3:20
indirect discourse 4:743
predication 7:666
proper names 7:752–4, 7:755,
8:685
singular terms
Evans, G. 3:459, 3:460
Frege, G. 3:459–60
thought
Frege, G. 8:686
truth-values 8:686
sense-data **8:694–8**
see also qualia; sense perception;
senses
acquaintance 3:379
colour 8:596, 8:597
dualism 3:135–6
empiricism 3:300, 3:301
fallibility 7:296–8
foundationalism 5:269
non-conceptual content
(Broad, C.D.) 2:24
observation statements (Ayer, A.J.)
1:616–17
perception 7:287–8, 7:289–91
phenomenal consciousness
2:592
phenomenalism 7:331

philosophical analysis
(Moore, G.E.) 6:497
sensibilia (Russell, B.A.W.)
8:399–400
senses
see also experience; perception;
sensation; sense perception; sense-
data
adaptability (Diderot, D.) 3:64
beauty
naturalistic conception 1:682
consciousness relationship
Sarvāstivāda Buddhism 2:57
Yogācāra Buddhism 2:72
doubt (Descartes, R.) 3:6–7
external
Ibn Bajja 4:607
Islamic philosophy 9:41, 9:42
Ikhwan al-Safa' 4:687
inaccuracy of
Indian Buddhism 2:97
internal
Ibn Bajja 4:607
Islamic philosophy 9:41–2
intuitive cognition (Duns
Scotus, J.) 3:166
knowledge (Nietzsche, F.W.) 6:849
Mahābhārata
Nyāya-Vaiśeṣika 7:59
Molyneux problem 6:467–8
objects of (Hobbes, T.) 4:469
receptivity (Schleiermacher, F.)
8:534–5
stimulation
qi (Yangzhu) 9:822
subjectivity of
Vasubandhu 9:585
unreliability of 8:493–4
sensibility
Baumgarten, A.G. 1:671
sensible world
Neoplatonism (Plotinus) 7:457
soul relationship (Plotinus) 7:459
sensory atoms
perception (Mach, E.) 4:52
sensory deprivation
religious experiences 6:631
sensory elements
Gestalt complexity (Ehzanfels, C.
Von) 4:52
sensory experience
eliminativism 3:264
Ramsey, I.T. 8:50
religious 8:250, 8:251
credulity 8:252
religious experience comparison
8:252–5

sensory properties
conceptual role semantics 8:655
sensualism
Feuerbach, L.A. 3:635, 3:636
hedonism critique 9:553
sensuality
Aquinas, T. 1:338
sensus divinitatis (Calvin) 8:216
sentences **7:787–8**
constituent structure 9:247–8
of definition
Indian philosophy 2:850
glossary 5:808
logical atomism (Wittgenstein, L.)
9:757
logical form 5:782–3
logical truths (Wittgenstein, L.)
9:759–60
meaning
Hindu philosophy 4:436
Indian theories of 6:242
Mīmāṃsā 6:380
Patañjali 7:248–9
potentiality
Indian theories of 7:607
testimony in Indian philosophy
9:315–17
paraphrasis (Bentham, J.) 1:722–3
picture theory of meaning
(Wittgenstein, L.) 9:759
schema
model theory 6:436–7
simple objects (Wittgenstein, L.)
9:760
structure
Frege, G. 3:765, 3:767–9,
3:771–2
predication 7:666
syntactic categories 9:247–8
utterances distinction 7:625
word order 9:246–7
sentencing
penal theory 2:705, 2:708–9
sentential logic
Łukasiewicz, J. 5:862
predicate calculus 7:659–61
sentience
see also consciousness
panpsychism 7:194–5
sentimentalism
see also moral sentiments
moral approval 6:548
moral sense 6:548
Shaftesbury, Third Earl of 8:730,
8:731–2
sentiments
moral *see* moral sentiments

passions (Hume, D.) 4:549–50
Sepänmaa, Y. 6:735
separability thesis
    belief and knowledge 1:706, 1:708
separation, axiom of 5:798
separation-individuation
    psychoanalysis
        post-Freudian 7:820
separatism
    legal concepts
        critique of substantialism 5:495
Septimus, B. 6:650
sequent calculus **6:676–82**
    Gentzen, G.K.E. 3:704–5, 4:24,
        6:604, 7:747
    proof theory 7:747
Serafine, M. 6:614
Serapion 4:333–4
Serene, E. 1:296
Sereno, M. 2:579
Serequeberhan, T. 1:107
Sergeant, John **8:698–9**
seriality
    Whitehead, A.N. 9:713–14,
        9:716–17
Serjeant, R.B. 8:565
Sermoneta, G. 4:433, 4:710, 5:131
Serrano, S.J. 5:308
Serre, Jean de 7:441
Serres, Michel 3:334–5, 3:336, 3:785,
    3:786
Servetus, Michael 2:178
Service, Robert
    Lenin, V.I. †5:564–7
Servius Sulpicius Rufus 8:343–4
Sesardić, Neven 9:53, 9:55
Sessions, G. 3:336, 4:165
Sessions, R. 6:614
Sestili, G. 8:778
Sesvara 6:378
set theory **8:700–9**
    see also sets; Zermelo-Fraenkel set
        theory
    abstract objects 1:34
    axiom of choice 1:612–14
    axiomatization of 8:711–15
        Löwenheim-Skolem theorem
            and non-standard models
            5:846–51
        Zermelo, E. 9:853–4
    Cantor's theorem 2:196–7,
        2:199–200
    dialogical logic (Lorenzen, P.)
        5:826–7
    early twentieth century 5:735
    forcing 5:802–3
    free logics 3:742

God
    existence of 4:91–2
    independence proof
        Boolean algebra 1:845–6
        continuum hypothesis 2:654,
            2:656–7
    intensional entities 4:804
        Quine, W.V. 8:9
    lambda calculus 5:348
    logicism (Quine, W.V.) 8:7
    mereology distinction 6:317, 6:319
    model theory 6:439–40
    Neumann, J. von 6:810
    numbers 7:51–2
    paradoxes **7:214–21**
    Royce, J. 8:380
    Russell's paradox 8:394
    second-order logic 8:602–3
    systems of **8:709–16**
    universals 9:540–1, 9:542–3
Setaro, F.C. 7:610
Seth, A. 4:300
Seth, J. 4:185
Sethi, I.K. 2:579
Seton, John 5:770–1
sets
    see also set theory
    algebra of
        Boolean algebra 1:844–5
    constructible 4:755
    elementary theory of the category
        of (ETCS) 2:233–5
    extensionality 4:803
    inductively defined 4:753–5
    mass forms 6:169
    vagueness 9:564–5
Setschkareff, W. 8:522
Settar, S. 5:57
set-theoretic structures
    scientific theories
        semantic conception 9:344,
            9:348
        structuralism 9:344, 9:350–1
Setton, M. 2:343
Seuse, Heinrich *see* Suso, Henry
'seven feelings'/'four beginings'
    debate *see* Four–Seven Debate
Severino, E. 5:42
sex
    see also reproduction; sexuality
    erotic art 3:406–9
    pleasure (Antisthenes) 1:316
    purpose of (Musonius Rufus)
        6:616
    religious significance
        (Rozanov, V.V.) 8:383

sexism
    see also androcentrism; feminist
        philosophy
    feminism
        Latin America 3:625, 3:627
    oppression
        feminism 3:579–80
    pornography 7:544
    science
        resultant distortions 3:861–2,
            3:863–4
    sport 9:112, 9:114
    in traditional ethics 3:604–5
Sextus of Chaeronea 6:94
Sextus Empiricus **8:716–17**
    Aenesidemus 1:51
    Agrippa 1:129
    atomism 1:535
    Carneades 2:220
    Dialectical school 3:59
    dissoi logoi (twofold argument)
        3:106–7
    dogmatism
        natural law 6:686
    epistemic parity 8:829, 8:832
    Gorgias 4:146
    Hellenistic philosophy 4:337
    knowledge
        concept of 5:276
    logic 5:693
    Pyrrhonian Scepticism 7:850–2,
        7:853–4
    scepticism 3:373, 3:383, 8:499,
        8:501
        Mersenne, M. refutation
            6:326–8
    Stoicism 9:160
sexual abuse
    memory (Freud, S.) 3:787–8
sexual act
    definition of 8:718–20
    intergenerational 8:724
sexual ethics *see* sexuality
sexual selection
    evolutionary theory
        (Darwin, C.R.) 2:797
sexuality **8:717–30**
    see also heterosexuality;
        homosexuality; pornography;
        reproduction; sex
    concepts 8:717, 8:718
    difference (Irigaray, L.) 5:1–3
    difference (Kristeva, J.) 5:306–7
    ethics (Foucault, M.) 3:712
    female modesty (Hume, D.) 4:554
    feminism 3:580
    genealogy (Foucault, M.) 3:711

hedonism (Helvétius, C.-A.)
4:345–6
language and gender 5:362–3
linguistic discrimination 5:642
male dominance
feminist jurisprudence 3:608
masculine/feminine orientations
(Freud, S.) 2:259
metaphysics 8:717, 8:720–1
neutrality
subject
postmodern critique of 9:199
normative analysis 8:717–18
Aquinas, T. 8:721–2
consent 8:724–5
Kant, I. 8:722–3
Kantian ethics
conservative 8:724
libertarian 8:723–4
Vatican 8:724
love 8:726
sadomasochism 8:725–6
utilitarianism 8:725
primitivism (Diderot, D.) 3:65
psychic structure (Freud, S.) 3:792
Seyffert, Peter 6:588
Seyhan, A. 8:352
Sezeman, Vasilii 6:796, 6:797
Sezgin, F. 6:620
sGam-po-pa (Gamboba) 9:405
Sgard, J. 5:379
Shackle, G.L.S. 7:34
Shackleton, R. 6:494
shadow pricing 4:164
Shafer, B.E. 3:250
Shaffer, E.S. 3:267
Shaffer, Jerome A. 8:719, 8:729, 9:617
Shaffer, S. 2:630
Shaftesbury, Third Earl of (Anthony
Ashley Cooper) **8:730–2**
enthusiasm 3:331, 3:332
moral sense theories 6:545–6,
6:548
Shaftesbury, S. 1:684
Shah, N.J. 7:27
Shah Wali Allah (Qutb al-Din
Ahmad ibn 'Abd al-Rahim)
8:732–5
mystical philosophy 6:619
Shah Waliullah of Delhi *see* Shah
Wali Allah
al-Shahrastani, Muhammad ibn 'Abd
al-Karim 4:158
al-Shahrazuri, Shams al-Din 9:223
Shakespeare, William 8:141, 9:449
de-Shalit, A. 2:471
shamanism 6:621

shame
Buddhism
Indian 2:95
embarrassment distinction 3:282,
3:283
guilt contrast 6:567–9, 8:139
moral sentiments 6:549–50
self-punishment
conscience 2:580
Shand, J. 5:153
Shaner, D.E. 3:111, 5:320
Shang tangsakba *see* Zhang Thang
sag pa
Shang Yang 5:532, 5:535, 5:538
Shangshu see Shujing
Shanker, S.G. 1:6
Shanks, N. 4:567
Shanley, M.L. 8:859
Shannon, Claude E.
computability and information
2:482
information theory 4:782, 4:789
semantics
informational 8:662
Shannon, T.A. 2:228–9
Shanzer, D.R. 3:309
Shao Yong 4:450, 6:767–8, **8:736–7**
Shapere, Dudley
incommensurability †4:732–6
Kuhn, T.S. 5:318
matter †6:192–6
observation 7:86
scientific theories 9:354
Shapin, S. 1:857, 2:630, 9:2
Shapiro, B. 5:435
Shapiro, Ian
human nature †4:520–6
Shapiro, J. 2:532
Shapiro, Michael J. 5:645, 8:822
Shapiro, Stewart
Church's thesis †2:351–5
logical laws 5:789
mathematics
foundations of 6:192
second-order logic 8:595,
†8:599–604
Shapley, L.S. 2:835
shari'a (God's law) 5:457–8
Shari'ati, Ali 5:19, 5:21
Sharma, A. 3:568
Sharma, B.N.K. 6:32
Sharma, D. 9:514
Sharma, N.K. 8:451
Sharma, S.K. 1:517
Sharp, D.E. 8:312, 9:376
Sharp, L. 2:287
Sharpe, F.C. 2:753

Sharpe, L. 8:529
Sharples, R.W.
Alexander of Aphrodisias
†1:169–76
Hellenistic philosophy 4:337
Peripatetics †7:304–5
Strato †9:161–4
Sharrat, P. 8:55
Shastri, D.N. 3:76, 7:67
Shatz, David
prophecy †7:767–71
Shaver, Robert
enthusiasm †3:330–2
Shavlik, J. 2:578, 2:579
Shaw, G. 4:599
Shaw, I. 3:250
Shaw, R. 7:214
Shayegan, Y. 1:386, 4:159, 6:808
Shea, W.R. 3:19
Shearmur, J. 7:539
Sheehan, Thomas
Heidegger, M. †4:307–23
Rahner, K. 8:39
Sheets-Johnstone, M. 2:777
Sheffer, H.M. 1:846, 2:434, 7:575,
7:665
Shehadi, F. 4:68
Shein, L. 8:746
Shelah, S. 3:696, 6:439
Sheldon, G.W. 5:85
Sheldon-Williams, I.P. 3:405, 7:808
Shelley, C. 1:359
Shelley, P.B. 7:477
Shem Tov family 5:89, **8:737–40**
Shen Buhai 5:534–5, 5:536, 5:537,
5:538
Shen Dao (Tao) 5:533, 5:534, 5:538
Shendongbas *see* gzhan-stong-pa
Shenhui 8:620
Shenxiu 7:398–9
Shepard, J. 6:278
Shepard, R. 4:704–5
Sheppard, H.J. 1:158–9
Sheppard, S. 6:654
Sher, G. 3:27, 5:780–1, 5:789, 7:665
Sher, R.B.
Blair, H. †1:781–2
Enlightenment, Scottish 3:330
Ferguson, A. 3:633
Oswald, J. 7:170
Sherburne, D.W. 7:715
Sherif, M. 4:68
Sherman, N. 3:231, 6:564, 9:631
Sherover, C. 9:416
Sherwin, O. 6:474
Sherwin, Susan 3:604, 3:606
Sherwood, E. 4:16

Shestov, Lev (Yehuda Leib Shvartsman) **8:740–6**
Nietzsche, F.W.
impact on Russian thought 6:864
religious existentialism 8:741, 8:744–5
Schellingianism 8:522
shi (authoritative power) 4:219, 5:531, 5:533–4, 9:230–1
Shi'a
see also Isma'ilism; Twelver Shi'ism
justice
al-Tusi 9:506
philosophy–religion relationship 5:8
political leaders 5:27
theological disputes
'ilm al-kalam 5:26, 5:27–8
Shiach, M. 2:374
Shibles, W. 6:337
Shieber, S. 9:495
Shiel, J. 1:813
Shields, Christopher
language
ancient philosophy of †5:356–61
Shields, Rob
Lefebvre, H. †5:489–91
al-Shifa see Ibn Sina
Shih Hsiao-yen 1:74
Shi'ism *see* Shi'a
Shiji see Sima Qian
Shijing (Book of Songs) 2:309, 2:310, 2:311, 2:314
Shiloah, A. 4:710
Shils, E. 9:447
Shim Jae-Ryong 2:118, 2:332
Shimony, A. 1:716, 7:890
shin see kokoro
Shin, S.J. 5:746, 8:672
Shin, S.S. 9:442
Shin (True Pure Land School)
Buddhism 5:72–3
Shiner, R. 5:468, 7:41
Shingon Buddhism 2:102, 5:71, 5:318–19
shinjin (entrusting mind/heart) 5:73
Shinn, R.L. 9:412
Shinran 5:73, **8:746–8**
Shintō **8:748–51**
Buddhism relationship 2:103–4, 8:750–1
Confucianism assimilation 2:552–3
East Asian Philosophy 3:195

influence of Japanese philosophy 5:69, 5:70
Japanese aesthetics 1:82, 1:85
Motoori Norinaga 6:588–9
Nō (Zeami) 9:840
Tominaga Nakamoto 9:440
al-Shirazi, Sadr al-Din Muhammad
see Mulla Sadra
Shiva, V. 3:868, 7:525
Shklar, J. 1:753, 6:494, 8:377
Shklovskii, Viktor 8:410, 8:413
Shkurinov, P.S. 7:564
Shlomo ben Yehoshua *see* Maimon, Salomon
Shoah see Holocaust
Shobin, E.J. 2:394–5
Shoemaker, Sydney
Butler, J. 2:160
causation 2:251
colour and qualia 2:427
consciousness 2:596
dualism 3:138
functionalism 3:813
introspection 4:842, 4:843–4, 4:846
materialism 6:178
mental states
phenomenal consciousness 2:593–4
personal identity
bodily criterion 7:307–8, 7:314
qualia 7:867
soul 9:48
time 9:414, 9:416–17
Shoenfield, J.R. 4:378, 7:30, 8:709, 9:502
Shoesmith, D.J. 6:84, 6:91, 6:604
Shoham, Y. 7:34
Shope, Robert K.
Gettier problems †4:54–9
knowledge
causal theory of 5:266
concept of 3:383, 5:276
defeasibility theory 5:279
Shore, R. 9:502
short-term memory (STM) 4:845
Shōtoku Constitution 5:70, **8:752–4**
Confucianism 2:550
Shotter, J. 1:695
Shōwa Study Group 6:358
Showalter, E. 3:614
showing
meaning (Wittgenstein, L.) 9:757, 9:761
Shpet, Gustav Gustavovich **8:754–8**
Herzen, A.I. 4:410
Russian Neo-Kantianism 6:797

Shrader-Frechette, Kristin
ecology 3:205
risk †8:331–4
technology and ethics 9:282, 9:284
Shrager, J. 3:103
shu (deference)
Chinese Legalism 4:219, 5:534–5, 5:536, 5:537
Confucianism
Daoism comparison 2:785, 2:787–93
Shu Xiang 5:446
Shue, H. 4:833, 5:157
Shuger, D.K. 4:507
Shujing (Book of Documents) 2:309, 2:310, 2:311, 2:314
history, Chinese theories of 4:452
Legalist philosophy 5:532
Shukman, A. 6:587–8, 8:413
Shun Kwong-Loi
Mencius 6:304
Wang Yangming †9:682–4
Shushigaku School 5:75
Shusterman, Robert M.
poetry †7:472–8
Shuttleworth, S. 3:267
Shvartsman, Yehuda Leib *see* Shestov, Lev
Shweid, E. 4:499
Siauve, S. 6:33
Sibley, Frank
aesthetic concepts 1:56–7, 1:58, 1:59
art criticism 1:463
taste
artistic 1:511, 1:513
Sicily
Empedocles **3:293–8**
Gorgias **4:144–6**
Siddhārtha Gautama *see* Buddha
Siddhasena Divākara 4:764, 5:51–2, 5:54–5, 5:57
Sidelle, Alan
essentialism 3:421
necessary truth and convention †6:747–50
Sider, David 1:254
Sider, Robert D. 9:309
Siderits, Mark
Buddhist nominalism 7:27
Nāgārjuna †6:638–41
testimony in Indian philosophy 9:319
Sidgwick, A. 8:764
Sidgwick, E.M. 8:764
Sidgwick, Henry **8:758–64**
consequentialism 2:606

desert and merit 3:27
dualism of practical reason
  8:760–1
egoism and altruism 3:246, 3:248
ethics 3:473
  economics 3:211
  evolution 3:476
  intuitionism 9:555, 9:557
  gratitude 8:138, 8:141
  Grote, J. 4:185
  happiness 4:228, 4:229
  hedonism 4:259
  international relations 4:828–9,
    4:833
  pleasure 7:449, 7:451
  praise and blame 7:647
  rational choice theory 8:65
  reciprocity 8:132
  right and good
    ancient/modern distinction
      8:322, 8:323–4, 8:325
  theory and practice 9:359
  truthfulness 9:483, 9:485
  utilitarianism 8:758, 8:759–61,
    8:762
  Moore, G.E. 6:496
Sidner, C. 3:98, 7:631
Sidney, Algernon 8:281
Sidney, Sir Philip 7:478, 9:449
Siedentop, L.A.
  state 9:123
  Tocqueville, A. de †9:423–5
Sieg, Wilfried
  Church's thesis 2:355
  Hilbert's programme and
    formalism 4:429
  mathematics
    foundations of 6:192
  primitive recursive functions
    †2:482–91
  proof theory †7:742–5
  Turing machines 9:499
Siegel, D.M. 6:210
Siegel, H. 3:234, 3:240
Siegel-Causey, D. 9:276
Siep, L. 8:134
Sierpiński, W. 7:495, 7:499
Sierra, Justo 5:653, 7:567, 7:570
Sigal, R. 2:496
Siger of Brabant **8:764–8**
  Aristotle 1:400, 8:765
  Averroism 1:595, 1:596, 1:598
  John of Jandun 5:107
  Liber de causis 5:598
  medieval natural philosophy 6:705
  monopsychism
    Averroism 1:596

sight *see* vision
Sigmund, P.E. 1:349, 6:838
signals
  information theory 4:786–7
signatures
  deconstruction (Derrida, J.) 2:899
  glossary 5:808–9
significance test
  statistics and social science 9:130
signification
  see also semiotics; signs
  Albert of Saxony 1:143
  Aristotle 5:359–60, 5:390
  Berkeley, G. 5:375–6
  Brinkley, R. 2:20
  Buridan, J. 2:132
  of concepts
    Renaissance 5:412
  connotations 5:397–8
  imposition 5:389, 5:390, 5:391–2
  Indian philosophy 6:241
  Kilwardby, R. 5:247
  language
    Renaissance philosophy of
      5:411–12
    Leibniz, G.W. 5:376
    linguistic rhythms (Kristeva, J.)
      5:305
    linguistic structuralism 9:185,
      9:186–7
    Locke, J. 5:374–5
  medieval theories of 5:389,
    5:390–3, 5:397–8
    Brito, R. 2:21, 2:22
  modism 5:393–4
  paronymy (Anselm of Canterbury)
    1:289–90
  propositional
    Renaissance 5:412
  psychology of (Abelard, P.) 1:12
  Roscelin of Compiègne 8:356–7
  signatures (Derrida, J.) 2:899
  structuralist linguistics (Lacan, J.)
    5:337
  supposition distinction 5:392–3,
    5:397–8
  transitivity of 5:391, 5:392
  truth
    Anselm of Canterbury 1:290
    Aristotle 1:416–17
    William of Sherwood 9:748
    Wodeham, A. 9:774
sign-inferences
  scientific method
    Epicureanism 3:345
Signposts movement **8:768–74**
  Marxism-idealism shift 8:769

neo-idealism 8:421
  Russian liberalism 5:608
  Utopianism versus humanism
    8:769–70
signs
  see also semiotics; signification;
    symbols
  Bacon, R. 1:635
  classification of (Soto, D. de) 5:412
  demythologization of (Barthes, R.)
    1:656–7
  doctrine of (John of St Thomas)
    5:118–19
  formal negation of (Báñez, D.)
    1:648
  interpretation of (Peirce, C.S.)
    7:278–9
  linguistic
    Saussure, F. de 8:481–2
    structuralism 9:185, 9:187
    universals (Stewart, D.) 9:138
  natural/artificial (Lessing, G.E.)
    5:575–6
  nominalist natural reason
    (Gerson, J.) 4:46
  referential relations (Major, J.)
    6:54
  Renaissance theories of 5:411–12
  the symbolic (Lacan, J.) 5:337
  systematicity 8:678
  types of 8:677–8
al-Sijistani, Abu Sulayman
    Muhammad **8:774–6**
  al-Farabi 3:557
  Presocratic philosophy
    Islamic 4:158
Sikdar, J.C. 5:57
Sikora, A. 7:488
Sikora, R.I. 3:822, 7:543
Sikorski, R. 1:846, 4:853, 7:498–9
Silburn, L. 1:19
Sileo, L. 3:169
Silla Vijñānavāda School of
  Buddhism 2:110
Silloi (Mockeries) 9:419
Silman, Y. 4:213
Silva Lisboa, José da 2:9
Silver, D.J. 6:48
Silverberg, M. 5:660
Silverstein, M. 8:473
Silverthorne, M.
  Carmichael, G. †2:206–8
Silvestri, Francesco **8:776–8**
Silvestris, Bernardus *see* Bernard of
  Tours
Silz, W. 8:352, 8:531
Sima Guang 4:450

Sima Qian 4:448–9, 4:452
Sima Tan 2:784
similarity
　Chinese language theories 5:702–3
　Hellenistic medical epistemology
　　4:334
　species classification 9:78
simile
　metaphor comparison 6:335–6
Simkin, C. 7:539
Simmel, Georg **8:778–80**
　historicism 4:446
　Lebensphilosophie 5:489
　Ortega y Gasset, J. 7:166
　Schiller, J.C.F. 8:529
　Schopenhauer, A. 8:554
　society
　　concept of 8:889
Simmonds, N.E.
　Blackstone, W. †1:780–1
　law and morality †5:438–42
Simmons, A. John
　authority 1:586
　consent †2:596–9
　contractarianism 2:665
　obligation
　　political †7:76–80
Simmons, J. 8:132
Simmons, P.M. 2:654
Simon, Herbert A.
　causation 2:251
　cognitive architecture 2:393
　consciousness 2:595
　discovery
　　logic of 3:102–3
　introspection, psychology of 4:843,
　　4:845
　language of thought hypothesis
　　5:407
　practical reasoning/rationality
　　8:96, 8:103
　rationality 8:64
　Turing machines 9:499
　unconscious mental states 9:524,
　　9:526
Simon, J. 2:692
Simon, L. 4:193
Simon, Lawrence H.
　rationality and cultural relativism
　　†8:80–6
Simon, U. 4:613
Simoncioli, F. 7:97–6
Simons, M.A. 1:687
Simons, Peter
　Brentano, F. †2:12–17
　identity of indiscernibles
　　†4:678–81

Leśniewski, S. 5:574
Meinong, A. †6:282–6
　mereology 6:320
　predication 7:667
Simonutti, L. 2:744, 6:168
simple type theory *see* types, theory of
simples
　logical atomism (Wittgenstein, L.)
　　9:757, 9:760–2, 9:764
　monads (Leibniz, G.W.) 5:547
simplicity
　inference to the best explanation
　　4:768
　pragmatic virtue 9:341, 9:342
　in scientific theories **8:780–3**
　theories (Schlick, F.A.M.) 8:540
simplicity, divine 4:98, **8:783–8**
　Aquinas, T. 6:760
　arguments for 8:785–6
　challenges to 8:786
　immutability 4:712
　necessary being 6:744–5
　omnipresence 7:106
　omniscience 7:108
　perfect goodness 4:142
　religious language 8:259
Simplicius **8:788–91**
　Aristotelianism 1:408
　Aristotle commentators 1:436
　Damascius 2:772
　Diogenes of Apollonia 3:88
　ethics 8:789
　Eudoxus 3:453
　mathematics 8:790
　physics 8:789–90
　Zeno of Elea 9:846, 9:852
Simpson, A.W.B. 2:442, 2:446, 8:365
Simpson, D. 4:44
Simpson, E. 3:490
Simpson, R. 1:509
Simpson, S.
　see also Simpson's theorem
　Gödel's theorems 4:118
　Hilbert's programme and
　　formalism 4:429
　proof theory 7:747, 7:751
　Turing reducibility and Turing
　　degrees 9:502
Simpson, T.M. 1:231, 1:234
Simpson's theorem 9:502
simulation
　child's theory of mind 6:385, 6:388
　folk psychology 3:687
Simultaneists 9:405–6
simultaneity
　conventionality thesis 8:194–6
　eternity 3:423, 3:424, 3:425–6

relativity theory 8:193
sin **8:791–6**
　see also original sin; sinners; vices
　actual 8:791–3
　Augustine 1:548, 1:552, 1:554–5
　conditions for (Abelard, P.) 1:13
　consequence 8:450
　deadly
　　Eastern Orthodoxy 8:455
　evolutionary process (Teilhard de
　　Chardin, P.) 9:290–1
　freedom of choice (Anselm of
　　Canterbury) 1:290–1
　God
　　natural knowledge of 8:216–17
　grace 4:147, 4:149, 4:150
　grave
　　'ilm al-kalam 5:26, 5:27
　Hebrew Bible 1:768
　hell 4:329, 4:331, 4:332
　intermediate position (Mu'tazila)
　　1:520–1
　Manicheism 6:74, 6:76
　Pelagianism 7:284–5, 7:286
　predestination 7:653–4, 7:655–6
　purgatory 7:836–8
　reasoning (Bacon, R.) 1:634
　reprobation 8:272–3
　satisfaction doctrine (Anselm of
　　Canterbury) 1:293–4
　sexual acts (Aquinas, T.) 8:721–2
　social effects 6:842–3
Singer, B. 8:470
Singer, D. 9:27
Singer, D.W. 2:39
Singer, Ira
　morality and identity †6:571–6
Singer, Irving 8:729
Singer, Isadore 6:812
Singer, J. 3:285
Singer, L. 1:687
Singer, M.B. 8:141
Singer, Peter
　civil disobedience 2:369
　democracy 2:872
　ethics 3:437
　　animals 1:276
　　applied 1:325
　　bioethics 1:574–5, 1:580,
　　　1:583–4, 1:776
　　development ethics 3:44
　　nursing 7:57
　　population and 7:543
　　universalism in 9:539
　help and beneficence 4:344
　impartiality 4:715, 4:717

justice
 international 5:157
 moral standing 6:554
 responsibilities of scientists and
  intellectuals 8:290
Singh, J. 1:19
Singh, R.J. 5:57
Singh, S.P. 1:569–1:10
Single Circular System 2:681, 2:683
singular propositions
 glossary 5:809
singular terms *see* reference
singularity of form
 Gilbert of Poitiers 4:69–70
Sinha, J. 3:413, 8:694
Sinha, S. 4:867–8
Sinisi, V. 1:138
Sinkler, Georgette
 Bacon, R. †1:632–6
Sinn und Bedeutung see sense and
 reference
Sinnema, D.W. 8:275–6
sinners
 see also sin
 justification by faith (Luther, M.)
  6:2
 status of
  'ilm al-kalam 5:26, 5:27
Sinnott-Armstrong, W. 3:182, 6:520,
 6:545
Sintonen, M. 9:669
Siorvanes, L.
 Chaldaean Oracles †2:273–4
 Hypatia †4:596–7
 Iamblichus †4:598–9
 Neoplatonism †6:797–803
 Porphyry †7:545–50
 Proclus †7:723–31
Sipfle, David A.
 Meyerson, É. †6:348–51
Sipset, M. 2:476
al-Sirafi, Abu Sa'id 5:707, 6:237
Siraisi, N.G. 7:208
Sirat, C.
 Abravanel, I. 1:23
 Albo, J. 1:154–5
 Averrroism
  Jewish 1:602
 Duran, P. 3:171
 Duran, S. 3:172
 Ibn Ezra, A. 4:613
 Ibn Falaquera 4:617
 Ibn Gabirol, S. 4:620
 Karaism 5:209
 Shem Tov family 8:740
 voluntarism
  Jewish 9:667

Sircello, Guy 1:683, 1:684, 3:409
sirhak (practical learning) 2:341–2,
 2:558, **8:796–8**
Sirhindi, Shaykh Ahmad 8:733
Sitskin, L. 4:617
situation ethics **8:798–9**
situation semantics **8:669–72**
Śiva *see* Śaivism
'six marks' 9:516
Skagestad, P. 7:284
Skelton, P. 4:375, 7:170
Skilling, H.G. 6:166
skills
 type of knowledge 5:267
Skinner, A.S. 3:329, 8:821, 8:822
Skinner, Burrhus Frederick
 8:799–802
 analytic behaviourism 1:692–3
 Chomsky, N. 2:341
 learning 5:487
 operationalism 7:135
 psychology
  theories of 7:829
 scientific behaviourism 3:266
  logical positivist approach
   1:696–7, 1:699
 social science
  methodology of 8:868
Skinner, Q.
 absolutism 1:32
 Aristotelianism
  Renaissance 1:413
 Keckermann, B. 5:225
 Machiavelli, N. 6:22
 political philosophy
  history of 7:517
 public interest 7:835
 religion and political philosophy
  8:229
 republicanism 8:283
 social science
  history of philosophy of 8:859
 social sciences
  theory and observation 9:356
 state 9:123
 Vitoria, F. de 9:645
Skirbekk, Gunnar 7:648, 7:649,
 8:492, 9:613
Sklar, Lawrence
 natural laws 5:475
 Poincaré, J.H. 7:482
 probability, interpretations of
  7:705
 reduction
  problems of 8:149

relativity theory
 philosophical significance of
  8:199
 theoretical/epistemic virtues 9:343
 thermodynamics †9:366–9
 time †9:413–17
Sklare, D.E. 5:209
Skolem function 5:849
Skolem, Thoralf
 see also Löwenheim-Skolem
 theorem; Skolem function;
 Skolem's paradox
 constructivism in mathematics
  2:636, 2:638–9
 Gödel's theorems 4:118
 logic
  early twentieth century 5:734
  first-order 5:730, 5:731, 5:734
 logicism 5:817
 nonstandard analysis 1:216
 set theory 8:716
 Zermelo, E. 9:854, 9:855
Skolem's paradox 5:850–1, 7:219,
 8:708
Skolimowski, H. 7:489
Skorupski, John
 African traditional religions 1:118,
  1:121
 Coleridge, S.T. 2:406
 Mach, E. 6:16
 Mill, J.S. †6:360–75
 morality and ethics †6:564–71
 rationality and cultural relativism
  8:86
Skoss, S. 8:440
Skovoroda, Hryhorii Savych 8:419,
 8:802–3
Skrupskelis, I.K. 5:68
Skyrms, B.
 causal theory of knowledge 5:266
 confirmation theory 2:535
 decision and game theory 2:835
 induction 4:752
 inductive inference 4:759
 modal operators 6:436
 natural laws 5:475
 rational choice theory 8:75
Slater, R.H.L. 7:11
Slaught, R.L. 4:59
Slaughter, M.M. 5:379, 9:535
slavery **8:803–7**, 8:804
 Africans in Brazil 2:8–9
 anti-slavery movement 1:210,
  7:191–2
 exploitation (Locke, J.) 5:681
 halakhah 4:205

liberty comparison (Price, R.)
7:678
natural equality argument
(Hutcheson, F.) 4:591–2
natural law argument 7:512
postcolonial studies 7:580–1
slave–master dialectic (Kojève, A.)
5:289–90
Slavophilism **8:807–11**
ecclesiology 8:809–10
history
philosophy of 8:808–9
Schellingianism 8:522
ideological evolution 8:810–11
messianism
Russian philosophy 8:419
Russian Hegelianism 4:305
Solov'ëv, V.S. 9:28, 9:30
Slawson, D.A. 1:90
sleep
dreaming 3:127, 3:128
Sleeper, R. 3:51
Sleigh, R.C. 5:562
Sleigh, R.C., Jr 1:448
Slemon, S. 7:583
Slesinski, Robert
Florenskii, P.A. †3:679–82
Sleszynski, J. 7:495, 7:499
slingshot argument 3:536–7
Sloan, D. 9:757
Sloan, P. 2:122
Sloane, N.J.A. 4:786
Sloboda, J. 6:614–15
Slote, Michael
concepts 2:517
moral psychology †6:531–4
practical reasoning/rationality
8:97, 8:103
virtue ethics 9:625
virtues and vices 9:631
Sloterdijk, P. 2:759, 5:854
Slovakia **8:811–13**
National Revival movement
8:812–13
Reform School 8:812
Slovic, P.
probabilism 7:711
probability, interpretations of
7:705
reasoning
rationality of belief 8:87, 8:88,
8:89
risk 8:334, 8:337, 8:338
slovo ('the word') 8:756–7
Sluga, H. 8:688
Słupecki, J. 5:863, 7:493, 7:499

Small, Robin
Dühring, E.K. †3:147–9
Smalley, Beryl 4:479, 5:111
Smart, A. 8:141
Smart, C. 3:610, 3:611
Smart, John Jamieson Carswell
8:813–15
Australian materialism 1:579
colour and qualia 2:427
consciousness 2:596
consequentialism 2:606
Gödel's theorems 4:118
identity theory of mind 6:399
impartiality 4:717
materialism 6:173, 6:178
reductionism, philosophy of mind
8:153
scientific realism and antirealism
8:581, 8:584
time 9:417
utilitarianism 9:557
Smart, Ninian
causation
Indian theories of 2:257
mysticism, history of 6:626
reincarnation 8:186
salvation 8:451
Smelser, N. 9:256
Smetana, Augustin 2:766
Smethurst, M. 9:841
Smiley, Timothy J.
ancient logic 5:691–2, 5:693
consequence †2:599–603
many-valued logics 6:84, 6:91
multiple-conclusion logic †6:602–4
paraconsistent logic 7:211
Smith, A.D.
primary–secondary distinction
†7:684–7
secondary qualities 8:599
supervenience of mind 6:178
Smith, Adam **8:815–22**
Chinese Legalism 5:533, 5:538
commercial society
political philosophy
history of 7:513
conscience 6:547, 6:548
division of labour 9:795
economics
philosophy of 3:211, 3:222
Enlightenment 3:316
free market
conservatism 2:611–12
freedom of labour 8:820
historical jurisprudence 5:138,
5:141
Hutcheson, F. 4:592, 4:594

imaginative order 8:817–18
impartiality 4:717
influence of
Burke, E. 9:445–6
Marx, K. 7:516
*An Inquiry into the Nature and
Causes of the Wealth of Nations*
8:816, 8:817
economics, philosophy of 3:211,
3:222
freedom of labour 8:820
law and politics 8:819–21
libertarianism 5:618
Mandeville, B. 6:74
market
ethics of the 6:110
moral theory 8:818–19
needs and interests 6:755
rational choice theory 8:66, 8:75
religion 8:816–17
social science
history of philosophy of 8:851,
8:859
social theory
Enlightenment, Scottish 3:328,
3:330
state intervention
Bentham, J. comparison 1:721
sympathy
morality 6:561–2, 6:564
Smith, Andrew 7:550
Smith, B. 1:612, 6:16, 6:170, 6:320
Smith, Barry
Gestalt psychology †4:51–4
Husserl, E. 4:587
Reinach, A. †8:180–2
Twardowski, K. 9:509
Smith, Barry C.
language
conventionality of †5:368–71
social nature of †5:415–19
meaning and rule-following
†6:214–19
Smith, B.K. 4:256
Smith, C.U.M. 4:238
Smith, D.E. 3:593, 3:868
Smith, D.W. 4:348, 4:587
Smith, E. 2:516, 2:517
Smith, F. 1:530
Smith, Frederick M.
heaven
Indian concepts of †4:253–7
Smith, George E.
Newton, I. †6:823–8
Smith, G.W.
limits of law †5:460–4
toleration 9:432

Smith, H. 1:530, 8:264
Smith, J.C. 7:609
Smith, J.E. 3:245, 7:640
Smith, John 2:185
Smith, K., Jr 8:737, 9:831
Smith, L.D. 7:135
Smith, M.
    al-Ghazali 4:68
    Jhering, R. von 5:101
    mysticism, history of 6:626
    objectivity 7:75
Smith, Michael
    desire 3:33
    emotivism †3:291–3
    moral motivation 6:528
    reasons and causes †8:124–7
Smith, Nicholas D.
    slavery †8:803–7
    wisdom †9:752–5
Smith, Nicholas J.J.
    epiphenomenalism †3:351–4
Smith, N.V. 7:632
Smith, Peter
    Broad, C.D. †2:23–6
    chaos theory 2:280
    mind, philosophy of 6:407
Smith, Q.
    creation and conservation
        religious doctrine of 2:700
Smith, Quentin
    tense and temporal logic †9:303–7
Smith, Ralph 8:728
Smith, R.G. 1:838, 4:217
Smith, S.B. 8:807
Smith, W.D. 7:656
Smith, Wilfred Cantwell 8:261, 8:264
Smitherman, G. 5:645
Smolensky, P. 2:576, 2:578, 2:579,
    5:407–8
Smoliatich, Klim see Klim Smoliatich
Smorynski, C. 4:118, 4:429, 4:853,
    7:797
Smulders, P. 9:291
Smullyan, A.F. 3:24
Smullyan, R. 4:118, 7:30
Smyth, D. 4:594
Snare, Francis 4:562
Sneath, P.H.A. 9:275
Sneed, J.D. 4:672, 6:259, 9:350–1,
    9:354
Snelders, H.A.M. 6:743
Snell, B. 4:441, 4:502
Snellgrove, D. 6:417
Snow, D.E. 8:520
Snowdon, Paul F.
    Strawson, P.F. †9:168–74
Snyder, J. 7:381

Snyder, L. 2:866–7
Snyder, W. 4:378
Sô Kyôngdôk 2:557
Soames, S.
    intentionality 4:821
    proper names 7:757
    propositional attitudes 7:779,
        7:786
    situation semantics 8:672
Soare, R.I. 2:491, 9:502
Sober, Elliott
    concepts 2:517
    evolutionary theory 3:482–3
        and ethics †3:472–6
        and social science †3:483–7
    functional explanation 3:804,
        3:805
    genetics 4:16
    innate knowledge †4:794–7
    simplicity (in scientific theories)
        †8:780–3
    social science
        methodology of 8:868
        sociobiology 8:896
        taxonomy 9:275
    theoretical/epistemic virtues 9:343
Soble, Alan
    sexuality †8:717–30
Sobociński, B. 5:863, 6:320, 7:494,
    7:499
sobornost' (catholicity/conciliarity)
    5:830, 8:426, 8:809–10
Sobrino, Jon 5:615, 5:617
Sochor, Z.A. 1:820
social action 8:822–4, 8:869, 8:886
    explanation in social science
        3:529–30
    intentionality (Reinach, A.)
        8:181–2
    joint action 8:822–3
    joint intention 8:822–3
    understanding (Weber, M.)
        9:695–6
social anthropology
    behaviourism in the social sciences
        1:694, 1:695
social arithmetic
    Condorcet, M.J.A.N. 2:528,
        2:529–30
social behaviour
    cognitive development 2:394, 7:385
    evolutionary theory
        (Darwin, C.R.) 2:798
social choice 8:824–6
    aggregation 8:824–5
    criticism of 8:825–6
    economics 3:209, 8:826

general will 4:11
    impossibility theorems 8:824
    interpretation 8:824–5
social class see class
social conflict
    Latin American literature 5:653–4
social constructionism
    sexuality 8:719–20
    social reality 9:355
social constructivism 2:624–5
    ethics 2:630–1
    technology and ethics 9:283
social contract
    see also contractarianism
    agreement 2:658
    autonomy
        ethical 1:587
    conservatism 2:610
    conventionalism 2:661
    democratic 2:661–3
    equality condition (Rawls, J.)
        8:106–7
    general will 4:10
    Hobbes, T. 2:657–8
    Hobbesian views
        contemporary 2:660–1
    interest-based 2:659, 2:663–4
    liberalism 5:603–4
    Locke, J. 5:680–2
    natural law 5:465–6
    natural right
        political philosophy
            history of 7:512–13
    political authority
        legitimacy of 5:539
    republicanism 8:282, 9:57–8
    right-based 2:663–4
    Rousseau, J.-J. 7:514, 8:368,
        8:371–2, 9:57–8
    Slavophilism 8:809
    sovereignty (Rousseau, J.-J.) 7:514
social control
    African socialism (Nyerere, J.)
        1:101
    Mozi 6:452, 6:453
social convention
    D.K.Lewis' account 8:834
    justice (Hume, D.) 4:553, 4:554
    society
        concept of 8:887
social Darwinism
    see also European positivism
    Spencer, H. 9:88
social democracy 8:827–8
    Kautsky, K.J. 5:222–3
    socialism conflict 8:880

social discounting
    green economic critique 4:164
social diversity 8:836
    continuities 8:837
    historical diversity 8:837
social ecology 3:200–1
social engineering
    legal policy
        Petrażycki, L. 7:329, 7:330
social epistemology **8:828–32**
    collective knowledge 8:830–1
    Hume, D. 4:549
    justified belief 5:163–4
    knowledge construction 8:831
    organization of cognitive labour
        8:830
    social construction of knowledge
        8:831
    testimony 8:828–30
social facts
    Durkheim, É. 3:175
    explanation in history and social
        science 3:526–7
    holism in social science 4:483
social functionalism **3:813–18**
    biological functions 3:815–16
    critique of 3:815
    rational choice 3:813–14
    structuralism relationship
        3:814–15
social injury
    feminist jurisprudence 3:609
social intelligence
    democracy (Dewey, J.) 3:49–50
social interaction 8:886–7
    see also social action; sociality;
        symbolic interaction
    Simmel, G. 8:779
    subject/object differentiation
        (Taylor, C.) 9:276–7
    sympathy (Smith, A.) 8:815, 8:818
social justice
    see also justice, distributive
    agricultural ethics 1:126–7
    feminist jurisprudence 3:607–8
    liberalism 7:502
    violence 9:615–16
social laws **8:832–4**
    see also social theory
    antecedents/consequents 8:833
    causal laws 8:832–3
    definition 8:832–3
    psychological laws 8:833
    reduction 4:485
    social properties 8:833
social morphology
    Lambriola, A. 5:335

social norms **8:834–6**
    definition 8:834
    reciprocity 8:130–1
    social convention
        D.K.Lewis' account 8:834
    social rules 8:834–5
    society
        concept of 8:887, 8:888
social order
    Confucius
        harmony 5:443, 5:445
        influence in Japan 5:70
    harmony of
        law and ritual, China 5:443,
            5:445–6
    society
        concept of 8:886, 8:887
social organization
    science of (Saint-Simon) 8:446–7
social pathologies
    Durkheim, É. 3:176
social philosophy
    Vaz Ferreira, C. 3:625–7
social physiology
    Saint-Simon 8:446
social policies
    multiculturalism 6:600–1
social positivism
    Latin America 7:565, 7:566, 7:567
        evolutionary positivism
            conflicts 7:567–8
social practices
    genres of discourse 8:844
    theory of knowledge 8:844–5
social psychology
    behaviourism in 1:693–4
    Freud, S. 3:792
social recognition
    rights 8:325, 8:327–8
social reform
    Masaryk, T.G. 6:165
social relations
    see also social interaction; sociality
    egoist conception of (Stirner, M.)
        9:141
    freedom of consciousness
        (Sartre, J.-P.) 8:475–6
    gender (Wollstonecraft, M.)
        9:789–90
    independence (Proudhon, P.-J.)
        7:792
    individual distance
        (Emerson, R.W.) 3:271
    Stoicism (Hierocles) 4:422
    unity of (Marcel, G.) 6:92
social relativism **8:836–8**
    see also cultural relativism; moral

relativism
    idealism 8:837–8
    social diversity 8:836, 8:837
social responsibility
    business ethics 2:152–3
social revolution
    Marcuse, H. 6:96, 6:97
social roles
    responsibility 8:287–8, 8:289–90
social rules *see* rules, social
social science **8:868–71**
    see also anthropology; society;
        sociology
    behaviourism in **1:693–6**
    contemporary philosophy of
        8:838–47
    critical theory
        functionalism 3:732
    development ethics 3:39–42
    empiricism (Neurath, O.) 6:814
    evolutionary theory **3:483–7**
    experiments in **3:518–20**
    explanation in **3:525–31**
    feminism **3:588–93**
    functionalism in **3:813–18**
    history of philosophy of **8:847–59**
    holism in **4:482–8**
    individualism in **4:482–8**
    legal realism 5:523
    methodology of **8:859–68**
    natural science comparison 8:870
    naturalism **6:717–21**
    Neo-Kantianism (Lange, F.) 5:353
    operationalism 7:131, 7:134
    political legitimacy 5:540–1
    positivism **7:558–61**
    post-structuralism **7:600–4**
    prediction in **8:871–2**
    risk assessment 8:336
    scientific realism **8:584–9**
    statistics **9:127–33**
    structuralism in **9:184–9**
    systems theory **9:253–6**
    technology and ethics 9:280, 9:283
    theory and observation **9:355–6**
    value judgments in **9:575–80**
    Verstehend (interpretive approach)
        (Habermas, J.) 4:195–6
social space
    theory of (Lefebvre, H) 5:490
social stability
    etiological theory of biological
        function 3:816
social status *see* status, social
social structures
    influence on African philosophy
        ethnophilosophy 3:448

social theory
  see also social laws; society;
    sociology
  Bourdieu, P. 1:848–50
  communicative action
    (Habermas, J.) 4:194, 4:195–6
  critical see critical theory
  epistemes (Foucault, M.) 4:3
  justice (Weil, S.) 9:700
  law 8:872–9
    Critical Legal Studies 2:714,
      2:716
    Enlightenment ideas 8:873
    models of practice 8:877
    postmodernism 8:873, 8:878
    scientific rationalism 8:874
    Western Marxism 8:875–6
  modernity
    transition to 8:874
  natural law 6:687
  para-critical 8:843
  positivism (Habermas, J.) 4:194–5
  scientific explanation
    Enlightenment, Scottish
      3:327–9
  the 'social' 8:873–4, 8:876–7
'social theory of reality' 9:478–9
social values
  art (Plato) 1:479
  postcolonial philosophy of science
    7:575–6
  privacy 7:690–1
socialism 8:879–86
  see also communism; Marxism
  African 1:98, 1:99–1:101, 1:111
  associational 8:884
  Bernstein, E. 1:758–9
  Christian (Barth, K.) 1:651–2
  critiques of
    feminism 8:883–4
    Hayek, F.A. 4:245–6, 4:247,
      4:248–9
  definitions 8:879–81
  distributive justice 8:884
  economic planning 8:881–2
  Engels, F. 3:310–11
  environmentalist perspective 8:885
  ethical 4:414
    Cohen, H. 6:781
  ethics of (Sorel, G.) 9:34–5
  evolutionary
    Marxism (Bernstein, E.)
      6:142–3
  feminism 3:614, 3:617–18
  psychoanalysis 3:586
  future of 8:884–5
  Hess, M. 4:413–15

Kautsky, K.J. 5:222–3
Lassalle, F. 5:419–20
Latin America 6:160, 6:161, 6:162,
  6:163
legal theory (Renner, K.) 8:267
market 8:881, 8:884–5
market ethics 6:108–9
Marx, K. 6:118, 6:130–1
  political philosophy
    history of 7:516
Mises, L. von 4:247
personalistic (Berdiaev, N.A.)
  1:730
populist (Lavrov, P.L.) 5:435–8
Proudhon, P.-J. 7:791–2
revolution 8:303
rule-of-law (Hessen, S.I.) 4:415,
  4:417–18
Russian (Herzen, A.I.) 4:405–6,
  4:408–9, 5:607
Schumpeter, J.A. 8:555–6
scientific (Engels, F.) 3:309, 3:311
social democracy 8:827
solidarity 9:23–4
utopian 9:557, 9:558–9
  Belinskii, V.G. 1:711
  Hessen, S.I. 4:417, 4:418
  Zionism 9:868–9
socialist realism
  aesthetics (Lunacharskii, A.)
    8:407–8
sociality
  ethical autonomy 1:589
  human communication
    (Mead, G.H.) 6:210–11
  language relationship
    Wittgensteinian ethics 9:772
  moral relativism 6:540, 6:541
  morality
    Mead, G.H. 7:642–3
    Voltaire 9:659
  person (Il'enkov, E.V.) 4:688, 4:690
  practices
    critical theory 9:358
    promising 7:740–2
  reciprocity 8:131
  'taking the role of the other'
    (Mead, G.H.) 6:210–11
society
  see also anthropology; citizenship;
    civil society; class; political
    philosophy; public; sociology
  art and morality 1:455–6
  artificial distinctions
    (Wollstonecraft, M.) 9:788,
      9:789–90
  atonement 1:536–7

bourgeois (Hegel, G.W.F.) 4:274–5
cerebral chart (Comte, A.) 2:503–4
civic humanism (Ferguson, A.)
  3:631
civil rights (Burke, E.) 2:139
civilized
  Enlightenment, Scottish 3:329
classification (al-Farabi) 3:557
commercial
  political philosophy
    history of 7:513–14
commercial (Smith, A.) 8:815
communalism
  African 1:98–9
concept of 8:886–9
  communication 8:887–8
  game theory 8:887, 8:888
  social interaction 8:886–7
  social order 8:887
concern for (Xenophanes) 9:808
concrete identity (Taylor, C.)
  6:574–5
Confucianism 2:320, 2:538, 2:542
consumer culture (Baudrillard, J.)
  1:662–3
critical theory 2:722–8, 3:731
Daodejing 2:781
differentiation in (Habermas, J.)
  4:196
elite–masses relationship (Ortega y
  Gasset, J.) 7:167
existentialism 3:498
family as basic unit 3:550
Fascist actualism (Gentile, G.) 4:22
happiness of
  al-Farabi 3:557
  Ibn Rushd 4:641–2
harmony
  Chinese philosophy 2:315, 2:324
    common language 2:323
    syncretism 2:324
  Daoism 2:321, 4:513
  de 2:809–10
historical patterns of
  Smith, A. 8:819–20
  Vico, G. 9:599–600, 9:602–4
holism
  Marxist philosophy of science
    6:148
holistic conception of 8:851
human nature (Diderot, D.) 3:67–8
India
  Arya Samaj reform movement
    1:517
India (Kauṭilya) 5:220–1
individual interaction (Watsuji
  Tetsurō) 9:691–2

individual relationship
    political institutions 6:646
individual relationship (Marcus
    Aurelius) 6:94
individualistic conception of
    8:850–1
intercultural comparisons
    Ramakrishna Movement 8:40
Islamic sociology (Ibn Khaldun)
    4:623, 4:624–5
lawful behaviour (Hobbes, T.)
    4:459–60
Mosaic
    Jewish philosophy
        (Abravanel, I.) 1:21–2
mutual aid (Kropotkin, P.A.)
    5:314
natural environment
    Daoism 2:321
objectivity
    Marxist philosophy of science
        6:149–50
origins of inequality (Rousseau, J.-
    J.) 8:370
philosophers in
    Islamic philosophy 7:519
philosophy relationship (Hume, D.)
    4:549, 4:558
physis and *nomos* debate
    ancient philosophy 1:302–3,
        7:381–2
pluralist conception of
    (Anderson, J.) 1:268
polis (Aristotle) 7:506
political (Hobbes, T.) 2:659
pragmatism
    Dewey, J. 7:634
    liberal democracy 7:637–8
professional roles
    responsibility 8:287–8
public interest 7:832–4
public virtues (Smith, A.) 8:820
rationalization in (Habermas, J.)
    4:196
religion
    belief (Troeltsch, E.P.W.) 9:462
    Ibn Khaldun 4:626
    transition to reason (Vico, G.)
        9:604–5
rights (Smith, A.) 8:819
risk 8:331, 8:332–3
ritual
    China 2:327
    Xunzi 2:324
scientific attitude (Neurath, O.)
    6:814

self-cultivation
    Chinese philosophy 8:613,
        8:615, 8:625
    Zhongyong 9:862
sin
    Frank, S.L. 3:728–126
    Niebuhr, R. 6:842–3
social contract theory
    (Rousseau, J.-J.) 8:368, 8:371–2
socialism
    African 1:101
socioeconomics
    development ethics 3:39–42
solidarity 9:23, 9:24
state relationship 9:120
status
    feminist jurisprudence 3:607–8
suicide 9:226–7
symbolic interactionism 9:243,
    9:244–5
technology 9:284–5, 9:286–7
temporal development
    political philosophy
        Indian 7:522
threats to
    risk assessment 8:334–7
typology according to legal
    systems
    historical jurisprudence 5:140–1
unilinear development (Millar, J.)
    6:376
virtues and vices (La Mettrie, J.O.
    de) 5:334
Society of Jesus *see* Jesuits
Society for the Support of Islam *see*
    Anjuman-e-Himayat-e-Islam
Socinianism **8:889–92**
    Astell, M. critique 1:528
    atonement 1:539
sociobiology 3:483, **8:892–6**
    see also Darwinism; evolution
    assessment of 3:484–5
    family ethics 3:549
    functionalism in social science
        3:815–17
    genetic determinism 3:485
    variation
        explanation of 3:485
socioeconomics
    development ethics 3:39–42
sociological jurisprudence
    Pound, R. 7:609
sociology
    behaviourism in 1:694
    domination (Weber, M.) 9:4
    hermeneutic theory 9:3, 9:4

history
    comparison (Lavrov, P.L.)
        5:437–8
    Holocaust explanation 4:496
    Kantian functionalism 9:5
    of knowledge **9:1–2**
        anti-positivism
            Latin America 1:306–7
    method (Durkheim, É.) 3:174–6
    positivism (Comte, A.) 2:500
    presuppositional studies 9:3–4
    Russian positivism 7:563–4
    science, demarcation problem
        2:864–5
    structural-functionalism 9:5
    subjective (Lavrov, P.L.) 5:436–7
    theories of **9:2–8**
        hermeneutical 9:4
        presuppositional 9:3–4
sociopolitical order
    Confucianism 2:324
        Guanzi 4:186
        li 2:542
        fa 3:532
        Han Feizi 4:219
Sockratikoi logoi see Socratic
    dialogues
Socrates **9:8–19**
    see also Socratic dialogues;
        Socratic schools
    akrasia 1:139–40
    analytic interpretation (Vlastos, G.)
        9:652
    aretē 1:373, 9:10–11, 9:14–15
    asceticism (al-Razi, Abu Bakr)
        8:111
    character of
        Plato's dialogues 7:405
    death sentence
        Plato's dialogues 7:406, 7:407
    defence of
        Plato's dialogues 7:404–5, 7:408
    educational philosophy 3:223
    elenchus (refutation) 9:11–14
    esotericism (Strauss, L.) 9:167–8
    evil 3:464
    Hypatia 4:597
    influence of 1:263, 9:17–18
        Antisthenes 1:314–15, 1:316–17
        Aristotle
            virtues 9:628
        Enlightenment (Nietzsche, F.W.)
            6:846–7
    Islamic moral philosophy 3:438–9
    method of refutation (Vlastos, G.)
        9:652
    moral education 6:508

personality of 9:16–17
Plato (Vlastos, G.) 9:652
political philosophy
  history of 7:506
Presocratics 7:671
Prodicus 7:731
al-Razi, Abu Bakr 8:110
self-knowledge 9:112, 9:115–16
Sophists 9:33, 9:34
substances
  medieval philosophy 6:273
trial of 9:8, 9:9, 9:11
Socratic dialogues **9:19–21**
see also Plato, Socratic dialogues;
  Xenophon
background to 9:8, 9:9
chronology
  dubious nature of 9:19, 9:20
common themes 9:20
external form 9:20
fictional nature of 9:19–20
interpretation of 9:9–9:10
Xenophon 9:811–12
Socratic schools **9:21–3**
ancient philosophy 1:263
diversity of teaching 9:22–3
Megarian 6:279
Sodipo, J.O. 1:103–4, 1:106, 9:834
sodomy
conservative position 8:724
Thomism 8:722
Sohravardi (al-)Suhrawardi
Soja, E. 5:491
Sokal, R.R. 9:276
Sokol, M. 9:27
Sokolow, N. 9:870
Sokolowski, R. 4:587, 7:342
soku 5:326–7, 5:713–14
Solana, M. 2:408, 3:690, 9:40, 9:435
Solari, G. 8:364
solidarity **9:23–5**
Durkheim, É. 3:176
social
  Lavrov, P.L. 5:437
solipsism **9:25–6**
see also methodological solipsism;
  other minds; physical world,
  knowledge of
definition 8:493
innate anti-solipsism 4:796
Wittgenstein, L. 2:711, 9:757
Solitaires 7:551
solitude
of philosophers (Ibn Bajja) 4:605,
  4:606, 4:607
Thoreau, H.D. 9:389
Sölle, D. 9:333

Sollers, P. 9:293
Solmsen, F. 2:383, 3:298, 4:413
Solomon, E. 6:181
Solomon ibn Gabirol *see* Ibn
  Gabirol, Solomon
Solomon, M. 8:832
Solomon, Robert C.
business ethics 2:153
emotions
  nature of †3:281–5
  philosophy of †3:285–90
existentialism 3:502
German idealism 4:45
honour 4:504
morality and emotions 6:564
Solomonoff, R.J. 2:482, 2:496
Solomos, J. 8:21
Solovay, R.
computer science 2:496
Solovay, Robert M.
see also Solovay's completedness
  theorem
computability and information
  2:482
computational complexity 2:475
forcing 3:695, 3:697
provability logic 7:797
Solovay's completedness theorem
  7:795–6
Soloveitchik, Joseph B. **9:26–8**
Jewish philosophy
  contemporary 5:95
Solov'ëv, S.M. 9:32
Solov'ëv, Vladimir Sergeevich
9:28–33
All-Unity 8:420, 9:28–9
ecumenism (Chaadaev, P.I.) 2:272
history
  Schellingianism 8:522
idealism
  Signposts movement 8:770
Nietzsche, F.W.
  impact on Russian thought
  6:864
Russian liberalism 5:608
Slavophilism 8:811, 9:28, 9:30
Sophiology 9:29–30
Solow, R. 3:220–1
Soltan, K.E. 2:621
solvable problems 2:472, 9:498
Solzhenitsyn, Aleksandr 8:773
Soman, A. 2:290
Somerset, Fiona
Dietrich of Freiberg †3:69–71
Gerbert of Aurillac †4:40–1
John of Mirecourt †5:111–13
Thomas of York †9:375–6

Sommerfeld, A. 3:260
Sommers, F. 2:232–3
Sommerville, Johann P.
absolutism 1:32
Filmer, R. †3:677–9
Hobbes, T. 4:476
Sommerville, S.T. 8:404
Sommervogel, C. 2:408
Son, I.S. 9:828
Sôn Buddhism 2:110–14
see also Chan; Zen
Chinul 2:329–31
Sôsan Hyujông 2:115–16, 9:36
Sonderegger, E. 8:791
Soni, Jayandra
Jaina philosophy †5:48–5
manifoldness †6:77–81
Mahāvīra †6:33–5
Sonoda, K. 8:753–4
Sontag, F. 4:102
Soper, Kate
critical realism 2:722
nature and convention †6:735–7
Sophia 4:85
Sophiology
Bulgakov, S.N. 2:124–5
Florenskii, P.A. 3:681
Lossky, N.O. 5:836
Solov'ëv, V.S. 9:29–30
sophism
glossary 5:809
sophismata 5:747, 5:748–9
Heytesbury, W. 4:419–20
Kilvington, R. 5:244–5
Oxford Calculators 7:180–1
Paul of Venice 7:265
sophistical syllogisms
Islamic philosophy 5:710
Sophists 1:262, 1:263, **9:33–4**
Antiphon 1:301–3
Antisthenes 1:314–15, 1:316
Chinese 2:322
dissoi logoi (twofold argument)
  3:106–7
educational philosophy 3:223
Gorgias 4:144–6
Hippias 4:440–1
logos 5:818
nature and convention 6:713–14,
  8:847, 8:848–9
political philosophy
  history of 7:505–6
Prodicus 7:731–3
Protagoras 7:789–90
Socrates 9:8
Thrasymachus 9:397–8
Thucydides 9:398

Sorabji, Richard
  animal language and thought
    1:273
  Aristotelianism
    medieval 1:404
  Aristotle 1:434, 1:435
    commentators †1:435–7
  atomism, ancient 1:535
  Augustine 1:559
  Boethius, A.M.S. 1:813
  eternity of the world
    medieval views of 3:429
  immutability 4:714
  intentionality 4:821
  natural philosophy
    medieval 6:707
  Parmenides 7:234
  Philoponus 7:377
  Porphyry 7:550
  Simplicius 8:791
  Strato 9:163
  Zeno of Elea 9:852
Sorai see Ogyū Sorai
Sorai School see Ken'en School of
    Confucianism
Sorel, Georges 9:34–6
  fascism 3:562
  Mariátegui, J.C.
    Latin American Marxism 6:163
  syndicalism 6:143
Sorell, Tom
  business ethics †2:150–4
  Hobbes, T. †4:459–76
Sorensen, R.A. 9:396–7, 9:566
sorites paradox 3:822, 9:564, 9:566
  glossary 5:809
Sorkin, D. 3:323–4
Sorley, W.R. 4:375
Sorokin, P.A. 5:438, 7:564
Soroush, Abdul 5:19–20
Sorrentino, S. 8:538
Sortais, Gaston 1:391–3, 2:120
sortal terms see count terms
Sosa, Ernest
  concept of knowledge 5:276
  epistemology 3:365
    ethics 3:370
    justification 5:165
  foundationalism †3:718–23
  imperative logic 4:721
  mental causation 6:311
  metaphysics 6:341
  reliabilism 8:209, 9:619, 9:622
Sôsan Hyujông 2:115–16, 9:36–7
Sosnowski, L. 4:792
soteriological exclusivism
  definition 8:260

Soto, Domingo de 9:37–40
  signs 5:412
  Spain, philosophy in 9:71, 9:77
Sōtō Zen Buddhism
  Dōgen 3:109–10
  Zeami 9:839–40
Souffrin, P. 6:705, 7:157
soul 9:44–8
  see also ātman; Great Soul;
    Physical Soul; psychē; Soul
    (hypostasis); World-Soul
  action
    Indian fatalism 3:567
  active principles (Telesio, B.)
    9:298–9
  activity of
    Ibn Tzaddik, J. 4:661
    Schleiermacher, F. 8:534–12
  afterlife
    Jewish philosophy
      Hillel ben Samuel of Verona
        4:432–3
      Ibn Tzaddik, J. 4:660, 4:662
  agent intellect (Ibn Bajja) 4:606
  air analogy (Anaximenes) 1:261
  alchemy 1:157
  animal (Le Grand, A.) 5:480
  Aquinas, T. 1:335
  Aristotelianism
    Albert the Great 1:147–8
    al-Ghazali's refutation of 4:641
  atomist psychology (Democritus)
    2:875
  Augustine of Hippo 7:260
  Averroism (Paul of Venice) 7:266
  body relationship 9:44–8
    Aristotle 1:424–5
      Alexander of Aphrodisias
        1:171
    death 2:818, 2:819, 2:820, 2:821
    descent to body
      Kabbalah (Herrera, A.
        Cohen de) 4:399
      Neoplatonism 6:801
      Proclus 7:728
    Epicureanism 3:344
    al-Ghazali 4:65–6
    Ibn Miskawayh 4:631
    Ibn Sina 4:651–2
    Ikhwan al-Safa' 4:687
    Islamic philosophy 9:40, 9:41
      al-Ghazali 4:65–6
      Ibn Miskawayh 4:631
      Ibn Sina 4:651–2
      Ikhwan al-Safa' 4:687
      al-Sijistani 8:775

  Jewish philosophy
    Abravanel, J. 1:25–6
    Ibn Gabirol, S. 4:618
    John of Jandun 5:107
    Knutzen, M. 5:288
    La Forge, L. de 5:331
    Neoplatonism (roclus) 7:727,
      7:728–9
    Peter Lombard 5:821
    Porphyry 7:547
    Proclus 7:727, 7:728–9
    psychological dualism
      medieval 6:274
    Rāmānuja 8:43
    Renaissance Aristotelianism
      1:408–9
    al-Sijistani 8:775
  as corporeal substance
    (Leibniz, G.W.) 5:547–8,
    5:555–6
  creation of
    Jewish philosophy (Judah ben
      Moses of Rome) 5:129
  definition of (Ailly, P. d') 1:134
  divine relationship
    Madhva 6:31–2
    Marius Victorinus 6:106
    Rāmānuja 8:43
  division of (Ibn 'Adi) 4:600
  doctrine of (Aristotle) 1:407
  dualism (Wolff, C.) 9:782
  emanationism
    Mir Damad, Muhammad Baqir
      6:409
    al-Tawhidi 9:271
  embodied
    Iamblichus 4:598–9
    Simplicius 8:789
  essence of
    rational psychology (Wolff, C.)
      9:782
  eternal principle of (al-Razi, Abu
    Bakr) 8:111
  evolution of the
    Ramakrishna Movement 8:41
  evolutionary theory
    problems raised by 2:797–8
  existence of
    empirical psychology (Wolff, C.)
      9:782
    Islamic philosophy 9:40
  faculties
    Ibn Sina 1:76
    Jewish philosophy 4:608–9
  four dimensions of
    Early Platonism 7:425

free will
   Cudworth, R. 2:742
   Origen 7:258–9
God
   obedience to
      Jewish pietism 4:635
      unity with (Iamblichus) 4:599
   Homeric hero allegory (Porphyry)
      7:548
hypostasis Soul and World-Soul
   distinctions (Plotinus) 7:459
illumination
   Jewish philosophy (Israeli, I.)
      5:33
imaginal world (Mulla Sadra)
   6:598
immaterialism (Clarke, S.) 2:378–9
immortality of 2:821, 2:822, 9:44,
   9:46–8
   Ailly, P. d' 1:134
   Alcmaeon 1:160
   Alexander of Aphrodisias
      1:171–2
   al-'Amiri 1:207, 1:208
   Aquinas, T. 9:45
   Averroist debate
      Vernia, N. 9:597
   Cajetan 2:171, 2:172–3
   Charleton, W. 2:286
   Collins, A. 2:417
   denial of
      Blasius of Parma 1:784,
         1:785
      Ibn Rushd 4:641
      Overton, R. 7:175, 7:176
   Digby, K. 3:71, 3:72, 3:73
   Ficino, M. 3:653–4, 3:656–7
   Gassendi, P. 3:854–5
   Hegel, G.W.F. 4:273
   Helmont, F.M. van 4:341
   Ibn Miskawayh 4:631
   Ibn Sina 4:651–2
   Islamic philosophy 9:40, 9:43
      (al-'Amiri) 1:207, 1:208
      Ibn Miskawayh 4:631
      Ibn Sina 4:651–2
   Jewish philosophy
      Alemanno, Y. 1:163
      Mendelssohn, M. 6:305
   John of St Thomas 5:119
   Kant, I. 9:46–7
   Mīmāṃsā 6:379
   More, H. 6:576, 6:577
   natural
      Aquinas, T. 9:46
      Plato 9:46

Plato 3:414, 8:294–5
   Meno 7:409–10
   Phaedo 7:412–13
   Pythagorean doctrine 7:400
   Symposium 7:412
Platonism 7:425
Pythagoras 7:855–6
Pythagoreanism 7:857, 7:860
Renaissance Aristotelianism
   1:409–10
   Pomponazzi, P. 7:529–30
Renaissance philosophy 8:266
resurrection 3:416
Siger of Brabant 8:765
Strato 9:163
Suárez, F. 9:191–2
Zoroastrianism 9:873
importance of (Socrates) 9:8
impurities in (Vallabhācārya)
   9:574–5
Indefinite Dyad
   Early Platonism 7:424
indigenous people
   Jesuits in Brazil 2:8
indivisibility (Ibn Sina) 4:651
innate ideas (More, H.) 6:578
intellect relationship (Matthew of
   Aquasparta) 6:201
intellective
   Godfrey of Fontaines 4:119,
      4:121
   Grosseteste, R. 4:179
   Vernia, N. 9:597
Islamic philosophy 9:40–4
karma and rebirth
   Indian conceptions of 5:212–13,
      5:215
knowledge
   of God (Bonaventure) 1:831,
      1:832–3
   Ibn Sina 4:649
   Ikhwan al-Safa' 4:687
   Jainism 5:51
   Jewish philosophy (Ibn
      Falaquera) 4:616
Madhva 6:31
materialism (Locke, J.) 5:677–8
metaphysical illusion (Kant, I.)
   5:188
mind distinction (Plutarch of
   Chaeronea) 7:467–8
as monad
   Jainism 5:49
monopsychism
   Averroism 1:596

moral philosophy
   Ibn Miskawayh 3:440–1, 4:631,
      4:632
   Ibn Sina 3:440
   al-Razi 3:439
mortality of
   Epicureanism 3:348–9
Native American philosophy 6:665
natural motion (Malebranche, N.)
   6:63
nature of 9:44–6
   Byzantine philosophy 2:162
   Denys the Carthusian 2:885
   Isaac of Stella 5:4
   Islamic philosophy 5:15, 9:40–2
   James of Viterbo 5:58, 5:59
   Jewish philosophy
      Bar Hayya, A. 1:649–50
      Hillel ben Samuel of Verona
         4:431, 4:432
      Kabbalah 4:399
      Saadiah Gaon 8:438
   John of La Rochelle 5:110–11
   Kabbalah
      Herrera, A. Cohen de 4:399
   Kilwardby, R. 5:248
   Meister Eckhart 6:287
   Nemesius 6:763–4
   Neoplatonism 6:800–1
   Pecham, J. 7:267–8
   personal identity 6:571–2, 7:306
   Peter of Spain 7:325
   Posidonius 7:556
   Proclus 7:728
   Richard Rufus of Cornwall
      8:316
   Richard of St Victor 8:312–13
   Tauler, J. 9:270
   Thomas of York 9:375
non-rational
   Islamic philosophy 9:40–2, 9:43
nous
   Aristotle 7:43–4
   Plato 7:43
objective
   Islamic philosophy 9:40, 9:42–3
ontological categories
   Indian philosophy 7:127
perfection quest (Philo of
   Alexandria) 7:360
persons 7:318
Plato
   chariot metaphor 3:286
   knowledge 3:371
   Phaedo 7:412–13
Platonic dualism
   Plotinus 7:461–2

rejection of
  Aristotle 1:424–5
Platonism
  Islamic philosophy 7:430
  medieval 7:433, 7:434
pneuma (Strato) 9:162–3
powers of
  Augustinianism 1:562
pre-existence
  Glanvill, J. 4:82
  Nemesius 6:764
punishment and reward (Ibn Sina)
  4:652
rational
  Active Intellect (Judah ben
    Moses of Rome) 5:129
  Descartes, R. 3:16
  irrational distinction
    (Numenius) 7:55
  Islamic philosophy 3:386, 9:40,
    9:42, 9:43
  Suárez, F. 9:191
resurrection 8:294–5
  Islamic philosophy (al-Ghazali)
    4:65
science of the
  Jewish philosophy (Rosenstock-
    Huessy, E.) 8:360
self-control (Plato) 8:611, 8:612
as self-moving number
  (Xenocrates) 9:807
singularity of (Wodeham, A.)
  9:773
spirit
  Ibn Massara 4:629
  More, H. 6:579–80
substance of (Heraclides of
  Pontus) 4:363–4
temporality
  Neoplatonism (roclus) 7:727
thought (Voltaire) 9:658–9
transcendence
  Indian fatalism 3:566–7
transmigration of
  Numenius 7:55
  Orphism 7:164
  Proclus 7:729
  Pythagoreanism 7:855–6, 7:857,
    7:860
tripartite conception of (Galen)
  3:833
universal
  Thales 9:323
universals
  Islamic philosophy 3:386–7
virtue 1:833
  Ibn Miskawayh 4:631

voluntary motion (Elisabeth of
  Bohemia) 3:268
Soul (*hypostasis*)
  Plotinus
    hierarchy of principles 7:457
    individual soul and World-Soul
      distinctions 7:459
    sensible world relationship
      7:459
'soul' mysticism
  Zaehner, R.C. 6:630
soul-making
  evil, problem of 3:469–70
soundness (of an argument)
  glossary 5:809
soundness (of a logical calculus)
  glossary 5:809
soundness (of a theory)
  glossary 5:809
sounds
  language
    potentiality, Indian theories of
      7:607
Sousa, R. 4:567
Souslin/Kleene theorem 8:144
South America *see* Latin America
South, James
  Renaissance Aristotelianism
    †1:404–13
South Slavs **9:48–56**
  hermeneutics 9:49
  neo-Marxism 9:49, 9:52
  praxis 9:52
  Soviet Marxism-Leninism 9:49,
    9:52
Southern, R.W.
  Anselm of Canterbury 1:296
  Chartres, school of 2:290–1, 2:292
  Grosseteste, R. 4:183
  Platonism
    medieval 7:439
  Thierry of Chartres 9:373
Southgate, Beverley
  Sergeant, J. †8:698–9
  White, T. †9:712–13
Southwest German School of Neo-
  Kantianism 6:776–7, 6:784–8
  Rickert, H. 6:777, 6:785–6, 6:791
  Windelband, W. 6:776, 6:781,
    6:784–5, 6:791
sovereignty **9:56–9**
  absolutism 1:30
  authority 9:56–7
    Hobbes, T. 8:227
  commonwealth (Hobbes, T.)
    4:459–60, 4:471–3
  confederalism 3:572, 3:573

constitutionalism 2:618–19
contract theory (Rousseau, J.-J.)
  7:514
Erasmus, D. 3:396, 3:398
federalism 3:572
Filmer, R. 3:678
general will
  social contract theory 8:371
God
  Edwards, J. 3:240, 3:241–2
  Niebuhr, H.R. 6:839
independence 9:58
legal norms (Austin, J.) 7:39
legislative (Dicey, A.V.) 3:62
limitations of (Hooker, R.) 4:506
nationalism 6:658–9
public law (Bodin, J.) 1:796
republicanism 9:57–8
self *see* autonomy
Shintō 8:751
social contract 2:659
state 4:829
  political philosophy
    history of 7:511
theology
  political (Schmitt, C.) 9:331
Tocqueville, A. de 9:424
utility 9:56
Soviet Marxism *see* Marxism,
  Russian/Soviet
Soviet Union (USSR)
  see also Lithuania; Russia; Russian
    Revolution; Ukraine
  Asmus, V.F. **1:523–7**
  Il'enkov, E.V. **4:688–92**
  Mamardashvili, M.K. **6:66–71**
  Moscow-Tartu school **6:583–8**
  Vygotskii, L.S. **9:671–5**
  Vysheslavtsev, B.P. **9:675–7**
Sowa, J. 5:746
Sowden, L. 8:101
Soyinka, W. 1:107, 1:121
Sozialtheologie see theology, political
Spaapen, B. 9:374
space **9:59–66**
  absolute
    classical mechanics 6:253
    Kant, I. 5:182
    Newton, I. 2:678, 6:253
  Aristotelian
    cosmology
      medieval natural philosophy
        6:702
    Simplicius corollary 8:789–90
  Euclidian
    classical mechanics 6:251–3
    Newton, I. 2:678

geometric
  bodies distinction
    Epicureanism 3:340, 3:341–2
  corporeal extension
    (Philoponus) 7:373
  Daoism 2:786
  divisibility of
    Kant, I. 5:181
    Zeno of Elea 9:847–51
  mathematical logic (Royce, J.)
    8:380
  nature of
    Neoplatonism 6:801–2
    Reichenbach, H. 8:168–9
  relational theory (Poincaré, J.H.)
    7:480
  science of 4:30–2
motion
  Newton, I. 6:825, 9:59, 9:60–1
non-sentient substance
  Jainism 5:49
place
  Neoplatonism 6:801–2
  Philoponus 7:373
  Proclus 7:729
  Strato 9:162
place-void definitions
  Stoicism 9:148
that-which-is (Parmenides) 7:231
time
  the Absolute 1:28
  abstract objects 1:32, 1:33
  duration (Bergson, H.-L.) 1:733
  eternity 3:424
  infinity
    Crescas, H. 2:701–2
    Melissus 6:294
  metaphysics 6:339
  personalism (Bowne, B.P.) 7:316
  al-Razi, Abu Bakr 8:111
  space-time differences 9:413
space hierarchy theorem
  computational complexity 2:472–3
spacetime 9:66–70
  Alexander, S. 1:168
  causation (Reichenbach, H.) 8:169
  classical mechanics 6:253
  co-reality of
    relativity theory 8:193
  Einstein, A. 2:678
  energy-momentum
    (Heisenberg, W.) 4:328
  general relativity 4:5–6
  Kantian reaction 4:6–7
  Kant, I. (Maimon, S.) 6:36
  knowledge of (Kant, I.) 5:182,
    5:184–5

time travel 9:418
Spade, P.V.
  Ailly, P. d' 1:135
  Brinkley, R. 2:21
  logic
    medieval 5:758, 5:759
  Platonism
    medieval 7:439
  Porphyry 7:550
  universals
    medieval debate 9:543–4
  Wodeham, A. 9:776
  Wyclif, J. 9:804, 9:805
Spae, J.J. 2:555, 5:44
Spain 9:70–7
  Abravanel, I. 1:19–23
  Albo, J. 1:152–5
  Arama, I. 1:350–1
  Báñez, D. 1:647–9
  Bar Hayya, A. 1:649–51
  Crescas, H. 2:700–4
  Duran, P. 3:170–1
  Duran, S. 3:171–2
  Generation of 1898 9:70, 9:73
  Generation of 1914 9:73–4
  Halevi, J. 4:207–13
  Ibn al-'Arabi 4:601–5
  Ibn Bajja 4:605–8
  Ibn Daud, A. 4:608–11
  Ibn Ezra, A. 4:611–13
  Ibn Ezra, M. 4:613–15
  Ibn Falaquera 4:615–17
  Ibn Gabirol, S. 4:617–20
  Ibn Hazm 4:620–1
  Ibn Massara 4:627–30
  Ibn Paquda, Bahya 4:633–6
  Ibn Rushd 4:638–46
  Ibn Sab'in 4:646–7
  Ibn Tufayl 4:657–9
  Ibn Tzaddik, J. 4:659–62
  institutionism 9:73
  Islamic philosophy 5:14
    see also Ibn al-'Arabi; Ibn Bajja;
    see also Ibn Rushd; Ibn Tufayl
    Aristotelianism 1:384
    Greek philosophy influence
      4:158–9
    mysticism 6:618
  Judaeo-Arabic philosophy see
    Abravanel, I.; Abravanel, J.;
    Albo, J.; Arama, I.; Bar
    Hayya, A.; Crescas, H.;
    Duran, P.; Halevi, J.; Ibn Daud;
    Ibn Ezra, A.; Ibn Ezra, M.; Ibn
    Falaquera; Ibn Gabirol, S.; Ibn
    Paquda; Ibn Tzaddik;

Maimonides, M.; Shem Tov
    family
  Judah Halevi 4:207–13
  Krausist idealism 9:72–3
  Llull, R. 5:662–4
  Maimonides, M. 6:40–9
  Middle Ages 9:70
  Nahmanides, M. 6:647–51
  Novatores (renovators) movement
    9:72
  Ortega y Gasset, J. 7:165–8
  Peter of Spain 7:324–5
  philosophy in exile 9:74–5
  Renaissance 9:70–1
  Santayana, G. 8:467–70
  scholasticism 9:71, 9:72
  School of Translators of Toledo
    9:70
  Seneca, L.A. 8:679–82
  Shem Tov family 8:737–40
  Soto, D. de 9:37–40
  Suárez, F. 9:189–96
  Toletus, F. 9:433–5
  Unamuno y Jugo, M. De 9:519–22
  Vitoria, F. de 9:643–5
  Vives, J.L. 9:645–50
Spanish conquest
  Mexican philosophy 6:345
  pre-Columbian thought 5:429,
    5:430
Spanish Netherlands
  Lipsius, J. 5:650–2
Spanneut, M. 2:385, 9:309
Sparham, G. 2:75
Sparks, S. 6:654
Sparshott, F. 1:468, 1:472, 2:777,
    6:615
Spartacus group 6:7
spartan argument
  theoretical/epistemic virtues
    9:341–2
spatial concepts
  see also space
  absolutism
    Leibniz/Newton debate 5:556–7
  Clarke/Leibniz debate 2:379
  Epicurean atomism
    Gassendi, P. 3:852
  Gassendi, P.
    Bernier, F. critique 1:757
  infinite (More, H.) 6:576, 6:580
  mitigated scepticism (Bayle, P.)
    1:674
  Molyneux problem 6:467–8
spatial length see extension

spatiality
divine
omnipresence 7:103, 7:105
spatio-temporal continuity
material objects 2:652–3
Spaventa, Bertrando
Gentile, G. 4:21
Gioberti, V. 4:80
Hegelianism 4:300
Italian Renaissance
origin of modern philosophy
5:37–8, 5:42
speaker's intention see
communication, intention
Speas, M. 4:745
special relativity theory
Bridgman, P.W. 2:18
Einstein, A. 3:254, 3:255
philosophical significance of
8:191, 8:192–6
positivism 4:5
twin paradox 8:193–4
species **9:78–81**
see also Darwin, Charles;
evolutionary theory; speciesism
afterlife of (Ibn Rushd) 4:641
biological concept 9:78–9
classification of 9:273
Linnaeus, C. von 5:647–8, 5:649
continuity across
language 1:269–70
evolutionary theory 3:477–8
Darwin, C.R. 2:796–7
individuation (Duns Scotus, J.)
3:165
intelligible
Renaissance Aristotelianism
1:408
logic of (Tanabe Hajime) 5:715,
9:261, 9:262
monogenetic anthropology
(Buffon, G.L.L.) 2:122
natural kinds 6:683
new 4:26
normative nature
differentiated (Han Wŏnjin)
4:221
Yi Kan 9:825
origin of (Anaxagoras) 1:250
phylogentic concepts 9:78, 9:79–80
procreative ability (Buffon, G.L.L.)
2:120, 2:121–2
solidarity
moral standing 6:552
species-being
alienation (Marx, K.) 6:118, 6:122

speciesism
animals and ethics 1:273, 1:275
Singer, P. 1:580
Speck, F. 6:671
Speck, S. 1:498
Specker, E.P. 1:716, 7:884, 7:886
Spector, C. 7:143, 7:747, 7:751–2
spectrality
Marx, K. (Derrida, J.) 2:900
spectroscopy
Bohr, N.
optics 7:138
speculation
action relationship (Comte, A.)
2:498–9
speculative empiricism
Herzen, A.I. 4:405
speculative metaphysics
Whitehead, A.N. 9:714, 9:716–17
speculative philosophy
critical distinction (Broad, C.D.) 2:24
speech
see also speech acts
child development (Vygotskii, L.S.)
9:673
essential–crude distinction
(Blanchot, M.) 1:783
figures of
medieval language theories
5:400
freedom of **3:762–5**
primacy over writing
Rabbinic theology 9:335–6
production
split brain studies 9:108
reported see indirect discourse
semiotic rhythms
Kristeva, J. 5:305–6
utterance distinction
Stoics 5:360
writing distinction
Derrida, J. 2:896, 2:898
speech acts 7:621, **9:81–7**
see also illocutionary acts;
locutionary acts; performatives;
perlocutionary acts; utterances
ambiguity 1:199
contextual implications 7:621–2
emotive meaning 3:290–1
fiction 3:661
intention 2:456–8
intentionality
Searle, J. 8:589
meaning
non-truth-conditional 7:622–3
metaphors 6:337
open texture 7:624

social acts comparison
(Reinach, A.) 8:181–2
Speer, Albert 8:632
Speilberg, H. 5:298
Spelke, E.S. 2:391–2, 2:394, 2:395,
6:675
Spelman, E.V. 5:645
Spence, K.W. 7:134
Spencer, Herbert 8:571, **9:87–9**
see also Spencerianism
Comte, A. 2:505
European positivism 7:565–6,
7:570
evolutionary theory 4:455, 9:87–8
Mikhailovskii, N.K. critique
6:356
humour 4:564, 4:567
individual existence (Unamuno y
Jugo, M. De) 9:519
influence of
Ramakrishna Movement 8:40–1
Latin American philosophy 5:427
science, nineteenth century
philosophy of 8:568, 8:572
social science
history of philosophy of 8:854,
8:859
Spencer, S. 6:626–7
Spencerianism
Brazil 2:10
Spener, Philip Jacob 7:393–4, 7:395
Spengler, Oswald 2:748, 2:750, 4:453,
4:459
Sperber, D.
anthropology
philosophy of 1:299
implicature 4:725
Lévi-Strauss, C. 5:585
pragmatics 7:632
rationality of belief 8:90
structuralism 9:177
Spero, S. 9:27
Sperry, R.W. 9:107, 9:109, 9:110
Spettmann, H. 7:269
Speusippus **9:89–91**
spheres of being
knowledge (Scheler, M.F.) 8:507
religion (Scheler, M.F.) 8:507
sphere-sovereignty
Dooyeweerd, H. 3:113
sphoṭa theory 4:436, 5:379, 5:382–3,
7:249
Spiegel, S. 4:213
Spiegelberg, Herbert
Husserl, E. 4:587–8
intentionality 4:821

phenomenological movement
7:342
Reinach, A. 8:182
Scheler, M.F. 8:509
Spiel see play
Spink, J.S. 5:622, 9:663
Spinka, M. 4:574
Spinner, J. 2:365
Spinoza, Benedict de **9:91–107**
see also Spinozism
awe 8:339
biblical authority 9:92, 9:106
body (Deleuze, G.) 2:857–8
contingency 2:650, 2:652
Descartes, R. 3:16
dualism (Vygotskii, L.S.) 9:673
emotions 3:287, 3:290, 9:101–2
error 7:204
Ethica Ordine Geometrico
Demonstrata (Ethics
Demonstrated in a Geometrical
Manner)
emotions 9:101–3
geometrical method 9:91,
9:92–3
God
love for 9:103–4
nature identification 9:95–7
knowledge 9:99–9:101
mind-body monism 9:97–9
moral theory 9:102–3
substance-monism 9:93–5
evil 3:465, 3:466, 7:204–5
free will 3:752, 7:204
geometrical method 9:91, 9:92–3
God
anthropomorphism
Leibniz, G.W. critique 5:545
love for 9:103–4
nature
identification with 9:91,
9:95–7
hermeneutics 4:389
Herrera, A. Cohen de comparison
4:399
hope 4:510
Ibn Ezra, A. 4:611, 4:613
immortality 7:204
influence of
Goethe, J.W. von 4:127, 4:129
Jewish philosophy 5:91, 5:93,
5:95
Schelling, F.W.J. von 8:514
Jewish Enlightenment 3:322–3
knowledge 3:375–6, 3:383, 9:92–3,
9:99–101
of God 9:91, 9:103

virtue relationship 9:102
love 5:843, 5:844, 5:846
mind-body monism 9:97–9
monism 6:474, 6:475
moral psychology
Hume, D. comparison 4:551
moral theory 9:102–3
morality and emotions 6:560,
6:564
necessary being 6:743, 6:745, 6:747
necessity 5:550
omnipresence 7:107
pantheism 4:100, 7:202, 7:203–4,
7:205
politics 9:104–6
prophecy 7:769, 7:771
rationalism 8:80
substance 9:206, 9:210–11
substance-monism 9:93–5
Spinozism
Lessing, G.E. (Jacobi, F.H.) 5:45–6
pantheism (Herder, J.G.) 4:382–3
Régis, P.-S. 8:165
spirit
body relationship (Isaac of Stella)
5:4
existence of (More, H.) 6:578–80
explanation of human faculties
(Wallace, A.R.) 9:679
extension (More, H.) 6:579
Hegel, G.W.F. 1:179
Hegelian idealism (Croce, B.)
2:728–9, 2:731
indiscerpibility (More, H.) 6:578–9
matter relationship (More, H.)
6:579
of nature (More, H.) 6:580
nature (*priroda*) relationship
(Berdiaev, N.A.) 1:727
objective
systems of reciprocal influence
(Dilthey, W.) 3:81
philosophy of (Hegel, G.W.F.)
4:264, 4:273–7
pneuma **7:470–2**
self-realization (Jaspers, K.) 5:80
soul
Ibn Massara 4:629
More, H. 6:579–80
spirits
see also daemons; spiritualism
communication with
(Swedenborg, E.) 9:241, 9:242–3
fear of as social control (Mozi)
6:454
immortal intellect (Telesio, B.)
9:299

literal belief in
African traditional religions
1:117, 1:118
spiritualism
see also neo-spiritualism; spirits
African ethical systems 3:431–2
eclectic
Argentina, philosophy in 1:376
French (Boutroux, É.) 1:850, 1:851
spirituality
see also mysticism
Chinese philosophy
tian 9:401
Christianity (Luther, M.) 8:456–7
consciousness (Santayana, G.)
8:469
Edwards, J. 3:243–4
growth
Christian 8:456
Protestantism 8:457
Hasidism 4:244
humanism (Frank, S.L.) 3:728
Jewish mysticism 6:623
kami
Japanese philosophy 5:69
neo-Confucianism (Shao Yong)
6:767
nirvāṇa 7:8–11
Spirtes, Peter
causation 2:251
statistics and social science
†9:127–33
Spitz, L.W. 6:292
Spitz, Renée 7:819–20, 7:824
Spitzer, A.B. 2:692
Spivak, Gayatri Chakravorty
Derrida, J. 2:901
feminist literary criticism
†3:611–14
Le Doeuff, M. 5:479
political philosophy
Indian 7:524
postcolonialism 7:582, 7:583
split brains **9:107–10**
critique of dualism 3:134
splitting
psychoanalysis (Klein, M.) 7:818
Spohn, W. 2:215, 3:222
Sponberg, Alan
Ambedkar, B.R. †1:196–7
spontaneous acts
classification of (Reinach, A.)
8:181
spontaneous generation 5:633–4,
9:641
sport **9:112–16**
art analogy 1:455

ethics **9:110–12**
mind–body problem 9:112–13, 9:116
'nature versus nurture' 9:114
self-knowledge 9:112, 9:115–16
society 9:112, 9:113–15
Sprague, R.K.
  Antiphon 1:303
  dissoi logoi (twofold argument) 3:107
  Gorgias 4:146
  Hippias 4:441
  Prodicus 7:732–3
  Protagoras 7:791
  Sophists 9:34
  Thrasymachus 9:398
Sprat, T. 1:632
Sprigge, T.L.S.
  the Absolute †1:27–9
  Bradley, F.H. 1:863
  idealism †4:662–9
  James, W. 5:68
  panpsychism †7:194–7
  Santayana, G. 8:470
  sense-data 8:698
Sprinchorn, E. 7:131
The Spring and Autumn Annals see Chunqiu
Sprinker, M. 1:195
Sprintzen, David A.
  Camus, A. †2:194–6
sprit
  objective 3:81
Sprockoff, J.F. 6:30
Sprott, S.E. 9:230
Spruit, L. 1:413, 2:39
Sprung, M. 2:64
Squadrito, K.M. 1:530
Squires, R. 6:300
Sri Aurobindo *see* Aurobindo Ghose
Śrīharsa 6:477–8, 6:479
Srinivasachari, P.N. 9:594
Srinivasachari, S.M. 8:44
Śrīsampradāya School of Vaishnava 8:42
Srubar, I. A. 8:561
Srzednicki, J.T.J. 5:574, 6:320, 7:499
Staal, J.F. 4:766, 5:57, 9:319
Stabb, M.S. 1:307, 5:657
stability
  ecology 3:203
  political
    corruption 2:675
    federations 3:573
    justice as fairness 8:108
Stace, Walter T. 6:628, 6:629, 6:630, 6:633–4

Stachel, J. 3:258, 4:9, 8:198
Stachniak, Z. 5:574
Stack, George J.
  Lange, Friedrich Albert †5:352–4
  materialism †6:170–3
stadium paradox *see* Dichotomy argument
Stadler, F.
  Hempel, C.G. 4:352
  Neurath, O. 6:815
  Vienna Circle †9:606–14
Staël-Holstein, Anne-Louise-Germaine, Mme de **9:116–18**
Stafford, B.M. 3:320
Stafleu, F.A. 5:650
sTag tshang lõ tsa ba (Daktsang lodzawa) 9:405
Stahl, Georg Ernst
  aesthetic concepts 1:59
  analytical philosophy in Latin America 1:234
  chemistry
    philosophical aspects of 2:296
Stair, James Dalrymple, Viscount **9:118–20**
  Roman law/civilian tradition 8:347
Stair-Douglas, M. 9:711
Stairs, Allen
  parapsychology †7:224–7
  quantum logic 7:886
  quantum mechanics, interpretation of †7:890–5
stakeholders
  see also employees
  business ethics 2:150, 2:151, 2:153
  social responsibility 2:152–3
Stalder, R. 9:804
Stalin, Iosif V. 6:155–6, 7:239–40, 7:241
  see also Stalinism
Stalinism
  see also totalitarianism
  Marxist defence of 6:145
  Soviet Marxism 6:155–6
  Trotsky, L. opposition to 9:464
Stalker, D. 4:140
Stallman, Richard 4:779
Stålmarck, G. 6:682
Stalnaker, Robert
  see also Stalnaker-Lewis semantics
  analytic philosophy 1:229
  belief 1:706
  concepts 2:517
  conditionals 6:433, 8:665
    counterfactual 2:686–7, 2:688
    indicative 4:741, 4:743
  intensional entities 4:807

Lewis, D.K. 5:591, 5:593–4
  possible worlds semantics 8:667–8, 8:669
  pragmatics 7:632
  presupposition 7:675
  propositional attitudes 7:787
  propositions 7:788
  semantics
    informational 8:662
Stalnaker-Lewis semantics 7:33–4
Stambaugh, J. 6:594
Stammler, H. 8:385
Stammler, R. 5:512, 5:514
Stampe, D. 8:662
standards
  normative
    society
      concept of 8:888
standpoints (*nayavāda*)
  manifoldness, Jaina theory of 6:77, 6:79–81
Stanford, D. 7:299
Stanhope, Charles 5:744
Stankevich, Nikolai 4:302
Stanley, J.C. 3:520
Stanley, J.L. 9:36
Stanley, L. 3:593
Stanosz, B.
  Kotarbiński, T. †5:293–6
Stanton, Elizabeth Cady 3:579
Stanton, W.L. 1:280
Stanwood, P.G.
  Law, W. †5:468–70
Stapp, H.P. 4:329
Star, S.L. 8:728
Stark, Cynthia A.
  self-respect †8:635–8
Starkey, P. 6:675
Starobinski, J. 6:494, 8:377
state **9:120–3**
  see also government; nation; obligation, political; political representation; politics; sovereignty
  abolishment of the (Herder, J.G.) 4:383–4
  absolutism 1:31
  administration (Schleiermacher, F.) 8:536–7
  anarchism 1:244–7
  atomization 9:424
  authority
    individual liberty 4:829–30
    Suárez, F. 9:192–3

autonomy of
Renaissance philosophy 8:849,
8:850
political 7:509
Chinese philosophy
fa 3:532
church relationship
Calvin, J. 2:180–1
political philosophy
history of 7:504, 7:507–8
civil condition (Oakeshott, M.J.)
7:72
communitarianism 4:829–30
constraints on
rule of law 8:388
Gramsci, A. 4:152–3
Hayek, F.A. 4:248–9
Hegel, G.W.F.
Marx, K. critique of 6:121
Hegelian concept of
(Rosenzweig, F.) 8:358
intervention (Bentham, J.) 1:721
Islamic philosophy 5:14–15
justification of
political philosophy
history of 7:513
libertarianism 5:617, 5:618, 5:619
medieval concepts of (Marsilius of
Padua) 6:112
morality 4:826–7, 4:828–30
enforcement of 5:438–42
as myth (Cassirer, E.) 2:225–6
neutrality 6:818–20
nightwatchman theory
(Spencer, H.) 9:87
Nozick, R. 7:45–6
people relationship
Slavophilism 8:809
philosophy–theology relationship
(Ibn Rushd) 4:642
property rights (Kant, I.) 5:191,
5:195
punishment 2:705, 2:709
realization of the universal
(Tanabe Hajime) 9:261
religion relationship
Hobbes, T. 4:462, 4:472–3
Judaism (Leibowitz, Y.) 5:562–4
political philosophy
Indian 7:521, 7:522–3
revolution (Kant, I.) 5:195
Russian Hegelianism
Belinskii, V. 4:304
Kavelin, K. 4:304–5
separation of powers
rule of law 8:388–9, 8:390
social logic (Bosanquet, B.) 1:847

society relationship (Ibn Khaldun)
4:624
sovereignty
political philosophy
history of 7:511
theory of (Hegel, G.W.F.) 4:275
state of nature
autonomy
ethical 1:587
Hobbes, T. 4:470–1
pre-sovereign 9:56
libertarianism 5:618–19
liberty (Locke, J.) 5:681
social contract 5:603–4
war 9:685, 9:689–90
statements **7:787–8**
factual–moral distinction
logic of ethical discourse
5:759–61
religious 8:255–9
state-protection Buddhism
Korea 2:116–17
states
physical
determinism 3:37–9
superposition of
quantum mechanics 7:891–2
statistical explanation
covering-law model
Salmon, W. critique 3:523
statistical mechanics 9:366
statistics **9:123–7**
probability (Keynes, J.M.) 5:233–4
random number generatorss
bias dangers 8:56–7
and social science **9:127–33**
causal models 9:130–2
positivist influence 7:559
probabilistic models 9:128–30
summary type of 9:127–8
uses of 9:127
statistical dynamics (Maxwell, J.C.)
6:208
Statman, Daniel
moral luck †6:520–2
status
social
Akan philosophical psychology
1:138
feminist jurisprudence 3:607–8
Hindu philosophy 4:437
statutes
common law distinction 2:441,
2:443
real/personal distinction (Bartolus
of Sassoferrato) 1:658
Staudenmaier, J.M. 9:288

Staum, M.S. 2:168
Stcherbatsky, T. 2:58, 3:53, 4:766,
6:758
Stead, Christopher
Eusebius †3:456–8
Gnosticism †4:83–5
logos †5:817–19
patristic philosophy 7:261
pneuma (spirit) †7:470–2
steady-state cosmology 2:679, 8:233
Stearns, R.E. 2:475
Steck, M. 5:352
Stecker, R.
art
artistic expression 1:498
definition of 1:466, 1:468
fiction
semantics of 3:662
Reid, T. 8:180
Stedman Jones, G. 3:313, 5:859
Steel, C. 2:772, 4:599, 6:803, 7:439
Steel, T.B., Jr 8:3
Steenson, G.P. 5:224
Stefanini, L. 4:80
Steffan, T.G. 3:332
Steger, M. 3:313
Stegmann, J. 8:891
Stegmüller, F. 2:408
Stegmüller, W. 2:535–6, 3:222, 8:509,
9:354
Stein, E.
epistemic relativism 3:362
Husserl, E. 4:588
linguistic discrimination 5:645
phenomenology 7:342–3
sexuality 8:729
Stein, H.
Newton, I. 6:828
relativity theory
philosophical significance of
8:199
spacetime 9:69–70
time 9:417
Stein, Howard
Dedekind, J.W.R. †2:839–42
logicism †5:811–17
Stein, M. 5:135
Stein, Peter
Carmichael, G. 2:208
historical jurisprudence †5:138–41
justice, equity and law 5:153
Justinian 5:169
legal hermeneutics 5:510
Stair, J.D. 9:119–20
Steinberg, A. 1:779–80, 8:746
Steinberg, L. 3:409
Steinbock, B. 5:630

Steindl, H. 1:541
Steindler, L. 4:572
Steiner, G. 9:452
Steiner, H. 5:619, 9:89
Steiner, M. 5:266
Steiner, P. 8:413
Steiner, Rudolf **9:133–4**
Steinkellner, Ernst
    Buddhist nominalism 7:27
    Dharmakīrti †3:51–3
    karma and rebirth
        Indian theories of 5:218
    momentariness
        Buddhist doctrine of 6:473
Steinmann, W. 6:107
Steinmetz, D.C. 2:182, 6:5
Steinmetz, P. 7:557–8
Steinschneider, M. 1:602, 4:159,
    4:623, 5:131
Steitz, J.A. 4:16
Steklov, Y.M. 2:306
Stemberger, G. 6:355
Stenberg, C. 7:822
Stenheim, Solomon Ludwig 5:98,
    5:100
Stenius, Erik 4:721, 7:632, 8:492
Stenlund, S. 2:434, 5:349
Stent, G. 6:459, 6:460
Stepelevich, Lawrence S.
    Bauer, B. †1:663–7
    Cieszkowski, A. †2:360–2
    Hegelianism 4:298
Stephen, James Fitzjames 5:440,
    5:441, 5:442
Stephen, L. 2:160, 2:419, 9:423, 9:493
Stephenson, B. 5:232–3
Stephenson, H. 5:128
Stępień, Antoni B.
    Ingarden, R.W. †4:789–93
    Poland †7:483–9
Stepun, Fëdor 6:796
Sterelny, Kim
    genetics 4:16
    language 5:411
    reductionism, philosophy of mind
        †8:149–53
    reference 8:163
    semantics
        teleological 8:675
    species †9:78–81
    unconscious mental states 9:526
stereotypes
    see also nominal essence
    discrimination 3:103, 3:104
        linguistic 5:642–3

sexual
    feminist jurisprudence 3:607,
        3:609
Stern, C. 4:16
Stern, D. 7:824
Stern, Josef
    Arama, I. †1:350–1
    Nahmanides, M. †6:647–51
Stern, J.P. 5:624
Stern, Robert
    Hegel, G.W.F. 4:279
    Hegelianism †4:280–302
    McTaggart, J.M.E. 6:28
Stern, S.M. 4:630, 5:253
Sternberg, R.J. 9:754–5
Sternglass, E.J. 1:669
Sternhell, Z. 3:563
Stevens, P.F.
    Linnaeus, C. von †5:646–50
Stevens, S.S. 4:846, 7:133, 7:134,
    7:135
Stevenson, Charles Leslie **9:134–5**
    analytic ethics 1:223
    emotive meaning 3:291
    emotivism 3:293, 7:740, 9:134–5
    good, theories of the 4:135
    human nature 4:522, 4:525–6
    moral knowledge 6:520
    moral relativism 6:542
    moral scepticism 6:545
    prescriptivism 7:671
Stevenson, Dan
    Zhiyi †9:859–61
Stevin, Simon 9:393
Steward, H.
    akrasia †1:139–42
Stewart, Dugald **9:135–40**
    Common Sense School 2:448,
        9:135–9
        ethics 2:450, 2:451
    human agency 9:137
    influenced, by Reid, T. 9:136
    nominalism, eighteenth century
        9:138
    scientific hypotheses 9:138–9
    Smith, A. 8:822
Stewart, F. 3:44
Stewart, I. 5:521
Stewart, J.A. 2:185
Stewart, John B. 4:562
Stewart, M.A.
    Enlightenment, Scottish 3:330
    Oswald, J. †7:168–70
    Turnbull, G. 9:504
Stewart, R.M. 8:729
Sthiramati 9:217

Stich, Stephen P.
    belief management 6:728
    child's theory of mind 6:389
    cognitive pluralism †2:395–8
    concepts 2:517
    connectionism 2:578, 2:579
    content
        wide and narrow 2:646
    Dennett, D.C. 2:884
    eliminativism 1:708, 3:266
    epistemic relativism †3:360–2
    epistemology
        advisory 7:38
        normative 6:726
        objections to 7:709, 7:711
    folk psychology 1:709, †3:686–7
    holism
        mental and semantic 4:493
    innate knowledge 4:797
    language of thought hypothesis
        5:408
    modularity of mind 6:450, 6:451
    nativism 6:675–6
    propositional attitudes 7:787
    rationalism 8:80
    rationality 8:64
        of belief 8:90
    unconscious mental states 9:524,
        9:527
Stietencron, H. von 4:256–7
stigmatization 5:642–3
stillness
    Chinese philosophy *see jing*
Stilpo of Megara 6:279
stimulus
    adequacy of
        nativist–empiricist debate
            6:672–3
    poverty of
        nativist–empiricist debate
            6:672–3
stimulus-response (S-R) theory
    5:484–5, 8:800
Stinchcombe, A.L. 9:7
Stirling, J.H. 4:300
Stirner, Max **9:140–1**
    anarchism 1:245, 1:248
    liberated self 4:284
    nihilism 7:2, 7:5
Stites, R. 7:8
Stitskin, L. 1:651
Stob, M. 5:487
Stock, B. 1:756
Stock, G. 1:862, 1:863
Stocker, Michael
    moral pluralism 6:530, 6:531
    moral psychology 6:533

morality and emotions 6:564
virtue ethics 9:626
Stocking, G.W. 4:501
Stockman, N. 8:587
Stockmeyer, L. 2:476
Stoeffler, F.E. 7:395
Stoelen, A. 2:887
Stoicism 1:263, **9:141–61**
  see also neostoicism
  Abelard, P. 1:12–13, 1:14
  agency 9:721
  alchemy 1:157
  Alcinous 1:159
  apprehensive appearance (Philo of
    Larissa) 7:362–3
  archē 1:360
  Ariston of Chios 1:380–2
  Aristotle 1:431
  Blair, H. 1:782
  Chrysippus 2:345–6
  Cleanthes 2:382–3
  Cleomedes 2:385
  cognitive certainty debate
    Academic sceptics 7:849, 9:142,
      9:151–2
  conscience (Peter Lombard) 5:822
  critiques of
    Arcesilaus 1:353
    Carneades 2:216, 2:217–18
    Galen 3:833
    moralistes 6:556
    Philo of Larissa 7:362–3
    Plutarch of Chaeronea 7:465,
      7:466
    Valla, L. 9:570–1
  Cynicism (Antisthenes) 1:315
  determinism (Pomponazzi, P.)
    7:531
  educational philosophy 3:224–5
  emotions 3:285, 3:287
  Epictetus 3:337–9
    Simplicius commentary 8:789
  epistemology 3:373
  evil 3:465
  Hierocles 4:421–2
  history of school 9:143–4
  individual philophers
    guide to 9:143
  influence of
    Heraclitus 4:368–9
    Islamic philosophy 3:439, 4:158,
      5:251–2, 5:710
    Middle Platonism 7:424
  language
    philosophy of 5:357, 5:360
  Lipsius, J. 5:651

logic 5:687, 5:690–1, 5:750
  Dialectical school 3:58
  Encyclopedists, medieval 3:306
  Islamic philosophy 5:710
logos 5:817, 5:818, 5:819
love 5:843
Marcus Aurelius 6:93–5
matter 6:194
Middle (Panaetius) 7:188–90
morality
  Cicero, M.T. 2:358
  emotions 6:558, 6:560
  Wollaston, W. 9:787
Musonius Rufus 6:615–16
oikeiōsis 9:153–4
Old Academy syncretism
  (Antiochus) 1:300
omnipresence 7:103–4
ontological classifications 9:147–8
optionality 3:756
pantheism 4:100, 7:202
perfect-being theology 4:96, 4:97
personal property (al-Kindi)
  5:251–2
pneuma (spirit) 7:470, 7:471
political philosophy
  history of 7:511
Posidonius 7:555–7
providence 7:797
psychē (soul) 7:810
rationality of world
  design argument 9:142
Roman 9:143, 9:159
Seneca, L.A. 8:679–81
suicide 9:224
syllogism 5:690–1
theology (Cicero, M.T.) 2:357–8
three main topics of 9:144
vocabulary development 1:262
Zeno of Citium 9:841–2
Stojanovic, S. 9:55
Stoker, Valerie
  Madhva †6:31–3
Stokes, M.C.
  Hesiod 4:413
  Melissus 6:296
  Parmenides 7:234
  Xenophanes 9:810
  Zeno of Elea 9:853
Stokhof, M. 1:243, 3:98, 8:3
Stolnitz, J. 1:55, 1:187
Stolz, A. 1:296
Stone, C. 6:554–5
Stone, J. 5:101, 5:514, 8:22–3, 8:483
Stone, L. 7:693
Stone, M.W.F.
  casuistry †2:227–9

Stone, R.H. 6:844
Stone representation theorem
  1:844–5
Stonequist, E.V. 6:101
Stopper, M.R. 7:848
Störring, G. 9:322
Story Tellers
  Lushi chunqiu 5:864–5
story telling
  narrative 6:654–6
Stoudt, J.J. 1:801
Stouffer, S. 3:520
Stough, C.L. 7:854
Stout, G.F. 7:22, 7:23
Stove, D. 3:642, 7:539–40
Stöve, E. 2:175
Stoy, J. 5:349
Strack, F. 6:743
Straight, G.A. 7:610
Strakhov, Nikolai 7:6–7
Strassen, V. 2:496
strategies
  evolutionarily stable strategy
    (ESS) 2:831
  game theory 2:825–9, 8:66–8
  prisoner's dilemma 2:831
Strato **9:161–4**
  Aristotelian doctrines
    attitude to 9:161–3
  Lyceum decline 9:161
Stratton-Lake, Philip
  hope †4:507–10
Strauss, David Friedrich **9:164–7**
  Bauer, B. 1:664, 1:667
  Cieszkowski, A. 2:362
  Eliot, G. 3:267
  Hegelianism
    religion 4:282
Strauss, Leo **9:167–8**
  Judah Halevi 4:213
  Machiavelli, N. 6:22
  Maimonides, M. 6:48–9
  Xenophon 9:814
Stravinsky, Igor 6:615
Strawson, Galen
  free will †3:743–5
  Hume, D. 4:562
  materialism 6:178
  unconscious mental states 9:525,
    9:527
Strawson, Peter Frederick **9:168–74**
  see also Strawsonian
    presupposition
  aesthetics and ethics 1:68
  analytic behaviourism 1:692
  analytic philosophy 1:229, 1:239
  art criticism 1:463

Austin, J.L. debate
  correspondence theory of truth
    9:170
bundle theory of mind 6:385
communication and intention
  2:459
conceptual analysis 2:522
descriptions 3:22–3, 3:24
  definite 9:168, 9:169
doubt 3:125
dualism 3:138
formal logic
  speech relationship 9:168,
    9:169–70
Grice, H.P. 4:177
imagination 4:708
individuals 7:238
induction 4:752
Kant, I. 5:200
mass terms 6:170
meaning and understanding 6:229
metaphysics
  revisionary/descriptive 7:237
moral sentiments 6:550
ordinary language philosophy
  7:147, 7:152, 7:153
perception 7:299
performative theory of truth
  9:476–7, 9:478
persons
  as primitive concept 9:171–2
pragmatics 7:632
praise and blame 7:647
presupposition 7:673–4, 7:675
proper names 7:757
propositions 7:788
reference 8:164
speech acts 9:86
statements
  sentence distinction 7:787
substance 9:207–8, 9:211
testimony 9:314
transcendental arguments 9:454
truth conditions 9:170
Strawsonian presupposition 7:673–4
stream of consciousness
  existential phenomenological
    ontology (Ingarden, R.W.)
    4:790
  multiple-drafts model
    (Dennett, D.C.) 2:883
Streeten, Paul 3:44, 3:211
Streminger, Gerhard 4:562
Stremoukhoff, D. 9:32
Streng, F.J. 2:64, 2:80, 6:641
strength
  equality 3:393

Strenski, I. 3:263
Strickberger, M. 4:16
Striedter, J. 8:413–14
Strike, K. 3:240
Striker, G.
  Arcesilaus 1:354
  Carneades 2:220
  Hellenistic philosophy 4:337
  practical reason and ethics 7:619
Ströker, E. 4:588
Stroll, A. 7:147
Stromberg, R.N. 2:856
Strosberg, M. 6:264
Strotz, J. 9:133
Stroud, Barry
  bundle theory of mind 6:385
  conceptual analysis 2:521, 2:522
  contextualism
    epistemological 2:649–50
  doubt 3:125
  Hume, D. 3:383, 4:562
  Moore, G.E. 6:499
  Strawson, P.F. 9:174
  transcendental arguments 9:454
Stroumsa, C.G. 5:25
Stroumsa, Sarah
  al-Baghdadi 1:638
  Ibn ar-Rawandi 4:638
  al-Muqammas, D. †6:604–6
Stróżewski, Władysław 7:253, 7:487
structural ambiguity *see* scope,
  ambiguity of
structural-functionalism
  explanation in social science 3:815
  systems theory 9:254
structuralism **9:174–7**
see also neo-structuralism; post-
  structuralism
  African reconstructionist
    philosophy (Mudimbe, V.) 1:113
  anti-Platonist realism 8:122
  arithmetic 1:440
  art works
    ontology of 1:480
    type/token distinction 1:482–3
  classical 9:185–7
    social science 9:185–7
  Czech Republic, philosophy in
    2:767
  dialectical method (Hessen, S.I.)
    4:416
  functionalism relationship
    3:814–15
  global (Quine, W.V). 8:9–10
  hermeneutics (Ricoeur, P.)
    8:319–20

  as ideological restriction
    (Lyotard, J.-F.) 6:8
  influence on legal discourse 5:498
  Lévi-Strauss, C. 5:582, 5:583,
    5:584
  limitations (Foucault, M.) 7:597
  linguistic 9:174–5, 9:176, **9:177–81**
    Barthes, R. 1:656–7
    influence on Lévi-Strauss, C.
      5:583
    literary theory 9:181, 9:182
    Lyotard, J.-F. 6:8
    Moscow-Tartu school 6:583,
      6:584
    Saussure, F. de 8:481
    social science 9:184–5
    the symbolic (Lacan, J.) 5:337
  in literary theory 6:655, 9:175,
    9:181–4
    features 9:182
    history 9:181–2
    language usage 1:513
    Todorov, T. 9:425–6
  Marxism (Althusser, L.) 6:145
  mathematical (Benacerraf, P.)
    6:188
  method
    French anti-postmodernism
      7:593–4
    new 9:187–8
    psychoanalytic feminism 3:584,
      3:585
    Sartre, J.-P. 8:474
    social science 3:527–8, 7:600–1,
      9:184–9
    synchronic vs. diachronic analysis
      9:176
  Tel Quel school 9:292–3
structure
  glossary 5:809
*The Structure of Scientific
  Revolutions see* Kuhn, Thomas
  Samuel
Strugnell, A. 3:69
Strunk, O. 7:131
Struve, Pëtr B. 5:609, 8:770, 8:771
studia humanitatis
  humanism 4:528, 4:529
Stulmitz, J. 4:37
Stumme, J.R. 9:413
Stump, David J.
  Poincaré, J.H. †7:478–83
  scientific realism and antirealism
    8:584
  unity of science 9:532–3
Stump, Eleonore
  Aquinas, T. †1:326–50

atonement 1:541
Boethius, A.M.S. 1:813
divine simplicity 8:787
eternity †3:422–7
eternity of the world
    medieval views of 3:429
evil, problem of 3:472
hell 4:333
justification doctrine 5:168
Kilvington, R 5:245
logic
    medieval 5:758, 5:759
omniscience 7:112
perfect goodness 4:144
prayer 7:653
prophecy 7:771
religion
    history of philosophy of 8:247
    and morality 8:224
    philosophy of †8:248–50
sanctification 8:458
William of Champeaux 9:730
Štúr, L'udovít 8:812–13
Sturgeon, Nicholas L.
    Butler, J. 2:160
    naturalism in ethics †6:713–17
Sturm, Johan 8:53
Sturm und Drang 4:214
Sturrock, J. 1:516, 7:600
Sturt, H. 4:669
Sturtevant, A.H. 4:15
Sturtevant, W. 6:671
Styazhkin, N.I. 5:722, 5:729, 5:746
style
    art history 1:506
    artistic **1:505–9**
        definition 1:505–6
        expression 1:505–6, 1:507–8
        film aesthetics 3:673–5
        form 1:506–7
        history 1:506
        intention 1:513–15
        personality 1:508–9
        signature 1:507
    categories 1:508
    contemporary analysis 1:506–7
    determinist theories of change
        1:507–8
    formal elements 1:507
    Hegel, G.W.F. 1:506
    nature of 1:507
    rhetoric 1:506
    Romanticism 1:506
Styles, Scott C.
    Stair, J.D. †9:118–20

Suárez, Francisco 9:72, 9:77,
    9:189–96
    absolutism 1:30, 1:32
    applied ethics 1:325
    evil, problem of 3:469
    Latin America, colonial thought in
        5:422, 5:426
    law 9:192–3
    metaphysics 9:190–1
    Molinism 6:466, 9:189–90
    rational soul 9:191–2
    School of Sagres (Portugal) 2:8
    substance 9:211
    Thomism 9:382–3
Suarism 9:72
subconscious mind
    James, W. 5:62
Subitists 9:405–6
subject
    alterity
        postmodernism 1:187
    identity philosophy
        (Schelling, F.W.J. von)
        8:511–13, 8:515, 8:516
    imagery (Le Doeuff, M.) 5:477
    masculine
        Irigaray, L. critique 5:1
    object distinction
        phenomenology 7:343, 7:344,
        7:345–7
        Western poetry 1:69
    object unity (Marcuse, H.) 6:97–8
    postmodern critique of **9:196–201**
    predicate distinction
        (Strawson, P.F.) 9:170–1
    syntax 9:246, 9:247
    transcendental idealism
        (Schopenhauer, A.) 8:547,
        8:548–9
    verisimilitude (Lacoue-
        Labarthe, P.) 5:341
subjective colour 2:419–20, 2:421,
    2:424
    neurophysiology 2:422–3
subjective culture
    objective culture distinction
        (Simmel, G.) 8:779
subjective idealism *see* absolute
    idealism
subjectivism
    see also anti-subjectivism
    aesthetic
        beauty 1:681, 1:683
        art criticism 1:460, 1:463
        bodily sensations 1:793–4
    Cārvāka
        causation 2:251, 2:253

colour, theories of 2:428–9
critiques of
    Hägerström, A.A.T. 4:202
    Plekhanov, G.V. 7:453
ethical 9:580–1
    genetic arguments 3:474
individuality (Mikhailovskii, N.K.)
    6:355
innateness of ideas (Rosmini-
    Serbati, A.) 8:362
Lavrov, P.L. 5:436–7
libertarianism 5:619
objectivity 7:73–4
pleasure
    Cyrenaics 2:759–60
    Protagoras 7:790
values 9:582
subjectivity
    see also intersubjectivity;
    objectivity
    aesthetic 1:55, 1:56
        nature 6:734
    Chinese Marxism 6:133, 6:140
    free (Fichte, J.G.) 3:642
    goodness 4:132
    Hegel, G.W.F. 4:271–2
    imaginary (Lacan, J.) 5:336–7
    knowledge
        Bridgman, P.W. 2:18
        Lichtenberg, G.C. 5:623
    liberalism
        law and morality 5:439
    mental causation 6:310
    objectivity distinction
        Hegel, G.W.F. 4:263–4
        Nagel, T. 6:643–6
    Other relationship (Levinas, E.)
        5:580–1
    religious belief (Kierkegaard, S.)
        5:236, 5:240–2
    structuralism (Foucault, M.) 7:601
    the symbolic (Lacan, J.) 5:337
    transcendence of (Bataille, G.)
        1:660
subjunctive conditionals *see*
    counterfactual conditionals
sublimation
    moral life (Vysheslavtsev, B.P.)
        9:676
    symbolism (Freud, S.) 3:790
sublime, the **9:201–5**
    beauty
        Kant, I. 5:194
        Reid, T. 8:176–7
    nature 6:731, 6:732
    postmodernist interpretation
        (Lyotard, J.-F.) 6:9

power of (Burke, E.) 2:136,
2:137–8
Schiller, J.C.F. 8:525–6
subsistences
singularity of forms (Gilbert of
Poitiers) 4:69
substance **9:205–11**
see also matter; properties;
substance-pluralism
accidents
Duns Scotus, J. 3:154, 3:159
Godfrey of Fontaines 4:120–1
Aristotle 1:424, 5:687, 9:205–6,
9:210
categories 2:230
nature of 1:418–19, 1:422
primary form 1:422–3
primary-divine substance
relationship 1:424
Ash'ariyya–Mu'tazila comparison
1:520
atomism
Democritus 2:872–4
Vaiśeṣika 6:197, 6:198–9
Cartesian view
Leibniz, G.W. rejection 5:546,
5:555
category of
Nyāya-Vaiśeṣika ontology
7:60–1
Chinese philosophy *see ti*
conceptualism 9:205, 9:207–8
corporeal (Leibniz, G.W.) 5:555–6
divine (Aristotle) 1:424
dualism (Brown, T.) 2:27
essence distinction (Locke, J.)
5:665, 5:673–4
'everything in everything' doctrine
(Anaxagoras) 1:250–2
extension (Descartes, R.) 3:1–2,
3:14
feminist theology 3:623
forms (Ikhwan al-Safa') 4:686
human
Akan philosophical psychology
1:138–9
ideas (Locke, J.) 5:665, 5:672
immutability
Islamic fundamentalism 5:10
Indian conceptions of inherence
7:125–6
Indian conceptions of
inherence 7:124–5
Nyāya-Vaiśeṣika ontology
7:60–1
ontological categories 7:120–2
qualities 6:31

qualities 7:122–3
self-nature of 7:126
types 7:118–19
universals 9:545–6
indiscerpibility (More, H.) 6:578–9
indivisibility (Kant, I.) 5:181
infinite divisibility of
(McTaggart, J.M.E.) 6:26–7
inherence
Indian philosophy 7:124–6
interaction (Knutzen, M.) 5:288
Jainism 8:449
Jewish philosophy
Ibn Gabirol, S. 4:618–19
Ibn Tzaddik, J. 4:660
Leibniz, G.W.
Arnauld, A. critique 1:447
mass nouns 6:169–70
medieval doctrines of 6:273–4
mind–body problem
(Descartes, R.) 3:11
modal transmutations
(Conway, A.) 2:670
monads (Leibniz, G.W.) 5:547–8
nature of (Aristotle) 1:418–19,
1:422
ontological categories
Indian philosophy 7:120–2
particulars 7:235
primary
air as (Anaximenes) 1:259,
1:260, 1:261
divine substance relationship
(Aristotle) 1:424
form (Aristotle) 1:422–3
qualities
difference between (Madhva)
6:31
inherence
Indian philosophy 7:122–3
realism 9:208–9
reincarnation 8:183, 8:184
self-nature of
Indian philosophy 7:126
Spinozism (Régis, P.-S.) 8:165
successive states of
perception (Kant, I.) 5:187
types of
Indian philosophy 7:118–19
universals
Indian theories of 9:545–6
substance pluralism
critique by Spinoza B. de 9:93–5
substance-monism
Spinoza, B. de 9:93–5
substance-pluralism
Nyāya 6:197

Sāṅkhya-Yoga 6:197, 6:199–200
Vaiśeṣika 6:197, 6:198–9
substantia
Trinity 9:458–7
substantial form
natural philosophy, medieval
6:696–7
nature of
Aristotle 1:422–3
Richard of Middleton 8:310–11
unity of (Giles of Rome) 4:73–4
substantial motion
Mulla Sadra 6:596–7
substantialism
legal concepts 5:494–5
space 9:61–2
substitution
atonement 1:537, 1:539–40
substitution of identities, law of
4:807, 4:809
substitutional quantifiers 7:878–80
substitutional theory
paradoxes
Russell, B.A.W. 8:395
substitutivity *see* intersubstitutability
subsumptive model of moral
reasoning
logic of ethical discourse 5:762–3,
5:764
subversion
invention (Certeau, M. de) 2:268–9
succession
see also diadochai
teacher-pupil
ancient Greece 3:125–6
succession of forms theory
Burley, W. 2:141
succession principle
ordinal logics 7:141
Suchocki, Marjorie
feminist theology †3:621–5
Suchon, Gabrielle **9:211–13**
Suderman, J.M.
Campbell, G. †2:191–3
suffering **9:213–15**
Book of Job (Aquinas, T.)
1:329–30
Buddhism **9:215–19**
Ābhidharmika Schools 2:53,
2:54
attachment 2:90–1
canonical accounts 9:215–16
causation
Indian theories of 2:252
cessation of
nominalism 7:23
impermanence 6:592

Mādhyamika School 9:217
scholastic interpretation
9:216–17
Shintō comparison 8:750
Tsong kha pa Blo bzang grags
pa 9:488
Yogācāra School 9:217–18
divine (Bonhoeffer, D.) 1:835–6
evil, problem of
evidential argument 3:471
human condition
Jainism 5:50
human (Horkheimer, M.) 4:510
redemption (Shestov, L.) 8:743–4
suicide 9:226
sufficient reason, principle of
cosmological argument for the
existence of God 8:241
Democritus 2:874
Kant, I. critique 5:181
Leibniz, G.W. 5:545–6
Wolff, C. 9:781
Sufism
Aristotelianism (al-'Amiri) 1:207
four journeys (Mulla Sadra)
6:597–8
al-Ghazali 4:61–3, 4:65
Ibn Massara 4:629
Ibn Sab'in 4:646–7
Ibn Taymiyya critique of 4:655–6
'ilm al-kalam 5:30
influence on Jewish mysticism
Ibn Paquda 4:635
Kabbalah 5:174–5
Maimonides, A. 6:38–9
modern Islamic philosophy 5:20
mysticism 6:618, 6:619, 6:625–6
revelation (al-Ghazali) 4:66
science 8:564
Sugar, A. 9:353
Sugden, R. 7:834, 8:102, 9:705
Sugiyama, C. 8:822
al-Suhrawardi, Shihab al-Din Yahya
9:219–24
existence–quiddity relationship
6:596
Illuminationist philosophy 4:701,
4:703, 6:806, 9:219, 9:220–3
Ibn Kammuna 4:622
imaginal world 6:598
modern Islamic philosophy 5:16
mystical philosophy 6:617–18,
6:620, 9:219–23
Neoplatonism 6:805–6
suicide 9:224–30
Augustine 1:556
Durkheim, É. 1:694, 1:695, 3:176

euthanasia comparison 5:628
Jewish bioethics 1:777–8
legal punishment 9:228
Masaryk, T.G. 6:165
meaning of life 5:631
nihilism 7:3
offence
against nature 9:227
spiritual 9:225–6
Suika Shintōism
Yamazaki Ansai 2:552
Suits, B. 9:113, 9:116
Suklalji, P. 5:57
Suleiman, S.R. 9:293
Sullivan, A. 8:729
Sullivan, David
Lotze, Rudolph Hermann
†5:838–42
Sullivan, J.W.N. 6:615
Sullivan, M.W. 1:326
Sullivan, R.E. 8:891, 9:429
Sullivan, R.J. 3:231
Sulloway, Frank
psychoanalysis
methodological issues in
7:811–12, 7:814, 7:815, 7:817
Summa contra gentiles see Aquinas,
Thomas
Summa philosophiae see Pseudo-
Grosseteste
Summa theologiae see Aquinas,
Thomas
Summers, M. 3:818
Summers, R.S.
Fuller, L.L. 3:802
legal reasoning and interpretation
5:531
Pound, R. 7:610
Wróblewski, J. 9:798
summum bonum (highest good)
4:507–8, 9:47
see also telos
Sumner, B.H. 7:201
Sumner, Claude
African philosophy, Anglophone
1:107
Ethiopian philosophy †3:442–5
Sumner, L.W. 4:229, 8:331, 9:215
Sumner, W.G. 8:838
sun
pre-Columbian religions 5:429,
5:430
Sun Bin
Sunzi 9:230, 9:231
Sun Pin see Sun Bin
Sun Wu 9:230–1
Sun Yirang 5:696–7, 6:591

Sundaram, P.K. 5:285
Sundholm, G. 6:682
Sûngnang 2:107–8
Sungtaek Cho
Buddhism, Korea †2:106–18
sunnah Allah 2:243
Sunni Islam
see also Ash'ariyya
philosophy/religion
incompatibility 5:8
Sun-tzu see Sunzi
śūnyatā see emptiness
Sunzi (The Art of Warfare) 9:230–2
super-ego
see also ego; id
Freud, S. 3:791–2
supererogation 9:232–5
beneficence 4:343
superhuman see Übermensch
superimposition
Advaita Vedānta 4:435, 4:438
superiority theory
laughter 2:435
supernatural
see also magic; witchcraft
apparitions (More, H.) 6:580
in biblical explanation
(Strauss, D.K.) 9:164–5
grace 4:147–8
miracles 6:411–16
miracles (Arama, I.) 1:351
prophecy 7:767, 7:768, 7:769
religious experience (Oman, J.W.)
7:97
superorganisms
ecology 3:203
superposition
quantum mechanics 7:891–2
superstition
fatalism 3:564
'superstructuralism' 9:176
supersubstantivalism
relativity theory 8:198
supervaluational semantics
Fraassen, B.C. van 3:739, 8:646
supervenience 9:235–8
aesthetic realism 1:57–8
colour
on physical properties 2:430–1
composition
contrast with 9:236
dualism/reductionism 9:237–8
epistemic 3:719–21
formal foundationalism 3:719
ethics (Moore, G.E.) 6:496
holism in social science 4:484
materialism 6:175–6

of the mental **9:238–40**
mental causation 6:309–10
moral realism 6:536
psychophysical anomalism
  (Davidson, D.) 1:279
reductionism 8:147, 8:148
strong versus weak 9:237
varieties of 9:236–7
Suppe, Frederick
  Bridgman, P.W. †2:17–19
  models 6:446
  natural laws 5:475
  operationalism †7:131–6
  positivism in the social sciences
    7:561
  scientific theories †9:343–55
Suppes, Patrick
  causation 2:251
  definition 2:849
  explanation 3:525
  measurement, theory of †6:243–9
  models 6:446
  Montague, R.M. 6:485
  Nagel, E. 6:643
  scientific theories 9:353, 9:354–5
supplemented equivalence theory
  indicative conditionals 4:742
supposition theory 5:398–9
  Buridan, J. 2:132
  medieval logic 5:747, 5:749,
    5:753–4
  natural philosophy 6:701–2
  realism 2:20
  Renaissance 5:411
  William of Sherwood 9:748–9
supraclassicality
  non-monotonic logic 7:33
Supracosmic Principle 5:836
surjection
  glossary 5:809
Surma, S.J. 5:574, 7:499–500
surplus
  general economy (Bataille, G.)
    1:660
surprise examination paradox 7:211,
  7:213
surrogacy 8:276, 8:277–9
Surtz, E.L. 2:464
surveys
  social
    experiments in social science
      3:518–19
survival value
  evolutionary theory
    teleology 8:673
Susiluoto, I. 1:820
Suso, Henry **9:240–1**

suspicion
  hermeneutics of 4:393
sustainability
  green political philosophy 4:160
Suszko, R. 7:496
Sutherland, K. 8:821
Sutherland, N.S. 7:827, 7:829
Sutherland, R.D. 3:109
Sutlić, Vanja 9:52, 9:55
suum 7:94
Suun *see* Tonghak
Suvchinskii, Pëtr Petrovich 3:454
Suzuki, D.T. 5:293, 7:399
Suzuki, Yoshijirō 9:822
Svabhāva 9:404
Svartvik, J. 6:170
Svarvervud, R. 5:103
Svātantrika School of Buddhism
  2:60, 2:61, 9:403–4
Svatoš, M. 2:440
Svenneby, E. 8:491
Svetambara Jainism *see* Jaina
  philosophy
Svozil, K. 2:482
Swaaningen, R. van 2:710
Swabey, M. 4:567
Swain, Marshall
  internalism–externalism
    distinction 4:826
  justification 3:383
  knowledge
    causal theory of †5:263–6
    defeasibility theory of 3:383,
      †5:276–80
Swanson, P. 2:75, 2:92, 9:861
Swanton, C. 3:757, 6:533
Swartz, R.J. 7:293, 8:698
Swedberg, Richard
  Schumpeter, J.A. †8:554–6
Sweden 8:485–6
  Hägerström, A.A.T. **4:202–4**
  Linnaeus, C. von **5:646–50**
  Nygren, A. **7:68–9**
  Olivecrona, K. **7:94–5**
  Swedenborg, E. **9:241–3**
Swedenborg, Emanuel **9:241–3**
Sweeney, L. 5:598
Sweet, W. 1:848
Swerdlow, N.M. 2:672
Swiderski, E. 6:160
Swift, A. 2:471
Swift, Jonathan 3:332
Swijtink, Zeno
  Beth's theorem and Craig's
    interpolation theorem †1:760–4
Swinburne, Richard
  atheism 1:534

atonement 1:541
dualism 3:138
eschatology 3:417
evil, problem of 3:472
faith 3:543, 3:544
God
  arguments for the existence of
    4:93, 6:709, 8:242–3
  probabilistic 9:302
God, concepts of 4:102
hell 4:333
induction 4:752
miracles 6:416
monotheism 6:481, 6:483
mysticism 6:634, 8:252
natural theology 6:713
omnipresence 7:104, 7:107
original guilt 8:795, 8:796
prayer 7:653
religion
  and epistemology 8:218
  history of philosophy of 8:247
  religious experience 8:255
revelation †8:296–300
soul †9:44–8
Tennant, F.R. 9:303
theological virtues 9:331
Trinity 9:457, 9:458–9, 9:461
Swineshead, Richard 7:179–80
Swineshead, Roger 5:757, 7:182
Switzerland
  Barth, K. **1:651–6**
  Bonnet, C. **1:838–40**
  Brunner, E. **2:30–4**
  Constant de Rebecque, H.-B.
    2:615–18
  Einstein, A. **3:254–8**
  Jung, C.G. **5:132–5**
  Le Clerc, J. **5:475–6**
  Paracelsus **7:205–8**
  Piaget, J. **7:383–6**
  Rousseau, J.-J. **8:367–77**
  Saussure, F. de **8:479–82**
Swoboda, Philip
  Frank, S.L. †3:726–30
Swoboda, W. 1:595
Swoyer, C. 5:475
syāt (viewpoint) 6:78
Sydenham, Thomas 6:265, 6:269
Sykes, S. 1:655–6
Sylla, Edith
  Bradwardine, T. †1:863–7
  Burley, W. †2:140–4
  Heytesbury, W. 4:421
  medieval natural philosophy
    †6:690–707
  Oresme, N. 7:157

Oxford Calculators †7:179–83
syllogism
  Aristotelianism
    Islamic philosophy 5:706,
      5:710–11
  Aristotle 5:688–9, 5:691–2
    formal logic 3:702, 5:781–2
  assent
    Islamic philosophy 5:709
  categorical
    demonstrative method
      (Wolff, C.) 9:781
  categorical 5:809
  critique of
    Bacon, F. 1:628
  De Morgan, A. 2:813, 2:814
  definition of (Philoponus) 7:372
  demonstrative
    scientific knowledge 3:372,
      3:373–4
  disjunctive 5:809
  distributed terms 5:801–2
  eighteenth century 5:719
  figures 5:802
  Greek 9:572
  hypothetical
    counterfactual conditionals
      2:686–7
  hypothetical 5:809–10
  inferential logic
    Stoicism 9:150–1
  intelligibles (Ibn Sina) 4:649
  Islamic philosophy 4:649, 4:652,
    5:706, 5:709, 5:710–11
    Aristotelianism 5:706, 5:710–11
    assent 5:709
    Ibn Sina 4:649, 4:652
  logical laws 5:786
  medieval logic 5:750–2
  modal 5:810
  momentariness
    Buddhist doctrine of 6:472
  perfect 5:751
  poetic language (Ibn Sina) 4:652
  practical
    Aristotelian 8:91
  Renaissance logic 5:771
  seventeenth century logic 5:717
  Stoics 5:690–1
  Theophrastus 5:689–90
  Venn, J. 9:594–5
Sylvan, Richard 1:584, 3:336, 8:204
Sylvester, Francis, of Ferrara see
  Silvestri, Francesco
Sylvester, R.P. 6:499
the symbolic
  semiology (Kristeva, J.) 5:307

structuralist linguistics (Lacan, J.)
  5:337
symbolic forms
  Cassirer, E. 2:223–5
symbolic interactionism 9:243–5
  language matrix 9:243–4
  reflexivity 9:244
  self 9:243, 9:244
  society 9:244–5
symbolic logic see mathematical logic
symbolic representations
  child development
    pre-operational stages
      (Piaget, J.) 7:383
symbolic utility
  Nozick, R. 7:47
symbolism
  alchemy 1:156
  anthropological
    African traditional religions
      1:117, 1:118
  art works (Langer, S.K.K.)
    5:354–5
  Christianity (Tillich, P.) 9:411
  erotic art 3:408
  hermeneutics
    biblical 4:393
  Kant, I. (Helmholtz, H. von) 4:339
  letters
    Kabbalah 5:173
  mysticism (Bonaventure) 1:830
  psychoanalysis (Lacan, J.) 7:821
  rationality and cultural relativism
    8:84–5
  religious language
    Ibn Tufayl 4:657, 4:658–9
    Tillich, P. 9:409–11
  Russian
    Nietzscheanism 6:862–3
    Russian religious-philosophical
      Renaissance 8:422, 8:423,
      8:425–6
symbolisticism
  religious language 8:258
symbols
  see also signs
  aesthetics 4:137–8
  computer
    meaning acquisition 6:392
  Goodman, N. 4:135–6, 4:138–9
  incomplete (Russell, B.A.W.)
    8:397–8
  interpretation of (Peirce, C.S.)
    7:278–9
  logical analysis (Langer, S.K.K.)
    5:354

media culture (Baudrillard, J.)
  1:662–3
pictorial depiction 2:893–4
psychoanalysis (Freud, S.) 3:790
reference 4:138
semiology dialectic (Kristeva, J.)
  5:305–6
symmetry
  conservation principles 2:607
sympathy
  see also compassion
  medicine (Digby, K.) 3:73
  moral motivation 6:525–6
  moral obligations (Hume, D.)
    6:546–7
  morality
    Christian view 6:561–2
  passions (Hume, D.) 4:550–1
  Scheler, M.F. 8:504, 8:507
  Schopenhauer, A. 8:546, 8:552
  social interaction (Smith, A.)
    8:815, 8:818
symptom interpretation
  psychoanalysis
    methodological issues in
      7:813–14
Synan, E.A. 1:835, 2:294, 3:174
syncategorematic terms
  see also categorematic terms
  adverbs 1:46
  categorematic terms distinction
    7:19
  conceptual analysis 2:519
  Locke, J. 5:375
  medieval logic 5:747, 5:754–5
    sophistimata 5:749
  Oxford Calculators 7:181
  William of Sherwood 9:749
synchronic analysis
  structuralism 9:176
synchronicity
  Jung, C.G. 5:133–4
synchrony
  Lévi-Strauss, C. 5:584
syncretism
  Buddhism/Shintō 8:750
synderesis 2:580
syndicalism
  revolutionary militancy
    Sorel, G. 6:143
synechism
  Peirce, C.S. 7:270, 7:280
synecholgy
  Herbart, J.F. 4:370
Synesius 4:597
Synge, Edward 6:468, 6:469

synonymy
 intensional logic 2:212, 4:810
 logical truths (Quine, W.V.)
  8:10–11
syntactic consequence
 model theory 6:438–9
syntactic entities
 propositional attitudes 7:782
syntax **9:246–53**
 see also grammar
 ambiguity 1:198–9, 1:200
 anaphora 1:239–40
 binding theory
  anaphoric expressions 1:239–40
 Boethius of Dacia 1:814–15
 categories 9:247–8
  Ajdukiewicz, K. 1:137
  Chomsky, N. 5:408
 compositionality 2:476–7
 computers
  Chinese room argument 2:328
  Turing test critique 9:494
 Encyclopedists, medieval 3:305,
  3:307
 logic distinction (Kilwardby, R.)
  5:246–7
 logical constants 5:779–80
 meaning 9:246–7
 medieval theories of language
  5:402
  Marsilius of Inghen 6:111
 metalanguage (Carnap, R.)
  2:210–12
 modism 5:393, 5:397, 5:402
 natural language (Chomsky, N.)
  8:649

paronymy (Anselm of Canterbury)
 1:289–90
predication **7:665–7**
Priscian 5:389
semantic interpretation
 computational theories of mind
  6:392
semantics relation 6:392
sense (Dummett, M.A.E.) 3:150
structuralist literary theory
 (Todorov, T.) 9:426
transformational (Chomsky, N.)
 2:337
truth theories 6:221
synteresis see synderesis
synthesis
 explanation (Ravaisson-
  Mollien, F.) 8:104, 8:105
 reality (Krause, K.) 5:299
synthetic a priori knowledge 4:665,
 5:183–4
synthetic truth
 conservation laws (Meyerson, É.)
  6:349, 6:350–49
synthetic–analytic distinction
 Kant, I. 1:234
Sypnowich, C. 8:886
Syria
 Antiochus **1:299–301**
 Damascius **2:771–2**
 al-Farabi **3:554–8**
 Ibn Taymiyya **4:655–6**
 John of Damascus **5:105–6**
 Lucian **5:853–4**
 al-Muqammas, Daud **6:604–6**
 Nemesius **6:763–4**
 Numenius **7:54–6**

Posidonius **7:555–8**
Syriac
 Greek translations to 4:156
Syrianus 4:155–6
systematic ambiguity of existence *see*
 tashkik al-wujud
systematic philosophy
 Rorty, R. 7:599–600
systematic realism
 Anderson, J. 1:266–7
Systematics *see* Philippo-Ramist
 school of logic
systems
 logic of (Comte, A.) 2:501–2
 of meaning 7:588, 7:589
 physical
  determinism 3:36–7
systems theory
 functionalism relationship
  3:814–15
 Keckermann, B. 5:225
 in social science **9:253–6**
Szabó, A. 4:34
Szabó, Zoltán Gendler
 language
  early modern philosophy of
   †5:371–9
Szaniawski, K. 5:295, 7:489, 9:353–4
Szasz, K. 6:314
Szczepańska, A. 4:792
Szczerba, L.W. 7:877, 9:264–5
Szczucki, L. 7:488, 7:489
Szkice filozoficzne Romanowi
 Ingardenowi w darze 4:792
Sznajder, M. 3:563
Sztompka, P. 9:7
Szumilewicz-Lachman, I. 7:500

T

Ta Hsüeh see Daxue
Tabarroni, A. 3:174, 5:758
Taber, John A.
  duty and virtue
    Indian conceptions of †3:183–7
  Mīmāṃsā †6:376–81
  universals
    Indian theories of †9:544–8
tableau systems **6:676–82**
taboos
  African ethical systems 3:431
tabula rasa
  Bonaventure 1:832
Tachau, K.H.
  Aureol, P. 1:566
  Crathorn, W. 2:694
  Gregory of Rimini 4:172
  John of Mirecourt 5:113
  natural philosophy
    medieval 6:707
  William of Ockham 9:748
  Wodeham, A. 9:776
Tachibana no Toshitsuna 1:81
Tachikawa, M. 9:514
tacit knowledge
  mental imagery 4:705
  Polanyi, M. 7:489, 7:490–1
Tae-Hung, Ha 2:118
Taftazani, A. 4:647, 6:620
Tager-Flusberg, H. 6:389
Tagliacozzo, G. 9:606
Tagore, Debendranath 2:6
Tagore, Rabindranath **9:257–8**
Tahafut al-falasifa (The Incoherence
  of the Philosophers) *see*
  (al-)Ghazali
Tahafut al-tahafut (The Incoherence
  of the Incoherence) *see* Ibn Rushd
Tai Chen *see* Dai Zhen
Tai xuan jing (Canon of Supreme
  Mercy) *see* Yang Xiong
taiji (Supreme Ultimate) 6:768, 6:770,
  9:862
Taine, Hippolyte-Adolphe **9:258–60**
Taira, Satō 5:716
Tait, A.L. 8:409
Tait, P.G. 6:259
Tait, W.W. 2:639, 4:772, 7:752
Tajfel, H. 1:695–6

Takakusu, M. 8:467
Takasaki, J. 2:75, 9:219
Takeuchi Yoshinori 5:324, 5:330
Takeuti, G. 3:706, 4:117
Talgyurwa School Prāsaṅgika School
Taliaferro, C. 8:250
Tallon, A. 8:39
Talmon, Jacob 3:316
Talmud
  halakhah 4:206
  philosophy relationship 2:861
  providence 7:797–8
  Rabbinic theology 9:333–6
  scholarship 9:26
  suicide 9:224–5
Talon, H. 5:470
Talon, Omer 8:502
Tamás, G.M. 4:572
Tamayo Herrera, José 7:350, 7:352–0
Tambiah, S.J. 8:86
Tamburrini, Guglielmo
  Turing machines †9:495–9
Taminiaux, J. 4:323, 4:482
Tamir, Y. 6:661–2
Tanabe Hajime **9:261–2**
  Kyoto School 5:78, 5:79, 5:323–9
  logic 5:715, 5:716
Tanahashi, Kazuaki 3:111
Tang, C. 9:857
Tanizaki Jun'ichirō 1:89, 1:90–1,
  5:659
Tankó, B. 4:572–3
Tannen, D. 5:367–8
Tanner, A. 6:671
Tanner, Michael
  aesthetics and ethics †1:65–8
  art and morality †1:452–6
  music
    aesthetics of 6:615
  opera
    aesthetics of †7:128–31
Tannery, P. 4:353–4, 7:51, 9:653–4
Tannsjo, T. 2:614–15
Tantra
  Āryan tradition
    Tsong kha pa Blo bzang grags
      pa 9:487, 9:488, 9:489–90
  Hindu
    Abhinavagupta 1:17–18

    language 5:381
  voidness
    Jo-nang-pa School 9:403
Tantrism *see* Tantra
tao see dao
Tao Qian 1:70
Tao Te Ching see Daodejing
Taoism *see* Daoism
Tappenden, J. 3:772, 3:778
Tarán, L. 4:369
Tarasti, E. 6:614, 8:679
Tardieu, M. 8:791
Tarentum
  Archytas **1:367–9**
Tarkatīrtha, V. 3:827
Tarrant, H. 7:363, 7:429
Tarski, Alfred **9:262–5**
  see also Banach-Tarski paradox;
    Tarskian paradigm; Tarski's
    definition of truth
  Beth's theorem and Craig's
    interpolation theorem 1:761,
    1:763
  Bolzano, B. 1:827
  consequence 2:601–2, 2:603
  definition of truth 2:848, 2:849,
    9:265–9
  formal languages and systems
    3:706
  geometry 4:34
  infinitary logic 4:772
  intuitionism 4:850
  logic
    constants 5:777–8, 5:781
    early twentieth century 5:738
    forms 5:785
    laws 5:786, 5:789
    modal 6:433
    non-monotonic 7:34–5
    Polish 7:494–5, 7:498, 7:500
      axiom of choice 7:495
      Leśniewski, S. 7:494
      post-war influence 7:496
  Löwenheim-Skolem theorem and
    non-standard models 5:851
  meaning and verification 6:236
  models 6:437, 6:441, 6:442, 6:446
  non-constructive rules of inference
    7:30

predicate calculus 7:665
quantifiers 7:871, 7:873
scientific theories 9:353
semantic paradoxes and theories
    of truth 8:643, 8:648
    metalanguage 8:642, 8:643,
    8:644
truth theory (Davidson, D.) 8:31–2
truth-functional contexts 6:429
use/mention distinction 9:551
Tarskian paradigm
    logical constants 5:776–7
Tarski's definition of truth **9:265–9**
    model theory 6:440–1
Tartu School *see* Moscow-Tartu
    School
Tasan *see* Chông Yagyong
tasawwur (conceptualization)
    3:384–5, 5:708–9
Taschek, W. 7:757
tasdiq (assent)
    conceptualization distinction
    5:708–9
    to knowledge 3:384–5
    syllogistic theory 5:710, 5:711
tashkik al-wujud (gradation of being)
    Shah Wali Allah 8:734
tashkik al-wujud (systematic
    ambiguity of existence)
    Mulla Sadra 6:596, 6:597
Tasioulas, John
    justice, equity and law †5:147–53
Tassin, E. 7:254
Tasso, Torquato 9:449
taste
    aesthetic 1:55–7
        Alison, A. 1:185–6
        Gerard, A. 4:36
    artistic 1:505, **1:509–13**
        aesthetics 1:60, 1:511
        Hume, D. 1:510–11
        Kant, I. 1:511
        Sibley, F. 1:511
        definition 1:509–10
        judgments of 1:511–12, 5:193
        Kant, I. 5:193
    literary
        Blair, H. 1:782
        Reid, T. 8:176–7
Tatacharya, N.S.R. 3:846
Tatacharya, Ramanuja 3:412–13
Tatakis, B.N. 2:165
Tate, W.R. 4:395
Tathāgatagarbha
    Huayan Buddhism 3:568–9
    Yogācāra Buddhism 2:66, 2:83–4

Tathāgatas
    suffering
        Buddhist views of origination of
        9:216
Tatia, N. 5:57
Taton, R. 3:133
Tatum, J. 9:814
Tatz, M. 2:75
Taub, Liba
    Eudoxus †3:452–3
    Ptolemy 7:832
Tauler, John **9:269–71**
Tauscher, H. 9:490
tautologies
    constructivism (Lorenzen, P.)
    5:827
    conventionalism (Wittgenstein, L.)
    6:748
    evolutionary theory 3:480–1
    glossary 5:810
    mathematical propositions
        (Ramsey, F.P.) 8:45
    picture theory (Wittgenstein, L.)
    9:759–60
Tavard, G.H. 9:713
Tavares, S. 2:408
Tavuzzi, Michael
    Cajetan 2:175
    Capreolus, J. †2:200–2
    Pomponazzi, P. 7:532
    Silvestri, F. †8:776–8
al-tawahhud see solitude
al-Tawhidi, Abu Hayyan **9:271–2**
    al-Farabi 3:557
    al-Sijistani 8:774, 8:776
Tawney, R.H. 4:234
taxonomy **9:272–6**
    see also classification; species
    evolution 2:796–7
Tay, A. 5:454
Taylor, A.E. 1:863
Taylor, Barry
    Dummett, M.A.E. †3:149–53
Taylor, C.C.W.
    Democritus †2:872–8
    epistemology 3:383
    eudaimonia †3:450–2
    Eudoxus 3:453
    hedonism 4:259
    Leucippus †5:578–9
    pleasure 7:451
Taylor, Charles **9:276–9**
    axiology 1:611, 1:612
    community and
        communitarianism 2:471
    concrete identity 6:574–5
    culture 2:750

Enlightenment, continental 3:316
German idealism 4:45
Hegel, G.W.F. 4:279
history
    philosophy of 4:457, 4:459
libertarianism 5:619
MacIntyre, A. 6:24
moral agents 6:500, 6:504
multiculturalism 6:602
nature and convention 6:737
neutrality
    political 6:820, 6:821
obligation
    political 7:80
postmodernism and political
    philosophy 7:592
power 7:613
public interest 7:835
self-realization 8:635
Shaftesbury, Third Earl of 8:732
social science
    holism and individualism 4:488
    methodology of 8:868
teleology 9:297
tradition and traditionalism 9:447
Taylor, F.K. 6:269
Taylor, G. 6:550, 6:571
Taylor, Harriet 3:616, 3:620, **9:279–80**
Taylor, Isaac 3:332
Taylor, Jacqueline A.
    moral sense theories †6:545–8
Taylor, Jeremy 3:332
Taylor, John R. 6:249
Taylor, Kenneth A.
    propositional attitude statements
    †7:771–9
Taylor, Mark C. 7:585, 7:586
Taylor, Michael 2:389, 8:75, 9:89
Taylor, Paul
    art and truth †1:456–9
    artist's intention †1:513–16
Taylor, P.W.
    agricultural ethics 1:126, 1:128
    ecological philosophy 3:202
    moral standing 6:555
Taylor, R.
    Alexander of Aphrodisias 1:176
    fatalism 3:564
Taylor, R.C.
    Liber de causis 5:598
Taylor, Richard
    meaning of life 5:631, 5:633
Taylor, S. 6:728
Taylor series 1:217
Taylor, V. 1:541
T-biconditional 9:265–6
te see de

teaching
 see also education
 ancient Greece
  teacher-pupil succession
   3:125–6
 educational concepts 3:232
techné
 existential anxiety 6:358
technocracy
 theory/practice distinction 4:194
technology **9:284–8**
 see also computer science;
 computers; engineering ethics;
 information technology
 artifacts 9:285
 autonomy of 9:286–7
 change 9:286–7
 critical theory 2:723
 ethics **9:280–4**
  Anglo-American tradition
   9:280, 9:282–3
  Continental tradition 9:280,
   9:281–2
 feminist approaches 3:865–6
 green political philosophy 4:161
 as knowledge 9:285–6
 Losev, A.F. critique 5:830–1
 medical ethics 6:260–1
 nihilism
  Heidegger, M. 4:317
 privacy 7:691
 transfer of 3:102
Tedlock, B. 6:671
Tedlock, D. 6:671
Teetaert, A. 1:566, 7:269
Teeuwen, P. 2:887
Teichgraeber, R.F. 8:822
Teichmann, Jenny 1:282
Teilhard de Chardin, Pierre 8:249,
 9:288–91
 creation doctrine 2:699
 optimism 9:289–90
 phenomenology 9:289
tektology
 organizational science 1:818
Tel Quel school **9:291–4**
teleological argument *see* God,
 existence of
teleological ethics **9:294–5**
 see also consequentialism;
 hedonism; perfectionism;
 utilitarianism
 negative duties 3:179
 practical reason 7:614
 virtues
  Aristotle 9:627
teleological semantics **8:672–5**

teleology **9:295–7**
 see also teleological ethics
 autonomy
  Kant, I. 5:194–5
 biology 8:862–3
 creation
  Jewish philosophy 4:48
 divine
  Jewish philosophy 5:309
 final cause 3:802
 justice 5:142, 5:143
 mechanism 9:161–2
 morality
  Mill, J.S. 6:372
 nature 3:833
 Naturphilosophie (Kant, I.) 6:737
 processes 7:721
 social science 3:486
 technology 9:285
 theosophy 9:364–5
telepathy
 paranormal phenomena 7:221
Teles 2:756
Telesio, Bernardino **9:297–300**
 Campanella, T. 2:187
Telfer, Elizabeth 3:796, 3:797, 8:285,
 8:286
Telfer, W. 6:764
Teller, P.
 parapsychology 7:227
Teller, Paul
 field theory, quantum †3:670–3
telos (highest goal)
 Alexandrian Platonism 7:426
 Carneades 2:217
 Stoicism 9:155–6
Temesvári, Pelbárt 4:568
Temkin, O. 3:835
Tempels, Placide
 African philosophy 1:107
  Bantu Philosophy 1:110, 1:111,
   1:116
 ethnophilosophy 3:449
temperance
 self-control 8:612
Tempier, Bishop Étienne
 Paris condemnations
  Aristotelianism 1:400–1
  Averroism 4:159
  Boethius of Dacia 1:813
  Giles of Rome 4:73
  natural philosophy 6:700
  Siger of Brabant 8:764
Temple, William **9:300–1**
Templeton, A. 9:81

temporal anaphora
 Discourse Representation Theory
  3:94–5, 3:97
temporal duration
 relativity theory 8:193–4
temporal judgment
 Kant, I. 5:187
temporal logic **9:303–7**
 see also tense
 conditionals (Diodorus Cronus)
  3:83, 3:84–5
 master argument (Diodorus
  Cronus) 3:84, 3:85–6
 possible worlds semantics 8:665
 Prior, A.N. 7:688
temporal parts theory
 continuants 2:653–4
temporality
 see also time
 biblical hermeneutics
  Rabbinic theology 9:335
 eternity
  Jewish philosophy relationship
   4:48
 eternity relationship 3:422–3
 human 3:495
  Dasein 4:307, 4:309, 4:310–11
 infinity 6:293, 6:294
 literary genres 1:643–4
 omniscience 3:425
 paradoxes
  relativity theory 8:193–4
 phenomenological being 4:790
 religious statements 8:258
 revelation
  Jewish philosophy 8:359–60
temptations
 inner life
  moral agents 6:501–2
Ten, C.L. 6:375
Ten Eyck Perry, H. 2:263
'ten mindsets'
 Kūkai 5:319
Ten Modes of Scepticism 7:850–1
 Aenesidemus 1:50–1
 Agrippa 1:129
Tendai Buddhism
 see also Lotus Sūtra; Tiantai
 buddhahood 2:102
 enlightenment 3:109
 Saichō 5:71
Tennant, Frederick Robert **9:301–3**
 religion, history of philosophy of
  8:247
Tennant, N. 4:863, 7:665
Tennyson, G.B. 2:206
Tenorth, H.-E. 6:792

tense
   see also temporal logic; tense logic
   Discourse Representation Theory
      3:94–5
   indexicality 2:878
   language
      temporality 9:413–14
   Montague Grammar 3:92
   time
      theory of 2:653
         continuants 2:653–4
tense logic 7:687, 7:688, **9:303–7**
Tenth Intellect
   see also Active Intellect
   al-Farabi 3:557
Terdiman, R. 2:269
Teresa of Avila 6:625, 7:653
terminism
   logic
      adverbs 1:46
      Buridan, J. 2:132
terminology
   development of
      scientific methods 8:579–80
   logical 5:795–811
   mathematical 5:795–811
   technical
      ordinary language philosophy
         7:149, 7:150–1
terms
   coreferring see intersubstitutability
   general
      free logics 3:742–3
   logical see logical constants
   logico-linguistic signs 6:54
   William of Ockham 9:739–40
Ternero, E. 4:630
Terrace, Herbert S. 1:271, 1:273
Terras, Victor
   Belinskii, V.G. †1:709–12
   Schellingianism †8:520–2
Terrasson, Jean 3:251, 3:253, 3:254
terror
   the sublime 9:202
Tersteegen, Gerard 7:395
Tertullian, Quintus Septimus Florens
   9:307–9
   materialistic theology 7:257
   omnipresence 7:107
   religious belief 8:245
   resurrection 8:296
   satisfaction doctrine 1:538
   supererogation 9:232, 9:235
   Trinity 9:457–8, 9:461
   wisdom 9:755
Tessier, G. 5:113
Tessitore, F. 9:606

testability
   social sciences 8:860–1
   theoretical/epistemic virtues 9:341
testimony **9:309–14**
   credulity (Hume, D.) 4:548
   epistemology 3:363
      autonomy 9:310–12
      empiricist 3:301–2
      feminist 3:601
      justification 5:164
      social 8:828–30
   Indian philosophy **9:315–19**
      conditions of understanding
         9:316–17
      Hinduism 3:860, 4:436, 7:63–4,
         8:465
      sentential meaning 9:315–16
      truth and falsity 9:317–18
   moral judgment 8:177
   natural theology 6:710
   as pramāṇa
      Nyāya-Vaiśeṣika 7:63–4
   reductionism 9:310–12
   reliability of
      inductive inference 4:756
   Sānkhya 8:465
   verbal
      as pramāṇa 7:63–4
   verification 9:312
Tetens, Johann Nicolaus **9:319–22**
   cognition 9:320–1
   transcendentalism 9:320
Tetragrammaton
   emanation
      Kabbalah 4:397, 4:398
tetraktys
   numerology
      Pythagoreanism 7:858
Teubner, G. 2:720
textual analysis 1:502–3
   Barthes, R. 1:657
   Jewish philosophy
      Averroism 1:599
      Jewish Enlightenment 3:321
      midrash 6:353–4
      medieval scholastic method
         6:269–70, 6:272
   Ricouer, P. 8:320
   underdetermination
      Rabbinic theology 9:335–6
Thagard, P.R. 1:492, 9:343
Thaiss, L. 6:388, 6:389
Thakur, A.L. 7:67
Thaler, B. 9:786
Thales 1:262, 1:263, **9:322–4**
   Anaximander 1:257, 1:259

Egyptian influence on ancient
   Greek thought 3:251
Presocratic philosophy 7:671–2
Thal-'gyur-ba School see Prāsaṅgika
Thapar, R. 7:525
Tharp, L. 5:781
'that-which-is' see being
Thayer, H.S. 7:640
theatre
   see also Nō
      nōh
         kokoro 5:292
Thébaud, J.-L. 7:592
Theerman, P. 6:828
Theiler, W. 7:558
theism
   see also agnosticism; atheism;
      evidentialism; God; religious belief
   Christian (Lewis, C.S.) 5:589–90
   classical 4:98–100
      immutability 4:710–11
      omnipotence 7:101–2
      process theism comparison
         7:716, 7:717–19
   creation
      Jewish philosophy 8:436–7
   di-polar
      Holocaust 4:498
   evil, problem of 3:466–7
   idealism relationship 2:67
   Indian
      Brahman 2:4
      monism 6:478–9
   natural philosophy (Cudworth, R.)
      2:739–41
   personalism 7:317
   philosophy relationship 8:248–9
   prayer 7:651
   sacramentality of the universe
      8:444–5
   Supracosmic principle
      (Lossky, N.O.) 5:833, 5:835–6
   Uddyotakara 9:514
   universality of 1:532
   Vedānta 9:590, 9:591–2
   will to truth 6:852
thematic adverbs 1:47–9
thematic unity
   Baumgarten, A.G. 1:671
Themistius **9:324–6**
theocentrism
   Philo of Alexandria 7:359
theocracy
   free
      triune authority 9:30
theodicy
   see also evil, problem of

Abelard, P. 1:13–14
definition of 7:651
Helmont, F.M. van 4:341
karma
    Japanese Buddhism 2:104–5
Leibniz, G.W. 5:545
    Bayle debate 1:675–6
Malebranche, N. 6:56–7, 6:63–4
    Bayle debate 1:672, 1:674–5
    critiques of
        Arnauld, A. 1:446–7
        Leibniz G.W. 6:64
natural theology 6:711
providence 9:659–61
religious experience 3:680–1
Theodore of Antioch 5:22
Theodorians
eudomonism
    Cyrenaics 2:760, 2:762–3
Theodulf of Orleans 2:223
theogony
    Orphism 7:163–4
Theologia see Abelard, Peter
theological discourse
    transpositions
        Gilbert of Poitiers 4:70–1
theological materialism
    Tertullian, Q.S.F. 9:308
theological virtues **9:326–31**
    faith 9:326, 9:327–9
    hope 9:326, 9:327, 9:329–30
    love 9:326, 9:327, 9:329–30
theology
    see also feminist theology; negative
        theology; process theology;
        religion; theism
    Abelard, P. 1:9
    agnosticism 7:788–9, 7:790
    anthropological 2:30, 2:31–2
    Aristotelianism 6:751
    Aristotle 1:424
    Boyle, R. 1:855
    Cartesianism 8:342
    casuistry 2:227–8
    Christianity
        Nygren, A. 7:67–8
        Philoponus 7:374–6
        right and good 8:323–4
    civic 9:428
    clarificatory 6:711–12
    common sense 7:168–9
    concordism (Pico della
        Mirandola, G.) 7:386, 7:387,
        7:388–90
    covenant
        political philosophy 7:510–11

of crisis
    Brunner, E. 2:30–1
critical realism 5:824–5
critiques of
    Bauer, B. 1:664
    Kant, I. 5:189
of the cross
    Bultmann, R. 2:129
cultural context 9:370
'depth'
    Judaism 4:411
Duhem, P.M.M. 3:144–5
eristic 2:31
eschatological (Bultmann, R.)
    2:129
essence–energy relations 5:829–30
existentialist **3:505–9**, 5:81
faith (Luther, M.) 6:1, 6:2
first-cause 4:95–6
free choice (Dostoevskii, F.M.)
    3:116
Hindu Tantra 1:17–18
human condition (Pascal, B.)
    7:241, 7:244–5
of humility
    Luther, M. 6:1–2
irenicism 6:326
Islamic **5:25–31**
    see also 'ilm al-kalam
    fundamentalism 5:9–5:12
    influence on Jewish philosophy
        6:604–5
    philosophy relationship 5:14–15
        Ibn al-'Arabi 4:602–3
        Ibn Rushd 4:642, 4:643
        al-Razi, Fakhr al-Din
            8:112–13
liberal 8:232
liberation **5:613–17**
    Latin American literature 5:655
Lutheran
    forensic justification 6:289
medieval philosophy 6:269, 6:271,
    6:272, 6:275–6
    political 7:508–9
method (Luther, M.) 6:3
natural **6:707–13**
    Aristotle 6:708
    Brunner, E. 2:31
    Cicero, M.T. 2:357–8
    Clarke, S. 2:378
    critiques of 6:710–11
    Paley, W. 7:186–7
    Wolff, C. 9:782–3
natural history 6:750, 6:751

natural philosophy
    medieval 6:693, 6:694, 6:703
        angels 6:692, 6:694
        Christianity and science
            6:698–701
        creation 6:699
        voluntarism 6:703
naturalistic
    Democritus 2:875–6
Newton, I. 6:827
obligation/supererogation
    distinction 9:232
pagan
    Christianity 3:655–6
    Neoplatonic interpretation
        7:388
    Theophrastus 9:339
patriarchal 3:622
perfect-being 4:93, 4:95–8, 4:99
philosophia Christi (Erasmus, D.)
    3:399
philosophy relationship 8:248
    Alexander of Hales 1:176, 1:177
    Aquinas, T. 1:341–4
    Barth, K. 1:654
    Brunner, E. 2:30, 2:32
    Byzantine 2:160–1
    Damian, P. 2:772–3
    Maritain, J. 6:102
Platonism
    Early and Middle 7:425–6
political **9:331–3**
positive science 8:535
postmodern **7:583–6**
Primordial One 5:831
public 6:841, 6:842
Rabbinic *see* Rabbinic theology
rational
    Kant, I. critique 5:189
rationality relationship
    Jewish Averroism 1:601–2
Reformation
    political philosophy
        history of 7:510–11
rule of faith debates 8:698, 8:699
Russian Orthodox 2:125
scholastic (Biel, G.) 1:769–71
science **8:230–6**
    Galilei, G. 3:839–40
    Holcot, J. 4:477–8
    Troeltsch, E.P.W. 9:461–2
scriptural
    Renaissance humanism 4:538–9
Socinianism 8:889–92
Stoicism 9:146–7
understanding
    Jewish pietism 4:634

university subject 7:68
William of Ockham 9:742–3
theology
  of the Word
    Barth, K. 1:651, 1:653–4
Theology of Aristotle 1:75–6, 1:384,
  5:24, 6:804
theonomies
  Tillich, P. 9:411–12
theophany
  Voegelin, E. 9:655
Theophilos of Antioch 7:257
Theophrastus **9:337–40**
  doxography 3:126
  ethics 9:339
  first principles 9:338–9
  logic 5:689–90
    syllogisms 9:337–8
  metaphysics 9:338–9
  Metaphysics
    first principles 9:338–9
  psychology 9:338
  science 9:339–40
  theology 9:339
theoretical entities
  psychology 7:344–5
theoretical intellect
  Islamic philosophy 3:386–7
  rational soul 9:40, 9:42–3
theoretical virtues *see* virtues,
  theoretical/epistemic
theoreticism
  Bakhtin, M.M. rejection of
  1:641–2
theories
  axiomatic 5:798
  categorical 5:798–9
  construction
    ordinary language philosophy
    7:149–50, 7:152
  folk psychology 8:151
  Galen 3:834
  glossary 5:810
  method
    scientific
      Epicureanism 3:345
  ontological commitment
    (Quine, W.V.) 8:7–8
  Ramsey sentences 8:45, 8:47–8
  scientific **9:343–55**
    analysis of
      idealizations 4:672
    Campbell, N.R. 2:193
    concepts distinction 3:781–2
    construction of
      measurement 6:245
    crucial experiments 2:735

determinism-indeterminism
  3:35–9
  evidence
    underdetermination
    9:527–30
  experiment 3:514, 3:515–17
  falsification 5:317
  incommensurability 3:640,
    4:732–6
  interlevel
    molecular biology 6:459,
    6:460
  model distinction 6:445
  observation 7:81, 7:82–4, 7:86
  philosophy of science 8:573–4
  proliferation 3:641
  reduction
    Nagel model 8:146, 8:148
  restrictive nature of 4:224
  simplicity **8:780–3**
  Stewart, D. 9:138–9
  taxonomy conflicts 9:275
  testing
    observation 7:81
  simplicity 8:540
  systematization 4:350
  unobservable entities (Ramsey, F.)
    3:806–7
theory
  see also critical theory
  choice
    social epistemology 8:831
  concept of
    Frankfurt School 2:723–4
  critique of
    Nietzsche, F.W. 6:846–7
  definition 9:357
  fitness model 3:486
  indirect description (Mach, E.)
    6:14
  observation distinction 6:724,
    6:728
  observation relation 8:870
  ontological commitments of
    7:113–14, 7:115
  practice relationship
    Beattie, J. 1:679
    ethics **9:356–9**
    Lenin, V.I. 5:566
  social sciences **9:355–6**
    positivism 9:356
    scientific realism 9:355–6
    standard view 9:355
  tests of (Mozi) 6:454–5
  use of term 7:113–14, 7:115
theory of types *see* types, theory of

theory-ladenness
  archaeology 1:356–7
  observation 7:81, 7:82–4
    experiment 3:515
    Hanson, N.R. 4:224
  science
    gender-based analyses 3:862
    Heidegger, M. 4:325–6
    medicine 6:266
theosophy **9:363–6**
  Boehme, J. 1:800
  Steiner, R. 9:133–4
  Theosophical Society 9:364–5
  traditional 9:363–4
therapy
  genetics and ethics 4:17–18
  medical
    evaluation of 6:267
  psychology
    theories of 7:828–9
Theravāda School of Buddhism
  Abhidharma 2:54
  asceticism 1:518
  reincarnation 8:184
  salvation 8:448
thermodynamics **9:366–9**
  chemistry 2:297–8
  Duhem, P.M.M. 3:142, 3:143
  irrationals 6:349
  Planck, M.K.E.L. 7:396
Théry, G. 9:518
Thesleff, H. 6:809, 7:421
Thessaly
  Philo of Larissa **7:361–3**
Theunissen, M.
  Buber, M. 2:48
  critical theory 2:728
  Hegel, G.W.F. 4:279–80
  Hegelianism 4:295, 4:298
theurgy 4:599, 6:800
Thévenaz, P. 7:470
Thevenot, L. 9:7
Thibaut, G. 6:479, 8:44, 9:594
Thiel, Udo
  Overton, R. †7:175–7
Thielen-Wilson, L. 3:593, 3:868
Thielicke, H.
  religion, critique of 8:238
Thielicke, Helmut **9:370–1**
  Teilhard de Chardin, P. 9:291
Thieme, P. 2:4–5
Thierry of Chartres **9:371–3**
  Chartres school 2:290, 2:291
  Platonism
    medieval 7:432
Thijssen, J.M.M.H.
  Buridan, J. 2:136

eternity of the world
        medieval views of †3:427–30
    Gregory of Rimini 4:172
    Henry of Harclay 4:363
Thinès, G. 7:829
'thing'
    Henry of Ghent 4:355–6
things
    thing–event contrast 3:462
things-in-themselves
    Kant, I. 4:664–6
    ontology 7:117, 7:118
    Schopenhauer, A. 4:666–7
thinking
    representations 5:405
Thinley, K. 6:353
third man argument 9:541, 9:651,
    9:652
Third Master, the see Mir Damad,
    Muhammad Baqir
Third World see development ethics
Thirouin, L. 7:247
Thiselton, Anthony C.
    hermeneutics
        biblical †4:389–95
Thistlethwaite, S.B. 3:625
Thistlewaite, P.B. 8:204
Thody, P. 2:196
Thom, P. 1:472, 6:615
Thom, Paul
    ancient logic †5:687–93
Thomas à Kempis 9:373–5
Thomas de Vio see Cajetan
Thomas of York 9:375–6
Thomas, Alan
    MacIntyre, A. †6:22–4
    values †9:581–3
Thomas, Barry Smithalan
    axiology †1:608–12
Thomas, C. 6:654
Thomas, Christian see Thomasius,
    Christian
Thomas, D. 4:118
Thomas, David Oswald 7:679
Thomas, Donald 3:109
Thomas, E.J. 2:53
Thomas, G. 4:170
Thomas, G.F. 7:205
Thomas, J.A.C. 7:609
Thomas, K. 3:818
Thomas, L. 3:105, 8:638, 9:469
Thomas, N. 7:583
Thomas, O.C. 9:301
Thomas, W.
    infinitary logic 4:771
    model theory 6:442

paradoxes of set and property
    7:220
second- and higher-order logics
    8:595
Thomas, W.E.S.
    Mill, J. 6:360
Thomasius, Christian 9:376–80
    justice 9:378
    morality 9:378–9
    reason 9:378
    voluntarism 9:377–8
Thomason, B.
    Schütz, A. 8:561
Thomason, R.H.
    common-sense reasoning 2:453
    deontic logic 2:890
    modal logic 6:426
    Montague, R.M. 6:485
    provability logic 7:797
Thomason, S.K. 6:84
Thomism 9:380–8
    see also Aquinas, Thomas; Neo-
        Thomism
    colonial philosophy
        Latin America 5:422, 5:424
    critique of
        Durandus of St Pouçain 3:172,
            3:173
        Dominicans 9:381–2, 9:383–4
        Garrigou-Lagrange, R. 3:847
        Jesuits 9:382–3
        John of St Thomas 5:117, 5:118,
            5:119–20
        Maritain, J. 6:101–3
    matter
        Aristotelianism 1:388–9
    natural law
        contemporary philosophy 8:228
    Neo-Thomism 9:381, 9:383–6
    objective right 9:614
    place
        Aristotelianism 1:389
    Poland 7:485, 7:487
    Rahner, K. 8:36
    reprobation 8:275
    Roman Catholicism 9:380–6
    Silvestri, F. 8:776–7
    Soto, D. de 9:37–9
    Suárez, F. 9:189
    Transcendental 9:384
Thompson, Edward P. 1:195–6
Thompson, Evan 1:492
Thompson, F. 8:149, 9:238
Thompson, J.
    Elisabeth of Bohemia 3:269
    Kierkegaard, S. 5:244
    state 9:123

Thompson, J.B.
    Habermas, J. 4:199
    ideology 4:685
    Ricoeur, P. †8:318–22
Thompson, K. 3:177
Thompson, Kirill Ole
    Chinese theories of language 5:706
    Zhang Zai †9:856–7
    Zhou Dunyi †9:862–3
    Zhu Xi †9:863–5
Thompson, Michael
    Anscombe, G.E.M. †1:280–3
Thompson, P. 9:355
Thompson, R.F. 1:65
Thompson, W. 6:259
Thomson, A. 3:634–5, 5:335
Thomson, G. 6:755
Thomson, J.J. 3:182–3, 6:542
Thomson, S.H. 4:183, 9:803
Thomson, W.R. 9:805
Thoreau, Henry David 9:388–92
    American philosophy in the
        eighteenth and nineteenth
        centuries 1:202
    Cavell, S. 9:390
    transcendentalism 9:389–90
Thorndike, Edward Lee 5:484, 8:800,
    8:802
Thornhill, Christopher
    historicism †4:443–6
thought
    see also cognition; ideas; mental
        states; mind; reason; reasoning
    absolute prepositions 2:411, 2:413
    abstract 5:583
    abstract (Frank, S.L.) 3:727
    action unity
        Confucianism, Japanese 2:553
    addition to matter 1:822, 1:823
    animals 1:269–73, 1:272, 2:804
    being
        logic of origin 2:399
    bodily character 6:652
    cogito argument (Descartes, R.)
        3:7–8
    cognitive development 2:394
    cognitive impression
        Stoicism 3:373
    cognitive stages 9:320–1
    concepts 2:505–14
    concrete predication (Brentano, F.)
        2:14
    conscious/unconscious
        connection principle
            (Searle, J.R.) 2:328
    content 6:405
        wide and narrow 2:643–6

definition
  language of thought hypothesis
    5:405
  distinguished from thinking
    3:769–70
  doubt 3:124
  economy of 6:14
  epistemic realism 5:840
  Fregean 3:769–70, 7:772
  halakhah–aggadah relationship
    4:411
  ideality 4:690
  identity philosophy 8:513
  indexical content of **2:639–40**
  indivisibility (Ibn Sina) 4:651
  intellect relationship
    Averroist monopsychism 1:596
  language **5:404–8**
    Aristotle 5:359
    cognition 5:404–7
    Condillac, É.B. de 5:376–7
    Derrida, J. 2:898
    Dummett, M.A.E. 3:149–50
    Fodor, J.A. 3:684
    Hamann, J.G. 4:215–16
    Heidegger, M. 2:897
    language of thought hypothesis
      5:405–7
    propositional attitudes 5:405–6
    Sapir-Whorf Hypothesis
      8:470–3
    Sellars, W.S. 8:638, 8:639–40
    Vygotskii, L.S. 9:673–4
  laws of
    Boole, G. 1:841–2
    Cohen, H. 6:781
    Mill, J.S. 6:360, 6:361–74
  life relationship 3:533, 3:534–5
  linguistic discrimination 5:641
  logical categories 5:839–40
  mental language 9:732
  mind–body problem
    (Descartes, R.) 3:11
  non-verbal
    language of thought hypothesis
      5:406
  normativity of 2:413
  object relationships 3:460–1
  objective
    Frege, G. 3:770
    Hegelian Concepts 4:270–1
  preconditions of 9:453
  problem-centred 6:92
  productive intellect (Aristotle)
    1:426
  rational
    religious suppositions 3:113–14

reflective
  Nishida Kitarō 7:13–14
  Ryle, G. 8:428, 8:431
self distinction 9:761
sensation 9:163
sense and reference 3:460
transcendental idealism 8:511–12
thought experiments **9:392–7**
see also twin earth thought
  experiments
  Condillac, É.B. de 2:524–5
  fission of persons
    personal identity 7:306,
      7:309–12
  Galilei, G. 3:838
  indiscernibility experiments 4:680
  'inverted spectrum'
    colour and qualia 2:424
  Tiles, J.E. 9:397
Thrace
  Protagoras **7:788–91**
Thrasyllus
  Platonic writings
    arrangement of 7:402–3
Thrasymachus **9:397–8**
'three natures' theory
  Tibetan Buddhism
    Jo-nang-pa School 9:403
    Yogācāra Buddhism 9:792
Three Treatise (Sanlun) School of
  Buddhism
  China 2:82–3
threefold path
  self
    Indian theories of 8:607
Throne (Qur'an)
  Ibn Massara 4:628
Thrower, J. 1:534
thrownness (*Geworfenheit*) 2:225–6,
  4:308–9, 4:312
Thucydides **9:398–9**
  corruption 2:675, 2:677
Thuillier, R. 6:331
Thulstrup, N. 4:301–2, 5:244
Thurman, R.A.F. 9:793
Thwaites, R.G. 6:671
ti (substance)
  Chinese philosophy **9:400**
tian (Heaven)
  Chinese philosophy **9:400–2**
  Chông Yagyong 2:342
  Confucius 6:455–6
  Dong Zhongshu 3:111–12
  Legalism 5:537
  Mozi 6:453, 6:454, 6:455–6
  order 2:325
  Xunzi 9:819

Tiantai School of Buddhism
  see also Tendai
  China 2:86–7, 2:91
  Saichō 5:71
  Zhiyi 9:859, 9:860–1
Tibawi, A.L. 4:688
Tibet
  see also Tibetan philosophy
  Buddhism *see* Buddhist
    philosophy, Tibet
  Great Debate of bSam-yas 9:405–6
  language
    pronunciation 4:739–40
  Mi bskyod rdo rje **6:351–3**
  mKhas grub dge legs dpal bzang
    po **6:416–17**
  rGyal tshab dar ma rin chen
    8:304–5
  Sa skya paṇḍita **8:433–5**
  Tsong kha pa Blo bzang grags pa
    9:487–90
  Yogācāra Buddhism 2:66
Tibetan philosophy **4:736–40,
  9:402–9**
  epistemology 9:407
  logic 9:407
  Mādhyamika School of Buddhism
    2:58–64, 9:402–5
  spiritual realization 9:405–6
  universals 9:406–7
Tibor Gašparíková 8:813
Ticci Viracocha 5:430
Tice, T.N. 8:538–9
Tichý, P. 8:3
Tiefel, H.O. 4:499
t'ien see tian
Tienson, J. 2:577–8
Tierno, Enrique Galván 9:75–6, 9:77
Tiffin, H. 7:578–9, 7:581
Tikhomirov, Lev 7:452–3
Tiles, J.E.
  pragmatism in ethics †7:640–4
  thought experiments 9:397
Tiles, Mary E.
  Bachelard, G. †1:620–4
  Cantor's theorem †2:199–200
  continuum hypothesis †2:654–7
  French philosophy of science 3:786
Tillemans, Tom J.F.
  Tibetan philosophy †9:402–9
  Tsong kha pa Blo bzang grags pa
    †9:487–90
Tillers, P. 5:505–6
Tillich, Hannah 9:413
Tillich, Paul **9:409–13**
  atheism 1:531
  ethics 9:411

existentialist theology 3:508, 3:509
faith 3:540, 9:410–11
God
    concepts of 4:102
    definition of 6:480
nihilism 7:5
ontology 9:410
religious language 8:258, 8:260
revelation 9:410
social philosophy 9:411–12
utopianism 9:562
Tilliette, X. 5:84, 8:520
Tillman, Hoyt Cleveland
    Cheng Hao †2:300–2
    Cheng Yi †2:302–3
    Lu Xiangshan 5:852–3
Tilton, T. 8:828
Timasheff, N. 7:330
time 9:413–17
    see also atemporality; change;
    duration; *saṃsāra*; spacetime;
    temporality
    as a priori concept 1:637
    absolute
        Newton, I. 2:678, 6:825
        relativity theory 8:193
    absolute idealism 1:28
    abstract objects 1:32, 1:33
    anti-determinism
        (Dostoevskii, F.M.) 3:116,
        3:117, 3:118–19
    Aristotelian paradoxes 8:790
    asymmetry
        thermodynamics 9:368–9
    being in (Ingarden, R.W.) 4:790
    being-time (Dōgen) 6:593–4
    causality 6:409
    contingency (Tolstoi, L.N.)
        9:436–7
    continuants 2:652–4
    continuity 9:162
    cosmology
        Indian theories of 2:683
        medieval natural philosophy
        6:702
    creation
        Augustine 4:712
        Ibn Rushd 4:639–40
    Daoism 2:786
    definition of 7:459
    dependency on change
        Epicureanism 3:341
    direction of
        thermodynamics 9:369
    discrete 4:74–5
    divisibility of
        Aristotle 1:420–1

Zeno of Elea 9:849–51
    ecological 3:204
    eternal principle of Bakr 8:111
    eternity 3:422–7
        present 7:230–1
    eternity of the world
        medieval theories of 1:832,
        3:427–9
    existence 9:413–14
    existential 1:728
    experience 1:168–9
    extension
        Buddhist critique of 7:23–4
    as fourth dimension 8:814
    God
        Augustine 1:550–1
        al-Ghazali 4:64–5
    hierarchy theorem
        computational complexity
        2:473
    homogeneous/heterogeneous 3:261
    identity philosophy 8:513
    incorporeality of
        Stoicism 9:148
    infinity 8:315–16
    knowledge of (Kant, I.) 5:182,
        5:184–5
    metaphysics 6:339–40
    motion
        Hellenistic philosophy 5:251
    multiplicity 2:856, 2:857
    nature of
        Neoplatonism 6:801
    non-sentient substance
        Jainism 5:49–50
    personalism 7:316
    reality/unreality of 9:413–14
    relativity theory 6:448, 8:169,
        8:193–4
    sacred 3:260
    serial/pure duration distinction
        4:865
    space 6:36
    tense logic 7:688
    tensed theory of 2:25, 2:653,
        9:303–6
    tenseless theory of 2:653–4, 2:653
    trilateral conception (Mir Damad,
        Muhammad Baqir) 6:408,
        6:409–10
    unreality of 2:275, 6:25–6
time travel 9:417–19
timelessness
    divine simplicity 8:785
Timmons, Mark
    duty 3:182

logic of ethical discourse
    †5:759–64
moral knowledge 6:520
moral scepticism 6:545
universalism in ethics 9:539
Timon 9:419–20
    Pyrrho 7:846–7
    Pyrrhonism 7:848, 7:849
Tindal, Matthew 9:420–3
    deism 2:855, 2:856
Tinder, G. 9:433
Tipler, F.H. 2:651
Tipton, Ian
    Berkeley, G. †1:737–50
Tirosh-Samuelson, Hava (neé Tirosh-
    Rothschild)
    Messer Leon †6:331–5
    Shem Tov family †8:737–40
Tiruchelvam, N. 3:43
Tissa Moggalīputta 2:96, 2:99
Tissot, C.J. 2:168
Titchener, E.B. 7:826, 7:829–30
Tiuryn, J. 3:191
Tkachëv, Pëtr Nikitich 7:452, 8:417
Tlacaelel 5:430–1
Tobin, T.H. 7:361
Tocqueville, Alexis de 9:423–5
    civil society 2:369, 2:372
    democracy 2:868–9, 2:872
    federalism and confederalism
        3:574
Toda, K. 1:74
Todd, C.L. 5:122
Todd, Robert B. 9:326
    Cleomedes †2:385–6
Todd, S. 1:492
Todd, William Mills III
    Moscow-Tartu school †6:583–8
Todhunter, I. 9:711
Todorov, Tzvetan 9:425–7
    Lévi-Strauss, C. 5:585
    Saussure, F. de 8:482
    structuralism 9:177
    structuralism in linguistics 9:181
T'oegye *see* Yi Hwang
Toews, J. 4:302
token *see* type/token distinction
token identity theory
    mental causation (Davidson, D.)
        6:308–9
Toksvig, S. 9:243
Toland, John 9:427–9
    deism 2:854, 2:856
Toledo, Francisco de *see* Toletus,
    Franciscus
Toledo, School of Translators of 9:70

tolerance
  logical 2:208, 2:211
toleration **9:429–33**
  see also freedom of speech;
    multiculturalism; neutrality,
    political
  concept of 9:430–1
  justification 9:431–2
  law and morality 5:438–42
  multiculturalism 6:601
  pluralism 7:464
  political philosophy
    history of 7:511
  pornography 7:544
  postmodernism 7:592
  religious
    Collins, A. 2:418
    divinity 8:224
    Enlightenment 8:228
    Latitudinarianism 5:433
    Locke, J. 5:676–7, 8:227
    More, H. 6:576, 6:581
    pluralism 8:260–1
    Port Royal 7:552
    Radhakrishnan, S. 8:24
Toletus, Franciscus **9:433–5**
  Aristotelianism
    seventeenth century 1:387,
      1:388
  Renaissance logic 5:767, 5:771,
    9:434
Tolman, E.C. 7:133–4, 7:135, 8:802
Tolman, R.
  thermodynamics 9:369
Tolmer, L. 4:518
Tolstoi, Lev Nikolaevich **9:435–40**
  aesthetics
    morality relationship 9:438–9
  anarchism 1:245, 1:248
  art
    and morality 1:456
    value of 1:478, 1:480
  evil
    passive resistance to 9:439
  history
    uncertainty 9:437–8
  meaning of life 5:633
  Shestov, L. critique 8:742
Tolstoy, Leo
  poetry 7:478
Tolstykh, V.I. 6:159
Tomabechi, T. 9:490
Tomasoni, F. 3:639, 3:640
Tomberlin, J.E. 5:766
Tomiche, A. 6:12
Tominaga Nakamoto **9:440–1**
Tomlinson, G. 1:133

Tomm, W. 3:593
Tonelli, G. 2:739
Tong, Rosemarie
  feminist ethics †3:602–6
Tonghak (Eastern Learning) **9:441–2**
Tönnies, Ferdinand 5:140, 5:141,
  8:874, 8:879
Tonry, M. 2:710
Tooby, J. 3:487, 8:88, 8:89
Tooley, Michael 5:475, 5:630
top down inductive decision trees
  (TDIDT)
  connectionist networks
    backpropagation comparison
      studies 2:574–5
top-down causation
  divine action 8:234
topics
  humanist logic 5:769–70
    Boethius, A.M.S. 5:769, 5:770
    Ramus, P. 8:52
  judgment 9:601
Topics see Aristotle
topoi (commonplaces)
  legal reasoning 5:527
topos
  see also logic of place
  category theory 2:234–5, 2:237,
    2:238
Torah
  astrology 4:612
  decontextualization of
    Rabbinic theology 9:335
  divine transcendence 6:46
  halakhah 4:204–6
  intellectual study
    Rabbinic theology 9:333–4
  Jewish Averroism 1:601
  knowledge 3:170, 3:171
  rhetoric 6:331, 6:332
Toraldo di Franca, G. 9:352
Torchia Estrada, Juan Carlos
  Argentina, philosophy in †1:374–9
Tormey, A. 1:498, 6:615
Torok, M. 2:900
Torrance, John
  Marx, K. 6:133
  Marxism
    Western †6:141–7
Torrell, J.-P. 1:349
Torres, L. 3:593
Torretti, Roberto
  analytical philosophy in Latin
    America 1:234
  geometry 4:34
  Poincaré, J.H. 7:483

relativity theory
  philosophical significance of
    8:199
  space †9:59–66
  spacetime †9:66–70
Torrey, N.L. 2:376, 3:69
torts
  Coase Theorem 5:456–7
Tosaka Jun *see* Kyoto School
tosim (mind of *dao*)
  insim (human mind) relationship
    9:826
totalitarianism **9:442–4**
  see also dictatorship; fascism;
    Nazism; Stalinism
  Arendt, H. 1:369–70
  community 1:783
  critical theory 2:726–7
  Dostoevskii, F.M., prediction of
    3:116
  ecology relationship
    environmental ethics 3:334
  family system ethics 9:692
  Hayek, F.A. 4:245
  historicism 4:445
  Plato 7:533, 7:536–7
totality
  Buddhism
    Kegon School 2:102
  Marxist 1:193–4
totalization
  historical
    Lyotard, J.-F. critique 6:8–9
totemism
  Lévi-Strauss, C. 5:583
Touati, C. 2:704, 4:51
Toulmin, Stephen E.
  casuistry 2:228
  examples in ethics 3:490
  legal reasoning 5:527, 5:531
  matter 6:196
  Melbourne University 1:584
  moral scepticism 6:545
  rhetoric 8:310
  scientific theories 9:355
Touraine, A. 2:372
Towa, Marcien 1:112, 1:116
Towell, G. 2:578, 2:579
Towes, J.E. 1:667
Townsend, Dabney
  Alison, A. †1:185–7
  Gerard, A. †4:36–7
Trabant, J. 8:679
Tracey, J. 3:401
trade unions
  social democracy 8:827

tradition **9:445–7**
  Confucianism 2:541–6
  Greek philosophy
    Lucian 5:853
    Socrates 9:9
traditionalism **9:445–7**
  see also antitraditionalism
tragedy **9:447–52**
  comedy comparison 2:434–5,
    2:436
  emotional response to art 3:278–9
  England 9:449–50
  faith (Shestov, L.) 8:743–4
  France 9:449
  Germany 9:450
  Greek 9:447–8
  Hamlet analysis 9:673
  irrationality 5:218
  Italy 9:449
  katharsis (Aristotle) 5:218–19
  law and literature movement
    (Nussbaum, M.) 5:150
  meaning (Shestov, L.) 8:742–3
  Nietzsche, F.W. 6:844
  origins of 9:447–8
  Plato's dismissal of 1:479
  poetics 1:431
  poetry 7:474
  salvation 8:551
  Schiller, J.C.F. 8:525–6
  twentieth century 9:450–1
trairism
  Eliade, M. 3:261
traits
  see also properties
  innate 4:795
Traniello, F. 8:364
Tranøy, Knut Erik 8:490, 8:492
tranquility
  Epicureanism 3:347
  moral life 8:818
transcendence
  as absolute dimension of being
    5:81
  divine
    Eriugena, J.S. 3:403
    Hebrew Bible 1:767
  feminist theology 3:622–3
  imagery relationship 5:477
  inclusivism 8:261
  karma and rebirth
    Mādhyamika Buddhism 5:214
  the Sacred (Bataille, G.) 1:659–60
transcendental apperception
  Kant, I. 5:186
transcendental arguments **9:452–4**
  conceptual analysis 2:520

eliminativism 3:264–5
  private language argument 9:452–3
  Stroud, B. critique 2:521
  substance 9:207–8
  verification principle 9:453–4
transcendental deduction
  Kant, I. 2:231, 5:186
transcendental idealism
  defence of (Schopenhauer, A.)
    8:548–9, 8:550
  Kant, I. 4:664–5, 5:182, 5:184–5,
    5:192, 5:196
  original representing 1:688
  self 2:67
transcendental realism *see* critical
  realism
Transcendental Thomism 9:384
transcendentalism
  Concord Transcendentalists
    1:202–3, 9:389–90
  ego
    epistemic issues in
      phenomenology 7:346
  logic
    unity of cultural consciousness
      (Cohen, H.) 2:399
  metaphysical concepts
    (Tetens, J.N.) 9:320
  Naturphilosophie (Schelling, F.W.J.
    von) 8:509, 8:511–12
  phenomenology
    constitutive (Husserl, E.)
      7:336–7
    of perception (Merleau-
      Ponty, M.) 6:321–3
  Rahner, K. 8:37
  scepticism (Strawson, P.F.) 9:172–3
transcendentals
  Nifo, A. 6:870
  Philip the Chancellor 7:356
  univocity
    Duns Scotus, J. 3:154, 3:157–8
    Henry of Ghent 4:358–9
  Valla, L. 9:571
transfer condition
  epistemic paradoxes 7:211–12
transference
  psychoanalysis (Freud, S.)
    3:789–90
transfinite induction
  glossary 5:810
transfinite numbers 7:50–1
  Cantor, G. 2:197–8, 2:199, 2:656,
    8:702–5
  paradoxes 7:52
transformation
  myths 5:584

Sāṅkhya-Yoga
  causation 2:251, 2:252, 2:253–4
transformational syntax 9:249
trans-generational community
  obligations to future generations
    3:820–1
transgenics
  ethics 4:16, 4:18–19
transgression
  morality and ethics 6:569
transience
  Chinese philosophy *see mujō*
transignification
  sacramental 8:444
transition
  to the similar
    Hellenistic medical
      epistemology 4:334
transitive particularity
  aesthetic attitude 1:54
transitivity
  monism
    Schelling, F.W.J. von 8:512–13
translation
  see also interpretation
  creative incorporation 3:443
  cultural relativism (Davidson, D.)
    8:80, 8:83
  holism
    mental/semantic 4:491–2
  incommensurability (Kuhn, T.S.)
    4:734–5
  indeterminacy of (Quine, W.V.)
    8:12–13, 8:26–9
  intentionality (Brentano, F.)
    4:576–7
  logical form 5:782–3
  meaning 6:213, 6:222
  moral traditions 6:23
  ontological commitment 7:115–16
  proxy functions 8:9–8:10
  radical **8:25–35**
    charity principle 2:283
    indeterminacy of 8:26–9
    indeterminacy of reference
      8:29–31
    Quine, W.V. 8:12–13
    radical interpretation 8:31, 8:34
    truth theory 8:31–4
translations
  Arabic
    to Hebrew 5:23–4
    to Latin 5:22–3, 9:455
    Gerard of Cremona **4:37–8**
    medieval natural philosophy
      6:692–3, 6:698

Greek
  to Arabic 4:156–7
  to Latin 3:653, 3:654, 9:455–6
Latin America
  Nahuatl thought 6:345
  pre-Columbian thought 5:429,
    5:430–1
medieval
  of Aristotle 1:393–4, 1:395–8,
    1:400
Renaissance
  humanist logic 5:769
translators 9:455–7
  Boethius, A.M.S. 1:805
  Gerard of Cremona 4:37–8
transmigration
  karma
    Japanese Buddhism 2:104
  self
    Indian theories of 8:607–8
  of souls
    Numenius 7:55
    Orphism 7:164
    Proclus 7:729
    Pythagoreanism 7:855–6, 7:857,
      7:860
transparency thesis
  photography 7:379–80
transpersonalism
  legal institutionalism
    (Gurvitch, G.) 4:800
transplantation
  human organs
    Jewish bioethics 1:779
transposition
  theological discourse (Gilbert of
    Poitiers) 4:70–1
transubstantiation
  Descartes, R.
    Arnauld, A. critique 1:445
  John of Paris 5:114
  Wyclif, J. 9:802, 9:803
Trapezountios, George *see* George of
  Trebizond
Trapp, A.D. 4:172
trauma
  Wagnerian opera 7:130–1
Travis, C. 4:752, 7:632
Traweek, S. 3:868
treatment outcomes
  psychoanalysis
    methodology problems
      7:812–13
Treichler, P.A. 5:367
Trejo, W. 1:230–1, 1:234
Trend, J. 1:23

Trendelenburg, Adolf 4:298, 5:729,
  6:779, 6:791
Trent, Council of *see* Council of
  Trent
Trentman, J.A. 9:388
Treserra, F. 9:376
Trevarthan, C. 2:392, 9:110
Trevisani, F. 2:382, 5:138
Trevor-Roper, H. 2:309
triage
  Jewish bioethics 1:777, 1:778
Tribus, M. 4:786
Tricker, R.A.R. 3:260
Trickster
  Native American philosophy
    6:668–9
Trifogli, Cecilia
  Giles of Rome †4:72–8
Trigger, B.G. 1:359
Trimpi, W. 8:310
Trinity 9:457–61
  see also God; Jesus Christ
  Abelard, P. 1:9, 1:10, 1:11
  Anselm of Canterbury 1:285,
    1:292–3
  Augustine 1:548
  Bernard of Clairvaux
    Abelard conflict 1:754
  Boehme, J. 1:800
  Boethius, A.M.S. 1:807, 1:808
  Byzantine philosophy 2:161
  Chatton, W. (Wodeham, I.A.)
    2:293
  distinction of persons
    Holcot, R. 4:478
    John of Damascus 5:105
  divine essence distinction
    Francis of Meyronnes 3:724
    Joachim of Fiore 5:104
  divine relations 4:75
  divine simplicity 8:784
  divine union 6:287
  history analogy 5:103–4
  human knowledge of 4:75
  Jesus Christ
    Socinianism denial 8:890
  kenoticism 4:729–30
  logical predication 9:774
  Neoplatonic conception of
    6:105–6
  Origen 7:161–2
  Platonic analogy 9:731
  pneuma (spirit)
    New Testament usage 7:472
  as polytheism
    Swedenborg, E. critique 9:242
  relative identity 9:459–61

Richard of St Victor 8:312
Roscelin of Compiègne 8:356
Socinianism denial 8:890
soul relationship 5:4
Tertullian, Q.S.F. 9:308
Thierry of Chartres 9:371–2
tritheism 7:375–6
unity of God 4:600–1
Trinkaus, C. 4:541, 9:573
Tristán, Flora 3:625, 3:628
tritheism
  Philoponus 7:375–6
Trivers, R. 8:896
Troelstra, A.S.
  constructivism in mathematics
    2:639
  formal languages and systems
    3:706
  intuitionism 4:850, 4:853
  linear logic 5:641
  mathematics
    foundations of 6:192
Troeltsch, Ernst Peter Wilhelm 4:446,
  9:461–4
Troisfontaines, R. 6:93
Troitskii, Matveii 7:562–3
tropes 7:22
  particulars 7:237
  rhetoric 8:305, 8:308–9
Trotsky, Leon 9:464–6
  art
    understanding of 1:475
  New Left Movement 6:145
Trotter, Catherine *see* Cockburn,
  Catharine
Trubachev, A. 3:682
Trubetskoi, E.N. 9:32
Trubetskoi, Prince Nikolai Sergeevich
  3:454–5
Trubetskoi, Prince Sergei 9:31–2
Trubetzkoy, N.S. *see* Trubetskoi,
  Prince Nikolai Sergeevich
true causes, principle of
  geology
    philosophy of 4:26
true law *see* natural law
True Pure Land Buddhism *see* Shin
  Buddhism
Truesdell, C. 6:259
Truman, N.E. 6:53
trust 9:466–70
  see also promising; reciprocity
  professional ethics 7:735
  truthfulness and deception 9:484
trustworthiness
  Chinese philosophy *see* xin

truth
  see also analytic truth; bivalence;
    logical truth; necessary truth
  a posteriori 1:1
  a priori 1:3–5, 1:4
  absolute 4:665
  acceptance of
    Judaism 4:616
  adequacy 9:99
  adequacy (Spinoza, B. de) 9:99
  aesthetic experience 3:828
  analytic ethics 1:222
  analyticity **1:234–9**
  appearances 2:218
  Aristotelianism 4:74
  art **1:456–60**
    interpretation 1:505
    Japanese 1:85–6
  axiomatic 6:577–8
  belief theory 8:44–5
  Buddhism 2:107–8
  Christianity
    Dostoevskii, F.M. 3:118
    Frank, S.L. 3:728
  claims 8:523
  classical 3:150–2
  cognition of (Hegel, G.W.F.)
    4:269–70
  coherence theory of **9:470–2**
    circularity 9:471
    coherence theory of justification
      distinction 5:253–6, 5:257–8
    consistency 9:470–1
    mutual entailment 9:470–1
    'pure' truth 9:470–1
    scepticism 9:471–2
    Schlick, F.A.M. critique 8:542
  common sense (Buffier, C.)
    2:119–20
  conceptual
    contingency of 2:521
    modal thesis 2:519–20
  conceptual schemes 5:587
  confirmation theory
    (Hempel, C.G.) 4:348–50
  consciousness 5:339
  context
    Dōgen 5:74
    Foucault, M. 8:844–5
  contingent
    infinite analysis 5:554
  by convention 8:10
  correspondence theory of **9:472–5**
    congruence 9:472–3
    conventions 9:473
    correlation 9:472–3
    facts 3:536

  James, W. 9:479–80
  knowledge by acquaintance/
    description 5:261–2
  Prior, A.N. 7:688–9
  protocol sentences 8:542
  tense logic 9:305–6
  Yoruba epistemology 9:832–3
criteria of
  Gassendi, P. 3:852
  Huet, P.-D. 4:516
  Pyrrhonism 7:852
  Stoicism 9:152–3
dao 2:778, 9:858
deflationary theories of **9:475–8**
  eliminativism 3:264–5
  gratuity thesis 9:475, 9:476–7
  Ramsey, F.P. 8:46
  sentential operators 9:477
  Tarski, A. 9:268–9
degrees of 9:564–5, 9:566
democracy 2:869–70
Descartes, R. 4:515
divine
  Llull's Great Art 5:662–3
divine illumination 9:572
divine immutability 4:713
doxastic theory (Brentano, F.) 2:15
embodiment of essence 8:468–9
Enlightenment humanism 4:530
epistemological pluralism
  political philosophy
    Indian 7:522
as event 3:828
existentialist theology 3:506–7
facts
  as truth-makers 3:535, 3:536–7
  Wittgenstein, L. 6:339
first principles 8:178–9
forms of experience 2:413–14
freedom of speech 3:762–3
game-theoretic semantics 8:657
Gandhi, M.K. 3:842–3
God
  existence arguments
    Bonaventure 1:831
    Descartes, R. 3:9
  Henkin semantics 8:593–2
historical theory of 9:600–1
identity theory of 1:860
independence of 3:770
indeterminacy of translation 8:27
indexicals 2:879, 2:880
induction
  Russell, B.A.W. 8:401
  Wright, G.H. von 9:667
inference to the best explanation
  4:766–9

'intuition-discursion'
  (Florenskii, P.A.) 3:680–1
intuitive
  common sense 2:454
justice conflict 7:603
knowledge of
  Henry of Ghent 4:357
  William of Auvergne 9:726
language
  Hamann, J.G. 4:216
  substitutional 7:881
law of excluded middle 8:118–19
logical 5:781, 8:591–2, 9:267
  conventions 7:689
  negation 9:759–60
  objective harmony 2:145
  picture theory of meaning
    (Wittgenstein, L.) 9:759
  reference 8:7
and meaning *see* meaning, and
  truth
'metaphysics of presence'
  (Derrida, J.) 2:896, 2:898
mimēsis 5:340, 5:341
model theory 6:437, 6:440–1
moral
  natural law 6:687
  scepticism 6:543–4
  Wollaston, W. 9:787–8
natural theology 6:708
naturalism 6:847
necessity
  modal logic 6:427–8
objective
  language 6:323
partial
  manifoldness, Jaina theory of
    6:77, 6:79–81
philosophical/prophetic
  Islamic philosophy 3:387
poetry 7:473
postmodernism 7:589
as practice
  Russian Marxism 1:818
pragmatic theory of **9:478–80**
pragmatism 7:635–7
  James, W. 5:60, 5:65
  Peirce, C.S. 7:273
  Ramsey, F.P. 8:46
preconception
  Epicureanism 3:345
radical interpretation
  (Davidson, D.) 8:31–4
realism/antirealism 8:116, 8:117
  in mathematics 8:118
reason
  fact distinction 5:552–3

Judaism 5:96
  relationship with 4:372–3
redundancy theory of 9:475, 9:476
relativism 8:189, 8:190
  Mikhailovskii, N.K. 6:355
  Protagoras 7:790
  Ramakrishna Movement 8:40
  Twardowski, K. 9:509
religion–science relationship
  Judaism 4:610
religious 8:255–6
  Kierkegaard, S. 5:241–2
  philosophical truth distinction
    Jewish Averroism 1:601
  symbolism 4:657, 4:658–9
Renaissance scepticism 3:398
respect for
  intellectual responsibility
    8:288–9
  scientific responsibility 8:289
science
  Islamic philosophy 8:562–3
  method
    Epicureanism 3:345
  theory
    crucial experiments 2:735–6
    Whewell, W. 9:710
self-evident 3:714
sense perception
  Epicureanism 3:344–5
sentential
  testimony in Indian philosophy
    9:317–18
signification 1:290
Strauss, L. 9:168
success semantics 8:46–7
synthetic
  a priori knowledge 1:4
synthetic a priori judgments
  (Kant, I.) 5:183–4
Tarski, A. **9:265–9**
technology as 9:281
theories of 6:221–2, **8:642–8**
  extension 8:645
  identity theory 1:860
  Kripke, S. 8:644–6
  language 6:221–2, 8:644–5
  liar paradox 8:642–4, 8:645
  substitutional language 7:881
truthfulness distinction 9:481–2
unitary
  Buddhism 9:793
universal designation 8:539
universals 1:442–3
verification transcendent 6:233–4
virtues
  theoretical/epistemic 9:342

zhi 9:858
truth bearers 7:787–8
  presupposition 7:673–4
truth lemma
  method of forcing 3:694, 3:696–7
truth-conditions
  context 6:224
  counterfactual conditionals 2:685
  de relde dicto belief 2:815, 2:816
  epistemic logic 3:355
  indicative conditionals 4:741–2
  intuitionistic logic 4:856
  language–world connection 5:410
  meaning 6:219–20, 6:222–3
    declarative sentences 6:220–1
  semantics 8:650
  truth theories 6:221–2
  understanding 4:861, 6:226–8
truthfulness **9:480–5**
  deception contrast 9:480–4
  journalism ethics 5:127
  justification 9:482–3
  line drawing 9:483–4
  self-deception 8:631
  truth distinction 9:481–2
truth-functionality
  glossary 5:810
  imperatives 4:718
  indicative conditionals 4:740–1
  logic gates 1:486
  modal operators 6:433
  quantifiers 6:429, 7:870–1
  three-valued
    many-valued logic 6:84, 6:85–6,
    6:88
truth-preservation
  imperative logic 4:717, 4:718–19
Truths
  Four Noble
    Buddha
      dependent origination
      9:215–16
truths
  three
    Zhiyi
      Chinese Buddhism 2:86–7
truth-tables
  dialogical logic 5:827
  glossary 5:810
  intuitionistic logic 4:856, 4:858
  Łukasiewicz, J. 6:84–8
  predicate calculus 7:660
truth-tracking theory
  Nozick, R. 7:46
truth-value gaps
  Kripke, S. 8:642–3, 8:646

truth-values
  Boolean algebra 1:845–6
  compositionality 2:476
  de relde dicto belief 2:815
  free logics 3:740, 3:742–3
  glossary 5:810
  improper terms 3:20
  sense and reference 3:768–9, 8:686
  sentential logic
    predicate calculus 7:659–60,
    7:661–3
Tschirnhaus, Ehrenfried Walther von
  9:485–7
Tsiv'ian, T.V. 6:588
Tsohatzidis, S.L. 7:632, 9:86–7
Tsong kha pa Blo bzang grags pa
  (Dzongkaba) 9:403–5, **9:487–90**
  Great Debate of bSam-yas 9:405
  influence of
    mKhas grub dge legs dpal
      bzang po 6:416
    Mādhyamika Buddhism 2:62–3
    Mi bskyod rdo rje critique of
      6:351, 6:352
    Wŏnch'ŭk 9:792
Tsouna, Voula
  Aristippus the Elder †1:379–80
  Cyrenaics †2:759–63
  Socratic schools †9:21–3
Tsubouchi Shōyō 5:658
Tsuji, Tatsuya 7:91–2
Tsung-mi *see* Zongmi
Tsunoda, Ryusaku 2:555, 5:79, 9:441
Tu Wei-ming
  aesthetics
    Chinese 1:75
  Chinese Confucianism 2:549
  Daxue †2:807–9
  neo-Confucianism 6:776
  self-cultivation †8:613–26
  Wang Yangming 9:684
  Zhongyong †9:861–2
Tu Wei-ming Yi Yulgok 9:827
Tubero, Orasius 5:621
Tübingen school
  Plato
    interpretation of dialogues
    7:406
Tucci, G. 9:219, 9:408
Tuck, A.P. 6:641
Tuck, R.
  Grotius, H. 4:186
  Hobbes, T. 4:476
  Pufendorf, S. 7:836
  rights 8:331
  Selden, J. 8:605

Tucker, Abraham **9:490–3**
　associationism 9:491
　motivation 9:490–2
Tucker, A.W.
　prisoner's dilemma 8:67–8
Tucker, B. 1:248
Tucker, G.A. 1:776
Tucker, John Allen
　Fujiwara Seika †3:799–801
　Itō Jinsai †5:42–4
　Ogyū Sorai †7:90–2
　Tominaga Nakamoto †9:440–1
Tucker, Mary Evelyn
　Confucianism, Japanese 2:555
　Kaibara Ekken †5:176–7
Tucker, S.I. 3:332
Tudor, Henry
　Bernstein, E. †1:758–60
　Kautsky, K.J. †5:222–4
　Lassalle, F. †5:419–21
　Luxemburg, R. †6:5–7
Tudor, J.M. 1:760
Tufts, J. 7:643
Tugwell, S. 1:349
Tull, H.W. 5:218
Tulloch, H. 2:42
Tulloch, J. 2:185, 2:752, 5:435
Tullock, G. 8:73
Tully see Cicero
Tully, J. 4:389, 7:761, 9:279
Tung Chung-shu' see Dong
　Zhongshu
Tunikabuni, M.M. 6:411
Tunisia
　Ibn Khaldun 4:623–7
　Israeli, Isaac ben Solomon 5:31–4
　Tertullian, Q.S.F. 9:307–9
　Themistius 9:324–6
Tuomela, Raimo
　Beth's theorem and Craig's
　　interpolation theorem 1:763
　Finland, philosophy in 8:488
　holism and individualism in
　　history and social science 4:488
　meaning and communication
　　6:213–14
　social action †8:822–4
Tupi-Guarani thought
　Brazil 2:7
-tuple
　glossary 5:810
Tur, R. 5:227, 5:521
Tur, Richard 7:736, 7:737
Turgenev, I. 7:1, 7:5, 7:8
Turi, G. 4:23
Turing, Alan Mathison **9:493–5**
　see also Church-Turing thesis;

Turing degrees; Turing machines;
　Turing test; Turing's thesis
　computability theory 2:485, 2:489
　computer science 2:491–4, 2:496
　effectiveness 2:350
　ordinal logics 7:139, 7:141–2, 7:143
Turing degrees **9:499–502**
　recursion-theoretic hierarchies
　　8:143
Turing machines 9:493–4, **9:495–9**
　Church's thesis 2:351, 2:354
　cognitive architecture 2:393
　computability theory 2:472,
　　2:485–7, 2:492–4
　computational theories of mind
　　6:391, 6:392
　glossary 5:810
　language of thought hypothesis
　　5:405
　oracle machines 2:475
　universal
　　computer science 2:493–4
Turing reducibility **9:499–502**
Turing test 9:494
　Chinese room argument 2:328,
　　2:329
　criticisms of 9:494–5
　inductive interpretation of 9:495
Turing's thesis 9:495, 9:498
Turkestan
　al-Farabi **3:554–8**
Turkey
　Anaxagoras **1:249–54**
　Arcesilaus **1:351–4**
　Chrysippus **2:345–6**
　Cleanthes **2:382–3**
　Diodorus Cronus **3:83–6**
　Diogenes Laertius **3:86–7**
　Diogenes of Oenoanda **3:89–90**
　Galen **3:832–5**
　Heraclides of Pontus **4:363–4**
　Heraclitus **4:364–9**
　Simplicius **8:788–91**
　Thales **9:322–4**
Turkle, S. 9:201
Turnbull, C. 1:299
Turnbull, George 7:170, **9:502–4**
Turnbull, G.H. 2:440
Turnbull, H.W. 1:726
Turner, B.S.
　sociology
　　theories of 9:8
Turner, R. 4:807, 7:766, 7:767
Turner, S. 4:340
Turner, Stephen P.
　Durkheim, É. 3:177
　Weber, M. †9:693–8

Turquette, A.R. 6:84
Tushnet, Mark 2:718, 2:720
al-Tusi, Khwajah Nasir **9:504–7**
　ethics 3:441, 3:442
　Islamic theology 5:31
　al-Razi, Fakhr al-Din 8:113
Tversky, A.
　decision and game theory 2:834
　probability 7:705, 7:711
　rationality 8:64, 8:95, 8:102
　rationality of belief 8:87, 8:88,
　　8:89, 8:90
　risk 8:334, 8:337
Twambley, P. 3:701, 8:141
Twardowski, Kazimierz **9:507–9**
Tweedale, Martin M.
　Abelard, P. †1:8–15
　Alexander of Aphrodisias 1:176
　medieval logic 5:759
　Roscelin of Compiègne †8:356–7
　William of Champeaux †9:729–30
Twelve Tables
　legal hermeneutics 5:506
Twelver Shi'ism
　al-Tusi 9:505–6
Tweney, R.D. 9:801
Twersky, I. 4:613, 6:49
Tweyman, S. 9:788
twin earth thought experiments
　see also methodological
　　individualism
　content
　　wide and narrow 2:643, 2:644–5
　criticism of 2:644–5
　Putnam, H. 4:491, 7:840–1
　　concepts 2:513–14
　　mental causation 6:309
　reference 8:157
twin prime conjecture
　number theory 2:353
Twining, William
　Kelsen, H. 5:227
　legal evidence and inference 5:505,
　　5:506
　legal positivism 5:521
　legal realism 5:525
　Llewellyn, K.N. †5:661–2
two-factor theories
　concepts 2:506
twofold argument *see dissoi logoi*
Tye, Michael
　adverbial theory of mental states
　　†6:314–17
　consciousness 2:596
　mental imagery †4:703–5
　vagueness †9:563–6
Tyler, S. 7:590

Tylor, Sir Edward 8:84
Tymieniecka, A.T. 4:792
Tynianov, Iu. 8:411, 8:412–13, 8:414
type theory
    simple 9:360, 9:361
type/token distinction **9:509–11**
    ambiguity 1:199
    art works
        ontology of 1:482
    concepts 2:507
    dance 2:775
    existence of types 9:510
    indexical content of thought 2:640

occurrence 9:510
use/mention distinction 9:549
typed lambda calculus 5:348–9
types
    Being
        Lacoue-Labarthe, P. 5:340
    theory of 5:730, **9:359–62**
        intensional logic 4:808–9
        nonstandard analysis 1:213
        paradoxes 7:218–19, 8:714
        property theory 7:765
        Russell, B.A.W. 5:733, 8:395–7
        Wittgenstein, L. 9:759

typology
    archaeological 1:356
tyranny
    costs/benefits of 9:813
    eighteenth-century British politics
        4:558
    justification for killing 5:116
    property rights 4:553–4
Tyre
    Porphyry **7:545–50**
Tyrš, Miroslav 2:766
Tzimtzum
    creation of worlds 4:397, 4:398

U

Übel, T. 2:215
Übermensch (the overhuman)
  Nietzsche, F.W. 6:856–7, 6:858
Udayana **9:512–14**
  God
    arguments for the existence of
      4:435
    Indian and Tibetan philosophy
      4:738
    Nyāya-Vaiśeṣika 7:58
Uddyotakara **9:514–16**
  heaven 4:255
  Indian and Tibetan philosophy
    4:738
  inference 4:764–5, 4:766
  universals 9:546, 9:548
Uebel, T.E. 5:795, 6:816, 8:544, 9:613
Uebele, W. 9:322
Ueda Makoto 1:91, 5:293
Ueda Shisuteru 5:324, 5:330
Ueda, Yoshifumi 8:748
Uehlein, F.A. 2:406
Uehling, T.E. 5:304, 8:209, 9:631
Ui, H. 2:75–6
Ûich'ŏn 2:111
Ûisang **9:516–17**
  Hwaôm Buddhism
    Korea 2:109–10
Ukraine
  see also Russia; Soviet Union
  Berdiaev, N.A. **1:726–32**
  Ha'am, Ahad **4:192–3**
  Shestov, L. **8:740–6**
  Shpet, G.G. **8:754–8**
  Skovoroda, H.S. **8:802–3**
Ulam, S. 6:813
Ulich, R. 3:231
Ullian, J.S. 5:276, 9:343
Ullman, J.D. 2:475, 3:706
Ullman, S. 9:638
Ullman, W. 1:659, 7:517
Ullman-Margalit, E. 7:35, 8:836,
  8:889
Ulman, H.L. 1:15
Ulrich of Strasbourg **9:517–18**
ultimate causes
  Liber de causis 5:595–6
ultimate reality
  emptiness 6:351–2

God's role 4:94–5
  Nāgārjuna 6:638–40
  religious pluralism 8:260–2
'Ulysses Contract'
  medical ethics 6:262
Umaba *see* dBu ma pa
Umāsvāti 2:684, 5:48, 5:54, 5:57
Umehara, T. 8:754
Una Juarez, A. 2:144
Unamuno y Jugo, Miguel De
  9:519–22
  cultural identity 2:746
  Spain, philosophy in 9:73, 9:77
  tragedy 9:451, 9:452
uncertainty
  see also certainty
  Chinese philosophy
    warfare 9:231
  practical reasoning 8:98
  principle of 7:841
  Bohr, N. 1:820–1
  Heisenberg, W. 4:327–8
unconscious
  see also dreaming; non-conscious
  phenomena; unconscious mental
  states
  conscious distinction
    perception 5:542
  fantasies (Freud, S.) 3:790–1
  Hartmann, K.R.E. von 4:239
  structuralism in social science
    9:186
  as subject–object gap (Lacan, J.)
    5:336
  teleological view of (Jung, C.G.)
    5:132–3
  thought accessibility (Searle, J.R.)
    2:328
unconscious mental states **9:522–7**
  see also dreaming
  Chomsky, N. 9:524–5
    free association (Freud, S.)
      3:787–8
  Freud, S. 9:523
  introspection 4:843
  self-deception 8:627
    sublimation (Freud, S.) 3:790

uncountability
  Löwenheim-Skolem theorem
    5:850–1
  natural numbers 8:708
undecidability
  computability theory 2:488–9
  lambda calculus 5:347–8
  method of forcing 3:694, 3:695
underdetermination **9:527–30**
  biblical exegesis
    Rabbinic theology 9:335–6
  conventionalism 7:480
  criteria 9:527–8
  deductive and ampliative 9:528
  Duhem, P.M.M. 3:142, 3:144
  holistic ('D-thesis') 9:528–9
  scientific theories
    fallibilism 3:546
    realism 8:582
  social epistemology 8:831
  sociology of knowledge 9:1
underdevelopment *see* development
  ethics
Underhill, E. 6:634
understanding
  aesthetic judgment (Kant, I.)
    5:193, 5:194
  categories of (Kant, I.) 5:185–6
  cognitive stages 9:321
  common notions 4:371, 4:373
  conditional platform of
    (Oakeshott, M.J.) 7:71–2
  conditions of
    testimony in Indian philosophy
      9:316–17
  hermeneutics
    biblical 4:391
    Dilthey, W. 4:386–7
    Gadamer, H.-G. 3:827, 3:828–9
    Heidegger, M. 4:312
    Schleiermacher, F. 8:535–6
  knowing distinction
    testimony in Indian philosophy
      9:317
  knowledge
    private states 7:700
  language 4:861
  meaning **6:226–9**
    Dilthey, W. 3:81

metaphysical illusions (Kant, I.)
5:188
mind–language connection 5:409
objective spirit 3:77, 3:81
realist versus antirealist models
6:226–7
religious
Jewish pietism 4:634
scientific realism
social sciences 8:586
social action (Weber, M.) 9:695–6
transcendentalism 9:320
truth as event 3:828
Vernunft distinction 2:404
Verstehen distinction 3:79–80,
6:213
virtue epistemology 9:621
unenlightenment
Awakening of Faith in Mahāyāna
1:603–4
Ungar, A.M.
Herbrand's theorem †4:375–8
natural deduction, tableau and
sequent systems †6:676–82
Ungar, S. 1:784
Unger, Peter
certainty 2:266, 2:267
content
wide and narrow 2:646
help and beneficence 4:344
morality and identity 6:575
personal identity 7:314
scepticism 8:498
Unger, Richard 4:482
Unger, Roberto 2:720, 5:140–1
Ungerer, G.A. 9:801
Ungrund ('the groundless')
divine creation (Berdiaev, N.A.)
1:727–8
Uniacke, Suzanne
double effect principle †3:119–22
UNICEF *see* United Nations
International Children's
Emergency Fund
uniformitarianism
geology 4:25–7
unique composition axiom
mereology 6:318–19
uniqueness
divine simplicity 8:785
measurement theory 6:244–5
unity distinction
dao 2:778
unitarianism *see* Arianism;
Socinianism
United Kingdom *see* Great Britain
United Nations International

Children's Emergency Fund
(UNICEF) 5:157
United Nations (UN)
decade of the woman 3:625
war 9:686–7
United States of America
absolute idealism 4:667
Baumgardt, D. 1:667–9
Bowne, B.P. 1:852–3
Bridgman, P.W. 2:17–19
Cavell, S. 2:257–60
Chisholm, R.M. 2:332–5
Chomsky, N. 2:335–41
Church, A. 2:346–9
colonial America 1:201–2
Common Sense School 2:446–7
Critical Legal Studies 2:714,
2:715–16
Davidson, D. 2:801–6
Dennett, D.C. 2:882–4
Dewey, J. 3:44–51
Dworkin, R. 3:187–9
Edwards, J. 3:240–5
eighteenth and nineteenth century
1:201–7
Einstein, A. 3:254–8
Emerson, R.W. 3:269–72
feminist literary criticism 3:612
Fodor, J.A. 3:684–6
Frank, J. 3:725–6
Franklin, B. 3:737–8
Frei, H. 3:778–9
Fuller, L.L. 3:801–2
Goodman, N. 4:135–40
Hanson, N.R. 4:224–6
Hegelianism 4:287–8, 4:292,
4:295–6
hermeneutical phenomenology
7:339–40
Hohfeld, W.N. 4:476–7
Holmes, O.W. 4:493–5
James, W. 5:60–8
Jefferson, T. 5:84–5
Johnson, A.B. 5:120–2
Johnson, S. 5:124–6
Kaplan, M. 5:204–6
Kripke, S.A. 5:301–5
Kuhn, T.S. 5:315–18
legal realism 5:521, 5:522–4
Lewis, C.I. 5:585–9
Lewis, D.K. 5:590–4
Llewellyn, K.N. 5:661–2
Mead, G.H. 6:210–12
modern constitutionalism
2:619–20
moral realism 6:535–6
Nagel, E. 6:641–3

Nagel, T. 6:643–7
Native American philosophy
6:662–7
Niebuhr, H.R. 6:838–41
Niebuhr, R. 6:841–4
Nozick, R. 7:44–7
Paine, T. 7:184–6
Peirce, C.S. 7:269–84
personal idealism 4:668
pietism 7:394
Post, E.L. 7:573–5
post-structuralism 7:596,
7:599–600
Pound, R. 7:609–10
pragmatism 7:633–40
psychoanalysis
post-Freudian 7:819–21
Putnam, H. 7:839–44
Quine, W.V. 8:3–14
Rand, A. 8:55–6
Rawls, J. 8:106–10
Rorty, R. 8:352–6
Royce, J. 8:377–81
Santayana, G. 8:467–70
Searle, J. 8:589–91
Sellars, W.S. 8:638–42
Shütz, A. 8:559–61
Skinner, B.F. 8:799–802
social freedom 8:40
Soloveitchik, J.B. 9:26–8
Strauss, L. 9:167–8
theosophy 9:364
Thoreau, H.D. 9:388–92
Tillich, P. 9:409–13
War of Independence
republican liberty 7:514
unity
of being *see* wahdat al-wujud
changeless 6:294–5
common nature 3:164
of conscience *see* wahdat al-shuhud
diachronic
bundle theory of mind 6:384
diversity contrast problem
Neoplatonism 7:723–4, 7:725–6
divine
Giles of Rome 4:75
Proclus 7:726
Ṛg Veda 4:102–3
of existence
Ibn al-'Arabi 4:601
Sufism
Ibn Sab'in 4:646, 4:647
of experience
process theism 7:717
free 9:29

of God
  Ash'ariyya/Mu'tazila
    comparison 1:519, 1:521–2
  Ibn 'Adi 4:599–601
  al-Kindi 5:251
  hierarchy of principles (Plotinus)
    7:457
  intellect
    Cajetan of Thienne 1:409
    Giles of Rome 4:74
  metaphysics 2:202–3
  mind–body (Descartes, R.)
    3:11–12
  multiplicity 2:857
  mystical experiences 6:629,
    6:631–2
  nature (Hegel, G.W.F.) 4:264
  of opposites 4:364, 4:366–7
  personal 7:315–16
  plurality relationship 9:846
  poetry/philosophy 7:475–6
  reason (Hegel, G.W.F.) 4:259,
    4:262–3, 4:267–8
  of science 9:530–3
    reductionism 8:145
  sobornost'
    Slavophilism 8:809–10
  social 6:92
  substantial form 4:73–4
  synchronic
    bundle theory of mind 6:384
  taiji
    neo-Confucianism
      China 6:768–9
  total 3:727–8
  uniqueness distinction
    dao 2:778
  virtues (Aristotle) 9:628
  world
    Daoism 2:792
universal
  dialectical 7:14
universal characteristic
  logical language (Leibniz, G.W.)
    5:553–4
universal consent see consensus
    gentium
Universal Declaration of Human
    Rights 4:832, 5:127, 6:103–4
universal generalization 7:868
  glossary 5:811
Universal Grammar (UG)
  Chomsky, N. 2:335–6, 2:337–8
    algorithmic learning procedures
      5:486
    innateness of language 4:51–2
    unconscious mental states 9:524

universal hylomorphism
  angelic intelligences 5:247–8
  potentiality 1:832
universal instantiation
  glossary 5:811
universal intellect
  Ibn Massara 4:628, 4:629
  revelation
    Islamic mysticism 6:618
universal language 9:533–5
Universal Law, Formula of (Kant, I.)
    5:190
universal nature
  humanism
    Chinese Marxism critique
      6:138–9
universal science (scientia universalis)
  influence on Chinese philosophy
    2:316
Universal Soul
  Ikhwan al-Safa' 4:686, 4:687
universal specification, principle of
  free logics 3:739–40
universal Turing machines see Turing
    machines
universality
  see also ethical universalism;
    nonuniversalism
  discourse ethics 4:196
  epistemic norms 3:367–8
  ethical norms 3:367
  ethics discourse 5:762–3
  feminist aesthetics 3:594
  genetics 4:14
  innate belief 4:795
  political 7:525–6
    relativism debate 7:501
  rights 8:328–9
  scientific theories 3:548, 7:576–7
  theism 1:532
  vocality
    medieval language 5:392, 5:393
universalizability
  legal reasoning 5:527–8, 5:529–30
  postmodernist discourse 6:9
  prescriptivism 4:230
  self-perfection 2:752–3
universals 9:539–44
  see also nominalism
  Abelard, P. 1:11
  abstract objects 1:33
  Active Intellect 4:650
  Albert the Great 1:146–7
  ante rem/in rebus 9:540
  Baumgarten, A.G. 1:670
  Boethius, A.M.S. 1:806, 7:18

Buddhism
  Dharmakīrti 7:24–5
  Tibet 9:406–7
category of
  Nyāya-Vaiśeṣika ontology 7:61
conceptualist theory of 1:566
Crathorn, W. 2:692–3
debate
  medieval Platonism 7:434–5
essence relationship 8:468
essentialism 1:172
existence of 9:540, 9:541
  extramental 4:360–1
identification through contrasts
    5:229
imagination 4:650
immanent–transcendent
  distinction 7:547
independent reality 9:513
Indian theories of 7:126, 8:692,
    9:544–8
individuals relationship
  Kilwardby, R. 5:247
  ontology in Indian philosophy
    7:126
individuation 3:154, 3:163–5
infinite regress 9:541
instantiation 9:540, 9:541, 9:543
intensional entities 4:803
intentional objects 4:403
language 8:175–6
Latin American colonial
    philosophy
  defence of Plato 5:424
logic of place 7:14
mathematics 9:540, 9:542
medieval epistemology 6:274
metaphysics 6:338–9
Mīmāṃsā 6:379
moderate realism 8:304–5
Navya-Nyāya theory of definition
    2:850
  relations 2:850–1
nominalism 7:18
  Buridan, J. 2:131, 2:132–3
  Peter Lombard 5:821
  William of Ockham 9:732,
    9:734–7
Nyāya 9:515
objects 9:715
ontological categories
  Indian philosophy 7:123–4
particulars 7:235
  Stoicism 9:142, 9:149–50
Peirce, C.S. 7:279–80
Peter of Spain 7:324
productive intellect 1:426

properties 9:540–1, 9:542–3
Ramsey sentences 8:48
real entities 8:433
realism
    antirealism distinction 8:116–17
    Armstrong, D.M. 1:442–3
    Brinkley, R. 2:20
    Duns Scotus, J. 3:154, 3:163
    nominalism debate 9:138
    Paul of Venice 7:265–6
reality of
    Aristotle 1:423
    Wyclif, J. 9:802–3
Richard of Middleton 8:311
Roscelin of Compiègne 8:356–7
samenesses/differences 9:540–1
set theory 9:540–1, 9:542–3
third man argument 9:541
type/token distinction 9:510
William of Champeaux 9:729
William of Ockham 7:19–20
universally free logics 3:740
universe
    see also cosmogony; cosmology
    Anaximenes 1:259, 1:261–2
    Aristotle
        Simplicius commentary 8:789
    concept of
        pre-Columbian thought 5:429,
            5:430, 5:431
    'episodic'
        Speusippus
            Aristotle critique 9:89–90
    eternity of 8:767
    God 7:104–5
        fine tuning argument for the
            existence of 4:90–1
        al-Sijistani 8:774, 8:775
    indestructability of
        Jewish philosophy 4:49
    Indian theories of 2:681–4
    infinity of
        Epicureanism 3:342
    love
        Jewish philosophy 1:26
    matter 6:193–4, 6:196
    mechanical philosophy 1:725
    neo-Confucianism
        China 6:764–5, 6:767–9
    Neoplatonism
        Chaldaean Oracles 2:273
    order
        design argument 4:558–9
    permanence of
        Epicureanism 3:341
    regularities 8:736
    sacramentality of 8:444–5

teleology 8:730
    threefold division of 7:468
universe-models
    anthropic 2:679
    Big-Bang theory 2:679–80
    Einstein, A. 2:678–9
    Hubble expansion 2:679
    inflationary model
        Guth, A. 2:679–80
    many-universe 2:679
    steady-state 2:679
universities
    establishment of
        effect on medieval philosophy
            6:272–3
University of Coimbra see Collegium
    Conimbricense
University of Paris see Paris,
    University of
univocality
    Aquinas, T. 6:760
    Henry of Harclay 4:361
univocity 8:258–9
    Duns Scotus, J. 2:293, 3:154,
        3:157–60
    eternity 3:423
    Henry of Ghent 4:358–9
    transcendental concepts 3:157–8
Unno, Taitetsu
    Kyoto School 5:330
    logic in Japan 5:716
    Nishitani Keiji 7:17
    Shinran †8:746–8
    Tanabe Hajime 9:262
unpredictability
    human desire of 3:116–17
unreason
    madness (Foucault, M.) 3:709–10
unsolvability
    degrees of see Turing degrees
Upadhye, A.N. 6:34–5
Upaniṣads
    see also Veda
    Advaita Vedānta 8:610
    authority of 5:283–4
    awareness 1:605
    Brahman 2:1, 2:2–3, 2:5, 6:622
    causation 2:251
    cosmology and cosmogony 2:682,
        2:684
    inference 4:761–2, 4:766
    interpretation 4:835–6
    karma and rebirth 5:210,
        5:211–12, 5:217
    mind 6:399–401
    monism 6:478, 6:479
    mysticism 6:621–2

pantheism 7:202
renunciation
    duty and virtue 3:185
self
    theories of 8:606, 8:607, 8:611
    Vedānta 4:437–8, 9:589–91, 9:592,
        9:594
Uranga, Emilio 6:346, 6:348
Urbach, E.E. 9:336–7
Urbach, P. 1:632, 5:475, 9:126
Urban II, Pope 1:284
Urbancic, I. 9:55
Ureña, E.M. 5:301
Urmson, J.O.
    analytic philosophy 1:229
    Austin, J.L. †1:571–4
    Chinese Confucianism 2:549
    emotive meaning 3:291
    logical atomism 5:775
    ordinary language philosophy
        7:153
    perception 7:299
    Prichard, H.A. 7:682
    Ross, W.D. 8:367
    supererogation 9:235
Urquhart, Alasdair
    computational complexity
        †2:471–6
    many-valued logics 6:84, 6:91
    Russell, B.A.W. 8:404
Urry, J. 8:587, 8:858
Uruguay
    feminism 3:625–7
    phenomenology 7:350
    positivism 7:568
Urvoy, D. 1:386, 4:646, 5:664
use theories
    poetry 7:475
use/mention distinction **9:548–51**
    compositionality 2:476
Usener, H. 3:350
ushin
    Buddhism
        kokoro 5:292
Usigli, Rodolfo 5:655
Uspenskii, B.A. 6:585–7, 6:588
Uspensky, V.A. 2:490
USSR see Soviet Union
usul al-fiqh (roots of jurisprudence)
    Islamic law 5:457, 5:458–9
Utechin, S.V. 8:409
utilitarianism **9:551–7**
    see also utility
    act-utilitarianism 8:814–15, 9:551,
        9:554
        see also utilitarianism, rule
    anarchism 1:244–5

animals and ethics 1:274
arguments for 9:555
autonomy 1:590
beneficence 4:343–4
Bentham, J. 1:718–19, 1:720–4,
    8:100
business ethics 2:151, 2:152
common good 2:752–3
critiques of 3:187
    Collingwood, R.G. 2:414
    Green, T.H. 4:168
    Grote, J. 4:183
    Prichard, H.A. 7:680
    Williams, B.A.O. 9:751
democracy 2:870
economic efficiency 5:454
egoism 3:246, 8:760–1
emotions 6:559
Enlightenment, continental 3:318
ethnophilosophy relationship
    3:447
external preferences 5:441–2
friendship 3:796
golden rule (Mill, J.S.) 9:537
happiness 4:227–8
harm principle (Mill, J.S.) 5:440
human nature 4:521–2
ideal
    Moore, G.E. 2:604, 6:496
    Rashdall, H. 8:59–60
impartiality 4:715
individualism 5:600
intuitionism 8:759–60
Japan 7:12
Jewish bioethics 1:778
justice 5:143
Kantian ethics synthesis
    (Baumgardt, D.) 1:668–9
Mill, J.S 6:361–75
moral motivation 6:525–6
moral psychology 6:532
moral recipients 6:499
moral standing 6:553
morality
    and religion 8:220
Mozi 6:455
negative 3:140
obligations to future generations
    3:819–20
paternalism 7:250–1
perfectionism comparison 7:300

political obligation 7:79
political philosophy
    history of 7:515
population ethics 7:541
practical reason
    instrumentalism 7:615
praise and blame 7:644–5
prescriptivism 4:230
problems for 9:555–6
professional ethics 7:736
progressive hedonism comparison
    3:140
promising 7:741
property 7:758–9
public interest 7:832, 7:833, 7:834
rational choice theory 8:64, 8:72–3
respect for persons 8:285
right and good 8:324
rights 8:329
risk 8:332, 8:333
rule-utilitarianism 8:815, 9:554–5
    see also utilitarianism, act
sexuality 8:725
Sidgwick, H. 8:758, 8:759–61,
    8:762
Singer, P. 1:580
situation ethics 8:798–9
slavery 8:805
Smart, J.J.C. 1:580
toleration 9:431–2
Tucker, A. 9:491–2
utility concepts 9:552–3
virtue ethics contrast 9:623
utility
    see also expected utility theory;
    utilitarianism
desire
    utilitarianism 9:553
expected
    decision and game theory
        2:824–5
    'famous fire cause' (Godwin, W.)
        4:123
ideal
    utilitarianism 9:553
pleasure
    utilitarianism 9:552–3
principle of (Mill, J.S.) 6:360,
    6:371, 6:372
property 7:757, 7:760

rationality
    economics 3:206
    social choice 8:825
    theory test 6:454
    welfare 3:206–7, 9:703
utopianism **9:557–62**
    anti-utopianism 9:559
    Bloch, E.S. 1:788–9
    Campanella, T. 2:186
    critiques of
        Dostoevskii, F.M. 3:116
        Tillich, P. 9:412
    Frankfurt School 6:144
    free theocracy (Solov'ëv, V.S.) 9:30
    hope 4:508
    humanism debate
        Signposts movement 8:770
    imagery 5:477
    liberation philosophy
        Latin America 5:612
    Marxist 4:417
    Nozick, R. 7:45–6
    politics 9:842
    relative 2:195
    Renaissance humanism 8:15–16
    social theory 9:559–60
    socialism
        Hessen, S.I. 4:417, 4:418
        socialité 1:711
    visions of
        Latin America 5:654
Uttara Mīmāṃsā see Vedānta
utterances
    analytic philosophy 1:226, 1:227
    conversational implicature
        (Grice, H.P.) 4:173–5
    double voiced (Bakhtin, M.M.)
        1:641
    expressive 5:587
    language units (Bakhtin, M.M.)
        1:640
    locutionary force (Austin, J.L.)
        1:571, 1:573
    performatory (Austin, J.L.) 1:571,
        1:572–3
    sentences distinction 7:625
    speech distinction
        Stoics 5:360
utterer's intention see
    communication, intention
Uzín Fernández, Oscar 5:655, 5:657

V

Vacca, Giovanni 1:761
Vacherot, E. 4:159
vacuum
    nature's abhorrance of (Strato)
        9:162
    scientific method (Pascal, B.)
        7:241, 7:242
Vadet, J.C. 1:208
Vādidevasūri 5:55, 5:57–8
vagueness **9:563–6**
    ambiguity 1:199
    computability 2:353
    concepts 2:508, 2:512–13
    fuzzy logic 3:823
    prediction
        chaos theory 2:276, 2:278
Vahek, J. 9:181
Vahid, S.A. 4:867–8
Vaibhāṣika School of Buddhism
    2:77–8, 2:79, 9:584–5
Vaidya, Chimanlal M. 9:575
Vaihinger, Hans **9:566–8**
    Dühring, E.K. 3:149
    fictionalism 3:667–8
    Kant, I. 5:200
    Lange, F. 5:354
Vaillot, R. 3:133
Vaiśeṣika 4:438–9
    see also Nyāya-Vaiśeṣika;
        Vaiśeṣikasūtra
    atomism 6:197, 6:198–9
    karma and rebirth 5:212, 5:213
    self
        theories of 8:608
    universals 9:545–6
    Vedānta School critique 9:591
Vaiśeṣikasūtra
    inference 4:766
    Nyāya-Vaiśeṣika 7:58, 7:60–1,
        7:64, 7:67
    ontology 7:128
    universals 9:548
Vaisey, J. 8:828
Vaishnava 8:42
Vaiṣvānara *see* Vallabhācārya
Vājapyāyana 9:544
Vajda, G.
    Bar Hayya, A. 1:651
    Ibn Paquda 4:636

Ibn Tzaddik, J. 4:662
Jewish Averroism 1:602
al-Muqammas, D. 6:606
Saadiah Gaon 8:440
Vajirañāṇa, P.M. 7:11
Vākyapadīya see Bhartṛhari
Valdés, M.J. 8:322, 9:521–2
Valentinus 4:84–5
Valenza, P. 8:189
Valera, Jerónimo de 5:422
validation
    critique (Bacon, F.) 1:627–8
validity
    see also consequence
    degrees of
        Bolzano, B. 1:825–6
    glossary 5:811
    intrinsic
        Mīmāṃsā 6:378, 6:379
    logic
        formal and informal 3:702
        laws 5:786–7, 5:788–9
        second-order 8:592
        predicate calculus 7:658–9
Valla, Lorenzo 1:124–5, 4:537–8,
    9:568–73
Vallabha Bhaṭṭa *see* Vallabhācārya
Vallabhācārya **9:574–5**
    heaven 4:255–6
    Indian and Tibetan philosophy
        4:738
    nondualism 4:438
Vallance, J. 4:335
Vallejo, César 5:655, 5:657
Vallentyne, P. 5:475
Vallooran, A.D. 9:594
Valsiner, J. 9:675
valuation
    glossary 5:811
value
    see also value pluralism; value
    theory; value-neutrality; values
    artistic 1:60, **1:476–80**, 3:707–8
        aesthetic distinction 4:790–1
        expressiveness 1:497–8
        interpretation 1:504
        morality 1:454–5
        truth 1:459

works of 3:706–7
    epistemological (Bachelard, G.)
        1:621
    evil 4:143
    fact distinction **3:537–8**, 9:770–1
    goodness distinction 4:131–2
    hedonism 4:257–8
    Humean projection
        Grice, H.P. 4:175–6
    individuality (Mikhailovskii, N.K.)
        6:355–6
    intrinsic
        Chisholm, R.M. 2:333
        extrinsic distinction 9:582
        goodness 4:131–2
    liberalism 5:600
    of life 5:625–6
    life 6:656
    love 5:844–5
    moral 9:582–3
    moral pluralism 6:529, 6:530
    moral realism 6:537
    ontological status of **9:580–1**
        error theory 9:580
        objective 9:580
        properties 9:580–1
    of persons 4:133, 8:285
    right/good distinction 4:133
    systemic view 4:161–2
    utilitarianism (Bentham, J.) 1:721
    value theory
        axiology 1:610–11
value judgments
    economics 3:213
    fact distinction (Weber, M.) 6:686
    al-Juwayni 5:170
    linguistic discrimination 5:643
    in social science **9:575–80**
        advocacy 9:577–8
        bias problem 9:577
        codes of conduct 9:578–9
        praxis-methodological
            distinction 9:576
        scientific methodology 9:577
        strength-of-evidence 9:578
value pluralism
    see also moral pluralism
    Berlin, I. 1:750, 1:751–2

value theory
  Brentano, F. 2:15–16
  Meinong, A. 6:284
  personal identity 7:306, 7:312–14
  rational choice theory 8:72–3
  Scheler, M.F. 8:504, 8:506
value-neutrality
  feminist epistemology 3:597–8,
    3:599
  modern science 7:576
values **9:581–3**
  absolutism (Lossky, N.O.) 5:833,
    5:837
  aesthetic 1:62–3, 1:64, 1:466
  aesthetics (Alexander, S.) 1:168
  art
    abstract 1:450–1
  ascetic ideal (Nietzsche, F.W.)
    6:845, 6:851
  authentic
    self-deception 8:629–30
  axiology **1:608–12**
  conceptual vacuum
    information technology 4:779
  conflict of
    professional ethics 7:734, 7:736
  critique of (Mackie, J.) 6:538
  cultural
    Cohn, J. 6:787–8
    postcolonial philosophy of
      science 7:575–6, 7:577
    proverbs 3:432
  democracy 2:868–9
  desert 3:25
  ethics 1:774, 4:779, 7:734, 7:736
    autonomy 1:589–90
    development 3:42
    existentialist 3:503
    sports 9:111
  feminism and social science 3:591
  God
    Niebuhr, H.R. 6:840
    Nietzsche, F.W. 6:852
  happiness (Hobbes, T.) 4:470
  law relationship 5:466–7
  liberal
    socialism 8:883
  libertarianism 5:619
  medical concepts 6:266
  morality (Nietzsche, F.W.) 6:855–6
  naturalism (Nietzsche, F.W.) 6:847
  naturalistic fallacy (Moore, G.E.)
    6:495
  nihilism 7:2, 7:4
  nihilism (Nietzsche, F.W.)
    6:853–60
  objective (James, W.) 5:60, 5:62

  ontology (Hartmann, N.) 4:241–2
  political 8:843
  power 7:611–12
  practical functions (Husserl, E.)
    4:581
  social
    Daodejing 2:779, 2:780–1
    Epicureanism 3:347–8
  socialist 8:880
  spiritual (Santayana, G.) 8:469
  sport 9·112, 9:113–14
Van Damme, W. 1:65
Van de Vall, R. 1:509
Van den Eynde, D. 4:520
van der Veer, R. 9:675
Van Deusen, N.C. 9:300
Van Dijk, R.T.M. 9:374
Van Eck, C. 1:509
Van Engen, J. 9:374
Van Ess, J. 1:523
van Gelder, T. 1:492, 2:579–7
Van Gelderen, M. 7:517
Van Geytenbeek, A.C. 6:616
Van Gulick, R.
  Chinese room argument †2:328–9
  colour and qualia 2:427
  Searle, J. 8:591
van Gulick, R.H.
  aesthetics
    Chinese 1:75
Van Helmont, Francis Mercurius *see*
  Helmont, Franciscus Mercurius
  van
Van Inwagen, Peter
  being 1:702
  fiction
    fictional entities 3:666, 3:667
    semantics of 3:662
  free will 3:753
  Incarnation and Christology
    †4:725–32
  Lewis, D.K. †5:590–4
  resurrection †8:294–6
  Trinity †9:457–61
Van Leeuwen, H.G. 2:308, 4:83, 5:435
Van Neste, R. 5:113
Van Norden, Bryan W.
  Mencius †6:302–4
Van Peursen, C.A. 9:487, 9:786
Van Steenberghen, F. 1:349, 1:404,
  1:598, 8:768
Van Straaten, Z. 9:174
Van Valen, L. 9:81
Van Veldhuijsen, P. 8:312
Vanberg, V. 3:220
Vancourt, R. 6:53
Vander Haeghen, V. 4:61

Vander Nat, A. 1:3, 1:6, 3:365
Vander Waerdt, P.A. 9:23, 9:814–15
Vanderjagt, A.J. 1:126, 2:376
Vandermeersch, L.
  Chinese Legalist philosophy 5:538
Vanderveken, D. 4:721
VanDeVeer, D. 1:776
Vane, Sir H. 4:234
Vanhoozer, K.J. 8:322
Vannoy, R.C. 8:729
Varadachari, K.C. 8:44
Vardhamāna *see* Mahāvīra
Vardi, Moshe Y. 3:359
Varela, F.J. 1:492, 3:202
Vargas-Lozano, G. 6:348
Vargish, T.
  modernism †6:447–9
variability
  measurement theory 6:244,
    6:247–9
variables
  experimental analysis
    social science 3:518–19
  generalization of
    (Whitehead, A.N.) 9:714
  glossary 5:811
  relations
    Navya-Nyāya theory of 2:851
Var'iash, A. 1:524, 1:527
variation
  classical mechanics 6:256
  genetic 4:15
Varley, Paul
  bushi philosophy †2:146–50
  Shintō †8:748–51, 8:752
Varma, V.P. 7:525
varṇa
  caste system
    political philosophy 7:523
    duty 3:183, 3:184
Varro 3:305
Vartainian, A. 5:335
Vasconcelos, José
  Latin America
    anti-positivism 1:304, 1:306,
      1:307
    literature 5:654, 5:657
Vasoli, C.
  Agricola, R. 1:126
  Melanchthon, P. 6:292
  Ramus, P. 8:55
  Renaissance logic 5:772
  Vernia, N. 9:599
Vasubandhu **9:583–7**
  Abhidharmakośa 9:584–5
  Ābhidharmika Schools of
    Buddhism 2:58

cosmology 2:681, 2:683
illusion 3:410
Indian and Tibetan philosophy
    4:738
inference 4:762, 4:763–4
Japanese Buddhism 2:101
karma 7:606, 7:608
mind 6:403
momentariness 6:472, 7:605–6
sense perception 8:692
suffering
    Buddhist views of origination of
        9:216, 9:217, 9:219
    Yogācāra Buddhism 2:65, 2:75–6
Vatican 8:724
Vatican Council 5:613
Vatke, Wilhelm 4:282, 4:298
Vātsīputrīya-Sāṃmatīya School of
    Buddhism 5:214
Vātsyāyana **9:587–8**
Indian and Tibetan philosophy
    4:738
inference 4:764, 4:766
Nyāya-Vaiśeṣika 7:64
veridicality 3:411
Vattanky, J. 7:67
Vattel, E. de 4:833
Vattimo, Gianni 1:192, 5:39, 5:42
Vaughn, S.N. 1:285, 1:296–7
Vaught, R. 5:851
Vaz Ferreira, Carlos
Latin America
    analytical philosophy 1:230,
        1:234
    anti-positivism 1:304, 1:305,
        1:307
    feminist thought in 3:625–7,
        3:628
Veatch, Robert M. 1:776, 7:735, 7:737
Veber, Franz (Franz Weber) 9:51,
    9:55
Veblen, Oswald 1:761, 4:34, 5:738
Veblen, T. 3:222
vectors
    connectionist networks 2:572,
        2:573
Veda
    see also Upaniṣads
    Arya Samaj 1:516–17
    authority of
        Mīmāṃsā 4:439
    Brahman 2:1
    causation 2:251
    cosmology and cosmogony
        2:681–2
    critiques of
        Buddha 2:93

Dharmakīrti 2:97
epistemology 3:390–1
fallibility of
    Dignāga 3:75
God as author of
    Mīmāṃsā School rejection of
        4:103
heaven 4:253–4
Hinduism
    Indian and Tibetan philosophy
        4:737
inference 4:760–1
interpretation 4:833–6
karma and rebirth 5:210, 5:211–12
linguistic power 7:607
meaning 6:240, 6:243
Mīmāṃsā 6:376–7, 6:378,
    6:379–80, 8:609–10
mysticism 6:621–2
self
    theories of 8:606–7
Vedānta 4:437–8, **9:588–94**
    see also Advaita Vedānta;
    Bhedābheda; Dvaita; Viśiṣṭādvaita
    Advaita–theistic Schools conflict
        9:590, 9:591–2
    Brahmansūtra 9:590–1
    contemporary India 9:592–3
    God
        concepts of 4:103–4
    Indian and Tibetan philosophy
        4:737
    individual eschatology 3:414
    karma and rebirth 5:213
    mysticism 6:622
    Neo-Vedānta movement 9:592–3
    Rāmānuja 8:42–3
    Śaṅkara 8:458–61
    self
        theories of 8:609–10
    theists
        Brahman 2:2–3
        Vallabhācārya 9:574–5
Vedas see Veda
Védrine, H. 2:39
vegetarianism
    ethics 1:273–4, 1:275
    Porphyry 7:545, 7:546
    Theophrastus 9:339
Veideman, Aleksandr 6:796, 6:797
Veitch, E.W. 5:746
Veitch, J. 2:208, 4:219
Veith, G.E., Jr 8:458
Vekhi see Signposts movement
Velazco y Trianosky, Gregory
    Shaftesbury, Third Earl of 8:732
    supererogation †9:232–5

Velkeley, R. 7:619
Velmans, M. 9:527
velocity
    al-Baghdadi 1:637
    Oresme, N. 7:154, 7:155
    quantification of
        Oxford Calculators 7:180
    ratios of (Bradwardine, T.) 1:863–4
Vendler, Z. 1:273
Venerable Bede 6:692
Venevitinov, D.V. 8:522
Venezuela
    analytical philosophy 1:232
    phenomenology 7:351
Venn diagrams 5:740, 5:742–3,
    9:594–5
Venn, John **9:594–5**
    chains of reasoning 5:502
    logic 5:722, 5:729
    machines and diagrams 5:746
Ventura, M. 8:440
Venturelli, A. 3:149
Venturi, F. 3:319–20
Vera, A. 4:299
Vera Cruz, Alonso de la 5:422, 5:423,
    5:426
verbalization (vyavahāra)
    knowledge
        Indian views of 5:280
Verbeek, Theo
    Aristotelianism
        seventeenth century 1:391–3
    Clauberg, J. 2:382
    Descartes, R. 3:19
    Geulincx, A. †4:59–61
    Le Clerc, J. †5:475–6
    Regius, H. 4:354
    Rohault, J. †8:341–3
Verbeke, G. 7:377, 7:472
verbs
    see also adverbs; predication
    mass/count terms 6:169
    phrases
        constituent structure 9:247,
            9:248
    propositional attitude
        recursion 9:249–50
    sentential 9:249–50
    transitive/intransitive 9:248
Verdon, T. 7:392
Verdonk, J.J. 8:55
Verene, Donald Philip
    Cassirer, E. †2:223–7
    sexuality 8:729
    Vico, G. 9:606
Veres, I. 4:573

veridicality
  criteria for
    Indian philosophy 3:409,
      3:411–12
  reliabilism
    Nyāya 3:388, 3:389–90, 3:391
  self-certificationalism
    Mīmāṃsā 3:388, 3:391
  sense perception
    Indian philosophy 8:691
verifiability theory of meaning *see*
  verificationism
verification
  criteria 2:712, 8:255, 8:257
  epistemic paradoxes 7:212–13
  identity of belief and knowledge
    1:707
  intuitive knowledge (Sidgwick, H.)
    8:761
  law of excluded middle 8:118
  meaning 4:860, 4:861–2, **6:230–6**
  phenomenalism 7:332
  pragmatism 5:65
  principle of
    transcendental arguments 9:453–4
  testimony 9:312
  Yoruba epistemology 9:833
verificationism **6:230–6**
  analytic behaviourism 1:690
  atheism
    Holocaust 4:496
  Ayer, A.J. 1:614, 1:615–16
  confirmation theory
    (Hempel, C.G.) 4:350–1
  critiques of 6:230, 6:233, 8:11
  legal positivism (Ross, A.) 8:365
  logical positivism 6:230
  meaning 4:860, 4:861–2
  moral knowledge 6:517–18
  omniscience objection 6:234–5
  Schlick, F.A.M. 8:541–2
  Vienna Circle 2:210
  Wittgenstein, L. 9:762
Verma, R.R. 9:174
Vermazen, B. 1:498
Vermes, G. 6:355
Vermes, P. 2:48
Vernadskii, Georgii Vladimirovich
  3:455–6
Verneaux, R. 8:270
Vernia, Nicoletto **9:596–9**
  Renaissance Aristotelianism 1:406,
    1:407, 1:409
Verniére, P. 5:476
Vernon, Richard
  federalism and confederalism
    3:574

Proudhon, Pierre-Joseph †7:791–3
Verona
  Hillel ben Samuel of **4:431–3**
Verra, V. 5:48
Verri, P. 5:42
Verrycken, K. 1:210, 7:377
Verständigung (agreement)
  language 2:459
Verstehen see understanding
Verucci, Guido
  Rosmini-Serbati, A. †8:362–4
Vesey, G.N.A. 7:295, 7:299
Vesley, R.E. 4:852
Vetö, M. 9:701
Vetter, T. 3:53
Vetterling-Braggin, M. 5:368
via negativa see negative philosophy
Viano, C.A. 5:42
Viatges, K. 8:438
vices
  see also sin
  Augustine 1:555
  Buddhism
    Indian 2:95
  coexistence with righteousness
    (Abelard, P.) 1:13
  evil 3:463, 3:464, 3:465–6
  sexual acts (Aquinas, T.) 8:721–2
  Stoicism 9:142, 9:157
  supererogation 9:232, 9:233–4
  and virtues **9:626–31**
vicious circles
  paradox 7:219, 9:359
Vick, G.R. 5:378
Vickers, B. 7:208
Vico, Giambattista **9:599–606**
  Croce, B. 2:730
  history
    humanism 5:35–6, 5:42
    knowledge 9:604
    philosophy of 4:459, 9:602–4
  poetry 7:478
  rationality and cultural relativism
    8:86
  rhetoric 8:308–9, 8:310
  social science 8:841, 8:847, 8:851,
    8:859
Vidal, C. 2:279
Vidyābhūṣaṇa, Baladeva 3:858–9,
  4:766
Vidyāraṇya 6:29–30
Viehweg, Theodor 5:527
Vienna Circle **9:606–14**
  see also Ayer, A.J.; Carnap, R.;
    Lvóv-Warsaw School; Neurath, O.;
    Schlick, Friedrich; Wittgenstein, L.
  analytic philosophy 1:225

logical positivism 5:789–90,
  5:792–3, 9:531
meaning and verification 6:231
science
  language and method 6:814–15
  naturalized philosophy of 6:729
Vierheller, E.J. 9:682
Vieu, L. 3:98
viewpoints *see* standpoints
Vignaux, P. 1:566, 3:725, 4:47
Vigrahavyāvartanī (Averting the
  Disputes) *see* Nāgārjuna
Vihan, P. 4:25
Vijñānavāda School of Buddhism,
  Korean 2:110
Viktorin Kornel of Všehrdy 2:765
Vilar, P. 9:77
Villanueva, E. 1:233
Ville, J. 2:482
Villegas, A. 6:348
Villey, Michel **9:614–15**
Villey, P. 6:489
Villoro, Luis 6:346
Villoslada, R. 6:56
Vimuktisena 2:61–2
Vincent, A. 4:170, 9:123
Vincent, R.J. 4:833
Vincenti, W.G. 9:288
vindication
  justification (Sellars, W.S.) 8:641
Vineis, E. 5:404
Vinogradoff, Sir Paul 5:141
Vinti, C. 5:298
Vio, Thomas de *see* Cajetan
violence **9:615–17**
  anti-colonialism
    Fanon, F. 1:112
    moral legitimacy of 1:101
  domestic
    feminist jurisprudence 3:608–9,
      3:610
  proletarian (Sorel, G.) 9:34, 9:35
  rejection of
    Jainism 6:34
Violi, C. 1:792
Virasoro, M.A. 3:514
Virchow, Rudolf 6:265, 6:266, 6:269
virtù
  princely (Machiavelli, N.) 6:17,
    6:18–19
virtue
  see also aretē; honour; virtue
    epistemology; virtue ethics; virtues
  abstract/practical distinction
    (Price, R.) 7:678
  actions/agents distinction
    (Price, R.) 7:677–8

agricultural ethics 1:127–8
ambiguity of (Xenophon)
   9:812–13
Aristotelian definition 3:287, 7:427
Aristotle 1:428–9
benevolence (Witherspoon, J.)
   9:756
Buddhism
   Indian 2:95
of character *(ēthikē aretē)*
   (Aristotle) 1:427–8
Chinese philosophy
   see also de
   qi 7:862–3
choice
   Aristotle 1:428
Christian Epicureanism (Valla, L.)
   9:569–70
civic 3:737, 8:282
duties of (Kant, I.) 5:190
education
   Aristotle 3:224
   Locke, J. 3:226
   Plato 3:223–4
   Socrates 3:223
ethics
   Antisthenes 1:316
   of character
      Aristotle 1:427–8
   Indian conceptions of **3:183–7**
eudaimonia 3:450–1, 4:134
   see also virtue, happiness
freedom (Kant, I.) 5:181–2
gender roles (Wollstonecraft, M.)
   9:789–90
good, theories of the 4:132
Greek political philosophy 7:505–6
happiness 3:557, 4:227, 7:426–7
   see also virtue, *eudaimonia*
highest good (Kant, I.) 5:192
human good (Aristotle) 1:429
human nature relationship
   (Butler, J.) 2:154–5
Ibn Miskawayh 4:631
Indian conceptions of **3:183–7**
Islamic moral philosophy 3:440,
   3:441
justice 9:506
knowledge (Spinoza, B. de) 9:91–2,
   9:102
morality 6:548, 9:103, 9:104
motivation (Locke, J.) 5:679–80
Neoplatonism 6:799–800
perfectionism 7:301
potentiality
   Indian theories of 7:606–7
promising 7:741

prudence (Aristotle) 1:428
rational agents (Aristotle) 1:427
renunciation
   Indian philosophy 3:183,
      3:185–7
Stoicism 2:382–3, 9:142, 9:154
teleological ethics 9:294
trust 9:468
truthfulness 9:482
unity of (Ariston of Chios) 1:380,
   1:382
virtue epistemology 3:364, 3:368–9,
   9:617–22
virtue ethics 9:618–20
virtue ethics **9:622–6**
   Anscombe, G.E.M. 1:281, 9:623
   antitheory
      moral particularism 6:528
   Chinese philosophy
      Confucianism 2:538–40,
         2:542–3
      Mencius 6:303
   honour 4:503
   impartiality 4:716–17
   MacIntyre, A. 6:22–4, 9:624
   moral luck 6:521
   moral psychology 6:533
   professional ethics 7:736
   virtue epistemology 9:618–20
   will 9:722–3
virtue theory *see* virtue ethics
virtues
   see also virtue; virtue
   epistemology; virtue ethics
   Aquinas, T. 1:340
   artificial
      Hume, D. 4:551, 4:554–5
         chastity and modesty 4:554
         justice 4:553–4
         promises 4:554
   Augustine 1:555
   cardinal
      Panaetius 7:190
      prudence 7:802
      Smith, A. 8:818–19
   Chinese philosophy (Mencius)
      6:303
   classification of (Porphyry) 7:548
   Confucianism
      xin 9:816
   definitions of (Socrates) 9:14
   doctrine of (Bonaventure) 1:833–4
   education (Socrates) 9:10
   egoism 3:247–8
   forms of knowledge (Socrates)
      7:408
   Gerard of Odo 4:39

hierarchy of (Plotinus) 7:462
imperfect duties (Kant, I.) 5:201
intellectual
   social epistemology 9:619
Jewish pietism (Ibn Paquda)
   4:634–6
medieval ethics 6:274
moral education 6:507–8
moral sentiment (Hume, D.) 4:555
moral theory (Shaftesbury, Third
   Earl of) 8:731–2
moral/theological distinction
   (Kilwardby, R.) 5:248
natural (Hume, D.) 4:551–3
nature of (Socrates) 9:8
negative 8:815, 8:819, 8:821
   positive distinction 8:819
Nietzsche, F.W. 6:854–61, 6:855–6,
   6:859
positive (Smith, A.) 8:819, 8:820
professional ethics 7:736
rational choice theory 8:65–6
self-cultivation
   Chinese philosophy 8:614
social (Smith, A.) 8:820
society (La Mettrie, J.O. de) 5:334
soul relationship (Socrates) 9:8
theological **9:326–31**
   faith 9:326, 9:327–9
   forgiveness and mercy 3:697–9,
      3:700
   hope 9:326, 9:327, 9:329–30
   love 9:326, 9:327, 9:329–30
theoretical/epistemic **9:340–3**
unity of
   Socrates 9:14–15
   Stoicism 9:155
and vices **9:626–31**
William of Auxerre 9:728
wisdom 9:752, 9:753, 9:754
vis viva (living force)
   Leibniz, G.W. 5:555–6
Vischer, F.T. 4:298
vision **9:631–8**
   Aristotelian sensibles (Ptolemy)
      7:830–1
   atomism
      Epicureanism 3:344
   colour and qualia 2:420–1, 2:425
   computation
      connectionist networks 2:574,
         2:575
      methodological individualism
         6:342–3
      models 9:632, 9:634–7
   computational theories 6:405
   Epicureanism 3:340, 3:344–5

geometric models 9:632
Gestalt theories 9:633
Illuminationist philosophy (al-
  Suhrawardi) 9:222
modularity of mind 6:450–1
Molyneux problem 6:467–8
optics 7:137
perception
  direct versus indirect 9:632–3
  infant cognition 2:390
  Reid, T. 8:172–3
perceptual processing 9:631–2,
  9:636
phenomenal consciousness
  2:590–1
psychology of (Berkeley, G.)
  1:740–1
split brains 9:107–8
vision in God doctrine
  Arnauld, A. 1:446
  Malebranche, N. 6:56, 6:58–61
    Leibniz, G.W. critique 5:552
  Norris, J. 7:42
visions
  see also mysticism
  religious (Hildegard of Bingen)
    4:429–30
Viśiṣṭādvaita 4:102, 4:104, 9:592
Viṣṇu 4:438, 6:31
Viṣṇudāsācārya 6:33
Viṣṇu-Nārāyaṇa 3:566
Viṣṇupurāṇa
  Rāmānuja 8:44
Visser, Albert
  provability logic †7:793–7
Viśvambhara Miśra see Caitanya
Viśvanātha Pañcānana 4:766, 7:67
Viśveśvara (Bhaṭṭa) 5:218
Viswanathan, Gauri 7:583
Viswanathan, Meera
  Japanese aesthetics †1:79–91
  kokoro †5:291–3
  Kuki Shūzō 5:321
Visweswaran, K. 7:583
vita activa
  Arendt, H. 1:370–1
vita contemplativa
  Arendt, H. 1:371–2
Vital du Four 9:638–9
vital reason
  Ortega y Gasset, J. 7:165, 7:166–7
Vitali, M.C. 5:109
Vitalis de Furno see Vital du Four
vitalism 9:639–43
  French philosophy of science 3:782
  historicism 4:444
  Le Roy, É.L.E.J. 5:481

life, origin of 5:634
Vitányi, P.M. 2:482, 2:496
Vitoria, Francisco de 9:643–5
  Spain, philosophy in 9:71–2, 9:77
Vitruvius 1:361–3, 1:366
Vivekananda 8:39–41, 8:42, 9:592–3
Vives, Juan Luis 9:645–50
  logical notation 5:739
  Spain
    philosophy in 9:71, 9:77
Vizenor, Gerald 6:669, 6:671
Vlačić, Matija (Mattias Flacius
  Illyricus) 9:49, 9:55
Vlastos, Gregory 9:650–4
  Democritus 2:878
  equality 3:396
  Heraclitus 4:369
  love 5:846
  Plato 7:421
  slavery 8:807
  Socrates 9:18–19
  Xenophon 9:815
  Zeno of Elea 9:853
Vleeschauwer, H.J. de 2:411, 4:61
vocation
  happiness (Skovoroda, H.S.) 8:803
Voegelin, Eric 9:654–7
Vogel, H. 7:398
Vogel, Jonathan
  inference to the best explanation
    †4:766–9
  scepticism 8:498
Vogler, Candace A.
  Taylor, H. †9:279–80
'voice'
  in discourse (Le Doeuff, M.) 5:477
void
  Aristotelian mechanics 6:249,
    6:251
  Aristotelian physics 7:373
  atomic motion
    Epicureanism 3:343
  categories of (Gassendi, P.)
    3:852–3
  creative nothingness (Nishitani
    Keiji) 7:17
  Epicureanism 3:341, 3:342, 3:343
  microscopic (Strato) 9:162
  motion (Melissus) 6:295
  space
    Stoicism 9:148
  within bodies
    Epicureanism 3:342
voidism
  Mahayana Buddhism
    reincarnation 8:183, 8:184

voidness
  see also emptiness
  Tibetan philosophy
    Jo-nang-pa School 9:402–3
Voigt, G. 4:532, 4:541
Voitle, R. 8:732
volition
  see also will
  action 1:37, 1:39–40
  individual choice
    paternalism 7:251–2
  moral luck 6:521
Völkerpsychologie (cultural
  psychology)
  Wundt, W. 9:799–800
Volksgeist
  German historical school of law
    5:139
Vollert, C. 1:349, 3:429
Volodin, A.I. 4:307
Voloshinov, V.N. 6:155, 6:160
Volotskii, Iosif 6:278
Volpe, Galvano della 6:147
Voltaire (François-Marie Arouet)
  9:657–63
  cosmology 9:659–60
  critique of (Rousseau, J.-J.) 8:373
  deism 2:855
  Du Châtelet-Lomont, É. 3:132
  freedom 9:661
  hope 4:510
  humanism 4:529
  Leibniz, G.W. 5:562
  liberalism 5:602, 5:605
  metaphysics 9:658–9
  Montesquieu, C.L. 6:492
  morality 9:659
  optimism 9:660–1
  suicide 9:230
  teleology 9:297
  toleration 9:430
voluntarism 9:663–4
  see also antivoluntarism
  Chinese Marxism 6:134–5
  Epicureanism (Gassendi, P.) 3:851
  evolution (Lossky, N.O.) 5:836–7
  Gerard of Odo 4:38, 4:39
  Henry of Ghent 4:359
  human freedom (Gassendi, P.)
    3:855
  Jewish 5:87, 9:664–7
    creation 4:619, 6:45
    emanation 5:32–3
  Mohist philosophy 6:452, 6:453,
    6:457
  morality 8:219, 8:792, 9:377–8
  natural law 2:750–1, 5:465

natural philosophy
    medieval 6:703
natural religion (Paley, W.) 7:187
political obligation 7:78–9
structuralism
    social science 9:185
voluntary action
    desire (Aristotle) 1:426–7
voluntas see will
Volynskii, A. 6:797
von Cieszkowski, August *see*
    Cieszkowski, August von
von Hartmann, Edouard *see*
    Hartmann, Karl Robert Eduard
    von
von Helmholtz, Hermann *see*
    Helmholtz, Hermann von
von Humboldt, Wilhelm *see*
    Humboldt, Wilhelm von
von Jhering, Rudolf *see* Jhering,
    Rudolf von

von Neumann-Bernays-Gödel class
    theory 8:709, 8:712–13
Von Wright, Georg Henrik 5:624,
    9:667–9
    causation 2:251
    epistemic logic 3:359
    explanation in history and social
        science 3:531
    holism and individualism in
        history and social science 4:488
    social science
        contemporary philosophy of
            8:847
Vonèche, J.J. 7:829
Vorgriff
    Rahner, K. 8:37, 8:38
Vorgrimler, H. 8:39
Vorländer, Karl 6:143
vortex
    theory of (Descartes, R.) 3:14–15
Vorverständnis 4:391, 5:527

Vosagine, Jacobus de 6:631–3
Voss, S. 3:19
Vossenkuhl, W. 9:454
voting systems 8:64, 8:69–70, 8:825,
    8:826
Voutsinas, D. 6:53
voyeurism 3:408
Vrijer, M.J.A. de 4:354
Vucinich, A. 1:820, 6:797
Vuillemin, J. 1:297, 3:19
Vuk-Pavlović, Pavao 9:51, 9:55
vulnerability **9:669–71**
Vvedenskii, Aleksandr 6:793–4, 6:797
Vyādi 9:544
Vygotskii, Lev Semënovich **9:671–5**
    cognitive development 2:394
    influence on Russian Marxism
        6:155, 6:160
Vyrubov, Grigory 7:562
Vysheslavtsev, Boris Petrovich
    9:675–7

W

Wachtel, H.I. 6:816
Wachterhauser, B. 3:831
Wacks, R. 7:693
Wada, H. 1:244, 3:99
Wada, T. 7:67
Waddington, C. 8:55
Wade, I.O. 2:376, 3:133, 3:320, 9:663
Waelhens, A. de 6:325
wager, Pascal's *see* Pascal's wager
Wagner, C. 7:711, 8:832
Wagner De Reyna, A. 3:514
Wagner, G. 5:842
Wagner, H.R. 8:561
Wagner, Richard 6:846, 7:130–1
Wagner, S. 5:789
wahdat al-shuhud (unity of conscience) 8:733, 8:734
wahdat al-wujud (oneness of existence/unity of being) 4:655–6, 6:806, 8:733, 8:734
Wahl, F. 9:177
Wahl, Jean
    existentialism 3:502
    Hegelianism 4:293, 4:299
    Koyré, A. 5:298
    Whitehead, A.N. 9:719
wahm (estimation) 4:650
Wain, J. 5:123
Wainwright, H. 3:614
Wainwright, William J.
    Edwards, J. †3:240–5
    miracles 6:416
    mysticism 6:634
    omnipresence 7:107
    original guilt 8:795, 8:796
    religious experience 8:255
Waismann, F. 5:795, 7:632–3
Wajcman, Judy 3:865–6, 3:868
wajib al-wujud see necessary being
Wakeling, E. 3:109
Wakoff, Michael B.
    theosophy †9:362–6
Walbridge, J. 4:703, 9:223–4
Walcott, Derek 6:100
Wäldä Heywåt 3:444, 3:445
Waldenfels, H. 7:17
Waldron, Jeremy
    justice 5:147
    liberalism †5:598–605

multiculturalism 6:602
neutrality
    political †6:818–21
    property 7:761
Proudhon, P.-J. 7:793
rights 8:331
Walens, S. 6:671
Wales
    Price, R. **7:675–9**
Waley, A. 2:549, 2:781, 2:795
Walicki, Andrzej
    Chaadaev, P.I. †2:269–73
    Chernyshevskii, N.G. †2:303–6
    Hegelianism
        Russian †4:302–7
    Hessen, S.I. †4:415–19
    Lavrov, P.L. †5:435–8
    liberalism
        Russian 5:610
    Mikhailovskii, N.K. †6:355–7
    Neo-Kantianism
        Russian 6:797
    Pan-Slavism 7:201
    Plekhanov, G.V. 7:455–6
    positivism
        Russian †7:561–4
    religious-philosophical
        Renaissance
        Russian 8:428
    Russian philosophy 8:422
    Slavophilism †8:807–11
    Solov'ëv, V.S. †9:28–33
Walker, A.D.M. 6:571, 7:80
Walker, A.K. 5:470
Walker, J.R. 6:671
Walker, L. 6:505
Walker, N. 2:711
Walker, Nicholas
    Hegelianism †4:280–302
    Hölderlin, J.C.F. †4:479–82
Walker, Paul E.
    al-Razi, Abu Bakr †8:110–12
Walker, Ralph C.S.
    contingency †2:650–2
    Kant, I. 5:198
    Strawson, P.F. 9:174
Wall, P.D. 9:215
Wall, R. 6:435
Wallace, A.F.C. 6:672

Wallace, Alfred Russel **9:678–9**
    evolution, theory of 3:476, 3:483
Wallace, G. 6:571
Wallace Hadrill, J.M. 8:229
Wallace, J. 2:646
Wallace, J.D. 2:581
Wallace, R.
    Socinianism 8:891–2
Wallace, R. Jay
    moral motivation †6:522–8
    moral sentiments †6:548–50
Wallace, R.J., Jr
    social science 8:867, 9:579
Wallace, W.
    Hegelianism 4:300
Wallace, W.A.
    Dietrich of Freiberg 3:71
    Galilei, G. 3:841
    Renaissance Aristotelianism 1:413
    Renaissance logic 5:772
    Soto, D. de 9:40
    Zabarella, J. 9:839
Wallace, William
    Aristotelianism
        seventeenth century 1:391–3
Wallace-Hadrill, D.S. 3:458
Wallacker, B. 4:514
Walli, K. 3:568
Wallis, John 4:468
Wallis, R.T. 6:803
Wallman, Joel 1:272, 1:273
Wallner, I.M. 1:689
Walls, J.L. 4:333, 7:838, 7:839
Wallwork, E. 3:177
Walraff, C.F. 5:84
Walsh, A. 8:729
Walsh, C. 5:590
Walsh, D. 1:801
Walsh, J.J. 2:136, 4:39
Walsh, W.H. 4:459, 7:682
Walter, M.L. 2:19, 7:135–6
Walter, S. 8:387
Walters, G.J. 5:84
Walters, L. 8:867, 9:579
Walters, R.L.
    Du Châtelet-Lomont, É. †3:131–3
Walters, R.S. 5:475
Walton, C. 6:66

Walton, Douglas N.
  action 1:41
  dialogical logic 3:61–2
  fallacies †3:544–5
  formal and informal logic
    †3:701–3
Walton, Kendall
  aesthetics 3:281
    music 6:615
    photography 7:381
  art
    abstract 1:450, 1:452
    ontology of 1:484
  pictorial depiction 2:896
    understanding of 1:475
  fiction
    fictional entities 3:665–6, 3:667
    semantics of 3:663
Waltz, K. 9:256
Waltz, K.N. 9:691
Walzel, O. 8:352, 8:531
Walzer, Michael
  citizenship 2:365
  community and
    communitarianism 2:471
  consent 2:599
  conventionalism 5:142
  equality 3:396
  ethics
    applied 1:325
    market 6:110
  international relations 4:833
  justice 5:147, 5:154, 5:157
  moral relativism 6:539, 6:542
  political philosophy
    nation and nationalism 6:662
    nature of 7:528
    and religion 8:229
    war and peace 9:691
  work
    philosophy of 9:797
Walzer, R. 1:386, 4:159, 7:160, 7:430
Wang Bi 2:782, 5:594, 9:400,
    9:829–30, 9:831
Wang Chong 9:679–80
Wang Chuanshan see Wang Fuzhi
Wang Ch'ung see Wang Chong
Wang Fu-chih see Wang Fuzhi
Wang Fuzhi 6:774, 9:680–2
Wang, H. 2:637, 2:639, 4:118–19
Wang, H.P. 4:220, 5:537, 5:538
Wang, L. 9:858
Wang Ruoshui 6:139–40
Wang Su 9:857
Wang Xizhi 1:71
Wang Yangming 9:682–4
  Confucianism, Japanese 2:553

li 5:595
neo-Confucianism 6:772–3
self-cultivation 2:326, 8:623–4
xin 9:816
Wang, Zhouming 5:103
Wanner, E. 4:54
war 9:684–91
  China 6:455, 9:230–1
  conception of 9:685
  conduct 9:687–8
  ethics of killing
    Augustine 1:542, 1:556
    Roman Catholicism 4:798
  international relations 4:827
  just 9:686–7
    Aquinas, T. 8:226
    Augustine 1:542, 1:556
    Chinese philosophy
      Lushi chunqui 5:864
    Grotius, H. 4:185
    Mozi 6:453, 6:455
    rights of conquest 9:644–5
    slavery
      Locke, J. 8:805
    Suárez, F. 9:192
  justification 9:685–7
  pacifism 9:688
  pre-morality of (Croce, B.) 2:732
  rights of conquest (Vitoria, F. de)
    9:644–5
  slavery (Locke, J.) 8:805
  state of nature (Hobbes, T.) 4:460,
    4:470–1, 4:475
  Toletus, F. 9:434
  violence 9:615
war crimes
  Arendt, H. 1:371
Warburton, W. 2:419
Ward, C. 1:248
Ward, Keith 5:200
Ward, R. 6:583
Ward, W.R. 7:395–6
Warder, A.K. 2:99, 3:76, 8:694
Wardy, R.
  categories †2:229–33
warehouse consciousness
  Yogācāra Buddhism 2:73
Warfield, T.A. 2:578, 2:579, 2:646
Wargo, R.J.J. 5:716
Warminski, A. 4:482
Warner, R. 4:177
Warnick, B. 1:782
Warnke, G. 3:831, 9:8
Warnock, G.J.
  Austin, J.L. 1:574
  emotivism 3:293

ordinary language philosophy
  †7:147–53
Warnock, Mary
  applied ethics 1:325
  existentialism 3:502
  ethics 3:505
  imagination 4:708
  Sartre, J.-P. 8:479
warrant 5:268–72, 7:36–7
  a posteriori 1:1
  belief 9:619
  certainty 2:265–7
  coherentism 1:1–2
  contextualism 2:265–6
  epistemic paradoxes 7:211–12
  foundationalism 1:2–3
  God's role 7:37
  justification distinction 5:268
  truth-concepts
    Dummett, M.A.E. 3:150–1
Warren, Austin 5:470
Warren, H.C. 8:186
Warren, K.J. 3:336
Warren, S. 7:693
Warrier, A.G.K. 2:5
Warrington, R. 2:719, 5:499,
    5:509–10
warrior way, Japanese philosophy see
    bushi philosophy
Warsaw school of logic 7:492
Wartofsky, Max W.
  Feuerbach, L.A. 3:640
  Hegelianism 4:301, 4:302
  models 6:446–7
  Naturphilosophie 6:740
  quantum mechanics,
    interpretation of 7:894
Washington, Corey
  use/mention distinction †9:548–51
Wason, P.C. 8:86–7, 8:88, 8:90
Wasserman, E.A. 1:698, 5:487
Waszink, J.H. 2:176
Watanabe, S. 2:106
water
  as primary substance 9:322–3
Waterland, D. 9:423
Waterlow, S. 1:435
Waters, C.K. 4:16
Waters, E. 7:822
Waters, R.H. 7:135
Watkin, D. 1:366
Watkins, John 3:222
Watkins, J.W.N. 8:859
Watling, J. 8:404
Watner, C. 7:177
Watson, A. 8:347
Watson, B. 2:549, 4:452, 5:852, 5:865

Watson, F. 4:395
Watson, G. 3:33, 6:533
Watson, James
    DNA discovery
        molecular biology 6:458–9,
        6:460
    genetics 4:16
    life, origin of 5:635
Watson, J.B.
    analytic behaviourism 1:693
    eliminativism 3:263
    learning 5:487
    psychology
        theories of 7:826, 7:830
    scientific behaviourism 1:696,
        1:697, 1:699
    Skinner, B.F. 8:800, 8:802
Watson, Jean 7:57
Watson, P.J. 1:359
Watson, P.S. 7:287
Watson, R.A. 3:718, 5:481, 8:166
Watsuji Tetsurō **9:691–3**
    Confucian ethics 5:78, 5:79–80
    Japanese aesthetics 1:90
    Japanese philosophy 5:79–80
        in modern literature 5:659
Watt, W.C.
    semiotics †8:675–9
Watt, W.M. 4:68, 6:411
Wattjes, J.G. 4:286–7
Wattles, J. 9:539
Watts, I. 8:796
Wayland, Francis 2:448
Wayman, A. 9:219
weak saturation condition
    nonstandard analysis 1:213
weakness of will *see akrasia*
Weale, Albert
    consent 2:599
    equality †3:392–6
    needs and interests †6:752–5
    public interest 7:834
    welfare †9:702–6
wealth
    equality 3:394
    market economy 8:820
Wealth of Nations see Smith, Adam
Weaver, C.E. 2:482
Weaver, W. 8:662
web of belief
    conventionalism (Quine, W.V.)
        2:667
    mental/semantic holism 4:488,
        4:489
    underdetermination 9:528–9
Webb, B. 5:637–8
Webb, C.C.J. 4:375, 6:713

Webb, J. 4:119, 4:429
Webb, M.E. 4:238
Webb, R.K.
    Martineau, Harriet †6:116–17
Webber, B.L. 1:244
Webelhuth, G 2:341
Weber, Franz *see* Veber, Franz
Weber, Max **9:693–8**
    adequate causation 9:694–5
    asceticism 1:519
    authority 1:584–5, 1:586
    Brahmo Samaj 2:7
    bureaucracy 9:3
    economics 3:222
    ethics 9:696
    fact–value distinction 6:686
    Habermas, J. 4:199–200
    intention 9:696
    legitimacy 5:541, 9:695
    Marx, K. comparison 9:697
    power 7:610, 7:613
    Protestant ethic 9:696–7
    social science
        contemporary philosophy of
            8:847
        functionalism 3:818
        methodology of 8:868
        philosophy of history 8:854,
            8:859
        society 8:886, 8:889
        sociology 9:8
        value judgments 9:576, 9:580
    social theory
        law 8:876, 8:879
            historical 5:140, 5:141
    understanding (*Verstehen*) 9:695–6
Weber, Samuel 5:338, 6:12
Weber, T. 7:890, 7:894
Webster, C. 1:632, 2:287, 7:208
Webster, J. 1:656
Wedberg, Anders 5:496, 8:492
Weed, D. 9:580
Weeks, A. 1:801, 9:366
Weems, B.B. 9:442
Wegener, W. 9:694
Wehrli, F. 4:364, 7:305, 9:163–4
Wei Furen 1:71
Weier, W. 2:382
Weierstrass, Karl 1:218, 1:219–20,
    7:51
Weil, A. 4:34
Weil, E. 4:299
Weil, Simone **9:698–701**
    being in the world 9:699
    decreation 9:699–700
    grace 9:700
    justice 9:700

Weiler, G. 1:23, 6:206
Weinberg, B. 4:541
Weinberg, F.M. 8:18
Weinberg, G. 1:379
Weinberg, J. 2:773–4
Weinberger, Ota **9:701–2**
    legal positivism 5:521
    neo-institutionalism 4:801–2
Weyr, F. †9:707–9
Weindling, Paul
    Haeckel, E.H. †4:200–1
Weiner, A.M. 4:16
Weiner Kreis see Vienna Circle
Weingart, R.E. 1:541
Weingartner, R.H. 8:780
Weinreb, L.L. 5:521
Weinsberg, L. 4:662
Weinsheimer, J. 3:831
Weinstein, D. 6:101, 8:780
Weinstein, L. 9:260
Weinstein, M. 8:780
Weinstein, Michael A.
    anti-positivism
        Latin America †1:303–7
    cultural identity 2:746
    marginality 6:101
    violence 9:617
Weinstein, S. 5:487, 9:861
Weinstein, W.L. 3:756
Weinstock, Daniel M.
    moral pluralism †6:529–31
Weinstock, J. 5:650
Weintraub, E. 3:222
Weishaupt, A. 4:696–7
Weisheipl, J.A.
    Albert the Great 1:152
    Aquinas, T. 1:349
    Bradwardine, T. 1:866–7
    Burley, W. 2:144
    Heytesbury, W. 4:421
    medieval natural philosophy 6:707
    Oxford Calculators 7:183
Weiskel, T. 9:205
Weiskrantz, Lawrence
    blindsight
        phenomenal consciousness
            2:590–1, 2:596
        unconscious mental states
            9:522, 9:524, 9:525, 9:527
Weiss, J. 4:245, 4:415
Weiss, P. 9:113, 9:116
Weiss, R. 4:541
Weisser, C.D. 9:412
Weisskopf, V.F. 4:329
Weithman, P. 8:729–30

Weithman, Paul J.
  religion and political philosophy
    †8:224–30
Weitz, M. 1:464–5, 1:468, 7:478
Weizenbaum, J. 4:781–2
Welbon, G.R. 7:11
Welbourne, M. 9:314
Welby, V. 7:284
welfare **9:702–6**
  see also interests; needs; wellbeing
  as capabilities 9:702, 9:705
  child
    reproduction ethics 8:278–9
  happiness 4:228–9
  market efficiency 6:107, 6:108
  moral agents 6:502
  moral agents (Hume, D.) 6:502
  objective accounts 9:702, 9:704–5
  as preference 3:206–7, 9:702,
    9:703–4
  social democracy 8:827
  utilitarianism 9:551, 9:552, 9:553
welfarism
  social choice 8:824, 8:825
wellbeing
  see also eudaimonia; interests;
    needs; welfare
  alternative views 3:207–8
  classification of
    development ethics 3:42
  happiness relationship 4:226,
    4:227, 4:228–9
  preference satisfaction theories
    3:207
  socialism 8:882–3, 8:885
Wellbery, D.E. 5:578
Welling, M. 4:802
Wellman, C. 1:519
Wellman, H.M. 2:392, 6:387–8, 6:390
Wellman, K.
  La Mettrie, J.O. de †5:332–5
Wellmer, A. 2:460–1, 2:462
well-ordering
  glossary 5:811
well-ordering principle
  constructible universe 2:623
Wells, C. 8:294
Wells, G.A. 4:129
Wells, N.J. 2:175, 9:196
Weltalter philosophy 8:514–15
Weltanschauung 1:111
wen 1:68–9
Wendel, F. 2:182
Wensinck, A. 5:31
Werhane, P.H. 8:822
Werner, Heinz 2:394
Wernham, J. 8:746

Wertheimer, A. 2:389, 3:104, 3:106,
  8:730
Wertheimer, Max 4:53
Wertsch, J.V. 9:675
Wertz, D.C. 4:19
Wesen see eidos
Wesensschau (essential insight) 4:579
Wesley, Charles 7:395
Wesley, John
  pietism 7:393, 7:394–5
  sanctification 8:457
Wessell, L.P. 1:672
West, C. 1:207, 7:640
West, D.C. 5:105
West, M.L. 7:165
West, T.H. 1:790
Westberg, D. 1:349, 9:631
Westerink, L.G. 1:210, 6:803
Westermann, C. 2:700
Westermarck, E.A. 8:488, 9:230
Western culture
  developing countries
    marginality 6:99–100
  identity 2:745–6
  imperialism
    Latin American Marxism 6:162,
      6:163–4
Western Marxism *see* Marxism,
  Western
Western philosophy
  Chinese philosophy comparison
    2:315
    being 9:834–5
    Daodejing 2:780
    ethics 2:537–8
    order 2:316–17
    social harmony 2:323
  cultural identity 2:744, 2:744–5
  dichotomies
    feminist critique of 3:601
  East Asian Philosophy
    comparison 3:192–3, 3:194,
      3:195
  Europe
    cultural dominance
      postcolonial philosophy of
        science 7:575–6
    expansionism
      postcolonial philosophy of
        science 7:575, 7:576–7
    Jewish Enlightenment 3:320,
      3:322–3
  influence of
    Chinese Marxism 2:326
  Islamic philosophy
    influence of 4:653

  relationship with 5:16–18,
    5:19–20, **5:21–5**
  Orientalism **7:158–60**
  science and religion
    history 8:230
Westerståhl, Dag
  quantifiers
    generalized †7:873–7
    situation semantics 8:672
Westfall, R.S. 6:828, 8:571
Westin, A.F. 4:781
Westkott, M. 3:593
Westman, R. 2:672
Westminster Confession of Faith 7:657
Westminster Shorter Catechism 7:657
Weston, M. 5:244
Westphal, Merold
  phenomenology of religion
    †7:352–5
  postmodern theology †7:583–6
Wetherbee, Winthrop
  Bernard of Tours †1:755–6
  Chartres school 2:292
  Isaac of Stella †5:4–5
  Platonism
    medieval 7:439
Wetherell, M. 1:695
Wetherick, N.E.
  psychology
    theories of †7:824–30
Wetlesen, J. 6:637
Wetter, G. 3:58, 5:567
Wettersten, J. 7:539, 7:540
Wettstein, H.K. 5:304, 8:209, 9:631
Wettstein, Howard
  ritual †8:338–41
Wetzel, J. 1:559
Wetzel, Linda
  type/token distinction †9:509–11
Weyl, Hermann **9:706–7**
  Cantor, G. 2:198–9
  conservation principles 2:608
  constructivism in mathematics
    2:637–8, 2:639
  Einstein, A. 3:258
  geometry 4:32, 4:34
  Hilbert's programme and
    formalism 4:429
  Kronecker, L. 5:313
  mathematics
    foundations of 6:192
  proof theory 7:752
Weyr, František **9:707–9**
Weyuker, E. 2:496
Wezler, A. 7:63, 7:67
Whately, R. 1:843, 5:729
Wheatley, S.C. 2:621

Wheeler, J.A. 7:890, 8:200, 9:68–9
Whelan, Frederick 4:562
Whewell, William **9:709–11**
common-sense ethics 2:451
induction
inference 4:759
science, nineteenth century
philosophy of 8:567, 8:568
Maxwell, J.C. 6:207
Mill, J.S. 6:365, 6:375
science 8:578
knowledge 8:578
method 8:581
nineteenth century philosophy
of 8:565–6, 8:569, 8:570–1,
8:572
science, demarcation problem
2:864, 2:867
Whichcote, Benjamin 2:185
Whicher, S. 3:272
Whiston, W. 2:419
Whitaker, M.A.B. 4:329
Whitbeck, Caroline 3:606
White, A.D. 8:236
White, A.R.
Butler, J. 2:160
duty 3:183
Hohfeld, W.N. 4:477
ordinary language philosophy
7:152, 7:153
White, F.C. 8:554
White, H. 6:657, 8:310
White, H.V. 9:606
White, James D.
Plekhanov, G.V. †7:451–6
White, John
moral education †6:505–9
White, K. 2:201, 7:323
White, M. 6:352, 6:643
White, M.G. 7:640
White, M.J. 1:535, 3:86, 9:853
White, Morton 1:239
White, P.A. 4:846
White, S.
conceptual role semantics 8:654,
8:655–7
content
wide and narrow 2:645, 2:646
Habermas, J. 4:199–200
White, Stephen A.
Cicero, M.T. †2:355–60
eudaimonia 3:452
Panaetius †7:188–90
White, Stephen K.
postmodernism and political
philosophy †7:590–3
White, Thomas **9:712–13**

White, V. 1:541
Whitehead, Alfred North **9:713–20**
Carnap, R. 2:215
consequence 2:603
constructivism in mathematics
2:639
definition 2:846, 2:849
descriptions 3:24
ecological philosophy 3:202
educational philosophy 3:231
Gödel's theorems 4:108, 4:119
Hempel, C.G. 4:352
intensional entities 4:807
lambda calculus 5:349
Lewis, C.I. 5:589
logic 5:733, 5:738, 5:782, 5:785
logical positivism 5:792, 5:795
logicism 5:817, 9:714–15
Russell, B.A.W. 8:394
mathematics 6:192
mereology 6:320
modal logic 6:419
panpsychism 7:197
Post, E.L. 7:575
predicate calculus 7:665
Principia Mathematica
consequence 2:603
constructivism in mathematics
2:639
definition 2:846, 2:849
descriptions 3:21–2, 3:24
Gödel's theorems 4:108, 4:119
intensional entities 4:807
lambda calculus 5:349
logic in the early twentieth
century 5:733, 5:738
logical form 5:782, 5:785
logical positivism 5:792, 5:795
logicism 5:817
logicism 8:394, 9:714–15
mathematics
foundations of 6:192
modal logic 6:419
Post, E.L. 7:573, 7:575
predicate calculus 7:665
scientific theories 9:346
semantic paradoxes and
theories of truth 8:643–4,
8:648
theory of types 9:362
process philosophy 4:669,
7:712–13, 7:715–16
perception/'prehension'
7:713–14
process theism 7:716, 7:720
processes 7:723
Quine, W.V. 8:14

Ramsey, F.P. 8:49
religion, history of philosophy of
8:247
scientific theories 9:355
scope 8:589
semantic paradoxes and theories
of truth 8:643–4, 8:648
sense experience 9:715–16
speculative metaphysics 9:714,
9:716–17
types, theory of 9:362
Whitehead, J.H.C. 4:34
Whiteley, Peter
Native American philosophy
†6:662–7
Whiteside, D.T. 6:828
Whitford, F. 1:452
Whitford, Margaret 3:583–8, 3:602,
5:3–4, 9:201
Whitmore, C.E. 4:185
Whittaker, E.T. 3:260, 3:670, 6:210
Whittaker, J. 7:429
wholly other
Derrida, J. 2:897
Whorf, Benjamin Lee 6:664, 6:672,
8:471–2
Whyte, J.T. 8:49
Whyte, L. 2:596, 9:527
Whyte, L.L. 9:55
Wickens, G.M. 2:807
Wicki, N. 7:357
Widdicombe, R.T. 9:562
Wider, K. 4:597
Widmann, J. 3:653
Wieacker, F. 5:101–2, 8:347–8
Wiechens, P. 1:661
Wiedebach, H. 2:402
Wiedenhofer, S. 6:292
Wieder, N. 5:209, 6:40
Wiedman, F. 2:17
Wiehl, R. 9:719
Wielgus, Stanisław
Poland, philosophy in †7:483–9
Wielockx, R. 7:269
Wiener, J.M. 6:264
Wiener, N. 5:738
Wierenga, E. 7:103, 7:112, 7:771
Wiesenthal, Simon 8:136–7, 8:141
Wiggershaus, R. 3:737
Wiggins, D.
Heraclitus 4:369
justice, equity and law 5:153
personal identity 7:314
Wiggins, David
analytic ethics 1:223
axiology 1:612
meaning of life 5:632, 5:633

moral realism 6:538
substance 9:211
universalism in ethics 9:539
value 9:583
Wiggins, D.R.P
  essentialism 3:421
  identity 4:678
  indiscernibles 4:681
Wigmore, John Henry 5:501, 5:502–3
Wigner, E.P. 2:608, 7:890
Wigoder, Geoffrey
  Bar Hayya, A. †1:649–51
Wikler, Daniel
  medical ethics †6:259–64
Wilbur, E.A. 8:891–2
Wilcocks, R. 8:479
Wild, J. 6:818, 8:807
Wildavsky, A. 8:334, 8:337
Wildberg, Christian
  Ammonius, son of Hermeas
    †1:208–10
  Philoponus †7:371–8
  Simplicius †8:788–91
Wilde, Oscar 9:485
Wilder, R.L. 2:200
wilderness
  environmental ethics 3:335
Wilders, N.M. 9:291
Wildi, H.M. 1:656
Wildt, A. 8:134
Wiles, P.J.D. 2:464
Wiley, E.O. 9:81, 9:276
Wilkerson, T.E. 6:684–5
Wilkes, C. 1:850
Wilkes, K.V. 9:110–09
Wilkie, J.S. 2:122–3
Wilkins, Barry 3:43
Wilkins, Burleigh T. 2:140, 9:617
Wilkins, E.H. 7:329
Wilkins, John 9:534, 9:535
Wilkins, K.S. 2:120
Wilkinson, E.M. 8:529
Wilkinson, R. 4:224, 5:20
Wilkosz, W. 7:495
Wilks, M. 5:117
will 9:720–5
  see also akrasia; free will; self-
    control; volition; voluntarism
  Abelard, P. 1:13
  ability/motivation distinction
    (Anselm of Canterbury) 1:291
  action (Arendt, H.) 1:372
  aesthetic judgment (Herbart, J.F.)
    4:370
  affections
    Duns Scotus, J. 3:155, 3:167
    Lachelier, J. 5:339

Aquinas, T. 1:338–9
Augustine 1:548–9
autonomy 1:588
bodily movement (Reid, T.) 8:174
character relationship
  good, theories of the 4:132–3
  in cognition (Locke, J.) 5:676
  control of (Elisabeth of Bohemia)
    3:268
  development of (Natorp, P.) 6:783
divine
  creation
    Ibn Gabirol, S. 4:618–19
    Ibn Tzaddik, J. 4:661
  as source of law 5:465–6
  emotions (Spinoza, B. de) 9:101
  as freedom
    Jewish voluntarism 9:665–6
  freedom of
    compatibilism
      Dennett, D.C. 2:882–3
      Kant, I. 5:191–2
      paradigm case argument 7:151
      Schopenhauer, A. 8:552
  general see general will
Godfrey of Fontaines 4:121
good relationship
  Thomasius, C. 9:378–9
human nature 4:522–3
intelligence relationship
  Matthew of Aquasparta 6:202
  Weil, S. 9:699
introspection (Maine de Biran, P.-
  F.) 6:49, 6:51–2
justice (Anselm of Canterbury)
  1:292
legal norms (Austin, J.) 7:39
to life (Schopenhauer, A.)
  8:549–50, 8:552–3
misery (Schopenhauer, A.) 8:550–1
moral virtue (Gerard of Odo) 4:39
morality
  Duns Scotus, J. 3:154–5,
    3:166–7
  Seneca, L.A. 8:680
motivation (Schopenhauer, A.)
  8:548
necessity contrast
  Jewish voluntarism 9:666
passions (Hume, D.) 4:551
phenomenology (Ricoeur, P.) 8:319
as a power for opposites (Duns
  Scotus, J.) 3:154–5, 3:166–7
prescriptivism 7:669
primacy of (Richard of
  Middleton) 8:311

reason relationship
  Descartes, R. 3:9–10
  law 5:464
  Matthew of Aquasparta 6:202
  structure of (Buridan, J.) 2:134
  universal causation
    (Hartmann, K.R.E. von) 4:239
  utility principle (Mill, J.S.)
    6:369–70
  voluntarism 9:663, 9:799
  weakness of (Socrates) 9:15–16
will
  as world (Schopenhauer, A.) 8:545,
    8:546, 8:549–50
Will, D. 2:722
Will, F. 2:692
will to believe
  epistemic judgments
    (Ducasse, C.J.) 3:140–1
will to power
  life (Nietzsche, F.W.) 6:857–8
will to truth
  Nietzsche, F.W. 6:852–9
Willard, Charity Cannon
  Pizan, C. de †2:343–5
Willard, D. 5:842
Willey, T. 6:792
William II, King of England 1:284
William of Auvergne **9:725–7**
William of Auxerre **9:727–9**
William of Champeaux **9:729–30**
  Abelard, P. 1:8
  Parisian theology 4:519
  Platonism
    medieval 7:434
  universals
    realism 7:18–19
William of Conches **9:730–1**
  Chartres school 2:290, 2:291
  Platonism
    medieval 7:435–6, 7:439
William de la Mare 9:388
William of Luna 5:22
William of Militona 1:177, 1:178
William of Moerbeke 5:748, 7:436,
  9:456
William of Ockham **9:732–48**
  see also Ockhamism; Ockham's
    Razor
  Ailly, P. d' 1:134
  Albert of Saxony 1:143
  Aristotelianism 1:394, 1:401
  Biel, G. 1:770
  categorematic/syncategorematic
    distinction 7:19
  Chatton, W. 2:292–3

concepts
　as signs 5:412
divine foreknowledge 8:243–4
epistemology 3:374, 3:383
Gregory of Rimini 4:171
intentionality 4:403, 4:404
justification doctrine 5:166
Kilvington, R. 5:244–5
Marsilius of Inghen comparison
　6:110–11
natural philosophy 6:700, 6:703
nominalism 7:18, 7:19–20, 7:23
　motion 2:141
Pelagianism 7:285–6, 7:287
poverty controversy 9:732, 9:733–4
propositions 9:739
religion, history of philosophy of
　8:247–8
reprobation 8:274, 8:276
rights 8:328
signification 5:391, 5:392, 5:398,
　5:401
substance 9:211
supposition theory 5:754
universals 3:154, 3:163
voluntarism 9:663, 9:664
Wodeham, A. 9:773, 9:774–5
William of Sherwood 9:748–9
Williams, Alan
　Zoroastrianism †9:872–4
Williams, Bernard Arthur Owen
　9:749–52
analytic ethics 1:223
analytic philosophy 1:227, 1:228,
　1:229
applied ethics 1:325
Berlin, I. †1:750–3
consequentialism 2:606
death 2:818, 2:821, 2:823
Descartes, R. 3:19
duty 3:183, 4:674, 4:675
economics and ethics 3:211
epistemology 3:383–4
equality 3:396
help and beneficence 4:344
Homer 4:502
impartiality 4:715, 4:717
imperative logic 4:721
infinity 4:778
Kantian ethics 5:204
morality 6:564–5, 6:569, 6:571
　concrete identity 6:574
　moral expertise 6:511
　moral luck 6:520, 6:522
　moral motivation 6:528
　moral pluralism 6:530, 6:531
　moral psychology 6:534

moral sentiments 6:550
opera, aesthetics of 7:131
personal identity 7:314
practical reason 7:619, 8:103
praise and blame 7:647
professional ethics 7:737
prudence 7:804
rectification and remainders 8:141
relativism 8:190
responsibility 8:294
Sidgwick, H. 8:764
theory and practice 9:359
transcendental arguments 9:454
universalism in ethics 9:539
utilitarianism 9:556, 9:557
virtue ethics 9:626
virtues and vices †9:626–31
Williams, C.J.F.
deflationary theories of truth
　9:476, 9:478
existence 3:492, 7:118
Prior, A.N. †7:687–90
Williams, D.
Condorcet, M.J.A.N. †2:527–32
Voltaire †9:657–63
Williams, D.C. 7:22, 7:236–7, 7:238
Williams, D.E. 7:540
Williams, G. 2:389, 9:230
Williams, G.C. 8:896
Williams, G.H. 8:892
Williams, Glanville 5:515, 5:521
Williams, Howard 5:199
Williams, M. 6:813
Williams, Michael
contextualism
　epistemological 2:647, 2:650
　deductive closure principle 2:845
　doubt †3:122–5
Feyerabend, P.K. †3:640–2
Williams, N.P. 8:796
Williams, P. 7:583
Williams, Paul
Ābhidharmika Schools of
　Buddhism 2:58
Buddhist philosophy
　emptiness †2:76–80
　in India 2:99
Mi bskyod rdo rje †6:351–3
mKhas grub dge legs dpal bzang
　po 6:417
nirvāṇa 7:11–12
Tibetan philosophy 9:408
Williams, R.
recognition 8:134
social science
　history of philosophy of 8:859
tragedy 9:452

Weil, S. †9:698–701
Williams, R.C. 8:409
Williams, R.M. 9:69
Williams, S. 3:109
Williams, S.G.
　truth and meaning †6:219–26
Williams, Sylvester 7:193
Williams, Thomas
　Farrer, A.M. †3:560–1
Williams, W.H. 9:557
Williamson, Timothy
　epistemic paradoxes 7:214
　identity †4:675–8
　meaning and verification 6:236
　vagueness 9:566
willing
　concept of (Schelling, F.W.J. von)
　　8:514
Willm, J. 5:301
Wills, G. 1:207, 5:85
Wilmott, M.J. 7:265
Wilshire, B. 5:68
Wilson, A. 9:447
Wilson, A.D. 6:743
Wilson, A.M. 3:69, 3:304
Wilson, B.R. 2:398, 6:721, 8:86, 8:838
Wilson, C.
　Heytesbury, W. 4:421
　Islamic philosophy, transmission
　　into Western Europe 5:25
　natural philosophy
　　medieval 6:707
　Newton, I. 6:828
　Oxford Calculators 7:183
Wilson, Daniel J. 6:731
Wilson, Deirdre 4:725, 7:632
Wilson, E. 3:475–6, 9:719–20
Wilson, E.O. 3:818, 8:892, 8:896
Wilson, F. 6:375
Wilson, G. 7:870
Wilson, G.D. 7:816
Wilson, George M. 3:677
Wilson, H.H. 4:105
Wilson, J.A. 1:769
Wilson, J.H. 3:607, 3:611
Wilson, J.S. 3:285
Wilson, L.S. 2:608
Wilson, Mack 3:772, 3:778
Wilson, Mark
　field theory, classical †3:668–70
　mechanics, classical †6:251–9
　natural laws 5:475
Wilson, M.D. 1:528, 1:530, 3:19
Wilson, N. 8:35
Wilson, R. 2:834–5, 6:344
Wilson, R.M. 4:85

Wilson, T.D.
  consciousness 2:595–6
  folk psychology 3:687
  introspection, psychology of 4:843,
    4:844–5, 4:846
  psychoanalysis
    methodological issues in 7:817
    unconscious mental states 9:523–4,
      9:527
Wilson, Thomas 8:822
Wilson, W.J. 1:94
Wiltshire, S.F. 7:693
Wimmer, F.M. 9:612
Wimmer, H. 6:386, 6:389, 6:390
Wimsatt, W. 3:103, 4:16, 6:447
Wimsatt, W.K. 1:475, 1:513, 1:516
Winant, H. 8:21
Winch, D. 8:822
Winch, P.
  anthropology 1:299
  explanation in history and social
    science 3:531
  practical reason and ethics 7:619
  private language argument 7:698
  rationality and cultural relativism
    8:86
  responsibilities of scientists and
    intellectuals 8:290
  social science
    contemporary philosophy of
      8:847
    methodology of 8:868
    naturalism in 6:721
    theory and observation 9:356
  Weil, S. 9:701
Windelband, Wilhelm
  Hegelianism 4:298
  Neo-Kantianism 6:776, 6:781,
    6:784–5, 6:791
Wing, L. 6:390
Wingren, G. 8:458
Winkler, Kenneth P.
  Berkeley, G. 1:750
  Browne, P. †2:29–30
  Collier, A. †2:408–11
  Collins, A. †2:415–19
  Hutcheson, F. 4:594
  language
    early modern philosophy of
      5:379
  More, H. †6:576–83
Winkler-Oswatitsch, R. 5:635
Winner, Langdon 9:284
Winnicott, Donald Woods 7:819,
  7:824
Winnie, John
  computer science †2:491–6

winning
  sport ethics 9:110, 9:111
Winslow, G. 7:737
Winslow, O.E. 3:245
Winston, D. 7:361
Winter, E. 2:402–3, 9:487
Winternitz, J. 4:6–7, 4:9
Winternitz, M. 5:222
Wintrobe, R. 8:73
Wippel, John F.
  Aquinas, T. 1:349–50
  Augustinianism 1:565
  Godfrey of Fontaines †4:119–22
  James of Viterbo 5:59
  Siger of Brabant †8:764–8
Wiredu, Kwasi
  African philosophy
    Anglophone †1:97–1:108
    Francophone 1:116–17
  Akan philosophical psychology
    †1:138–9
  ethnophilosophy, African 3:448,
    3:450
  traditional religions
    African 1:119, 1:121
  Yoruba epistemology 9:834
Wirszubski, C. 7:392
wisdom 9:752–5
  Chinese philosophy (Mencius)
    6:303
  comedy 2:436–7
  cultivation of (Vico, G.) 9:599,
    9:600–1
  divine
    creation 1:756
  educational objective
    Augustine 3:225
    Descartes, R. 3:226
  Ethiopian philosophy 3:444, 3:445
  goodness
    Stoicism 9:155
  happiness (Confucius) 2:568
  Hellanistic Judaism 7:255
  of Moses (Philo of Alexandria)
    7:358–9
  paradox
    Stoicism 9:156
  philosophic/theological distinction
    (Denys the Carthusian) 2:885
  Plato 7:412
  potentiality for
    Indian philosophy 7:607
  practice of
    Porphyry 7:548
  pursuit of
    Jewish philosophy
      Ibn Paquda 4:633–6

self-cultivation
  Chinese philosophy 8:620
  Socrates 9:10–11
  virtue epistemology 9:621
Wisdom, J.O. 7:540
Wise Club see Aberdeen
  Philosophical Society
Wise, S. 3:593
Wiseman, J. 1:776
Wiseman, J.A. 6:627
wish-fulfilment
  Freud, S.
    desire 3:788–90, 3:791
    religious belief 8:214–15
Wiśniewski, A. 8:3
Wissenschaftslehre (theory of science)
  3:642, 3:645–6, 3:647–9
Wisser, R. 5:83, 5:84
Wissink, J.B.M. 3:429–30
Wiszniewski, Michał 7:486, 7:489
witchcraft
  see also magic; supernatural
  Agrippa von Nettesheim, H.C.
    1:130, 1:131
  irrationalism 3:641
  natural phenomena 4:80, 4:82
Wither, G. 7:177
Witherspoon, G. 6:672
Witherspoon, John 9:755–7
witnesses
  testimony 9:311
Witt, B.S. de 7:894
Witt, C. 1:435, 3:602
Witt, R.E. 1:159–60
Wittenborn, A. 9:865
Wittgenstein, Ludwig Josef Johann
  9:757–70
  see also Wittgensteinian ethics;
    Wittgensteinianism
  a priori 1:5
  aesthetic attitude 1:54, 1:55
  analytic philosophy 1:225, 1:229
  animal language and thought
    1:270, 1:273
  antirealism
    mathematics 1:311, 7:740
  arithmetic 1:441
  art
    understanding of 1:475–6
  Augustine 1:542, 1:545, 1:559
  behaviourism
    analytic 1:693
  bodily sensations 1:795
  Cantor's theorem 2:200
  certainty 2:265, 2:267
  cognitive architecture 2:393

communal justification 8:830–1, 8:832
concepts 2:517
  conceptual role 2:506, 2:512, 8:657
  confusion elimination 4:401–2
  family resemblances 2:506, 2:512
contextualism
  epistemological 2:650
contradiction 8:61
conventionalism 6:748, 6:750
criteria 2:258, **2:711–14**
doubt 3:125
eliminativism 3:266
emotions 3:285
ethics
  fact-value distinction 9:770–1, 9:772
  language games 9:770, 9:771
  practical reason and 7:617, 7:619–20
facts 6:339
family resemblances 2:506, 2:512, 7:23
folk psychology 3:686, 3:687
general terms 7:21
Hanson, N.R. 4:224, 4:225–6
Hempel, C.G. 4:352
ideology 4:684–5
imagination 4:708
induction 4:751, 4:752
infinity 4:776, 4:778
influence of
  Australian philosophy 1:574, 1:578
  Schlick, F.A.M. 8:540–1
language games 5:419, 9:757, 9:762–3
logical analysis
  Moore, G.E. opposition 6:497
logical atomism 5:773–4, 5:775, 9:757
  saying and showing 9:761
  simples 9:760–1
  world picture 9:763, 9:764
logical form 5:785
logical positivism 5:795
Mauthner, F. 6:205–6
meaning
  rule-following 6:214–16, 6:219
  sceptical paradox
    Kripke, S.A. 6:216
    McDowell, J. 6:216–17
neutral monism 6:818
numbers 7:53–4
Nygren, A. 7:69

ordinary language philosophy 7:147, 7:148–9, 7:150, 7:153
other minds 7:173
perception 7:297
Philosophical Investigations
  language games 9:762–3
  private language argument 7:693, 7:695–6
  rule-following 9:763–4
philosophy as therapy 7:640
picture theory of meaning 7:150, 9:758–9, 9:761
pragmatics 5:408–9, 7:633
predication 7:666, 7:667
private language argument 7:693–7, 7:698
  qualia 2:426
property theory 7:767
Ramsey, F.P. 8:49
rationality and cultural relativism 8:85, 8:86
rule-following 7:75, 9:763–4
  ethics 9:770, 9:771–2
  meaning 6:214–16, 6:219
  sceptical paradox
    Kripke, S.A. 6:216
    McDowell, J. 6:216–17
Russell, B.A.W. 8:397, 8:398–9, 8:404
scepticism 8:498, 9:768
  Cavell, S. 2:258
  language 5:409–10
Sellars, W.S. 8:638
social science
  methodology of 8:864, 8:868
solipsism 5:647, 9:25, 9:761
substance 9:211
syntax 9:253
Tractatus Logico-Philosophicus
  conventionalism 6:748, 6:750
  logical atomism 5:773–4, 9:757, 9:761, 9:763, 9:764
  ordinary language philosophy 7:150
  solipsism 9:761
unconscious mental states 9:527
Wright, G.H. von 9:667–8
Wittgensteinian ethics **9:770–3**
  practical reason 7:617
Wittgensteinianism
  faith 3:543
  language of thought hypothesis 5:406–7
Witzel, M. 4:257, 4:766
Włodkowic, Pawel z 7:484
Wodeham, Adam **9:773–6**
  Chatton, W. 2:293, 2:294

Gregory of Rimini 4:171
  language 9:773–4
Woeam *see* Yi Kan
Wójcicki, R.
  formal languages and systems 3:706
  Łukasiewicz, J. 5:863
  many-valued logics 6:91
  Polish logic 7:496, 7:500
  scientific theories 9:353–4
Wojcik, J.W. 1:857
Wojtyła, Karol (Pope John Paul II) 7:487, 8:724, 8:730
Wokler, R.
  Buffon, G.L.L. †2:120–3
  Diderot, D. †3:63–9
  Enlightenment, continental †3:315–20
  Monboddo †6:473–4
  Rousseau, J.-J. 8:377
Wold, H. 9:133
Woleński, J.
  Ajdukiewicz, K. †1:135–8
  Kotarbiński, T. 5:295–6
  Leśniewski, S. †5:571–4
  Łukasiewicz, J. †5:859–63
  Poland 7:489, 7:498, 7:500
  Twardowski, K. †9:507–9
Wolf, Friedrich August 4:385, 4:389
Wolf, Susan
  free will 3:753
  meaning of life †5:630–3
  morality and identity 6:575–6
  supererogation 9:235
Wolff, C. von 5:719
Wolff, Christian **9:776–86**
  critiques of (Kant, I.) 5:179
  Crusius, C.A. 2:737
  division of philosophy 9:780–1
  international relations 4:833
  Knutzen, M. 5:287–8, 5:289
  Mendelssohn, M. 6:304–5, 6:306
  metaphysical doctrines 9:781–3
  method 9:777, 9:781
  natural philosophy
    mathematics 9:486
Wolff, Janet 3:596
Wolff, Jonathan
  libertarianism †5:617–19
  Nozick, R. †7:44–7
  political philosophy 7:503
Wolff, M. 7:377–8
Wolff, Robert Paul
  anarchism 1:244, 1:248
  authority 1:585, 1:586
  Kant, I. 5:198, 5:200

obligation
  political 7:80
solidarity 9:25
state 9:123
toleration 9:433
violence 9:617
Wölfflin, H. 1:506, 1:509
Wolf-Gazo, E. 7:723, 9:719
Wolfram, S. 6:685
Wolfson, E.R. 4:613, 5:176, 6:651
Wolfson, H.A.
  Crescas, H. 2:704
  divine simplicity 8:787–8
  Gersonides 4:51
  Ibn Rushd 4:646
  Ibn Tzaddik, J. 4:662
  Islamic philosophy, transmission
    into Western Europe 5:25
  Jewish philosophy
    contemporary 5:95
    voluntarism 9:667
  Karaism 5:209
  logic in Islamic philosophy 5:713
  natural philosophy
    medieval 6:707
  patristic philosophy 7:261
  Philo of Alexandria 7:361
  resurrection 8:296
  Shem Tov family 8:740
  Spinoza, B. de 9:107
Wolheim, R. 7:817
Wollaston, William **9:787–8**
Wollgast, S. 9:487
Wollheim, Richard
  aesthetic attitude 1:54, 1:55
  art
    artist's intention 1:516
    depiction 2:894, 2:896
    erotic 3:409
    expression 1:498
    ontology of 1:484
    style and personality 1:508
    understanding of 1:473, 1:476
  Bradley, F.H. 1:863
  democracy 2:869, 2:872
  Freud, S. 3:794
  type/token distinction 9:511
Wollschlägen, C. 5:101–2
Wollstonecraft, Mary **9:788–92**
  feminism 3:578, 3:583, 3:615–16,
    3:621
Wolman, B.B. 7:830
Wolter, A.B. 3:169–70, 8:325, 9:664
Wolters, G. 2:215, 5:352, 8:572
Wolterstorff, Nicholas
  art works
    ontology of 1:484–5

Calvin, J. 2:182
  divine simplicity 8:788
  faith †3:538–44
  fictional entities 3:663, 3:666,
    3:667
  Frei, H. †3:778–9
  hermeneutics
    biblical 4:395
  music
    aesthetics of 6:615
  Reformed epistemology 6:709,
    6:713
  religion and political philosophy
    8:229–30
  type/token distinction 9:511
women
  see also feminist philosophy;
  feminist theology; gender
  economic role
    family 3:550
  education
    Chinese classics 2:313
    Masham, D. 6:167
    Schurman, A.M. van 8:557–8
  feminist ethics **3:602–6**
  in government (Plato) 7:414
  Hindu repression of
    Brahmo Samaj critique 2:5–6
  Latin America 3:626–7, 5:655
  Mandeville, B. 6:71
  modesty within marriage
    (Hume, D.) 4:554
  moral education
    (Wollstonecraft, M.) 9:789–90
  Renaissance humanism 4:540
  rights
    reproduction ethics 8:277–8
  Russian nihilism 7:6
  science
    role in research 3:864
  sexual consent 8:724–5
  sexual differences (Irigaray, L.)
    5:1–3
  subordination of
    feminist ethics 3:604–5
  theology **3:621–5**
Wŏnch'ŭk **9:792–3**
  Yogācāra Buddhism 2:110
Wong, David B.
  moral relativism †6:539–42
Wŏnhyo **9:793–4**
  syncretic Buddhism 2:108–9, 2:117
Wood, Allen W.
  alienation †1:178–81
  dialectical materialism †3:53–8
  Fries, J.F. †3:797–9
  Hegel, G.W.F. 4:279–80

Kant, I. 5:200
  Marx, K. 6:133
  naturalism in ethics 6:717
  self-control 8:613
Wood, David 8:322
Wood, Dennis
  Constant de Rebecque, H.-B.
    †2:615–18
Wood, G.S. 2:622
Wood, J.C. 8:822
Wood, O.P. 8:432
Wood, Paul
  Aberdeen Philosophical Society
    †1:15
  Beattie, J. †1:677–80
  Turnbull, G. †9:502–4
Wood, R. 2:48
Wood, Rega
  Brinkley, R. 2:21
  Burley, W. 2:144
  Crathorn, W. 2:694
  Duns Scotus, J. 3:170
  Richard Rufus of Cornwall
    †8:314–18
  Wodeham, A. †9:773–6
Wood, T.E. 6:641, 8:451
Woodcock, G. 1:248, 5:314, 7:793
Woodfield, Andrew
  teleology †9:295–7
Woodger, J.H. 7:500
Woodhouse, C.M. 2:165
Woodruff, G. 6:386, 6:390
Woodruff, P. 8:648
Woodruff, Paul
  Aenesidemus 1:51
  Thucydides †9:398–9
Woodruff Smith, D. 4:587
Woods, John 3:663
Woods, Julian F.
  Indian fatalism †3:564–8
Woods, M. 7:804
Woods, R. 6:634
Woods, W. 8:657
Woodward, A. 8:470
Woodward, J. 3:517, 3:518, 7:86
Woodward, James
  statistics †9:123–7
Woodward, R.L. 7:570
Woodward, W.H. 3:231, 3:401
Woodward, W.R. 5:842
Woolf, C.N.S. 1:659
Woolf, Virginia 2:263
Woolgar, Steve 2:626–7, 2:630, 3:517
Woolnar, H. 7:177
Woolston, Thomas 2:854–5, 2:856
Wootton, D. 5:605, 7:177, 8:892
Woozley, A.D. 1:708, 1:709

Worczyna, Pawełz 7:484
Word
    mysticism of (Abhinavagupta) 1:17
word association test
    Jung, C.G. 5:132, 5:134
words
    eternality of
        Mīmāṃsā 6:377, 6:380
        universals 9:544–5
    knowledge relationship
        testimony in Indian philosophy
            9:315
    meaning 9:246–7
        Bacon, R. 1:635
        Indian theories of 6:240, 6:241
        Patañjali 7:248–9
        Navya-Nyāya theory of definition
            2:852
Wordsworth, W. 7:478
Worek, J. 4:172
work
    see also business ethics; employees;
    labour; professional ethics
    expressive 9:390
    as necessity 9:699
    philosophy of **9:794–7**
    socialism 8:882
working classes
    Marxism
        Latin America 6:160, 6:162,
            6:163
Workman, H.B. 9:805
world
    see also Dasein; earth; eternity of
    the world; external world; *kosmos*;
    possible worlds
    Brahman relationship
        Upaniṣads 2:2
    contingency of 2:650–1
    cyclical recurrence of
        Stoicism 9:146
    demystification 4:408
    destruction of the 2:703
    dialectical universal 7:14
    as dynamic set of relations
        4:311–12
    evolutionary 1:568
    existence of 8:509
    human construction of 3:270
    immaterialism 2:408, 2:409–10
    ladder of nature (*scala natura*)
        (Bruno, G.) 2:37
    language relationship
        (Wittgenstein, L.) 9:764
    logical structure (*Aufbau*)
        (Carnap, R.) 2:209

macrocosm/microcosm doctrine
    (Paracelsus) 7:205, 7:206
mechanistic view 5:542
nature of
    Stoicism 9:144–5
pantheism 7:202
physical
    Platonism (Plutarch of
        Chaeronea) 7:467
    Stoicism (Cleomedes) 2:385
rationality of
    Stoicism 9:141–2, 9:146–7
scientific concept of
    Vienna Circle 9:609–10
as will (Schopenhauer, A.) 8:545,
    8:549–50
world order
    reasonable politics (Jaspers, K.)
    5:81–2
world state
    peace 9:689–90
worlds
    plurality of 2:703
    possible **7:570–3**
    spacetime
        alternative structures 9:68
world-soul
    Alcinous 1:159
    beneficent-maleficent dualism
        (Plutarch of Chaeronea) 7:467
    four dimensions of
        Early Platonism 7:425
    hypostasis Soul and individual soul
        distinctions (Plotinus) 7:459
    Jewish philosophy
        (Formstecher, S.) 5:98
    nature of
        Middle Platonism 7:426
        Neoplatonism (Proclus) 7:727
    Xenocrates 9:806
worldview
    Cartesian 3:197–8
    cosmogonic/non-cosmogonic
        Chinese philosophy 9:817
    early modern 8:230–1
    ecological 3:198–9
    historical consciousness
        (Dilthey, W.) 3:82
    language effect on
        Chinese 2:778
    'ten mindsets' 5:319
    morality 8:219, 8:221–3
    Newtonian 3:197
    personalism 7:315–16
Worrall, John
    Lakatos, I. †5:342–5
    science, philosophy of †8:572–6

Worringer, W. 1:449, 1:452
Worster, D. 4:166
Wren, T. 3:240
Wright, A. 2:92, 8:828, 8:886
Wright, Crispin J.G.
    abstract objects 1:35
    American philosophy 1:207
    antirealism
        mathematics 1:311
    arithmetic 1:440, 1:441
    Ayer, A.J. 1:618–19
    constructivism 2:639
    Dummett, M.A.E. 3:153
    Frege, G. 3:778
    Freud, S. 3:793
    intuitionistic logic 4:863
    meaning and truth 6:225–6
    moral realism 6:537, 6:539
    objectivity 7:74, 7:75–6
    private states and language 7:701
    realism/antirealism 8:119
    rule-following
        extension 6:218–19
    Wittgenstein, L. 9:770
Wright, E. 3:584, 3:588, 5:368
Wright, Georg Henrik Von *see* Von
    Wright, Georg Henrik
Wright, J. 3:593
Wright, John P. 4:562
Wright, John S.
    Amo, A.W. †1:210–11
Wright, Kathleen
    Gadamer, H.-G. †3:827–31
Wright, L.
    explanation 3:525
        functional 3:803, 3:805
    mental illness
        concepts of 6:314
    semantics
        teleological 8:675
    teleology 9:297
Wright, M.R. 3:298
Wright, Tamra
    Buber, M. †2:42–8
Wright, Terence R. 3:267
Wrightsman, L.S. 1:696
writing
    hieroglyphics
        pre-Columbian cultures 5:428–9
    language relationship (Barthes, R.)
        1:656–7
    speech relationship
        Derrida, J. 2:896, 2:898
        Rabbinic theology 9:335–6
Wróblewski, Jerzy **9:797–8**
Wrong, D.H. 7:613

wrongdoing
  forgiveness 8:135–7
  mercy 8:135, 8:137–8
  transgression 6:569
Wroński, A. 6:91
Wrywa, D. 2:385
Wu, Emperor 2:310
wu forms
  Daoist philosophy
    wuyu 2:790–1
Wu, J.C.H. 3:533
Wu Kuang-ming 2:795, 9:867
wu (nonbeing) 2:316, **9:834–5**
  li 5:594

wu-forms
  Daoist philosophy 2:787–91
    wuwei (non-action) 2:789–90,
      5:448
    wuzhi (no-knowledge) 2:788–9
    wuyu (no-desire) 2:790–1
wuhua (transformation of things)
  2:791–4
wuji (utmost of nonbeing) 6:768,
  9:862
Wundt, E. 9:801–2
Wundt, M. 2:739, 3:653, 9:196
Wundt, Wilhelm **9:798–802**
  psychology
    theories of 7:825–6, 7:830

Wurtz, J.-P. 9:487
wuxing (five elements) 6:768
Wyatt, D.J. 8:737, 9:831
Wyclif, John **9:802–5**
  Hus, J. 4:573
Wykstra, S.J. 3:472, 8:218
Wylie, Alison
  archaeology †1:354–9
  feminism and social science
    †3:588–93
  gender and science 3:868
Wyller, Egil 8:490
Wyner, A.D. 4:786
Wynn, K. 6:676, 8:209
Wyschogrod, M. 4:499, 5:95

X

Xenocrates **9:806–7**
Xenophanes **9:807–10**
  natural science 9:809
  pantheism 7:202
  religion 9:808–9
  social criticism 9:808
  theory of knowledge 9:809–10
xenophobia *see* racism
Xenophon **9:810–15**
  agricultural ethics 1:127, 1:128
  Antisthenes 1:314–15, 1:317
  Apology
    Socrates 9:9, 9:10, 9:19
  Aristippus the Elder 1:380
  Cynics 2:754, 2:759
  Cyrenaics 2:763
  Memorabilia
    Socrates' defence 9:10
  moral education 9:812–13
  Prodicus 7:733

  self-sufficiency 9:813–14
  Socratic dialogues 9:8, 9:16, 9:19, 9:811–12
  virtue 9:812–13
Xia, Z. 3:39
Xiangshan *see* Lu Xiangshan
Xiaojing (Book of Filial Piety) 2:309, 2:312, 2:314
Xie He 1:72
Xie Lingyun 1:70
xin (heart-and-mind) **9:815–16**
  Confucianism 2:546
  self-cultivation 8:614–15, 8:616, 8:623–4
xin (trustworthiness) **9:816–17**
  cheng 2:300
  Confucianism 2:546
Xin shu see Jia yi
xing (human nature)
  Chinese philosophy **9:817–18**

xinxue (learning of the mind) 6:770
Xiong Shili 8:624, 8:625
Xu Shen 9:857
Xuanzang 2:76, 2:85, 9:792
Xun Kuang *see* Xunzi
Xun Qing *see* Xunzi
Xunzi 2:543–5, **9:818–20**
  basic terms 2:537
  cheng 2:300
  Chinese classics 2:310
  Confucian philosophy 2:323–4
  historical appeal 2:545–7
  history, theories of 4:448
  language theories 5:694, 5:704–5
  law and ritual 5:448, 5:449–50
  li 2:541, 2:542, 5:594
  self-cultivation 8:616–17, 8:626
  yi 2:541

Y

Yablo, Stephen
  essentialism †3:417–22
  mental causation 6:311
Yack, B. 5:153
Yādavaprakāśa 8:42
Yaglom, I.M. 4:34
Yahweh see God
Yalom, I.D. 3:502
Yamaga Sokō 2:149, 2:553
Yamamoto Tsunetomo 2:149, 2:150
Yamasaki, Taikō 5:320
Yamashita, S.H. 5:44, 7:91, 9:827
Yamauchi, E. 4:85
Yamazaki Ansai 2:552
Yamazaki Masakazu 1:90, 9:841
Yamin, G.S., Jr 9:464
Yampolsky, P.B. 2:92, 7:399
Yāmunācārya 8:42–3
Yan Hui (Yan Yuan) 2:568, 6:774
Yan, Lingfeng 6:591
Yan Shoucheng, W.F. 9:682
Yan Yuan *see* Yan Hui
Yanagita, S. 5:646
Yanal, R. 3:281
Yandell, Keith E.
  Bowne, B.P. †1:852–3
  Hastings †8:59–61
  Hume, D. 4:562
  Inge, W.R. †4:793–4
  Loisy, A. †5:819–20
  mysticism 6:634
  Oman, J.W. †7:97–8
  Otto, R. †7:173–5
  pantheism †7:201–5
  personalism †7:314–18
  Ramsey, I.T. †8:49–51
  reincarnation †8:182–6
  religious experience 8:255
  salvation †8:447–51
  Steiner, R. †9:133–4
  Teilhard de Chardin, P. †9:288–91
  Temple, W. †9:300–1
  Thielicke, H. †9:370–1
yang see yin-yang
Yang Chu *see* Yangzhu
Yang Guang 9:860
Yang Hsiung *see* Yang Xiong
Yang Xiong **9:821–2**
Yangzhu **9:822–3**

Yaofu *see* Shao Yong
Yāska
  interpretation 4:834–5, 4:837
  language 5:379, 5:380
  Patañjali 7:250
Yaśovijaya 4:766, 5:55, 5:58
Yasuda, K. 9:841
Yates, F.A.
  Agrippa von Nettesheim, H.C.
    1:133
  Bruno, G. 2:39
  Hermetism 4:397
  Llull, R. 5:664
  Renaissance Platonism 7:447
Yates, Robin D.S.
  Mozi †6:590–1
Yayshay wangbo *see* Ye-shes dbang-
  po
Yearley, L.H. 6:304
Yerushalmi, Yosef Hayim 9:335,
  9:337
Ye-shes dbang-po (Yayshay wangbo)
  9:406
Yessenin-Volpin, A.S. 2:637
yi (appropriateness) 2:320, 2:540–1,
  2:544, 2:545
Yi, B.D. 9:828
Yi Hwang **9:823–5**
  Four–Seven Debate 2:556,
    2:557–8, 2:560–2
Yi I *see* Yi Yulgok
Yi, J.H. 9:828
Yi Kan **9:825–6**
  Horak Controversy 2:563, 2:564
Yi, Ton-hwa 9:442
Yi, Urho 2:343
Yi Yulgok **9:826–8**
  Four-Seven Debate 2:556, 2:557–8,
    2:561–2
Yi Zhi 6:457
Yijing (Book of Changes) **9:828–31**
  Chinese classics 2:309, 2:310,
    2:311, 2:314
  dao 2:778
  Dharmakīrti 3:53
  self-cultivation 8:619
  Shao Yong 6:767, 8:736
Yili (Ceremony and Rites) 2:309,
  2:311–12, 2:314, 9:857

yin-yang **9:831–2**
  correlative thinking 2:318
  Daoist philosophy 2:793
  East Asian Philosophy 3:194
  five phases
    Zhou Dunyi 9:862
    qi 7:862
    Yijing 2:311, 9:830
Yixuan 8:621
Yob, I. 5:356
Yoder, J.H. 9:691
yoga
  duty 3:183, 3:185, 3:186
  Eliade, M. 3:261
  India 6:621, 6:622
  sense perception 8:693
  soul–non-soul interaction
    Jainism 5:50
Yoga 4:439
  see also Sāṅkhya-Yoga; *Yogasūtra*
  awareness
    dualism 1:605
    perception 1:605–6
  karma and rebirth 5:212
  Sāṅkhya School contrast 8:462,
    8:464
  self
    theories of 8:608–9
  self-realization 4:102, 4:104
Yogācāra School of Buddhism
  2:64–76
  see also Yogācāra-Vijñānavāda
  School
  asceticism 1:518
  awareness
    idealism 1:606–7
  Buddha
    nature of 2:96
  causation
    Indian theories of 2:256
  consciousness
    eight types of 2:72–4
  dependent origination
    Vasubandhu 9:217–18
  emptiness 2:79
  enlightenment path
    five stages of 2:74
  epistemology 3:388–9
    inference/perception 5:283

primacy of 2:68–9
role of 2:67–8
history of 2:65–6
idealism contrast 2:66–7
illusion 3:410–11, 3:412
karma 2:69–71
Korea 2:110
Mādhyamika Buddhism
  comparison
    China (Wŏnch'ŭk) 9:792
matter 2:71–2
momentariness 6:471
self-nature
  three types of 2:74
sense perception 8:691
Vasubandhu 9:585–6
voidness
  Tibetan philosophy 9:402–3
Yogācāra-tathāgatagarbha debate
  China 2:83–4
Yogācāra-Vijñānavāda School of
  Buddhism 5:214
Yogasūtra 4:439
yogocracy 7:523–4
Yôksa hakhoe 8:798
Yolton, J.W.
  a posteriori 1:3
  Burthogge, R. 2:146
  Clarke, S. 2:380
  Enlightenment, continental 3:320
  logic
    seventeenth and eighteenth
      century 5:722
  perception 7:293
Yōmeigaku ('Yangming studies')
  2:553

Yonan, E. 3:263
yong (function) **9:399–400**
Yoruba philosophy
  aesthetics 1:61–2, 1:63–4
  epistemology **9:832–4**
    hermeneutical interpretation of
      1:103–4
Yosha, N.
  Herrera, A. Cohen de †4:397–400
Yoshikawa, Kōjirō 5:44, 6:590, 7:91–2
Yoshimizu, C. 9:409, 9:490
Young, B.W. 5:470
Young, George M.
  Fëdorov, N.F. †3:574–6
Young Hegelians 4:280, 4:284
  see also Feuerbach, L.;
  Strauss, D.F.
  Bauer, B. 1:663–5
  critique of Hegel, G.W.F.
    metaphysical 4:284–5
    political 4:284
    religious 4:282–3
  history (Cieszkowski, A.) 2:360,
    2:361
  Marx, K. 6:120–1, 6:123
  religion 6:118, 6:120
  Ruge, A. 8:385
Young, Iris Marion
  citizenship 2:365
  desert and merit 3:27
  equality 3:396
  feminist political philosophy
    3:620, 3:621
  multiculturalism 6:602
  postmodernism and political
    philosophy 7:593

Young, J. 6:861, 8:554
Young, M.J.L. 8:565
Young, Robert 1:505, 7:583, 9:201
Young, Robert M. 2:798, 4:238
Young, Thomas 7:136
Young-Bruehl, E. 1:372, 5:84
Young-Eisendrath, P. 5:135
Yourgrau, P. 2:881, 6:226, 9:417,
  9:418–19
you-wu (being/nonbeing) 2:316,
  2:786, **9:834–5**
Yovel, Yirmiahu 5:95, 6:48
Ypma, E. 5:59–60
Yu Chai shin
  Buddhism, Korean 2:118
Yu, C.S. 9:793
Yu, P. 1:75
Yu Wôn-dong 8:798
Yu Ying shi (Yü Ying-shih)
  Cheng Yi 2:303
  Dai Zhen †2:770–1
Yuanjue jing (Scripture of Perfect
  Enlightenment)
  Zongmi 9:870, 9:871
Yuasa Y. 5:321
Yuejing (Book of Music) 2:310
Yugoslavia see South Slavs
Yukio Kachi
  Shōtoku Constitution †8:752–4
Yulgok see Yi Yulgok
Yun, Sasoon 9:825
Yusa, Michiko
  Zeami †9:839–41
Yushkevich, A.P. 1:220

Z

Zabarella, Jacopo **9:836–9**
logic
    method 5:772
    logical eclecticism 5:717
    Renaissance Aristotelianism 1:406,
    1:407, 1:410
Zabell, S.L. 2:536
Zac, S. 6:38
Zadeh, Lofti 2:517, 3:823–4, 9:566
Zaehner, R.C.
    mysticism 6:627, 6:628, 6:630,
    6:634
    negative theology 6:762–3
Zagzebski, Linda
    concept of knowledge 5:276
    epistemology and ethics 3:370
    eternity 3:427
    goodness, perfect †4:140–4
    heaven †4:249–53
    limbo †5:635–8
    purgatory †7:836–9
    virtue epistemology †9:617–22
Zahar, E.G. 5:345
Zahar, Z. 6:351
Zahirite school 4:620
Zai Yu 2:569
Zainaty, G. 4:608
Zaitchik, D. 6:388, 6:390
Zajac, A. 7:139
Zajonc, A. 7:139
Zajonc, R.B. 1:696
Zakariyya, Fu'ad 5:17
Zakydalsky, Taras D.
    Shestov, L. 8:746
    Skovoroda, H.S. †8:802–3
Zakzouk, M.
    al-Ghazali 4:68
Zallen, D. 6:459, 6:461
Zalta, E.N. 4:807, 4:810, 6:747
Zambelli, P. 1:133, 5:298
Zanardo, A. 8:387
Zander, L. 2:126
Zangari, M. 2:680–1
Zanier, G. 7:532–3
Zank, M.
    Cohen, H. †2:398–403
Zar'a Ya'ecob
    African philosophy 1:96

Ethiopian philosophy 1:104–5,
    1:108
    The Treatise of Zar'a Ya'ecob
    3:443–4, 3:445
Zarathushtra
    Zoroastrianism 9:872, 9:873
Zarka, Y. 4:476
Zaunick, R. 9:487
Zavalloni, R. 8:312
Zawirski 7:486–7, 7:489
Zea, Leopoldo
    Latin America
        anti-positivism 1:304, 1:306–7
        feminist thought 3:627, 3:628
        literature 5:655, 5:657
        marginality 6:100, 6:101
        Mexican philosophy 6:344,
        6:346
        positivism 7:570
Zeami **9:839–41**
    Japanese aesthetics 1:84, 1:88
    kokoro 5:292, 5:293
Zedler, B. 3:269
Zeevat, H. 1:244, 3:99
Zeh, H.-D. 9:369, 9:417
Zeilinger, Z. 1:716
Zeitlin, I. 9:425
Zeitlin, S. 8:440
Zeldin, M.B.
    Frank, S.L. 3:729
    Mikhailovskii, N.K. 6:357
    Russian religious-philosophical
    Renaissance 8:427
    Slavophilism 8:811
Zeleny, J. 3:531
Zeller, E. 6:280, 9:19, 9:23
Zeller, Eduard 4:298, 6:779, 6:780,
    6:792
Zelliot, E. 1:197
Zemach, E. 3:281
Zeman, Zybnek A.B. 6:166
Zemer, M. 4:207
Zen Buddhism
    see also Chan; Rinzai; Sôn; Sōtō
    Dōgen 3:109–10, 5:73–4
    language
        ritual use of 2:100
    mysticism 6:622–3
    neo-Confucianism 2:551

Nishida Kitarō 7:13–15
Nishitani Keiji 7:16–17
    sport 9:112, 9:115
Zengzi 2:540
Zenkovsky, V.V.
    Berdiaev, N.A. 1:732
    Fëdorov, N.F. 3:576
    Florenskii, P.A. 3:682
    Frank, S.L. 3:729–30
    Hessen, S.I. 4:419
    Leont'ev, K.N. 5:570
    Losev, A.F. 5:833
    Lossky, N.O. 5:835, 5:838
    Russian philosophy 8:422
        medieval 6:278–9
        Neo-Kantianism 6:797
        positivism 7:564
        religious-philosophical
        Renaissance 8:428
    Skovoroda, H.S. 8:803
    Solov'ëv, V.S. 9:33
    Vysheslavtsev, B.P. 9:677
Zeno of Citium **9:841–3**
    Ariston of Chios 1:380–1
    perfect-being theology 4:96
    politics 9:842
    scepticism
        Augustine 1:544
    Stoicism 1:263, 9:141–2, 9:143,
    9:144, 9:151–2
Zeno of Elea 1:263, **9:843–53**
    infinity 4:773
    motion 7:722
        arguments against 9:843,
        9:847–51
    motion paradox (Bergson, H.-L.)
    1:732, 1:733–4
    paradoxes
        Anaxagoras comparison 1:250,
        9:843–52
    plurality
        arguments against 9:843,
        9:847–51
    space (Bayle, P.) 1:674
Zerachja, B. Izsak 5:597
Zermelo, Ernst **9:853–5**
    see also Zermelo-Fraenkel set
    theory
    axiom of choice 1:612–13

decision and game theory 2:835
infinitary logic 5:734–5
logicism 5:817
paradoxes of set and property
7:217, 7:219–20
set theory 8:709, 8:716
Zermelo-Fraenkel set theory 8:700,
8:706, 8:707–8, 8:711–12
ETCS distinction 2:233, 2:234
transfinite numbers 7:52
Zermelo-König paradox 7:218
Zernov, N.N. 8:428
Zeus
obedience to (Epictetus) 3:338
Orphism 7:163–4
pneuma (spirit) 7:471
providence 7:797
rule of (Hesiod) 4:412–13
Zeyl, D. 1:265
Zhang Thang sag pa 9:404
Zhang Xuecheng 4:450–1
Zhang Zai 6:768–9, **9:856–7**
Zhang Zhidong 9:400
Zhang-Tshal-pa 9:405
Zhao Lun see Sengzhao
Zhao Mengfu 1:73
Zheng Xuan **9:857–8**
zhi **9:858**
Zhi Dun **9:859**
Zhili 2:91
Zhiyan 3:568–9
Zhiyi 2:86–7, **9:859–61**, 9:860–1
Zhong Bing 1:72
Zhongyong (Doctrine of the Mean)
2:300, 8:619, **9:861–2**
Zhou Dunyi 6:768, 8:622, **9:862–3**
Zhouli (Rites of Zhou) 2:309,
2:311–12, 2:315, 9:857
Zhu Xi 2:312, 2:325–6, **9:863–5**
Cheng Hao 2:301
Cheng Yi 2:302
Confucianism 2:543–5
Chinese 2:549
quan 2:545
ren 2:539
critiques of
Itō Jinsai 5:43
Daxue 2:807, 2:808
history, theories of 4:450
influence of
Confucianism, Japanese 2:549,
2:551, 2:552
li 5:595
neo-Confucianism 6:769–71, 6:772
Korean 2:556
self-cultivation
neo-Confucianism 8:623

Wang Yangming 9:683
ti/yong 9:400
wuji 9:862
xin 9:816
Yijing 9:829–30
Zhuangzi **9:865–7**
dao
self-cultivation 8:618–19
history, theories of 4:448
language theories 5:694, 5:702–4
li 5:594
Zhuangzi 9:865
Chinese classics 2:310
Daoist philosophy 2:795
Daoist philosophy 2:787
li 5:594
order 2:321
wu-forms 2:790–2
wuhua 2:792, 2:793–4
xin (heart-and-mind) 9:815,
9:816
Zi Mozi *see* Mozi
Ziai, Hossein
Illuminationist philosophy
†4:700–3
Mulla Sadra 6:599
mystical philosophy in Islam 6:620
al-Suhrawardi 9:224
Ziegler, K. 7:470
Ziegler, T. 2:51
Ziff, P. 3:291
zig-zag theory
paradoxes 7:218, 8:395
Zijing *see* Lu Xiangshan
Zilu 2:568–9
Zimand, M. 2:481
Zimmerman, David 2:389
Zimmerman, Michael E. 3:336,
4:323, 4:327
Zimmerman, M.J. 3:183, 8:294
Zimmerman, W.D. 1:838
Zimmermann, A. 1:152, 1:350
Zimmermann, F.W. 5:713
Zimmermann, R. 8:348
Zimring, F.E. 7:545
Zinn, G.A. 1:835, 8:314
Zinn, H. 2:369
Zintzen, C. 7:429
Zinzendorf, Nikolaus Ludwig Graf
von 7:394
Zionism **9:867–70**
anti-Semitism 1:313–14
Buber, M. 2:42–3, 9:869
cultural
Buber, M. 2:42–3

cultural (Ha'am, Ahad) 4:192,
4:193
Hess, M. 4:414, 9:867
Hibbat-Zion 9:867–8
Holocaust relationship 4:497
Jewish philosophy 5:87
Judah Halevi 4:208, 4:212
Klatzkin, J. 9:868
opposition to (Rosenzweig, F.)
8:360
political definition (Leibowitz, Y.)
5:563
reconstructionism (Kaplan, M.)
5:205
religious
Leibowitz, Y. critique 5:563
secular 5:563
socialist 9:868–9
ziran (self-so-ing) 9:401
Zirk-Sadowski, Marek
Wróblewski, J. †9:797–8
Zisi 9:861
Zita, J.N. 5:645
Ziwo *see* Zai yu
Žižek, Slavoj 5:338, 9:53, 9:55–6,
9:205
Zohar: Mishnat ha-Zohar (text) 5:176
Zohar, N.
halakhah †4:204–7
Jewish bioethics †1:776–80
Zöller, G.
Lambert, J.H. †5:350–2
Lichtenberg, G.C. †5:622–5
Tetens, J.N. †9:319–22
Zöllner, Johann Friedrich 3:317
Zolo, D. 6:816
Zongmi **9:870–2**
Zonta, M. 4:617, 5:25
Zorn's lemma 8:701–2
glossary 5:811
Zoroaster *see* Zarathushtra
Zoroastrianism **9:872–4**
dualism 6:75
Illuminationist philosophy 9:222
Zou Yen 5:864
Zoubov, V. 4:40
Zschokke, Heinrich 3:322
Zubiri, Xavier 9:74, 9:77
Zuckerkandl, V. 6:615
Zuckert, M. 1:207
Zuidervaart, L. 1:46
Zumr, Josef
Comenius, J.A. †2:438–40
Czech Republic, philosophy in
†2:763–9
Masaryk, T.G. †6:165–6
Patočka, J. †7:252–4

Permission acknowledgements

The publishers thank the copyright holders of the following material (listed by publisher in alphabetical order) for permission to reproduce extracts and artwork in the *Routledge Encyclopedia of Philosophy*.

Academic Press, Inc., USA.
Artwork: 'Wakan: Plains Siouan Concepts of Power' (by DeMallie and Lavenda), from *The Anthropology of Power: ethnographic studies from Asia, Oceania, and the New World*, edited by R.D. Fogelson and R.N. Adams (1977).

Cambridge University Press, England.
Extracts from: *Philosophical Papers, F.P. Ramsey*, edited by D.H. Mellor (1990);
The Philosophical Writings of Descartes, volumes I and II, translated and edited by J. Cottingham, R. Stoothoff and D. Murdoch (1985);

The Philosophical Writings of Descartes, volume III, translated and edited by J. Cottingham, R. Stoothoff, D. Murdoch and A. Kenny (1991).

Lawrence Erlbaum Associates, Inc., USA.
Artwork: 'A Simple Connectionist Network', from *The Symbolic and Connectionist Paradigms: Closing the Gap*, edited by J. Dinsmore (1992).

G. Olms Publishers, Germany.
Extracts from: *Die Fragmente der Vorsokratiker* (Fragments of the Presocratics), edited by H. Diels and W. Kranz (1952).

Princeton University Press, USA.
Extracts from: *A Source Book in Chinese Philosophy*, translated and edited by Chan Wing-tsit (1963).

455